Extract of the Rejected Applications of the Guion Miller Roll of the Eastern Cherokee

Volume 1

Jo Ann Curls Page

HERITAGE BOOKS
2006

HERITAGE BOOKS
AN IMPRINT OF HERITAGE BOOKS, INC.

Books, CDs, and more—Worldwide

For our listing of thousands of titles see our website
at
www.HeritageBooks.com

Published 2006 by
HERITAGE BOOKS, INC.
Publishing Division
65 East Main Street
Westminster, Maryland 21157-5026

Copyright © 1999 Jo Ann Curls Page

Other books by the author:
Index to the Cherokee Freedmen Enrollment Cards of the Dawes Commission, 1901-1906
Extract of Rejected Applications of the Guion Miller Roll of the Eastern Cherokee, Volume 2
Extract of Rejected Applications of the Guion Miller Roll of the Eastern Cherokee, Volume 3

All rights reserved. No part of this book may be reproduced or transmitted in any form or by any means, electronic or mechanical, including photocopying, recording or by any information storage and retrieval system without written permission from the author, except for the inclusion of brief quotations in a review.

International Standard Book Number: 978-0-7884-1315-5

Table of Contents

Introduction v

How to use this Index ix

Rejected Applicants 1

Extract of the Rejected Applications of the Guion Miller Roll of the Eastern Cherokee

Introduction

The Cherokee Nation filed three lawsuits against the United States Government for funds due them under their treaties of 1835, 1836, and 1845. The United States Court of Claims decided in favor of the Cherokee. As a result of this decision, over one million dollars was awarded to the Eastern Cherokee.

The Guion Miller Roll was created to distribute the funds from these three lawsuits among each Eastern Cherokee person who was alive on 28 May 1906. The criteria to qualify was to prove membership in the Eastern Cherokee Nation at the time of the treaties of 1835, 1836 and 1845, or to prove descendancy from a member of the tribe.

The United States Department of Interior assigned Mr. Guion Miller as a special agent to identify those eligible to receive the warrant of $133.18 that was given to each person. The Guion Miller Roll is on 348 rolls of microfilm. Most rolls contain 150 applications. There are a number of published works on applicants that were approved for the Guion Miller Roll. These books include the information that I am extracting plus much more. The only works on the rejected applicants are a name and residence index. My intent is to give the descendants of rejected applicants access to more information without having to look at all 348 rolls of microfilm.

Over 45,000 applications were filed representing 90,000 individuals. Only 30,840 individuals were found to be eligible. Almost 60,000 individuals were rejected, many of them African Americans. Some of the African American applications were rejected with a notation that this person was a former slave or descendant of a slave. While others were rejected as "Old Settlers" (Cherokee who came west before 1835); some were identified as members of another tribe (Creek, Choctaw, etc.); and others failed to prove relationship to an ancestor on an earlier Cherokee roll; and some were identified as "white."

Each applicant was asked such information as name, residence, age, place of birth, name of husband/wife, names of children, place of birth and date of death of parents and grandparents, names and ages of brothers and sisters, and names and residence of grandparents' children. The completed applications on file are rich in genealogical information.

Many applicants filed incomplete information. Some did not name their parents or grandparents. Others did not list the dates and places of birth of their parents and grandparents. It is not known why they omitted this information, but it is assumed that they didn't know and there were no records available to show the information.

These applications filed by many individuals are excellent sources for the researcher who has Cherokee lineage in his/her family history. For example, some applicants submitted pictures to show how Indian their ancestor looked. Other applicants submitted pedigree charts and family group sheets. These applications are also excellent sources for those who do not know if they have Indian ancestry because many people applied that could not prove any Indian heritage.

This book is based on my family research which began over five years ago. Family tradition tells that I am a descendant of the Cherokee tribe. Looking at the General Index to Eastern Cherokee Applications (NARA: M1104, Roll 1) I noticed the name "Moses Riley". I am related to a great uncle with that name, so I sent for the roll of microfilm that contained his application. Examining the application form closely, along with other information that I had researched, proved that the Moses Riley listed on this application was indeed my great uncle.

Moses gave the names of his maternal and paternal grandparents along with the names of their children on his application. This was all new information that I had not known. Using this additional information, I searched the entire roll to see if any other applicants had listed any of these same people. Subsequently, ten more applicants were found that were also related to my great uncle Moses Riley.

This new discovery led me to search all 348 rolls of microfilm, looking for additional relatives. Searching for female relatives is difficult especially if the maiden name is unknown. Looking at the names of the parents and grandparents helps to locate unknown female relatives.

I decided to copy all the information for African Americans so that I would not have to repeatedly send for the same rolls. Be aware of such pit falls as you continue to do more research, and are constantly finding new relatives as you could end up searching some of the same rolls over and over again.

Many of the African Americans were not identified as African American (in 1906, the terminology was slaves, Negroes, Blacks, or colored but not African American). It was my desire to compile information on all of the applicants that were rejected, which would include most African Americans.

This is volume one of two. The extract of rejected applications from the first 195 rolls of microfilm are included in volume one (half of the applications or 23000 applications). Volume two will be completed at a later date. It will contain rejected applications from rolls 196 to 348 (applications 23001 to 45857).

Hopefully, this extract of information from the Guion Miller Roll of Eastern Cherokee will help you find missing relatives as it has helped me to find many of my missing or unknown relatives.

Sources:

National Archives Microfilm Publication, *Eastern Cherokee Applications of the U.S. Court of Claims, 1906-1909.* M1104. Rolls 1-195.

Buswell, Carol Anne, "The Guion Miller Roll of 1906-1909: Cultural Geography of late 19th and early 20th century Cherokees" (Gilroy, California: Indian Scout Publications, 1997

National Archives and Records Service, *Guide to Genealogical Research in the National Archives.* (Washington: National Archives Trust Fund Board, 1983.

How to use this Index

This index consists of a table with nine columns. Column one has the roll number of the applicant. Column two has the name of the applicant. Column three has the state of residence of the applicant. Column four has the date of birth of the applicant. Column five has the name of the spouse of the applicant. Column six has the name of the father of the applicant. Column seven has the name of the mother of the applicant. Column eight has the name of the paternal grandparents of the applicant. Column nine has the name of the maternal grandparents of the applicant.

Every applicant does not have information in all nine columns. If there is a blank space, the information was not given or in some cases the applications are so light that they are not readable.

An asterisk after the applicant's name indicates that the applicant stated that he was Negro or Colored or some of his relatives stated that fact.

This index is arranged alphabetically by the surname of the applicant. Every effort was made to copy the names exactly as they were written, but because of the difficulty of reading the handwriting, there might be some mistakes.

EASTERN CHEROKEE ENROLLEES - REJECTED

National Archives Microfilm M1104, Rolls 1 - 195 completed

*Indicates African American Enrollees

Application #	Name	State	Birth	Spouse	Father	Mother	Paternal Grandparents	Maternal Grandparents
17787	Aaron, Thomas	GA	1872	Sarah Aaron		Elizabeth Lively		Joseph & Mary Lively
20895	Abbott, Jeff	NC	1861	Fannie Abbott	William Abbott	Nancy Scott	Jeff & Tildy Abbott	Wm & Betsie Harris
11001	Abercrombie, Willis	GA	34yrs	Gwhe Abercrombie	William Abercrombie	Mary Abercrombie		
9530	Abernathy, Daniel	GA	1882	Daisy Abernathy	John Abernathy	Delphia Tidwell	Daniel Abernathy	Francis Tidwell
9527	Abernathy, Delphia	GA	1855	John Abernathy	Francis Tidwell	Margaret Gravitt	John Langley & Sallie Tidwell	
19281 *	Abernathy, Judy	GA	80yrs	Rufus Abernathy	Sharp McClellan	Caty Stinson	Sharp & Rody McClellan	
2632	Abernathy, Marion	GA	1873	Bell Abernathy	Zephenia Abernathy	Ophelia Tidwell		Margaret Tidwell
15379	Abernathy, Minnie	GA	1872		Jeffrey Beck	Mandy Loggins	Coleman Davis & Elmira Beck	
9528	Abernathy, Ruth	GA	1877	none	John Abernathy	Delphia Tidwell	Daniel Abernathy	Francis Tidwell
9529	Abernathy, William	GA	1884	none	John Abernathy	Delphia Tidwell	Daniel Abernathy	Francis Tidwell
8544	Able, Melvina	TN	1863	Robert Able	Able Pennington	Emly Blevins	Andrew & Hester Pennington	
8543	Able, William	TN	1879	Sally Able	Robert Able	Malvina Pennington		Able & Emly Pennington
22046	Abney, Ida	TX	1903	none	Charles Abney	Tessie Sloan	Sandford Sloan	Annie Sloan
22048	Abney, Lessie	TX	1884	Charles Abney	S.H. Sloan	Annie Davis	Absalom Sloan	Mary Sloan
12254	Absher, Rebecca	NC	1886	Mac Absher	Curtis Brooks	Polly Wagoner		Henry & Charlotte Wagoner
21643 *	Adair, Benjamin	OK	1868	Lizzie Adair	George Adair	Celia Stover	Abram Ward	Charity Stover
12483	Adair, Bettie	OK	1842	J B Adair	Joe Clening	Katie Fields	Sally Clenning	Charles & Wuttie Fields
16204	Adair, Joe	OK	1879	Minnie Adair	George Adair	Lucinda Hardy	Henry & Sallie Adair	
3721	Adair, Samuel, gdn	OK	1866	widower	Wilson Morris	Ellen Powell	Su-wa-gee- & Co-lee-chee	
16629	Adair, Susan	OK	1830		John Bean	Ruth Starr		Caleb & Nancy Starr
11398	Adams, Ada	NC	22yrs		James Adams	Anna Barnett	John & Oma Adams	Thos & Elizabeth Barnett
154	Adams, Adolphus	GA	1875	Lou Adams	Richard Adams	Docia Sharp	David & Clarinda Adams	Richard & Elizabeth Sharp
11385	Adams, Albert	NC	21yrs		Joseph Adams	Lucretia Taylor	Posey & Jane Adams	David & Anna Taylor
582	Adams, Allen	GA	1863		David Adams	Clerinda Parker	Price Adams	Jathen & Ona Parker
22389	Adams, Allen for minors	GA			Allen Adams	Ellia Hudson	David & Claudia Adams	Mary Hudson
22296 *	Adams, Andrew	OK	1870	Edith Adams	Harve Martin	Fanny Martin	Adam & Chollote Martin	Harry & Nancy Martin

19533	Adams, Barney	TN	1896		John Adams	Anna Long	John & Nancy Adams	Cornelius & Luraney Long
22386	Adams, Bertha	MO	1885	James Adams	John Lomas	Dicy Fender		Michael & Anna Fender
12439	Adams, Catharine	VA	1844	Riley Adams	Jackson Lewis	Nancy Caldwell		Joseph & Cathrine Caldwell
10349	Adams, Charley	OK	1871	May Adams	George Adams	Louise Rogers		Henry & Mariah Rogers
5996	Adams, Dicey	MO	1864	Thomas Adams	Michael Fender	Martha Wallis	Daniel & Dicey Fender	Jeptha & Nancy Wallis
19992	Adams, Disa	GA	1850	Spencer Adams	Russell Jones	Ellen Perdue	Bartley & Disa Jones	Ruth Perdue
19534	Adams, Edmond	TN	1899		John Adams	Anna Long	John & Nancy Adams	Cornelius & Luraney Long
3341	Adams, Ellen	AL	21yrs	none	William Adams	Alice Gibson	William & Peggy Adams	W D & Peggy Gibson
9723	Adams, Frank	AR	1875		George Adams	Louise Rogers		Henry & Mariah Rogers
20250	Adams, Herman	TN	1889		Ab Adams	Mary Lane		John & Louisa Lane
19034	Adams, Isabell	GA	1876	Fayett Adams	Thomas Allison	Sarah Roberts	Ben & Beckey Allison	Wm & Rosa Roberts
12437	Adams, Jackson	VA	1866		Riley Adams	Catharine Caldwell		Joseph & Cathrine Caldwell
844	Adams, James	NC	1857	Eliza Adams	John Adams	Leomy Parker	David & Elizabeth Adams	Johnathan & Leomy Parker
7038	Adams, James	TX	1862	none	Gidian Adams	Lucinda Jackson		Isaac Jackson & Elizabeth Brock
12106	Adams, James	NC	27yrs	Tallie Adams	Joseph Adams	Lucretia Taylor	Posey & Jane Adams	David Taylor & Anna Adams
8581	Adams, Jesse	VA	1855		Henry Adams	Susan Fuget		Winney Fuget
1773	Adams, John	OK	1855	Margret Adams	David Adams	Clerinda Parker	Price & Elizabeth Adams	Joathon & Oma Parker
9111	Adams, John	OK	1863	Emma Adams	Frank Adams	Mary Parker	Price & Elizabeth Adams	Jonathan & Ona Parker
12278	Adams, John	NC	30yrs	Delphia Adams	James Adams	Anna Barnett	John & Oma Adams	Thos & Elizbeth Barnett
12438	Adams, John	NC	1868	Elisabeth Adams	Riley Adams	Catharine Caldwell		Joseph & Cathrine Caldwell
15378	Adams, Lillie	GA	1889	Lee Adams	Charles Brown	Martha Ivey	Clete & Winnie Brown	Milton & Eliza Ivey
21540	Adams, Margaret	GA	1852	Mathew Adams	Foster Hughes	Docia Fowler	George & Margaret Hughes	Thomas & Basche Fowler
18935	Adams, Margarett	TN		Giles Adams	Willis Carroll	Mary Crofford	Millie Carroll	Ellish Crofford
4069	Adams, Martha	NC		Ace Adams	Henry Moss	Martha Rogers		Robert & Jane Rogers
2450	Adams, Mary	OK	1852	Robert Adams	David Adams	Clerinda Parker	Price & Elizabeth Adams	Jothan & Omie Parker
17969	Adams, Mary	GA	1880	Charlie Adams	James Patterson	Maggie Ward	Samuel & Nancy Patterson	John & Sarah Ward
21075	Adams, Mary	GA	1886	A.Adams	Joe Etses	Lydia Etses	Noble Etses	Nina Cordell
18234*	Adams, May	GA	1871	John Adams	Henry Findley	Fanny Vann		Pate & Viley Vann
3324	Adams, Mrs William	AL		William Adams	Bart Gibson	Ann Moniac	Gibson	Moniac

3331	Adams, Mrs Wm	AL	25yrs	William Adams	William Adams	Alice Gibson	Jack McGhee & Mariah Adams	
11383	Adams, Oma	NC	24yrs		James Adams	Anna Barnett	John & Oma Adams	Thos & Elizabeth Barnett
153	Adams, Richard	GA	1848	Docia Adams	David Adams	Clerinda Parker	Jonathan & Ona Parker	
10089	Adams, Robert	OK	1866	none	Frank Adams	Mary Parker	Brice & Lizzie Adams	Joniehan & Ona Parker
22463	Adams, Robert	OK	1874	Nannie Adams	John Adams	Margaret Adams	David & Clarinda Adams	
22390	Adams, Ross	OK	1884	Mattie Adams	John Adams	Margret Moody	David & Clerenda Adams	Isaac & Elender Moody
22300*	Adams, Sam	OK	1866	Hattie Adams	Harvin Martin	Fannie Martin	Adam & Charlotte Martin	Jack Bean & Mary Martin
6347	Adams, Sarah	AL	25yrs	none	Bill Adams	Nancy Rollin	Peggy McGhee	Jack & Polly Rollin
10360	Adams, Simon	OK	1873		George Adams	Louise Rogers		Henry & Mariah Rogers
11390	Adams, Will	NC	23yrs	Minnie Adams	Joseph Adams	Lucretia Taylor	Posey & Jane Adams	David & Anna Taylor
3368	Adams, William	AL	27yrs	Lizzie McGhee	William Adams	Alice Gibson	William & Peggy Adams	W D & Peggy Gibson
18601	Addington, Hessie	TN	1885	J.W. Addington	Peter Thomas	Eliza Landers	Peter & Pattie Thomas	John & Vienna Landers
21463	Addison, Thomas	AR	1878	Joedello Addison	Alex Addison	Adelia Evans	Eldridge Addison	Thomas Evans
13061	Adison, George	TN	1882		John Adison	Sarah Pressley		
12464	Adkins, Mary	OK	1849	Marry Adkins	Mike Dooling	Polly Stevens		Jack Stevens
17931	Adkins, Mary	TN	1831		King Burgess	Betsie Alford		Richard & Millie Alford
7523	Adkins, Morris	OK		Mary Adkins	William Adkins	Susan Cooper	Morris & Jane Adkins	Isac & Mahala Cooper
6372	Adkins, Mrs John	AL	1855	John Adkins	Elijah Boone	Visa Hathcock	John & Rena Boone	Thos Hathcock & Elisabeth Marlow
13638	Adkins, Rosie	WV	1880	Ansel Adkins	Major Adkins	Susan Sizemore		Owen & Rosie Sizemore
8893	Admire, Martha	TX	1870	Levy Admire	Hamilton Wilson	Elisabeth Maney	Paul Wilson	Martin Maney
11692	Adolph, Pairlee	MO	1869	William Adolph	Ezekel Snible	Frances Collins	Wm & Ellen Snible	
13785	Agnew, Tamer	GA	1853	Nim Agnew	Tom Cunningham	Eliza Valentine		Jack & Tamer Valentine
13610	Ah ma su gee, Nancy	OK	22yrs		Ah ma su ga	Sussie Coon ha	Stee lee chee & Jennie Deerskin	Coon ha & Mollie
14459	Akers, Cozette	WV	1887	T J R Akers	John Cook	Margret Stewart	Thos & Rebecca Cook	George & Peggie Stewart
14454	Akers, Eva	WV	1889	Jacob Akers	John Cook	Margret Stewart	Thos & Rebecca Cook	
17308	Akers, Lawrence	WV	1903		John Cook	Margaret Stewart		
15377	Akin, Mary	GA	1870	Jeff Akin	James Spears	Francis Dupree	Josiah & Martha Spears	
20824	Akins, Mary	GA	1889	Thomas Akins	John Whitlock	Lounitha Fowler	Wm & Caroline Whitlock	E. & Susan Fowler
16755	Alberty, Elias	OK	1860	Sue Alberty	James Alberty	Martha Wright	John Alberty & Susan Wicket	Cornelius Wright & Hattie
2123	Alberty, Gibson	OK	1873	none	Jesse Alberty	Charitie Collins	John & Mary Alberty	Joseph & Nancy Collins

1105	Albright, Ida	KS	1872	Lewis Albright	Orvil Cavin	Margaret Burns	Wm & Bettie Cavin	Robert & Maria Burns
21918 *	Alexander, Causada	TN	1854		Bartley Horton	Melie Green	Peter & Sallie Horton	
18971	Alexander, Elizabeth	FL	53yrs	J.E. Alexander	Richard Taylor	Susan Hosford	Jacob & Martha Taylor	Daniel & Patsy Hosford
21575	Alexander, Ella	TN	1878	Daniel Alexander	Erve White	Liddie Hargrove	Dempsy & Nancy White	James & Serena Hargrove
5966	Alexander, James	OK	1841	Louisa Schrimsher	James Alexander	Sina Alexander		
17592 *	Alexander, Jefferson	TN	1860	Georgia Alexander	Jefferson Green	Deaby Alexander		
18972	Alexander, Martha	FL	20yrs		J.E. Alexander	Elizabeth Taylor	Alonzo & Susan Alexander	Richard & Susan Taylor
1193	Alexander, Mary	OK	1883		James Stephens	Mary Hall	Green & Nancy Stephens	Alfred & Mahala Hall
18929	Alexander, Mary	GA		Newton Alexander	Martin Loggins	Laura Loggins	Sam & Betsy Loggins	Jenny Loggins
9469	Alexander, Minnie	OK	1873	Reuben Alexander	Fleming Green	Margarite Clung		
22201	Alford, Alice	TX	1887					
3079	Alford, Andrew	OK	1842	Sarah decd	M E Alford	Nancy Orrick		William & Cela Orrick
22439	Alford, Dora	TX	1887	J.D. Alford	Walter Bell	Janie Pancake		John & Marthey Pancake
11620	Allen Jinnie	NC	35yrs	Jim Allen	Charlie Colbert	Addie McClelland		Sharp & Katie McClelland
6350	Allen, Ada	AL	1881	Warren Allen	Alex Boone	Minervy Moniac		Davie Moniac & Catherine Hale
20825	Allen, Addie	GA	1880	Haze Allen	Jeff Strickland	Margaret Strickland	Matt & Cinda Strickland	Alfred & Jane Summerhour
20732	Allen, Almer	GA	1899		James Allen	Almer Goins	Harrison & Bettie Allen	Wm & Delia Goins
20733	Allen, Almer	GA	1879	James Allen	Wm Going	Delia Cole	Wm & Nancy Going	John & Betsy Cole
20826	Allen, Andrew	GA	1856	Lizzie Allen	Thomas Allen	Linda Minion	J. & Fannie Allen	Thomas & Nancy Minion
19338	Allen, Anslom	GA	1863		Thomas Allen	Linda Minion	Jay & Fannie Allen	Thomas & Nancy Minion
18416	Allen, Attie	CA	1882	Robert Allen	Griffin Oxcudine	Perline Lowery		Mary Lowery
10838	Allen, Charles	IN	1882	Minnie Allen	Thomas Allen	Mary Stout	John & Martha Allen	Robert Stout & Jane Pierce
21939	Allen, Cora	TN	1882	Francis Allen	Elijah Lower	Louisa Hufsletter	John & Ellen Lower	Wm & Lucinda Hufsletter
21478	Allen, Cornelia	OK	1878	James Allen	Thomas Walker	Sarah Burnett	Samuel & Cathren Walker	John & Deliah Burnett
14683	Allen, Elizabeth	NC	1854	Thomas Allen	William Martin	Miriam Hauser	John & Jenanie Martin	John & Elizabeth Hauser
21772	Allen, Elvirtie	OK	1883	William Allen	James Moore	Martha Parsons	John & Mary Moore	Hiram & Martha Parsons
17890	Allen, Emma	OK	1882		James Allen	Sarah Barker	Daniel & Louisa Allen	Alex & Sarah Barker
19447	Allen, Emma	GA	1888	Earl Allen	Enoch Patterson	Lou Smith	Samuel & Nancy Patterson	Jonah & Bettie Smith
19830	Allen, Emma	OK		Oscar Allen	David Shook	Amanda Colvard	Eli & Sara Shook	Wm Colvard & Emily Campbell
19339	Allen, Erastus	GA	1859	Mary Allen	Thomas Allen	Linda Minion	Jay & Fannie Allen	Thomas & Nancy Minion
19340	Allen, Haze	GA	1878	Addie Allen	Benj Allen	Jane Sexton	Jay & Fannie Allen	John & Polly Sexton

5470	Allen, Ida	NC	23yrs	Jaames Allen	Allen Loudermilk	Josephine Thomas	Jacob & Sarah Loudermilk	Nancy Thomas
8400	Allen, James	TN	1882	Ida Allen	Perry Allen	Julia Ledford		Elbert Ledford
14966	Allen, James	OK	1844	Sarah Allen	Daniel Allen	Louisa Curtis	John & Martha Allen	James & Sarah Curtis
7043	Allen, Jesse	KS	21yrs	Viola Allen	Louis Allen	Sarah Corban	Joseph Jr. & Margaret Allen	
7040	Allen, John	KS	1865	widower	Joseph Allen	Margaret Logan	Joseph & Kate Allen	Wm & Matilda Logan
10837	Allen, John	OK	1879		Thomas Allen	Mary Stout		
14362	Allen, John	OK	1875	Rosa Allen	James Allen	Sarah Barker	Daniel & Loisa Allen	Alex & Sarah Barker
14959	Allen, John	GA	1844	Nancy Allen	John Allen	Eddie Johnson		
15376	Allen, John	GA	1840	Nancy Allen	Hol Allen	Edie Johnson		John &Rebecca Johnson
11243	Allen, John (decd)	IN	1864	Ellen Allen	John Allen	Nancy Brower	John & Martha Allen	
6400	Allen, Jonathan	TN	1842	Martha Allen	Willis Parker	Martha Allen	Jonathan & Leoma Parker	James & Pheba Allen
2555	Allen, Julia	TN	1859		Elbert Leadford	Elisa Robertson	Levy Leadford	Jrutha Pitman
14361	Allen, Julius	IN	1838	Lizzie Allen	John Allen	Nancy Brower	John & Martha Allen	
7042	Allen, Leonard	KS	1858	Effie Allen	Lewis Allen	Margaret Logan	Joseph & Catharine Allen	Wm & Matilda Logan
7041	Allen, Louis	KS		Sarah Allen	Joseph Allen	Margaret Logan	Joseph & Kate Allen	Wm & Matilda Logan
15612	Allen, Lucy	NC	1863	G W Allen	Payton Owens	Eliza Marion	Thomas & Pollie Owens	Jerry & Mary Marion
7044	Allen, Margaret	KS	1834	Joseph Allen	William Logan	Matilda Thaxton	Zachariah & Margaret Logan	
20298	Allen, Mollie	TX		Joe Allen	A.J. Avants	Rebecca Welch		
6322	Allen, Mrs. James	AL	48yrs	James Allen	Wah Taylor	Mary Colbert		David & Cealy Colbert
14858	Allen, Nathan	IN	1838	widower	Herman Allen	Ann Clark	John & Rachel Allen	Daniel & Mary Clark
20734	Allen, Odessa	GA	1901		James Allen	Almer Goins	Harrison & Bettie Allen	Wm & Delia Goins
21485	Allen, Rebecka	OK	1867	John Allen	George Marshall	Margaret Russell	Andrew & Mary Marshall	Joe Russell
2556	Allen, Sarah	NC	1868	Elisha Allen	Elbert Leadford	Leuisa	Leviy Leadford	John Robinson
18876	Allen, Sarah	NC	1857	John Allen	Benj Pettitt	Nancy Flynn	Benj & Charlotte Pettitt	Thos & Jennie Flynn
20898	Allen, Selia	NC	1866	M.A. Allen	? Hamby	Mary Hudson		
10885	Allen, Stella	KS	1878		Elias Allen	Menerva Pierson	Samuel & Martha Allen	
6328	Allen, Susan	AL	20yrs	George Allen	John Boone	Lavittia Moniac	John Boone & Martha Poston	Sam & Susan Moniac
20735	Allen, Thomas	GA	1905		James Allen	Almer Goins	Harrison & Bettie Allen	Wm & Delia Goins
20827	Allen, Thomas	GA	1861	Mary Allen	Ben Allen	Jane Sexton	J. & Fannie Allen	John & Polly Sexton
9022	Allen, William	IN		Mary Allen	Samuel Allen	Martha Henley	John & Martha Allen	

#	Name	State	Year					
20011	Allison, Conyer	GA	1880	Janey Allison		Jane Allison		
20258	Allison, Emma	GA	1888		W.J. Allison	Mary Hester	Hamilton & Katie Allison	Alfred & Polly Hester
20009	Allison, Jane	GA	1860	J. Farmer	J.B. Allison	Mary Gauch		Tillman & Elizabeth Gauch
18466 *	Allison, John	NC	1872		Wallace Allison	Nancy Stitt	Joe & Nancy Wallace	Sallie Stitt
14681	Allison, Martha	GA	1883	Thomas Allison	William Powell	Lucinda Lail	Abe Powell	James Lail
20008	Allison, Mary	GA	1837	J.B. Allison	Tillman Gouch	Elizabeth Justice	John & Sally Gouch	Billy & Sally Justice
22916	Allman, Julia	NC	33yrs	Daniel Allman	Bailey Palmer	Sallie McDonald		Jonathan & Haritt McDonald
2665	Alloway, Delila	OK	1865	Christopher Alloway	Neely Denton	Catherine McDaniel	Alford & Rhoda Denton	
16205	Allred, William	OK	1895		Lee Allred	Arzona Dawson	F M & Sarah Dawson	
20314	Ambrose, Fred	MO			Lafayet Ambrose	Miza Herrell		Emerson & Clarisa Herrell
9537	Amburn, Julia	TN	1876	John Amburn	Newton Cole	Malinda Gwinn	Wm & Sarah Cole	Almon & Sarah Gwinn
2019 *	Amis, Mary	OH	33yrs	George Amis	Isaac McClelland	Minerva Harshaw	Ross & Dorcas McClelland	Samuel & Charlott Harshaw
304	Anderson Jr., William	NC	33yrs	Samantha Anderson	Robert Anderson	Mary Kitchens	Lazrus & Nancy Anderson	John & Elizabeth Kitchins
13156	Anderson, Amanda	GA	1874	S E Anderson	Simpson Burrell	Rebecca Burleson	Jesse Burrell & Marning Barnes	Andy & Maruny Brown
18092	Anderson, Angie	GA	1889	John Anderson	Cicero Wheeler	Izabella Helton	Richard & Mary Wheeler	Clark & Mary Helton
306	Anderson, Barnett & Oma	NC	18yrs 15yrs		John Anderson	Eliza Cowart	Lazrus & Nancy Anderson	Jason & Hannah Cowert
15375	Anderson, Cora	GA	1897		Mose Anderson	Tennessee Morris	Mose & Susie Anderson	
288	Anderson, Docia	NC	23yrs	none	Robert Anderson	Mary Ann Kitchins	Lazrus & Nancy Anderson	John & Elizabeth Kitchins
950	Anderson, Dock	NC	21yrs	none	Robert Anderson	Mary Kitchens	Lazarus & Nancy Anderson	John & Elizabeth Kitchens
15374	Anderson, Dock	GA	1893		Mose Anderson	Tennessee Morris	Mose & Susie Anderson	
6737	Anderson, Drucy	VA	1851	Malvin Anderson	Hugh Peck	Marga Hart		George & Polly Hart
9989	Anderson, Earl	VA	1901		Welden Anderson	Sarah Hash	Linvill & Ludemy Anderson	Harvey & Milly Hash
18235	Anderson, Edie	GA	1865	Will Anderson	Josiah Burnett	Louisa Roland		George & Edie Roland
15373	Anderson, Ella	GA	1887		Mose Anderson	Tennessee Morris	Mose & Susie Anderson	
21285	Anderson, Ettie	TX	1874	James Anderson	James Stone	Jemima Coe	George & Delpha Stone	Andrew & Rhoda Coe
5424	Anderson, Hannah	NC	1868	Lenshes Anderson	Joseph Hughs	Martha Hampton	James & Anna Hughs	George & Mary Hampton
17486	Anderson, Ida	GA	1872	Farish Anderson	Caeb Whitfield	Rosalee Crow	W.G. & Anna Whittfield	Anna Crow
3234 *	Anderson, Isabella	GA	1876	Charley Anderson	Henderson Abernathey	Hariett Moore		Jerry & Manerva Moore
959	Anderson, James	NC	1840	Mary Anderson	Lazrus Anderson	Nancy Maney	Lazrus & Franky Anderson	James Maney & Barbara Barrett

6523	Anderson, Jessie	OK	1886	Claud Anderson	James Tittle	Annie Prather	Danel & Rosanner Tittle	Robert & Caroline Prather
15372	Anderson, Joe	GA	1880		Mose Anderson	Tennessee Morris	Mose & Susie Anderson	
13477	Anderson, John	NC	1879		Robert Anderson	Mary Kitchens	Lazrus & Nancy Anderson	John & Elizabeth Kitchens
15371	Anderson, John	GA	1882	Mamie Anderson	Mose Anderson	Tennessee Morris	Mose & Susie Anderson	
18091	Anderson, John	GA	1905		John Anderson	Angie Wheeler	John & Arminda Anderson	Cicero & Izabella Wheeler
15370	Anderson, Lela	GA	1873	Ben Anderson	David Wallis	Ann Turner	Jess & Liza Wallis	
292	Anderson, Linkeron	NC	28yrs	Ava Anderson	Robert Anderson	Mary Kitchins	Lazrus & Nancy Anderson	John & Elizabeth Kitchins
4112	Anderson, Louisa	OK	1865	Albert Anderson	Wilson Cordery	Nannie Hall	David & Charlotte Cordery	
19357	Anderson, Malinda	GA	1859	John Anderson	Robert Galaway	Mahala Pearson		Aphraim & Nancy Pearson
7049	Anderson, Mamie	MO	1885	W H Anderson	John Karr	Mary Williams	John & Susan Karr	John & Mary Williams
10337	Anderson, Manda	NC	1900	none	Enos Anderson	Dora Wagoner		Eli & July Wagone
18350	Anderson, Martha	WI	1880	Arthur Anderson	Elijah Bass	Elizabeth Bass	Elijah & Matilda Bass	Drewery & Emily Arnold
12972	Anderson, Mary	NC	1852	William Anderson	Balzamore Henslee	Sarah Morgan	Benj Henslee	George Morgan
18004	Anderson, Mary	NC	1848	Ab Anderson	Robert Poindexter	Martha Ward	Robert & Charlotte Poindexter	Wiley & Polly Ward
7512	Anderson, Matilda	AR	1882	A. A. Anderson	John Cornette	Jennie Fox	Cullen Cornette	
7039	Anderson, Maude	OK	1885	widow	Walter Bays	Francis Robison	Joseph & Carry Bays	Wm & Ellen Robison
15369	Anderson, Mose	GA	1862	Tennessee Morris	Mose Anderson	Susie Corban		John & Delila Corban
6332	Anderson, Mrs Charles	AL	1876	Charles Amderson	Charles Weatherford	Martha Staples	Chas Weatherford & Elisabeth Stiggins	James & Margaret Staples
956	Anderson, Nancy	NC		widow	James Maney	Barbara Barrett	Martin Maney & Kinziar Van	Wm & Betsy Barrett
12965	Anderson, Naomy	WV	1869	Thomas Anderson	Calaway Pennington	Nancy Privette	Andrew & Hetty Pennington	
15644	Anderson, Neter et al	GA			W R Anderson	Katherine Gibbs	J E & Lucy Anderson	Thos & Jane Gibbs
15368	Anderson, Octavia	GA	1889		Mose Anderson	Tennessee Morris	Mose & Susie Anderson	
13478	Anderson, Oma, Paul, John	NC			Lazarus Anderson	Nancy Maney	James & Frankey Anderson	James Maney & Barbere Berrett
305	Anderson, Patience	NC	55yrs	none	Lazrus Anderson	Nancy	James Anderson & Frank Swimlin	James Maney & Barbara Berrett
15367	Anderson, Richard	GA	1885		Mose Anderson	Tennessee Morris	Mose & Susie Anderson	
284	Anderson, Robert	NC	57yrs	Mary Anderson	Largrus Anderson	Nancy Maney		James Sr. & Barbara Maney
291	Anderson, Robert gdn.	NC					James & Franky Anderson	James & Barbara Berrett
8603	Anderson, Sallie	GA	1870	James Anderson	Marion Reece	Elisabeth Newman	James & Mary Reece	James & Sarah Newman
15366	Anderson, Sam	GA	1883		Mose Anderson	Tennessee Morris	Mose & Susie Anderson	

9996	Anderson, Sarah	VA	1884		Harry Hash	Milly Young		Wm & Catharine Young
8170	Anderson, Sulvanner	WV	1872	Jennie Anderson	Malvin Anderson	Drucy Peak		Hugh & Marga Peak
15365	Anderson, Susie	GA	1842	Mose Anderson	John Corban	Delila Whitmire		Samuel & Polly Whitmire
276	Anderson, Tobitha gdn.	NC		Link Anderson	Lazrus Anderson	Nancy Maney	James Anderson	James Maney Sr.
295	Anderson, William	NC	55yrs	Jane Anderson	Lazrus Anderson	Nancy Maney	James Anderson Franky Smerlin	James Maney & Barbara Berrett
18645	Andrews, Alonza	NC	1885		James Andrews	Malinda Baker	Meredith & Tamsey Andrews	Harrison & Francis Baker
18644	Andrews, Elmay	NC	1890		James Andrews	Malinda Baker	Meredith & Tamsey Andrews	Harrison & Francis Baker
5181	Andrews, Sarah	GA	1849	Cole Andrews	Barker	Polly Pinion		Nancy Pinion & Pryor Tally
6554	Angel, Abraham	GA	1869	Lisa Angel	James Gi	Arener Angel		Sopha Siler
689	Angel, Alice	NC	1869	Joseph Angel	Andrew Wall	Rebeca Delozier		Edward & Elizabeth Delozier
16401	Angel, Julia	NC	1880	Emory Angel	Sanford Nichols	Cornelia Spainhour	William & Julia Nichols	Theopholus & Elvira Spainhour
2658	Anglen, Samuel	MO	1851	widow	John Anglen	Vilettie Brown		Tom & Polly Brown
14520	Anglin, William	GA	1888		John Anglin	Mary Hinkle	Mary Anglin	Clark Helton & Nancy Hinkle
16480 *	Anthony, Elizabeth	NC	1823	James Anthony	Benj Evans	Lucy M?		
14883	Apperson, Edward	NC	1859	Alice Apperson	William Apperson	Mary Edwards	Bennett & Nancy Apperson	Edward & Matilda Edwards
14824	Apperson, Laura	NC	1856	Peter Apperson	Wm Miller	Catharine Martin	John & Elizabeth Miller	Samuel & Elizbeth Martin
14885	Apperson, Lesetta	NC	1867		William Apperson	Mary Edwards	Bennett & Nancy Apperson	Edward & Matilda Edwards
15895	Apperson, Mary	NC	1865		William Apperson	Mary Edwards	Bennett & Nancy Apperson	Edward & Matilda Edwards
12065	Appleman, Margaret	OK	1868	widow	B H Curry	Sarah Elmore		Anderson Elmore
14806	Arch, Nancy	OK	1866	Willie Arch	Johnson James	Judie Teehee		
9719	Arch, Semahoyah (decd)	OK	21yrs	Lem Hilderbrand	John Arch	Sindy Tutonsiemgee		
5220	Archer, Anna	OK	1878	Thomas Archer	Abrah Meek	Alfa Schrimsher	Wm & Maria Meek	Isac & Armanda Schrimsher
18025	Archibald, Maggie	LA	1863	J.T. Archibald	Ellison Mayfield	Stella Slatten	Enos & Sarah Mayfield	John & Nancy Slatten
21177	Ark, James	TN	1886		John Ark	Eliza Decker	Fields Ark	Darcus Decker
17489	Ark, John	TN	1850	Seiza Ark	Fields Ark	Dareus Daker	Elijah Ark	
22362	Ark, John	TN			Fields Ark	Darens Decker	Elijah Ark	Jenni Decker
21176	Ark, William	TN	1883		John Ark	Eliza Decker	Fields Ark	Darcus Decker
4892	Arledge, Minta	TN	1887	Charles Arledge	Henry Nelms	Rebecca Wilson	Wm & Margaret Nelms	Thomas & Rebecca Wilson
9268	Armerteskey, Lizzie	OK		none	Tauncece	Carnhawker		
13535 *	Arms, Mary	WI	1863	Mary Arms	Ishamel Roberts	Delaney Revels	Benj & Sarah Roberts	McCaga & Mornon Revels

2666	Armstrong, John	OK	1883	none	Pat Armstrong	Dorcus Fawling		John Fawling
22536 *	Armstrong, Minnie	IN			John Locust	Angeline Hardman	Moses Locust	John Hardman
20896	Armstrong, Mollie	MS	1883	J.T. Armstrong	J.R. McCutchen Jr.	Catharine Loveless	J.R. Sr. & Mary McCutchen	A.P. & Nancy Loveless
20897	Armstrong, Nancy	MS	1885	G.W. Armstrong	J.R. McCutchen Jr.	Catharine Loveless	J.R. Sr. & Mary McCutchen	A.P. & Nancy Loveless
2981	Armstrong, Thomas	KS	1875	Ellen Armstrong	P F Armstrong	Dorcas Falling		John & Leecey Falling
14053	Armstrong, William	TN	1861	Martha Armstrong	James Armstrong	Harriet Blair	Buck & Emmaline Rivers	Billy & Rachel Blair
19098	Arnett, Effie	TX	1890	H.S. Arnett	T.W. Dean	C.E. Hughes	James & Mary Dean	J.F. & C.E. Hughes
18236 *	Arnold, Emma	GA	1864	Alec Arnold	Upson Allen	Lizzie Tuck		
12292	Arnold, George	GA			G T Arnold	Sally		S S & M C Garrett
21382	Arnold, Ida	TX	1879	William Arnold	William Hagar	Lucindia Franklin		Anderson Franklin
12356	Arnold, James	GA	1905		G T Arnold	Sally Garrett		I S & M C Garrett
12355	Arnold, Lula	GA	1897		G T Arnold	Sally Garrett		I S & M C Garrett
11306	Arnold, Sally	GA	1875	G.T. Arnold	J S Garrett	Margret Dempsey		Porter & Charlotta Dempsey
22204	Arnold, Susan	TX	1873	James Arnold	Lewis Ledbetter	Nancy Johnson	William & Malinda Ledbetter	Massey & Susan Jackson
6410	Arp, Georgia	GA		William Arp	Joseph Bailey	Nancy Legueire	Benjamin Bailey	Miner Leguire
842	Arrawood, Louisa	NC	1847	James Arrawood	Willis Parker	Adaline Vanoy	Jonathan & Leomy Parker	Joel & Elizabeth Vanoy
3366	Arrington, Louisa	AL	1856	Lude Arrington	James Looksy	Vicey Shemoy		John Shemoy
18380	Arrington, Mrs. Monroe	AL	17yrs	Monroe Arrington	Clarence Brazile	Eliza Murphy	Daniel & Cally Brazile	George & May Murphy
294	Arrowood, Lillie	GA	22yrs	James Arrowood	Lazrus Chadwick	Martha Maney	Abe Chadwick & Rosa Carroll	James Maney & Betsy Owensby
21804	Artis, Fannie & Mint Mitchell	AL	1882 1880	John Artis	Montgomery Mitchell	Adline Cloud		
15849	Arundale, Naomi	KS	1872	John Arundale	Benj Williamson	Martha Logan	James Williamson	William Logan
9536	Ash, Emma	GA	1878	George Ash	Mart Williamson	Margret Ledford		John & Nancy Ledford
9502	Ash, George	GA	1867	Emma Ash	David Ash	Elisabeth Davenport		John & Elisabeth Davenport
17347	Ash, Harvey	GA	1887	Caroline Ash	David Ash	Nancy Foster	David & Elisabeth Ash	
2610	Ash, John	GA	1856	Sarah Ash	David Ash	Elisabeth Davenport		John & Elisabeth Davenport
4169	Ash, Lillie	NC	1876	E J Ash	James Davis	Lurana McDonald	Reason & Sevilla Davis	James & Minia McDonald
14407	Ash, M A	GA	1875	Seney Ash	David Ash	Elisabeth Davenport		John & Elisabeth Davenport
4353	Ash, Maggie	NC	1879	J M Ash	G W Doris	Mary McDonald	Reason & Sorila Doris	James & Jemina McDonald
4760	Ash, Sarah	NC	1864	Milton Ash	Eli Dockery	Catherine McCloud	James & Tabatha Dockery	James & Sarah McCloud

20043	Ashburn, Nonnie	NC	1887		W.J. Bayler	Carrie Stone	John & Susan Bayler	Frank & Sarah Stone
5448	Ashe, Ellen	NC	1873	John Ashe	Wm Bunyarren	Sarah Allen		Joseph & Tabitha Allen
5468	Ashe, Elvira	NC	1865	William Ashe	Adolphus Welch	Sarah Sawyer	Joseph & Cathrine Welch	Joel & Esther Sawyer
3597	Ashe, Rebecca	NC	1883	N B Ashe	Asbury Gibbs	Martha Cox	William Gibbs	Levi Cox
10552	Atherton, Leila	GA	1880	Glenn Atherton	Edward Prather	Mary Wofford	James & Parthenia Prather	
15485	Atkins, Albert	GA	1891		Calvin Atkins	Victoria Morris	Berryman & Martha Atkins	
15491	Atkins, Amanie	GA	1897		Ben Atkins	Malinda Cowart	Berryman & Martha Atkins	
10550	Atkins, Benjamin	GA	1864	Malinda Atkins	Berryman Atkins	Martha Corban		John & Delila Corban
10551	Atkins, Berry	GA	1849	Fanny Atkins	Berryman Atkins	Martha Corban		John & Delila Corban
15501	Atkins, Berry	GA	1898		Frank Atkins	Martha Smith	Berryman & Martha Atkins	
10549	Atkins, Calvin	GA	1854		Berryman Atkins	Martha Corban		John & Delila Corban
20596	Atkins, Caroline	TN	1841		John Craven	Letha Stokes		
15490	Atkins, Charley	GA	1899		Ben Atkins	Matilda Cowart	Berryman & Martha Atkins	
15489	Atkins, Della	GA	1896		George Atkins	Viney Smith	Berryman & Martha Atkins	
15488	Atkins, Dessa	GA	1900		George Atkins	Viney Smith	Berryman & Martha Atkins	
15487	Atkins, Dock	GA	1896		Calvin Atkins	Victoria Morris	Berryman & Martha Atkins	
15486	Atkins, Emaline	GA	1905		George Atkins	Viney Smith	Berryman & Martha Atkins	
15495	Atkins, Florence	GA	1885		Ben Atkins	Malinda Cowart	Berryman & Martha Atkins	
12040	Atkins, Francis	GA	1882		Webster Atkins	Malinda Carney	Berryman & Martha Atkins	Edmond & Elizabeth Carney
15494	Atkins, Freeman	GA	1893		George Atkins	Viney Smith	Berryman & Martha Atkins	
10548	Atkins, George	GA	1868	Vina Atkins	Berryman Atkins	Martha Corban		John & Delila Corban
15493	Atkins, George	GA	1887		Calvin Atkins	Victoria Morris	Berryman & Martha Atkins	
14921	Atkins, Harriet	GA	1842	Wm Atkins	Davis Sinard	Sarah Ellenberg	James & Margaret Sinard	John & Alice Ellenberg
15364	Atkins, Homer	GA	1896		Jim Atkins	Mary Haynes	Webster & Malinda Atkins	
11309	Atkins, James	GA	1869	Mary Atkins	Webster Atkins	Malinda Carney	Berryman & Martha Atkins	Edmond & Elizabeth Carney
11308	Atkins, John	GA	1882	Lela Atkins	Webster Atkins	Malinda Carney	Berryman & Martha Atkins	Edmond & Elizabeth Carney
15492	Atkins, Joseph	GA	1880		Calvin Atkins	Victoria Morris	Berryman & Martha Atkins	
15509	Atkins, Lester	GA	1887		Ben Atkins	Malinda Cowart	Berryman & Martha Atkins	
15508	Atkins, Lillie	GA	1894		Calvin Atkins	Victoria Morris	Berryman & Martha Atkins	
19967	Atkins, Louella	NC	1883	Cornelius Atkins		Augustus Williams		L.W. & Martha Williams
15507	Atkins, Mahala	GA	1876		Calvin Atkins	Victoria Morris	Berryman & Martha Atkins	

15506	Atkins, Marion	GA	1897		George Atkins	Viney Smith	Berryman & Martha Atkins	
15363	Atkins, May	GA	1894		Jim Atkins	Mary Haynes	Webster & Malinda Atkins	
15505	Atkins, Ola	GA	1899		Frank Atkins	Martha Smith	Berryman & Martha Atkins	
15362	Atkins, Olin	GA	1901		Jim Atkins	Mary Haynes	Webster & Malinda Atkins	
15504	Atkins, Patsy	GA	1898		George Atkins	Viney Smith	Berryman & Martha Atkins	
15503	Atkins, Pearl	GA	1904		Frank Atkins	Martha Smith	Berryman & Martha Atkins	
15502	Atkins, Perry	GA	1882	Ada Atkins	Calvin Atkins	Victoria Morris	Berryman & Martha Atkins	
15500	Atkins, Rosa	GA	1894		George Atkins	Viney Smith	Berryman & Martha Atkins	
15361	Atkins, Roy	GA	1906		John Atkins	Lela Harmon	Webster & Malinda Atkins	
15499	Atkins, Sallie	GA	1884		Calvin Atkins	Victoria Morris	Berryman & Martha Atkins	
15498	Atkins, Sam	GA	1900		Frank Atkins	Martha Smith	Berryman & Martha Atkins	
21401	Atkins, Sarah	AL	1862	William Atkins	James Faught	Mariah Sides	Samuel & Elizabeth Faught	
12041	Atkins, Solomon	GA	1877		Webster Atkins	Malinda Carney	Berryman & Martha Atkins	Edmond & Elizabeth Carney
11367	Atkins, Spartan	GA	1874		Webster Atkins	Martha Carney	Berryman & Martha Atkins	Edmond & Elizabeth Carney
15497	Atkins, Stephen	GA	1886		William Atkins	Harriet Sinyard	Berryman & Martha Atkins	
15496	Atkins, Thomas	GA	1873	Mary Atkins	Calvin Atkins	Victoria Morris	Berryman & Martha Atkins	
15484	Atkins, Velvie	GA	1889		Calvin Atkins	Victoria Morris	Berryman & Martha Atkins	
10547	Atkins, Webster	GA	1847	Malinda Atkins	Berryman Atkins	Martha Corban		John & Delila Corban
10546	Atkins, William	GA	1845	Hattie Atkins	Berryman Atkins	Martha Corban		John & Delila Corban
12382	Atkins, William	GA	1851	Dovey Atkins	Joseph Atkins	Martha Evans		Pleasant & Mahala Evans
4981	Atkinson, Julia	GA	1883	Albert Atkinson	John Pope	Sarah Jones		John & Lucinda Jones
6673	Atkinson, Maud	MO	1881	George Atkinson		Charlotte Sweaney		Levi & Myra Sweaney
8576	Atwood, Edward	VA	1876	Amanda Atwood	Nathaniel Atwood	Mary Osborn		David & Nancy Orsborn
8577	Atwood, Garnet	VA	1875	Louia Atwood	Nathaniel Atwood	Mary Osborn		Daniel & Nancy Orsborn
17932	Atwood, Mary	GA	1872	Z.T. Atwood	Enoch Newberry	Mary Aurburn		Alex & Mary Aurburn
17358	Auburn, Elizabeth et al	TN			John Auburn	Julia Cole	Samuel & Mary Auburn	Newton & Malinda Cole
11979	Audd, Flora	OK	1869	Richard Audd	Joseph Coodey	Mary Hardage	Joseph Coodey & Jane Ross	Joe & Muskogee Hardage
17979*	Austell, Ada	TN	1847	George Austell	Nathan Beavers	Hager Clausell		
17982*	Austell, Carrie	TN	1853	Rufus Austell	Cato Livoly	Manerva Joyce		Lucinda Joyce
17984*	Austell, George	TN	1832	Ada Austell	Morris Austell	Elizabeth Austell		

#	Name	State	Year	Spouse	Father	Mother	Paternal GP	Maternal GP
580	Austin, Edith	OK	1875	Clifford Austin	Daniel Janeway	Rachel Freeman	John & Nancy Janeway	Elijah & Nancy Freeman
14548	Austin, Marilda	GA	1864	Wm Austin (decd)	Thomas McClure	Amanda Millwood	J J & Marilda McClure	Hugh & Miram Millwood
14962	Austin, Nancy	TN	1876	George Austin	Lafayette Ogle	Jane Parten		Eli & Elizabeth Parten
14369	Auten, Tiney	NC	1884	Jac Auten	Green	Lucindy Dyson		Solomon & Polly Dyson
20296	Avants, A.J.	OK	1868	Ella Avants	Jack Avants	Becky Welsh		
17730	Avants, Calley	OK	1873	Nancy Avants	Thomas Avants	Frances Stovall	Peter Avants	Peter Stovall
22955	Avants, Charles	OK	1876	Ara Avants	James Avants	Susan Armstrong	Thos & Frances Avants	James & Susan Armstrong
7045	Avants, Eliza	OK	1879	William Avants	John Smith	Margaret Avants	John Smith	Joe Avants
923	Avants, James	AR	1851	Susan Avants	Thomas Avants	Francis Stovall	Peter Avants	Thomas Stovall
22820	Avants, James	OK	1884		James Avants	Susan Armstrong	Thomas & Fransis Avants	James & Susan Armstrong
7047	Avants, Jimmie	TX	1885	none	John Avant	Annie Rich	Thomas & Francis Avants	Leroy & Edith Rich
7046	Avants, John	TX	1850	Annie Avants	Thomas Avants	Francis Stovall	Peter Avants	
7050	Avants, Sterling	TX	1882	none	John Avants	Annie Rich	Thomas & Francis Avants	Leroy & Edith Rich
8201	Avants, Thomas	OK	1866	Amanda Avants	Thomas Avants	Frances Stovall		
3222	Avants, W.W.	OK	1842	Missouri Avants	John Avants	Elisebeth Sharp	Peter & Ellen Avants	John & Ellen Sharp
7048	Avants, William	OK	1869	Eliza Avants	Isaac Avants	Melinda Blanton	John Avants	John & Kisiah Blanton
15885	Avary, Alvin	TX	1887		John Avary	Harriett Whitter	W W & Tilitha Avary	Joel & Nancy Whitter
2323	Avary, Charlie	TX	1875	Josie Avary	John Avary	Harriett Whitten	Wilson & Telithie Avary	Joel & Nancy Whitten
2330	Avary, Harriett	OK	1846	John Avary	William Avary	Telitha Thomes	Jesse & Myram Avary	Luke & Polly Crumpton
10484	Avary, Robert	OK	1824	Sallie Avary	Jessie Avery	Myrom Crumpton	Robert & Gidy Avery	Luke & Pollie Crumpton
20598	Avery, Allen	TN	1873	Katie Avery	Allen Avery	Agnis Purcell	John & Susan Avery	John & Charity Purcell
20555	Avery, Christopher	GA	1883	Laura Avery	Allen Avery	Agnes Purcell	John & Susan Avery	John & Charity Purcell
14642	Avery, Isaac	TX	1841		Jessie Avery	Myron Crumpton		Luke Crumpton & Polley Duke
20557	Avery, John	TN	1871		Allen Avery	Agnes Purcell	John & Susan Avery	John & Charity Purcell
3507	Avery, Samuel	AL	1853	Josie Avery	Robert Avery	Sallie	Jessie Avery & Mirane Crumpton	John Thomas & Ruthie Cobb
13338	Ayers, Laura	GA	1879	Walter Ayers	Joseph Mason	Sarah Mason	John & Polly Mason	
374	Ayres, Bettie	OK	1857	widow	P.M. Buckner	Emily Weathersby		Geo Weathersby Betty Middleton
6382	Backus, Lottie	WV	1875	Alex Backus	Solomon Osburn	Susan Nichols	Elias & Sally Osburn	Wm Nichols & Betsy Boggs
6381	Backus, Mary	WV	1873	Johnathan Backus	Solomon Osburn	Susan Nichols	Elias & Sally Osburn	Wm Nichols & Betsy Boggs

10850	Bacon, Mattie	TX	1862	Charles Bacon	Ezra Morrison	Sophia Griffin	Wm & Nancy Morrison	Wm & Delilah Griffin
4114	Badger, Lottie	NC	1882	Felix Badger	James Thompson	Malvine Sullivan	Samuel & Marget Thompson	
21600	Badgett, Burrell	NC	1847	Martha Badgett	James Badgett	Elizabeth Winfrey	Abram & Mickey Badgett	Caleb & Mary Winfrey
21601	Badgett, Early	NC	22yrs		B.W. Badgett	Martha Pilson	James & Elizabeth Badgett	Moses & Betsy Pilson
20828*	Bagby, Mary	GA	1854	Richard Bagby	Squire Strickland	Harriet Fields	George & Joyce Tassell	Sylla Fields
19025	Baggle, Daniel	TN	1865	Louisa Baggle	Daniel Baggle	Annie Gallimor	Samuel Baggle & Lizzie Scott	David Gallimore & Susan Dupree
19024	Baggle, John	TN	1852	Louisa Baggle	Daniel Baggle	Annie Gallimor	Samuel Baggle & Annie Scott	David Gallimore & Susan Dupree
19026	Baggle, Thomas	TN	1856	Mary Baggle	Daniel Baggle	Annie Gallimor	Samuel Baggle & Lizzie Scott	David Gallimore & Susan Dupree
1019	Bagley, Clara	KS	1885	John Bagley	William Jones	Mary Stamper	Wm & Martha Jones	Eli & Susanna Stamper
1018	Bagley, Lota	KS	1906		John Bagley	Clara Jones	John & Eliza Bagley	Wm & Mary Jones
13879	Bagley, Mary	GA	1857	John Bagley	Jehu Streetman	Gilliam Bagley	John & Francis Streetman	Francis & Lucretia Strickland
10488	Bailey, Anna	WV	1855		Thomas Cook	Rebecca Sizemore		Ned Sizemore & Annie Bolden
756	Bailey, Arbazine	TX	43yrs	widow	Caleb Gaines	Sallie Alberty		Alberty
20289	Bailey, Artis	GA	1854	Margaret Bailey	James Bailey	Sarah Deverill	Zachariah & Malissa Bailey	John & Mary Deverill
13833	Bailey, Emma	OK	1885	James Bailey	Willie Smith	Addie Hendricks	Ned & Susie Smith	Joe & Ruth Goldeman
20290	Bailey, Francis	GA	1860	Alice Bailey	James Bailey	Sarah Deverill	Zachariah & Malissa Bailey	John & Mary Deverill
11823	Bailey, Frankie	TX	1852	C W Bailey	Numa Walker	Adline Sizemore	Chas Walker & Frankey Peters	John Sizemore & Franky Arms
12979	Bailey, J.B.	NV	1876		C W Bailey	F J C Walker	J & P Bailey	Numa & Adoline Walker
20291	Bailey, James	GA	1863	Lucy Bailey	James Bailey	Sarah Deverill	Zachariah & Malissa Bailey	John & Mary Deverill
6402	Bailey, Joseph	GA	62yrs	Benjamin Bailey			Joseph Baddy	
6405	Bailey, Julius	GA	27yrs	Amandy Bailey	Joseph Bailey		Benjamin Bailey	Joseph Braddy
19092	Bailey, Lela	MO	1880	W.T. Bailey	J.T. Johnson	Mary Holt		James Holt
17355	Bailey, Mary	MS	1846	Wm Bailey	John Morris	Didamie Trout	James & Katie Morris	James & Annie Trout
12981	Bailey, Melvin	TX	1885	Nora Bailey	C W Bailey	F J C Walker	J & P Bailey	Numa & Adoline Walker
6406	Bailey, Phillip	GA	25yrs	Dovey Bailey		Nancy Lequire	Benjamin Bailey	Joseph Braddy
12980	Bailey, W W	TX	1872	Clara Smith	C W Bailey	F J C Walker	J & P Bailey	Numa & Adoline Walker
21691	Baird, Mary	OK	1842	William Baird	John DeHart	Rebecca Seabolt		Adam & Annie Seabolt
21724	Baird, Willie et al	OK			Charles Baird	Mary Cockrell	Mary DeHart Baird	
16208	Baize, James	OK	1875	Maggie Baize	D P Baize	P M Hundley	J L & Mary Baize	Joseph & Mary Hundley
22123	Baize, Melvina	OK	1879	Hiram Baize	James Taylor	Annie Davison	Zebadee & Mary Taylor	Armstrong & Louisa Davison

16206	Baize, Patiashant	OK	1849	Peter Baize	Joseph Hundley	Mary Phelps	Jordan & Betsy Hundley	James & Nancy Phelps
9603	Baker, Benjamin	VA	1867	Josephine Baker	Peter Baker	Jane Goins	Benj & Tabitha Baker	Fed & Rhodie Goins
21291	Baker, Ellen	TX	1868	T.M. Baker	George Biddy	Edna McDonald	Elvin & Elizabeth Biddy	Tillman & Louise McDonald
12949	Baker, Elmira	GA	1859	William Baker	Jacob Cox	Delila McCaslin	Jacob Cox	
21875	Baker, Georgia	TN	1872	Thomas Baker	Thomas Colwell	Mary Glover	Joseph & Sarah Colwell	Wm & Clara Glover
19513	Baker, Grace	AR	1873	Samuel Baker	T.C. Hart	Ellen Quick		Nathan & Bettie Quick
15649	Baker, Harriet	GA	1850	D D Baker	Hudson Greenwood	Sophia Humphrey	Keowee Greenwood	Jane Humphrey
21050	Baker, Irene	MN	1890		James Baker	Elizabeth Duvall	Walter Baker & Susan Wanidisher	Thos & Hester Duvall
14285	Baker, John	NC	1852	Mary Baker	Absalom Baker	Peggie Poindexter	William Baker	John Poindexter
16937	Baker, John	NC	1876	Bettie Baker	John Baker	Mary Scales	A C & Peggie Baker	Joseph & Louisa Scales
21237	Baker, Laura	TX	1868	Elbert Baker	George Biddy	Edna McDonald	Elvin & Elizabeth Biddy	Tillman & Louise McDonald
3682	Baker, Martha	NC	1854	A M Baker	John Shook	Rebeca Nichelson		Amanna Nichelson
12219	Baker, Martha	NC						
22148	Baker, Matilda	AR	1858	George Baker	Peter Stout	Elizabeth Umphries	Sarah Prentice	Rebecah Fitsgerald
17985 *	Baker, Mattie	TN	1862	Ben Baker	Thomas Davidson	Julia Wildman	Ned & Meely Smith	Vina Winton
22869	Baker, Minnie	TN	1882	Luther Baker	William Headrick	Ella Haynes	Andrew & Eliza Headrick	Albert & Martha Haynes
9080	Baker, Sintha	NC	1876	W G Baker	James Blevins	Sarah Baker	George & Lydia Blevins	
13430	Baker, Thomas	TN	1884	Margaret Baker	A M Baker	Martha Shook	Samuel & Salinia Baker	John & Jane Shook
22311 *	Baldridge, Dick	OK	1885	Artie Baldridge	Jack Baldridge	Nancy Berlow	Kalooka Baldridge	Mary Baldridge
22317 *	Baldridge, John	OK	1886	none	Jack Baldridge	Nancy Barlow	Taloka Baldridge & Lettie Vann	John Barlow
11933	Baldridge, Sarah	KS	1841	John Baldridge	John Hudgins	Elizabeth Roe		
7968	Baldriedge, Charlie	NC	1894	none	Will Baldriedge	Juley Maney	Joseph Baldriedge	George & Elisebeth Maney
7967	Baldriedge, Juley	NC	1879	Will Baldriedge	George Maney	Elisebeth Anderson	John & Poley Maney	Jackson & Poley Anderson
3574	Baldwin, Alice	VA	1878	none	William Baldwin	Rosey Osborn	William & Margret Baldwin	
3569	Baldwin, Boyd	VA		none	William Baldwin	Rosy Osborn	William & Margret Baldwin	George & Catherine Osborn
13984	Baldwin, C.C.	NC	1876	Margret Baldwin	John Baldwin	Francis Kilby	Wm & Margret Baldwin	
2404	Baldwin, Cicero	VA	1860	Mattie Baldwin	Noah Baldwin	Mahala Blevins	Wm & Margaret Baldwin	Elisha & Elizabeth Blevins
13985	Baldwin, F.H.	NC	1861		John Baldwin	Francis Kilby	Wm & Margret Baldwin	
3571	Baldwin, George	VA			William Baldwin	Rosey Osborn	William & Margret Baldwin	George & Catharine Osborn
13988	Baldwin, J N	NC	1865	Rebecca Baldwin	John Baldwin	Francis Kilby	Wm & Margret Baldwin	

2914	Baldwin, James	VA	1861	Victoria Baldwin	Hiram Baldwin	Julia Osborn	W D & Margret Baldwin	James & Rachel Osborn
3572	Baldwin, Jasa	VA	1884	R B Baldwin	Jesse Baldwin	Caroline Kilby	Joseph Baldwin	Hilery Kilby
2875	Baldwin, Jefferson	VA	1861	Mary Baldwin	Hiram Baldwin	Julia Osborn	James & Rachel Osborn	Wm & Margaret Baldwin
3513	Baldwin, Jesse	NC	1855	A C Baldwin	J R Baldwin	Marilda Jones	Wm & Margaret Baldwin	
3511	Baldwin, John	VA	1865		Kiram Baldwin	Julia Osburn	W D & Margret Baldwin	James & Rachel Osburn
13989	Baldwin, John	NC	1837	Frances Baldwin	William Baldwin	Margret Stringer	Joseph Baldwin	Catherine Hart
3515	Baldwin, Joseph	NC	1831	Marilda Baldwin	William Baldwin	Margret Stringer	Joseph Baldwin	Catherine Hart
2876	Baldwin, Julia	VA	70yrs	Hiram Baldwin	James Osborn	Rachel Blevins	Elias & Salley Osborn	
1854	Baldwin, Martha	VA	50yrs	R.K. Baldwin	James Osborn	Rachel Blevins	Elias & Sallie Osborn	
5923	Baldwin, Martha	MO	1850		Caleb Hubbard		Hardy Hubbard	
3616	Baldwin, Mary	NC	1861		T J Baldwin	Elizabeth Jones	Wm & Margaret Baldwin	
19058	Baldwin, Mary	VA	1885	Wiley Baldwin	Wm Roop	Mary Finley	Wm & Margaret Baldwin	
2403	Baldwin, Myrtle	VA		none	Cicero Baldwin	Mattie Garris	Noah & Mahala Baldwin	Wiley & Rebecca Garris
22548	Baldwin, Neola	NC	1886	none	Jesse Baldwon	Caroline Kelly	J R & Matilda Baldwin	
3464	Baldwin, Plymouth	NC	1868	Etta Baldwin	T J Baldwin	Elizabeth Jones	W D & Marget Baldwin	Regin & Polly Jones
1529	Baldwin, Polly	MO	1859	widow	William Brown	Lucinda Swadley	Isom Brown	Matilda Tindle
3617	Baldwin, Rachel	NC		none	T J Baldwin	Elizabeth Jones	Wm & Margaret Baldwin	
3512	Baldwin, Reason	NC		Martha Baldwin	J R Baldwin	Marilda Jones	Wm & Margaret Baldwin	
3570	Baldwin, Reece	VA				Rosey		George Osborn
5075	Baldwin, Robert	VA	1871	Nancy Baldwin	William Baldwin	Rosey Osborn	Wm & Margret Baldwin	Geo & Catharine Osborn
3517	Baldwin, Roby	NC		Malinda Baldwin	J R Baldwin	Marilda Jones	Wm & Margaret Baldwin	
3573	Baldwin, Rosa	VA	1843	William Baldwin	George Osborn	Catherine Taylor	Elias & Salley Osborn	
5077	Baldwin, Rosa	VA	1880	Wiley Baldwin	Marion Weaver	Frona Roten	Wm & Catharine Weaver	W. & Catharine Roten
1853	Baldwin, Ruben	VA	1852	Martha Baldwin	Wm Baldwin	Margret Stamper	Joseph Baldwin & Catharine Holt	
3620	Baldwin, Thos	NC	1837		Wm Baldwin		Joseph Baldwin	Catharine Hart
13986	Baldwin, W.S.	NC	1863	Celie Baldwin	John Baldwin	Francis Kilby	Wm & Margret Baldwin	
1855	Baldwin, Wiley	VA						

5078	Baldwin, Wiley	VA	37yrs	Rosa Baldwin	Wm Baldwin	Rosa Osborn	Wm & Margret Baldwin	Geo & Catharine Osborn
3514	Baldwin, William	NC		Ellin Baldwin	J R Baldwin	Marilda Jones	Wm & Margret Baldwin	
3568	Baldwin, William	VA	1845	Roby Baldwin	William Baldwin	Margret Stringer	Joseph Baldwin	Catherine Hart
20467	Bales, Alison	TN	1881	Mary Bales	Joseph Bales	Evaline Cagle	John & Fannie Bales	Peter & Elizabeth Cagle
18233	Bales, Evaline	TN	1851	Joseph Bales	Peter Cagle	Elizabeth Henson	Jacob & Ruthy Cagle	Thomas & Nancy Henson
20466	Bales, Joseph	TN	1872	Malinda Bales	Joseph Bales	Evaline Cagle	John & Fannie Bales	Peter & Elizabeth Cagle
20678	Bales, Rebecca	TN	1876	William Bales	William Reed Jr.	Nancy Murray	McKenzie & Nancy Reed	James & Jane Murray
11179	Bales, Jefferson et al	OK			David Bales	Matilda Dew	Caleb & Jincy Bales	
19074	Ball, Ida	TX	1857	S.L. Ball	W.A. Crawford	M.L. Starr		Joshua
16219	Ballard, Emily	OK	1859	Mathew Ballard	Alex Brownfield	Mary Sameritan	Sam	Tarrie
14423	Ballard, Mira	NC	1850	R T Ballard	Robert Holcomb	Sallie Maney	Henry & Fanny Holcomb	John & Polly Maney
22073	Ballard, R.B.	OK		none	Willie Ballard	Mittie Toliver	Mathew Ballard	Emer Ballard
22072	Ballard, Willie	OK	1877	Presilla Ballard	Mathew Ballard	Emly Brownfield		
10624	Ballew, Eliza	GA	1860	K A Ballew		Nancy Good		Eliza Good
22790	Ballew, Louiza	GA	1884		John Mathis	Loucinda Coggins	Jane Mathis	
10203	Ballou, Thomas	VA	1859	Sallie Ballou	Hugh Ballou	Eliza Stamper	Blake & Patsy Ballou	Eli & Susanna Stamper
1014	Bange, Jim	TN	1869	Maggie Bange	William Bange	Susan Gallimore	John Bange	Tom & Nancy Gallimore
4756	Banks, Jane	GA	1854	Brice Banks	U.H. Summany	Mary Helton		Hile & Clarissa Helton
5408	Banks, Jane	GA		Brice Banks	Henry Summey	Mary Helton	George & Barbra Summey	Jake & Clerecy Helton
17736	Bankson, Matilda	TN	1851	John Bankston	Eli Corbin	Dinelia Rogers	Thos Corbin	
20294	Banta, J.F.	TX	1885		Jeff Banta	Mollie Avants	Isaac Banta	A.J. Avants
13273	Bar nos ky, Darnie	OK	1885	Consene Bar nos ky	Mohawk Beaver	Mollie Simmons	Runabout & Cah le so ya sky	Go lee cha
8385	Barbee, Della	OK		John Barbee	Wesley Boyd	Sallie Yeates		Benj & Elizabeth Yeates
20292	Barber, Amanda	OK	1874	W.A. Barber	J.A. Short	Mary McFarber	Michael Short	
2368	Barber, Austin	WA	1859	Ida Barber	J J Barber	Joanah Petty		
5449	Barber, George	OK	1884	Birdie Barber	Joel Barber	Attie Swinney	Isaac & Joanah Barber	
2012	Barber, James	OK	1877	Ida Barber	Isaac Barber	Joanah Petty		Elizabeth Petty
1306	Barber, Joanah	TX	1835	Isaac Barber	John Petty	Elizabeth Dawson		Samuel Dawson & Polly Rogers
2014	Barber, Joel	OK	1856	Attie Barber	Isaac Barber	Joanah Petty		
17643	Barber, Johnson	OK	1855	Jennie Barber	Peter Barber	Ge-yo-he		

5397	Barber, Tol	OK	1882	Vella Barber	Joel Barber	Attie Swinney	Isaac & Joanah Barber	
18504	Barber, William	CO						
9024	Barbour, Claire	IN		Ruskin Barbour	William Allen	Hannah Stephens	Samuel & Martha Allen	
6342	Barclay, Elisabeth	AL	1867	J W Barclay	Ben Bryars	Lucretia Miles		Nellie Miles
11816	Bare, Canyada	NC	1869	John Bare	Ephrim Osborne	America Osborne	Jesse & Cyntha Osborne	Joseph & Susie Bare
6880	Bare, Mary	VA	1885	Nelson Bare	Wilburn Parker	Mary Lewis		Andrew & Biddy Lewis
11094	Bare, Meca	VA	1856	Noah Bare	Jessie Blevins	Catherine Pennington	Eli & Millie Blevins	
6163	Barker, Alice	NC	1871	Alfred Barker	William Jones	Nancy Phipps	Thos & Elisabeth Jones	Ahart & Maryan Phipps
4577	Barker, Eli	NC	1850	Mary Barker	William Barker	Betty Blevins	Edward & Vina Barker	Eli & Milly Blevins
16899	Barker, Elvira	OK		William Barker	? Mayfield	Sarah Starr		
9579	Barker, Ettie	VA	1873	Calvin Barker	Robert Phipps	Emily Price	Ahart & Maryann Phipps	Alfred & Tildy Price
5005	Barker, Jennie	OK	1881	none	William Barker	Sallie Christie		Bill & Betsey Christie
11241	Barker, John	IN	1861		Elihu Barker	Hannah Allen		John & Martha Allen
2607	Barker, Lizzie	GA	1880	Jalish Barker	Drury Campbell	Rebecca Earley	Henderson & Susanah Campbell	
6138	Barker, Lyddia	NC	1875	Hampton Barker	James Blevins	Louisa Sullen	Eli & Milly Blevins	Joseph & Malinda Sullen
4827	Barker, Lydia	NC	1835	Montgomery Barker	Allen Clark	Betsey Blevins		James & Lydia Blevins
2093	Barker, Martha	NC	1874	L C Barker	G D Blevins	Celia Parsons	Daniel & Anna Blevins	Wm & Rutha Parsons
8564	Barker, Mary	NC	37yrs	decd	Thomas Barker	Mary Blevins		Daniel & Amy Blevins
6139	Barker, Meacy	NC	1860	W F Barker	Alfred Blevins	Marjary Sheets	James & Meacy Blevins	Joseph & Elisebeth Hudler
10969	Barker, Minnie	NC	1877	C C Barker	John Spencer	Martha Anderson	Solomon & Nellie Spencer	
20767*	Barker, Polline	GA	1880		H. Barker	Sarah Ledbetter		Jack & Linda Ledbetter
4578	Barker, Reece	NC	1885		Eli Barker	Mary Porter	Wm & Betty Barker	Riley & Melyndia Porter
15360*	Barker, Sarah	GA	86yrs	Hamp Barker	Josh Ledbetter	Lindy Limous	Nancy Ledbetter	July Limous
21606	Barker, Susannah	NC	1845	Solomon Barker	Kennie Hale	Celie Hale	Katie Clark	Jennie Hale
20687	Barks, Maggie	FL	1876	Joe Barks	Jacob Taylor	Malissa Kimbrough	Richard & Susan Taylor	Hiram & Nancy Kimbrough
22917	Barlow, Arthur	AR	1881		Ransom Barlow	Mary Robertson	Samuel & Sarah Barlow	Thos & Hepsey Robertson
17705	Barlow, Mary	AR	1851	Ransom Barlow	Thomas Robertson	Hopsey Surles		Betsy Surles
22502*	Barlow, Mintie	OK	1833	John Barlow	Andrew Johnson	Eliza Vann		
11093	Barlow, Nancy	VA	1844	Mikel Barlow	Jessie Blevins	Catherine Pennington	Eli & Millie Blevins	

14359	Barnard, George	MO	1850	Senora Barnard	Sterling Barnard	Nancy Mason	John Barnard & Betsy Griffin	John & Elizabeth Mason
14360	Barnard, Joseph	MO		widower	Sterling Barnard	Nancy Mason	John Barnard & Betsy Griffin	John & Elizabeth Mason
3753	Barnard, Robert	OK	1856	Alice Barnard	Sterling Barnard	Nancy Mason	John Barnard	
8430	Barnes, Annie	MO	1864	George Barnes	R. Wilson Fender	Louisa Wallace	Daniel & Dicie Fender	
4971	Barnes, Artemincy	GA	1880	Charley Barnes	Wade Ross	Margaret		
18796	Barnes, Delilah	AL	1844	Wm Barnes	Benj Raines	Fannie Raines	Nancy Raines	John & Delilah Raines
19968	Barnes, Effie	NC	23 yrs	Walter Barnes	Haywood Fulk	Rebecca Randleman	Leonard & Nancy Scott	John Randleman
13387	Barnes, Ellen	OK	1842	Dock Barnes	Mullen			
14721	Barnes, Ellen	OK	1875	John Barnes	Isaac Boyd	Ellen Justice	Frank Boyd	Isaac Justice & Charity Mason
20427	Barnes, Henry	TN	1872	Ada Barnes	Doc Barnes	Ellen Mullinax		
20428	Barnes, Jacob	TN	1861	Clora Barnes	Doc Barnes	Ellen Mullinax		
15982	Barnes, James	OK	1861	Mary Barnes	W M Barnes	Charlotte Gafford	John & Tempie Barnes	Nancy Gafford
4967	Barnes, Louisa	GA	1885	Brit Barnes	George Blaylock	Marsha Taylor	D K Blaylock	Manba Taylor
21475	Barnes, Macy	TX	1886	J.W. Barnes	James Graham	? Fullbright		
6750	Barnett, Alman	OK	1875	Minnie Barnett	Jesse Barnett	Salina Foreman		Joe & Lethia Foreman
21240	Barnett, Anna	OK	1848	William Barnett	James Slater	Margaret Moore	Jeremiah Slater	Margaret Moore
21241	Barnett, Charles	OK	1872		William Barnett	Anna Slater		James & Margaret Slater
12478	Barnett, George	OK			Jesse Barnett	Salina Forman		Joe & Letha Forman
5141	Barnett, James	AR	1873	Laura Barnett	Jessie Barnett	Salina Foreman	John & Nancy Barnett	Joseph & Letha Foreman
14547	Barnett, John	GA	1872	Lula Barnett	E C Barnett	Haley Evans		Robt & Sallie Evans
20829	Barnett, Marcus	GA	1880	Jessie Barnett	Ebenezer Barnett	Haley Evans		Robert & Sallie Evans
20830	Barnett, Margaret	GA	1885		Ebenezer Barnett	Haley Evans		Robert & Sallie Evans
20831	Barnett, Riley	GA	1870	Annie Barnett	Ebenezer Barnett	Haley Evans		Robert & Sallie Evans
10887	Barnett, Robert	OK		Sarah Barnett	Jessie Barnett	Salina Foreman	John & Nancy Barnett	Joseph & Leatha Foreman
20832	Barnett, Robert	GA	1878	Annie Barnett	Ebenezer Barnett	Haley Evans		Robert & Sallie Evans
19341	Barnett, Roy	GA	1905		Riley Barnett	Annie Wimberly	Ebeneezer & Haley Barnett	Talmage Wimberly
20833	Barnett, William	GA	1868	Mattie Barnett	Ebenezer Barnett	Haley Evans		Robert & Sallie Evans
6098	Barns, Julie	NC	1871	Edward Barns	Robbert Phipps	Caroline Yates	Benjamin & Ruthy Phipps	Eli & Nancy Yates
20768	Barnwell, Ann	GA	1862	Floyd Barnwell	James Whitmire	Jane Cagle	Chris & Nancy Whitmire	
20769	Barnwell, Bunyon	GA	1894		Floyd Barnwell	Ann Whitmire		James & Jane Whitmire
20770	Barnwell, Claud	GA	1883		Floyd Barnwell	Ann Whitmire		James & Jane Whitmire

20771	Barnwell, Edna	GA	1900		Floyd Barnwell	Ann Whitmire		James & Jane Whitmire
20772	Barnwell, Ethel	GA	1890		Floyd Barnwell	Ann Whitmire		James & Jane Whitmire
20773	Barnwell, Eunice	GA	1903		Floyd Barnwell	Ann Whitmire		James & Jane Whitmire
20774	Barnwell, Gordon	GA	1887		Floyd Barnwell	Ann Whitmire		James & Jane Whitmire
20775	Barnwell, Mattie	GA	1897		Floyd Barnwell	Ann Whitmire		James & Jane Whitmire
20776	Barnwell, Millard	GA	1882		Floyd Barnwell	Ann Whitmire		James & Jane Whitmire
20777	Barnwell, Willie	GA	1892		Floyd Barnwell	Ann Whitmire		James & Jane Whitmire
7071	Barrett, W. R.	TX	1873	Clemma Barrett	V C Barrett	Delpha Williams		Louis & Lucinda Williams
4986	Barrett, Addie	GA	1876	Thomas Barrett	John Pope	Sarah Jones		John & Lucinda Jones
13608	Barrett, Addie	GA	1906		Thomas Barrett	Addie	John Poe	John Watley
7083	Barrett, Alice	OK	1869	none	V C Barrett	Delpha Williams	Louis & Lucinda Williams	
14744	Barrett, Blackburn	WV	1877	Martha Barrett	James Barrett	Phoebe Sizemore		Wilburn & Clarinda Sizemore
15359	Barrett, Carrie	GA	1881	Carl Barrett	William Dover	Margaret Evans	Wm & Alantha Dover	
14358	Barrett, Delpha	OK	1849	V C Barrett	Louis Williams	Lucinda Privett	Marten Williams	Naoma Privett
15358	Barrett, Emily	GA	1834	Andrew Barrett	Christopher Whitmire	Nancy Reece	Samuel & Polly Whitmire	Jacob Reece
9779	Barrett, Joel	NC	1866	none	Jackson Barrett	Mary Hensley	Thos & Kaziah Barrett	John Brigmond & Lucinda Hensley
7069	Barrett, Katey	OK	1880	none	V C Barrett	Delpha Williams		Louis Williams
9780	Barrett, Kittie	NC	1876	none	Jackson Barrett	Mary Hensley	Thos & Kaziah Barrett	John Brigmond & Lucinda Hensley
19754	Barrett, Laura	GA	1885	Author Barrett	Milton Loggins	Lizzie Hughes	Martin & Laura Loggins	Nathen & Viney Hughes
20154	Barrett, Mary	GA	1889	Henry Barrett	Pink Brown	Eliza McAllister	Bill & Martha Brown	Charley & Nancy McAllister
7070	Barrett, Nancy	TX	1871	Lee Baltimore	V C Barrett	Delpha Williams		Louis & Lucinda Williams
15357	Barrett, Ollie	GA	1879	Melvin Barrett	John Edge	Sarah Spears		Josiah & Martha Spears
18870	Barrett, Sallie	GA	1876	Saul Barrett	William McCauley	Amanda Toldeu		
10434	Barrett, William	NC	1873		Jackson Barrett	Maryan Hensley	Thos & Keziah Barrett	Lucinday Hensley
22697	Barron, Eli	AL	1852	Mandy Barron	Jim Barron	Martha Walls		Billy & Becky Walls
4450	Barry, Lizzie	OK	1879	Kidder Barry	S L Hughes	Gracie Tidwell	J R & Mahala Hughes	John & Lucecy Tidwell
17704	Barthell, Emely	OK	1856	Joseph Barthell	George Lloyd	Jane Turner	Thos & Susan Lloyd	Wm & Margret Turner
13987	Barton, Effie	WV	1874	James Barton	John Baldwin	Francis Kilby	Wm & Margret Baldwin	
21492	Barton, Zelma	TX	1883	J.R. Barton	? Fletcher	Martha Colston		Mary Colston
14052	Bass, Charles	WI			Samuel Bass	Elija Murphy	Elija & Tilda Bass	George & Becky Murphy

17569	Bass, Clifford	WI	1884		Samuel Bass	Eliza Murphy	Elijah & Matilda Bass	George & Becka Murphy
17657	Bass, Elijah Jr.	WI	1835	Elizabeth Bass	Elijah Bass	Matilda Dutton	Willis & Olive Bass	Zachariah & Mary Dutton
17660	Bass, Elizabeth	WI	1842	Elijah Bass Jr.	Dewey Arnold	Emily Peters	Docia Arnold	Emily Peters
7078	Bass, James	OK	1864	Theodicia Bass	James Bass	Margaret Miller		
7079	Bass, James	OK	1827	Maggie Bass	Samuel Bass	Mary Stockton		Joseph Stockton
17659	Bass, Mansfield	WI	1870	Hilda Bass	Elijah Bass	Elizabeth Arnold	Elijah & Matilda Bass	Drewry & Emily Arnold
17656	Bass, Martha	WI	1878	William Bass	Samuel Bass	Eliza Murphy	Elijah & Matilda Bass	George & Rebeca Murphy
18015	Bass, Ransom	WI	1862	Myrtle Bass	Elijah Bass	Elizabeth Arnold	Elijah & Matilda Bass	
19825	Bass, Rosa	WI			Samuel Bass	Elisa Murphy	Elijah & Matilda Bass	George & Rebecky Murphy
17661	Bass, William	WI	1864	Martha Bass	Elijah Bass	Elizabeth Arnold	Elijah & Matilda Bass	Drewry & Emily Arnold
18222	Bass, William	TN	1872		Joseph Bass	Martha Grimes		Allen & Caroline Grimes
19594 *	Bassett, Louetta	IN	1882	Ithamer Bassett	Henry Marshall	Elizabeth Milton	Henry Marshall & Polly Roper	Bolden Milton & Elizabeth Scott
21014	Bassett, Nancy	CA	1861		Vance Evans	Mahala Joy		
21266	Bateman, Cora	TX	1867	William Bateman	Frank Jeter	Adlia Thompson	G.w. Jeter & Mary Coplin	
19712	Bateman, Etta	TN	1871	Dovy Bateman	Thomas Hooper	Ritty Hatcher		Robert & Mary Hatcher
5826	Bateman, Jacob	NC	1849	Celia Bateman	A. Bateman	Mahala Tramel		William Tramel
5825	Bateman, Thomason	NC	1874	Moley Bateman	J N Bateman	Tildie Jones	A & Mahala Bateman	Jacob Tramel & Pollie Hogs
21911 *	Bates, Alexander	TN	1874	Fannie Bates	Nathan Bates	Rebecca Scott		Abram & Fanny Scott
21927 *	Bates, Lee	TN	1876		Rubin Scott	Fany Parks	Nathan & Rebecca Bates	Annie Parks
22189	Bates, Malinda	TX	1867	Thomas Bates	David Ward	Nancy Martin	Lee & Nancy Ward	James & Elizabeth Martin
21931 *	Bates, Oliver	TN	1886	Cinnie Bates	Nathan Bates	Rebecca Scott		Abram & Fannie Scott
20286	Bates, Pheoby	TX	1872	Irie Bates	James Mayden	Nancy Christman	Lewis & Pheoby Mayden	
20066 *	Bates, Sim	TN	1851	Sarah Bates	Nathan Bates	Becky Scott	George	Abraham & Fanny Scott
16894	Battle, Ada	OK	1841	H A Battle	John Tidwell	Lucresa Temperence	Young Deer	
18176	Baublits, Anna	CO	1884	Raymond Baublits	Thomas Cordill	Sally Baker		Lucy Huff
7051	Baughman, Lela	TX	1884	John Baughman	James Stone	Sarah Hunter		Willy & Sarah Hunter
9023	Baunhofer, Mary	OK	1877	Louis Baunhofer	Elicy Stillwell	Abigal Elmore		Anderson Elmore
9095	Baxter, Elizabeth	WV	1873	John Baxter	Samuel Mullens	Rebecca Pain	Samuel Mullen	James Pain
15045 *	Baxter, Jane	GA	75yrs	widow	Bush Lowry	Jane Sims		
10290	Bayne, Cora	OK	1875		George Price	Julia Rushing	Joseph Price	James & Cormelia Rushing
8223	Bays, David	OK	1836	Precious Bays	Joshua Bays	Emley Burch	Josia & Letta Bays	Joseph & Mila Burch

12085	Bays, David	OK	1872	Maggie Bays	David Bays	Precious Jones	Joshua & Emley Bays	Samuel & Susan Jones
7072	Bays, Ella	OK	42yrs	Wm Bays (decd)	Walter Bays	Francis Robison	Joseph & Carrie Bays	Wm & Ellen Robison
20121	Bays, Fred	NE	1891		Alfred Bays	Eva Hawes	Josiah & Leta Bays	
20236	Bays, George	KS	1877	Ida Bays	Alfred Bays	Josephine Polly	Josiah Bays & Letta Mays	
14357	Bays, James	IN	1845	Ibby Bays	Jackson Bays	Elizabeth Hutchins	Joe & Lettie Bays	
21058	Bays, James	NV	1872	none	Alfred Bays	Josephine Polly	Joshua & Letta Bays	
6986	Bays, Joshua	MO	1844	Emma Bays	Joshua Bays	Embley Burch	Josiah & Lettie Bays	Joseph & Millie Burch
8224	Bays, Josiah	IL	1875	Lizzie Bays	Neal Bays	Sarah Bilyen	Joshua & Elizabeth Bays	John & Elizabeth Bilyen
12084	Bays, Lizzie	CO	1877		Nemal Bays	Sarah Bilyen	Joshua & Emley Bays	John & Elizabeth Bilyen
7074	Bays, Walter	OK	1844	Francis Bays	Joseph Bays	Carrie Burch	Josiah & Letta Bays	Joseph & Millie Burch
7073	Bays, Wiley	OK	1878	Mary Bays	Walter Bays	Francis Robison	Joseph & Carrie Bays	Wm & Ellen Robison
21444	Beacham, Mertie	TX	1875	J.B. Beacham	Joseph Litchfield	Sarah Elder		
6551	Beal, David	GA	1853		John Beal	Nancy Proctor	Jad Proctor	
6547	Beal, Joseph	GA	1849		John Beal	Nancy Proctor		Joe Proctor
20943	Beam, Amanda et al	AL	1889		David Beam	Mary Wilabay		Elizabeth Davidson
21011	Beam, Christopher	AL	1885		David Beam	Mary Wilabay		Elizabeth Davidson
19075	Beam, Elizabeth	AR	1830	David Beam	Hilliard Davis	Becca Tonie		Elizabeth Tonie
21010	Beam, John	AL	1875	Dicy Beam	David Beam	Mary Wilabay		Elizabeth Davidson
9573	Beam, Mary	AL	1855	David Beam	John Wilabay	Rebecca Davidson		James & Elizabeth Davidson
21009	Beam, William	AL	1876	Mary Beam	David Beam	Mary Wilabay		Elizabeth Davidson
22175	Beaman, Florence	AL	1867	James Beaman	Richard McGee	Victoria Weaterford	Billy McGee	Alex & Polly Weatherford
9281	Beamer, Sam	OK		none	Oohelook	Orlstertee		
22210 *	Bean Leander	OK	1850	Phyllis Bean	Jack Bean	Mary Martin		Harry Martin
22494 *	Bean, Arthur	OK	1841	Louisa Bean	Sandy Bean	Rachel Adair		George & Aniky Martin
22407 *	Bean, Frances	OK	1850	widow	Simon Sanders	Sarah Chambers	Daniel Sanders	
22275 *	Bean, Ida	OK	1867	John Bean	Wilson Martin	Patsy Martin	Charles & Mary Martin	Ezekiel Belin & Lydia Cochran
22498 *	Bean, Joseph	OK	1842	Amy Bean	Sandy Bean	Rachel Adair		George & Aniky Martin
17042	Bean, Mariah	AR		David Bean	Hiliar Davis	Tonie Davis		Elizabeth Tonie
20234 *	Bean, Richard	TN	1847	Matilda Bean	Belser Largen	Susan Bean		
1785	Bean, Susan	OK	56yrs	Jack Bean	Watt Sanders	Betsy Sanders	Sanders	Jennie
22337 *	Bean, Tobias	NC	1837	Jane Bean	Sandy Bean	Rachel Martin		George & Annaka Martin

14719	Bear Wool, George	OK	1879		Sine Bear Wool	Betsy Youngbird		
18624	Beard, Martha	TN	1852	Henry Beard	George Payne	Patsy Hayden	George & Sallie Payne	Dennis & Susan Hayden
21890	Bearden, Flora	GA	1887	Selemon Bearden	Timothy Miller	Mary Haggard	John & Charity Miller	David & Martha Haggard
14867	Bearden, Sarah	GA	1839	Williby Bearden	Jesse Burrell	Mourning Brown	W & Rebecca Burrell	Andy Brown
19960	Beasley, Charley	NC	1891		Mat Beasley	Lear Goins	Thomas Beasley	James Goins & Miley Moran
21008	Beasley, Emaly	AL	1842	James Beasley	John Sims	Mary Scisom	John & Elizabeth Sims	Joe Cisom
20320	Beasley, James	NC	1887		Mat Beasley	Lear Goins	Thomas Beasley	James & Miley Goins
21012	Beasley, Sarah	AL	1869		James Beasley	Emley Sims	Wm & Liza Beasley	John & Mary Sims
13283	Beaver, Ah lee che	OK	1890		Mohawk Beaver	Mollie Simmons	Runabout & Cah le so ya sky	Go lee cha
13153	Beaver, Dora	OK	1890		Lemuel Beaver	Lucy Simmons	Beaver	Jess Simmons
13111	Beaver, Eliza	OK	1883		Lemuel Beaver	Lucy Simmons		Jess Simmons
13130	Beaver, Lesley	OK	1883	Susie Beaver	Mohawk Beaver	Mollie Simmons	Runabout & Cah lee as ya sky	
15850	Beaver, Louisa	MO		H A Beaver	Robert Buler	Penelope Shelton		
13220	Beaver, Lucy	OK	1858	Lemuel Beaver	Jess Simmons	La sah	Woxe Simmons	
13221	Beaver, Maggie	OK	1896		Lemuel Beaver	Lucy Simmons	Beaver	Jess Simmons
13803	Beaver, Mollie	OK	1847	Mohawk Beaver	Wilson	Nancy		
13217	Beaver, Sallie	OK	1882	Clem Beaver	J Hully	Polly	Jess Simmons	Ah da yo le
13154	Beaver, Sam	OK	1891		Lemuel Beaver	Lucy Simmons	Beaver	Jess Simmons
13282	Beaver, Washington	OK	1874		Mohawk Beaver	Mollie Simmons	Runabout & Cah le so ya sky	Go lee cha
2609	Beavers, Bascom	GA	1874	Effie Beaver	John Beaver	Mary Davenport		John & Elisabeth Davenport
2608	Beavers, Columbus	GA	1867	Rosey Beavers	John Beaver	Mary Davenport		John & Elisabeth Davenport
21408	Beavers, John	OK	1861	Minnie Beavers	Barry Beavers	Ann Watson	John Beavers	John Watson
10623	Beavers, Josephine	GA			James Flood	Margaret Tyler		Daniel & Elisabeth Tyler
2606	Beavers, Mary	GA	1836	John Beaver	John Davenport	Elisabeth Long		Josiah & Nancy Long
21409	Beavers, Minnie	TX	1874	John Beavers	William Heaton	Mary Phillips		
19514	Beck, Alberta	AR	1884	G.H. Beck	T.O. Hill	Ellen Quick		Nathan & Bettie Quick
22256	Beck, Ben	OK	1846	Bettie Beck	George Drumgene	Sarah Muskrat		
15356	Beck, Cooper	GA	1886		Jeffrey Beck	Mandy Loggins	Coleman Davis & Elmira Beck	
18960	Beck, Ida	AR	1877	Butterford Beck	Hamilton Burtin	Elizabeth Maney		Martin & Polly Maney
15355	Beck, Jeffrey	GA	1879		Jeffrey Beck	Mandy Loggins	Coleman Davis & Elmira Beck	
15354	Beck, Johnie	GA	1891		Jeffrey Beck	Mandy Loggins	Coleman Davis & Elmira Beck	

11341	Beck, Martin	GA	1849	Wilma Beck	Coleman Davis	Elmira Beck	Daniel & Rachel Davis	
15353	Beck, Namon	GA	1885		Jeffrey Beck	Mandy Loggins	Coleman Davis & Elmira Beck	
18237	Beck, Solomon	GA	1853	Sarah Beck	Jesse Beck	Ellen League		
18758	Beck, William	AR	1847	Nannie Beck	William Beck	Mary Long		
13537*	Becks, Maria	MI	1862	Thornton Becks	Alfred Weaver	Charity Revels	Bird & Sarah Weaver	McCagy & Mornon Revels
19464	Bedwell, Jessey	TN	1895	Sarah Bedwell	Jessey Bedwell	Darus Collins	John Bedwell	
14242	Bedwell, Pleasant	TN	1843	Marry Bedwell	Jessie Bedwell	Darcus Foamens		
17889	Beeler, Bertha	MO			Robert Beeler	P.J. Shelton	Daniel & Larina Beeler	Ralph & Anna Shelton
20293	Beeler, J.W.	MO	1877	Eva Beeler	Robert Beeler	P.J. Shelton		
14951	Beeler, Penelope	MO		Robert Beeler	Ralph Shelton	Anna Taylor		
11834	Beeman, Wm et al	GA	1879		Joseph Jones	Rachel Phillips		
7085	Beeson, Luella	TX	1887	Joseph Beeson	William Rowell	Martha Terral	David Rowell & Mary Fountain	Joseph & Matilda Terrell
11618	Belcher, Cora	WV	1888	Robert Belcher	Augustus Bailey	Annie Cook	Floyd & Zelpha Bailey	Thos & Rebecca Cook
17855	Belcher, John	WA	1856	Louisa Belcher	Benj Belcher	Susanah Lester	Wm Belcher & Asa Kingery	Abner Lester & Rebecca Whitt
3893	Belew, Govnor	OK	1833	Maggie Belew	Sam Belew	Mary Bryant		John Bryant
19664	Bell, America	OK				Emily Bell		
14245	Bell, Benjamin	AR	1856	Maggie Bell	William Bell	Nancy Harison	Duke Flax	Ned Harison & Lucinda Wilks
21139*	Bell, Charles	AL	1882	Queeny Bell	Thomas Bell	Mintu Thompson	Norham & Mary Bell	
15345	Bell, Cleveland	GA	1885	Retter Bell	Martin Bell	Hulda Dover		Wm & Alantha Dover
1661	Bell, Columbus	TN	1855	Mary Bell	David Bell	Alzira Williams	Robert & Sallie Bell	Wm & Polly Williams
15344	Bell, George	GA	1895		Martin Bell	Hulda Dover		Wm & Alantha Dover
22192*	Bell, George	OK	1860	Margaret Bell	Armstarel Phillips	Anica Thompson		July Lynch & Hanah Thompson
15343	Bell, Geranie	GA	1893		Martin Bell	Hulda Dover		Wm & Alantha Dover
22814	Bell, Green	AL	1882	Mollie Bell	Lafayett Bell	Nancy Halcomb		Wm & Sara Halcomb
15342	Bell, Hulda	GA	1870	Martin Bell	William Dover	Alantha Chambers		Jim & Polly Chambers
10796	Bell, J H	GA	1877	Gustie Bell	J S Bell		Jim & Elizebeth Bell	Henry Ditmore
2833	Bell, James	NC	1843	Mary Bell	David Bell	Alzira Williams	Robert & Sally Bell	William & Polly Williams
17284	Bell, James	TX	1866	Julia Bell	Robert Bell	Lucinda Hampton	J.M. & Ellisibeth Bell	G.W. & Mary Hampton
22156	Bell, James	AL	1874	Claudie Bell	Lafayette Bell	Nancy Holcomb	Ira & Jane Bell	William & Sarah Holcomb
17494	Bell, John	AR	1867	Martha Bell		Marie Bell		Wm & Nancy Bell
20834*	Bell, John	GA	1874	Eva Bell	Jack Bell	Eliza Roe	Jesperson & Omly Dobbs	Richard & Caroline Roe
22347*	Bell, July	OK	45yrs	none	Umph Cunningham	Annaka Cunninham		Hannah Cunningham
15341	Bell, Lizzie	GA	1883		Martin Bell	Hulda Dover		Wm & Alantha Dover

22236	Bell, Lorenzo	AL	1880	Cora Bell	Lafayett Bell	Nancy Holcomb	Ira & Jane Bell	William & Sarah Holcomb
15340	Bell, Lucillus	GA	1891		Martin Bell	Hulda Dover		Wm & Alantha Dover
19663	Bell, Luther	OK	1884		J.S. Bell	Emily Ditmore	J.M. & Elisabeth Bell	H.W. & Elisabeth Ditmore
22075	Bell, Magnolia	OK	1894	none	Ben Bell	Mary Ballard	Mathew Ballard	Emly Ballard
13365	Bell, Mattie	OK	1865	James Bell	Jesse Murphy	Pheby Allen	Polly Whiplash	
15339	Bell, Naomi	GA	1889		Martin Bell	Hulda Dover		Wm & Alantha Dover
7884	Bell, Pinkney	TN	1845	Elisabeth Bell	Daniel Bell	Alzora Williams	Robert & Salley Bell	Wm & Polley Williams
3353	Bell, Queen	AL	1886	Sylvester Bell	Thomas Boon	Arthureen Dees	L & Vicie Boon	Thomas & L H Dees
21758	Bell, Robert	TX	1882		J.S. Bell	Emily Ditmore	J.M. & Elisabeth Bell	Hen & Elisabeth Ditmore
5111	Bell, Salina	AR	1876	Tilden Bell	Robbert Foreman	Annie Trusdall	Joseph & Letha Foreman	
22237	Bell, Sarah	AL	1872	none	Lafayett Bell	Nancy Holcomb	Ira & Jane Bell	William & Sarah Holcomb
15338	Bell, Tom	GA	1897		Martin Bell	Hulda Dover		Wm & Alantha Dover
15337	Bell, Velvie	GA	1899		Martin Bell	Hulda Dover		Wm & Alantha Dover
19662	Bell, W.T.	OK	1882		J.S. Bell	Emily Ditmore	J.M. & Elisabeth Bell	H.W. & Elisabeth Ditmore
22155	Bell, Wallace	AL	1876	Nancy Bell	Lafayette Bell	Nancy Holcomb	Ira & Jane Bell	William & Sarah Holcomb
4454	Bell, William	TN	1847	Altha Bell	David Bell	Alzira Williams	Robert & Sally Bell	Wm & Polly Williams
17596	Bell, William	TX	1869	Julia Bell	Robert Bell	Lucindy Hampton	James & Mary Bell	George & Maryan Hampton
7052	Belt, Leta	MO	1887	Charles Belt	George Crowly	Fannie Holman	Wm & Margaret Crowly	George & Willie Holman
1270	Beltch, Lovie	KS	1880	U.C. Beltch	James Wilkerson	Rebeca White	Richard & Nancy Wilkerson	James & Cynthia White
13490	Benbow, Martha	NC	1890	Wm E Benbow	Robert Poindexter	Martha Ward	Robert & Charlotte Poindexter	Wiley & Polly Ward
20399*	Benjamin, Jane	TN	1846		George Moseley	Rachel Mitchel	James & Nancy Moseley	Jeff & Sarah Mitchel
10177	Bennett, Arch	GA	50yrs	Sidney Bennett	Oliver Bennett	Gracey Smith	Archibald Bennett	
15352	Bennett, Archie	GA	1884		Monroe Bennett	Carrie Wallace		Jesse & Liza Wallace
15351	Bennett, Carrie	GA	1858	Monroe Bennett	Jesse Wallace	Eliza Whitmire		Chris & Nancy Whitmire
15350	Bennett, Delmer	GA	1881	Jamie Bennett	Monroe Bennett	Carrie Wallace		Jesse & Liza Wallace
10176	Bennett, Elinder	GA		Joseph Bennett	William Davenport	Margret Falls	Thos & Elizabeth Davenport	Gilbert & Elinder Falls
15349	Bennett, Emory	GA	1889		Monroe Bennett	Carrie Wallace		Jesse & Liza Wallace
18839	Bennett, Hannah	KS	1851		Martin Hammonds	Mary Elmore		Hannah Elmore
20644	Bennett, James	TN	1874	Mollie Bennett	Charles Bennett	Delaney Willard	Moses & Delaney Bennett	Jesse & Levisa Campbell
15348	Bennett, Jewel	GA	1893		Monroe Bennett	Carrie Wallace		Jesse & Liza Wallace
15347	Bennett, Lyman	GA	1898		Monroe Bennett	Carrie Wallace		Jesse & Liza Wallace

15346	Bennett, Nancy	GA	1855	Webster Bennett	Elias Whitmire	Louisa Owen	George & Mary Whitmire	
1658	Bennett, Sallie	OK	1854	Wm Bennett	John Buckingham	Martha Lasley	Thos & Betsy Buckingham	Jim & Patsy Lasley
18840	Bennett, Samuel	MO	1857	Jennie Bennett	James Bennett	Lucinda Williams	Noah & Esther Bennett	
18897	Bennett, Winnie	GA		T.J. Bennett	James Kelley	Malinda Beck	Wm & Winnie Kelley	Solomon & Millie Beck
17324	Bennette, Nancy	GA	1849	J.D. Bennette	William Wheeler	Mary Lite		Olie & Mary Lite
15967	Benson, Frank	AL	1873	Sarah Benson	Billey Benson	Mary Bondo		Billey & Matt Bondo
17330 *	Benson, Oliver	GA	1826	Celie Benson	Jacob Mochess	Ibby Benson		
22727	Benton, Angus	TX	1884		T.J. Benton	E.E. McLeod		
17786	Benton, Mary	KY	1863	Price Benton	John Wright	Anna Evans	Shelton & JoeAnna Wright	John & Anna Evans
16217	Benton, Thomas	TX	1858		Jobe Benton			
22796	Berry, Cora	TN	1876	Tom Berry	James Helton	Martha Clark	Daniel & Patsy Helton	John & Peggy Clark
19320 *	Berry, Elisabeth	IN	1854	George Berry	Bolden Milton	Elizabeth Scott	Willis & Anna Milton	Hubbard & Sally Scott
8881	Berry, Elizabeth	OK	1849	Thomas Berry	Thomas Ross	Annie Seabolt	Akie Latimer	Adam & Annie Seabolt
2913 *	Berry, Nicktiye	MO					Philip Dare	
21694	Berryhill, Jane	AL	1819	Andy Berryhill	Suisou Scott	Millie Campbell		Thomas Campbell
7606	Beshears, Sarah	GA	1876	Harris Beshears	Evereese Brinyard	Lois Brown		
13848	Beshears, William	GA	1849	Cordelia Beshears	James Beshears	Elizabeth Roper		Isaac & Sarah Roper
20287	Best, Jennie	OK	1866	George Best	Samuel Goodwin	Agnes Yeargin		John & Martha Yeargin
3134	Betts, Evander	MO	1846	Sarah Betts	William Betts	Ede Bird	John & Ruthie Betts	John & Nancy Bird
21495	Bevers, Georgia	CO	1877	George Bevers	William Page	Emily Wall		Drury Wall
7076	Bickham, Annah	TX	1875	L W Bickham	Jacob Keith	Sarah Watson	Eli Keith & Elizebeth Week	Wm Watson & Nelly Caldwell
7075	Bickham, Attie	TX	1869	E D Bickham	Jacob Keith	Sarah Watson	Eli Keith & Elizibeth Week	Wm Watson & Nelly Caldwell
18485	Biddy, Annie	GA	1886		Elijah Biddy	Georgian Anderson		
16529	Biddy, Elias	GA	1851	Zilpha Biddy	Elias Biddy	Mary Brooks	Meshack & Nancy Biddy	David & Susannah Brooks
7815	Biddy, Elijah	GA	1848	Georgia Diddy	John Diddy	Sallie Haron	Mr. Posey	Mr. Harron
21290	Biddy, George	TX	1876		George Biddy	Edna McDonald	Elvin & Elizabeth Biddy	Tillman & Louise McDonald
21332	Biddy, George	TX	1852	Barbara Biddy	James Biddy	Delila McDonald	Elvin & Lisie Biddy	Grancer Rogers
21312	Biddy, Henry	OK	1858	Minnie Biddy	George Biddy	Edna McDonald	Elvin Biddy	
21234	Biddy, Hughell	TX	1878		George Biddy	Eleen McDonald	Elvin & Elizabeth Biddy	Tillman & Louise McDonald
21315	Biddy, James	TX	1855	Martha Biddy	George Biddy	Edna McDonald	Elvin & Elizabeth Biddy	Tillman & Louise McDonald
21317	Biddy, James	TX	1829	Delila Biddy	Elvin Biddy	Elizabeth Rogers	Edmund Biddy	David & Ruthy Rogers

21326	Biddy, James	TX	1876	Birtie Biddy	George Biddy	Barbara Hampton	James & Delila Biddy	Henry & Mollie Hampton
21329	Biddy, James	TX	1865	Sallie Biddy	James Biddy	Delila McDonald	Elvin & Lisie Biddy	Grancer Rogers
14562	Biddy, John	GA	1853	Elizabeth Biddy	Elias Biddy	Polly Brooks	Mashack & Nancy Biddy	
16531	Biddy, John	GA	1840	Susan Biddy	Mashack Biddy	Nancy Ledbetter		John & Polly Ledbetter
21316	Biddy, John	TX	1871	Seler Biddy	James Biddy	Delila McDonald	Elvin & Lisie Biddy	Grancer Rogers
21331	Biddy, Lon	TX	1880	Mamie Biddy	Robert Biddy	Sallie Renfro	James & Delila Biddy	
15458	Biddy, Newton	GA	1875	Bessie Biddy	Elija Biddy	Georgia Anderson	John Biddy	John Anderson
16526	Biddy, Noah	GA	1838	Harriet Biddy	Mashack Biddy	Nancy Ledbetter	Mary Biddy	Pollie Ledbetter
21327	Biddy, Oliver	TX	1875	Addie Biddy	James Biddy	Delila McDonald	Elvin & Lisie Biddy	Grancer Rogers
21236	Biddy, Robert	TX	1857	Sallie Biddy	James Biddy	Delila Donald	Elvin & Lissie Biddy	Grancer Rogers
16528	Biddy, Ruthey	GA	1848		Elias Biddy	Polly Brooks	Meshack & Nancy Biddy	David & Susannah Brooks
21314	Biddy, Sadie	TX	1885		James Biddy	Martha Graham	George & Edna Biddy	Wm & Sallie Graham
16534	Biddy, Sarah	GA	1856		Elias Biddy	Polly Brooks	Meshack & Nancy Biddy	David & Susannah Brooks
21313	Biddy, Thomas	OK	1871	Mary Biddy	George Biddy	Edna McDonald	Elvin Biddy	
15459	Biddy, William	GA	1880	Mattie Biddy	Elija Biddy	Georgia Anderson	John Biddy	John Anderson
21292	Biddy, William	OK	1864	Cleopatra Biddy	George Biddy	Edna McDonald	Elvin & Elizabeth Biddy	Tillman & Louise McDonald
21318	Biddy, William	TX	1867	Dora Biddy	James Biddy	Delila McDonald	Elvin & Lisie Biddy	Grancer Rogers
3443	Biggs, Mollie	AL		James Biggs	Adam Hollinger	Elizabeth Lomax	Jeff & Elizabeth Hollinger	Sidney & Mary Lomax
20569	Biggs, Thomas	TN	1861	Mary Biggs	James Biggs	Leander Furgesson		
14396	Bigham, Tolithia	CA	1860	Lewis Bigham	Jones Evans	Mahala Ivey		
15764	Bililes, William	WV	1842	Janlinia Bililes	Alex Bililes	Jennie Guyans	William Bililes	Johnson Guyans
13582*	Billings, Frank	GA	50yrs	Sallie Billings		Vicey Roskee		Iona Roskee
13384	Billips, Elsie	WV	1879		John Billips	Rebecca Harman	Edwood Billips & Mary Sizemore	Wm & Nancy Harman
9127	Billips, James	WV	1857	Belle Phillips	Kirah Billips	Iramin Sizemore		George Sizemore
13972	Billips, Kiah	VA	1872		Kiah Billips	Arenia Sizemore	James & Nancy Billips	George & Jennie Sizemore
13973	Billips, Robert	VA	1856	Mary Billips	Kiah Billips	Arenia Sizemore	James & Nancy Billips	George & Jennie Sizemore
6275	Bilyen, Ethel	MO	1888	none	Sampson Bilyen	Carrie Bays	Peter & Elizabeth Bilyen	Newel & Carrie Bays
12083	Bilyen, Rebbeca	OK	1865	Isaac Bilyen	D C Bays	Precious Jones	Joshua & Embley Bays	Samuel & Susan Jones
14356	Bingham, James	KS	1860	Elizabeth Bingham	Edward Bingham	Eliza Olinger	Frederic & Bida Bingham	John & Clara Olinger
14950	Bingham, John	CA	1857	Hester Bingham	Edward Bingham	Eliza Olinger	Frederic & Bida Bingham	John & Clara Olinger
18722	Bingham, Martha	TN	1843	Joel Bingham	Willis Guy	Mahala Gibson	Edmund & Judie Guy	George & Viney Gibson

7082	Bingham, Mary	OK	1873	John Bingham	Daniel Jackson	Epnetious Whatley	Isaac & Elizabeth Jackson	
19699	Binkley, Kizzie	TN	1874	Lee Binkley	Nathan Curtis	Susan Collier	Joshua & Elizabeth Curtis	
21250	Bird, Daisy	TX	1870	C.O. Bird	S.E. Blair	E.J. Penn	Hiram & Adeline Blair	Sanford & Elizabeth Penn
4654	Bird, George	TN	1857	Carrie Bird	David Bird	Amanda Jenkins		Solomon & Fannie Aikens
8039	Bird, Henry	OK	1870	none	White Red Bird	Ger za jeh	Unknown	Unknown
10862	Bird, Martha	WV	1879	Willard Bird	Jessie Sizemore	Nancy Walker	Hiram & Jane Sizemore	Milton & Martha Walker
13289	Bird, Nellie	OK	19yrs	Andrew Bird	Lewis Simmons	Lizzie Smith	Sam & Rachel Simmons	Smith & Chu wo cha ga
14372	Birmingham, Mary	AL		W G Birmingham	John Otts	America Newell	Joseph & Delphia Otts	Mathis & Rebecca Newell
15569 *	Birse, Crockett	GA	1897		William Birse	Mary Houston	Harry & Susan Birse	Wm & Sarah Houston
15568 *	Birse, William	GA	1895		William Birse	Mary Houston	Harry & Susan Birse	Wm & Sarah Houston
11068	Bishop, Alice	VA	1880	Andrew Bishop	William Dolinger	Selah Edmondson		Isaac & Martha Edmondson
21521	Bishop, Allen	TX	1863	Luella Bishop	Joseph Bishop	Averilla Bowles		Allen & Averilla Bowles
12350	Bishop, Ella	GA	1880	Frank Bishop	William Fowler	Mary Otwell	Wm & Eliza Fowler	Joseph & Amanda Otwell
21428	Bishop, John	TX	1860	Amy Bishop	Joseph Bishop	Avarilla Bowles		Allen Bowles
528	Bishop, Lillie	NC	1860	Calvin Bishop	Blue Syms	Catherine Jordan	unknown	unknown
12345	Bishop, Mary	GA	1905		Francis Bishop	Ella Fowler	Nevill & Evalyn Bishop	Wm & Mary Fowler
3425	Bishop, Mrs Joe	AL	1877	Joe Bishop	Alex Rollin	Mary Hathcock	Jack & Polly Rollin	John & Rosa Hathcock
19965	Bishop, Nannie	NC	1880	Frank Bishop	Henry Flippin	Lockey Owens	John & Catherine Flippin	Jesse Owens
19077	Bishop, R.R.	AR	1844	C.A. Bishop	J.R. Bishop	Lucy Price		
18372	Bishop, Rebecca	KS	1857	Robert Bishop	John Brock	Rebecca Langley	James & Sarah Brock	Matthew Langley
2635	Bishop, Rosanna	GA	1863	William Bishop	John Adams	Leomy Parker		Jonathan & Leomy Parker
10132	Bishop, Sarah	WV	1885	Crocket Bishop	Greensberry Green	Mary Perdew	Nancy Green	Nathaniel & Sallie Perdew
16816 *	Bitting, William	NC	1853	Isabelle Bitting	Benj Bitting	Rhoda Tucker	Soloman Bonner	Kate Mathews
2778	Bivins, David	KS	1875	none	Lewis Bivins	Catherine Cheek		Betsey Cheek
2779	Bivins, Walter	OK	1878	none	Lewis Bivins	Catherine Cheek		Betsey Cheek
7065	Black, J. Elliott	TX	1878	none	William Black	Eliza Jackson		John Jackson & Elizabeth Caldwell
18425	Black, Clifford	MO	1906		Morris Black	Vada Graham	James & Francis Black	Jeff & Sarrie Graham
7066	Black, Della	OK	1882	none	William Black	Eliza Jackson		John Jackson & Elizabeth Caldwell
7067	Black, Eliza	OK	1844	William Black	John Jackson	Elizabeth Caldwell		Andrew Caldwell & Corene Sevier

7064	Black, Forrest	TX	1877	Addie Black	William Black	Eliza Jackson		John Jackson & Elizabeth Caldwell
11251	Black, John	OK	1806	Mary Black	Henley Black	Judith Carter		Rudolph & Frankie Carter
7068	Black, Kennie	OK	1880	none	William Black	Eliza Jackson		John Jackson & Elizabeth Caldwell
10430	Black, Martha	OK	1844	George Black	John Stover	Charlotte Ward		George & Lucy Ward
17299	Black, Nancy	AL	1873	J.M. Black	James Sizemore	Mary Black	Daniel & Anna Sizemore	J.C. & Elizabeth Black
18424	Black, Vada	MO	1887	Elmer Black	Jeff Graham	Sarrie Gillstrap	Alex & Margret Graham	Jerry & Margret Gillstrap
196	Blackbird, Rebecca	OK	1845	Ciffus Blackbird	Tom Swimmer	Lottie Rowe		Arch & Jennie Rowe
6007	Blackburn, Andrew	OK	1846	Maria Blackburn	Andrew Blackburn	Francis Eddings	John & Elsie Blackburn	John & Elizabeth Eddings
7060	Blackburn, Benjamin	IL	1846	Sarah Blackburn	James Blackburn	Elizabeth Gray		
7063	Blackburn, Earl	OK	1884	Lillie Blackburn	Thomas Blackburn	Sarrah Stamper	James & Elizabeth Blackburn	Wm & Annie Stamper
45	Blackburn, James	CA		Maggie Blackburn	John Blackburn	Sarah Miller	Andrew & Frances Blackburn	
11941	Blackburn, James	GA	1843	Francis Blackburn	John Blackburn	Fannie Brown	Allen Blackburn	Jimmy & Peggy Brown
5997	Blackburn, John	CA	1834	Martha Blackburn	Andrew Blackburn		John & Elsie Blackburn	John & Elizabeth Eddings
6392	Blackburn, Pleasant	IL	1848	Caroline Blackburn	Andrew Blackburn	Francis Eddings	John & Elsie Blackburn	John & Elizabeth Eddings
6377	Blackburn, Robert	IL	1876	Ella Blackburn	George Blackburn	Julia Collins	Andrew & Francis Blackburn	
2098	Blackburn, Susannah	NC	1872	Roby Blackburn	Cicero Blevins	Elisabeth Childers	Daniel & Anna Blevins	Franklin & Susannah Childers
6005	Blackburn, Thomas	IL	1876	Nola Blackburn	Pleasant Blackburn	Caroline Farris	Andrew & Francis Blackburn	
7062	Blackburn, Thomas	OK	1850	Sarah Blackburn	James Blackburn	Elizabeth Gray	Benjamin Blackburn	
4176	Blackburn, William	OK	1874	Rachel Blackburn	John Blackburn	Sarah Miller	Andrew & Francis Blackburn	Henry & Rhody Miller
6006	Blackburn, William	OK	1838	Mary Blackburn	Andrew Blackburn	Francis Eddings	John & Elsie Blackburn	John & Elizabeth Eddings
7061	Blackburn, William	OK	1848		James Blackburn	Elizabeth Gray	Benjamin Blackburn	
17648	Blackledge, Nancy	GA	1861	Franklin Blackledge	Joseph Sosebee	Francis Dixon	Jerry & Elizabeth Ward	Martin & Elizabeth Dixon
15869*	Blacksmith, Fannie	TN	1867	John Blacksmith	Newt Stroud	Amanda Smith	Peggy Stroud	Frances Smith
5450	Blackwelder, Ida	NC	1890	none	Thomas Blackwelder	Sallie Wilson		Jeptha & Cyntha Wilson
7526	Blackwelder, Sally	NC	39yrs	Thomas Blackwelder	Jeptha Wilson	Cynthia Mason		Johnnie & Polly Mason
1989	Blackwell, Annie	OK	1844		John Hooper	Hariet Ratliff	John Hooper	Henry Turner Ratliff
18723	Blackwell, Emer	TN	1871	Roy Blackwell	Andrew Guy	Polly Bingham	Willis & Mahala Guy	Joel & Lydia Bingham

9556	Blackwell, Franklin	GA	1855	Nancy Blackwell	Joseph Blackwell	Maryann Ridley		Bill & Mary Ridley
2542	Blackwell, Joseph	SC	1861	Jane Blackwell	Joseph Blackwell	Mary Ridley		Wm Ridley & Mary Yearby
9557	Blackwell, Joseph	NC	1883		Frank Blackwell	Tabitha Speed	Joseph Blackwell	Mary Ridley
10836	Blackwell, Julia	TX	1871	William Blackwell	John Lewis	Almeda Onsbey	John & Luan Lewis	Wm & Martha Onsbey
2543	Blackwell, Mary	GA	1834	Joseph Blackwell	Bill Ridley	Mary Yearby		
16157	Blackwell, Parthenia	GA	1854	James Blackwell	Edward Tatum	Rebecca Carver	John & Jennie Tatum	James & Nancy Carver
16532	Blackwell, Ruthey	GA	1862	Thomas Blackwell	Louis Biddy	Elizabeth Jackson	Wm & Ruthey Allen	
12957	Blackwell, Sarah	OK	1883	William Blackwell	Jefferson Manier	Ardenie Miller	Wm Manier & Sallie Lowery	
22118	Blagg, Henry	KS	1880	Nelle Blagg	Dick Blagg	Leddie Folk	William Blagg	Benwal & Hettie Folk
748	Blair, Amanda	IL	1855	Y.Y. Blair	John Hadden	Mary Robinson	James & Rachel Hadden	John & Jane Robinson
3133 *	Blair, Henderson	KS		Narcissa Blair	Sam Grimmitt	Matilda Grimmitt	Judah Grimmitt	Duncan & Grimmitt
12829	Blair, John	GA		Lizzie Blair	Blair			Williams
21878	Blair, Mary	TN	1866	Ell Blair	Joseph Dedmon	Martha Black	Jesse & Hannah Dedmon	John & Jane Black
20288	Blair, Naoma	MO	7yrs			Lucy Blair	Lovel Ward	
21379	Blair, Soloman	TX	1847	Betty Blair	Hiram Blair	Sarah Hewitt		Soloman Hewitt
3321	Blair, Syrana	KS	1866	John Blair	Reuben Moore	Catherine Cook		Thomas Barnes & Delaney Cook
22557	Blair, William	KS	1895		John Blair	Syrana Moore	Rhuben Moore	Cathrine Moore
18238 *	Blake, Molly	GA	1871	Dilmus Blake		Rachel Gambol		Jennie Gambol
10452	Blakely, Hiram	WV	1833	Mary Blakely	Wiley Blakely	Kedie Robinson	Wiley & Crissilla Blakely	Rudy & Kedie Robinson
13796	Blakely, Susanah	NC	1846	George Blakely	Absalom Matthews	Amitta Poindexter	Aaron & Mary Matthews	Wm & Elizbeth Poindexter
19296	Blalock, Arnold	GA	1884	Norah Blalock	Wm Blalock	Denie Kelley	Robert & Margaret Blalock	
19293	Blalock, Carlton	GA	1884		Calvin Blalock	Josephine Freeman	Wm & Katie Blalock	
19107	Blalock, Emma	AR	1876	Adam Blalock	Joseph McGavack	Harriet Evans	America McGavack	Malachi & Sarah Evans
21025	Blalock, Francis	GA	1874	Sarah Blalock	Calvin Blalock	Josephene Freeman	Wm & Catherine Blalock	Alex & Sarah Freeman
19295	Blalock, Luidora	GA	1872		Calvin Blalock	Josephine Freeman	Wm & Katie Blalock	
19763	Blalock, Newton	GA	1868	Delila Blalock	Calvin Blalock	Josephine Freeman	Wm & Katie Blalock	
19294	Blalock, Stella	GA	1886		Calvin Blalock	Josephine Freeman	Wm & Katie Blalock	
14354	Bland, Elizabeth	IN	1863	Roland Bland	Edward Bingham	Eliza Olinger	Frederic & Lida Bingham	John & Clara Olinger
21649	Blankenship, Frank	NC	1880	Rebecka Blankenship	James Blankenship	Lorena Maney		Martin & Matilda Maney
21651	Blankenship, G. Zeb	NC	1887		James Blankenship	Lorina Maney		Martin & Matilda Maney
21650	Blankenship, George	NC	1870	Tricie Blankenship	James Blankenship	Lorena Maney		Martin & Matilda Maney
21653	Blankenship, J. Merit	NC	1873	Etta Blankenship	James Blankenship	Lorina Maney		Martin & Matilda Maney

21648	Blankenship, John	NC	1875		James Blankenship	Lorena Maney		Martin & Matilda Maney
14427	Blankenship, Lorina	NC	1844	James Blankenship Jr	Martin Maney	Matilda Holcombe	John & Polly Maney	
14418	Blankenship, Matilda	NC		John Blankenship	Robert Holcomb	Sallie Maney	Henry & Fanning Holcomb	John & Polly Maney
21652	Blankenship, Millerd	NC	1868	Ales Blankenship	James Blankenship	Lorina Maney		Martin & Matilda Maney
21645	Blankenship, Robert	NC	1878	Harriett Blankenship	James Blankenship	Gima Maney		Martin & Matilda Maney
5999	Blankenship, Rosa	IL	1864		Jesse Mayberry	Eliza Blackburn		Andrew & Francis Blackburn
1769	Blaylock, George	GA	1855	Louise Rice (decd)	Isham Blaylock	Martha Taylor		George Taylor
13602	Blaylock, George	GA	1888	Lizzie Blaylock	Geo Blaylock	Georgia Rice	I.K. & Martha Blaylock	G W & Amanda Rice
13600	Blaylock, Joe	GA	1875	Beele Blaylock	Geo Blaylock	Georgia Rice	I.K. & Martha Blaylock	G W & Amanda Rice
13601	Blaylock, Pink	GA	1876	Lula Blaylock	Geo Blaylock	Georgia Rice	I.K. & Martha Blaylock	G W & Amanda Rice
14403	Bleckley, Julia	GA	1873	Logan Bleckley		Mary Ridley		Wm & Mary Ridley
19322	Bledsoe, Martha	NC	1838	Tyrell Bledsoe	Tyrell Poindexter	Matilda Overby	John & Mary Poindexter	Wm & Susan Overby
4129	Blevins, Ada	NC	1839	Shubal Blevins	John Thompson	Polly Blevins		James & Lydia Blevins
6904	Blevins, Ala	VA	1855	A.J. Blevins	Armstrong Clark	Mary Miller		Elizabeth Blevins
6876	Blevins, Alfred	VA	1861	Martha Blevins	Edward Blevins	Nancy Blevins	James & Lydia Blevins	
11050	Blevins, Alice	VA	1863	William Blevins	Isaac Edmondson	Martha Blevins		Wells & Elizabeth Blevins
4466	Blevins, Allen	VA	22yrs	Mary Blevins	Eli Blevins	Betty Blevins	Tobias & Susan Blevins	
6873	Blevins, Allen	VA	1830	Rachel Blevins	Wells Blevins	Elizabeth Blevins	James & Lydi Blevins	
11096	Blevins, Alley	VA	23yrs	Manuel Blevins	Mack Stamper	Kesiah Stamper	Wiley & Eliza Stamper	
12553	Blevins, Alsander	NC	1881		Leander Blevins	Peggy Osborne	Granville & Polly Blevins	David & Nancy Osborne
8587	Blevins, Ambroes	VA	1872	none	W H Blevins	Nancy Davis	Armstrong & Catharine Blevins	Jordan & Seany Davis
6162	Blevins, Andrew	VA	1866	Mary Blevins	Wilburn Blevins	Martha Lewis		Andrew & Biddy Lewis
6852	Blevins, Andrew	VA	1852	Ala Blevins	James Blevins	Margaret Edmondson	Wells & Elizabeth Blevins	
7961	Blevins, Andrew	NC	1865	Susan Blevins	Wesley Blevins	Nancy Brown	Daniel & Annie Blevins	
8479	Blevins, Andrew	WA	1858	Alice Blevins	Isam Blevins	Ann Edmondson	George & Lydia Blevins	
8546	Blevins, Annie	VA	31yrs	T C Blevins	John Hall	Martha Blevins	Lexington & Nancy Hall	Andrew & Susan Blevins
22187	Blevins, Armes	OK	1844		Jack Blevins	Susanne Schultz	Dick Blevins	Jones
10103	Blevins, Arthur	VA	1880	Bartie Blevins	Levi Blevins	Evaline Hart	Ned & Nancy Blevins	
11448	Blevins, Bartie	VA		Author Blevins	John Blevins	Sousie Blevins	Eli Blevins	James & Margret Blevins

6127	Blevins, Bartlet	NC	1845	Rhoda Blevins	Eli Blevins	Milly Brinegar	James & Lyddia Blevins	Adam & Polly Brinegar
3655	Blevins, Benjamin	VA	44yrs	Elisabeth Blevins	Armstrong Blevins	Catherine Blevins	James Blevins	Lydda Blevins
5372	Blevins, Bertha	VA	1893	E Still Blevins	Allen Clark	Clara Welch	Allen & Elisabeth Clark	James & Nancy Welch
18623	Blevins, Bertie	VA	1880	Irving Blevins	Levi Haga	Martha Faircloth	David & Rebecca Haga	T.A. & Christina Faircloth
18159	Blevins, Birtie	VA	1889			Malvina Blevins		Riley & Agga Blevins
4896	Blevins, Bonnie	VA	1885	Charley Blevins	William Miller	Evaline Blevins	Isaac & Bashabe Miller	Riley & Agnes Blevins
6874	Blevins, Calvin	VA	1844	Mary Blevins	James Blevins	Mecy Pennington	James & Lydia Blevins	
8494	Blevins, Caney	VA		Harrette Blevins	Noah Blevins	Catharine Dolinger	Allen & Fannie Blevins	John & Betty Dolinger
6133	Blevins, Carie	NC	1877	Sarahan Blevins	James Blevins	Louisa Sullen	Eli & Milly Blevins	
8497	Blevins, Catharine	VA	1853	Noah Blevins	John Dolinger	Betty Colwell		Joseph & Catharine Colwell
2092	Blevins, Charley	NC	1878	none	G D Blevins	Celia Parsons	Daniel & Anna Blevins	Wm & Rutha Parsons
6872	Blevins, Christopher	KY	1881	Lillie Blevins	Eli Blevins	Mary Hill	Armstrong & Catharine Blevins	Franklin & Abaline Hill
6902	Blevins, Christopher	VA	39yrs	Annie Blevins	Allen Blevins	Rachel Williams	Wells & Elizabeth Blevins	Miles & Mary Williams
6180	Blevins, Crumpler	NC	1871	Mertie Blevins	George Blevins	Almedia Jones	Eli & Molly Blevins	Thomas & Elisebeth Jones
7959	Blevins, Daniel	NC	1861	Isabell Blevins	Wesley Blevins	Nancy Brown	Daniel & Annie Blevins	
8461	Blevins, Darthulia	VA	1882	William Blevins	Solomon Lewis	Martha Huffman	A J & Biddy Lewis	Will & Elisabeth Blevins
6105	Blevins, David	NC	1850	Rebeca Blevins	Jackson Blevins	Sarah Allen	James & Sarah Blevins	Elisibeth Alen
6186	Blevins, David	NC	1866	Alice Blevins	Bartet Blevins	Ealine Carter	Eli & Milley Blevins	Daniel & Milly Carter
6845	Blevins, David	VA	1860	Louisa Blevins	James Blevins	Margree Edmondson	Wells & Elizabeth Blevins	
7633	Blevins, David	VA	1880	Rachel Blevins	Wm Blevins	Mary Thompson	Daniel & Annie Blevins	James & Caroline Thompson
9053	Blevins, Dellia	VA		Clayborne Blevins	Noah Blevins	Catharine Dolinger	Allen & Fanny Blevins	John & Betty Dolinger
8537	Blevins, Dora	VA	1877	Wels Blevins	Wels Miller	Matilda Phipps	Isac & Basha Miller	
19970	Blevins, Early et al	NC	20 yrs			Mary Blevins		John & Mary Blevins
9084	Blevins, Edward	VA	31yrs	Ella Blevins	Janus Blevins	Mary Blevins	Ned & Nancy Blevins	Levi & Ada Blevins
17990	Blevins, Elbert	VA	1871	Lydda Blevins	Riley Blevins	Olive Ham	Eli & Milly Blevins	Larkin & Rebecca Ham
8552	Blevins, Elcaney	VA	1888	none	Eli Blevins	Margarett Ruper	Shubal & Ada Blevins	
4468	Blevins, Eli	VA	47yrs	Elisabeth Blevins	Tobias Blevins	Susan Blevins	Eli Blevins	Milly Blevins

4894	Blevins, Eli	VA	1855	Nancy Blevins	Riley Blevins	Agney Barker	Eli Blevins	Milley Brineger
6870	Blevins, Eli	KY	1846	Mary Blevins	Armstrong Blevins	Catharine Hart	James & Lydia Blevins	
8231	Blevins, Eli	VA	1891	none	Eli Blevins	Margarett Ruper	Shubal & Ada Blevins	
8471	Blevins, Eli	KY	1869	Flawrence Blevins	Edward Blevins	Susan Blevins	Armstrong Blevins	Catharine Blevins
6861	Blevins, Elijah	KY	1848	Rachel Blevins	Armstrong Blevins	Catharine Hart	James & Lydia Blevins	
3654	Blevins, Elisabeth	VA	38yrs	B F Blevins	Calvin Farmer	Bethany Thompson	Sam & Margret Thompson	
4469	Blevins, Elisabeth	VA	44yrs	Eli Blevins	Calton Blevins	Nancy Blevins	Wells & Nancy Blevins	Eli & Jennie Blevins
11066	Blevins, Elizabeth	VA	1846	Leander Blevins	John Hart	Polley Caldwell	George & Polley Hart	Joseph & Catharine Caldwell
11089	Blevins, Elizabeth	VA	1851	W M Blevins	James Blevins	Margaret Edmondson	Wells & Elizabeth Blevins	Andrew & Susan Blevins
4318	Blevins, Ellen	NC	1884	none	David Sullivan	Mary Roop		King & Louisa Roop
12961	Blevins, Elzina	VA	1868	F.M. Blevins	Jessie Blevins	Catherine Pennington	Eli & Millie Blevins	Able & Lydia Pennington
11053	Blevins, Emanuel	VA	1882	Allie Blevins	William Blevins	Alice Edmondson		Isaac & Martha Edmondson
11078	Blevins, Estelle	VA	1878	Bertha Blevins	Ephram Blevins	Sarah Hart		John & Polly Hart
6131	Blevins, Esther	NC	1866	none	Alfred Blevins	Margary Sheets	James & Mecy Blevins	
6130	Blevins, Ettie	NC	1877	Thomas Blevins	Benjamin Phipps	Rebecca Plummer	Ahart & Maryan Phipps	Joseph Plummer
11095	Blevins, Ettie	VA	1877	Robert Blevins	Mack Stamper	Ettie Stamper	Wiley & Eliza Stamper	
6121	Blevins, Eugene	NC	1872	Eminor Blevins	Alfred Blevins	Margary Sheets	James & Mary Blevins	
6900	Blevins, Eulala	VA	1878	none	Harvy Blevins	Malinda Blevins	Tobias Blevins	Susan Blevins
3590	Blevins, Fannie	VA	23yrs		Shade Blevins	Naomy Blevins	Andy & Charity Blevins	Tobias & Susan Blevins
21018	Blevins, Flem	NC	1860	Malvina Blevins	Granville Blevins	Polly Reeves	Wm & Rhoda Blevins	Enoch & Gracy Reeves
8475	Blevins, Francis	KY	1858	Jenny Blevins	Ned Edward Blevins	Susan Blevins	Armstrong Blevins	Catharine Blevins
12963	Blevins, Franklin	VA		Elzina Blevins	James Blevins	Margaret Edmonds	Wells & Elizabeth Blevins	
2097	Blevins, G.D	NC	1844	Celia Blevins	Daniel Blevins	Anna Dickson	James & Lydia Blevins	Douglas & Jenney Dickson
5114	Blevins, George	VA	1875	Alyena Blevins	Riley Blevins	Alie Ham	Eli Blevins	Milly Blevins
6126	Blevins, George	NC	1829	Almedia Blevins	Eli Blevins	Milly Brinegar	James & Lyddia Blevins	Adam & Polly Brinegar
9074	Blevins, George	NC	1848	Cynthia Blevins	George Blevins	Lydia Blevins	James Blevins	Lydia Blevins
9075	Blevins, George	NC	1872	Dora Blevins	James Blevins	Sarah Baker	George & Lydia Blevins	
11079	Blevins, George	WV	1867	Clara Blevins	Wilborn Blevins	Rosey Farmer	Washington Hart & Elizbeth Blevins	

6187	Blevins, George Jr.	NC	1885	Ines Blevins	Bartect Blevins	Ealine Carter	Eli & Milley Blevins	Daniel & Milley Carter
4476	Blevins, Gipson	VA	5yrs	none	Amanuel Blevins	Sarah Hogston	Tobias & Susan Blevins	Will & Martha Hogston
11092	Blevins, Gorden	VA			Eli Blevins	Eliza Bare	Jessie & Catharine Blevins	James & Ansley Bare
8538	Blevins, Green	NC	1875	Hanniah Blevins	Alford Blevins	Marjary Sheets	James Jr & Nancy Blevins	Joseph & Elisebeth Huddler
11062	Blevins, Green	VA	28yrs	Hulda Blevins	John Blevins	Martha Hall	Andrew & Susan Blevins	Lexington & Nancy Hall
11071	Blevins, Henry	VA	1877	Sinsilla Blevins	Leander Blevins	Elizabeth Hart		John & Polley Hart
9059	Blevins, Hiram	NC	1871	Cora Blevins	Wells Blevins	Catharine Baker	George & Lydia Blevins	
8521	Blevins, Holly	WA	1882	none	Andrew Blevins	Betty Blevins	Isham Blevins	Ann Blevins
6842	Blevins, Horton	VA	1870	Nancy Blevins	Alen Blevins	Rachel Williams	Wells & Elizabeth Blevins	Miles & Mary Williams
11060	Blevins, Irving	VA	22yrs		Eli Blevins	Eliza Bare	Jessie & Catharine Blevins	James & Angela Bare
14749	Blevins, Isaac	VA	1876	Dora Blevins	Calvin Blevins	Mary Simmons	James & Meacy Blevins	James & Anna Simmons
6104	Blevins, Jackson	NC	1880	none	David Blevins	Rebeca Clark	Jackson & Sarah Blevins	Allen & Roda Clark
8457	Blevins, Jacob	VA	1879		Wilburn Blevins	Martha Davis	Wells & Elizabeth Blevins	
3465	Blevins, James	VA	1868	Dory Blevins	Alfred Blevins	Margia Huddler	James & Mecy Blevins	Joseph & Elizabeth Huddler
5836	Blevins, James	VA						
6111	Blevins, James	VA	1851	Mary Blevins	Edward Blevins	Nancy Blevins	James & Lydia Blevins	
6179	Blevins, James	NC	1858	Louisa Blevins	Eli Blevins	Milly Brinegar	James & Lyddia Blevins	Adam & Polly Brinegar
6183	Blevins, James	NC	1885	none	Shade Blevins	Cilia Hurley	George & Almedia Blevins	
6858	Blevins, James	VA	1873	Martha Blevins	Shubal Blevins	Ada Thompson		John & Polly Thompson
8491	Blevins, James	VA	1877	Mary Blevins	Calvin Blevins	Mary Simmons	James & Mecie Blevins	James & Annie Simmons
8496	Blevins, James	LA	1858	Laura Lewis	Allen Blevins		Wells & Elizabeth Blevins	
9045	Blevins, James	NC	1845	Sarah Blevins	George Blevins	Lydia Blevins	James Blevins	Lydia Blevins
9051	Blevins, James	NC	1871	Rilda Blevins	George Blevins	Cynthia Baker	George & Lydia Blevins	
8472	Blevins, Jane	OH	1865	Edward Blevins	Ned Blevins	Susan Blevins	Armstrong Blevins	Catharine Blevins
9061	Blevins, Jehue	NC	1850	Alice Blevins	Jehue Blevins	Alice Billings	James & Lydia Blevins	
12468	Blevins, Jessie	NC	1879		Leander Blevins	Peggy Osborne	Granville & Polly Blevins	David & Nancy Osborne
18774	Blevins, Joe	OK	1857		Jack Blevins	Annie Gibbs		Margarett Gibbs
6106	Blevins, Joel	NC	1884	none	David Blevins	Rebeca Clark	Jackson & Sarah Blevins	Allen & Rhoda Clark

2099	Blevins, John	NC	1873	Lucy Blevins	Cicero Blevins	Elisabeth Childers	Daniel & Anna Blevins	Franklin & Susannah Childers
8512	Blevins, John	VA	41yrs	Susa Blevins	Eli Blevins	Betsey Sturgill	Wells & Elizabeth Blevins	
8588	Blevins, John	VA	1874	Eliza Blevins	W H Blevins	Nancy Davis	Armstrong & Catharine Blevins	Jordan & Seany Davis
10766	Blevins, John	NC	1871	Mary Blevins	Wesley Blevins	Nancy Brown	Daniel & Annie Blevins	Wm & Patsy Brown
11075	Blevins, John	VA	1883		Ephram Blevins	Sarah Hart		John & Polly Hart
6124	Blevins, Joseph	NC	1861	Nancy Blevins	Alfred Blevins	Margera Sheets	James & Meacy Blevins	Joseph & Elizabeth Huddler
6860	Blevins, Joseph	VA	1870	Octava Blevins	Shubal Blevins	Ada Thompson		John & Polly Thompson
8553	Blevins, Joseph	VA	1885		Eli Blevins	Margarett Ruper	Shubal & Ada Blevins	
8474	Blevins, Josephine	KY		Ned Blevins	Ned Blevins	Josephine Carter	Armstrong Blevins	Catharine Blevins
11058	Blevins, Josephine	VA	31yrs	Harvey Blevins	John Blevins	Martha Hall	Andrew & Susan Blevins	Lexington & Nancy Hall
9592	Blevins, Levi	VA	1872	Eliza Blevins	Lee Blevins	Bethany Blevins	Jess & Catie Blevins	Ned & Nancy Blevins
6838	Blevins, Lottie	VA	1884	Sherman Blevins	Eli Hart	Jennie Sheets	Stephen & Rebecca Hart	Andrew & Catharine Sheets
12962	Blevins, Loyd	VA	1862	Elisa Blevins	Jessie Blevins	Catherine Pennington	Eli & Millie Blevins	Able & Lydia Pennington
6905	Blevins, Lydia	VA	1871	Shade Blevins	Eli Pennington	Emily Allen	Andrew & Hetty Pennington	
9289	Blevins, Maggie	VA	1884	Arthur Blevins	Joseph Hart	Jane More	Riley & Emily Hart	Wm & Isabella More
10102	Blevins, Major	VA	1878	Ona Blevins	Levi Blevins	Evaline Hart	Ned & Nancy Blevins	
6893	Blevins, Malinda	VA	1859	Harvy Blevins	Tobias Blevins	Susan Blevins		Eli & Milly Blevins
11098	Blevins, Manerva	VA	1879		William Blevins	Elizabeth Blevins	Jessie & Catherine Blevins	James & Margret Blevins
12964	Blevins, Marcilia	VA	1861		Jessie Blevins	Catherine Pennington	Eli & Millie Blevins	Able & Lydia Pennington
6848	Blevins, Martha	VA	33yrs	W.R. Blevins	John Blevins	Martha Hall	Andrew & Susan Blevins	Livington & Nancy Hall
6875	Blevins, Martha	VA	1863	Alfred Blevins	William Lewis	Nancy Lewis		Andrew & Biddy Lewis
6901	Blevins, Martha	VA	29yrs	none	Allen Blevins	Rachel Williams	Wells & Elizabeth Blevins	Miles & Mary Williams
8459	Blevins, Martha	VA	1847	Wilburn Blevins	Andrew Lewis	Biddy Blevins		Wells & Biddy Blevins
11057	Blevins, Martha	VA	51yrs	John Blevins	Lexington Hall	Nancy Childers	Owin & Juda Hall	John & Nancy Childers
11562	Blevins, Martha	VA	1866	Monroe Blevins	Eli Blevins	Elizabeth Sturgill	Wells & Elizabeth Blevins	
5559	Blevins, Mary	VA	1878	Solomon Blevins	Harrison Cook	Mary Tucker		David & Mahala Tucker
6103	Blevins, Mary	NC		William Blevins	Allen Blevins	Rachel Williams	Wells & Elizabeth Blevins	Miles & Mary Williams
11097	Blevins, Mary	VA	1881		William Blevins	Elizabeth Blevins	Jessie & Catherine Blevins	James & Margret Blevins

14949	Blevins, Mary	NE		John Blevins	Edward Bingham	Eliza Olinger	Frederic & Bida Bingham	John & Clara Olinger
4473	Blevins, Masourie	VA		none	Tobias Blevins	Susan Blevins	- - - Blevins	Eli & Milley Blevins
6907	Blevins, Miles	VA	1865		Allen Blevins	Rachel Williams	Wells & Elizabeth Williams	
8539	Blevins, Minie	VA	1887	Wilburn Blevins	Elexander Huffman	Emeline Penington	Elexander & Celie Huffman	Samuel & Sarah Penington
11063	Blevins, Minter	VA	21yrs	Bessie Blevins	John Blevins	Martha Hall	Andrew & Susan Blevins	Lexington & Nancy Hall
11563	Blevins, Monroe	VA	1858	Martha Blevins	Edward Blevins	Nancy Blevins	James & Lydia Blevins	
17749	Blevins, Nancy	VA	72yrs	Calton Blevins	Eli Blevins	Jennie Lunkin	James & Lydda Blevins	James & Nancy Lunkin
4475	Blevins, Naomy	VA	51yrs	Shade Blevins	Tobias Blevins	Susan Blevins	Eli Blevins	Milley Blevins
6867	Blevins, Nicholas	KY	1867	Amanda Blevins	Elijah Blevins	Rachel Felty	Armstrong & Cathrine Blevins	
8510	Blevins, Noah	VA	1853	Catharine Blevins	Allen Blevins	Fanny Privette	Wells & Elizabeth Blevins	Noah & Naoma Privette
6956	Blevins, Oney	VA	1888	Mojas Blevins	Haywood Blevins	Lydia McGrady	Ely & Betty Blevins	Jacob & Jinney McGrady
6866	Blevins, Peter	KY	1873	Lucy Blevins	Elijah Blevins	Rachel Felty	Armstrong & Cathrine Blevins	Nicholas & Susan Felty
6844	Blevins, Poindexter	VA	34yrs	Matilda Poindexter	Alen Blevins	Rachel Williams	Wells & Elizabeth Blevins	Miles & Mary Williams
14759	Blevins, Rachel	KY	1844	widow	Solomin Blevins	Elizabeth Quinley	Elisha Blevins & Rachel Osborn	
14723	Blevins, Reace	WV	1870	Hiry Blevins	Calvin Blevins	Mary Simmons	James & Mecy Blevins	James & Anna Simmons
6102	Blevins, Rebeca	NC	1845	none	Jackson Blevins	Sarah Allen	James & Sarah Blevins	Elisibeth Allen
6107	Blevins, Rhoda	NC	1882	none	David Blevins	Rebeca Clark	Jackson & Sarah Blevins	Allen & Rhoda Clark
5113	Blevins, Riley	VA	1824	Alie Blevins	Eli Blevins	Milly Brineger	James & Lyda Blevins	
6849	Blevins, Robert	VA	1884	Etta Blevins	W.F. Blevins	Alice Edmondson		Isaac & Martha Edmondson
2090	Blevins, Roby	NC	1871	Elizabeth Blevins	G.D. Blevins	Celia Parsons	Daniel & Anna Blevins	Wm & Ruthey Parsons
4128	Blevins, Roby	NC	1867	Ellen Blevins	Shubal Blevins	Ada Thompson		John & Polly Thompson
14707	Blevins, Roby	WV	1881		Calvin Blevins	Mary Simmons	James & Necy Blevins	Jonas & Anna Simmons
21016	Blevins, Rufus	NC	1884		Leander Blevins	Peggy Osborne	Granville & Polly Blevins	David & Nancy Osborne
19966	Blevins, Sam	NC		Emer Blevins		Mary Blevins		Mary Wall
3615	Blevins, Sarah	NC	46yrs	none	Armstrong Blevins	Catherine Blevins	James & Lydda Blevins	Betsy Blevins
8458	Blevins, Sarah	VA	1876	Granvill Blevins	William Lewis	Nancy Lewis		Andrew & Biddy Lewis
8591	Blevins, Sarah	VA	1868	William Blevins	William Holaway	Louisa Waters		William & Zilpha Waters
11074	Blevins, Sarah	VA	1852	Ephraim Blevins	John Hart	Polley Caldwell	George & Polley Hart	Joseph & Catharine Caldwell

6132	Blevins, Sarahan	NC	1888	Carie Blevins	Wily Hurley	Malicy Blevins		John & Caroline Blevins
6182	Blevins, Shade	NC	1856	Cilia Blevins	George Blevins	Almedia Jones	Eli & Molly Blevins	Thomas & Elizabeth Jones
4471	Blevins, Susan	VA	70yrs	Tobis Blevins	Eli Blevins		James & Lydda Blevins	
6865	Blevins, Susan	KY	1867	Burbage Blevins	Elijah Blevins	Rachel Felty	Armstrong & Cathrine Blevins	Nicholas & Susan Felty
8532	Blevins, Susie	VA		John Blevins	James Blevins	Margaret Edmondson	Wells & Elizabeth Blevins	
6181	Blevins, Thomas	NC	1870	Ettie Blevins	George Blevins	Almedia Jones	Eli & Molly Blevins	Thomas & Elisabeth Jones
6868	Blevins, Thomas	KY	1871	Venie Blevins	Elijah Blevins	Rachel Felty	Armstrong & Cathrine Blevins	Nicholas & Susan Felty
6846	Blevins, Wells	VA	1856	Kisiah Blevins	Allen Blevins	Fanny Privette	Wells & Elizabeth Blevins	
9073	Blevins, Wells	NC	1873	none	George Blevins	Cynthia Baker	George & Lydia Blevins	
8460	Blevins, Wilburn	VA	1844	Martha Blevins	Edward Blevins	Nancy Blevins	James & Lyddia Blevins	
8484	Blevins, Wilburn	VA	1887	Minie Blevins	Wilburn Blevins	Martha Lewis	Edward & Nancy Blevins	Jackson & Biddy Lewis
4893	Blevins, Wiley	VA	1876	Lieza Blevins	Eli Blevins	Nancy Hams	Riley & Agney Blevins	
9054	Blevins, Wiley	VA	29yrs	Denna Blevins	James Blevins	Mary Blevins	Ned & Nancy Blevins	Levi & Ada Blevins
6101	Blevins, William	NC	1870	Mary Blevins	Jackson Blevins	Sarah Allen	James & Sarah Blevins	Elizabeth Allen
6184	Blevins, William	NC	1882		Shade Blevins	Cilia Hurley	George & Almedia Blevins	
6814	Blevins, William	NC	1886	Mandie Blevins	James Blevins	Louisa Sullen	Eli & Milly Blevins	Joseph & Malinda Sullen
6863	Blevins, William	VA	1876	Mary Blevins	Shubal Blevins	Ada Thompson		John & Polly Thompson
7634	Blevins, William	VA	1866	Rosa Blevins	James Blevins	Margaret Oson	Wells & Elizabeth Blevins	
8462	Blevins, William	VA	1877	Dartualia Blevins	Wilburn Blevins	Martha Lewis	Wells & Elizabeth Blevins	
8473	Blevins, William	KY	1875	Nancy Blevins	Ned Blevins	Susan Blevins	Armstrong Blevins	Catharine Blevins
8584	Blevins, William	VA	1840	Nancy Blevins	Armstrong Blevins	Catharine Hart	James & Lydia Blevins	
8586	Blevins, William	VA	1870	Sarah Blevins	W H Blevins	Nancy Davis	Armstrong & Catharine Blevins	Jordan & Seany Davis
9082	Blevins, William	NC	1867	Marth Blevins	George Blevins	Cynthia Baker	George & Lydia Blevins	
11087	Blevins, William	VA	1847	Elizabeth Blevins	Jessie Blevins	Catherine Pennington	Eli & Millie Blevins	Able & Lydia Pennington
11811	Blevins, William	NC	1889	Peggy Blevins	Leander Blevins	Peggy Osborne	Granville & Polly Blevins	David & Nancy Osborne
12966	Blevins, William	VA	1873	Martha Blevins	William Blevins	Elizabeth Blevins	Jessie & Catherine Blevins	James & Margaret Blevins
4474	Blevins, Willie	VA	20yrs	Sarah	Eli Blevins	Elisabeth Blevins	Tobias & Susan Blevins	Callon & Nancy Blevins

16320 ½	Bloodworth, Laura	AL	1864	M P Bloodworth	J W Morris	Didamia Trout		
7500	Bluejacket, Carrie	MO	1858	Charles Bluejacket	William Foreman	Lucinda McLain	Joseph & Narcissa Foreman	
16974	Bluejacket, Jennie	KS	1871		Keller Coody	Nancy Jenkins		
22335 *	Bly, Minnie	OK	1883	Henry Ridge	Art Williams	Abby Bly	Peggy Lynch	George & Annake Martin
7055	Boatright, Charles	KS		none	William Boatright	Isabel Clark	James & Rebecca Boatright	George & Sally Clark
7056	Boatright, Emmett	OK	1881	none	John Boatright	Fannie Wylie	Benj & Julia Boatright	Harvey & Ruth Wylie
16200	Boatright, Jesse	OK	1830	Evaline Boatright	William Boatright	Sallie Gater	Benj & Elizabeth Boatright	
7058	Boatright, John	OK	1843	Fannie Boatright	Benjamin Boatright	Julia Patterson	Benj & Elizabeth Boatright	John & Rhoda Patterson
7053	Boatright, John Jr.	KY	1879	Clara Boatright	John Boatright	Fannie Wylie	Benj & Julia Boatright	Harvey & Ruth Wylie
19090	Boatright, Lela	MO	1881	John Boatright	Benj Looney	Etna Eaves	Wm & Malissa Looney	James & Violetta Eaves
7059	Boatright, Morris	OK	1869	Sallie Boatright	John Boatright	Fannie Wylie	Benj & Julia Boatright	Harvey & Ruth Wylie
7057	Boatright, Robert	OK	1884	none	John Boatright	Fannie Wylie	Benj & Julia Boatright	Harvey & Ruth Wylie
7421	Boatright, Roy	OK	1877	none	James Boatright	Ella Winston	J J & Emeline Boatright	Wm & Martha Winston
7054	Boatright, Samuel	MO	1869	Lizzie Boatright	William Boatright	Isabel Clark	James & Rebecca Boatright	Thomas Clark
7080	Boen, Ed	MO	1858		James Boen	Pheobe Boggs	Zaza & Mary Boen	Ed & Elizabeth Boggs
14251	Bogue, Martha	IN	1842	widow	Herman Allen	Ann Clark	John & Rachel Allen	Daniel & Mary Clark
14256	Bogue, Sibbie	IN	1836	Josiah Bogue	Herman Allen	Ann Clark	John & Rachel Allen	Daniel & Mary Clark
19537	Bohanan, Charles	TN	1846	Amanda Bohanan	Ozahs Bohanan	Sarah Wade	William Bohanan	Edward & Elizabeth Wade
20162	Bolding, Julia	GA	1854	Thompson Bolding	Ephriam Sosebee	Sarah Church	Wm & Nancy Sosebee	Timothy & Mary Church
19519	Boling, Emma	TN	1872	Preston Boling	Andrew Davis	Sarah Goins		Sanford & Charity Goins
10786	Boling, Jerrymine	GA	1841	Amanda Boling	James Boling	Letty Christopher	Elliot Boling	Mattie Bridges
19518	Boling, Preston	TN	1858	Emma Boling	Pleasant Boling	Elizabeth Goins	Ezekiel & Nancy Boling	Carter & Cynthia Goins
7088	Bollinger, Emma	MO	1885	Perry Bollinger	James Morgan	Dartha Furguson	Nathan & Anna Morgan	Josiah & Arthusa Furguson
9551	Bolt, Mary	SC	1859	Henry Bolt	E B Knox	Mary Wall		Wm & Rebecca Wall
17350	Bolt, Mary	SC	1857	Henry Bolt	E.B. Knox	Mary Wall		Wm & Rebecca Wall
14279 *	Bommer, Robert	TN	1854	Eleanor Bommer	Dennis Tilley	Mary Bommer		
12039	Bone, Albert	GA	1903		Lee Bone	Lou Lawrence		Robert & Eliza Lawrence
12038	Bone, Bessie	GA	1906		Lee Bone	Lou Lawrence		Robert & Eliza Lawrence
8391	Bone, Easter	AR	1888	A S Bone	Thompson Wood	Eliza Martin	Johnson & Margaret Wood	Wm & Susan Martin

12037	Bone, Lou Etta	GA	1886	Lee Bone	Robert Lawrence	Eliza Brown		John & Loduska Brown
8485	Bone, Mary	VA	1850	John Bone	Armstrong Blevins	Catherine Blevins	James Blevins	Lydia Blevins
8508	Bone, Shady	WV	1878	Martha Bone	John Bone	Elizabeth Blevins		Armstrong & Catharine Blevins
8449	Bone, William	VA	1880	none	John Bone	Mary Blevins		Armstrong & Catharine Blevins
5366	Bonham, Elisabeth	VA	1862	James Bonham	Allen Clark	Lydda Blevins	Allen & Elisabeth Clark	Samuel & Annie Blevins
5791	Bonner, Annie	AR	1871	Andy Bonner	Milton Monroe	Henrietta Livengood	Wm & Rebecca Monroe	Daniel & Sarah Livengood
5786	Bonner, Saria	AR	1861	Jacob Bonner	Milton Monroe	Henrietta Livengood	Wm & Rebecca Monroe	Daniel & Sarah Livengood
13020	Booker, Mary	AL	1881	Charles Booker	James Hightower	Mary Houss	James & Nancy Hightower	Gilbert & Levitia Houss
2402	Booker, Neoma	VA	1864	Philip Booker	Noah Baldwin	Mahala Blevins	Wm & Margaret Baldwin	Elisha & Elizabeth Blevins
6942	Bookout, Flora	TN	1878	Henry Bookout	George Edmunds	Susan Gibbs	Mathew Edmunds	Linnville Gibbs
10726	Boon, Zadie	AL	1857	Thomas Boon	Jason Staples	Margarette Powell		
6333	Boone, Daniel	AL	23yrs	Callie McClelland	John Boone	Vicey Moniac	John & Nancy Boone	Sam & Susan Moniac
18576	Boone, Frank	AL	38yrs	Bettie Boone	Origin Boone	Susan Hathcock	John Boone	Thos & Betsey Hathcock
22711	Boone, James	AL	1849	Ms Lindsay				
6375	Boone, John	AL	27yrs	Lina Allen	Alex Boone	Minervy Moniac		David Moniac & Catherine Hale
18571	Boone, John	AL	26yrs	Maggie Boone	John Boone	Vicie Moniac	John Boone	Sam & Susan Moniac
6351	Boone, Mrs Alex	AL	1860	Alex Boone	David Moniac	Catherine Hale		Sam & Susan Moniac
6373	Boone, Mrs. Elijah	AL	1835	Elijah Boone	Thomas Hathcock	Elisabeth Marlow		
6367	Boone, Wm Thomas	AL	1861	Florence Allen	Elijah Boone	Vina Hathcock	John & Rena Boone	Thomas & Elisabeth Hathcock
19963	Booth, Ben	NC	1862	Elizabeth Booth	Benj Booth	Fannie Smith	Jacob Booth	
19961	Booth, James	NC	1870	Louisa Booth	Benj Booth	Fannie Smith	Jacob Booth	
19962	Booth, Joseph et al	NC			James Booth	Luider Brown	Benj & Fannie Booth	
19971	Booth, Lula et al	NC	40yrs		Ben Booth	Elizabeth Brown	Jacob Booth	William Smith
18239*	Boozeley, Adeline	GA	1858	Joe Boozeley	Tommy Benningham	Becca Crankfield	Tommy & Judy Benningham	Bob & Millie Crankfield
18240*	Boozeley, Lousiana	AL	1888		Joe Boozeley	Adaline Benningham		Tommy & Rebecca Benningham
18241*	Boozeley, Richard	GA	1871	Lula Boozeley	Joe Boozeley	Adaline Benningham		Tommy & Rebecca Benningham
12978	Borders, Rosa	TX	1874	John Borders	C W Bailey	F J C Walker	J & P Bailey	Numa & Adoline Walker
20330*	Borders, Walter	GA	1851	Caroline Borders	Tom Hargroves	Fannie Borders		Dave & Sooky Indian
18684	Borras, Margarette	FL	1839	John Borras	Thomas Robinson	Mary Harvel		Elizabeth Harvel
21017*	Boss, Annie	NC	1868	James Boss	George Foster	Polly Foster	Peter Bryan	Anie Bryan

16155	Bostwick, Matilda	WI	48yrs	Syrus Bostwick	Samuel Bass	Eliza Murphy	Elijah & Matilda Bass	Washington & Rebecky Murphy
7087	Boswell, Lucina	KS	1883	Nelon Boswell	Jasper Wade	Lucinda Allen		Joseph & Margaret Allen
19093	Boucher, Robby	KS	1890		Peter Boucher	Rebeca Holt		
6916	Boudinet, Caroline	OK	1830	W.P. Boudinet	Thomas Fields	Nancy Downing	Richard & Susanna Fields	John Downing & Ollie Crittenden
14812	Boudinot, Elias	AR	1859	Clara Boudinot	Elias Boudinot	Harriette Gold	Oo wa tie & Susannah	
996	Boulder, Sarah	OK	1845	widow	Nathan Goins	Mary McGill	Jim & Rhody Goins	Bill & Hannah McGill
21740	Bounds, Ida	LA	1859		? Jeter	Jane		
3506	Bowar, Annie	TX	1883	James Bowar	Jeff Moore	Emma Bower	Eppie Moore	Isaac & Janah Bower
15614	Bowen, Henry	NC	1877	Carrie Bowen	Lewis Bowen	Elvira Scott	Harrison & Elizabeth Bowen	Henry & Mary Scott
16472	Bowen, Henry & Nellie	GA	1896 1898		Mack Bowen	Milda Bettes	William Bowen	Leroy & Nancy Bettes
19064	Bowen, Jettie	NC	1881		Lewis Bowen	Elvira Scott	Harrison & Elizabeth Bowen	Henry & Mary Scott
16398	Bowen, John	NC	1884	Luella Bowen	Lewis Bowen	Elvira Scott	Harrison & Elizabeth Bowen	Henry & Mary Scott
19063	Bowen, Lewis	NC	1885		Lewis Bowen	Elvira Scott	Harrison & Elizabeth Bowen	Henry & Mary Scott
16772	Bowen, Permelia	TN	1864	N D Bowen	J G Trulove	Flora Butner	Austin & Pattie Trulove	Bettie Butner
22097	Bowen, Selela	AR	1878	J.H. Bowen	T.K. Frost	Mary Rogers	J.B. & Ursula Frost	J.A. & Mary Rogers
22099	Bowerman, Mariah	TX	1866		Joseph Rogers	Mary Hodges	Henry & Mariah Rogers	Jemima Hodges
7084	Bowers, Carrie	OK	1874	Willard Bowers	Walter Bays	Frances Robison	Joseph & Carrie Bays	Wm & Ellen Robison
18359	Bowers, Daniel	GA	1846	Martha Bowers	David Bowers	Tilda Mathis	George Bowers	Wm Mathis & Elizabeth Henson
6728	Bowers, Effie	OK	1883	Lon Bowers	Jemy Tittle	Annie Prather	Don & Rozener Tittle	Robert & Carline Prather
8366	Bowers, Ida	OK	1861	Fred Bowers	George Rogers	Elizabeth Foster	Robert Rogers	
12191	Bowers, Lillie	NC	1873	Thomas Bowers	John Osborn	Polly Stamper	Jesse & Cynthia Osborn	Jobe & Elizabeth Stamper
12189	Bowers, Mary	NC	1876	widow	John Osborn	Polly Stamper	Jessey Osborn	Jobe & Elizabeth Stamper
18599	Bowers, Rosco	NC	1894		Alex Bowers	Mary Osborn	Jyles & Laurina Bowers	Jess & Polly Osborn
18111	Bowers, Thomas	NC			Thomas Bowers	Lillie Osborn	Gil & Louisa Bowers	Johnathan Osborn
21013	Bowlan, Mattie	AL	1870	David Dowlan	Daniel Sizemore	Rebecca Markham	Joel Sizemore	Andrew Markham
21523	Bowles, Allen	TN	1854	Ella Bowles	Elexander Bowles	Lettie Bishop	Allen Bowles	
21515	Bowles, Charles	OK	1869	Mattie Bowles	James Bowles	Malinda Nutt	Allen & Arraville Bowles	
18562	Bowles, Frank	OK	1861	Matilda Bowles	James Bowles	Melinda Nutt	Allen Bowles	Anevetta Broack
21524	Bowles, James	OK	1857	Fannie Bowles	James Bowles	Malinda Nutt	Allen Bowles	Abie Broach
13980	Bowles, Mattie	OK	1871	Charles Bowles	Thomas Horn	Nelly July	Jeremiah Horn	July & Towne
18573	Bowles, Sebron	OK	1873	Maggie Bowles	James Bowles	Malinda Nutt	Allen Bowles	Averrilla Broach

ID	Name	State	Year	Col5	Col6	Col7	Col8	Col9
18003	Bowlier, Eliza	OK	1859	Emil Bowlier	Nathan Swift	Adaline Holt		Berry & Susanna Holt
12475	Bowlin, Susan	NC	1866	James Bowlin	James Osborne	Clemmenzy Bare	David & Nancy Osborne	Joseph & Sousie Bare
22169	Bowling, Alvin	GA	1872		Thomas Bowling	Sallie Haney	John & Elizabeth Bowling	Joe Haney & Elizzie Kines
7814	Bowling, Annie	GA	1902		George Bowling	Amanda Kinnett	George & Harriett Bowling	Alonzo & Annie Kinnett
7813	Bowling, George	GA	1879	Amanda Bowling	George Bowling	Harriett Bowling	Alexander Bowling	John & Elizabeth Bowling
7811	Bowling, Geroge	GA	1906		George Bowling	Amanda Kinnett	George & Harriett Bowling	Alonzo & Annie Kinnett
8709	Bowling, Hester	TN	1865	Joe Bowling	John Mann	Barbara Owens		Henry & Mary Owens
22168	Bowling, Josep	GA	1875	Lena Bowling	Thomas Bowling	Sallie Haney	John & Elizabeth Bowling	Joe Haney & Elizabeth Kines
7815	Bowling, Lillie	GA	1899		George Bowling	Amanda Kinnett	George & Harriett Bowling	Alonza & Annie Kinnett
22071	Bowling, Thadeus	AL	1854	Mary Bowling	Martin Bowling	Virginia Mitchel	Preston Bowling	Carter Bowling
17534	Bowling, William	GA	1845	Pocahuntus Bowling	Elexander Bowling	Elizabeth Kines		Martin & Elizabeth Kines
17887	Bowman, Estella	IL		Charles Bowman	Alfred Bays	Josephine Polly		
14429	Bowman, Genie	AL	1878	T U Bowman	J Stanley Todd	Missouri Morris	John & Lucinda Todd	John & Didamie Morris
5422	Bowman, John	OK	1862	Anna Bowman	Jason Bowman	Desdemo-na McGraw	James & Rachel Bowman	John & Martha McGraw
12139	Bowman, Margaret	VA	1850		Kith Billips	Irene Sizemore	James & Nancy Billips	George Sizemore
13655	Bown, Saphronia	ID	1862	Herbert Bown	Caleb Duncan	Mary Hudson	Charles & Mahala Duncan	
13444*	Bowyer, Nettie	WI		Thomas Bowyer	Mark Revels	Kneel Winchel	McCaga & Mornon Revels	James & Jane Winchel
22234	Box, John	AL	1876		H.T. Box	- Warren		J.W. & Fannie Warren
21015	Box, Martha	AL	1856	Henry Box	John Warren	Faney	Abil Green	Christian Hyte
8388	Boyd, Charley	OK	1867	Blanch Boyd	Wesley Boyd	Sallie Yeates		Benj & Elizabeth Yeates
19964	Boyd, Mahala	NC	1851	Floyd Boyd	Jessie Hooker	Betsy Arrington	Sam Hooker	Mary Gibson
21026	Boyd, Ora	GA	1861	Robert Boyd	Calvin Blalock	Josephene Freeman	Wm & Catherine Blalock	Alex & Sarah Freeman
7759	Boyd, William	OK	1850	Allie Boyd	William Boyd	Elizabeth Oxford		Abram & Edith Oxford
8383	Boyd, William	OK	1871	Sallie Boyd	Wesley Boyd	Sallie Yeates		Benj Yeates
7539	Boyle, Francis	AZ	1862	William Boyle	Joseph Jourdan	Sarah Blackburn	Aquilla & Betsey Jourdan	Andrew & Francis Blackburn
7536	Boyle, Frank	AZ	1882	Mabel Boyle	William Boyle	Francis Jourdan		Joseph & Sarah Jourdan
14085	Bozeman, James	GA	1858	Delphia Bozeman	John Bozeman	Sarah Darby	Amos & Nancy Bozeman	Charles & Nancy Darby
16278	Bozeman, Lincoln	GA	1864	Nancy Bozeman	John Bozeman	Sarah Darby	Amos & Nancy Bozeman	Charles & Nancy Darby
14086	Bozeman, Sarah	GA	1841	widow	Charles Darby	Nancy Biddy	Charles & Nancy Darby	Jonathan & Mary Biddy
16277	Bozeman, William	GA	1866	Annie Bozeman	John Bozeman	Sarah Darby	Amos & Nancy Bozeman	Charles & Nancy Darby

8023	Bracket, Sarah	OK	1851	Daniel Bracket	Allen Mathews	Jane McDanell		Sally Raper
15483	Bradford, Harriet	GA	1847	R I Bradford	Joe Pearson	Arminda Darby		Charlie & Nancy Darby
3 *	Bradford, Nancy	MO	1805	widow	Tom Sanders	Mary Samuels		
9365	Bradford, Nettie	OK	1877	Homer Bradford	Charlie Schumaker	Judith McBee		John & Katie McBee
18154	Bradish, Maggie	IL	1882	Edgar Bradish	William Graham	Hormana Dale	Alex & Margret Graham	John & Carline Dale
17783	Bradley, Alice	IN	1854			Nancie Goins		
12433	Bradley, Cynthia	OK	1855	George Bradley	Jesse Sanders	Caroline Catron	George & Jennie Sanders	John & Margret Catron
14649	Bradley, Dorothy	GA	1816	Jefferson Bradley	James Moss	Dorothy Jackson	Henry & Malinda Moss	Margaret Jackson
20525	Bradley, Johnnie	GA	1904		John Bradley	Mary Lane	John Sr. & Elizabeth Bradley	Samuel & Caroline Lane
19426	Bradley, Laura	TN	32yrs	W.B. Bradley	Thomas Hooper	Rittie Hatcher	James Hooper	James Hatcher
7757	Bradley, Margaret	OK	1875		Andrew Gambill	Mary Hulsey	Wm & Sallie Gambill	
546	Bradley, Margret	TX	1874	Wm Bradley	Francis Housman	Mary Garrett	James & Srophana Housman	Hezkiah & Margret Garrett
567	Bradley, Mary	TX	1874	John Bradley	Marcis Housman	Mary Garrett	James & Srophana Housman	Hezkiah & Margrett Garrett
20554	Bradley, Mary	GA	1872	John Bradley	Samuel Lane	Caroline Tallent	Wilson & Martha Lane	Russell & Mary Tallent
18575	Bradley, Ora	GA		G.C. Bradley	General Stephens	Jane Ledford	Canon Stephens	Silas & Armindia Ledford
18678	Bradley, Peter	FL	1878	Emma Bradley	M. Bradley	Harriett Monk		John & Silva Monk
22705	Bradley, Robinson	KY	1857	Alice Bradley	James Bradley	Frances		
20524	Bradley, Rosa	GA	1899		John Bradley	Mary Lane	John Sr. & Elizabeth Bradley	Samuel & Caroline Lane
20556	Bradley, Sallie	GA	1903		John Bradley	Mary Lane	John Sr & Elizabeth Bradley	Samuel & Caroline Lane
22998 *	Bradley, Sim	TN	1832	Jane Bradley	Thomas Skelton	Tilda Goss		
1464	Bradley, Thomas	OK	1850	Emly Bradley	Richard Bradley	Nancy Foushudeman	Mary Bradley	Mary Fike
20551	Bradley, Vicie	GA	1905		John Bradley	Mary Lane	John Sr & Elizabeth Bradley	Samuel & Caroline Lane
18323	Bradshaw, Featherston	MS	1869	Mary Bradshaw	Sanford Bradshaw	Patie Busby	Stephen Bradshaw	Nathan & Willy Busby
18813	Bradshaw, George	MS	1864	Mary Bradshaw	Sanford Bradshaw	Patie Busby	Stephen Bradshaw	Nathan Busby
18121	Bradshaw, Levie	NC	22yrs	Harve Bradshaw	Elisha Smith	Amanda Anderson	Wm & Polly Smith	Lazrus & Nancy Anderson
22627	Bradshaw, Sanford	MS	1882		Sanford Bradshaw	Patie Busby	Stephen Bradshaw	Willie & Nathan Busby
9545	Bradshaw, Susan	NC	1852	N V Bradshaw	Lafayette Underwood	Margaret Jackson	Joseph Vanoy & Delia Underwood	Moses & Sarah Jackson
17850	Brady, Mary	TN	1861	J.T. Brady	Wm Paine	Martha Neal	Thos Paine & Maranda Watson	Wm & Harriet Neal
13188	Brady, Robert	NC	1868	Priscilla Brady	Marcus Powell	Nancy Brady		Dow & Debby Brady
13656	Bragdon, Emily	CA	1871	Edwin Bragdon	Caleb Duncan	Mary Hudson	Charles & Mahala Duncan	

9342	Braig, Arabella	MO	1881	John Braig	Jarner Poe	Sarah Harralson		Vincent & Martha Harralson
8225	Brainard, Hannah	OK	1855	Alvah Brainard	William Hammond	Eliza Woodward	Moses & Dorcas Hammond	Abraham & Elizabeth Woodward
9350	Brainard, Walter	OK	1883	none	A O Brainard	Hannah Hammond	DeWitt & Sallie Brainard	Wm & Eliza Hammond
15336	Bramlett, Charley	GA	1888		William Bramlett	Margarett Moore	Wesley & Many Bramlett	
15335	Bramlett, Clinton	GA			William Bramlett	Margarett Moore	Wesley & Many Bramlett	
15334	Bramlett, John	GA	1892		William Bramlett	Margarett Moore	Wesley & Many Bramlett	
12218	Bramlett, Josie	NC	1880	Ervin Bramlett	? Baker		Samuel Baker	
15333	Bramlett, Laura	GA	1896		William Bramlett	Margarett Moore	Wesley & Many Bramlett	
15332	Bramlett, Lena	GA	1902		William Bramlett	Margarett Moore	Wesley & Many Bramlett	
12354	Bramlett, Lucy	GA	1892		Robert Bramlett	Mary Turner	Wesley & Polly Bramlett	Mack & Arie Turner
17756	Bramlett, Margaret	GA	1864	Wm Bramlett	Bennett Moore	Aley Butler	James & Sallie Moore	Joel & Mattie Butler
12353	Bramlett, Robert	GA	1855	Mary Bramlett	Wesley Bramlett	Polly Howell	Miles & Annie Bramlett	Jackson & Catharine Howell
12051	Bramlett, Tilda	GA	1880		Murray Bramlett	Nancy Blalock	Miles & Annie Bramlett	George & Jane Blalock
15331	Bramlett, Wiliam	GA	1866	Margarett Bramlett	Wesley Bramlett	Mary Howell	Miles & Annie Bramlett	Jack Howell
15230	Bramlett, William	GA	1898		William Bramlett	Margarett Moore	Wesley & Mary Bramlett	
22356	Branch, J.T.	TN	1865	Mollie Branch	Jessie Branch	Ruthie Howard		Mollie Canoot
15879*	Branham, Amanda	GA	1865	Levi Branham	Lewis McDade	Judy Bailey	Mary McDade	Wm & Martha Bailey
17999	Brannan, S.H.	TN	1845	Octavia Brannan	George Brannan	Rebekah Samples	Tom & Phoebe Brannan	Charley & Mary Samples
17361	Brannock, Mollie	WV	1876	James Brannock	Howard Smith	Elizabeth Toffie	Pollie Smith	John & Judia Toffie
18146	Branstetter, Josephine	GA	1879	James Branstetter	John Brown	Loduskey Tidwell		John & Loucrecy Tidwell
17853	Brashears, Catherine	OK	1873	Wm Brashears	W.A. Williams	Mary Haynes	Joseph & Catharine Williams	
12811	Braswell, Lizzie	GA	1844	Derrell Braswell	Henry Guess	Jerusha Swimmers	Abner Guess	Alford Swimmers
18441	Bray, Eddy	NC	1871	Mary Bray		Martha Bray		Martha Poindexter
20046	Bray, Henrietta	NC	1902		Eddy Bray	Mary Loggins	Martha Bray	Sanders & Henrietta Loggins
20045	Bray, Ira	NC	1905		Eddy Bray	Mary Loggins	Martha Bray	Sanders & Henrietta Loggins
10846	Bray, Julia	NC	36yrs		Billy Meacham	Helen Morse		Jesse & Littie Morse
17689	Bray, Malinda	TN	1862	Charles Bray	William Goss	Sarah Johnson	Riley & Sarah Goss	Daniel & Nancy Johnson
18442	Bray, Martha	NC	1846		Henry Bray	Martha Poindexter		
22446	Bray, Parlee	OK	1869	John Bray	Edward Morris	Eliza Drummond	Jefferson Morris & Nancy Jones	Freeman & Nancy Drummond
17677	Bray, Thomas	NC	1860	Sarah Bray	William Bray	Martha Poindexter	Henry & Martha Bray	Robert & Martha Poindexter
20018	Bray, William	NC	1900		Eddy Bray	Mary Loggins	Martha Bray	Sanders & Henrietta Loggins

19124	Braziel, Edward	GA	1867	Anna Braziel	James Braziel	Seleta Doss		Edward & Seleta Doss
15229	Braziel, Floyd	GA	1876	Della Braziel	James Braziel	Seleta Doss		Edward & Seleta Doss
6497	Braziel, Robert	OK	1842	Nancy Braziel	Wm Braziel	Margret Proctor		
19125	Braziel, Robert	GA	1869	Lula Braziel	James Braziel	Seleta Doss		Edward & Seleta Doss
19126	Braziel, Seleta	GA	1844	James Braziel	Edward Doss	Seleta Parker		Jesse & Lizzie Parker
19127	Braziel, Tandy	GA	1879	Lillie Braziel	James Braziel	Seleta Doss		Edward & Seleta Doss
19521	Brazier, Alton	TN	1905		Johnathan Brazier	Annie Marshall	Thomas & Lucy Brazier	Hayden & Chick Marshall
19525	Brazier, Charles	TN	1868	Winnie Brazier	Thomas Brazier	Lucy Kelly	Wm & Pauline Brazier	Charles & Lucy Kelly
19523	Brazier, Edward	TN	1893		Johnathan Brazier	Annie Marshall	Thomas & Lucy Brazier	Hayden & Chick Marshall
19522	Brazier, Holland	TN	1900		Johnathan Brazier	Annie Marshall	Thomas & Lucy Brazier	Hayden & Chick Marshall
19527	Brazier, Nathan	TN	1884		Thomas Brazier	Lucy Kelly	Wm & Pauline Brazier	Charles & Lucy Kelly
19637	Brazier, Obediah	TN	1880	Tennie Brazier	Thomas Brazier	Lucy Kelly	Wm & Pauline Brazier	Charles & Lucy Kelly
19526	Brazier, Robert	TN	1877	Lizie Brazier	Thomas Brazier	Lucy Kelly	Wm & Pauline Brazier	Charles & Lucy Kelly
19524	Brazier, Thomas	TN	1870	Jennie Brazier	Thomas Brazier	Lucy Kelly	Wm & Pauline Brazier	Charles & Lucy Kelly
22302 *	Breakbill, Sophia	OK	1865	J.J. Breakbill	Lewis Rowe	Chaney Landrum	Jesse & Delila Rowe	Clora Landrum
16045	Breeding, Joel	OK	1841	Sophia Breeding	Stephen Breeding			
12990	Brendle, Patsy	NC		J D Brendle	Asberry Burns Jr.	Sarah Morris	Uriah & Sallie Burns	
7086	Brenner, Hattie	KS	1879	A F Brenner	Laken Davis	Mary Cunningham	Henry & Harriet Davis	
6278	Brewer, Carrie	MO	1866	Samuel Brewer	Newell Bays	Carrie Heaton	Joshua & Emily Bays	David Heaton
12679	Brewer, Cherokee	OK	1839	George Brewer	Richard Ratcliff	Nancy Fields	Martha Ratcliff	George & Sallie Fields
8589	Brewer, Dora	VA	1885	John Brewer	William Blevins	Nancy Davis	Armstrong & Catharine Blevins	Jordan & Seany Davis
685	Brewer, Eliza	OK	1849	divorced	William Betts	Ede Bird	John & Ruthie Betts	John & Nancy Bird
20942 *	Brewer, Eliza	NC	1865	George Brewer		Mary Brown		Pollie Brown
3256	Brewer, Emma	OK	1851	George Brewer	Tom Ross	Annie Seabolt	David & Alcey Ross	Adam & Annie Seabolt
18353	Brewer, James	AR	1868	Mary Brewer	George Brewer	Susan Denham		Caroline Denham
22062	Brewer, Minnie	MO	1888	Harvey Brewer	Zachriah West	Lula Smith	Isaac & Nancy West	Henry & Saviah Smith
8590	Brewer, Nancy	VA	1888	William Brewer	William Blevins	Nancy Davis	Armstrong & Catharine Blevins	Jordan & Seany Davis
17633 *	Brewer, Seenie	OK	60yrs		Jack Gilbreath	Dorothy Carter		
20139	Brewton, Josephine	FL	1867	N.J. Brewton	Valentine Fillingim	Sarah Dukes	Robert & Ester Fillingim	Thomas & Ann Duke
18710	Briars, Ula	MS		B.F. Briars	Marion Franklin	Francis	Ellis & Laplata Franklin	John & Martha Lawson

12082	Brigance, Sarah	TX	1854	Melvin Brigance	Wm Gambill	Susan Ribble	Wm & Sarah Gambill	
7963	Brigmon, Effie	NC	1893	none	John Brigmon	Margret Maney	Van & Tilday Brigmon	George & Elisebeth Maney
7973	Brigmon, Margret	NC	1873	John Brigmon	George Maney	Elisebeth Anderson	John & Poley Maney	Jackson & Poley Anderson
19976	Brigmon, Matilda	NC	1883	Charley Brigmon	James Blankenship	Lorina Maney		Martin & Matilda Maney
7974	Brigmon, Zetta	NC	1898	none	John Brigmon	Margret Maney	Van & Tildey Brigmon	George & Elisebeth Maney
21221	Briley, Mittie	OK	1882	Elwin Briley	James Sampson	Sarah Lumpkin	Wm & Mary Sampson	Bushsod & Mary Lumpkin
8203	Brindle, Josephine	NC	1861	John Brindle	Asbury Burns	Adaline Morris	Uriah & Sallie Burns	
9096	Brinegar, Daniel	WV		none	David Brinegar	Sarah Osborne	Jacob & Sheba Brinegar	Jesse Osborne
9088	Brinegar, Edward	WV		Nellie Brinegar	David Brinegar	Sarah Osborn	Jacob & Shebe Brinegar	Jesse Osborn
9097	Brinegar, J L	WV	1878	Sallie Brinegar	Adam Brinegar	Jane Hoppers	Jacob & Sheba Brinegar	Daniel & Sintha Hoppers
9091	Brinegar, John	WV	1861	Margaret Brinegar	Adam Brinegar	Jane Hoppers	Jacob & Sheba Brinegar	Daniel & Sintha Hoppers
13008	Brinegar, Leroy	NC	1849	Martha Brinegar	Jacob Brinegar	Sheby Sizemore	Jacob Brinegar	Ned & Mahala Sizemore
6148	Brinegar, Mary	NC	1879	Robbert Brinegar	Eli Phipps	Jeston Phipps	Benjamin & Rutha Phipps	Ahart & Maryan Phipps
9105	Brinegar, William	WV	1868	Mary Brinegar	Adam Brinegar	Jane Hoppers	Jacob & Sheba Brinegar	Daniel & Sintha Hoppers
21607	Brinkley, Clarisa	NC	1843	R.W. Brinkley	James Badgett	Elizabeth Winfrey	Abram & Mickey Badgett	Caleb & Mary Winfrey
18363	Brock, James	OK	1854	Minnie Brock	John Brock	Rebecca Langley	Sarah Brock	Matthew Langley
2331	Brock, Lillian	GA		James Brock	William Matheson	Malissa Hampton	John & Hannah Hampton	Eli & Annie Matheson
11528	Brock, Mary	OK	1877	Hugh Brock	Joel Kieth	Susan McClure	Mathey & Elizbeth Kieth	James & Rebecca McClure
18523	Brock, Orthey	GA	1871	Wesley Brock	A.J. Smith	Martha Bowen	Elijah Smith	Margaret Smith
14988	Brogdon, John	AL	1866	Ella Brogdon	B. Cloud	Mary Brogdon		
2260	Brogdon, Lillie	GA	1872	C B Brogdon	R R Bell	Lucinda Hampton	J M & Elizabeth Bell	G W & Mary Hampton
18793	Brooks, Christine	GA	1886		Hiram Brooks	Louisa Yother		Adam & Celia Yother
11215	Brooks, Elizabeth	MO	1859		Sterling Banard	Nancy Mason	Betsy Griffin	John Mason & Mary Moore
6154	Brooks, Ellen	NC	1879	Author Brooks	William Jones	Nancy Phipps	Thomas & Elizabeth Jones	Ahart & Maryan Phipps
2902	Brooks, Henry	OK	1855	Mary Brooks	Jessie Brooks	Sallie King	John Brooks & Aggie Knott	Jack King & Olive Price
18794	Brooks, Louisa	GA	1842		Adam Yother	Celia Holyfield	Adam Yother	Isaac Holyfield
15567*	Brooks, Loula	GA	1866	Elias Brooks	Ephraim Gregory	Caroline Burge	Joe & Clay Witt	Toney & Clarissy Burge
14968	Brooks, Lucetta	OK	1882		Jack Rainey	Lunetta Caldwell		Joseph & Polly Caldwell
10412	Brooks, Manda	NC	1874	Larkin Brooks	William Osborn	Sirena Lewis		Ephrim & Abbie Roark

15725*	Brooks, Mary	GA	1853	Andrew Brooks	William Mack	Hannah Hog		Frank & Tena Hog
21768	Brooks, Mary	AL	1889	F.C. Brooks	W.F. Cryor	Mary Givens		
6349	Brooks, Mrs T.J.	AL	1887	T J Brooks	Alex Boone	Minerva Moniac		David Moniac & Catherine Hale
17487	Brooks, Phoeba	GA	1874	James Brooks	Caeb Whitfield	Rosalee Crow	W.G. & Anna Whittfield	Anna Crow
10213	Brooks, Polly	NC	1855	Curtis Brooks	Henry Wagoner	Charlottte Sizemore		Owen & Rebecha Sizemore
10433	Brooksher, Nancy	GA	1865	Beverly Brooksher	Robert Hulsey	Mary Wacaster	Wesley & Lucy Hulsey	John & Peggy Blasingame
7616	Brookshier, Permelia	GA	1842	Tilman Brookshier	John Gates	Elizabeth Hood		Martie Richard-son Hood
18242	Broom, May	GA	1873	J.S. Broom	John Cook	Mary Ragar		James & Louvica Cook
18899	Brooms, William	AR	1858	Maldona Brooms	John Brooms	Emiline Gullett	Lewis & Bettie Brooms	Russ Gullett
21957	Brothers, Mary	TN	1872	none	Dock Brothers	Martha Nipper		Cosby & Polly Cox
20233	Brought, Cynthia	OK	1863	Cloid Brought	Rainey Chastain	Judah Watts	John & Marth Chastain	Pleasant & Polly Watts
8623	Broughton, Martha	OK	1861	Andrew Broughton	James Howard	Lidda Crabtree	Arington & Elizebeth Howard	Isaac & Mary Crabtree
4548*	Brown, Alice	MO	1865	G H Browne	Wilburne Taylor	Harriet Williams	John & Elizabeth Taylor	Allen & Alice Williams
19030	Brown, Alice	AL	1896		William Brown	Sarah Goins		Nathan & Charlotta Goins
19670	Brown, Amanda	TN	1869	George Brown	Robbert Hatcher	Mary Hooper	John & Henrietta Hatcher	Dency & Elizabeth Hooper
21385	Brown, Amanda	TX	1845	D.O. Brown	? Graham	? Glass		
21372	Brown, Andrew	TX	1846	Luvina Brown	Burrell Brown	Nancy Hoyle	William Brown	
21373	Brown, Andrew	TX	1871	Susan Brown	Andrew Brown	Easter Cobin	Burrell Brown & Nancy Hoyle	
12183	Brown, Anna	WV			Calvin Blevins	Mary Simmons	James Blevins	James Simmons
56	Brown, Annie	MO	1857	Frank Brown	L. Byron Boynton	Laura Rider		Austin Rider & Polly Starr
15941*	Brown, Annie et al	GA	1896		Monroe Brown	Lizzie Castleberry	Gilford & Mary Chandler	
6552	Brown, Barnabas	IL	1857		Zedirck Brown	Fannie Blackburn	Barney & Nance Brown	Andrew & Francis Blackburn
12036	Brown, Barum	GA	1865	Carry Brown	Barum Brown	Sarah Foster	Jim & Cary Brown	John & Nancy Foster
21553	Brown, Becca	GA	1855	Joe Brown	Harrison Cooley	Adaline Jones		Harriette Jones
13858	Brown, Bell	NC	1866	W J Brown	James Redmon	Bell Redmon	Morgan Redmon	Sonsan Redmon
7713	Brown, Carrie	OK	1863	Carl Brown	William Trotter	Louisa Pittsenborger		John & Cathrine Pittsenborger
17433	Brown, Carrie	GA	1865	Barum Brown	Jim Brown	Sarah Summers	Jim & Cary Brown	
5451	Brown, Charles	KS	1880	Ella Brown	Nelson Brown	Melvina Blair		
18593	Brown, Charles	OK	1854	Mary Brown	Joseph Brown	Nancy Ward		Charles Ward
19032	Brown, Cora	AL	1897		William Brown	Sarah Goins		Nathan & Charlotta Goins
19760*	Brown, Cora	TN		William Brown	James Johnson	Betty Johnson		
1137	Brown, Daniel	MO	1855	Flora Brown	William Brown	Lucinda Swadley	Isom Brown & Matilda Tindle	Thomas Swadley & Annie Fanning

7625	Brown, David	GA	1841	Massoura Brown	Alexander Brown	Poley Marco	Sallie Rainwater	
12056	Brown, Donia	WV	1856	George Brown	William Williams	Mary Sizemore	Wm & Mary Williams	Hiram & Jane Sizemore
21288	Brown, Dora	TX	1870	Burson Brown	John Bishop	Avarillo Bowles		
12034	Brown, Eddie	GA	1886		C H Brown	Martha Ivey	Clete & Winnie Brown	Milton & Eliza Ivey
22154	Brown, ElDora	AL	1878	D.M. Brown	Layfayett Bell	Nancy Holcomb	Ira & Jane Bell	William & Sarah Holcomb
2334	Brown, Elias et al	MO			Jade Brown	Mollie Hensley	William & Mary Brown	William & Sarah Hensley
22977	Brown, Elihu	VA	1863	Laura Brown	Wesley Brown	Sarah Stamper	Oesley & Lettie Brown	Eli & Susanna Stamper
9839	Brown, Eliza	WY	1865	J C Brown	John Buttry	Margret Martin	Wm & Luvisa Buttry	Wm & Susan Martin
20174	Brown, Eliza	GA	1845	Pink Brown	Charley McAllister	Nancy Stiwinter	Jeff & Martha McAllister	
20589	Brown, Elsie	TN	1899		James Brown	Mary Cross	Wm & Nancy Brown	Absalom & Susan Cross
4759	Brown, Elvin	MO	1883	none	Nelson Brown	Melvina Blair	Tom & Mary Brown	
11283	Brown, Elzina	NC	1864	Shadrick Brown	Calvin Osborne	Martha Sheets	Jesse & Cynthia Osborne	Jacob & Sally Sheets
7714	Brown, Enoch	OK	1864	Eliza Brown	Smith Brown	Elizabeth Bricker	Smith Brown	William Bricker
16388	Brown, Evan	TX	1845	Callie Brown	Aaron Brown	Elizabeth McIntire		
21762	Brown, Ewell	TX	1867		Ephraim Brown	Julia Watson	John & Hannah Brown	Wm & Harriett Watson
18553	Brown, Fannie	TN	1864	William Brown	David Cate	Jane McCrary		Pegy Oxford
505	Brown, Floid	MO	1892	none	Elijah Eaves	Emma Brown	James Eaves	Villitty Hambelton
13730*	Brown, Frank	GA	1855	Rose Brown	Ned Brown	Martha Bly	Cue & Tilla Tiffens	Wilkerson & Hannah Bly
17917	Brown, Frank	MO	1852	Martha Brown	William Brown	Mary Stives	Tom & Polly Brown	Balis & Reoby Stives
13732*	Brown, Frank gdn	GA			Ned Brown	Martha		
13580*	Brown, Frank Jr.	GA	1884	Bessie Brown	Frank Brown	Rose Tompson	Ned & Martha Brown	George & Mary Tompson
20391*	Brown, George	TN	1844	Silver Brown	George Brown	Mariah Jabount	Benj & Emma Brown	Harry & Easter Duncan
19694	Brown, Grady	TN	1895		George Brown	Amanda Hatcher		Robert & Mary Hatcher
11954*	Brown, Henry C.	GA	1864	Julia Brown	Loyd Brown	Rebecca Schey	Stephen Brown	
3315	Brown, Ida May	NC	21yrs	S N Brown	Joel Crisp	Nancy Delozier	Pendleton & Nancy Crisp	Edward & Elizabeth Delozier
12033	Brown, Inez	GA	1898		Charlie Brown	Martha Ivey	Clete & Winnie Brown	Milton & Eliza Ivey
4280	Brown, J., C., & B.	OK			James Brown	Nancy Fountain	John & Lodusky Brown	
7812	Brown, James	GA	1906		James Brown	Mary Richardson	John & Sarah Brown	Nathan & Delilah Richardson
19081	Brown, James	OK	1841	Margaret Brown				Wm & Adeline Downing
22613	Brown, James	OK	1860	Mary Brown	William Brown	Nancy Heatherly	James & Sally Brown	James & Rebecca Haines

125 *	Brown, Jessie	NC	1876	William Brown	Jacob Candler	Nancy Russell	Randall & Nancy Russell	Canada & Beckie Cheek
2326	Brown, Jessie	MO	1888	none	Jade Brown	Mollie Hensley	William & Mary Brown	William & Sarah Hensley
21389	Brown, Jessie	TX	1881	General Pitcher	David Brown	Amanda Graham		
17432	Brown, Jim	GA	1820	Sarah Brown	Jim Brown	Cary Addington		
2367 *	Brown, John	NC	1885	none	Lee Brown	Lena Gaither	Robert & Lizzie Brown	Lorenzo & Classie Gaither
5567	Brown, John	OK	1839	none	Isham Brown	Matilda Tindal	Alex Brown & Sarah Canoe	
7628	Brown, John	GA			Alex Brown	Poley Marco	Sallie Rainwater	
12035	Brown, John	GA	1867	Mary Brown	Barnum Brown	Sarah Foster	Jim & Cary Brown	John & Nancy Foster
13578 *	Brown, John	GA	1858	Lidia Brown	Ned Brown	Martha Bly	Cue & Tella Tippins	Wilkerson & Hannah Bly
15228	Brown, John	GA	1867	Mary Brown	Barum Brown	Sallie Forester	Jim & Cary Brown	
13733 *	Brown, John gdn	GA			Ned Brown	Martha		
16042	Brown, Joseph	OK	1863	Kittie Brown	George Brown	Elizabeth Steedley		
22499 *	Brown, Joseph	OK	1881	none	Charles Brown	Sarah Scoot		
22847	Brown, Josephine	TX	1880	Joe Brown	Lewis Gaines	Elizabeth Baxter	Caleb & Sallie Gaines	
21371	Brown, Lafayette	TX	1880	Ema Brown	Andrew Brown	Easter Cobin	Burrell Brown	
12032	Brown, Laura	GA	1893		Charlie Brown	Martha Ivey	Clete & Winnie Brown	Milton & Eliza Ivey
2076 *	Brown, Lena	NC	1867	widow	Lorenzo Gaither	Classie Irving	Abe & Florry Gaither	Lacona & Larina Irving
20590	Brown, Leonard	TN	1898		James Brown	Mary Cross	Wm & Nancy Brown	Absalom & Susan Cross
22348 *	Brown, Lettie	OK	1868	Ellis Warren	Charley Pee	Susan Vann		Taloke & Lettie Vann
17813	Brown, Lillie	GA	1867	John Brown	Huston Clark	Sarrah Brown	Lula Hawkins	Big Black & Mary Big Black
7622	Brown, Littleton	GA	1826	Georgia Brown	William Brown	Francis Lyons		Francis Lyons
10215	Brown, Lousana	NC	1850	Presley Brown	Henry Wagoner	Charlotte Sizemore		Owen & Beckie Sizemore
13579 *	Brown, Lucius	GA	1875	Mary Brown	Frank Brown	Rose Tompson	Ned & Martha Brown	George & Mary Tompson
15674 *	Brown, Mack	GA	1869		Gilford Chandler	Mary Brown	Stokes & Hannah Chandler	Jenkins & Martha Hammonds
818	Brown, Martha	OK	1858	Wm C. Brown	Charles Fleetwood	Lucinda Morgan		Hosea & Frankie Morgan
2033	Brown, Martha	GA	1858	Eliza Brown	Anderson Franklin	E Jane Bryant	Abram & Elizabeth Franklin	
19691	Brown, Martha	TN	1893		George Brown	Amanda Hatcher		Robert & Mary Hatcher
19711	Brown, Martha	TN	1877	Perry Brown	Thomas Hooper	Ritty Hatcher		Robert & Mary Hatcher
21582	Brown, Martha	GA			Henry Roach	Martha Willbanks	Jim & Elizabeth Roach	
19661	Brown, Martina	TX	1868	John Brown	Marvin Biggerstaff	Bettie	Matt Biggerstaff	

4477	Brown, Mary	VA	1874	Joseph Brown	David Sullivan	Mary Roop		King & Louisa Roop
7823	Brown, Mary	GA	1866	James Brown	Nathan Richardson	Delilah Gibson	James & Nancy Richardson	John & Sarah Gibson
12952	Brown, Mary	GA	1847	James Brown	Jacob Cox	Delila McCaslin	Jacob Cox	
18759	Brown, Mary	OK	1865		Damon Snyder	Nancy Miller		
18764	Brown, Mary	GA	1875	James Brown	Wm McGaha	Peggy Norton	Richard & Rebecca McGaha	Sam & Rhoda Norton
19128 *	Brown, Mary	GA	1860	James Brown	Alfred Nickelson	Margratte Riddlespluger		Missouri Dean
19668	Brown, Mary	TN	1889		George Brown	Amanda Hatcher		Robert & Mary Hatcher
10868	Brown, Melissia	WV	1880	Wm Brown	John Osburn	Louana Keith	Solomon & Marth Osburn	Guy & Rachel Keith
4740	Brown, Melvina	MO	1856	widow	Alexander Blair	Mahala Clark	Alexander Brown	
21328	Brown, Mollie	TX	1872	W.M. Brown	George Biddy	Barbara Hampton	James & Delila Biddy	Henry & Mollie Hampton
15647 *	Brown, Monroe	GA	1867	Lizzie Brown	Gilford Chandler	Mary Brown	Stokes & Hannah Chandler	Jenkins & Martha Hammonds
663	Brown, Nancy	OK	1840	William Brown	James Heatherly	Betsy Ivins	James Heatherly	Walter & Rachel Ivins
17912 *	Brown, Nancy	MS	1840	George Brown	Anthony Derert	Charity Thorp		Sallie Thorp
18795	Brown, Nancy	GA	1852	Joe Brown	Ambros Anderson	Rebeca Mann	Noble & Elizabeth Anderson	Elizabeth Mann
20153	Brown, Nancy	GA	1888		Pink Brown	Eliza McAllister	Bill & Martha Brown	Charley & Nancy McAllister
22464	Brown, Nancy	MO	1881	Walter Choate	Daniel Brown	Flory Swadley	William & Flory Brown	
18778	Brown, Nannie	GA	1889	Miner Brown	John Patterson	Eliza Mauldin	Samuel & Nancy Patterson	John & Caroline Mauldin
19129	Brown, Oliver	GA	1865	Mary Brown	Harp Brown	Sophia King		Ollie King
10863	Brown, Rebecca	WV	1882	Charles Brown	Abraham Keith	Sarah Osburn	Guy & Rachel Keith	Solomon & Marth Osburn
22191 *	Brown, Richard	OK			Edward Brown	Elliott Best	James Brown & Phillis Brown	
4960	Brown, Robert	OK	1840	Esther Brown	Isom Brown	Matilda Tyndal	Alexander Brown	
19713	Brown, Robert	TN	1888		George Brown	Amanda Hatcher		Robert & Mary Hatcher
22465	Brown, Robert	OK	1840		Isom Brown	Matilda	Alexander Brown	
14176	Brown, Rosa	TN	1886		John Rich	M A Welch	Elisha & Mary Rich	
18413	Brown, Rosa	FL	1868	C.C. Brown	W.Y. Miles	Sarah Leatherwood	Thomas & Betsy Franklin	W.H. & Susanah Leatherwood
3034	Brown, Samuel	MO	1857	Lucinda Brown	William Brown	Lucinda Swadley	Isom & Matilda Brown	Thomas & Annie Swadley
9037	Brown, Sarah	WV	1871	David Brown	Wilburn Osburn	Permelia Dunford	Solomon & Martha Osburn	Thomas & Honor Dunford
19794	Brown, Sarah	AL	1845	O.B. Brown	Sanford Goins	Charity Helton	James & Rhoda Goins	Hamon & Sarah Helton
21947 *	Brown, Sarah	TN	1856	Samuel Brown	Jarrett McNair	Martha Maglothlis	Fannie McQueen	
20373 *	Brown, Silver	TN	1858	George Brown	Gill Cade	Flora Coleman	Thomas & Julia Cade	Hugh Saxon & Silvey Ford
15935	Brown, Susie	GA	1881		Yancy Barmon	Elizabeth Cunningham		Tom & Eliza Cunningham

6396	Brown, Thomas	OK	1875	Rutha Brown	Jahew Brown	Fannie Blackburn	Barney Brown	Andrew & Francis Blackburn
19775 *	Brown, Thomas	GA	1856	Jane Brown	James Freeman	Monie Freeman		Sarah Hattoct
2081	Brown, Tom	MO	1861	Ada Brown	Wm Brown	Mary Stives	Tom & Hollie Brown	Botts & Fesby Stives
9344	Brown, Tom	OK	1861	Adah Brown	Isam Brown			
19029	Brown, Vandora	AL	1866	W.T. Brown	Nathan Goins	Charlotta Goins	Sanford & Charity Goins	Shade & Orpha Goins
20591	Brown, Vecey	TN	1889		James Brown	Mary Cross	Wm & Nancy Brown	Absalom & Susan Cross
20602	Brown, Walter	TN	1883		James Brown	Mary Cross	Wm & Nancy Brown	Absalom & Susan Cross
20260	Brown, Wesley	GA	1884	Flo Brown	Pink Brown	Eliza Allister	Bill & Martha Brown	Charley & Nancy McAllister
22190 *	Brown, Willa	OK	1893	none	Richard Brown	Rosa Clayton	Edward Brown	Mary Cox
3033	Brown, William	MO	1862	Sarah	William Brown	Lucinda Swadley	Isom & Matilda Brown	Thomas & Annie Swadley
3648	Brown, William	TX	1852	Annie Brown	Aaron Brown	Elizabeth McIntire	Aaron & Polly Brown	John McIntire
7717	Brown, William	OK	1855	none	Smith Brown Jr.	Elizabeth Bricker	Smith Brown	William Bricker
10354	Brown, William	GA	1866	Marsha Brown	John Brown	Dicey Springfield	William Brown	
19031	Brown, William	AL	1889		William Brown	Sarah Goins		Nathan & Charlotta Goins
19692	Brown, William	TN	1891		George Brown	Amanda Hatcher		Robert & Mary Hatcher
20593	Brown, William	TN	1891		James Brown	Mary Cross	Wm & Nancy Brown	Absalom & Susan Cross
21369	Brown, William	AR		Anna Brown	William Brown	Susan Downs	David & Rhoda Brown	Thomas & Rachel Downs
21390	Brown, William	TX	1868	Ada Brown	David Brown	Amanda Graham		
1217	Brown, Zenia	OK	1867	Gold Brown	Wiley Vann	Mary McCoy		Daniel & Margaret McCoy
1747	Browning, Enoch	OK	1849	Mahulda Browning	Sam Browning	Pheraby Horn	John Browning	Bettie Moore
7632	Browning, Enoch	OK	1849	Mary Browning	Sam Browning	Feriby Horne	John & Bettie Browning	
5170 *	Broyles, Sidney	GA	1838	Frank Broyles	Long Jack	Dilcey Nash		
14836	Bruce, Amanda	TN	1857	Green Bruce	John Chappell	Lucy Howell	Drury Chappell	Samuel & Nancy Howell
19779	Bruce, Emma	TN	1907		Green Bruce	Amanda Choppell	Ellie Bruce	John & Lucy Choppell
19299	Bruce, Fannie	GA	1869	Berry Bruce	Hardy Bryant	Winnie Tatum	Wm & Fannie Bryant	James & Susie Tatum
18366	Bruce, Margret	TN	1875		Samuel Graves	Mahala Payne		Samuel & Charlotta Payne
13895	Brummet, James	CO	1862	Maggie Brummet	Preston Brummet	Narcissus Cole		Anna Cole
21709	Bruner, Ida	OK	1880	Nathan Bruner	A.T. Gallaway	Mary Harrell		Clarissa Loveless
16131	Bruner, Rider	OK	1870	Jane Bruner	Lewis Bruner	Jane Miller		Rider Fields
679	Bruner, Rose	OK			Jack Roe	Siney Roe		

19998	Bryan, Barney	GA	1871	Emma Bryan	John Bryan	Martha Johnson	James & Elizabeth Bryan	Wm & Elizabeth Blake
4745	Bryan, Frances	MO		Marion Bryan	William Doke	Sarah Hambelton	Merick & Mary Doke	Isaiah & Martha Hambelton
19994	Bryan, Martha	GA	1875		John Bryan	Martha Johnson	James & Elizabeth Bryan	Wm & Elizabeth Blake
20157	Bryan, Martha	GA	1843	John Bryan	Albert Stephens	Mary Lyle	John & Nelia Stephens	John & Sarah Turner
20057	Bryan, Victoria	TX	1865	Thomas Bryan	Thomas Griffis	Margaret Faucett	Wm & Sarah Griffis	Wm & Elizabeth Faucett
15227	Bryan, William	GA	1864	Nancy Bryan	John Bryan	Martha Johnson		Hugh & Elizabeth Johnson
15231	Bryan, Winson	GA	1866	India Bryan	John Bryan	Martha Johnson		Hugh & Elizabeth Johnson
14561	Bryant, Amanda	GA	1877	Frank Bryant	John Hubbard	Sarah Haynes	Patrick & Margaret Hubbard	Hopper & Rutha Haynes
19828	Bryant, Anna	TN	1884	David Bryant	Allen Bowles	Ella Griffin		
18981	Bryant, Audrey	GA	1894		James Bryant	Rebecca Shirley	Hardy & Winnie Bryant	Andrew & Sarah Shirley
19418	Bryant, B.F.	TN			David Bryant	Nancy Bryant	Hezekiah Bryant	Mary Bryant
6320	Bryant, Clara	AL	1882	Ausphera Bryant	John Steadham	Mary McGhee	Ned Steadham	Nancy McGhee
122	Bryant, Dicey	MO	1864	James Bryant	Thomas McGuire	Sarah Fender	Thomas McGuire	Alexander Brown
6084	Bryant, Fannie	GA	1880	Thomas Bryant	Alpheus Key	Minerva Hembree	William Key	Reubin Hembree
18520	Bryant, Frankie	MO	1843	Asa Bryant	James Crook	Nancy Wills	John & Nellie Crook	James & Nancy Wills
19439	Bryant, George	TN		Dora Bryant	D.J. Bryant	Nancy Bryant	Hezekiah Bryant	Mary Bryant
18878	Bryant, Hardy	GA	1861	Emma Bryant	Hardy Bryant	Winnie Tatum	Wm & Fanny Bryant	James & Susie Tatum
18879	Bryant, James	GA	1864	Rebecca Bryant	Hardy Bryant	Winnie Tatum	Wm & Fanny Bryant	James & Susie Tatum
19419	Bryant, James	TN	44yrs		David Bryant	Nancy Bryant	Hezekiah Bryant	Mary Bryant
18471	Bryant, Joseph	GA	1882	Genia Bryant	William Bryant	Mary Hinton	Wm & Fannie Bryant	
15566 *	Bryant, Louvester	GA	1880		Peter Bryant	Mary Killian	Calvin & Sookey Bryant	Frank & Eliza McConnell
16043 *	Bryant, Luelza	OK	18 ?	R H Bryant	Dofet Cripp	Mary Friend		George Friend
14546 *	Bryant, Mary	GA	1834	Peter Bryant (decd)	Frank McConnell	Eliza Bedford	Jim & Mary Shackelfoot	Jim & Sookey Bedford
22345 *	Bryant, Minnie	OK	1876	Lim Nash	Ephram Bryant	Flora Gott	Abram Ward & Amelia Bryant	Sandy Bean
3787	Bryant, Nancy	NC	1879	William Bryant	James Forester	Martha Mason		John & Polly Mason
4763	Bryant, Nellie	MO	1879	George Bryant	William Ellis	Mary Palmer	Alexander & Mary Ellis	Wm & Luereany Palmer
18475	Bryant, Pinkney	GA	1873	Safrona Bryant	William Bryant	Mary Hinton	Wm & Fannie Bryant	
19301	Bryant, Susie	GA	1871		Hardy Bryant	Winnie Tatum	Wm & Fannie Bryant	James & Susie Tatum
21059	Bryant, Thomas	GA	1851	Lucy Bryant	William Bryant	Fannie Green	Thomas & Catherine Bryant	Isaac & Betsy Green
18472	Bryant, Wesley	GA	1879	Bessie Bryant	William Bryant	Mary Hinton	Wm & Fannie Bryant	
18473	Bryant, William	GA	1849		William Bryant	Fannie Green		Daniel & Fannie Green
18945	Bryant, Willie	GA	1880	Annie Bryant	Hardy Bryant	Winnie Tatum	Wm & Fannie Bryant	James & Susie Tatum

18944	Bryant, Winnie	GA	1875		Hardy Bryant	Winnie Tatum	Wm & Fannie Bryant	James & Susie Tatum
18415	Bryars, Benjamin	AL	31yrs		Benj Bryars	Lucretia Miles	Charles & Margaret Bryars	James & Ellen Miles
18408	Bryars, Burgess	AL	29yrs	E.S. Bryars	Ben Bryars	Lucretia Miles	Charles & Margaret Bryars	James & Ellen Miles
1148	Bryars, Charles	AL	1861	Henrietta Bryars	B.H. Bryars	Lucretia		
21823	Bryars, Gertrude	FL	1879	J.R. Bryars	H.B. Evans	Mollie Williams	Josh Evans	James & Margaret Williams
1150	Bryars, Henrietta	AL	29yrs	Charles Bryars	Elijah Boon	Louisa Heathcock	John Boon	Betsey Heathcock
6316	Bryars, Leucetia	AL		B H Bryars	Miles	Elen Franklin		Thomas Franklin
15065 *	Bryson, Catharine	TN	1885	Skelp Bryson	Harrison Houston	Catharine Abington	George & Elsy Houston	Clem & Ruth Abington
8431	Bryson, James	NC		Jane Bryson	John Bryson	Margarett Ingham	Andrew Bryson	
18217 *	Bryson, Josephine	TN	1854		Green Bryson	Harriet Buck		Tom & Louisa Buck
19595	Bryson, Napoleon	TN	1882		Napoleon Bryson	R. Wilson	Goldman & Susana Bryson	
20005 *	Bryson, Sallie	NC	1877	Jack Bryson		Fannie Moore		Allen & Betsie Garner
3016	Bryson, Samuel	NC	1823	Mary Bryson	John Bryson	Margaret Ingram	Andrew Bryson	Goldman & Jemima Ingram
3319	Buchanan, Dora	NC	23yrs	Wiley Buchanan	Joel Crisp	Nancy Delozier	Pendleton & Nancy Crisp	Edward & Elizabeth Delozier
4777	Buchanan, Elma	OK	1879	Lewis Buchanan	George Edmisten	Sally Kirby		Nancy Robison
22128	Buchanan, Esau	VA	1864	Parthena Buchanan	George Buchanan	Sally Hamilton	Arter & Tempy Buchanan	Hamilton & Dotson
17492	Buckhanan, George	WV	1879		George Buckhanan	Amy Sizemore	Arthur & Isabel Buckhanan	John & Jennie Sizemore
2994	Buckner, Jane	AR	1870	Robert Buckner	James Groomes	Delita Ramsey	Milley Groomes	Thomas Ramsey
7081	Buffington, Anna	OK	1869	Lewis Buffington	Walter Bays	Frances Robison	Joseph Bays	Wm & Ellen Robison
22259 *	Buffington, Gus	OK	1825	Mary Buffington		Lucy Buffington		
2527 *	Bugg, Perrie	GA		Amanda Bugg	Benjamin Bugg	Elizabeth Williams		
18692	Bullard, Emma	FL	1863	Charles Bullard	Alex Stapleton	Mima Tigner		Charles & Mima Tigner
15751	Bullard, Etty	IL	1881	Jessie Bullard	Aquilla Jourdan	Mary Boyles	Joseph & Sarah Jourdan	
16044	Bullard, Sion	OK	1833	Sallie Bullard	Benj Bullard	Syneth Barns	Sion & Rachel Bullard	Jerry & Frankie Barns
17440	Bullett, Lucy	OK	1865	James Bullett	Sam Car-ler-sar-yah-ha	Ar nu wagee Sam	Gar ler sar yo ha	So gee nee
21337	Bullock, Addie	TX	1887	Joe Bullock	Henry Jeter	Mary Fortson	Elyazer & Martha Jeter	Elijah & Arrilla Fortson
19131	Bullock, Dovie	GA	1871	J.M. Bullock	James Braziel	Seleta Doss		Edward & Seleta Doss
10795	Bullock, Ora	TX	1878	William Bullock	John Carnes	Amelia Morrison	Joshua & Nancy Carnes	Ezra & Sophia Morrison
22032	Bumb, Maie	TX	1876	Frank Bumb	John Prator	Ava Crawford	Henry & Carry Prator	Watson & Margarite Crawford
19506	Bunch, Jane	MO	1848		John Bunch	Nancy Talley		John & Jane Talley

#	Name	State	Year					
20778	Bunch, Ora	GA	1887	James Bunch	John Cook	Mary Ragan	James Cook & Louvica Carns	
9351	Bunch, Ruhamie	AR	1846	Charles Bunch	Thomas McCollough	Lovicie Bays	Moses McCollough	Letta Bays
20295	Burchell, Leah	AR	1875		William Hughes	Mary Welkerson	William Hughes	Harmon Welkerson
12467	Burchett, Ellen	VA	1866	Ezekiel Burchett	Jacob Pruitt	Nancy Orsburn	Bedney Pruitt	David Orsburn
13784 *	Burdell, George	GA	1843	Mary Burdell	Jeff Neel	Jennie Reid	Mack Neel & Lizzie Reece	Abraham & Prue Reid
18313	Burden, Arthur	IN	1879	Emilie Burden	Oliver Burden	Addie Peterson	Thornton Elexander	Perlina Peterson
18314	Burden, Frances	IN		Oliver Burden	Mymaduke Winburn	Timpie Brooks		Gilford & Dicie Brooks
22241	Burden, Leota	IN	1872	W.M. Burden	Dudley Roberts	Elizabeth Hamands		Derbany & Mamas Hamands
15888 *	Burden, Marcia	IN	1880	Jasper Burden	James Pettiford	Sarah Gulliford	Osborn Giles & Clarinda Pettiford	Green & Martha Gulliford
18900	Burdyshaw, Virgie	AR	1888	Henny Burdyshaw	Wm Brooms	Maldona Hardy	John & Emiline Brooms	John & Mary Hardy
15565 *	Burge, Charity	GA	1856	Ezra Burge	Isaac Avery	Susan Kemp	Green & Sarah McConnell	Sam & Lena Mansel
20835 *	Burge, Mary	GA	1854	Henry Burge	Squire Strickland	Harriet Fields	George & Joyce Tassell	Sylla Fields
19742	Burge, Sarah	GA	1865	Jerry Burge	Robert Evans	Margaret Barnett	Robert & Sallie Evans	Richard & Rhoda Barnett
21528	Burger, Charley	GA	1852	Nancy Burger	Jim Burger	Delila Phillips	Charley & Malinda Burger	Sarah Phillips
115 *	Burgess, Alpha	NC	1870	Richard Burgess	Jessie Lowry	Elizabeth Sheppard		Lee Sheppard
14545	Burgess, James	GA	1881	Agnes Burgess	Edward Burgess	Mary Evans		Robt & Sallie Evans
64	Burgess, Jesse	OK	1836	Elizabeth Burgess	William Burgess	Mary Vann	Elizabeth Burgess	John & Mary Vann
22108 *	Burgess, John	OK	1859	Jennie Burgess	Burgess Foreman	Sophia Lipe	Rodie Gunter	Kate Solomon
8688 *	Burgess, Julius	NC	1856	Dolow Burgess	Ben Burgess	Matilda Ross	William Burgess	James & Nancy Ross
16577	Burgess, Lester	WA	1894		Early Burgess	Olie Fender		Middleton & Elizabeth Fender
7 *	Burgess, Richard	NC	1866	Altha Burgess	Benjamin Burgess	Mariah Goode		
18845	Burk, Margaret	GA	1849	John Burk	John Ledford	Elisa Griffin	Solom & Ana Ledford	Isac & Margret Griffin
21870	Burk, Rebecca	TN	1860	Jonas Burk	Joseph Dedmon	Martha Black	Jesse & Hannah Dedmon	John & Jane Black
18388	Burk, Viola	FL	24yrs	Adam Burk	John Steadham	Levy Boone	John & Mary Steadham	Gugon & Susan Boone
22629	Burk, Wildie	GA	1879	Frank Burk	Calvin Blalock	Josephine Freeman	Wm & Katie Blalock	
11402	Burke, Lula	OK	1883	John Burke	Elijah Webb	Malissa Cook	Elijah & Sylina Webb	Jacob & Delana Cook
17945	Burkett, Sarah	TN	1851	Jackson Burkett	Wiley Burnett	Mary Looney	John & Susan Burnett	Arter & Annie Looney
20425	Burkett, William	GA	1858	Mary Burkett	Isaac Burkett	Evaline Tyner		
21301	Burks, Everett	KS	1880	Olive Burks	Evan Burks	Maggie Clemmons	Wm & Eliza Burks	Williamson & Parzadia Clemmons
14355	Burks, Nora	OK	1873	A M Burks	C C Hudson	Martha Hazlewood		Thos & Mary Hazlewood

14632	Burley, Addie	GA	1898		C M Burley	Angeline Wesbrooks		Marion & Amena Wesbrooks
14631	Burley, Angeline	GA	1861	CM Burley	Marion Wesbrooks	Amena Holland		Wm & Susan Holland
14630	Burley, Cora	GA	1895		C M Burley	Angeline Wesbrooks		Marion & Amena Wesbrooks
14629	Burley, George	GA	1887		C M Burley	Angeline Wesbrooks		Marion & Amena Wesbrooks
14628	Burley, James	GA	1878	Estelle Burley	C M Burley	Angeline Wesbrooks		Marion & Amena Wesbrooks
14627	Burley, Louisa	GA	1900		C M Burley	Angeline Wesbrooks		Marion & Amena Wesbrooks
14626	Burley, Marion	GA	1885		C M Burley	Angeline Wesbrooks		Marion & Amena Wesbrooks
14625	Burley, Mary	GA	1891		C M Burley	Angeline Wesbrooks		Marion & Amena Wesbrooks
10275	Burnett, David	AR	1868	Alma Burnett	William Burnett	Nancy Howery		
3938	Burnett, H.L.	GA	1884		Ells Burnett	Lucy Sisson		James & Barb Sisson
21341	Burnett, James	AR	1861	Nannie Burnett	John Burnett	Lydia Griffith	John & Susan Burnett	Arden & Delila Griffith
21795	Burnett, Madeline	TX	1873	Francis Burnett	Solomon Blair	Bettie Penn	Sarah Hueitt	
10233	Burnett, Myrtie	WV	1888	George Burnett	N C C Walker	Sarah Wood	Newma & Adaline Walker	German & Nancy Wood
10277	Burnett, Ruben	AR	1872	Minnie Burnett	William Burnett	Nancy Howery		
22665	Burnett, Tressi	TN	1883	Milton Burnett	James Helton	Martha Clark	Daniel & Martha Helton	
10276	Burnett, William	AR	1870	Mittylene Burnett	William Burnett	Nancy Howery		
21480	Burnett, William	AR		Bessie Burnett	John Burnett	Lydia Griffith	John & Susan Burnett	Arden & Delilah Griffith
7758	Burnette, Mary	OK		Frank Burnette	Andrew Gambill	Mary Hulsey	Wm & Sallie Gambill	
7077	Burns, Alice	OK	1868	Luther Burns	Robert French	Sarah Stephenson		James & Elizabeth Stephenson
15214	Burns, Henervee	GA		George Burns	Jeffrey Beck	Mandy Loggins	Coleman Davis & Elmina Beck	
18090	Burns, Henervee	GA	1880	George Burns	Jeffrey Beck	Mandy Loggins	Coleman Davis & Elmira Beck	
15215	Burns, Jack	GA	1904		George Burns	Henervee Beck		Jeffrey & Mandy Beck
3007	Burns, Lucinda	TN	1863	William Burns	Solomon Morgan	Omie Wallace		John & Sally Wallace
15218	Burns, Marie	GA	1900		George Burns	Henervee Beck		Jeffrey & Mandy Beck
15225	Burns, Mary	GA	1906		George Burns	Henervee Beck		Jeffrey & Mandy Beck
11006	Burns, Samuel	TN	1849	Roxanna Burns	Uriah Burns	Sallie Birchfield	Hezikiah & Betsy Burns	
6917	Burrell, Jesse	GA	1841	Elvina Burrell	Jesse Burrell	Marviny Barus	Andy Brown	Maruicy Barus
18008	Burrell, Jesse	GA	1872	Emmer Burrell	Jesse Burrell	Elvira Haygood	Jesse & Mariny Burrell	Andy & Mariny Brown
13157	Burrell, Jessee	GA	1879	Sousan Burrell	Simpson Burrell	Rebecca Burleson	Jesse Burrell & Marning Barnes	Andy & Maruny Brown
4649	Burrell, Mary	NC	1847	W.T. Burrell	James Maney	Margaret Corn	John & Mary Maney	Adam & Hannah Corn

12524	Burrell, Oscar	GA	1884		Simpson Burrell	Rebecca Burleson	Jessee Burrell	Anda & Mariecy Brown
12523	Burrell, Seeborn	GA	1881	Bunia Burrell	Simpson Burrell	Rebecca Burleson	Jessee Burrell	Anda & Mariecy Brown
12525	Burrell, Simpson Jr.	GA	1872	Dacia Burrell	Jessee Burrell	Elevira Haygood	Jessee Burrell & Mariecy Brown	Osborn & Lida Haygood
17581	Burrell, T. T.	GA	1847	Josie Burrell	Kinneous Burrell	Elisabeth McClure	Jessee Burrell	Mariney Burrur
10348	Burrell, W T	GA	1861	Sarah Burrell	Jessee Burrell	Elvira Haygood	Jessee & Marlily Burrell	
14353	Burroughs, Rose	TX			James Jackson	Sarah Maloney	John & Elizabeth Jackson	
21239	Burrow, Mary	OK	1876	Daniel Burrow	William Barnett	Anna Slater		James & Margaret Slater
22212	Burrows, Cinda	OK	1873	Monroe Burrows	William Reed	Nancy Murray	McKenzie & Nancy Reed	James & Jane Murray
18040 *	Burse, Nelson	GA	61yrs	Mary Burse	Mortomer Burse	Mahaly Brown	Madison & Milly Burse	Nelson & Mariah Brown
19781	Burton, Jonathon	NC	1845	Margret Burton		Ligthie Whitaker		Bollie & Jesey Whitaker
21725	Busby, Robert	TX	1873	Emma Busby	Robert Busby	Elizabeth Chewning		George & Ersula Chewning
21352	Bush, Louisiana	TX	1858	Willie Bush	William Knight	Sarah Tekell		
21350	Bush, Willis	TX	1858	Louisiana Bush		Vica Cooper		
54	Butler, Carolina	GA	1869	John Butler	Phenias Tompkins	Hannah Ross	Isaac & Helen Tompkins	Templin & Eliza Ross
22730	Butler, Elizabeth	LA	1882	Alex Butler	T.J. Benton	E.E. McLeod		
2844	Butler, Manny	OK	1860	Anna Butler	Edward Butler	Elizabeth Reeder	Hogskin	Reeder
15745 *	Butler, Mattie	GA	1859	Harvey Butler	Daniel Pratt	Kissie Pratt		Edward & Eve Pratt
11780	Butler, Robert	OK	1866	Carrie Butler	Edward Butler	Elizabeth Reeder	Goo-coo & Te cah nut ste skee	
18578	Butner, Augusta	NC	1857	Augustin Butner	Benj Pettitt	Nancy Flint	Benj & Charlott Pettitt	
13794	Butner, Martha	NC	1851	William Butner	John Hauser	Elizabeth Poindexter	Adam & Margaret Hauser	Robert & Miriam Poindexter
5427	Buttry, Audie	AR	1882	Minta Buttry	Joab Buttry	Mary Miller	John & Margret Buttry	Davidson & Elizabeth Miller
5426	Buttry, Author	AR	1878	Lottie Buttry	Joab Buttry	Mary Miller	John & Margret Buttry	Davidson & Elizabeth Miller
4258	Buttry, Caldonia	AR	1860	L M Buttry	Joh Buttry	Margret Martin	Wm & Luvisa Buttry	Wm & Susan Martin
4250	Buttry, Claudis	AR	1885	none	L M Buttry	Caldonia Buttry		John & Margret Buttry
5406	Buttry, Dolly	AR	1885	none	William Buttry	Elizabeth Patterson	John & Margret Buttry	John & Susan Patterson
5428	Buttry, Joab	AR	1850	Mary Muttry	John Buttry	Margret Martin	Wm & Luvisa Buttry	Wm & Susan Martin
3786	Buttry, John	AR	1868	Cordelia Buttry	John Buttry	Margaret Martin		Susan Martin
10615	Buttry, Louis	OK		Emma Buttry	John Buttry	Margaret Wolf		Wm & Susan Martin
581	Buttry, Margaret	AR	1830	John Buttry (decd)	Wm Martin	Susan Wolf	Thomas & Elizabeth Martin	Dennis & Polly Wolf
9833	Buttry, Stella & Hattie	AR	1898 1901		James Buttry	Ella Myers	John & Margarett Buttry	Wm & Susan Myers

5402	Buttry, William	AR	1858	Elizabeth Buttry	John Buttry	Margret Martin	Wm & Luvisa Buttry	Wm & Susan Martin
16158 *	Butts, Amy	WI	1867	Benj Butts	Aaron Roberts	Martha Stewart	Ismael & Delany Roberts	Waldin & Hetty Stewart
8610	Buyess, Mary	GA	1864	David Buyess	Marion Reece	Elizabeth Newman	James & Mary Reece	James & Sarah Newman
6747	Byars, Louisa	MO	1870	Walter Byars	John Hudler	Tamsy Stitt		Jacob & Hiley Stitt
15226	Byars, Louvenie	GA	1879	Ben Byars	William Vernon	Nancy Philips	Archie & Jane Vernon	
11366	Byars, Sarah	GA	1858	Jim Byars	Robert Ray	Rachel Davis		Wm & Annie Davis
17541	Byers, Ida	NC	1876	Agnew Byers	Henry Ditmore	Elizabeth Hampton	John & Eliza Ditmore	George & Mary Hampton
4007	Byrd, Edward	OK	1843	widower				
15482	Byrd, Isaiah	GA	1839	Savannah Byrd	Isaiah Byrd	Margaret Locklear		Jesse & Margaret Locklear
20026	Byrd, Laura	TN	1875		John Layman	Catherine Morgan	Henry & Mary Layman	Wm & Millie Morgan
8	Byrd, Mary	AR	1873	Robert Byrd	Samuel Denton	Nancy Snelgrove	Jonathen Denton & Caty Armstrong	Billy Snelgrove & Eliza Meeds
11365 *	Byrd, Millie	GA	1840	Joe Byrd	Alonzo Moon	Mary Davis	Jim & Becca Hulsey	
1405	Byrd, Susan	OK	1881	B B Byrd	George Mills	Martha Chambers		Grief & Didamay Chambers
12275	Byron, Nettie	OK	1873	Dennis Byron	Benjamin Courtney	Matilda Fender	Wm & Matilda Courtney	Daniel & Dicy Fender
7607	Cabe, Robert	GA			Samuel Cabe	Mary Howard		Wm & Jennie Howard
12342	Cagle, Henry	GA	1904		Columbus Cagle	Mary Sams	Henry & Sarah Cagle	Columbus & Susan Sams
20437	Cagle, Henry	TN	1853		Peter Cagle	Elizabeth Henson	Jacob & Rutha Cagle	Thomas & Nancy Henson
20463	Cagle, Jacob	TN	1862	Emer Cagle	Peter Cagle	Elizabeth Henson	Jacob & Rutha Cagle	Thomas & Nancy Henson
21895	Cagle, James	TN	1884		Henry Cagle			
20443	Cagle, John	TN	1860	Mattie Cagle	Peter Cagle	Elizabeth Henson	Jacob & Rutha Cagle	Thomas & Nancy Henson
19362	Cagle, Lois	GA	1907		Columbus Cagle	Mary Sams	Henry & Sallie Cagle	Columbus & Susan Sams
12341	Cagle, Mary	GA	1884	Columbus Cagle	Columbus Sams	Susan Mills	Wm & Mahaley Sams	Joseph & Annie Mills
20533	Cagle, Mattie	TN	1886	John Cagle	Jesse Hughes	Mary Copeland	Jesse Sr & Fronia Hughes	Samuel & Jane Morelock
15481	Cagle, Rosa	GA	1870	Lewis Cagle	S T Townsend	Catharine Morris	Zeke & Annie Townsend	Joseph & Halie Morris
20438	Cagle, William	AL	1869	Daisey Cagle	Peter Cagle	Elizabeth Henson	Jacob & Rutha Cagle	Thomas & Nancy Henson
18901	Cain, Alcey	AR	1862	John Cain	John Brooms	Elizabeth Dickens	Lewis & Bettie Brooms	George & Emiline Dickens
14544	Cain, Anie	GA	1878	Charlie Cain	Thomas McClure	Amanda Millwood	J J & Marilda McClure	Hugh & Miram Millwood
19440	Cain, John	GA	1857	Aminthia Cain	William Cain	Rachel Dowda	Ransom Cain & Elizabeth Bryant	Robert Dowda & Polly Davis
20950	Cain, John	GA	1850	Elizabeth Cain	Harrison Cain	Elizabeth Jett	Elisha Cain	Stephen Jett
19989	Cain, Louella	GA	1871	Samuel Cain	Francis Owen	Sarah Whitmire	Wiley & Mary Owen	James & Cassie Whitmire
19427	Cain, Mary	GA	1868		William Cain	Rachel Dowda	Ransom Cain & Elizabeth Bryant	Robert Dowda & Polly Davis

19441	Cain, Mathew	GA	1866	Uarka Cain	William Cain	Rachel Dowda	Ransom Cain & Elizabeth Bryant	Robert Dowda & Polly Davis
21943 *	Calaway, Johnnie	TN	1876	William Calaway	Harrison Hood	Mary Coker	Amey Hood	Martin Coker
14757	Caldiron, Elizabeth	OH	1872	Peter Caldiron	Isaac Speaks	Rachel Blevins	Musentine Speaks	Nancy Blevins
11578	Caldwell, Andrew	KY	1861	Prissilla Caldwell	Freland Caldwell	Elizabeth Shoemaker	Sallie Caldwell	Wm & Phebe Shoemaker
11582	Caldwell, Catherine	KY	1863	Thomas Caldwell	Jonas Smith	Sarah Baker	Crabtree & Martha Smith	Elijah & Margaret Baker
9056	Caldwell, Celia	NC	1858	William Caldwell	John Hash	Sarah Hash	Robery Hash	Margrey Hash
1659	Caldwell, David	VA	1861			Nancy Caldwell		
14750	Caldwell, James	VA	1863	Matilda Caldwell	Freeland Caldwell	Elizabeth Shoemaker	Sallie Caldwell	Wm & Pebe Showmaker
11580	Caldwell, Louisa	KY	1861	William Caldwell	Jonas Smith	Sarah Baker	Crabtree & Martha Smith	Elijah & Margaret Baker
11585	Caldwell, Luther	KY	1884	Edna Caldwell	William Caldwell	Louisa Smith	Freland & Elizabeth Caldwell	Jonas & Sarah Smith
1749	Caldwell, Mary	VA	1866	David Caldwell	Noah Osborn	Nancy Balinger	James & Rachel Osborn	
9769	Caldwell, Matilda	VA	1864	James Caldwell	Calaway Pennington	Nancy Privit	Andrew & Hesther Pennington	Noah & Naoma Privitt
11581	Caldwell, Thomas	KY	1859	Catherine Caldwell	Freland Caldwell	Elizabeth Shoemaker	Sallie Caldwell	Wm & Phebe Shoemaker
961	Caler, Allie	NC	1871	none	Thomas Caler	Martha Pace		Stephen & Dovey Pace
1066	Caler, Raleigh	TN	1865	Lucy Caler	Thomas Caler	Martha Pace		Stephen & Dovey Pace
20133	Calhoun, Clemontine	AL	1854	L.L. Calhoun	Eser Killam	Caroline Weatherford	John Killam	John Weatherford & Martha Dye
2546	Calhoun, Lillie	GA		Fred Calhoun	W C Norton	Malissie Dockins	Edward & Elizabeth Norton	Benj & Amanda Dockins
20143	Caliway, Fannie	GA	1848	Isic Caliway	Joseph Graham	Celie Lathem	Smart & Mariah Belton	
11593	Call, Calvin	GA	1884		Joseph Call	Elizabeth Teague	John & Nancy Call	Isaac & Rachel Teague
11588	Call, John	GA	1879	Emma Call	Joseph Call	Elizabeth Teague	John & Nancy Call	Isaac & Rachel Teague
11596	Call, John	GA	1899		John Call	Emma Young	Joseph & Elizabeth Call	
14981	Call, Joseph (decd)	GA		Elizabeth Call	John Call	Nancy Montgomery		Polly Sanders
19456	Call, Katie	FL	1882	Willie Call	Robert Holland	Eliza Moore		Eliza Mayo
5053	Callahan, Austrilla	GA	37yrs		Taylor Pool	Julian Carver	John & Susie Pool	
15977	Callaway, Harriett	OK	1835		Samuel Fergisen	Amie Larkins		
21850 *	Callaway, Solomon	TN	1880	Lillian Callaway	John Benson	Jensy Callaway		James & Sarah Callaway
4358	Callis, Martha	AR	1872	John Callis	William Warren	Katherine Martin	George & Susan Warren	William & Susan Martin
21860 *	Calwell, Sarah	TN			Thomas Calwell	Mary Glover	Joseph & Sarah Calwell	Wm & Clara Glover
5321	Calwell, Sirena	GA	1872		Eliott Boling	Sarah Teague	Thomas Boling	Annie Teague

ID	Name	State	Year					
18996*	Cameron, Amanda	IL		Blake Cameron	Edward Revels	Silvy Roberts	McCaga & Monon Revels	Kinchen Roberts
17896*	Cameron, Elsie	AL	1881		Blake Cameron	Amanda Revels		Edward & Silvey Revels
12595	Cameron, Lizzie	OK			Charlie Nofire	Lizzie Batt	No wah to nuh & Ga to yo eh	
16220	Cameron, Mary	OK	1872	D. Cameron	Samuel Craft	Sarah Monday		Benj & Mary Monday
19043	Camp, Jessie	GA	1869	A.H. Camp	Joseph Lumpkin	Susan Lloyd		Thomas & Susan Lloyd
21232	Camp, Ollie	TX	1883	Will Camp	R.B. Graham	Mittie Sisk		James & Martha Graham
6019	Campbell, Dessie	MO	1883	William Campbell	Hugh Presley	Ollie Fender	Hugh & Deliah Presley	Michael & Martha Fender
2603	Campbell, Drury	GA	1857	Rebecca Campbell	Henderson Campbell	Susy Davenport		John & Elisabeth Davenport
2605	Campbell, John	TN	1861	Marthey Campbell	Henderson Campbell	Susy Davenport		John & Elisabeth Davenport
9206	Campbell, Mary	NC	1877	Alexander Campbell	William Head	Nancy Woody	John & Ann Head	Ky & Mary Woody
2604	Campbell, William	GA	1882	Addie Campbell	Drury Campbell	Rebecca Campbell	Henderson & Susanah Campbell	
9503	Campbell, Z.H.	TN	1880	Roenia Campbell	John Campbell	Martha Earley	Henderson & Susey Campbell	
1465	Candill, Arthur	NC	1881	none	William Candill	Elizabeth Thompson	Wiley & Amandy Thompson	Samuel & Mary Candill
1466	Candill, Elizabeth	NC	1862	William Candill	Wesley Thompson	Amandy Powers	Jhon(sic) & Polly Thompson	
110*	Candler, Nancy	NC	1854	Jacob Candler	Randall Russell	Celia Cheek	John & Nancy Russell	Canada & Beckie Cheek
164	Candy, Samuel	OK	1840	none	Thomas Candy	Susan Graves	Samuel & Elizabeth Candy	
18479*	Cannada, Florine	GA	1855	Alec Cannada	Dary Cannada	Julia Swinney	Norris & Cely Cannada	Mary Swinney
10436	Cannafax, Josephine	OK	1850	widow	George Healey	Abigal Rhea	George & Juvica Haley	Linney Rhea
20027	Cannefax, Ceryal	OK	1903		George Cannefax	Clara Binner	George & Margret Cannefax	Robert & Tennie Binner
13806	Cannefax, Clyde	OK	1877		George Cannefax	Margret Haley	Joseph & Sarah Cannefax	George & Abbie Haley
12522	Cannefax, George	OK	1874	Clara Cannefax	George Cannefax	Margaret Haley	Joseph & Sarah Cannefax	George & Abigail Haley
20028	Cannefax, Ruthie	OK	1900		George Cannefax	Clara Binner	George & Margret Cannefax	Robert & Tennie Binner
22459	Cannon, Dora	WA	1869	James Cannon	James Brown	Margaret Suggs	Silas & Surrlldla Brown	John & Ruth Suggs
14129	Cannon, Lee	TN	1840	Harritt Cannon	Bill Cannon	Mila Smith	Bill Cannon	
21330	Cansler, Ida	TX	1888	Joe Cansler	Robert Biddy	Sallie Renfro	James & Delila Biddy	
15937*	Cantrell, Fannie	GA	1878	Andrew Cantrell	Aaron Frazier	Clora Banks	Bob Frazier	
19130	Cantrell, Samantha	GA	1861	W.W. Cantrell	Francis Bradford	Sarah Bradley	Lucy Bradford	
21057	Capper, Emmeline	PA	1865	widow	Edward Quinn	Arriana Jones	Edward & Emiline Quinn	Samuel & Eliza Jones
18341	Carden, Fannie	TN	1856	Cornelius Carden	Goldman Bryson	Susan Payne		John & Polly Payne

ID	Name	State	Year					
21986	Cardill, Sallie	MO	1851	Thomas Cardill	Seth Baker	Lucy Huff	Alpheus & Marietta Baker	Huff
18343	Cardin, Mary	TN	1868	Stone Cardin	James Cheek	Sarah Sexton	Joseph & Malinda Cheek	Jessie & Violet Sexton
3361	Cardwell, Frances	AL	39yrs	Wil Cardwell	William Dees	Annie Parte	Wm Dees & Hetty Shemack	Mary Parte
6108	Carelton, Ida	VA	23yrs	Eugene Carelton	Alexander Dixon	Julia Pugh		Stephen & Sarah Pugh
15082	Carey, Ann	OK	1874	Thomas Carey	John Elmore	Ann Beamen	Thos & Hannah Elmore	Jessie & Rachel Beamen
22428	Carey, Annie	TN	1865	John Carey	Russell Tallent	Mary Saunders		Betsey Saunders
22792*	Carlock, Mandie	TN	1886	Dempsy Carlock	Bob Melton	Nancy Wimberly	Moses & Amanda Melton	Doss Johnson
9987	Carlton, Matilda	TN	1863	James Carlton	Norman Mansfield	Jane Haney	Wm & Susanna Mansfield	William Haney
10851	Carnes, Amelia	TX	1848	John Carnes	Ezra Morrison	Sophia Griffin	Wm & Nancy Morrison	Wm & Delilah Griffin
8156	Carnes, Dora	WV	1865	A C Carnes	Hiram Sizemore	Frances Morton	Owen & Rebecca Sizemore	Thos & Millie Morton
10859	Carnes, Edward	TX	1871		John Carnes	Amelia Morrison	John & Nancy Carnes	Ezra & Sophia Morrison
10852	Carnes, Maude	TX	1883		John Carnes	Amelia	Joshua & Nancy Carnes	Ezra & Sophia Morrison
20030	Carnes, Wilbern	GA	1849	Olivia Carnes	Wells Carnes	Clara Herring	Richard & Delphia Carnes	William Herring
17386	Carnett, Ellen	GA	1874	Samuel Carnett	John Leadford	Lizey Griffin	Solomon & Ann Leadford	
15216	Carney, Aaron	GA	1844	Nancy Carney	Edmond Carney	Elizabeth King	Lot Carney	Stephen & Clara King
14624	Carney, Almer	GA	1897		Cisero Carney	Susan Reece		John & Elizbeth Reece
19385	Carney, Almer	GA	1881	Greeley Carney	John Mayfield	Francis Johnson	Hamp & Arie Mayfield	
14623	Carney, Bettie	GA	1906		Cisero Carney	Susan Reece		John & Elizbeth Reece
12030	Carney, Cicero	GA	1870	Lula Carney	Lewis Carney	Nancy Owen	Edmund & Elizabeth Carney	Stephen & Clara King
19386	Carney, Dewey	GA	1912		Greeley Carney	Almer Mayfield		John & Francis Mayfield
14622	Carney, Dora	GA	1900		Cisero Carney	Susan Reece		John & Elizbeth Reece
19387	Carney, Ethel	GA	1899		Greeley Carney	Almer Mayfield		John & Francis Mayfield
12029	Carney, Freeman	GA	1881		A P Carney	Nancy Owen	Edmund & Elizabeth Carney	Stephen & Clara King
14621	Carney, George	GA	1904		Cisero Carney	Susan Reece		John & Elizbeth Reece
15213	Carney, Gordon	GA	1887		A P Carney	Nancy Owen	Edmond & Elizabeth Carney	Reuben & Jennie Owen
14620	Carney, Luther	GA	1892		Cisero Carney	Susan Reece		John & Elizbeth Reece
14619	Carney, Rosa	GA	1890		Cisero Carney	Susan Reece		John & Elizbeth Reece
14618	Carney, Sam	GA	1902		Cisero Carney	Susan Reece		John & Elizbeth Reece
11364	Carney, Scott	GA	1887		Lewis Carney	Nancy Owen	Edmond & Elizabeth Carney	
11363	Carney, Silas	GA	1852	California Carney	Edmond Carney	Elizabeth King		Stephen King
11362	Carney, Susan	GA	1871	Cisero Carney	John Reece	Elizabeth Pool		John & Susan Pool

22133 *	Carpening, Callie	NC	1880	Vance Carpening	James Powell	Laura Gather	Richard & Emerline Powell	James & Vinie Gather
4397	Carpenter, Amanda	OK	1848	Robert Carpenter	Lindsay Carter	Jona Jones	Leonard & Lydia Carter	
21464	Carpenter, Etta	AR	1866	C.C. Carpenter	Alex Addison	Adelia Evans	Eldridge Addison	Thomas Evans
20484	Carpenter, Nancy	TN	1862	Phillip Carpenter	William Gibson	Nancy Dethero	Ramsey & Polly Gibson	Jacob Dethero
15480	Carr, Laura	GA	1875	Albert Carr	John Cook	Mary Ragan	James & Louvica Cook	
19336	Carrell, Viane	GA	1833	Andrew Carrell	Julian Parker	Ceilia Moss	Wm & Edith Parker	Fannie Moss
21898	Carroll, Charles	TN			Silas Carroll	Lucinda Haynes	James & Lucinda Carroll	Jos & Matilda Haynes
22715	Carroll, Cristerfer	TN	1869	America Carroll	Absalum Carroll	Rebecca Leadford	Daniel Carroll	Jessie Leadford
21909	Carroll, Elizabeth	TN	1875		Silas Carroll	Lucinda Haynes	James & Lucinda Carroll	Joseph & Matilda Haynes
14410	Carroll, Emily	GA	1885	R C Carroll	Boscom Ash	Nancy Foster	David & Elisabeth Ash	
22806	Carroll, Emma	IL	1885	Lee Carroll	James Curtis	Elizabeth Nelson	John & Martha Curtis	Penelton & Ruthie Nelson
7115	Carroll, Frances	MO	1838	Prudence Carroll (decd)	James Carroll	Polly Bond	Wiliam Carroll	
20302	Carroll, Gertrude	MO	1876	James Carroll	Lafayet Ambrose	Miza Herrell		Emerson & Clarisa Herrell
21554 *	Carroll, Ida	GA	1878	Jordan Carroll	William Hancock	Mat Thrash	Jane Smith	
7095	Carroll, John	MO	1857	none	Sterling Carroll	Jane Clendenon	James & Polly Carroll	
21866	Carroll, John	TN			Silas Carroll	Lucinda Haynes	James & Lucinda Carroll	Jos & Matilda Haynes
21894	Carroll, Lee	TN			Silas Carroll	Lucinda Haynes	James & Lucinda Carroll	Jos & Matilda Haynes
21952	Carroll, Lucinda	TN	1853	Silas Carroll	Trusten Haynes	Matilda McCorkle	Ira & Rebecca Haynes	Samuel & Tena McCorkle
676	Carroll, M. C.	TN	1842	widower	Phillips	Cynthia Dupee		
16886	Carroll, Mary	OK		John Carroll	Sam Russell	Susie Cockran	Watt Russell & Patchecy	
15891	Carroll, Mary Ann	GA	1827		Elisha Crawford	Nancy Stephens	Moses & Nancy Crawford	Obediah & Elizabeth Stephens
21910	Carroll, Onslow	TN	1884		Silas Carroll	Lucinda Haynes	James & Lucinda Carroll	Joseph & Matilda Haynes
7093	Carroll, Oscar	MO	1883	none	Samuel Carroll	Eliza Thomas	Sterling & Jane Carroll	Francis & Jane Thomas
21092	Carroll, Randolph	TN			Silas Carroll	Lucinda Haynes	James & Lucinda Carroll	Jos & Matilda Haynes
7092	Carroll, Richard	MO	1860	Emma Carroll	Sterling Carroll	Jane Clendenon	James & Polly Carroll	
7091	Carroll, Samuel	MO	1851	Eliza Carroll	Sterling Carroll	Jane Clendenon	James & Polly Carroll	
7094	Carroll, William	MO	1848	Nissa Carroll	Sterling Carroll	Jane Clendenon	James & Polly Carroll	
9201	Carson, Patsy	NC	1820	widow	Robert Hayden	Susan Chavers		Burl Chavers
9593	Carter, Charles	OK	1868	Ada Carter	Benj Carter	Serena Guy	David & Jennie Carter	

14412	Carter, Amanda	GA	1887		David Ash	Nancy Foster	David & Elisabeth Ash	
20227*	Carter, Benjiman	GA	1847	Fannie Carter	Anderson Carter	Sylvia King		
14617	Carter, Billy	GA	1879	Nellie Carter	John Carter	Jane McMain	Thomas & Nellie Carter	
13917	Carter, Caroline	NC	1903		L T Carter	Ella Lowe	Benj Lowe & Martha Hooks	
10913	Carter, Clement	CA	1875	Dora Carter	John Carter	Rebecca Duncan		Charles & Mahala Duncan
9522	Carter, Dora	NC	1888	none	Nathan Carter	Tildy Ledford	Thos & Fannie Carter	Elbert & Louisa Ledford
19887*	Carter, Dorcas	TN	59yrs	James Carter	Evry Montgomery	Rachel Julian		
3025	Carter, Earnest	AR	1876	Agnes Carter	Albert Carter	Luvisa Buttry	John & Elizabeth Carter	John & Margret Buttry
9523	Carter, Elbert	NC	1873	Mary Carter	Nathan Carter	Tildy Ledford	Thos & Fannie Carter	Elbert & Louisa Ledford
20120	Carter, Eliza	NE	1852	James Carter	John Uland	Mary Bays	Betsy Bingham	Josiah & Letty Bays
14411	Carter, Elizabeth	GA	1883	Henry Carter	David Ash	Nancy Foster	David & Elisabeth Ash	
13922	Carter, Ella	NC	1905		L T Carter	Ella Lowe		Benj Lowe & Martha Hooks
5185	Carter, Elzina	NC	1877	B M Carter	William Hart	Martha Miller	Stephen & Rebecca Hart	
10914	Carter, George	CA	1860	Effie Carter	John Carter	Rebecca Duncan		Charles & Mahala Duncan
32	Carter, Hicks	GA			Nathan Carter	Nelly Yarberry	Wm & Rebecca Carter	
14616	Carter, Hicks	GA	1884		John Carter	Jane McMain	Thomas & Nellie Carter	
19886	Carter, James	TN	1850	Dorcas Carter	Joseph Carter	Susan Thomas		John & Susan Thomas
33	Carter, Jane	GA			Nathan Carter	Ellender Yarberry	Wm & Rebecca Carter	
2316	Carter, John	GA	1867	Billy Carter	John McClvy	Jane Carter		Nathan & Nellie Carter
12063	Carter, John	CA	1826	Rebecca Carter	George Carter	Elizabeth	Charles Duncan	
15479	Carter, John	AL	1856	Jane Carter	Thomps Carter	Nellie Yarberry	Billie Carter	
12948	Carter, Laura	GA	1857	James Carter	Jacob Cox	Delila McCaslin	Jacob Cox	
3029	Carter, Louisa	AR	1854	Albert Carter	John Buttry	Margaret Martin	Wm & Luvisa Buttry	Wm & Susan Martin
11494*	Carter, Luke	OK	1852	Ellen Carter	Richard Carter	Mary Carter	Dave & Jane Duckleg	Riley & Annie Carter
13916	Carter, Lula	NC	1885	Lazarus Carter	Benj Lowe	Martha Hooks	Nelson Lowe	Martha McDuffee
8450	Carter, Meacy	VA	1873	Samuel Carter	William Sammons	Mary Blevins		Armstrong & Catharine Blevins
10911	Carter, Millard	CA	1858		John Carter	Rebecca Duncan		Charles & Mahala Duncan
21635	Carter, Mollie	AR	29yrs	James Carter	William Ridling	Minerva Parrish	Henry & Margaret Ridling	Garland & Jane Parrish
19111	Carter, Olive	AR	1886	James Carter	Joseph McGavack	Harriet Evans	America McGavack	Malachi & Sarah Evans
10912	Carter, Robert	CA	1863	Catharine Carter	John Carter	Rebecca Duncan		Charles & Mahala Duncan

4251	Carter, Thomas	NC	1852	Mary Carter	Nelson Carter	Vina Gibson	Nelson & Billie Carter	John & Morning Gibson
1228 *	Carter, William	GA	1835	Susan Carter	Fred Carter	Peggie Reed		
21174 *	Carter, Willis	GA	1878	Sallie Carter	Jeff Carter	Julia Richardson	Anderson & Queen Carter	
14639	Carver, Charley	GA	1879	Mary Carver	Charley Carver	Passey Pool	Wiley & Polly Carver	Marion & Matilda Pool
15191	Carver, Jacob & Marion	GA	1881 1884	Elizabeth Carver	Charley Carver	Passey Pool	Wiley & Polly Carver	Marian & Matilda Pool
21132	Carver, Mary	TN	1846	Samuel Carver	Benjaman Laster	Louisa Cooper	John & Jennie Laster	Joel & Fannie Cooper
12282	Carver, Possey	GA	1857	C E Carver	Marion Pool	Matilda Childers	Moses & Martha Pool	Robert & Pacient Childers
16373	Case, Henry	OK	1859	Rebecca Case	George Case	Lucinda Still	George & Shalottie Case	Jacob & Rachel Still
16150	Case, Robert	OK	1872	Lillie Case	George Case	Lucinda Stull	George Case	Jacob & Lottie Stull
932	Casey, Mary Jane	TN	1860	Newton Casey	Andy Phillips	Cathrion Evans	John & Polly Phillips	Jess & Susie Evans
18957 *	Cash, Charles	GA	1889		Larry Cash	Lizie Dunn	Charles & Rebecca Cash	
18956 *	Cash, Dan	GA	1852		Charles Cash	Rebecca Wofford	Dan Scism & Rachel Cash	
11952 *	Cash, Larry	GA	1856	Cordie Cash	Charles Cash	Rebecca Wofford	Dan Sisson & Rachel Cash	
14831	Cash, Mirchie	TN	1865		Joseph Goode	Mahala Swansen	Andrew & Barbery Goode	Joshua & Elizabeth Swansen
20483	Cash, Sarah	TN	1844		Daniel Coleman	Mary Johnson	Daniel Coleman	Dempsy & Hannah Johnson
17840	Cashman, May	GA	1891		Charlie Cashman	Dora Davis		Frank & Trecy Davis
13821	Cass, Mary	AL	1860	John Cass	John Canes	Sarah Martin		Thomas Martin
17326	Cassell, Emma	GA	1890		Calvin Cassell	Ella Johnson		Wm & Mary Johnson
18089	Castill, Mary	GA	1876	Joseph Castill	Solomon Sosebee	Sarah Millwood	Solomon & Polly Sosebee	Hugh & Miriam Millwood
21514	Castleberry, Laura	GA	1871	John Castleberry	James Jenkins	Permelia Hargis	Wm & Francis Jenkins	Jackson & Mary Hargis
7719	Casto, James	OK	1869	Eva Casto	William Casto	Mary McCabe		Wm & Mary McCabe
7718	Casto, John	OK	1867	Lulie Casto	William Casto	Mary McCabe		Wm & Mary McCabe
7720	Casto, Mary	OK	1842	William Casto	William McCabe	Mary Pittsenborger		John & Cathrine Pittsenborger
18327 *	Cate, Jerry	TN	1851	Rose Cate	Jackson Cate	Grace Matlock	Jack Walker	
2311	Cathey, Victoria	GA	1879	Virgel Cathey	William Matheson	Malissa Matheson	John & Hannah Hampton	Eli & Annie Matheson
21603	Catus, William	NC	55yrs	Ella Catus		Sally Catus		Wm & Marina Catus
10406	Caudle, Louisa	OK	1862	William Caudle	James Terry	Amanda Pearson	Curtis & Elizabeth Terry	Joseph & Tempie Pearson
1643	Caulk, Milton	OK	1848	Malinda Caulk	Elebian Caulk	Rhoda Schimsher		John & Edith Schrimsher
13409	Caulk, Pleasant	OK	1862	Dora Caulk	Elebian Caulk	Rhoda Schrimsher	Henry Caulk	John & Edith Schrimsher
22028	Caulkins, Leatha	OK	1883	Jesse Caulkins	Alexander Terry	Arminda Carroll	William & Mary Terry	
20140	Cautharn, Emely	FL	1859	James Cautharn	Valentine Fillingim	Sarah Dukes	Robert & Ester Fillingim	Thomas & Ann Duke

6664	Cave, Minora decd	OK	1873	W T Cave	James Tittle	Anna Prather	Daniel & Rosaner Tittle	
1106	Cavin, Wm & Lewis	KS	1888	none	Orvil Cavin	Margaret Burns	Wm & Bettie Cavin	Robert & Maria Burns
1086	Caylor, William	TX	1867	Mattie Caylor	Thomas Caylor	Martha Pace		Stephen & Dovey Pace
17524	Cearley, Huldah	NC	1858	Kimsey Cearley	H.J. Sparks	Elizabeth Thomas	Allen & Martha Sparks	Wm & Nancy Thomas
4352	Cears, Tallie	GA	1885	Virgil Cears	James Reece	Loduska Helton	Aaron & Nancy Reece	John & Mary Helton
2374	Chadwick, Lillie	GA	1873	Math Chadwick	Henry Cordell	Lucinda Maney	John & Angeline Cordell	John Maney & Polly MadCap
14865	Chadwick, Louis et al	GA			Math Chadwick	Lillie Cordell	Ealine Chadwick	H & Lucinda Cordell
14916	Chadwick, Luther et al	GA			Abe Chadwick	Sarah Wilson	A & Evaline Chadwick	George & Pessie Wilson
14919	Chadwick, Sarah	GA	1872	Abe Chadwick	George Wilson	Passie Parker	Samuel & Elizabeth Wilson	Julia & Celia Parker
8520	Chambers, Elisabeth	VA	1849	Solomon Chambers	Stephen Hart	Rebecca Powers	John & Nancy Hart	
20465	Chambers, Hannah	TN	1874	Jugh Chambers	Joseph Bales	Evaline Cagle	John & Fannie Bales	Peter & Elizabeth Cagle
8519	Chambers, James	VA	1886	Saba Chambers	Solomon Chambers	Elisabeth Hart		Stephen & Rebecca Hart
8513	Chambers, Jesse	WV	1876	none	Solomon Chambers	Elisabeth Hart		Stephen & Rebecca Hart
15892	Chambers, John Jr.	GA	1874	Nancy Chambers	William Chambers	Martha Nichols	John & Elizabeth Chambers	Charles Nichols
16093	Chambers, L.D.	OK	65yrs	Elsie Chambers	Sam Chambers	Nancy ?		Sam Jordan
16372	Chambers, Laura	NC	31yrs	Samuel Chambers	David Haney	Elizabeth Ledford	James Haney & Caroline Burnet	Jessie Ledford & Polly Pressley
18300 *	Chambers, Mary	GA	1872	Lewis Chambers	Charlie Anderson	Becky Hendrick		
5466	Chambers, Ruth	NC	1830	Philip Chambers	Joel Sawyer	Esther Thompson	Wm & Betsy Sawyer	Nathan & Hester Thompson
2565	Chambers, Vaner	AL	1880	Edmund Chambers	G W Sizemore	Mary Nobles	Wm & Elizabeth Sizemore	Marion & Martha Nobles
8789	Chambers, Vann	OK	1850	Jennie Crabtree	Henry Chambers	Nancy Hendricks	Maxwell & Elsie Chambers	Wm & Susie Hendricks
3471	Chambers, William	TN	1869	Sarah Chambers	William Chambers	Martha Wells	John & Bettie Chambers	Alexander & Nasa Wells
22361 *	Champion, Nettie	OK	1849	James Champion	Cullins Manley	Malinda Jones		
19132 *	Champion, Will	GA	1870		Henry Champion	Anna King		
11174	Chance, Della	GA	1876	Charles Chance	Joseph Neighbors	Elizabeth Helton		
16046	Chance, James	OK	1847	Mary Chance	Ezekiel Chance	Nancy Thomas		Joseph & Martha Thomas
17300	Chandler, Ada	AL	18??		W.J. Hankins	Louisa		
21615	Chandler, Mary	NC	1866	Z.E. Chandler	Joseph White	Mary May	Joseph & Clara White	Prior & Rachel May
21596	Chandler, Mattie et al	NC			J.E. Chandler	Mary White	P.G. & Aly Chandler	Joseph & Mary White
19974	Chandler, Phirson	NC	1826	Julia Chandler	James Chandler	Lucinda Barker	Wm & Nancy Chandler	

22143	Chandler, Virginia	AL	1873	Lee Chandler	Ace Gibbs	Jane Hale	Jim & Hannah Hale	
21599	Chandler, Z.E.	NC					James & Luenda Chandler	Ezekial Ives
16737	Chaney, John	OK	1885		Jasper Chaney	Ellen Ragsdale		Isaac & Mary Ragsdale
7105	Chaney, Mattie	TX	1874	John Chaney	John Avants	Selah Doshier	Thomas & Francis Avants	Samuel & Sarah Doshier
4889	Chaney, Minerva	TN	1859	Joseph Chaney	Thomas Wilson	Rebecca Hampton	Thomas & Sarah Wilson	Sarah Hampton
15037	Chapman, Effie	GA	1879	A E Chapman	John Sard	Sarah Key	Curtis & Bettie Sard	Dina Hembree
21066	Chapman, John	TN		Maldine Chapman	Chapman	Malindy Morgan	Gola & Saley Morgan	
15478	Chapman, Polina	GA	1873	Scott Chapman	Jackson Elrodd	Sarah Dover	Peter & Kate Elrodd	Wm & Alantha Dover
20568	Chapman, Sallie	TN	1868	Joseph Chapman	Fields Chapman	Margaret Hultse	George & Harriet Chapman	Robert Hultse
21147	Chappel, Wade	TN	1882	Ednie Chappel	Charley Chappel	Frances Moore	John Chappel	John & Lucy Moore
14835	Chappell, D B	TN	1857	Agnes Chappell	John Chappell	Lucy Howell	Drury Chappell	Samuel & Nancy Howell
14819	Chappell, Charles	TN	1855		John Chappell	Lucy Howell	Drury Chappell	Samuel & Mary Howell
18607	Chappell, Fell	TN	1885		D.B. Chappell	Aggie Climer	John Chappell & Lucy Howell	Gane Climer
18882	Chappell, J.B.	TN		Mollie Chappell	John Chappell	Lucy Howell	Drury Chappell	Samuel Howell
14822	Chappell, Joe	TN	1851	Pallastine Chappell	John Chappell	Lucy Howell	Drury Chappell	Samuel & Nancy Howell
14821	Chappell, Thomas	TN	1844	Virginia Chappell	John Chappell	Lucy Howell	Drury Chappell	Samuel & Nancy Howell
10464	Charles, Sallie	WV	1859	William Charles	John Christian	Clemie Horman	Moses & Mary Christian	Charles & Betsey Horman
20666	Chase, Cecil	GA	1902		James Chase	Sarah Carlock	Nathan & Narcissa Chase	John & Narcissa Carlock
20663	Chase, James	GA	1871	Sarah Chase	Nathan Chase	Narcissa Roper	Chester Chase	Noah & Minerva Roper
2474	Chase, Narcissa	TN	1842	widow	Noah Roper	Minerva Taylor	Thomas & Jane Roper	Hudson & Sallie Taylor
20634	Chase, Nola	TN	1879		Nathan Chase	Narcissa Roper	Chester Chase	Noah & Minerva Roper
20559	Chase, Thelma	GA	1900		James Chase	Sarah Carlock	Nathan & Narcissa Chase	John & Narcissa Carlock
20648	Chase, William	GA	1873		Nathan Chase	Narcissa Roper	Chester Chase	Noah & Minerva Roper
8211	Chastain, Aron	GA	1855	Senthie Chastain	Eligah Chastain	Elizabeth Burrell	Wm & Annie Chastain	Mart Burrell & Hulda Hooper
13747	Chastain, Eli	GA	1838			Nancy Chastain		Billey Chastain
14900	Chastain, Elvira	GA	1881	J D Chastain	C C Kelly	Rebecca Chastain	Richard & Frances Kelly	Wm & Elizabeth Chastain
8209	Chastain, James	GA	1862	Mary Chastain	Elijah Chastain	Elizabeth Burrell	Wm & Annie Chastain	Mart Burrell & Hulda Hooper
19014	Chastain, Jinnet	GA	1857	David Chastain	Larkin Jones	Winnie Rapier	Wm & Jinnet Jones	Wm & Jimima Rapier
14899	Chastain, Mahala	GA	1854	Samuel Chastain	R T Kelly	Frances Combs	Richard & Mahala Kelly	Edward & Martha Hash
8207	Chastain, Mark	SC	1858	Adeline Chastain	Elijah Chastain	Elizabeth Burrell	Wm & Annie Chastain	Mart Burrell & Hulda Hooper
12518	Chastain, Mary	GA	1876	James Chastain	Jerry Kincaid	Susan Davenport	James & Martha Kincaid	Thos & Elizabeth Davenport

ID	Name	State	Year	Spouse	Father	Mother	Paternal Grandparents	Maternal Grandparents
19272	Chastain, Nancy	TN	1845	Wm Chastain	Cleveland Cordell	Sallie Hammond		
17899	Chastain, Pary	GA	1851		Eliga Chastain	Elizabeth Burrell	Wm & Annie Chastain	Mark & Hulche Burrell
18162	Chastain, Ruhamey	GA	1889		Elija Chastain	Elizabeth Burrell	Wm & Annie Chastain	Mary & Huldie Burrell
16573	Chastain, Sarah	GA	1876	Charley Chastain	William Ray	Malinda Dotson	Warren & Nancy Ray	Nathaniel & Elizabeth Dotson
8206	Chastain, Thomas	GA	1861	Seruphie Chastain	Elijah Chastain	Elizabeth Burrell	Wm & Annie Chastain	Mart Burrell & Hulda Hooper
14393	Chastang, Jerome	AL	1830	Mollie Chastang	Sustang Chastang	Cecelia Wetherford		Nancy Fisher
4470	Chatman, Lucretia	VA	24yrs	Sam Chatman	Eli Blevins	Elisabeth Blevins	Tobias & Susan Blevins	Callon & Nancy Blevins
2921	Chattin, Addelia	GA	1859	none	Hery Chattin	Rachel Bird	Robert & Sarah Chattin	John Davis & Nancy Bird
2922	Chattin, Jesse	GA	1866	Ella Chattin	Henry Chattin	Rachel Bird	Robert & Sarah Chattin	John Davis & Nancy Bird
2923	Chattin, John	GA	1879	Sallie Chattin	Henry Chattin	Rachel Bird	Robert & Sarah Chatten	John Davis & Nancy Bird
1788	Chattin, Rebecca	GA	1846	Thomas Chattin	James Dooley	Ruthia Anderson	James & Liensindy Dooley	Josiah & Hannah Anderson
15720 *	Che ca you ee or Ross	OK	1857		Tet lah Ya ho lo	Celia Ya ho lo	Ah kil lar ne car	
48	Cheney, Ross	OK		Mary Cheney	Dick Cheney	Minnie Tucker	Noel & Mary Poter	Ben Tucker
11371	Cherry, Amanda	IL	1865	Jefferson Cherry	Jesse Eddings	Mary Middleton	John & Francis Eddings	Joel & Elisabeth Middleton
16780	Cherry, Bettie	MO	1853	W H Cherry	George Haley	Abigail Rhea	George & Lucisa Haley	
21378	Childers, Audrey	TX	1881	T.W. Childers	Solomon Blair	Elizabeth Penn	Hiram & Sarah Blair	Sanford & Elizabeth Penn
7090	Childers, Laura	OK	1879	Jim Childers	William Boyd	Sofrona Gregg	Wm & Elisebeth Boyd	
520	Childers, Levi	OK	31 yrs	Mary Childers	John Childers	Rachel Whygle	unknown	unknown
18893 *	Childress, Berry	TN	1833	Hanah Childress	Alford Childress	Roadia Flint		
14045	Chilson, Edna	KS	1881	Arthur Chilson	John Hill	Elizabeth Allen		Herman Allen
21542 *	Chism, Bill	GA	1852	Avery Chism	Jonas Chism	Sarah Hunter	Isaac & Sophia Chism	Joe & Hannah Hunter
18032 *	Chitwood, Sallie	TN	1843		Nathan Moore	Hannah Wyatt		
2062	Choate, Wm (dec'd)	OK	1859	Martha Choate	John Choate	Anna Bushyhead		Isaac Bushyhead
17325	Christian, Adolphos	GA	1886	Carrie Christian	Thos Christian	Tank Waters	James & Cit Christian	Jason & Fannie Waters
1457	Christie, Jennie	OK	1850	widow	George Ben	Nancy	Oo-thal-hah	Ah-mah-chu-lu-lau
6059	Christie, Rachel	OK	1871		Henry Christie	Nancy	Rachel Christie	
8147	Christie, Rachel	OK		none	Henry Christie	Que-di-ni	Rachel	Lizzie
19463	Christopher, Charles	IN	1864	Malinda Christopher		Flora Axendine		Louis Axendine
21436	Christopher, Clara	OK	1890		John Christopher	Francis Rimare	John Christopher & Mary Siddall	Binion Rimare & Francis Marshall

21435	Christopher, John	OK	1887		John Christopher	Francis Rimare	John Christopher & Mary Siddall	Binion Rimare & Francis Marshall
21483	Christopher, Louis	OK	1873	Delcer Christopher	John Christopher	Francis Rimare	John Christopher & Amelia Siddall	Binion & Francis Rimare
6407	Christopher, Millie	GA	33yrs	Zack Christopher	George Glase		George Glase	Sophronia McDonald
21484	Christopher, Nancy	OK	1865	Abner Christopher	Binion Rimare	Francis Marshall		
19556	Christy, Amanda	IN	1857	John Christy	Ruffin Stewart	Martha Manuel	Abel & Jency Stewart	Wyatt & Charlotte Manuel
19555	Christy, Meta	IN	1895		John Christy	Aminda Stewart	Wm & Maria Christy	Ruffin & Martha Stewart
21193	Christy, Oran	CO	1880	none	John Christy	Aminda Stewart	William & Maria Christy	Ruffin & Martha Stewart
21407	Clarida, John	OK	1876	Laura Clarida	Henry Clarida	Samantha Grams		
5368	Clark, Allen	VA	1839	Clara Clark	Allen Clark	Elisabeth Blevins		James & Lydda Blevins
16478	Clark, Amanda	GA	1877	George Clark	Leroy Bettes	Nancy Thompson	Wm Lattiner & Nancy Bettes	
21518	Clark, Arthur	TX	1881	Maude Clark	John Clark	Mary Bishop	Joseph Clark	Averilla Bishop
5365	Clark, David	WV	1872	Mary Clark	Allen Clark	Lydda Blevins	Allen & Elisabeth Clark	Samuel & Annie Blevins
4822	Clark, Dora	NC	1887	Garfield Clark	Asa Miller	Nancy Byrd	Marion & Betty Miller	Major & Paulina Byrd
21774	Clark, Elisebeth	TX	1873	Roland Clark	Martin Adams	Mollie Teate		
15224	Clark, Eula	GA	1876	Alvin Clark	David Wallis	Ann Turner	Jesse & Liza Wallis	
13515	Clark, Gabriel	TN	1864	Ida Clark	Gabriel Clark	Elizabeth Wofford	Andersen & Isabel Clark	Alford & Nancy Wofford
4823	Clark, Garfield	NC	1880	Dora Clark	Monroe Clark	Martha Sexton	Armstrong & Mary Clark	
8558	Clark, Harvey	NC	1860	Rachel Clark	Armstrong Clark	Mary Miller	Elizabeth Blevins	
21517	Clark, Iredell	TX	1878	Myrtle Clark	John Clark	Mary Bishop	Joseph Clark	Averilla Bishop
12031	Clark, J.P.	GA	1851	Catharine Clark	Jim Clark	Tasey Brewer	Patrick & Susie Clark	George & Tempie Brewer
5364	Clark, James	WV	1868	Sarah Clark	Allen Clark	Lydda Blevins	Allen & Elisabeth Clark	Samuel & Annie Blevins
7106	Clark, James	IN	1854	Anna Clark	Roland Clark	Mary Baugh	James & Mildred Clark	Wm & Susan Baugh
4826	Clark, Jane gdn.	NC	1874	widow	John Clark	Jane Greer	Alen & Lydia Clark	Ellick & Rebecca Greer
11981	Clark, Laura	OK	1879	Elias Clark	Richard Puffer	Margret Bolton		Uri & Lucinda Bolton
22531	Clark, Lydia	TN	1867	Isham Clark	Perry Hayden	Sallie Hubbard		Betsey Hubbard
13866	Clark, Margaret	MO	1866	Zachriah Clark	William Brown	Lucinda Swadley	Isam Brown & Matilda Twidle	Thos Swadley & Annie Fanning
19745	Clark, Margaret	GA	1884	William Clark	Robert Evans	Harriet Sutton	Robert & Sallie Evans	Abe & Eliza Sutton
22081	Clark, Martha	GA		John Clark	Henry Johnson	Nancy Loring	Billie & Ibie Johnson	Calvin & Elizabeth Loring
3900	Clark, Mary	GA	1873	David Clark	Andrew York	Mary Rogers	John & Sarah York	Samuel Rogers
21519	Clark, Mary	TX	1858	John Clark	Joseph Bishop	Averilla Bowles		Allen & Sarah Bowles
4825	Clark, Monroe	NC	1858	Martha Clark	Armstrong Clark	Mary Miller	Elizabeth Blevins	

4891	Clark, Omnette	TN	1885	William Clark	Henry Nelms	Rebecca Wilson	Wm & Margaret Nelms	Thomas & Rebecca Wilson
8557	Clark, Rachael	NC	1861	Harvy Clark	Isaac Edmondson	Martha Blevins		Wells & Elizabeth Blevins
5370	Clark, Rebecka	VA	1882	none	Allen Clark	Clara Welch	Allen & Elisabeth Clark	James & Nancy Welch
13340	Clark, Susan	AL	1856	John Clark	James Helton	Torrassaa Sexton	John & Easter Helton	Russell & Ruth Sexton
7107	Clark, Thomas	IN	1856	Alice Osborn	Roland Clark	Mary Baugh	James & Mildred Clark	Wm & Susan Baugh
5369	Clark, Tolbert	VA	1866	Docia Clark	Allen Clark	Lydda Blevins	Allen & Elisabeth Clark	Samuel & Annie Blevins
4824	Clark, William	NC	1866	Callia Clark	Armstrong Clark	Mary Miller	Elizabeth Blevins	
4640	Clay, Nancy	OK	1837	Nicholas Clay decd	William Matoy	Martha Smith	James & Polly Matoy	
16309	Clayton, Maggie	GA	1883	Monroe Clayton	David Davenport	Lucind Bradford	Thomas & Elizabeth Davenport	Moses & Nancy Bradford
19012 *	Cleag, Will	OK	1880	Lillie Cleag	Cleag	Susie Hassler		
4750	Clement, Bessie	AR	1888	Berton Clement	James Buttry	Ella Myers	John & Margaret Buttry	
19329	Clement, Jennie	TX	1888		Leroy Clement	Nannie Mayfield	Andy & Mollie Clement	Pink & Nancy Mayfield
14054 *	Clemmons, Felix	TN	1874	Lillie Clemmons	George Clemmons	Eliza Starks	Granville & Sylvia Clemmons	Moses Starks
12050 *	Cleveland, Goerge	GA	1868	Viola Cleveland	Quill Cleveland	Mariah Butts	Charley Waters	Sophia Butts
13585	Cleveland, Mary	GA	1857	P C Cleveland	Jim Hicks	Nicey Tiffins	Bill & Betsy Hicks	Que & Tilla Tiffins
19342 *	Cleveland, Viola	GA	1865	George Cleveland	Cyrus Gusham	Tempie McAfee	Cyrus & Nancy Gusham	Wade & Violet McAfee
7109	Clevenger, Jesse	MO	1883	none	James Clevenger	Mary Goldsbury	Benj & Margaret Clevenger	Wm & Mary Goldsbury
7108	Clevenger, Kate	MO	1879	Arch Clevenger	John Reynolds	Mary Morgan	George & Elizabeth Reynolds	Nathan & Anna Morgan
12277	Clevinger, Virginia	WV	1858	Joseph Clevinger	Nathaniel Perdew	Salley Sizemore	Jessey & Sarrah Perdew	Ned & Anna Sizemore
17416	Clifford, George	MS	1867	Pauline Clifford	Goodridge Clifford	Peggy Reed		Thos Reed & Centhy Roberson
11169	Clifford, William	FL	1869	Josephine Clifford	G C Clifford	Peggy Reed	Samuel & Cordelia Clifford	Thos Reed & Cinthia Robertson
15166	Clifton, Jane	WV	1849	John Clifton	Bige Baldwin	Mahala Sizemore	Annie Baldwin	Ned Sizemore
4558	Cline, Amanda	NC	1851	Jack Cline	Uriah Burns	Sallie Birchfield	Hezekiah & Betsey Burns	
12340	Cline, Garrison	GA	1905		Rheno Cline	Jane Sams	George & Rhodia Cline	Columbus & Susan Sams
9038	Cline, George	WV	1859	Clara Cline	Moses Cline	Virginia Sizemore	Henry & Nancy Cline	George & Virginia Sizemore
9043	Cline, Henry	WV	1861	decd	Moses Cline	Virginia Sizemore	Henry Cline	George Sizemore
6425	Cline, James	NC	1850	Josephine Cline	Mike Cline	Catherine Hyde		Ben & Elizabeth Hyde
10119	Cline, James	WV	1877	Minnie Cline	Moses Cline	Virginia Sizemore	Henry & Nancy Cline	Geo & Virginia Sizemore

12339	Cline, Jane	GA	1886		Columbus Sams	Susan Mills	Wm & Mahaley Sams	Joseph & Annie Mills
17285	Cline, John	VA	1870		John Cline	Louisa Sizemore	John & Polly Cline	Franklin & Polly Sizemore
9085	Cline, Polly	WV	1872	Mitten Cline	John Sizemore	Lucy Clay	John & Jane Sizemore	Henry & Polly Clay
9042	Cline, Virginia	WV	1836	Moses Cline	George Sizemore	Jinney Bauldin	Geo & Elizabeth Sizemore	John & Virginia Bauldin
12338	Cline, William	GA	1903		Rheno Cline	Jane Sams	George & Rhodia Cline	Columbus & Susan Sams
17287	Cline, William	VA	33yrs	Bertha Cline	John Cline	Louisa Sizemore	John & Polly Cline	Franklin & Polly Sizemore
19423	Clingman, Jane	NC	1851		John Clingman	Camilla Cash	Jacob & Jane Clingman	Francis & Harriet Cash
19501	Clingman, John	NC	1853	Cora Clingman	John Clingman	Camilla Cash	Jacob & Jane Clingman	Francis & Harriet Cash
19433	Clingman, Thomas	NC	1856	Belle Clingman	John Clingman	Camilla Cash	Jacob & Jane Clingman	Francis & Harriet Cash
15201	Cloer, Ann	GA	1823	George Cloer	William Swanson	Millie Pool	Phillip & Sarah Swanson	
15197	Cloer, Dawson	GA	1855	Josephine Cloer	George Cloer	Ann Swanson		Wm & Millea Swanson
17159	Cloer, Marion	GA	1852	Laura Cloer	George Cloer	Jane Swanson	Nichollis Cloer	Wm Swanson & Millie Poole
10778	Clouse, Martha	TN	1862	J W Clouse	John Everett	Elizabeth Barger	George & Easter Everett	Robert & Ellen Barger
14869	Clouts, Hannah	GA	1857	John Clouts	Vann Wright	Mary Smith	Jesse & Lovicie Wright	David & Lucy Smith
4963	Clouts, James	TN	1857	Lugretia Clouts	John Clouts	Mahala Hembree		James Hembree
4973	Clouts, John	GA		Hannah Wright	John Clouts	Mahala Hembree		James Hambree
15004	Clouts, Lucy	TN	1862	James Clours	Vann Wright	Mary Smith	Jesse & Lovicie Wright	David & Lucy Smith
4969	Clouts, Mahala	GA	1829	John Clouts decd	James Hambree	Nancy Floyd	Abram & Winnie Hambree	Thos & Sallie Floyd
4966	Clouts, Polly	TN	1881	none	James Clouts	Lucy Clouts		
4968	Clouts, Samuel	GA		Nancy Clout	Samuel Clout	Mahala Hembre		James Hembree
13605	Clouts, Sarah	GA	1859		John Clouts	Sarah Hembree	Christian & Peggy Clouts	James & Nancy Hembree
21811	Cloyd, Dappy	KY	1877	Moses Cloyd	Oliver Hutchins	Settil Martin	John & Elizabeth Hutchins	David & Lousinda Martin
15607	Clugman, Richard	NC	1865	Edna Clugman	John Clugman	Camilla Cash	Jacob Clugman & Jane Poindexter	
18872*	Coats, Sofronia	OK		Julios Coats	Spencer Bell	Patsy Butler	Charles Martin	Harry Butler & Nancy Lynch
15936*	Cobb, Eula	GA	1879	Henry Cobb	Arthur Wolding	Clarisy Mohair	Swept Cox	Charity Cash
21067	Cobb, John	TN	1857	Catherine Cobb	Stephis	McDullen	Jess Cobb	
2998	Cobb, Lydia	MO	1873	Will Cobb	James Eaves	Villetty Hambelton	Patric & Polley Eaves	Elijah & Salley Hambelton
18816*	Cobb, Permelia	SC	1853		Sam Mansell	Matilda Mansell		
17662	Cobb, Richard	OK	1852	Cherne Cobb	Samuel Cobb	Margaret Turner	Henny Cobb	
22414	Cochran, Callie	TN	1869		James Payne	Annice Parks	John & Mary Payne	

22050	Cochran, James	GA	1833	Susan Cochran	William Cochran	Susan Shilmett	Cochran	Bates
8426	Cochran, Laura	NC	1859	Andy Cochran	Asbury Burns	Adaline Morris	Uriah & Sallie Burns	
20995	Cochran, Mary	GA	1859	William Cochran	Franklin Orten	Tilda Rufty		
8772	Cochran, Ollie	OK	45yrs	Rufus Cochran	Gunzalis	Dela Adair		Polly Adair
16672	Cochran, Thomas	OK	1877		Luna Cochran	Jane Sanders	Arch & Katy Cochran	
19022	Cochrum, Polly	TN	1856	David Cochrum	Daniel Baggle	Annie Gallimor	Samuel Baggle & Lizzie Scott	David Gallimore & Susan Dupree
11372	Cockrum, John	OK	1877	Edith Cockrum	John Cockrum	Mary Eddings	James Cockrum	Richard Eddings
22476	Coda, Dora	TN	36yrs		William Metcalf	Martha Hensley	Hiram & Jane Metcalf	Wm & Sela Hensley
18952	Coe, Andrew	OK	1885		James Coe	Virginia Howell	Andrew & Rhoda Coe	Thomas & Rachel Howell
21441	Coe, Cleveland	TX	1885		J.D. Coe	Melissa Hestand	Rhoda Coe	Dicie Hestand
19047	Coe, Euler	OK	1870	Florence Coe	William Coe	Mary Smith	Andrew & Rhoda Coe	James Smith
18954	Coe, Herschell	OK	1882	Jonalle Coe	James Coe	Virginia Howell	Andrew & Rhoda Coe	Thomas & Rachel Howell
18953	Coe, James	OK	1852	Virginia Coe	Andrew Coe	Rhoda Morton	Chove & Lucindy Coe	John Morton
21439	Coe, John	TX	1859	Melissa Coe	Andrew Coe	Rhoda Martin	Andrew & Cherlis Coe	Rhoda Martin
19233	Coe, Robert	TX	1874	Malissa Coe	William Coe	Mary Smith	Andrew & Rhoda Coe	James Smith
19046	Coe, William	OK	1844	Mary Coe	Andrew Coe	Rhoda Martin	Charles & Lucindy Coe	John Martin
19048	Coe, William	OK	1883		William Coe	Mary Smith	Andrew & Rhoda Coe	James Smith
397	Coffey, Malissie	NC	1880	Barney Coffey	Thos J Wilson	Josephine Pace	Jack & Isabella Wilson	Stephen & Dovey Pace
21238	Coffey, Minnie	TX	1874	Robert Coffey	George Biddy	Edna McDonald	Elvin & Elizabeth Biddy	Tillman & Louise McDonald
16566	Cogar, Julia	WV	1842	Archibald Cogar	Jacob Brinegar	Sheba Sizemore	Jacob Brinegar	Ned Sizemore & Anna Baldwin
22520	Coggs, Mary	OK	1877		George McDaniel	Dora Lunsford	Redbird McDaniel	Polly Thornton
17794	Cohard, Mary	NC	1850	Charlie Cohard		Judah McLelland		Sharpe & Katie McLelland
7110	Coker, John	MO	1841	Jane Coker	Demps Coker	Lucy Ratcliff	Joseph Coker & Cyntha Rogers	
21876	Colbaugh, Ada	TN	1878		James Colbaugh	Mary Williams	Henry & Mary Colbaugh	John & Louiza Williams
21863	Colbaugh, Fred	TN	1898		James Colbaugh	Mary Williams	Henry & Mary Colbaugh	John & Louiza Williams
21913	Colbaugh, George	GA	1850		Henry Colbaugh	Mary Williams	Henry & Polly Colbaugh	Samuel & Tenna McCorkle
21858	Colbaugh, Glennie	TN	1895		James Colbaugh	Mary Williams	Henry & Mary Colbaugh	John & Louiza Williams
21877	Colbaugh, James	TN	1862	Mary Colbaugh	Henry Colbaugh	Mary Williams	Henry & Polly Colbaugh	Samuel & Tenna McCorkle
21859	Colbaugh, John	TN	1889		James Colbaugh	Mary Williams	Henry & Mary Colbaugh	John & Louiza Williams
21855	Colbaugh, Lafayett	TN	1891		James Colbaugh	Mary Williams	Henry & Mary Colbaugh	John & Louiza Williams
21857	Colbaugh, Lemont	TN	1892		James Colbaugh	Mary Williams	Henry & Mary Colbaugh	John & Louiza Williams

21856	Colbaugh, Lionel	TN	1905		James Colbaugh	Mary Williams	Henry & Mary Colbaugh	John & Louiza Williams
21871	Colbaugh, Naomi	TN	1902		James Colbaugh	Mary Williams	Henry & Mary Colbaugh	John & Louiza Williams
21864	Colbaugh, Sam	TN			James Colbaugh	Mary Williams	Henry & Mary Colbaugh	John & Louiza Williams
21914	Colbaugh, William	GA	1880	Georgia Colbaugh	George Colbaugh	Velma Davis	Henry & Mary Colbaugh	Wm & Dicey Davis
6357	Colbert, David	AL	45yrs	Betty & Rhody	William Colbert	Mary Moniac	William Colbert	Sam & Susan Moniac
3435	Colbert, Henry	AL	45yrs	Huston Colbert	William Colbert	Mary Moniac	Bill & Cely Colbert	Sam & Susan Moniac
3436	Colbert, James	AL	37yrs	Florence Colbert	William Colbert	Mary Moniac	Bill & Cealy Colbert	Sam & Susan Moniac
46	Colbert, Jennie	GA	35yrs	separated	Jack Thompson	Patty Chitwood	Charley & Sally Thompson	
14352	Colbert, Josephine	MO	1860		James Boatright	Rebecca Williford	Benj & Elizabeth Boatright	Samuel & Elizabeth Williford
3434	Colbert, Louisa	AL	38yrs	none	William Colbert	Mary Moniac	Bill & Cely Colbert	Sam & Susan Moniac
18385	Colbert, Mack	AL	26yrs	Addie Colbert	Henry Colbert	Aurelia Taylor	Wm Colbert	Wiley Taylor
3433	Colbert, Mary	AL	33yrs	W D Colbert	Kila Williams	Susan Hale		
8410 *	Colbert, Mary	NC	35yrs	John Colbert	Greenberry Willis	Elvira Abernathy		Henderson & Harriett Abernathy
6358	Colbert, Mrs W L	AL		W L Colbert	Wash Williams	Edy Lofton		
18396	Colbert, Mrs. James	AL	34yrs	James Colbert	Joe Walker	Creacy McGhee		Richard & Betsy McGhee
10835	Colbert, Rebecca	MO	1880		Andrew Colbert	Josephine Boatwright		James & Rebecca Boatwright
6365	Colbert, Walter	AL	35yrs	Louisa Williams	William Colbert	Mary Moniac	William Colbert	Sam & Susan Moniac
20024	Colder, John	AR	1890		Moses Colder	Mary Nelson	Peter & Liza Colder	Simon & Annie Nelson
20429	Coldwell, Mary	TN	1853		William Glover	Clara Cooley		Jacob & Hannah Autry
14439	Cole, Abraham	NC	1883	Lu Cole	Newton Cole	Malinda Gwinn	Wm & Sarah Cole	Almon & Sarah Gwinn
22837	Cole, Bettie	TN	1878	Zollie Cole	William Rayder	Margaret Lynn	Harvey & Katie Rayder	Jonas & Demerisa Lynn
13820	Cole, Darthula	VA	1851	Linder Cole	John Weaver	Celia Pennington		Sam & Elizabeth Pennington
4338	Cole, George Sr.	NC	1838		Benjamin Cole	Mary Walker		
9539	Cole, James	TN	1872	Medie Carrett	Newton Cole	Malinda Gwinn	Wm & Sarah Cole	Almon & Sarah Gwinn
14437	Cole, Jasper	TN	1880		Newton Cole	Malinda Gwinn	Wm & Sarah Cole	Almon & Sarah Gwinn
9538	Cole, John	TN	1874	Hattie Cole	Newton Cole	Malinda Gwinn	Wm & Sarah Cole	Almon & Sarah Gwinn
8813	Cole, Mary	GA	1869	Arlando Cole	Pickens Corley	Martha Whitemore		Spencer & Melissa Whitemore
14543	Cole, Mary	GA	1846	John Cole (decd)	Robert Evans	Sallie Christopher	Robt & Haley Evans	Anbrous & Sallie Christopher
19331	Cole, Mary	TX	1885	Ernest Cole	Bomerman	Mariah Rogers		Joseph & Mary Rogers

21280	Cole, Mary	OK	1850	William Cole	Lewis Anderson	Nancy Hopkins	Abraham & Rachael Anderson	Stephen & Rachal Hopkins
12337	Cole, Noah	GA	1843	Mary Cole	John Cole	Betsy Whitlock	Samuel & Nancy Cole	James & Sallie Whitlock
16346	Cole, Shepherd	KY	1849	Mary & Deemas Cole	Charles Cole	Charlotte Cole	Wm Campbell & Louana Cole	Wm Cole & Biddy Collins
12336	Cole, Thomas	GA	1881		Noah Cole	Mary Wimpy	John & Betsy Cole	Hensley & Bettie Wimpy
14440	Cole, Thomas	NC	1878	Lizzie Cole	Newton Cole	Malinda Gwinn	Wm & Sarah Cole	Almon & Sarah Gwinn
14438	Cole, William	TN	1869	Delia Cole	Newton Cole	Malinda Gwinn		Almon Gwinn & Sarah Lillard
3104	Coleman, Charley	MS	1880	Sue Coleman	Jerry Coleman	Mary Hobgood		Charles & Martha Hobgood
12989 *	Coleman, Harrison	NC	1853	M E Coleman	Cow su yoh kee Littlejohn	Becky Coleman	Littlejohn & Jennie Littlejohn	
20146 *	Coleman, J.F.	GA	1872	Lula Coleman	Ransom Coleman	Lucy Rankins	Bass & Chaney Erbey	
3103	Coleman, James	MS	1880	Lena Coleman	Jerry Coleman	Mary Hubgood		Charles & Martha Hobgood
3102	Coleman, Mary	MS	1856	Jerry Coleman	Charles Hobgood	Martha Lowe		Thomas & Annie Lowe
8689 *	Coleman, Morning	NC	1856	Harrison Coleman	Washington Gibson	Peggy Carter	Ransom Welch & Rhoda Gibson	Thomas & Morning Carter
4781	Coleman, Ora	NC	1882	George Coleman	James Dockery	Malissa Williamson	Eli & Catherine Dockery	James & Betsey Williamson
15881	Coles, Willie Ross	KS	1893		John Johnston	Mary Kimberman	Thomas & Mary Johnston	George & Mary Kimberman
6380	Collet, Joseph	TN	1837	Jane Collet	Joel Collet	Betsy Raburn		
12289	Collet, Martha	GA	1863	John Collet	Caleb Henry	Martha Dickey	Alexander Sour John	
20031	Collett, Archibald	GA	1846	Susannah Collett	John Collett	Jensie Darby	Greenberry & Sallie Collett	Charles & Nancy Darby
14541	Collett, Clarence	GA	1906		James Collett	Amanda Howard	Archibald & Susanna Collett	John & Sarah Howard
14540	Collett, Clyde	GA	1906		James Collett	Amanda Howard	Archibald & Susanna Collett	John & Sarah Howard
14539	Collett, Grady	GA	1902		James Collett	Amanda Howard	Archibald & Susanna Collett	John & Sarah Howard
14070	Collett, James	GA	1878	Amanda Collett	Archibald Collett	Susannah Herndon	John & Jensie Collett	Enoch Herndon
20729	Collett, James	GA	1883	Mary Collett	Jesse Collett	Mary Glass	John & Caroline Collett	Wm & Ellen Glass
14072	Collett, Jesse	GA	1862	Mary Collett	John Collett	Jane Darby	Green Collett	Charles & Nancy Darby
14073	Collett, John	GA	1856	Callie Collett	John Collett	Jane Darby	Green Collett	Charles & Nancy Darby
20032	Collett, John	GA	1870	Winnie Collett	Archibald Collett	Susannah Herndon	John & Jensie Collett	Enoch & Susannah Herndon
14071	Collett, Lennie	GA	1882	Samantha Collett	Archibald Collett	Susannah Herndon	John & Jensie Collett	Enoch Herndon
14542	Collett, Lennier	GA		Samantha Collett	James Collett	Amanda Howard	Archibald & Susanna Collett	John & Sarah Howard
14538	Collett, Luther	GA	1904		James Collett	Amanda Howard	Archibald & Susanna Collett	John & Sarah Howard
17680	Collier, Ella May	OK	1877	Will Collier	Duncan McKeller	Louisa Miller	Timothy Keller & Catherine McLane	Christy Miller & Permelia Williams
11471 *	Collier, John	GA	87yrs	Vinie Collier	Seaborn Mays	Eva Collier		

16218	Collier, Lewis	OK	1859		John Collier	Elizabeth Ruth		Hopkin & Millie Ruth
18757	Collier, Mary	AL	1854	James Collier	Richard Hall	Amanda Harris	Willis & Mary Hall	Peter & Elizie Harris
21145	Collier, Mary	TN	1867	H.C. Collier	Thomas Akin	Louisa Bryant	William & Nancy Akin	Jackson & Matilda Bryant
10545	Collins, Fannie	GA	1877	H L Collins	Thomas Loyd	Elisabeth Mathis	Thos & Susanna Loyd	Lewis & Elizabeth Matthews
15650*	Collins, George	GA	1893		Israh Collins	Margaret Smith		Ansel & Nancy Smith
7102	Collins, Guy	OK	1883	none	John Collins	Thyrza McKaeig	Edward & Mary Collins	John McKaeig
17902	Collins, J.B.	FL	1867		Wm Haggerty	Mary Vaughn	John & Mary Haggerty	Ambrose & Josephine Vaughn
7103	Collins, John	OK	1854	Theodosia Collins	Edward Collins	Mary Hammack	John & Nancy Collins	Daniel & Annie Hammack
22490	Collins, Laura	TN	1867	B.H. Collins	Joseph Collett	Lucretia Watson	Joe & Betsy Collett	Thomas & Martha Watson
21710	Collins, Maggie	OK	1863	Thomas Collins	? Rowe	Rachel Fields		George Fields
17603	Collins, Margaret	OK	1850		A.W. Brown	Elizabeth Harris	Joshua Brown	Ned Harris
15723*	Collins, Margarette	GA	1864	Isah Collins	Ansel Smith	Nancy Jenkins	Frank & Tena Hog	Sam & Lucy Jenkins
5037	Collins, Morgan	OK		Sarah Collins	James Collins	Martha Catton		
18699	Collins, Pauline	FL	1868	Augustus Collins	Peter Reeache	Nancy Vaughn		Ambrose & Tabitha Vaughn
13736	Collins, Sallie	GA	1861	I.T. Collins	Andrew Whitlock	Eliza Rowson	George & Nancy Whitlock	Elija & Millie Rowson
4964	Collis, Letty	GA	1882	Maney Collis	Wade Ross	Margaret Clouts		Mahala Clouts
21261	Colston, Joseph	TX	1877	S.D. Colston	Thomas Colston	Mary Graham		
21263	Colston, Mary	TX	1840	Thomas Colston	? Graham	? Glass		
21720	Colstone, Anna	TX	1881	Henry Colstone	Richard Graham	Mittie Sisk	James & Martha Graham	
19490	Colter, James	MO	1879	Nancy Colter	James Colter	Adinza Mallicoat	George & Mary Colter	Daniel Mallicoat & Malinda Whittenberg
19492	Colter, John	MO	1888		James Colter	Adinza Mallicoat	George & Mary Colter	Daniel Mallicoat & Malinda Whittenberg
16207*	Colton, Flutana	OK	1882		Joseph Colton	Emeline Andrews		Allen & Lucinda Andrews
16232*	Colton, Joseph	GA		Lula Colton	Joseph Colton	Emeline Andrews		Allen & Lucinda Andrews
16237*	Colton, Willie	AL	1876		Joseph Colton	Emeline Andrews		Allen & Lucinda Andrews
17679	Colvard, San Juan	KS	1848		Andrew Colvard	Myra King	John Colvard & Elizabeth Welch	James King & Rebecca Ratcliff
13197	Colvin, William	TN	1878		Thomas Colvin	Dolly Meeb		
21862*	Colwell, Mabell	TN			Thomas Colwell	Mary Glover	Joseph & Sarah Colwell	Wm & Clara Glover
21849*	Colwell, Robert	TN			Thomas Colwell	Mary Glover	Joseph & Sarah Colwell	Wm & Clara Glover
21583*	Colwell, Sampson	GA	1874	Mary Colwell	Thomas Colwell	Mary Glover		Clara Glover
17696*	Colyer, Anna	TN	1865	William Colyer	Richard Banks	Merilla Williams		Lottie Williams

13328	Combes, Elvira	WV	1881	Sisro Combes	Sam Mitchem	Nazomy Sizemore	Franklin & Christena Mitchem	Owen & Nancy Sizemore
21325	Combest, Mollie	TX	1874	Obe Combest	George Biddy	Barbara Hampton	James & Delila Biddy	Henry & Mollie Hampton
4159	Combs, Abbie	MO	1888	Alf Combs	Benjamin Sweckard	Martha Hambleton	Samuel & Albigail Sweckard	Isiah & Martha Hambleton
22640	Combs, Annie	MO	1882	Carlos Combs	William Miller	Ellen Sloan	W.G. Sr. & Mary Miller	A.C. & Mary Sloan
6887	Combs, Bertie	VA	1885	Eli Combs	Alexander Huffman	Emaline Pennington	Alex & Sealy Huffman	Samuel & Sarah Pennington
6116	Combs, Jenetty	VA	1874	Alvin Combs	Samuel Pennington	Sarah Huffman	Andrew & Hetty Pennington	
22440	Combs, Lucretia	TX	1834	K.C. Combs	Robin McGee	Ester Berry	William McGee	Thomas & Hannah Berry
22378	Combs, Mittie	NC	1887	E.S. Combs	Jessie Isaacs	Mary Scott	Joseph & Frankie Isaacs	Benjamin & Bettie Scott
16242	Comer, Celia	OK	1851	J S Comer	Caleb Balies	Jensie Craig		John Craig
17882	Comsilk, Emaline	NC	1887		Armstrong Comsilk	Anna Kieger	Neggi Comsilk	
21406	Comstock, William	AL	1872	Missouri Comstock	William Comstock	Cenia Stanson		
14351	Condit, Emma	MO	1886	Roy Condit	William Boatright	Isabella Clark	James & Rebecca Boatright	Thomas & Sarah Clark
8683	Condrey, Sterling	OK	1845	Charity Condrey	William Condrey	Louisa Barnett		Betsey Griffin
19332	Conley, George	AR	1874		Jim Conley			
2432	Conley, Lydia	GA	1866	J L Conley	W J Mason	Susie Benfield	John & Pollie Mason	Tom & Lydie Benfield
3314	Conley, Mary	NC	28yrs	Willard Conley	Joel Crisp	Nancy Delozier	Pendleton & Nancy Crisp	Edward & Elizabeth Delozier
8691 *	Conley, Mary	NC	1869	Thomas Conley	Washington Gibson	Peggy Carter	Ransom Welch & Rhoda Gibson	Thomas & Morning Carter
18939	Connelly, Sarah	VA		James Connelly	John Kingsbury	Eliza Chapman	John Kingsbury	
13894	Conner, Emmeline	OK	1861	Arthur Conner	Brummett	Nersis Cole		Anna Cole
4651	Conner, Margaret	NC	1864	D.F. Conner	James Maney	Margaret Corn	John & Mary Maney	Adam & Hannah Corn
76	Connors, Ellen	SC	1852	Charles Connors	Phineas Tompkins	Hannah Ross	Isaac Tompkins & Helen Backus	Templin Ross & Eliza Sevier
10594	Conrad, Elizabeth	OK		John Conrad	Jesse Davis	Manervia Martin		Samuel & Sallie Martin
2017	Constant, James	NC	1882	Hettie Constant	John Constant	Elizabeth Delozier		Ed & Elizabeth Delozier
2015	Constant, William	NC		Laura Constant	John Constant	Elizabeth Delozier		Ed & Elizabeth Delozier
20136	Conway, Anna	FL	1861	John Conway	Valentine Fillingim	Sarah Dukes	Robert & Ester Fillingim	Thomas & Ann Duke
16241	Conway, Polly	TX	1856	H A Conway	George Williams	Nancy Stephens	George & Nancy Williams	George & Pollie Stephens
20137	Conway, Trammell	FL	1886		John Conway	Anna Fillingim	Wm Conway & Amgeline Phenelphy	V. & Sarah Fillingim
12360	Coodey, William	OK	1873	Lavena Coodey	Joseph Coodey	Mary Hardage	Joseph & Jane Coodey	Joe & Muskogee Hardage
12365	Coody, Sarah	OK	1859		Joseph Coodey	Mary Thornberry	Joseph & Jane Coodey	
14465	Cook, A E	WV	1873	Bellzora Cook	Charles Cook	Mary Cook	R M & Polly Cook	Thos & Rebecca Cook

#	Name	State	Year					
17310	Cook, A.E. et al	WV	1875				Thos & Rebecca Cook	
18243	Cook, Albert	GA	1852	Emma Cook	James Cook	Louvica Carner		Polly Carner
14615	Cook, Caleb	GA	1848	Sarah Cook	George Cook	Jane Page	Alex & Patsy Cook	
12486	Cook, Calla	GA	1883	Samuel Cook	Hick Carter	Polly Cochran	N T & Nellie Carter	Henry & Deliah Cochran
14614	Cook, Carrie	GA	1884		Caleb Cook	Sarah Cook	George & Jane Cook	
19392	Cook, Charles	GA			William Cook	Jane Coker	Richard & Sarah Cook	
18244	Cook, Charlie	GA	1874	Roma Cook	Albert Cook	Emma Cumming	James & Louvica Cook	
18088	Cook, Chilie	GA	1851	Carrie Cook	Major Cook	Eliza Bowen		Austin & Rose Bowen
15477	Cook, Clayton	GA	1885		John Cook	Mary Ragan	James & Louvica Cook	
6815	Cook, David	VA			Harrison Cook	Mary		
14537 *	Cook, E.G.	GA	1865	Texas Cook	Major Cook	Eliza Bowen		Austin & Rose Bowen
7098	Cook, Edna	KS	1873	Robert Cook	Rilley Allen	Caurissia Heaps	Lewis & Margaret Allen	Thomas & Betsy Heaps
10230	Cook, Edward	VA	1872	Angie Cook	Calvin Cook	Rebecca Bailey	Thos Cook & Rebecca Sizemore	Jamison Bailey & Polly McConnas
17306	Cook, Edward	WV	1872	Marinda Cook	John Cook	Margarett Stewart	Thos Cook & Rebecca Sizemore	George & Peggie Stewart
19805	Cook, Ellen	GA	1881		James Cook	Laura Cantrell	Richard & Sarah Cook	
12938	Cook, Ellis	WV	1874	Icie Cook	Calvin Cook	Rebecca Bailey	Thos & Rebecca Cook	Jamison & Polly Bailey
14613	Cook, Elter	GA	1889		Caleb Cook	Sarah Cook	George & Jane Cook	
15476	Cook, Felton	GA	1877	Della Cook	John Cook	Mary Ragan	James & Louvica Cook	
19388	Cook, George	GA	1861	Jane Cook	Richard Cook	Sarah Land	John Tucker	
19806	Cook, Gladdis	GA	1906		John Cook	Annie Cook	Isaac & Martha Cook	
14449	Cook, H. Ingram	WV	1875	Mandy Cook	John Cook	Margaritte Stewart	Thos Cook & Rebecca Sizemore	George & Peggie Stewart
19390	Cook, Ida	GA	1885		William Cook	Jane Coker	Richard & Sarah Cook	
19807	Cook, James	GA	1859	Laura Cook	Richard Cook	Sarah Land	John Tucker	
21747	Cook, James	OK	1874	Nellie Cook	Thomas Walker	Sarah Burnett		Lydia & John Burnett
17301	Cook, Jamison	WV	1870		Calvin Cook	Rebecca Bailey	Thos Cook & Rebecca Sizemore	Jamison Bailey & Polly
19389	Cook, Jane et al	GA			George Cook	Jane Denson	Richard & Sarah Cook	
16071	Cook, Jeff	OK	1861	Eler Cook	Henry Cook	Edey Moore	Bill Cook	Colim Moore
15223	Cook, John	GA	1844	Mary Reagan	James Cook	Louvisa Carnes	John & Poer Cook	
19809	Cook, John	GA	1850	Jane Cook	Richard Cook	Sarah Land	John Tucker	
19811	Cook, John	GA	1875	Annie Cook	Isaac Cook	Martha Turner	Richard & Sarah Cook	
20779	Cook, John	GA	1892		John Cook	Mary Ragan	James Cook & Louvica Carns	
20781	Cook, Lawton & Elmer	GA	1903 1905		Willie Cook	Lula Samples		Wesley & Francis Samples
20780	Cook, Lula	GA	1884	Will Cook	Wesley Samples	Francis Gaines	Thomas & Sallie Samples	

21917*	Cook, Margaret	TN	1843		Charles Butler	Devy McMahan		Fannie McMahan
5560	Cook, Mary	VA	1840	Harrison Cook	David Tucker	Mahala Blevins		Wells & Elizabeth Blevins
20782	Cook, Mary	GA	1890		John Cook	Mary Ragan	James Cook & Louvica Carns	
14478	Cook, May	WV	1879		Charles Cook	Mary Cook	R W Cook & Polly Goins	Thos Cook & Rebecca Sizemore
2557	Cook, Mrs. Vennor	GA	1884	Poley Cook	F M Russell	Mary Leadford		Jason Leadford
17311	Cook, R. Beecher	WV	1881	Leona Cook	Charles Cook	Mary Cook	R.M. & Polly Cook	Thos & Rebecca Cook
17312	Cook, R. Beecher	WV	1904				Thos & Rebecca Cook	
15222	Cook, Richard	GA	1829	Sarah Cook	John Tucker	Martha Cook		Tom & Polly Cook
12453	Cook, Robert	WV	1870	Bettie Cook	John Cook	Margaret Stewart	Thomas & Rebecca Cook	George & Peggie Stewart
14662	Cook, Robert	WV	1881		Elijah Cook	Harriet Sizemore	James & Sarah Cook	Franklin & Polly Sizemore
19810	Cook, Roscoe et al	GA			John Cook	Jane Nations	Richard & Sarah Cook	
20783	Cook, Sallie	GA	1883	William Cook	J.R. Edwards	Martha Crow	Wm & Catherine Edwards	
9093	Cook, Sarah	WV	1866	Dan Cook	Calvin Sizemore	Mary Brinegar	John & Jane Sizemore	Jacob & Sheba Brinegar
19808	Cook, Sarah et al	GA			James Cook	Laura Cantrell	Richard & Sarah Cook	
11077	Cook, Susan	VA	1879	Alonzo Cook	Andrew Widener	Mary Blevins		Isham & Anna Blevins
10490	Cook, Thomas	WV	1859	Lovesa Cook	Thomas Cook	Rebecca Sizemore	Wm Cook & Catharine Stewart	Ned Sizemore & Annie Bolden
19812	Cook, Vernon & Sarah	GA			Richard Cook	Laura	James & Laura Cook	
17309	Cook, W. Sherman	WV	1868	Nancy Cook	John Cook	Margaret Stewart	Thos & Rebecca Cook	George & Peggie Stewart
10139	Cook, William	WV	1840	Mary Cook	Thomas Cook	Rebecca Sizemore	Wm & Catherine Cook	Ned & Annie Sizemore
15475	Cook, William	GA	1880	Sarah Cook	John Cook	Mary Ragan	James & Louvica Cook	
19391	Cook, William	GA	1863		Richard Cook	Sarah Land	John Tucker	
19813	Cook, William	GA	1881	Minnie Cook	George Gook	Jane Denson	Richard & Sarah Cook	
19814	Cook, William & Jane	GA			William Cook	Minnie Futon	George & Jane Cook	
3933	Cooksey, Thomas	OK	1848	Maggie Goins	John Cooksey	Margarett Doolin		
17340	Cooley, Nancy	VA	1847	George Cooley	Wm Smith	Temperance Todd	David Smith	Levi Todd
108	Coon, Bernard	OK	1879	Sarah Coon	Solomon Coon	Catherine Smith		John & Polly Smith
12509	Coon, Deekilasky	OK	1855	Jennie Coon (decd)	Coon	Che ner que		Che ner que
21213	Cooper, Arthur	OK	1874		John Cooper	Emma Simpson	J.W. & Elizabeth Cooper	Wm & Jemima Simpson
7097	Cooper, Fielden	TX	1856	Sarah Cooper	John Cooper	Yonny Blood		
18910	Cooper, Georgie	AR	1886	Willie Cooper	James Reeder	Mary Glenn		James & Nancy Parrish
4914	Cooper, Iza	OK	1866	James Cooper	Silas McMillan	Rosana Pippin		Thomas & Dicie Pippin

17764	Cooper, James	TN	1875	Annie Cooper	Francis Cooper	Julia Mansfield	John & Eliza Cooper	Thomas & Susan Mansfield
19199	Cooper, John	OK	1885		W.T. Cooper	Sary Woods	J.W. Cooper & Elizabeth McAdams	J.W. Woods
21218	Cooper, John	OK	1847		J.W. Cooper	Elizabeth McAdam	James Cooper & Delilah Simpson	James & Rachel McAdams
21210	Cooper, Joshua	OK	1874		J.W. Cooper	Embly Pierce	James Cooper & Delilah Simpson	James & Rachel McAdams
7096	Cooper, Mary	TX	1839	Charles Cooper (decd)	John Pearce	Nancy Allen		
19589	Cooper, Peter	AL	1843	Malindee Cooper	William Cooper	Susan Burks	Isaac & Jane Cooper	Johnathan & Nancy Burks
20023	Cooper, Priscilla	AR	1883		Moses Colder	Mary Nelson	Peter & Liza Colder	Simon & Annie Nelson
8183	Cooper, Riley	MO	1836	Butley Cooper	Lemuel Cooper	Cynthia Riley	Henry Cooper	James Riley
19185	Cooper, Samuel	OK	1883	Nellie Cooper	W.T. Cooper	Sary Woods	J.W. Cooper & Elizabeth McAdams	J.W. Woods
21211	Cooper, Samuel	OK	1858	Ella Cooper	J.W. Cooper	Elizabeth McAdam	James Cooper & Delilah Simpson	James & Rachel McAdams
18841	Cope, John	OK	1859	Missouri Cope	Rheubin Cope	Jane Brock		James Brock & Sarah Arick
18453	Cope, Merideth	OK	1856	Mary Cope	Reubin Cope	Jane Brock		
18842	Cope, Missouri	OK	1864	John Cope	Paul Maze	Martha Isbell	Wm & Mary Maze	Pincelton Isbell
5167	Cope, Mont	OK	1885	none	William Cope	Josie Waddle	Paris	Ed & Sallie Ingram
16371	Cope, Parile	NC	17yrs	Pauli Cope	David Haney	Elizabeth Ledford	James Haney & Caroline Burnet	Jessie Ledford & Polly Pressley
8600	Cope, Sallie	NC	1876	Elbert Cope	John Bateman	Matildie Jones	Archibald & Mahala Bateman	
18625	Cope, Stanley	OK	1849	Eliza Cope	Rheubin Cope	Jane Brock		James Brock & Sarah Arick
21481	Cope, Sue	OK	1855		John Burnett	Lydia Griffith		
9041	Copeland, Adline	WV	1861	James Copeland	Wilburn Osburn	Permelia Dunford	Solomon & Martha Osburn	Thos & Honor Dunford
22208	Coray, Martha	OK	1861	Bob Cora	Jacob Creason	Martha Creason	Walter & Mary Creason	Elijah & Elizabeth Creason
14390	Corban, Ellender	GA	1843	widower	Ezekiel Townsend	Annie Patterson	Eddie & Annie Townsend	Roly Patterson
11361	Corban, John	GA	1856	Arie Corban	Joe Corban	Elinder Townsend	John & Delila Corban	
14453	Corbett, Elizabeth	AL	1831		Daniel Sizemore	Anna Hankins	Wm & Mary Sizemore	
17313	Corbett, Mathey	AL	1862	O.L. Corbett	Sizemore	Black	Daniel Sizemore	Ana Hankins
20885	Corbin, Ellender	GA	1843		Ezekiel Townsend	Annie	Edward & Annie Townsend	
14954	Corbitt, Amos	OK	1878		Wm Corbitt	Marth Tucker	Wm & Mary Corbitt	
14946	Corbitt, Edith	OK	1859	Charles Corbitt	Wm Corbitt	Mary Conley		Archable & Mary Conley
17303	Corbitt, Mary	OK	1867	James Corbitt	Daniel Sizemore	Margarett Woods	Daniel & Anna Sizemore	Thomas & Juda Woods
14948	Corbitt, Robert	OK	1880		W N Corbitt	Martha Tucker	Wm & Mary Corbitt	
14945	Corbitt, William	OK	1876		Wm Corbitt	Martha Tucker	Wm & Mary Corbitt	
14947	Corbitt, William	OK	1854	Martha Corbitt	Wm Corbitt	Mary Conley	Mary Corbitt	Archable & Mary Conley
18331	Cordell, Eff Allen	GA	1845	Margaret Cordell	Jeremiah Cordell	Mary Whisenant	Stephen Cordell	Adam & Jania Whisenant

7116	Cordell, Elsworth	MO	1890		Jacob Cordell	Amanda Van Trump		Josiah & Susan Van Trump
19505	Cordell, Ezekiel	GA	1841	Mary Cordell	Jeremiah Cordell	Mary Whisanunt	Stephen Cordell	
19503	Cordell, George	GA	1848	Mary Cordell	Jeremiah Cordell	Mary Whisanunt	Stephen Cordell	
2365	Cordell, Green	GA	1864	Missario Cordell		Lucinda Maney		John Maney & Polly Madcap
9896	Cordell, Harrison	TN	1873	Jane Cordell	John Cordell	Margurite Elrod	Benett Cordell & Marthy Dukes	
19504	Cordell, Henry	GA	1881		Ezekiel Cordell	Eliza McDaniel	Jeremiah Cordell	
7588	Cordell, James	GA	1827	Ellen	Bennett Cordell	Martha Barten		Lewis & Martha Barten
9597	Cordell, John	GA	1834	Sarah Cordell	Cooper Cordell	Martha Duke		Thomas Duke
10268	Cordell, John	GA	1867	Marthy Cordell	John Cordell	Margarite Elrod	Benett Cordell	Marthy Dukes
14914	Cordell, Lera	GA	1905		Willard Cordell	Caldonia Prather	Columbus & Passie Cordell	T S & Amanda Prather
14864	Cordell, Lillie et al	GA			Green Cordell	Missouri Gravitt	Lucinda Maney	B F & Martha Gravitt
21479	Cordell, Nancy	AR	1859	James Cordell	John Burnett	Lydia Griffith	John & Susan Burnett	Arden & Delilah Griffith
14904	Cordell, Passie	GA	1851	Columbus Cordell	Julian Parker	Celia Moss	Wm & Edith Parker	
14915	Cordell, Walter et al	GA			Columbus Cordell	Passie Parker	John & Angeline Cordell	Julian & Celia Parker
14918	Cordell, Willard	GA	1885	Caldonia Cordell	Columbus Cordell	Passie Parker	John & Angeline Cordell	Julian & Celia Parker
9897	Cordell, William	TN	1869	Amanda Cordell	John Cordell	Margurite Elrod	Bennett Cordell & Marthy Dukes	
18506	Corey, William	UT	1853	Julie Corey	Howard Corey	Jane Burn		
8810	Corley, Robert	GA	1876	Flora Corley	Pickens Corly	Martha Whitemore		Spencer & Melissa Whitemore
8811	Corley, William	GA	1867	Laura Corley	Pickens Corley	Martha Whitemore		Spencer & Melissa Whitemore
8809	Corly, Samuel	GA	1893	Lena Corley	Pickens Corly	Martha Whitemore		Spencer & Melissa Whitemore
11336	Corn, Bessie	GA	1889		George Corn	Ida Perry	John & Caroline Corn	
19774	Corn, Earl	GA	1881	Lula Corn	Henry Corn	Mollie Lesser	John & Caroline Corn	Samuel & Caroline Lesser
9448	Corn, Edwin	GA	1855	Julia Corn	John Corn	Caroline Davis	Wm & Phebee Corn	John Davis & Nancy Bird
11340	Corn, George	GA	1867	Ida Corn	John Corn	Caroline Davis		John & Nancy Davis
11337	Corn, Henry	GA	1893		George Corn	Ida Perry	John & Caroline Corn	
13853	Corn, John	GA	1862	Julia Corn	John Corn	Caroline Davis	Wm & Phebee Corn	John Davis & Nancy Bird
17509	Corn, John	GA	1880	Jannie Corn	Edwin Corn	Julia Nunn	John & Caroline Corn	Seabom & Luitie Nunn
11338	Corn, Sudie	GA	1895		George Corn	Ida Perry	John & Caroline Corn	
15285	Cornet, Montie	GA	1884	LeRoy Cornet	George Spears	Mary Adams	Josiah & Martha Spears	
11291	Cornett, Benjman	GA	1859	Mary Cornett	Cornett	Elizabeth Helton	George Cornett	J C Helton

19744	Cornett, Hulda	GA	1882	Cary Cornett	Robert Evans	Margaret Barnett	Robert & Sallie Evans	Richard & Rhoda Barnett
2602	Cornett, Margret	GA	1879	Furt Cornett	Drury Campbell	Rebecca Early	Henderson & Susanah Campbell	
2313	Cornwell, Nancy	NC	1857	W H Cornwell	Eli Dockery	Catherine McLoud	James & Bitha Dockery	Harve & Sallie McLoud
22248	Corrie, Ophelia	IL		Lafayett Corrie	John Blackburn	Sarah Miller	Andrew & Francis Blackburn	Henry & Rhody Miller
10781	Corvin, Plesant	TN	1846		Philo Corvin	Margret Teague	Thomas & Margret Corvin	Allen & Peggy Teague
21394	Cory, Tiletha	TX	1870	Marshall Cory	Thomas Marshall	Tiletha Martindale	Andrew Marshall	Mary Russell
17459	Costly, Joseph	AR	1822	Elizabeth Costly	Castly	McIntyre		
127	Cothren, Alice	NC	1885	Gudger Cothren	Jake Rowland	Martha Pace		Stephen & Dovey Pace
126	Cothren, Anna	NC	1880	Levi Cothren	Jake Rowland	Martha Pace		Stephen & Dovey Pace
17952	Cotter, Catharine	GA	1847	J.C.K. Cotter	John Hubbard	Polly Edwards	John & Catharine Hubbard	Henry & Peggy Edwards
21195	Cottingham, Mary	AR	1873	Henry Cottingham	John Williams	Patience Man		Frederick & Sarah Man
16399	Couch, Amanda	OK	1884	John Couch	Isaac Herrington	Allie Vann		Wiley & Mary Vann
4006	Couch, Marian	OK	1842	Mary Couch				
17009	Couch, William	OK	1856	Mary Couch	Peter Couch	Mary Couch	Jacob Couch	Andy & Mary Couch
21260	Coulston, Anna	TX	1881	Henry Coulston	Richard Graham	Mittie Sisk		
21427	Coulston, James	OK	1868	Abbie Coulston	Thomas Coulston	Mary Grayham	Elex Coulston	James & Martha Grayham
21264	Coulston, John	TX	1871	Lillie Coulston	T.B. Coulston	Mary Graham	Aleck Coulston	James & Patsy Graham
21262	Coulston, William	TX	1863	Emma Coulston	T.B. Coulston	Mary Graham	Aleck Coulston	James & Patsy Graham
7104	Courter, Lucinda	KS		Peter Courter	William Boatright	Isabell Clark	James & Rebecca Boatright	George & Sally Clark
22247	Courtland, Elizabeth	NC	1842	John Courtland	Edward DeLozier	Elizabeth Poindexter	Jesse & Posey DeLozier	Pledge & Elizabeth Poindexter
12274	Courtney, Isham	OK	1866	Eva Courtney	Benjamin Courtney	Matilda Fender	Wm & Matilda Courtney	Daniel & Dicy Fender
18404	Courtney, Jane	AL	21yrs	Early Courtney	James Seals	Louisa Hadley	Wm & Lucy Seals	Simon & Caroline Hadley
12094	Courtney, Mary	OK	1871		Benjamin Courtney	Matilda Fender	Wm & Matilda Courtney	Daniel & Dicy Fender
1515	Courtney, Matilda	OK	1842	Benj Courtney	Daniel Fender	Dicey Brown	Michael & Winnie Fender	Alex & Violetta Brown
14648	Courtney, William	OR	1867	Prescilla Courtney	Benj Courtney	Matilda Fender	Wm & Matilda Courtney	Daniel & Dicy Fender
20347*	Covington, Artice	GA	1900		S.F. Covington	Belle Williams	Franklin & Mariah Covington	David & Adaline McFarland
20413*	Covington, Belle	GA	1861	Scot Covington	David McFarland	Adaline Jones	Carrie McFarland	Green & Malissa Henry
20350*	Covington, Charles	GA	1883		Scott Covington	Belle Williams	Franklin & Mariah Covington	Wm & Adaline Williams
20414*	Covington, D.Forrest	GA			Scot Covington	Belle Williams	Frank & Mariah Covington	David & Adaline McFarland
20351*	Covington, Dewitt	GA			Scott Covington	Belle Williams	Franklin & Mariah Covington	David & Adaline McFarland

20363*	Covington, Effie	GA			S.F. Covington	Belle Williams	Franklin & Mariah Covington	David & Adaline McFarland
12335	Covington, Hattie	GA	1879	Frank Covington	Samuel Hillhouse Jr	Augusta Cole	Samuel & Annie Hillhouse	John & Betsy Cole
20656*	Covington, James	GA			Scott Covington	Belle Williams	Frank & Mariah Covington	David & Adaline McFarland
3779	Covington, Mary	OK	1882	John Covington	John Avary	Hariett Whitten	W W & Tilitha Avary	Joel & Nancy Whitten
15564	Covington, Mary	GA	1884	Young Covington	Francis Southerlen	Cinthia Owensby	Cas & Patsy Southerlen	Ephraim & Sally Owensby
20349*	Covington, Pluma	GA	1881		Scott Covington	Belle Williams	Franklin & Mariah Covington	Wm & Adaline Williams
14705	Cowart, Mary	GA	1853	A W Cowart (decd)	Rinderall Burrell	Elisabeth McClure	Jesse & Maring Burrell	Sarah Better
20324*	Cowen, Isaac	GA	1829	Virginia Cowen	Dock Cowen	Viola Cowen	Caesar Cowen	
11021	Cowen, Isadora	OK	1875	John Cowen	Jeremiah Deen	Louisa Braden		John & Genetta Braden
18122	Cowert, Connie	NC	24yrs		Columbus Cowert	Elizabeth Anderson	Luke & Sarah Cowert	Lazrus & Nancy Anderson
18119	Cowert, Jane	NC	22yrs		Columbus Cowert	Elizabeth Anderson	Luke & Sarah Cowert	Lazrus & Nancy Anderson
18124	Cowert, Modena et al	NC	18yrs		Columbus Cowert	Elizabeth Anderson	Luke & Sarah Cowert	Lazrus & Nancy Anderson
17714	Cox, Bertie	GA	1873	Stephen Cox	James Mann	Anna Patterson	Harrison Mann & Polly Lovelace	Hix & Sally Patterson
12945	Cox, George	GA	1854	Nancy Cox	Jacob Cox	Delila McCaslin	Jacob Cox	
21730	Cox, George	TN	1868	Maggie Cox	Robert Cox	Angeline Starling	Edward & Mary Cox	John Starling
8821	Cox, Gertrude	MO	1876	Charles Cox	Danial Dougherty	Telitha McBee	William & Mary Dougherty	John & Katie McBee
21732	Cox, Green	TN	1879		Robert Cox	Angeline Starling	Edward & Mary Cox	John Starling
12947	Cox, James	GA	1865	Callie Cox	Jacob Cox	Delila McCaslin	Jacob Cox	
12261	Cox, John	NC			Alex Cox	Martha Osborn	John & Sunie Cox	Calvin & Martha Osborn
12953	Cox, John	GA	1851	Mary Cox	Jacob Cox	Delila McCaslin	Jacob Cox	
20886	Cox, Kemper	NC	1894		Alex Cox	Martha Osborne	John & Sally Cox	Calvin & Mary Osborne
7112	Cox, Lillie	OK	1876		Thomas Terry	Cerene Jackson	James Terry	John & Elizabeth Jackson
18963	Cox, Lucy	TN	1874	Alford Cox	George McGill	Delila Goins	Rolan & Eliza McGill	Solomon & Elisabeth Goins
12255	Cox, Martha	NC	1859	Alexander Cox	Calvin Osborne	Martha Sheets	Jesse & Cyntha Osborne	Jacob & Sally Sheets
19104	Cox, Mary	OK	1872	T.D. Cox	William Casto	Mary McCabe		Mary Reed
20439*	Cox, Mary	TN	1880	J.H. Cox	Nathaniel Berry	Lucinda Sabaston		Mose & Margret Kimbrough
19801	Cox, Robert	NC	1881		Columbus Cox	Sarah Black		
20083	Cox, Sarah	TN	1890	Elmer Cox	Neel Dameworth	L.E. Smith	Henry & Nancy Dameworth	Eli & M.J. Smith
8812	Coyle, Mary	GA		B.C. Coyle	Obedyer Whitemore	Millie Shubert		
7114	Crabtree, Emma	MO	1860	Leonard Crabtree	Francis Carroll	Prodence Wade	James & Polly Carroll	John & Nancy Wade
4996	Crabtree, Willie	OK		John Crabtree	William Warspeaker	Ida Herrod	Wm & Diana Warspeaker	

11305	Craft, Charley	GA	1888		George Craft	Emma Helton	Ira & Sallie Craft	Robert & Eliza Helton
12956	Craft, Ella	OK	1882	Harry Craft	Benj Courtney	Matilda Fender	Wm & Matilda Courtney	Daniel & Dicy Fender
11304	Craft, Lula	GA	1890		George Craft	Emma Helton	Ira & Sallie Craft	Robert & Eliza Helton
11303	Craft, Thomas	GA	1892		George Craft	Emma Helton	Ira & Sallie Craft	Robert & Eliza Helton
5412	Crafton, Caddie	OR	1869	A J Crafton	William Fisher	Elisabeth Wood	Abraham & Martha Fisher	
13427	Craig, Andrew	TN	1877	Elisabeth Craig	Daniel Craig	Hanna Coons	Ellis & Margaret Craig	Andrew & Sarah Coons
13429	Craig, Eliza	TN	1880	George Craig	Daniel Craig	Hanna Coons	Ellis & Margaret Craig	Andrew & Sarah Coons
19675	Craig, Frances	TN	1867	Loren Craig	Robbert Hatcher	Mary Hooper	John & Henrietta Hatcher	Dency & Elizabeth Hooper
9418	Craig, Frank decd	OK	1854	Catherine Craig	Samuel Craig	Eliza Harlan		Ezekiel & Hannah Lewis
13382	Craig, Georgie	TN	1882		A.M. Baker	Martha Shook	Samuel & Salina Baker	John & Jane Shook
19491	Craig, Mary	MO	1886	E.C. Craig	James Colter	Adinza Mallicoat	George & Mary Colter	Daniel Mallicoat & Malinda Whittenberg
19693	Craig, Mary	TN	1895		Loren Craig	Frances Hatcher	Loren & Frances Craig	Robert & Mary Hatcher
19667	Craig, Maud	TN	1897		Loren Craig	Francis Hatcher		John & Henrietta Hatcher
17885	Crane, Annie	NE	1883		E. W. Crane	Elizabeth Bays	Nathaniel & Phebe Crane	James & Rachel Bays
17884	Crane, Blanche	NE	1888		E. W. Crane	Elizabeth Bays	Nathaniel & Phebe Crane	James & Rachel Bays
18061	Crane, Frances	GA	65yrs		Charley Craine	Katie Waycaster		Jake & Peggy Waycaster
22816	Crane, Henry	OK	1880	Salie Crane	John Crane	Louisa Thompson		Jack & Elizabeth Thompson
14022	Crane, Lizzie	GA	1885	Jim Crane	Columbus Loggins	Mandy Farmer	Wm & Nancy Loggins	Reuben & Sarah Farmer
4217	Crane, Louisa	OK	1844	widow	Jack Thompson	Elizabeth Griffin	Betsy Thompson	James & Nancy Griffin
9446	Crane, Rachel	GA	1865	Francis Crane	John Corn	Caroline Davis	Wm & Phebee Corn	John Davis & Nancy Bird
17886	Crane, Wiley	NE	1879		E. W. Crane	Elizabeth Bays	Nathaniel & Phebe Crane	James & Rachel Bays
17910	Cranon, Catanna	MO	1859	Ina Cranon	Manlove Cranon	Eleanor Lee	Thomas Cranon	Elisabeth Little
17995	Cranor, James	MO	1857	Carrie Cranor	Harvey Cranor	Mary Copeland	Manlove Cranor & Eleanor Lee	Wesley Copeland & Malinda Mitchell
17911	Cranor, William	MO	1847		Manlove Cranor	Eleanor Lee	Thos & Elizabeth Cranor	
21636	Crapo, Lewis	OK	62yrs	Linda Crapo	Robin Crapo	Katy	George & Susanah Crapo	Gau-le-cha-he
7113	Craven, Frances	MO	1863	Franklin Craven	Nathan Morgan	Anna Massengale	James & Martha Morgan	Blakely & Polly Massingale
20599*	Craven, Monroe	TN	1839		Frank Craven	Charity Craven		John & Gemima Craven
20565*	Cravens, Emma	TN	1884	William Cravens	Henry Holmes	Adaline Quillan	Nathan & Lucy Holmes	Ned & Zilpha Hutchison
7761	Crawford, Charles	KS	1869	Mary Crawford	Arthur Crawford	Elizabeth Perkins		Aaron & Cilia Perkins
18352	Crawford, Cynthia	NC	1851	S.M. Crawford	Benj Hyde	Cynthia Sherrice	Benj Hyde	Elizabeth Leatherwood

945	Crawford, Ed L.	OK	1860	Zouvia Crawford	Russell Crawford	Nancy Yeates	Joseph & Mary Crawford	Larkin & Nancy Yeates
21471	Crawford, Frank	TX			Watson Crawford	Margaret Starr	Watson Crawford	Caleb Starr
14678	Crawford, Manda	GA	1862	George Crawford	Mitchel Davy	Martha Morrow	Dova Davy	William Morrow
12665	Crawford, Mary	WV	1876	Asbery Crawford	George Sizemore	Elizabeth Mitchum	Owen & Nancy Sizemore	Francis & Christiana Mitchum
19515	Crawford, Rhoda	TN	1834	John Goins & John Crawford	Sanford Goins	Charity Helton	James & Rhoda Goins	Harmon Helton & Sarah Morgan
7760	Crawford, Sarah	MO		none	Watkins Crawford	Elisebeth Perkins		Aaron & Cealy Perkins
21469	Crawford, Thaddeus	TX	1876	Carry Crawford	Frank Crawford	Nannie Cole	Watson & Margaret Crawford	
15188	Crawford, Thomas	GA	1848	Lucinda Crawford	Thomas Crawford	Mary Ritchie		
21470	Crawford, Thomas	TX	1879	Nannie Crawford	Frank Crawford	Nannie Cole	Watson & Margaret Crawford	
4260	Creasman, Ida	NC	1862	Philip Creasman	Twitt Edwards	Bettie Parker		Jonathan Parker
19216	Credill, Mattie	AL	1874	Reuben Credill	Joe Byers	Rhoda Keyton	Ham & Polly Byers	Clifton & Sookie Keyton
20317	Creech, Eliza	MO		John Creech	Emerson Herrell	Clarisa Scruggs	Michael & Lucy Herrell	Lewis & Anne Scruggs
8382	Crisp, Mary	GA	1867	none	Mat Crisp	Elisabeth Dee	Matt Crisp	
3313	Crisp, Robert	NC	25yrs	Texanah Crisp	Joel Crisp	Nancy Delozier	Pendleton & Nancy Crisp	Edward & Elizabeth Delozier
5396	Crisp, Robert	NC	1887		John Crisp	Mary Delozier		Edward & Elizabeth Delozier
5418	Crisp, Tina	NC	45yrs	John Crisp	Green Payne	Fannie Harkins	John Payne	Fannie Scisoms
19972	Crissman, John et al	NC			John Crissman	Lizzie Donathan	Aaron & Betty Crissman	Frances & Sally Donathan
19973	Crissman, Sarah	NC	1878	J.H. Crissman	Francis Donathan	Sally Key	Larkin & Vina Donathan	Linsay & Nancy Key
3552	Crittenden, Martha	OK	1836	Aaron Crittenden	Campbell Wood	Mary Hubbard	William & Lottie Wood	Uriah & Nellie Hubbard
17241	Crittenden, Nannie	OK			Richard Crittenden	Mary Proctor	Joe Crittenden & Martha Dry	Tom & Sallie Proctor
2830	Crocker, Ella	OK	1876	Felix Crocker	Samuel Hughes	Gracie Tidwell	John Hughes	John & Lucrecia Tidwell
20442*	Crockett, Mary	1851	TN		Andy Winton	Fannie Winton	Neil & Esther Cunningham	George & Agnes Winton
18370	Croffard, Manda	TN	1882	Barnett Croffard	Samuel Graves	Mahala Newman		Samuel & Charlotta Newman
22699	Cromwell, Mary	IN	1884	James Cromwell	Thomas Hammonds	Armesa Winburn	Mark & Delaney Hammonds	Louis & Sarah Winburn
7089	Cromwell, Minnie	TX	1886	Marcius Cromwell	James Stone	Sarah Hunter		Willis & Sarah Hunter
18518	Crook, Susan	MO	1890		Wm Crook	Ann Teage	James & Nancy Crook	Joe & Mary Teage
18519	Crook, Thomas	MO	1884	Minnie Crook	James Crook	Jocibene Hodge	James & Nancy Crook	Collay & Febie Hodge
18524	Crook, Wallace	WI	1861	Minnie Crook	Rufus McKinney	Diania Welsh		
18444	Crooks, Amy	MO	1872	Henry Crooks	John Mandy	Mahala Corbett	Samuel & Bettie Mandy	

18448	Crooks, Ethel	MO	1889		Henry Crooks	Amy Mandy		John & Mahala Mandy
18446	Crooks, Mabel	MO	1894		Henry Crooks	Amy Mandy		John & Mahala Mandy
18445	Crooks, Raymond	MO	1898		Henry Crooks	Amy Mandy		John & Mahala Mandy
18447	Crooks, Royce	MO	1901		Henry Crooks	Amy Mandy		John & Mahala Mandy
18478	Crosby, Tracy	OK	1871	May Crosby	Thomas Whitman	Vina Price		
504	Cross, Sarah	TN	1845	J H Cross	Daniel Helton	Martha Walker	Peter & Jennie Helton	Wm & Katie Walker
12571	Cross, Sarah	AR	65yrs	J M Cross	Wm Crosson	Francie Hood	Lewis & Susan Crosson	Seymour & Alice Rosier
19335	Cross, Wallie	GA	1885		Robert Landers	Lucy Partian	George & Elizabeth Landers	Henry & Nancy Partian
17000	Crossland, Samuel	OK	188?		Samuel Crossland		Crossland	
13424	Crossland, William	OK	1855	Mollie Crossland	Richard Crossland	Amanda Riley		
21431	Crosslin, Lucinda	TX	1852	J.C. Crosslin	James Graham	Martha Glass		Richard & Pliny Glass
18728	Crouse, Bunyan	NC	1896		I.W. Crouse	Martha Scott	Henry & Henrietta Crouse	W.P. & Amy Scott
18729	Crouse, Curtis	NC	1892		I.W. Crouse	Martha Scott	Henry & Henrietta Crouse	W.P. & Amy Scott
18821	Crouse, Iggie	NC	1871	Thos Crouse	Thomas Webb	Sarah Kirk		
18464	Crouse, Martha	NC	1855	I.W. Crouse	William Scott	Amy Hunt	Henry & Polly Scott	James & Loupy Hunt
19460	Crouse, T.V.	NC	1875	Sarah Crouse	T.W. Crouse	Martha Scott	Henry & Henrietta Crouse	W.P. & Amy Scott
20211	Crouse, William	NC		Minnie Crouse	J.W. Crouse	Martha Scott	Henry & Henrietta Crouse	W.P. & Amy Scott
20883	Crow, Abraham	AL	1879		John Crow	Nancy Talbert	Abraham Crow	Isabelle Talbert
11951	Crow, Alfred	GA	1864	Nancy Crow	Alfred Crow	Cassie Cash	Samuel & Mariah Farrow	Jordan & Martha Sisson
15668	Crow, Ann	GA	1844	J H Crow	Nathan Wilkins	Lindia Thomas	Isaac Wilkins & Elizabeth Green	C C Thomas & Jimania Whiscant
22135	Crow, Arthur	AL	1882	Estelle Crow	John Crow	Nancy Talbert	Abraham & Phoebe Crow	Isabell Talbert
13906 *	Crow, Bell	GA	1886	Nathaniel Crow	Frank McClaughton	Rendy Simpson	Francis & Narcisia McClaughton	
21140	Crow, Charles	GA	1880	Louiza Crow	James Crow	Ann Wilkins	James & Ome Crow	Nathan & Linda Wilkins
9748	Crow, Clark (decd)	AR		Josie Crow	John Crow	Maranda Rogers		Henry & Mariah Rogers
2637	Crow, Dock	NC	1852	Mary & Hester Crow	Alfred Crow	Cassie Moss	George Ax	
8395	Crow, Dock	NC	1852		A Crow	Cassy Moss	George & Sophia Axe	Marurvill Crow
22101	Crow, George	AR	1876	none	John Crow	Maranda Rogers		Henry & Mariah Rogers
10395	Crow, James	OK	1857	Sarah Crow	John Crow	Marandy Rogers		Henry & Mariah Rogers
22134	Crow, James	AL	1877	Emeline Crow	John Crow	Nancy Talbert	Abraham & Phoebe Crow	Isabell Talbert
8601	Crow, Jesse	NC	1892	none	Severe Crow	Laura Maney		Jim Maney
2525	Crow, Laura	GA	1846	D H Crow	Josephus Early	Jane Odel	Elizabeth Chapman	James Odel

18365	Crow, Lillie	TN	1884	Joseph Crow	Ruphis Kirkland	Mary Donley	Jessie & Bettie Kirkland	Wm & Adry Donley
11955	Crow, Manda	GA	1867		Alfred Crow	Cassie Cash	Samuel & Mariah Farrow	Jordan & Martha Sisson
11382	Crow, Milley	GA	1830	William Crow	Surrey Donaldson	Mary Ellison	Wm & Elizabeth Donaldson	Joseph & Margaret Ellison
22007*	Crow, Nancy	GA	1860	Alfred Crow	Wimbaly McMellon	Philis Cook	Toney Griffin	July Jordan
11944	Crow, Nathaniel	GA	1878	Laura Crow		Lizzie Crow		Alfred & Sophie Crow
20884	Crow, Thomas	AL	1874	Anna Crow	John Crow	Nancy Talbert	Abraham Crow	Isabelle Talbert
20867	Crow, Viola	AL	1862	K.C. Crow	? Townsend	? Kurle	Edward & Anna Townsend	
10359	Crow, William	OK	1865	Dozie Crow	John Crow	Marandy Rogers		Henry & Mariah Rogers
11949	Crow, William	GA	1862	Louisa Crow	Alfred Crow	Cassie Cash	Samuel & Mariah Farrow	Jordan & Martha Sisson
21543	Crowder, Rebecca	GA	1851	James Cryder	Wesley Bramlett	Mary Howell	Miles & Annie Bramlett	Jack & Katie Howell
7099	Crowley, Eva	MO	1884	W J Crowley	J A Hyder	Catharine Van Trump	William & Emily Hyder	Josiah & Susan Van Trump
7100	Crowley, George	MO	1858	Fannie Crowley	William Crowley	Margaret Miller	Isham & Elizebeth Crowley	Wm & Susan Miller
7101	Crowley, James	MO	1840	Adoliza Crowley	William Crowley	Margaret Miller	Isham & Elizebeth Crowley	Wm & Susan Miller
8829	Crowley, Margaret	MO	1862	S G Crowley	Lemuel Cooper	Cynthia Riley	Henry Cooper	James & Margaret Riley
20784	Croy, Laura	GA	1867	Webb Croy	John Godfrey	Margrete Findley	Jim Godfrey	M. & Linda Findley
20785	Croy, Sam	GA	1903		Webb Croy	Laura Godfrey		John & Margaret Godfrey
9499	Crumby, Kansas	GA	1866	Isah Crumby	David Ash	Elisabeth Davenport		John & Elisabeth Davenport
7111	Crumley, Sallie	TN	1856	H J Crumley	Wm Hammond	Eliza Woodard	Moses & Dorcus Hammonds	Abraham & Betty Woodard
21633	Crumpton, Ara	AR	21yrs	Carry Crumpton	William Ridling	Minerva Parrish	Henry & Margaret Ridling	Garland & Jane Parrish
6389	Crutchfield, Artie	OK	1881	Claud Crutchfield	Jesse Mayberry	Eliza Blackburn	James & Nancy Mayberry	Andrew & Francis Blackburn
2320	Crutchfield, Eli et al	OK	1899		Thomas Crutchfield	Saran Piersall	Joseph & Lizzie Crutchfield	
16194	Crutchfield, John	TX	1822	Emma Crutchfield	Joseph Crutchfield	Amgelin ?		
12166	Cry, John	TN	1862	Mary Cry	James Cry	Nancy Kimbrough	Wm & Elizabeth Cry	Brad & Margret Kimbrough
21356	Cryer, Henry	AL	1877		William Cryer	Mary Givens	Joseph Cryer	Betsy Parham
21355	Cryer, Ida	AL	1884		William Cryer	Mary Givens	Joseph & Elizabeth Cryer	James & Eliza Givens
21354	Cryer, Ora	AL	1881		William Cryer	Mary Givens	Joseph & Elizabeth Cryer	James & Eliza Givens
21357	Cryer, William	AL	1857	Mary Cryer	Joseph Cryer	Elizabeth Parham	Furgeson & Annie Cryer	Elisha & Sarah Parham
14612	Culberson, Charles	GA	1881		Columbus Culberson	Mary Holland	Martin & Seney Culberson	Wm & Susan Holland
14611	Culberson, Columbus	GA	1877		Columbus Culberson	Mary Holland	Martin & Seney Culberson	Wm & Susan Holland
14610	Culberson, James	GA	1868		Columbus Culberson	Mary Holland	Martin & Seney Culberson	Wm & Susan Holland
21046	Culberson, Johnson	GA	1870	Ida Culberson	Columbus Culberson	Mary Holland		Susan Holland

11360	Culberson, Mary	GA	1842	Columbus Culberson	William Holland	Susan Posey		John & Susan Posey
15610	Culler, Cephus	NC	1860	Lenora Culler	Constantine Culler	Martha Scott	Solomon & Mary Culler	Henry & Pollie Scott
15023	Culler, John	NC	1859	Martha Culler	C W Culler	Martha Scott	Solmon & Polly Culler	Henry & Polly Scott
18463	Culler, Joseph	NC	1875	Lara Culler	Wm Jackson	Permelia Scott	Henry & Polly Scott	Leonard & Nancy Scott
14825	Culler, Lenora	NC		Cephus Culler	Solomon Hauser	Louisa Poindexter	Samuel & Nancy Hauser	Denson & Sarah Poindexter
19627	Culler, Martha	NC	1856	John Culler	Simon Poindexter	Nancy Wooley	John & Nancy Poindexter	Johnathan & Matilda Wooley
18572	Culler, Vance	NC	1883	Florence Culler	John Culler	Margaret Scott	Constantine & Elizabeth Culler	Hamphie & Elizabeth Scott
21230	Culpepper, Bettie	OK		Stephen Culpepper	William Graham	Martha Faulkner		
20951	Culver, George	AL	1866	Margarett Culver	J.M. Culver	Nancy Harris	Wm & Sinthy Culver	
2526	Culver, Margaret	AL	1872	George Culver	John Jacoups	Misauri Beaty		
670	Cummins, Anna	MO	1875	Frank Cummins	Orvil Cavin	Margaret Burns	Wm & Bettie Cavin	Robert & Maria Burns
668	Cummins, Helen, Margaret	MO	1901 1903	none	F W Cummins	Anna Cavin	Cummins	Cavin
13475	Cummins, Lizzie	OK	1865	J W Cummins	Charles Stinson	Victoria Rogers	Track & Jennie Stinson	John & Paulina Rogers
12081	Cundiff, Louvina	OK	1867	W Y Cundiff	John Smith	Catharine Elmore		Anderson Elmore
18566	Cundiff, Lucy	NC	1859	William Cundiff	William Poindexter	Mary Apperson	Thos & Amelia Poindexter	Thos & Luvitha Apperson
18038 *	Cundiff, Minerva	NC	1850	Wm Cundiff	Solomon Sawyers	Tabitha Evans		Ben & Lucy Evans
12381 *	Cunningham, Amanda	TN	1851	Solomon Cunningham	John Hardigan	Sina Jackson		Henry & Judy Bibb
17381	Cunningham, Annie	GA	1860	Robert Cunningham	H.M. Paris	Anna Townsend		Ezekiel Townsend
18037 *	Cunningham, Emma	TN	1864	Jack Cunningham	George Hams	Dyna Hill		
5447	Cunningham, Lydia	MO	1886	Allen Cunningham	William Eddings	Emma Snow	James & Roda Eddings	Thomas & Mary Snow
18914	Cunningham, Mathew & Cornelius	GA	1845			Willie Watts		William Watts
18983	Curd, Senie	TN	1856		William Price	Mary Ball	Thomas & Telitha Price	Osborn & Martha Ball
13789 *	Curry, Ella & Lillian	GA			Lee Curry	Addie Blackwell	Cintha & Henry Curry	Frank & Cornelia Blackwell
12080	Curry, Robert	OK	1871	Rosy Curry	B H Curry	Sarah Elmore		Anderson Elmore
12079	Curry, Rosy	OK	1876	Robert Curry	William Corbitt	Martha Tucker	Wm & Mary Corbitt	
12078	Curry, Sarah	OK	1844	B H Curry	Anderson Elmore	Margret Modral	David & Elizabeth Elmore	
20704	Curtis, Bessie	TN	1894		John Curtis	Narcis Dameworth	Joshoway & Elizabeth Curtis	Henry & Nancy Dameworth
19436	Curtis, Cora	TN	1887	S.A. Curtis	Rufus Hatcher	Sarah Curtis	John Hatcher & Mary Sizemore	Ezekiel Curtis & Arlean Wheeler
19720	Curtis, Cyrus	TN	1880	Daisy Curtis	J. Curtis	Elizabeth Patrick	Joshua & Elizabeth Curtis	
20016	Curtis, Eady	TN	1860	Charley Curtis	Eli Smith	Mary Curtis	Gibson & Edith Smith	Joshua & Elizabeth Curtis

20075	Curtis, Earl	TN	1893		John Curtis	Sarah Hooper	John & Manda Curtis	Clark & Amogine Hooper
22636	Curtis, Edward	IL	1869	Mable Curtis	James Curtis	Elizabeth Wilson	John & Martha Curtis	Penelton & Ruthe Wilson
19688	Curtis, Eli	TN	1882	Leonie Curtis	J. Curtis	Elizabeth Patrick	Joshua & Elizabeth Curtis	
21161	Curtis, Eli	TN	1872	Lula Curtis	Nathan Curtis	Susan Colyar	Joseph & Rebecca Curtis	
22193	Curtis, Eli	TX	1845	Kezeiah Curtis	Josh Curtis	Elizabeth Hatcher		Elizabeth Hatcher
20725	Curtis, George	TN	1874	Sadie Curtis	John Curtis	Amanda Hatcher	Joshua & Elizabeth Curtis	Wm & Betsie Hatcher
20707	Curtis, Henry	TN	1894		John Curtis	Narcis Dameworth	Joshoway & Elizabeth Curtis	Henry & Nancy Dameworth
19705	Curtis, J.Burl	TN	1848	Elizabeth Curtis	Joshua Curtis	Elizabeth Hatcher		John & Henrietta Hatcher
4218	Curtis, James	IL	1836	Elizabeth Curtis	John Curtis	Martha Reed	Henry & Polly Curtis	Riley Reed
10798	Curtis, James	TN		Elizie Curtis	Joshua Curtis	Elizebeth Hatcher		John & Henryetta Hatcher
19883	Curtis, James	TN	1886		Charles Curtis	Eudora Smith	Joshua & Lucinda Curtis	Eli & Mary Smith
20073	Curtis, James	TN	1887		John Curtis	Louella Wheeler	John & Manda Curtis	Gallant & Abagail Wheeler
19697	Curtis, John	TN	1874	Georgia Curtis	J. Curtis	Elizabeth Patrick	Joshua & Elizabeth Curtis	
19707	Curtis, John	TN	1871	Mary Curtis	Nathan Curtis	Susan Collier	Joshua & Elizabeth Curtis	
20076	Curtis, John	TN	1861		John Curtis	Manda Hatcher	Josh & Elisabeth Curtis	Wm & Elisabeth Hatcher
20705	Curtis, John	TN	1896		John Curtis	Narcis Dameworth	Joshoway & Elizabeth Curtis	Henry & Nancy Dameworth
22194	Curtis, John	TX	1873	Sallie Curtis	James Curtis	Sallie Wheeler	Joshua & Elizabeth Curtis	
21146	Curtis, Joshua	TN	1880		James Curtis	Sarah Wheeler	Joshua & Elizabeth Curtis	Robert & Sarah Wheeler
20077	Curtis, Joshuaway	TN	1857	Martha Curtis	John Curtis	Manda Hatcher	Josh & Elisabeth Curtis	Wm & Elisabeth Hatcher
22773	Curtis, Louis	IL	1866	Nettie Curtis	James Curtis	Elizabeth Nelson	John & Martha Curtis	Penillon & Ruthie Nelson
19687	Curtis, M.A.	TN	1881	Joshua Curtis	Rufus Hatcher	Sarah Curtis	John Hatcher & Mary Sizemore	Ezekiel Curtis & Ardicie Wheeler
10237	Curtis, Mary	TX	1867	D C Curtis	Flemming Green	Margrette Clung	John Green	R J Clung
20702	Curtis, Miranda	TN	1892		John Curtis	Narcis Dameworth	Joshoway & Elizabeth Curtis	Henry & Nancy Dameworth
20017	Curtis, Mollie	TN	1886	Tom Curtis	James Curtis	Sarah Wheeler	Joshua & Elizabeth Curtis	Robert & Sarah Wheeler
19702	Curtis, Nathan	TN	1847	Susan Curtis	Joshua Curtis	Elizabeth Hatcher		John & Henrietta Hatcher
19704	Curtis, Newton	TN	1884	Gertie Curtis	J. Curtis	Elizabeth Patrick	Joshua & Elizabeth Curtis	
21162	Curtis, Perry	TN	1876	Mattie Curtis	Nathan Curtis	Susan Colyar	Joshua & Rebecca Curtis	
19435	Curtis, Silas	TN	1875	Janie Curtis	James Curtis	Sarah Wheeler	Joshua & Elizabeth Curtis	Robert & Sarah Wheeler
21078	Curtis, Thomas	TN	1902		John Curtis	Narsis Damworth	Joshua & Elizabeth Curtis	Henry & Nancy Dameworth
20015	Curtis, Tom	TN	1880	Mollie Curtis	Charley Curtis	Eudora Smith	Joshua & Lucinda Curtis	Eli & Mary Smith
18797	Cusler, Dora	GA	1884	Isam Cusler	James Evans	Nancy Rainwater	Robert & Sallie Evans	John & Julia Rainwater

20222	Cuthreel, Effie	IN	1872	John Cuthreel	Richard Elmore	Rachel Reed	John & Mary Elmore	Isaac & Hannah Reed
7133	Dagley, Allen	MO	1864	Amanda Dagley	Joseph Dagley	Hariet Goodwin	Salie Dagley	Allen & Emeline Goodwin
7132	Dagley, Amanda	MO	1870	Allen Dagley	John Reynolds	Mary Morgan	George & Elizabeth Reynolds	Nathan & Anna Morgan
7764	Dagley, Elias	MO	1850	Lois Dagley	Alvis Dagley	Nancy Wilson	Elias & Hannah Dagley	William Wilson
7131	Dagley, Joseph	IL	1853	Mary Dagley	Joseph Dagley	Celina Keeney	Elias & Hannah Dagley	Wm & Elisabeth Keeney
13769	Daizer, John	GA	1878		Alfred Daizer	Nancy Strickland	Henry & Isie Days	Ester Sander
13767	Daizer, Ruth	GA	1883	Clara Daizer	Alfred Daizer	Nancy Strickland	Henry & Isie Days	Andy Strickland & Ester Sander
6082	Dale, Missouri	GA	1886	Thomas Dale	Alpheus Key	Minerva Hembree	William Key	Reubin Emery
8942	Dalinger, Calvin	VA	1881	none	Wiley Dalinger	Marilda Weaver	John & Catharine Dalinger	
8452	Dalinger, Calvinbia	VA	1878	Harrison Dalinger	Abel Penington	Sarah Abee	Andrew & Hester Penington	Leander Abee
4427	Dalinger, Freelin	VA	1866	Polley Dalinger	John Dalinger	Elisabeth Caldwell	Wm & Catherine Dalinger	Joseph & Catherine Caldwell
4428	Dalinger, Polly	VA	1866	Freelin Dalinger	Noah Baldwin	Mahala Blevins	Wm & Margaret Baldwin	Elisha & Elizabeth Blevins
8941	Dalinger, Wiley	VA	1855	Marilda Dalinger	John Dalinger	Elisabeth Caldwell		Joseph & Catharine Caldwell
22042	Dalrymple, China	AR	1870	Robert Dalrymple	John Stewart	Sarah Stewart	John Stewart	Sarah Stewart
10834	Dalton, Martha	OK	1876	Tinvil Dalton	Wm Rowell	Martha Terral	David Rowell & Mary Fountain	
20712	Dameworth, Eli	TN	1900		Neil Dameworth	L.E. Smith	Henry & Nancy Dameworth	Eli & Mary Smith
20710	Dameworth, George	TN	1897		Neil Dameworth	L.E. Smith	Henry & Nancy Dameworth	Eli & Mary Smith
20699	Dameworth, Henry	TN	1905		C.N. Dameworth	L.E. Smith	Henry & Nancy Dameworth	Elie & Mary Smith
20708	Dameworth, Lula	TN	1902		Neil Dameworth	L.E. Smith	Henry & Nancy Dameworth	Eli & Mary Smith
20711	Dameworth, Ollie	TN	1891		Neil Dameworth	L.E. Smith	Henry & Nancy Dameworth	Eli & Mary Smith
20709	Dameworth, Thedocia	TN	1895		Neil Dameworth	L.E. Smith	Henry & Nancy Dameworth	Eli & Mary Smith
11019	Damson, Francis	MO	1844		Josiah Dorris	Margaret Bly		Robert & Fannie Revelle
17543	Dando, Sarah	AR	1873	Richard Dando	James Hamilton	Anna Denny	Wm & Matilda Hamilton	James & Margaret Denny
12194	Daney, Mary	NC	1861	Enos Daney	Calvin Osborn	Martha Sheets	Jesse & Cynthia Osborn	Jacob Sheets
7612	Dangler, Riley	GA	1854	Mary Dangler	Nathaniel Dangler	Eliza Jourdan		
3528	Daniel, John	OK	1842	Nancy Daniel	Stan Watie	Sarah Bell	Daniel & Susanna Watie	
18245*	Daniel, Lucius	GA	1877	Abner Daniel	Isom Daniel	Jane Ware		
20356	Daniel, Malinda	GA		Thomas Daniel	John Mulkey	Cornelia Wallace	John & Cindie Mulkey	Sookey Wootten
21887*	Daniel, Malinda	TN	1843	Green Daniel	Thomas Wynn	Dinah Glenn	Jada Wynn	

16943	Daniel, William	OK	1853	L.D. Daniel	John Daniel	Mary Jeffreys		
22258 *	Daniels, George	OK	1855	Francis Daniels	Tony Daniels	Cynthia	Henry Blackburn & Betsy Daniels	Griffin & Celia Daniels
17682	Daniels, Mary	OK		Walter Daniels	Henry Cob	Mattie Tate	Isaah & Sealey Cob	
18830	Danley, John	TN	1852	Amanda Danley	Wm Danley	Adry Henson	Patsey Danley	Loyd Henson
16944	Dansby, Julia	TX	1873	W. Dansby	Abraham Ellington	Jane Music	Wm & Martha Ellington	
16527	Darby, Bailey	GA	1890		Henry Darby	Margaret Sams	Reuben & Frances Darby	James & Caroline Sams
14079	Darby, Charles	GA	1860	Cassie Darby	Reuben Darby	Francis Mason	Charles & Nancy Darby	John & Polly Mason
14082	Darby, Farish	GA	1895		James Darby	Martha Bradford	James & Caroline Darby	Ranson & Harriet Bradford
14081	Darby, Henry	GA	1858	Susan Darby	Reuben Darby	Francis Mason	Charles & Nancy Darby	John & Polly Mason
16533	Darby, Minerva	GA	1858		James Darby	Caroline Hudgins	Charles & Nancy Darby	Jacob & Elizabeth Hudgins
14074	Darby, Newton	GA	1842	Clarinda Darby	Charles Darby	Nancy Biddy	Charles & Mary Darby	Jonathan & Mary Biddy
14080	Darby, Thomas	GA	1875	Dora Darby	Reuben Darby	Francis Mason	Charles & Nancy Darby	John & Polly Mason
21786	Darity, Doshaphene	OK	1873	Ben Darity	Simeon Slusher	Kizzie Salyers		
8923	Darnall, Wade	NC	1882	none	Lewis Darnall	Marget Peak	Wm & Sally Darnall	Huah & Margie Peak
8619	Darnel, Margret	NC	1850	Lewis Darnel	Hugh Peak	Margie Hart		George & Polley Hart
13426	Darnell, Cora, Elbert, Charles	OK			Lorenzo Darnell	Sanora Matoy		Wm & America Matoy
4322	Darnell, Hilay	NC	1851	W H Darnell	Thomas Jones	Tamsy Thompson	Jonathan & Nancy Jones	Chris & Salley Thompson
8620	Darnell, J.C.	NC	1881	Daisy Darnell	Lewis Darnall	Margie Peak	Wm & Sally Darnall	Hugh & Margie Peak
21144	Darnworth, Nancy	TN	1884	Henry Darnworth	John Smith	Thedocia Cowen	Eli & Jane Smith	Umphrey & Ann Cowen
11583	Darrall, Flora	KY	1859	W H Darrall	Jonas Smith	Sarah Baker	Crabtree & Martha Smith	Elijah & Margaret Baker
11584	Darrell, Willie	KY	1885		Harlan Darrell	Flora Smith	Henry & Rebecca Darrell	Jonas & Sarah Smith
19599	Daughton, Emorie	NC			Robert Daughton	Boyd Greer		Lottie Greer
17348	Davenport, B.M.	GA	1868	Mary Davenport	John Davenport	Sarah Ross	John & Elisabeth Davenport	
18139	Davenport, Brook	GA	1877		Wm Davenport	Margaret Falls	Thos & Elizabeth Davenport	Gilbert & Rutha Falls
14414	Davenport, C T	GA	1884		John Davenport	Sarah Ross	John & Elisabeth Davenport	
2601	Davenport, David	GA	1872	Mary Davenport	Drury Davenport	Piety Watson	John & Elisabeth Davenport	
14406	Davenport, Druey	GA	1877	Missouri Davenport	John Davenport	Sarah Ross	John & Elizabeth Davenport	
2599	Davenport, Drury	GA	1843	Piety Davenport	John Davenport	Elisabeth Long	Josiah & Nancy Long	
2600	Davenport, Drury	GA	1875	Parteley Davenport	Drury Davenport	Piety Watson	John & Elisabeth Davenport	
16061	Davenport, Edward	AL		Mattie Davenport	John Davenport	Elizabeth Martin	Wm & Polly Davenport	Ebeneyer & Elizabeth Martin

16308	Davenport, Eliza	GA	1879	James Davenport	I D Falls	Mary Garland	David Davenport	Moses & Sinda Bradford
308	Davenport, Harvey	NC	22yrs	Adelie Davenport	James Davenport	Sallie Moss	Martin & Polly Davenport	Milton & Rebecca Moss
16190	Davenport, Isaac	AL	1857	Sarah Davenport	John Davenport	Elizabeth Martin	Wm & Polly Davenport	Ebenezer & Elizabeth Martin
303	Davenport, Jennie	NC	25yrs	none	James Davenport	Sallie Moss	Martin & Polly Davenport	Milton & Rebecca Moss
2598	Davenport, John	GA	1883	Sallie Davenport	Drury Davenport	Piety Watson	John & Elisabeth Davenport	
9501	Davenport, John decd	GA		Julia Davenport	John Davenport	Sarah Ross	John & Elisabeth Davenport	
300	Davenport, Louola	NC	28yrs	Theodore Davenport	Benjamin Garrett	Rena Maney	William & Nancy Garrett	John & Jennie Maney
21272	Davenport, Lucy	MO	1859	Thomas Davenport	James Gordan	Deborah McAdams		Joseph & Delilah McAdams
14405	Davenport, Missouri	GA	1880	D M Davenport	David Lovell	Fannie Long		Wm & Annie Long
10180	Davenport, Nancy	GA		none	David Davenport	Lucinda Bradford	Thos & Elizabeth Davenport	Moses & Nancy Bradford
11201	Davenport, Pleasant	GA	1877	Theodocia Davenport	David Davenport	Lucinda Bradford	Thos & Elizabeth Davenport	Nancy Bradford
21278	Davenport, Walter	MO	1883	Eva Davenport	Thomas Davenport	Lucy Gordon		James & Deborah Gordon
9318	Davenport, William	GA	1840	Margret Davenport	Thomas Davenport	Elizabeth Smith	Ausbom Davenport	William Smith
16231	Davenport, William	AL	1851	Ginsey Davenport	John Davenport	Elizabeth Martin	Wm & Polly Davenport	Ebenezer & Elizabeth Martin
21273	Davenport, Winnie	MO	1866		James Gordan	Deborah McAdams	Hugh & Eliza Gordon	Joseph & Delilah McAdams
21945 *	Davey, Maggie	TN	1841	Thomas Davey	Aaron Donaldson	Hannah Jackson	Aaron Jackson	John & Mary Carter
622	Davidson, Georgia	CA	1867	Wallace Davidson	Taylor Ridley	Vianna Pope	James Ridley & Louisa Shomate	John Pope & Jane Shomate
20562	Davidson, Mary	TN			John Davidson	Martha Whitice	John & Elizabeth Davidson	W.A. & Eliza Whitice
21883	Davis, Addie	TN	1860	Thomas Davis	William Pasley	Elizabeth Black	William Pasley	Martha Black
21487	Davis, Albert	TX	1877	Ura Davis	Benj Davis	Amanda Rimare	Martin Davis	Binion & Francis Rimare
3370	Davis, Alexander	AL	59yrs	Fannie Bryars	- Davis	Susan		
21043	Davis, Alice	KS			Alex Davis	Mary Stephenson		John & Sarilda Stephenson
12028	Davis, Allen	GA	1903		Henry Davis	Millie Young	John & Nancy Davis	
10685	Davis, Allison	OK	1861		Jesse Davis	Manervia Martin		Samuel & Sallie Martin
19005	Davis, Alwilda	NC	1856	J. Davis	Wm Martin	Mariam Hansen	John & Jennie Martin	John & Elizabeth Hansen
9818	Davis, Angeline	NC	1852	Avery Davis	James Murphy	Polly McMillan	Polly Murphy	Joe & Millie McMillan
21626 *	Davis, Angeline	GA	1843	Eben Davis	Charles Jackson	Delpha Brooks		
43	Davis, Arvaline	GA	1890	William Davis	James Kell	Mary Carter	Week & Lucinda Kell	Ellick & Mary Carter
15672	Davis, Augusta	NC	1857	Widow	Thomes Hauser	Lucinda Sprinkle	Samuel & Nancy Hauser	Thomes & Elizabeth Sprinkle

17481	Davis, Becky	NC	1851	Joe Davis	Charlie Hornbuckle	Pollie Wilks		
11212	Davis, Benjamin	GA	1881	Mary Davis	Mitchell Davis	Marsha Morrow	Wm & Annie Davis	Morgan & Dovey Morrow
8454	Davis, Bethany	VA	1845	Jorden Davis	Ned Blevins	Nancy Blevins	James Blevins	Lydia Blevins
9595	Davis, Betsey	OK	1853	Jug Davis	Nick Porter	Sallie King	William Porter	Jackson King
10108	Davis, Birdie	VA	1878	James Davis	Sidney Tucker	Malvinia Blevins	David & Mahaley Tucker	
12027	Davis, Bulah	GA	1896		Henry Davis	Millie Young	John & Nancy Davis	
18068	Davis, Calvin	NC	1881	Laura Davis	C.C. Davis	Matilda Pennington	Jordan & Sinie Davis	Andrew Pennington & Hettie Blevins
7119	Davis, Carrie	KS	1885	none	William Davis	Hulda Haines	James & Mary Davis	
2596	Davis, Catharine	GA	1868	James Davis	William Postell	Disey Davenport		John & Elisabeth Davenport
10096	Davis, Clem	NC	1863	Sarah Davis	James Davis	Lurane McDonald	Reason & Sevilla Davis	James & Vina McDonald
8050	Davis, Cosley	WV	1873	James Davis	Ned Sizemore	Jane Workmin	George & Jiney Sizemore	Joe & Betty Workmin
15027	Davis, Della	NC	1885	John Davis	Thomas Allen	Elizabeth Martin	James & Rebecca Allen	Wm & Margrett Martin
14857 *	Davis, Dora	IN	1865	Frances Davis	Boulden Melton	Elizabeth Scott	Mills & Anna Melton	Hubert & Sallie Scott
699	Davis, Elizabeth	OK	1843	widow	John Thornton	Rhodie York	Davis & Susan Thornton	
19219	Davis, Elizabeth	MO	1863	Grant Davis	James Sizemore	Mary Abbott	Richard & Elizabeth Sizemore	Eliza Abbott
8562	Davis, Ella	NC	1882	George Davis	Elijah Tucker	Ida Foster	David & Mahala Tucker	Edward & Ellen Foster
6834	Davis, Ellis	VA	1880	Rosy Davis	Jordan Davis	Naomi Blevins		Armstrong & Catharine Blevins
22057 *	Davis, Ema	OK	1859	William Davis	Isac Glass	Betsy Whitmire	Suckie Glass	Daniel & Tempy Sanders
6832	Davis, Estel	VA	1877	Aley Davis	Jordan Davis	Naomi Blevins		Armstrong & Catharine Blevins
7124	Davis, Eugene	OK	1881	Fanie Davis	Richard Davis	Martha Holcomb		W J Holcomb & Louisa Berry
8567	Davis, Eula	VA	1884	W C Davis	Elijah Tucker	Ida Foster	David & Mahala Tucker	Edward & Ellen Foster
22585	Davis, Euphenia	TN	1851		George Hodge	Rebecca Smote	James & Rebecca Hodge	Jesse & Elizabeth Smote
9607	Davis, Evaline	VA	1861	Jesse Davis	Riley Hart	Emily Powers	John & Nancy Hart	Major & Mary Powers
18071	Davis, Ezera	NC	1883	Sinie Davis	Calvin Davis	Matilda Pennington	Jordan & Sinie Davis	Andrew & Hettie Pennington
7930	Davis, Fannie	VA	1885	Hampton Davis	Eligha Hart	Amanda Blevins	Stephen & Rebecca Hart	
5818	Davis, Felix	NC	1881	Annie Davis	James Davis	Lourena McDonald	Reson & Savilla Davis	James & Maria McDonald
5819	Davis, Festus	NC	1884	Ellie Davis	James Davis	Lourena McDonald	Resen & Savilla Davis	James & Maria McDonald
22587	Davis, Francis	TN	1871		William Davis	Euphenia Hodge	Alex & Sallie Davis	George & Rebecca Hodge

5504	Davis, Frank	VA	1857	Mollie Davis	Robert Davis	Darthula Weiss	Samuel & Jennie Davis	
2882	Davis, George	GA	1830	Martha Davis	William Davis	Annie Cross		Joseph & Sarah Cross
7721	Davis, George	OK	1849	Mazzpa Davis	George Davis	Elizabeth Whitecotton		George Whitecotton
9283	Davis, George	GA	1840	Etta Davis	Isaac Davis	Rhoda James	Mashack & Lydia Davis	
14944	Davis, Gertrude et al	MO			James Davis	Mary Martin		Daniel Martin & Sally Elmore
12026	Davis, Gussie	GA	1893		Henry Davis	Millie Young	John & Nancy Davis	
22147	Davis, Harvey	ID	1898	none	James Davis	Mary Warton		
14870	Davis, Haseltine	AL	1860	William Davis	Vann Wright	Mary Smith	Jesse & Lovicie Wright	David & Lucy Smith
22441	Davis, Hattie	IN	1868	Hawley Davis	Levi Winburn	Martha Roberts	Harry & Keziah Winburn	Stephen & Mary Roberts
10544	Davis, Henry	GA	1851	Millie Davis	John Davis	Nancy Adcooson		John & Sallie Adcooson
22367*	Davis, Henry	OK	1840	Emma & Annie	Tom Davis	Pricilla Davis		
18072	Davis, Jackson	VA	1879	Lizza Davis	Calvin Davis	Matilda Pennington	Jordan & Sinie Davis	Andrew & Hettie Pennington
2879	Davis, James	GA	1872	Nancy Davis	George Davis	Martha Brookshire	William & Annie Davis	James & Eliza-beth Brookshire
5820	Davis, James	NC	1867	Sarah Davis	James Davis	Lourena McDonald	Resen & Savilla Davis	James & Maria McDonald
17571	Davis, James	GA	1832	Matilda Davis	Wm Davis	Ann Cross	Mashack & Lyda Davis	Joseph & Sarah Cross
6146	Davis, Johannah	NC	1844	Elisha Davis	Soloman Spencer	Nellie Hash	Isaac & Johannah Spencer	Robert & Margery Hash
2240	Davis, John	GA	1841	Jane Davis		Caroline Davis		Isaac Davis & Rhoda James
6176	Davis, John	NC	1872	Cora Davis	Elisha Davis	Johannah Spencer	John & Sallia Davis	Solomon & Nellie Spencer
7881	Davis, John	GA	1858	Mary Davis	George Davis	Martha Brookster	Wm & Anna Davis	James & Elizabeth Brookster
8561	Davis, John	NC	1846	Enice Davis	Thomas Barker	Mary Blevins		Daniel & Amy Blevins
9407	Davis, John	OK	1872		Charlie Davis	Dora Shelton	John & Nellie Davis	Jesse Shelton
15026	Davis, John	NC	1881	Della Davis	Samuel Davis	Augusta Hauser	Thos & Anna Davis	Thos & Lucinda Hauser
15221	Davis, John	GA	1884	Lillian Davis	Henry Davis	Millie Young	John & Nancy Davis	
21803	Davis, John	OK	1840	Lizzie Davis	James Davis	Sallie Davis		Redding & Dorcas Davis
8563	Davis, John (for 2 orphans)	NC	1846	Eunice Davis	Thomas Barker	Mary Blevins		Daniel & Amy Blevins
17572	Davis, Joseph	GA	1839	Taletha Davis	Wm Davis	Ann Cross	Mashack & Lyda Davis	Joseph & Sarah Cross
7121	Davis, Larkin	KS	1839	Mary Davis	Henry Davis	Harriett Baker		
20212	Davis, Laura	OK	1893		A.H. Scott	Ann Hunt	Leonard & Sally Scott	James & Temperance Hunt
12025	Davis, Lillie	GA	1898		Henry Davis	Millie Young	John & Nancy Davis	

21925	Davis, Lula	TN	1873	Nathan Davis	John Nunnly	Hannah Reneau		Benj & Mary Reneau
4167	Davis, Lurane	NC	1848	James Davis	James McDonald	Minia Deaton	Anguish & Sallie McDonald	John & Sallie Deaton
19246	Davis, Margarette	NC	1842		Henry Martin	Margaret Hauser	Samuel & Elizabeth Martin	Adam & Margaret Hauser
7122	Davis, Martha	OK	1840	Richard Davis	William Holcomb	Louisa Berry	Benj & Sara Holcomb	Hiram & Sara Berry
4166	Davis, Mary	NC	1851	G W Davis	James McDonald	Minca Deaton	Anguish & Sallie McDonald	John & Sallie Deaton
16535	Davis, Mary	TN	1869	Ancil Davis	John Bozeman	Sarah Darby	Amos & Nancy Bozeman	Charles & Nancy Darby
21039	Davis, Mary	KS	1850	Alex Davis	John Stephenson	Sarilda Ritchie		Zachriah Ritchie & Elizabeth McDanial
18070	Davis, Matilda	NC	1842	C.C. Davis	Andrew Pennington	Hettie Blevins		James & Lydia Blevins
21964	Davis, Mollie	TN	1876	William Davis	John Hansard	Catherine Cook	Sidney & Margret Hanssard	William & Eliza Cook
7126	Davis, Nancy	MO	1845		Andrew Roberts	Eliza Blackburn	Wm & Margaret Roberts	John & Elizabeth Blackburn
13807	Davis, Nancy	GA	1863	Marion Davis	White Lindsay	Cyrenia Crow	George & Jane Lindsay	Abraham & Phoebe Crow
19237	Davis, Nancy	NC	1850	Eli Davis	Richard Marion	Margaret Hauser	Adam & Sallie Marion	Samuel & Nancy Hauser
6835	Davis, Naomy (decd)	VA	1856	Jordan Davis	Armstrong Blevins	Catharine Hart	James & Lydia Blevins	
10543	Davis, Oscar	GA	1891		Henry Davis	Millie Young	John & Nancy Davis	
21488	Davis, Owen	TX	1867	Laura Davis	Benj Davis	Amanda Rimare	Martin Davis	Binion & Francis Rimare
566	Davis, Pare Lee	GA	1869	R. H. Davis	Rundler Leachford	Elisa Robertson	Burton Leadford	Johney Robinson
12024	Davis, Pearl	GA	1889	Homer Davis	Henry Davis	Millie Young	John & Nancy Davis	
6831	Davis, Redaford	VA	1885	Mary Davis	Jordan Davis	Naomi Blevins		Armstrong & Catharine Blevins
9990	Davis, Robert	NC	1868	none	Henderson Davis	Caroline Spencer		Solomon & Nellie Spencer
21769	Davis, Robert	TX			Benj Davis	Amanda Rimare	Martin Davis	Binion & Francis Rimare
6147	Davis, Rosa	NC	1866	none	Elisha Davis	Johannah Spencer	John & Sallie Davis	Solomon & Nellie Spencer
6833	Davis, Rosey	VA	1882	Ellis Davis	William Holaway	Louisa Waters		Wm & Zilpha Waters
2758	Davis, Ross	OK	1853	Jennie Davis		Tse-yo-se		
7123	Davis, Rufus	OK	1868	Flora Davis	Richard Davis	Martha Holcomb		W J Holcomb & Louisa Berry
19591	Davis, Samuel	NC	1867	Lula Davis	Alvis Davis	Margaret Martin	Thomas & Malinda Davis	Henry & Elizabeth Martin
2312	Davis, Sarah	NC	1864	Clem Davis	Nute Nicholson	Melvina McDonald	Alfred & Polly Nicholson	Sallie McDonald
8184	Davis, Sarah	KS	1866	William Davis	William Boatwright	Isabella Clark	James & Rebecca Boatwright	Thos & Sarah Clark
18069	Davis, Sinie	NC	1843	Ezra Davis	Eli Miller	Aley Hart	Isaac & Brashie Miller	Steven & Betsie Hart
19286	Davis, Soloman	NC			William Davis	Jane Gibson	Isaac Davis & Rhoda Jones	Solomon Gibson & Betsy Millsaps

10097	Davis, W.Frank	NC	1861	Celia Davis	James Davis	Lurane McDonald	Reason & Sevilla Davis	James & Vina McDonald
17883	Davis, Walker	AR	1872	Minnie Davis	James Davis	Mary Martin		Sallie Martin
7120	Davis, William	KS	1858	Hulda Davis	James Davis	Mary Baker	Franklin & Docia Davis	Benj & Mary Baker
7125	Davis, William	OK	1860	Sara Davis	Richard Davis	Martha Holcomb		W J Holcomb & Louisa Berry
11211	Davis, William	GA	27yrs	Arvaline Davis			Wm & Anna Davis	Morgan & Dovey Morrow
10600	Davis, Willis	OK	1851	none	Jesse Davis	Manervia Martin		Samuel & Sallie Martin
10408	Davison, John	OK	1850	Mary Davison	Isaac Davison	Mary Conley	Elizabeth Toney	
9266	Davison, William	OK	1847	Sarah Davison	Isaac Davison	Mary Conley	Jim & Elizabeth Davison	
19095	Dawson, Frances	OK		Katy Dawson	Robert Dawson	Jane Watkins	Samuel & Polly Dawson	Isa Watkins
19678	Dawson, Sarah	TN	1841	John Dawon	Davis House	Mariah King	Martha Stocky	John & Cassie King
4259	Day, Della	AR	1887	none	W M Day	Martha Buttry	Mat & Bettie Day	John & Margret Buttry
7137	Day, Dora	OK	1887	C W Day	T J Blackburn	Sarah Stamper	James & Elisebeth Blackburn	Wilburn & Annie Stamper
13822	Day, John	AL	1857	Emma Day	Fletcher Day	Rebeca Smith		
7471	Day, Vinita	OK	1878	R.L. Day	John Matoy	Martha Gibson	Mike & Eliza Matoy	John & Polly Gibson
8958	Day, William	OK	1827	Mary Day (decd)	Isaac Day	Marthy Johnson		
21048*	Days, Nancy	GA	1850	Alfred Days	Andrew Stricklin	Esther Sanders		James Hayden & Thenia Sanders
13911*	Daysor, Clara	GA	1887	Ruff Daizer	Pearce Knox	Alice Rucker	Albert Knox & Minerva Terrell	Alfred Rucker & Rose Smith
20003	Deakins, Loria	TN	1905		J.F. Deakins	Tennie Lane	Robert & Jane Deakins	John & Louise Lane
19975	Deakins, Tennie	TN	1883		John Lane	Louise Phillips	Lindsey & Rebecca Lane	George & Mary Phillips
21966	Dean, Avery	GA	1905		William Dean	Josephine Pilgrim	Abraham & Margaret Dean	John & Emma Pilgrim
20010	Dean, B.P.	GA	1847	Caroline Dean	Cornelius Dean	Sophie Humphries	Cornelius & Phenie Dean	Hudson & Nancy Greenwood
21968	Dean, Earnest	GA	1891		William Dean	Josephine Pilgrim	Abraham & Margaret Dean	John & Emma Pilgrim
13741	Dean, James	GA	1868	Martha Dean	John Dean	Elizabeth Williams	Jackson & Sofie Greenwood	Absalom & Lucy Williams
2109	Dean, John	GA	1846	Elizabeth Williams	Elisha Dean	Sopham Umpharee		Jackson Greenwood & Jame Umpharee
21969	Dean, Josephine	GA	1881	William Dean	John Pilgrim	Emma Haynes	Martin & Nancy Pilgrim	Hezekiah & Julia Haney
21967	Dean, Lorena	GA	1897		William Dean	Josephine Pilgrim	Abraham & Margaret Dean	John & Emma Pilgrim
19217	Dean, Mary	KS	1874	L.L. Dean	James Sizemore	Mary Abbott	Richard & Elizabeth Sizemore	Eliza Abbott
13337	Dean, Samuel	TN	1840	Martha Dean	Thomas Dean	Nancy Hood	Rider	Toterkie
3334	Deaux, Corine	AL	34yrs	William Deaux	Elijah Boon	Levisa Hathcock	John & Ramie Boon	Thos & Elizabeth Hathcock
18399	Deaux, Henry	AL	30yrs	Lizzie Deaux	Joseph Deaux	Adell Miles	Joseph & Amilia Deaux	Frances & Nancy Miles
1144	Deaux, Joseph	AL		Corine Deaux	Joe Deaux	Adella Myers	French	Stiggons

6362	Deaux, Mrs Joseph	AL	1850	Joseph Deaux	Frances Miles	Nancy Stiggens	William Miles	George & Elisabeth Stiggins
2371	Deavers, Vinie	GA	1873	Will Deavers	James McKinney	Cisco Adams	Allison & Fannie McKinny	David & Clerinda Adams
8529	Deboard, Margret	VA	1867	Crede Deboard	Elisha Roop	Mandy Osborn		James & Rachel Osborn
6172	Deboard, Wiley	NC	1885	Sarah Deboard	John Deboard	Martha Gaultney	Benjamin & Elisabeth Deboard	Cartins & Lucretie Gaultney
6140	Debord, Charley	NC	1874	Cynthia Debord	Benjamin Debord	Elizabeth Phipps	Elijah & Mary Debord	Benjamin & Ruth Phipps
6145	Debord, Creed	VA	1866	Margaret Debord	Benjamin Debord	Elizabeth Phipps	Elijah & Mary Debord	Benjamin & Ruth Phipps
6141	Debord, Elijah	NC	1871	none	Benjamin Debord	Elizabeth Phipps	Elijah & Mary Debord	Benjamin & Ruthy Phipps
6135	Debord, Elizabeth	NC	1868	none	Benjamin Debord	Elizabeth Phipps	Elijah & Mary Debord	Benjamin & Ruth Phipps
6149	Debord, John	NC	1861	Florence Debord	Benjamin Debord	Elizabith Phipps	Elijah & Mary Debord	Benjamin & Ruthy Phipps
11359	Debord, John	GA	1884	Jessie Debord	Elisha Debord	Rachel Dover	Thos & Ibbie Debord	Dillan & Betsy Dover
6142	Debord, Robert	NC	1858	Mary Debord	Benjamin Debord	Elizabeth Phipps	Elijah & Mary Debord	Benjamin & Ruth Phipps
2522	Deck, Boyd	NC	1872	Mintie Deck		Mary Hayden		Pattsee Carson
4956	Deckard, Ephram	OK	1884	none	George Deckard	Matilda Brown	Ephram & Rachel Deckard	Robert & Esther Brown
20182	Deckard, George	MO	1826	Margaret Deckard		Charity Maw		
4958	Deckard, Matilda	OK	1860	George Deckard	Robert Brown	Esther Snodgrass	Isom & Matilda Brown	Wm & Nancy Snodgrass
4955	Deckard, Robert	OK	1884	none	George Deckard	Matilda Brown	Ephram & Rachel Deckard	Robert & Esther Brown
5678	Deckard, William	OK	1882	none	George Deckard	Matilda Brown	Loram & Rachel Deckard	Robert & Esther Brown
13412	Decker, Alice	CA	1864	O.B. Decker	Taylor Ridley	Vianna Pope	James & Lue Ridley	John & Jane Pope
21956	Dedmon, John	TN	1868	Margaret Dedmon	Joseph Dedmon	Martha Black	Jesse & Mary Dedmon	John & Jane Black
21955	Dedmon, Joseph	TN	1870	Bettie Dedmon	Joseph Dedmon	Martha Black	Jesse & Mary Dedmon	John & Jane Black
18189	Dedmon, Martha	TN	1834		John Black	Jane Henderson	Robert & Jane Black	Wm & Jane Nichols
3680	Deere. Lucy	OK		Jim Deere (decd)	Ok-ha-Na-Wie	Nancy		
3340	Dees, Jane	AL	1872	none	William Dees	Annie Parte	William & Hettie Dees	Mary Parte
17408	Dees, Margaret	AL	1843		Wm Dees	Hettie Semi		John & Nancy Semi
3427	Dees, Nancy	AL		none	William Dees	Lallie McGhee		Richard McGhee
3326	Dees, Vicey	AL	1874	none	William Dees	Anne Parte	William & Hetty Dees	Mary Parte
1155	Dees, William	AL	1840	Annie Pace	William Dees	Hetty Symac		John & Nancy Symac
17406	Dees, Willie	AL	1890			Jane Dees		Wm Dees & Ann Arington

14113 *	Delaney, Effie	WI	1855	William Delaney	McCaga Revels	Mornon Jakop	Stephen & Delilah Revels	Johnathan & Elizabeth Jakop
13536 *	Delaney, Jesse	WI	1861	Emma Delaney	Robert Delaney	Sarah Jakop		Johnathan & Nanny Jakop
14049 *	Delaney, John	WI	1856	Sarah Delaney	Robert Delaney	Sarah Jakop		Johnathan & Nanny Jakop
14111 *	Delaney, William	WI	1846	Effie Delaney	Robert Delaney	Sarah Jakop		Johnathan & Nanny Jakop
19240	Delano, Charles	OK	1859	Molly Delano	Young Duck	Maria Corntassel		Oonuchuste
21071	Delk, Jane	TN	1854	widow	Stephens	Saley Crockett	Jess Cobb	
21069	Delk, Nancy	TN		Eddie Delk	Samuel Cobb	Catherine Evans	Jesse Cobb	Nathaniel Evans
1164	DeLong, Altha	GA	1875	Griffin DeLong	Allen Hyde	Malissa Raines	Ansel & Elizabeth Hyde	Wesley & Talitha Raines
2078	Delozier, Amanda	NC	1887		Jesse Delozier	Mary Stilwell	Ed & Elizabeth Delozier	W.H. & Mariah Stilwell
20078	Delozier, Charles	KY	1865	Nancy Delozier	J.S. Delozier	Samantha Spilleman		
20089	Delozier, George	KY	1882	George Delozier				
2636	Delozier, Jesse	NC	1878	none	Jesse Delozier	Mary Stillwell	Edward & Elizabeth Delozier	Wm & Maria Stillwell
2633	Delozier, John	NC	1884	none	Jesse Delozier	Mary Stillwell	Edward & Elizabeth Delozier	Wm & Maria Stillwell
19576	Delozier, John	WV	1872	Lucy Delozier	T.L. Delozier	Elisabeth Hillman		
2634	Delozier, Lillie	NC	1880	none	Jesse Delozier	Mary Stillwell	Edward & Elizabeth Delozier	Wm & Maria Stillwell
2086	Delozier, Mary	NC	1850	Jesse Delozier				
2077	Delozier, Thomas	NC	1874	Sara Delozier	Jesse Delozier	Mary Stilwell	Ed & Elizabeth Delozier	Wm & Mariah Stilwell
12842	Delp, Ennice	NC	1881	Henry Delp	John Petty	Catherine Osborne		David & Lucy Osborne
18019	Dempsey, Effie	IN	35yrs	Harry Dempsey	Dudley Roberts	Mary	Thomas & Ailany Hammonds	
22698	Dempsey, Eliza	IN	1831	John Dempsey	King Tanner	Serrah Larence		Samuel & Lizey Larence
11302	Dempsey, Elvin	GA	1857	Louise Dempsey	Porter Dempsey	Charlotta Seipers	Moses & Olley Dempsey	
19554	Dempsey, Harvey	IN			James Dempsey	Malinda Watkins	James & Beccy Dempsey	James & Martha Watkins
12023	Dempsey, Jerry	GA	1878	Eliza Dempsey	Elven Dempsey	Louisa Bram	Porter Dempsey	
10900	Dempsey, Minnie	IN	1800		Wm Kelley	Margret Smith	Anderson & Elizabeth Kelley	
19553	Dempsy, Cyrus	IN		Mary Dempsy	James Dempsy	Rebecca Terry	Thomas Dempsy	Patsy Terry
22450	Dempsy, George	IN	1843	Ellen Dempsy	James Dempsy	Rebecca Terry		David Terry
7134	Denham, Edward	ID	1868	Lurlin Denham	Thomas Denham	Sarah Sanders	Martin & Sarah Denham	Samuel & Sarah Sanders
7135	Denham, Samuel	ID	1873	Margaret Denham	Thomas Denham	Sarah Sanders	Martin & Sarah Denham	Samuel & Sarah Sanders
19949	Dennis, Francis & Jacob	NC	1892 1889		John Dennis	Mary Womble	John & Mary Dennis	Wm & Elizabeth Womble
19945	Dennis, James	NC	1874	Etta Dennis	John Dennis	Mary Womble	John Dennis	Sampson & Polly Coble

19951	Dennis, William	NC	1857	Ruth Dennis	Arthur Dennis	Betsy Cobb	John Dennis	Sampson Cobb
5561	Dennison, Margret	VA	1868	S L Dennison	Noah Baldwin	Mahaley Baldwin	W D & Margret Baldwin	
19498	Denny, Alma	NC	1900		O.J. Denny	Manerva Pell		
19497	Denny, Annie	NC	1901		O.J. Denny	Manerva Pell		
19443	Denny, Cleo	NC	1897		O.J. Denny	Manerva Pell	Gabril & Sarah Denny	James Pell & M.J. Owens
20213	Denny, Columbus	NC	1869	Mollie Denny	Gabriel Denny	Sarah Stone	Joel & Nancy Denny	Frank & Sarah Stone
19613	Denny, Doctor	NC	1888			Sarah	Joel Denny	Sarah Poindexter
19444	Denny, Edith	NC	1906		O.J. Denny	Manerva Pell	Gabril & Sarah Denny	James Pell & M.J. Owens
19615	Denny, Emery	NC			Gabriel Denny	Sarah	Joel & Nancy Denny	
19445	Denny, Gabriel & James	NC			O.J. Denny	Manerva Pell	Gabril & Sarah Denny	James Pell & M.J. Owens
19640	Denny, Mary	NC	1882		Gabriel	Sarah		
20949 *	Denny, Mary	NC	1873	John Denny	Henry Mebary	Betsy Halder	Hawk	
19496	Denny, Oliver	NC	1871	M.E. Denny	Gabriel Denny	Sarah Stone	Joel & Nancy Denny	Frank & Caroline Stone
19617	Denny, Roxey	NC	1892		Gabriel Denny	Sarah	Joel & Nancy Denny	Sarah Stone
19614	Denny, Sallie	NC				Sarah		
19616	Denny, Sidney	NC	1886			Sarah	Joel & Nancy	
19446	Denny, William	NC	1903		O.J. Denny	Manerva Pell	Gabril & Sarah Denny	James Pell & M.J. Owens
19393	Denson, Ada	GA	1880	Sam Denson	Gazaway Cook	Nellie Reinhards	Richard & Sarah Cook	
12202	Denson, Ella	TN	1883	James Denson	Henry Cogle	Cathrine Brown	Henry Cogle	
19394	Denson, Griffin	GA	1898		Sam Denson	Ada Cook		Gazaway & Nellie Cook
19395	Denson, Mattie	GA	1901		Sam Denson	Ada Cook		Gazaway & Nellie Cook
19396	Denson, Walter	GA	1903		Sam Denson	Ada Cook		Gazaway & Nellie Cook
19397	Denson, Will	GA	1899		Sam Denson	Ada Cook		Gazaway & Nellie Cook
6268	Denton, Lina	VA	1873	John Denton	Joseph Lewis	Ransa Hart	Jessie & Sarah Lewis	Eliazer & Nancy Hart
952	Denton, Maggie	GA		Frank Denton	Benjamin Garrett	Rena Maney	Willie & Nancy Garrett	John & Jennie Maney
11429	De-qua-de-he, Browstan	OK	1894		Lancle	Jinnie Summerfield		Will Summerfield
5140	Desbozo, Tennessee	OK	1857		Watkins	Lizzie Sneed	Josiah Watkins	
9021	Deshazo, Nancy	OK		J A Deshazo	Martin Bobbitt	Elizabeth	Martin Many	
20411 *	Detheredge, Amanda	TN	1858	James Detheredge	Sampson Steward	Lucy Weed	Lydia Tillery	Betty Weed
21979 *	Dethridge, Boston	TN	1885	none	John Dethridge	Martha Ragland	Henry & Sarah Ragland	Creassie Ragland
21978 *	Dethridge, James	TN	1861	Amanda Dethridge	John Dethridge	Martha Ragland	Henry & Sarah Ragland	Creassie Ragland
3400	Dewise, Levia	AL		William Dewise	Richard Rollin	Levina Rollin	Jack Coons	Polly Rollin
3401	Dewise, William	AL	58yrs	Levia Rollin	Peter Dewise	Peggy Pigeon		Charles & Peggy Pigeon

20603	Deyhle, Mattie	TN	1885	John Deyhle	John Walker	Lucinda Robinson	Wm & Elizabeth Walker	Eli & Tempe Robinson
14536 *	Dial, Bertha	GA	1877	James Dial	Taylor Scudders	Rosa Summerhour	Kitty Scudders	
22090	Dial, Eddie	AL	1868	Richard Dial	Andy Berryhill	Jane Scott	Billie & Annie Berryhill	Simon & Millie Scott
14535 *	Dial, Josephine	GA	1906		James Dial	Bertha Scudders	Danial & Mariah Fowler	Taylor & Rosa Scudders
14534 *	Dial, Mary	GA	1904		James Dial	Bertha Scudders	Danial & Mariah Fowler	Taylor & Rosa Scudders
17545	Diamond, Stella	WV	1897		John Diamond	Jennie Smith		Andrew & Easter Smith
17491	Diamond, Vernon	WV	1895		John Diamond	Jennie Smith		Andrew & Easter Smith
13590	Dias, Jane	AR		Marcus Dias	Joseph Cooper	Jane Dupriest		
21816	Dick, Ellen	FL	1894		W.T. Dick	Lucy Bryars	John & Laura Dick	J.L. & Lizzie Bryars
21820	Dick, Leone	FL	1895		W.T. Dick	Lucy Bryars	John & Laura Dick	J.L. & Lizzie Bryars
9322	Dickerson, Hendie	GA	1847	W L Dickerson	Ira Ledbetter	Nellie Thomas		Thomas Thomas
10435 *	Dickerson, Mary	TN	1867	Tom Dickerson	Jack Maston	Jane Boyd		
7127	Dickey, Carrie	MO	1873	none	Thomas Dickey	Jane Morgan	John & Martha Dickey	Nathan & Anna Morgan
7129	Dickey, Jane	MO	1845	Thomas Dickey	Nathan Morgan	Anna Messingale	James & Martha Morgan	Blakely & Polly Messingale
7130	Dickey, Lotie	MO	1878	none	Thomas Dickey	Jane Morgan	John & Martha Dickey	Nathan & Anna Morgan
7128	Dickey, Myrtle	MO	1882	none	Thomas Dickey	Jane Morgan	John & Martha Dickey	Nathan & Anna Morgan
14955	Dicks, Allen	IN	1860	Mary Dicks	Nathan Dicks	Nancy Allen	Job & Hannah Dicks	Herman & Ann Allen
15068	Dicks, Gurney	KS	1859		Nathan Dicks	Nancy Allen	Job & Hannah Dicks	Herman & Ann Allen
13406	Dicks, Nancy	KS	1831	Nathan Dicks (decd)	Herman Allen	Ann Clark	John & Rachel Allen	Daniel & Mary Clark
2096	Dickson, Mary	NC	1864	Urvin Dickson	Alford Blevins	Marjary Sheet	James & Macy Blevins	Joe & Elizabeth Hudler
10437	Dickson, Rettie	NC	1875	C M Dickson	Elihu Tucker	Sarah Blevins	David & Rena Tucker	Eli & Susana Blevins
3450	Dilbeck, Martin	OK	1875	Emma Dilbeck	Marion Dilbeck	Eliza Bates		
21198	Dillahunty, Emily	AR	1852	Adolphus Dillahunty	John Williams	Patience Mann		Fredrick & Susan Mann
21200	Dillahunty, H.T.	AR	1876	Nettie Dillahunty	Adolphus Dillahunty	Emily Williams	Francis & Susan Dillahunty	John & Patience Williams
21201	Dillahunty, Nora	AR	1886		Adolphus Dillahunty	Emily Williams	Francis Dillahunty	John & Patience Williams
21194	Dillahunty, Robert	OK	1878	Sallie Dillahunty	Adolphius Dillahunty	Emily Williams	Francis & Susan Dillahunty	John & Patience Williams
12625	Dillard, Octavia	GA		Robert Dillard	Taylor Green	Nancy Lequire	Henry Green	Minor & Rena Lequire
19318	Dillard, Serena	IN	1864	John Dillard	Ruffin Stewart	Martha Manuel	Able & Jency Stewart	Wyatt & Charlotte Manuel
9225	Dillingham, Sarah	GA		James Dillingham	Elisha Thomas	Pollie Lee	Aaron & Sallie Thomas	
9224	Dillingham, William	GA		Callie Dillingham	James Dillingham	Sary Thomas	John & Pollie Dillingham	Elisha & Pollie Thomas

19280	Dills, Bettie	NC	1869	Charles Dills	Elick Holdbrooks	Nancy Roach		Jerry & Polly Roach
6159	Dinkins, Margart	VA	1877	Harvey Dinkins	Marion Miller	Mary Horn	Isaac & Bashabe Miller	Joshaway & Elizebet Horn
260	Ditmore, Charles	NC	1872	none	Charles Ditmore	Mary Hampton	John Ditmore	George & Maryan Hampton
1527	Ditmore, John	OK	1866	Lara Ditmore	Henry Ditmore	Elisabeth Hampton	John & Elisa Ditmore	George & Mary Hampton
259	Ditmore, Ples. Henry	NC	1869	Ida Ditmore	Charles Ditmore	Mary Hampton	John Ditmore	George & Maryan Hampton
257	Ditmore, Sarah	NC	1866	none	Charles Ditmore	Mary Hampton	John Ditmore	George & Maryan Hampton
258	Ditmore, Ulysses	NC	1878	Annah Ditmore	Charles Ditmore	Catharine Hampton	John Ditmore	George & Maryan Hampton
6859	Dixon, Alex	WA	1849	Julia Dixon	Stephen Pugh	Sarah Hash	James & Sarah Pugh	
4252	Dixon, Benj	GA	1875	Ida Dixon	Sam Dixon	Allie Coleman	Geo Dixon	Malinda Trusty
18214	Dixon, Carrie	TN	1876		Fleming Latty	Jane Jones	Emery & Nancy Latty	Wiley & Elizabeth Jones
14397	Dixon, Elizabeth	NC	1846	Harbey Dixon	Jim Scott	Delia Underwood	George & Abbie Scott	Lewis & Nancy Underwood
21192	Dixon, Elizabeth	MO	1844	Ben Dixon	John Stephenson	Sarah Ritchie	Elizabeth McDaniel	Zachriah Ritchie
9877	Dixon, Ida	GA	1881	Ben Dixon	William	Elizabeth Helton		Joseph Helton
12457	Dixon, James	GA	1864	Jane Dixon	George Dixon	Malinda Trusty		Trusty
5398	Dixon, John	GA	1873	Margret Dixon	Sam Dixon	Allie Colman	George & Malinda Dixon	Thomas & Lida Colman
12458	Dixon, Monroe	GA	1863		G W Dixon	Malinda Trusty		Trusty
11377	Dixon, Sam	KY	1847	Aldie Dixon	George Dixon	Malinda Trusty		
17733	Dixon, Sarah	TN	1859	James Dixon	Wm Coatney	Elizabeth Barger	Sarah Coarney	Wiley & Christiana Barger
4253	Dixon, Thomas	GA	1879	Annie Dixon	Sam Dixon	Alllie Coleman	Geo Dixon	Malinda Trusty
15639	Dobbins, W S	GA	42yrs	J B Dobbins	Drurey Dobbins	Harriet Grant	Drurey Dobbins	
15563	Dobbs, Ada	GA	1876	Richard Dobbs	John Reece	Martha Helton	Aaron & Nancy Reece	James & Camely Helton
15562	Dobbs, Agnes	GA	1902		Richard Dobbs	Ada Reece	Alfred & Rebecca Dobbs	John & Martha Reece
7816	Dobbs, Anna	GA	1876	Joseph Dobbs	John Reese	Martha Helton	Aaron & Nancy Reese	James & Camely Helton
10553	Dobbs, Edna	GA	1895		Joseph Dobbs	Anna Reece	Cicero & Mary Dobbs	Wesley & Martha Reece
15559	Dobbs, Era	GA	1904		Richard Dobbs	Ada Reece	Alfred & Rebecca Dobbs	John & Martha Reece
15560	Dobbs, Eva	GA	1904		Richard Dobbs	Ada Reece	Alfred & Rebecca Dobbs	John & Martha Reece
10556	Dobbs, Fannie	GA	1905		Joseph Dobbs	Anna Reece	Cicero & Mary Dobbs	Wesley & Martha Reece
10555	Dobbs, Leslie	GA	1899		Joseph Dobbs	Anna Reece	Cicero & Mary Dobbs	Wesley & Martha Reece
10554	Dobbs, Mattie	GA	1897		Joseph Dobbs	Anna Reece	Cicero & Mary Dobbs	Wesley & Martha Reece

15401	Dobson, Austin	GA	1906		Neely Dobson	Jane Mason	David & Mary Dobson	Bloop & Caroline Mason
15400	Dobson, Neely	GA	1881	Jane Dobson	David Dobson	Mary Eaton	Washington & Margret Dobson	Andrew & Caroline Eaton
7570	Dobson, Sarah (decd)	OK	1834	Leonidas Dobson	John Ross	Mary Staples		
14635	Doby, Charley	NC	1863		Thomas Doby	Eda Winkler	Alice Doby	
19088	Doby, James	WA	1862		Thomas Doby	Eda Winkler		
15171	Doby, John	VA	1857		Thomas Doby	Eda Winkler	Alce Doby	
15178	Doby, William	NC	1851		Thomas Doby	Eda Winkler	Alce Doby	
17283	Dockery, Alvin	NC	1873	Sally Dockery	A. J. Dockery	Martha McCloud	James & Tabitha Dockery	Harvey McCloud & Sally McDonald
5824	Dockery, Andrew	NC	1879	Eler Dockrey	William Dockrey	Martha McDonald	James & Tabitha Dockrey	James & Mima McDonald
4771	Dockery, Baily	NC	1888	none	James Dockery	Malissa Williamson	Eli & Catherine Dockery	James & Bekey Williamson
2302	Dockery, Ben	NC	1871	Jane Dockery	A J Dockery	Martha McLoud	James & Bitha Dockery	Harve & Sallie McLoud
10857	Dockery, Benjaman	NC	1871	Maxem Dockery	Wm Dockery	Martha McDonald	James & Bitha Dockery	James & Mima McDonald
18503	Dockery, Callie	NC	1890		Wm Dockery	Martha McDonald	James & Tabitha Dockery	James & Levina McDonald
1305	Dockery, Catherine	NC	1837	Eli Dockery	Harve McLoud	Sallie McDonald		Anguish & Sallie McDonald
4779	Dockery, Charlie	NC	1885	none	James Dockery	Malissa Williamson	Eli & Catherine Dockery	James & Betsey Williamson
4265	Dockery, Columbus	NC	1882	Eva Dockery	William Dockery	Martha McDonald	James & Tabitha Dockery	James & Mima McDonald
4266	Dockery, Eligah	NC	1885	none	John Dockery	Hepsey Lair	Andrew & Martha Dockery	Eligah & Susan Lair
2363	Dockery, Jacob	NC	1860	Martha Dockery	A J Dockery	Martha McLoud	James & Bitha Dockery	Harve & Sallie McLoud
4783	Dockery, James	NC	1855	Malissa Dockery	Eli Dockery	Catherine McCloud	James & Tabitha Dockery	James & Sarah McCloud
15192	Dockery, James	NC	1869	Lillie Dockery	A J Dockery	Martha McCloud	James & Tabitha Dockery	Harvey & Sally McCloud
2329	Dockery, Joseph	NC	1872	Nora Dockery	Eli Dockery	Catherine McLoud	James & Bitha Dockery	Harve & Sallie McLoud
19101	Dockery, Joshua	NC	1885	Hattie Dockery	Jacob Dockery	Manta Kephart	Jack & Manta Dockery	
4773	Dockery, Julia	NC	1886	none	James Dockery	Malissa Williamson	Eli & Catharine Dockery	James & Betsy Williamson
1304	Dockery, Martha	NC	1840	A.J. Dockery	James McLoud	Sallie Daniel	Catherine McLoud	Anguish & Sallie McDonald
4267	Dockery, Martha	NC	1848	William Dockery	James McDonald	Mima Deyton	Johnathan Blythe	John Deyton
18502	Dockery, Mimy	NC	1888		Wm Dockery	Martha McDonald	James & Tabitha Dockery	James & Levina McDonald
5417	Dockery, Nancy	NC	1842	John Dockery	Jonathan McDonald	Harrit Davidson	Anguish & Sallie McDonald	
2314	Dockery, Phoebe	NC	1862	none	Eli Dockery	Catherine McLoud	Jim & Bitha Dockery	Harve & Sallie McLoud
4268	Dockery, Riley	NC	1876	none	William Dockery	Martha McDonald	James & Tabitha Dockery	James & Mima McDonald
5821	Dockery, Robert	NC	1888	none	William Dockery	Martha McDonald	James & Tabitha Dockery	James & Mima McDonald

17454	Dockery, Robert	NC		Callie Dockery	Eli Dockery	Catherine McLoud	Jim & Bitta Dockery	Harve & Sallie McLoud
4780	Dockery, Rollin	NC	1892	none	James Dockery	Malissa Williamson	Eli & Catherine Dockery	James & Betsey Williamson
4264	Dockery, Tabitha	NC	1887	none	John Dockery	Hepsey Lair	Andrew & Martha Dockery	Elijah & Susan Lair
15190	Dockery, Thomas	NC	1867	Ella Dockery	A J Dockery	Martha McCloud	James & Tabitha Dockery	Harvey & Sallie McCloud
22127	Dockery, Wiley	NC	1893	none	Benjamin Dockery	Sary Dinkins	Andrew & Marthy Dockery	
4772	Dockery, Willie	NC	1892	none	James Dockery	Malissa Williamson	Eli & Catharine Dockery	James & Betsy Williamson
18486	Dockery, Willis	GA	1847	Jane Dockery	George Dockery	Margret Garret		
5822	Dockrey, Jacob	NC	1878	Elizabeth Dockrey	William Dockrey	Martha McDonald	James & Tabitha Dockrey	James & Mima McDonald
9878	Dockrey, Lillie	GA	1877	Nelson Dockrey	W J Smith			
20635	Dodd, Delie	TN	1867	Elizabeth Dodd	Madison Dodd	Annie Maples	Berry Dodd	
3784	Dodd, Martha	MO	1867	Maddinri Dodd	Samul Richards	Amandy Harralston	Martin & Lucy Richards	Vincent & Martha Harralston
20072	Dodd, William	TN	1856	Sophronia Dodd	Madison Dodd	Annie Maples	Jane Dodd	Wilson & Annie Maples
4001	Dodson, Ella	KS	1866	Meander Dodson	David McCracken	Sarah Wilson	John & Allsey McCracken	Arch & Hulda Wilson
16221	Dodson, Harriet	OK	1862	Levi Dodson	I M Robinson	Caroline Jones		James Jones
7118	Dodson, Mary	OK	1877	Henry Dodson	Joel Massey	Laura Holcomb	Ephram & Mary Massey	Wm & Louisa Holcomb
7117	Dodson, Nancy	TX	1879	Charley Dodson	John Shields	Sarah Hunter		Willis & Sarah Hunter
13392	Doherty, Louella	OK			Dennis Gonzales	Rachel Pettit		Charles & Charlotte Pettit
12465	Doke, Henry	MO	1874	Minnie Doke	James Doke	Jackey Harralson		Vincent & Marth Harralson
4744	Doke, Isaiah	MO	1875	Cora Doke	William Doke	Sarah Hambelton	Merick & Mary Doke	Isaiah & Martha Hambelton
2427	Doke, Jockey	MO	1854	James Doke	Vinson Harralson	Martha Hambelton	David & Peachy Harralson	Elijah & Sarah Hambelton
4743	Doke, Sarah	MO	1847	William Doke	Isaiah Hambelton	Martha Maney	Elijah & Sarah Hambelton	
5080	Dolinger, Andrew	VA	1869	Catharine Dolinger	John Dolinger	Elizabeth Caldwell	Wm & Catharine Dolinger	Joseph & Catharine Caldwell
5079	Dolinger, Catharine	VA		A.J. Dolinger	Noah Baldwin	Mahala Blevins	Wm & Margret Baldwin	
13004	Dolinger, Frank, John	VA			John Dolinger	Canzady Davis	John & Elisabeth Dolinger	
8173	Dolinger, Frulin	VA	1885	none	William Dolinger	Nancy Blevins	John & Elisabeth Dolinger	
6818	Dolinger, Isaac	VA	1878	Maggie Dolinger	William Dolinger	Selah Edmandson		Isaac & Martha Edmandson
6267	Dolinger, Lydia	VA	1860	Thomas Dolinger	Isaac Miller	Boshebe Blevins	Isaac & Eva Miller	Wells & Elisabeth Blevins
6908	Dolinger, Lydia	VA	29yrs	Roby Dolinger	Allen Blevins	Rachel Williams	Wells & Elizabeth Blevins	Miles & Mary Williams

#	Name	State	Year					
6955	Dolinger, Lydia	VA	1861	Haywood Blevins & Jesse Dolinger	Jacob McGrady	Jiney Blevins	Peter & Polly McGrady	George & Lydia Blevins
8511	Dolinger, Marth decd	VA		Wesley Dolinger	Edward Blevins	Nancy Blevins	James & Lydie Blevins	
11049	Dolinger, Selah	VA	1858	William Dolinger	Isaac Edmondson	Martha Blevins		Wells & Elizabeth Blevins
11051	Dolinger, Wilda	VA	1882		William Dolinger	Selah Edmondson		Isaac & Martha Edmondson
8172	Dolinger, William	VA	1850	Nancy Dolinger	John Dolinger	Elisabeth Caldwell	Wm & Catharine Dolinger	Joseph & Catharine Caldwell
1135	Donahoo, Mary	OK	1854	Sam Donahoo	Hiram Ross	Margaret Mackfalls	George & Rachel Ross	Arthur & Margaret Mackfalls
1134	Donahoo, Samuel	OK	1848	Mary Donahoo	John Donahoo	Nancy Howard		Ben & Sarah Howard
7136	Donaldson, Lenora	MO	1867	none	Milus Fuller	Ann Spenser	Andrew Fuller	John & Nancy Spenser
19947	Donathan, Frances	NC	58yrs	Sally Donathan	Lark Donathan	Viney Holyfield	Jacob & Nancy Donathan	Voley & Sally Holyfield
19948	Donathan, Jacob	NC	1879	Mary Donathan	Jacob Donathan Jr	Pathena Donathan	Lige & Hannah Donathan	Lark & Viney Donathan
19946	Donathan, Mary	NC	1881	Jacob Donathan	Frances Donathan	Sally Key	Lark & Sally Donathan	Vina
19944	Donathan, Thomas	NC				Eliza Donathan		Ben Donathan & Rena Mitchell
19950	Donathan, W.B.	NC	1875	Louesa Donathan	Frank Donathan	Mary Hutchins	Wm & Mary Donathan	
19940	Donathon, Alice & Colonel	NC	1902 1905		Jacob Donathan	Mary Donathan	Jacob & Parthena Donathan	Frances & Sally Donathan
11250	Doncarlos, Frank	OK	1881	Luella Doncarlos	Frank Doncarlos	Mary Cornwell		Issie & Mary Cornwell
9109	Donley, Martha	TN	1848	none	William Donley	Adra Henson		Lloyd & Sallie Henson
9112	Donley, Nancy	TN	1857	none	William Donley	Adra Henson		Lloyd & Sallie Henson
10446	Donoho, Minerva	TN	1858	P S Donoho	Andrew Harrison	Rachel Mathis	Samuel & Rosa Harrison	A P & Easter Mathis
14533 *	Dooley, Kitty	GA	1881	Harrison Dooley	Madison Scudders	Julia Looper	Kitty Scudders	Thursday Looper
1007	Dooley, Sarah Jane	GA	1860	widow	Augustus Williams	Sarah Ledbetter	John & Rhoda Williams	Johnston & Nancy Ledbetter
10260	Dorris, John	KS	1851	none	Josiah Dorris	Margarett Bly		Robert Revelle & Fannie Bly
19285	Dorsett, Ellen	NC	1852	Elias Dorsett	Solomon Spainhour Jr.	Polly Scott	Solomon & Nancy Spainhour	Chesly & Rebecca Scott
13725 *	Dorsey, Emma	GA	1870		Ed Dorsey	Tilla Brown	Joe Standford & Selie Dorsey	Ned & Martha Brown
13726 *	Dorsey, Fletcher	GA	1871	Martha Dorsey	Ed Dorsey	Tilla Brown	Joe Standford & Selie Dorsey	Ned & Martha Brown
15683	Dorsey, Hannah	GA			Ed Dorsey	Tilla Brown	Joe Standford & Sallie Dorsey	Ned & Martha Brown
19471 *	Dorsey, Ida	GA	1885	Charly Dorsey		Babe Brown		Mary Brown
20013 *	Dorsey, Lila	GA	1864	Dock Dorsey	Ron Sulton	Francis Welch		Joe & Millie Welch
13728 *	Dorsey, Susie	GA	1865	Dave Dorsey	Ron Sutton	Francis Welch		Joe & Millie Welch
13724 *	Dorsey, Tilla	GA	1852	Ed Dorsey	Ned Brown	Martha Bly	Cue & Tilla Tiffens	Wilkerson & Hannah Bly

6877	Doss, James	VA	1879	Mary Parish	William Parish	Ada Waters		Wm & Zilpha Waters
19959	Doss, Malisa	NC	1878	John Manor	John Blevins	Mary Blevins	John Blevins	William Wall
6879	Doss, William	VA	1870	Zilpha Doss	William Parish	Ada Waters		Wm & Zilpha Waters
777	Dotson, Amanda	GA	1878	none	Nathaniel Dotson	Ellen Willwood		
20517*	Dotson, Amelia	TN	1880	Rufus Dotson	Oscar Wilson	Mary Owens	James Foeman & Millie Coffin	Harry & Sally Owens
775	Dotson, Nancy	GA	1874	widow	Nathaniel Dotson	Ellen Millwood		
2372	Dotson, Nancy	NC	1847	Franklin Dotson	Elisha Thomas	Mary Lee	Aaron & Sarah Thomas	John & Elizabeth Lee
22770*	Dotson, Susie	OK	1883	Wilson Dotson	Frank Keyes	Malinda Moore	Ely Keyes	Julia Brown
9214	Doublehead, Alsey	OK	40 yrs	none	Dakatak	Arnarn		
10725	Doublehead, Bird	OK	61yrs	Maggie Doublehead	Bird Doublehead			
14295	Doublehead, Isaac	OK	1858		Eli Doublehead	Ah nee Ooleeciegee	Doublehead & Mattie Doublehead	Jessie Ooleeciegee
7763	Dougherty, Telitha	KS	1850		John McBee	Katie Hames	William McBee	John & Katie Hames
7762	Dougherty, William	KS	1879	Rosa Dougherty	Daniel Dougherty	Lelitha McBee	Wm & Mary Dougherty	John McBee & Katie Hames
20601	Douglas, Lillie	TN	1887	Robert Douglas	James Brown	Mary Cross	Wm & Nancy Brown	Absalom & Susan Cross
17762*	Douglass, Annie	TN	1870	Edward Douglass	John Knox	Laura Ware	Isaac Knox	Dafney & Beverly Ware
21490	Douglass, Dollie	TX	1884	Oscar Douglass	Adrian Bonds	Martha Galleher	Wm & Margaret Bonds	Charles & Eliza Galleher
13336	Douthet, Dock	GA	1889		Samuel Douthet	Florida Weaver	Samuel Douthet	Poley Tomotley
8381	Douthet, Frank	GA	1877	none	Samuel Douthet	Florid Weavers	Samuel Douthet	Poley Tomathey
13334	Douthet, Isaac	GA	1871		Samuel Douthet	Florida Weaver	Samuel Douthet	Poley Tomotley
13339	Douthet, Timothy	GA	1885		Samuel Douthet	Florida Weaver	Samuel Douthet	Poley Tomotley
8407	Douthit, Montraville	GA	1869		Samuel Douthit	Floria Weaver	Samuel Douthit	Poley Tomathey
15220	Dover, Alantha	GA	1819	William Dover	Jim Chambers	Polly Buff		
20476	Dover, Alice	TN	1870		William Dover	Mary Whitice	John & Elizabeth Dover	Wm & Eliza Whitice
15219	Dover, Andrew	GA	1895		Richard Dover	Sarah Lemley	Wm & Alantha Dover	Elias Lemley
15217	Dover, Benjamin	GA	1885		Richard Dover	Sarah Lemley	Wm & Alantha Dover	Elias Lemley
15207	Dover, Carl	GA	1898		Richard Dover	Sarah Lemley	Wm & Alantha Dover	Elias Lemley
15208	Dover, Charley	GA	1898		William Dover	Margarett Evans	Wm & Alantha Dover	
20736	Dover, Delia	GA	1902		Lewis Dover	Nancy Goins	Gus & Sally Dover	Wm & Delia Goins
15209	Dover, Eddie	GA	1879	Rachel Dover	William Dover	Margarett Evans	Wm & Alantha Dover	
20737	Dover, Effie	GA	1905		Lewis Dover	Nancy Goins	Gus & Sally Dover	Wm & Delia Goins
15210	Dover, Elmira	GA	1891		William Dover	Margarett Evans	Wm & Alantha Dover	

16169	Dover, Francis	KS	1846	I L Dover	James Norton	Rhoda Dennis	Wm & Jane Norton	
15211	Dover, Frederic	GA	1889		William Dover	Margarett Evans	Wm & Alantha Dover	
20479	Dover, George	TN	1882	Erma Dover	William Dover	Mary Whitice	John & Elizabeth Dover	Wm & Eliza Whitice
13868	Dover, Josephine	GA	1870	Jim Hayes	Linch Dover	Sabrah Franklin		John Franklin & Sarah Swimmey
20738	Dover, Lafayette	GA	1899		Lewis Dover	Nancy Goins	Gus & Sally Dover	Wm & Delia Goins
18955 *	Dover, Larra	GA	1872	Sandy Dover	Bird Cash	Harrett Cash		Charles & Rebecca Cash
20506	Dover, Lillie	TN	1878		William Dover	Mary Whitice	John & Elizabeth Dover	Wm & Eliza Whitice
15202	Dover, Lizzie	GA	1893		Richard Dover	Sarah Limley	Wm & Alantha Dover	Elias Lemley
15203	Dover, Maggie	GA	1884		William Dover	Margarett Evans	Wm & Alantha Dover	
18027	Dover, Mary	TN	1846	Wm Dover	Wm Whitice	Eliza Read	Wm & Mary Whitice	Josiah Read
20513	Dover, Mary	TN	1888		William Dover	Mary Whitice	John & Elizabeth Dover	Wm & Eliza Whitice
20739	Dover, Nancy	GA	1877	Lewis Dover	Wm Going	Delia Cole	Wm & Nancy Going	John & Betsy Cole
13779 *	Dover, Nellie	GA	1876	Louisa Dover	Jim Dover	Harriet Hughes		Ester McMillon
20512	Dover, Raymond	TN	1890		William Dover	Mary Whitice	John & Elizabeth Dover	Wm & Eliza Whitice
15204	Dover, Richard	GA	1861	Sarah Dover	William Dover	Alantha Chambers		James Chambers & Polly Buff
15205	Dover, Rose	GA	1887		Richard Dover	Sarah Limley	Wm & Alantha Dover	Elias Lemley
13768 *	Dover, Sandy	GA	1864	Laura Dover	Jim Dover	Harriet Hughes		Ester McMillan
15206	Dover, Sarah	GA	1894		William Dover	Margarett Evans	Wm & Alantha Dover	
15212	Dover, Viola	GA			William Dover	Margarett Evans	Wm & Alantha Dover	
15160	Dover, William	GA	1854	Margarett Dover	William Dover	Alantha Chambers		Jim & Polly Chambers
18221	Dover, William	TN	1872	Rosa Dover	William Dover	Mary Whitice	John & Elizabeth Dover	Wm & Eliza Whitice
18591	Dovy, Virgie	TN	1881	Elijah Dovy	Benj Holland	Izora Tidwell		Wm & Matilda Tidwell
21837	Dowdy, Francis	GA	1853	J.R. Dowdy	J.C. Swancy	Mary Grizzel		
21222	Dowdy, Ina	OK	1878	Franklin Dowdy	James Sampson	Sarah Lumpkin	Wm & Mary Sampson	Bushsod & Mary Lumpkin
17577	Dowdy, Laura	NC	1860	D.J. Dowdy	Isaac Sneed	Sarah Sneed	Ezekiel & Nancy Sneed	James & Elizabeth Sneed
21951	Dowdy, Lena	TN	1874	William Dowdy	William Perin	Manerva Chaney	Baty & Elizabeth Perin	Easter Chaney
21223	Dowdy, Mary	OK	1880	Clarence Dowdy	James Sampson	Sarah Lumpkin	Wm & Mary Sampson	Bushsod & Mary Lumpkin
21035	Dowell, Claude	OK	1885	Leora Dowell	Eugene Dowell	Mattie McCoy		John & Catherine McCoy
18844	Dowell, Dovie	TN	1868		James Dowell	Vicia Redman		Richard Redman & Vicia Buse
22292 *	Downing, Elias	OK	1852	Mary Downing	Ruben Downing	Jennie Martin		George Adair
22299 *	Downing, Jennie	OK	1860	Zebedee Downing	Joseph Powell	Rosa Chissell		Mike Waity
13839	Downing, Louis	OK	1875	Mamie Downing	Samuel Downing	Neppie Wolf	Louis & Lydia Downing	Thomas & Manervia Wolf
22295 *	Downing, Martha	OK	1870	Alex Downing	Louis Rowe	Chaney Landrum	Jesse & Delila Rowe	Clora Landrum

2083	Downing, Sarah	OK	1846	Woodsey Downing	Oscar Harrison	Mary Maney	Robert Harrison	Wm Maney
22625	Downs, Thomas	TN	1872	Jennie Downs	Zack Downs	Amanda Welch	Alex & Cathrine Downs	Thomas & Amanda Welch
17915	Doyee, Samuel	MO	1872	Annie Doyee	Isaac Doyee	Mary Morrison		Samuel Morrison & Sarah Gildow
13347	Doyle, Benckley	TN		Ada Doyle	Jacob Doyle	Malisa Pagin		Jane Wall
18246	Dozier, Martha	GA	1827	Buck Dozier	Lewis Bates	Rhoda		
3076	Drake, Josephine decd	OK	1853	Drake, John	Clement McNair	Susie Bigby	David & Delila McNair	James & Catherine Bigby
21682	Dreadfulwater, Lydia	OK	1850		Ah-ten-ku-do-gu	Ko-he-ni		
5157	Drew, Benjamin	OK	1879	Annie Drew	Perlan Drew	Jane Zowago	George Drew	
21434	Duboise, Francis	OK	1855	J.W.C. Duboise	William Hill	Mary Douthil	James & Francis Hill	
15187	Dubry, Charlotte	MI	1840	Peter Dubry	John Ansell	Mary Everett		
18823	Ducket, Mosuria	TN	1871	Jess Ducket	Daniel Harris	Mosurie Kirkland	James & Elizabeth Harris	James & Joisie Kirkland
18168 *	Duckworth, Ida	WI	1885	Wm Duckworth	Matthew Revels	Alice Murphy	Aaron & Elizabeth Revels	Berlie & Elizabeth Murphy
16811	Duckworth, William	TN	1837	Arena Duckworth	William Duckworth	Mary Hill	Thomas Wicker	___ Snow
9549	Dudley, Charley	GA	1873	Adas Dudley	David Dudley	Jinetta Tidwell	Millory Dudley	
2549	Dudley, Hiram	GA	1863	Martha Dudley	David Dudley	Jennette Tidwell	David Dudley	John & Betsy Tidwell
2630	Dudley, Jennette	GA	1838	David Dudley	John Tidwell	Betsy Brantt	John Tidwell	Betsey Grantt
9548	Dudley, Jinetta	GA	1839	David Dudley	John Tidwell	Winnie Tidwell	Lovis Love Deer	
17346	Dudley, Mattie	GA			David Dudley	Ginetta Tidwell	David Dudley	John Tidwell
19768	Duffield, James	TN	1853	Mary Duffield	Landon Duffield		George & Lottie Duffield	
17158	Dugger, Sarah	GA	1847	Joel Dugger	Linville Holloway	Elizabeth Brooks	Wm & Elizabeth Holloway	Vincell & Sally Brooks
20894 *	Dula, Laura	NC	1868	Ed Dula	Jerry Perkins	Semptsom Miller		Perry & Winnie Miller
20948 *	Dula, Mary	NC	1844		Losen Jones	Emley Witherspoon	Joe & Hannah Jones	
20102 *	Dumas, John	GA	1839	Katie Dumas	Cuffey Dumas	Mary Harvy		Huston Harvy
9143	Dunagan, Sarrah	GA	1841		Geter Bryant	Sarah Frost		
18496	Dunagan, Tinie	GA	1882	George Dunagan	Jack Patterson	Sinda Chalmurs	Samuel & Nancy Patterson	Jophes & Sarah Chalmurs
18622	Duncan, Elmira	GA	1828	Early Duncan	Abraham Kirkendol	Elizabeth Alton		
13653	Duncan, Ernest	CA	1891		Alfred Duncan	Lucy Murphy	Caleb & Mary Duncan	
13648	Duncan, George	CA	1882		Alfred Duncan	Lucy Murphy	Caleb & Mary Duncan	
8694	Duncan, Leonidas	CA	1843	Mary Duncan	Charles Duncan	Mahala Abecrombia		
13654	Duncan, Lucy	CA	1847	Alfred Duncan	Caleb Duncan	Mary Hudson	Charles & Mahala Duncan	

21384	Duncan, Nannie	TX	1876	Nathan Duncan	Edward Martin	Luan Hill		
13645	Duncan, Ora	CA	1887		Alfred Duncan	Lucy Murphy	Caleb & Mary Duncan	
13649	Duncan, R.L.	CA	1866		Caleb Duncan	Mary Hudson	Charles & Mahala Duncan	
13538	Duncan, Robert	ID	1837	Sophia Duncan	Charles Duncan	Mahala Abercrombie	Gordon & Darcas Duncan	Mahala Abercrombie
13657	Duncan, William	CA	1879	Mattie Duncan	Alfred Duncan	Lucy Murphy	Caleb & Mary Duncan	
16191	Dunham, John	TX	1871	Mary Dunham	Elija Dunham	Anie Pitman	Richard & Comfort Dunham	Danil Pitman
9196	Dunlap, Lela	OK	1886	Carl Dunlap	Kinchen Matthews	Mary McBee	Lagrus & Jane Matthews	John & Katie McBee
22673	Dunlop, Ora	IN	1881	Clarence Dunlop	Frank Henderson	Victoria Hammonds		Thomas & Delaney Hammonds
13722*	Dunn, Amanda	GA	1849	Sam Dunn	Ned Brown	Martha Bly	Cue & Tilla Tiffens	Wilkerson & Hannah Bly
13723*	Dunn, Charley	GA	1870	Soffie Dunn	Carl McKinney	Amanda Brown	Bose & Huldy McKinney	Ned & Martha Brown
8478	Dunn, Elihu	WV	1867	Susan Dunn	Junius Dunn	Milley Blevins	Armstrong Blevins	Catharine Blevins
20665*	Dunn, Jennie	TN	1865	Richard Dunn	More Map	Sulla King		Kelly & Hettie King
16057	Dunn, Laura	TX	1880	C H Dunn	Doctor Baize		Joseph & Mary Baize	Joseph & Mary Hundley
8476	Dunn, Lee	WV	1880	Amy Dunn	Junia Dunn	Milley Blevins	Armstrong Blevins	Catharine Blevins
15730*	Dunn, Lucinda	GA	1846	Edward Dunn	Isaac Waters	Millie Waters		Mollie ?
21061	Dunn, Mae	GA	1872	Ida Dunn	William Dunn	Mary Weathers	Daniel Dunn	Mac & Rosa Weathers
19218	Dunn, Maudie	KS	1885	W.W. Dunn	Grant Dons	Elizabeth Sizemore		James Sizemore
21838	Dunn, Nancy	TN	1879	Thomas Dunn	Joshua Colville	Harriett Ware		
6713	Dunn, Rachel	OK	1845	William Dunn	Samuel Wood	Elizabeth Bennett	Johnathan Wood & Mary Bryant	Hardy Bennett & Mittie York
20362*	Dunn, Richard	TN	1856	Jennie Dunn	Isaac Dunn	Martha Billips		George & Lucy Billips
8477	Dunn, Roby	WV	1873	Lucinda Dunn	Junia Dunn	Milley Blevins	Armstrong Blevins	Catharine Blevins
5500	Dunn, Teney	AR	1860	Osbemy Dunn (decd)	Calloway Sizemore	Nancy Davis	Edward & Polly Sizemore	
6712	Dunn, William	OK	1847	Rachel Dunn	Allen Dunn	Emiline McCamish	Wm Dunn & Rebecca Hedrick	Robt McCamish & Mary Moore
21915	Dunning, Laura	TN	1882	Berry Dunning	George Colbaugh	Velma Davis	Henry & Mary Colbaugh	Wm & Dicey Davis
22455	Dunsmore, Joseph	TN	1820	Lydia Dunsmore	William Dunsmore	Margeret Myers	Samuel & Lizzie Dunsmore	Christopher Myers
22456	Dunsmore, Lydia	TN	1830	Joseph Dunsmore	Thomas Roper	Kate Sinocs	William & Muky Roper	John & Ginsey Sinocs
14532	Dupree, Charley	GA	1871	Isabella Dupree	Thad Dupree	Francis Cole	Griffin & Juda Dupree	John & Betsy Cole
14531	Dupree, John	GA	1869	Susan Dupree	Thad Dupree	Francis Cole	Griffin & Juda Dupree	John & Betsy Cole
14530	Dupree, Joshua	GA	1873	Hester Dupree	Thad Dupree	Francis Cole	Griffin & Juda Dupree	John & Betsy Cole
14529	Dupree, Marion	GA	1860	Amanda Dupree	Thad Dupree	Francis Cole	Griffin & Juda Dupree	John & Betsy Cole

#	Name	State	Year					
14528	Dupree, Oscar	GA	1880	Martha Dupree	Thad Dupree	Francis Cole	Griffin & Juda Dupree	John & Betsy Cole
21970	Durham, Annie	GA	1883	Thomas Durham	John Pilgrim	Emma Haynes	Harlin & Nancy Pilgrim	Hezekiah & Julia Haney
21972	Durham, Carrie	GA	1901		Thomas Durham	Annie Pilgrim	Martha Durham	John & Emma Pilgrim
21973	Durham, John	GA	1903		Thomas Durham	Annie Pilgrim	Martha Durham	John & Emma Pilgrim
20720	Durham, Malissa	TN	1878	George Durham	John Smith	Thedocie C ?	Eli & Jane Smith	
17755	Durham, Nancy	GA	1875	Wade Durham	John Holt	Manerva Baker	Rhoda Holt	James & Charlotte Baker
21971	Durham, Robert	GA	1906		Thomas Durham	Annie Pilgrim	Martha Durham	John & Emma Pilgrim
20186	Durham, Ruthey	AL		Frances Durham	Hezakiah Haney	Juliann Wilson	James & Matilda Haney	Wm & Caroline Wilson
17013	Duval, Charley	OK	16yrs		Oscar Duval	Ahle wee dah	Joe & Polly Duval	Ah le wee dah & Lucy
6136	Duvall, Cora	NC	1883	William Duvall	Robbert Debard	Mary Sexton	Benjamin & Elizabeth Debord	Rubin & Easter Sexton
15052	Duvall, Fannie	OK	1895		Jo Duvall	Francis Roberts	Logan & Nellie Duvall	Wm & Magie Roberts
15051	Duvaul, Jessie	OK	1898		Joe Duvall	Nancy Olaughlien	Logan & Nellie Duvall	James & Maggie Olaughlien
17273	Dye, Amanda	VA		Charles Dye	R. T. Taylor	Mary Lyles	Robert & Catherine Taylor	George & Margaret Lyles
7540	Dye, Dora	OK	1877	Lee Dye	Joseph Jourdan	Sarah Blackburn	Aquilla & Betsey Jourdan	Andrew & Francis Blackburn
13857	Dye, Laura	WV		John Dye	Kiah Billips	Rena Sizemore	James & Nancy Billips	George & Jenny Sizemore
21555	Dykes, Joseph	GA	1871	Annie Dykes	Spencer Dykes	Nancy Redmond	Solomon & Polley Dykes	Sandy Redmond
15159	Dykes, M.W.	GA	1869	Lou Dykes	Spencer Dykes	Nancy Redmon	Solomon & Charlotte Dykes	Sandy & Mary Redmon
2541	Dyson, Cyntha	NC	1850	none	Jacson Dyson	Eada Malbba	William & Polley Dyson	
2537	Dyson, Elizabeth	NC	1853	John Dyson	Solman Dyson	Polley Malbba	William & Polley Dyson	
2538	Dyson, James	NC	1885	Villet Dyson	John Dyson	Elizabeth Dyson	Solmar & Polley Dyson	Jacson & Miley Dyson
2532	Dyson, John	NC	1854	Elizabeth Dyson	Jackson Dyson	Miley Malba	William & Polly Dyson	
2540	Dyson, John	NC	1854	Elizabeth Dyson	Jacson Dyson	Miley Molba		
14368	Dyson, Lindsey	NC	1883		Jacson Dyson	Elizabeth Dyson	Solomon & Polly Dyson	Jackson & Milly Dyson
2533	Dyson, Lousinda	NC	1847	none	Solomon Dyson	Polley Mallba	William & Polly Dyson	
2535	Dyson, Marcus	NC	1884	none	John Dyson	Merry Dyson	Salmar & Polly Dyson	Jacson & Milly Dyson
9568	Dyson, Mary	NC	1862	none	Solman Dyson	Polley Marble	Wm & Polley Dyson	
2534	Dyson, Susan	NC	1886	none	James Andrews	Lucinda Dyson		
2536	Dyson, Violet	NC	1887	James Dyson	Bartlett McGee	Lucinda Dyson		Solmon & Poley Dyson
2539	Dyson, Zero	NC	1879	none	John Dyson	Elizabeth Dyson	Salmar & Polley Dyson	Jacson & Miley Dyson

ID	Name	State	Year					
19995	Eades, Carrie	GA	1880	Edgar Eades	John Bryan	Martha Johnson	James & Elizabeth Bryan	Wm & Elizabeth Blake
16173	Eades, Isaac	OK	1850	Alice Eades	John Eades	Nancy Durham	John & Dolotha Eades	
13841 *	Ealey, Chainey	OK	68yrs	Henry Ealey	Mitchel Cherokee	Sallie		
13840 *	Ealey, Henry	OK	75yrs	Chainy Ealey	George Ealey	Ann Hudson		
13362	Earl, Sadia	KS	1862	Lincoln Earl	James Perry			
2592	Early, Amanda	GA	1879	John Early	John Beaver	Mary Davenport		John & Elisabeth Davenport
13539	Early, Mattie	AR	1872	John Early	Cyrus Hathaway	Cenie Bell	Cyrus & Ann Hathaway	Wm & Nancie Bell
436 *	Earnest, Mary E.	IL	1855	Robert Earnest	Square Williamson	Harriett Adams	Elisha & Charity Williamson	Tony Adams
19953	East, Alpha	NC	1886		Ben Booth	Alphia Booth	Ben Booth	Elizabeth Booth
19952	East, Cary	NC	1884	William East	William Revels	Caroline Pace	Jordan Revels	Polly Bryant
19133	East, Charlie	GA	1877	Annie East	Francis East	Peggy Chitwood	Daniel East	
18247	East, Francis	GA	1851	Jane East	Daniel East	Betsy Eubanks	Harvey East	
19134	East, James	GA	1872	May East	Francis East	Peggy Chitwood	Daniel East	
19135	East, William	GA	1875	Bell East	Francis East	Peggy Chitwood	Daniel East	
8555	Eastep, Lillie	VA	1889	George Estep	Eli Blevins	Margarett Ruper	Shubal & Ada Blevins	
18041 *	Easterling, Bertha	GA	1870	Jim Easterling	Robert Sharks	Sylva Coleman	Robert & Bertha Sharks	Gil Code & Flora Coleman
18161 *	Easterling, William	GA	1833	Rebecca Easterling	Isaac Furlow	Isabella Easterling		
14560	Eaton, Jesse	GA	1854	Biltha Eaton	Andrew Eaton	Rutha Biddy	James Eaton	Mashack & Nancy Biddy
22333 *	Eaton, Nettie	OK	1869	Thomas Eaton	Stephen Lynch	Peggie Christy	Henry & Judy Blackburn	Esseck
22349 *	Eaton, Thomas	OK	1861	Nettie Eaton	Phil Barker	Rachel Eaton	Ezekel Eaton	
509	Eaves, Coy	MO	1887	none	Elijah Eaves	Emma Brown	James Eaves	Vitely Hambelton
35	Eaves, Elijah	MO	1863	widower	James Eaves	Viletty Hamletton	Palie & Pollie Eanes	Elijah & Sally Hamletton
506	Eaves, Lester	MO	1895	none	Elijah Eaves	Emma Brown	James Eaves	Villetty Hambelton
507	Eaves, Lillie	MO	1889	none	Elijah Eaves	Emma Brown	James Eaves	Villetty Hambelton
10430	Eaves, Rosa	OK	1880	Jack Eaves	Jefferson Latta	Harriet Robinson		Emsi Robinson
3200	Eaves, William	MO	1868	Oxlena & Lola Eaves	James Eaves	Vilety Hambeliton	Patric & Polly Eaves	Elijah & Sally Hambeliton
15744 *	Eberhart, Sallie	GA	1840	Van Eberhart	Joe Hollands	America Hughes		Sandy & Lucinda Hughes
14303 *	Eccles, Wesley	NC	1862	Ellen Eccles	Alexander Eccles	Lucinda London	Elija & Nancy Eccles	James & Susan London
21205	Echols, Elijah	AL	1833	Emma Echols	Bradley Echols	Betsy Peak		
21207	Echols, Emma	AL	1871	Elijah Echols	William Wright	Lettie Tyler		Gabrel Tyler & Celia Johnson
21206	Echols, Ida	AL	1868	Joseph Echols	William Wright	Lettie Tyler		Gabrel Tyler & Celia Johnson

1672	Eddings, Andrew	OK	1840	widower	Evan Eddings	Malinda Culp	John & Elizabeth Eddings	Joseph & Hettie Culp
8836	Eddings, James	IL	1850		James Eddings	Roda West	John & Francis Eddings	James West
11369	Eddings, James	IL	1856	Mariah Eddings	Jesse Eddings	Mary Middleton	John & Francis Eddings	Joel & Elisabeth Middleton
7529	Eddings, Jasper	KS	1883	none	William Eddings	Emma Snow	James & Roda Eddings	Thomas & Mary Snow
5829	Eddings, Jesse	IL	1856	Eliza Eddings	James Eddings	Roda West		
8837	Eddings, John	IL	1843	none	James Eddings	Roda West	John & Francis Eddings	James West
22765	Eddings, John	KS	1877	May Eddings	Josiah Eddings	Polly Myser	Richard & Elizabeth Eddings	Henry & Mary Myser
1671	Eddings, Josiah	OK	1844	Polly Eddings dec'd	Richard Eddings	Betsy Melton	John & Elizabeth Eddings	John & Marie Melton
2370	Eddings, Levi	OK	1836		Juan Eddings	Malinda Culp	John & Elizabeth Eddings	
7769	Eddings, Maggie	OK	1877	W C Eddings	Isaac Hobbs	Ava Oxford	James & Mary Hobbs	
11376	Eddings, Newton	IL	1850	Delily Eddings	Jesse Eddings	Mary Middleton	John & Francis Eddings	Joel & Elisabeth Middleton
11373	Eddings, Wesley	IL	1867	Mary Eddings	Jesse Eddings	Janie Middleton	John & Francis Eddings	Joel & Elisabeth Middleton
11370	Eddings, William	IL	1858	Mary Eddings	Jesse Eddings	Mary Middleton	John & Francis Eddings	Joel & Elisabeth Middleton
17523	Eddleman, Mary	OK	1848	D.J. Eddleman	James Daugherty	Eleanor McGeehee	Wm & Sallie Daugherty	
19060	Edelman, Isabella	OK	1866	B. Edelman	Henry Barnes	Sarah Clark	A.O.W. & Sophronie Barnes	Samuel & Lucindy Clark
20149	Edge, Arey	GA	1866	John Edge	A.J. Smith	Patsey Bowen	Elija & Margret Smith	Nat & Jennie Swaney
14998	Edge, Harry	OK	1874	Millie Edge	Sah dus cut	Une nut	Jah ah she	Bill Chisholm
15158	Edge, Isaac	GA	1866	Ida Edge	John Edge	Sarah Spears		Josiah & Martha Spears
15157	Edge, Richard	GA	1875	Louisa Edge	John Edge	Sarah Spears		Josiah & Martha Spears
15156	Edge, Sarah	GA		John Edge	Josiah Spears	Martha McKissiah	James & Docia Spears	
15000	Edge, Stanley	OK	1873	Pauline Edge	Sah dus cut	Une not	Jah ah she	Bill Chisholm
15155	Edge, Thomas	GA	1877	Missouri Edge	John Edge	Sarah Spears		Josiah & Martha Spears
17557	Edmason, Ider	TN			Bennett Franklin	Ider Franklin	Gardner Green	
5403	Edmisten, George	MO	1850	Julia Edmisten	Rufus Edmisten	Nancy Robinson		Betsey Elliott Robinson
5521	Edmisten, Lockie	VA	1871	Jesse Edmisten	Charles Blevins	Millie Ham	James & Margret Blevins	Joshua & Elizabeth Ham
18982	Edmonds, Febie	TN	1846	Bart Edmonds	William Price	Mary Ball	Thomas & Telitha Price	Osborn & Martha Ball
215	Edmonds, Susannah	MO	1843	Henry Edmonds	Joseph England	Sabra Coapis	Bill & Susan England	Benjamin Coapis
11099	Edmondson, Delila	VA	1876	Thomas Edmondson	William Blevins	Elizabeth Blevins	Jessie & Catherine Blevins	James & Margret Blevins
11056	Edmondson, Isaac	VA	1884		Isaac Edmondson	Milly Blevins		Jessee & Catharine Blevins
19254	Edmondson, James	WV		Luvena Edmondson	Isaac Edmondson	Martha Blevins	Andrew & Susan Edmondson	Wells & Elizabeth Blevins

9052	Edmondson, John	TN	1870	Mary Edmondson	Isaac Edmondson	Martha Blevins		Wells & Elizabeth Blevins
8492	Edmondson, Kern	WA	1878	Hulda Edmondson		Milley Blevins		Jesse & Catharine Blevins
11055	Edmondson, Lucinda	VA	1890		Isaac Edmondson	Milly Blevins	Andrew & Susan Edmondson	Jessee & Catharine Blevins
19255	Edmondson, Luvenia	WV		J.W. Edmondson	Calvin Blevins	Mary Simmons	James & Necy Blevins	James & Anna Simmons
11054	Edmondson, Rhoda	VA	1886		Isaac Edmondson	Milly Blevins	Andrew & Susan Edmondson	Jessee & Catharine Blevins
6847	Edmondson, William	VA	1868	Evaline Edmondson	Isaac Edmondson	Martha Blevins	Andrew & Susan Edmondson	Wells & Elisabeth Blevins
15871*	Edmonson, Puss	TN	1835	Rubin Canady	Gilbert Vanleer	Violet Vanleer		
15474	Edwards, Abraham	GA	1868	Lula Edwards	William Edwards	Catherine Dowdy	Thomas & Agnes Edwards	Robert & Polly Dowdy
15473	Edwards, Alfred	GA	1859	Cintha Edwards	William Edwards	Catherine Dowdy	Thomas & Agnes Edwards	Robert & Polly Dowdy
20786	Edwards, Andrew	GA	1892		A.L. Edwards	Sarah Cook	Wm & Catherine Edwards	John & Mary Cook
18248*	Edwards, Celantha	GA	1877	Will Edwards	Henry Findley	Fanny Vann		Pate & Miley Vann
4096	Edwards, Celia	VA	1887				Washington & Elisabeth Finley	Elisha & Nancy Hart
12248	Edwards, Doska	NC	1873	H P Edwards	Aaron Osborne	Martha Garel	John & Polly Osborne	
15472	Edwards, Forest	GA	1880	Minnie Edwards	Alfred Edwards	Cintha Crow	Wm & Catharine Edwards	
20787	Edwards, Henry	GA	1862	Emma Edwards	William Edwards	Catherine Dowdy	Thomas & Agnes Edwards	Robert Dowdy
20788	Edwards, Henry	GA	1880	Mamie Edwards	Joseph Edwards	Marthie Crow	Wm & Catharine Edwards	Miles & Sallie Crow
20789	Edwards, James	GA	1895		A.L. Edwards	Sarah Cook	Wm & Catherine Edwards	John & Mary Cook
20790	Edwards, John	GA	1890		A.L. Edwards	Sarah Cook	Wm & Catherine Edwards	John & Mary Cook
21376	Edwards, John	OK	1861	Mary Edwards	George Edwards	Loana Lumpkins	James & Elizabeth Edwards	Bushnod & Mary Lumpkins
15471	Edwards, Joseph	GA	1856	Martha Edwards	William Edwards	Catherine Dowdy	Thomas & Agnes Edwards	Robert & Polly Dowdy
21460	Edwards, Joseph	OK	1885	Silva Edwards	John Edwards	Mary Houston	George & Loenie Edwards	Joseph & Martha Houston
13038	Edwards, Julia	OK	1867	J W Edwards	Arch Martin	Rachel Sanders	Joseph & Julia Martin	Isaac & Jane Sanders
15470	Edwards, Lewis	GA	1878	Ora Edwards	Alfred Edwards	Cintha Crow	Wm & Catharine Edwards	
10481	Edwards, Lilly	GA	1861	Jasper Edwards	John Robinson	Lucindy Leatherwood		Saml & Lizbeth Leatherwood
21375	Edwards, Loana	OK	1840	George Edwards	Bushnod Lumpkin	Mary Martin	George & Mary Lumpkin	Joshua & Sarah Martin
15154	Edwards, Martha	GA	1871	Berry Edwards	John Edge	Sarah Spears		Josiah & Martha Spears
20214	Edwards, Naomi	NC	1873	Rufus Edwards	Gabriel Denny	Sarah Stone	Joel & Nancy Denny	Frank & Sarah Stone
10833	Edwards, Nettie	IN		J A Edwards	Thomas Allen	Mary Stout	John & Martha Allen	Robert Stout & Jane Pierce
966	Edwards, Rachel	OK	1827	none	Richard Wilkerson	Nancy Powell		
13969	Edwards, Sarah	OK	1865	Paul Edwards	William Cathey	Martha Clary	George & Pollie Cathey	

20791	Edwards, Sarah	GA	1871	A.L. Edwards	John Cook	Mary Ragan	James Cook & Louvica Carns	
21459	Edwards, Silvie	OK	1889	Joseph Edwards	William Riggs	Samantha Wattman	James & Louisa Riggs	Johnson & Martha Wattman
1398	Edwards, Stephen	OK	1854		Abraham Edwards	Minervia Fleetwood		Chas & Lucinda Fleetwood
1249	Edwards, Susanna	MO	1849	Henry Edwards	Joseph England	Satsa Coapes	Bill & Susa England	Ben & Patty Coates
20792	Edwards, W.H.	GA	1888		A.L. Edwards	Sarah Cook	Wm & Catherine Edwards	John & Mary Cook
15469	Edwards, William	GA	1825	Catherine Edwards	Thomas Edwards	Agnes Carnes	Joseph & Joycey Edwards	Hubbard Carnes
1011	Edwardy, Mrs. Albert	GA	1890	Cecil Edwardy	Jeramiah Pilgrim	May Stoffregen	Elijah & Rhoda Pilgrim	H G & Henrietta Stoffregen
14999	Edye, Mary	OK	1895		Chah pony	Une nut		Bill Chisholm
1467	Eggers, Amanda	NC	1879	Jackson Eggers	William Candill	Elizabeth Thompson	Samuel & Mary Candill	Wesley & Amandy Thompson
2020	Eggers, Emma	NC	1875	J C Eggers	John Constant	Elizabeth Delozier		Ed & Elizabeth Delozier
8501	Eggers, Etta	LA	1869	Abner Eggers	Noah Blevins	Catharine Dolinger	Allen & Fanny Blevins	John & Betty Dolinger
7144	Eidson, Ben	TX	1880	Beulah Eidson	James Eidson	Virginia Avants		Thomas & Francis Avants
7768	Eidson, Fannie	TX	1886	none	James Eidson	Jinnie Avants	Orn & Mary Eidson	Thomas & Francis Avants
7143	Eidson, George	TX	1878	none	James Eidson	Jinnie Avants	Orn & Mary Eidson	Thomas & Francis Avants
7139	Eidson, James	TX	1851	Jennie Eidson	Isom Eidson	Mary Herring	James Eidson & Rhoda Blakely	Y. Herring
7765	Eidson, Jinnie	TX	1861	James Eidson	Thomas Avants	Francis Stovall	Peter Avants	
7767	Eidson, Nora	TX	1884	none	James Eidson	Jinnie Avants	Orn & Mary Eidson	Thomas & Francis Avants
7766	Eidson, William	TX	1877	Mattie Eidson	James Eidson	Jinnie Avants	Orn & Mary Eidson	Thomas & Francis Avants
15717	Eiffert, Susan	OK	1851	Henry Eiffert	Richard Thompson	Elizabeth Thornton	William Thompson	Amos Thornton
21760	Eldridge, John	AR	1883	Lizzie Eldridge	Louis Eldridge	Nannie Derossette	Ransom & Mary Eldridge	Sam & Martha Derossette
21761	Eldridge, Louis	AR	1859	Susie Eldridge	Ransom Eldridge	Mary Andrews		
7141	Eldridge, Lula	OK	1885	James Eldridge	William Stripling	Louisa Davis		Richard Davis & Martha Holcomb
13386	Elk, Samuel	OK	22yrs	Nannie Elk	William Elk	Mary Harly	Elk	Creek Charley & Marley
4313	Eller, Celia	NC	1864	Joshua Eller	Thomas Jones	Tamsey Thompson	Johnathan & Nancy Jones	Christopher & Salley Thompson
492	Eller, Daisy	NC	1878	John Eller	Jesse Plummer	Frances Stamper	Plummer	Stamper
15153	Elliot, Almeda	GA	1861	James Elliot	Archie Vernon	Jane Hayes	Nehemiah & Elizabeth Vernon	Stephen & Nancy Hayes
18136	Elliott, Andrew	TN			Thomas Elliott	Sarah Morrison	John & Mary Elliott	F. & Mary Morrison
18135	Elliott, Arthur	TN	1903		Thomas Elliott	Sarah Morrison	John & Mary Elliott	F. & Mary Morrison

5169	Elliott, Helen	VA	1851	Henry Elliott	Phinea Tompkins	Hannah Ross	Isaac Tompkins & Helen Backus	Templin Ross & Eliza Sevier
8833	Elliott, Jacob	MO	1866	Sarah Elliott	John Elliott	Rebecca Willson	Jonas & Nancy Elliott	Soloman & Elizabeth Willson
18133	Elliott, James	TN	1905		Thomas Elliott	Sarah Morrison	John & Mary Elliott	F. & Mary Morrison
20268	Elliott, James	OK			Francis Elliott	Lenora Grow		
3593	Elliott, Julia	NC	1877	Drury Elliott	George Fritts	Melvina Thompson	Rubin & Kissey Fritts	Wesley & Amanda Thompson
7140	Elliott, Lenora	OK	1840		Annois Grow	Sallie Helterbrand		
17881	Elliott, Lota	OK			Francis Elliott	Linora Grow		
16394	Elliott, Lottie	OK	1864	John Elliott	George Case	Lucinda Stull	George & Lottie Case	Jacob & Rachel Stull
18167*	Elliott, Malissa	WI	1871	John Elliott			McCaga & Norman Revels	Mike & Polly Waldon
18134	Elliott, Marion	TN	1906		Thomas Elliott	Sarah Morrison	John & Mary Elliott	F. & Mary Morrison
15655	Elliott, Mary	GA	1880	W A Elliott	Jeff Lathem	Sufrona Bryant	George & Jane Lathem	Geten & Sallie Bryant
18131	Elliott, Mary	TN	1897		Thomas Elliott	Sarah Morrison	John & Mary Elliott	F. & Mary Morrison
18130	Elliott, Minnie	TN	1899		Thomas Elliott	Sarah Morrison	John & Mary Elliott	F. & Mary Morrison
7770	Elliott, Orra	OK	1880	Mary Elliott	Francis Elliott	Lenora Gum		
18132	Elliott, Samuel	TN	1895		Thomas Elliott	Sarah Morrison	John & Mary Elliott	F. & Mary Morrison
10109	Elliott, Stephen	WV	1885	Gussie Elliott	W R Elliott	Lydia Sizemore	John & Sarah Elliott	Jessie & Nancy Sizemore
18137	Elliott, Thomas	OK	1874	Sarah Elliott	John Elliott	Mary Phillpott	John & Nancy Elliott	Barton & Catharine Phillpott
2010	Ellis, Alfred	MO	1862	Minnie Ellis	Eleander Ellis	Mary Martin	Wm Martin	Susan Wolf
5419	Ellis, Alfred	MO	1862	Winnie Ellis	Alexander Ellis	Mary Martin	Isaac Ellis	Wm & Susan Martin
6783	Ellis, Etta	MO	1870	Alfred Ellis	Jim Stephens	Mary Hall	Green & Nancy Stephens	Alfred & Mahala Hall
16768	Ellis, Francis	OK	1873		J H Bowens	Malinda Sutton		Mary Sutton
19467	Ellis, Harvy	GA	1869	Elizabeth Ellis	Thomas Ellis	Margret Shaffer	John Tucker	
4093	Ellis, Ida	VA	51yrs	James Ellis	Armstrong Blevins	Catherine Blevins	James Blevins	Lydda Blevins
3998	Ellis, Lizzie	OK	35yrs	John Ellis		Mary Jumper		
11282	Ellis, Mary	NC	1881	William Ellis	Curtis Brooks	Polly Wagoner		Henry Sizemore
20595	Ellis, Nancy	TN	1873		Samuel Ellis	Frankie Lecroy	Moses & Rachel Ellis	Jackson & Martha Lecroy
20605	Ellis, Robert	TN	1867	Lucinda Ellis	Husee Ellis	Frankie Lecroy	Moses & Rachel Ellis	Jackson & Martha Lecroy
20433	Ellis, Thomas	TN	1858	Sarah Ellis	Hersey Ellis	Frankie Lecroy	Moses & Rachel Ellis	Jackson & Martha Lecroy
4762	Ellis, William	AR	1852	Mary Ellis	Alexander Ellis	Mary Martin	Isaac Ellis	Wm & Susan Martin
20641	Ellis, Winslow	TN	1870	Margaret Ellis	John Ellis	Elizabeth Bush	Moses & Rachel Ellis	Calvin & Elizabeth Bush

11959*	Ellison, Amanda	GA	1845	widow	Anderson Jones	Clarah Hay		Frank & Penninie McCluster
17777	Ellison, Mary	TN	1869		Shade Lofte	Martha Killian		Wm Killian
7138	Elmore, Dovey	MO	1868	none	John Elmore	Sally Harris	James & Sallie Elmore	Alfred & Polly Harris
20221	Elmore, Earl	IN	1875	Cleo Elmore	Richard Elmore	Rachel Reed	John & Mary Elmore	Isaac & Hannah Reed
12077	Elmore, Jesse	KS	1880		John Elmore	Grace Wilson	Jesse & Jane Elmore	Andrew & Mary Wilson
8227	Elmore, John	KS	1847	Grace Elmore	Jesse Elmore	Jane Newman	Archelis & Nancy Elmore	Jarred & Margaret Newman
9352	Elmore, Newman	KS	1885	none	John Elmore	Grace Wilson	Jesse & Jane Elmore	Andrew & Mary Wilson
20019	Elmore, Richard	IN	1851	Rachel Elmore	John Elmore	Mary Mills	Thomas Elmore	Nathan & Betsey Mills
8226	Elmore, Walter	MO	1876	none	John Elmore	Grace Wilson	Jesse & Jane Elmore	Andrew & Mary Wilson
20793	Elrod, Augustus	GA	1870	Mary Elrod	Joseph Elrod	Jane Davis		Wm & Alantha Davis
20794	Elrod, Charles et al	GA	1889		Augustus Elrod	Mary Edge	Joseph & Jane Elrod	
20795	Elrod, George	GA	1879	Bessie Elrod	Joseph Elrod	Jane Davis		Wm & Alantha Davis
20087	Elrod, John & Jeanette	GA	1903 1905		Joseph Elrod	Berta Stubbs	Joseph & Jane Elrod	
20086	Elrod, Joseph	GA	1876	Berta Elrod	Joseph Elrod	Jane Davis		Wm & Alantha Davis
20796	Elrod, Mack	GA	1904		George Elrod	Bessie McEvie	Joseph & Jane Elrod	
17431	Elrod, Nancy	GA	1862	Jesse Elrod	Jim Brown	Sarah Summers	Jim & Cary Brown	
11751	Elrod, Samuel	TN	1859	Lousina Elrod	Jacob Elrod	Mausioury Benton	Samuel Elrod	Patsey Benton
15468	Elrodd, Goodman	GA	1890		Jackson Elrodd	Sarah Dover	Peter & Kate Elrodd	Wm & Alantha Dover
15467	Elrodd, Marlin	GA	1892		Jackson Elrodd	Sarah Dover	Peter & Kate Elrodd	Wm & Alantha Dover
15466	Elrodd, Richard	GA	1886		Jackson Elrodd	Sarah Dover	Peter & Kate Elrodd	Wm & Alantha Dover
15465	Elrodd, Sarah	GA	1848	Jackson Elrodd	William Dover	Alantha Chambers		James Chambers & Polly Buff
15464	Elrodd, William	GA	1875		Jackson Elrodd	Sarah Dover	Peter & Kate Elrodd	Wm & Alantha Dover
18207	Embrey, George	AL	1862	Mary Embrey	George Embrey	Elizabeth Sutton	James Embrey	John Sutton
19603	Embrey, John	AL	1874	Vicie Embrey	George Embrey	Elizabeth Sutton	Daniel Embrey	John & Patsey Sutton
2967	Emerson, Sarah	VA	1886	Dewit Emerson	James Hart	Franky Gaultney	Hugh & Easter Hart	Carpus & Creasy Gaultney
11244	Emery, Ida	IN	1871	Newton Emery	John Allen	Nancy Brower	John & Martha Allen	
20112*	Emline Carlton & Mary Butler	GA	1842 1857	Guss Carlton & Mathew Butler	Jack Fain	Patsie Heard		Buck & Patsie Heard
20594	Emory, Charlotte	TN	1862	Thomas Emory	Samuel Ellis	Frankie Lecroy	Moses & Rachel Ellis	Jackson & Martha Lecroy
3092	Engell, Mattie	MS	1870	Willie Engell	Jacob Kinerd	Martha Hobgood		Charles & Martha Hobgood
4638	England, Lucy	OK	1848	Charles England	Isaac Ragsdale	Mary Sanders	John & Ellen Ragsdale	Alex & Margarite Sanders

3225	England, Rebecca	OK	1850	widow				
3920	English, Mary	NC	1881	William English	Henry Metcalf	Sarah Crawford	Hiram & Jane Metcalf	Benson & Eda Crawford
6526	Enloe, Hugh	MO	1847	Harriette Enloe	Enoch Enloe	Jane Murray		
13892	Enloe, James	MO	1838	widower	Enoch Enloe	Jane Murray	James Enloe	Thomas Murray
13893	Enloe, John	MO	1858	Sarah Enloe	Enoch Enloe	Jane Murray	James Enloe	Thomas Murray
3437	Enzor, Joseph	AL	1869	Florence House	Jessie Enzor	Sallie Pardon	James & Betsy Enzor	Jones Pardon
19455	Enzor, Levitia	AL	1896		Joseph Enzor	Florence House	Jesse & Sallie Enzor	Wm & Martha House
19454	Enzor, Martha	AL	1899		Joseph Enzor	Florence House	Jesse & Sallie Enzor	Wm & Martha House
19450	Enzor, William	AL	1894		Joseph Enzor	Florence House	Jessie & Sallie Enzor	Wm & Martha House
22939	Epperson, Mary	OK	1897		James Epperson	Mattie Wood		John & Susan Wood
22940	Epperson, Mary	OK	1882	James Epperson	John Wood	Susan Gentry	Mary Wood	Mary Millen
17875	Erickson, Pheba	KS	1876	John Erickson	E.W. Crane	Elizabeth Bays		Josiah Bays & Letta Mays
18230	Erwin, Ella	TN	1853		W.A. Whitice	Eliza Reed	Wm & Mary Whitice	Josiah Reed
20836	Erwin, Joseph	GA	1852	Mary Erwin	Alex Erwin	Mary Horolel	Bill Erwin	Holmon Hearrell
20416	Erwin, Ruth	TN	1854		Andrew Erwin	Ella Whitice	Benj & Dicy Erwin	William & Eliza Whitice
20560	Erwin, William	TN	1877	Myrtle Erwin	Andrew Erwin	Ella Whitice	Benj & Dicey Erwin	Wm & Eliza Whitice
7142	Estes, John	OK	1863	Delia Estes	Cicero Estes	Adelia Miller	Joel Estes	
18147	Etis, Martha	GA	1867	Rubin Etis	Cader Stancel	Eliza Corbin	Jesse & Annie Stancel	
19723	Etres, Joe	GA	1861	Lidia Etres	Robert Etres	Mima Cordell		
20679	Etter, Hazel	GA			Owen Etter	Norah Brundage	Andrew & Julia Etter	William & Sarah Brundage
17943	Etter, Owen	GA	1871	Norah Etter	Andrew Etter	Julia Stancel	Peter & Frankie Etter	John & Sarah Stancel
16671	Eubanks, Birta	GA	1894		A R Eubanks	Polly Roy	John & Elvira Eubanks	Thomas & Julia Roy
16669	Eubanks, Lee	GA	1892		A R Eubanks	Polly Roy	John & Elvira Eubanks	Thomas & Julia Roy
16667	Eubanks, Lela	GA	1886		A R Eubanks	Polly Roy	John & Elvira Eubanks	Thomas & Julia Roy
16668	Eubanks, Marion	GA	1888		A R Eubanks	Polly Roy	John & Elvira Eubanks	Thomas & Julia Roy
5236	Eubanks, Polly	GA	1869	A R Eubanks	Thomas Roy	Julious Worly	Wm & Antha Roy	Federal Jackson & Elisabeth Worley
11339	Eubanks, Thomas	CA	1828	Charlotte & Jane	Johnathan Eubanks	Polly Pool		Clabom & Martha Pool
16670	Eubanks, Will	GA	1890		A R Eubanks	Polly Roy	John & Elvira Eubanks	Thomas & Julia Roy
17399	Evans, Abraham	TN	1851	Nannie Evans	Pleasant Evans	Mahala Caroer	William Evans	Wm & Agnes Caroer
22438	Evans, Ada	GA	1864	Jasper Evans	Joseph Parker	Irene Hardin	Johnathan & Oma Parker	Jacob & Millie Hardin
14527	Evans, Alonzo	GA	1878	Leona Evans	Ambrous Evans	Deranda Barnett	Robert & Sallie Evans	Richard & Rhoda Barnett
15152	Evans, Amos	GA	1886		Jim Evans	Polly Dover		Wm & Alantha Dover
15558 *	Evans, Anna	GA	1867	Louis Evans	Charles Morris	Cenie Webb	Joel & Rachel Morris	Dock Morris & Mira Webb

18012*	Evans, Bettie	TN	45yrs	Henry Evans	Albert Hamilton	Edith Ward	Matilda Hamilton	Berger Ward
21792	Evans, David	TN	1859	Florence Evans	Samuel Evans	Deborah Cobb		Fannie Coker
19747	Evans, Ebb	GA	1890		Robert Evans	Harriet Sutton	Robert & Sallie Evans	Abe & Eliza Sutton
18670	Evans, Eden	GA	1869	Wilce Evans	William Wade	Elizabeth Sosebee	David & Charity Wade	Wm & Nancy Sosebee
15174	Evans, Edith	OK	1864	Isaac Evans	Goerge Lloyd	Mary Wanslee	Thos & Susan Lloyd	Nathan & Izzie Wanslee
12267	Evans, Ellen	NC	1871		David Haney	Elizabeth Ledford	James Haney	Caroline Burnett
19108	Evans, George	AR	1849	Nancy Evans	Malachi Evans	Sarah Scarborough	Thomas Evans	
19736	Evans, George	GA	1880	Martha Evans	Robert Evans	Margaret Barnett	Robert & Sallie Evans	Richard & Rhoda Barnett
20893	Evans, George	OK	1849		Willis Evans	Mary Evans	J.H. Evans	
18801	Evans, Hattie	GA	1883		James Evans	Nancy Rainwater	Robert & Sallie Evans	John & Julia Rainwater
19748	Evans, James	GA	1874	Nancy Evans	Robert Evans	Margaret Barnett	Robert & Sallie Evans	Richard & Rhoda Barnett
20085	Evans, Jamima	NC	1861	Granville Evans	Zadok Osborn	Catherine Hoppers	Jesse & Cynthia Osborn	Jacob & Ekissie Hoppers
20025	Evans, Jesse	TN	1861	Dan Evans	Sam Evans	Deborah Cobb	Nathan Evans & Mary Storie	Jesse Cobb & Nettia Stephens
19746	Evans, John	GA	1872		Robert Evans	Margaret Barnett	Robert & Sallie Evans	Richard & Rhoda Barnett
21797	Evans, John	TN	1857	Meg Evans	Sam Evans	Deborah Cobb	Nathan Evans	
15151	Evans, Lien	GA	1878		Jim Evans	Polly Dover		Wm & Alantha Dover
14526	Evans, Marion	GA	1855	Ellie Evans	Robert Evans	Sallie Christopher	Robert & Haley Evans	Ambrous & Sallie Christopher
8605	Evans, Martha	GA	1878	Lester Evans	Marion Reece	Elizabeth Newman	James & Mary Reece	James & Sarah Newman
17845*	Evans, Martha	TN	1875	Charles Evans	Jack Mason	Jane Boyd		
18173*	Evans, Martha	TN		Charles Evans	Randle Moss	Rosie Toka		Sindy & Pashion Toka
17398	Evans, Martin	NC	1830			Polly Evans		
17382	Evans, Mary	GA	1873	Thomas Evans	H.M. Paris	Anna Townsend		Ezekiel Townsend
15150	Evans, Mary (Polly)	GA	1858	Jim Evans	William Dover	Alantha Chambers		Jim & Polly Chambers
15149	Evans, Matilda	GA	1888		Jim Evans	Polly Dover		Wm & Alantha Dover
10477	Evans, Minnie	AZ	1880	John Evans	George Lloyd	Mary Wanslee	Thos & Susan Lloyd	Nathan & Izzie Wanslee
21822	Evans, Mollie	FL	1860	Holden Evans	James Williams	Margaret Miles		James & Ellen Miles
17396	Evans, Nannie	TN	1859	Abraham Evans	James Kelley	Charlotta Evans	Wm & Nancy Kelley	Meeley Evans
21064	Evans, Nathaniel	TN		Emma Evans	Joshua Evans	Jane Cobb	Nathaniel Evans	Jess Cobb
14514	Evans, Rhoda	GA	1861	John Evans	Ambros Evans	Deranda Barnett	Robert & Sallie Evans	Richard & Rhoda Barnett
19741	Evans, Rhoda	GA	1861		Robert Evans	Margaret Barnett	Robert & Sallie Evans	Richard & Rhoda Barnett
19737	Evans, Richard	GA	1877	Sissy Evans	Robert Evans	Margaret Barnett	Robert & Sallie Evans	Richard & Rhoda Barnett
18802	Evans, Robert	GA	1881		James Evans	Nancy Rainwater	Robert & Sallie Evans	John & Julia Rainwater

19743	Evans, Robert	GA	1840	Harriet Evans	Robert Evans	Sallie Christopher	Robert Evans & Mahaly Welcher	Ambrose & Priscilla Christopher
21065	Evans, Samuel	TN	1865	Vania Evans	Joshua Evans	Jane Cobb	Nathun Evans	Jess Cobb
16123	Evans, Sarah	GA	1880	Jesse Evans	I M Minton	Jane Bailey	Riley & Betheny Minton	Isaac & Mandy Bailey
16175	Evans, Sarah	OK	1848	N E Evans	George Still	Jane Morgan	Andrew Still & Sally Bryant	Armstead Morgan & Delilah Moore
18182	Evans, Tennessee	TN	1870	George Evans	William Walker	Margaret Calvin	Bird & Frankie Walker	Thomas & Esther Calville
19740	Evans, Thomas	GA	1893		Robert Evans	Harriet Sutton	Robert & Sallie Evans	Abe & Eliza Sutton
16482 *	Evans, Washington	NC		Matilda Evans		Lucy M?		
15148	Evans, Wilce	GA	1883	Rachel Evans	Jim Evans	Polly Dover		Wm & Alantha Dover
19738	Evans, Will	GA	1895		Robert Evans	Harriet Sutton	Robert & Sallie Evans	Abe & Eliza Sutton
4572	Everett, George	TN	1834		George Everett	Easter White	Wm & Nancy Everett	John & Polley White
10780	Everett, Joseph	TN	1883	none	Joseph Everett	Kitty Jordan	George & Easter Everett	Susan Jordan
17161	Evett, Joseph	GA	1872	Ida Evett	William Evett	Margaret Williams		John & Jane Williams
13581 *	Fagan, Mary	GA	1881	J T Fagan	Frank Brown	Rose Tompson	Ned & Martha Brown	George & Mary Tompson
13731 *	Fagan, Mary gdn	GA	1881	J T Fagan	Frank Brown	Rose	Ned & Martha Brown	Georgia Brown
20106 *	Fain, Corine	GA	1865	Virgil Fain	Henry Bass	Catherine Anderson		Mariah
20105 *	Fain, Wiley	GA	1852	Georgia Fain	Jack Fain	Patsie Heard		Buck & Patsie Heard
4542	Faircloth, Christina	VA		F A Faircloth	George Hart	Polly Blevins	James & Catharine Hart	
8504	Faircloth, Franklin	KY	1863	Tennessee Faircloth	Thelbert Franklin	Cristeen Hart		George & Dolly Hart
8503	Faircloth, Jarvis	VA		Nancy Faircloth	Thelbert Faircloth	Cristeen Hart		George & Sally Hart
4544	Faircloth, Leanza	VA	1865	none	F A Faircloth	Christina Hart		George & Polly Hart
8507	Faircloth, Lemuel	KY	1853	Mary Faircloth	Thelbert Faircloth	Cristeen Hart		George & Sally Hart
4543	Faircloth, Millard	VA		Della Faircloth	F A Faircloth	Christina Hart		George & Polly Hart
18947	Faister, Lucy	GA	1879	Alfred Faister	William Parker	Marcena Mears	Abner & Millie Parker	Marion & Lucy Mears
20891	Falkner, Nancy	AL	1856	Issac Falkner	John Warren	Abigil Green		
17410	Fallen, Samuel	OK	1878		Alex Fallen	Dolly Hinsley	Ellis & Elizabeth Fallen	Samuel Hinsley
19850	Fallen, Willie et al	NC	1900		W.L. Fallen	Alice Donathan	Henry Fallen	
19942	Fallin, Mary	NC		M.L. Fallin	Henry Fallin	Emly Oshborn	Lark Donathan	Vina Holyfield
9797	Falling, Wilson	OK	1852	Katie Falling	Garle-gar-loaskie	Nelly		
18766	Falls, Nancy	GA	1874	Agustus Falls	Nathaniel Dotson	Ellen Willwood		
17098	Falls, Thomas et al	TN	1887		Robert Falls	Nancy Melton	Thomas & N.L. Falls	John & Sarah Melton
22772 *	Fambro, Francis	GA	1844	Martin Fambro	Barney Smith	Mary Collins		Abram & Edith Collins

22920	Fargo, Isaac	OK	1881	Maud Fargo	Charles Fargo	Narcicia Pernell		
22800	Fargo, Robert	OK	1872		Charles Fargo	Narcicia Parnell		
11818	Farington, Susie	NC	1874	William Farington	Ephram Osborne	America Osborne	Jesse & Syntha Osborne	Joseph & Susie Bare
7245	Farland, Lizzie	KS	1874	J M Farland	Lakin Davis	Mary Cunnengham	Henry & Hariett Davis	
9090	Farley, Cansas	WV	1866	M G Farley	David Brinegar	Sarah Osborn	Jacob & Sheba Brinegar	Jesse Osborn
9098	Farley, Emiline	WV	1863	J H Farley	David Brinegar	Sarah Osborn	Jacob & Sheba Brinegar	Jesse Osborn
7597	Farley, Martha	NC	37yrs	Willie Farley	Joel Payne	Nancy Holingshead	Asa & Nancy Payne	
10229	Farley, N E C	WV	1872	J A Farley	Newma Walker	Adaline Sizemore	Chris Walker & Frankie Peters	John Sizemore & Frankie Arms
10136	Farley, Nancy	WV	1849	James Farley	Nathaniel Perdew	Sallie Sizemore	Sallie Blankenship	Ned Sizemore & Annie Baldwin
9767	Farmer, Arthor	VA	1883	Carrie Farmer	Wiley Farmer	Lydia Miller	Henry & Nancy Farmer	Israel & Bashebe Miller
19936	Farmer, Arthur, Elin	NC	1901 1903		Rufus Farmer	C.V. Hicks	Patrick & Ana Farmer	Pless & Leta Gibson
19512	Farmer, Charles	AR	1874	Rosa Farmer	William Farmer	Eliza Hart	Pleas & Sarah Farmer	Anthony & Francis Hart
6843	Farmer, Deemy	VA	32yrs	J.H. Farmer	Calvin Davis	Matilda Pennington		Andrew & Hesther Pennington
4091	Farmer, Harrison	WV	1884	Sallie Farmer	Marshal Farmer	Tamsy May	Calvin & Bethany Farmer	John & Nancy May
19957	Farmer, James	NC	1876	Letta Farmer	Patrick Farmer	Smira Gibson	Daniel & Polly Farmer	Pess & Litha Gibson
4828	Farmer, Lydia	VA	1872	Noah Farmer		Bethany Thompson		Samuel & Marget Thompson
4092	Farmer, Marshal	WV	42yrs	Tamsy Farmer	Calvin Farmer	Bethany Thompson	Catherine Farmer	Sam & Margaret Thompson
19935	Farmer, Rufus	NC	1879	C.V. Farmer	Patrick Farmer	Smira Gibson	Daniel Farmer & Polly Jackson	Pless & Letha Gibson
19958	Farmer, Susan	NC	1903		James Farmer	Letta Nelson	Patrick & Smira Farmer	Ples & Litha Gibson
7880	Farmer, Tilda	GA	1855	Henry Farmer	Franklin Orton	Tilda Rufty	Caroline Orton	
9768	Farmer, Wiley	VA	1888	Delia Farner	Wiley Farmer	Liddie Miller	Henry & Nancy Farmer	Isaac & Basha Miller
22086	Farrington, Champ	NC			William Farrington	Susie Orshorn	Milton & Saly Farrington	Ephraim & Morita Orshorn
11048	Farris, Laura	VA		Robert Farris	Isaac Edmondson	Milly Blevins	Andrew & Susan Edmondson	Jessee & Catharine Blevins
19226	Faucett, Ethel	MO	1901		James Faucett	Margret Sharp	Robert & Mary Faucett	Henry & Charlotta Sharp
19229	Faucett, Louise	MO	1898		James Faucett	Margret Sharp	Robert & Mary Faucett	Henry & Charlotta Sharp
19230	Faucett, Margret	MO	1872	James Faucett	Henry Sharp	Charlotta Auxies	Anderson & Martha Sharp	John & Nancy Auxies
19228	Faucett, Nannie	MO	1896		James Faucett	Margret Sharp	Robert & Mary Faucett	Henry & Charlotta Sharp
19227	Faucett, Nora	MO	1895		James Faucett	Margret Sharp	Robert & Mary Faucett	Henry & Charlotta Sharp
19224	Faucett, Onis	MO	1893		James Faucett	Margret Sharp	Robert & Mary Faucett	Henry & Charlotta Sharp

ID	Name	State	Year	Spouse	Father	Mother	Paternal Grandparents	Maternal Grandparents
19225	Faucett, Ralph	MO	1903		James Faucett	Margret Sharp	Robert & Mary Faucett	Henry & Charlotta Sharp
20055	Faucett, Robert	TX	1869		Miles Faucett	Sallie Griffis	Wm & Elizabeth Faucett	Wm & Mary Griffis
20051	Faucett, Sallie	TX	1843	Miles Faucett	Wm Griffis	Mary Aldridge	Wm & Sarah Griffis	
21410	Faught, Hugh	OK	1871	Lucindy Faught	James Faught	Mariah Sides	Samuel & Elizabeth Faught	
21413	Faught, James	AL	1837	Mariah Faught	Samuel Faught	Elizabeth Brown	John & Marilla Faught	John & Hannah Brown
21399	Faught, Jerry	OK	1871	Sophie Faught	John Faught	Altie Pike	Samuel Faught & Elizabeth Brown	
21416	Faught, Jess	OK	1875		Samuel Faught	Sarah Cowart	John & Alta Faught	Tom & Lyda Cowart
21412	Faught, John	OK	1864	Sarah Faught	John Faught	Alta Pike	Samuel & Elizabeth Faught	
21685	Faught, John	MO	1882	Ida Faught	Samuel Faught	Sarah	John Faught	
21686	Faught, John	OK	1866	Martha Faught	James Faught	Mariah Sides	Samuel & Elizabeth Faught	
21414	Faught, Rutherford	OK	1880	Ida Faught	James Faught	Mariah Sides	Samuel & Elizabeth Faught	
21398	Faught, Samuel	OK	1853	Sarah Faught	John Faught	Altie Pike	Samuel Faught & Elizabeth Brown	
21411	Faught, Samuel	AL	1864	Docia Faught	James Faught	Mariah Sides	Samuel & Elizabeth Faught	David & Sallie Sides
21415	Faught, Samuel	TX	1884	Bessie Faught	Samuel Faught	Sarah Cowart		
21400	Faught, Ulysses	AL	1872	Grace Faught	James Faught	Mariah Sides	Samuel & Elizabeth Faught	
19939	Faulk, Rosa et al	NC	19yrs		Martan Faulk	Augusta Stone	Aaron & Sarah Faulk	Francis & Sarah Stone
15968	Faulkenberry, Manerva	GA		John Faulkenberry	William Flippins			
16683	Faulkenberry, Manerva	GA	1870	John Faulkenberry	William Flippins	Mary Palmer	Jefferson Flippins	
19479	Faulkner, Amanda	AL	1859		H.L. Ward	Caroline Turner	Ely & Rebecca Ward	H.W. & Jensie Turner
8622	Faulkner, Mary	OK	1848	John Faulkner	Tom North	Cathrine Pettit	Martin & Nancy North	Wm & Nancy or Jane Pettit
17785	Fawling, Sarah	OK			Elis	Elizabeth		
2106 *	Feilds, Annie	OK	1861	James Fields (decd)	Henry Bolden	Camelia Geter	Moses Bolden	Judia Jeader
18662 *	Felker, Lewis	GA		Lucindy Felker	Charley Ivins	Easter Felker		
13847	Felmet, Martha	TX	1842	widow	Nelson Carter	Elizabeth Carter	Wm & Rebecah Carter	Henry & Martha Carter
10720	Felts, Jennie	NC	1872	John Felts	Owen Wagoner	Polly Sturgill	Henry & Charlotte Wagoner	John & Virgina Sturgill
2328	Fender, Asa	MO	1857	none	Asa Fender	Charlotte Tuck	Daniel & Dicie Fender	William & Anna Tuck
14647	Fender, Curtis	OK	1877		Middleton Fender	Elizabeth Johnston	Daniel & Dicy Fender	Thomas & Eliza Johnston
12273	Fender, Elizabeth	OK	1854	Middleton Fender	Thomas Johnston	Eliza Bancom	Thomas & Mary Johnston	Thos & Elizbeth Bancom
4163	Fender, John	MO	1847	Margee Fender	Daniel Fender	Dicie Brown	Michael & Winnie Fender	Alex & Vilelly Brown
4162	Fender, Joseph	MO	1880	none	John Fender	Margee Wallis	Daniel & Dicie Fender	Sarah Wallis
4161	Fender, Luther	MO	1876	Cora Fender	John Fender	Margee Wallis	Daniel & Dicie Fender	Sarah Wallis

#	Name	State	Year	Spouse	Father	Mother	Paternal Grandparents	Maternal Grandparents
5828	Fender, Martha	MO	1834	Michael Fender	Jeptha Wallis	Nancy Stevenson	Mathew & Sarah Wallis	James & Jane Stevenson
3017	Fender, Michael	MO	1829	Martha Fender	Daniel Fender	Dicie Brown	Michael & Winnie Fender	Alex & Viletty Brown
3977	Fender, Middleton	OK	1844	Elizabeth Fender	Daniel Fender	Dicey Brown	Michael & Winnie Fender	Alex & Violetta Brown
2303	Fender, Sarah	MO	1855	none	Asa Fender	Charlotte Tuck	Daniel & Dicy Fender	William & Anna Tuck
5463	Fender, William	MO	1850	Alva Fender	Daniel Fender	Dicie Brown	Michael & Winnie Fender	Alex & Viletty Brown
13349	Fender, William	OK	1880		Middleton Fender	Elizabeth Johnston	Daniel & Dicy Fender	Thomas & Eliza Johnston
1176	Fenley, Mary	GA	1865	Ed Fenley	Wesley Raines	Talitha Rakestraw	Lila Raines	
22238	Ferguson	GA			Kin Prince	Synthia Keith	Gilbert & Pollie Prince	
17893	Fery, Vina	OK	1883	W.S. Fery	Jerimah Gilstrap	Mary Grayham		Alex & Margaret Grayham
4764	Fielding, Luereany	AR	1884	James Fielding	William Ellis	Mary Palmer	Alex & Mary Ellis	Wm & Luereany Palmer
16059	Fields, Agnes	OK	1888		Jefferson Fields	Amanda Vines	Jason & Susan Fields	Calvin & Jane Vines
7643	Fields, Cynthia	OK	1859	James Fields -decd				
16235	Fields, James	OK	1860		Jason Fields	Susan Jones	Obediah & Lydia Fields	John & Kizzie Jones
16234	Fields, Jefferson	OK	1858	Amanda Fields	Jason Fields	Susan Jones	Obediah & Lydia Fields	John & Kizzie Jones
16684	Fields, Margaret	OK	1826		Thomas Fields	Nancy Downing	Richard Fields & Susanna Emery	John Downing & Ollie Crittenden
13191	Fields, Martha	KS		Thomas Fields				
18946	Fields, Minnie	GA	1873	John Fields	Hardy Bryant	Winnie Tatum	Wm & Fannie Bryant	James & Susie Tatum
20526	Fields, Norah	TN	1863		Winfield Scott	Talula Shewwaters		Chief & Talula Bottlewash
21036	Fields, William	OK	1851	Mattie Fields	John Henderson	Charlott Fields		Tim Fields
20141	Fillingim, Jacob	FL	1870	Lennie Fillingim	Valentine Fillingim	Sarah Dukes	Robert & Ester Fillingim	Thomas & Ann Duke
15146	Findley, A.Webb	GA	1872	Mattie Findley	Henry Findley	Mary Whorton	Francis & Linnie Findley	
15147	Findley, Alma	GA	1887		Henry Findley	Mary Whorton	Francis & Linnie Findley	
15145	Findley, Daisy	GA	1881		Henry Findley	Mary Whorton	Francis & Linnie Findley	
15143	Findley, Francis	GA	1895		Henry Findley	Mary Whorton	Francis & Linnie Findley	
15008	Findley, George	GA	1874		Henry Findley	Mary Whorter	Frances & Luise Findley	
15007	Findley, Harley	GA	1896		Henry Findley	Mary Whorter	Frances & Luise Findley	
11358	Findley, Henry	GA	1849	Alice Findley	Francis Findley	Linnie Whitmire	James & Katie Findley	Samuel Whitmire
15257	Findley, Henry	GA	1877	Villa Findley	Webb Findley	Sarah Newberg	James & Katie Findley	
15280	Findley, Jeff	GA	1907		Henry Findley	Mary Whorton	Francis & Linnie Findley	
15279	Findley, Jim	GA	1876		Henry Findley	Mary Whorton	Francis & Linnie Findley	

15278	Findley, John	GA	1886		Henry Findley	Mary Whorton	Francis & Linnie Findley	
17994	Findley, John & Harrison	GA	1855 1860	Edna Findley	Mansee Findley	Lina Corder		Shodrick Corder
18249 *	Findley, Lamar	GA	1869		Henry Findley	Fanny Vann		Pate & Miley Vann
15277	Findley, Lee	GA	1901		Henry Findley	Villa	Webb & Sarah Findley	
15276	Findley, Leomer	GA	1898		Henry Findley	Villa	Webb & Sarah Findley	
15275	Findley, Linnie	GA	1898		Henry Findley	Mary Whorton	Francis & Linnie Findley	
15274	Findley, Linton	GA	1896		Henry Findley	Villa	Webb & Sarah Findley	
18250 *	Findley, Oliver	GA	1882		Henry Findley	Fanny Vann		Pate & Miley Vann
15273	Findley, Ruby	GA	1899		Henry Findley	Mary Whorton	Francis & Linnie Findley	
19708	Finley, Arthur	TN	1902		Gideon Finley	R. Fredonia Hatcher		Robert & Mary Hatcher
19696	Finley, Dave	TN	1890		Gideon Finley	R. Fredonia Hatcher		Robert & Mary Hatcher
19671	Finley, Harrison	TN	1889		Gideon Finley	Ritty Hatcher		Robert & Mary Hatcher
4099	Finley, Ider	VA	1859	James Finley	Eliazer Hart	Nancy Ingram	Washington & Elisabeth Hart	Richard & Jennie Ingram
4098	Finley, Jerome	VA	1887	none	James Finley	Ider Hart	Washington & Elisabeth Finley	Elisha & Nancy Hart
19709	Finley, John	TN	1887		Gideon Finley	Ritty Hatcher		Robert & Mary Hatcher
19690	Finley, Rittie	TN	1860	Gideon Finley	Robert Hatcher	Mary Hooper	John & Henrietta Hatcher	Demie & Elizabeth Hooper
19669	Finley, Willie	TN	1886		Gideon Finley	Ritty Hatcher		Robert & Mary Hatcher
21456	Finney, Effie	TX	1869		Frank Jeter	Adelia Thompson	George & Mary Jeter	
2362	Fisher, Ishmael	TX	1860	Burnie Fisher	Richard Fisher	Evelyn Berry	Abraham & Martha Fisher	Thomas & Mary Barry
5413	Fisher, John	OR		Sary Fisher	William Fisher	Elisebeth Wood	Abraham & Martha Fisher	
8509	Fisher, Malinda	VA	1854	John Fisher	Wiley Stamper	Eliza Anderson	George & Naomi Stamper	James & Mary Anderson
1771	Fisher, Mayfield	MO	1852	Sadie Fisher	Henry Fisher	Eliza Hopkins	Abram & Martha Fisher	Daniel & Nancy Hopkins
21623	Fisher, Ralph	Phil. Is.	1878		George Fisher	Francis Goff	Richard & Martha Fisher	
22245	Fisher, Stephen	OR	1877	H.B. Fisher	W.J. Fisher	Elizabeth Fisher	Abraham & Martha Fisher	Martha Durham
14995	Fisher, Thomas	VA	1880	Martha Fisher	John Fisher	Malinda Stamper	Levi & Nancy Fisher	Wiley & Eliza Stamper
1761	Fisher, Vasse	OK	1890	George Fisher	John Eller	L.C. Manney	W,M, & Martha Eller	Martin & Jane Manney
3970	Fisher, William	OR	1842	Elizabeth Fisher	Abraham Fisher	Martha Durham	Calep & Pollie Fisher	Henry & Sarah Durham
19764 *	Fitzgerald, Anna	TN	1854		Samuel Johnson	Eliza West		Clara West
11332	Fitzsimmons, Leila	GA	1882	W H Fitzsimmons	John Reece	Elizabeth Pool		John & Susan Pool
15272	Fitzsimmons, William	GA	1905		W H Fitzsimmons	Lela Reece		John & Elizabeth Reece

10864	Fitzwater, William	WV	44yrs	Catherine Fitzwater	William Fitzwater	Catherine Keith	Telemis & Sabrina Fitzwater	Abraham & Sarah Keith
20890*	Flack, Iserfana	NC	1852	Squire Flack	Sandy Francis	Jane Ledbetter		
17874	Flader, Mary	NE	1864	Tilman Flader	Davis Burch	Millie Bays		Josiah & Elizabeth Bays
16149	Flanders, Cynthia et al	OK	1895		Henry Flanders	Lizzie Martin	George & Cynthia Flanders	David & Susie Martin
17809*	Flanigan, Catharine	GA	1865	George Flanigan	Albert Pealer	Margaret Loggins	Allen & Edie Pealer	Peter & Catherine Loggins
8187	Flatt, Belle	AR	1877	C A Flatt	John Taylor	Kate Noland		
10918	Fleetwood, Edward	OK	1846	Malinda Fleetwood	Charles Fleetwood	Lucinda Morgan		Hoseah & Awee Morgan
11894	Fleetwood, Eljerry	OK	1856	Sarah Fleetwood	Charles Fleetwood	Lucinda Morgan		Hoseah Sr. & Awee Morgan
6042	Fleming, Annie	OK	1870	Plyander Fleming	James Tittle	Annie Prather	Danel & Rosanner Tittle	Robert & Caroline Prather
15399	Fleming, Case	GA	1906		Homer Fleming	Clifford Roberts	Buddy & Sallie Fleming	Wm & Sarah Roberts
15398	Fleming, Clifford	GA	1884	Homer Fleming	William Roberts	Sarah Harris	Joshua & Mary Roberts	Gillison & Martha Harris
18426	Fleming, Margret	NC	1843	Calvin Fleming	Adam Hauser	Kathrine Scott	Adam & Margaret Hauser	Daniel & Kathrine Scott
9367	Fletcher, Jinnie	OK	1873	John Fletcher	Caleb Wright	Ruthie Collins		Joseph & Angeline Collins
14896	Fletcher, Lucy	NC	1872	William Fletcher	Wm Apperson	Mary Edwards	Bennett & Nancy Apperson	Edward & Matilda Edwards
17872	Fletcher, Maggie	KS	1869	J.B. Fletcher	J.S. Franks	Fannie Todd	Wm Franks & Kitty Winn	Charles Todd & Becca Winn
9842	Flinn, Kina	MO	1878	George Flinn	James Poe	Sarah Harralson		Vincent & Martha Harralson
19937	Flippin, Emily	NC	1870		Henry Flippin	Locky Owens		
19941	Flippin, Floid	NC	1865	Liler Flippin	Henry Flippin	Locky Owens	John & Catherine Flippin	Jesse & Mary Owens
19881	Flippin, Henry	NC	1832	Laeky Flippin	John Flippin	Catherine Pell	Joseph & Anis Flippin	Henry & Sally Pell
19882	Flippin, J.F.	NC	1867	Christopher Flippin	Henry Flippin	Cathen Owens	John & Cathen Flippin	Jesse & Mary Owens
19938	Flippin, Jessie	NC	1874		Henry Flippin	Locky Owens		
19934	Flippin, John	VA	1863	Rosa Flippin	Henry Flippin	Luckey Owens	John & Catherine Flippin	Jesse & Mary Owens
19955	Flippin, William	NC	1868		Milton Flippin	Ruth Rodgers		William Rodgers
16690	Flippins, John	MS	1856	Mattie Flippins	Flippins	Lizzie King	Jefferson Flippins	Martin King
10621	Flood, Albert	GA	1867	Jan Flood	James Flood	Margaret Tyler		Daniel & Elisabeth Tyler
21628	Flood, Edna	TX	1880	Patrick Flood	George Fisher	Francis Goff	Richard & Martha Fisher	
21104	Flournoy, Comer	AL	1882		Joseph Flournoy	Rachel Stow	William & Sarah Flournoy	A.R. & Frances Stow
21472	Flowers, Mamie	KS	1875	Samuel Flowers	James Croslin	Loveinda Grayham		
17400	Flowers, Mary	TN	1865	Jeno Flowers	Andrew Brown	Mary Evans		Pleasant & Mahala Evans
21520	Flowers, Mary	OK	1882	Eugene Flowers	George Wyatt	Mattie Bowles	Ruben & Mary Wyatt	James & Hawkins Bowles
14001	Flowers, Mollie	AR	1876	William Flowers	Cyrus Hathaway	Cinie Bell	Cyrus & An Hathaway	Wm & Nancy Bell
2523	Floyd, Dorah	NC	1866	Felix Floyd	Joe Ray	Lizzie Higgins	John & Melissa Ray	

22035	Floyd, Julia	AR	1862	John Floyd	G.A. Williams	Nancy Belt	James & Nancy Williams	Rufus & Elizabeth Belt
17566	Flynn, Sidney	NC	1871	Blanchie Flynn	James Flynn	Margaret Scott	Tom Flynn	Leonard Scott
17314	Flynn, Willie	AL	1887	Lue Flynn	William Middleton	Anna Sizemore	James & Sarah Middleton	Joel & Anna Sizemore
17558	Fogleman, Hattie	OK	1856		Watson Walker	Nancy Bushyhead		Isaac & Nancy Bushyhead
7153	Foley, Andrew	MO	1853	Dora Foley	James Foley	Rhoda Boatright		Benj & Elizabet Boatright
7148	Foley, Charles	CA	1871	Sarah Foley	Zachary Foley	Ellanora Miller	James & Rhoda Foley	Johnathan & Elizabeth Miller
7147	Foley, Guy	CA	1877	none	Zachary Foley	Ellanora Miller	James & Rhoda Foley	Jonathan & Elizabeth Miller
8185	Foley, Hugh	MO	1881	none	Zachary Foley	Ellanore Miller	James & Rhoda Foley	Jonathan & Elizabeth Miller
7145	Foley, James	MO	1846	Mary Foley	James Foley	Rhoda Boatwright	James Foley	Allen Boatwight & Elizabeth Blackburn
7771	Foley, James	MO	1873	Norah Hubbard	James Foley	Mary Osborn	James & Rhoda Foley	James Osborn & Nancy Lewis
7154	Foley, Olla	KS	1874	Ella Foley	Zachary Foley	Ellanora Miller	James Foley & Rhoda Boatright	Elizabeth Miller
7157	Foley, Walter	MO	1878	Lulu Foley	James Foley	Mary Osborn	James & Rhoda Foley	James Osborn & Nancy Lewis
7146	Foley, Zachariah	CA		Ellonore Foley	James Foley	Rhoda Boatright		Benj & Elizabet Boatright
20134	Forbes, Pat	FL	1864	Lizzie Forbes	James Forbes	Seney Snowden	Bill Hollinger	Tobitha Snowden
18977	Ford, Cynthia	MO	1848		Harden Williams	Jane Clemmons	Fredrick & Nancy Williams	
7155	Ford, Ellen	MO	1876	Edwin Ford	William Roberts	Eliza Dagley	Andrew & Eliza Roberts	Joseph & Calina Dagley
19041	Ford, Mary	GA	1875	Emory Ford	Joseph Lumpkin	Susan Lloyd		Thomas & Susan Lloyd
14055 *	Ford, Robert	TN	1837	Judy Clinton Ford	Abraham Ross	Winnie Porter		Billy & Sarah Smith
8186	Ford, Zina	OR	1881	Walter Ford	Ed Boen	Olie Stockwell	James & Phoebe Boen	Miller & Mary Stockwell
4976	Forde, Bessie	FL	1886	Joseph Forde	John Pope	Sarah Pope		
19327 *	Fore, William	TN	1875		Lorenzo Fore	Gemima McGill	Robert & Polly Hoyl	Rolan & Jane McGill
75	Foreman, George	OK	1865	Isabel Foreman	Jeremiah Foreman	Celeste Stidham	Stephen & Sallie Foreman	Creeks
13798	Foreman, Jennie	OK	17yrs		Charley Foreman	Polly Leaf	Tom & Ailsey Foreman	
22246	Foreman, Millie	OK	1867	Nathan Foreman	Joseph Parker	Irine Harden	Jonathan & Oma Parker	Jacob & Millie Harden
16981	Foreman, Richard	OK	1881	Annie Foreman	John Foreman	Louisa Mann	David Foreman	Cary & Elzia Mann
697	Foreman, Sarah	OK	1847	widow	Tom Ross	Betsy Shelton	Dave & Aky Ross	
11900	Foreman, Sis Ann	OK	1878	Richard Foreman	Harrison Hughes	Elmira Sylcox		Burton & Farribee Sylcox
16656	Foreman, Tom	OK	1891		James Foreman	A gin nisa	Oo yuh sta duh & Gar duh na sha	Tom Jones

4356	Forest, George	MO	1871	Drucilla Forest	Samuel Forest	Marinda Lantz	James & Arrillar Forest	Moses & Jerisha Lantz
3781	Forester, Addie	NC	1869	none	James Forester	Martha Mason		John & Polly Mason
11396	Forester, David	AR	1877	Lydia Forester	James Forester	Martha Mason		John & Pollie Mason
3780	Forester, James	NC	1873	Samantha Forester	James Forester	Martha Mason		John & Polly Mason
1316	Forrest, Clara	MD	1882	George Warring	Jeramiah Pilgrim	Mary Stoffregen	Elijah & Rhoda Pilgrim	H G & Henriette Stoffregen
18822	Forshey, Hirem	MO	1853	Charity Forshey	George Forshey	Narcissus Hanlin	Hiram & Sarah Forshey	James & Mary Hanlin
11757	Forsythe, Thursey	TN	1857		Joel Gothard	Elizabeth Corvin	Allen & Mariah Gothard	Thos & Easter Corvin
7608	Fortner, Louisa	GA	60yrs	L F Fortner	Joshua Howard	Mary Deal		Wm & Jennie Howard
531	Fortner, Sis	TN	1861	George Fortner		Catherine Jordan	unknown	unknown
16032	Fossett, Hannah	GA	1863	L T Fossett	Walter McArthur	Mary Russell	Eleazer & Rosa McArthur	Elisha & Nancy Russell
21100	Foster, Angeline	TN	1870	John Foster	Steve Grimes	Lucinda Looney	Arter Looney	
9844	Foster, Artie	GA	1882	Manson Foster	Wm Kuykendall	Sarah Forrist	Van & Caroline Kuykendall	
12451	Foster, Beulah	WV	1900		Edward Foster	Josie Osburn	Jonathan & Emma Foster	Jefferson & Mary Osburn
8710	Foster, Clarence	GA	1903	none	Clinton Foster	Minnie Reece	Paschal & Josie Foster	Wesley & Martha Reece
22157*	Foster, Ed	NC	1854		George Foster	Polly Lenoir		
9845	Foster, Ella	GA	1904	none	Manson Foster	Artie Kuykendall	Joel & Eva Foster	Wm & Sarah Kuykendall
20501	Foster, George	TN	1849		John Ellis	Elizabeth Bush	Moses & Rachel Ellis	Calvin & Elizabeth Bush
9846	Foster, Lee	GA	1906	none	Manson Foster	Artie Kuykendall	Joel & Eva Foster	Wm & Sarah Kuykendall
15383	Foster, Lester	GA	1878	John Foster	William Roberts	Sarah Harris	Joshua & Mary Roberts	Gillison & Martha Harris
14409	Foster, Mary	GA	1870	John Foster	John Davenport	Sarah Ross	John & Elisabeth Davenport	
7819	Foster, Minnie	GA	1884	Clinton Foster	John Reese	Martha Helton	Aaron & Nancy Reese	James & Camely Helton
12449	Foster, Ocal	WV	1903		Edward Foster	Josie Osburn	Jonathan & Emma Foster	Jefferson & Mary Osburn
22307*	Foster, Robert	OK	1849	Hester Foster	Bob Coody	Eliza Coody		Dilcy Coody
6011	Foster, Susan	OK	1831		Andrew Blackburn	Francis Eddings	John & Elsie Blackburn	John & Elizabeth Eddings
9179	Foster, Thomas	OK	1855	Mary Foster	William Foster	Susan Blackburn	John Foster	Andrew & Francis Blackburn
6010	Foster, Thomas Jr	OK	1876	Carrie Foster	B D Fosster	Surita Cornstuble	Susan Foster	
18606	Foster, William	OK	1861	Jeanie Foster	William Foster	Susan Blackburn		Francis Blackburn
18941*	Fountain, George	TN	1842	Amanda Fountain	Shepard Fountain	Nancy		
12334	Fowler, Alice	GA	1876		William Fowler	Mary Otwell	Wm & Eliza Fowler	Joseph & Amanda Otwell

20889	Fowler, Andrew	AL	1869	Lula Fowler	Dempsey Fowler	Mary Rodgers	Sam & Lucy Fowler	John & Sallie Rodgers
12333	Fowler, Arthur	GA	1892		William Fowler	Mary Otwell	Wm & Eliza Fowler	Joseph & Amanda Otwell
20740	Fowler, Bartow	GA	1892		James Fowler	Lou Harris		Gillison & Martha Harris
20741	Fowler, Byrd	GA	1894		James Fowler	Lou Harris		Gillison & Martha Harris
15453	Fowler, Charlie	GA	1887		John Fowler	Dora Hubbard		John & Sarah Hubbard
17839	Fowler, Charlie	GA	1900		Eli Fowler	Effie Grier	Martin & Elizabeth Fowler	Henry & Emily Grier
17838	Fowler, Clarence	GA	1898		Eli Fowler	Effie Grier	Martin & Elizabeth Fowler	Henry & Emily Grier
15456	Fowler, Dora	GA	1869	John Fowler	John Hubbard	Sarah Haynes	Patrick & Margret Hubbard	Hoffer & Rutha Haynes
17837	Fowler, Effie	GA	1880	Eli Fowler	Henry Grier	Emily Flanagan	Joshua & Susan Grier	Wiley Flanagan
18002	Fowler, Elizabeth	OK	1870	James Fowler	Nathan Swift	Adaline Holt		Berry & Susanna Holt
12320	Fowler, Emory	GA	1878	Sallie Fowler	William Fowler	Mary Otwell	Wm & Eliza Fowler	Joseph & Amanda Otwell
20742	Fowler, Esda	GA	1888		James Fowler	Lou Harris		Gillison & Martha Harris
12319	Fowler, Estelle	GA	1882		William Fowler	Mary Otwell	Wm & Eliza Fowler	Joseph & Amanda Otwell
15454	Fowler, Grady	GA	1874		John Fowler	Dora Hubbard		John & Sarah Hubbard
20888	Fowler, Henry	AL	1871	Fannie Fowler	Dempsey Fowler	Mary Rodgers	Sam & Lucy Fowler	John & Sallie Rodgers
12317	Fowler, Iler	GA	1884		William Fowler	Mary Otwell	Wm & Eliza Fowler	Joseph & Amanda Otwell
21541	Fowler, Iola	GA	1870	Joseph Fowler	Foster Hughes	Docia Fowler	George & Margaret Hughes	Thomas & Basche Fowler
21019	Fowler, Isaac	AL	1866	Veola Fowler	Dempsey Fowler	Mary Rodgers	Sam & Lucy Fowler	John & Sallie Rodgers
12332	Fowler, Joe	GA	1886		William Fowler	Mary Otwell	Wm & Eliza Fowler	Joseph & Amanda Otwell
15455	Fowler, Johnnie	GA	1901		John Fowler	Dora Hubbard		John & Sarah Hubbard
12318	Fowler, Julia	GA	1888		William Fowler	Mary Otwell	Wm & Eliza Fowler	Joseph & Amanda Otwell
21544	Fowler, Laura	GA	1861	William Fowler	Moses McCollum	Sarah Hughes	John & Amanda McCollum	George & Margaret Hughes
20743	Fowler, Lou	GA	1853	James Fowler	Gillison Harris	Martha Fowler	Lorenzo & Sarah Harris	
12322	Fowler, Lunie	GA	1890		William Fowler	Mary Otwell	Wm & Eliza Fowler	Joseph & Amanda Otwell
12055	Fowler, Mariah	WV	1868	Charley Fowler	William Williams	Mary Sizemore	Wm & Elizbeth Williams	Hiram & Jane Sizemore
19346	Fowler, Martha	GA	1849		Andrew Williams	Lucinda King	John & Sallie Williams	Wm & Mary King
12321	Fowler, Mary	GA	1853	Wiliam Fowler	Joseph Otwell	Amanda Samples	Madison & Millie Otwell	Jesse & Phoebia Samples
14078	Fowler, Mary	GA	1865	Richard Fowler	Reuben Darby	Francis Mason	Charles & Nancy Darby	John & Polly Mason
17836	Fowler, Paul	GA	1904		Eli Fowler	Effie Grier	Martin & Elizabeth Fowler	Henry & Emily Grier
18984	Fowler, Sarah	GA	1854	Denrell Fowler	Andrew Williams	Lucinda King	John & Sallie Williams	Wm & Mary King
14077	Fowler, Savannah	GA	1900	Thomas Fowler	James Darby	Martha Bradford	James & Caroline Darby	Ranson & Harriet Bradford

20887	Fowler, Thomas	AL	1861		Dempsey Fowler	Mary Rodgers	Sam & Lucy Fowler	John & Sallie Rodgers
12316	Fowler, Veneta	GA	1896		William Fowler	Mary Otwell	Wm & Eliza Fowler	Joseph & Amanda Otwell
12315	Fowler, Vernia	GA	1894		William Fowler	Mary Otwell	Wm & Eliza Fowler	Joseph & Amanda Otwell
9578	Fox, Mary	GA	1854	John Fox	George Whisenant	Malinda Cross	Nicholas Whisenant & Nancy Willson	Thos Cross & Rebeca Dovey
4599	Fox, Sarah	OK	1842	James Fox decd	Earl Cordrey	Charlotte Berryhill		Sam Berryhill
12818	Fox, Yillie	VA	1878	Walles Fox	William Dolinger	Nancy Blevins	John & Elisabeth Dolinger	
6080	Frady, Elsada	GA	1869	James Frady	Alphus Key	Minerva Hembree	William Key	Reubin Emery
21798	Fragge, Hanah	TN			Samuel Evans	Deborah Cobb		
8872	Fraley, Margaret	VA	1825	James Fraley	William Ramsey	Susan Bush	Polly Ramsey	Austin & Nancy Bush
5399	Framkum, Siro	NC	1844	Ellen Framkum	James Framkum	Lauria Indlish		John Indlish
12848	Francis, Elizabeth	TN	1869	Daniel Francis	Thomas Shepherd	Eliza Maney	John & Dartha Shepherd	Martan & Matilda Maney
17160	Francis, Emil	MO	1884		Thomas Francis	Margarett Maulder	Allie Green	
6164	Francis, Jerome	NC	1881	Ollie Francis	Robert Francis	Martha Spencer	Eli & Mahala Francis	Solomon & Nellie Spencer
3518	Francis, Margret	NC	1859	W P Francis	J R Baldwin	Marilda Jones	Wm & Margret Baldwin	
6169	Francis, Martha	NC	1850	Robert Francis	Soloman Spencer	Nellie Hash	Isaac & Johannah Spencer	Robert & Margery Hash
9060	Francis, Roby	NC	1873	Ida Francis	Robert Francis	Elisabeth Blevins		George & Lydia Blevins
3388	Franklin, A.	AL	21yrs	none	Ben Franklin	Frances Bryars		
3391	Franklin, Albert	AL	21yrs	none	Benjamin Franklin	Frances Bryars		
1774	Franklin, Anderson	GA	1823	Elizabeth Franklin	Abram Franklin	Elisabeth Anderson	Sarah Franklin	Abram & Linda Anderson
3389	Franklin, Ben	AL	62yrs	Frances Bryars	Thomas Franklin	Clarendy Powers		
19648	Franklin, Ben	TN	1892		William Franklin	Violen Morgan	Louis & Sarah Franklin	Elizabeth Morgan
8396	Franklin, Benjaman	TX	1868	Martha Franklin	Wm Franklin	Amy Ledford	Abram & Elisbeth Franklin	Benj & Grace Ledford
14820	Franklin, Caroline	GA	1861			Susaner Franklin		Wm & Elizbeth Franklin
2335	Franklin, Charley	GA	1868	Rosa Franklin	William Franklin	Susan		Sarah Green
19956	Franklin, Charlie	NC	1890		George Franklin	Mary King		Charity
19653	Franklin, Corbet	TN	1904		William Franklin	Violen Morgan	Louis & Sarah Franklin	Elizabeth Morgan
19815	Franklin, Elizabeth	GA	1869	William Franklin	George Henderson	Dovie Martin	Harper & Margaret Henderson	Daniel Rogers
21848 *	Franklin, Ella	TN	1863		Henry Clay	Charlotte		

11617	Franklin, Evvie	TX	1888		Abraham Franklin	Lizzie Tapp	Anderson & Elisebeth Franklin	Hugh & Agnes Tapp
19880	Franklin, George	NC	1843	Mary Franklin		Charity Franklin		Charity Franklin
6009	Franklin, Harriet	GA	1883	Burt Brown	James Franklin	Lizabeth Dunn	Wm & Josephus Franklin	Simon & Polly Dunn
21178	Franklin, Henry	TN	1850	Harret Franklin	John Franklin	Mary Mapels	Henry & Tibitha Franklin	Eliza Mapels
8401	Franklin, Ida	GA	1876	W McEntire	Wm Franklin	Josephine Witzel	John Franklin & Sarah Swinney	Ebinezer Witzel
4034	Franklin, Jacob	NC	1836	Adeline Franklin decd	Joseph Martin	Mary Hunt	John Martin	
10860	Franklin, Jacob	TN			Elias Franklin	Manervy Frankllin	Aberham Franklin	Jacob Franklin
6378	Franklin, James	GA		Elizabeth Franklin	Wm Franklin	Jacy Witzel	John Franklin	Ebinezer Witzel
17422	Franklin, James	TN	1866		Elias Franklin	Harriet Franklin	Jacob Franklin	Abraham Franklin
22244	Franklin, James	NC	26 yrs		Leander Franklin	Minda Garrett	Laura English	Selia Unston
6415	Franklin, Jason	GA	1879	none	John Franklin Jr	Josephen Mull	Wm & Josephen Franklin	Jake & Olna Mull
3040	Franklin, John	NC	1866	Mary Franklin	Jacob Franklin	Adeline Martin		Joseph & Mary Martin
3904	Franklin, John	WA	1853	none	Anderson Franklin	Elisebeth Bryan	Abram Franklin & Elisebeth Anderson	Tarrene Bryan
6008	Franklin, John	GA	1860	Josephus Franklin	William Franklin	Josephus Witzel	John Franklin & Sarah Swinney	Ebenizer Witzel
8406	Franklin, John	WA	1853	none	Anderson Franklin	Elisebeth Bryan	Abraham & Elisebeth Franklin	Torrence Bryan
13875	Franklin, Joseph	TN	1855	Mollie Franklin	John Franklin	Manervia Franklin		
8409	Franklin, Juan	TX	1872	Sarah Franklin	Wm Franklin	Amy Ledford	Abram & Elisabeth Franklin	Benj & Grace Ledford
3533	Franklin, Julia	TN	1862	Wiliam Franklin	William Chambers	Martha Wells	John & Bettie Chambers	Alexander & Nasa Wells
10801	Franklin, Louis	TN	1849	Sarah Franklin	William Franklin	Mary Franklin	John & Sallie Franklin	Wm & Elisbeth Franklin
6390	Franklin, Luther	GA	1872	Lena Franklin	Wm Franklin	Josephen Witzel	John Franklin & Sarah Swinney	Ebinezer Witzel
17461	Franklin, Margaret	GA	1869	Wm Franklin	James Carter	Sarah Parker	Frederick & Margaret Carter	Pleasant & Jane Parker
18709	Franklin, Marion	FL	61yrs	Frances Franklin	Ellis Franklin	Laplaty Lawson	Thos & Bette Franklin	John & Martha Lawson
7540	Franklin, Mary	NC	1886	Nelson Franklin	Asburry Gibbs	Martha Cox	William Gibbs	Rebeca Cox
15942	Franklin, Mary	GA	1884	Cain Franklin	John Reaves	Lizzie Redman	Asel & Clara Reaves	Richard & Malinda Redman
3384	Franklin, Norman	AL	28yrs	Susan Daughtey	Ben Franklin	Frances Bryars	Thomas Franklin	
21214	Franklin, Rose et al	TX	1889		Daniel Franklin	Lizzie Cooper	Tucker Franklin	Wiley & Rebecca Cooper
6384	Franklin, Tary	GA	1870	Rody Franklin	Wm Franklin	Josephen Witzel	John Franklin & Sarah Swinney	Ebinezer Witzel
19642	Franklin, Violen	TN	1875	W.A. Franklin		Elizabeth Morgan		Jessa & Louisa Morgan

2249	Franklin, William	GA	1871	Mary Franklin	Anderson Franklin	Elizabeth Bryan	Abram & Elisbeth Franklin	Clarence Bryan
8287	Franklin, William	GA	1864	Amanda Franklin	Wm Franklin Sr	Josephine Witzel	John Franklin & Sarah Swinney	Ebinezer Witzel
8403	Franklin, William	TX	1866	Mary Franklin	Wm Franklin	Amy Ledford	Abram & Elisabeth Franklin	Benj & Grace Ledford
9566	Franklin, William	AL	1866		John Franklin	Puss Phillips	Phillemon Franklin	Lucy Simmons
18862	Franklin, William	TN	1869	Violen Franklin	Louis Franklin	Sarah Murrell	Wm & Mary Franklin	Ben & Topy Murrell
19647	Franklin, William	TN	1904		William Franklin	Violen Morgan	Louis & Sarah Franklin	Elizabeth Morgan
19816	Franklin, William	GA	1854	Elizabeth Franklin	Jacob Franklin	Adeline Martin	Jacob Franklin	Joseph Martin
6391	Franklin, Wm Jr.	GA	1883	none	John Franklin	Josephen Mull	Wm & Josephen Franklin	Jake & Edna Mull
20267	Franks, Charles	AR	1871	Betty Franks	John Franks	Fannie Todd	Wm Franks & Kitty Winn	Charles Todd & Betty Winn
17873	Franks, Edward	OK	1873	Emma Franks	John Franks	Fannie Todd	Wm Franks & Kitty Winn	Charles Todd & Betty Winn
14470	Franks, Emily	AL	1875	John Franks	D H Sizemore	M L Woods	Daniel & Anna Sizemore	Thos & Juda Woods
20266	Franks, John	OK	1876	Rosa Franks	John Franks	Fannie Todd	Wm Franks & Kitty Winn	Charles Todd & Betty Winn
5578	Franks, Lucinda	NC	1862	William Franks	James Forester	Martha Mason		John & Pollie Mason
8842	Franks, Maggie	NC	1878		T J Tramel	Rebeca Caler	Jake Tramel	
6759	Frankum, Hettie	NC	36yrs	widow	Monroe Frankum	Ann Judlis	John & Catherine Judlis	
6758	Frankum, Nellie	NC	27yrs	none	Monroe Frankum	Ann Judlis	John & Catherine Judlis	
17681	Frayser, Mary	OK	1851	Edward Frayser	William Vann	Lavinia Coster	Andy Vann	
13978	Frazier, Bettie	OK	1863	John Frazier	Wilson Boggs	Peggie Leek		Jesse Leek
19587	Frazier, Elizabeth	AL	1855	William Frazier	Thadius McJunkins	Martha Johnson	Samuel McJunkins & Elizabeth Carr	Jack Johnson & Permelia Patterson
7156	Frazier, Mary	OK		J M Frazier	Martin Holcomb	Sarah Hays	William Holcomb	John & Louisa Hay
21977	Fredrick, Mary	TN	1840	widow	Mose Copeland	Malinda Sammonds		
897	Freels, Mattie	TN	1862		Sam Goforth	Mary Lindly	Dave Goforth	Adams
18384	Freeman, David	AL	24yrs		Freeman	Laura Taylor		Matilda Taylor
4975	Freeman, George	GA	1869	Mosella Freeman	William Freeman	Phebe Jones		John & Lucina Jones
15726 *	Freeman, J P	AL	1837		Sam Freeman	Noveey Welch		Billy Welch
21799	Freeman, Jennie	TX	1875	Rufus Freeman	James Childers	Sarah Rice		George Rice
6348	Freeman, John	AL	1875	Sallie Well	William Freeman	Elisabeth ?Norwood?	Boswell & Rosanah Freeman	John ?Norwood?
18251 *	Freeman, Louisiana	GA	1860	William Freeman	Ceb Irving	Sarah Campbell		Major & Lucy Campbell
13842	Freeman, Louvisa	MO	1852	W T Freeman	George Haley	Abigail Rhea	George Sr & Lovisa Haley	
13891	Freeman, Martha	VA		James Freeman	James Heath	Sallie Thomas	Margret Heath	

21800	Freeman, Martha	TX	1858	John Freeman	Jesse Crain	Mary Gosnell		Jacob Gosnell
4349 *	Freeman, Mary	OK		John Freeman	Chille McIntosh	Jane Jones	Chille & Creesy McIntosh	Frank & Jane Jones
4984	Freeman, Phebe	GA	1843	William Freeman	John Jones	Lucinda Spence		
9369	Freeman, Polly	OK	1875	Lee Freeman	John Fields	Charlotte Deerhead	Scar-caty & Charlotte Ca-ta-yah	
3357	Freeman, Robert	AL	1859	Misouri Williams	Boswall Freeman	Rosanna Colbert	Boswell Freeman & Missource Williams	William & Celia Colbert
4978	Freeman, Robert	GA	1883	none	William Freeman	Phebe Jones		John & Lucinda Jones
20640	Freeman, Sarah	GA	1865	T.F. Freeman	Andrew Bailey	Lucinda Mullens	James & Phebe Bailey	Peas & Martha Mullens
3354	Freeman, Thomas	AL	1877	none	William Freeman	Martha Norwood	Boss & Rose Freeman	John Norwood
22039	Freeman, Toney	TX	1882	Sylvia Smith	John Freeman	Martha Freeman	Hiram & Dillie Freeman	Jesse & Mary Crain
3430	Freeman, William	AL	1852	Martha & Mattie	Boswell Freeman	Rosana Colbert		William & Cely Colbert
4977	Freeman, William	GA	1875	Nancy Freeman	William Freeman	Phebe Jones		John & Lucinda Jones
7820	Fremont, Russell	GA	1888			Sarah Helton		James & Camely Helton
13344	French, George	NC	37yrs	Wolla French	French Hawk	Annie Grease		
8421	French, William	SC	40yrs	Awee French	Frank French	Annie Grease		
5423	Fricks, Alice	NC	1875	James Fricks	James Dockery	Sarah McDonald		James & Numia McDonald
17773	Fricks, Alice	TN	1881	Carl Fricks	Edward Ellison	Sarah Lofte	Daniel & Jane Ellison	Shade & Martha Lofte
17349	Fricks, Arto	SC	1873	Alexzana Fricks	Alex Fricks	Mary Knox	Silus Fricks & Millie Calhoun	E.B. Knox & Mary Wall
13652	Friend, Viola	CA	1877		Alonzo Mathews	Julia Duncan		Caleb & Mary Duncan
6030	Fritts, Elzie	WA	1874	Sevilla Fritts	George Fritts	Melvina Thompson	Reuben & Kissiah Fritts	Wesley & Amanda Thompson
17352	Frix, Jasper	SC	1879	Sarah Frix	Alex Frix	Mary Knox	Silus Frix & Millie Calhoun	E.B. Knox & Mary Wall
21901	Frost, Charles	TN	1880	Beulah Frost	William Frost	Parlee Goins	John & Catharine Frost	Nathan & Sally Goins
21697	Frost, Henry	TN	1883		William Frost	Parilee Goins	John & Catherine Frost	Nathan & Sally Goins
22182	Frost, James	NC	1869		James Frost	Elizabeth Davis	James & Mary Frost	Horace & Mary Davis
21698	Frost, John	AL	1876	Sydney Frost	William Frost	Parilee Goins	John & Catherine Frost	Nathan & Sally Goins
19334	Frost, Mary	AR	1854	T.K. Frost	John Rogers	Mary Roe	Henry & Mariah Rogers	Thomas & Mary Roe
19793	Frost, Parlee	AL	1851	William Frost	Nathan Goin	Sally Goin	Jimmy Goin & Rhoda Demcan	Nancy Goin
21886	Frost, William	AL	1878	Artie Frost	William Frost	Paralee Goins	John & Catharine Frost	Nathan & Sally Goins
21680 *	Fry, Andy	OK	1833	Millie Fry	? Fry	Harriet Ross		
22262 *	Fry, Milly	OK	1836	Andy Fry	Washington Adair	Mary Martin	Rachel Adair	Harry & Nancy Martin

20265	Fryar, William	TX	1882	Maude Fryar	James Fryar	Margarett Yates	Isaac & Rebecca Fryar	Lewis & Elizabeth Yates
19879	Fulk, Augusta	NC	1860		Francis Stone	Sarah Poindexter	Enoch & Elizabeth Stone	Denson & Sally Poindexter
19954	Fulk, Bessie	NC	1895		William Fulk	Emma Thore	Aaron & Dolly Fulk	George & Margaret Thore
19943	Fulk, Rebecca	NC	1843	Haywood Fulk	Charles Scott	Rebecca Randleman	Leonard & Nancy Scott	John Randleman
7149	Fuller, Dora (decd)	MO	1877	none	John Fuller	Margaret Baldwin	Andrew & Mary Fuller	Alonzo & Rebecca Baldwin
17291	Fuller, Emiline	AL	1865	Charles Fuller				William Sizemore
7151	Fuller, Milus	MO	1836	Ann Fuller	Andrew Fuller	Mary Stanton	Richard Fuller	John Stanton
7150	Fuller, Robert	MO	1881	none	Milus Fuller	Ann Spencer	Andrew Fuller	John & Nancy Spencer
7152	Fuller, Sarah	MO	1875	none	Milus Fuller	Ann Spencer	Andrew Fuller	John Spencer & Nancy Crowley
16174	Fulsom, Missouri	OK	1882	Will Fulsom	Charlie Jetts	Annie Moore	William Jetts	Henry Moore
21233	Funderburgh, Sallie	TX	1882	W.H. Funderburgh	George Biddy	Eleen McDonald	Elvin & Elizabeth Biddy	Tillman & Louise McDonald
2685	Funderburk, James	MS	1859		Jonas Funderburk	Ellen Sweet	Abe & Rachel Funderburk	
6026	Funderburk, John	AL	1858	Pinana Funderburk	Jonas Funderburk	Ellenar Sweat	Abe & Rachel Funderburk	
4027	Funderburk, Noah	MS	1853	M E Collins	James Funderburk	Ellaner Sureat	Abe & Rachel Funderburk	
2684	Funderburk, William	MS	1845	Nancy Marina	James Funderburk	Elener Sweat	Abe & Rachel Funderburk	
17718	Gaddis, Amanda	GA	1878	T.B. Baddis	James Mann	Anna Patterson	Harrison Mann & Polly Lovelace	Hix & Sally Patterson
11357	Gaddis, Mary	GA	1859	A C Gaddis	John Pool	Susan Patterson	Clabom & Martha Pool	
18898	Gaddis, Sarah	GA	1837	Wm Gaddis	James Kelley	Malinda Beck	Wm & Winnie Kelley	Solomon & Millie Beck
12021	Gadfrey, Elinda	GA		W H Gadfrey	John Pool	Susan Patterson	Claborn & Martha Pool	
21821*	Gadsden, Tama	GA	1837	Lemerick Gadsden	Abraham Reid	Judia Swift	David & Lucinda Reid	Isaac & Lucinda Swift
20509*	Gadson, Anthony	TN	1844	Joseph Gadson	James Taddy	Rosa Willburn		
20114*	Gage, Sam	GA	1829	Mary Gage	Sam Gage	Jennie Royston		
591	Gage, Sarah	OK	1844	widow	Chesley Paggett	Eliza		
22961	Gaines, Elizabeth	TX	1884		Lewis Gaines	Elizabeth Baxter	Caleb & Sallie Gaines	
20333	Gaines, G.J.	GA	1847	Mattie Gaines	Allen Gaines	Katie Watts	John & Betsy Gaines	Bill & Mary Watts
22685	Gaines, George	GA	1883		Thomas Gaines	Martha Watkins	Allen Gaines & Katie Watts	Thomas Watkins
22846	Gaines, Gus	TX	1883	Lugene Gaines	Lewis Gaines	Elizabeth Baxter	Caleb & Sallie Gaines	
757	Gaines, Lewis	TX	1849	Winnie Gaines	Caleb Gaines	Sallie Alberty		Alberty
19210*	Gaines, Paul	TN	1876	Wesley Gaines	Samuel Gaines	Sarah Bohanan	Jerry & Polly McReynolds	
22963	Gaines, Rosa	TX	1886		Lewis Gaines	Elizabeth Baxter	Caleb & Sallie Gaines	

ID	Name	State	Year	Spouse	Father	Mother	Paternal Grandparents	Maternal Grandparents
14964	Gaines, Thomas	GA	1842	Martha Gaines	Alkie Gaines	Katie Watts		
22181*	Gains, John	TN	1879	Julia Gains	Samuel Gains	Sarah Bohanan	Jerry & Polly McReynolds	
19480*	Gaither, Jefferson	TN	42yrs	Florence Gaither	London Gaither	Janie Holmes	Dave & Vinie Pearson	Joe & Elee Holmes
20664*	Gaither, Josie	GA	1871	Charles Gaither	Richard Leach	Darkis McCamy		Aaron Montgomery
20319*	Gaither, Ruben	NC	1857	Frances Gaither	London Gaither	Janie Kokre	Vince & Cine Pearson	Joe & Celia Holmes
20566*	Gaither, Willie	GA			Charles Gaither	Josie Leach	Harry & Ellen Gaither	Richard & Darkis Leach
1013	Galimore, David	TN	1844	Sarah Gallimore	Jim Gallimore	Betsy Dupee	Jim & Nancy Gallimore	Susan Dupee
17732	Gallaher, Andrew	TN	1872	Annie Gallaher	Pleasant Gallaher	Elizabeth Bledsoe	Preston & Ruth Gallaher	Daniel & Margaret Bledsoe
21897	Gallimore, James	TN	1854	Sallie Gallimore	Tom Gallimore	Nancy Baggle	David & Polly Gallimore	Samuel & Elizabeth Baggle
19817	Galloway, Bell	GA	1887	James Galloway	George Cook	Jane Denson	Richard & Sarah Cook	
19818	Galloway, James & Ethel	GA			Jim Galloway	Bell Cook		George & Jane Cook
21529	Galloway, William	GA	1866	Mollie Galloway	William Galloway	Mahaley Ranson	John Galloway	
21360	Gambill, Alex	AR	1879	Mamie Gambill	John Gambill	Susan Rutherford	Aaron Gambill	James & Nancy Rutherford
7772	Gambill, Andrew	OK	1829	Minnie Gambill	William Gambill	Sallie Ward		John & Polly Ward
9353	Gambill, Benjamin	OK	1851	Lenora Gambill	William Gambill	Susan Ribble	Wm & Sarah Gambill	
9070	Gambill, Estes	NC	1880	Molly Gambill	Robert Gambill	Nancy Jones	Patsy Gambill	Samuel & Adaline Jones
7773	Gambill, George	OK	1869	Mary Gambill	A.J. Gambill	Mary Hulsey	Wm & Sallie Gambill	Marian & Malinda Hulsey
14350	Gambill, Josephine	OK	1866	Pauline Gambill	William Gambill	Susan Ribble	Wm & Sarah Gambill	
14943	Gambill, Thomas	OK	1856	Letitia Gambill	Wm Gambill	Susan Ribble	Wm & Sarah Gambill	
7774	Gambill, William	TX	1862	Ella Gambill	Benjamin Gambill	Mary Cooper	Wm Gambill	Milton & Charlotte Cooper
10824	Gambill, William	OK	1862	Mary Gambill	William Gambill	Susan Ribble	Wm & Sarah Gambill	
21143	Gamble, Mary	TN	1877	William Gamble	Parks Kelett	Jane Mathes	Cas & Ez Kelett	William & Nancy Mathes
20946	Gann, Dosia	AL	1880	Henry Gann	Daniel Sizemore	Rebecca Markham	Joel Sizemore	Andrew Markham
21007	Gann, Dosia	AL	1880	G.H. Gann	D.E. Sizemore	Rebecca Markham	Joel Sizemore & Catharine Webster	Anderson Markham & Mary Daniels
7776	Gann, Marthy	TX	1861	J M Gann	John Montgomery	Catharine Williams	Nathan & Martha Montgomery	Joseph & Catharine Williams
20426*	Gardenhire, George	TN	1870	Tricey Gardenhire	William Gardenhire	Mary Bellen	George Maddux & Mariah Cheek	Ezekial Ballen & Nancy Goins
7168	Gardner, Annie	TX	1885	none	William Gardner	Sarah Montgomery	J E & Ann Gardner	J W & Catharine Montgomery
8399	Gardner, Fannie	OK	1882	H S Tellinghast	Wm Gardner	Lucy Hick	Wm & Elizabeth Gardner	
7167	Gardner, Mary	OK		William Gardner	Richard Davis	Martha Holcomb		Wm & Louisa Holcomb

#	Name	State	Year					
7169	Gardner, Sarah	TX	1865	William Gardner	John Montgomery	Catharine Williams	Nathan & Martha Montgomery	Joseph & Catharine Williams
5570	Gardner, William	OK	1879	Minnie Gardner	William Gardner	Lucy Ellick	Wm & Elizabeth Gardner	
5576	Gardner, William	OK	1840	Lucy Gardner	William Gardner	Elizabeth Perrin		Thomas & Jane Perrin
8575	Garis, Sarah	VA	1844	John Garis	James Orsborn	Rachel Blevins	Elias & Sally Orsborn	
3688	Garland, Elisabeth	NC	76yrs		James Roper	Susanna McDonnal	Thomas & Catherine Roper	Eleckander & Susanna McDonnel
2878	Garland, Isaac	GA	1862	Mary Garland	Ezekiel Garland	Polly Davis		Isaac Davis
881	Garland, Johnanah	OK	1857	S.F. Garland	John Nivens	Deliah	Wilson Nivens	Rachel
14404	Garland, Mary	NC	1881	Albert Garland	Frank Blackwell	Tabitha Speed	Joseph & Mary Blackwell	
2880	Garland, Polly	GA	1821	Ezekiel Garland	Isaac Davis	Rhoda		
18140	Garland, Polly	GA	1867	A.B. Garland	Anderson Neal	Sarah Davis	Thomas & Polly Neal	Wm & Anna Davis
2084	Garlinghouse, Joanah	CA	1874	Owen Garlinghouse	Bryce Smart	Ailcy Barber	Wm & Polly Smart	Isaac & Joanah Barber
2521	Garren, Matilda	NC	1839	S N Garren	David Bell	Alzira Williams	Robert & Sallie Bell	William & Polly Williams
22158	Garrett, Eliza	AL	1877		Joseph Trussell	Fiba Liviston		
10242	Garrett, Ivey	GA		Isaac Garrett	George Owenby	Sarah Anderson	Minter Owenby	Lazarus & Nancy Anderson
13439	Garrett, Ivey	GA		Isaac Garrett	George Owenby	Sarah Owenby	Minter & Elander Owenby	Lazarus & Nancy Anderson
13442	Garrett, Ivey	GA	1872	Isaac Garrett	George Owenby	Sarah Anderson	Minter & Elander Owenby	Lazarus & Nancy Anderson
11307	Garrett, Margrett	GA	1837	J S Garrett	Porter Dempsey	Charlotta Seipers	Moses & Ollie Dempsey	
13440	Garrett, Martha	GA	1874	Elisha Garrett	George Owenby	Sarah Owenby	Minter & Elander Owenby	Lazarus & Nancy Anderson
17997	Garrett, Nora	GA	1877	W.R. Garrett	Hampton Watson	Hulda Chapman	Joseph & Martha Watson	Joseph & Rena Chapman
11319	Garrett, S.E.	GA	1866	Billy Garrett	J S Garrett	Margret Dempsey		Porter & Charlotta Dempsey
19136	Garrett, Sanford	GA	1871	Alma Garrett	Charlie Garrett	Mary Horton	Rebecca & Hansby Garrett	
21102*	Garrett, Sarah	NC		Walter Garrett	London Gaither	Janie Holmes	Dave & Vinie Pearson	Joe & Celere Holmes
17998	Garrett, Thomas	GA	1894		Wm Garrett	Nora Watson	Benj & Samantha Garrett	Hampton & Hulda Watson
16318	Garrett, Wm & Rebecca Childers	GA	1849 1838		M V Garrett	Lourena Dockery	Martin & Fanne Garrett	Thomas Dockery
129	Garrish, Martha	NC	1847	Samuel Garrish	Stephen Pace	Dovey Martin	William Pace	Joseph Martin & Mary Hunt
2243	Garrison, Alice, Myrtle	TX		none	Thomas Garrison	Augustia Sharp	David & Mary Garrison	
232	Garrison, Elmo	OK	1889	none	G W Garrison	Martha Hunter	David & Mary Garrison	
10146	Garrison, Frank	OK	1865		David Garrison	Mary Blasingame	Calop Garrison	Thos & Jennie Blasingame

#	Name	State	Year	Spouse	Father	Mother	Paternal GP	Maternal GP
233	Garrison, George dec'd	OK	1857	Cathalica Garrison	David Garrison	Mary Blasingame	Colop Garrison	Thomas & Jennie Blasingame
229	Garrison, Harvey	OK	1880	none	G W Garrison	Martha Hunter	Dave Garrison & Mary Blasingame	
230	Garrison, Hurbert	OK	1893	none	G W Garrison	Martha Hunter	David & Mary Garrison	
21298	Garrison, Lucy	AL	1878	William Garrison	Daniel Lamons	Delila Criscoe	James & Mary Lamons	G.W. & Emma Criscoe
3905	Garrison, Luevenia	MO	1850	widow	Henry Butler	Deliah Van	John & Nancy Butler	Isaac Van & Luvinia Schrimpsers
236	Garrison, Malven	OK	1886	none	G W Garrison	Martha Hunter	David & Mary Garrison	
234	Garrison, Pauline	OK	1897	none	G W Garrison	Martha Hunter	David & Mary Garrison	
2327	Garrison, Robt Frankie	OK		none	Frank Garrison		David & Mary Garrison	
231	Garrison, Sula	OK	1884	none	G W Garrison	Martha Hunter	David & Mary Garrison	
548	Garrison, Thos.	TX	1853	widower	David Garrison	Mary Blasingame	Calop Garrison	Thomas & Janie Blasingame
18316	Gaskin, Gertrude	IN	1869		Jessie Philips	Jane Varneal	Moses & Barbra Philips	
22707	Gaskin, James	IN	1865	Gertrude Gaskin	Cephas Gaskin	Lucy Pulley	James & Flora Gaskin	James & Lucy Pulley
22680	Gaskin, Lucy	IN	68yrs	Seppro Gaskin	James Pulley	Louise Weaver	James & Edie Pulley	
18667 *	Gaskin, William	IN	1876	Blanche Gaskin	David Gaskin	Deliah Milton	Cephas & Mary Gaskin	Bolden & Elizabeth Milton
14856	Gaskins, Delila	IN	1824	David Gaskin	Boulden Melton	Elizabeth Scott	Mills & Anna Melton	Hubert & Sallie Scott
13851 *	Gaskins, Harry	IN	1882	Myrtle Gaskins	Thomas Gaskins	Sarah Weaver	Seth & Mary Gaskins	Alfred Weaver & Charity Moore
4752	Gates, Parise	MO		Francis Gates	William Doke	Sarah Hambelton	Merick & Mary Doke	Isaiah & Martha Hambelton
8830	Gathings, Robert	TX	1874	none	George Gathings	Martha Smith	James & Jane Gathings	
21530	Gaydon, Messer	GA	1884	Belle Gaydon	Archie Gaydon	Nancy Come		John & Nancy Davis
11356	Gaydon, Nancy	GA	1860	Archie Gaydon	John Corn	Caroline Davis		John & Nancy Davis
21531	Gaydon, Spencer	GA	1883		Archie Gaydon	Nancy Come		John & Nancy Davis
21657	Gayler, Garland	KS	1883	Stella Gayler	C.M. Gayler	Mary Sisemore	Calvin & Casandra Gayler	Wm & Susannah Sisemore
21654	Gayler, Mary	KS	1888		C.M. Gaylor	Mary Sisemore	Calvin & Casandra Gaylor	Wm & Susannah Sisemore
13449	Gayler, Victoria	OK	1866	Samuel Gayler	James Chouteau	Sarah Alberty		
21659	Gayler, Wm & Margery	KS	1889 1897		C.M. Gayler	Mary Sisemore	Calvin & Casandra Gayler	Wm & Susannah Sisemore
18252	Gayton, Annie	GA	1880	John Gayton	Henry Roach	Martha Willbanks	Jim & Elizabeth Roach	
18253	Gayton, Cicero	GA	1901		John Gayton	Annie Roach		Henry & Martha Roach
18254	Gayton, Hattie	GA	1899		John Gayton	Annie Roach		Henry & Martha Roach
18255	Gayton, Julian	GA	1903		John Gayton	Annie Roach		Henry & Martha Roach

18256	Gayton, Theodore	GA	1905		John Gayton	Annie Roach		Henry & Martha Roach
7166	Gee, Alice	TX	1827	M L Gee	William Gambill	Sallie Ward	James & Alice Gambill	John & Allie Ward
17354	Genings, Ella	GA	1880	Chas Genings	A.T. McCollun		B.C. Pugh	
21556	Gentry, Agnes	GA	1874	Lemar Gentry	Joseph Elrod	Jane Dover		Wm & Alantha Dover
10847	Gentry, Annie	NC	1883		S C Gentry	Nancy Palmer		Johnathan & Harrett McDonald
21557	Gentry, Brewer et al	GA	1899		Lemar Gentry	Agnes Elrod		Joseph & Jane Elrod
19010	Gentry, Cora	TN	1881	Gus Gentry	Absalom Metcalf	Eveline Slagle	Hiram & Jane Metcalf	Jesse & Margarette Slagle
8518	Gentry, Dovie	VA	1884	James Gentry	Solomon Chambers	Elisabeth Hart		Stephen & Rebecca Hart
7175	Gentry, Mary	IN	1881	James Gentry	William Manning	Susan Clark	John & Emily Manning	Roland & Mary Clark
8464	Gentry, Solomon	VA	1877	Biddy Lewis	William Lewis	Nancy Lewis	A J Lewis	Biddy Lewis
11743	George Sizemore	WV	1870	Keziah Sizemore	George Sizemore	Elizabeth Mitchum	Owen & Nancy Sizemore	Francis & Christiana Mitchum
22103	George, Lena	AR	1871	L.C. George		Mary Rogers	J.B. Frost	Mary Rogers
10444	George, Pearl	OK	1888	Will George	Albert Linton	Elizabeth Davison		Elizabeth Toney
20070	Gerald, Joseph	TN	1850	Mary Gerald	Robert Gerald	Lurania Poe	John & Polly Gerald	
2341	Gerboth, Cora	OK	1884	F W Gerboth	Ruben Moore	Catherine Cook		Jacob & Delana Cook
19006	Gheeren, Lou	GA	1884	W.F. Gheeren	John Allison	Fannie Hester	Hamilton & Katie Allison	Alfred & Polly Hester
16117	Ghomley, David	OK	56yrs					
3509	Gibbs, Artha	OK	1886	Walter Gibbs	John Avery	Harriett Whitten	W W & Tibitha Avary	Joel & Nancy Whitten
7176	Gibbs, Lillie	OK	1887	Henry Gibbs	William Stripling	Louisa Davis	Richard Davis & Martha Holcomb	Wm Holcomb & Louisa Berry
21363	Gibbs, Nellie	TX	1882	Thomas Gibbs	John Jeter	Susan Thompson	Washington & Mary Jeter	Amos Thompson
20007	Gibbs, Simon	GA	1866	Catherine Gibbs	Tom Gibbs	Jane Dean	Cornelius & Sally Gibbs	Elisha & Sophie Dean
3275	Gibby, Susen	NC	1851	John Gibby	James Burress	Eliza Gibby	Margaret Wolf Bryson	
3405	Gibson, Mrs Henry	AL	21yrs	Henry Gibson	William Rollin	Elisa McGhee	Bart & Peggy Gibson	Jack & Polly Rollin
1159	Gibson, Bettie	AL	1857	Wm Gibson	Wm Henson	Ann Herseford		
19866	Gibson, D.D.	NC	1892			Myra Gibson	Norfleet Thore	Martha Gibson
1153	Gibson, David	AL	1863	Nancy Gibson	Wm Gibson	Peggy Monac		Dickson & Betsy Monac
18736	Gibson, Elizabeth	NC	1844	James Gibson	Richard	Elizabeth Clingman	John & Sarah	Jacob & Jane Clingman
21558 *	Gibson, Emma	GA	1869	Anderson Gibson	George Washington	Charlotte Fuller	Lizzie Washington	
6370	Gibson, Ernest	AL	1885	Jeffie Gibson	Wm Gibson	Bettie Henson	Wm & Peggy Gibson	
22630 *	Gibson, Ester	NC	1830	George Gibson	Alfred Pearson	Nancy Pearson	Ned & Ester Pearson	David Pearson & Bridget Garner
3329	Gibson, Frank	AL	31yrs	Annie	Thomas Lindsay	Dresylla Gibson		W D & Peggy Gibson

19867	Gibson, George	NC	1903		Robert Gibson	Daisy Hicks	Abner & Martha Gibson	Carl & Martha Hicks
7532	Gibson, Georgie	GA	1871	Allen Gibson	Richard McGaha	Rebecca Pool	Josiah & Deliah McGaha	Moses & Sarah Pool
6313	Gibson, Gid	AL	55yrs	Martha Moniac	Wm Gibson	Peggy Moniac		Sam & Susan Moniac
19273	Gibson, Hiram	TN	1867	Nannie Gibson	Gilbert Gibson	Cordelia Maxell	Hiram Gibson	Salley Maxell
6780	Gibson, Joe	NC	22yrs	none	Sol Gibson	Elizabeth Wright	John Gibson & Morning Carter	John & Margaret Wright
6778	Gibson, John	NC	20yrs	none	Sol Gibson	Elizabeth Wright	John Gibson & Morning Carter	John & Margaret Wright
5460	Gibson, Joseph	NC	1843	Rosalee Gibson	Isaac Gibson	Nancy Jordan	Nathan Gibson & Maria Barnes	John Jordan
8687 *	Gibson, Julius	NC			Washington Gibson	Peggy Carter	Ransom Welch & Rhoda Gibson	Thomas & Morning Carter
6772	Gibson, Martha	NC	1841	John Gibson (decd)		Nancy Chastain		Wm & Annie Chastain
13824	Gibson, Martha	AL	1862	Widow	Fletcher Day	Rebeca Smith		
19859	Gibson, Martha	NC	1854	A.T. Gibson	Norfleet Thore	Frances Boon		
3968	Gibson, Mary	GA	1835	John Gibson (decd)	Elisha Talley	Elizabeth Allen		
12049	Gibson, May	GA	1883	Thomas Gibson	Membry Bramlett	Nancy Blalock	Miles & Annie Bramlett	
3365	Gibson, Mrs. Frank	AL	1887	Frank Gibson	F T Cardwell	Annie Cardwell		William & Annie Dees
6311	Gibson, Mrs. Gid	AL	50yrs	Gid Gibson	David Moniac	Catherine Hale	Sam & Susan Moniac	Louis & Catherine Hale
1154	Gibson, Nettie	AL	1846	none	Wm Gibson	Peggy Monac		Dickson & Betsy Monac
8690 *	Gibson, Ransom	NC	1861	Hattie Gibson	Washington Gibson	Peggy Carter	Ranson Welch & Rhoda Gibson	Thomas & Morning Carter
6771	Gibson, Rhoda	NC	1874	none	John Gibson	Martha Chastain	Nancy Gibson	Nancy Chastain
9110	Gibson, Rhoda	GA	1865	D E Gibson	Lou Allen Gibson	Elizabeth Pool		Moses Pool
6312	Gibson, Robert	AL	21yrs	none	Gideon Gibson	Martha Moniac	Wm & Peggy Gibson	David & Catherine Moniac
19860	Gibson, Robert	NC	1878	Daisy Gibson	A.T. Gibson	Martha Thore	Plesant & Bessie Gibson	Norfleet & Frances Thore
21049	Gibson, Theodore	AL	1883		William Gibson	Bettie Horseford	Wm & Peggy Gibson	Wm & Ann Henson
21126	Gibson, Tobias	TN		Louisa Gibson	Jordan Gibson	Nancy Sprodlin	Tobias & Barber Gibson	Abraham & Sallie Sperodlin
1161	Gibson, William	AL	1859	Betty Gibson	Wm Gibson	Peggy Monac		Dickson & Betsy Monac
6764	Gibson, William	NC	31yrs	Ellen Gibson	Sol Gibson	Elizabeth Wright	John Gibson & Morning Carter	John & Margaret Wright
19099	Gibson, William	GA	1869	Shadie Gibson	Wm Gibson	Mary Hickman	Harrison Gibson	Rosy Weaver
19274	Gibson, William	TN	1872	Lona Gibson	Gilbert Gibson	Cordelia Maxell	Hiram Gibson	Salley Maxell
18383	Gibson, Zephie	AL	19yrs	Earnest Gibson	John Rollin	Rhody Taylor	John & Polly Rollin	Wash & Matilda Taylor
5054	Gifford, Lucinda	OK	66yrs		James Gifford	Malissa Newman	Isac & Sallie Gifford	Solomon & Elizabeth Newman

22268	Giger, Mary	TX	1873	D.B.Giger	Syrim Knight	Sarah Ott	Jack & Martha Knight	Abe & Mary Ott
488	Gilbert, Fannie	TN	1882	Leonard Gilbert	Jesse Plummer	Frances Stamper	Plummer	Stamper
20837	Gilleland, Annie	GA	1874	Samuel Gilleland	Ebenezar Barrett	Haley Evans		Robert & Sallie Evans
21933*	Gillespie, Ada	TN	1883	James Gillespie	Henry Holmes	Adaline Quillen	Nathan & Lucy Holmes	Ned & Vephie Hutchison
21242	Gilley, Jeff	AL	1860	Mary Gilley	Jorden Gilley	Ann Hill	Wm & Matilda Gilley	Mount & Susie Hill
15263	Gillham, Victoria	GA	1871	Roe Gillham	William Haynes	Nancy Green		Shade & Nancy Green
9633	Gilliam, Eliza	OK	1855	Morgan Gilliam	John Cooper	Elizabeth McAdams	James & Delilah Cooper	James & Rachel McAdams
21348	Gilliam, Elizabeth	TN	1857	William Gilliam	Alex Bowles	Lettie Bishop	Allen Bowles	
17259	Gilliam, Sarah	AR	1887	Lloyd Gilliam	Lawson Runyon		Robert Runyon	
18153	Gillis, Elizabeth	OK	70yrs		William Reed	Margaret Fortner	James & Harriet Reed	Ezekial & Margaret Fortner
5293	Gillis, Margarett	TN	1854		Joseph Murry	Nancy Hensley	Wm & Elizabeth Murry	Lewis & Elizabeth Hensley
10393	Gillispi, Sarah	GA	1853	James Gillispi	John Stousell	Rebeca Mathis		Wm & Rebeca Mathis
16052	Gillmore, George	MO	1878	Rhoda Gillmore	Sam Gillmore	Mary Hundley	Wm & Lucy Gillmore	Joseph & Mary Hundley
16056	Gillmore, Mary	MO	1845	Sam Gillmore	Joseph Hundley	Mary Phelps	Jerdan & Elizabeth Hundley	James & Nancy Phelps
18682	Gillroy, Emily	FL	1886		John Gillroy	Harriet Monk		John & Silva Monk
18683	Gillroy, Julia	FL	1888		John Gillroy	Harriet Monk		John & Silva Monk
17708	Gillstrap, Zimriph	OK	1884	Dora Webb	Jermiah Gillstrap	Mary Grayham		Alex & Margaret Grayham
21305	Gilly, Andrew	AL		Rebecca Gilly	Jorden Gilly	Ann Hill	Wm & Matilda Gilley	Mount & Susie Hill
17535	Gilly, Nancy	GA	1840	John Gilly	Jesse Locklear	Mary Turner		Moses Turner
21616	Gilmer, Emily	NC	53yrs	Marshall Gilmer	Absom Hale	Eliza Hale		Martha Hale
21386	Gilmore, Clara	TX	1884		? Gilmore	Julia Brown		David & Amanda Brown
21387	Gilmore, Julia	TX	1864	John Gilmore	D.O. Brown	Amanda Graham		
21374	Gilmore, Mattie	TX	1866	Jefferson Gilmore	David Brown	Amanda Graham		
20259	Gilstrap, Berthie	GA	1881	P.C. Gilstrap	Mose Myres	Emley Savage	Jimmina Hulsey & Elisebeth Savage	
60	Gilstrap, Lou	GA	1872	Homer Gilstrap	Lewis Williams	Mary Lovelady	Augustus & Sarah Williams	Andrew & Sarah Lovelady
8210	Gipson, Bright	GA	1855	Martha Gipson	John Gipson	Martha Chastain	Sam Gipson	Nancy Chastain
6774	Gipson, Cordelia	SC	1872		John Gipson	Martha Chastain	Nancy Gipson	Nancy Chastain
6775	Gipson, Elijah	NC	1870	widow	John Gipson	Martha Chastain	Nancy Gipson	Nancy Chastain
6779	Gipson, Francis	SC	1872	Joseph Gipson	Martin Chastain	Adeline Teague	Eliza Chastain	
14854	Gipson, George	GA	1843	Nancy Gipson	William Gipson	Matilda Rainey	Jacob & Parthenia Gipson	Woodson & Tempe Rainey

#	Name	State	Year					
6776	Gipson, Joseph	SC	1866	Francis	John Gipson	Martha Chastain	Nancy Gipson	Nancy Chastain
22043	Girty, Daniel	OK	35yrs	none	Snake Girty	Ka-ya-gus-fah		John Gah-stah-gah-lah
22044	Girty, Ned	OK		Caty Girty	Snake Girty	Ka-yah-gus-tah		John Gah-stah-gah-lah
2520 *	Givens, Henrietta	AL		William Givens	Jacob Harris	Tempie		
16494	Givens, Joseph	TN	55yrs	Parolee Givens	Anderson Givens	Haret McKeeymore		A B & Harett McKeymore
10773	Glad, Mary	OK	1862	Joseph Glad	Alex Robertson	Nellie Terrell		Jack & Lizzie Terrell
7172	Gladden, Estella	TX	1887	Fred Gladden	John Avants	Annie Rich	Thomas & Francis Avants	Leroy & Edith Rich
13864	Gladden, Scelia	GA	1852	Elias Gladden	Shan Nelson	Nancy Davis	Noah & Mary Nelson	
6945	Gladson, Campbell	TN			James Gladson	Margaret Johnson	John Gladson & Edna Raper	
6944	Gladson, Chas, Mattie, & Mandie	TN	1887 1894 1898		William Gladson	Jennie	John & Edna Gladson	
6943	Gladson, George	TN	1862	Mandy Gladson	John Gladson	Edna Raper		Thomas Raper & Katy Pitts
4658	Gladson, Mandy	TN	1881	George Gladson	James Rhea	Polly Hildebrand		John & Nicey Hildebrand
5159 *	Glass, John	OK	1865	Luella Glass	Ned Glass	Lucy Birt	George Glass	Abraham & Temmpy Birt
13280 *	Glass, John	OK	1880		Joe Glass	So kin ny		Dela gu sku & Rosie
21689	Glaze, Elizabeth	CO	1881	William Glaze	William Page	Emily Wall		Drury Wall & Elizabeth Moore
12363 *	Glenn, Bettie	NC		Noah Glenn	Loss Hansen	Louisa Payne	Miles Efison	
14130	Glenn, James	MO		Almeda Glenn	Robert Glenn	Martha Murry	James & Margret Glenn	Joshua & Polly Murry
12372 *	Glenn, Noah	NC	1859	Bettie Glenn	Brice Scales	Mary Hansen		Alice Hansen
21885 *	Glenn, Thomas	GA	1854	Carrie Glenn	Thomas Wynn	Dinah Glenn	Jada Wynn	
7178	Glockles, Luzenia	MO	1870	William Glockles	George McMillen	Mary Boatright	Jonathan & Mary McMillen	Wm & Sallie Boatright
1227	Glover, Celestia	OK	1883	Walter Glover	James Wilkerson	Rebeca White	Richard & Nancy Wilkerson	James & Cynthia White
21711 *	Glover, John	GA	1875	Maggie Glover	Henry Glover	Amanda Walker	Richard & Eliza Glover	
3525	Clover, Sarah	AR			George Sims	Jane Sinyard		Samp & Mary Sinyard
17002 *	Gober, Sarah	GA	1866		Mason Rucker	Liddie Flemming	Pleas & Alice Nails	Fred & Hannah Adams
18418	Goble, Rosalie	CA	1868	Charles Goble	Griffin Oxcudine	Perline Lowery		Mary Lowery
20945	Goddard, Charles	GA	1880	Mattie Goddard	John Goddard	Sarah Granitt	J.E. & Sarah Goddard	
20944	Goddard, Eddie	GA	1884		John Goddard	Sarah Granitt	J.B. & Laura Goddard	
18325	Goddard, George	OK	1847	Ellen Goddard	Jefferson Cordrey	Sallie Gravit	David & Sarah Cordrey	Obediah Gravit
8728	Goddard, James	GA	1844	Lucy Goddard	Early Goddard	Sarah Gravitt	David & Winnie Cordry	Obediah & Nancy Gravitt

20941	Goddard, John	GA	1844	Lorny Goddard	Jefferson Goddard	Sarah Granitt	John & Winnie Goddard	Olidie Granitt & Ella Goddard
9526	Goddard, Mary	GA	1879	John Goddard	John Abernathy	Delphia Tidwell	Daniel Abernathy	Francis Tidwell
21787	Goddy, Molly	AR	1870	N.T. Goddy	William Haynes	Jane Thompson	Sarah Haynes	Wm & Estes Thompson
14609	Godfrey, Amy	GA	1905		Charley Godfrey	Laura Tomberlin	W H & Elender Godfrey	
14608	Godfrey, Calvin	GA	1887		W H Godfrey	Elender Pool		John & Susan Pool
14607	Godfrey, Charley	GA	1874	Laura Godfrey	W H Godfrey	Elender Pool		John & Susan Pool
20798	Godfrey, Elmer	GA	1897		Samuel Godfrey	Minda Kelley	John & Margaret Godfrey	
20799	Godfrey, Ermy	GA	1895		Samuel Godfrey	Minda Kelley	John & Margaret Godfrey	
20800	Godfrey, Ernest	GA	1900		John Godfrey	Georgia Cavinter	John & Margaret Godfrey	
20801	Godfrey, Evie	GA	1905		Samuel Godfrey	Minda Kelley	John & Margaret Godfrey	
14606	Godfrey, Fannie	GA	1881		W H Godfrey	Elender Pool		John & Susan Pool
14605	Godfrey, Hubert	GA	1903		Charles Godfrey	Laura Tomberlin	W H & Elender Godfrey	
9837	Godfrey, James	GA	1861	Sallie Godfrey	Louallen Godfrey	Elizabeth Pool		Moses & Sarah Pool
14604	Godfrey, John	GA	1876	Lela Godfrey	W H Godfrey	Elender Pool		John & Susan Pool
20802	Godfrey, John	GA	1870	Georgia Godfrey	John Godfrey	Margarite Findley	Jim Godfrey	Manuel & Linda Findley
20803	Godfrey, Lonnie	GA	1899		Samuel Godfrey	Minda Kelley	John & Margaret Godfrey	
14603	Godfrey, Lou Ellen	GA	1903		John Godfrey	Lelia Howell	W H & Elender Godfrey	
20804	Godfrey, Loyle	GA	1901		Samuel Godfrey	Minda Kelley	John & Margaret Godfrey	
14602	Godfrey, Mamie	GA	1904		John Godfrey	Lelia Howell	W H & Elender Godfrey	
20805	Godfrey, Margarett	GA	1843	John Godfrey	Manuel Findley	Linda Whitmire		Chris & Nancy Whitmire
20806	Godfrey, Myrtie	GA	1895		John Godfrey	Georgia Cavinter	John & Margaret Godfrey	
20797	Godfrey, Onnie	GA	1898		John Godfrey	Georgia Cavinter	John & Margaret Godfrey	
14601	Godfrey, Oscar	GA	1889		W H Godfrey	Elender Pool		John & Susan Pool
15463	Godfrey, Partheny	GA	1862	J D Godfrey	Marian Johnson	Mary Prather		James & Partheny Prather
14600	Godfrey, Patterson	GA	1884		W H Godfrey	Elender Pool		John & Susan Pool
14599	Godfrey, Robert	GA	1878	Lula Godfrey	W H Godfrey	Elender Pool		John & Susan Pool
7596	Godfrey, Sallie	GA	1869	James Godfrey	John Gibson	Mary Tally		
20807	Godfrey, Samuel	GA	1869	Minda Godfrey	John Godfrey	Margarett Findley	Jim Godfrey	Manuel & Linda Findley
20808	Godfrey, Selmer	GA	1892		Samuel Godfrey	Minda Kelley	John & Margaret Godfrey	
11392	Godfrey, Warren	GA	1858	JoAnn Godfrey	Lou Allen Godfrey	Elizabeth Pool		Moses & Sarah Pool
20217*	Goens, Clemenie	IN	1879	Jefferson Goens	Elias Shoecraft	Jane White	Jeremiah & Patsey Shoecraft	
3601	Goines, Naomi	AR	1844	Jas Goines	George Hampton	Mary Barnes	George & Mary Hampton	
19363	Going, Albert	GA	1906		John Going	Octavia McPherson	Wm & Delia Going	Cicero & Fanny McPherson

19364	Going, Alonzo	GA	1900		Byers Going	Alver Chandler	Wm & Delia Going	Beverly & Georgia Chandler
20744	Going, Byers	GA	1876	Alver Going	Wm Going	Delia Cole	Wm & Nancy Going	John & Betsy Cole
20745	Going, Delia	GA	1857	William Going	John Cole	Betsy Whitlock	Samuel Cole	James & Sallie Whitlock
19365	Going, Dessie	GA	1902		Byers Going	Alver Chandler	Wm & Delia Going	Beverly & Georgia Chandler
14441	Going, Georgia	GA	1875	Lesley Going	Benj. Pugh	Sarah Chastain		
20746	Going, James	GA	1891		Wm Going	Delia Cole	Wm & Nancy Going	John & Betsy Cole
20747	Going, John	GA	1886		Wm Going	Delia Cole	Wm & Nancy Going	John & Betsy Cole
19366	Going, Lela	GA	1897		Byers Going	Alver Chandler	Wm & Delia Going	Beverly & Georgia Chandler
20748	Going, Maggie	GA	1884		Wm Going	Delia Cole	Wm & Nancy Going	John & Betsy Cole
19370	Going, William Jr.	GA	1905		Byers Going	Alver Chandler	Wm & Delia Going	Beverly & Georgia Chandler
18930	Goins, A. Jackson	TN	1853	Milly Goins	John Goins	Julia Goins	Thomas & Sarah Goins	Tilman & Diana Goins
10977	Goins, Albert	TN		Bertie Goins	James Goins	Melvina Goins	Granville & Polly Goins	Martin & Susan Goins
20564	Goins, Arch	TN	1874	Florence Goins	James Goins	Melvina Goins	Granville & Polly Goins	Martin & Susan Goins
10294	Goins, Asa	TN	1846	Sarah Goins	Jack Goins	Janie McGill	John Goins	Bittie Devies
11186	Goins, Benjaman	TX	1862		Josh James	Rachel Goins		Granvill & Pollie Goins
12203	Goins, Burk	TN	1873		Brad Goins	Mary Goins	Jackson Goins	Susan Goins
12480	Goins, Bush	OK	1882	Mary Goins	Jim Goins	Harriet Sizemore	Martin & Mandy Goins	
19529	Goins, Calvin	TN	1868	Sarah Goins	Nathan Goins	Charlotta Goins	Sanford & Charity Goins	Shade & Orpha Goins
14939	Goins, Charles	TN	1876	Nancy Goins	James Goins	Melvina Goins	Granville & Polly Goins	Martin & Susan Goins
19516	Goins, Colonel	TN	1877	Nellie Goins	Joshowey Goins	Katie Goins	Tilman & Diane Goins	Sanford & Charity Goins
21845	Goins, Edly	TN	1878			Tilda Goins		John Goins
14957	Goins, Elijah	TN	1872	Dora Goins	James Goins	Melvina Goins	Granville & Polly Goins	Martin & Susan Goins
19530	Goins, Erelda	TN	1840	Joshoway Goins	Nathan Goins Sr	Sarah Magill	James Goins	Wm Magill & Nancy Goins
10982	Goins, Francis	AL	1857	Mary Goins	Elijah Newton	Susan Goins		Nancy McGill
10440	Goins, George	OK	47yrs	Alice Goins	Martin Goins	Manda	James & Rhoda Goins	Malinda Bolin
20561	Goins, Granville	TN	1869		Dotson Goins	Serilda Goins	Granville & Polly Goins	Nathan & Sallie Goins
19796	Goins, Harvey	TN			Nathan Goins	Charlotta Goins	Sanford & Charity Goins	Shade & Orpha Goins
11187	Goins, Henry	TN	1836	Elizabeth Goins	Jack Goins	Safronia McGill	John Goins	William Driver
21155	Goins, James	TN	1861		Dodson Goins	Erelda Goins	Granvelle & Polly Goins	Nathan & Sarah Goins
21639	Goins, Jennie	TN	1883		Bradford Goins	Mary Newton	Jackson & Susan Goins	James Goins & Eliza Newton
3710	Goins, John	OK		Zona Goins	John Goins	Melissa McGill	Nathaniel & Mary Goins	Wm & Sallie McGill
10295	Goins, John	TN	63yrs		Martin Goins	Susan Goins		Nancy Goins
19543	Goins, John	TN	1872		Nathan Goins	Charlotta Goins	Sanford & Charity Goins	Shade & Orpha Goins
19795	Goins, Joshoway	TN	1838	Katie, Sippie Goins	Tilman Goins	Diana Helton	Laban & Ellie Goins	Hamon & Sarah Helton
2645	Goins, Lena	OK	1867	Benj Paden	Martin Jones	Mary Carpenter		

20184	Goins, Marshel	TN	1883		Joe Goins	Sallie Goins	Nathan & Charity Goins	Bird & Julie Irwin
6290	Goins, Martha	TN	1859	W.V. Goins	Elijah Newton	Susan Goins		Wm McGill & Nancy Goins
6288	Goins, Mary	AL	1860	F M Goins	Joshua Jones	Rachel Goins		Granville & Polly Goins
19531	Goins, Mary	TN	1871	William Goins	Nathan Goins	Charlotta Goins	Sanford & Charity Goins	Shade & Orpha Goins
22913	Goins, Mattie	AR	1882	Tom Sides	James Goins	Naoma Hampton	Wm & Liza Goins	George & Mary Hampton
10779	Goins, Miller	TN	1842	Nany Goins	Tilman Goins	Siana Helton	Labomy Goins	
18931	Goins, Milly	TN	1854	Andrew Goins	Nathan Goins	Charlotta Goins	Sanford & Charity Goins	Shade & Orpha Goins
9761	Goins, Milo	OK	33yrs	Mary Goins	James Goins	Francis McGill	Martin Goins & Manda Bowlin	William McGill
12481	Goins, Minnie	OK	1886		Jim Goins	Harriet Sizemore	Martin & Mandy Goins	
19541	Goins, Myrtle	TN	1883	Harvey Goins	Henry Goins	Fannie Bolden	Labron & Zeya Goins	Artenie & Nancy Goins
19544	Goins, Nathan	TN	1832	Charity Goins	Sanford Goins	Charity Helton	James & Rhoda Goins	Hanson & Sarah Helton
19520	Goins, Nelly	TN	1877	Colonel Goins		Polly Goins		James & Rhoda Helton
21696	Goins, Noah	TN	1867	Jane Goins	Dobson Goins	Eeraldy Goins	Granville Goins	Sarah Right
19540	Goins, Polly	TN	1855	John Goins	James Helton	Rhoda Goins	Joshoway & Polly Helton	Sanford & Charity Goins
8067	Goins, Riley	OK	1867	decd	Martin Goins	Amanda Bollin	James Goins	Malinda Bolin
21164	Goins, Samuel	TN	1871	Mary Goins	Dotson Goins	Erelda Goins	Granville & Polly Goins	Nathan & Sarah Goins
21156	Goins, Sarah	TN		George Goins	Spencer Goins	Edie Morrison	Tilman & Diana Goins	
19532	Goins, Sippie	TN	1870	Joshoway Goins		Paulina Goins		Thomas & Orpha Goins
8068	Goins, Taylor	OK	1855	Mary Goins	Martin Goins	Amanda Bollin	James Goins	Malinda Bollin
18932	Goins, Thomas	TN	1872		Jackson Goins	Merva Goins	John Goins	Eliza Goins
21852	Goins, Thomas	TN	1880	Annie Goins	Alfred Goins	Haley Goins	Thomas Goins	Granville & Polly Goins
22602	Goins, Vestie	TN	1887	Bircy Goins	John McEwin	Sarah Helton		Daniel & Martha Helton
6289	Goins, W.V.	TN	1848	Martha Goins	Nathan Goins	Marvilla Goins	John Goins	Laborn & Ella Goins
10980	Goins, William	TN	1848	Martha Goins	Nathan Goins	Marilla Goins	John Goins	Layburn Goins
19028	Goins, William	AL	1865		Nathan Goins	Charlotta Goins	Sanford & Charity Goins	Shade & Orpha Goins
19542	Goins, William	TN	1875	Mary Goins	Albert Goins	Polly Goins		James Helton & Rhoda Goins
20364	Goins, William	TN	1873		Joshua Goins	Catharine Goins	Tillman & Dinah Goins	Sanford & Charity Goins
22174	Goins, William	TN	1846	Nancy Goins	Solomon Goins	Betsy Shellhouse	Goins	Monday & Chariot Prescot
22910	Goins, William	AR	1879	May Goins	James Goins	Naoma Hampton	Wm & Liza Goins	George & Mary Hampton
2548	Golden, Nancy	GA	1871	N G Golden	Martan Williamson	Margaret Leadford		John & Nancy Leadford
7161	Goldsbury, Jesse	MO	49yrs	Sallie Goldsbury	William Goldsbury	Mary Blackburn		Jesse Blackburn

7163	Goldsbury, Orval	MO	1885	none	Jesse Goldsbury	Sallie Smith	Wm & Mary Goldsbury	Benage & Elizabeth Smith
7162	Goldsbury, Sallie	MO	52yrs	Jesse Goldsbury	Benage Smith	Elizabeth Blackburn		James & Nancy Blackburn
12435	Gonzales, Caleb	OK	1878		Dennis Gonzales	Rachel Pettit		Charles & Charlotte Pettit
16666	Gonzales, Frank	OK			Dennis Gonzales	Rachel Pettit		Charles & Charlotte Pettit
12815	Gonzales, John	OK	1876	Lucinda Gonzales	Dennis Gonzales	Rachel Pettit		Charles & Charlotte Pettit
16377	Gonzalis, Spencer	OK	1870	Sarah Gonzalis	Gunzlias	Deely Adair		George Hughes & Betsey Rowe
17742	Gonzalos, Mary	TN	1840		Tyree Kelley	Delila Emry	Johnathan & Mary Kelley	James & Nancy Emry
20035	Goodgion, Azilee	GA	1887	William Goodgion	William Fleming	Elizabeth Kirby	Gilbert & Caroline Fleming	James & Tabitha Kirby
20147 *	Goodin, Sarrah	GA	30 yrs	James Goodin	Joseph Brooks	Lueser Davis	George Steels & Mollie Brooks	
10981	Goodman, Charles	TN	1849	Katie Goodman	Thomas Goodman	Polly Hickman		
21045	Goodman, Genevieve	AL	1886	Crawford Goodman	Robert Holland	Eliza Moore		Eliza Mayo
22959	Goodman, Ida	OK	37yrs	Joseph Goodman	Charles Fargo	Narcicia Parnell		
22582	Goodman, Kate	TN	1882	Charles Goodman	John Hubbard	Martha Graves	James & Renna Hubbard	Silas & Mary Graves
6857	Goodman, Martha	VA	1879	Thomas Goodman	Abal Blevins	Ada Thompson		John & Polly Thompson
20482	Goodrich, Mary	TN	1841	James Goodrich	Godfrey Mathias	Mary Sloan	Mary Mathias	Annie Sloan
22162	Goodson Myra							
20940	Goodson, Alice	AL	1878	George Goodson	John Goddard	Sarah Granitt	J.B. & Laura Goddard	
17155	Goodwin, C.J.	TN	1859	W.T. Goodwin	George Cloer	Ann Swanson	Wm N. Cloer	Elizabeth Nicholes
10854	Goodwin, Cora	TX	1877	Wm Goodwin	Daniel Lawrence	Angeline Snow		Solomon Snow
22112	Goodwin, John	GA	57 yrs	Vera Goodin	John Goodin	Ellen Costtoe	Harrison & Harriet Goodin	Edward & Sarah Costtoe
6434	Goodwin, Kate	OK	1880	none	George Knight	Elizabeth Scott	Susan Knight	
22188	Goodwin, Lewis	GA	1863	widower	John Goodwin	Ellen Costlow	Elizabeth Goodwin	Edward & Sarah Costlow
11586	Goolsby, John	GA			John Goolsby	Sarah Ridley	Tanda & Jane Goolsby	Joseph & Emiline Ridley
11594	Goolsby, Sarah	GA	1870	John Goolsby	Joseph Ridley	Emiline Butler	Bill Ridley	
21277	Gorden, Abe	MO	1874	Mattie Gorden	James Gordan	Deborah McAdams	Hugh & Eliza Gordon	Joseph & Delilah McAdams
18892	Gorden, Albert	TN	1842	Eller Gorden	Cafitin Jim	Martha Jim		
21722	Gorden, Charles	TX	1869	Hulda Gorden	J.C. Gorden	Deborah McAdams	Hugh & Eliza Gorden	Joseph & Delila McAdams
7173	Gordon, Clara	KS	1875	John Gordon	Charles Shrim	Matilda Allen		Louis & Maggie Allen
22817	Gordon, Daisy	IL	1873	Samuel Gordon	John Irwin	Amanda Hadden	John Irwin & Amy Horner	John Hadden & Mary Robinson
22537	Gordon, John	IN	1840	Amy Gordon	George Gordon	Clarissa Williams		Joshua & Lucy Williams
5383	Gordon, Mary	MO		Embre Gordon	John Sweaney	Mary Loveall	Levi & Myra Sweaney	Stephen & Amanda Loveall
18950 *	Gordon, Robert	GA	1834	Rosa Gordon	Charles Rumph	Louisa Manning		Joe & Mary Manning

ID	Name	State	Year					
17327*	Gosa, Alson	AL			R.L. Gosa	N.A. Mole	J.W. & Lavina Gosa	Andy & Matildy Mole
17397*	Gosa, James	AL	1893	Lisey Gosa	Levi Gosa	Nancy Mots	James & Lavena Gosa	
17328*	Gosa, Robert	AL	1852		J.W. Gosa	Lanney Ivins	James Gosa	
20838*	Goss, Harriett	GA	1868	James Goss	Squire Strickland	Harriet Fields	George & Joyce Tassell	Sylla Fields
19137*	Goss, John	GA	1851	Jane Goss	Snute Eye	Ann Goss		Benj Stately
3611	Goss, Laura	NC	1878	F M Goss	Wilson Thompson	Eda Eldrith	Wesley & Amanda Thompson	John & Sarah Eldrith
3612	Goss, Maria	NC		Winfield Goss	Wilson Thompson	Eda Eldrith	Wesley & Amandy Thompson	John & Sarah Eldrith
14349	Goss, Mary	KS	1874	D H Goss	George Wetzel	Josephine Logsdon	Henry & Elizabeth Wetzel	
2597	Goss, Rufiny	GA	1854	Joseph Goss	David Ash	Elisabeth Davenport		John & Elisabeth Davenport
17737	Gossett, Rillie	TN	1884	H.M. Gossett	Hezekiah Posey	Viney Goodwin	Hezekiah & Patsey Posey	
21595	Gotts, Ruth	NC	1862		David Watson	Nancy King		John & Katie King
14127	Gough, Amittia	NC	1840		William Poindexter	Mary Taylor	Wm & Elizabeth Poindexter	Mart & Susanah Taylor
18843	Gough, Lethia	NC	1885	W.H. Gough	J.W. Culler	M.E. Scott	Constatin & Bettie Culler	Hampton & Bettie Scott
21888*	Gowdy, Harriet	TN	1859		Oliver Gowdy	Margaret Gowdy		
17586	Graham, Ada	KS	1892		Asa Graham	Barbra Graham	Charles & Margret Graham	Alex & Margret Graham
18054	Graham, Albert	MO	1884		Thomas Graham	Loucretia Gapp	Alex & Margaret Graham	James & Lorena Gapp
17587	Graham, Alonzo	KS	1880	Mamie Graham	Asa Graham	Barbra Graham	Charles & Margret Graham	Alex & Margret Graham
17589	Graham, Barbra	KS	1853	Asa Graham	Alex Graham	Margret Golden	Benj & Mary Graham	Wm & Darkas Golden
18584	Graham, Capitola	MO	1906		Jeff Graham	Lessie Cherry	Alex & Margret Graham	Jess & Lusenda Cherry
18096	Graham, Charles	MO	1880	Eliza Graham	William Graham	Hormana Dale	Alex & Margret Graham	John & Carline Dale
21476	Graham, Charles	TX			James Graham	Martha	James & Martha Graham	
21477	Graham, Charles	TX	1856	Mary Graham	? Graham	? Glass		
20231	Graham, Charlie	TN		Eliza Graham	Austin Graham	Easter Graham		
10489	Graham, Cherry	WV	1882	Henry Graham	John Walker	Nancy Bailey	Numa & Martha Walker	Floyd & Z S Bailey
18583	Graham, Earl	MO	1898		Jeff Graham	Susie Cherry	Alex & Margret Graham	Jess & Lusenda Cherry
18066	Graham, Ella	MO	1878	Otis Ingram	Thomas Graham	Loucretia Gapp	Alex & Margaret Graham	Jean & Lorena Gapp
18586	Graham, Elsie	MO	1902		Jeff Graham	Lessie Cherry	Alex & Margret Graham	Jess & Lusenda Cherry
18770	Graham, Flocy	MO	1906		Sid Dixon	Ina Graham	Edgar & Lisezebeth Dixon	Thos & Lucrecia Graham
21311	Graham, George	TX	1875	Alice Graham	William Graham	Jane Faulkner	James & Martha Graham	
17590	Graham, Harvey	KS	1876	Pearl Graham	Asa Graham	Barbra Graham	Charles & Margret Graham	Alex & Margret Graham
18059	Graham, Ina	MO	1890	Sidney Dixon	Thomas Graham	Loucretia Gapp	Alex & Margaret Graham	Jean & Lorena Gapp

18106	Graham, Ivy	MO	1889	Jess Taylor	William Graham	Hormana Dale	Alex & Margret Graham	John & Carline Dale
18058	Graham, James	MO	1872	Nora Graham	Thomas Graham	Loucretia Gapp	Alex & Margaret Graham	Jean & Lorena Gapp
18298	Graham, James	OK	1892	Siopa Graham	Alex Graham	Margret Golden	Peter & Mary Graham	Wm & Darbis Golden
21306	Graham, James	TX	1848	Martha & Amanda	James Graham	Martha		Richard Glass
18588	Graham, Jeff	MO	1860	Lessie Graham	Alex Graham	Margret Golden	Benj & Mary Graham	Wm & Darkis Golden
18420	Graham, John	MO	1872	Dollie Graham	Wm Graham	Martha Thorn	Alex & Margret Graham	Bill & Mary Thorn
21229	Graham, John	TX	1861	Eliza Graham	James Graham	Martha Glass		
18095	Graham, Joie	MO	1906		Charles Graham	Eliza Reagan	Wm & Hermana Graham	Robert & Evaline Reagan
21307	Graham, Joseph	TX	1883		William Graham	Sarah Faulkner		
18055	Graham, Lelia	MO	1894		James Graham	Nora Maxwell	Thomas & Lucretia Graham	Wm Maxwell & Sarah Bristow
18589	Graham, Lessie	MO	1869	Jeff Graham	Jess Cherry	Lucenda Golden	Bill & Sarah Cherry	Wm & Darkis Golden
17654	Graham, Lula	OK	1884		Asa Graham	Barbra Graham	Charles & Margret Graham	Alex & Margret Graham
19223	Graham, Madge	KS	1887	Fred Graham	Grant Davis	Elizabeth Sizemore		James Sizemore
1586	Graham, Martha	OK	1885			Margaret Golden		William Golden
3123	Graham, Martha	MS	1867	John Graham	James Hobgood	Martha Stuart	Charles & Martha Hobgood	
1585	Graham, Mary	OK				Margaret Golden		William Golden
9821	Graham, Mary	NC	1865		James Murphy	Polly McMillan	Polly Murphy	Joe & Millie McMillan
12022	Graham, Mary	GA	1842	James Graham	James Prather	Parthenia Pool		Claborn & Martha Pool
13519	Graham, Mary	GA	1842	widow	James Prather	Parthana Pool	Edward & Mary Prather	Martha Pool
19258	Graham, Mary	KS	1903		Harvy Graham	Leanisa Payton	Asa & Barbra Graham	John & Sarah Payton
19259	Graham, Mary	KS	1904		Lanza Graham	Mamie Laird	Asa & Barbra Graham	Isaac & Elizabeth Laird
18108	Graham, Maud	MO	1903		William Graham	Hormana Dale	Alex & Margret Graham	John & Carline Dale
19260	Graham, Mildred	KS	1906		Lanza Graham	Mamie Laird	Asa & Barbra Graham	Isaac & Elizabeth Laird
19257	Graham, Miram	KS	1905		Harvy Graham	Leanisa Payton	Asa & Barbra Graham	John & Sarah Payton
18107	Graham, Nellie	MO	1893		William Graham	Hormana Dale	Alex & Margret Graham	John & Carline Dale
18056	Graham, Nina	MO	1899		James Graham	Nora Maxwell	Thomas & Lucretia Graham	Wm & Sarah Maxwell
18094	Graham, Orville	MO	1901		Charles Graham	Eliza Reagan	Wm & Hermana Graham	Robert & Evaline Reagan
18093	Graham, Paul	MO	1903		Charles Graham	Eliza Reagan	Wm & Hermana Graham	Robert & Evaline Reagan
18423	Graham, Pearl	OK	1885		Jeff Graham	Sarrie Gillstrap	Alex & Margret Graham	
17588	Graham, Philip	NE	1874	Myra Graham	Asa Graham	Barbra Graham	Charles & Margret Graham	Alex & Margret Graham
21227	Graham, Richard	TX	1859	Mittie Graham	James Graham	Martha Cambline		Richard & Pliny Glass

22198	Graham, Stacy	TN	1853	N. Graham	William Murphy	Millie McMullen	Matoy & Rachel Riley	Joseph & Millie McMullen
18587	Graham, Thelma	MO	1900		Jeff Graham	Lessie Cherry	Alex & Margret Graham	Jess & Lusenda Cherry
18065	Graham, Thomas	MO	1849	Lucrecia Gaff	Alex Graham	Margret Golden	Benj & Mary Graham	Wm & Darkis Golden
18585	Graham, Walter	MO	1892		Jeff Graham	Lessie Cherry	Alex & Margret Graham	Jess & Lusenda Cherry
18067	Graham, Ward	MO	1887		Thomas Graham	Loucretia Gapp	Alex & Margaret Graham	Jean & Lorena Gapp
11393	Graham, William	TN	1855	Sarah Graham	William Graham	Mary Matoy		
17591	Graham, William	KS	1872		Asa Graham	Barbra Graham	Charles & Margret Graham	Alex & Margret Graham
18057	Graham, William	MO	1896		James Graham	Nora Maxwell	Thomas & Lucretia Graham	Wm & Sarah Maxwell
21228	Graham, William	TX	1886	Ida Graham	John Graham	Lena Copeland	James & Martha Graham	
21310	Graham, William	TX	1844	Sarah Graham	James Graham	Patsy Glass		Pliny Glass
21473	Graham, William	TX	1877	Lula Graham	William Graham	Jane Faulkner	James Graham	George Faulkner
22881	Graham, William	MO	1871	Effie Graham	Taylor Graham	Nancy Matay		Wm & Martha Matay
15265	Grambling, Ola	GA		Coleman Grambling	Jeffrey Beck	Mandy Loggins	Coleman Davis & Elmira Beck	
18087	Gramblling, Ola	GA	1884		Jeffrey Beck	Mandy Loggins	Coleman Davis & Elmira Beck	
8827	Grandstaff, Ulah	OK	1885	W C Grandstaff	William Davis	Sara Garison	Richard Davis	
19279	Grant, Amanda	NC	1876	Charles Grant	Samuel McMahan	Mary Mason		John & Pollie Mason
11389	Grant, Mary	NC	1876	Wilkie Grant	Joseph Mason	Caroline Mason	John & Pollie Mason	
22360	Grant, Minnie	TN	1878	Vassie Grant	Jeff Luthem	Sufrona Bryant	George & Jane Lathem	Geter & Sarah Bryant
19819	Grant, Ramoth	GA	1882	Clarence Grant	Isaac Cook	Martha Turner	Richard & Sarah Cook	
1434	Grant, Susannah	TN	1854	Thomas Grant	Jonas Linn	Demerisa Kirkland	Thomas Linn & Betsy Boston	Jim Kirkland & Susanah Boston
9113	Grant, Tiney	NC	1876	James Grant	James Martin	Elizabeth Caylor	Abigail Martin	
2285	Grass, Vennie et al	OK	18, 15, 8yrs		Benjamin Grass	Sarah & Eliza Grass	Jack & Katie Grass	
15271	Gravely, Dora	GA	1902		Bucker Gravely	Sallie Jordan		Noah Jr & Susan Jordan
15270	Gravely, Elbert	GA	1900		Bucker Gravely	Sallie Jordan		Noah Jr & Susan Jordan
11355	Gravely, Ellen	GA	1844	A. Gravely		Dorothy Kennedy		Lexington & Elizabeth Kennedy
15269	Gravely, Hubert	GA	1905		Bucker Gravely	Sallie Jordan		Noah Jr & Susan Jordan
11354	Gravely, J. Lemmuel	GA	1851	Martha Gravely	Jesse Gravely	Elizabeth Warren		Anderson & Betsy Warren
15268	Gravely, Jesse	GA	1896		Bucker Gravely	Sallie Jordan		Noah Jr & Susan Jordan
15267	Gravely, Jim	GA	1899		Bucker Gravely	Sallie Jordan		Noah Jr & Susan Jordan
10530	Gravely, Oscar	GA	1872		A. Gravely	Ellen Kennedy		Dorothy Kennedy
11353	Gravely, Prestor	GA	1869	Fannie Gravely	A. Gravely	Ellen Kennedy		Dorothy Kennedy

15264	Gravely, Sallie	GA	1877	Bucher Gravely	Noah Jordan Jr	Susan Ragsdale	Noah & Adaline Jordan	
10531	Gravely, Thomas	GA	1875	Lizzie Gravely	A. Gravely	Ellen Kennedy		Dorothy Kennedy
15262	Gravely, Wealthy	GA	1841		Jesse Gravely	Elizabeth Warren		Anderson & Betsy Warren
16361	Graves, Allen	TN	1866	Dollie Graves	Al Newman	Charlotie Payne	Samuel Graves & Simmi Newman	Shilottie Payne & Millie Graves
16362	Graves, Doshie	TN	1887		Samuel Graves	Mahalie Newman	Samuel Graves & Simmi Newman	Shilottie Payne & Millie Graves
22571	Graves, Ellen	OK	1870	Thomas Graves	William Vann	Lottie Willis	David & Nancy Vann	Hamp & Amanda Willis
18333	Graves, George	TN	1869		Samuel Jones	Mahala Newman		Samuel & Charlotta Newman
3274	Graves, Harriett	NC	1855	John Graves	James McDonald	Jemima Deaton	Anquish & Sallie McDonald	Johnathan & Sarah Deaton
19579	Graves, Kate	MI	1876	Ervin Graves	Lark Robinson	Rebecca Roots		Rubin Roots
12460	Graves, Luther	NC	1879	Ada Graves	John Graves	Harriet McDonald	William Graves	James McDonald
18335	Graves, Mahala	TN	63yrs	Samuel Graves	Samuel Newman	Charlota Payne		John & Jane Payne
18332	Graves, Press	TN		Sillie Graves	Samuel Graves	Mahala Newman	Allen Jones	Samuel Newman & Charlota Payne
18334	Graves, Samuel	TN	1867	Manda Graves	Samuel Jones	Mahala Newman		Samuel & Charlotta Newman
18337	Graves, Samuel	TN	1832	Mahala Graves	Allen Jones	Mahala Graves		Benj & Rachel Graves
18505	Graves, Tennessee	NC	1889		John Graves	Harett McDonald	Wm & Amy Graves	James & Mary McDonald
14513	Gravit, Dovie	GA	1897		John Gravit	Mira Brookshir	Luke & Celia Gravit	Levi & Jane Brookshir
14512	Gravit, John	GA	1836	Mira Gravit	Luke Gravit	Celia Tidwell	Obediah & Nancy Gravit	John Tidwell
14511	Gravit, Leila	GA	1893		John Gravit	Mira Brookshir	Luke & Celia Gravit	Levi & Jane Brookshir
14510	Gravit, Lewis	GA	1880	Lizzie Gravit	John Gravit	Mira Brookshir	Luke & Celia Gravit	Levi & Jane Brookshir
14509	Gravit, Mancel	GA	1882	Mollie Gravit	John Gravit	Mira Brookshir	Luke & Celia Gravit	Levi & Jane Brookshir
21006 *	Gravitt, Maggie	GA	1870	C.C. Gravitt	George Wilson	Mary Morgan	Eliga & Martha Wilson	Elizabeth Morgan
14508	Gravitt, Melvin	GA	1889		John Gravit	Mira Brookshir	Luke & Celia Gravit	Levi & Jane Brookshir
14507	Gravitt, Nelia	GA	1895		John Gravit	Mira Brookshir	Luke & Celia Gravit	Levi & Jane Brookshir
16035	Gravley, Lovie	GA	1855	L W Gravley	W B Swann	Polly Kelly	James & Rebecca Swann	
10394	Gray, Amy	OK	1872	Samuel Gray	John Crow	Marandy Rogers		Henry & Mariah Rogers
16477 *	Gray, Charley	GA	1845	Mariah Gray	Toney Craft	Eliza Saddler		Peter & Rachel Baily
20299	Gray, Clara	OK	1878	Bunk Gray	Andrew Avants	Rebeckie Welch		
20004	Gray, Ellen	TN	1859	James Gray	Samuel Newman	Mary Elison		Abe & Austin Elison
21353	Gray, Sam	TX	1881		E.A. Gray	Lela Burton	Jim Gray	John Burton
7171	Gray, Theodore	OK	1869	Gertrude Gray	Hinchen Gray	Sarah Biggers		Wm Biggers & Cynthia Nicholson
20341 *	Gray, William	TN	1845	Flora Gray	- Gray	Anica -		

3618	Graybeal, Martha	NC	1871	W S Graybeal	T J Baldwin	Elizabeth Jones	Wm & Margaret Baldwin	
17054	Grayson, Katie	OK	40yrs	Eli Grayson	Sup sie	Ros sie		Ca nuch ee & Jennie
3449	Grayson, Samuel gdn	OK			Sam Grayson	Kate Ross		Richard & Lizzie Ross
17121	Greece, Betsey	OK			Tom Candy	Susan Graves	John & Betsey Candy	John Ca nee ta
21846	Green, Amanda	TN	1868	Joe Green	William Russell	Marenia Spivey	Mathew & Annie Russell	Halliday & Susan Spivey
10144	Green, Arnold	WV	1895	none	Greensberry Green	Mary Perdew	Nancy Green	Nathaniel & Sallie Perdew
10143	Green, Calvin	WV	1886	Nancy Green	Greensberry Green	Mary Perdew	Nancy Green	Nathaniel & Sallie Perdew
1136	Green, Catherine	OK	1857	Robert Green	James Green	Elvira Perrin		Thomas & Jane Perrin
18896	Green, Donie	NC	44yrs	W.T. Green	William Giles	Adaline Battle		Watson & Saley Battle
18417	Green, Ellen	CA	1870	William Green	Griffin Oxcudine	Perline Lowery		Mary Lowery
19138	Green, Essie	GA	1879	Amber Green	James Braziel	Seleta Doss		Edward & Seleta Doss
19885	Green, Feriba	TN	1878	C.N. Green	Nathan Curtis	Susan Collier	Joshua & Elizabeth Curtis	
15851	Green, George et al	OK	1859		John Green	Emily Langford		Robt Langford & Lucinda Randolph
22579	Green, Irvin	TN	1849		John Green	Mary Freeman	John & Jane Green	Obediah & Elizabeth Freeman
5739	Green, James	OK	1859	Ruthey Smalley	Fleming Green	Margarite Clung	John Green	R J Clung
20417	Green, Jane	TN	1858		Willis Prescott	Ellen Haney		Jackson & Rachel Haney
17966 *	Green, Jesse	GA	1833		Coleman Green	Louisa Singleton	Jesse & Dolly Green	Ab & Louisa Singleton
9697	Green, John	OK	1865	Emma Green	Flemings Green	Margaret Clung	John Green	R J Clung
17967 *	Green, John	GA	1844	Malissa Green	Jesse Green	Hulda Reid	Coleman & Louisa Green	
19674	Green, Laura	TN	1875	James Green	Wallace Medcalf	Victory Hatcher	Joel & Susan Medcalf	Wm & Elisabeth Hatcher
16386	Green, Lucinda	OK	1885	John Green	Jackson Kelley	Rachel Young Squirl	Wm & Catherine Kelley	James & Annie Young Squirl
1027	Green, Lucy	KY	1855	none	James Green	Elvira Perrin		Thomas & Jane Perrin
16347	Green, Mariah	TN	1849	Joseph Green	John Dunahoo	Nancy Howard	John Dunahoo	Wm Howard & Sallie Sixton
5155	Green, Marian	TN	1849	Lydia Green	Stantun Green	Temperance Eaton		Wm & Marian Eaton
17672	Green, Marinda	GA			Luke Gravett	Celia Tidwell	Obediah & Nancy Gravett	John & Sallie Tidwell
9558	Green, Marion	NC	1851	Mercy Green	Benj Green	Dicey Prichard	Ely & Saly Green	Jessey & Dart Prichard
11205	Green, Marion	GA	1864	Sallie Green	John Green	Mary Stone	Balis & Myra Green	Archabel & Mary Stone
10287	Green, Martha	GA	1881	Ira Green	David Davenport	Lucinda Bradford	Thos & Elizabet Davenport	Aaron & Nancy Bradford
18202	Green, Martha	TN	1859		Allen Grimes	Caroline Scott	Hattie Grimes	Jeney Scott
21419	Green, Meady	TX	1877	J.S. Green	William Meadows	Maggie Meadows	Emly Meadows	

10127	Green, Nathaniel	WV	1882	Lou Green	Greensberry Green	Mary Perdew	Nancy Green	Nathaniel & Sallie Perdew
9560	Green, Richard	NC	1848	none	Berry Green	Duck Pritchard	Eley & Salley Green	Jessey & Dart Pritchard
2980	Green, Sabray	MO	1845	widow	John Woodall	Annie Halcomb	John & Causby Woodall	John & Sarah Halcomb
7601	Green, Samuel	GA	1845	Nancy Green	John Green	Elmyra Parker	John & Mary Green	
10134	Green, Sanna	WV	1884	Nellie Green	Greensberry Green	Mary Perdew	Nancy Green	Martelia & Sallie Perdew
18915	Green, Thomas	GA		Emma Green		Mary Green		Rolin Green
20284	Green, Tinie	OK	1884	Frank Green	T. Welch	Annie Beeler	Henry & Annie Welch	Robert & P.J. Beeler
8429	Green, William	NC	1865	Dona Green	William Hyde	Jane Green	William Tomas	Cathren Rogers
9569	Greene, Francis	AL	1878	Anna Greene	David Greene	Levina Martan		Joseph Martan
18811	Greenham, Mande	TX	1886	Ottis Greenham	Henry Speer	Sarah Tekell		Niper & Eliza Tekell
21073	Greenway, George	AL	1847		William Greenway	Rhoda Jennings	John Greenway	James Jennings
8937	Greer, Bertie	TN	1904	none	Henry Greer	Mina Geiler	J Greer & Eugenia Parker	John Geiler & Elizabeth Danneberg
10764	Greer, Callie	OK	1880	Luther Greer	Lewis Powell	Rebecca Hinchee		Benjamin & Annie Hinchee
3575	Greer, Elzina	NC	1881	Harrison Greer	Wilson Thompson	Eda Eldrith	Wesley & Amanda Thompson	John & Sarah Eldrith
3592	Greer, Emmaline	NC	1872	Benjamin Greer	George Fritts	Melvina Thompson	Rubin & Kissey Fritts	Wesley & Amanda Thompson
8935	Greer, Frank	TN	1883	none	J Munson Greer	Eugenia Parker	Newton Greer	Willis Parker & Adeline Vanoy
8936	Greer, Grace	TN	1888	none	J Munson Greer	Eugenia Parker	Newton Greer	Willis Parker & Adeline Vanoy
8939	Greer, Henry	TN	1881	Nuna Greer	J Munson Greer	Eugenia Parker	Newton Greer	Willis Parker & Adeline Vanoy
15069	Greer, Lelia	OK	1882	William Greer	Benjamin Stone	Emma Murphy		Jess & Phoeba Murphy
8933	Greer, Lewis	TN	1874	Rose Greer	J Munson Greer	Eugenia Parker	Newton Greer	Willis Parker & Adeline Vanoy
8934	Greer, Lula	TN	1875	none	J Munson Greer	Eugenia Parker	Newton Greer	Willis Parker & Adeline Vanoy
20188	Greer, Reuben	TN	1858	Mary Greer	David Greer	Anna Watson	Samuel Greer & Sara Church	Thos Watson & Gracey Owasa
8938	Greer, Vanoy	TN	1893	none	J Munson Greer	Eugenia Parker	Newton Greer	Willis Parker & Adeline Vanoy
20038	Gregory, Barney	OK	1903		James Gregory	Susan Graham	James & Margaret Gregory	Asa & Barbara Graham
17578	Gregory, Chrustiana	NC	1870	A.J. Gregory	Isaac Sneed	Sarah Sneed	Ezekiel & Nancy Sneed	James & Elizabeth Sneed
18803 *	Gregory, Claude	GA	1885	Mattie Gregory	John Gregory	Fannie Kemp	Ephraim & Caroline Gregory	
15557 *	Gregory, Eunice	GA	1883	George Gregory	Sam Smith	Rhoda Jinks	Pink & Lizzie Smith	Joe Jinks & Elizabeth Morris
15555 *	Gregory, Georgia	GA	1884	Wesley Gregory	Allen McConnell	Julia Rump	Frank & Eliza McConnell	Tol & Hannah Rump
20040	Gregory, Harold	OK	1906		James Gregory	Susan Graham	James & Margaret Gregory	Asa & Barbara Graham

20039	Gregory, Hazel	OK	1905		James Gregory	Susan Graham	James & Margaret Gregory	Asa & Barbara Graham
15556*	Gregory, Henry	GA	1852	Etta Gregory	Ephraim Gregory	Caroline Burge	Joe & Clay West	Roney & Clarisy Burge
15548*	Gregory, Jack	GA	1882		Ephraim Gregory	Mary Fields	Joe & Clay Witt	
11516	Gregory, Jane	MO	1851	William Gregory	Enoch Euloe	Jane Murray		Thos & Burhart Murray
18858	Gregory, Lucinda	TN	1859	John Gregory	John Elliott	Mary Phillpott	John Elliott & Nancy Brumet	Barton Phillpott & Cathran Burk
10475	Gregory, Mary	MO	1884	Robert Gregory	Alfred Ellis	Mary Sikes	Alex & Mary Ellis	Benj & Elizabeth Sikes
19535	Gregory, Mary	TN	1866	Samuel Gregory	Cornelius Long	Luraney Shoemake		John & Mary Shoemake
14506*	Gregory, Mattie	GA	1892	Claude Gregory	Madison Scudders	Julia Looper	Kitty Scudders	Thursday Looper
15547*	Gregory, Oliver	GA	1888		Ephraim Gregory	Caroline Burge	Joe & Clay Witt	Toney & Clarisy Burge
15546*	Gregory, Seaborn	GA	1882	Lena Gregory	Ephraim Gregory	Caroline Burge	Joe & Clay Witt	Toney & Clarisy Burge
17653	Gregory, Susan	OK	1878	James Gregory	Asa Graham	Barbra Graham	Charles & Margret Graham	Alex & Margret Graham
13874	Gribble, Georgia	TX	1875	James Gribble	Robert Bell	Lucindy Hampton	James & Elizabeth Bell	George & Mary Hampton
14505	Grier, Belle	GA	1898		Robert Grier	Lula Grovitt	Joshua & Nannie Grier	John & Francis Grovitt
14549	Grier, Bessie	GA	1908		Robert Grier	Lula Gravitt	Joshua Grier	John & Francis Gravitt
14525	Grier, Carrie	GA	1885	William Grier	George Millwood	Amanda New	Hugh & Miriam Millwood	Joel & Mary New
17835	Grier, Henry	GA	1857	Emily Grier	Joshua Grier	Susan Dogget		
15545	Grier, Jane	GA	1878	Henry Grier	Frank Richardson	Susan Philipps	James & Nancy Richardson	Elijah & Lucinda Philipps
14524	Grier, Jesse	GA	1904		Robert Grier	Lula Gravit	Joshua & Nannie Grier	John & Francis Gravit
14523	Grier, Lessey	GA	1900		Robert Grier	Lula Gravit	Joshua & Nannie Grier	John & Francis Gravit
11318	Grier, Lula	GA	1872	Robert Grier	John Gravit	Francis Tyler	Luke & Celia Gravit	Jim & Susan Tyler
17834	Grier, Roxie	GA	1883		Henry Grier	Emily Flanagan	Joshua & Susan Grier	Wiley Flanagan
15544	Grier, Ruby	GA	1004		Henry Grier	Jane Richardson	Thos & Mary Grier	Frank & Susan Richardson
14522	Grier, Walter	GA	1896		Robert Grier	Lula Gravit	Joshua & Nannie Grier	John & Francis Gravit
17833	Grier, William	GA	1888		Henry Grier	Emily Flanagan	Joshua & Susan Grier	Wiley Flanagan
11352	Griffies, Thomas	GA	1866	Nancy Griffies	William Griffies	Louisa Freeman	Isham & Nancy Griffies	
6463	Griffin, Martha	OK	1848	Ignatious Griffin	Wm Braziel	Margaret Prater	Sarah Brazile	Aaron & Susan Prater
16142	Griffin, Edna	TX	1882	Anderson Griffin	William Henson	Josephine Mabry	Henry Henson & Mary Hardman	Joseph Mabry & Hester Adkins
10321*	Griffin, Emaline	GA	69yrs	George Griffin	Thomas Thumb	Hannah Townsend		
18348	Griffin, Loony	OK	1861	Mary Griffin	Jack Griffin	Lila Petitt	Thomas Griffin	
20050	Griffin, Ruth	TX	1884	Singleton Griffin	Miles Faucett	Sallie Griffis	Wm & Elizabeth Faucett	Wm & Mary Griffis
20060	Griffin, Vera	TX	1880	Marshall Griffin	Miles Faucett	Sallie Griffis	Wm & Elizabeth Faucett	Wm & Mary Griffis
20054	Griffis, Joe	TX	1873	Anna Griffis	Thomas Griffis	Margaret Faucett	Wm & Sarah Griffis	Wm & Elizabeth Faucett
20053	Griffis, William	TX	1854		Thomas Griffis	Margaret Faucett	Wm & Sarah Griffis	Wm & Elizabeth Faucett

11942 *	Griffith, Albert	GA	1845	Nancy Griffith	William Griffith	Addaline Griffith		
12746	Griffith, Mary	TN	1848	John Griffith	James Ford	Elizabeth Mantooth		Thos Mantooth & Lettie Dillon
2663	Griffitts, Jessie	MO	1882	Perry Griffitts		Asa Fender		Asa & Charlotte Fender
9354	Grigg, Sarah	AR	1856	Jasper Grigg	Thomas McCollough	Lovicie Bays	Moses McCollough	Letta Bays
2554	Griggs, Tina Tidwell	GA	1881	Jasper Griggs	John Tidwell	Susan Abernathy	Francis Tidwell	Margaret Tidwell
19757	Grimes, Highley	TN	1840		John Hicks	Polly Medling	Cager & Mary Hicks	
14282 *	Grimes, Patsy	TN	1861	Bill Grimes	Sam Grimes	Hager Jackson	Bob & Katie Blacksmith	
17296	Grimm, Emily	AL	1883	Mary Grimm	William Sizemore	Margarett Black	Joel Sizemore	Sinthe Webster
18783 *	Grimmett, Easter	OK		Dan Williams	Jack Ratliff	Silvia Ratliff	Harry Bloodworth	Judia Grimmett
18152	Grindle, Martha	GA	1873	James Grindle	Jesse Stancel	Annie Brown	John & Millie Stancel	
14219	Grisham, Martha	TN	1851	Thomas Grisham	Andrew Headrick	Eliza Jestus	John & Mary Headrick	Martin & Polly Jestus
5253	Gritts, Nancy	OK	32yrs	George Gritts	Ah-ne-loh-geh-yah	Alsie Bear		
8435	Grizzle, Malinda	GA	1831	James Grizzle	Jacob Helton	Elizabeth Swain	John & Dicie Helton	Levi & Nancy Swaine
17424	Grose, Cordelia	WV	1845	G.W. Grose	John Brown	Susan Neal	Alex Brown	John Neal
17871	Grow, Harry	OK	1883		Wm Grow	Mahalia Wethers	Amos & Sallie Grow	
7775	Grow, Robert	OK	1856	Maria Grow	Annias Grow	Sallie Hilterbrand		Henry & Mary Hilterbrand
7164	Grow, William	OK	1874	Laura Grow (decd)	William Grow	Mahalie Weather	Ananias & Sallie Grow	
7165	Grow, William	OK	1848	Ellie Grow	Annias Grow	Sallie Hilterbrand		
14348	Grubb, Fanny	OK	1880	Samuel Grubb	James Allen	Sarah Barker	Daniel & Louisa Allen	Alex & Sarah Barker
16815	Grubbs, Isabella	NC	1874	Thomas Grubbs	Henry Farrus	Deana Whitehead	John & Candess Farrus	James & Hannah Whitehead
18033 *	Gude, Charles	TN	1870	Lucinda Gude	Richard Gude	Elizabeth Mee		Charles & Harriet Mee
11023	Guess, Nannie	VA	1858	Mathuslia Guess	John Tester	Sarah Mofield		James Dolison & Polly Mofield
17844	Guest, Sina	GA	1882	Joseph Guest	James Patterson	Maggie Ward	Samuel & Nancy Patterson	John & Sarah Ward
17593	Guffey, Cynthia	NC	1856	Thomas Guffey	Samuel Leatherwood	Hazy Robertson	Samuel & Sallie Leatherwood	Thomas & Annie Robertson
21003	Guinn, Abraham	TN	1890		Newton Guinn	Forest Kimsey	Jack & G. Guinn	Humphrey Kimsey
22140	Guinn, Abraham	TN	1828		Almond Guinn	Sarah Lillard		
7177	Guinn, Caleb	OR	1867	Eva Guinn	Isaac Guinn	Mary Smith	William Guinn	Benage & Elizabeth Smith
21004	Guinn, Charles	TN	1885		Newton Guinn	Forest Kimsey	Jack & G. Guinn	Humphrey Kimsey
22092	Guinn, George	TN	1862	Louisa Guinn	Abraham Guinn	Cornelia Crawford	Almond Guinn	Thomas Crawford
16404	Guinn, John	TN	1857	Margaret Guinn	Abraham Guinn		Allman Guinn	
21005	Guinn, Owen	TN	1893		Newton Guinn	Forest Kimsey	Jack & G. Guinn	Humphrey Kimsey

21002	Guinn, William	TN	1882		Newton Guinn	Forest Kimsey	Jack & G. Guinn	Humphrey Kimsey
7170	Gun, Martha	OK	1845	Jodie Gumm	Ananais Grow	Sally Hilderbrand		
19649	Gunn, Louisa	TN	1844	A..J. Gunn	Thomas Crofford	Elizabeth Edner	George & Pattey Crofford	Mrs. Harper
22950*	Gunter, Rachel	OK	63yrs	Lewis Gunter	Parlor Drew	Katie Mackey		Joshua & Lucy Vann
18315	Guthery, Nancy	IN	50yrs		James Guthery	Margret Bowman		Edger & Abigail Bowman
17678	Guthrey, Dickson	CO	1859	Emma Guthrey	William Guthrey	Francis Lee	Robert & Mary Guthrey	J.A. & Sarah Lee
17916	Guthrey, John	CO	1862	Laura Guthrey	Wm Guthrey	Frances Lee	Robert & Mary Guthrey	J.C. & Sarah Lee
18360	Guthrey, Lena	TN	1868		Wm Guthrey	E.Frances Lee	Robbert Guthrey & Mary Hardin	J.C. & Sarah Lee
18357	Guthrey, Lyetta	TN	1879		Wm Guthrey	E.Frances Lee	Robbert Guthrey & Mary Hardin	J.C. & Sarah Lee
18361	Guthrey, William	TN	1871	Lillian Guthrey	Wm Guthrey	E.Frances Lee	Robbert Guthrey & Mary Hardin	J.C. & Sarah Lee
21166	Guthrie, Charlie	TN	1884	John Guthrie	Harold	Isabelle Goins		Nathan & Sallie Goins
21642	Guthrie, Stella	TN	1882	George Guthrie	Jeff Goins	Isabella Goins		Nathan & Sally Goins
669	Guy, Aaron	IN	1856	Ora Guy	Henry Guy	Kizziah Mitchell	Henry & Betsy Guy	
16574	Guy, Adaline	GA	1861	J A Cash	Daniel Guy	Mary Forster		
13812	Guy, George	TN	1855	Josephine Guy	John Wolf	Juda Guy	Squirrel	
18725	Guy, Henry	TN	1869	Cordia Guy	Andrew Guy	Polly Bingham	Willis & Mahala Guy	Joel & Lydia Bingham
18718	Guy, Isaac	TN	1854	Maggie Guy	Willis Guy	Mahala Gibson	Edmund & Judie Guy	George & Viney Gibson
7174	Guy, Jessie	MO	1875	John Guy	John Fuller	Margaret Baldwin	Andrew & Mary Fuller	Alonzo & Rebecca Baldwin
16567	Guy, Joseph	GA	1866	Lillie Guy	Daniel Guy	Mary Foster	Jessey Guy & Betsey Merriett	Sam Foster
16570	Guy, Lou	GA	1872		Daniel Guy	Mary Forester	Jerry Guy & Betsey Merit	Sam Forester
16576	Guy, Maggie	GA	1874	John Green	Daniel Guy	Mary Foster	Jessie Guy & Bettie Merrett	Sam Foster
18717	Guy, Mary	TN	1838		Willis Guy	Mahala Gibson	Edmund & Judie Guy	George & Viney Gibson
18724	Guy, Millard	TN	1857	Annie Guy	Willis Guy	Mahala Gibson	Edmund & Judie Guy	George & Viney Gibson
18719	Guy, Sarah	GA	1852		Willis Guy	Mahala Gibson	Edmund & Judie Guy	George & Viney Gibson
2629	Guyton, Fannie	GA	1880	William Guyton	J T Abernathy	Delpha Tidwell	David Abernathy	Francis Tidwell
21001	Guyton, Isabelle	MS	1847	J.T. Guyton	C.M. Marler	H.C. Clearmon	T.B. & Matilda Marler	Van & Peggie Clearmon
17290	Guyton, Marget	AL	1872		Harrison Hollis	Mary Wright	& M.L. Hollis	& Martha Wright
14481	Gwinn, Anna	AL	1870	widow	Daniel Sizemore	Margaret Woods	Daniel Sizemore & Anna Hawkins	
7158	Gwinn, Dovie	MO	1873	William Gwinn	Lewis Turner	Alice Dagley	George & Sarah Turner	Joseph & Harriet Dagley
7160	Gwinn, Mary	MO		Isaac Gwinn	Benage Smith	Elizabeth Blackburn		James & Nancy Blackburn
7159	Gwinn, William	MO	1870	Dova Gwinn	Isaac Gwinn	Mary Smith	Wm & Hannah Gwinn	Benage & Elizabeth Smith

18530	Gwyn, Carmelia	NC	1870		Alex Martin	Betty Hartgrove	John & Jennie Martin	Wm & Ann Hartgrove
272	Haddock, Levarie	CA	1859	William Haddock	John Blackburn	Sarah Miller	Andrew & Frances Blackburn	Henry & Rhody Miller
3394	Hadley, Charley	AL	46yrs	Maggie Parker	Simon Hadley	Caroline Hollinger		
6363	Hadley, Joshua	AL	53yrs	Martha Cartute	Simon Hadley	Caroline Hollinger	Benjaman Hadley	Jeff Hollinger
3387	Hadley, Simon Jr.	AL	28yrs	Mary & Virginia	Simon Hadley	Caroline Hollinger		
3398	Hadley, Walter	AL	44yrs	Harriett Hadley	Simon Hadley	Caroline Hollinger		
6816	Haga, Hetty	VA	1869	Thomas Haga	Eli Pennington	Emily Allen	Andrew & Hetty Pennington	
8498	Haga, Ida	VA	1884	James Haga	Noah Blevins	Catharine Dolinger	Allen & Fanny Blevins	John & Betty Dolinger
6113	Haga, James	VA	1862	Mary Blevins	Tobias Blevins	Susan Blevins	Eli & Milley Blevins	
4834	Haga, John	VA	1886	Julia Haga	Henry Haga	Margret Dalinger		John & Elisabeth Dalinger
4833	Haga, Margret	VA	1863	Hnery Haga	John Dolinger	Elisabeth Caldwell		Joseph & Catharine Caldwell
1802	Haga, Martha	VA	1854	Levi Haga	T.A. Faircloth	Christina Hart		George & Polly Hart
6889	Haga, Nancy	VA	1880	J.W. Haga	Hiram Pennington	Margaret Huffman	Andrew & Hetty Pennington	
6112	Haga, Sarah	VA	1869	David Haga	Samuel Pennington	Sarah Huffman	Andrew & Hettie Pennington	
6888	Haga, Selah	VA	1887	Noah Haga	Isaac Haze	Geroma Pennington		Hiram & Margaret Pennington
5575	Hagar, Charles	MO	1877	Elizabeth Hagar	William Hagar	Sarah Fullerton	Anthony & Sarah Hagar	Taylor & Mary Fullerton
9029	Hagar, Earl	MO	1880	none	William Hagar	Sarah Fullerton	Anthony & Sarah Hagar	Taylor & Mary Fullerton
17901	Hagerty, Mary	FL		Wm Hagerty	Ambrose Vaughn	Josephine Reyer	Wilson & Nancy Vaughn	
18693	Haggerty, Charles	FL	1869		Wm Haggerty	Mary Vaughan	John & Mary Haggerty	Josephine Vaughan
6394	Hagler, Adar	TN			France Hagler	Nancy Reed	France & Nancy Hagler	John & Nancy Reed
6393	Hagler, Thomas	TN			France Hagler	Nancy Reed	France & Nancy Hagler	John & Nancy Reed
7200	Hagler, Virginia	TX	1879	Robert Hagler	Jacob Kieth	Sarah Watson	Eli Keith & Elizabeth Meek	
4472	Hagston, Lilley	VA	34yrs	John Hagston	Tobias Blevins	Susan Blevins	Eli Blevins	Milley Blevins
4467	Hagston, Rachel	VA	26yrs	Lee Hagston	Eli Blevins	Elisabeth Blevins	Tobias & Susan Blevins	Calton & Nancy Blevins
15510	Haines, Tinie	GA	1879	Sam Haines	Solomon Sosebee	Sarah Millwoods	Solomon & Polly Sosebee	Hugh & Miram Millwoods
17770	Hale, Emma	TN	1875	George Hale	Shade Lofte	Martha Killian		Wm Killian
11962	Hale, George	TN	1857	Mariah Hale	Henry Hale	Sarah Bullard	Michael Hale	
22700	Hale, John	AL	1858	Josie Hale	James Hale	Hanah Hale	John & Eliza Hale	
17692	Halkom, Richard	TN	1858		James Holkom	Elizabeth		Lucy Holkom

15642	Hall, Alice	GA	1889		Joe Hall	Alice Hall	Joe Thompson	Lindis & Betsey Ashworth
18438	Hall, Avalon	NC	1900		S.W. Hall	Mattie Johnson		Thos Poindexter & Betty Pledge
19203*	Hall, Burt	TX	1884	Charles Hall	Tom Stone	Ann Stell		Charley Stell & Burby Marshall
9601	Hall, Charles	GA	1837		Meshack Hall	Elvina Thompson		Robert & Lovevina Thompson
18439	Hall, Charlie	NC	1895		S.W. Hall	Mattie Johnson		Thos Poindexter & Betty Pledge
21235	Hall, Dora	TX	1883	Howard Hall	Robert Biddy	Sallie Renfro	James & Delila Biddy	
149	Hall, Drayton	TN	1861	Georgia Hall	Levi Hall	Kizerah Skelton	Wm Hall & Susie Davis	Jerry Skelton & Annie Hughes
17624	Hall, Ercle	OK	1897		Thomas Hall	Eva Cordell		Sally Cordell
3069	Hall, Eva	OK	1880	Louis Hall	Isaac Owens	Rachel Segraves		Wm & Tabia Segraves
17626	Hall, Eva	OK	1873	Thomas Hall	Thomas Cordell	Sallie Baker		Lucy Huff
11059	Hall, Franklin	VA	32yrs	Martha Hall	John Hall	Martha Blevins	Lexington & Nancy Hall	Andrew & Susan Blevins
17623	Hall, Gladys	OK	1894		Thomas Hall	Eva Cordell		Sally Cordell
255	Hall, Henry	OK	1886	none	H.C. Hall	Margaret Caulk		Elmer & Roda Caulk
13374	Hall, Henry	GA	1883	Lindie Hall	Joe Hall	Lizer Thompson		Joe & Lindie Thompson
18440	Hall, James	NC	1904		S.W. Hall	Mattie Johnson		Thos Poindexter & Betty Pledge
6782	Hall, John	MO	1860	Martha Hall	Alfred Hall	Mahala Martin	John & Lois Hall	Wm & Susan Martin
11061	Hall, John	VA	51yrs	Elizabeth Hall	Lexington Hall	Nancy Childers	Owin & Juda Hall	John & Nancy Childers
18436	Hall, Johnson	NC	1893		S.W. Hall	Mattie Johnson		Thos Poindexter & Betty Pledge
3505	Hall, Julia	MO	1871	Noah Hall	James Proctor	Francis Pace	Ransome & Rutha Proctor	John & Jane Pace
18754	Hall, Kizzy	AL	1858		Richard Hall	Amanda Harris	Willis & Mary Hall	Peter & Elizie Harris
18435	Hall, Lawrence	NC	1902		S.W. Hall	Mattie Johnson		Thos Poindexter & Betty Pledge
12167	Hall, Leander	NC	1885		Leander Hall	Jane Fuguette		Esom Fuguette
12606	Hall, Lizer Jane	GA	1852	Joe Hall	Joe Thompson	Lizer Ashworth		
18434	Hall, Locksley	NC	1899		S.W. Hall	Mattie Johnson		Thos Poindexter & Betty Pledge
17627	Hall, Mannilla	OK	1898		Thomas Hall	Eva Cordell		Sally Cordell
14221	Hall, Mattie	NC	1865	S W Hall	John Johnson	Sue Poindexter	John & Sarah Johnson	Robert & Charlotte Poindexter
18437	Hall, Mattie Sue	NC	1897		S.W. Hall	Mattie Johnson		Thos Poindexter & Betty Pledge
21700	Hall, Newton	OK	1875	Anna Hall	Henry Hall	Margrett Caulk	R.M. Hall	Elenezer & Rhoda Caulk
11542	Hall, Rachel	TN	1845	John Hall	William Matoy	Millie McMillian		Joseph & Nellie McMillian
14346	Hall, Sarah	IN	1846	John Hall	Jackson Bays	Elizabeth Holcomb	Joe & Lettie Bays	
2406	Hall, Susan	OK	1888	Frank Hall	Jeff Balew	Nancy Gass	John & Agnes Belew	Robert & Rachel Gass
11252	Hall, William	OK	1850	Alice Hall	Joe Hall	Becky Burns		Clarisy Burns

#	Name	State	Year/Age	Spouse	Father	Mother	Paternal GP	Maternal GP
16313	Hallaway, James	GA	38yrs	Mahala Hallaway	Thomas Halloway	Safronia Lundsford	Sidney Langley	
16312	Hallaway, Mahalie	AL	26yrs	J E Hallaway	Willis Dockery	Jane Wilkins	Geo & Pegie Dockery	
20144	Hallman, Henry	GA	1832	Annie Hallman	John Hallman	Sarah Hallman		
12102	Halsey, Cathaney	WV		Robert Halsey	Franklin Sizemore	Polly Workman	George & Jinney Sizemore	Joseph & Elizabeth Workman
21781	Ham, Emily	OK	1856	Henry Ham	Marlin Deen	Louisa Hodges	Ebenezer Deen	Granville Hodges
18073	Ham, Francis	NC	1869	Jackson Ham	Calvin Davis	Matilda Pennington	Jordan & Sinie Davis	Andrew & Hettie Pennington
3741	Ham, Lunda	NC	1883	Rosa Ham	Solomon Ham	Mary Blevins	Solomon Sr & Mary Ham	Riley & Agnes Blevins
3744	Ham, Mary	NC	1849	Solomon Ham	Riley Blevins	Agnes Barker	Eli Blevins & Milley Brineger	Edward & Catharine Barker
6851	Ham, Mary	VA	1854	Alfred Ham	Abram Roop	Catherine Hart		George Hart & Polly Blevins
21782	Ham, Millard	OK	1881	Dela Ham	Henry Ham	Emily Deen	Eber & Elizabeth Ham	Martin & Louisa Deen
10106	Ham, Winfield	NC	1879	Alice Ham	Nelson Ham	Elisabeth Blevins	Larkin & Rebeckey Ham	Riley & Agnes Blevins
2031	Hambelton, John	MO	1859	none	Isaiah Hambelton	Martha Moxie	Elijah & Sarah Hambelton	
3318	Hambelton, Elijah	MO	1842	Nancy Hambelton	Isaiah Hambelton	Martha Maxie	Elijah & Sarah Hambelton	Wm & Nancy Maxie
2009	Hambelton, Isaiah	MO	1862	Margaret Hambelton	Isaiah Hambelton	Martha Moxie	Alex & Vilitty Brown	
2023	Hambelton, James	MO	1845	Florence Hambelton	Isaiah Hambelton	Martha Maxie	Alex Brown & Viletty Barton	
3778	Hambelton, Oliver	MO	1868	Mellisi Hambelton	Elijah Hambelton	Fario Hicks	Isiah & Martha Hambelton	Hiram & Mary Hicks
997	Hambie, Cloie	OK	1870	widow	John Goins	Melissia McGill	Nathan & Sarah Goins	Bill & Manry McGill
2022	Hambleton, Sidney	MO	1864	Elender Hambleton	Isaiah Hambleton	Martha Maxey	Elijah & Sarah Hambleton	Maxey
20869	Hamby, Calvin	NC	1855	M.E. Hamby	Thomas Hamby	Mary Hudson	Simpson & Elizabeth Hamby	Joseph & Elizabeth Hudson
20938	Hamby, James	NC	1857	America Hamby	? Hamby	Mary Hudson		Joseph Hudson
20868	Hamby, John	NC	1851		Thomas Hamby	Mary Hudson	Simpson & Elizabeth Hamby	Joseph & Elizabeth Hudson
20934	Hamby, Mary	NC	1849		? Hamby	Mary Hudson		Joseph Hudson
20935	Hamby, Nancy	NC	1860		? Hamby	Mary Hudson		Joseph Hudson
6724	Hamby, Olney	TN	1885		Rance Helton	Jenny Smith	Daniel & Jennie Hellon	
22159	Hamby, Rebecca	NC	1853	none		Mary Hudson		
8875	Hamelton, Martha	OK	1867	widow	Jack Simmons	Agness Buffington		Percilla Buffington
17925	Hamill, Neaty	GA	1879	Frank Hamill	Thomas Heatherly	Rebecca Thornton	James & Elizabeth Heatherly	Thomas & Ruth Thornton
22426	Hamilton, Annie	TN	1887	none	Newton Hamilton	Mary Payne		John & Polly Payne
22454	Hamilton, Charles	TN	1877	Martha Hamilton	J. Newton Hamilton	Mary Payne		John Payne
15176	Hamilton, Leonah	TN	1870	W R B Hamilton	Ophua Powell	Lourah Jordan		

19561	Hamilton, Mary	TN	1848	Newton Hamilton	John Payne	Mary	John & Jane Payne	Jake & Jane Hamentru
17948*	Hamilton, Sallie	TN	1864	Sandy Hamilton	Frank Wycoff	Oma Wilson	James Garrett & Nancy Montgomery	Joseph & Hannah Wycoff
17542	Hamilton, Samuel	MO	1869	Nellie Hamilton	James Hamilton	Anna Denny	Wm & Matilda Hamilton	James & Margaret Denny
16224*	Hamlett, Walter	OK	1887		William Hamlett	Elizabeth Hamilton	John Hamlett	Wilberty Hamilton
7203	Hamm, Lena	KS	1863	Jacob Hamm	Hiram Johnson	Minerva Miller	Merritte & Emily Johnson	Isaac & Elizabeth Miller
18859	Hammett, Fanny	GA	36yrs	James Hammett	Wm Massey	Mary Mahow	James & Patsy Massey	James & Milley Mahow
21502	Hammock, Maud	AR	1884	J.C. Hammock	Reuben Marcum	Sarah Berry	Robert & Polly Marcum	Wm & Nancy Berry
21506	Hammock, Rupert	TX	1877	George Hammock	Elyazer Jeter	Martha Bentley	George & Mary Jeter	
7204	Hammond, John	TN	1870	Ethel Hammond	James Hammond	Virginia Shipman	Wm & Alizzia Hammond	Abrham & Betty Woodard
8228	Hammond, John	OK	1849	none	William Hammond	Eliza Woodward	Moses & Dorcas Hammond	Abraham & Elizabeth Woodward
21662	Hammond, Rosa	TN	1871	Frederick Hammond	Almon Guinn	Sophia Arthur	Almon & Sarah Guinn	
18752	Hammonds, Birtha	TX	1885	Arthur Hammonds	I.D. Harwell	Annie Davis	James Harwell & Nancy Payne	
22470	Hammonds, Cassius	IN	1859	Cordelia Hammond	Thomas Hammond	Delma Brown	Mark & Kathrine Hammond	John Smothers
17988*	Hammonds, Julia	TN	1840			Viney Duncan		Beddy Duncan
17797*	Hammonds, Kizzie	TN		Madisan Hammonds	Peter Sligar	Nancy Cazby		Jack & Rizzie Cazby
22696	Hammonds, Thomas	IN	1847	Armisa Hammonds	Thomas Hammonds	Delaina Brown	Mark & Betsie Hammonds	
20810	Hammons, Alice et al	GA	1888		Jesse Hammons	Martha Padget	Henry & Susanna Hammons	
20809	Hammons, Jesse	GA	1862	Martha Hammons	Henry Hammonds	Susana Cox		Wm & Nancy Cox
157	Hampton, Alex	GA	1853	Indianna Hampton	John Hampton	Hannah Montieth	George & Maryan Hampton	George & Vina Montieth
7722	Hampton, Della	OK		William Hampton	William Casto	Mary McCabe		Wm & Mary McCabe
21874	Hampton, Delphy	TN	1893		William Hampton	Sarah Hughes		Jesse & Mollie Hughes
22408	Hampton, Dewit	MO	1859	Jennie Alexander	Hodge Hampton	Nancy Farris		John Farris & Jennie Gunter
1520	Hampton, Eddie	TN	1888	none	Francis Hampton	Eliza Cunningham	Geo & Mary Hampton	Robt & Rachel Cunningham
3316	Hampton, Henry	OK	1827	none	George Hampton	Mary Blythe		Johnathan & Annie Blythe
371	Hampton, James	GA	1854	Roxie Hampton	John Hampton	Hannah Montieth	George & Maryan Hampton	George & Nina Montieth
1512	Hampton, James	TN	1874	Callie Hampton	Francis Hampton	Eliza Cunningham	Geo & Mary Hampton	Robt & Rachel Cunningham
3976	Hampton, John	NC	1872	Julia Hampton	Harrison Hampton	Rinda Roberson	George & Mary Hampton	John & Cuida Roberson
726	Hampton, Jonathan	NC	1862	Pasly Hampton	John Hampton	Hannah Montieth	George & Mary Hampton	George & Vesia Montieth
8502	Hampton, Laura	VA	1877	Thomas Hampton	Noah Blevins	Catharine Dolinger	Allen & Fanny Blevins	John & Betty Dolinger

1519	Hampton, Monte	TN	1879	Zona Hampton	Francis Hampton	Eliza Cunningham	Geo & Mary Hampton	Robt & Rachel Cunningham
13884	Hampton, Renny	GA	1849	William Hampton	John Robinson	Lucindy Leatherwood		Samuel & Elizabeth Leatherwood
1511	Hampton, Robert	GA	1871	Halie Hampton	Francis Hampton	Eliza Cunningham	Geo & Mary Hampton	Robt & Rachel Cunningham
1201	Hampton, Ruth	IL	1849	none	George Stewman	Malinda Voils	Daniel Shehorn	James & Ruth Voils
20530	Hampton, Sarah	TN	1883	Will Hampton	Jesse Hughes	Mary Copeland	Jesse Sr & Fronia Hughes	Samuel & Jane Morelock
944	Hampton, W.H.	GA	1847	Renvy Hampton	George Hampton	Mary Blythe	George Hampton	Mary Ann Blythe
10473	Hampton, William	GA	1847	Reuney Hampton	George Hampton	Mary Blythe		Ann Blythe
10866	Hamrick, Arminta	WV	1870	Elisha Hamrick	Willburn Osburn	Melia Dunford	Solomon & Martha Osburn	Thomas & Honor Dunford
12090	Hand, Josie	VA	1877	James Hand	William Parish	Ada Waters		W P & Zilpha Waters
17832 *	Hanes, Ann	GA	1839		Jerry Wright	Sallie Harmon		
19139 *	Hanes, Charlie	GA	1867	Mary Hanes	Henry Hanes	Ann Wright		Jerry & Sallie Wright
19140 *	Hanes, Gadson	GA	1876	Anne Hames	Henry Hanes	Ann Wright		Jerry & Sallie Wright
238	Haney, Alford	NC	1833	Sarah Haney	James Haney	Carline Burnett	Sam Haney	
12268	Haney, Ambros	NC	1872		David Haney	Elizabeth Ledford	James Haney	Caroline Burnett
21693	Haney, Columbus	AL	1877	Myrtle Haney	Hezakiah Haney Sr.	Juliann Wilson	James Haney	William Wilson
16370	Haney, Frank	NC	19yrs		David Haney	Elizabeth Ledford	James Haney & Caroline Burnet	Jessie Ledford & Polly Pressley
18232	Haney, Harvey	GA	1879	Mary Haney	Jurd Haney	Mary Lively	James & Gracie Haney	Gilliam & Jane Lively
21692	Haney, Hezakiah Jr.	AL	1874	Lena Haney	Hezakiah Haney Sr.	Juliann Wilson	James Haney	William Wilson
20490	Haney, Hezekiah	AL	1839	Julian Haney	James Haney	Matilda McClure	James & Matilda Haney	Joseph & Nancy McClure
219	Haney, John	NC	1849	Harriett Haney	James Haney	Caroline Bennett	Sam Haney	
15543	Haney, John	GA	1876		J S Haney	Kate Spears	Timothy & Sarah Haney	John & Margret Spears
20494	Haney, Julian	AL	1843	Hezekiah Haney	William Wilson	Caroline Spencer	Andrew & Mary Wilson	Abram & Sarah Spencer
15542	Haney, Kate	GA	1845	J S Haney	Jehu Spears	Margaret Foster	Hezekiah & Christine Spears	Josiah & Polly Foster
21699	Haney, Lawrence	AL		Nettie Haney	Hezekiah Haney Sr.	Juliann Wilson	James Haney	William Wilson
12269	Haney, Mark & Alice	NC			David Haney	Elizabeth Ledford	James Haney	Caroline Burnett
15541	Haney, Nancy	GA	1843	Jacob Haney	Jehu Spears	Margaret Foster	Hezekiah & Christine Spears	Josiah & Polly Foster
14521 *	Haney, Robert	GA	1843	Arvenie Haney	Henry McMahan	Hannah Haney	Hetty McMahan	Nathaniel & Millie Foster
22767	Haney, Sarah	NC	1881	Napolean Haney	John Haney	Hattie Grant	James & Caroline Haney	John & Mary Grant
19036	Hanie, Jane	GA	1865	C.A. Hanie	Thomas Allison	Sarah Roberts	Ben & Beckey Allison	Wm & Rosa Roberts
19302	Hanil, Nettie	GA	1882	B.V. Hanil	John Hicks	Bettie Cole	Joe & Martha Hicks	Thomas & Amanda Cole

ID	Name	State	Year	Spouse	Father	Mother	Paternal Grandparents	Maternal Grandparents
9507	Hankins, Annie	AL	1892		Mathew Newell	Rebeca Branon		Amanda Branon
9510	Hankins, C.L.	AL	1888	none	W J Hankins	Louisa Newell		Rebeca Newell
17475	Hanks, Belle Miller	OK						
18465	Hanks, John	TN	1862	Belle Hanks	Alfred Hanks	Lydia Crabtree	John & Susie Hanks	Thomas Crabtree
6871	Hanner, Malissa	KY	1872	John Hanner	Eli Blevins	Samantha Carter	Armstrong & Catharine Blevins	Daniel & Miley Carter
14792	Hannon, Andrew	OK	1857	Jennie Hannon	Ned Hannon	Melissia Tadpole		Harriett Tadpole
17758	Hansard, Catharine	TN	1856		Wm Cooke	Eliza Mullins	Henry Cooke	John & Elizabeth Mullins
12368*	Hansen, Jerry	NC	1859	Tissue Hansen	Lawson Hansen	Louisa Payne	Miles Efison	
12370*	Hansen, Wiley	NC	1870	Luma Hansen	Lawson Hansen	Louisa Payne	Miles Efison	
20579	Hanssard, James	TN	1881		John Hanssard	Catharine Cook	Sidney & Margaret Hanssard	Wm & Eliza Cook
21900	Hanssard, Katie	TN	1885		John Hanssard	Catharine Cook	Sidney & Margaret Hanssard	Wm & Eliza Cook
20578	Hanssard, Samuel	TN			John Hanssard	Catharine Cook	Sidney & Margaret Hanssard	Wm & Eliza Cook
13845	Hardgrave, James	OK	1859	Cynthia Hardgrave	James Hardgrave	Louisa McKee		
19358	Hardin, Allie	GA	1882	Thomas Hardin	John Anderson	Malinda Galaway	John & Emily Anderson	Robert & Mahala Galaway
19359	Hardin, Jamie	GA	1906		Thomas Hardin	Allie Anderson	James & Elizabeth Hardin	John & Malinda Anderson
11622	Hardin, Lura	SC	28yrs	Oliver Hardin	James Adams	Anna Barnett	John & Ana Adams	Thos & Elizabeth Barnett
16151	Hardin, Saidie	GA	1859	John Hardin	Francis Bradford	Sarah Bradley	Thomas & Lucy Bradford	
19360	Hardin, Sam	GA	1905		Thomas Hardin	Allie Anderson	James & Elizabeth Hardin	John & Malinda Anderson
19361	Hardin, Tranquilla	GA	1903		Thomas Hardin	Allie Anderson	James & Elizabeth Hardin	John & Malinda Anderson
18318	Harding, Cornelia	IN	1835	Wilson Harding	James Guthery	Margret Bowman		Edger & Abigail Bowman
22310*	Hardrick, Eliza	OK		none	Moses Ross	Patience Ross	Silas & Winnie Ross	Isaac & Mary Ross
22271*	Hardrick, Mary	OK	1871	Nelson Hardrick	Jack Baldrige	Lettie Woffard	Tuloka Baldrige & Lettie Vann	Ben Whitmore
21447	Hardt, Oma	OK	1884	Fred Hardt	Joseph Litchfield	Sarah Elder	Joseph & Jane Litchfield Sr.	Ben & Nancy Elder
21965	Hardy, Margaret	TN	1837	widow	Pleasant Slay	Manerva Mills	Peabin & Manerva Slay	David & Adaline Mills
15930	Hargis, Agnes	TN	1892		J W Hargis	Frances Beasley	Jackson & Mary Hargis	Jesse & Matilda Beasley
15927	Hargis, Dora	TN	1883		J W Hargis	Frances Beasley	Jackson & Mary Hargis	Jesse & Matilda Beasley
17748	Hargis, Hugh	TN	1857	Sarah Hargis	Jackson Hargis	Mary Uhlis	Wm Hargis & Jennie Jacobs	
15929	Hargis, Ida	TN	1890		J W Hargis	Frances Beasley	Jackson & Mary Hargis	Jesse & Matilda Beasley
15928	Hargis, J.W.	TN	1852	Frances Hargis	Jackson Hargis	Mary Uhles	Wm Hargis & Jennie Jacobs	Richard Uhles
15931	Hargis, Wilson	TN	1888		J W Hargis	Frances Beasley	Jackson & Mary Hargis	Jesse & Matilda Beasley
8229	Hargrove, Bessie	OK	1880	decd	George Wetzel	Josephine	Henry & Elizabeth Wetzel	

7723	Hargrove, Nancy	OK		J S Hargrove	Isaac West	Nancy Owens	Rachel West	
21226	Harkey, Laura	TX	1869	Richard Harkey	James Sampson	Sarah Lumpkin		
19333	Harkey, M. J.	AR	1875	Rosa Harkey	Moses Harkey	Hester Conley	Levi & Julia Harkey	Isaac & Sally Conley
20410 *	Harland, John	TN	1835	Julia Harland	Buck Craig	Celia Center		Newman & Bettie Ealy
20409 *	Harland, Julia	TN	1855	John Harland	Newman Parice	Mary Yoe		Charles & Charlotte Yoe
6306	Harmon, Margaret	OK	1859	John Harmon (decd)	John Turpen	Mary Miller		
8202	Harmon, Mary	MO	1880	Alfonso Harmon	W G Miller	Ellen Sloan	William Miller	Mary Sloan
22132	Harp, Nancy	AL	1851	Winton Harp	William Holcomb	Sarah Lane	Massis & Mary Holcomb	
13994	Harper, Amanda	OK		Isaac Harper	William Redding	Eliza Ross	John & Fannie Redding	Joe & Percilla Ross
20872 *	Harper, Annie	NC	1819	Louis Harper	Randall Kent	Delphia Parish		
14010	Harper, Dee	GA	1861	David Harper	Rollin Pardue	Lissie Loggins	Albert & Ruth Pardue	James & Dicie Loggins
21405	Harper, George	TX					Mary Harper	David Martin
17698	Harper, William	GA	1845	Caroline Harper	Douglas Harper	Martha Brown	Henry Harper	Allen & Patty Brown
2429	Harralson, James	MO	1860	none	Vinson Harralson	Martha Hambelton	David & Peachy Harralson	Elijah & Sarah Hambelton
3030	Harralson, John	MO	1878	Lizzie Harralson	Nathan Harralson	Margaret Kirby	Vinson & Marth Harralson	Henry & Rebecca Kirby
3026	Harralson, Nathan	MO	1852	Margaret Harralson	Vinson Harralson	Martha Hambelton	David & Peachey Harralson	Elijah & Sarah Hambelton
3018	Harralson, Vince	MO	1863	Sarah Harralson	Vinson Harralson	Martha Hambelton	David & Pearly Harralson	Elijah & Sarah Hambelton
8684	Harrell, Sarah	OK	1848	William Harrell	William Condrey	Louisa Barrett		Betsey Griffin
22400	Harrill, Anna	TN	1864	widow	A J Saiunders	Margaret Crowder	Bittsey Saunders	S & Karney Crowder
12810	Harris, Adaline	TN	1868	Jason Harris	Murray	Nancy Hensley	Wm & Elizbeth Murray	Lewis Hensley
1076	Harris, Chas. L.	OK	1873	Lou Harris	Bird Harris	Ellen Rogers	Wm & Susan Harris	Robert & Mary Rogers
1077	Harris, Cheasquah	OK	1873	Nellie Harris	Bird Harris	Ellen Rogers	Wm & Susan Harris	Robert & Mary Rogers
16733	Harris, Chrosha	TN	1864	John Harris	Daniel Freeman	Nancy Ivey	James Ivey	Elizabeth Chavls
1075	Harris, Ellen	OK	1840	Red Bird Harris	Robert Rogers	Mary Balish	John & Sarah Rogers	Annie Detish
19500	Harris, Emily	AR	1870	James Harris	William Farmer	Eliza Hart		
22993	Harris, Hettie	OK	1883	Asa Harris	Ruben Mullins	Elizabeth Gibson	John & Mahala Mullins	Keener & Hetty Gibson
6398	Harris, Ina	MO	1882	Dave Harris	Frank Lewis	Amanda Mayberry		Jesse & Eliza Mayberry
14965	Harris, John	GA	1856	Mattie Harris	Ben Harris	Charlotte McDaniel		Alex & Abagail McDaniel
19141 *	Harris, Laura	GA	1863	John Harris	Henry Hanes	Ann Wright		Jerry & Sallie Wright

ID	Name	State	Year	Col5	Col6	Col7	Col8	Col9
12116	Harris, Malinda	KY	1848	Rusel Harris	Andrew Harrison	Rachel Mathews	Samuel & Rosa Harrison	A.J. & Easter Mathews
6559	Harris, Margaret	AR	1868	L W Harris	Thompson Wood	Eliza Martin	Johnson & Margaret Wood	Wm & Susan Martin
1960	Harris, Mary	KS	1882	George Harris	Harry Slaughter	Sarah Mongrain	Alban & Eunice Slaughter	Chas & Martha Mongrain
22420	Harris, Nannie	TN	1878	none	William Harris	Susan Payne	John & Mary Payne	
18181	Harris, Rachel	AL	1866	Hillard Harris	John Tims	Martha Colisky	John Tims	Wm & Betsy Colisky
21594	Harris, Robert	NC	1847		William Harris	Elvina Davis	Robert & Dicie Harris	David & Polly Davis
22901	Harris, Robert	TX	1876		William Harris	Fannie Harrell	Peggy Tankersly	
22422	Harris, Sarah	TN	1884	none	William Harris	Susan Payne	John & Mary Payne	
22417	Harris, Susan	TN	1855	William Harris	John Payne	Mary Hamentree	John & Jane Payne	Jacob & Jane Hamentree
22419	Harris, Susan for 3 children	TN	1855					
18661	Harris, Texanna	TN	1849	Jacob Harris	James Overton	Ann Ellison	Moses & Polly Overton	
11496	Harris, Thomas	OK	1855	Nancy Harris (decd)	William Harris	Lydia		
11508	Harris, Thomas	OK	1839	Martha Harris	Charles Harris	Sallie Collins		Parker & Nannie Collins
16070	Harris, W G	TX	1856	Lou Harris	W G Harris	Sarah Smith	Benj Harris & Peggy Tankersby	Henry Smith & Caroline Fulcher
20331*	Harris, Wade	GA	1851	Tiny Harris	John Harris	Parthenia Thompson	Spencer & Fannie Harris	Warren & Harrett Thompson
20680	Harris, William	TN	1884	Adda Harris	William Harris	Elizabeth Kittle	Wiliam & Mary Harris	Francis & Ann Kittle
1074	Harris, Wm R.	OK	1863	Leila Harris	Bird Harris	Ellen Rogers	Wm & Susan Harris	Mary Batish
21494	Harrison, Emily	CO	1885	James Harrison	William Page	Emily Wall		Drury Wall
739	Harrison, George	OK	1863	Elizabeth Harrison	Oscar Harrison	Mary Maney	Robert Harrison	William Maney
19325	Harrison, George	TN	1870	Mary Harrison	James Harrison	Elizabeth Henslee	Rubin & Margrett Harrison	Ralzemore & Sarah Henslee
10823	Harrison, Louisa	MO	1846	William Harrison	Sterling Barnard	Nancy Mason	John Barnard & Betsy Griffin	John & Elizabeth Mason
3445	Harrison, Vicie	AL	1878	Robert Harrison	Adam Hollinger	Elizabeth Lomax	Jeff & Elizabeth Hollinger	Sidney & Mary Lomax
1799	Hart, Amanda	NC	1860	Elijah Hart	L.H. Blevins	Beca Dollinger	John & Nancy Hart	
5183	Hart, Amanda	NC	1880	none	William Hart	Martha Miller	Stephen & Rebecca Hart	
6837	Hart, Andrew	VA	1850	Rebecca Hart	Elisha Hart	Nancy Stringer	George & Polly Hart	
3740	Hart, Bashey	NC	1877	James Hart	Solomon Ham	Mary Blevins	Solomon Sr & Mary Ham	Riley & Agnes Blevins
1798	Hart, Biddy	NC	1869	none	Stephen Hart	Celia Blevins	John & Nancy Hart	Will & Elizabeth Blevins
11629	Hart, Caroline	NC	1841		David Hart	Nancy Taylor	Edward & Nancy Hart	Richard & Millie Taylor
11450	Hart, Cathrine	NC	1829		John Hart	Nancy Floyd	James & Cathrine Hart	
11083	Hart, Celey	NC	1832	Stephen Hart	Wills Blevins	Elizabeth Blevins	James & Lydia Blevins	
11609	Hart, Cynthia	NC	1880			Melia Hart		Sonia Hart

5184	Hart, David	NC	1881	none	William Hart	Martha Miller	Stephen & Rebecca Hart	
9604	Hart, Drury	VA	1859	Laurinda Hart	Riley Hart	Emily Powers	John & Nancy Hart	Major & Mary Powers
8522	Hart, Eli	VA	1850	Jinnie Hart	Stephen Hart	Rebecca Powers	John & Nancy Hart	
6841	Hart, Elisha	VA	1878	Gertrude Hart	Andrew Hart	Rebecca Pennington	Elisha & Nancy Hart	Andrew & Hesther Pennington
6740	Hart, Enoch	VA	1854	Edy Hart	Stephen Hart	Rebecca Powers	John & Nancy Hart	
13466	Hart, Fred	NC	1886		Otto Hart	Maggie Cox	David & Nancy Hart	Solomon & Mary Cox
4880	Hart, G.W.	VA		Mary Hart	John Hart	Polley Caldwell	George & Polley Hart	Joseph & Catharine Caldwell
12960	Hart, Harvey	VA	1882		Andrew Hart	Rebecca Pennington	Elisha & Nancy Hart	Andrew & Hesther Pennington
11073	Hart, Hugh	VA	1877	Bennie Hart		Sarah Hart		John & Polley Hart
8550	Hart, Ira	NC	1881	Daisy Hart	Stephen Hart	Celey Blevins	John & Nancy Hart	Wells & Elizebeth Blevins
4094	Hart, Isaiah	VA	1882	none	James Hart	Jeroma Huffman	Elisha & Nancy Hart	Uriah & Delinda Huffman
3743	Hart, James	NC	1873	Basha Hart	Stephen Hart	Celey Blevins	John & Nancy Hart	Wells & Elisabeth Blevins
4095	Hart, James	VA	1857	Jeroma Hart	Elisha Hart	Nancy Davis	George & Polly Hart	John & Sallie Davis
4879	Hart, John	VA	1820	Polly Hart	George Hart	Polly Blevins	James & Catharine Hart	
11007	Hart, John	VA	1872	Minnie Hart	Stephen Hart	Selah Blevins	John & Nancy Hart	Wells & Elizabeth Blevins
11451	Hart, John	NC	1859	Cora Hart		Cathrine Hart		John & Nancy Hart
2965	Hart, Joseph	VA	1878	Bertie Hart	James Hart	Franky Gaultney	Hugh & Easter Hart	
7518	Hart, Joseph	VA	1863	Jane Hart	Riley Hart	Emily Powers	John & Nancy Hart	Major & Mary Powers
4881	Hart, Milley	VA		none	John Hart	Polley Caldwell	George & Polley Hart	Joseph & Catharine Caldwell
11694	Hart, Nan	NC	1860			Emelia Hart		David & Nancy Hart
7197	Hart, Nina	KS	1871	Frank Hart	Jonathan Miller	Mary Foley	Wm & Susan Miller	James & Rhoda Foley
3614	Hart, Rachel	NC	1859	James Hart	Riley Hart	Emily Powers	John Hart	Nancy Floyd
6836	Hart, Rebbecca	VA	1850	Andrew Hart	Andrew Pennington	Hesther Blevins		James & Lydia Blevins
18604	Hart, Rosey	VA	1879	James Hart	Harvy Hash	Milly Young		Wm & Catherine Young
6839	Hart, Samuel	OK	1880	none	Andrew Hart	Rebbecca Pennington	Elisha & Nancy Hart	Andrew & Hesther Pennington
1524	Hart, Sarah	AL	1878	William Hart	John Graves	Harriet McDonald		James & Sarah McDonald
8548	Hart, Wells	NC	1878	Minnie Hart	Stephen Hart	Celey Blevins	John & Nancy Hart	Wells & Elizabeth Blevins
9605	Hart, Wesley	WV	1858	Malissey Hart	Riley Hart	Emily Powers	John & Nancy Hart	Major & Mary Powers

4875	Hart, William	VA		Laura Hart	John Hart	Polley Caldwell	John & Polly Hart	Josep & Catharine Caldwell
5186	Hart, William	NC	1846	Martha Hart	Stephen Hart	Rebecca	John & Nancy Heart	
12959	Hart, William	VA	1876	Mary Hart	Andrew Hart	Rebecca Pennington	Elisha & Nancy Hart	Andrew & Hesther Pennington
20163	Hart, Winnie	FL	1841		John Taylor	Lucinda Warhoochee		
3083	Hartless, Nevada	OK	1887	L M Hartless	Michael Young	Mary Young	James & Mary Young	Elisha & Nancy Young
7605	Hartley, Lum	GA	28yrs	Orla Hartley	Wilks Hartley	Renia Nichols	Fredrick Hartley	
6266	Hartley, Martha	VA	1875	Creed Hartley	Jerome Hash	Nancy Peak	John & Sally Hash	Uriah & Carnelia Peak
22614	Hartman, Celia	OK	1868	H. A. Hartman	William Brown	Nancy Heatherly	James & Sally Brown	James & Rebecca Haines
7205	Hartman, Jim	TX	1871	Mamie Hartman	George Hartman	Bill Jordan	John & Susan Hartman	Daniel & Susan Jordan
2357	Hartsell, Jackson	AR	1852	Margret Hartsell	Jonas Hartsell	Mary Morton	Jacob & Lucy Hartsell	Joseph & Margret Morton
2358	Hartsell, Jonas	AR	1876	Margret Hartsell	Jonas Hartsell	Mary Morton	Jacob & Lucy Hartsell	Joseph & Margret Morton
2356	Hartsell, Margret	AR	1871	Jonas Hartsell	Leonard Tucker	Margret Morton	Lewis & Patsy Tucker	Joseph & Margret Morton
1510	Harvey, Euphemia	TX	1865	Horatie Harvey	James Smith	Eliza Perrin	Benj Smith & Ellin Hill	Thomas & Euphemia Perrin
10486	Harvey, Leona	WV		Clowney Harvey	M C C Walker	Sarah Wood	Neoma Walker	German Wood
3101	Harvey, Vallie	MS	1874	John Harvey	Benjamin White	Kibbie Hobgood		Charley & Martha Hobgood
3699	Harvison, Annie	OK	1862	Wm Harvison	William Mackey	Nannie Drew	Samuel & Sallie Mackey	
18751	Harwell, I.D.	TX	46yrs	Annie Harwell	James Harwell	Nancy Payne	Ambrose Harwell & Polie Brown	Thomas Payne
18753	Harwell, J.S.	OK	1882	Bessie Harwell	I.D. Harwell	Annie Davis	James Harwell & Nancy Payne	
7623	Hasford, Elijah	GA	48yrs		James Hasford	Eliza Brown		Robert & Francis Lyons
8500	Hash, Bonnie	VA	1888	Winfield Hash	Noah Blevins	Catharine Dolinger	Allen & Fanny Blevins	John & Betty Dolinger
22965	Hash, Charlie	VA	1878	Elisabeth Hash	Jerome Hash	Nancy Peak	John & Sallie Hash	Uriah & Cornelia Peak
10015	Hash, Fields	NC	1865	Eliza Hash	John Hash	Elizabeth Hawks	Robert & Marga Hash	
10013	Hash, Lee	NC	1868	Ettie Hash	John Hash	Elizabeth Hawks	Robert & Marga Hash	
10014	Hash, Luetta	NC	1875	Lee Hash	Franklin Porter	Catherine Blevins	Jackson & Jinee Porter	George & Lyda Blevins
6819	Hash, Mary	VA	1878	Calvin Hash	Abel Pennington	Sarah Abel	Andrew & Hetty Pennington	
10340	Hash, Milly	VA		Harvy Hash	William Young	Catharine Hash		Robert & Marja Hash
10012	Hash, Omega	NC	1882	Thomas Hash	John Spencer	Martha Anderson	Solomon & Nellie Spencer	
20207	Hash, Riley	VA	1853	Martha Hash	John Hash	Polly Andrews	Robert & Polly Hash	William Andrews

10016	Hash, Thomas	NC	1879	Omega Hash	John Hash	Elizabeth Hawks	Robert & Marga Hash	
19282	Hash, Walter	VA	1875	Martha Hash	John Hash	Elizabeth Hawks	Robert & Margaret Hash	Wm & Rebecca Hawks
19834	Hash, Walter	VA	1875	Martha Hash	John Hash	Elizabeth Hox	Robert & Margry Hash	Wm & Elizabeth Hox
19276	Hash, William	VA	1864	Rosa Hash	John Hash	Elizabeth Hawks	Robert & Margaret Hash	Wm & Rebecca Hawks
20044	Hash, William	VA	1864	Rosa Hash	John Hash	Elizabeth Hax	Robert & Margaret Hash	Wm & Elizabeth Hax
20285	Haste, Dora	LA	1877	James Haste	James Davis	Mary Martin		
18483	Hasten, Dora	NC	1866	Julius Hasten	Pinkney Stafford	Eliza Hendrix	Zeddock & Polly Stafford	David & Hannah Hendrix
4208	Hastings, Belle	AR	1879	William Hastings	Hamilton Wilson	Elisabeth Maney	Paul Wilson	Martin Maney
19831	Hatcher, Alfred	TN	1877	Emma Hatcher	James Hatcher	Mary Halbrook	John Hatcher & Louisa Craft	Joseph & Catherine Halbrook
3991	Hatcher, Betsy	GA	1837	widow	Aaron Parris	Celie Tidwell		John & Celie Tidwell
20726	Hatcher, Charlotte	TN	1823	James Hatcher	Ezekial Craft	Sarah Thaxton		
20689	Hatcher, Christopher	TN	1842	Mary Hatcher	William Hatcher	Elizabeth Hooper	John & Ritta Hatcher	
21128	Hatcher, Earl	TN	1900	none	Alfred Hatcher	Emma Triplett	James & Mary Hatcher	
20718	Hatcher, Earnest	TN	1898		James Hatcher	Mary Halbrook	John & Eliza Hatcher	Joseph & Catherine Halbrook
21082	Hatcher, Effie	TN	1891	Howard Hatcher	John Curtis	Narsis Damworth	Joshua & Elizabeth Curtis	Henry & Nancy Dameworth
20724	Hatcher, Elisha	TN	1902		James Hatcher	Mary Halbrook	John & Eliza Hatcher	Joseph & Catherine Halbrook
21130	Hatcher, Evonne	TN	1905		Alfred Hatcher	Emma Triplett	James & Mary Hatcher	
20721	Hatcher, Frances	TN	1887		James Hatcher	Mary Halbrook	John & Eliza Hatcher	Joseph & Catherine Halbrook
20693	Hatcher, George	TN	1869	Minnie Hatcher	Chris Hatcher	Mary McCartey	Wm & Elizabeth Hatcher	
17651	Hatcher, Henry	GA			Henry Hatcher	Betsey Parris	Wm & Charlotte Hatcher	Aaron Parris & Celia Tidwell
20691	Hatcher, Howard	TN	1874	Effey Hatcher	Chris Hatcher	Mary McCartey	Wm & Elizabeth Hatcher	
19115	Hatcher, James	TN	1856	Mary Hatcher	John Hatcher	Louisa Croft	John & Henrietta Hatcher	E. & Louisa Croft
19689	Hatcher, James	TN	1878	Sarah Hatcher	Rufus Hatcher	Sarah Curtis	John Hatcher & Mary Sizemore	Ezekiel Curtis & Ardicie Wheeler
20722	Hatcher, James	TN	1890		James Hatcher	Mary Halbrook	John & Eliza Hatcher	Joseph & Catherine Halbrook
20690	Hatcher, John	TN	1872		Chris Hatcher	Mary McCartey	Wm & Elizabeth Hatcher	
20719	Hatcher, Lemuel	TN	1905		James Hatcher	Mary Halbrook	John & Eliza Hatcher	Joseph & Catherine Halbrook
21129	Hatcher, Lester	TN	1903	none	Alfred Hatcher	Emma Triplett	James & Mary Hatcher	
19112	Hatcher, Mary	TN	1826	Robert Hatcher	Demcy Hooper	Elizabeth Hooper	Baily & Frances Hooper	Clarence & Mary Hooper
19666	Hatcher, Mary	TN	1858		Robbert Hatcher	Mary Hooper	John & Henrietta Hatcher	Dency & Elizabeth Hooper
20723	Hatcher, Maudie	TN	1894		James Hatcher	Mary Halbrook	John & Eliza Hatcher	Joseph & Catherine Halbrook
21077	Hatcher, Osburn	TN	1906		William Hatcher	Maggie Singleton	James & Mary Hatcher	

20695	Hatcher, Peter	TN	1877		Chris Hatcher	Mary McCartey	Wm & Elizabeth Hatcher	
21076	Hatcher, Riley	TN	1903	none	William Hatcher	Maggie Singleton	James & Mary Hatcher	
20694	Hatcher, Ritty	TN	1868		Chris Hatcher	Mary McCartey	Wm & Elizabeth Hatcher	
18608	Hatcher, Rufus	TN	1858	Sarah Hatcher	John Hatcher	Mary Sizemore	John & Henrietta Hatcher	James & Sarah Sizemore
19686	Hatcher, Sarah	TN	1879	J.M. Hatcher	James Curtis	Sarah Wheeler	Joshua & Elizabeth Curtis	Robert & Sarah Wheeler
19621	Hatcher, Silas	TN	1883	Bessie Hatcher	Rufus Hatcher	Sarah Curtis	John & Mary Hatcher	Ezekiel & Ardelia Curtis
21127	Hatcher, Thurston	TN	1898	none	Alfred Hatcher	Emma Triplett	James & Mary Hatcher	
17649	Hatcher, William	GA	1874	Lula Hatcher	Henry Hatcher	Betsey Parrish	Wm & Charlotte Hatcher	Aaron Parrish & Celia Tidwell
20692	Hatcher, William	TN	1865	Alice Hatcher	Chris Hatcher	Mary McCartey	Wm & Elizabeth Hatcher	
20727	Hatcher, William	TN	1883	Maggie Hatcher	James Hatcher	Mary Halbrook	John & Louiza Hatcher	
21080	Hatcher, William	TN	1859	Lucinda Hatcher	John Hatcher	Luize Craft	John & Henrietta Hatcher	
10169	Hatchet, Aggie	OK	1841	Tom Hatchet	Oce Hothouse	Jennie Yoon Cult	Oo loo chie	Yoon Cult & Chi au see
12076	Hatfield, Daisy	OK	1879	Lawrence Hatfield	Allie West	Nann Rutherford	Isaac & Nancy West	
16410	Hathaway, Cyrus	AR	1862	Nannie Hathaway	Cyrus Hathaway	Cenie Bell	Cyrus & Ann Hathaway	Wm & Nancy Bell
13952	Hathaway, Jim	AR	1878		Cyrus Hathaway	Cenie Bell	Cyrus & Ann Hathaway	Wm & Nancy Bell
3336	Hathcock, Carmen	AL		Mary Hathcock	John Hathcock	Rosa McGhee	Thomas & Betsey Hathcock	Richard & Elizabeth McGhee
6368	Hathcock, Silas	AL	1874	Leona Hathcock		Rhoda Hathcock		Wash & Matilda Taylor
17848	Haulbrook, Minnie	GA		Frank Haulbrook			Rosy Biddy	
15618	Hauser, Alice	NC	1877	Solomon Hauser	S Allen	Elizabeth Martin	James & Rebecca Allen	Wm & Margret Martin
16413	Hauser, Calvin	NC	1853	Emma Hauser	Adam Hauser	Catherine Scott	Adam & Margaret Hauser	Daniel & Margret Scott
19198	Hauser, Emma	NC		James Hauser	Solomon Hauser	Louisa Poindexter	Samuel & Louisa Hauser	Sarah Poindexter
15609	Hauser, John	NC	1870	Nettie Hauser	Solomon Hauser	Eliza Poindexter	Samuel & Nancy Hauser	Denson & Sarah Poindexter
16491*	Hauser, Lawson	NC	1827		Mi Eperson	Bettesy Coe		Wm & Nancy Kirby
16414	Hauser, Louis	NC	1860	Louise Hauser	Adam Hauser	Catherine Scott	Adam & Margaret Hauser	Daniel & Margret Scott
19195	Hauser, Louisa	NC			James Hauser	Sarah Hauser	Solomon & Nerve Hauser	Loussa & Biddie Hauser
16489*	Hauser, Mary	NC	1859	Doc Hauser	Moses Shores	Patsey Davis	Free Bill Sheppard	Friday & Phoebe Davis
14879	Hauser, Roby	NC	1865	Letha Hauser	Solomon Hauser	Louise Poindexter	Samuel & Nancy Hauser	Denson & Sarah Poindexter
16490*	Hauser, Sandy	NC	1851	Malliss Hauser	Jerry Hauser	Amanda Evans	Sam & Darkus Shanell	Henry Kapp & Anna Evans
18649	Hauser, Sanford	NC	1883		Dock Hauser	Mary Shore	Loss & Harriet Hauser	Mose & Patsy Shore
14880	Hauser, Solomon	NC	1833	Laura Hauser	Samuel Hauser	Nancy Martin	Adam & Peggie Hauser	Lenard & Nancy Scott
15025	Hauser, Solomon	NC	1872	Allice Hauser	Thomas Hauser	Lucinda Spinkle	Nancy Hauser	

14088	Hauser, Thomas	NC	1854	Charlotte Hauser	John Hauser	Elizabeth Poindexter	Adam & Margeret Hauser	Robert & Miriam Poindexter
21854	Haussard, Lula	TN	1859		John Haussard	Catharine Cook	Sidney & Margaret Haussard	Wm & Eliza Cook
5453	Haviland, Effie	KS	1881	Frank Haviland	Nicholas Mitchell	Martha Martin	Charles & Nancy Mitchell	Willman & Susan Martin
18115	Hawk, Eda	AL	1874	John Hawk	George Sanders	Mary Hollingsworth	George & Harriet Sanders	Eli & Mary Hollingsworth
20113 *	Hawkins, Alexander	GA	1831	Francis Hawkins	Ridge	Fanny Riles		Robert & Mary Mitchell
21559 *	Hawkins, Augustus	GA	1861	Louisa Hawkins	Alex Hawkins	Francis Gardener	John & Martha Ridge	
8578	Hawkins, Eliza	VA	1882	Commadore Hawkins	Alford Reeves	Sarah Orsborn		James & Rachel Orsborn
9547	Hawkins, Hattie	GA	1880	U.C. Hawkins	David Dudley	Jinetta Tidwell	David Dudley	John Tidwell
20020	Hawkins, Ida	AR	1879	Thomas Hawkins	Enoch Brown	Mary Towns	John & Sallie Brown	Richard Towns
18036 *	Hawkins, James	TN	1882		Tennessee Hawkins	Mattie Marsh	Wm & Mary Hawkins	Martha Marsh
8582	Hawkins, Jesse	VA	1865	Matilda Hawkins	Jesse Hawkins	Ludema Fuget	Ned & Debbie Hawkins	Winnie Fuget
18257 *	Hawkins, Joshua	GA	1854	Malissa Hawkins	Parker Hawkins	Harriet Stone		
14480	Hawkins, Mary	MS	1856	Daniel Hawkins	Joel Sizemore	Cynthia Webster	Daniel Sizemore & Anna Hawkins	
18035 *	Hawkins, Nelson	TN	1860	Mattie Hawkins	Wm Hawkins	Mary Hawkins		Armstead & Mariah Johnson
18626	Hawkins, Roxie	OK	1854	John Hawkins	Leander Hall	Rebeca Bond	Enoch & Nancy Hall	
20052	Hawkins, Sallie	TX	1878	Thomas Hawkins	Miles Faucett	Sallie Griffis	Wm & Elizabeth Faucett	Wm & Mary Griffis
18940	Hawks, Alice	VA		Osborn Hawks	John Kingsbury	Eliza Chapman	John Kingsbury	
9185	Hayden, Andrew	NC		Molly Hayden	Robert Hayden	Susannah Chavis		Burl & Sooky Chavis
22055 *	Hayden, Mariah	OK	1861	Henry Hayden	Martin Whitmire	Peggie Downing	Harrison & Philis Whitmire	Jubia & Polly Bryant
9555	Hayden, Michael	NC	1836	Caroline Hayden	Michael Hayden	Mariah Mills	Bob Hayden & Succa Chavus	Isaac McGee & Jennie Mills
10634	Hayes, Lew	GA	1847	Myra Hayes	Sampson Hayes	Martha Carter	Lew & Hannah Hayes	Jesse & Elizabeth Carter
9050	Hayes, Lydda	VA	25yrs	James Hayes	Wilburn Blevins	Susan Lewis	Ned & Nancy Blevins	Jackson & Biddy Lewis
15266	Hayes, Mary	GA	1857	Bill Gasaway	Elias Whitmire	Louisa Owen	George & Mary Whitmire	
17450	Hayes, Mary	GA	1826		Sampson Hayes	Hannah Weeks	Samuel & Susan Hayes	Wm & Rachel Weeks
18880	Hayes, Nannie	NC	1874	Roland Hayes	Isaac Roberts	Emma Martin		Thos Martin & Ann Poindexter
10088	Hayes, Rinda	NC	1868	Tom Hayes	Green Payne	Fannie Harkins	Acey & Nancy Payne	
15261	Haygood, Carrie	GA		Robert Haygood	Jeffrey Beck	Mandy Loggins	Coleman Davis & Elmira Beck	
18086	Haygood, Carrie	GA	1878		Jeffrey Beck	Mandy Loggins	Coleman Davis & Elmira Beck	
14862	Haygood, John	GA	1875	Nancy Haygood	Thomas Haygood	Julia Burrell	Osborn & Lydia Haygood	Jesse & Mourning Burrell
12262	Haynes, Alice	NC	1877	L. Haynes	James Stamper	Sally Wagoner	William Stamper	Henry & Charlotte Wagoner

ID	Name	State	Year	Spouse	Father	Mother	Paternal GP	Maternal GP
21742	Haynes, Arch	AR	1862	Aseinth Haynes	William Haynes	Jane Thompson		Easter Thompson
21959	Haynes, Arthur	TN	1888		Clinton Haynes	Mary Grubb	Joseph & Matilda Haynes	Elder & Nancy Grubbs
21958	Haynes, Clinton	TN	1855	Mary Haynes	Joseph Haynes	Matilda McCorkle	Ira & Rebecca Haynes	Samuel & Katee McCorkle
20336	Haynes, Elizabeth	TN	1875	George Haynes	Theopholis DeLozier	Samantha Spillman		Charles & Ferriba Spillman
21953	Haynes, Frank	TN	1885	none	Clinch Haynes	Mary Grubbs	Ira & Matilda Haynes	Elder & Nancy Grubbs
14347	Haynes, George	NE	1853		James Haynes	Elizabeth Obinger		John & Cloe Obinger
12020	Haynes, Hulda	GA	1879	Jim Haynes	Webster Atkins	Malinda Carney	Berryman & Martha Atkins	Edmond & Elizabeth Carney
21790	Haynes, James	AR	1877	Betty Haynes	William Haynes	Jane Thompson	Sarah Haynes	Wm & Estes Thompson
21351	Haynes, Jane	AR	1844		William Thompson	Ester Parsley	Zack & Chasty Thompson	Steve & Jane Parsley
15260	Haynes, Ollie	GA	1902		Jim Haynes	Huldy Atkins		Webster & Malinda Atkins
15022	Haynes, Sarah	NC	1848	James Haynes	Leonard Scott	Sallie Hauser	Leonard & Nancy Scott	Adam & Margaret Hauser
21785	Haynes, Zack	AR	1874	Altie Haynes	William Haynes	Jane Thompson	Sarah Haynes	Wm & Estes Thompson
21088	Hays, J.Norman	GA	1873	Normancy	Louis Hayes	Nancy Pope	Samson & Marthy Hayes	Gabril & Kattie Pope
18755	Hays, Mary	KS	1842	James Hays	John Burk	Zelphy Williams	James & Lucy Burk	John Williams
6895	Haze, Fanny	VA	1883	William Haze	Hiram Pennington	Margaret Huffman	Andrew & Hetty Pennington	
6884	Haze, Geroma	VA	1870	Isaac Haze	Hiram Pennington	Margaret Huffman	Andrew & Hetty Pennington	
6854	Haze, Rebecca	NC	1878	Eugene Haze	Samuel Pennington	Sarah Huffman	Andrew & Hetty Pennington	
6117	Haze, Wm & Sarah	VA			William Haze (decd)	Sarah Pennington		Samuel & Sarah Pennington
17720	Hazelwood, Mary	TN	1873	A.B. Hazelwood	W.G. Tidwell	Matilda Paine	W.G. Tidwell & Martha Shelton	Thos Paine & Miranda Watson
22889	Hazlewood, John	TX	1863	Nannie Hazlewood	William Hazlewood	Betsie Man	William Hazlewood	Spencer
17724	Hazlewood, Mattie	TN	47yrs	A.W. Hazlewood	W.G. Tidwell	Matilda Paine	W.G. Tidwell & Martha Shelton	Thos Paine & Miranda Watson
21560	Head, Annie	GA	1883	Gypson Head	John Warsham	Nancy Edwards		Wm & Catherine Edwards
15462	Head, Maggie	GA	1869	Thomas Head	John Cook	Mary Ragan	James & Louvisa Cook	
17774	Head, Martha	TN	1873	Wm Head	John Brumih	Lucy Archer		Felix & Jane Archer
3774	Head, Nealie	GA	1884	C D Head	J F Perdew	Julia Davis	Walt & Ruth Perdew	John Davis & Nancy Bird
22868	Headrick, Artie	TN	1880	Salie Headrick	William Headrick	Ella Haynes	Andrew & Eliza Headrick	Albert & Martha Haynes
22870	Headrick, Eddie	TN	1884	Pearl Headrick	William Headrick	Ella Haynes	Andrew & Eliza Headrick	Albert & Martha Haynes
22867	Headrick, Oscar	TN	1879		William Headrick	Ella Haynes	Andrew & Eliza Headrick	Albert & Martha Haynes
4660	Headrick, William	TN	1853	Ella Headrick	Andrew Headrick	Eliza Jestus	John & Mary Headrick	Polly Jestus
18023	Heagpath, Christina	IN	1849	Frank Heagpath	Dudley Roberts	Mary Roberts		Thomas Hammonds

7196	Heape, Charley	KS	1869	Julia Heape	John Heape	Matilda Allen		Louis & Maryan Allen
21545 *	Heard, Nancy	GA	1863	Lou Heard	Frank Palmour	Agnes Owensby	George & Millie ?	Joe & Violet Owensby
15743 *	Heard, Sallie	GA	1859	Jerre Heard	Edmond Roberson	Virginia Morgan		Joe & America Hollands
22165	Hearing, P.L.	GA			P.L. Hearing	Mary Woody		
20877	Heart, C.	GA	1873	Bell Heart	C.F. Heart	Mary Andress	Mike & Lizzie Heart	Willie Andress & Bettie Guess
20876	Heart, James	GA	1870	Mary Heart	C.F. Heart	Mary Andress	Mike & Lizzie Heart	Willie Andress & Bettie Guess
16276	Hearth, Mary	GA	1851	James Hearth	James Darby	Caroline Hudgins	Charles & Nancy Darby	Jacob & Elizabeth Hudgins
14994	Heath, J. William	VA	1871	Ida Heath	Scott Heath	Martha Rouse	John & Alcey Heath	Isaac & Peggie Rouse
10971	Heath, Charles	VA	1882		John Heath	Sarah Thomas	Margret Heath	Presley & Patsey Thomas
14083	Heath, Elizabeth	GA	1844	Robert Heath	William Heath	Isie Darby	Benjamin Heath	Charles & Nancy Darby
14084	Heath, Elizabeth	GA	1869	Caleb Heath	Russell Arrows	Manerva Darby		Charles & Nancy Darby
9244 ½	Heath, Ellen	VA	1859	Thomas Heath	George Blevins	Almedia Jones	Eli & Milly Blevins	Thomas & Elizabeth Jones
6185	Heath, George	NC	1879	Martha Heath	Thomas Heath	Ellen Blevins		George & Almedia Blevins
10974	Heath, John	VA	1858	Sarah Heath		Margret Heath		John & Alcie Heath
13890	Heath, Julie	VA	1878		John Heath	Sarah Thomas	Margret Heath	Presley & Patsy Thomas
10973	Heath, Lon	VA	1889		John Heath	Sarah Thomas	Margret Heath	Presley & Patsey Thomas
9240	Heath, Maggie	VA	1880	Marion Heath	McClelland Pennington	Mary Blevins		Jesse & Catharine Blevins
10970	Heath, Marion	VA	1883	Maggie Heath	Robert Heath	Jennie Luster	Margreat Heath	Wm & Nancie Luster
6137	Heath, Martha	NC	1898	George Heath	Elisha Hurley	Alpha Barker		Wm & Betty Barker
21117	Heath, Nancy	NC	1865	Lee Heath	William Eaton	Malinda Finlk	George & Elizabeth Eaton	Rob & Teany Finlk
21118	Heath, Nancy,gdn	NC						
12182	Heath, Robert	VA	1863	Jennie Heath		Margret Heath		John & Ailce Heath
14996	Heath, S T	VA	1854	Sarah Heath		Margarette Heath		John & Alcie Heath
12716	Heath, Scott	VA	1849		John Heath	Alcey Powers	John & Vina Heath	James & Mima Powers
3472	Heath, Selia	VA	1861		James Thompson	Caroline Head	John & Polly Thompson	Elexander & Liza Head
9244	Heath, William	VA	1884	none	Thomas Heath	Ellen Blevins	Wm & Polly Heath	George & Almedia Blevins
17951	Heatherly, Amanda	TN	1888		Thomas Heatherly	Rebecca Thornton	James & Elizabeth Heatherly	Thomas & Ruth Thornton
17939	Heatherly, Edward	TN	1882	Elizabeth Heatherly	Thomas Heatherly	Rebecca Thornton	James & Elizabeth Heatherly	Thomas & Ruth Thornton
17687	Heatherly, Mossie	TN	1884		Thomas Heatherly	Rebecca Thornton	James & Elizabeth Heatherly	
17949	Heatherly, Pearl	TN	1894		Thomas Heatherly	Rebecca Thornton	James & Elizabeth Heatherly	Thomas & Ruth Thornton
18528	Heckler, Lizzie	MO	1886	Arthur Heckler	John Woods	Melvina Forshey	John & Lizzie Woods	George & Narcissus Forshey

19706	Hedrick, Nancy	TN	1879	Anderson Hedrick	Nathan Curtis	Susan Collier	Joshua & Elizabeth Curtis	
8656	Hefner, Lula	OK	1874	John Hefner	James Tittle	Annie Prather	Dan & Rosana Tittle	Robbie & Eady Prather
841	Helm, Caroline	OK	1840	Sumner Helm	Thomas Perrin	Euphenia Travis	Charles & Catherine Perrin	Benjamin & Catherine Travis
840	Helm, Elna etc.	OK			Sumner Helm	Caroline Travis	James & Sarah Helm	Thomas & Euphenia Perrin
839	Helm, William	OK	1871	Delta Helm	Sumner Helm	Caroline Perrin	James & Sarah Helm	Thomas & Euphenia Perrin
10113	Helmadollar, Arminta	WV		James Helmadollar	Joel Rose	Virginia Sizemore	Frank & Abby Rose	Ned & Annie Sizemore
5156	Helmer, Mary	OK	1848	Joseph Helmer	John Harris	Katie Bear		Peter & Louisa Bear
8927	Helmer, Nora	OK	1877	Joseph Helmer	Thomas Mathews	Martha Brasuell		Samuel & Phebe Brasuell
10972	Helms, Ales	VA	1880		John Heath	Sarah Thomas	Margret Heath	Presley & Patsey Thomas
13936	Helms, Ida	NC	1875	Marshall Helms	George Moss	Mary Reider	James & Polly Moss	
16720	Helms, Mary	OK	1833	Elijah Helms	John Vanzandt	Sarah Wilson	John & Nancy Vanzandt	Ephriam & Mary Wilson
16403	Helpinstine, Ella	OK	1866	Samuel Helpinstine	George Case	Loucinda Stull	George & Marlottie Case	Jacob & Rachel Stull
18085	Helton, Claud	GA	1881		Lou Wiley	Clarkie Helton	Huey Wiley	Mary Helton
22591	Helton, Dock	TN	1885		James Helton	Martha Clark	Daniel & Patsy Helton	John & Peggy Clark
12462	Helton, Ervin	GA	1849	Lufenia Helton	James Helton	Tarrossa Sexton	John & Easter Helton	Russell & Ruth Sexton
503	Helton, James	TN	1840	Mary Helton	Daniel Helton	Martha Walker	Peter & Jennie Helton	Wm & Katie Walker
10261	Helton, James	GA	1849	Sarah Helton	James Helton	Camilla Southerland	Calvin & Sarah Helton	John & Marth Southerland
12942	Helton, James	GA	1862	Ola Helton	James Helton	Tarrassa Sexton	John & Easter Helton	Russell & Ruth Sexton
4573	Helton, John	TN	1881		Ransom Helten	Jennie Smith	Daniel Helton	Martha Walker
17546	Helton, Larkin	GA	1835	Caroline Helton	Jacob Helton	Elizabeth Swaim	John & Dicie Helton	Beecham & Nancy Helton
15746	Helton, Martin	GA	1844	Priccilla Helton	Jacob Helton	Elizabeth Swain		
595	Helton, Matilda	TN	1872	divorced	Silas Helton	Salina Francis	Daniel Helton	John Francis
22872	Helton, Maude	TN	1888		James Helton	Martha Clark	Daniel & Patsy Helton	John & Peggy Clark
3071	Helton, Rodolphus	GA	1859	Henrietta Helton	John Helton	Mary McElroy	James & Camilla Helton	
675	Helton, Samuel	TN	1868	Samantha Helton	Silas Helton	Salina France	Daniel Helton	John France
677	Helton, Silas	TN	1862	Kate Helton	Silas Helton	Luia France	David & Patsy Helton	Bill France
899	Helton, T.F.	TN	1868	Willie Helton	Jason Helton	Mary Wilson	Daniel & Pollie Helton	Tom Wilson
501	Helton, Thomas	TN	1858	Sanny Helton	Soloman Helton	Eliza Graves	Daniel & Martha Helton	Soloman & Nancy Graves
12461	Helton, Walker	GA	1860	Mary Helton	James Helton	Tarrossa Sexton	John & Easter Helton	Russell & Ruth Sexton

19142	Helton, Will	GA	1877	Anna Helton	Joe Helton	Linda Nations		Crecy & Jessie Nations
8711	Helton, William	GA	1868	Celia Helton	James Helton	Sarah Honen	James & Carnely Helton	Thomas & Priscilla Honen
22589	Helton, William	TN	1874	Flora Helton	James Helton	Martha Clark	Daniel & Patsy Helton	John & Peggy Clark
10178	Hembree, Monroe	GA	1887	none	Joseph Hembree	Magie Cornett	Andrew Hembree	Eldred & Rachel Cornett
12984 *	Hembree, Octavia	GA	1876	William Hembree	Edmond Kellogg	Elizabeth Allen	Edmond & Hanna Kellogg	David & Elizabeth Daniel
12982 *	Hembree, William	GA	1860	Octavia Hembree	Pressley Hembree	Amanda Howell		Caleb & Lucy Howell
9484 *	Hemmitt, London	OK	1849	Julia Hemmitt	John Hemmitt	Celia Law	John & Bedie Hemmitt	Isaac & Jennie Law
21072	Hemphill, Susan	GA	1837	widow	Elisha Sizemore	Fannie Burton		Elizabeth Burton
7192	Hemsell, Malinda	TX		William Hemsell	Joel James	Angeline Ryan	Johnathan & Amanda James	
636	Henderson, Bayless	TN	1872	Zilpha Henderson	Wash Henderson	Mary Rogers	Harper & Margaret Henderson	Daniel & Dovey Pace
8499	Henderson, Bertha	VA	1886	J W Henderson	N M Blevins	Catharine Dolinger	Allen & Fanny Blevins	John & Betty Dolinger
21511	Henderson, Bettie	AL	1874	Alfred Henderson	Louis Parham	Julia Watkins	Andrew Parham	Lucinda Barker
19449	Henderson, Edith	AL	1906		John Henderson	Mary House	John & Catherine Henderson	Wm & Martha House
15259	Henderson, Emma	AL		Marshall Henderson	Milton Ivey	Eliza Giles		Martha Giles
717	Henderson, Eva	NC	1886	none	James Pace	Susan Henderson		Wash & Mary Henderson
21513	Henderson, James	AL	1859	Selena Henderson	James Harbin	Lucindy Henderson	James & Polly Harbin	
11069	Henderson, Lottie	VA	1879	D E Henderson	Leander Blevins	Elizabeth Hart		John & Polley Hart
635	Henderson, Mary	NC	1842	Wash Henderson	Daniel Rogers	Dovey Martin	Enoch & Rachel Rogers	Joseph & Mary Martin
2966	Henderson, Mary	VA	1879	Charley Henderson	James Hart	Franky Gaultney	Hugh & Easter Hart	
3356	Henderson, Mary	AL	1871	John Henderson	William Houss	Martha Lambert	Gilbert & Levita Houss	Joseph & Mary Lambert
13749	Henderson, Nancy	GA	1859	E. V. Henderson	Andrew Whitlock	Eliza Rowson	George & Nancy Whitlock	Elija & Millie Rowson
637	Henderson, Susan	NC	1867	none	Wash Henderson	Mary Rogers	Harper & Margaret Henderson	Daniel Rogers & Dovey Pace
22674	Henderson, Victoria	IN	1862	Frank Henderson	Thomas Hammonds	Dilena	Mark Hammonds	
2318	Hendricks, Dona	OK	1884	Ben Hendricks	James Tanner	Susan Buttry		John & Margarett Buttry
18577	Hendricks, Hester	NC	1882	John Hendricks	Thomas Allen	Elizabeth Martin	James & Rebecca Allen	Wm & Margret Martin
17197	Hendricks, William	OK	1831	Ann Hendricks	William Hendricks	Susannah		
16244	Hendrix, Elias	OK	1830		J J Hendrix	Cisley Kelley		
16133	Hendrix, Hattie	GA	1871	A S Hendrix	Phillip Spoke	Tildy Henry	Samuel & Harriet Spoke	
20423	Henkel, Martha	TN	1858	Henry Henkel	Robert Kirkman	Caroline Murphy		Johnathan & Eliza Murphy
14345	Henley, Daniel	MO	1846	Elmyra Henley	John Henley	Mary Allen		

14343	Henley, Hezekiah	OK	1856	Mary Henley	John Henley	Mary Allen		Martha Allen
8230	Henley, John	IN		Elizabeth Henley	John Henley	Mary Allen		
14344	Henley, Samuel	MO	1862	Eleanor Henley	John Henley	Mary Allen		
9756	Henning, Mason	WV	1846	Sarah Neal	William Henning	Melinda Roberts	Thos Henning	Ann Grant
12285	Henry, Benjamin	GA	1855	Arona Henry	Caleb Henry	Martha Dickey	Alexander Sour John	
12287	Henry, Charley	GA	1850	Mary Henry (decd)	Caleb Henry	Martha Dickey	Alexander Sour John	
13859	Henry, Ellen	GA	1880	Charles Henry	Samuel Donthit	Florida Weaver	Samuel & Polly Donthit	Ellen Weaver
12286	Henry, Mary	GA	1861	Alford Lowry	Caleb Henry	Martha Dickey	Alexander Sour John	
477	Henry, Silas Wm	AL	1836	Wincy Henry	Isom Henry	Dorcus Williams	unknown	Hubard Williams
19213	Henry, Zella	TN					Sam Shoutz	
19572	Henslee, Charley	TN	1878		Feilders Henslee	Mary Ragle	Ralzey & Sarah Henslee	Henry & Mary Ragle
12207	Henslee, Feilden	TN	1842	Mary Henslee	Ralzamore Henslee	Sarah Morgan	Benjamin Henslee	George Morgan
19571	Henslee, James	NC	1881	Elvira Henslee	Feilders Henslee	Mary Ragle	Ralzey & Sarah Henslee	Henry & Mary Ragle
19573	Henslee, John	TN	1869		Feilders Henslee	Mary Ragle	Ralzey & Sarah Henslee	Henry & Mary Ragle
19569	Henslee, Martha	TN	1883		Feilders Henslee	Mary Ragle	Ralzey & Sarah Henslee	Henry & Mary Ragle
19574	Henslee, Robert	TN	1875		Feilders Henslee	Mary Ragle	Ralzey & Sarah Henslee	Henry & Mary Ragle
12209	Henslee, William	NC	1856	Dora Henslee	Ralzamore Henslee	Sarah Morgan	Benjamin Henslee	George Morgan
16813	Hensley, Alka	NC	1884	Rabern Hensley	Hiram Hensley	Harriett Riddle	Dolph & Malinda Hensley	Marvin & Rachel Riddle
14863	Hensley, Alta et al	GA			Barnett Hensley	Ona Simmons	Lucinda Maney	Wm & Nancy Simmons
20878	Hensley, Annie	TN	1877	Charles Hensley	Newton Gwinn	Forest Kimsey	Jack & Alucon Gwinn	Humphrey Kimsey
14827	Hensley, Arcemus	NC	1882	Tilda Hensley	Hiram Hensley	Harrett Riddle	Dolphos & Malinda Hensley	Thos & Kizah Barrett
11397	Hensley, Armeyetta	TN	1884	Arthur Hensley	John Crisp	Mary Delozier		Ed & Elizabeth Delozier
2428	Hensley, Barnette	GA	1860	Oney Hensley	William Hensley	Lucinda Maney		John Maney & Polly MadCap
21808	Hensley, George	OK	1879	Minnie Hensley	Daniel Hensley	Martha Dorsey	Amos & Margaret Hensley	John & Martha Dorsey
4576	Hensley, Hiram	TN	1862		Barnett Hensley	Lucinda Hensley	Wm & Mary Hensley	Lewis & Elizabeth Hensley
9778	Hensley, Hiram (decd)	NC	1861	Harrett Hensley	Dolfuss Hensley	Malinda Hensley	Wm & Sela Hensley	Thos & Kaziah Barrett
21807	Hensley, John	OK	1876	Birty Hensley	Daniel Hensley	Martha Dorsey	Amos & Margaret Hensley	John & Martha Dorsey
4139	Hensley, Joseph	TN	1847		Lewis Hensley	Elizabeth Metcalf	Benjamin & Nancy Hensley	Absalom & Nancy Metcalf
10256	Hensley, Lucinda	TN	50yrs	Wesley Hensley	Hiram Metcalf	Jennie Hensley	Abselum & Nancy Metcalf	
16248	Henson, Bettie	TX	1884		William Henson	Josephene Mabry		

ID	Name	State	Year					
16167	Henson, Henry	TX	1823	Susan Henson	James Henson	Elizabeth Talley	Wm Henson & Drucilla Motley	Mathias Tally & Elizabeth Pyron
16144	Henson, Jesse	TX	1876		William Henson	Josephine Mabry	Henry Henson & Mary Hardman	Joseph Mabry & Hester Adkins
6004	Henson, Mary	IL	1873	S C Henson	Pleasant Blackburn	Caroline Farris	Andrew & Francis Blackburn	
17116	Henson, Mattie	OK	42yrs	Scott Henson	John Thomas	Nancy Warren		
19186	Henson, Polley	OK		Boot Henson	Campbell Taylor	Peggie		
16143	Henson, Thomas	TX	1880		William Henson	Josephine Mabry	Henry Henson & Mary Hardman	Joseph Mabry & Hester Adkins
16141	Henson, William	TX	1850	Josephine Henson	Henry Henson	Mary Hardman	James Henson	Elizabeth Talley
1384	Herndon, Hattie	OH	1880	George Herndon	William Williamson	Emma Taborn	Square & Harriett Williamson	Chavors
20318	Herrell, Bert	MO	1886		James Herrell	Allice Douglas	Emerson & Clarisa Herrell	
20311	Herrell, George	MO			James Herrell	Allice Douglas	Emerson & Clarisa Herrell	John & Eliza Douglas
20308	Herrell, James	MO	1860	Alice Herrell	Emerson Herrell	Clarisa Scruggs		Louis & Ann Scruggs
22437	Herrill, Myrtle	TN	1890	none	George Herrill	Ann Saunders	Jack & Betsy Saunders	
20947	Herring, Posie	GA	1873	Mary Herring	E.R. Herring	Mary Leach	Ephrem & Mollie Herring	Jake & Resillie Leach
12799	Herron, Ruthie	MO	1882		George Cannefax	Margret Haley	Joseph & Sarah Cannefax	George & Abigail Haley
18924	Hester, Bessie	GA	1895		John Hester	Della Williams	Joseph & Rhoda Hester	Berry & Lou Williams
18916	Hester, Freddie	GA	1906		William Hester	Rena Scoggins	Joseph & Rhoda Hester	John & Margaret Scoggins
18925	Hester, Homer	GA	1901		John Hester	Della Williams	Joseph & Rhoda Hester	Berry & Lou Williams
18921	Hester, Jesse	GA	1894		John Hester	Della Williams	Joseph & Rhoda Hester	Berry & Lou Williams
18923	Hester, John	GA	1867	Della Hester	Joseph Hester	Rhoda Hester		Giddeon & Louiza Hester
18853	Hester, Rhoda	GA	1847	Joseph Hester	Giddeon Hester	Louiza Helton	Benj & Milly Hester	Joseph & Lillie Helton
13616	Hester, Rosa	IN	1877	William Hester	Henderson Phipps	Phedelia Hash		James & Marjory Hash
18920	Hester, Thomas	GA	1903		John Hester	Della Williams	Joseph & Rhoda Hester	Berry & Lou Williams
18917	Hester, William	GA	1879	Rena Hester	Joseph Hester	Rhoda Hester		Giddeon & Louiza Hester
18922	Hester, William	GA	1906		John Hester	Della Williams	Joseph & Rhoda Hester	Berry & Lou Williams
2809	Hewell, Kate	OK	1865	G W Hewell	Sizemore	Nancy Davis	Edward & Polley Sizomore	
13783*	Heywood, Mytle & Goldin	GA	1890 1892		John Heywood	Orzelia Whitaker		Henry Whitaker
13782*	Heywood, Orzelia	GA	1876	John Heywood	Henry Whitaker	Mahalia Man	John & Millie Kearklin	
19877	Hiatt, Greenville	NC	1845	Virginia Hiatt	Jacob Hiatt	Arminda Barker	William Hiatt	Thomas & Nancy Barker
2595	Hice, Charles & Ellen	GA		none	George Hice	Margret Davenport		John & Elisabeth Davenport
2593	Hice, Mary	GA	1872	William Hice	George Hice	Margret Davenport		John & Elisabeth Davenport
2594	Hice, Thomas	GA	1866	A E Hice	George Hice	Margret Davenport		John & Elisabeth Davenport

20342 *	Hickenbottom, Iona	TN	1870	Solomon Hickenbottom	Isaac McCarny	Mckie Thompson	Lindsay McCarny	Moses & Fashion Johnson
20340 *	Hickenbottom, Vivian	TN	1898		Solomon Hickenbottom	Jane McCarney	John & Mary Hickenbottom	Isaac & Mckie McCarney
17515	Hickman, Frederick	OK	1871	Kittie Hickman	J.A. Hickman	Sarah Hicks	Fred & Polly Hickman	Linsey Hicks & Catherine Miller
17517	Hickman, Ida	OK	1882		J.A. Hickman	Sarah Hicks	Fred & Polly Hickman	Linsey Hicks & Catherine Miller
18183	Hickman, Millie	TN	1857		Mordeca Cooper	Genette Hughes	Thomas & Susan Cooper	Wm & Mary Hughes
19304	Hicks, C.H.	GA	1885	Eula Hicks	John Hicks	Bettie Cole	Joe & Martha Hicks	Thomas & Amanda Cole
19618	Hicks, Charley	TN	1885	Ellie Hicks	Dave Hicks	Mary Morgan	Charley & Mary Hicks	Jesse & Louisa Morgan
19650	Hicks, Eveie	TN	1895		Dave Hicks	Mary Morgan	Charley & Mary Hicks	Jessa & Louisa Morgan
8895 *	Hicks, Franklin	AL	76yrs	Susan Hicks	William Franklin	Nellie Stephens		
19612	Hicks, Henry	TN	1895		Dave Hicks	Mary Morgan	Charley & Mary Hicks	Jessa & Louis Morgan
19652	Hicks, James	TN	1882		Dave Hicks	Mary Morgan	Charley & Mary Hicks	Jessa & Louisa Morgan
19305	Hicks, John	GA	1861	Bettie Hicks	Joe Hicks	Martha Carroll	Daniel & Annie Hicks	John Carroll
19651	Hicks, Leller	TN	1889		Dave Hicks	Mary Morgan	Charley & Mary Hicks	Jessa & Louisa Morgan
19861	Hicks, Lester	VA			Rufus Hicks	Martha Thore	Sarah Hicks	George & Margaret Thore
3027	Hicks, Lovinda	MO	1847	Jonathan Hicks	Vinson Harralson	Martha Hambleton	David & Peachey Harralson	Elijah & Sarah Hambelton
19874	Hicks, Martha	VA	30yrs	Rufus Hicks	George Thore	Margaret Joyce	Norfleet & Frances Thore	John & Louisa Joyce
14837	Hicks, Mary	TN	1851	Dave Hicks	Jesse Morgan	Louisa Franklin	Rub & Martha Morgan	Wm & Elizabeth Franklin
10478	Hicks, Noah	MO	1880	Lula Hicks	Johnathan Hicks	Lorinda Harralson	Hiram & Mary Hicks	Vincin & Martha Harralson
11375	Hicks, Strumlow	MO	1870	Abbie Hicks	Johnathan Hicks	Lorinda Haralson	Hiram & Mary Hicks	Vincin & Martha Haralson
22953	Hicks, Virginia	AR	1874	Robert Hicks	John Green	Sabray Woodall		John & Ann Woodall
19303	Hicks, Wilton	GA	1884		John Hicks	Bettie Cole	Joe & Martha Hicks	Thomas & Amanda Cole
8286	Higdon, Delia	GA	1884	Samuel Higdon	Albert Sisan	Nancy Key	Richard & Lucy Sisan	
16247	Higdon, Joseph	TX	1862	Emma Higdon	James Higdon	Rachel Freeland	Joseph & Marget Higdon	Howell & Zilpha Freeland
22731	Higdon, Joseph	TX	1869	Emma Higdon	James Higdon	Rachel Freeland	Joseph & Mary Higdon	H. & G. Freeland
596	Higdon, Rachel	OK	1840	James Higdon	Howell Freeland	Zilpha Campbell	Freeland	unknown
2835	Higgins, Fannie decd	OK	1866	William Higgins	William Russell	Susan Willis	James & Elizabeth Russell	William & Polly Willis
19759 *	Higgins, Isaac	TN	1852	Ida Higgins		Caroline Higgins		
4582	Higgins, Josephine	OK	1854	Charles Higgins	John Nivins	Dealla Stenson		
121	Higgins, Margaret	AR	1868	Albert Higgins	Thomas McGuire	Sarah Fender	Thomas McGuire	Alexander Brown
18203	Higgins, Texana	TN	1869	James Higgins	Fleming Latty	Jane Jones	Emery & Nancy Latty	Wiley & Elizabeth Jones

2628	Hight, Nancy	GA	1871	Samuel Hight	Linford Summing	Artilda Tidwell	Margaret Grantt	F M & Sallie Tidwell
20338 *	Hightower, Annie	TN	1860		Milo Steele	Mary Smith	Thomas & Betty Smith	Gilbert & Hagar Moore
4989	Hightower, Emma	GA	1889	Basil Hightower	Robert Pitts	Lena Sanders		Dianna Sanders
18538	Hightower, Ernest	AL	1886		James Hightower	Mary Houss	James & Nancy Hightower	Isaac & Levita Houss
3380	Hightower, Gustave	AL	1888	none	James Hightower Jr.	Mary Houss	James & Nancy Hightower	Gilbert & Levitia Houss
3371	Hightower, Isabella	AL	1870	none	James Hightower Jr	Mary Houss	James & Nancy Hightower	Gilbert & Levitia Houss
18539	Hightower, James Jr.	AL	1877		James Hightower	Mary Houss	James & Nancy Hightower	Isaac & Levita Houss
3358	Hightower, Mary	AL	1841	James Hightower Jr.	Gilbert Houss	Levita Hollinger		William & Levita Hollinger
3377	Hightower, Verdelia	AL	1873	none	James Hightower Jr	Mary Houss	James & Nancy Hightower	Gilbert & Levitia Houss
3379	Hightower, William	AL	1884	none	James Hightower	Mary Houss	James & Nancy Hightower	Gilbert & Levitia Houss
21687	Hilburn, Isham	AL	1864	Mary Hilburn	James Hilburn	Rebecca Kerbo		
21688	Hilburn, Mary	AL	1861	I.F. Hilburn	James Gordon	Bathsaba Bush	Charley & Sallie Gordon	George & Martha Bush
3008	Hildebrand, James	TN	1833	none	John Hildebrand	Nice Russell	Michael Hildebrand	Russell
3009	Hildebrand, John	TN	1837	Amanda	John Hildebrand	Nice Russell	Michael Hildebrand	Russell
9923	Hilderbrand, Lulah	OK	22yrs	Robert Hilderbrand	John Payne	Elisebeth Swindle	Elisha & Malisa Payne	
9887	Hilderbrand, Robert	OK	1882	Lulah Hilderbrand	Jeff Hilderbrand	Maggie Moore	Steve & Mandy Hilderbrand	Anderson & Hairot Moore
20322	Hill, Callie	GA	1877	William Hill	John Abbot	Jane Wood	John & Mary Abbot	
10609	Hill, Elizabeth	OK	1848	Johnny Hill	Herman Allen		Ann Allen	
22442	Hill, Emma	IN	1872	Henry Hill	Levi Winburn	Martha Roberts	Harry & Keziah Winburn	Stephen & Mary Roberts
21074	Hill, Fannie	GA	1872	C.W. Hill	George Greenway	Mary Williams	W.F. Greenway & Rhoda	Wesley Williams & Clara
14044	Hill, Hazel	KS	1886		John Hill	Elizabeth Allen		Herman Allen
13144	Hill, Margaret	OK	1850	William Hill	Robert McGenty	Nancy Couch	Johnethan & Deby McGenty	John & Charity Couch
14940	Hill, Margrett	OK	1893		Juneous Hill	Rose Hudson	Wm & Martha Hill	
17329	Hill, Mariah	GA	1837	Bonnie Hill	Allen Franklen	Sookey Franklen		
16240	Hill, Mary	OK	1841	Henry Hill	Louis Couch	Nancy Stowbaugh	John & Charity Couch	William Stowbaugh
12710	Hill, Rachel	MO	1863	Charles Hill	Daniel Murray	Tilitha Hines	Joshua & Mary Murray	Walter & Matilda Hines
13143	Hill, Rebecca	OK		Wm Hill				
12482	Hill, Richard	GA	1836		D B Hill	Eliza Chitwood		Patsy Chitwood
17841 *	Hill, Rosana	WI	1857	Abraham Hill	James Malone	Catherine Barber		Harry Barber
14942	Hill, Samuel	OK	1857	Amanda Hill	Wm Hill	Martha Allen		Martha Allen
10250	Hill, Sarah	OK	1874	R D Hill	John Carnes	Amelia Morrison	Joshua & Nancy Carnes	Ezra & Sophia Morrison
17768	Hill, Susan	TN	1842		Tyree Kelley	Delila Emry	Johnathan & Mary Kelley	James & Nancy Emry

20642	Hill, Tennessee	TN	1861	Westley Hill	Henry McKeil	Mariah Gann	Singleton McKeil	George & Eliza Gann
14941	Hill, William	OK	1884		Samuel Hill	Amanda Lindley	Wm & Martha Hill	
21546 *	Hill, William	GA	1840		Robin Hill	Caroline Barnes	Eddie & Annie Hill	Windson & Charlotte Barnes
16246 *	Hillery, Sarah	OK	1846	Tom Hillery	Amos Jefferson	Mollie Brown		
15397	Hillhouse, Albert	GA	1902		John Hillhouse	Kate Roberts	John & Francis Hillhouse	Wm & Sarah Roberts
14559	Hillhouse, Alexander	GA	1892		Joseph Hillhouse	Riller Brown	Samuel & Augusta Hillhouse	George & Mary Brown
9848	Hillhouse, Alice	GA	1901	none	Samuel Hillhouse	Mary Howard	Samuel & Augusta Hillhouse	Oliver & Susan Howard
12312	Hillhouse, Annie	GA	1897		Robert Hillhouse	Sarah McCollum	Samuel & Augusta Hillhouse	John & Elizabeth McCollum
10557	Hillhouse, Augusta	GA	1840	Samuel Hillhouse	John Cole	Betsy Whitlock		James & Sallie Whitlock
12314	Hillhouse, Belle	GA	1900		James Hillhouse	Mary Brown	Samuel Jr & Augusta Hillhouse	George & Mary Brown
9849	Hillhouse, Coleman	GA	1897	none	Samuel Hillhouse	Mary Howard	Samuel & Augusta Hillhouse	Oliver & Susan Howard
12306	Hillhouse, Elias	GA	1893		Robert Hillhouse	Sarah McCollum	Samuel & Augusta Hillhouse	John & Elizabeth McCollum
12311	Hillhouse, Ernest	GA	1900		Joshua Hillhouse	Olie Grier	Samuel & Augusta Hillhouse	Thomas & Tobie Grier
14558	Hillhouse, Ernest	GA	1895		Joseph Hillhouse	Riller Brown	Samuel & Augusta Hillhouse	George & Mary Brown
12310	Hillhouse, Ethel	GA	1904		Robert Hillhouse	Sarah McCollum	Samuel & Augusta Hillhouse	John & Elizabeth McCollum
12309	Hillhouse, Fannie	GA	1889		Robert Hillhouse	Sarah McCollum	Samuel & Augusta Hillhouse	John & Elizabeth McCollum
12308	Hillhouse, George	GA			James Hillhouse	Mary Brown	Samuel Jr & Augusta Hillhouse	George & Mary Brown
12305	Hillhouse, James	GA	1903		James Hillhouse	Mary Brown	Samuel & Augusta Hillhouse	George & Mary Brown
12307	Hillhouse, James	GA	1871	Mary Hillhouse	Samuel Hillhouse Jr	Augusta Cole	Samuel Sr & Annie Hillhouse	John & Betsy Cole
14557	Hillhouse, James	GA	1890		Joseph Hillhouse	Riller Brown	Samuel & Augusta Hillhouse	George & Mary Brown
9850	Hillhouse, Jesse	GA	1898	none	Samuel Hillhouse	Mary Howard	Samuel & Augusta Hillhouse	Oliver & Susan Howard
12304	Hillhouse, Jessie	GA	1886		Robert Hillhouse	Sarah McCollum	Samuel & Augusta Hillhouse	John & Elizabeth McCollum
12303	Hillhouse, Joseph	GA	1900		Robert Hillhouse	Sarah McCollum	Samuel & Augusta Hillhouse	John & Elizabeth McCollum
12302	Hillhouse, Joshua	GA	1875	Olie Hillhouse	Samuel Hillhouse	Augusta Cole	Samuel & Annie Hillhouse	John & Betsy Cole
12313	Hillhouse, Joshua	GA	1898		Joshua Hillhouse	Olie Grier	Samuel & Augusta Hillhouse	Thomas & Tobie Grier
15396	Hillhouse, Kate	GA	1880	John Hillhouse	William Roberts	Sarah Harris	Joshua & Mary Roberts	Gillison & Martha Harris
14556	Hillhouse, Lilly	GA	1897		Joseph Hillhouse	Riller Brown	Samuel & Augusta Hillhouse	George & Mary Brown
12301	Hillhouse, Maitie	GA	1904		Joshua Hillhouse	Olie Grier	Samuel & Augusta Hillhouse	Thomas & Tobie Grier
9851	Hillhouse, Mary	GA	1892	none	Samuel Hillhouse	Mary Howard	Samuel & Augusta Hillhouse	Oliver & Susan Howard
12299	Hillhouse, Melvin	GA	1902		Robert Hillhouse	Sarah McCollum	Samuel & Augusta Hillhouse	John & Elizabeth McCollum

9852	Hillhouse, Minnie	GA	1905	none	Samuel Hillhouse	Mary Howard	Samuel & Augusta Hillhouse	Oliver & Susan Howard
12291	Hillhouse, Robert	GA	1864	Sarah Hillhouse	Samuel Hillhouse	Augusta Cole	Samuel & Annie Hillhouse	John & Betsy Cole
9853	Hillhouse, Sallie	GA	1903	none	Samuel Hillhouse	Mary Howard	Samuel & Augusta Hillhouse	Oliver & Susan Howard
9847	Hillhouse, Samuel	GA	1868	Mary Hillhouse	Samuel Hillhouse	Augustas Cole	Samuel & Annie Hillhouse	John & Betsy Cole
9854	Hillhouse, Samuel	GA	1893	none	Samuel Hillhouse	Mary Howard	Samuel & Augusta Hillhouse	Oliver & Susan Howard
14555	Hillhouse, Samuel	GA	1888	Eva Hillhouse	Joseph Hillhouse	Riller Brown	Samuel & Augusta Hillhouse	George & Mary Brown
12357	Hillhouse, Susan	GA	1895		Robert Hillhouse	Sarah McCollum	Samuel & Augusta Hillhouse	John & Elizbeth McCollum
12352	Hillhouse, Thomas	GA	1898		James Hillhouse	Mary Brown	Samuel & Augusta Hillhouse	George & Mary Brown
9855	Hillhouse, William	GA	1895	none	Samuel Hillhouse	Mary Howard	Samuel & Augusta Hillhouse	Oliver & Susan Howard
12351	Hillhouse, William	GA	1891		Robert Hillhouse	Sarah McCollum	Samuel & Augusta Hillhouse	John & Elizbeth McCollum
17769	Hilliard, John	TN	1872	Elizabeth Hilliard	George Hilliard	Jane Mantooth	Wesley Hilliard	Calvin & Vina Mantooth
7202	Hilton, Lucy	KS	1873		John Boatright	Fannie Wylie	Benj & Julia Boatright	Harvey & Ruth Wylie
11845	Hinchee, Ford	KY			Samuel Hinchee	Jennie Ashbrooke	James Hinchee & Margret Smith	
10993	Hinchee, Jonah	OK	1874	Henry Hinchee	Bengman Hinchee	Annie Walker	James & Margret Hinchee	
12800	Hinchee, Miller	KY	1880		Samuel Hinchee	Jane Ashbrook	James & Margret Hinchee	
10797	Hinchee, Samuel	OK	1880	Susie Hinchee	Benjamin Hinchee	Euphemia Hill	Jonnes & Margret Hinchee	
11511	Hinchee, Samuel	KY	1829	Lizzie Hinchee	Jonas Hinchee	Margaret Smith	Morris & Polly Hinchee	
11844	Hinchee, Samuel	KY	1875	Winona Hinchee	Samuel Hinchee	Jane Ashbrooke	James Hinchee & Margret Smith	
3000	Hines, Joseph	OK	1889	none	Joe Hines	Cinthy Ragzel	Isaac & Mary Ragzel	
3001	Hines, Mary	OK	1893	none	Joe Hines	Cinthy Ragzel	Isaac & Mary Ragzel	
22733	Hinkle, Burl	MO	1885		Sidney Hinkle	M.A. Tuck	Jacob & Sarah Hinkle	Henry & Mary Tuck
2510	Hinkle, Dennis	MO	1875	Delia Hinkle	Sidney Hinkle	M A Tuck	Jacob & Sarah Hinkle	Henry & Mary Tuck
3964	Hinkle, Henry	MO	1877	Louise Hinkle	Sidney Hinkle	Alzanio Tuck	Jacob & Sarah Hinkle	Henry & Mary Tuck
20305	Hinkle, John	MO	1872	Mary Hinkle	Daniel Hinkle	Lucy Herrell	John & Cynthia Hinkle	Emerson & Clarissa Herrell
22735	Hinkle, Kitty	MO	1888		Sidney Hinkle	M.A. Tuck	Jacob & Sarah Hinkle	Henry & Mary Tuck
2511	Hinkle, Leonora	MO	1867	Jacob Hinkle	Jacob Hinkle	Sarah Hambelton	Jesse & Hannah Hinkle	Elijah & Sarah Hambelton
20315	Hinkle, Lucy	MO	1850		Emerson Herrell	Clarisa Scruggs	Michael & Lucy Herrell	Lewis & Anne Scruggs
22734	Hinkle, Ora	MO	1882		Sidney Hinkle	M.A. Tuck	Jacob & Sarah Hinkle	Henry & Mary Tuck
2509	Hinkle, Sidney	MO	1854	M A Hinkle	Jacob Hinkle	Sarah Hambelton	Jesse & Hannah Hinkle	Elijah & Sarah Hambelton

6366	Hinson, William	AL	25yrs		John Hinson	Bettee Hathcock	Bill Hinson	John Hathcock & Rosa McGhee
12137	Hipes, Adeline	VA	1865	J M Hipes	Kith Billips	Jane Sizemore	Jessie Billips	George Sizemore
197 *	Hitchcock, Dove	NC	1843	widow	Ned Graham	Dorcas McLelland		
198 *	Hitchcock, John	NC	1873		Glenn? Hitchcock	Dove Goins	Dave Crowder	Gerrett Crowder
20939	Hite, James	GA	1867	Henryetta Hite	Marion Helton	Jane Hite	Peter Helton & Gabrel Hite	Sarah Hite
15258	Hitt, Jeff	GA	1875	Emma Hitt	Thomas Hitt	Elizabeth Carney		Lem & Katie Carney
15256	Hitt, Robert	GA	1883		Thomas Hitt	Elizabeth Carney		Lem & Katie Carney
19027	Hix, Lou	TN	1880	Robert Hix	George Hilliard	Jane Mantooth	John Hilliard	
3095	Hobgood, Allie	MS	1883	Thomas Hobgood	John Hobgood	Mattie Coleman	Charles & Martha Hobgood	
3096	Hobgood, Charles	MS	1883	none	Charles Hobgood	Evie Henderson	Charles & Marlha Hobgood	
3100	Hobgood, Charles	MS	1852	Willie Hobgood	Charles Hobgood	Martha Lowe		Thomas & Annie Lowe
3106	Hobgood, Charles	MS	1873	Daisey Hobgood	James Hobgood	Martha Stuart	Charles & Martha Hobgood	
18258	Hobgood, Cleo	GA	1901		Lewis Hobgood	Delia Atkins	Lewis & Nancy Hobgood	Webster & Malinda Atkins
15255	Hobgood, Delia	GA	1870	Lewis Hobgood	Webster Atkins	Malinda Carney	Berryman & Martha Atkins	Ed & Elizabeth Carney
18259	Hobgood, Edward	GA	1890		Lewis Hobgood	Delia Atkins	Lewis & Nancy Hobgood	Webster & Malinda Atkins
18260	Hobgood, Etta	GA	1905		Lewis Hobgood	Delia Atkins	Lewis & Nancy Hobgood	Webster & Malinda Atkins
18261	Hobgood, George	GA	1899		Lewis Hobgood	Delia Atkins	Lewis & Nancy Hobgood	Webster & Malinda Atkins
3091	Hobgood, James	MS	1839	Martha & Ella Hobgood	Charles Hobgood	Martha Lowe		Thomas & Annie Lowe
3098	Hobgood, James	MS	1875	Agnes Hobgood	James Hobgood	Martha Stuart	Charles & Martha Hobgood	
3099	Hobgood, James	MS	1871	Lessie Hobgood	John Hobgood	Mattie Coleman	Charles & Martha Hobgood	
3097	Hobgood, John	MS	1850	Mattie Hobgood	Charles Hobgood	Martha Lowe		Thomas & Annie Lowe
18262	Hobgood, Nancy	GA	1892		Lewis Hobgood	Delia Atkins	Lewis & Nancy Hobgood	Webster & Malinda Atkins
3107	Hobgood, Temple	MS	1884	Ethel Hobgood	James Hobgood	Martha Stuart	Charles & Martha Hobgood	David Stuart
3094	Hobgood, Thomas	MS	1877	Allie Hobgood	Charles Hobgood	H Evie Henderson	Charles & Martha Hobgood	
12246	Hobgood, Thomas	MS	1882		James Hobgood	Martha Stuart	Charles Hobgood	Thomas & Patty Low
18263	Hobgood, Thomas	GA	1895		Lewis Hobgood	Delia Atkins	Lewis & Nancy Hobgood	Webster & Malinda Atkins
3122	Hobgood, Virgil	MS	1877	Mary Hobgood	James Hobgood	Martha Stuart	Charles & Martha Hobgood	
22691	Hobson, Connie	NC	1877	Dalles Hobson	Isaac Poindexter	Mary Hauser	Denson & Sarah Poindexter	Samuel & Nancy Hauser

7201	Hockett, Agnes	OK		F J Hockett	Samuel Goodwin	Agnes Yeargin		Martha Yeargin
18050	Hodge, Annie	TN	1899		Wm Hodge	Callie Oxendyne	Sarah Hodge	John & Mary Oxendyne
18051	Hodge, Susie	TN	1893		William Hodge	Callie Oxendyne	Sarah Hodge	John & Mary Oxendyne
9755	Hodges, Amey	OK	1849	John Hodges	Henry Rogers	Mariah Rodgers	Joseph Rogers	
1157	Hodges, Sallie	AL	1879	Robert Hodges	Wm Gibson	Bettie Henson	Wm & Peggy Gibson	Wm & Ann Henson
21020*	Hogan, Manda	TN	1853	Scot Hogan		Amy Cowan		
2516	Hogan, Sarah	GA	1867	W.C. Hogan	Moses Anderson	Susan Corbin		John & Delilah Corbin
20230*	Hoge, Andrew	TN	1839	Mary Hoge	Bob Kerry	Sarah Hoge	Bob Vann	Silva Belcher
296	Hogseed, Iler	NC	21yrs	James Hogseed	R L Anderson	Mary Kitchens	Lazrus & Nancy Anderson	John & Elizabeth Kitchins
9760	Hogtoter, Nancy	OK	56yrs	Sandy Hogtoter	oo-dau-lah-ner	qua-ku-Justice		noo & Rachel Justice
4729	Hogue, Missouri	OK	1862	H.H. Hogue	Edward Williams	Winfred Stout	John & Nancy Williams	
2254	Holbrook, Amanda	GA	1876	J M Holbrook	William Mason	Susie Benfield	John & Pollie Mason	Thomas & Lydia Benfield
15395	Holbrook, Berta	GA	1870	Landrum Holbrook	Gillison Harris	Martha Fowler	Lorenzo & Sarah Harris	Wm & Lucy Fowler
15394	Holbrook, Frank	GA	1895		Landrum Holbrook	Berta Harris	Frank & Catherine Holbrook	Gillison & Martha Harris
2321	Holbrook, Julia	GA	1879	J H Holbrook	W J Mason	Susie Benfield	John & Pollie Mason	Tom & Lydie Benfield
15393	Holbrook, Paul	GA	1903		Landrum Holbrook	Berta Harris	Frank & Catherine Holbrook	Gillison & Martha Harris
16177	Holbrook, William	OK	1843	Samantha Holbrook	Jessie Holbrook	Mary Sewell	Jessie Holbrook	Joshua Sewell
14760	Holbrooks, Isabell	KY	1862	Green Holbrooks	Solmon Blevins	Elizabeth Quinley		
18211*	Holcomb, Alice	GA	1872	John Holcomb	Jurd Haney	Mary Lively	James & Gracie Haney	Gilliam & Jane Lively
7777	Holcomb, Annie	OK	1875	none	Marten Holcomb	Sarah Hayes	Wm & Louisa Holcomb	John & Louisa Hayes
15679*	Holcomb, Carr	GA	1860		Paul Holcomb	Lottie Noble		Catie Noble
20881	Holcomb, Charles	NC	1890		James Holcomb	America McPheters	Robert & Sallie Holcomb	Chas & Betsie McPheters
20281	Holcomb, Cleo	GA	1882		Holcomb	Swisher	W.J. Holcomb	
20879	Holcomb, Dock	NC	1888		James Holcomb	America McPheters	Robert & Sallie Holcomb	Chas & Detsie McPheters
4755	Holcomb, Elizabeth	GA	1861	Thomas Holcomb	Masiah Smith	Mary Smith	Christopher Smith	Nancy Smith
14444	Holcomb, Genarch	GA	37yrs	Mack Holcomb	P. Bohanon	Mary Keith		
14442	Holcomb, Georgia	GA		Benj Holcomb	P. Bohanon	Maryan Keith		
7187	Holcomb, Harvey	OK	1885	none	Martin Holcomb	Sarah Hays	Wm & Louisa Holcomb	John & Louisa Hays
3075	Holcomb, Henry	TX	1851	Martha Holcomb	Asa Holcomb	Polly Townsend	Henry & Betty Holcomb	Edward & Annie Townsend

15254	Holcomb, Hix	GA	1858	Annie Holcomb	Asa Holcomb	Polly Townsend		Edward & Anna Townsend
17775	Holcomb, James	TN	1854	Mary Holcomb	Joshua Holcomb	Malinda Gutch	Bennett Holcomb	Sallie Tillman
7186	Holcomb, John	OK	1883	none	Martin Holcomb	Sarah Hays	Wm & Louisa Holcomb	John & Louisa Hays
20282	Holcomb, John	GA	1874	Cora Holcomb	W.A. Holcomb	Swisher	W.J. Holcomb	Harry Swisher
20880	Holcomb, Lizzie	NC	1891		James Holcomb	America McPheters	Robert & Sallie Holcomb	Chas & Betsie McPheters
20874	Holcomb, Lyaergus	NC	1882		James Holcomb	America McPheters	Robert & Sallie Holcomb	Chas & Betsie McPheters
14421	Holcomb, Margaret	NC	1857	John Holcomb	Bob Holcomb	Sallie Maney	Henry & Fanny Holcomb	John & Polly Maney
7189	Holcomb, Martin	OK	1846	Sarah Holcomb	William Holcomb	Louisa Berry	Benj & Sarah Holcomb	Hiram & Sarah Berry
9588	Holcomb, Mary	WV		James Holcomb	Amon Sizemore	Nancy Backhouse	Hiram & Jane Sizemore	John & Pheeby Backhouse
20875	Holcomb, Milton	NC	1853	Osie Holcomb	Robert Holcomb	Sallie Maney	Henry & Fanny Holcomb	John & Polly Maney
7188	Holcomb, Thomas	GA	1880	Lucinda Holcomb	Martin Holcomb	Annie Swisher	Benj Holcomb	Sarah Nicholson
13780 *	Holcomb, Will	GA	1864	Cornelia Holcomb	Paul Holcomb	Lottie Noble		Catie Noble
20882	Holcomb, Willard & Nellie	NC	1898		James Holcomb	America McPheters	Robert & Sallie Holcomb	Chas & Betsie McPheters
14341	Holcomb, William	GA	1846	Louisa Holcomb	W J Holcomb	Louise Shook		
20839	Holcombe, Allie	GA	1884	Frank Holcombe	William Reeves	Martha Whitlock	Mat & Neeby Reeves	Wm & Caroline Whitlock
14417	Holcombe, James	NC	1848	Emaline Holcombe	Robert Holcombe	Sally Maney	Henry & Fanning Holcombe	John & Polly Maney
21437	Holden, Beulah	TX		Edward Holden	Thomas Mulinax	Susan Galleher	Peter & Elizabeth Mulinax	Charles & Eliza Galleher
2127	Holden, Nathaniel	NC	1882	none	John Holden	Samantha Martin		Joseph & Adeline Martin
4767	Holden, Samantha	TN	1859	John Holden	Joseph Martin	Adeline Moose	Joseph & Mary Martin	
15044	Holden, Sarah	GA	1847	William Holden	James Suggs	Mary Cox	James & Polly Scruggs	
18377	Holder, Eliza	AL	37yrs	John Holder	George Murphy	Mary Allen	Nat & Mariah Murphy	James & Nancy Allen
14963	Holder, Lemuel	GA	1865	Lizzie Holder	Sam Holder	Lucresia Moreland	Jim & Frankie Holder	Cynthia Moreland
10259	Holder, Ruth	TN	1838	widow	Hiram Vann	Susan Biggs	Dempsey Vann & Ruthy Reece	Dempsey Biggs
19876	Holeyfield, Henrietta	NC	1864	Jeff Holeyfield	Arthur Dennis	Betsey Cobb	John Dennis Sr.	
7198	Holis, Pearl	TX	1884	J W Holis	W P Parsly	Mattie Boatright		
5165	Holland, Isabella	OK	1858	Louis Baptiste	Francis Watkins	Nancy Jones	John & Hazier Watkins	Wm & Sarah Jones
18603	Holland, Izora	TN	1862	Benj Holland	William Tidwell	Matilda Pane	Gasaway Tidwell	Thos Pane & Maranda Watson
7603	Holland, James	GA	1842	Martha & Minnie	William Holland	Susie Posey		John Posey
11937 *	Holland, Jennie	AL	1876	John Holland	Samuel Sapp	Mary Broyles		Sidney Broyles
18597	Holland, Minnie	TN	1883		Benj Holland	Izora Tidwell		Wm & Matilda Tidwell

14342	Holland, Nancy	OK	1862	A O Holland	Anderson Musgrave	Millie Young	Thos & Sallie Musgrave	John & Millie Young
17739 *	Holland, Winnie	TN	1838		William Ray	Martha Smith		Edie
8534	Hollaway, George	VA	1872	Rosa Hollaway	William Hollaway	Louisa Waters		Wm & Zilpha Waters
8535	Hollaway, Louisa	VA	1856	William Hollaway	William Waters	Zilpha Thompson		John & Polley Thompson
19557	Hollenshead, Harriett	NC	1858	W.H. Hollenshead	Andrew Payne	Elizabeth Murry	John & Jane Payne	
20048	Holley, Lena	TX	1866	William Holley	Miles Faucett	Sallie Griffis	Wm & Elizabeth Faucett	Wm & Mary Griffis
17609 *	Hollie, George	TN	1834	Bettie Hollie	Peter Alexander	Ann Gardner	Simon & Easter Alexander	John & Lydia Gardner
15638	Hollifield, Nancy	GA	50yrs	W H Hollifield	Drurey Dobbins	Harriet Grant	Drurey Dobbins	
3442	Hollinger, Adam	AL	1857	Mary Hollinger	Jeff Hollinger	Elizabeth Harris		John & Vicie Harris
3376	Hollinger, Elizabeth	AL	1882	J S Biggs	Adam Hollinger	Elizabeth Lomax	Jeff & Elizabeth Hollinger	Sidney & Mary Lomax
3342	Hollinger, Josephine	AL	1848	William Hollinger	George Sizemore	Elizabeth Harris	Absent & Susan Sizemore	John & Levita Harris
3352	Hollinger, Josephine	AL	1880		Adam Hollinger	Elizabeth Lomax	Jeff & Elizabeth Hollinger	Sidney & Mary Lomax
19871	Hollingsworth, Thena	NC	1834	C.H. Hollingsworth	Martha Reid	Jula Glass	John & Nancy Reid	James & Jula Glass
18264 *	Hollins, Sam	GA	1849	Jane Hollins	George McArver	Mary Hart		Charlie & Charlotte Berry
17302	Hollis, John	AL	1880	F.M. Hollis	Brunson Hollis	Mary Wright	Berry & Mittie Hollis	John & Martha Wright
17307	Hollis, Lonnie	AL	1883	M.J. Hollis	Brunson Hollis	Mary Wright	Berry & Mittie Hollis	John & Martha Wright
20865	Hollis, Sterling	AL	1878	Mary Hollis	Brunson Hollis	Mary Wright	Berry & Mittie Hollis	John & Martha Wright
13413	Hollister, Cora	CA	1872	J W Hollister	Taylor Ridley	Vianna Pope	James & Lue Ridley	John & Jane Pope
112 *	Holloway, Armstrong	NC	1871	widower	Joe Holloway	Julia Russell	Randall & Nancy Russell	Canada & Beckie Cheek
111 *	Holloway, Edgebert	NC	1885	none	Joe Holloway	Julia	Randall & Nancy Russell	Canada & Beckie Cheek
13187	Holloway, Joseph	NC	1885	Amanda Holloway	Thomas Holloway	Elissie Postell	J J & Matilda Holloway	James & Elissie Postell
113 *	Holloway, Julia	NC	1852	Joe Holloway	Randall Russell	Celia Cheek	John & Nancy Russell	Canada & Beckie Cheek
10318	Holloway, Martha	NC	1880	Den Holloway	Thos Holloway	Lucilla Postill		James & Malissa Postill
19873	Hollyfield, Bessie et al	NC			Jeff Hollyfield	Henrietta Dennis		Arthur & Betsy Dennis
18550	Holman, Inna	OK	1871	David Holman	William Holt	Susan McNeeley	James Holt & Martha Stark	Friar Neeley & Annie Marlowe
18663 *	Holmes, Adaline	TN	1855		Hutchinson	Zilpha Chipley		Leah Chipley
474	Holmes, Archibald	TN		none	Geo. Holmes	Mary Plummer	Holmes	Plummer & Ned Sizemore
20415 *	Holmes, Benjamin	TN	1878		Henry Holmes	Adaline Quillen	Lucy Cox	Henry & Leah Chipley
21547	Holmes, Hilliard	GA	1851	Loula Holmes	John Holmes	Harriet Collins	Tarp Minn & Lucy Reynolds	Amos & Gorph Collins

487	Holmes, Mary Etta	TN	1873	George Holmes	Jesse Plummer	Frances Stamper	Plummer	Stamper
11608	Holmes, Nancy	GA	1874	Alfred Holmes	Jesse Blair	Salina Woodell		
21891*	Holmes, Robert	TN			Henry Holmes	Adaline Quillen		
21893*	Holmes, Rossie	TN	1887		Henry Holmes	Adaline McQuillen		
20132	Holt, Adell	AL	1855		Eser Killam	Caroline Weatherford	John Killam	John Weatherford & Martha Dye
21170	Holt, Belle	TX	1890		James Holt	Anna Rogers	Berry Holt	Susan Driskill
22354*	Holt, Bettie	OK	1846	Dennis Hicks widow	Jesse Hicks	Easter Holt		Nellie Campbell
4491	Holt, Brunettie	NC	1852	M M Holt	Reuben Leatherwood	Salle Spivey	Samuel Leatherwood & Betsey Tucker	Josiah Spivey
20127	Holt, Clyde	AL	1895		William Holt	May Holt	James & Adelle Holt	
18548	Holt, Earl	TX	1887		William Holt	Susan McNeeley	James Holt & Martha Stark	Friar Neeley & Annie Marlowe
21053	Holt, Elmira	AL	1857	Thomas Holt	Robert Daniel	Jane Daniel	Crawford & Elizabeth Daniel	Elias & Delilah Daniel
18164	Holt, Fannie	GA	1871	D.M. Holt	John Green	Lucinda Davis	Rolin Green	
19084	Holt, George	KS	1882	Maud Holt	Napolian Holt	Sarah White	George & Sarah Holt	Silas & Susah White
18533*	Holt, George Jr.	MO	1862	Mary Holt	George Holt	Sarah McKean	Berry & Susana Holt	Nathanial & Mary McKean
20128	Holt, Hillary	AL	1906		Robert Holt	Lula Holt	James & Adelle Holt	
20730	Holt, J.W.	TX	1872	Flora Holt	John Holt	Manerva Baker	Rhoda Holt	
18590	Holt, James	MO	1860		James Holt	Martha Stark	Berry & Susanah Holt	
20130	Holt, James	AL	1882	Fannie Holt	James Holt	Adell Killiam	W. & Polly Holt	Eser & Caroline Killiam
18547	Holt, Jesse	TX	1867	Nellie Holt	William Holt	Susan McNeeley	James Holt & Martha Stark	Friar Neeley & Annie Marlowe
22342*	Holt, Joshua	OK	1848	Jane Holt	Jhonas Pack	Easter Holt		Nellie Campbell
17745	Holt, Louiza	GA	1870		John Holt	Manerva Baker	Noogen & Rhoda Holt	James & Charlotte Baker
18975	Holt, Mabel	KS	1887		Napolean Holt	Sarah White	George & Sarah Holt	Silas & Susan White
19864	Holt, Mary	VA	1887		George Thore	Margaret Joyce	Norfleet & Frances Thore	John & Lovisa Joyce
19009	Holt, Minnie	KS	1889		Napoleon Holt	Sarah White	George & Sarah Holt	Silas & Susan White
18177	Holt, Napoleon	OK	1857	Sarah Holt	George Holt	Sarah McKean	Berry & Susana Holt	
18889	Holt, Newton	MO	1860	Mollie Holt	George Holt	Sarah McKeon	Berry & Susana Holt	Nathaniel & Mary McKeon
21169	Holt, Oscar	TX	1892		James Holt	Annie Rogers	Berry Holt	Susan Driskill
20129	Holt, Robert	FL	1884	Lula Holt	James Holt	Adell Killiam	W. & Polly Holt	Eser & Caroline Killiam
20056	Holt, Sarah	TX	1863	Sam Holt	Thomas Griffis	Margaret Faucett	Wm & Sarah Griffis	Wm & Elizabeth Faucett
16193*	Holt, Thadeus	OK	1831	Rainey Holt	James Holt	Sarah Graves		Levi Edwards & Sabie Roundtree
19007	Holt, Thet	KS	1896		Napoleon Holt	Sarah White	George & Sarah Holt	Silas & Susan White
18545	Holt, Thomas	OK	1875		William Holt	Susan McNeeley	James Holt & Martha Stark	Friar Neeley & Annie Marlowe

20505	Holt, Virginia	TN	1884	James Holt	Joseph Bales	Evaline Cagle	John & Fannie Bales	Peter & Elizabeth Cagle
20131	Holt, William	AL	1880	May Holt	James Holt	Adell Killiam	W. & Polly Holt	Eser & Caroline Killiam
18549	Holt, William Jr.	TX	1864		William Holt	Susan McNeeley	James Holt & Martha Stark	Friar Neeley & Annie Marlowe
18546	Holt, William Sr.	TX	1845	Susan Holt	James Holt	Martha Stark		
494	Honney, William	MO	1846	Mary Honney	John Honney	Lucinda Katreen	John Honney	John & Agnes Katreen
5414	Hood, Ellen	OR	1871	W R Hood	William Fisher	Elisabeth Wood	Abraham & Martha Fisher	
15253	Hood, F. Catherine	GA	1860		Elias Whitmire	Louisa Owen	George & Mary Whitmire	
10476	Hood, Julia	OR	1879	Frank Hood	William Fisher	Elizabeth Wood	Abraham Fisher	
11879	Hood, Louisa	OK	1844	James Hood	Sam Morgan	Hannah Nicholson	Wesley Morgan	Alfred & Mary Nicholson
19784	Hood, N.W.	GA	1880		Henry Wood	Nancy Sosebee	Jerry Wood & Elizabeth McMillan	Joseph & Nancy Sosebee
13373*	Hood, Sallian	GA	1830	Daniel Hood	John Dodd	Sarah Dodd	Dodd	
3596	Hooker, Emaline	MO	1831	widow	James Mason	Nancy Wood		Absalom & Monday Wood
19878	Hooker, James	VA	1881	Ruth Hooker	Thomas Hooker	Martha Carter	Samuel & Martha Hooker	
19869	Hooker, Juda	NC	1888		Thomas Hooker	Martha Oaster	Thomas & Ann Hooker	
19872	Hooker, Lucinda	VA	1892		Thomas Hooker	Martha Carter	Sam & Lucinda Hooker	
19862	Hooker, Perrin	VA	1865	Harriet Hooker	Jessie Hooker	Betsy Arrington	Sam & Mary Hooker	
19870	Hooker, Robert	VA	1855	Jothina Hooker	Jessie Hooker	Betsy A.	Sam Hooker & Mary Gibson	
19865	Hooker, Samuel	NC	1838	Francis Hooker	Jesse Hooker	Betsy Arrington	Sam & Mary Hooker	John & Polly Arrington
3090	Hooks, Jewell	MS	1887	William Hooks	Jacob Kinerd	Martha Hobgood		Charles & Martha Hobgood
13877	Hooks, Winnie	GA	1844	Austin Hooks	Elihu Randolph	Martha McGhahu	Robert & Nancy Randolph	Wm & Rhody McGhahu
19703	Hooper, Clara	TN	1889	James Hooper	J. Curtis	Elizabeth Patrick	Joshua & Elizabeth Curtis	
19710	Hooper, Eli	TN	1865	Alice Hooper	Thomas Hooper	Ritty Hatcher		Robert & Mary Hatcher
22104	Hooper, Ellen	OH	1837	Allen Abney	John Hooper	Harriet Rattlif	Hooper	Rattlif
19425	Hooper, James	TN	1864		Thomas Hooper	Rittie Hatcher	James Hooper	James Hatcher
20706	Hooper, Manda	TN	1881	William Hooper	Joshoway Curtis	Martha Wheeler	John & Manda Curtis	Gallant & Abagil Wheeler
19434	Hooper, Noah	TN		Nancy Hooper	Thomas Hooper	Pattie Hatcher	James Hooper	James Hatcher
21160	Hooper, Susan	TN	1869	J.A. Hooper	Nathan Curtis	Susan Colyar	Joshua & Rebecca Curtis	
367	Hooper, William	OK	1839	Mary Hooper	John Hooper	Harret Turner	Hooper	James & Fox Turner
19438	Hooper, William	TN	1867	Lennie Hooper	Thomas Hooper	Rittie Hatcher	James Hooper	James Hatcher
6903	Hoosier, Lenora	VA	1872	John Hoosier	Edward Blevins	Nancy Blevins	James & Lydia Blevins	
21432	Hoover, Lula	CO	1869	J.M. Hoover	William Hussey	Mary Pitts	Thomas & Aletha Hussey	Johnathan & Elizabeth Pitts

ID	Name	State	Year					
13770	Hopkins, Jasper	GA	1836	Sue Hopkins	Green Nutt	Clary Tate	Jim & Sarah Nutt	Thomas & Enia Tate
4348	Hopkins, John	GA	1853	Emma Hopkins	John Hopkins	Eliza Roberts	George Hopkins	John & Elisabeth Roberts
14363	Hopkins, Lizzie	GA	1885	Bill Hopkins	Martin Page	Martha Norton		Edward & Elizabeth Norton
20108*	Hopkins, Lizzie	GA	1847		Eli Keith	Violet Caldwell		Spencer & Lizzie Scott
8487	Hopkins, Minta	VA	1864		Wiley Stamper	Eliza Anderson	George & Naomi Stamper	
21392	Hopper, Francis	OK	1883	James Hopper	John Christopher	Francis Rimare	John & Amelia Christopher	Binion & Francis Rimare
20239	Hopper, George	OK	1844	Louisa Hopper	John Hopper	Mary Self		Pressly & Annie Self
14402	Hopper, Josie	GA	1878	James Hopper	Isaac Ramey	Martha Blackwell		Joe & Mary Blackwell
11693	Hoppers, Elon	NC	1845	Martin Hoppers		Emilia Hart		David Hart & Nancy Taylor
15040	Horalson, James	GA	1870	Sallie Horalson	Thomas Horalson	Mary Logan	James & Sarah Horalson	Frank & Hulda Logan
21950	Horn, Jennie	TN			Charles Horn	Minnie Smith	Hiram & Lou Horn	Wm Smith & Margaret Hardy
21629	Horn, Josephine	OK	11yrs		John Horn	Maggie Moore	James & Cynthia Horn	
21974	Horn, Lillie	TN	1898		Charles Horn	Minnie Smith	Hiram & Lou Horn	William Smith & Margaret Hardy
17962	Hornbuckel, J.H.	OK	1848	Margaret Hornbuvkel	Charley Hornbuckel	Nancy Hawkins		Abner & Alkine Hawkins
19658	Hornbuckle, Peter	NC	1847	Mary Hornbuckle	Charlie Hornbuckle	Pollie Wilks		
17405	Horseford, Bill	AL	1872	Lela Horseford	Jake Horseford	Ann Werth	Jabe & Catherine Horseford	
3328	Horseford, Mrs Wm	AL	1883	William Horford	William Cardwell	Frances Dees		William & Ann Dees
20871	Horton Patsey	NC	1833		James Scott	Lila Barnett		John & Sally Barnett
20870*	Horton, Isabel	NC	1842		John Horton	Sinthia Horton		
14422	Horton, Martha	NC	1878	Elija Horton	James Hurst	Polly Maney	John & Patty Hurst	John & Elisabeth Maney
12939	Horton, Mary	WV	1853	J W Horton	Thomas Cook	Rebecca Sizemore	Wm & Katharine Cook	Ned & Annie Sizemore
17436	Hosea, Joe	OK	1852	Katy Hosea	Joe Hosea	Sara Hogshooter		
7199	Host, Bertha	KS	1891	Frank Host	Charles Shimm	Matilda Allen		Louis & Margaret Allen
6869	Houck, Ida	OH	1880	Isom Houck	Eli Blevins	Mary Hill	Armstrong & Cathrine Blevins	Franklin & Avaline Hill
15252	House, Hugh	GA	1894		B.D. House	Rhoda Carmichael		Joe & Mary Carmichael
2369	House, Irena	CO	1863	W J House	Isaac Barber	Joanah Petty		
3444	House, Isaac	AL	28yrs	none	William House	Martha Lambert	J J & Levitia House	Joe & Mary Lambert
3439	House, J P	AL	21yrs	none	William House	Martha Lambert	J G & Levitha House	Joseph & Mary Lambert
15251	House, Joe	GA	1902		B.D. House	Rhoda Carmichael		Joe & Mary Carmichael
15250	House, Lawrence	GA	1899		B.D. House	Rhoda Carmichael		Joe & Mary Carmichael

15249	House, Lettie	GA	1897		B.D. House	Rhoda Carmichael		Joe & Mary Carmichael
19452	House, Lillie	AL	1889		William House	Martha Lambert	Gilbert & Livitia House	Joseph & Mary Lambert
21281	House, Maggie	OK	1876	J.W. House	William Burgess	Mollie Matey	Sterling Burgess	Jerimiah Matey & Sarah Finley
17956	House, Mrs. J.G.	AL	1885	J.G. House	Sidney Lomax	Rosetta Boone	Sidney & Matilda Lomax	John & Martha Boone
15248	House, Rhoda	GA		B D Hubbard	Joe Carmichael	May Spears		Josiah & Patty Spears
19453	House, Verdelia	AL	1887		William House	Martha Lambert	Gilbert & Livitia House	Joseph & Mary Lambert
3440	House, William	AL	1848	Marth Lambert	J G House	Malissa Hollinger		Wm & Hettie Hollinger
3441	House, William	AL	1886	none	William House	Martha Lambert	J G & Levitha House	Joseph & Mary Lambert
732	Houseman, Robert	TX	1872	none	Francis Houseman	Mary Garrett	James & Sophana Houseman	Hezekiah & Margrett Garrett
8547	Houser, Nancy	VA		William Houser	Wilburn Blevins	Martha Lewis		A J & Biddy Lewis
23000 *	Houston, Dana	TN	1891		Jack Houston	Fanna Welch		Wm & Sarah Welch
15540 *	Houston, Elmer	GA	1882	Loula Houston	William Houston	Sarah Allen	Elijah & Sarah Jones	Ben & Jane Allen
17703 *	Houston, Hartwell	OK	1834	Narcissus Houston	Almon Joyner	Anna Brown	Billy & Bettie Joyner	John & Winnie Brown
22999 *	Houston, Jackson	TN	1850	Nancy Houston	George King	Margaret Huston	Liddie Armstrong	
15539 *	Houston, John	GA	1888		William Houston	Sarah Allen	Elijah & Sarah Jones	Ben & Jane Allen
19347	Houston, Sarah	GA	1859		Ben Allen	Jane Sexton	Jay & Fannie Allen	John & Polly Sexton
2355	Houston, Tom decd	OK	1845	Martha Houston	Tom Eli	Charlott Houston		
21738	Houx, Cora	TX	1869	J.B. Houx	Calvin Sides	Elsie Tetrick	Mack Sides & Malinda Chusher	George Tetrick & Permelia Middleton
7604	Howard, Ellen	GA	1865	W N Howard	William Eller	Isabella Barns		Ellenor Barns
375	Howard, Emma	AR	1868	B W Howard	David Garreson	Mary Blasingame	Calop Garrison	Thomas & Janie Blasingame
22177	Howard, Georgia	AR	1895	none	B.W. Howard	Emma Garrison		David & Mary Garrison
11737	Howard, Harriett	TX		David Elliott	David Elliott	Nancy Childers	James Elliott	
20840	Howard, Harriett	GA	1873	William Harrlett	William Chester	Ellen Clark	John & Nancy Chester	Levy & Elizabeth Clark
7626	Howard, Henry	TN		Mary I Ioward	Joshua Howard	Mary Deal	Wm & Jane Howard	
5638	Howard, Isaac	OK	1857	Rhoda Howard	James Howard	Lidda Crabtree	Arington & Elizabeth Howard	Isaac & Mary Crabtree
8624	Howard, John	OK	1855	Jane Howard decd	James Howard	Lidda Crabtree	Arington & Elizebeth Howard	Isaac & Mary Crabtree
17699	Howard, Joseph	TN	1853	Elen Howard	Joseph Howard	Martha Newsom	Billie Howard	
16387	Howard, Lila	OK	1880	Edward Howard	Waity Foreman	Lucinda Young Squirl		James & Annie Young Squirl
22819	Howard, Maggie	OK	1878	E.J. Howard	James Avants	Susan Armstrong	Thomas & Fransis Avants	James & Susan Armstrong

12349	Howard, Samuel	GA	1882	Jimmie Howard	Oliver Howard	Susan Hillhouse	Samuel & Polly Howard	Samuel & Augusta Hillhouse
10558	Howard, Susan	GA	1860	Oliver Howard	Samuel Hillhouse	Augusta Cole	Samuel & Annie Hillhouse	John & Betsy Cole
7602	Howard, William	GA	1849	Ellen Howard	Joshua Howard	Mary Deal	Wm & Jinnie Howard	
15537	Howell, Oscar	GA	1878	Annie Howell	Elijah Howell	Sarah	Frederic & Martha Howell	Wm & Martha Dukes
18265	Howell, Cora	GA			Jesse Beck	Sophrona Cook	Jesse & Ellen Beck	
2100	Howell, Cordelia	NC	1884	Judson Howell	G D Blevins	Celia Parsons	Daniel & Anna Blevins	Wm & Ruth Parsons
15179	Howell, Elenore	TN	1906		Charles Howell	Emily Payne	Archibald & Emily Howell	J H & Mary Payne
15538	Howell, Elijah	GA	1845	Sarah Howell	Frederick Howell	Martha Grier	David & Nancy Howell	Aquilla & Beshavia Grier
7190	Howell, Ellen	TX	1840	G W Howell	Jerry Ward	Nancy Freeman	John Ward	Polly Madole
9783	Howell, Isaac	GA	1871	Mary Howell	Thomas Howell	Catherine Ingram	Jackson & Catherine Howell	Isaac Ingram
4579	Howell, Lura	NC	1878	Cicero Howell	Eli Barker	Mary Porter	Wm & Betty Barker	Riley & Melyndia Porter
4113	Howell, Mary	GA	1846	John Howell	Jeremiah Barker	Polly Pinyam		Stokes Pinyam
12100	Howell, Moses	TX	1862	Addie Howell	John Howell	Belinda Qualls		David & Martha Qualls
6345	Howell, Norq	AL		John Howell	Benjaman Franklin	Frances Bryars		
2518	Howell, William	GA	1854	Margaret Howell	Andrew Howell	Jane Edwards		
22153	Howers, C.H.	GA		Annie Howers	Andy Howers	Sarah Grant	George & Mahaly Howers	Radford & Mary Grant
22151	Howers, Josep	GA	1875	Ella Howers	Andy Howers	Sariejane Grant	George & Mahaly Howers	Radford & Mary Grant
20071	Hoxworth, Margaret	TN	1854	James Hoxworth	Madison Dodd	Annie Maples	Jane Dodd	Wilson & Annie Maples
18962 *	Hoyle, Hattie	TN	1878	James Hoyle	General Cardin	Hester Eskridge	Esaw & Easter Cardin	Edmund & Matilda Eskridge
18966 *	Hoyle, Henderson	TN	1847	Mary Hoyle	Lawson Hoyle	Mary Love	Robert Hoyle	
17567	Hoyt, Cyrena	OK		Will Hammurus	Milo Hoyt	Hariet Fulsom	Milo & Lydia Hoyt	Jacob Fulsom
22675	Hubbard, Alfred	MO	1851		William Hubbard	Amanda Chenoweth	Joseph Hubbard	
6470	Hubbard, Calvin	AL	1844		Peter Hubbard	Flora Teal		Winnie Teal
15247	Hubbard, Emily	GA	1884		John Hubbard	Mary Bennett	Isiah & Nancy Hubbard	
4347	Hubbard, Frank	OK	1867		Caleb Hubbard		Hardy Hubbard	
4458	Hubbard, Gamaliel	MO	1847		Joseph Hubbard		Hardy Hubbard	
8219 *	Hubbard, George	OK	1858	Patsy Hubbard	George Hubbard	Jane Reece	George Frost	Johnson Reece
1983	Hubbard, Hairet	OK	1823	Wilkerson Hubbard	Wm Thomas	Jemima Thomas		
4457	Hubbard, Henry	MO	1845		Joseph Hubbard		Hardy Hubbard	

17532	Hubbard, Hettie	GA	1856	John Hubbard	Wm Whitmire	Eliza Campbell	Wm Whitmire	Eliza Campbell
4456	Hubbard, James	OK			Caleb Hubbard		Hardy Hubbard	
3297	Hubbard, Jeremiah	OK	1837		Joseph Hubbard	Matilda Johnson	Hardy Hubbard	
14554	Hubbard, John	GA	1845	Sarah Hubbard	Patrick Hubbard	Margaret Cobb	John & Nancy Hubbard	Thos & Sallie Black
15246	Hubbard, John	GA	1847	Mary Hubbard	Isaiah Hubbard	Nancy Kildees	Johnie & Teany Hubbard	Abram & Katie Childers
3298	Hubbard, Joseph	OK	1852	Angie Hubbard	Joseph Hubbard		Hardy Hubbard	
15245	Hubbard, Leander	GA	1870	Kate Hubbard	John Hubbard	Mary Bennett	Isiah & Nancy Hubbard	
5235	Hubbard, Martin	CA	1849	Emma Hubbard	Caleb Hubbard		Hardy Hubbard	
15244 ½	Hubbard, Maxey	GA	1873	Tourie Hubbard	John Hubbard	Mary Bennett	Isiah & Nancy Hubbard	
16222 *	Hubbard, Patsy	OK		George Hubbard	Wyley Jones	Sineans Kennerdy		
5519	Hubbard, Simeon	OR	1854		Caleb Hubbard		Hardy Hubbard	
14553	Hubbard, Thomas	GA	1849	Eliza Hubbard	Patrick Hubbard	Margaret Cobb	John & Nancy Hubbard	Thos & Sallie Black
15244	Hubbard, William	GA	1866	Ann Hubbard	John Hubbard	Mary Bennett	Isiah & Nancy Hubbard	
14076	Hudgins, Eliza	GA		William Hudgins	John Bozeman	Sarah Darby	Amos & Nancy Bozeman	Charles & Nancy Darby
21632	Hudgins, Martha	AR	31yrs	Holder Hudgins	William Ridling	Minerva Parrish	Henry & Margaret Ridling	Garland & Jane Parrish
9071	Hudler, Charlie	NC	1881	Mannie Hudler	Isaac Hudler	Adaline Simmons	John & Tamsey Hudler	
9076	Hudler, Ira	NC	1860	Sarah Hudler	John Hudler	Tamsy Stitt		Jacob & Hiley Stitt
9072	Hudler, Isaac	NC	1859	Adaline Hudler	John Hudler	Tamsey Stitt		Jacob & Hiley Stitt
9063	Hudler, James	NC	1877	Sally Hudler	John Hudler	Tamsey Stitt		Jacob & Hiley Stitt
9079	Hudler, Joseph	NC	1874	Ellen Hudler	John Hudler	Tamsey Stitt		Jacob & Hiley Stitt
9062	Hudler, Minnie	NC	1882		John Hudler	Tamsey Stitt		Jacob & Hiley Stitt
9048	Hudler, Robert	NC	1880	Zenia Hudler	John Hudler	Tamsy Stitt		Jacob & Hiley Stitt
9047	Hudler, Tamsey	NC	1845	John Hudlor	Jacob Stitt	Hiley Thompson		Christopher & Sally Thompson
17418	Hudler, Wiley	VA	1866	Myrtie Hudler	John Hudler	Tamsy Stitt		Jacob & Hiley Stitt
9077	Hudler, William	NC	1872	Lettie Hudler	John Hudler	Tamsey Stitt		Jacob & Hiley Stitt
19017	Hudson, Belle	TN	1885	Lem Hudson	George Hilliard	Jane Mantooth	John Hilliard	
17580	Hudson, Frances	TX	1837	Henry Hudson	James Allard	Nancy Weaver		David Weaver & Frances Womack
19015	Hudson, John	TN	1877		Henry Hudson	Sarah Rector	John & Rachel Hudson	Mort Rector
14340	Hudson, Joseph	OK	1879	Mary Hudson	Charles Hudson	Martha Hazelwood		Thos & Mary Hazelwood

19016	Hudson, Lem	TN	1886	Belle Hudson	Henry Hudson	Sarah Rector	John & Rachel Hudson	Mort Rector
20262	Hudson, Margaret	TX	1859		Lewis Yates	Elizabeth Gambill	Thomas & Avis Yates	Wm & Sallie Gambill
14339	Hudson, Martha	OK	1841	C C Hudson	Thomas Hazelwood	Mary Randolph	Blairy Hazelwood	Henry Randolph
21930	Hudson, William	TN	1884		Jack Hudson	Mary Pockholt	Sallie Hudson	Frank & Susan Pockholt
13521	Huff, Ellen	NC	1856	J.G. Huff	Robbert Poindexter	Martha Ward	Robbert & Charlotte Poindexter	Wiley & Polly Ward
17620	Huffaker, Sarah	GA	1852	F.L. Huffaker	James Phipps	Elizabeth Helton		
6115	Huffman, Alexander	VA	1862	Emaline Huffman	Alexander Huffman	Selah Blevins		Wells & Elizabeth Blevins
6114	Huffman, Emaline	VA	1867	Alexander Huffman	Samuel Pennington	Sarah Huffman	Andrew & Hetty Pennington	
18760	Huffman, Luvenia	TN	1876	George Huffman	William Grant	Ruth Brown	Archibald & Mary Grant	Wm & Mary Brown
19348	Huggins, Margaret	GA	1869	John Huggins	James Rakestraw	Delilah Rains	Wm & Telitha Rakestraw	Benj & Fannie Rains
16536	Huggins, Margerie	GA	1860	Cicero Huggins	John Bozeman	Sarah Darby	Amos & Nancy Bozeman	Charles & Nancy Darby
13624	Hughes, Allen	OK	1870	Mary Hughes	Harrison Hughes	Elmira Sylcox		Burton & Farribe Sylcox
11896	Hughes, Charles	OK	1865	Cora Hughes	Harrison Hughes	Elmira Sylcox		Burton & Farribee Sylcox
3713	Hughes, George	OK	1884	none	S L Hughes	Gracie Tidwell	J R & Mahala Hughes	John & Lucrecy Tidwell
13625	Hughes, Harrison	OK	1867	Jane Hughes	Harrison Hughes	Elmira Sylcox		Burton & Farribe Sylcox
104	Hughes, Heb	NC	1883	Bessie Hughes	John Hughes	Rebecca Thomas	John & Rebecca Hughes	David & Jane Thomas
3715	Hughes, James	OK	1870	none	S L Hughes	Gracie Tidwell	J R & Mahala Hughes	John & Lucui Tidwell
11901	Hughes, James	OK	1884		Harrison Hughes	Elmira Sylcox		Burton & Farribee Sylcox
3714	Hughes, Jennie	OK	1887	none	S L Hughes	Gracie Tidwell	J R & Mahala Hughes	John & Lourisa Tidwell
17936	Hughes, Jesse	TN	1848	Mary Hughes	Jesse Hughes / Muse	Safrona Branner		
21879	Hughes, Jessee May	TN	1893		Samuel Hughes	Martha May	Jesse & Mollie Hughes	Wm & Elizabeth Todd
3822	Hughes, John	OK	1871	Clara Hughes	S. Hughes	Gracie Tidwell	J R & Mahala Hughes	John & Lucrecie Tidwell
20283	Hughes, John	AR	1871		William Hughes	Mary Wilkerson	William Hughes	Harron Wilkerson
21548	Hughes, John	GA	1850		Foster Hughes	Docia Fowler	George & Margaret Hughes	Thomas & Basche Fowler
4451	Hughes, Lee	OK	1872	Ida Hughes	S L Hughes	Gracie Tidwell	J R & Mahala Hughes	John & Loucre Tidwell
3823	Hughes, Louis	OK	1880	Lizzie Hughes	S L Hughes	Gracie Tidwell	J R & Mahala Hughes	John & Lucrece Tidwell
8822	Hughes, Mary	AR	1833		Hiram Wilkerson	Nancy Bowers		Lenora Bowers
105	Hughes, Rebecca	NC	1843	John Hughes	David Thomas	Jane Morrison	William Morrison	
20532	Hughes, Samuel	TN	1885	Posey Hughes	Jesse Hughes	Mary Copeland	Jesse Sr & Fronia Hughes	Samuel & Jane Morelock

21549	Hughes, Smith	GA	1868		Foster Hughes	Docia Fowler	George & Margaret Hughes	Thomas & Basche Fowler
4449	Hughes, William	OK	1869	Marry Hughes	S L Hughes	Gracie Tidwell	J R & Mahala Hughes	John & Lucreca Tidwell
13622	Hughes, William	OK	1862	Lizzie Hughes	Harrison Hughes	Elmira Sylcox		Burton & Farribe Sylcox
2144	Hughs, Charley	OK	1849	Ellen Hughs	John Hughs	Mary Rowe	Barney & Sallie Hughs	
4757	Hughs, James	NC	1858	Jane Hughs	Joseph Hughs	Martha Hampton	James & Anna Hughs	George & Mary Hampton
4765	Hughs, Martha	NC	1840	Joseph Hughs (decd	George Hampton	Mary Blythe		Johnathan & Anna Blythe
4747	Hughs, Maud	NC	1884	none	Joseph Hughs	Martha Hampton	James & Anna Hughs	George & Mary Hampton
2088	Hughs, Rebecca	OK		widow	Wilson Layfett	Jackson	Wilson	Jackson
17877	Hughs, Sarah	GA	1841	Thos Hughs	N.H. Cochran	Aultin Griffin	Robert & Celie Cochran	Sarah & Hardy Griffin
4746	Hughs, William	NC	1866	none	Joseph Hughs	Martha Hampton	James & Anna Hughs	George & Mary Hampton
15893	Hulsey, William	GA	1874	Martha Hulsey	Robert Hulsey	Mary Blassingame	Charles & Margaret Hulsey	John & Peggie Blassingame
1689	Humanstriker, Nellie	AR	1859	Wm Humanstriker	Danial Arch	Sallie Jack	Arch & V-si-gi	Oo-see-nee-tah & Ah-li
7191	Humbard, Lizabeth	MO	1861	William Humbard	Minter Williams	Sarah Martin	Beniah & Nancy Williams	Thomas & Lydia Martin
22425	Humbird, Charity	MO	1847	widow	David Williams	Jennie Bunk	Solomon Williams	Josephus & Polly Bunk
19238	Humphrey, Ida	NC	1845	Lottie Humphrey	Henry Clingman	Emily Magee	Peter Clingman & Anne Poindexter	Edward Magee & Harriet Meer
12732	Humphrey, Martha	TN	1854	William Humphrey	Lemuel Michael	Mary Irvin	Jacob Michael	George & Phoebe Irvin
19473	Humphries, Cassie	GA	1869	Wm Humphries	John Whitmire	Sarah Moore	James & Cassie Whitmire	Watson & Charity Moore
14005	Humphries, Dicie	GA	1872	James Humphries	Rollin Pardue	Lissie Loggins	Albert & Ruth Pardue	James & Dicie Loggins
17628*	Humphries, Emily	OK	93yrs	Stephen Ross	Sam Russel	Anna Russel		Cleora
4761	Humphries, Octavia	NC	1874	Jesse Humphries	John Graves	Harrett McDonald	Wm & Annie Graves	James & Mina McDonald
1008	Hunkler, Henrietta	GA	1886	Wm Hunkler	Jeramiah Pilgrim	Mary Stoffregen	Elijah & Rhoda Pilgrim	H G & Henrette Stoffregen
21907	Hunley, Susan	TN	1883	Robert Hunley	Silas Carroll	Lucinda Haynes	James & Lucinda Carroll	Joseph & Matilda Haynes
20552	Hunt, Addie	GA	1874	William Hunt	Richard Wofford	Eliza Quillen	Moses & Phoebe Berry	Zilpha Quillen
22388	Hunt, Attie	OK	1867	widow	Isaac Barber	Joanah Petty	Joe & Celia Barber	John & Elizabeth Petty
21028	Hunt, Callie	GA	1868	F.C. Hunt	Harrison Riley	Eliza Johnson	Joseph Riley	Wm & Elizabeth Blake
19863	Hunt, Elmer	NC	1881		Thomas Hunt	Sarah Wall	James & Temp Hunt	Robert & Mary Scott
20749	Hunt, Julia	GA	1881	Ervin Hunt	Wm Going	Delia Cole	Wm & Nancy Going	John & Betsy Cole
19420	Hunt, Mary	NC	1852	Leander Hunt	Thomas Martin	Ann Poindexter	Samuel & Elizabeth Martin	Francis & Rosanna Poindexter
20750	Hunt, Minnie	GA	1877	Robert Hunt	James Parr	Annie Goddard	Wm & Mary Parr	John & Edie Goddard
22580	Hunt, Mollie	TN	1850	Albert Hunt	Alex Reeder	Julia Boswell	Sarah Reeder	Wm & Sally Boswell

4531	Hunt, Ora	OK	1858	Lemuel Hunt	Orrell Couch	Nannie Wilson	John Couch	William Wilson
19868	Hunt, Sarah	NC	1857	Thomas Hunt	Isriah Wall	Martha Scott		Robert & Mary Scott
18342	Hunt, Susan	TN	1861	William Hunt	Goldman Bryson	Susan Payne		John & Polly Payne
3221	Hunter, Athie	OK	1847	Isac Hunter (decd)	John Avants	Elisebeth Sharp	Peter & Ellen Avants	John & Ellen Sharp
20477*	Hunter, Avery	TN	1878	John Hunter	George Allen	Georgia Law	Friday Allen	Sampson & Mary Law
13846	Hunter, Bertha	OK	1890		Benj Hunter	Mattie Cannefax	Ben & Isabella Hunter	George & Margret Cannefax
13843	Hunter, Clarence	OK	1886		Benj Hunter	Mattie Cannefax	Ben & Isabella Hunter	George & Margret Cannefax
7181	Hunter, Daniel	OK	1877	none	Willis Hunter	Sarah Cantrell	Daniel & Patsy Hunter	Hozel & Cynthia Cantrell
20873*	Hunter, David	MO	1875		Horace Hunter	Harriett Hill		David Hill
21180	Hunter, et al	GA			William Right	Lowenda Shope		Sarah Wright
20377*	Hunter, Ethalena	TN	1906		John Hunter	Avery Allen	James & Adaline Hunter	George & Georgia Allen
15019	Hunter, Frances	NC	1844	widow	Thomas Poindexter	Jane James	John & Sarah Poindexter	James & Jane James
20382*	Hunter, George	TN			John Hunter	Avery Allen	James & Adaline Hunter	George & Georgia Allen
13805	Hunter, Georgia	OK	1893		Benj Hunter	Hattie Cannefax	Ben & Clisabella Hunter	George & Margret Cannefax
16280	Hunter, Hattie	OK	1870	Benj Hunter	George Cannefax	Margret Haley	Joseph & Sarah Cannefax	George & Abbiegail Haley
7183	Hunter, Hazle	OK	1874	Mollie Hunter	Willis Hunter	Sarah Cantrell	Daniel & Patsy Hunter	Hazel & Cynthy Cantrell
20384*	Hunter, Jennie	TN			John Hunter	Avery Allen	James & Adaline Hunter	George & Georgia Allen
7184	Hunter, John	OK	1879	Mary Hunter	Willis Hunter	Sarah Cantrell	Daniel & Patsy Hunter	Hazel & Cynthia Cantrell
20385*	Hunter, John	TN			John Hunter	Avery Allen	James & Adaline Hunter	George & Georgia Allen
20475*	Hunter, John	TN	1872	Avery Hunter	James Hunter	Adaline Hutson	James & Sophia Ervin	James Hutson
20751	Hunter, Lether	GA	1881	Charles Hunter	James Parr	Annie Goddard	Wm & Mary Parr	John & Edie Goddard
19215	Hunter, Luvitha	NC	1837	James Hunter	Thomas Apperson	Luvitha Vest	Wm Apperson & Elizabeth Carr	Isam Vest & Nancy Pledge
13854	Hunter, Mable	OK	1887		Benj Hunter	Mattie Cannefax	Benj & Isabella Hunter	George & Margret Cannefax
21093	Hunter, Maggie	TN	1866	James Hunter	Daniel Boman	Martha Rods	John & Jennie Boman	Tensly & Fannie Rods
19875	Hunter, Mahala	NC	1871	John Hunter	James Pike	Elizabeth Hooker	Isaac & Rebecca Pike	Sam & Letha Hooker
20378*	Hunter, Maire	TN			John Hunter	Avery Allen	James & Adaline Hunter	George & Georgia Allen
7179	Hunter, Samuel	TX	1862	Nora Hunter	Willis Hunter	Sarah Cantrell	Daniel & Patsey Hunter	Cozel & Cynthia Cantrell
7182	Hunter, William	TX	1869	Ida Hunter	Willis Hunter	Sarah Cantrell	Daniel & Patsy Hunter	Hazel Cantrell
7180	Hunter, Willis	OK	1838	Sarah Hunter	Daniel Hunter	Patsie Brumley	Daniel Hunter	Willis & Sallie Brumley
7185	Hunter, Willis	OK	1872	Rebecca Hunter	Willis Hunter	Sarah Cantrell	Daniel & Patsie Hunter	Hazel & Cynthia Cantrell

11744	Hurd, George	OK	1872	Clara Hurd	Charles Hurd	Amerillis Jones		Squire & Lucy Jones
22445	Hurd, Richard	OK	1846	Mary Hurd	William Hurd	Eliza Neel		
18062	Hurley, Birdie	NC	1886	Wm Hurley	Wm Starlin	Tamsy Powers	Abraham & Sarah Starlin	
4429	Hurley, Birtha	VA	1885	John Hurley	F H Dalinger	Polley Baldwin	John & Elisabeth Dallinger	
489	Hurley, Elizabeth	NC	1844	widow	Eli Stamper	Susanne Stamper	Stamper	Stamper
22960	Hurley, Ira	VA	1868	Alice Hurley	Leander Hurley	Elizabeth Stamper	Thos & Percilla Hurley	Eli & Suanna Stamper
5523	Hurley, John	NC	1881	Sarah Hurley	Wiley Hurley	Malicy Blevins	Thomas & Barbry Hurley	John & Carolina Blevins
6153	Hurley, Mollie	NC	1875	William Hurley	Benjamin Phipps	Rebecca Plummer	Ahart & Maryan Phipps	Joseph Plummer
6100	Hurley, William	NC	1868	Mollie Hurley	Elisha Hurley	Alpha Barker		Wm & Bettie Barker
14420	Hurst, Creek	NC	1880	Aney Hurst	James Hurst	Polley Maney	John & Patty Hurst	John & Elisabeth Maney
14428	Hurst, Daniel	NC	1876	Arzilar Hurst	James Hurst	Polley Maney	John & Polly Hurst	John & Elisabeth Maney
17870	Hurst, Laura	OK	1866	Jim Hurst	John Franks	Fannie Todd	Wm Franks & Kitty Winn	Charles Todd & Betty Winn
15631	Hurst, Sarah	AL	1852	Lemel Hurst	Tobias Woodard	Tinizar Burges		William Burges
10099	Huse, Roda	NC	1866	Sam Huse	Green Payne	Fannie Harkins	Acey & Nancy Payne	
333	Huskins, James R.	NC	1840	Ellen Huskins	Arch Murphy	Nancy Huskins	Jubilee Huskins	Polly Huskins
21501	Hussey, Judiah	OK	1848	Louisa & Lucy	Thomas Hussey	Aletha Benbow	Judiah Hussey & Agatha Henly	
15243 *	Hutcheson, Ellen	GA	1841	James Hutcheson	Ray Dickerson	Lucy Dickerson		
20001 *	Hutchins, Alex	GA	1876	Ella Hutchins	John Hutchins	Adline Garvin	Washington Byrd & Eady Charman	Harriet Garvin
17100 *	Hutchins, Emmaline	TN		Alex Hutchins	John Thurston	Susan Whearhousa		
20000 *	Hutchins, John	GA	1844	Adline Hutchins	Washington Byrd	Eady Haynes		Nancy Haynes
21443	Hutchins, Loucette	KY	1853	Oliver Hutchins	David Martin	Lucinda Coe	John & Sidney Martin	Charles & Lucy Coe
2657	Hutchinson, Birdie	MO	1881	Alex Hutchinson	Samuel Anglen	Nancy Kirby	John & Vilettie Anglen	Henry & Rebecca Kirby
18756	Hutchison, May	OK	33yrs		Edward Morris	Eliza Drumond	Nancee Morris	Eliza Drumond
14059 *	Hutton, William	TN	1848	Eliza Hutton	William Hillman	Charlotte Hutton	Conway	
12808	Hyatt, Harvey	NC	1864	Emma Hyatt	Abel Hyatt	Sarah Moody	Nathan Hyatt & Rutha Sherrill	
12432	Hyatt, Norah	NC	1878	M.S. Hyatt	Thomas Shepherd	Eliza Maney	John & Dartha Shepherd	Martin & Matilda Maney
15757	Hyatt, Ora	NC	1877	May Hyatt	Albirto Hyatt	Darkey Montieth	Nathan Hyatt	Samuel Monteith
12266	Hyatt, Reuben	NC	1861	Minnie Hyatt	Abel Hyatt	Sarah Moody	Nathan & Rutha Hyatt	
13255	Hyde, Emily	NC	1860		Ervin Hyde	Nancy Sherrill	Benj & Elisabeth Hyde	
8701	Hyde, James	OK	1846	Jane Hyde	Benjamin Hyde	Cynthia Sherrell	Elizabeth Walker Hyde	

1271	Hyde, Lawrence	GA	1877	Marietta Jenkins	Allen Hyde	Malissa Rains	Ansel & Elizabeth Hyde	Wesley & Talitha Rains
3908	Hyde, Robert	CA			William Hyde			
2079	Hyde, Sarah	NC	1882	John Hyde	Jesse Delozier	Mary Stillwell	Ed & Elizabeth Delozier	Wm & Mariah Stillwell
13254	Hyde, William	NC	1861		Ervin Hyde	Nancy Sherrill	Benj Hyde & Elisebeth Leatherwood	
500	Hyde, Wm P	NC	1843	Parsie Hyde	Wm Thomas	Catharine Hyde		Leatherwood
17965	Hyden, J. Catherine	GA	1863	A.M. Hyden	Joseph Sosebee	Frances Dixon	Wm & Nancy Sosebee	Martin & Elizabeth Dixon
7193	Hyder, Catharine	MO	1856	J A Hyder	Josiah Van Trump	Susan Heffly	John & Elizabeth Van Trump	Samuel & Mary Heffly
7194	Hyder, Maurice	MO	1882	Clara Hyder	John Hyder	Catharine Van Trump	Wm & Emily Hyder	Josiah & Susan Van Trump
7195	Hyder, Medici	MO	1865	Marshal Hyder	Reuben Van Trump	Dyanna Carries	John & Elizabeth Van Trump	Daniel Carries
13224	Ice, Lucinda	OK	1870	Lewis Ice	Mohawk Beaver	Mollie Simmons	Runabout	
15242	Ideson, Lou	GA		Andrew Ideson	Elexander Bowling	Elizabeth Kines		Martin & Elizabeth Kines
17772*	Igou, Thomas	TN	1841		Seabourn Yarnell	Betsie Spicer		
17763*	Igou, William	TN	1843	Fannie Igou	Thomas Spicer	Betsie Spicer		
1195	Ihrig, Mahala	OK	1872	Francis Ihrig	James Stephens	Mary Hall	Green & Nancy Stephens	Alfred & Mahala Hall
14663	Ingle, Ida Mae	NC	1883	Collet Ingle	Thomas Morse	Lillie Sandford	Jessie & Littie Morse	
9355	Inman, Asenath	IN	1862	C F Inman	Samuel Allen	Martha Henley	John & Martha Allen	Elias & Jane Henley
20514	Inman, Edna	TN	1862	William Inman	George Ellis	Malinda Millsaps		Mary Millsaps
11934	Inscore, Emma	NC	1865	William Inscore	Thomas Doby	Edy Hinkley	John Doby	
6286	Irwin, Burty	TN	1893		W T Irwin	Mary Goins	E H & Betsie Irwin	Alfred & Halie Goins
19683	Irwin, Cora	TN	1869	James Irwin	Abner Sayers	Nancy Scales	James Sayers	Nicholas & Mary Scales
6285	Irwin, Floyd	TN	1888		W T Irwin	Mary Goins	E H & Betsie Irwin	Alfred & Halie Goins
22861	Irwin, Fred	IL	1879		John Irwin	Amanda Hadden	John Irwin & Amy Horner	John Hadden & Mary Robinson
6287	Irwin, Leaner	TN	1892		W T Irwin	Mary Goins	E H & Betsie Irwin	Alfred & Halie Goins
8705	Irwin, Mollie	TN	1871	William Irwin	James Goins	Melvina Goins	Granville & Polly Goins	Martin & Susan Goins
6284	Irwin, Oriah	TN	1889		W T Irwin	Mary Goins	E H & Betsie Irwin	Alfred & Halie Goins
22862	Irwin, Walter	IL	1881		John Irwin	Amanda Hadden	John Irwin & Amy Horner	John Hadden & Mary Robinson
22467	Isaacks, Arwell	VA	1873	Flora Isaacks	Jesse Isaacks	Mary Scott		Benjamin Scott
22328	Isaacks, Mary	NC	1842	Jennie Isaack	Benjamin Scott	Elizabeth Norman	Thomas & Dannuel Scott	Wm & Delia Norman
22322	Isaacs, J. Melvin	NC		Lucinda Isaacs	Jessie Isaacs	Mary Scott	Joseph & Frankie Isaacs	Benjamin & Betsy Scott

22325	Isaacs, Bettie	NC	1872	none	Jessie Isaacs	Mary Scott	Joseph & Frankie Isaacs	Benjamin & Betsy Scott
22382	Isaacs, Elisha	NC	1867	Margaret Isaacs	Jessie Isaacs	Mary Scott	Joseph & Frankie Isaacs	Benjamin & Bettie Scott
22383	Isaacs, Jesse	NC	1875	Nancy Isaacs	Jesse Isaacs	Mary Scott	Joseph & Frankie Isaacs	Benjamin & Bettie Scott
16637	Isaacs, Roxanna	OK	1888	James Isaacs	Joe Hines	Synthia Ragsdal		Isaac & Mary Ragsdal
12361	Island, Minnie	OK	1880	John Island	Joseph Coodey	Mary Hardage	Joseph & Jane Coodey	Joe & Muskogee Hardage
9115	Ivester, Callie	NC	1880	John Ivester	T J Tramel	Rebeca Caley	Jakey Tramel	Pollie Hogsed
3777	Ivester, Martha	NC	1872	J P Ivester	James Forester	Martha Mason		John & Polly Mason
16732	Ivey, Edley	TN	1868		Daniel Freeman	Nancy Ivey		
19214	Ivey, Johnnie	TN			Edley Ivey	Annie	Dan Freeman	Annie Angel
21610	Ivie, J. Hugh	GA	1863	Sinia Ivie	John Ivie	Joicie Evans	Thomas & Bettsie Ivie	Davie & Mary Evans
16731	Ivy, Edley	TN	1875		John Ivy	Malinda Ivy		
3758	Ivy, John	TN	1855	Laura Ivy	Harrison Vilett	Mary Ivy		Absalom Ivy
15	Jack, Sally	TN	18??	Thomas Jack	James Sexton	Sally Lambeth	William & Nancy Sexton	Nancy & John Lambeth
15239	Jackson, Albert	GA	1883		James Jackson	Nancy Wallis		Jesse & Liza Wallace
18614	Jackson, Albert	TN	1882		Samuel Jackson	Martha Westmorland	Shadrock & Katie Jackson	P.M. & Katherine Westmorland
20183*	Jackson, Amanda	TN	27yrs	Charles Jackson	Howard McDay	Abbie Coeson	Judie McDay	
7210	Jackson, Andrew	OK	1840	Sallie Jackson	John Jackson	Elizabeth Caldwell	Elliott & Sally Jackson	Andrew & Cerene Caldwell
20900	Jackson, Andrew	AL	1856		Zophers Jackson	Louisa Jackson	William Jackson	Andrew Jackson
16473*	Jackson, Berry	GA	1874	Etta Jackson	Colonel Jackson	Judy Mye	Mollie Glasgow	John & Edie Anderson
7778	Jackson, Charles	TX	1867	Valeria Jackson	James Jackson	Sarah Maloney	John & Elizabeth Jackson	
18610	Jackson, Charles	TN	1877	Lou Jackson	Samuel Jackson	Martha Westmorland	Shadrock & Katie Jackson	P.M. & Katherine Westmorland
21794	Jackson, Claud	TX	1877	Will Jackson	Solomon Blair	Bettie Penn		
7211	Jackson, Daniel	OK	1852	Emetious Jackson	Isaac Jackson	Elizabeth Brock	Elza Jackson	Margaret Brock
15238	Jackson, Ebie	GA	1885		James Jackson	Nancy Wallis		Jesse & Liza Wallace
20902	Jackson, Elizabeth	AL	1853		Zophers Jackson	Louisa Jackson	William Jackson	Andrew Jackson
21999	Jackson, Emma	TN	1852	none	James Jackson	Julia Bowles	John Jackson	Allen Bowles
20924	Jackson, Francis	AL	1844		Zopher Jackson	Louisa Jackson	William Jackson	Andrew Jackson
18612	Jackson, George	AL	1857	Jenny Jackson	Shadrock Jackson	Katie Copeland	Martin Jackson	James Copeland
21522	Jackson, George	FL	1844		James Jackson	Juilan Bowles		Allen Bowles
14335	Jackson, Georgia	TX			James Jackson	Sarah Maloney	John & Elizabeth Jackson	
9543	Jackson, Harper	NC	1850	Rebecca Jackson		Harriet Jackson		Moses & Sarah Jackson

18492	Jackson, Hattie	AR		Z.H. Jackson	Silus Simpkins	Isabella Thurman		Wm & Laney Thurman
18613	Jackson, Henry	TN	1874	Eva Jackson	Samuel Jackson	Martha Westmorland	Shadrock & Katie Jackson	P.M. & Katherine Westmorland
14336	Jackson, James	OK		Bessie Jackson	James Jackson	Sara Maloney	John & Elizabeth Jackson	
14338	Jackson, James	TX	1834	Sara Jackson	John Jackson	Elizabeth Caldwell		Andrew & Cerene Caldwell
15009	Jackson, James	NE	1836	Ruth Jackson	Isaac Jackson	Elizabeth Brock	Eliza Jackson	John & Margaret Brock
21998	Jackson, James	TN		none	John Jackson	Mary Calhoun	James & Julia Jackson	James & Julia Calhoun
13619*	Jackson, Jerry	IL	1857	Mahala Jackson	William Jackson	Mary Carper		Nicholas Carper
15240	Jackson, Jessie	GA	1906		James Jackson	Nancy Wallis		Jesse & Liza Wallace
7221	Jackson, John	OK	1878	Eva Jackson	Daniel Jackson	Epnetious Dohatley	Isaac Jackson	Elzera Marsley
19911	Jackson, John	NC	1852	Mahera Jackson	Alison Jackson	Sarah Thore	Amer & Bea Jackson	Norfleet & Frances Thore
22000	Jackson, John	TN	1841	Mary Jackson	James Jackson	Julia Bowles	Allen Bowles	
22815	Jackson, Josiah	AL	1864	Nancy Jackson	Zof Jackson	Luisa Jackson	Andrew Jackson	Claborn & Sallie Jackson
17003	Jackson, Judy	GA			John Anderson	Edy Feed	Charles Anderson	
18615	Jackson, Lawrence	TN	1880	Maggie Jackson	Samuel Jackson	Martha Westmorland	Shadrock & Katie Jackson	P.M. & Katherine Westmorland
7212	Jackson, Luella	MO	1883	Orbah Jackson	Zachary Foley	Elanora Miller	James & Rhoda Foley	Elizabeth Colley
15241	Jackson, Lula	GA	1890		James Jackson	Nancy Wallis		Jesse & Liza Wallace
17430	Jackson, Martha	GA	1849	Andrew Jackson	Jim Brown	Sarah Summers	Jim & Cary Brown	
20965*	Jackson, Martha	MS	1862	Henry Jackson	Dick Marshall	Mary Thomas		Tamar Thomas
7629	Jackson, Mary	GA	49yrs		Alex Brown	Poley Marco	Sallie Rainwater	
13620*	Jackson, Michael	IL	1855	Almira Jackson	William Jackson	Mary Carper		Nicholas Carper
15237	Jackson, Nancy	GA	1868	Jim Jackson	Jesse Wallace	Eliza Whitmire		Chris & Nancy Whitmire
15613	Jackson, Nancy	NC	1858	A L Jackson	Payton Owens	Eliza Marion	Thomas & Pollie Owens	Jerry & Mary Marion
13618*	Jackson, Nicholas	IL	1851		William Jackson	Mary Carper		Nicholas Carper
15236	Jackson, Pauline	GA	1895		James Jackson	Nancy Wallis		Jesse & Liza Wallace
20899	Jackson, Robert	AL	1859		Zophers Jackson	Louisa Jackson	William Jackson	Andrew Jackson
19926	Jackson, Rosa et al	NC	1892		W.N. Jackson	Loura Sinnons	Peter & Sarah Jackson	Gabriel & Emma Sinnons
21726	Jackson, Sadie	TN	1881	Burton Jackson	William Frost	Parilee Goins	John & Catherine Frost	Nathan & Sally Goins
7220	Jackson, Sally	OK	1880	none	Andrew Jackson	Sarah Eastman	John & Elizabeth Jackson	James & Mary Eastman
18611	Jackson, Samuel	TN	1840	Martha Jackson	Shadrock Jackson	Katie Copeland	Martin Jackson	James Copeland
14399	Jackson, Squire	NC	1846	Melinda Jackson		Margaret Jackson		Moses & Sarah Jackson
21997	Jackson, Tressa	TN		none	John Jackson	Mary Calhoun	James & Julia Jackson	James & Julia Calhoun

19915	Jackson, W.L. et al	NC			John Jackson	Sarah Thore	Olison & Sarah Jackson	Norfleet & Francis Thore
19912	Jackson, William	NC	43yrs	Laura Jackson	Peter Jackson	Sarah Thore	Amer & Betsy Jackson	Wm & Frances Thore
20922	Jackson, William	AL	1850		Zopher Jackson	Louisa Jackson	William Jackson	Andrew Jackson
19143 *	Jacobs, Nora	GA	1887	Will Jacobs	Henry Findley	Fanny Vann		Pate & Viley Vann
18266	Jacobs, Pink	GA	1831		Isaac Stanford	Edie Wylie		
9575 *	Jacoups, James	AL	1854	Mary Jacoups		Margret Jacoups		
16066 *	Jamerson, Caroline	OK	1852	Mims Jamerson	Henry Albertie	Hannah Albertie		
16041	James, Alice	OK	1868	Eli James	Ramy Chastain	Juda Watts	John Chastain	William Watts
10441	James, Girty	OK	20yrs	Tom James	James Goins	Maggie Turnham	Nathan & Mary Goins	David & Mary Turnham
15461	James, H.F.	GA	1876	Eliza Reece	William James	Rhodia Dillard	Selena James	Wm & Nancy Dillard
7213	James, Isaac	TX	1845		Marton James	Delila Thraser		
7214	James, Joel	TX	1848		John James	Agnes Chambers	Johnithan & Amanda James	
13976	James, Louisa	OK	1873	J W James	Nathan Goins	Louisa Goins	John & Nancy Goins	
15443	James, M.F.	GA	1874	Eliza James	W.W. James	Rhodia Dillard	Selena James	Wm & Nancy Dillard
15460	James, Mack	GA	1863	Laura Crow	William James	Rhodia Dillard	Selena James	Wm & Nancy Dillard
7519	James, Mary	VA	1889	William James	Joseph Hart	Jane More	Riley & Emily Hart	Wm & Isabellia More
4554	James, William	GA	1837	Rhoda	Johnson Alberty	Salena James		Sheord & Dicey James
7528 *	Jamison, Sherman	NC	43yrs	Candus Jamison	Tom Jamison	Mary ?	Anthony Jamison & Phebe Murphy	Grayson
10986	Janeway, Esther	TN	1876	J L Janeway	David Ridge	Martha Baily	Thomas Ridge	Thomas & Nancy Baily
574	Janeway, Marcus	OK	1867	Fanny Janeway	Daniel Janeway	Rachel Freeman	John & Nancy Janeway	Elijah & Nancy Freeman
10983	Janeway, Mary	TN	1861	L L Janeway	David Ridge	Martha Baily	Thomas Ridge	Thomas & Nancy Baily
18868	Janson, M.E.	AL	1875	J.W. Janson	J.C. Vincent	A.C. Sammons	J.C. & Eliza Vincent	Oliver & Elizabeth Cleveland
19417	Jarratt, Ellen	NC	1839	Isaac Jarratt	Richard Puryear	Elizabeth Clingman	John & Sarah Puryear	Jacob & Jane Clingman
18129	Jarrell, Polly	TX	1833	H.L. Jarroll	George Maddox	Rachel Maddox	William Maddox	Quilla Van
14236 *	Jarrett, Henry	GA	1827	Lizzie Jarrett	Ned Elston	Fannie Jarrett	Seata	Long Will
17629 *	Jarrett, Malinda	NC	1880	Richard Jarrett	Jerry Hutchins	Laura Williams		David & Fillis Williams
21608 *	Jarvis, Dolphus	NC	17yrs		Riley Jarvis	Rosa Revels	Nici Gilmer	Elias & Emily Revels
20958	Jarvis, Nancy	NC	1870		William Smith	Elizabeth Taffie	Wm Hardin & Nancy Smith	
20220	Jeek, Ena	IN	1880		Richard Elmore	Rachel Reed	John & Mary Elmore	Isaac & Hannah Reed
22141	Jeffery, Nancy	OK		John Jeffrey				

18226	Jeffres, Dean	GA	1875	Aler Jeffres	Alex Jeffres	Margaret Goins	Jerry & Sarah Jeffres	Smith Goins
18228	Jeffres, Eugene	AL		Fannie Jeffres	Alex Jeffres	Margaret Goins	Jerry & Sarah Jeffres	Smith Goins
18227	Jeffres, Stanley	GA	1871	Pollie Jeffres	Alex Jeffres	Margaret Goins	Jerry & Sarah Jeffres	Smith Goins
20435	Jeffrey, Delarn	AL	1866	Martha Jeffrey	Alex Jeffrey	Margaret Goins	Sarah Jeffrey	Smith Goins
15235	Jeffrey, Susie	GA	1861	Bennett Jeffrey	Columbus Culberson	Mary Holland	Martin & Sency Culberson	Wm & Susan Holland
20683	Jeffrey, Thomas	TN	1869	Alice Jeffrey	Alex Jeffries	Margaret Goins	Jerry Wilson & Sarah Jeffries	Benith & Betsie Goins
16053	Jeffreys, Elizia	AL	1856	Solliman Jeffreys	Colman Conner	Lizzie Henley	Henry & Lillie Conner	
7215	Jeffries, Sallie	MO	1870	Francis Jeffries	Thomas Dickey	Jane Morgan	John & Martha Dickey	Nathan & Anna Morgan
19146	Jemes, Jim	GA	1844	Mandy Jemes	Bob Jemes	Nancy Cash		Billy Cash
20508 *	Jenkins, Amanda	TN	1868	Lorenzo Jenkins	Calvin Benson	Matilda Routt		
21217	Jenkins, Callie	OK	1881	Sam Jenkins	John Cooper	Emma Simpson	J.W. & Elizabeth Cooper	Wm & Jemima Simpson
14283	Jenkins, Claborn	TN	1860	Agnes Jenkins	Henry Jenkins	Octavia Hightower	Henry & Dilsey ?	Dave & Mary Hightower
21985 *	Jenkins, Henry	TN	1858	Lula Jenkins	James Jenkins	Lavinia Jacobs		William & Kitty Jacobs
19677	Jenkins, Lucinda	TN	1827		James Ledbeter	Mary Cockrun		John & Agnes Cockrun
20180	Jenkins, Mary	TN	1866	J.F. Jenkins	Alford Hanks	Lieia Crabtree	John & Bettie Hanks	Thomas & Susie Crabtree
4556	Jenkins, Nancy	NC	1858	Henry Jenkins	Uriah Burns	Sallie Birchfield	Hezekiah & Betsey Burns	
19829	Jenkins, Prudence	OK	1889	William Jenkins	David Shook	Amanda Colvard	Eli & Sara Shook	Wm Colvard & Emily Campbell
3751	Jenkins, Ruth	NC	1848	F M Jenkins	Ben Hyde	Sinthy Sherrill	Ben Sr & Elizabeth Hyde	
10121	Jenkins, Sallie	WV	1888		Edward Mullens	Martelia Perdew	Richard & Sallie Mullins	Nathan & Sallie Perdew
20404	Jenkins, Susan	GA	1878		William Jenkins	Elizabeth Hargis	Samuel & Ruth Jenkins	Jackson & Mary Hargis
21248	Jenkins, William	GA	1868	Susan & Margarite	James Jenkins	Parmelia Hargis	Wm Jenkins & Francis Davis	Jackson Hargis & Caline Uhles
19323	Jennings, Edward	NC	1855	Cora Jennings	Jasper Overly	Polly Jennings		
5876	Jennings, Elzira	VA	1871	C D Jennings	Joseph Lewis	Rausa Hart	Jessie & Sarah Lewis	Eliazer & Nancy Hart
21209	Jennings, Sallie	AL	1888		John Jennings	Charly Lamascus	Saul & Georgia Jennings	
3382	Jernigan, Louisa	AL	1848	Seals & Jernigan	Simon Hadley	Caroline Hollinger	Hadley	Funstall & Hollinger
7219	Jessee, Eva	MO	1874	Samuel Jessee	David Preston	Nancy Roberts		Andrew & Eliza Roberts
21453	Jeter, Aaron	TX	1876		Frank Jeter	Adelia Thompson	George & Mary Jeter	
21365	Jeter, Brook	LA	1882	Velma Jeter	John Jeter	Susan Thompson	Washington & Mary Jeter	
21368	Jeter, Dickson	LA	1869	Mattie Jeter	John Jeter	Susan Thompson	Washington & Mary Jeter	
21449	Jeter, Ealy	TX	1875	Katie Jeter	Henry Jeter	Mary Fortson	Ealy & Martha Jeter	Elijah & Arrilla Fortson
21362	Jeter, Ed	TX	1872		Elia Jeter	Martha Bentley		

21451	Jeter, Frank	TX	1844	Adelia Jeter	George Jeter	Mary West		
21455	Jeter, Guss	TX	1880		Frank Jeter	Adelia Thompson	George & Mary Jeter	
21339	Jeter, Henry	TX	1854	Mary Jeter	Elyazer Jeter	Martha Pollard	George & Mary Jeter	
21505	Jeter, Tom	TX	1855	Mollie Jeter	Elyazer Jeter	Martha Pollard	George & Mary Jeter	
21450	Jeter, William	TX	1885		Henry Jeter	Mary Fortson	Ealy & Martha Jeter	Elijah & Arrilla Fortson
21338	Jeter, Willis	TX	1880	Ethel Jeter	Henry Jeter	Mary Fortson	Elyazer & Martha Jeter	Elijah & Arrilla Fortson
495	Jetter, Allen	OK	1849	Martha Jetter	Aurtor Jeter	Mary Bumbley	Buck & Sally Jeter	Wm & Elisebeth Bumbley
21258	Jetton, David	AL	1868	Alice Jetton	D.M. Jetton	Susanna Bush		George & Martha Bush
21257	Jetton, Joseph	AL	1870	Willie Jetton	D.M. Jetton	Susanna Bush		George & Martha Bush
7216	Jetton, Louisa	TX	1841	F B Jetton	John Pearce	Nancy Allen		
21256	Jetton, Montgomery	AL	1865	Sarah Jetton	D.M. Jetton	Susanna Bush		George & Martha Bush
17451	Jewell, Nellie	WV	1859	J.M. Jewell	Thomas Cook	Rebecca Sizemore	Wm & Catherine Cook	Ned & Anna Sizemore
9994	Jinnings, Ella	VA	1872	Lorans Jinnings	Columbus Peak	Caroline Spencer	Hugh & Marga Peak	Solomon & Nellie Spencer
19144	Johns, Allice	GA	1878	Henry Johns	Dudley McIntosh	Lizzie Jones	Alex & Martha McIntosh	
13290	Johns, Mary	OK	1878	William Johns	Mohawk Beaver	Mollie Simmons	Runabout & Cah le so ya sky	Go lee cha
14270	Johns, William	OK	1877	Mary Johns	Jar nah ju le	Martha		
14597	Johnson, C L	GA	1906		C L Johnson	Clemmie Tidwell		John & Rachel Tidwell
4738	Johnson, Addie	NC	1887	Joseph Johnson	John Graves	Harrett McDonald	Wm & Annie Graves	James & Minna McDonald
19094	Johnson, Albert	KS	1876	Ana Johnson	John Johnson	Mary Holt	T.J. Johnson	James & Martha Holt
17928	Johnson, Alexander	TN	1869		Thomas Johnson	Eliza Robison		Mat Anderson & Polly Robison
15870 *	Johnson, Alfred	TN	1854	Angeline Johnson	Thomas Johnson	Creasy Baker	Richard ?	Ned & Shebia Bell
17927	Johnson, Andrew	TN	1869	Alice Johnson	Thomas Johnson	Eliza Robison		Mat Anderson & Polly Robison
15234	Johnson, Annie	GA	1896		W J Johnson	Lizzie Spears		Joe & Mary Carmichael
18455 *	Johnson, Anthony	MS	1860	Sessom Johnson	George Young	Ann Thorp	Anthony Desset	Maraly Johnson
14213	Johnson, Archie	NC	1870	Lela Johnson	John Johnson	Susan Poindexter	John & Sarah Johnson	Robert & Charlotte Poindexter
3850	Johnson, Bell	TX	1887	Norman Johnson	James Trent	Lou Miner		Joseph & Mariah Miner
19145 *	Johnson, Betty	GA	1865	Ben Johnson	John Hall	Margratte Riddlespugler	Abe Hall	Missouri Richardson
15232	Johnson, Carl	GA	1898		W J Johnson	Lizzie Spears		Joe & Mary Carmichael
9245 *	Johnson, Carrie	MO		Charley Johnson		Phillis Salling		Tommy & Benis Sallings
15233	Johnson, Carrie	GA	1903		W J Johnson	Lizzie Spears		Joe & Mary Carmichael
20436 *	Johnson, Charity	TN	1837		Jerry McLocklin	Dafney Hanson		Peter & Katie Hanson

13389	Johnson, Charles	OK	1871		Tsu gino tsu ga	Tsi nu nu		
17986 ½	Johnson, Charles	TN	1891	H. Davis	John Johnson	Matilda Staten	Marion & Hannah Johnson	Anderson & Mary Staten
14222	Johnson, Charlie	NC	1866		John Johnson	Sue Poindexter	John & Sarah Johnson	Robert & Charlotte Poindexter
18998	Johnson, Clara	KS	1887		John Johnson	Mary Holt		
22255 *	Johnson, Clara	OK	1855	Julius Johnson	George Landrum	Cassie Muskrat	Jack Dixon & Charity Trunk	Lucy Muskrat
14598	Johnson, Clemmie	GA	1883		John Tidwell	Rachel Langford	John & Lucreasy Tidwell	
22355 *	Johnson, Dave	OK		Frances Johnson	Gulve Starr	Jane Johnson		Reuben Johnson
19767 *	Johnson, Eliza	TN	1832	Samuel Johnson	Mathew Clark	Clara West		
16065	Johnson, Elmira	OK	1849	James Johnson	James Norton	Roda Dennis	John & Jane Norton	
20728	Johnson, Esther	GA	1887	J.O. Johnson	Samuel Lathun	Sallie Reynolds	Richard & Rillis Lathun	Rufus & Mary Reynolds
18761	Johnson, Fannie	FL	1870	Quincy Johnson	Stephus Banks	Mima Tigner		Robt & Mima Stiggins
21625	Johnson, Florence	TN	1866	W. H. Johnson	John Bloodworth	America Hulsey		
15330	Johnson, Floyd	GA	1906		W J Johnson	Lizzie Spears		Joe & Mary Carmichael
17986	Johnson, Fredrick	TN	1889	H. Davis	John Johnson	Matilda Staten	Marion & Hannah Johnson	Anderson & Mary Staten
18454 *	Johnson, George	MS	1847	Anna Johnson	Anthony Diarut	Cherity Thorps		Salie Thorps
14755	Johnson, Georgia	NC	1893		Thomas Johnson	Victoria Martin	Elisha & Susan Johnson	Doc & Betty Martin
20173	Johnson, Grover	KS			John Johnson	Mary Holt		
22357 *	Johnson, Hannah	OK		widow	Jess Gunter	Sophia Campbell		
15054	Johnson, Harvey	TN	1887		Harvey Johnson	Mary Burch	Nathaniel & Nancy Johnson	Joseph & Pollie Burch
672	Johnson, Hattie	NC	1886	Anderson Johnson	Robt, Rowland	Margaret Pace		Stephen & Dovey Pace
15329	Johnson, James	GA	1868	Hassie Johnson	William Johnson	Martha Smith	Hugh & Elizabeth Johnson	
19242	Johnson, James	MO	1867	Mollie Johnson	John Johnson	Mary Holt		
19766 *	Johnson, James	TN	1845	Betty Johnson	Henderson Johnson	Cynthia West	James & Eliza Johnson	Edward & Clara West
19773 *	Johnson, James	TN		Sarah Johnson	Huston Johnson	Eliza West		Clarisa
3446	Johnson, Jane	AL	32yrs	Mr. Johnson	Simon Hadley	Caroline Hollinger		
19977 *	Johnson, Jane	GA	1844	William Johnson	Joshua Crow	Martha Johnson		
7207	Johnson, Jennie	TX	1869	Emmet Johnson	John Jolly	Amanda Ward	Wm & Martha Jolly	Jerry & Nancy Ward
20497 *	Johnson, Jesse	TN	1881		Columbus Johnson	Chaney Griffin	Ned & Sarah Johnson	John & Katie Griffin
4151	Johnson, John	NC	1889	Minnie Johnson	Aaron Johnson	Margaret Martin		William Martin
13517	Johnson, John	NC	1861	Mary Johnson	John Johnson	Susan Poindexter	John & Susan Johnson	Robert & Charlotte Poindexter
14408	Johnson, John	GA	1870	Mary Johnson	Harvey Johnson	Marinda Burch		Josiah & Polly Burch

19624	Johnson, John	NC	1830	Naomi Johnson	Robert Poindexter	Charlotte Poindexter		Thomas & Elizabeth Poindexter
14679	Johnson, Joseph	TN	1877		Harvey Johnson	Mary Burch	Nathaniel & Nancie Johnson	Joseph & Pollie Burch
18171 *	Johnson, Julia	TN		Sim Johnson	Randle Moss	Rosie Toka		Sindy & Pashion Toka
13888	Johnson, L.E.J	WV	1882	Wint Johnson	W W Walls	Emeline Peak	Parks & Jane Walls	Hughie & Margie Peak
19765 *	Johnson, Lewis	TN	1861	Jennie Johnson	Samuel Johnson	Eliza West		Clara West
15328	Johnson, Lizzie	GA	1869	W J Johnson	Joe Carmichael	Mary Spears		Josiah & Patty Spears
8480	Johnson, Lockey	WV	1883	Sherman Johnson	Elisha Roop	Nancy Poter	Aberham & Catherine Roop	James & Rebecka Poter
200	Johnson, Lucy	OK		James Johnson	James Wright	Mary Morgan		Richard & Kansas Morgan
19718	Johnson, Lucy	TN	1886	Elvin Johnson	J. Curtis	Elizabeth Patrick	Joshua & Elizabeth Curtis	
20344 *	Johnson, Luella	GA	1870	Greene Johnson	Isaac McCarny	Mckie Thompson	Lindsay McCarny	Moses & Fashion Johnson
4256	Johnson, Luverna	AR	1856	James Johnson	John Buttry	Margret Martin	Wm & Luvisa Buttry	Wm & Susan Martin
19495	Johnson, Mabrie	MO	1870	Samantha Johnson	John Johnson	Mary Holt		
15327	Johnson, Madie	GA	1901		W J Johnson	Lizzie Spears		Joe & Mary Carmichael
22818	Johnson, Maggie	NC	1874	Archie Johnson	Samuel Martin	Lishie Marion		
22332 *	Johnson, Mandy	OK	1832	Dick Vann widow	Andrew Johnson	Eliza Vann		Nellie
21550	Johnson, Martha	GA	1836	Wootson Johnson	Harris Sorrow	Adeline Kidd	Randall & Jennie Sorrow	Absalom & Elizabeth Kidd
8189	Johnson, Mary	TX	1874	James Johnson	J H Webb	Mary Gambell	Pleas Webb	A J & Mary Gambell
18487	Johnson, Mary	OK	1862	Samuel Johnson	George Brezee	Eunice Overacker	Jacob & Mary Brezee	Chris & Adaline Overacker
18817	Johnson, Mary	KS	1847	John Johnson	James Holt	Martha Stark	Telberey Holt	Susannah Driskill
20065 *	Johnson, Mary	TN	1854	Taylor Johnson	Ben Bates	Nellie Vandergriff		Susan Vandergriff
20124	Johnson, Mary	OK	1863	Simon Johnson	Jesse Garnette	Dannah	John Garnette	
15326	Johnson, Mattie	GA	1891		W J Johnson	Lizzie Spears		Joe & Mary Carmichael
17987	Johnson, Mattie	TN	1896		John Johnson	Matilda Staten	Marion & Hannah Johnson	Anderson & Mary Staten
14754	Johnson, McKenzie	NC	1889		Thomas Johnson	Victoria Martin	Elisha & Susan Johnson	Doc & Betty Martin
18395	Johnson, Mrs. William	AL	26yrs	Wm Johnson	James Seals	Louisa Hadley	Wm & Lucinda Seals	Simon & Caroline Hadley
18997	Johnson, Nancy	GA	1884	John Johnson	Berry Spearman	Hester Stevenson	John Spearman & Elizabeth Cameron	Joe Stevenson & Sibbie Thompson
22466	Johnson, Nancy	TN	1870	J.E. Johnson	Jonathen Allen	Martha Davidson	Willis Parker & Martha Allen	Wm & Malinda Davidson
21817	Johnson, Phillip	FL	1855		Phillip Johnson	Ann Chechee		Lydia Franklin Chechee
5160 *	Johnson, Pollie	OK	46yrs	James Johnson	Wiley Jones	Sirenia Skenidy	Skiszia Hayd & Umphry Jones	Charles & Jennie Skenidy
3959	Johnson, Robert	NC	1887	none	Aaron Johnson	Margaret Martin		Wm Martin & Harriett Trammel

21847	Johnson, Robert	WA	1872	Mellie Johnson	John Johnson	Mary Holt		
14596	Johnson, Ruth	GA	1902		C L Johnson	Clemmie Tidwell		John & Rachel Tidwell
20403	Johnson, Ruth	GA	1869	E.N. Johnson	William Jenkins	Elizabeth Hargis	Samuel & Ruth Jenkins	Jackson & Mary Hargis
18681	Johnson, Silva	FL	1883	Charles Johnson	John Gillroy	Harriet Monk		John & Silva Monk
15055	Johnson, Thomas	TN	1879		Harvey Johnson	Mary Burch	Nathaniel & Nancy Johnson	Joseph & Pollie Burch
7206	Johnson, Thursetta	MO	1865	Charles Johnson	James Foley	Mary Osborne	James & Rhoda Foley	James & Nancy Osborne
13525	Johnson, Victoria	NC	1868	Thomas Johnson	Doc Martin	Bettie Hartgrave	John & Jennie Martin	Wm & Ann Hartgrave
19577	Johnson, Walter	KS	1882	May Johnson	John Johnson	Mary		
3229	Johnson, William	TN	1857	Josephine Johnson	Francis Johnson	Lydia Roberts	Jefferson & Rosie Johnson	Roberts & Buckner
14415	Johnson, William	GA	1875	Janie Johnson	Harvey Johnson	Mary Burch		Josiah & Polly Burch
20458 *	Johnson, William	TN	1859	Eva Johnson	Henry Williams	Mariah Jordan		
14641	Johnston, Isaac	MO	1877		Thomas Johnston	Margaret Presley	Thomas Jr & Eliza Johnston	Isaac & Martha Presley
8416	Johnston, John	MO	1858	none	Thos Johnston Jr	Eliza Bancum	Thos & Mary Johnston	Thos & Elizabeth Bancum
21739	Johnston, Nelia	TX	1883	John Johnston	Thomas Jeter	Lalla Jeter	Ealyazer & Marthy Jeter	
13346	Johnston, Nellie	OK	1879	Cyrus Johnston	Benj Courtney	Matilda Fender	Wm & Matilda Courtney	Daniel & Dicy Fender
7209	Jolley, Amanda	TX	1843	John Jolly	Jerry Ward	Nancy Freeman	John & Polly Ward	Richard & Nellie Freeman
2531	Jolly, Lucy	NC	1884	Silas Jolly	John Dyson	Elizabeth Dyson	Salamar & Polley Dyson	Jackson & Miley Dyson
2530	Jolly, Silas	NC	65yrs	Lusey Jolly	John Dyson	Elizabeth Dyson	Lusey Jolly	
7208	Jolly, William	TX	1860	Hettie Jolly	John Jolly	Amanda Ward		Jerry & Nancy Ward
8188	Jones, Agnes	TX	1880	Walter Jones	Thomas Yates	Cordelia Womack	Henrietta Ward Yates	
1024	Jones, Alice	KS	1903		Wade Jones	Annie Dugas	Wm & Mary Jones	Joseph & Johanna Dugas
22131 *	Jones, Annie	NC	1874	Samuel Jones	Simptson Corpening	Tillie Corpening	Calvin Foney	Sarrah Patterson
15177	Jones, Arthur	IL	1876	Mable Jones	Lafayette Jones	Mary Eddings	Thompson & Lucinda Jones	James & Roda Eddings
18648	Jones, Augusta	NC	1852	Joseph Jones	Archibald Poindexter	Elizabeth Ward	Robert & Mariann Poindexter	Wiley & Polly Ward
1310 *	Jones, Belle	NC	1873	Dan Jones	Benjamin Burgess	Mariah Goode	Wm Burgess	
17857	Jones, Belle	NE	1874	John Jones	E.W. Crane	Elizabeth Bays		Josiah Bays & Letta May
9069	Jones, Benjamin	NC	1852	Matilda Jones	Samuel Jones	Adaline Hart	Isaac & Sallie Jones	Ned & Nancy Hart
1016	Jones, Boyd	KS	1893	none	Wm Jones	Mary Stamper	Wm & Martha Jones	Eli & Susanna Stamper
22555	Jones, Callie	TN	1874	Rob. Jones	Joe Collett	Lucresia Watson	Joel Collett & Betsy Raburn	Thos Watson & Martha Patterson

ID	Name	State	Year	Col5	Col6	Col7	Col8	Col9
12955	Jones, Cally	GA	1871	George Jones	Jacob Cox	Delila McCaslin	Jacob Cox	
1023	Jones, Charles	KS			Wade Jones	Annie Dugas	Wm & Mary Jones	Joseph & Johanna Dugas
19176	Jones, Charlie	GA	1879	Alice Jones	Jim Jones	Mary Cash		Billy Cash
4589	Jones, Clarinda	OK	1846	John Jones	Isham West	Elzada Perry	Japtha West & Millie Gentry	
18773	Jones, Claude	MO	1894		George Jones	Dora Batey	John & Sarah Jones	George & Pearline Batey
19996	Jones, Cora	GA	1873	Andrew Jones	Francis Owen	Sarah Whitmire	Wiley & Mary Owen	James & Cassie Whitmire
18772	Jones, Daisy	MO	1900		George Jones	Dora Batey	John & Sarah Jones	George & Pearline Batey
20573 *	Jones, David	TN	1840		Jerry Bryson	Delpha Johnson		
10856	Jones, Delora	TX	1882	John Jones	Daniel Lawrence	Angeline Snow		Solomon Snow
2250	Jones, Dovie	OK	1879	James Jones	Reuben Moore	Katherine Cook		
2309	Jones, Dovie	OK	1879	James Jones	Ruben Moore	Catherine Cook		Jacob & Delana Cook
20006	Jones, Edward	GA	1860	Laura Jones	Russell Jones	Ellen Perdue	Bartley & Disa Jones	Ruth Perdue
10182	Jones, Elisabeth	GA	1858	W A Jones	John Helton	Delila Hester	Joseph Helton & Letta Spradly	Benj Hester & Milla Aires
673	Jones, Eliza	NC	1874	James Jones	Robert Rowland	Margaret Pace		Stephen & Dovey Pace
6558	Jones, Eliza	AR	1883	John Jones	Thompson Wood	Eliza Martin	John & Margaret Wood	Wm & Susan Martin
20960	Jones, Eliza	NC	1858	Cyrus Jones	William Scott	Bethia Witherspoon		Sallie Scott
15442	Jones, Elizabeth	GA	1872	Joe Jones	W.W. James	Rhodia Dillard	Selena James	Wm & Nancy Dillard
7217	Jones, Ella	MO	1878	B G Jones	Jeremiah Williams	Sarah Worthington	Beniah & Nancy Williams	Francis & Sarah Worthington
16710	Jones, Ellias	SC	1843	Sheraba Jones	Ellias Jones	Rachel Brady	Ellias Jones	Rachel Brady
15916 *	Jones, Elmer	IN	1862	Etta Jones	Alex Jones	Jane Mitchell	John & Rebecca Jones	Alex & Rebecca Mitchell
3032	Jones, Emma	MO	1872	J A Jones	Jeremiah Sloan	Mary Lemmon	A C & Mary Sloan	
19580	Jones, Emma	KS	18		Wade Jones	Anne Dugas	W.B. & Mary Jones	Joseph & Johanna Dugas
5404	Jones, Eva	MO	1869	John Jones	James Proctor	Francis Pace	Ransom & Ruth Proctor	John & Jane Pace
1015	Jones, Fadina	KS	1880	none	Wm Jones	Mary Stamper	Wm & Martha Jones	Eli & Susanna Stamper
1025	Jones, Florence	KS	1901		Wade Jones	Annie Dugas	Wm & Mary Jones	Joseph & Johanna Dugas
18098	Jones, George	MO	1871	Dora Batey	John Jones	Sarah Cowan	George & Earsley Jones	Steve & Betsie Cowan
21561	Jones, Isom	GA	1857	Lou Jones	Harrison Cooley	Adaline Jones		Harriette Jones
10183	Jones, J. Martin	GA	1879		William Jones	Elisabeth Helton	Leander & Elisabeth Jones	John & Delila Helton
13274	Jones, J.B.	GA	1883		William Jones	Elisabeth Helton	Leander & Elisabeth Jones	John & Delila Helton

2524	Jones, James	GA	1842	Sarah Jones	Wilson Jones	Ellender Thomas	John & Lettie Jones	John & Nancy Thomas
15513	Jones, James	GA	1870		Allison Jones	Hester Prather		James & Parthenia Prather
21181	Jones, James	GA	39 yrs	Mary Ann Jones	James Jones	Nancy Cordell	Allen Jones	Lewis Cordell
21684 ½	Jones, Jane	AR		Alfred Jones	Alex Clingman	Ann Clingman	Peter & Ann Clingman	Alex & Mary Clingman
10635	Jones, Jesse	SC	1855	none	Elias Jones	Rachel Brady		John & Sally Brady
21532	Jones, Jim	GA	1812	Sarah Jones	Jim Jones	Sarah Lowry		
20328	Jones, Joe	GA	1853		Sol Jones	Martha Pace		
1030	Jones, John	KS	1897	none	Wade Jones	Annie Dugas	Wm & Mary Jones	Joseph & Johanna Dugas
14238 *	Jones, John	GA	1812		Jim Jones	Sarah Jones		
19147	Jones, John	GA	1871	Lella Jones	Jim Jones	Mary Cash		Billy Cash
20903 *	Jones, John	NC	1852	Linda Jones	Ross Witherspoon	Betsy Jones	John & Milly Gorden	
21060	Jones, Jonas	TN	1862	Margaret Jones	Jacob Jones	Jane Burns	Robert & Susan Jones	John Burns
11831	Jones, Joseph	GA	1852	Rachel Jones	Elias Jones	Rachel Brady		
14855 *	Jones, Laura	GA	1850	Stephen Jones	? Jenkins	Sarah McKinyer		Jesse & Hannah McKinyer
4340	Jones, Leanzy Alice	NC	1864	Jessie Jones	Elisha Pennington	Jane Anderson	Samuel & Bettey Pennington	Jessie & Amandy Anderson
20961 *	Jones, Lelah	NC	1855	Greene Jones	Perry Miller	Winnie Miller	Bille Brokins	Tenner Miller
22512	Jones, Lillie	MO	1881	Thomas Jones	John McGuire	Judy Pendergrass	Jesse & Elizabeth McGuire	John & Martha Pendergrass
20904 *	Jones, Lina	NC	1854	John Jones	Joe Horwood	Mary Witherspoon		Stephen & Betsy Witherspoon
22513	Jones, Lorain	MO	1902	none	Thomas Jones	Lillie McGuire	Marian & Martha Jones	John & Judy McGuire
20440 *	Jones, Lucinda	TN	1832	David Jones	Moses Kimbrough	Margaret Sabaston		
17930	Jones, Lula	TN	1868		Elder Neifhbors	Millie Henning	Grant & Elizabeth Neighbors	
6099	Jones, Lura	VA	1872	William Jones	William Phipps	Mary Mathena	Benjamin & Ruthy Phipps	David & Pheba Mathena
21731	Jones, Martha	TN	1846	W.P. Jones	Bies Wines	Jemima Horner	Abslum & Bettie Abbott	C. & Mary Horner
2239	Jones, Mary	NC	1873	James Jones	Joseph Martin	Mary Moose	Joseph & Mary Martin	Jacob & Sallie Moose
10636	Jones, Mary	SC	1842	none	Elias Jones	Rachel Brady		John & Sally Brady
13166	Jones, Mary	OK	1846	Charles Jones	John Wilkerson	Nancy Blankenship	John & Annie Wilkerson	
16198 *	Jones, Mary	OK	1832	Carter Jones	Joseph Cotton	Emeline Andrews	Allen Clapp & Lucinda Chambers	Allen & Lucinda Andrews
18776	Jones, Mary	MO	1885	Corbet Vanderpool	John Jones	Sarah Cowen	George & Earsley Jones	Steve & Betsie Cowen
1017	Jones, Mary Jane	KS		(too light	to read)		John & Sally Stamper	Solomon & Betsy Stamper
22556	Jones, Mattie	TN	1877	W.L. Jones	Joe Collett	Lucresia Watson	Joel Collett & Betsy Raburn	Thos Watson & Martha Patterson
6152	Jones, Nancy	NC	1841	William Jones	Ahart Phipps	Maryan Hash	Wm & Nancy Phipps	Robert & Margery Hash
19298	Jones, Nancy	GA	1877	Robert Jones	Hardy Bryant	Winnie Tatum	Wm & Fannie Bryant	James & Susie Tatum
21598	Jones, Nancy	NC	1849	W.M.L. Jones	Allen Oakley	Frances Brown	Wm & Nancy Oakley	John & Fannie Brown

1926	Jones, Neil	KS	1900		Wade Jones	Annie Dugas	Wm & Mary Jones	Joseph & Johanna Dugas
22726	Jones, Ollie	TX	1886	Tom Jones	T.J. Benton	E.E. McLeod		
19462	Jones, Perlina	IN	1834	Alfred Jones	James Bear	Polly Smith		James & Nancy Smith
11746	Jones, Russell	GA	1834	Rachel Jones	Alfred Jones	Mary Perdue	Bartlet Jones	Lucinda Perdue
2091	Jones, Rutha	NC	1869	W C Jones	G D Blevins	Celia Parsons	Daniel & Anna Blevins	Wm & Rutha Parsons
9058	Jones, Samuel	NC	1861	Jinnie Jones	Samuel Jones	Adaline Hart	Isaac & Sallie Jones	Ned & Nancy Hart
10281	Jones, Samuel	TN	1871	Mary Jones	James Jones	Nancy Cordell	Allen Jones	Martha Cordell
19788	Jones, Samuel	NJ	1837	Sophia Jones	Samuel Jones	Eliza Cook		
1834	Jones, Sarah	OK	1881	James Jones		Catherine Cook		Jacob Cook
11833	Jones, Sarah	SC	1883		Joseph Jones	Rachel Phillips		
19319	Jones, Silas	IN	1854	Ollie Jones	John Jones	Rebecca Shoecraft	William Jones	Silas & Mary Shoecraft
22273 *	Jones, Sophia	OK	1852	Hemstead Jones	George Landrum	Peggy Landrum	Moses & Lucy Walker	Charity Trunk
15441	Jones, Thad	GA	1894		Jim Jones	Venie Atkins		Frank & Nancy Atkins
6151	Jones, Thomas	NC	1877	none	William Jones	Nancy Phipps	Thos & Elizabeth Jones	Ahart & Maryan Phipps
8838	Jones, Thomas	IL	1871	none	Lafayet Jones	Mary Eddings	Thompson & Lucinda Jones	James & Roda Eddings
11889	Jones, Thomas	GA	1889		William Jones	Elizabeth Helton	B.L. & Elisabeth Jones	John & Delila Helton
15440	Jones, Venie	GA	1883	Jim Jones	Frank Atkins	Nancy Hill	Berryman & Martha Atkins	
1029	Jones, Vera	KS	1898	none	Wade Jones	Annie Dugas	Wm & Mary Jones	Joseph & Johanna Dugas
1031	Jones, Wade	KS	1876	Annie Jones	Wm B. Jones	Mary Stamper	Wm & Martha Jones	Eli & Susanna Stamper
15439	Jones, Walter	GA	1906		Jim Jones	Venie Atkins		Frank & Nancy Atkins
11836	Jones, William	GA	1840	Elizabeth Jones	Elias Jones	Rachel Brady		Rachel Brady
20160	Jones, William	GA	1865	Lizzie Jones	Benj Jones	Sarah Garrett	William Jones	Wells Garrett
6150	Jones, Winfield	NC	1875	none	William Jones	Nancy Phipps	Thos & Elizabeth Jones	Ahart & Maryan Phipps
15848	Jordan, Abe Lewis	VA	1884	Lula Jordan	Thomas Jordan	Ellen Hartbarger	Daniel Jordan & Susan James	Wm & Kittie Hartbarger
20752	Jordan, Alonzo	AL	1877	Lizzie Jordan	Jackson Jordan	Wiley Sharp	Noah & Adaline Jordan	Red & Culie Sharp
530	Jordan, Amanda	NC	1854	none		Catherine Ward	unknown	unknown
14519	Jordan, Annie	GA	1888	Travis Jordan	George Millwood	Amanda New	Hugh & Miriam Millwood	Joel & Mary New
20753	Jordan, Beatrice	AL	1902		Alonzo Jordan	Lizzie Walker	Jackson & Wiley Jordan	Isaac & Emma Walker
17761 *	Jordan, Callie	TN	1867		John Knox	Laura Ware	Isaac Knox	Dafney & Beverly Ware
15325	Jordan, Elector	GA	1886		Noah Jordan Jr	Susan Ragsdale	Noah & Adaline Jordan	
20754	Jordan, Etta	AL	1906		Alonzo Jordan	Lizzie Walker	Jackson & Wiley Jordan	Isaac & Emma Walker
20756	Jordan, Isaac	AL	1900		Alonzo Jordan	Lizzie Walker	Jackson & Wiley Jordan	Isaac & Emma Walker

10559	Jordan, Jackson	AL	1854	Luvisse Jordan	Noah Jordan	Adaline Clements	Nathan & Annis Jordan	
7218	Jordan, James	TX	1854	Ruth Jordan	Daniel Jordan	Susan James	Sarrah Jordan	Johnathan & Amanda James
20755	Jordan, James	AL	1898		Alonzo Jordan	Lizzie Walker	Jackson & Wiley Jordan	Isaac & Emma Walker
22532	Jordan, Jasper	NC	1883	none	Calvin Bishop stepfather	Lillie Jordan		Katy Jordan or Ward
15324	Jordan, Jefferson	GA	1881		Noah Jordan Jr	Susan Ragsdale	Noah & Adaline Jordan	
8712	Jordan, Julia	GA	1874	Rochelle Jordan	Preevely Gravitt	Francis Tyler	Lula Gravitt	James & Susan Tyler
15323	Jordan, Louisa	GA	1891		Noah Jordan Jr	Susan Ragsdale	Noah & Adaline Jordan	
18513	Jordan, Mary	AL	1867	Gordan Campbell	John Terry	Catherine Jordan		Charles Ward
7822	Jordan, Noah Jr.	GA	1853	Susan Jordan	Noah Jordan	Martha Hopper	Nathan Jordan	John Wyatt
7821	Jordan, Noah Sr.	GA	1815	Martha Jordan	Nathan Jordan	Annis Wyatt		
20757	Jordan, Pearllie	AL	1904		Alonzo Jordan	Lizzie Walker	Jackson & Wiley Jordan	Isaac & Emma Walker
7824	Jordan, Samuel	GA	1861	Susan Jordan	Noah Jordan	Adaline Clements	Nathan & Annis Jordan	
10777	Jordan, Tennessee	TN	1863	George Jordan	James Corvin	Sarah Fox	Thomas & Easter Corvin	Sandy & Polly Fox
19619	Jordan, Theodia	TN	1885	William Jordan	Rufus Hatcher	Sarah Curtis	John & Mary Hatcher	Ezekiel & Ardelia Curtis
7825	Jordan, Thomas	GA	1870	Fannie Jordan	Noah Jordan	Martha Hopper	Annis Jordan	
1528	Jordan, W. Clark	NC	1849	L L Jordan	Gaston Suit	Catherine Jordan		Charles Ward
7537	Jourdan, Albert	IL	1875	Effa Jourdan	Joseph Jourdan	Sarah Blackburn	Aquilla & Betsey Jourdan	Andrew & Francis Blackburn
7541	Jourdan, Allen	IL	1882	Lena Jourdan	Joseph Jourdan	Sarah Blackburn	Aquilla & Betsey Jourdan	Andrew & Francis Blackburn
8843	Jourdan, Aquilla	IL	1857	Mary Jourdan	Joseph Jourdan	Sarah Blackburn	Aquilla & Betsey Jourdan	Andrew & Francis Blackburn
8394	Jourdan, John	MO	1868	Lucy Jourdan	Joseph Jourdan	Sarah Blackburn	Aquilla & Betsey Jourdan	Andrew & Francis Blackburn
8844	Jourdan, Thomas	IL	1883	none	Aquilla Jourdan	Mary Boyles	Joseph & Sarah Jourdan	
7533	Jourdan, William	IL	1870		Joseph Jourdan	Sarah Blackburn	Aquilla & Betsey Jourdan	Andrew & Francis Blackburn
22145*	Joyce, April	GA	1844	Louisa Joyce	Jack Joyce	Anna Dukes		Kugole
14711	Joyner, Pattie	NC	1857	J G Joyner	J G Trulove	Flora Butner	Austin & Pattie Trulove	J & Bettie Butner
21921	Julian, Pacients	TN	1829		Indian Sow	Mary Gann		Samuel & Chaney Gann
14203	Jumper, Jack	OK	1866	Berta Jumper	Jumper	Lizzie Swimmer	Tarnastele	
11673	Justice, George	OK	1878		Richard Justice	NeGi Burntwood	Polly Justice	Qui Gi de ga li ga
10450	Kane, Lizzie	GA	1867	Frank Kane	Joseph Lumpkin	Susan Lloyd		Thos & Susan Lloyd
7228	Karr, Mary	MO	1864	John Karr	John Williams	Mary Nichols	Minter & Frankie Williams	Henry & Mary Nichols

6304	Kaufman, Alice	MO	1858	Robert Kaufman	Milton Monroe	Henrietta Livengood	Wm & Rebecca Monroe	Daniel & Sarah Livengood
8495	Kavanaugh, Della	LA	1886	Patrick Kavanaugh	James Blevins	Laura Lewis	Allen Blevins	
17496	Kayson, Susie	OK	1856	Packard Kayson	Joe Wolf	Malinda Smith		Peter & Dinah Smith
21906	Keef, Mary	TN	1880	John Keef	Ab Phillips	Sarah Cogburn	George & Mary Phillips	Moses & ?abel Cogburn
17514	Keefer, Julia	OK	1882	James Keefer	J.A. Hickman	Sarah Hicks	Fred & Polly Hickman	Linsey Hicks & Catherine Miller
11180	Keeffe, Elizebeth	GA	1862	Neal Keeffe	George Waddle	Lottie Cox		John Cox
15438	Keel, Georgia	GA	1859	Love Keel	William James	Rhoda Dillard	Selena James	Wm & Nancy Dillard
19116 *	Keene, Bertha	IN	1885	Bert Keene	Henry White	Mary Weaver	Denson & Parthenia White	Alfred & Charity Weaver
22312	Keene, Nellie	KS	1886	Joseph Keene	Thomas Cordill	Sallie Baker		Seth & Lucy Baker
4972	Keener, Harriet	GA	1877	William Keener	Wade Ross	Hariet		
17921	Keener, Martha	TN	1855		Engle Gudeson	Belza Painter		Jake & Bettie Painter
20970	Kees, Solomon	NC	1836	Elizabeth Kees	John Kees	Sarah Keller		
9092	Keith, Benjamin	WV	1876	Chessie Keith	Abraham Keith	Sarah Osburn	Guy & Rachel Keith	Solomon & Martha Osburn
7225	Keith, Bertie	TX	1884	none	Jacob Keith	Sarah Watson	Eli & Elizabeth Keith	Wm & Nelly Watson
20547	Keith, Calvin	TN	1887		Calvin Keith Sr.	Sarah Wilson	Rufus & Nancy Keith	Wm & Caroline Wilson
1040 *	Keith, Dan	GA	1867	Annie Keith	Tom Rogers	Leah Riley	Jack Rogers	Dan Wakely
7224	Keith, George	TX	1873	Emma Keith	Jacob Keith	Sarah Watson	Eli Keith & Elizabeth Meek	Wm Watson & Nelly Caldwell
10875	Keith, Guy	WV	1881		Abraham Keith	Sarah Osburn	Guy & Rachel Keith	Solomon & Martha Osburn
7223	Keith, Jake	TX	1877	none	Jacob Keith	Sarah Watson	Eli & Elizabeth Keith	Wm Watson & Nelly Caldwell
10466	Keith, Mathew	OK	1877	Mamie Martin	Joel Keith	Susan McClure		James & Rebecca McClure
681	Keith, Melissa	AR	1850	Alfred Keith widow	Henry Guy	Elizabeth Burns	Henry & Betsy Guy	
18525 *	Keith, Saminth	TN	48yrs	Will Keith	Thomas Lane			
7222	Keith, Sarah	TX	1839	Jacob Keith	William Watson	Nelly		Andrew & Sereny Caldwell
10865	Keith, Sarah	WV		Abraham Keith	Solomon Osburn	Martha Arms	Elias Osburn & Sarah Sizemore	Robert & Martha Arms
19221	Keith, Sarah	KS	1853	A.W. Keith	James Sizemore	Mary Abbott	Richard & Elizabeth Sizemore	Eliza Abbott
20397	Keith, Sarah	TN	1855		William Wilson	Caraline Spencer	Andrew & Mary Wilson	Abram & Sarah Spencer
17106	Keith, Victoria	OK	36yrs	John Keith	Andrew Martin	Sarah Kimbling	Jack & Mattie Martin	Wm & Pauline Johnson
2820	Keith, William	AR	1853	Ella Keith	David Keith	Mary Parker	James Keith	
221	Kell, Charles	CA	1845	Temperance Kell	David Kell	Darcas Duncan	Alick Kell	C.G. Duncan

21191*	Kell, Katie	OK	1849	widow		Lucy Rider		
3343	Keller, Mrs. James	AL	1868	James Keller	Sidney Lomax	Matilda Moniac		Sam & Susan Moniac
15053	Keller, Alice	TN	1873	John Keller	Harvey Johnson	Mary Burch	Nathaniel & Nancy Johnson	Joseph & Pollie Burch
21865*	Keller, Harry	TN	1873		William Manuel	Ellan Clay	George & Matilda Manuel	Henry & Charlotte Clay
21944*	Kelley, Albert	TN	1825	Daisy Kelley	Steave Kelley	Jincy Colvin		Aubny & Fanny White
8560	Kelley, Cora	NC	1868	John Kelley	Elisha Davis	Johanah Spencer		Solomon & Nella Spencer
20518	Kelley, Jane	TN	1855	Edward Kelley	Ned Osburn	Jane Partrage		Nancy Partrage
11290	Kelley, Jasper	TN	1866	Laura Kelley	James Kelley	Charlotta Evans	Wm & Nancy Kelley	Meeley Evans
8559	Kelley, John	NC	1863	Cora Kelley	Peter Kelley	Margrey Hash	William & Jane Kelley	
11289	Kelley, Leander	TN	1864	Sabria Kelley	James Kelley	Charlotta Evans	Wm & Nancy Kelley	Meeley Evans
18647*	Kelley, Mary	NC	1861		Lum Kelley	Mary Winfrey	Jefferson & Nancy Kelley	
20357	Kellogg, Edward	TN	1859	Lulla Kellogg	Isom Kellogg	Harriet Woodliff	Edward & Hannah Kellogg	Old Rock & Cela Woodliff
15512	Kellogg, Lizzie	GA	1852	Edward Kellogg	David Daniel	Elizabeth Allen		Hugh & Francis Allen
18402	Kellum, John	FL	54yrs	Minera Kellum	E.H. Kellum	Caroline Weatherford		John & Martha Weatherford
22469	Kelly, Alexander	IN	1847	none	Anderson Kelly	Betsey Jacobs	John & Nancy Kelly	John Jacobs
9519	Kelly, Lola	TN	1882	V L Kelly	C.N. Ledford	Eliza Alexander	Ealbert & Eliza Ledford	
13198	Kelly, Margret	TX	1858	Jacob Kelly	John Everett	Elizabeth Barger	George & Easter Everett	Robert & Ellen Barger
14909	Kelly, Narcissus	GA	1858		R T Kelly	Frances Combs	Richard & Mahala Kelly	Edmund & Martha Harp
18784	Kelly, Sabra	OK	1836	Andrew Kelly	David England	Susanna Fields		Santie Fields
15536*	Kemp, Green	GA	1854	Sylvia Kemp	Isaac Avery	Susan Kemp Mausel	Green & Sarah McConnell	Sam & Lena Mausel
15535*	Kemp, Minnie	GA	1885		Jim Kemp	Savannah McConnell	Frank Kincaid & Fannie Gregory	Peter & Mary Bryant
7229	Kendrick, Ruie	TX	1873	John Kendrick	Richard Davis	Martha Holcomb		W J Holcomb & Louisa Berry
18978	Kenedy, Martha	MO	1876	J.A. Kenedy	Sidney Ford	Cynthia Williams	Elijah & Martha Ford	Harden & Jane Williams
22228	Kennedy, Estella	CO	1901	none	John Kennedy	Etta Cordill	John & Sarah Kennedy	Thomas & Sallie Cordill
22227	Kennedy, Etta	CO	1881	John Kennedy	Thomas Cordill	Sallie Baker	Rufus & Nancy Cordill	Seth & Lucy Baker
7226	Kennedy, Lucinda	KS	1860	W T Kennedy	Joseph Allen	Margaret Logan	Joseph & Kate Allen	Wm & Matilda Logan
22226	Kennedy, Mandella	CO	1901	none	John Kennedy	Etta Cordill	John & Sarah Kennedy	Thomas & Sallie Cordill
18191	Kennedy, Mary	TN	1867	Ambrose Kennedy	Thomas Carter	Amandy Norton	Fred & Peggie Carter	
19148*	Kennemore, Adaline	GA	1847	Howard Kennemore		Ezzebella Wood		Captain Dan & Jennie
13518	Kennemur, Amanda	GA	1870	J K Kennemur	Stephen Kirby	Mary Mann	Richard Kirby & Amy Muse	John & Malinda Mann
15057	Kennicott, Alice	IL	1874		Flint Kennicott	Agnes Bramnon		Wm & Susan Bramnon

15058	Kennicott, Grace	IL	1884		Flint Kennicott	Agnes Bramnon		Wm & Susan Bramnon
15056	Kennicott, Harold	IL	1886		Flint Kennicott	Agnes Bramnon		Wm & Susan Bramnon
14230 *	Kenon, Lewis	GA	1857	Florence Kenon	Brown Kenon	Phoebe Kenon		Archaluke -Georgia Angel
14229 *	Kenon, Michael	GA	1859	Nancy Kenon	Brown Kenon	Phoebe Kenon		Archaluke -Georgia Angel
2655	Kephart, Andrew	NC	1883	none	James Kephart	Dorcus Dockery	Andy & Dorcus Kephart	A J & Martha Dockery
2252	Kephart, Dorcus	NC	1858	James Kephart	A J Dockery	Martha McLoud	James & Bitha Dockery	Harvie & Sallie McLoud
2430	Kephart, Jacob	NC	1880	Mollie Kephart	J F Kephart	Dorcus Dockery	A & Dorcus Kephart	A J & Marthy Dockery
16195	Kerby, Martha	AL		James Kerby	Ebeneyer Martin	Marinda Fowler	Luster & Creacy Martin	John Fowler
22059 *	Kernl, Katie	OK	1837	widow	John Vann	Harrett Vann		
4659	Kerr, Martha	TN	1869	Henry Kerr	James Ray	Polly Hildebrand		John & Nicey Hildebrand
19629	Kersey, Malinda	IN	57yrs	John Kersey	Mathew Morgen	Nancy Bass		Joseph & Jenny Bass
1432	Ketcher, John	OK	1877	Ruth Ketcher	John Ketcher	Margaret Chambers	Big & Sallie Te-cah-ne-ye-skee	James & Patsy Chambers
19924	Key, Abby	NC	1887	Deaman Key	John Dennis	Mary Wamble	Arthur & Elizabeth Dennis	
6083	Key, Allen	GA	1875	Fannie Key	Alpheus Key	Minerva Hembree	William Key	Reubin Hembree
6079	Key, Enoch	GA	1881		Alpheus Key	Minerva Hembree	William Key	Reubin Emery & Sarah Lard
3939	Key, Fanie	GA	1879	A D Key	Ells Burnett	Lucy Sisson		James & Barb Sisson
6081	Key, Henry	GA	1883		Alpheus Key	Minerva Hembree	William Key	Reubin Emery
6086	Key, Mary	GA	1867		Alpheus Key	Minerva Hembree	William Key	Reubin Emery
6078	Key, Minerva	GA	1845	Alpheus Key	Reubin Emery	Sarah Lard	Nancy Emery	Curtis & Betsie Lard
6087	Key, Pinkney	GA	1877		Alpheus Key	Minerva Hembree	William Key	Reubin Emery
3937	Key, Polly	GA	1875	H R Key	Ells Burnett	Lucy Sisson		James & Barb Sisson
22771	Keyes, Alice	OK	1888		Frank Keyes	Malinda Moore	Ely Keyes	Julia Brown
5702	Keys, Amanda	OK		Richard Keys				
15003	Keys, Dora	OK	1882		George Keys	Alice Sturm	Polly Noon	J J Sturm
8973	Keys, Dudley (decd)	OK	1872	Manda Keys	James Keys	Mary Smith	Samuel & Mary Keys	William & Ollie Smith
3932 *	Keys, Frank	OK	44yrs	Lourena Keys	Eli Keys	Junia Page		Tom & Lucinda Page
19820	Keys, Mary	GA	1879		James Cook	Laura Cantrell	Richard & Sarah Cook	
22405	Keys, Mary	GA	1846	widow	George Stuman	Malinda Voils	Nat & Nancy Stuman	James & Ruthie Voils

5703	Keys, Samuel	OK	1855	none	Richard Keys	Amanda Walker	Isaac & Elizabeth Keys	Samuel & Amelia Walker
3176	Keys, Sarah	OK	1854	Paul Fornburg	Richard Keys	Mary Hays	Samuel & Mary Keys	Charles & Ann Hays
19149*	Keyton, Fanney	GA	1865	Mayson Keyton	Miles Favors	Julia ?ack	Mary Toles	
19065	Kiger, Mary	NC	1874	Henry Kiger	Lewis Bowen	Elvira Scott	Harrison & Elizabeth Bowen	Henry & Mary Scott
5187	Kilby, Celia	VA	1830	W G Kilby	Samuel Pennington	Elisabeth Anderson	Andrew & Hattie Pennington	
21474	Kilcrease, Lena	TX	1880	Thomas Kilcrease	Charles Graham	Francis Adkison		
19676	Killgore, Abe	TN	1834	Rebeca Killgore	John Killgore	Elizabeth Copeland	Stephen & Rebecca Killgore	James Copeland
13869	Killgore, Evaline	GA	1847	Abner Killgore	Nicholas Leatherwood	Caroline Dodson	Samuel & Elizabeth Leatherwood	
18401	Killiam, Mrs. C.M.	AL	85yrs	Esau Killiam	John Weatherford	Martha Dyer	Chas Weatherford & Sheley McGilroy	Mary Dyer
4739	Killian, James	NC	1883	Sarah Killian	Benjamin Killian	Sarah McDonald	Daniel Killian	James & Minna McDonald
12281	Killian, Melissa	NC	1841	Ben Killian (decd)	James McDonald	Jemima Deyton	Anguish & Sarah McDonald	John & Sallie Deyton
4741	Killian, Sarah	NC	1841	Benjamin Killian	James McDonald	Minnie Deyton	Anguish & Sarah McDonald	John & Sallie Deyton
11368	Killingworth, Birtie	MO	1837	Lester Killingworth	James Doke	Jackey Harralson	Merritt & Mary Doke	Vince & Martha Harralson
18381	Killpatrick, Cora	AL	17yrs	E.K. Killpatrick	John Boone	Vicie Moniac	John Boone Sr.	Sam & Susan Moniac
18561*	Kimber, Alexander	NC	1863	Bettie Kimber	Live Kimber	Emeline Pearson	Matt Harding	Dollie Golding
18560*	Kimber, Frederick	NC	1853	Laura Kimber	Live Kimber	Emeline Pearson	Matt Harding	Dollie Golding
18011*	Kimbro, Laura	NC	1862	Fred Kimbro	David Williams	Phillis Williams		Anthony & Susan Hayes
21189	Kimmons, Charlie	KS	1892	none	James Kimmons	Jane Mondy	Jack & Alcie Downing	John & Mahala Mandy
18791	Kimmons, Jane	KS	1871	James Kimmons	John Mondy	Mahala Corbett	Samuel & Bettie Mondy	Wm & Mary Corbett
21190	Kimmons, Mamie	KS	1897	none	James Kimmons	Jane Mondy	John & Mahaly Mondy	Jack & Alcie Downing
14861	Kincaid, Charlie & Dolly	GA	20yrs 17yrs		James Kincaid	Mourning Haygood	James & Amanda Kincaid	T G & Julia Haygood
10288	Kincaid, James	GA	1883	none	J S Kincaid	Susa Davenport	James & Martha Kincaid	Thos & Elizabet Davenport
11202	Kincaid, Robert	GA	1874	B. Kincaid	Jerry Kincaid	Susan Davenport	James & Martha Kincaid	Thos & Elizabeth Davenport
12517 ½	Kincaid, William	GA	1878	Maud Kincaid	Jerry Kincaid	Susan Davenport	James & Martha Kincaid	Thos & Elizabeth Davenport
3110	Kinerd Jr., Jacob	MS	1881	Laura Kinerd	Jacob Kinerd	Martha Hobgood		Charles & Martha Hobgood
3109	Kinerd, Charley	MS	1879	Alma Kinerd	Jacob Kinerd	Martha Hobgood		Charles & Martha Hobgood
3093	Kinerd, John	MS	1876	Lelia Kinerd	Jacob Kinerd	Martha Hobgood		Charles & Martha Hobgood
3108	Kinerd, Martha	MS	1854	Jacob Kinerd	Charles Hobgood	Martha Lowe		Thomas & Annie Lowe
3111	Kinerd, Willard	MS	1872	Lizzie Kinerd	Jacob Kinerd	Martha Hobgood		Charles & Martha Hobgood

18267	King, Alice	GA	1867	L.L. King	John Cook	Mary Ragan	James & Louvica Cook	
20841	King, Cornelius	GA	1861	Nina King	George King Sr.	Phylis Williams		
20142 *	King, Emily	NC		Isaac King	London Gaither	Jenie Holmes	Dave & Vinee Pearson	Joe & Celia Holmes
1435	King, Francis	MO	1886	Sarah King	Johnson King	Mary Ridge	William King	William Ridge
16476	King, George et al	GA	16yrs		Thomas King	Louisa Bettes	John King	Leroy Bettes
6016	King, Henry	NC	1881	Ellen King	Nathaniel King	Rachel Cearley	Mary King	Newton Cearley
9033	King, Lawrence	GA	1884		Nathiel King	Rachel Cearly	George & Mary King	Newton Cearly
8817	King, Morgan	GA		Salena King	George King	Mary Gray	John & Elisabeth King	Samuel Gray & Pollie Laudermilk
6331	King, Mrs Charles	AL	1863	Charlels King	Joseph Shims	Mary Wheaden	Joseph & Rosanna Shoms	James & Mary Wheaden
9032	King, Nathaniel	GA	1887		George King	Mary Rider	John & Bettie King	Guy Rider & Polly Price
8819	King, Silas	GA		Salena King	George King	Mary Gray	John & Elisabeth King	Samuel Gray & Pollie Laudermilk
21602	Kingsbury, Edmond	NC	1844	Mary Kingsbury	John Kingsbury	Eliza Chapman	John & Sarah Kingsbury	Wm & Elizabeth Chapman
17831 *	Kinnemore, Howard	GA	1836		Bymun Kinnemore	Mary Baldwin		
20223 *	Kinney, Adaline	IN	1853		James Kane	Mary White		Dangerfield & Charlotte White
14007	Kinsey, Eddie	GA	1884	Lillie Kinsey	Felix Kinsey	Annie Gunter	James & Maney Kinsey	Levi & Lisa Gunter
14013	Kinsey, Felix	GA	1862	Annie Kinsey	James Kinsey	Nancy Loggins	Joseph & Maney Kinsey	James & Dicie Loggins
14033	Kinsey, Mat	GA	1864	Lizzie Kinsey	Mat Kinsey	Nancy Loggins	Joseph & Nancy Kinsey	James & Dicie Loggins
14011	Kinsey, Nancy	GA	1842	James Kinsey	James Loggins	Dicie East	Sam & Sallie Loggins	Stephens East
17193	Kinsey, Rebecca	GA	1848	John Kinsey	William Smith	Sarah Sluder	Henry & Nancy Smith	Wm & Labora Sluder
14008	Kinsey, William	GA	1863	Nannie Kinsey	James Kinsey	Nancy Loggins	Joseph & Maney Kinsey	James & Dicie Loggins
20312	Kinsley, Bertha	MO	1886	William Kinsley	James Herrell	Allice Douglas	Emerson & Clarisa Herrell	John & Eliza Douglas
7230	Kinsley, Mattie	OK	1871	William Kinsley	Walter Bays	Frances Robinson	Joseph & Carrie Bays	Wm & Ellen Robinson
12377	Kinyoun, Sarah	NC	1843	Lemuel Kinyoun	William Hartgrave	Ann Poindexter	James & Nancy Hartgrave	Robt & Miriam Poindexter
9192	Kiper, Nancy	OK	1852	B.H. Kiper	Luke Wood	Mary Thornton		Nancy Poe
10112	Kirby, Florence	WV	1887	Rufus Kirby	B U Morgan	Elizabeth Smith	Jonathan & M E Morgan	David & Lydia Smith
19655 *	Kirby, Jim	TN	1857			Lucy Kirby		John & Lucy Waters
19656	Kirby, John	TN	1855	Kate Kirby	John Waterlizard	Nancy		
18034	Kirby, Mary	TN	1859	Wm Kirby	John King	Mary Marler	Wm & Mary King	Alex & Mary Marler
12983 *	Kirk, Amanda	GA	1875	John Kirk	Pressley Hembree	Amanda Howell		Caleb & Lucy Howell
20631 *	Kirk, Calvin	TN	1834	Susan Kirk	Jeff Kirk	Mary Fields	John Kirk	

14156	Kirk, Martha	NC	60yrs	James Kirk	Thomas Poindexter	Amelia Dull	Wm & Bettie Poindexter	
20445*	Kirk, Susan	TN	1847	Calvin Kirk	Ezekial Piner	Tennie Etherage		Jeffrey & Clora Church
19100	Kirkes, Albert	OK	1885	Mira Kirkes	Thomas Kirkes	Mary Trenary	R.M. & Martha Kirkes	Wm Trenary & Margret Swager
19091	Kirkes, Lemuel	OK	1882	Sarah Kirkes	Thomas Kirkes	Mary Trenary	Robert & Martha Kirkes	Wm & Margrite Trenary
17157	Kirkes, Thomas	TX	1861	Mary Kirkes	Robert Kirkes	Martha Lay	Curtis	
18268	Kirkham, Alonzo	GA	1849	Mary Kirkham	Henry Kirkham	Martha Brown	Robert & Elizabeth Kirkham	
18269	Kirkham, Grover	GA	1892		Alonzo Kirkham	Mary Quarles	Henry & Martha Kirkham	
18270	Kirkham, Walter	TN	1881	Minnie Kirkham	Alonzo Kirkham	Mary Quarles	Henry & Martha Kirkham	
8597	Kirkland, Andy	TN	1851	Marth Kirkland	Ben Kirkland	Caroline Kirkland	Jack Kirkland & Powhattan's daughter	Jim Kirkland & Sussie Buston
18828	Kirkland, Callie	TN	21yrs	John Kirkland	Levi Duckett	Polly Underwood	Wm & Elizabeth Duckett	Joel & Sency Underwood
18825	Kirkland, Caroline	TN	1836		James Kirkland	Josie Belcher	James & Susan Kirkland	Jacob & Clary Belcher
18827	Kirkland, James	TN	1844	Sarah Kirkland	James Kirkland	Josie Belcher	James & Susan Kirkland	Jacob & Clary Belcher
18826	Kirkland, Martha	TN	1840		James Kirkland	Josie Belcher	James & Susan Kirkland	Jacob & Clary Belcher
18829	Kirkland, Mattie	TN	1884		Ruphis Kirkland	Mary Danly	Jess & Bettie Kirkland	Wm & Adry Danly
18824	Kirkland, Mosuria	TN	1851		James Kirkland	Josie Belcher	James & Susan Kirkland	Jacob & Clary Belcher
18368	Kirkland, Robert	TN	1878		Ruphis Kirkland	Mary Donley	Jess & Bettie Kirkland	Wm & Arbry Donley
14689	Kirkman, Martha	NC	1878	Rores Kirkman	John Poindexter	Nancy Allen	Thos & Amelia Poindexter	James & Rebecca Allen
11631	Kirksey, Fanney	AL		J W Kirksey	Louis Tyner	Mary Johnson	Reuben & Biddie Tyner	
20842	Kirkwood, Sarah	GA	1876	J.D. Kirkwood	Ebenezer Barrett	Haley Evans		Robert & Sallie Evans
6409	Kiser, Lola	WV	1879	Louis Kiser	James Osburn	Ellen Dorsey	Solomon & Patsy Osburn	James & Margaret Dorsey
19925	Kiser, Loranzy	NC	1862		Nicholas Kiser	Catherine Kiser		Wm & Betsey Kiser
19923	Kiser, Mike	NC	1863	Elsie Kiser	Nicholas Kiser	Catherine Kiser		Wm & Elizabeth Kiser
18229	Kiser, Mollie	GA		D.J. Kiser	Alex Jeffres	Margaret Goins	Jerry & Sarah Jeffres	Smith Goins
19932	Kiser, Naoma et al	NC		Martha Kiser	Nicholas Kiser	Catherine Kiser		Billy Bennett
19931	Kiser, Oliver	NC	1853	Temperance Kiser	William Kiser	Elizabeth Hooker	Philip & Peggy Kiser	Sam Hooker
19930	Kiser, Philip	NC	1862		Nicholas Kiser	Catherine Kiser	William Kiser	Betsy Hooker
19933	Kiser, Willie	NC	1884		Phillip Kiser	Martha Bennett	Nicholas & Catherine Kiser	Betsy
20604	Kitsmiller, Alexander	TN	1835		Jonas Devault	Jennie Reece		Peter & Easter
8279	Klaus, Robert Sr	OK	1839	Bettie Klaus		Polly Sanders		
21438	Knapp, Fannie	AR	1863	Blueford Knapp	Watson Crawford	Margaret Starr		Joshua Starr
13914*	Knox, Albert et al	GA	1888 1900		P.K. Knox	Alice Rucker	Albert Knox	Minerva Terrell

13771*	Knox, Alice	GA	1859	P.K. Knox	Alfred Rucker	Rose Smith	Pleas Nails	
13912	Knox, Mathew	GA		Lovey Knox	P.K. Knox	Alice Rucker	Albert Knox & Minerva Terrell	Alfred Rucker & Rose Smith
13907*	Knox, Pierce	GA	1853	Alice Knox	Albert Knox	Minerva Terrell		Frank & Jenne Terrell
16197	Knox, William	OK		A. Knox	John Knox	Amanda ?		
22052	Knuckles, Calvin	TN	1855	Luthena Knuckles	Obidiah Knuckles	Susan Johns		Yarlton & Eliza Johns
20972*	Kolb, John	AL	1861	Julia Kolb	Nelson Kolb	Harriet Ussery	Paulina Wheeler	Jesse & Jane Lay
18837	Koons, Mary	KS	1872	Adam Koons	Henry Neff	Hannah Hammonds		Martin Hammonds & Mary Elmore
7227	Kurtz, Ada	OK	1869	Oscar Kurtz	Christopher Williams	Martha Blackburn	James Williams	James & Nancy Blackburn
9856	Kuykendall, Effie	GA	1885	none	Wm Kuykendall	Sarah Forrist	Van & Caroline Kuykendall	
7829	Kuykendall, Franklin	GA	1893		William Kuykendall	Sarah Forrist	Van & Caroline Kuykendall	Jack & Jane Forrist
10560	Kuykendall, Georgia	GA	1874	Robert Kuykendall	Robert Wheeler	Isabella Helton	Wm & Polly Wheeler	Clark & Mary Helton
9871	Kuykendall, Orville	GA	1880	none	William Kuykendall	Sarah Forrist	Van & Caroline Kuykendall	
10832	Kuykendall, Polly	OK	1880	Key Kuykendall	Thomas Avants	Francis Stovall	Peter Avants	Thomas Stovall
7828	Kuykendall, Raymond	GA	1890		William Kuykendall	Sarah Forrist	Van & Caroline Kuykendall	Jack & Jane Forrist
7830	Kuykendall, Tyson	GA	1899		William Kuykendall	Sarah Forrist	Van & Caroline Kuykendall	Jack & Jane Forrist
7827	Kuykendall, Wiley	GA	1888		William Kuykendall	Sarah Forrist	Van & Caroline Kuykendall	Jack & Jane Forrist
7826	Kuykendall, William	GA	1859	Sarah Kuykendall	Van Kuykendall	Caroline Newman	Thos & Tilda Kuykendall	James & Sarah Newman
21462	Lackey, Lennie	OK	1886	William Lackey	William Riggs	Samantha Wattman	James & Louisa Riggs	Johnson & Martha Wattman
21458	Lackey, William	OK	1883	Lennie Lackey	James Lackey	Mary Burnette	James & Sarah Lackey	John Burnette
15878	Ladd, Josephine	IL	1868		Lafayett Jones	Mary Eddings	Thompson & Lucinda Jones	James & Roda Eddings
18943	LaDue, Clark	TN	1871	Francis La Due	Marion Winters	Nancy Pate		Overton Pate
18338	Lafave, Victoria	MS	1846	Charles Lafave	Ambrose Vaughan	Josephine Reyes	Nelson & Nancy Vaughan	John & Sarah Reyes
7240	Laffoon, Annie	MO	1872	Robert Laffoon	Isaac Gwinn	Mary Smith	Wm & Hannah Gwinn	Benage & Elizabeth Smith
7243	Laidlow, Emma	OK	1878	Daniel Laidlow	William Rowell	Martha Terral	David Rowell & Mary Fountain	
15616	Lakey, Plutina	NC	1856	Abraham Lakey	Wm Poindexter	Lucinda Davis	Denson & Sarah Poindexter	Thos & Elizabeth Davis
21776	Lamb, Katie	FL	1877	A.M. Lamb	George Jackson	Harriet Samford	James & Julia Jackson	James & Virginia Samford
7237	Lamb, Mattie	MO	1885		James Clevenger	Mary Goldsbury	Benj & Margaret Clevenger	Wm & Mary Goldsbury
10245	Lambert, Annie	NC	1857	Peter Lambert	John Barnes	Mary Ponder		Jeremiah & Sallie Ponder
14745	Lambert, Johnnie	OK	1867	John Lambert	Richard Peak	Susan	James & Judy Peak	

#	Name	State	Year	Spouse	Father	Mother	Paternal Grandparents	Maternal Grandparents
57	Lambert, Missouri	TX	1867	George Lambert	Constantine Harris	Edna Lacey	Osborn & Sallie Harris	Wm & Martha Lacey
18397	Lambert, Mrs. Ellis	AL	19yrs	Ellis Lambert	Joseph Deaux	Adell Miles	Robert & Amelia Deaux	Francis & Nancy Miles
21321	Lamons, Cassia	AL	1882		Mike Lamons	Sarah Prince	James & Mary Lamons	David & Sarah Prince
21422	Lamons, Eligah	AL	1862		James Lamons	Mary Parham	Mardocia & Sarah Lamons	Elisha & Sarah Parham
21320	Lamons, Grover	AL	1886	Ella Lamons	Mike Lamons	Sarah Prince	James & Mary Lamons	David & Sarah Prince
19008	Lamons, Houston	AL	1877	Ola Samons	James Lamons	Mandy Willis	James & Mary Lamons	
19197	Lamons, James	AL	1846	Amanda Lamons	James Lamons	Mary Parham	Mordica Lamons	Elisha & Sarah Parham
21420	Lamons, John	AL	1843		James Lamons	Mary Parham		Elisha & Sarah Parham
21299	Lamons, Lula	AL	1892		Daniel Lamons	Delila Criscoe	James & Mary Lamons	G.W. & Emma Criscoe
21421	Lamons, Mary	AL	1845		James Lamons	Mary Parham		Elisha & Sarah Parham
21323	Lamons, Mike	AL	1853	Sarah Lamons	James Lamons	Mary Parham		Elisha & Sarah Parham
21423	Lamons, Nancy	AL	1860		James Lamons	Mary Parham		Elisha & Sarah Parham
21324	Lamons, Sarah	AL	1849		James Lamons	Mary Parham		Elisha & Sarah Parham
21322	Lamons, Simie	AL	1883	Fanny Lamons	Mike Lamons	Sarah Prince	James & Mary Lamons	David & Sarah Prince
21319	Lamons, William	AL	1888	Bell Lamons	Daniel Lamons	Delila Criscoe	James & Mary Lamons	George & Emma Criscoe
14334	Lamphere, Elizabeth	NE	1836	Orlando Lamphere	John Olinger	Cloe Bays	J. Olinger	Josiah & Letta Bays
17555	Lance, Julia	GA	1873	George Lance	J.F. Perdew	Julia Bird	Whit & Matilda Perdew	John Davis & Nancy Bird
4140	Lance, Margaret	GA	1838	R W Lance (decd)	Enoch Swain	Cintha Griffies	John & Nancy Swain	Isum & Nancy Griffies
20969	Landers, Claten	GA	1844	Mary Landers	Bonnie Landers	Louise Lanson		Jesse Lanson
14367	Landers, James	NC	1851	Marry Landers	John Landers	Vianah Roberts	Barney & Prudy Landers	
10092	Landers, Robert	GA	1857	L M Landers	George Landers	Elizabeth Ramsey	Louis Landers	Thomas Ramsey
18180	Landers, Thomas	GA	1877	Alice Landers	Robert Landers	L.M. Pastian	George & Betsey Landers	Henry & Nancy Pastian
22253*	Landrum, Arch	OK	1827	Winnie Landrum	Lewis Ratcliff	Winnie Ratcliff		Tom & Polly Ratcliff
22308*	Landrum, Caroline	OK	1832	none	Griffin Danels	Celia		Rachel Danels
4222	Landrum, Elizabeth	OK	1833	Benjamin Landrum	George Woodall	Ellen Moore		Charles & Colocha Moore
22350*	Landrum, George	OK	1845	none	Dave Landrum	Hannah Muskray		Charley & Lucy Muskrat
22254*	Landrum, James	OK	1840	Margaret Landrum	George Landrum	Peggie Muskrat	Jack Dixon & Charity Trunk	Lucy Muskrat
14166	Landrum, Janie	OK	1875	Pete Landrum	James Lee	Leizzie Gun	Walkie & Lucinda Lee	Wm Gun & Jenie Brown
22004*	Landrum, John	OK		Mary Landrum	George Landrum	Peggie Walker	Jack Dickson & Charity Landrum	Lucy Walker
22343*	Landrum, Sam	OK	1866	Ferriby Landrum	Dan Landrum	Jane Ross	Sam & Peggie McNair	
22272*	Landrum, Spencer	OK	1854	widower	Arch Landrum	Winnie Walker	Jesse Landrum & Winnie Ratcliff	Moses & Lucy Walker

22274 *	Landrum, Winnie	OK	1838	Arch Landrum	Moses Walker	Lucy Walker		
17710	Lane Lindsey	GA	1879	Minnie Lane	John Lane	Louizia Phillips		George & Mary Phillips
20365	Lane, Caroline	TN	1849	Samuel Lane	Russell Tallent	Mary Sanders	Jepha & Elizabeth Tallent	Elisabeth Sanders
2258	Lane, Charles	OK	1872	Elizabeth Lane	John Lane	Mary Avary	James & Narsicia Lane	Wm & Telitha Avary
19979	Lane, Emer	TN	1896		George Lane	Kitty McCarry	John & Louise Lane	Thomas & Lou McCarry
20002	Lane, Evelyn	TN	1901		George Lane	Kitty McCurry	John & Louisa Lane	Thomas & Lou McCurry
18271	Lane, Fannie	GA		Samuel Lane	Alonzo Kirkham	Mary Quarles	Henry & Martha Kirkham	
19978	Lane, George	TN	1871	Kitty Lane	John Lane	Louisa Phillips	Lindsey & Rebecca Lane	George & Mary Phillips
586	Lane, Hattie	TN	1864	James Lane	Jonos Lim	Derronias Kirkland	Thomas Lim & Betty Boston	Jim Kirkland & Susan Boston
2029	Lane, James	OK	1873	Bessie Lane	John Lane	Mary Avary	J & Narcissus Lane	C W & Telitha Avary
18733	Lane, Martha	NC	1874	Shale Lane	B. Richardson	Mary Stamper	Clayburn & Nancy Richardson	Johnathan & Matilda Stamper
744	Lane, Mary	OK	1852	J.C. Lane	William Avary	Telitha Thomas	Wm Duke & Jessie Avary	John & Ruth Thomes
12095	Lane, Mary	OK	1850	J E Lane	Urain Avary	Tilith Thomas	Jesse & Myra Avary	John & Rutha Thomas
20388	Lane, Nancy	TN	1890		Samuel Lane Sr.	Caroline Tallent	Wilson & Martha Lane	Russell & Mary Tallent
9078	Lane, Naoma	VA	1874	Lee Lane	James Blevins	Sarah Baker	George & Lydia Blevins	
17711	Lane, Samuel	GA	1884	Fannie Lane	John Lane	Louizia Phillips		George & Mary Phillips
20519	Lane, Samuel	TN	1888		Samuel Lane Sr.	Caroline Tallent	Wilson & Martha Lane	Russell & Mary Tallent
18272	Lane, Thelma	GA	1906		Samuel Lane	Fannie Kirkham	John & Louizia Lane	Alonzo & Mary Kirkham
13030	Lane, Urbana	VA	1866	James Lane	John Weaver	Celia Pennington		Samuel & Elizabeth Pennington
20200	Laney, Cordelia	OK	1855	Thos. Laney	Josiah Davidson	Elisabeth Gilstrap	Mary Davidson	
11102	Lang, John	OK	56yrs	Nancy Lang	John Lang	Polly Webber	John & Celia Lang	Sam Webber
17508	Langford, Caroline	OK	1880	G.M. Langford	John Brown	Loduska Tidwell		John & Lucrecia Tidwell
18771	Langford, Catherine	GA	1840		Chamblin	Hannah		
9546	Langford, Josephine	GA	1878	Richard Langford	David Dudley	Jenetta	David Dudley	Lovlis Love Dear
19803	Langford, Nancy	GA	1865	Sam Langford	Robert Etres	Mina Cordell		
353	Langley, Jane	OK	1842	Lack Langley	John Langley	Susan Dougherty		James & Mary Dougherty
21370	Langley, Lue Ann	TX	1873	William Langley	Andrew Brown	Easter Cobin	Burrell Brown	
20381 *	Langston, Bertha	TN	1881	Charles Langston	Albert Smith	Clarissa Hunter	David Pledger	James & Lucy Hunter
17830 *	Langston, Fannie	GA	1847	Jerry Langston	Pate Van	Miley Van	Davie & Sallie Van	
17829 *	Langston, Jerry	GA	1830	Fannie Langston	Pouch	Mahilda Pouch		

11333	Lanier, Birdie	GA	1897		Earnest Lanier	Sarah Brookshire		Tilman & Amelia Brookshire
11334	Lanier, Minnie	GA	1900		Earnest Lanier	Sarah Brookshire		Tilman & Amelia Brookshire
11335	Lanier, Ola	GA	1895		Earnest Lanier	Sarah Brookshire		Tilman & Amelia Brookshire
11328	Lanier, Robert	GA	1888		Earnest Lanier	Sarah Brookshire	Tilman & Liza Lanier	Tilman & Amelia Brookshire
11351	Lanier, Sarah	GA	1871	Earnest Lanier	Tilman Brookshire	Amelia Gates	James & Patsy Brookshire	
22583*	Lanier, William	TN	1854	Alice Lanier	Wade Foote	Lettie Mariney	Isaac Foote	Harry & Rosette Mariney
19482	Lankford, Alfred	TN	1867	Lanora Lankford	William Lankford	Rebeckey Morgan		George Morgan
12201	Lankford, Marion	TN	50yrs	Calline Lankford	William Lankford	Rebeckey Morgan		George Morgan
2578	Lanning, G W A	GA	1861	M E Lanning	Fidella Lanning	Mary Davenport		John & Elisabeth Davenport
2579	Lanning, J E F	GA	1862	Amy Lanning	Fidella Lanning	Mary Davenport		John & Elisabeth Davenport
2577	Lanning, Laura	GA	1884	none	Geo. W A Lanning	M E Foster	Fidella Lanning	
18010	Lantz, Pearl	OK	1886	Wm Lantz	Morgan Gilliam	Eliza Cooper	Morgan & Sarah Gilliam	John & Lizzie Cooper
15868*	Larkins, Mary	TN	1832	Sam Larkins	Philip Demoss	Dinah Dillshunty	Stephen & Hagar Dillshunty	
15595	Larrance, Mary	ID	1830	Jesse Larrance	Herman Allen	Ann Clark	John & Rachel Allen	Daniel & Mary Clark
7231	LaRue, Ellen	KS	1883	Joseph LaRue	J F Williams	Julia Hubbard		Bridget Conway
9030	LaRue, Martha	KS	1872	James LaRue	Johnson Wood	Martha Martin	Thompson Wood	Wm & Susan Martin
16814*	Lash, Willis	NC	1830	Vina Lash	Sam Shovell	Darkus Martin		
12226	Laskey, Plutina	NC	1856	A R Laskey	William Poindexter		Denson Poindexter	
16238	Lasley, Thomas	NM	55yrs	Elizabeth Lasley	George Lasley	Martha Clark	Bill & Polly Lasley	
18765	Laster, Mary	GA	1861	Thomas Laster	John Brown	Dicey Springfield	Esther Busbee	Mary Millbanks
18569	Lathem, Arthur & Joseph	GA	1892 1896		Samuel Lathem	Sarah Reynolds	Richard & Rillus Lathem	Rufus & Mary Reynolds
18568	Lathem, Atticus	GA	1883		Samuel Lathem	Sarah Reynolds		Rufus & Mary Reynolds
16305	Lathem, Ira	GA	1886		Sam Lathem	Sallie Randles	Richard & Rillur Lathem	Rufus Randles
15653	Lathem, Jennie	GA	1884		Jeff Lathem	Sufrona Bryant	George & Jane Lathem	Gethen & Sallie Bryant
15654	Lathem, Mitchel	GA	1867	Alma Lathem	Jeff Lathem	Sufrona Bryant	George & Jane Lathem	Getey & Sallie Bryant
5271	Lathem, Sufrona	GA	1846	J H Lathem	Geter Bryant	Sarrah Frost	John Bryant & Jincy Pinion	W W Frost & Ruth Turner
169	Latta, Allen	OK	1843	Emily Latta	George Latta	Peggy Wakea		Karsefeld
22664	Latta, George	OK	1867	Rebecca Latta	Allen Latta	Emily Colbert		
21380	Latta, John	OK	1876		James Latta	Mary Gilbert	John & Fannie Latta	Felix & Nancy Gilbert
21417	Latta, Mary	AR	1855	James Latta	John Latta	Francis Conner		

16431	Latta, Thomas	OK	1872		Jefferson Latta	Harriet Robinson		Emsi Robinson
18231 *	Lattimore, William	GA		Sallie Lattimore	Peter Lattimore	Julia Calaway	Benj Lattimore	William Wright
18204	Latty, Florence	TN	1878		Fleming Latty	Jane Jones	Emery & Nancy Latty	Wiley & Elizabeth Jones
18209	Latty, Jennette	TN	1867		Fleming Latty	Jane Jones	Emery & Nancy Latty	Wiley & Elizabeth Jones
19432	Latty, Rhoda	GA	1838	Alex Latty	Calvin Sanders	Sarah Milner	Elias Plummer	
18210	Latty, Thomas	TN	1857	Mary Latty	Fleming Latty	Jane Jones	Emery & Nancy Latty	Wiley & Elizabeth Jones
8220	Lauchner, Charles	OK	1839	Margaret Lauchner	Samuel Lauchner	Sally	Clemisthen Lauchner	
6727	Lauchner, William	OK	1863	Mary Lauchner	Charles Lauchner	Margaret Casto	Samuel & Sally Lauchner	Aaron & Sarah Casto
6864	Lawhorn, Levinia	KY	1879	Niles Lawhorn	Elijah Blevins	Rachel Felty	Armstrong & Cathrine Blevins	Nicholas & Susan Felty
8078	Lawing, Rene	TN	1856	W W Lawing	Joseph Murray	Hensley		
8397	Lawrence, Becky	OK	1852		William Adkins	Susan Cooper		Isaac & Malaha Cooper
14595	Lawrence, Bessie	GA	1890		Robert Lawrence	Eliza Brown		John & Loduska Brown
14594	Lawrence, Cinda	GA	1888		Robert Lawrence	Eliza Brown		John & Loduska Brown
14593	Lawrence, Eliza	GA	1868	Robert Lawrence	John Brown	Loduska Tidwell		John & Lucresy Tidwell
12018	Lawrence, Georgia	GA	1896		Robert Lawrence	Eliza Brown		John & Loduska Brown
14592	Lawrence, John	GA	1892		Robert Lawrence	Eliza Brown		John & Loduska Brown
17740 *	Lawrence, John T.	TN	1860		Charles Lawrence	Matilda Kirkland		John & Fannie Kirkland
12017	Lawrence, Josie	GA	1894		Robert Lawrence	Eliza Brown		John & Loduska Brown
21805	Lawrence, Katie	AL	1858	James Lawrence	John Hall	Martha Dunns	Elijah Hall	Acie Dunn
12016	Lawrence, Lizzie	GA	1902		Robert Lawrence	Eliza Brown		John & Loduska Brown
15886	Lawrence, Minnie	KS	1886	Gilbert Lawrence	John Johnston	Mary Kimberman	Thomas & Mary Johnston	George & Mary Kimberman
3963	Lawrence, Proctor	GA	1844	widower	Samuel Lawrence	Amanda Bolaw		
12019	Lawrence, Robert	GA	1899		Robert Lawrence	Eliza Brown		John & Loduska Brown
21784	Lawrence, Sallie	TX	1838	George Lawrence	Wyley Bryant	Sallie Brand	John & Elizabeth Bryant	Solomon & Penelope Brand
5433	Lawson, George	OR	1867	Sarah Lawson	W J K Lawson	Louisa Barnard	Drewey Lawson & Alia Dodson	Robert Barnard & Manila Carpenter
70	Lawson, Alvin	TN	1881	Mary Lawson	W. Lawson	Elizabeth Logan	Drewry Lawson	Alec Dodson
69	Lawson, Drewrey	TN	1878	Nancy Lawson	W. Lawson	Elizabeth Logan	Drewry Lawson	Alec Dodson
551	Lawson, Edwin	OK	1872	Nora Lawson	Wilkerson Lawson	Mahala Martin	Hennis & Jaley Lawson	Wm & Sarah Martin
67	Lawson, Elisha	TN	1873	Jane Lawson	W. Lawson	Elizabeth Logan	Drewy Lawson	Alec Dodson

68	Lawson, John	TN	1883	Vema Lawson	W. Lawson	Elizabeth Logan	Drewy Lawson	Alec Dodson
7232	Lawson, Lydia	OK	1847	Joshua Lawson	Isaac Jackson	Elizabeth Brock	Elza Jackson	
18321	Lawson, Mary	TN	1888		Wm Sutton	Ernestine Davis	Isham Sutton	Polly Barnard
66	Lawson, Robbin	TN	1831		Nathaniel Lawson	Leanah Morgan	Drewy Lawson	Hanah Potts
4	Lawson, William	TN	1842	Elizabeth Lawson	Drewry Lawson	Alcy Dotson	Drewry Lawson Sr.	
14474	Laxton, L.B.Z.	WV	1880	R. L. Laxton	John Cook	Margaret Stewart	Thos Cook & Rebecca Sizemore	George & Peggie Stewart
14458	Laxton, Nancy	WV	1883	Barnett Laxton	John Cook	Margret Stewart	Thos & Rebecca Cook	George & Peggie Stewart
19150	Lay, Arnetta	GA	1863	Henry Lay	Bob Daniel	Mary Cash		Billy Cash
22063	Layer, Luella	OK	1866	J.W. Layer	Thomas Pittenberger	Lizzie Hinote	John & Catherine Pittsenberger	
18904	Layman, Catherine	AR	1845	John Layman	William Morgan	Millie Brewer	Zacharier & Nancy Morgan	Abel & Mary Brewer
21062	Layman, David	MO	1881	Lola Layman	John Layman	Catherine Morgan	Henry & Mary Layman	William & Millie Morgan
18905	Layman, John	AR	1846	Catherine Layman	Henry Layman	Mary Birchfill	Christopher & Betsy Layman	Joseph & Susin Birchfill
19123	Layman, Robert	AR	1879	Rachel Layman	John Layman	Catherine Morgan	Henry & Mary Layman	Wm & Millie Morgan
19465	Laymon, William	AR	1893	Ella Laymon	John Layman	Catherine Morgan	Henry & Mary Layman	Wm & Millie Morgan
16281	Lazenby, Carlena	MO	1876	B F Lazenby	George Cannefax	Margret Haley	Joseph & Sarah Cannefax	George & Abbiegail Haley
18883	Lazenby, Celia	MO	1906		B.F. Lazenby	Celena Cunifax	John & Mary Lazenby	G.B. & Josephine Cunifax
16282	Lazenby, Lois	MO	1900		Benj Lazenby	Carlena Cannefax	John & Mary Lazenby	George & Josephine Cannefax
16283	Lazenby, Typhenia	MO	1898		Benj Lazenby	Carlena Cannefax	John & Mary Lazenby	George & Josephine Cannefax
17462	Leach, Peggie	OK	1867	Worster Leach	Money	Arly Money	Little Deer	
2550	Leadford Jr., Elbert	NC	36yrs	Miney Fair	Renold Leadford	Luvisa Robertson	Elbert Leadford	John Robertson
2553 1/2	Leadford, Elbert	NC		Leuvisa Leadford	Levviy Leadford	Jrutha Pitman	Peter Leadford	Tuckey
17387	Leadford, John	GA	1845		Soloman Leadford	Ann Sisson		Richard & Lucy Sisson
2553	Leadford, Julius	NC	1866	none	Elbert Leadford	Leuvisa Robinson	Levy Leadford	Jrutha Pitman
17388	Leadford, Ollie	GA	1878		John Leadford	Lizey Griffin	Solomon & Ann Leadford	
2551	Leadford, Pressfield	TN	1861	Mary Leadford	Elbert Leadford	Elisa Robinson	Levy Leadford	Jrutha Pitman
2552	Leadford, Richard	TN	1857	Adda Leadford	Elbert Leadford	Jrutha Robinson	Levy Leadford	Jrutha Pitman
17389	Leadford, Richard	GA	1844	Mary Leadford	Soloman Leadford	Ann Sisson		Richard & Lucy Sisson
18529	Leaisure, Tom	MO	1888	Mary Leaisure	Owen Leasure	Martha Hanlin	Gim & Sarah Leasure	James & Mary Hanlin
9345	Leary, Sarah	OK	1869	John Leary	Benjamin Courtney	Matilda Femder	Wm & Matilda Courtney	Daniel & Dicey Fender

6002	Leathers, Minnie	WA	1878	Onie Leathers	Pleasant Blackburn	Caroline Farris	Andrew & Francis Blackburn	
20496	Leatherwood, Nora	TN	1883	Robert Leatherwood	William Julian	Jane Osborne		Ned & Jane Osborne
20536	Lecroy, Hassel	GA			James Lecroy	Annie Pryor	John & Mattie Lecroy	Mitchel & Matilda Pryor
20420	Lecroy, John	GA	1846	Martha Lecroy	Thomas Lecroy	Susana Allen	John & Darcus Lecroy	Howard Allen
20537	Lecroy, Turie	GA			James Lecroy	Annie Pryor	John & Mattie Lecroy	Mitchel & Matilda Pryor
21622	Ledbetter, Andrew	TX	1879	Lela Ledbetter	Lewis Ledbetter	Nancy Jackson	Wm Ledbetter & Malinda Williams	Massey Jackson & Susan Johnson
22196	Ledbetter, Bunyun	TX		Juanita Ledbetter	Lewis Ledbetter	Nancy Jackson	William & Malinda Ledbetter	Mussey & Susan Jackson
6777	Ledbetter, Ezekial	GA	1865		Thomas Ledbetter	Nellie Thomas	Phoeba Ledbetter	Thos & Hannah Thomas
8205	Ledbetter, John	GA	1857	Mollie Ledbetter	Thos Ledbetter	Nellie Thomas	Phoeba Ledbetter	Thos & Hannah Thomas
22197	Ledbetter, Kirbin	TX		none	Lewis Ledbetter	Nancy Johnson	William & Malinda Ledbetter	Mussey & Susan Jackson
22199	Ledbetter, Lewis	TX	1840	widower	William Ledbetter	Malinda Williams	Johnson & Nancy Ledbetter	John & Rhoda Williams
22195	Ledbetter, Oswald	TX	1869	Kate Ledbetter	Lewis Ledbetter	Nancy Jackson	William & Malinda Ledbetter	Mussey & Susan Jackson
8208	Ledbetter, Van	GA	1853	decd	Thomas Ledbetter	Nellie Thomas	Phoeba Ledbetter	Thos & Hannah Thomas
6773	Ledbetter, William	GA	1855	Annie Ledbetter	Thomas Ledbetter	Nellie Thomas	Phoeba Ledbetter	Thos & Hannah Thomas
9776	Ledford, Andrew	GA	1855	Nancy Ledford	Silas Ledford	Eliza Boling		Thos Boling & Polly McDonald
18117	Ledford, Annie	NC	1880	Vincen Ledford	Milton Moss	Rebecca Maney	Jeff Moss & Margret Henderson	James Maney Sr & Barbara Barrett
9518	Ledford, Ceth	TN	1847	Eliza Ledford	Elbert Ledford	Eliza Robinson	Levy & Jurenia Ledford	
283	Ledford, Elizabette	NC	31yrs	James Ledford	R L Anderson	Mary Kitchens	Dock & Nancy Anderson	John & Elizabette Kitchens
9520	Ledford, James	NJ	1871	Cora Ledford	C.N. Ledford	Eliza Alexander	Ealbert & Eliza Ledford	Wm & Resine Alexander
18123	Ledford, Margarett	NC	40yrs	Robert Ledford	Milton Moss	Rebecca Maney	Jeff Moss & Margaret Henderson	James Maney Sr & Barbara Barrett
11381	Ledford, Nancy	NC	1866	William Ledford	Joseph Tucker	Rachel Bell	Allen Tucker	
310	Ledford, Ranie	NC	23yrs	Frank Ledford	George Owenby	Sarah Anderson	Minter & Elender Owenby	Lazrus & Nancy Anderson
13479	Ledford, Rebecca	NC	1887	Jason Ledford	Robert Anderson	Mary Kitchens	Lazrus & Nancy Anderson	John & Elizebeth Kitchens
286	Ledford, Rilatine	NC	41yrs	Thadius Ledford	James Anderson	Mary Smith	James & Nancy Anderson	Wm & Margaret Smith
298	Ledford, Sallie	NC	39yrs	Buchanan Ledford	Betis Maney	Louisa Henson	James Maney & Barbara Barrett	Henry Henson & Mariah Wood
293	Ledford, Samantha	NC	34yrs	Farmin Ledford	Elisha Smith	Amanda Anderson	Billy & Mary Smith	Lazrus & Nancy Anderson
11175	Ledford, Saphronia	OK	1857	widow	John Tidwell	Lucresia White	Young Deer & Mary Tidwell	
9521	Ledford, William	TN	1869	Nannie Ledford	Ceth Ledford	Eliza Alexander	Ealbert & Eliza Ledford	

9599	Ledford, William	TN	1838	Turnettia Ledford	Levi Ledford	Corruttia Pitman	Peter Ledford	
22186	Ledletter, Alvarado	TX	1868	Belle Ledletter	Lewis Ledletter	Nancy Jackson	William & Malinda Ledletter	Massey & Susan Jackson
2425	Lee, Ada	NC	1871	Ephram Lee	Faister	Vina Redman	Faister	Willis
9924	Lee, Dora	OK	24yrs	Thomas Lee	John Payne	Elisebeth Swindle	Elisha & Malisa Payne	
19769	Lee, Katie	TN		Denton Lee	Coon Grimes	Lila Hicks	Ed & Rachel Grimes	
20968*	Lee, Mahaley	AL	1812	Ennos Lee		Freby Taylor		
17351	Lee, Mary	SC	1887		Alex Frix	Mary Frix	Silus Frix & Millie Calhoun	E.B. Knox & Mary Wall
19207	Lee, Mary	GA	1860	Samuel Lee	James Wright	Fannie Lingerfelt	John & Mary Wright	David & Barbary Lingerfelt
7241	Lee, Maude	MO	1880	John Lee	Franlin Craven	Frances Morgan	John & Nancy Craven	Nathan & Anna Morgan
21052	Lee, Pearlee	AR	1863	Zackariah Lee	Ben Mathews	Nancy Throer	Throer & Betty Throer	
19792	Lee, Thomas	OK	1871	Leelah Lee	James Lee	Elizabeth	Nellie Lee	Lucinda Brown
21051	Lee, Zackoriah	AL	1849	Peora Lee	Robert Lee	Matilda Shadrock	Zackariah & Nancy Lee	Charles & Cassy Shadrock
15589*	Leech, Carroll	TN	1842	Caroline Leech	William Goren	Hannah Reeves		
19013	Leemon, Thomas	AL	1843	Mary Leemon	S.G. Leemons	Sarah Merritt	Wm Leemons	James Merritt
4884	Lefler, Nealey	VA	1868	Henry Lefler	John Hart	Polley Caldwell	George & Polley Hart	
10871	Legg, Bertha	WV	1885	George Legg	John Osburn	Louana Keith	Solomon & Martha Osburn	Guy & Rachel Keith
21135*	Legg, Chaney	GA		Fortune Legg	Leon Few	Bettie Lowrey		Lottie & Chaney Lowrey
21936*	Legg, Emaline	TN	1834		Jerry Henderson	Lyda Arnold	Attie Henderson	Atny & Adaline Kemp
10861	Legg, John	WV	38yrs	Fanny Legg	John Legg	Fannie Keith	J C & Mary Legg	Abraham & Sarah Keith
9040	Legg, Lillie	WV	1879	B B Legg	Moses Cline	Virginia Sizemore	Henry & Nancy Cline	George & Virginia Sizemore
20178	Lemley, Belle	GA	1885	Gus Lemley	N.C. Tankersley	Eliza Lowe	Sarah Tankersley	
11759	Lemmons, Martha	TN	1878		Joseph Everett	Caroline Jourdan	George & Easter Everett	Oyras & Susan Jordan
19559	Lenderman, Salina	TN	1852	Crocket Lenderman	George Payne	Nancy Hooper	John & Jane Payne	Eanis & Margaret Hooper
20971*	Lenoir, Charlotte	NC	1838	Noah Lenoir	Perry Miller	Charlotte Sudderth	Billie Brockett	
17315	Leress, Mary	WV	1875	Perry Leress	Charles Cook	Mary Cook	R.M. & Polly Cook	Thos & Rebecca Cook
17734	Leroy, Amos	TN	1863	Cyntha Leroy	A.J. Leroy	Safrona Wilkey	Nancy Leroy	Frank & Emeline Wilkey
17735	Leroy, Oliver	TN	1878	Sallie Leroy	A.J. Leroy	Safrona Wilkey	Nancy Leroy	Frank & Emeline Wilkey
5367	Lester, Mollie	VA	1878	Ben Lester	Allen Clark	Clara Welch	Allen & Clara Clark	James & Nancy Welch
5371	Lester, Rhoda	VA	1880	James Lester	Allen Clark	Clara Welch	Allen & Clara Clark	James & Nancy Welch
18364	Letheve, Cathran	TN	1878	John Letheve	Samuel Graves	Mahala Payne		

10831	Lewis, Albert	TX	1865	Nannie Lewis	John Lewis	Almeda Onsbey	John & Luan Lewis	Wm & Martha Onsbey
5998	Lewis, Amanda	MO	1881	Frank Lewis	Jesse Mayberry	Eliza Blackburn		
11556	Lewis, Ambros	NC	24yrs	Minnie Lewis	Levi Lewis	Eliza Roaten	James & Hiley Lewis	
9922	Lewis, Carrie	OK	26yrs	Monro Lewis	John Payne	Elisebeth Swindle	Elisha & Malisa Payne	
20606	Lewis, Charles	TN	1877	Sarah Lewis	Warner Lewis	Matilda Crawford	John & Temperance Lewis	
22581	Lewis, Charles	TN	1874	Sarah Lewis	Warner Lewis	Matilda Crawford	John & Temperance Lewis	
12830	Lewis, Hettie	OK	1879	Albert Lewis	Henry Walkabout	Mary Hendricks		John & Precia Hendricks
8467	Lewis, Jacob	VA	1878	Sarah Lewis	William Lewis	Nancy Lewis		Andrew & Biddy Lewis
5347	Lewis, James	OK	1853	Sarah Lewis	Lewis Lewis	Ge go nella		
8468	Lewis, James	VA	1852	Sarah Lewis	Andrew Lewis	Biddy Blevins		Wells & Biddy Blevins
8493	Lewis, James	LA	1869	Mary Lewis	William Lewis	Nancy Lewis		Andrew & Biddy Lewis
6399	Lewis, Jesse	MO	1889	none	Frank Lewis	Amanda Mayberry		Jesse & Eliza Mayberry
8545	Lewis, Jessee	VA	1868	Sarah Lewis		Mary Lewis		Andrew & Biddy Lewis
11558	Lewis, John	NC	21yrs	Eliza Lewis	Levi Lewis	Eliza Roaten	James & Hiley Lewis	
18832*	Lewis, Jonah	OK	65yrs	Elizabeth Lewis	Rambo	Peggy Stanwate	Mr. Stanwate	
11555	Lewis, Levi	NC	53yrs	Eliza Lewis	James Lewis	Hiley Pennington	Eafrom & Abbia Roark	
19528	Lewis, Luanna	TN	1875	George Lewis	Thomas Brazier	Lucy Kelly	Wm & Pauline Brazier	Charles & Lucy Kelly
1804	Lewis, Manda	VA	1885	none	Wm Lewis	Mary Caldwell		Nancy Caldwell
8592	Lewis, Margaret	LA	1857	Franklin Lewis	William Blevins	Nancy Davis	Armstrong & Catharine Blevins	
8466	Lewis, Martha	VA	1861	Solomon Lewis	Alexandria Huffman	Celia Blevins		Wells & Elisabeth Blevins
1806	Lewis, Mary	VA	1849	Wm Lewis		Nancy Caldwell		Catherine Caldwell
6881	Lewis, Mary	SC	1873	William Lewis	William Lewis	Nancy Lewis		Andrew & Biddy Lewis
8465	Lewis, Mary	VA	1876	Andrew Lewis	William Lewis	Nancy Lewis	A. J Lewis	Biddy Lewis
16069*	Lewis, Mattie	OK	1868	John Lewis	George Hubbard	Jane Reece	George Frost	Johnson Reece
11557	Lewis, Rufus	NC	23yrs		Levi Lewis	Eliza Roaten	James & Hiley Lewis	
9700	Lewis, Sam	OK		none	Josiah	Asoothtee		A-sooth-tee
8463	Lewis, Solomon	VA	1857	Martha Lewis	Andrew Lewis	Biddy Blevins		Wells & Elisbeth Blevins
8469	Lewis, Solomon Jr	VA	1867	Eliza Lewis	William Lewis	Nancy Lewis		Andrew & Biddy Lewis

17383	Lewis, Susan	GA	1879	Charley Lewis	H.M. Paris	Anna Townsend		Ezekiel Townsend
6383	Lewis, Walter	MO	1886	Myrtle Lewis	Frank Lewis	Amanda Mayberry		Jesse & Eliza Mayberry
1801	Lewis, William	VA	1883	Alcy Lewis	W.P. Lewis	Mary Caldwell		Nancy Caldwell
10830	Lewis, William	TX	1863	Lillie Lewis	John Lewis	Almeda Onsbey	John & Luan Lewis	Wm & Martha Onsbey
6397	Lewis, Ira	MO	1879		Frank Lewis	Amanda Mayberry		Jesse & Eliza Mayberry
20645	Light, Rhoda	TN	1859		James Light	Sarah Pickett	Mike Light	Allen & Margaret Pickett
22130*	Lightfoot, Myra	NC	1822		Moses Patterson	Caroline Ackis		Lettie Ackis
21430	Lile, Selia	TX		Thomas Lile	James Crosslin	Lucinda Graham		James & Martha Graham
21634	Lilley, Arra	AR	25yrs	William Lilley	William Ridling	Minerva Parrish	Henry & Margaret Ridling	Garland & Jane Parrish
1009	Lindholm, Albert	GA	1903		Godfrey Lindholm	Rhoda Pilgrim		
22471	Lindley, Alice	IN	1866	widow	Thomas Hammonds	Delina Brown	Mark & Kathrine Hammond	John Smothers
12881	Lindsay, William	GA	1858	Mary Lindsay	Whire Lindsay	Cyrenia Crow	George & Jane Lindsay	Abraham & Phoebie Crow
21960	Lindsey, Willis	TN	1905		Willis Lindsey	Sallie Lewis	Hosey & Morning Lindsey	Isaac & Miriam Lewis
21861	Lindsey, Effie	TN	1884		Willis Lindsey	Sallie Lewis	Hosea & Mourning Lindsey	Isaac & Miram Lewis
21984	Lindsey, Ida	TN	1894		Willis Lindsey	Sallie Lewis	Hosea & Morning Lindsey	Isaac & Miram Lewis
19601	Lindsey, John	GA	1881	Rebecka Lindsey	W.E. Lindsey	Mary Lindsey		Serena Lindsey
21982	Lindsey, Lillie	TN	1896		Willis Lindsey	Sallie Lewis	Hosea & Morning Lindsey	Isaac & Miram Lewis
19602	Lindsey, Massener et al	GA			White Lindsey	Serena Crow	Jane Lindsey	Abraham & Rhoda Crow
21872	Lindsey, Nannie	TN	1892		Willis Lindsey	Sallie Lewis	Hosea & Mourning Lindsey	Isaac & Miram Lewis
2747	Lindsey, Nettie	OK		Joseph Lindsey	Nathaniel Stewart	Peggie Winters		Jno & Jennie Winters
21983	Lindsey, Ollie	TN	1900		Willis Lindsey	Sallie Lewis	Hosea & Morning Lindsey	Isaac & Miram Lewis
21981	Lindsey, Roberta	TN	1902		Willis Lindsey	Sallie Lewis	Hosea & Morning Lindsey	Isaac & Miram Lewis
21920	Lindsey, Sallie	TN	1865	Willis Lindsey	Isaac Lewis	Miram Buckner	David & Nancy Lewis	L.B. & Susan Buckner
21961	Lindsey, Sallie	TN	1865	Willis Lindsey	Isaac Lewis	Miram Buckner	David & Nancy Lewis	L.B. & Susan Buckner
1433	Linn, Andy	TN	1846	Mary Linn	Jonas Linn	Demerisy Kirkin		
21789	Linn, Donna	AR	1866	W.G. Linn	William Haynes	Jane Thompson	Sarah Haynes	Wm & Estes Thompson
13277	Linn, Eliza	TN	1832	William Linn	James Kirkland	Jossie Belcher	James Kirkland	Susan Boston
18961	Linn, Eliza	TN	1855	James Linn	Ray Shaw	Becca Kirkland		James & Susan Kirkland
10443	Linton, Isabelle	OK		Albert Linton	Isaac Davison	Mary Conley		Elizabeth Dawson
9656	Lipe, Henry	AR	1876		Henry Lipe	Susan Rogers	Sandy & Elizabeth Lipe	Henry & Mariah Rogers

10361	Lipe, Lola	OK	1894	none	Henry Lipe	Susan Rogers	Sandy & Elizabeth Lipe	Henry & Mariah Rogers
13017	Lipe, Maggie	OK	1849		Richard Thompson	Elizabeth Thornton		
19493	Lisenby, Norma	MO	1881	Rome Lisenby	James Colter	Adinza Mallicoat	George & Mary Colter	Daniel Mallicoat & Malinda Whittenberg
19190	Lissard, Susie	OK	1848		Dextask	Luce Qute		
8820	Lister, Susan	AL	1877	Josua Lister	Dan Lister	Minerva Payne	Richard & Susan Taylor	John & Pollie Payne
21445	Litchfield, Joseph	OK	1846	Sarah Litchfield	Joseph Lirchfield	Jane Robison		
21448	Litchfield, Joseph	TX	1870	Donie Litchfield	Joseph Litchfield	Sarah Elder		
15586	Little, Alice	GA	1868	Robert Little	Hampton Watson	Hulda Chapman	Joseph & Polly Watson	Joseph & Rena Chapman
17472	Little, Diana	GA	1838	Henry Little	Abram Crow	Feebie Townsend		Edward & Annie Townsend
17331	Little, Eula	GA	24yrs	Elonzo Little	H. Williams	Cora Boheman	Kitt Williams	Lilie Boheman
7238	Little, Francis	OK		J F Little	William Rowell	Martha Terrell	David Rowell & Mary Fountain	Joseph & Matilda Terrell
19592	Little, Isaac	GA	1885	Katie Little	Robert Little	Alice Watson	Isaac & Jane Little	Hampton & Hulda Watson
13787*	Little, Jasper	GA	1871	Lula Little	Crawford Little	Pink Wyley		Simon & Diana Moore
8190	Little, Lettie	CO		William Little	James Reed	Amanda Reed	Abraham Reed	
8573	Little, Rachel	VA	1876	John Little	William Blevins	Nancy Davis	Armstrong & Catharine Blevins	
17729	Littrell, Virgie	TN	1878	Jack Littrell	W.G. Tidwell	Matilda Paine	W.G. Tidwell & Martha Shelton	Thos Paine & Miranda Watson
15322	Lively, Amanda	GA	1865		Wiliam Stuart	Sarah Baswell	Austin Stuart	
7475	Liver, Eliza	OK	1832	Chu-leo Liver	George Jackson	Jennie Sevier	Nelly Jackson	Jack & Susie Sevier
18630	Livingston, Myrtle	KS	1883	Jinks Livingston	Napoleon Holt	Sarah White	George & Sarah Holt	Susan White
7242	Llafet, Erie	MO	1876	W B Llafet	Frances Preston	Sallie Smith	Gerusha Preston	Benaja & Elizabeth Smith
12394	Lloyd, Alice	GA	1861		Jasper Lloyd	Lolitha Leiser	Thomas & Susan Lloyd	
19040	Lloyd, Charles	GA	1851	Rebecca Lloyd	Jasper Lloyd	Tolitha Leiser	Thomas & Susan Lloyd	
10448	Lloyd, George	GA	1852	Mary Lloyd	James Lloyd	Temperance Modday	Thos & Susan Lloyd	
12396	Lloyd, James	GA	1854		Jasper Lloyd	Lolitha Leiser	Thomas & Susan Lloyd	
12397	Lloyd, James	GA	1862	Georgia Lloyd	James Lloyd	Temperance Maddey	Thomas & Susan Lloyd	
12392	Lloyd, Martha	GA	1849		Joseph Lloyd	Lolitha Leiser	Thomas & Susan Lloyd	
5831	Lloyd, Mattie	AZ	1880	W W Lloyd	Joel Barber	Tillie Summery	Isaac & Joanna Barber	
6352	Lloyd, Mrs H.G.	AL	1885	H G Lloyd	Alex Boone	Minervy Moniac		David & Catherine Moniac
12393	Lloyd, Virginia	GA	1865		Jasper Lloyd	Lolitha Leiser	Thomas & Susan Lloyd	
12395	Lloyd, Whitley	GA	1856	Cleo Whitley	Jasper Lloyd	Lolitha Leiser	Thomas & Susan Lloyd	

10853	Lloyd, William	AZ	1867	Mattie Lloyd	George Lloyd	Mary Wanslee	Thomas & Susan Lloyd	Nathan & Izzie Wanslee
7233	Lockard, Ida	MO	1868		Frank Preston	Sallie Smith	Doritha Preston	Benaja & Elizabeth Smith
7779	Lockard, Jacob	MO	1860	none	Jacob Lockard	Nancy Elliott	John & Mahala Lockard	Jonas & Elizabeth Elliott
7235	Lockard, John	MO	1867	Ida Lockard	Jacob Lockard	Nancy Elliott	John & Mahala Lockard	Jonas & Elizabeth Elliott
7234	Lockard, Nancy	MO	1822	Joseph Lockard	Jonas Elliott	Elizabeth Young	Archie & Nancy Elliott	James & Rhoda Young
20812	Lockeby, Clara	GA			Arch Lockeby	Martha Elrod		Joseph & Jane Elrod
20811	Lockeby, Martha	GA	1881	Arch Lockeby	Joseph Elrod	Jane Dover		Wm & Alantha Dover
17828*	Lockett, Samuel	GA	1872	Mary Lockett	George Lockett	Columbia Johnson	George Lockett	
14476	Lockhart, Dora	AL	1882	M.N. Lockhart	Danual Sizemore	Rebecca Markham	Joel Sizemore & Catharine Webster	Anderson Markham & Mary Danels
17827	Locklear, Dora	GA	1876		Frank Davis	Trecy Till	Wm & Susan Davis	
18273	Locklear, Patsy	GA	1867	John Locklear	John Halburn	Elizabeth Brown		John & Sallie Brown
9571	Locklear, Wesley	FL	1850	Martha Locklear	James Locklear	Allice Ballard	Robert Locklear	Jennie Ballard
18022*	Locus, Dillon	IN	1854		Simon Locus	Elizabeth Pettiford		
18018*	Locus, John	IN	1849	Nancy Locus	Simon Locus	Elizbeth Rettiford		
18017*	Locus, Mary	IN	1860		Charley Russell	Rachel Russell		Wm & Matilda Tompson
22538*	Locust, Myrtle	IN	1885	none	John Locust	Angeline Hardiman	Moses Locust	John Hardiman
21741	Logan, Ellen	OK	1883	Lon Logan	Henry Ham	Emily Deen	Eber & Elizabeth Ham	Martin & Louisa Deen
19349	Logan, Jacob	GA	1869	Octavia Logan	Lige Logan	Litha Brickstaff	Henry & Eliza Logan	Glass & Litha Brickstaff
22078	Logan, Leonard	OK	1884	none	David Logan	Mary Akin		
22082	Logan, Lester	OK	1884	none	Dave Logan	Mary Akin	Alexander & Eliza Logan	Samuel Akin
22080	Logan, Lonie	OK	1880	Ellen Logan	Dave Logan	Mary Akin	Thomas & Eliza Logan	Samuel Akin
22085	Logan, Mary	OK	1861	D.E. Logan	Samuel Akin	Ann Newkirk	Edward & Mary Akin	Henry & Lucy Newkirk
19350	Logan, Octavia	GA	1880	Jacob Logan	Ben Allen	Jane Sexton	Jay & Fannie Allen	John & Polly Sexton
7239	Logan, William	WA	1853	none	William Logan	Matilda Thaxton	Zacharia & Margaret Logan	
14026	Loggins, Bill	GA	1877	Minnie Loggins	Mat Loggins	Matilda Smallwood	Wm & Nancy Loggins	Wilkerson & Sarah Smallwood
14023	Loggins, Bud	GA	1883	Ada Loggins	Mat Loggins	Matilda Smallwood	Wm & Nancy Loggins	Wilkerson & Sarah Smallwood
19750	Loggins, Callie	GA	1870		Tom Loggins	Rebecky Purdy	Martin & Laura Loggins	George & Hannah Purdy
18854	Loggins, Caroline	GA	1845	Samuel Loggins	Giddeon Hester	Louiza Helton	Benj & Milly Hester	Joseph & Lillie Helton
14027	Loggins, Columbus	GA	1858	Mandy Loggins	William Loggins	Nancy Sears	James & Dicie Loggins	Bishop & Margrete Sears
14017	Loggins, Dillard	GA	1879	Mamie Loggins	John Loggins	Martha Vandiver	Wm & Nancy Loggins	Sofonsky Crain
22736	Loggins, Duncan	GA	1886		John Loggins	Marthie Vanduer	Wm & Nancie Loggins	Gafowlie Crane

20014	Loggins, George	GA	1874	Mary Loggins	Tom Loggins	Rebecka Purdy	Carlin & Laira Loggins	George & Hannah Purdy
18565	Loggins, Homer	SC	28yrs	Haty Loggins	Kimrey Loggins	Mary Smallwood	Wm & Nancy Loggins	Wilkson & Sary Smallwood
19751	Loggins, Ida	GA	1876		Tom Loggins	Rebecky Purdy	Martin & Laura Loggins	George & Hannah Purdy
19753	Loggins, James	GA	1878		Tom Loggins	Rebecky Purdy	Martin & Laura Loggins	George & Hannah Purdy
18926	Loggins, Jane	GA	1844		Martin Loggins	Laura Loggins	Sam & Betsy Loggins	Jenny Loggins
14025	Loggins, Joe	GA	1879	Mandy Loggins	Mat Loggins	Matilda Smallwood	Wm & Nancy Loggins	Wilkerson & Sarah Smallwood
14031	Loggins, Joe	GA	1881	Lillie Loggins	Kinsey Loggins	Sarah Smallwood	William & Nancy Loggins	Wilkenson & Sarrah Smallwood
14015	Loggins, John	GA	1856	Martha Loggins	William Loggins	Nancy Sears	James & Dicie Loggins	Bishop & Margrete Sears
18927	Loggins, Laura	GA	1820	Martin Loggins		Jenny Loggins		John & Polly Loggins
14029	Loggins, Lester	GA	1883	Mary Loggins	Columbus Loggins	Mandy Farmer	Wm & Nancy Loggins	Reuben & Sarah Farmer
14030	Loggins, Lewis	GA	1885		Kinsey Loggins	Marry Smallwood	William & Nancy Loggins	Wilkenson & Sarrah Smallwood
14021	Loggins, Lit	GA	1885	Annie Loggins	Mat Loggins	Matilda Smallwood	Wm & Nancy Loggins	Wilkerson & Sarah Smallwood
14018	Loggins, Loney	GA	1884		John Loggins	Martha Vandiver	Wm & Nancy Loggins	Sofonsky Crain
19752	Loggins, Lonnie	GA	1887		Milton Loggins	Lizzie Hughes	Martin & Laura Loggins	Nathen & Viney Hughes
14014	Loggins, Mary	GA	1850	Kinsey Loggins	Urich Smallwood	Sarrah Hamilton	Elijah & Sarah Smallwood	Simpson & Susan Hamilton
14032	Loggins, Mat	GA	1853	Matilda Loggins	William Loggins	Nancy Sears	James & Dicie Loggins	Bishop & Margrete Sears
19749	Loggins, Milton	GA	1855	Lizzie Loggins	Martin Loggins	Laura Loggins	Sam Loggins	Jerry Loggins
14012	Loggins, Rebecca	GA	1838		James Loggins	Dicie East	Sam & Sallie Loggins	Stephens East
14028	Loggins, Sandford	GA	1872	Emma Loggins	Kinsey Loggins	Marry Smallwood	William & Nancy Loggins	Wilkenson & Sarrah Smallwood
18928	Loggins, Sarah	GA	1848		Martin Loggins	Laura Loggins	Sam & Betsy Loggins	Jenny Loggins
19212	Logier, Mattie	TN	1877	S.G. Logier	J.R. Sanders	Phoebe Pate	James & Polly Sanders	
21468	Logwood, Maud	TX	1885	Orville Logwood	Frank Crawford	Nannie Cole	Watson & Margaret Crawford	
22639	Lomas, John et al	MO	1890		John Lomas	Dicy Fender	Wm & Ellen Lomas	Michael & Martha Fender
17955	Lomax, Estella	AL	1883		Sidney Lomax	Rosetta Boone	Sidney & Matilda Lomax	John & Martha Boone
6325	Lomax, Flora	AL	21yrs	none	Hillman Lomax	Monica Keller	Sid & Matilda Lomax	Hank & Elisabeth Keller
6326	Lomax, Maggie	AL	24yrs	none	Hillman Lomax	Minnie Keller	Sidney & Matilda Lomax	Hank & Elisabeth Keller
3374	Lomax, Matilda	AL	1827	Sidney Lomax	Dixon Moniac	Elisabeth Ellet		
17957	Lomax, Mattie	AL	1880		Sidney Lomax	Rosetta Boone	Sidney & Matilda Lomax	John & Martha Boone
3338	Lomax, Sidney	AL	1859	Rhet Boon	Sidney Lomax	Matilda Moniac		Sam & Susan Moniac
3372	Lomax, Tillmon	AL	1861	Mincy Feller	Sidney Lomax	Matilda Moniac		Sam & Susan Moniac

3770	Lombard, Albert	OK	1846	Hester Lombard	Robert Lombard	Agga Gore	Joseph Lombard	Samuel & Peggy Gore
2582	Long Jr., Wiley	GA	1851	Mary Long	William Long	Mary Johnson	Josiah & Nancy Long	
2587	Long, Alfred	GA	1854	none	Wiley Long	Magdalena Lingafelt	Josiah & Nancy Long	
9223	Long, Amanda	OK	1875	Lemuel Long	James Murphy	Isabelle Grayham	David & Caroline Murphy	Wm & Nancy Grayham
3896	Long, Clarence	OK	1890	none	Ed Long	Laura Smith	Daniel & Mary Long	John & Julia Smith
3895	Long, Darlene	OK	1895	none	Ed Long	Laura Smith	Daniel & Mary Long	John & Julia Smith
2586	Long, David	TN	1863	Minurvy Long	William Long	Mary Johnson	Josiah & Nancy Long	
3898	Long, Dorene	OK	1901	none	Ed Long	Laura Smith	Daniel & Mary Long	John & Julia Smith
2436	Long, James	KS	1871	Sarah Long	William Long	Lucena Cook		Jacob & Delana Cook
19536	Long, James	TN	1869	Mamie Long	Cornelius Long	Luraney Shoemake		John & Mary Shoemake
1685	Long, Laura	OK	1874	Edward Long	John Smith	Julia Taylor	Pleasant & Priscilla Smith	Wiley & Rosamond Taylor
7244	Long, Lee	TX		J G Long	W P Parsley	Mattie Boatright		J S Boatright
2373	Long, Lucena	OK	1848	William Long decd	Jacob Cook	Delana Epperson		Asa & Leah Epperson
11935	Long, Margaret	TN	1857	John Long	Samuel Reece	Mary Turner		David & Betsy Turner
2590	Long, Mary	GA	1867	none		Rosey Long		Wiley & Magdaline Long
21245	Long, Mollie	AL	1857	W.L. Long	Jorden Gilley	Ann Hill	Wm & Matilda Gilley	Mount & Susie Hill
19097	Long, Nancy	NC	1882		Wiley Long	Magdaleni Lingemfelt	Josiah & Nancy Long	
2589	Long, Rosey	GA	1839	none	Wiley Long	Magdalina Lingafell	Josiah & Nancy Long	
4965	Long, Sarah	TN	1885	Arthur Long	James Clouts	Lucy Clouts		
2588	Long, Stephen	FL	1876		Joseph Long	Sarah Simmons	Annetta Long	Percilla & Cornel Simmons
3897	Long, Vance	OK	1893	none	Ed Long	Laura Smith	Daniel & Mary Long	John & Julia Smith
2398	Long, Wiley	GA	1817	Magdalena Long	Josiah Long	Nancy Harris	Nancy Bird	
20470	Longwith, James	GA	1884	Ada Longwith	John Longwith	Rosa Roper	William Longwith	Noah & Minerva Roper
20069	Longwith, Martha	TN	1855	J.S. Longwith	Frank McAlister	Elizabeth Goin	John & Margaret McAlister	Ed & Sallie Goin
2006	Looney, Etna	MO	1859	Benjamin Looney	James Eaves	Violitty Hambleton	Patrick & Polly Eaves	Elijah & Sarah Hambleton
22643	Looney, Martha	MO	1887	James Looney	William Miller	Ellen Sloan	W.G. Sr. & Mary Miller	A.C. & Mary Sloan
20280	Loop, Livie	OK	1877	Augustus Loop	Robert Sims	Margaret Kennedy	James & Mary Sims	John & Lucinda Kennedy

2421	Lorence, Eliza	GA	37yrs		John Brown	Lodista Tidwell		John Tidwell
10317	Lotherow, Elizabeth	NC	1881	Alex Lotherow	John Postell	Sarah Head	James & Malissa Postell	
5474	Loudermilk, Ella	NC	25yrs	none	Allen Loudermilk	Josephine Thomas	Jacob & Sarah Loudermilk	Thomas Green & Nancy Thomas
22909	Loudermilk, Harrison	AR	1874	Rena Loudermilk	James Loudermilk	Naoma Hampton	Garner & Nancy Loudermilk	George & Mary Hampton
22911	Loudermilk, Jesse	AR	1876	Ella Loudermilk	James Loudermilk	Naoma Hampton	Garner & Nancy Loudermilk	George & Mary Hampton
1770	Loudermilk, Josephine	NC	45yrs		Thomas Green	Nancy Thomas		Jinney Thomas
22914	Loudermilk, Lucinda	AR	1865	William Clark	James Loudermilk	Naoma Hampton	Garner & Nancy Loudermilk	George & Mary Hampton
5476	Loudermilk, Lula	NC		none	Allen Loudermilk	Josephine Thomas	Jacob & Sarah Loudermilk	
22907	Loudermilk, Nancy	AR	1872	John Clark	James Loudermilk	Naoma Hampton	Garner & Nancy Loudermilk	George & Mary Hampton
3581	Loudermilk, Stonewall	OK	1883	none	Lee Loudermilk	Cyntha Ragsdale		Isaac & Mary Ragsdale
22912	Loudermilk, William	AR	1867	Dona Loudermilk	James Loudermilk	Naoma Hampton	Garner & Nancy Loudermilk	George & Mary Hampton
20493	Louise, Catie	TN			Jacob Louise	Narcise Dagan	Jacob & Rebecca Louise	Frank & Jane Dagan
20366	Louise, David	TN			Jacob Louise	Narcise Dagan	Jacob & Rebecca Louise	Frank & Jane Dagan
20491	Louise, Emma	TN			Jacob Louise	Narcise Dagan	Jacob & Rebecca Louise	Frank & Jane Dagan
20367	Louise, Jacob	TN			Jacob Louise	Narcise Dagan	Jacob & Rebecca Louise	Frank & Jane Dagan
20492	Louise, Narcise	TN	1857	Jacob Louise	Franklin Dagnan	Jane Keef	Patrick & Judah Dagnan	John & Betsie Keef
20500	Louise, Nevve	TN			Jacob Louise	Narcise Dagan	Jacob & Rebecca Louise	Frank & Jane Dagan
20480	Louise, Philip	TN			Jacob Louise	Narcise Dagnan	Jack & Rebecca Louise	Frank & Jane Dagnan
16483 *	Love, Bettie	NC	49yrs	Samuel Love	William Bowen	Anna Evans		Benj & Lucy Evans
3739	Love, Rebeca	NC	1870	Wagoner Love	Solomon Ham	Mary Blevins	Solomon Sr & Mary Ham	Riley & Agnes Blevins
8692 *	Love, Rhoda	NC	1859	Pink Love	Washington Gibson	Peggy Carter	Ransom Welch & Rhoda Gibson	Thomas & Morning Carter
9753	Loveall Jessie	MO	1890	none	D D Loveall	Ann Sweaney		
5313	Loveall, Ann	MO	1847	D D Loveall	Levi Sweaney	Myra Blackard		
5933	Loveall, J M	MO	1868	Emma Loveall	Daniel Loveall	Ann Sweaney		Levi & Myra Sweaney
13592	Loveall, Schyler	OK	1870	Maggie Loveall	Daniel Loveall	Anna Sweaney		Levi & Myra Sweaney
9288	Lovelace, Calley	VA	1886	Wiley Lovelace	Joseph Hart	Jane More	Riley & Emily Hart	Wm & Isabella More
17980 *	Lovelady, Eliza	TN	1869	Wm Lovelady	Cornelius Austin	Martha		
14387	Loveless, Alice	AL	1864		John Stanford	Nancy Wylie	John Stanford & Margarete Blare	John Wylie & Nancy Nelson
14392	Loveless, Antie	AL	1893		Dock Loveless	Alice Stanford	Abner & Nancy Loveless	John Stanford & Nancy Wylie

20905	Loveless, Barton	AL	1852	Susan Loveless	Abner Loveless	Nancy Townsand	Barton Loveless	Ned Townsand & Anna Taylor
17367	Loveless, Benjamin	AL	1856	Martha Loveless	Abmes Loveless	Nancy Townsand	Barton Loveless	Ned Townsand & Anna Taylor
14386	Loveless, Dock	AL		Alice Loveless	Abner Loveless	Nancy Townsand	Barton Loveless	Ned Townsand & Anna Taylor
14388	Loveless, Florence	AL			Dock Loveless	Alice Loveless	Abner & Nancy Loveless	
2325	Loveless, James	CA	1882	none	James Loveless	Levarie Blackburn	James & Martha Loveless	John & Sarah Blackburn
22160	Loveless, Jay	AL	1855	Elizabeth Loveless	Abner Loveless	Nancy Townsand	Barton Loveless & Miss Johnson	Ned Townsend & Annie Taylor
12720	Loveless, John	MS	1863	Mary Loveless	Loveless	Nancy Townsend	Barton Loveless	Ned Townsend & Ann Taylor
17368	Loveless, Martha	AL	1856	Ben Loveless	Abner Loveless	Nancy Townsand	Barton Loveless	Ned & Anna Townsand
14391	Loveless, Nancy	AL	1830	Abner Loveless	Ned Townsend			
12721	Loveless, Oscar et al	MS	1891 etc.		J M Loveless	Mary Presley	Abner Loveless & Nancy Townsand	Jim Presley & Elizabeth Bozeman
20307	Loveless, Peter	OK	1866	Ida Loveless	Jonathan Loveless	Clarisa Scruggs		Louis Scruggs & Ann Parker
22161	Loveless, Robert	AL	1865	Nancy Loveless	Abner Loveless	Nancy	Barton Loveless	Ned Townsend & Annie Taylor
12898	Loveless, Sam	MS	1883	Ellen Loveless	J M Loveless	Mary Presley	Loveless & Nancy Townsand	Jim & Elizabeth Presley
2581	Lovell, Fannie	GA	1845	David Lovell	William Long	Mary Johnson	Josiah & Nancy Long	
17647	Lovell, James	MO	1849		Edward Lovell	Ruth Barr	James & Sally Lovell	John & Anna Barr
2580	Lovell, John	GA	1882	none	David Lovell	Fannie Long	George Lovell	William & Mary Long
17646	Lovell, Sarah	MO	1854		Edward Lovell	Ruth Barr	James & Sally Lovell	John & Anna Barr
17645	Lovell, Thomas	MO	1848		Edward Lovell	Ruth Barr	James & Sally Lovell	John & Anna Barr
22373	Lovill, Grover	NC	1884	none	W W Lovill	Martha Jones	James & Betty Lovill	Francis & Mary Jones
22371	Lovill, James	NC	1880	none	W.W. Lovill	Martha Jones	James & Betty Lovill	Francis & Mary Jones
22376	Lovill, Joseph	NC	1883	none	W W Lovill	Martha Jones	James & Bettie Lovill	Francis & Mary Jones
22370	Lovill, Walter	NC	1853	Martha Lovill	James Lovill	Bettie Franklin	James & Sally Lovill	Wiley & Mary Franklin
22372	Lovill, Wiley	NC	1878	none	W W Lovill	Martha Jones	James & Betty Lovill	Francis & Mary Jones
22374	Lovill, William	NC	1881	none	Walter Lovill	Martha Jones	James & Betty Lovill	Francis & Mary Jones
17339	Lovin, Harriet	NC	1877	Wm Lovin	T.J. Ball	Margrett Maney	Daniel Ball	Martin Maney
11476*	Loving, Burletta	WI	1856	Andrew Loving	Samuel Waldron	Elizabeth Revels	Mike & Polly Waldron	Macaga & Mornon Revels
688	Lovingood, Harriet	NC	1853	G. Lovingood	UNK	Sallie McDonald	UNK	Anguish & Sallie McDonald
5569	Lovingood, Mary	NC	1870	Andy Lovingood	James Davis	Lou McDonald	Reason & Sovilla Davis	James & Mima McDonald
10561	Lovingood, Nora	GA	1888	Elmo Lovingood	Joseph Rice	Emily Cole	Wm & Alester Rice	John & Betsy Cole
22835	Lovingood, Sarah	NC	1859	Samuel Lovingood	James Davis	Luvena McDaniel		James McDaniel

1545	Lowe Lillie	NC	1888	John Lowe	Henry Martin	Allie Morgan	Joseph & Adeline Martin	
19698	Lowe, Addie	TN	1888	Halbert Lowe	J. Curtis	Elizabeth Patrick	Joshua & Elizabeth Curtis	
13938	Lowe, Benjamin	NC	1887		Benjamin Lowe	Martha Hooks	Nelson & Martha Lowe	George & Martha Hooks
13940	Lowe, Benjamin	NC	1850	Martha Lowe	Nelson Lowe	Martha McDuffe	Thomas & Annie Lowe	Daniel & Rebecca McDuffe
13924	Lowe, John	NC	1861	Louisa Lowe	Nelson Lowe	Martha McDuffee	Thomas & Annie Lowe	
13939	Lowe, Joseph	NC	1886		John Lowe	Louisa Hancock	Nelson & Martha Lowe	
9764	Lowe, Rhoda	OK	47yrs	Robert Lowe	Allen Sizemore	Malinda Sizemore		Ephram Sizemore
20398	Lowe, Rosa	TN	1878	John Lowe	Peter Scalf	Sarah Keller	Peter & Mary Scalf	Samuel & Katie Keller
13932	Lowe, Walter	NC	1894		John Lowe	Louisa Hancock	Nelson & Martha Lowe	
16040	Lowen, Addie	OK	1867	Noah Lowen	Richard McDaniel	Victoria Pittman	Richard & Matilda McDaniel	
22586	Lower, Louise	AL	1863	Elijah Lower	Wm Huffsteeter	Lucinda Luttrell	John & Stacy Huffsteeter	Silas & Garduehire Luttrell
22346*	Lowers, John	OK	1854	none	Jerry Towers	Winnie Walker	Ben & Mellie Danels	
21534	Lowery, Dave	GA	1849		Charley Lowery	Mary Strickland		Joseph & Sallie Strickland
3783	Lowery, James	OK	1855	Betsey Lowery	Isom Lowery	Cynthia Clayton	Charlie & Ann Lowery	Joseph Clayton & Hannah Bradshaw
18409	Lowery, Mrs O.R.	AL	39yrs	O.R. Lowery	Benj Bryars	Lucretia Miles	Charles & Margaret Bryars	James & Ellen Miles
18410	Lowery, Mrs. A.M.	AL	47yrs	A.M. Lowery	Benj Bryars	Lucretia Miles	Charles & Margaret Bryars	James & Ellen Miles
3218	Lowery, Nancy	OK	1869	George Lowery	Isac Hunter	Athie Avants	Robert & Winnie Hunter	John Avants & Elisebeth Sharp
3785	Lowrey, Betsy	OK	1853	James Lowrey	William Manar	Sally Lowrey		James & Sally Lowrey
4782	Lowrey, Isom	AR	1852		Isom Lowrey	Cyntha Clayton	Charles & Eudora Lowrey	Joseph & Hanar Clayton
22087	Lowrey, James	OK	1876	Jane Lowrey	James Lowrey	Betsy Mainor	Isom & Cyntha Lowrey	William & Sally Mainor
17694	Lowrey, Liley	TN	1877	Russel Lowrey	Thomas Heatherly	Rebecca Thornton	James & Elizabeth Heatherly	
19289	Lowrey, Mary	NC	1863	Bry Lowrey	Henry Gasoway	Millie Roach		Jerry & Polly Roach
17686	Lowrey, Sarilda	TN	1856	Houston Lowrey	Thomas Heatherly	Rebecca Thornton	James & Elizabeth Heatherly	
22088	Lowrey, William	OK	1875	Matilda Lowrey	James Lowrey	Betsy Mainor	Isom & Cyntha Lowrey	William & Sally Malnor
10542	Loyd, Bessie	GA	1887		James Loyd	Georgia Reynolds	James & Temperance Loyd	
10541	Loyd, George	GA	1852	Mary Loyd	James Loyd	Temperance Madry	Thos & Susanna Loyd	
10540	Loyd, Harper	GA	1881		James Loyd	Georgia Reynolds	James & Temperance Loyd	
10539	Loyd, Homer	GA	1889		James Loyd	Georgia Reynolds	James & Temperance Loyd	
20306	Loyd, Ida	MO		Larry Loyd	John Edmonds	Eliza Herrell		Emerson & Clarissa Herrell
10537	Loyd, James	GA	1893		James Loyd	Georgia Reynolds	James & Temperance Loyd	

10538	Loyd, James	GA	1862	Georgia Loyd	James Loyd	Temperance Grady	Thos & Susanna Loyd	
11330	Loyd, Mary	GA			Thomas Loyd	Clara Archer	George & Mary Loyd	
10536	Loyd, Nora	GA	1884		James Loyd	Georgia Reynolds	James & Temperance Loyd	
10535	Loyd, Robert	GA	1872	Ida Loyd	Thomas Loyd	Susanna Matthews	Thos & Susanna Loyd	Lewis & Elizabeth Matthews
5899	Loyd, Sarah	NC	1880		Samuel Shelton	Nancy Metcalf	Esaw & Sarry Shelton	James & Lurena Metcalf
11329	Loyd, Thomas	GA	1874	Clara Loyd	George Loyd	Mary Ivey	James & Temperance Loyd	
19466	Loze, Shrelda	GA	1846	Henderson Loze	James Heatherly	Elizabeth Ervins	John Heatherly & Nancy Wilson	Walter Ervins & Rachel Richerson
22678	Lucas, Dan	OK	1847		William Lucas	Sarah Duncil	Richard & Fanny Lucas	Wm & Millie Duncil
22270	Lucas, John	OK	1840	Mary Lucas	William Lucas	Sarah Duncil	Richard & Fanny Lucas	Wm & Millie Duncil
17750	Luffman, Martha	TN	1845		Wm Mills	Eliza Cunagin		Mary Eaton
19045	Lumpkin, Albert	VA	1858	Jennie Lumpkin	Joseph Lumpkin	Susan Lloyd		Thomas & Susan Lloyd
19044	Lumpkin, J. Frank	GA	1864	Amanda Lumpkin	Joseph Lumpkin	Susan Lloyd		Thomas & Susan Lloyd
3021	Lumpkins, Laura	OK	1886	Frank Lumpkin	Reuben Moore	Catherine Cook	Joseph Moore	Thomas & Leah Barnes
8160	Lusk, Jane	WV	1858	Jackson Lusk	Edward Sizemore	Malinda Workman	George & Jane Sizemore	Joseph & Betsy Workman
18810	Lusty, Caraell	TX	1877	James Lusty	Henry Speer	Sarah Tekell		Niper & Eliza Tekell
22717	Luther, Nancy	OK			William Huse	Mary Wilkison	William Huse	Hariman Wilkison
7236	Lutts, James	OK	1857	Martha Lutts	John Lutts	Jane Weatherford	Adam & Mariah Lutts	Joel & Nancy Weatherford
8198	Lutts, John	AL	1855		Alex Lutts	Margaret		Joel Weatherford
4464	Lyle, James	VA		Nancy Lyle	George Lyle	Margaret Hart		John & Nancy Hart
4465	Lyle, John	VA		none	George Lyle	Margaret Hart		John & Nancy Hart
11268	Lyle, John	VA	1884		James Lyle	Nancy Love	George & Margaret Lyle	Ransom & Susan Love
20658*	Lynch, Caroline	TN	1858		Joseph	Zil[pha Shipley		Leah Shipley
22265*	Lynch, Charley	OK	1861	Ara Lynch	Simon Lynch	Nancy Downing	Griffin & Cely Daniels	Lizzy Beck
21486	Lynch, Clara	TX	1894	Charles Lynch	Benj Davis	Amanda Rimare	Martin Davis	Binion & Francis Rimare
22353*	Lynch, Daniel	OK	1872	Mary Lynch	Stephen Lynch	Peggie Christy	Henry & Judy Blackburn	Esseck
22344*	Lynch, Edie	OK	1845	Simon Lynch		Viny Lynch		
13523*	Lynch, Ellen	OK	1859	W.M. Lynch	Rutherford Beck	Tempy Beck	Joseph Beck	
20667*	Lynch, Isom	TN			Harrison Lynch	Caroline Quillen	Isom & Drilla Stone	Joseph Thomas & Zilfer Quillen
22267*	Lynch, Louis	OK	1851	Lucinda Lynch	Isaac Lynch	Rachel	Wickliff	
7498	Lynch, Mary	OK	1875	Andrew Lynch	William Downing	Loutisha Ratlinggourd	John & Jennie Downing	Lund Rattlinggourd
22263*	Lynch, Simon	OK	1830	Edie Lynch	Griffin Daniels	Cely Daniels		Rachel Daniels

20432	Lynn, Mary	TN	1878	Fred Lynn	S. Houston Ellis	Rachel Lecroy	Moses & Rachel Ellis	Jackson & Martha Lecroy
22074	Lynn, Mary	OK	1875	none	Mathew Ballard	Emly Brownfield	Alexander Brownfield	Marry Brownfield
18336	Lynn, Millie	TN	1871	John Lynn	Samuel Graves	Mahala Newman		Samuel & Charlotta Newman
17528	Lyon, Esther	OK	1865	A.L. Lyon	John Wright	Anna Evans	Shelton & JoeAnna Wright	John & Anna Evans
22339 *	Lyons, Elias	OK	1866	none	Jeff Ross	Mahalia Danels	Lawrence & Liddie Ross	Mike Sanders
17536 *	Lyons, Phoeba	GA	1854		Sam Tutt	Patsy Elliott	Ben & Sophia Tutt	
12862	Mabe, Cicero et al	NC	1891 etc.		Rufus Mabe	Rosina Osborne		David & Sousie Osborne
3855	Mabe, Gloe	TX	1895	none	Frank Mabe	Lou Miner		Joseph & Mariah Miner
3849	Mabe, Irine	TX	1901	none	Frank Mabe	Lou Miner		Joseph & Mariah Miner
4131	Mabe, Katey	VA	1845	Marshall Mabe	Thomas Price	Cyntha Cox	John Price	Nancy Richardson
3847	Mabe, Lorane	TX	1901	none	Frank Mabe	Lou Miner		Joseph & Maria Miner
3848	Mabe, Lou	TX	1866	Frank Mabe	Joseph Miner	Mariah Miner	John Miner & Soukie Goins	Lewis Miner & Sallie Fields
3852	Mabe, Luther	TX	1897	none	Frank Mabe	Lou Miner		Joseph & Mariah Miner
3853	Mabe, Mattie	TX	1899	none	Frank Mabe	Lou Miner		Joseph & Mariah Miner
3854	Mabe, Maud	TX	1899	none	Frank Mabe	Lou Miner		Joseph & Mariah Miner
12863	Mabe, Rosina	NC	1872	Rufus Mabe	David Osborne	Susie Sheets	Elias Osborne	Jacob & Sally Sheets
12859	Mabe, Rufus	NC	1872	Rosina Mabe	Solomon Mabe	Margaret Evins	Ephram Mabe	Elizabeth Evins
3851	Mabe, Willie	TX	1905	none	Frank Mabe	Lou Miner		John & Mariah Miner
22720	Mabra, Queen	TX	1860	John Mabra	Henry Henson	Mary Hudman	James Henson & Martha Hudman	Hezekiah Hudman & Elizabeth Tally
20049	Mabry, Mary	TX	1873	Joseph Mabry	Miles Faucett	Sallie Griffis	Wm & Elizabeth Faucett	Wm & Mary Griffis
15742 *	Mack, Susie	GA	1878	Thos Mack	Ansel Smith	Nancy Jenkins	Frank & Tena Hog	Sam & Lucy Jenkins
16034	MacKenzie, Florence	IL	1880		Louis Jenks	Anna Brannon		Nathan Jordan & Annie Wyatt
22320 *	Mackey, Rosewell	OK	1855	none	Joshua Mackey	Malinda Phillips	Moses & Hannah Thompson	
22021	Madden, Malinda	OK		William Madden	David Rowe	Betsy Whitmire		Tempe Whitmire
6324	Madison, Elisa	AL		John Madison	Sam Moniac	Susan Marlow	Dixon & Betsy Moniac	James & Susan Marlow
3355	Madison, Pearl	AL	1879	Jim Arington	John Madison	Liezer Monac		Sam & Susan Monac
17959	Mahan, William	GA	1849	Nancy Mahan	James Mahan	Millie Allen	Robert Mahan	Howard Allen
12954	Mainer, Chas et al	OK	1889 etc.		Jefferson Manier	Ardenie Miller	Wm Manier & Sallie Lowery	
12946	Mainer, Henry	OK	1873	Laura Mainer	Gilbert Mainer	Mary Davis	Wm & Salie Mainer	
19499	Majors, Elizabeth	AR	1855	Sam Majors	William Farmer	Eliza Hart		

19284*	Malone, Ellen	GA	1859	Richard Malone	John Williams	Caroline Mills		
2245	Manar, James	OK	1876	Millie Manar	John Manar	Isabel Thompson	Wm & Sallie Manar	
532	Manar, John	OK	1849	Isabell, Manar	William Manar	Sallie Lowery	unknown	Lowery
2244	Manar, Walter	OK	1883	none	John Manar	Isabel Thompson	Wm & Sallie Manar	Willis Thompson
5475	Manchester, Sophronia	NC	1863	Frances Manchester	Anderson Franklin	Elisabeth Bryan	Abram & Elisabeth Franklin	Bryan
725	Mandley, Eliza	GA	1848	widow	Johney Robinson	Lucinda Leatherwood	Thomas Robinson	Sammie Forgenson
18449	Mandy, Mahala	MO	1847	John Mandy	Wm Corbitt		Wm Corbitt	
21621	Maner, Sarah							
299	Maney St., James	NC	44yrs	Sallie Maney	Betis Maney	Louisa Henson	James Maney & Barbara Barrett	Henry Henson & Mariah Wood
287	Maney, Albert	NC	31yrs		Rufus Maney	Susie Sellers	James & Barbara Maney	Dave & Clericy Sellers
21589	Maney, Alice	NC	1894		Garrett Maney	Alleghaney Blankenship	Martin & Matilda Maney	
21585	Maney, Bertha	NC	1887		John Maney	Consuela Banks	Martin & Matilda Maney	
290	Maney, Bettis	GA	1845	Louisa Maney	James Maney	Barbara Berrett	James Maney Sr.	Thomas Berrett
14866	Maney, Charles	GA	1873	Della Maney	Alfred Maney	Lucy Jones	James Maney	Samuel & Eliza Jones
21591	Maney, Charles	NC	1888		Garrett Maney	Alleghaney Blankenship	Martin & Matilda Maney	
297	Maney, Clingman	GA	31yrs	Add Maney	Betis Maney	Louise Henson	James Maney & Barbara Berrett	Henry Henson & Mariah Wood
21592	Maney, Clyde	NC	1896		Garrett Maney	Alleghaney Blankenship	Martin & Matilda Maney	
7975	Maney, Culberson	NC	1894	none	Robert Maney	Margret Ray	George & Elisebeth Maney	James & Roothey Ray
21671	Maney, Ella	NC	1878	Thomas Maney	John Maney	Consela Banks	Martin & Matilda Maney	
12781	Maney, Frank, Martha, Mary	NC			George Maney	Hester	James Maney & Margret Cosn	
14424	Maney, Garrett	NC	1857		Martin Maney	Matilda Holcomb	John & Polly Maney	Henry & Faney Holcomb
7970	Maney, George	NC	1834	Elisebeth Maney	John Maney	Poley Metcalf	Martin & Risar Maney	
22116	Maney, Hannah	NC						
307	Maney, Henry	GA	35yrs	Ermer Maney	Betis Maney	Louisa Henson	James Maney & Barbara Barrett	Henry Henson & Mariah Wood
949	Maney, Henry	NC	1855	Laveda Maney	James Maney Jr.	Betsy Owenby	James Maney & Barbara Berritt	Minter & Elender Owenby
13441	Maney, James	NC	1864	Talitha Maney	James Maney Jr	Betsy Owenby	James Sr & Barbera Maney	Minter & Elander Owenby
4647	Maney, Jasper	NC	1854	Josephine Maney	James Maney	Margaret Corn	John & Mary Maney	Adam & Hannah Corn
4646	Maney, John	NC	1850	Mary Maney	James Maney	Margaret Corn	John & Mary Maney	Adam & Hannah Corn
7969	Maney, John	NC	1897	none	Robert Maney	Margret Ray	George & Elisebeth Maney	James & Roothey Ray

ID	Name	State	Year	Spouse	Father	Mother	Paternal Grandparents	Maternal Grandparents
8418	Maney, John	NC	57yrs	Mary Maney	James Maney	Margaret	John & Mary Maney	
14425	Maney, John	NC	1814	Elisabeth Maney	John Maney	Polley Metcalf	Martin & Kaziah Maney	
14426	Maney, John	NC	1849	Marget Maney	Martin Maney	Matilda Holcombe	John & Polly Maney	Henry & Faney Holcombe
8835	Maney, Josephine	NC	1862	Jasper Maney	Mike Cline	Catherine Hyde		Ben & Elizabeth Hyde
4650	Maney, Leander	NC	1860	Sallie Maney	James Maney	Margaret Corn	John & Mary Maney	Adam & Hannah Corn
7965	Maney, Liley	NC	1874	none	George Maney	Elisebeth Anderson	John & Poley Maney	Jackson & Poley Anderson
22825	Maney, Marion	OK	1864	Mary Maney	John Maney	Jane Moss	James & Barbra Maney	Jeff & Peggie Moss
953	Maney, Martin	NC	1850	Samantha Maney	James Maney Jr.	Betsy Owenby	James Maney & Barbara Berrett	Minter & Edlender Owenby
4652	Maney, Martin	NC	1862	Elizabeth Maney	James Maney	Margaret Corn	John & Mary Maney	Adam & Hannah Corn
951	Maney, Milton	GA	1864	Bure Elle Maney	John Maney	Jenan Moss	James Maney	Jeff & Peggy Moss
7964	Maney, Robert	NC	1871	Margret Maney	George Maney	Elisebeth Anderson	John & Poley Maney	Jackson & Poley Anderson
21593	Maney, Robert	NC	1882		Garrett Maney	Alleghaney Blankenship	Martin & Matilda Maney	
21587	Maney, Verna	NC	1898		John Maney	Sue Ball	Martin & Matilda Maney	
21588	Maney, Vertie	NC	1891		Garrett Maney	Alleghaney Blankenship	Martin & Matilda Maney	
21647	Maney, Walter	NC	1880	Ida Maney	Garrette Maney	Aleghany Blankenship	Martin & Matilda Maney	
954	Maney, William	NC	1854	Sarah Maney	Rufus Maney	Jane Com	James Maney & Barbara Barrett	Adam & Farecie Com
955	Maney, William	GA	1833	widower	James Maney	Barbara Barrett	Martin Maney & Kinziar Van	Wm & Betsy Barrett
4648	Maney, William	NC	1868	Cordelia Maney	James Maney	Margaret Corn	John & Mary Maney	Adam & Hannah Corn
11633	Maney, William	NC		Martha & Bertha	Madison Maney	Mary Andrews	John & Polly Maney	
21590	Maney, Zora	NC	1901		Garrett Maney	Alleghaney Blankenship	Martin & Matilda Maney	
12951	Manier, James	OK	1835		Jefferson Manier	Ardenie Miller	Wm & Sallie Manier	
20964*	Maning, Emma	AL	1865	Isaac Maning	Henry Westmoreland	Mary Williams	George Wilson	George Williams
14281*	Manlove, Daphney	TN	1828			Harrlet Manlove		
10965	Mann, Albert & Julia	OK	1870 1868		Robert Mann	Ellar Wilson	Elizer & Cary Mann	Bird & Ellen Wilson
7920	Mann, John	GA		Rosa Mann	John Mann	Malinda Faister		Nancy Nalley
7786	Mann, Laura	TX	1876	W B Mann	Virgil Williams	Mattie McClain		
7921	Mann, Malinda	GA	1809		John Mann	Malinda Faister		Nancy Nalley
7922	Mann, Nancy	GA	1850		John Mann	Malinda Faister		Nancy Nalley

4790	Mann, Robert	OK	1842	Ellen Wilson (dec)				
1762	Manney, John	OK	1830	Jennie Manney	James Manney	Barbery Barrett	Martin Manney	Kisey Vann
14932	Manning, Cleveland	GA	1885	Jennie Manning	C B Manning	Mary Wright	Geo & Fannie Manning	Allen & Permelia Wright
14934	Manning, George	GA	1879		Charles Manning	Mary Wright	Geo & Fannie Manning	Allen & Permelia Wright
14925	Manning, Mary	GA	1858	Charles Manning	Allen Wright	Permelia Suddeth	Jesse & Lovicie Wright	James & Lizzie Suddeth
14924	Manning, Monroe et al	GA			Charles Manning	Mary Wright		Allen & Permelia Wright
7269	Manning, Oscar	IN	1879	Donna	William Manning	Susan Clark	John & Emily Manning	Roland & Mary Clark
7265	Manning, Susan	IN	1860	William Manning	Roland Clark	Mary Baugh	James & Mildred Clark	Wm & Susan Baugh
20688	Manning, Susan	FL	1878	John Manning	Jacob Taylor	Malissa Kimbrough	Richard & Susan Taylor	Hiram & Nancy Kimbrough
14931	Manning, Vernie	GA	1905		C C Manning	Jennie Teem	C B & Mary Manning	J C H & Manerva Teem
7266	Manning, Walter	IN	1884	Claudia Bowen	William Manning	Susan Clark	John & Emly Manning	Roland & Mary Clark
4350	Manous, Nancy	GA	1883	Joseph Manous	James Reece	Loduska Helton	Aaron & Nancy Reece	John & Mary Helton
7267	Mantonya, Bessie	KS	22yrs	Charles Mantonya	Louis Allen	Sarah Corbin	Joseph & Margaret Allen	
21122 *	Manuel, Nan	OK	1854	Hardy Manuel	George Landrum	Cassie Walker	Jack Dixon & Charity Landrum	Charley & Lucy Walker
20659 *	Map, Francis	TN			Isaac Ship	Sulla King	Nelie Shipp	Kelly & Nettie King
12075	Mapes, Mary	OK		D W Mapes	Charlie Shumaker	Judith McBee		John & Katie McBee
21617	Maples, Eva	KY	1882	Anderson Maples	George Guy	Jodie Ramsey	John Woolf & Judie Guy	Henry & Louisa Ramsey
19855	Marion Rachel et al	NC			Arthur Marion		R.E. & Margaret Marion	
19069	Marion, Ada	NC	1885		Samuel Marion	Johanna Butner	Richard & Margaret Marion	Edward & Mary Butner
19928	Marion, Adam	NC	1854	Virginia Marion	Richard Marion	Margrate Hooser	Adam & Sally Marion	Sam & Nancy Hooser
19856	Marion, Arthur	NC	1872	Elizabeth Marion	Richard Marion	Margaret Hooser		Samuel Hooser & Nancy Hause
19072	Marion, Carrie	NC	1874		Samuel Marion	Johanna Butner	Richard & Margaret Marion	Edward & Mary Butner
19312	Marion, Daniel	NC						
19073	Marion, Edward	NC	1877		Samuel Marion	Johanna Butner	Richard & Margaret Marion	Edward & Mary Butner
15989	Marion, John	NC	1856	Cora Marion	Frank Marion	Sally Hauser	Adam & Sally Marion	Samuel & Nancy Hauser
19929	Marion, Lela et al	NC			Adam Marion	Virginia Reeves	R.E. & Margrat Marion	James Reeves
19071	Marion, Lillian	NC	1884		S.H. Marion	J.H. Butner	Richard & Margaret Marion	Edward & Mary Butner
14877	Marion, Margaret	NC	1829		Samuel Hansen	Nancy Scott	Adam & Margaret Hansen	Len & Nancy Scott
19070	Marion, Mary	NC	1859		Richard Marion	Margaret Hauser	Adam & Sally Marion	Sanseal & Nancy Hauser
19969	Marion, Mary	NC	1849	John Marion	John Blevins	Mary Wall		William Wall
15990	Marion, Paul	NC	1877	Lutisha Marion	Frank Marion	Sally Hauser	Adam & Sally Marion	Samuel & Nancy Hauser

ID	Name	State	Year	Col5	Col6	Col7	Col8	Col9
15991	Marion, Samuel	NC	1859	Lizzie Marion	Frank Marion	Sally Hauser	Adam & Sally Marion	Samuel & Nancy Hauser
19067	Marion, Samuel	NC	1852	Johanna Marion	Richard Marion	Margaret Hauser	Adam & Sally Marion	Samuel & Nancy Hauser
19068	Marion, Samuel Jr.	NC	1881		Samuel Marion	Johanna Butner	Richard & Margaret Marion	Edward & Mary Butner
16014	Marion, Sanborn	NC	1860	Lucy Marion	Frank Marion	Sally Hauser	Adam & Sally Marion	Samuel & Nancy Hauser
19235	Marion, Sanburn	NC	1860	Lucy Marion	Frank Marion	Sallie Hauser	Adam & Sallie Marion	Samuel & Nancy Hauser
20036	Marion, Thomas	NC	1857	Dixie Marion	Frank Marion	Sallie Hauser	Adam & Sally Marion	Samuel & Nancy Hauser
19066	Marion, Wm et al	NC	1887		S.H. Marion	Johanna Butner	R.E. & Margaret Marion	E.I. & Mary Butner
2574	Markins, Margaret	GA	1872	C W Markin	Druey Davenport		John & Elisabeth Davenport	
9036	Markle, Lizzie	WV	1884	Elias Markle	George Cline	Clara Meadows	Moses & Virginia Cline	David & Polly Meadows
9563	Markle, Lula	AR	1869	John Markle	Andrew Smith	Laura Southern	Robert Smith	Warren & Mary Southern
14714	Marler, Henry	NC	1838	Bettie Marler	John Marler	Mary Poindexter	John & Wilmuth Marler	John & Sarah Poindexter
19422	Marler, Sallie	NC	1845	John Marler	Thomas Stimpson	Mary Poindexter	Rebecca Stimpson	Robert & Charlotte Poindexter
22217	Marler, William	NC	1839	Sarah Marler	John Marler	Mary Poindexter	John Marler	Jack & Mary Poindexter
21040	Marrow, Mrs. N.E.	TN	1859	Harvey Marrow	C.I. Simonds	Lucinda Johnson	Jonathan Simonds	Polley Wright
4753	Marsengill, Huldie	GA	1849	M.M. Marsengill	John York	Sary Chastain	Jefrey & Sallie York	Wm & Annie Chastain
302	Marsengill, Kizziar	GA	31yrs	John Marsengill	Betis Maney	Louisa Henson	James & Barbara Maney	Henry Henson & Mariah Wood
19927	Marsh, Della	NC	1877	W.H. Marsh	John Devis	Mary Wamble	Arthur & Betsy Devis	
12271	Marsh, Joseph	NE	1848		George Marsh	Adaline Powell	Wm Marsh & Nancy Harper	
20156 *	Marsh, Mary	GA	1860	Joe Marsh	Peter Adair	Molly Gann	Whitfield Adair	
21842	Marsh, Maude	KS	1880		Elijah Sloan	Lucy Mizener	Absalom & Mary Sloan	
22218 *	Marsh, Millie	GA	1821	widow	Joshua Penn	Sophia Penn		
19570	Marshall, Amanda	NC	1867	Ruffus Marshall	Feilders Henslee	Mary Ragle	Ralzey & Sarah Henslee	Henry & Mary Ragle
13249 *	Marshall, Ed	GA	1848	Polly Marshall	Henry Marshall	Lottie Ingersoll	Marshall & Hannah Jones	Ned Ingersoll & Becky Jones
20224 *	Marshall, Elmer	IN	1878	Audrey Marshall	Henry Marshall	Elizabeth Milton	Henry & Polly Marshall	Bolden & Elisabeth Milton
5164 *	Marshall, Shahaker	OK	28yrs	Author	Joseph Colton	Emeline Andrews		Lucinda Andrews
20226 *	Marshall, William	IN	1879	Marie Marshall	Henry Marshall	Elizabeth Scott	Henry & Polly Marshall	Bolden & Elisabeth Milton
17826	Marshell, Dock	GA	1852	Della Marshell	James Marshell	Zelfey Young		Viney Young
20111 *	Marshman, Catherine	GA		Stephen Marshman	Hewell Burns	Milly Ross		Chief Ross
13350	Martian, Sinthey	GA	1885	H M Martian	Wm McGaha	Adaline Reece	Richard & Rebecca McGaha	
9840	Martin, Adaline	NC	1871	David Martin	William Murphy	Lizzie Hipps	Wm & Martha Murphy	Creasman & Adeline Hipps

22289*	Martin, Addie	OK	1860	Alex White	Warren Martin	Jane McNair	Adam & Challotte Martin	Mariah McNair
18673	Martin, Alex	OK	1874	Bertia Martin	Ed Martin	Leean Hill	David Martin & Lucindy Coe	Thos Hill & Ellen Smith
5613	Martin, Alexander	OK		Minnie Martin	Joseph Martin	Julia Lombard	Jack & Nellie Martin	Lombard
552	Martin, Alfred	AR	1845	widower	Wm Martin	Susan Wolf	Thomas & Elizabeth Martin	Dennis & Polly Wolf
21924	Martin, Amanda	TN	1886	Fred Martin	Andrew Erwin	Ella Whitice	Benj & Dicey Erwin	Wm & Eliza Whitice
1311	Martin, Annie	TX	1868	C J Martin	J H Deane	Kattie Hirston		Richard Hirston & Mary Hill
6560	Martin, Arizona	AR	1874	John Martin	Thomspn Wood	Eliza Martin	Johnson & Margaret Wood	Wm & Susan Martin
22318*	Martin, Arter	OK	1849	Francis Martin	Charles Martin	Mary Martin		
19154	Martin, Barbara	GA	1873	W.D. Martin	Mart Evans	Mary Smith	Pleas & Mahala Evans	
13621	Martin, Betty	NC	1846	Doc Martin	William Hartgrave	Ann Poindexter	James & Nancy Hartgrave	Robert & Miriam Poindexter
19206	Martin, Carlis	OK	1878	Bertha Martin	Edwin Martin	Lean Hill	David & Lucinda Martin	Thomas Hill & Ellen Smith
5452	Martin, Charles	NC	1872	Mary Martin	James Martin	Elizabeth Caylor	Abigail Martin	
22447	Martin, Charles	TX	1875	Mollie Martin	Charles Martin	Elmyra Norton	James & Rebecca Martin	James & Rhoda Norton
20592	Martin, Cora	TN	1875	J.W. Martin	John Hanssard	Catharine Cook	Sidney & Margaret Hanssard	Wm & Eliza Cook
11485	Martin, Daniel	OK	1860	Fanney Martin		Mary Martin		Joe & Judie Martin
15194	Martin, Eliza	NC	1854	U L Martin	William Gibbs	Analine Batles		Watson & Saley Batles
14125	Martin, Elizabeth	NC	1858	Thomas Martin	John Trulove	Florina Butner	Austern Trulove	Patsey Poindexter
19785	Martin, Emory	GA	1881	Eva Martin	William Martin	Rhoda Wade		Wm & Elizabeth Wade
14724	Martin, Flora	NC	1869	W A Martin	John Poindexter	Nancy Allen	Thos & Amelia Poindexter	James & Rebecca Allen
19786	Martin, Hazel	GA	1905			Rhoda Wade		Elizabeth Wade
14726	Martin, Henry	NC	1850	Mary Martin	Henry Martin	Elizabeth Hauser	Samuel & Elizabeth Martin	Adam & Margrett Hauser
391	Martin, Henry B.	NC	1859	Alby Martin	Joseph Martin	Adeline Moose	Joseph & Mary Martin	Jacob & Sallie Moose
19287	Martin, J. M.	NC	1828	Sarah Martin	Henry Martin	Elizabeth Hauser	Samuel & Elizabeth Martin	Adam & Margret Hauser
1531	Martin, Jacob	NC	1868	Bitha Martin	Joseph Martin	Mary Moose	Joseph & Mary Martin	Jacob & Sallie Moore
5455	Martin, James	NC	1845	Elizabeth Martin		Abigail Martin		Joseph & Mary Martin
21941*	Martin, James	TN	1867	December Martin	James Martin	Nancy Martin	Jennie Martin	Hannah Martin
18768	Martin, Jerome	GA	1877	Lorena Martin	William Martin	Rhoda Wade	Milton & Syntha Martin	Wm & Elizabeth Wade
4357	Martin, John	AR	1870	Mary Martin	Alfred Martin	Louisa Tillman	William & Susan Martin	John & Lydia Tillman
8880	Martin, John	OK	1868	Minnie Martin	Ed Martin	Lea Ann Hill	David & Lucinda Martin	Thomas Hill
13554	Martin, John	NC	1852	Maggie Martin	William Martin	Margaret Hauser	John & Jennie Martin	John & Elizabeth Hauser
15075	Martin, John	IL	1860	Sarah Martin	Bennet Martin	Milliner Trulove	John & Jennie Martin	Austin & Martha Trulove

19424	Martin, John	NC	1845	Mary Martin	Thomas Martin	Ann Poindexter	Samuel & Elizabeth Martin	Francis & Rosanna Poindexter
14706	Martin, John Jr	NC	1883	Minerva Martin	Henry Martin	Elisabeth Houser	Samuel & Elisebeth Martin	Adam & Margret Houser
21940 *	Martin, Joseph	TN	1862	Nettie Martin	Joseph Martin	Nancy Martin	John & Jennie Martin	Hannah Martin
22309 *	Martin, Juno	OK	1810	Fred Martin widow	Jesse Ross	Fillis Ross	Jo & Juno Ross	Dick & Sarah Ross
22496 *	Martin, Katy	OK	1869	Louis Martin	Jeffrey Marcum	Lucy Vann		Ibby Vann
22315 *	Martin, Lula	OK	1876	James Martin	Jack Baldridge	Nancy Barlow	Taloka Baldridge & Lettie Vann	John & Eliza Barlow
10869	Martin, Manerva	GA	1881	Mack Martin	William McGaha	Rebecca Pool		Moses Pool
439	Martin, Marcus	NC	1881	none	Nathaniel Martin	Rachel Morgan	Joseph & Sarah Martin	
5612	Martin, Margaret	TX	1847	widower	James Brown	Lucinda Warren	Brown	Kemp
19236	Martin, Margaret	NC	1864	John Martin	Richard Marion	Margaret Hauser	Adam & Sallie Marion	Samuel & Nancy Hauser
4181	Martin, Martha	AL	1842	David Martin	William Pressley	Abbie Langley		
20029	Martin, Martha	GA	1886	Dawsey Martin	Charley Burger	Nancy Night	James Burger	Eligh & Minnie Night
4354	Martin, Mary	AR	1876	none	Alfred Martin	Louisa Tillman	William & Susan Martin	John & Lydia Tillman
22303 *	Martin, Mary	OK	1858	Howard Watson	Joshua Martin	Harriet Lynch	Charley & Mary Martin	
21533	Martin, Mattie	GA	1886	Dassie Martin	Charley Burger	Nancy Knight	Jim & Delila Burger	
22287 *	Martin, Mike	OK	1866	Ida Martin	Aaron Martin	Queen Downing	Mike Waity & Nellie Martin	Reuben Downing & Jennie Martin
13520	Martin, Minerva	NC	1863	John Martin	Robbert Poindexter	Martha Ward	Robbert & Charlotte Poindexter	Wiley & Polly Ward
22768	Martin, Minnie	TN	1878	Alfred Martin	William Bell	Eliza Hawkins	David & Alzira Bell	? Williams
14893	Martin, Nancy	NC	1830	Reps Martin	Denson Poindexter	Sarah Jones	Wm & Elizabeth Poindexter	Isaac & Basheba Jones
17780	Martin, Nancy	MO	1876	E.J. Martin	Nathan Swift	Adaline Holt		Berry & Susanna Holt
11064	Martin, Nannie	VA	1882	William Martin	Leander Blevins	Elizabeth Hart		John & Polley Hart
440	Martin, Nathaniel	NC	1857	Rachel Martin	Joseph Martin	Sarah Moose	Joseph & Mary Martin	Jacob & Sallie Moose
17198	Martin, Nathaniel	OK	1845	Callie Martin	John Martin	Rachel Arkinson	Sam Martin	
22497 *	Martin, Neda	OK	1838	William Martin, decd	Sandy Bean	Rachel Adair		George & Aniky Martin
18769	Martin, Olden	GA	1883		William Martin	Rhoda Wade	Milton & Syntha Martin	Wm & Elizabeth Wade
14676	Martin, Oliver	NC	1863	Kate Martin	Alexander Martin	Amittia Poindexter	John & Jennie Martin	Denson & Sarah Poindexter
22294 *	Martin, Peyton	OK	1848	Amanda Martin	Harry Martin	Celia Martin		Amy Martin
22334 *	Martin, Rachel	OK	1842	Joe Rucker	Elija Musgrove	Silvy Candy		
18551	Martin, Rhoda	GA	1850	William Martin	William Wade	Elizabeth Sosebee	David & Charity Wade	Wm & Nancy Sosebee
11662	Martin, Richard	OK	1858	Mary Martin	Jackson Cawn	Mary Martin		Joe Martin & Judy Roach

392	Martin, Richmond	NC	1870	Sarah Martin	Joseph Martin	Mary Moose	Joseph & Mary Martin	Jacob & Sallie Moose
12283	Martin, Rosa	GA	1888	C D Martin	William McGahu	Adaline Reece	Richard & Rebecca McGahu	Warsun & Manerva Reece
14873	Martin, Samuel	NC	1848	S V Martin	Henry Martin	Elizabeth Houser	Samuel & Elizabeth Martin	Adam & Margaret Houser
14872	Martin, Sarah	NC	1866	Thomas Martin	Ellis Norman	Octavia Poindexter	David & Milly Norman	Iverson & Sarah Poindexter
22261 *	Martin, Sina	OK	1826	widow	Beverly Martin	Hannah Martin		Pattie Martin
21196	Martin, Susie	AR	1882	William Martin	Adolphus Dillahunty	Emily Mann	Francis & Susan Dillahunty	John & Patience Williams
18637 *	Martin, Sylva	NC	1868	Alfred Martin	Louis Penland	Rheno Rona		Rona & Tilda Wilburn
14688	Martin, Tennessee	NC	1873	Luther Martin	John Poindexter	Nancy Allen	Thos & Amelia Poindexter	James & Rebecca Allen
8628	Martin, Thomas	OK		Lillie Martin	Ed Martin	Lea Hill	David & Lucinda Martin	Thomas Hill
11486	Martin, Thomas	OK	1874	Mandie Martin		Mary Martin		Joe & Judie Martin
15515 *	Martin, Thursday	GA	1872	Noah Martin	Madison Scudders	Julia Looper	Lew & Kitty Scudders	Thursday Looper
10975	Martin, Virginia	TN	1845	widow	Wm Jenkins	Eliza Woods	Henry & Francis Jenkins	John & Elizabeth Woods
22644	Martin, Walter	OK	1882	Eva Martin	Richard Martin	Delaney Ketchem	Mary Martin	W.H. Ketchem
14693	Martin, Wesley	NC	1862	Flora Martin	Bennette Martin	Mary Trulove	John & Virginia Martin	Austin Trulove & Patsy Poindexter
16054	Martin, William	AL	1869	Sarah Martin	John Martin	Lucinda Ogglesby	Ebenezer & Myrinda Martin	
21677	Martin, William	OK	1855	Jennie Martin	Hirkluse Martin	Parmelia Griffin		James & Nancy Griffin
22385	Martin, William	CA	1879	none	Charles Martin	Elmyra Norton		James & Rhoda Norton
18672	Martin, Willis	OK	1872	Annie Martin	Ed Martin	Leean Hill	David Martin & Lucindy Coe	Thos Hill & Ellen Smith
667	Martin, Wm Henry	NC	1836	Sally Martin	Joseph Martin	Mary Hunt	John Martin	
10579	Martindale, Sarah	OK	1853	John Martindale	Eli Sutton	Nellie McDaniel		Moses & Nancy McDaniel
664	Mashburn, Sarah	NC	1845	Andrew Mashburn	Edward Delozier	Elizabeth Poindexter	Jesse & Alsey Delozier	Pledge & Elizabeth Poindexter
4492	Masley, Julia	GA	1836	Albert Masley	John Mann	Elisabeth Smith	Benson Nalley	Nancy Nalley
18484	Mason, Ammer	GA	1883	Charlie Mason	Elijah Biddy	Georgia Anderson		
15392	Mason, Belle	GA	1904		Merrill Mason	Martha Dotson	Merrill & Sarah Mason	David & Mary Dotson
3782	Mason, David	NC	1882	none	Joseph Mason	Caroline Mason	John & Polly Mason	
11388	Mason, Dora	NC	1887		Joseph Mason	Caroline Mason	John & Pollie Mason	
12745	Mason, Dora et al	TN	1894 etc.		Thomas Mason	Addie Mason	John Mason	Thos & Lydia Benfield
15391	Mason, Effie	GA	1906		Merrill Mason	Martha Dotson	Merrill & Sarah Mason	David & Mary Dotson
15390	Mason, Garnia	GA	1902		Merrill Mason	Martha Dotson	Merrill & Sarah Mason	David & Mary Dotson
17332	Mason, J.A.	GA	1863		G. Willson	Becky Johnston	John & Creesie Jones	Jack & Mary Spratling
15675 *	Mason, Jessie	GA	1852	John Mason	Madison Shade	Caroline McCheston		Jake McCheston

6401	Mason, John	NC	1881	none	Joseph Mason	Sarah Mason	John & Pollie Mason	Joseph & Nellie Mason
2018	Mason, Joseph	NC	1847	Caroline & Cordie Mason	John Mason	Pollie Robinson		Aaron & Jane Robinson
22436	Mason, Josie	TN	1865	William Mason	Jack Saunders	Margaret Crossler	Bettie Saunders	
10858	Mason, Marian	NC	1868		W J Mason	Susie Benfield	John & Pollie Mason	Thomas & Lydia Benfield
13641	Mason, Martha	GA	1828	William Mason	Bennett Cordell	Martha Duke	Jesse & Patience Cordell	
15389	Mason, Martha	GA	1875	Merrill Mason	David Dotson	Mary Eaton	Washington & Margret Dotson	Andrew & Caroline Eaton
20962	Mason, Mollie	GA	1860	Thomas Mason	G.W. Mason	Nancy Worth	Larking & Maryan Mason	Malindia Willson
22233 *	Mason, Mollie gdn.	GA			Thomas Mason	Mollie North	G.W. & Mary Mason	Nancy North
4769	Mason, Oma	NC	1874	John Mason	Harmon Hampton	Rena Robertson	George & Mary Hampton	
15388	Mason, Orlene	GA	1898		Merrill Mason	Martha Dotson	Merrill & Sarah Mason	David & Mary Dotson
17641 *	Mason, Wiley	GA	1853		George Mason	Elmira Lemour	George Mason & Mary Waterhouse	Tom & Nancy McCoy
18274 *	Mason, Will	GA	1889		Wille Mayson	Allice Byrd	George & Elmira Mayson	
529	Mason, William	GA	1839	Susie Mason	John Mason	Pollie Robertson	Billie & Sallie Mason	Aaron & Pollie Robertson
17615	Mason, William	OK	1862	Ella Jane Mason	Wm Mason	Penelopia Green		Daniel Green
18275	Massengill, Annie	GA	1883	Robert Massengill	Willie Stinsion	Francis Turner		Thomas & Louvica Turner
7255	Massey, John	OK	1879	Emma Massey	Joel Massey	Laura Holcomb	Ephram & Mary Massey	Wm & Louisa Holcomb
7256	Massey, Laura	OK	1853	Joel Massey	William Holcomb	Louisa Berry	Benj & Sarah Holcomb	Hiram & Sarah Berry
7254	Massey, Tom	OK	1882	Sue Massey	Joel Massey	Laura Holcomb	Ephram & Mary Massey	Wm & Louisa Holcomb
18652	Masters, Mary	WV	1879	Charley Masters	Owen Sizemore	Lotty Belcher	Ned & Jane Sizemore	Wm & Polly Belcher
18685	Matamoras, Mary	FL	1835	John Matamoras	Thomas Robinson	Mary Harvel		Elizabeth Harvel
17954	Mathenie, Adren	TN	1878	Arthur Mathenie	R.L. Watson	Annettie Tidwell	James & Margaret Watson	Wm & Matilda Tidwell
2454	Matherly, Mary	MO	1876	Luther Matherly	Samuel Richards	Amanda Harralson	Martin & Lucy Richards	Martha & Vinson Harralson
156	Matheson, Malissia	GA	1855	William Matheson	John Hampton	Hannah Montieth	George & Maryan Hampton	George & Vina Montleth
13644	Mathews, Alonzo	CA		Julia Mathews	Caleb Duncan	Mary Hudson	Charles & Mahala Duncan	
13650	Mathews, Alonzo	CA	1888		Alonzo Mathews	Julia Duncan		Caleb & Mary Duncan
2575	Mathews, Clarissa	GA	1868	Thomas Mathews	George Hice	Margaret Davenport		John & Elisabeth Davenport
22216 *	Mathews, Edward	OK	1840	Carrie Mathews	Math Mathews	Ellen Mathews		Old Chief Bell Mathews
8930	Mathews, Frona	OK	1881	Charles Stanton	Thomas Mathews	Martha Brasuell		Samuel & Phebe Brasuell
8929	Mathews, George	OK	1884	none	Thomas Mathews	Martha Brasuell		Samuel & Phebe Brasuell

8928	Mathews, Martha	OK	1848	Thomas Mathews	Samuel Brasuell	Pheba Taylor	Wm & Elizebeth Brasuell	Wm & Elizebeth Taylor
7785	Mathews, Mary	OK	1843	none	John McBee	Katie Hames	Wm McBee & Rebecca Brannum	John & Katie Hames
8924	Mathews, Monroe	OK	1871	Dora Mathews	Thomas Mathews	Martha Brasuell		Samuel & Pheba Brasuell
8932	Mathews, Richard	OK	1879	Maggie Mathews	Thomas Mathews	Martha Brasuell		Samuel & Phebe Brasuell
8925	Mathews, Riley (decd)	OK	1874					
13651	Mathews, Robert	CA	1880		Alonzo Mathews	Julia Duncan		Caleb & Mary Duncan
20304	Mathews, Rosa	MO	1869	Seldon Mathews	Daniel Hinkle	Lucy Herrell	John & Cynthia Hinkle	Emerson & Clarissa Herrell
533	Mathews, Sam	OK	1881	Hettie Mathews	Lew Mathews	Artie Sanders	Samuel & Elizabeth Mathews	John & Nancy Sanders
8926	Mathews, Samuel	OK	1870	none	Thomas Mathews	Martha Brasuell		Samuel & Pheba Brasuell
8931	Mathews, Zachariah	OK	1883	none	Thomas Mathews	Martha Brasuell		Samuel & Phebe Brasuell
1557	Mathis, John	GA	1864		Allen Mathis	Jane McDaniel		
19854	Mathis, Nancy	NC	1836	Henderson Mathis	James Chandler	Lucinda Barker	Wm & Nancy Chandler	
19733*	Matlock, Jess	NC	1861	Lizzie Matlock	Jake Matlock	Nancy Ferguson		Adeline Ferguson
31	Matney, John	AR	1868	Elizabeth Matney	Joseph Matney	Sarah Stillwell	John & Catharine Matney	
1043	Matthews, Abraham	CO	1886	none	Martin Matthews	Francis Hardin		
7784	Matthews, Carl	OK	1879	Mabel Matthews	Kinchen Matthews	Mary McBee	Lezarus Matthews	John & Katie McBee
9835	Matthews, Carry	MO	1873	Albert Matthews	Jonathan Hicks	Lorinda Haralson	Hiram & Mary Hicks	Vincent & Martha Harralson
13572*	Matthews, Edward	OK	1840	Carrie Matthews	Matt Matthews	Elenor Matthews		Big Bill Matthews
1042	Matthews, Emma	CO	1884	none	Martin Matthews	Francis Hardin		
1041	Matthews, Florence	CO	1882	none	Martin Matthews	Francis Hardin		
13795	Matthews, Francis	NC	1838		Absalom Matthews	Amitta Poindexter	Aaron & Mary Matthews	Wm & Elizebeth Poindexter
22686	Matthews, Francis	NC	1860	Mary Matthews	Thomas Matthews	Sarah Jester	Absalom & Amittie Matthews	Jacob & Fannie Jester
22704	Matthews, Georgia	NC		John Matthews	William Miller	Nancy Apperson		
13407	Matthews, John	NC	1869	Georgia Matthews	John Matthews	Martha Warden	Abraham & Amitha Matthews	Bredell & Mary Warden
14115	Matthews, Joseph	NC	1848	Sarah Matthews	Absalom Matthews	Amitha Poindexter	Aaron & Mary Matthews	Wm & Elizebeth Poindexter
15924	Matthews, Julius	NC	1880	Pearl Matthews	John Matthews	Martha Warden	Absalom & Amithia Matthews	Oredell & Mary Warden
14680	Matthews, Lillie	NC	1875	Charlie Matthews	John Matthews	Martha Warden	Absalom & Amithia Matthews	Dredle & Mary Warden
16392	Matthews, Luther	NC	1882		John Matthews	Martha Warden	Absalom & Amithia Matthews	Predell & Mary Warden

13496	Matthews, Sanford	NC	1853	Nancy Matthews	Absalom Matthews	Amitha Poindexter	Aaron & Mary Matthews	Wm & Elizabeth Poindexter
13556	Matthews, Thomas	NC	1834	Lucinda Matthews	Absalom Matthews	Amittia Poindexter	Aaron & Mary Matthews	Wm & Elizabeth Poindexter
16402	Matthews, Virginia	NC	1866	James Matthews				
14385	Mattox, John	AL			William Mattox	Nancy Newman	John Mattox	Nancy Egnew
20992	Maughan, Clara	TN	1887	Charles Maughan	Newton Guinn	Forest Kinsey	Jack Guinn	Humphry Kinsey
19448	Mauldin, Laura	GA	1881	Minar Mauldin	Enoch Patterson	Lou Smith	Samuel & Nancy Patterson	Jonah & Bettie Smith
15173	Mauldin, Lourah	NC	1849	J A Mauldin	Alex Jordan	Catharine Ward		
21916	Mavity, Jesse	TN	1890		George Mavity	Tennessee Colbaugh	Andrew & Marvena Mavity	Henry & Mary Colbaugh
21954	Mavity, Tennessee	TN	1849	George Mavity	Henry Colbaugh	Mary Williams	Henry & Polly Colbaugh	Samuel & Tenna McCorkle
21613	Maxey, Eli	TN	1851	Sarah Maxey	John Maxey	Polly Nichols	Jabey Maxey	Molly Nichols
538	Maxwell, Nannie	OK	1849	Armstead Maxwell	Ellis Fawling	Elizabeth Griffin	Edmond & Nettie Fawling	
3598	Maxwell, Nora	OK	1880		J N Avary	Harriett Whitten	W W & Telitha Avary	Joel & Nancy Whitten
19695	May, M. Caroline	TN	1876	A.L. May	J. Curtis	Elizabeth Patrick	Joshua & Elizabeth Curtis	
10472	May, Mary	OK	1835		James Browning	Nancy Henderson	John & Rebeck Browning	Mary Reed
9116	May, Rachel	NC	1877	William May	Joseph Mason	Sarah Mason	John Mason	Pollie Mason
5454	May, Rosie	NC	1885	Milton May	Joseph Mason	Sarah Mason	John & Pollie Mason	
15624	May, Warner	MO	1868	Hattie May	William May	Susan Silvey		
6388	Mayberry, Calvin	OK	1883		Jesse Mayberry	Eliza Blackburn	James & Nancy Mayberry	Andrew & Francis Blackburn
6000	Mayberry, Charles	OK	1876	Olive Mayberry	Jesse Mayberry	Eliza Blackburn	James & Nancy Mayberry	Andrew & Francis Blackburn
5995	Mayberry, Eliza	OK	1841	Jesse Mayberry	Andrew Blackburn	Francis Eddings	John & Elsie Blackburn	John & Elizabeth Eddings
6386	Mayberry, Emmett	OK	1873	Flora Mayberry	Jesse Mayberry	Eliza Blackburn	James & Nancy Mayberry	Andrew & Francis Blackburn
6387	Mayberry, Franklin	OK	1871		Jesse Mayberry	Eliza Blackburn	James & Nancy Mayberry	Andrew & Francis Blackburn
6001	Mayberry, Harvey	OK	1869		Jesse Mayberry	Eliza Blackburn	James & Nancy Mayberry	Andrew & Francis Blackburn
6385	Mayberry, John	OK	1866		Jesse Mayberry	Eliza Blackburn	James & Nancy Mayberry	Andrew & Francis Blackburn
17866	Mayden, G.E.	TX	1880	Neomi Mayden	James Mayden	Nancy Christman	Lawrence Mayden	
4002	Mayfield, Isaac	OK	1822	Mary Mayfield	James Mayfield	Susan Dunn		
19398	Mayfield, John	GA	1857	Francis Mayfield	Hamp Mayfield	Arie Jackson		Peggy Jackson
19399	Mayfield, John	GA	1876	Anna Mayfield	John Mayfield	Francis Johnson	Hamp & Arie Mayfield	
22003	Mayfield, Josie	OK	1861	Alfred Mayfield	William Willburn	Rosilla Strong		
22336 *	Mayfield, Maggie	OK	1856	Charley Mayfield	Wash Ross	Jane Ross	Willis & Mareah Ross	

22288*	Mayfield, Nicy	OK	1832	widow	Ben Bean	Ibby		
5168	Mayhew, Charles	OK			James Mayhew	Tennesse Brawner		
12015	Mayhugh, Missie	GA		Oscar Mayhugh	Josiah Vernon	Evaline	Archibald & Jane Vernon	
21824	Mayo, Willie	AL	1884	F.A. Mayo	H.B. Evans	Mollie Williams	Josh Evans	James & Margaret Williams
22379	Mays, Sarah	NC	1876	J C Mays	Jessie Isaacs	Mary Scott	Joseph & Frankie Isaacs	Benjamin & Bettie Scott
22109	Mayson, Jane	GA	1865	M.F. Mayson	Calvin Pruitt	Elizabeth Rainwater	William & Dora Pruitt	Gabriel & Nancy Rainwater
18276	Maze, Elizabeth	GA	1840	Flemon Maze	Wallace Cornett	Mary Queen	Cullen & Sallie Cornett	
16049	Maze, Laura	TX	1864	G W Maze	John Nesmith	Rebeca Lancaster		
22111	McAbee, Amanda	GA	1854	Alfred McAbee	John Goodin	Ellen Costloe	Harrison & Harriett Goodin	Edward & Sarah Costloe
18303	McAdams, Florence	AL	1871	Peter McAdams	James O'Neal	Mary Hollinger		Wm & Hetty Hollinger
18304	McAdams, Hattie	AL	1905		Peter McAdams	Florence O'Neal		James & Mary O'Neal
18305	McAdams, James	AL	1897		Peter McAdams	Florence O'Neal		James & Mary O'Neal
18306	McAdams, Mary	AL	1899		Peter McAdams	Florence O'Neal		James & Mary O'Neal
22053*	McAlister, Elen	OK	1876	Andrew McAlester	Jesse Vann	Emma Riley	Billy Vann	Sam Riley
20068	McAlister, J.C.	TN	1860	Martha McAlister	Frank McAlister	Elizabeth Goin	John & Margaret McAlister	Ed & Sallie Goin
13814	McAllester, Henry	TN	1861	Margaret McAllester	John McAllester	Nancy Goins		Edward & Peggy Goins
21274	McAllister, Minnie	MO	1886	Victor McAllister	Thomas Davenport	Lucy		James & Deborah Gordon
17675	McAnalley, M.E.	AL	1841	David McAnalley	Ansel Fortner	Sarah Dood		Charles & Minnie Dood
9195	McAnally, Delphia	OK	1850	widow	Maston West	Malinda Parey	John & Delphia West	Campbell & Susan Posey
18109	McAnally, H.L.	AL	1880		David McAnally	M.E. Fortner	David McAnally	Ansel & Sarah Fortner
18110	McAnally, O.E.	AL	1885		David McAnally	M.E. Fortner	David McAnally	Ansel & Sarah Fortner
9142	McArthur, Mary	GA	1870	R.V. Mc Arthur	Simpson Burrell	Rebecca Burleson	Jesse & Maria Burrell	Isaac & Hanah Burelson
13739	McAvoy, Joanna	GA	1864	W R McAvoy		Sarah Whitlock		George & Nancy Whitlock
14971	McBee, Luta	MO	1866	J G McBee	Robert Beeler	P J Shelton		
14970	McBee, Sallie	MO	1869	J B McBee	Robert Beeler	P J Shelton		
5691	McBride, Susie	VA	1871	J W McBride	Calvin Thompson	Elizabeth Welch	Samuel & Margret Thompson	James & Nancy Welch
19062	McCain, Lula	OK	1876	Samuel McCain	Henry Sharp	Charlotta Auzies	Anderson & Martha Sharp	John & Nancy Auxies
18489	McCall, Adelaide	MI	1868	George McCall	Edward Davis	Martha Washington	Henry Davis & Sarah Kinney	Henry & Mary Washington
21136	McCall, Amy	SC	1888	S.B. McCall	J.W. Crouse	Martha Scott	W.P. & Amy Scott	Henry & Henrietta Crouse
19050	McCall, Effie	OK	1882	John McCall	Henry Sharp	Charlotta Auxier	Anderson & Martha Sharp	John & Nancy Auxier
19054	McCall, Elizabeth	OK	1904		John McCall	Effie Sharp	Olin & Arzela McCall	Henry & Charlotta Sharp

19051	McCall, Henry	OK	1899		John McCall	Effie Sharp	Olin & Arzela McCall	Henry & Charlotta Sharp
19053	McCall, John	OK	1906		John McCall	Effie Sharp	Olin & Arzela McCall	Henry & Charlotta Sharp
19052	McCall, Lillian	OK	1901		John McCall	Effie Sharp	Olin & Arzela McCall	Henry & Charlotta Sharp
14912	McCallister, Cicero	GA	1891		Wm McCallister	Lula Wilson	John & Polly McCallister	George & Passie Wilson
14913	McCallister, Lula	GA	1869	W H McCallister	George Wilson	Passie Parker	Samuel & Elizabeth Wilson	Julian & Celia Parker
16156	McCann, Delia	WI		C H McCann	Samuel Bass	Eliza Murphy	Elijah & Matilda Bass	George & Becky Murphy
20343 *	McCarny, Emma	TN	1868		Isaac McCarny	Mckie Thompson	Lindsay McCarny	Moses & Fashion Johnson
13010	McCartey, Ann	LA	1861	Henry McCartey	Van Buren McCellan	Licann Lewis	John McCartey	Robert Lewis
11940	McCarthy, Rosa	TN	1882	Tobe McCarthy	Wiilliam Thompson	Matilda Miller	James & Caroline Tucker	Marion & Elizabeth Miller
3521	McCartney, Mary	TN	1864	John McCartney	Benson Pack	Mary Evans	Benson & Hannah Pack	Charles & Julia Evans
21279	McCarty, Sadie	MO	1885	J.F. McCarty	Charles Davenport	Winnie Gordon	John & Elizabeth Davenport	James & Deborah Gordon
1141	McCauley, Emma	AL	41yrs	Fedrick McCauley	John Steadham	Mary McGhee	Ned Steadham	McGhee
21780	McClain, Lucinda	OK	1881	Wesley McClain	Robert Nicks	Nancy Puckett	Isaac & Nancy Nicks	James & Eliza Puckett
7251	McClarey, Maggie	KS	1882	J. McClary	Charles Shim	Matilda		Louis & Maggie Allen
13904 *	McClaughton, W.C.	GA	1879		Frank McClaughton	Rendy Simpson	Francis & Narcisia McClaughton	
13748 *	McClayton, Francis	GA	1848	Rindie McClayton	Frank McClayton	Narcissie Dayson		Joe & Delsie Dayson
9565	McClelland, Alice	AR	1879	J H McClelland	Andrew Smith	Laura Southern	Robert Smith	Warren & Mary Southern
7522	McClelland, Irena	NC	64yrs	none	Ned Grimes	Dorcas McClelland		
17360	McClelland, Lue et al	OK			D.C. McClelland	Emma Smith		A.J. & Laura Smith
6329	McClennan, Mrs. Harvy	AL		Harvy McClennan	John Boone	Lavittia Moniac	John Boone & Martha Poston	Sam & Susan Moniac
16525	McClesky, Eliza	GA	1867	George McClesky	Cue West	Mary Wright		Kansas Stalls
16524	McClesky, George	GA	1853	Eliza McClesky	Thos McClesky	Mary Reed	George McClesky	Downing Stall
2324	McClintock, Sarah	OK	1856	widow	Richard Fisher	Evelyn Berry	Abraham & Martha Fisher	Thomas & Mary Berry
18908	McCloughan, Annie	AR	1880		James Reeder	Mary Glenn		James & Nancy Parrish
12048	McClure, Amanda	GA	1849	Thomas McClure	Hugh Millwood	Miram Whitlock	Benj & Rachel Millwood	James & Sallie Whitlock
15527	McClure, Amanda	GA	1885		Robert McClure	Mary Millwood	Jack & Marilda McClure	Hugh & Miram Millwood
18118	McClure, Barbara	NC		T.D. McClure	Lazrus Anderson	Nancy Maney	James & Frankie Anderson	James Maney Sr & Barbara Barrett
15526	McClure, Henry	GA	1885		Robert McClure	Mary Millwood	Jack & Marilda McClure	Hugh & Miram Millwood
14518	McClure, James	GA	1885		Thomas McClure	Amanda Millwood	J J & Marilda McClure	Hugh & Mariam Millwood
15525	McClure, James	GA	1873	Dora McClure	Robert McClure	Mary Millwood	Jack & Marilda McClure	Hugh & Miram Millwood

18120	McClure, Louisa	NC	24yrs		T.S. McClure	Barbara Anderson	Andy & Margaret McClure	Lazrus & Nancy Anderson
22797	McClure, Marian	VA	1866	Henry McClure	John Blevins	Caraline Brown	Daniel & Annie Blevins	
11314	McClure, Mary	GA	1845	William McClure	Hugh Millwood	Miram Whitlock	Benj Malew & Rachel Millwood	Dock & Sallie Whitlock
15524	McClure, Murray	GA	1879	Naomi McClure	Robert McClure	Mary Millwood	Jack & Marilda McClure	Hugh & Miram Millwood
9320	McClure, Nancy	GA	1855	Cisero McClure	Thomas Davenport	Elizabeth Smith	Aurbon & Polly Davenport	Wm & Susan Smith
14517	McClure, Odie	GA	1891		Thomas McClure	Amanda Millwood	J J & Marilda McClure	Hugh & Mariam Millwood
15523	McClure, Samuel	GA	1872	Minnie McClure	Robert McClure	Mary Millwood	Jack & Marilda McClure	Hugh & Miram Millwood
7993	McClure, Susan	OK	1850	Joel Keith	James McClure	Rebeca Howell	Wm & Susan McClure	Mary Howell
15522	McClure, Walter	GA	1883		Robert McClure	Mary Millwood	Jack & Marilda McClure	Hugh & Miram Millwood
15521	McClure, Will	GA	1870	Ella McClure	Robert McClure	Mary Millwood	Jack & Marilda McClure	Hugh & Miram Millwood
14516	McClure, William	GA	1887		Thomas McClure	Amanda Millwood	J J & Marilda McClure	Hugh & Mariam Millwood
7246	McClusky, Alfradine	KS	1868	Robert McClusky	George McMillen	Mary Boatright	Johnathan & Mary McMillen	Wm & Sallie Boatright
9356	McCollough, Alexander	AR	1837	Sarah McCollough	Thomas McCollough	Lovicie Bays	Moses McCollough	Letta Bays
9357	McCollough, Andrew	AR	1849	Mary McCollough	Thomas McCollough	Lovicie Bays	Moses McCollough	Letta Bays
9358	McCollough, David	AR	1842	Permelia McCollough	Thomas McCollough	Lovicie Bays	Moses McCollough	Letta Bays
9359	McCollough, William	AR	1848	Ama McCollough	Thomas McCollough	Lovicie Bays	Moses McCollough	Letta Bays
15079	McCollum, Martha	OK	1859	Green McCollum	Samuel Orr	Christiana McDonald		Christiana Bailey
20279	McCollum, Ruby	OK	1887		Green McCollum	Marthie Orr	John McCollum	Christiana Orr
14443	McCollum, Sarah	GA	1872	Wm McCollum	Benj Pugh	Sarah Chastain	John Pugh	O L Chastain
20278	McCollum, Toy	OK	1884		Gun McCollum	Marthie Orr	John McCollum	Christiana Orr
14460	McComas, Nellie	WV	1869	E E McComas	W H H Cook	Mary Cooper	Thos Cook & Rebecca Sizemore	
20928	McComas, Oswald et al	WV	1892		Eli McComas	Nellie Cook	Archibald & Sorvilia McComas	W.H. & Mary Cook
10445	McComick, Sarah	KY	1850	Burel McComick	Andrew Harrison	Rachel Mathis	Samuel & Rosa Harrison	A P & Lucinda Mathis
12454	McCommis, Oca	WV	1877	Burl McCommis	Wilburn Osburn	Melia Dunford	Solomon & Martha Osburn	Thomas & Honor Dunford
15511 *	McConnell, Agnes	GA	1851	Bill McConnell	Joel Lay	Violet Lynch		Betsy Lynch
15520 *	McConnell, Benjamin	GA	1853	Georgia McConnell	Frank McConnell	Eliza Bedford	Jim & Mary Shackelfoot	Jim & Sookey Independent
17695 *	McConnell, Elsie	TN	1861	Harvy McConnell	Sandy Stubbs	Easter Jones	Robert & Chaney Stubbs	Redick & Alice Jones
15519 *	McConnell, Ephraim	GA	1885		Benj McConnell	Georgia Gregory	Frank & Eliza McConnell	Ephraim & Caroline Gregory
15518 *	McConnell, Georgia	GA	1863	Benj McConnell	Epraim Gregory	Caroline Burge	Joe & Clay Witt	Touny & Clarisy Burge
15517 *	McConnell, William	GA	1883		Benj McConnell	Georgia Gregory	Frank & Eliza McConnell	Ephraim & Caroline Gregory

#	Name	State	Year					
7252	McCorkle, Mary	OK	1885	Howard McCorkle	John Collins	Thyrza McKaeig	Edward & Mary Collins	John McKaeig
16239	McCormick, Mary	OK		Mathew McCormick	Alender Free	Nancy Gunter		James & Peggie Gunter
680	McCoy, Darthula	OK	1881	Henry McCoy	Wm Tucker	Matilda Green		Tom & Hester Green
17353	McCoy, Della	GA			Ben Holcombe	Georgia Bohemon	Elisha Holcombe	F. & Margaret Bohemon
14194	McCoy, Ezekiel	OK	17yrs		Alex McCoy	Akey Archillah		Archillah & Eliza Smith
14515	McCoy, Harriet	GA	1881	Harris McCoy	Thomas McClure	Amanda Millwood	J J & Marilda McClure	Hugh & Mariam Millwood
5430	McCoy, Mary	OK	1865	James McCoy	Jason Bowman	Desdemo-na McGraw	James & Rachel Bowman	John & Martha McGraw
7783	McCoy, Mary	KS	1885	Carl McCoy	Jonathan Miller	Mary Foley	Wm & Susan Miller	James & Rhoda Foley
12014	McCoy, Rebecca	GA	1855	Elijah McCoy	William Cook	Nancy Underwood	Katie Cook	Elijah & Nellie Underwood
6343	McCoy, Trudy	AL		R W McCoy	Ben Bryars	Lucretia Miles		Nellie Miles
19151*	McCoy, William	GA	1832	Julia McCoy		Mary McCoy		Millie
17553	McCracken, John	OK	1874	Oneida McCracken	Wm McCracken	Sarah Bullett	James & Charlotte McCracken	
7470	McCracken, Kelsey	OK	1862	none	David McCracken	Sarah Wilson	Johnnie & Ailsie McCracken	Arch & Huldie Wilson
5589	McCracken, Ollie	OK	1903	Joseph McCracken	Joseph McCracker	Ollie Deason	Wm & Taudora McCracken	Arch & Elizabeth Deason
14277	McCracken, Rufus	OK	1864	Mary McCracken	Wm McCracken	Ellen Alberty	Charlotte McCracken	
19631	McCrary, John	TN	1860	Mary McCrary	Bob McCrary	Lizzie Grissom	Samuel & Sallie McCrary	
19630	McCrary, Maybelle	TN	1888	Sam McCrary	John McCrary	Ritzie McCraig	Robert & Elizabeth McCrary	
17238	McCroskey, Mary	OK	1855	Samuel McCroskey	Francis Cox	Rebecca Evans	Wm & Rebecca Cox	Carter & Susan Evans
20430	McCullough, Leitha	TN	1831		William Armstrong	Betsy		
7250	McCullough, Mattie	MO	1867	Robert McCullough	Jesse Roberts	Mary Wylie	Andrew & Eliza Roberts	John & Elizabeth Blackburn
20392	McDade, Mary	TN	1846		Eli Robertson	Temperance Lewis	Wm & Mary Robertson	John & Temperance Lewis
7806	McDaniel, Grace	OK	1876	Willis McDaniel	Thomas Yates	Cordelia Womack		Henrietta Yates
14374	McDaniel, Henry	AL	1847	Sarah McDaniel	James McDaniel	Martha Moore	Aaron & Sallie McDaniel	
3966	McDaniel, James	OK	1885	none	George McDaniel	Dora Lunchford	Red Bird McDaniel	Polly Sixkiller
16037	McDaniel, Rebecca	GA	1837	James McDaniel	W B Swann	Polly Kelly	James & Rebecca Swann	
3273	McDonald, Alfred	NC	1860	Amanda McDonald	James McDonald	Jemima Deaton	Anquish & Sallie McDonald	Johnathan & Sarah Deaton
18009	McDonald, Alfred	GA	1861	Sarah McDonald	Lafayette McDonald	Sarah Bayett	Washington & Mary McDonald	Alfred Bayett & Nancy Jacobs
22682	McDonald, Birdie	TN	1885		William McDonald	Josie Hicks	James & Sarah McDonald	John & Rebecca Hicks
173	McDonald, Edward	OK	1840	Annie McDonald	James McDonald	Annie Baldridge	Goodeon & Susie McDonald	

222	McDonald, James	NC	1821	Jinna McDonald	Angus McDonald	Sallie Blythe		Jonathan & Annie Blythe
5573	McDonald, James	IL	1845	Elizabeth McDonald	Jonathan McDonald	Harriet Donaldson	Anquish & Sallie McDonald	
6757	McDonald, Jeptha	NC	44yrs	Sarah	James McDonald	Mina Deaton	Anguish & Sallie McDonald	
5425	McDonald, Jesse	GA	1840	Sallie McDonald	Jonathan McDonald	Harrit Davidson	Anguish & Sallie McDonald	
2662	McDonald, John	NC	1846	Malindy Killian		Sarah McDonald	Johnathan Blythe	Sallie Blythe
5416	McDonald, John	NC	1849	Mary McDonald	Jonathan McDonald	Harriet Davidson	Anguish & Sallie McDonald	
9449	McDonald, Josephine	GA	1861	Adelbert McDonald	John Corn	Caroline Davis	Wm & Phebee Corn	John Davis & Nancy Bird
13721*	McDonald, Mary	GA	1847	Clark McDonald	Ned Brown	Martha Bly	Cue & Tilla Tiffens	Wilkerson & Hannah Bly
20249	McDonald, Mary	TN			John Lane	Louisa Phillips	Lindsey & Rebecca Lane	George & Mary Phillips
20177*	McDonald, Mattie	TN		Joe McDonald	Mose Beassle	Winnie Boyd		
6334	McDonald, Mrs J.H.	AL	38yrs	J H McDonald	John Taylor	Minerva Paine	Richard & Susan Taylor	John & Mary Paine
15199	McDonald, Nathan	NC	1876		John McDonald	Malinda Killian	Sallie McDonald	Burl & Martha Killian
6763	McDonald, Newton	NC	1865	Savanah McDonald	James Mc Donald	Minnie Deaton	Anguish & Sallie McDonald	Jonathan Deaton & Sallie McKinney
15198	McDonald, Noah	NC	1880	Dovie McDonald	John McDonald	Malinda Killian	Sallie McDonald	Burl & Martha Killian
5415	McDonald, Thomas	NC	1856	Louisa McDonald	Jonathan McDonald	Harriet Davidson	Anguish & Sallie McDonald	
13555	McDonald, Thomas	KS	1854		Duncan McDonald	Lucinda Smith		James & Sanders Smith
22683	McDonald, Tully	TN	1883		William McDonald	Josie Hicks	James & Sarah McDonald	John & Rebecca Hicks
550	McDonald, William	TN	1866	Presilla McDonald	David McDonald	Rachel McNeill	Anguish & Sarah McDonald	James & Lucy McNeill
1513	McDonald, William	NC	1850	Flora McDonald		Sallie McDonald		Anguish & Sallie McDonald
13729*	McDonald, William	GA	1865		Clark McDonald	Mary Brown	Stoker Crow & Maria Moss	Ned & Martha Brown
19089	McDonald, William	TN	1861	Josephine McDonald	James McDonald	Sarah Selvage	Allen McDonald	
372	McDonald, Wm J.	TN	1866	Priscilla McDonald	David McDonald	Rachel McNeill	Anguish & Sarah McDonald	Joseph & Lucy McNeill
18721	McDowell, Amanda	TN	1845	Joseph McDowell	Willis Guy	Mahala Gibson	Edmund & Judie Guy	George & Viney Gibson
10656	McDuffie, Amelia	GA	1848	John McDuffie	Reuben Hill	Darkis Nubia		Winnie Nubia
15516	McDuffie, Robert	GA	1847	Marguerite McDuffie	Jim MacDuffie	Sallie Ross		
6958	McElhaney, Mary	OK	1876	Wiley McElhaney	Jasper Chaney	Ellen Ragsdale		Isaac & Mary Ragsdale
18014*	McElrath, Alice	TN		Louis McElrath	Hamilton	Caroline Keith	Matilda Ward	
3115	McElroy, Charles	MS	1869	Pattie McElroy	Ransom McElroy	Nancy Hobgood		Charles & Martha Hobgood

3114	McElroy, Nancy	MS	1845	Ransom McElroy	Charles Hobgood	Martha Lowe		Thomas & Annie Lowe
3113	McElroy, Ransom	MS	1878	Lottie McElroy	R L McElroy	Nancy Hobgood		Charles & Martha Hobgood
3112	McElroy, Robert	MS	1873	Florence McElroy	R L McElroy	Nancy Hobgood		Charles & Martha Hobgood
20096	McEntire, Indianna	GA	1886	W.M. McEntire	Pink Brown	Eliza McAllister	Bill & Martha Brown	Charley & Nanancy McAllister
17540	McFadden, Joseph	IN	1848	Mary McFadden	Wm McFadden	Elizabeth March	Wm McFadden	Wm & Nancy March
5312	McFall, Sarah	MO	1874	John McFall	Daniel Lovall	Ann Sweaney	Jonathen & Ruth Lovall	Levi & Myra Sweaney
17363 *	McFee, Ida Mae	GA	1877	W.A. McFee	A. Simalton	L. Moon	Geary & Ann Simalton	Jeony Wheeler
8218	McFerron, Sarah	MO	1850	Henry McFerron	Isaac West	Nancy Owens	Rachel West	
18371	McGaha, George	GA	1876	Pearl McGaha	William McGaha	Pagey Norton	Richard & Rebecca McGaha	Sam & Roda Norton
4170	McGaha, Rebecca	GA	1831	R D McGaha (decd)	Moses Pool	Sarah Owens	Wm & Bethany Pool	James & Any Owens
21562 *	McGahah, Harriette	GA	1847		Wesley Printis	Malinda Printis		
19109	McGavack, Harriett	AR	1855		Malachi Evans	Sarah Scarborough	Thomas Evans	
19106	McGavack, Robert	AR	1878	Mary McGavack	Joseph McGavack	Harriet Evans	America McGavack	Malachi & Sarah Evans
7782	McGee, Jesse	OK	1854	Jennie McGee	Robert McGee	Easter Berry	Holden McGee	
14333	McGee, Jessie Jr	OK		Mary McGee	Jesse McGee	Jennie Gardner	Robert & Easter McGee	
3362	McGee, Len	AL	29yrs		John McGee	- Gibson	Billy & Eliza McGee	
16474	McGee, Rosa	GA	1882	James McGee	Leroy Bettes	Nancy Thompson	Wm Lettiner & Nancy Bettes	
16945	McGeehon, W.B.	KS		Wilma	John McGeehon	Melvina Daniel		John & Mary Daniel
21269	McGehee, Leana	OK	1885	W.A. McGehee	J.T. West	Catherine Polk	M.C. West	C.A. & Arbella Polk
3421	McGhee, Mrs Frasier	AL	36yrs	Frasier McGhee	Alex Rollin	Julia McGhee	Jack & Polly Rollin	Jack & Mariah McGhee
3415	McGhee, Andrew	AL	28yrs	Bama McGhee	John McGhee	Polly Gibson	Richard McGhee & Elisabeth Henson	Bart Gibson & Peggy Moniac
3413	McGhee, Bama	AL		Andrew McGhee	William McGhee	Julia McGhee	Richard & Betsy McGhee	Jack & Maria McGhee
3412	McGhee, Bessie	AL	1883	Will McGhee	Elax Robbin	Mary Hathcock	Jack & Polly Robbin	John & Rosa Hathcock
3332	McGhee, Betsy	AL		none	Jack McGhee	Mariah Adams	Linn & Hettie McGhee	
3369	McGhee, Bettie	AL	20yrs	none	Will McGhee	Julia McGhee	Jack & Maria McGhee	Richard & Elizabeth McGhee
1156	McGhee, Carmen	AL	1867	Mary McGhee	John McGhee	Louise Gibson	Richard Mc Ghee & Elizabeth Hensen	Wm Gibson & Peggy Monac
3429	McGhee, Charles	AL	26yrs	Lucy Rollin	John McGhee	Polly Gibson	Richard McGhee & Elisabeth Henson	Bart Gibson & Peggy Moniac
1146	McGhee, David	AL	1875	none	John McGhee	Louisa Gibson	Richard & Elizabeth McGhee	Wm Gibson & Peggy Monac

1160	McGhee, Drucilla	AL	1848	John McGhee	Wm Gibson	Peggy Monac		Dickson & Betsy Monac
3337	McGhee, Hettie	AL	25yrs	Len McGhee	William Colbert	Mary Moniac	Bill & Cealy Colbert	Sam & Susan Moniac
3423	McGhee, Ida	AL	1879	Lee McGhee		Peggy Rollin		Jack & Polly Rollin
18394	McGhee, Ida	AL	22yrs	Neil McGhee	Man Woods	Mary Boatwright	John Woods & Sis Boone	
3339	McGhee, Jackson	AL	1885	none	John McGhee	Drucilla Gibson	Jack & Maria McGhee	William & Peggy Gibson
1139	McGhee, John	AL		Polly McGhee	Richard McGhee	Betsy Hinson	Richard McGhee	Elisabeth Hinson
3322	McGhee, John	AL	45yrs	Sylla Gibins	Jack McGhee	Mariah	Linn McGhee	
3424	McGhee, John	AL		John McGhee	Bart Gibson	Peggy Moniac		Sam & Susan Moniac
1158	McGhee, Lee	AL	1869	Ida McGhee	John McGhee	Louise Gibson	Richard McGhee & Elizabeth Henson	Wm Gibson & Peggy Monac
3422	McGhee, Margaret	AL	31yrs	none	Alex McGhee	Elisabeth Rollin	Jack & Maria McGhee	Jack & Polly Rollin
3330	McGhee, Mary	AL	35yrs	none	Jack McGhee	Mariah Adams	Linn & Hettie McGhee	
3335	McGhee, Mary	AL	25yrs	Robert McGhee	William Colbert	---- Taylor	William & Mary Colbert	Matilda Taylor
3325	McGhee, Mrs Thomas	AL	30yrs	Thomas McGhee	William Adams	Alcie Moniac	William & Peggy Adams	William & Peggy Gibson
3403	McGhee, Mrs. William	AL	49yrs	William McGhee	Jack Rollin	Polly Moniac		Betsey Moniac
1152	McGhee, Neal	AL	1876	Ida McGhee		Betsey McGhee		Jack & Maria McGhee
6369	McGhee, Oceola	AL	1882	none	Richard McGhee	Nettie Gibson	Jack & Maria McGhee	Wm & Peggy Gibson
3420	McGhee, Richard	AL		none	Richard McGhee	Betsy Hinson	Linn McGhee	
3364	McGhee, Robert	AL		Elizabeth Colbert	Alex McGhee	Elizabeth Rollin	Jack & Mariah McGhee	Jack & Polly Rollin
3426	McGhee, Roush	AL	1880	Charley McGhee	William McGhee	Julia McGhee	Richard & Betsy McGhee	Jack & Maria McGhee
6335	McGhee, Thomas	AL	30yrs	Georgia Adams	William McGhee	Julia McGhee	Jack & Mariah McGhee	Wm & Nancy McGhee
1140	McGhee, William	AL		Julia & Peggy McGhee	Richard McGhee	Betsey Hinson		
3406	McGhee, William	AL	1876	Bessie McGhee	William McGhee	Julia McGhee	Richard & Betsy McGhee	Jack & Maria McGhee
19999*	McGill, George	TN	68yrs	Delila McGill	Rolan McGill	Jane Dixon		Jim & Jemima Dixon
502	McGill, Mary	TN	1854	Robert McGill	Soloman Helton	Liza Graves	Daniel & Martha Helton	Soloman & Nancy Graves
19102	McGill, Rosa	KY	1864	George McGill	William Marsh	Christina Mazzett	Wm & Nancy Marsh	
17869	McGinnie, Stella	MO	1881	Oscar McGinnis	George Sims	Cora Waring	Robert & Margaret Sims	H.V. & Caroline Waring
8713	McGinnis, Charlie	GA	1891	none	William McGinnis	Jane Daniel	Martin & Minervia McGinnis	Sanford & Nancy Daniel

8714	McGinnis, Ethel	GA	1890	none	William McGinnis	Jane Daniel	Martin & Minervia McGinnis	Sanford & Nancy Daniel
10562	McGinnis, James	GA	1885	none	Lawson McGinnis	Isadore Pence	Martin & Minervia McGinnis	
10563	McGinnis, John	GA	1884		Lawson McGinnis	Isadore Pence	Martin & Minervia McGinnis	
10565	McGinnis, Lawrence	GA	1902		William McGinnis	Jane Daniel	Martin & Minervia McGinnis	Stanford & Nancy Daniel
2783	McGinnis, Manerva	GA	1833	widow	James Helton	Camilla Southerland	Calvin & Sarah Helton	John & Martha Southerland
8715	McGinnis, Riller	GA	1896	none	William McGinnis	Jane Damiel	Martin & Minervia McGinnis	Sanford & Nancy Daniel
8716	McGinnis, Sidney	GA	1898	none	William McGinnis	Jane Daniel	Martin & Minervia McGinnis	Sanford & Nancy Daniel
10564	McGinnis, William	GA	1862	Jane McGinnis	Martin McGinnis	Minervia Helton	James McGinnis	James & Camery Helton
14633	McGlothern, Sarah	NC	1849		Thomas Doby	Eda Winkler	Alice Doby	
4339	McGrady, Jinnie	NC	1834	Jacob McGrady	George Blevins	Lydia Blevins	James & Lydia Blevins	
10849	McGrath, Lillie	TX	1876	Daniel McGrath	John Carnes	Amelia Morrison	Joshua & Nancy Carnes	Ezra & Sophia Morrison
21300	McGraw, Maggie	OK	1858	John McGraw	Williamson Clemmons	Parzadia Childress		Ayers & Margaret Childress
21302	McGraw, Minnie	OK	1878	Sterling McGraw	Leland Burks	Maggie Clemmons		Williamson & Parazadia Clemmons
4431	McGuire, Causady	KY			Soloman Blevins	Elizabeth Quinley	Elisha Blevins	Eli Quinley
11615	McGuire, Helen	NC	32yrs	Bill McGuire	Bill Arwood	Louiza Parker	Lishey & Niney Arwood	Willis & Adaline Parker
22508	McGuire, Helen	MO	1906	none	James McGuire	Mary Setser	John & Judy McGuire	William & Mary Setser
22507	McGuire, James	MO	1884	Josephine McGuire	John McGuire	Judy Pendergrass	Jesse & Elizabeth McGuire	John & Martha Pendergrass
22505	McGuire, Jesse	MO	1876	Rosetta McGuire	John McGuire	Judy Pendergrass	Jesse & Elizabeth Mc Guire	John & Martha Pendergrass
22514	McGuire, John	MO	1855	Tedy McGuire	Jesse McGuire	Elizabeth Lunnia	John & Rachel McGuire	Arter & Mary Lunnie
18838	McGuire, Lizzie	KS	1874	M.A. McGuire	Henry Neff	Hannah Hammonds		Martin Hammonds & Mary Elmore
11374	McGuire, Loney	NC	32yrs	Joseph McGuire	James Adams	Anna Barnett	John & Oma Adams	Thos & Elizabeth Barnett
12200	McGuire, Margaret	NC	1854	Henry McGuire	Ralzamore Henslee	Sarah Morgan	Benjamin Henslee	George Morgan
22509	McGuire, Saide	MO	1906	none	Jesse McGuire	Rosetta Jones	John & Judy McGuire	Marian & Martha Jones
22511	McGuire, Tedy	MO	1893	none	John McGuire	Judy Pendergrass	Jesse & Elizabeth McGuire	John & Martha Pendergrass
16072	McGuire, Thomas	OK	1873	Emma McGuire	Jassie McGuire	Elizabeth Loonay	Jassie McGuire & Bettie Moore	Aurthur Loonay
22510	McGuire, William	MO	1896	none	John McGuire	Judy Pendergrass	Jesse & Elizabeth McGuire	John & Martha Penddergrass
22915	McGuire, William	OK	1862	Katie McGuire	Thomas McGuire	Sarah Fender	Thomas McGuire	Daniel & Dice Fender
414	McGuire, Wm D	OK	1862	Katie Buckles	Thomas McGuire	Sarah Fender	Thomas McGuire	Alexander Brown
17531	McHan, Arminda	GA	1846	Alfred McHan	Ancil Roe	Ara Tally	Ancil Roe	Horatio & Mary Tally

7547	McIntosh, Corda	OK	1885	Newt McIntosh	David Swadley	Mary Fannin		Joseph & Jane Fannin
19152	McIntosh, Dudley	GA	1849	Lizzie, Ellen McIntosh	Alex McIntosh	Martha Ross		
13957	McIntosh, Freeland	OK	1852	Kate McIntosh	Daiel McIntosh	Jane Ward	Susannah McIntosh	
12013	McIntosh, John	GA	1836	Susan & Sarah	John McIntosh	Jane Giles	Chilly McIntosh	
12696	McIntosh, John	OK	1840		Arch McIntosh	Ca la nus ke		
15182	McKay, William	GA	1874	Lou McKay	John McKay	Martha White		
9190	McKay, Wilson	OK		Liza McKay	Will McKay	Culleban		
12208	McKeehan, Sarah	TN	1843	A L McKeehan	Isaac Holcome	Rebecca Morgan	Benjamin Holcome	George Morgan
20380	McKeel, James	TN	1873	Laura McKeel	Henry McKeel	Mariah Gann	Mark McKeel	George & Eliza Gann
148	McKellar, Louisa	OK	1851		Christopher Miller	Permelia Williams	Abe Miller	Sam & Nancy Williams
22515	McKenzie, Alexander	TN	1882	none	William McKenzie	Sarah Hudson		William & Mary Hudson
16390	McKenzie, Maggie	CA	1877	Joseph McKenzie	Alfred Duncan	Lucy Murphy	Caleb & Mary Duncan	
17506	McKenzie, Mary	OK	1858	Henry McKenzie	Jesse Whitely	Elizabeth Harp	Samuel & Lucy Whitely	
9985	McKenzie, Sarah	TN	1850	W.M. McKenzie	William Hudson	Polly Lawson	Henry Hudson & Sarah Ross	Tye Lawson & Polly Hart
17926	McKeown, Sallie	TN	1850	William McKeown	Samuel McCamish	Mary Nyden		
746 *	McKiney, Alsie	NC	1855	Henry McKiney	Benjamin Burgess	Matilda Ross	William Burgess	
10181	McKinley, Caroline	GA		W R McKinley	John Helton	Delila Hester	Joseph Helton & Letta Spradly	Benj Hester & Milla Aires
1775	McKinney, Cisco	GA	1850	James McKinney	David Adams	Clerinda Parker		Jonathan & Oma Parker
2248	McKinney, David	GA	1875	Dora McKinney	James McKinney	Cisca Adams	Allen & Fannie McKinney	David & Clerinda Adams
15763	McKinney, George R.	WV			John McKinney	Jinney Sizemore	Samul & Betsy McKinney	Franklin & Polly Sizemore
6550	McKinney, Jinney	WY	1852	John McKinney	Franklin Sizemore	Polly Workman	George Sizemore	Joseph Workman
1033	McKinney, Malinda	GA	1861	G. McKinney	Dave Lambert	Sarah Sawyers		Charly & Patsy Sawyers
21646	McKinney, Martha	NC	1887	Sammie McKinney	Thomas Ball	Margarette Maney		Martin & Matilda Maney
19755	McKinnon, Laura	MS	1875		James Parker	Mary Ball		
1472	McKinzey, Simon	OK	1841	Emma McKinzey	Jeff McKinzey	Nancy Ookahyetah	Oosquut	Cheyowelah
10620	McKinzie, George	OK	1858	Ida McKinzie	Allen McKinzie	Sallie Green		James Green
223	McKinzie, Sarah	OK	1847	Lonzo McKinzie	Bill Taylor	Feby Kirk	William Monroe	
21806	McKown, William	OK	1864	Carrie McKown	S. McKown	Tabitha Box		W.B. Box
11350	McLain, Florence	GA	1863	R E McLain	Thomas Loyd	Susan Matthews	Thos & Susanna Loyd	Lewis & Elizabeth Matthews
16736	McLane, Lou	OK	1870	Austin McLane	Jasper Chaney	Ellen Ragsdale		Isaac & Mary Ragsdale

787	McLaughlin, Ezekiel	OK	1838	widower	Ezekiel McLaughlin	Polly McDaniel	Buffington	McDaniel
13450	McLaughlin, Nancy	OK	1864	William McLaughlin	James Chouteau	Sarah Alberty		
549 *	McLelland, Isaac	NC	1821	Lucy McLelland	Ned Grimes	Dorcus McLelland	unknown	unknown
2094	Mcloore, Ader	NC	1884	Arthur Mclore	Urvin Dickson	Mary Blevins		Alford & Marjary Blevins
6129	McLower, Maud	NC	1881	Samuel McClure	Alfred Blevins	Margary Sheets	James & Meacy Blevins	
19277	McMahan, Cora	NC	1882	Robert McMahan	Bry Lowery	Mary Gasoway		Henry & Millie Gasoway
19283	McMahan, James	NC	1880	Alice McMahan	Samuel McMahan	Mary Mason		John & Pollie Mason
19153	McMahan, John	GA	1852	Amanda McMahan	James McMahan	Sallie Little	Wm & Jane McMahan	
19290	McMahan, John	NC	1882	Callie McMahan	Samuel McMahan	Mary Mason		John & Pollie Mason
19245	McMahan, Martha	NC	1853	A.H. McMahan	William Miller	Catherine Martin	John & Ann Miller	Sammie & Elizabeth Martin
19278	McMahan, Robert	NC	1872	Cora McMahan	Samuel McMahan	Mary Mason		John & Pollie Mason
8427	McMahon, Louisa	NC	1856	Samuel McMahon	John Mason	Pollie Robinson		Aaron & Jane Robinson
20843 *	McMakin, Sylvia	GA	1856		Gloucester Garrett	Rinda Garrett	Gloucester & Rachel Cloud	
22008 *	McMellon, Monin	GA	1857	none	Wimbaly McMellon	Philis Cook	Toney Griffin	July Jordan
9199	McMickins, Mary	NC	54 yrs	Paul McMickins	Joshua Payne	Patsy Hayden	Leonard & Sally Payne	Robert & Susanna Hayden
21498	McMillan, Martha	TX		A. McMillan	John Stephens	Suburna Malicote	Benj & Elizabeth Stephens	
7247	McMillen, Dilsa	MO	1874	none	George McMillen	Mary Boatright	Jonathan & Mary McMillen	Wm & Sallie Boatright
7248	McMillen, Margaret	MO	1880	none	George McMillen	Mary Boatright	Jonathan & Mary McMillen	Wm & Sallie Boatright
7249	McMillen, Mary	MO	1844	George McMillen	William Boatright	Sallie Gates	Benj Boatright & Elizabeth Blackburn	Jacob & Susan Gates
7260	McMillen, William	MT	1867	Mary McMIllen	George McMillen	Mary Boatright	Jonathan & Mary McMillen	Wm & Sallie Boatright
20636	McNabb, William	TN	1871	Lillie McNabb	Henry McNabb	Sina Climes	Taylor & Mary McNabb	Antny & Edie Climes
8445	McNeill, James	OK	1849	widower	Joel McNeill	Margaret Skiller		John & Rebecca Skiller
18029	McNew, Robert	IN	1859	Mary McNew	Aaron McNew	Mary Alford	Elijah McNew	Wm & Millio Alford
17456	McNutt, Lizzie	MO	1872	John McNutt	Samuel Richards	Amanda Harralson	Martin & Lucy Richards	Vinson & Martha Harralson
20758	McPherson, Claude	GA	1906		Larkin McPherson	Mary Going	Cicero & Fanny McPherson	Wm & Delia Going
14747	McPherson, Harriet	OK	1832	Hugh McPherson	John Candy	Mary Watie	Samuel & Betsy Candy	
19380	McPherson, Lucy	GA	1884	Marshall McPherson	Newton Richardson	Bettie Jordan	James & Nancy Richardson	Noah & Martha Jordan
20759	McPherson, Mary	GA	1882	Larkin McPherson	William Going	Delia Cole	Wm & Nancy Going	John & Betsy Cole
541	McPherson, Polly	OK	1842	John McPherson	Isaac Ragsdale	Mary Sanders	John & Ellen Ragsdale	Elexander & Peggie Sanders

ID	Name	State	Year					
21932	McRoy, Annie	TN	1878	Jesse McRoy	Silas Carroll	Lucinda Haynes	James & Lucinda Carroll	Joseph & Matilda Haynes
21899	McRoy, Lue	TN	1880	John McRoy	Silas Carroll	Lucinda Haynes	James & Lucinda Carroll	Jos & Matilda Haynes
14761	McVey, Hiley	KY			Wells Blevins	Nancy Blevins	Wells Blevins	Elisha Blevins
18679	McVoy, John	FL		Dolly McVoy	W. McVoy	Harriet Monk		John & Silva Monk
18680	McVoy, Mary	FL	1877	W. McVoy	W. McVoy	Harriet Monk		John & Silva Monk
20698	McWhorter, Esther	TX	1883	Charlie McWhorter	Frank Hatcher	Elizabeth Collier	John Hatcher	
20697	McWhorter, Gena	TX	1883	F.M. McWhorter	Frank Hatcher	Elizabeth Collier	John Hatcher	
10839	Meacham, Helen	NC	1857	Billy Meacham	Jessie Morse	Liddie Lowe		Thomas & Annie Lowe
10840	Meacham, Jesse	NC	1876	Lula Meacham	Billy Meacham	Helen Morse		Jesse & Liddie Morse
6020	Meadows, Carrie	IL	1889	J E Meadows	James Jourdan	Lydia Friend	Joseph & Sarah Jourdan	
8845	Meadows, Daisy	IL	1886	William Meadows	Aquilla Jourdan	Mary Boyles	Joseph & Sarah Jourdan	
7534	Meadows, Joseph	IL	1888	none	Eli Meadows	Sarah Jourdan		Joseph & Sarah Jourdan
17688	Meadows, Matilda	TN	1848		Commodore Caldwell	Louisa Walters		Burton & Kiziah Coley
17289	Meadows, Polly	VA	25yrs		John Cline	Louisa Sizemore	John & Polly Cline	Franklin & Polly Sizemore
20323	Mealor, Lettie	GA	1834		Samuel Smith	Elsie Maddox	Abraham & Anna Smith	Bob Maddox
20959	Mealor, Roxie	SC	1864	Robert Mealor	Joseph Blackwell	Mary Ridley		Wm Ridley & Mary Early
13435	Measles, Jeff	OK	1856					
19673	Medcalf, V.A.	TN	1848	W.W. Medcalf	Wm Hatcher	Elisabeth Hooper	John & Henrietta Hatcher	Joseph & Rutha Hooper
19672	Medcalf, William	TN	1881	Hetty Medcalf	Wallace Medcalf	Victory Hatcher	Joel & Susan Medcalf	Wm & Elisabeth Hatcher
16479	Meeks, Hugh	GA	1851	Manda Meeks	Littleton Meeks	Francis Brown	Littleton & Polly Meeks	Robert Brown
19192	Meeks, Nancy	OK	1867	John Meeks	James Scott	Nancy Vann	Benj Scott	John & Sally Vann
10917	Meeks, William	OK	1879	Goldie Meeks	George Meeks	Delpheny Fleetwood		Charles & Lucinda Fleetwood
8826	Mellon, Belinda	MO		Joseph Mellon	John Elliott	Rebeca Wilson	Jonas & Nancy Elliott	Soloman & Elizabeth Wilson
21345	Melton, Haris	AR	1889		Henry Melton	Nancy Burnett	William Melton	John & Lydia Burnett
10289	Melton, Isabelle	OK	1857	Simpson Melton	William Graham	Nancy Matoy		Wm & Martha Matoy
21491	Melton, John	AR	1892		Henry Melton	Nancy Burnett	Wm Melton & Louveinda Rogers	John & Lydia Burnett
2897	Melton, Mary	NC	39yrs	Thomas Melton	William Martin	Sarah Rowland	Joseph & Mary Martin	Andrew & Polly Rowland
8121	Melton, Mary	OK	1838	S M Melton	William Matoy	Martha Smith		
18790	Mendenhall, Clarence	KS	1897		Wm Mendenhall	Delilah Lattur	Nancy Mendenhall	
18787	Mendenhall, Emma	KS	1901		Wm Mendenhall	Delilah Lattur	Nancy Mendenhall	
18788	Mendenhall, Enda	KS	1899		Wm Mendenhall	Delilah Lattur	Nancy Mendenhall	
18786	Mendenhall, Inez	KS	1903		Wm Mendenhall	Delilah Lattur	Nancy Mendenhall	
18789	Mendenhall, Willard	KS	1906		Wm Mendenhall	Delilah Lattur	Nancy Mendenhall	

18297	Mendenhall, William	KS	1868		Andrew Mendenhall	Nancy Colvard		
18785	Mendenhall, William Jr.	KS	1900		Wm Mendenhall	Delilah Lattur	Nancy Mendenhall	
17333	Merchant, Andrew	AL	1834	Lucinda Merchant	Wm Merchant	Lydia Bass	David Merchant	Bass Given
9777	Merck, Mattie	GA	1852	Joe Merck	Ambrose Payne	Sydney Posey	Thos Payne & Mary Mason	Patter Posey & Articia Chumley
16486*	Merrell, William	NC	1854	Louisa Merrell	Henry Merrell	Luzetta Hurley	Henry & Harriet Dishus	York & Asa Hurley
7840	Merritt, Charley	GA	1892		William Merritt	Clarka Helton	George & Lucinda Merritt	Clark & Mary Helton
7841	Merritt, Daisy	GA	1895		William Merritt	Clarka Helton	George & Lucinda Merritt	Clark & Mary Helton
61	Merritt, Rhoda	GA	1869	Frank Merritt	Elijah Pilgrim	Rhoda Ledbetter	Elijah & Betsy Pilgrim	Wm & Malinda Ledbetter
7842	Merritt, Twiggs	GA	1888		William Merritt	Clarka Helton	George & Lucinda Merritt	Clark & Mary Helton
17622	Mesinheimer, Lyda	OR	1873	Mose Mesinheimer	James Pratt	Louisa Musgrove		Elizabeth Musgrove
21454	Messick, Ura	TX	1882		Frank Jeter	Adelia Thompson	George & Mary Jeter	
3563	Metcalf, Absalom Jr	TN	1831		Hiram Metcalf Sr	Jane Hensley	Absalom & Nancy Metcalf	
22474	Metcalf, Amanda	TN	39yrs	none	William Metcalf	Martha Hensley	Hiram & Jane Metcalf	Wm & Sela Hensley
4478	Metcalf, Arphena	NC	1871	William Ramsey	Henry Metcalf	Sarah Crawford	Hiram & Jane Metcalf	Benson & Eda Crawford
12169	Metcalf, Cornelia	NC			Absalem Metcalf	Catherine Mitchell	Hiram & Jane Metcalf	John & Effsiha Mitchell
1577	Metcalf, Emerson	NC	1874	Zane Metcalf	Henry Metcalf	Sarah Crawford	Hiram & Jane Metcalf	Benson & Eda Crawford
3921	Metcalf, George	NC	1886	none	Henry Metcalf	Sarah Crawford	Hiram & Jane Metcalf	Benson & Eda Crawford
5294	Metcalf, George	NC	1886	none	Henry Metcalf	Sarah Crawford	Hiram & Jane Metcalf	Benson & Eda Crawford
3488	Metcalf, Henry	NC	1862		Enos Metcalf	Catherine Norton	Hiram & Jane Metcalf	Drew & Nancy Norton
12165	Metcalf, Hiram	NC	1854	Rachel Metcalf	Absalem Metcalf	Catherine Mitchell	Hiram & Jane Metcalf	John & Effsiha Mitchell
3524	Metcalf, Hiram Jr.	TN			Hiram Metcalf	Jane Hensley	Absalom & Nancy Metcalf	
9882	Metcalf, James	NC	1878	Ellen Metcalf	Henry Metcalf	Sarah Crawford	Hiram & Jane Metcalf	Benson & Eda Crawford
12164	Metcalf, John	NC	1865	Georgeana Metcalf	Absalem Metcalf	Catherine Mitchell	Hiram & Jane Metcalf	John & Effsiha Mitchell
22473	Metcalf, John	TN	1874			Margaret Metcalf		Wm & Martha Metcalf
3489	Metcalf, John Sr.	TN	1843		Hiram Metcalf	Jane Hensley	Absalom & Nancy Metcalf	
12170	Metcalf, Lee	NC	1882	Lucy Metcalf		Cornelia Metcalf		Absalem & Cathrine Metcalf
22475	Metcalf, Margarett	TN	52yrs	none	William Metcalf	Martha Hensley	Hiram & Jane Metcalf	Wm & Sela Hensley
22472	Metcalf, Mary	TN	41yrs		William Metcalf	Martha Hensley	Hiram & Jane Metcalf	
18443	Metcalf, Milton	TN	1879	Alice Metcalf	Hiram Metcalf	Loveda Pendley	Hiram & Jennie Metcalf	

14882	Metcalf, Nancy	NC	1875	Joe Roberson	Absalam Metcalf	Catharine Mitchell	Hiram Sr & Jinnie Metcalf	Johnie & Ethsiler Mitchell
19268	Metcalf, Robert	TN	1878	Margie Metcalf	Hiram Metcalf	Loveda Pendley	Hiram Metcalf & Jennie Hensley	
6254	Metcalf, Surena	GA			Lewis Hensley	Elizabeth Metcalf	Benjamin & Nancy Hensley	Absalom & Nancy Metcalf
8876	Metcalf, Thomas	NC	1857		Hiram Metcalf	Jane Hensley	Absalon & Nancy Metcalf	Benj & Nancy Hensley
17617	Metcalf, Wesley	NC	1854		Hiram Metcalf	Jane Hensley	Absalon & Nancy Metcalf	Benj & Nancy Hensley
1578	Metcalf, Wiley	NC	1869	Laura Metcalf	Henry Metcalf	Sarah Crawford	Hiram & Jane Metcalf	Benson & Eda Crawford
5179	Metcalf, Willard	TN	1871	Mary Metcalf	Abrah Metcalf	Catherine Mitchell	Hiram Metcalf	Jenie
389	Metcalf, William	TN	1833	Martha Metcalf	Hiram Metcalf	Jane Hensley	Absalon & Nancy Metcalf	
3564	Metcalf, William	TN			Enos Metcalf	Catharine Norton	Hiram & Jane Metcalf	
21802	Metzker, Martha	OK	1875	John Matzker	William Sparks	Mary Beaty	Rebecca Purvis	
20277	Meyers, Rozenia	AR	1881		William Hughes	Mary Wilkenson	William Hughes	Harnon Wilkenson
12735	Michael, Abraham	TN	1866	Nancy Michael	Lemuel Michael	Mary Irvin	Jacob Michael	George & Phoebe Irvin
12738	Michael, George	TN	1857		Lemuel Michael	Mary Irvin	Jacob Michael	George & Phoebe Irvin
12733	Michael, Jacob	TN	1873	Rosa Michael	Lemuel Michael	Mary Irvin	Jacob Michael	George & Phoebe Irvin
12736	Michael, John	TN	1864	Susan Michael	Lemuel Michael	Mary Irvin	Jacob Michael	George & Phoebe Irvin
12737	Michael, Mary	TN	1834	Lemuel Michael	George Irvin	Phoebe Lemmons		Jesse Lemmons
18737	Michem, Oney	WV	1888	Rife Michem	Calvin Sizemore	Kate Huffman	Ned & Jane Sizemore	George & Kathrine Huffman
18738	Michem, Rife	WV	1884	Omey Michem	Sam Mitchem	Omey Sizemore	Frank & Jean Mitchem	Owen & Nancy Sizemore
18871	Mickey, Eliza	NC	1864	Jory Mickey	Payton Owens Sr.	Eliza Marion	Leonard Sr. & Polly Scott	Jeremiah Marion & Mary Howard
16062	Mickle, Sarah	KS	53yrs	Zelus Eustee				
11400	Middleton, Charles	IL	1860	Maggie Middleton	George Middleton	Parthena Keel	Harris & Nancy Middleton	David & Martha Keel
18516	Middleton, George	NM	1874	Mattie Middleton	Charles Middleton	Mary Breeze	Wm & Nancy Middleton	
9824	Middleton, James	OK	1864	Mollie Middleton	Charles Middleton	Mary Breeze	Wm & Nancy Middleton	
6012	Middleton, John	AR	1836		William Middleton	Nancy Eddings		John & Elizabeth Eddings
13872	Middleton, Marion	OK	1871	Ida Middleton	Charles Middleton	Mary Breeze	William Middleton	
8447	Midkiff, Martha	WV	1831	widow	Johnithan James	Poly Bandy	William James	
17423	Mikel, Martha	OK	1875	R. Mikel	Benj Courtney	Matilda Fender	Wm & Matilda Courtney	Daniel & Dicey Fender
16539	Milam, J.G.	WV	1871	Grace Milam	Reece Milam	Mary Boman		
5788	Milam, Lemmer	OK	1878	Henry Milam	Milton Monroe	Henrietta Livengood	Wm & Rebecca Monroe	Daniel & Sarah Livengood
16538	Milam, R.L.	WV	1868	Louvina Milam	Russell Milam	Narcisas Sizemore		George Sizemore

ID	Name	State	Year/Age	Spouse	Parent 1	Parent 2	Grandparents 1	Grandparents 2
16877	Milem, John	WV	53yrs	Alice Milem	Russel Milem	Narcissus Sizemore	James & Nancy Milem	George & Jennie Sizemore
17453	Milem, Nancy	WV	55yrs		Rue Milem	Narcis Sizemore		
17867	Miles, Bobbie	OK			Noah Williams	Lewcinda Barton		Louis & Lucinda Williams
22444	Miles, Eller	OK	1887	W.E. Miles	Alford Greenhill	Parelee Morriss	Edward Morris	Eliza Drummond
3399	Miles, James	AL	1871	Georgia Benby	Wily Miles	Sarah Leatherwood		
13870	Miles, John	GA	1825	Martha Miles	Thomas Miles	Patsy Payton		Moses & Nancy Payton
18517	Miles, Sam	TN	1837	Lizzie Miles	Sam Miles	Jane Collins	Wm Miles	Jane Bowlin
18541	Miles, Usebia	TN	1844		Sam Miles	Jane Collins	Wm Miles	Jane Bowlin
18411	Miles, William	AL	57yrs	Mattie Miles	Benjis Miles	Frances Powell	Thomas & Betsy Franklin	
8571	Miller, Abram	NC	1865	Malinda Miller	Marion Miller	Betty Blevins		Betsey Blevins
11086	Miller, Aley	NC	1852	Eli Miller	Stephen Hart	Rebecca Powers	John & Nancy Hart	
6856	Miller, Allen	NC	1849	Marie Miller	Isaac Miller	Barhaly Blevins	Isaac & Eva Miller	Wills & Elizabeth Blevins
8566	Miller, Asa	NC	1862	Nancy Miller	Marion Miller	Betty Blevins		Betsey Blevins
10567	Miller, Augustus	GA	1893		William Miller	Harriett Bowling	Ben & Polly Miller	Alex & Elizabeth Bowling
6855	Miller, Basheba	NC	1869	none	Allen Miller	America Blevins	Isaac & Bathshib Miller	George & Lydia Blevins
11090	Miller, Binnie	NC	1890		Eli Miller	Ailey Hart		Stephen & Rebecca Hart
16128	Miller, Bluford	OK			Jacob Miller	Susan Fields		Rider Fields
16129	Miller, Charles	OK	1841		Jacob Miller	Susan Fields		Rider Fields
21889	Miller, Charles	GA	1879	Lena Miller	Timothy Miller	Mary Haggard	John & Charity Miller	David & Martha Haggard
11084	Miller, Charley	NC	1886		Eli Miller	Aley Hart		Stephen & Rebecca Hart
8524	Miller, Charlotte	NC	1879	Wilda Miller	Elisha Roop	Manda Osborn		James & Rachel Osborn
21882	Miller, Cicero	GA	1882		Timothy Miller	Mary Haggard	John & Charity Miller	David & Martha Haggard
4574	Miller, Claud	VA	1885	none	James Miller	Elizabeth Miller	Isaac & Abashia Miller	Abram & Elizabeth Miller
7263	Miller, Claude	KS	1883	Cora Miller	Jonathan Miller	Mary Foley	Wm & Susan Miller	James & Rhoda Foley
22319*	Miller, Dora	OK	1878	widow	William Richardson	Caroline Ratcliff		Lewis & Winnie Scott
3907	Miller, Dorah	VA	1880		James Osborn	Elisabeth Wingler	James Osborn	Elisabeth Wingler
10373	Miller, Eli	MO	1840	Silva Miller	Martin Miller	Polly Love	Henry Miller	James Love
11085	Miller, Eli	NC	1851	Aley Miller	Isaac Miller	Burhaley Blevins	Isaac & Eva Miller	Wells & Elizabeth Blevins
7584	Miller, Elihu	VA	1882	Maud Miller	James Miller	Elizabeth Miller	Isaac & Abasha Miller	Abram & Elizabeth Miller
34	Miller, Eliza	MO	1851	Josephus Miller	Evan Short	Nancy Jones	Reuben & Levina Short	Wm Jones & Sidanna Burks
10416	Miller, Elizabeth	NC	1871	none	Nathan Miller	Mary Privott	Abraham & Elizabeth Miller	

9843	Miller, Ellen	MO	1861	William Miller	A C Sloan	Mary Hambelton	Jeremiah Sloan	Sarah Hambelton
4897	Miller, Evaline	VA	1857	William Miller	Riley Blevins	Agnes Barker	Eli Blevins & Milley Brineger	Edward & Catherine Barker
8570	Miller, Evaline	NC	1863	none	Marion Miller	Betty Blevins		Betsey Blevins
7724	Miller, Flora	OK	1859	C W Miller	Wm Trotter	Louisa Pittsenborger		John & Cathrine Pittsenborger
15934*	Miller, Franklin	GA	1855	Jane Edmison	Spencer Miller	Sophie Davis		
15534	Miller, Genonia	GA	1885		Isaac Miller	Victoria Bond	Wm & Ann Miller	George & Sallie Bond
7262	Miller, George	KS	1869	Ida Miller	Jonathan Miller	Mary Foley	Wm & Susan Miller	James & Rhoda Foley
20383	Miller, Harriet	TN	1857	Clinton Miller	John Ellis	Elizabeth Bush	Moses & Rachel Ellis	Calvin & Elizabeth Bush
10566	Miller, Harriett	GA	1857		Alex Bowling	Elizabeth Kines	John Bowling	Martin & Elizabeth Kines
14237	Miller, Harriett	GA	1849		Green Redmond	Betsie Richards	John Redmond	Betsie Richards
4097	Miller, Ida	VA				Adeline Hart	Washington & Elisabeth Finley	Elisha & Nancy Hart
15533	Miller, Iona	GA	1890		Isaac Miller	Victoria Bond	Wm & Ann Miller	George & Sallie Bond
7261	Miller, James	KS	1879	Nellie Miller	Jonathan Miller	Mary Foley	Wm & Susan Miller	James & Rhoda Foley
14233*	Miller, James	GA	1859	Martha Miller	Newborn Jarrett	Vincy Jarrett	Jessie Jarrett	Lott Tabor
16073	Miller, James	OK	1870	Jessie Miller	James Miller	Mary Christman	David Miller	Stephen Christman
10568	Miller, Jennie	GA	1889		William Miller	Harriett Bowling	Ben & Polly Miller	Alex & Elizabeth Bowling
7583	Miller, Jessie	VA	1880	Lyddie Miller	James Miller	Elizabeth Miller	Isaac & Abash Miller	Abraham & Elizabeth Miller
7591	Miller, John	AR		Martha Miller	William Miller	Sally Rose		Samuel Rose & Sally Freeman
16000	Miller, John	NC	1861	Louraina Miller	William Miller	Catherine Martin	John Miller	Samuel & Elizabeth Martin
8517	Miller, Joicey	NC	1878	W A Miller	Solomon Chambers	Elisabeth Hart		Stephen & Rebecca Hart
20963*	Miller, Joseph	NC	1830	Jane Miller	Samuel Sumter	Tenner Miller		
20042	Miller, Larenza	NC	1865	John Miller	Thomas Hauser	Lucinda Sprinkle	Samuel & Nancy Hauser	Thomas & Betsy Sprinkle
5146	Miller, Laura	NC	1878	Caney Miller	Elijah Thompson	Malinda Testament	Samuel & Marget Thompson	James & Milley Testament
12986	Miller, Lavana	NC	1877	Harrison Miller	James Osborne	Clemmenzy Bare	David & Nancy Osborne	Joseph & Sousie Bare
4100	Miller, Lizzie	VA		Jackson Miller	James Finley	Ider Hart	Washington & Elisabeth Finley	Eliazer & Nancy Hart
3975	Miller, Louisa	MO	1871	Thomas Miller	Henry Poe	Martha Hambelton		Isiah & Martha Hambelton
6862	Miller, Maggie	WV	1876	Alfred Miller	Elijah Blevins	Rachel Felty	Armstrong & Catharine Blevins	Nicholas & Susan Felty
12985	Miller, Mamie et al	NC	1895 etc.		H K Miller	Lavana Osborne	Daniel & Ellen Miller	James & Clemmenzy Osborne

ID	Name	State	Year	Spouse	Father	Mother	Paternal Grandparents	Maternal Grandparents
10569	Miller, Marcus	GA	1897		William Miller	Harriett Bowling	Ben & Polly Miller	Alex & Elizabeth Bowling
6157	Miller, Marion	VA	1852	Mary Miller	Isaac Miller	Bashabe Blevins	Isaac & Eva Miller	Nell & Elisabeth Blevins
6155	Miller, Martha	VA	1864	Wells Miller	John Cakzort	Mary Peacock		
10105	Miller, Mary	NC	1854	Chamber Miller	Stephen Hart	Rebecca Powers	Stephen & Rebecca Hart	
10417	Miller, Mary	NC	1874	none	Abraham Miller	Cessa Banguess	Abraham & Elizabeth Miller	Richard & Polly Banguess
16001	Miller, Mary	NC	1848		William Miller	Catherine Martin	John & Elizabeth Miller	Samuel & Elizabeth Martin
11020	Miller, Matilda	MO	1844		Josiah Dorris	Margaret Bly		Robert & Fannie Revelle
6156	Miller, Mattie	VA	1874	none	Wells Miller	Matilda Phipps	Isaac & Bashabe Miller	
11449	Miller, Maudie	VA	1887	Elihu Miller	Wiley Farmer	Lydia Miller	Henry & Nancy Farmer	Israal & Bashebe Miller
12103	Miller, Mira	WV	1851	William Miller	Franklin Sizemore	Polly Workman	George & Jinney Sizemore	Joseph & Elizabeth Workman
6158	Miller, Monroe	VA	1879	Erica Miller	Marion Miller	Mary Horn	Isaac & Bashabe Miller	Jothaway & Elizebeth Horn
6374	Miller, Mrs John	AL	1857	John Miller	Elijah Boone	Visa Hathcock	John & Rena Boone	Thos Hathcock & Elisabeth Marlow
619	Miller, Nancy	OK	1866	J T Miller	John Brown	Loduska Tidwell	James & Nancy Brown	John & Lucretia Tidwell
14884	Miller, Nancy	NC	1857	William Miller	William Apperson	Mary Edwards	Bennett & Nancy Apperson	Edward & Matilda Edwards
6954	Miller, Netty	VA	1883	Wilson Miller	Haywood Blevins	Lydia McGrady	Ely & Betty Blevins	Jacob & Jeney McGrady
22433	Miller, Plattoff	OK	1847	Margrett Miller	Oliver Miller	Pollie Reese		
20464	Miller, Rebecca	TN	1864	John Miller	Peter Cagle	Elizabeth Henson	Jacob & Rutha Cagle	Thomas & Nancy Henson
8516	Miller, Rinda	NC	1874	Jerd Miller	Solomon Chambers	Elisabeth Hart		Stephen & Rebecca Hart
8572	Miller, Samuel	NC	1859	Jane Miller	Marion Miller	Betty Blevins		Betsey Blevins
17564	Miller, Sarah	OK		Robert Miller	James Stephens	Martha James	Henny Stephens & Lindia Belew	Thomas James & Elizabeth Strunk
4575	Miller, Trula & Minter	VA	1888 1870		James Miller	Elizabeth Miller	Isaac & Abasha Miller	Abram & Elizabeth Miller
15532	Miller, Victoria	GA	1862	I H Miller	George Bond	Sallie Dixon	Wiley & Fannie Bond	Seth & Elsie Dixon
10104	Miller, W.A.	NC	1872	Joyce Miller	Johnathan Miller	Louisa Blevins	Adam & Annia Miller	Danial & Annia Blevins
8565	Miller, Wilda	NC	1876	Elizabeth Miller	James Miller	Elizabeth Miller	Isaac & Abashia Miller	Abram & Elizaboth Miller
4895	Miller, William	VA	1855	Evaline Miller	Isaac Miller	Bashabe Blevins	Isaac & Eve Miller	Wells & Elizabeth Blevins
22553	Millikan, Arza	IN	1883		E. Millikan	Martha Barker		Elihu & Hannah Barker
11242	Millikan, Martha	IN	1858	Lewis Millikan	Elihu Barker	Hannah Allen		John & Martha Allen
20643	Milliken, Martha	TN	1868	Doc Milliken	John Ellis	Elizabeth Bush	Moses & Rachel Ellis	Calvin & Elizabeth Bush
20208	Mills, Cora	NC	1868	Robert Mills	Thomas Hauser	Lucinda Spinkle	Samuel & Nancy Hauser	Thomas & Betsy Spinkle

10222	Mills, E.G.	WV	1883	none	Aden Mills	Mahulda Walker	Robert & Lydia Mills	Newma & Adaline Walker
5471	Mills, Elvira	NC	1890	none	Tillman Mills	Montera Welch		Adolphus & Sarah Sawyer
10236	Mills, Hulda	WV	1859	Aden Mills	Newma Walker	Adaline Sizemore	Chris Walker & Frankie Peters	John Sizemore & Frankie Arms
19110	Mills, Ivy	AR	1883	Claud Mills	Joseph McGavack	Harriet Evans	America McGavack	Malachi & Sarah Evans
1406	Mills, Martha	OK	1837	George Mills	Grief Chambers	Didamay Tabor		Robert & Susanna Tabor
10123	Mills, Martha	WV	1862	J K Mills	Norma Walker	Martha Sizemore	Amos Walker & Frankey Peters	John Sizemore & Virginia Arms
10471	Mills, Martha	WV			J K Mills	Martha Walker	Robt Mills & Lydia Thompson	Neoma Walker & Martha Sizemore
16707	Mills, Mary	NC	1878	Arthur Mills	William Dorsey	Margaret Jenkins		John & Elizabeth Jenkins
1403	Mills, Miles	OK	1869	none	George Mills	Martha Chambers		Grief & Didamay Chambers
10232	Mills, Newma	WV	1885	N A Mills	Aden Mills	Mahulda Walker	Robert & Lydia Mills	Newma & Adaline Walker
10226	Mills, Sarah	WV	1881	Robert Mills	A J Bailey	Annie Cook	Floyd Bailey & Zilphy Mooney	Thos Cook & Rebecca Sizemore
10234	Mills, Viola	WV	1876	D B Mills	A T Bailey	Annie Cook	Floyd Bailey & Zilphy Mooney	Thos Cook & Rebecca Sizemore
10822	Mills, Virdie	WV	1885		J K Mills	Martha Walker	Robert Mills & Lydia Thompson	Noma Walker & Martha Sizemore
22453	Millsaps, James	TN	1879	Manda Millsaps	Ansel Millsaps	Lean Siglar		George & Nance Siglar
3359	Millstead, Jesie	AL	1884	none	Alen Millstead	- Woods	Jim Millstead	
14504	Millwood, Eula	GA	1900		George Millwood	Amanda New	Hugh & Miriam Millwood	Joel & Mary New
11315	Millwood, George	GA	1852	Amanda Millwood	Hugh Millwood	Miram Whitlock	Benj Malew & Rachel Millwood	Dock & Sallie Whitlock
14503	Millwood, James	GA	1906		George Millwood	Amanda New	Hugh & Miriam Millwood	Joel & Mary New
14502	Millwood, Jesse	GA	1839	Martha Millwood		Nicey Millwood		Fannie Millwood
11316	Millwood, John	GA	1856	Sallie Millwood	Hugh Millwood	Miram Whitlock	Benj Malew & Rachel Millwood	Dock & Sallie Whitlock
14501	Millwood, Leila	GA	1898		John Millwood	Sarah Hinkle	Hugh & Miriam Millwood	Pink & Nancy Hinkle
14500	Millwood, Ludie	GA	1895		George Millwood	Amanda New	Hugh & Miriam Millwood	Joel & Mary New
14499	Millwood, Nannie	GA	1894		John Millwood	Sarah Hinkle	Hugh & Miriam Millwood	Pink & Nancy Hinkle
14498	Millwood, Pauline	GA	1891		John Millwood	Sarah Hinkle	Hugh & Miriam Millwood	Pink & Nancy Hinkle
14497	Millwood, Robert	GA	1903		George Millwood	Amanda New	Hugh & Miriam Millwood	Joel & Mary New
14496	Millwood, Samuel	GA	1891		George Millwood	Amanda New	Hugh & Miriam Millwood	Joel & Mary New
14495	Millwood, Thomas	GA	1883	Gillia Millwood	George Millwood	Amanda New	Hugh & Miriam Millwood	Joel & Mary New
14494	Millwood, William	GA	1898		George Millwood	Amanda New	Hugh & Miriam Millwood	Joel & Mary New
20215*	Milton, Albert	IN	1870		George Milton	Dora Butley	Bolden & Elizabeth Milton	
19799*	Milton, David	IN	1876	Rhoda Milton	William Milton	Lydia Annin	Bolden Milton & Elizabeth Scott	John Annin & Phoebe Rankin
19583*	Milton, Frank	IN			Albert Milton	Rebecca Barrington	Boldene Milton & Elizabeth Scott	Richard Barrington & Martha Harvy

19919 *	Milton, John	IN	1879	J.M. Milton	William Milton	Lydia Annin	Bolden Milton & Elizabeth Scott	John Annin & Phoeba Rankin
17782	Mims, Myrtle	IN	1882	Andrew Mims	Robert Bradley	Matie Roberts		Willis & Malissia Roberts
12519	Minew, Rebecca	OK	1878	J P Flying (decd)				
6123	Mink, Matte	NC	1870	G S Mink	Allen Hash	Nancy Goins	John & Sally Hash	Thompson & Mary Goins
18640	Mink, Nellie	OK	1859		Mink	Gar-lon-na-ski		
4570	Minton Isaac	GA	1858	Jane Minton	William Minton	Mary Sellers	Nancy Minton	Isaac & Jane Sellers
19076	Minton, Jesse	GA	1871	Tilda Minton	Riley Minton	Mary Sellers		Isaac & Jane Sellers
16125	Minton, Joseph	GA	1885	Belle Minton	I M Minton	Jane Bailey	Riley & Betheny Minton	Isaac & Mandy Bailey
16126	Minton, Lilly et al	GA	1887		I M Minton	Jane Bailey	Riley & Betheny Minton	Isaac & Mandy Bailey
16124	Minton, Mary	GA	1876		I M Minton	Jane Bailey	Riley & Betheny Minton	Isaac & Mandy Bailey
18570	Minton, Mary	AL		Riley Minton	Isaac Sellers	Jane Gibson		Joe & Jemima Gibson
16132	Minton, William	GA	1878		I M Minton	Jane Bailey	Riley & Betheny Minton	Isaac & Mandy Bailey
10637	Mitcham, Louveny	WV	1861	Owen Mitcham	Ned Sizemore	Malinda Workman	George Sizemore & Jennie Edwards	James Workman & Bettie Reed
4312	Mitcham, Lula	OK	1868	John Mitcham	David McCracken	Sarah Wilson	John & Aelsia McCracken	Arch & Hulda Wilson
13738	Mitchel, Nancy	GA	1864	George Mitchel		Sarah Whitlock		George & Nancy Whitlock
5571	Mitchell, Alfred	KS	1887	none	Nicholas Mitchell	Martha Martin	Charles & Nancy Mitchell	Wm & Susan Martin
21990 *	Mitchell, Annie	AR	1860	William Mitchell	Frank Rutlage	Lucinda Roland		
5572	Mitchell, Charles	KS	1883	none	Nicholas Mitchell	Martha Martin	Charles & Nancy Mitchell	Wm & Susan Martin
21336	Mitchell, Dealtha	AR	1871	Thomas Mitchell	Robert Busby	Elizabeth Chewning		George & Ursula Chewning
18329	Mitchell, Hannah	NC	1854		John Mitchell	Effie Ayers	Josh & Betsy Mitchell	Gallant & Sallie Ayers
19351 *	Mitchell, James	GA	1838	Harriett Mitchell	Washington Mitchell	Ferraby Pollock	Indian & Nancy Guilleslee	Joe & Nancy Pollock
18344	Mitchell, Lousinda	TN	1839	Larkin Mitchell	Joel Underwood	Sency Loveless	Bill Doolen & Ann Underwood	Samuel & Anna Loveless
3028	Mitchell, Martha	KS	1841	Nicholas Mitchell	William Martin	Susan Wolf	Thomas & Elizabeth Martin	Dennis & Polly Wolf
18749	Mitchell, Martha	OK	1852	George Mitchell	Jermiah Nimby	Elizabeth Sercy	John Nimby	Robert Sercy
13876	Mitchell, Nancy	TX	1850	John Mitchell	Robert McGee	Esther Berry	Holden & Lucrecia McGee	Tommie & Hannah Berry
13333	Mitchem, Martela	WV	1879		Sam Mitchem	Nazoney Sizemore	Franklin & Christena Mitchem	Owen & Nancy Sizemore
13332	Mitchem, Naomi	WV	1851	Sam Mitchem	Owen Sizemore	Nancy Lambert	George Sizemore & Jennie Bolden	Garret Lambert & Roseann Hopkins
13330	Mitchem, Sarah	WV	1871		Sam Mitchem	Nazomy Sizemore	Franklin & Christena Mitchem	Owen & Nancy Sizemore
12664	Mitchum, Vicy	WV	1866	Henry Mitchum	George Sizemore	Martha Mitchum	Owen & Nancy Sizemore	Izah & Vicy Mitchum
17779	Mizee, Julia	MO	1874	L.P. Mizee	Nathan Swift	Adaline Holt		Berry & Susanna Holt
12188	Mobe, Charity	NC	1861	James Mobe	Johnathan Osborn	Polly Stamper	Jessey Osborn	Jobe & Elizbeth Stamper

12190	Mobe, Estel	NC	1885		James Mobe	Charity Osborn		Johnathan & Polly Osborn
19458	Mondy, John	CA	1872	Sula Mondy	John Mondy	Sula Hawkins	John & Mahalia Mondy	
19457	Mondy, Leonard	CA	1900		John Mondy	Sula Hawkins	John & Mahalia Mondy	
19459	Mondy, Ottis	CA	1902		John Mondy	Sula Hawkins	John & Mahalia Mondy	
2717	Mongrain, Rose	OK	1890	none	James Mongrain	Mary Higbee	Louis & Mary Mongrain	William & Sarah Higbee
1955	Mongrain, Stewart	OK	1852	Cornell Mongrain	Charles Mongrain	Elisabeth Fields	Noel Mongrain	George & Sarah Fields
6314	Moniac, Adeline	AL	1876	none	Jim Moniac	Mary	Sam & Susan Moniac	Wash & Jane Williams
14674	Monk, Merrell	LA	1872	Lizzie Monk	James Monk	Mary Robertson	Merrell Monk & Nancy Gray	Daniel Robertson & Lucrecia Tatum
7271	Monrgomery, Catherine	TX	1836	John Montgomery	Joseph Williams	Catharine Swofford	Edward Williams	Peggie Crittenden
21383	Monroe, Charity	OK	1854		William Thompson	Esther Parsley	Wm & Charity Thompson	Stephen & Jennie Parsley
5792	Monroe, Charles	AR	1865	Pauline Monroe	Milton Monroe	Henrietta Livengood	Wm & Rebecca Monroe	Daniel & Sarah Livengood
5789	Monroe, Columbus	OK	1870	Millie Monroe	Milton Monroe	Henrietta Livengood	Wm & Rebecca Monroe	Daniel & Sarah Livengood
5787	Monroe, James	OK	1872	Susie Monroe	Milton Monroe	Henrietta Livengood	Wm & Rebecca Monroe	Daniel & Sarah Livengood
17582	Monroe, Lee	TN	1849	Dora Monroe	John Monroe	Nancy Luttrell	Johnson Monroe	Nancy Hanks
7270	Monroe, Maggie	OK	1872	August Moore	Albert Williams	Rosanna Shippley	M B Williams	
5790	Monroe, Thomas	OK	1863	Eliza Monroe	Milton Monroe	Henrietta Livengood	Wm & Rebecca Monroe	Daniel & Sarah Livengood
21737	Montford, Emma	TX	1881	John Montford	Thomas Jeter	Lalla Sugg	Ealyazer & Marthy Jeter	
17483	Montgall, Elizabeth	OK	1850	Joseph Montgall	Jacob Miller	Sarah Fields		Rider & Margaret Fields
18028	Montgomery, Ary	TN	1852	Henry Montgomery	David Brown	Nancy Brown		
14720	Montgomery, Catherine	KY	1831		George Sizemore	Sallie Anderson	Henry Sizemore	Swamp Anderson
16216	Montgomery, Charles	OK	1884		Jonothan Montgomery	Ida Myers	John & Catherine Montgomery	Joe Myers
16147	Montgomery, Clara	OK	1886		Jonothan Montgomery	Ida Myers	John & Cathrine Montgomery	Joe Myers
17852	Montgomery, Grover	OK	1885		Jessie Montgomery	Bettie Curtis	John & Catherine Montgomery	D.B. & Eveline Curtis
16137	Montgomery, Jessie	OK	1859	Bettie Montgomery	John Montgomery	Catherine Williams	Nathan & Marth Montgomery	Joe & Catherine Williams
7272	Montgomery, John	TX	1867	Ocie Montgomery	John Montgomery	Catharine Williams	Nathan & Martha Montgomery	Joseph & Catharine Williams
19209 *	Montgomery, Martha	TN	1849		Jerry McReynolds	Polly		
10919	Montgomery, Mary	CA	1871	Thomas Montgomery	John Carter	Rebecca Duncan		Charles & Mahala Duncan
17944 *	Montgomery, Mary	TN	1856	Lewis Montgomery	Lewis Johnson	Caroline Myers		James & Vina Myers
19502	Montgomery, Zelma	TN	1890	R.V. Montgomery	Benj Holland	Izora Tidwell		Wm & Matilda Tidwell
13420	Moody, John	NC	1836		Reuben Moody	Mary Leatherwood		John & Sarah Leatherwood

#	Name	State	Year					
2512	Moody, Sarah	NC		William Moody	Washington Andrews	Kasiah Maney	Jackson & Sallie Andrews	John & Polly Maney
17359	Moody, Sarah	OK	1849	Alfred Moody	Abraham Guinn	Cornelia Crawford	Almon & Sarah Guinn	Thos & Pricilla Crawford
18903	Moody, Willie	AR	1889	John Moody	Asberry Parrish	Margarate Parrish	James & Nancy Parrish	
15939 *	Moon, Emaline	GA	1848		King Powers	Amy Powers	Peter & Betsy Grimes	Nathaniel & Nellie Holmes
22987	Mooney, Aaron	KS	1888		Lawson Mooney	Frances Mooney	James & Poley Mooney	Lazarus & Mary Mooney
22982	Mooney, Arta	MO	1901		Joseph Mooney	Matilda Sissel	Lawson & Frances Mooney	Mosses & Mary Sissel
22985	Mooney, Charley	KS	1884		Lawson Mooney	Frances Mooney	James & Poley Mooney	Lazarus & Mary Mooney
22984	Mooney, Emma	KS	1894		Lawson Mooney	Frances Mooney	James & Poley Mooney	Lazarus & Mary Mooney
22981	Mooney, Eva	MO	1903		Joseph Mooney	Matilda Sissel	Lawson & Frances Mooney	Mosses & Mary Sissel
22989	Mooney, Frances	MO	1854	Lawson Mooney	Lazarus Mooney	Mary Bevill	Joe & Betheny Mooney	Robert & Centha Bevill
22980	Mooney, Harry	MO	1899		Joseph Mooney	Matilda Sissel	Lawson & Frances Mooney	Mosses & Mary Sissel
22979	Mooney, Herschel	MO	1898		Joseph Mooney	Matilda Sissel	Lawson & Frances Mooney	Mosses & Mary Sissel
22986	Mooney, James	KS	1891		Lawson Mooney	Frances Mooney	James & Poley Mooney	Lazarus & Mary Mooney
20387	Mooney, Joseph	TN			John Mooney	Elizabeth Beddow	John & Elzine Mooney	Richard & Sarah Beddow
22983	Mooney, Joseph	MO	1875	Matilda Mooney	Lawson Mooney	Frances Mooney	James & Poley Mooney	Lazarus & Mary Mooney
20386	Mooney, Lillie	TN			John Mooney	Elizabeth Beddow	John & Elzine Mooney	Richard & Sarah Beddow
22978	Mooney, Ralph	MO	1905		Joseph Mooney	Matilda Sissel	Lawson & Frances Mooney	Mosses & Mary Sissel
2304 *	Mooney, Susan	NC	1877	Jule Mooney	Benjamin Burgess	Mariah Goade	William Burgess	
13381	Moore, Ada	TN	28yrs	D.N. Moore	A.M. Baker	Martha Shook	Samuel & Salina Baker	John & Jane Shook
9360	Moore, Adeline	AR	1851	Joseph Moore	Thomas McCollough	Lovicie Bays	Moses McCollough	Letta Bays
14398	Moore, Ann	NC	1843	William Moore	James Scott	Delia Underwood	George Scott	Lewis Underwood
2434	Moore, Candus	GA		Dave Moore	William Matheson	Malissa Hanpton	Eli & Anna Matheson	John & Hannah Hampton
3272	Moore, Catherine	OK	1849	none	Jacob Cook	Delana Epperson		Asa & Leah Epperson
12928 *	Moore, Charity	WI	1838	David Moore	Macaga Revels	Mornon Jacobs	Stephen & Delilah Revels	John Jacobs
3118	Moore, Dora	MS	1860	E G Moore	Charles Hobgood	Martha Lowe		Thomas & Annie Lowe
15680	Moore, Dora	GA	1876	Wash Moore	Yancy Barmon	Elizabeth Cunningham		Tom & Eliza Cunningham
22380	Moore, Dora	NC	1883	S E Moore	Jessie Isaacs	Mary Scott	Joseph & Frankie Isaacs	Benjamin & Bettie Scott
19103 *	Moore, Eliza	GA	1853	Harve Moore	Richard Glover	Emily McMullen		
10855	Moore, Elizabeth	NM	1855	George Moore	Alfred Hall	Mahala Martin	John Hall	Wm & Susan Martin
22297 *	Moore, Feriby	OK	1865	Thomas Moore	Jim Davis	Rhody Bean	Fred & Ellen Davis	Ben & Ibby Bean

2439	Moore, Francis	OK	1873	Martha Moore	Ruben Moore	Catherine Cook		Jacob & Delana Cook
1313	Moore, George	OK	1874	Susan Moore	Ruben Moore	Catherine Cook		Jacob & Delana Cook
14332	Moore, Gula	KS	1860	Samuel Moore	John Henley	Mary Allen		Martha Allen
22036	Moore, Henrietta	TX	1870	E.O. Moore	W.J. Mahony	Julia Smithhart		James & Mary Smithhart
1312	Moore, Ira	OK	1868	Sarah Moore	Ruben Moore	Catherine Cook		Jacob & Delana Cook
2756	Moore, John	OK	1869	none	Ruben Moore	Catherine Cook		Jacob & Delana Cook
3117	Moore, John	MS	1884	none	E G Moore	Dora Hobgood		Charles & Martha Hobgood
3119	Moore, Joseph	TX	1880	Blanche Moore	E G Moore	Dora Hobgood		Charles & Martha Hobgood
18951 *	Moore, Lucy	GA	1845	George Moore	Lonie Siler	Mariah Siler	Harry Lee & Lucy Siler	Levi & Caroline Siler
3070	Moore, Malisa	TN	1862	Angus Moore	Uriah Peak	Nealy Hart		George & Polly Hart
21744	Moore, Martha	OK	1862	James Moore	Hiram Parsons	Marthe Goode	Johnathan & Lydia Parsons	Nathan & Huldy Goode
7268	Moore, Mary	CO	1859	James Moore	Francis Carrel	Prudence Wade		
11601	Moore, Mary	GA	1838	M B Moore	William Nickolson	Eliza Orr	Issac Nickolson	Eliza Orr
21197	Moore, Mattie	AR	1887	Walter Moore	Adolphus Dillahunty	Emily Mann	Francis & Susan Dillahunty	John & Patience Williams
22291 *	Moore, Nelson	OK	1853	Rosa Moore	Anderson Taylor	Chaney Landrum	Abram & Nancy Taylor	Clora Landrum
19634 *	Moore, Richard	TN	1845		Marcus M?	Betey M?		
22286 *	Moore, Rosa	OK	1853	Nelson Moore	John Musgrove	Rachel Danels	John & Lucy Musgrove	Mile & Rachel Danels
1509	Moore, Ruben	OK	1880	Ula Moore	Ruben Moore	Catherine Cook		Jacob & Delana Cook
4262	Moore, Susan	OK	1858	Alvan Moore	Jesse Perkins	Emaline Mason	Jack Perkins	James & Nancy Mason
4262	Moore, Susan	OK	1858	Alvan Moore	Jesse Perkins	Emeline Mason	Jack Perkins	James & Nancy Mason
3116	Moore, Thomas	MS	1881	Mabel Moore	E G Moore	Dora Hobgood		Charles & Martha Hobgood
22298 *	Moore, Thomas	OK	1851	Feriby Moore	Anderson Taylor	Chaney Landrum	Abram & Nancy Taylor	Clora Landrum
12709	Moore, Vicinda	MO	1829	John Moore	Joshua Murray	Mary Spears	Christopher & Martha Murray	Mary Spears
19857	Moorefield, Eliza	NC		G.W. Moorefield	Allison Jackson	Sarah Thore	Amer & Betsey Jackson	William Thore
19858	Moorefield, Hessie et al	NC	1891		G.W. Moorefield	Eliza Jackson	John & Vina Moorefield	Pete & Sarah Jackson
2573	Moots, Nancy	GA		R P Moots	John Beaver	Mary Davenport		John & Elisabeth Davenport
20700	Moran, Edna	TN		Henry Moran	John Curtis	Louella Wheeler	John & Manda Curtis	Gallant & Abigil Wheeler
20703	Moran, Laura	TN	1895	Milton Moran	Joshoway Curtis	Martha Wheeler	John & Manda Curtis	Gallant & Abagil Wheeler
4080	Morehead, Polly	KS	1847	none	George Gentry	Amanda Gentry		

20925	Morgan, Alice	GA	1887		John Morgan	Mary Woods	Henory & Betsie Morgan	Beary & Mary Woods
12743	Morgan, Andrew	TN	1846	Mahala Morgan	Solomon Morgan	Omie Wallace	Solomon Morgan Sr.	
7258	Morgan, Annie	MO	1876	none	James Morgan	Elizabeth Dickey	Nathan & Anna Morgan	Lindsay & Martha Dickey
18891	Morgan, Annie	TN	1890			Elisabeth Morgan		Jesse & Louisa Morgan
7780	Morgan, Benjamin	MO	1853	Sophina Morgan	Nathan Morgan	Anna Massingale	James & Martha Morgan	Blakely & Polly Massingale
10998	Morgan, Elisabeth	TN	1849		Jesse Morgan	Louisa Franklin	Reed & Martha Morgan	Wm & Elisabeth Franklin
10114	Morgan, Elizabeth	WV		B U Morgan	David Smith	Lydia Sizemore		Ned & Annie Sizemore
10145	Morgan, Frankie	WV	1847	John Morgan	John Sizemore	Jane Arms	Ned & Annie Sizemore	
20926	Morgan, Henory	GA	1877	Fannie Morgan	John Morgan	Mary Woods	Henory & Betsie Morgan	Beary & Mary Woods
7257	Morgan, James	MO	1842	Dartha Morgan	Nathan Morgan	Anna Massingale	James & Martha Morgan	Blakely & Polly Massingale
14817	Morgan, James	TN	1854		Jesse Morgan	Louisa Franklin	Rul & Martha Morgan	Wm & Elizabeth Franklin
22163	Morgan, Jane	GA			John Morgan	Sallie Perkins	John & Mary Morgan	Bill & Nancy Perkins
21000	Morgan, Jasper	GA	1868	Mary Morgan	John Morgan	Mary Woods	John & Bettie Morgan	Beany & Nancy Woods
14833	Morgan, Jesse	TN	1831	Louisa Morgan	Rud Morgan	Marth Swaney	Rub Morgan	John & Hannah Swaney
20927	Morgan, Joe	GA	1879	Sallie Morgan	John Morgan	Mary Woods	Henory & Betsie Morgan	Beary & Mary Woods
22164	Morgan, Joseph	GA			John Morgan	Mary Perkins	John & Mary Morgan	Bill & Nancy Perkins
19700	Morgan, Lellie	TN	1903		William Morgan	M.Eviline Hatcher		Robert & Mary Hatcher
6741	Morgan, Maggie	VA	1883	William Morgan	Enoch Hart	Edy Dolinger	Stephen & Rebecca Hart	
8841	Morgan, Martha	IL	1853	William Morgan	James Eddings	Roda West	John & Francis Eddings	James West
19113	Morgan, Martha	TN	1865	Wm Morgan	Robert Hatcher	Mary Hooper	John & Henrietta Hatcher	Baily & Frances Hooper
19714	Morgan, Mary	TN	1895		William Morgan	Eviline Hatcher		Robert & Mary Hatcher
22427	Morgan, Modemi	TN	1868	Henry Morgan	Newton Hamilton	Mary Payne		John & Polly Payne
22150	Morgan, Rachel	GA			Henry Morgan	Mary Woods	John & Mary Morgan	William & Nancy Perkins
19701	Morgan, Robert	TN	1892		William Morgan	Eviline Hatcher		Robert & Mary Hatchor
20923	Morgan, Royed	GA	1874	Lillie Morgan	John Morgan	Mary Woods	Henory & Betsie Morgan	Beary & Mary Woods
7259	Morgan, Sarah	MO	1858	W A Morgan	Andrew Roberts	Eliza Blackburn	Wm & Margaret Roberts	John & Elizabeth Blackburn
18890	Morgan, Sarah	TN	1873			Elisabeth Morgan		Jess & Louisa Morgan
6055	Morgan, Solomon	OK	1839	Ruth Morgan	Griff Morgan	Anna Tadpole	Sam Morgan	Tadpole
7781	Morgan, Thomas	MO	1850	Mary Morgan	Nathan Morgan	Anna Massingale	James & Martha Morgan	Blakely & Polly Massingale
22152	Morgan, W.B.	GA			W.B. Morgan		John & Mary Morgan	

19715	Morgan, William	TN	1901		William Morgan	Eviline Hatcher			Robert & Mary Hatcher
20901	Morgan, William	GA	1864		John Morgan	Mary Woods	Henory & Bettie Morgan		Beary & Mary Woods
17625	Morris, Albert	OK	1840			Sarah Adams			
3447	Morris, Alice	AL	39yrs	Louis Morris	Bob Varcke	Mary Forbes	Hollinger & Fundall		Mary Forbes
15531*	Morris, Amanda	GA	1876	Steve Morris	Ephraim Gregory	Caroline Burge	Joe & Clay Witt		Tony & Clarisy Burge
15752	Morris, Christina	GA	1847	Poke Morris	Hiram Overby	Arminda Lewis	Freeman & Amanda Overby		
3386	Morris, Cornelia	AL	50yrs	Jerry Morris	Jim Hollinger	Leeny Snowden	William Hollinger		Bisey Dees
2069	Morris, Ellen	OK	1819	Wilson Morris (decd)	John Powel		Joe & Ellena Powell		
15530*	Morris, Essie	GA	1875	Fannie Morris	Jefferson Evans	Rhoda Jinks			Joe Jinks & Elizabeth Morris
21249	Morris, Gertrude	TX	1876	C.W. Morris	S.E. Blair	E.J. Penn	Hiram & Adeline Blair		Sanford & Elizabeth Penn
14434	Morris, James	AL	1857	Cornelia Morris	John Morris	Didamie Trout	James & Katie Morris		James & Annie Trout
14430	Morris, John	AL	1869	Claudia Morris	John Morris	Didamie Trout	James & Katie Morris		James & Annie Trout
17060	Morris, John	OK	44yrs	Lucy Morris	George Morris	Katie ?	Day gar sta ska		Ya ke
3383	Morris, Leone	AL		Charles Morris	John Woods	Mary Watherford	Woods		Watherford
15529*	Morris, Lina	GA	1860	Charles Morris	Frank McConnell	Eliza Bedford	Jim & Mary Shackelfoot		Jim & Sookey Independent
10117	Morris, Lydia	WV	1868	G W Morris	Jessie Sizemore	Nancy Walker	Hiram & Jane Sizemore		Milton & Martha Walker
11953*	Morris, Mary	GA	1863		Dan Cash	Harriett Moss	Dan Sisson		
13499	Morris, Robert	TN	1854	Vesta Morris	Isaac Morris	Sarah Pierce	Jesse Morris		Lewis Pierce & Mary Turk
17356	Morris, William	AL		Bettie Morris	John Morris	Didamie Trout	James & Katie Morris		James & Annie Trout
1522	Morrison, Ann	GA	1851	P E Morrison	J Summery	Mary Helton	George & Barbie Summery		Hugh Helton
1032	Morrison, Callie	RI	1881	George Morrison	Robert Rowland	Margaret Pace			Stephen & Dovey Pace
21199	Morrison, Mary	AR	1872	H.G. Morrison	Adolphus Dillahunty	Emily Williams	Francis & Susan Dillahunty		John & Patience Williams
13927	Morrison, Sarah	NC	1877	Clarence Morrison	John Poplin	Mary Moss	Thomas & Julia Poplin		James & Polly Moss
2032	Morrow, Susan	GA	1856	Alfred Morrow	Jacob Deal	Jane Welch			Isaac & Nellie Welch
10841	Morse, Ellis	NC		Annie Morse	Thomas Morse	Lillie Sandford	Jesse & Liddie Morse		
10842	Morse, Ettie	NC	1885		Thomas Morse	Lillie Sandford	Jesse & Liddie Morse		
10843	Morse, Nettie	NC	1885		Thomas Morse	Lillie Sandford	Jesse & Liddie Morse		
10844	Morse, Sherwood	NC	1851	Lillie Morse	Jesse Morse	Lydia Lowe	Wiley & Betsy Morse		Thomas & Annie Lowe
17868	Morton, Ada	MO	1884	Clyde Morton	John Sims	Florence Waring	Robert & Margaret Sims		H.V. & Caroline Waring
11538	Morton, Nancy	AL	1837	James Morton	William Nelson	Sarah Marten	E. Nelson		

16893	Mose, Lizzie	OK	56yrs	September Mose	Oo kah lah ga (Leaf)	Wutty Leaf		Kor tah quas ky
8393	Mosely, Minnie	MO	1873	John Mosely	John Buttry	Margret Martin	Wm & Luvisa Buttry	Wm & Susan Martin
19622	Moser, Aureylus	NC	1896		Francis Moser	Katie Hauser	E.A. & M.A. Moser	Solomon & Louisa Hauser
14828	Moser, Lovica	VA	1869	James Moser	Mike Barlow	Nancy Blevins	John Barlow	Jesse Blevins & Catharine Penington
14889	Moser, Therusophe	NC	1859	Basel Moser	Solomon Hauser	Louisa Poindexter	Samuel & Nancy Hauser	Denson & Sarah Poindexter
13480	Moss, Aelic	NC	1876	Alice Moss	Milton Moss	Rebecca Maney	Jeff & Margerett Moss	James & Barbere Maney
13476	Moss, Alice	NC	25yrs	Aelic Moss	Martin Maney	Samantha Spiva	James Maney & Betsy Owenby	Minter & Elander Owenby
13930	Moss, Annie	NC	1859		James Moss	Polly Lowe		Thos & Annie Lowe
18460	Moss, Bessie	MO	1901		Fred Moss	Nellie Mandy	Levi & Mary Moss	John & Mahala Mandy
13910 *	Moss, Bird	GA	1880	Etta Moss	Willis Moss	Mary Whittler	Sharp Scism & Maria Heard	Polly Whittler
18450	Moss, Edgar	MO	1900		Washington Moss	Stella Mandy		
13727 *	Moss, Ella	GA	1877	Calvin Moss	Ed Dorsey	Tilla Brown	Joe Standford & Selie Dorsey	Ned & Martha Brown
16317	Moss, Emaline	GA	70yrs		Merrel Collier	Mary Edwards	Merriel & Emoline Collier	Limael Edwards
11473 *	Moss, Emma	WI	1868	Jack Moss	Samuel Waldron	Elizabeth Revels	Mike & Polly Waldron	Macaga & Mornon Revels
13925	Moss, Emma	NC	1889		George Moss	Mary Reider	James & Polly Moss	
14908	Moss, Frances	GA	1866	L A Moss	C C Kelly	Rebecca Chastain	Richard & Frances Kelly	Wm & Elizabeth Chastain
13929	Moss, George	NC	1856	Mary Moss	James Moss	Polly Lowe		Thos & Annie Lowe
13933	Moss, George Jr	NC	1887		George Moss	Mary Reider	James & Polly Moss	
18456	Moss, Goldie & Earl	MO	1906		Fred Moss	Nellie Mandy	Levi & Mary Moss	John & Mahala Mandy
11943 *	Moss, Harrison	GA	1878	Ida Moss	Seth Moss	Charity Cash	Stokes & Mariah Crow	Charlie Cash & Rebecca Wofford
18457	Moss, Helen	MO	1902		Fred Moss	Nellie Mandy	Levi & Mary Moss	John & Mahala Mandy
18178 *	Moss, Henry	TN		Estter Moss	Randle Moss	Rosie Toka		Sindy & Pashion Toka
20204	Moss, Ida	GA	1881	Harrison Moss	Kimsey Cape	Annet Wynn		Austin & Liza Wynn
13934	Moss, James	NC	1877		George Moss	Mary Reider	James & Polly Moss	
347	Moss, James L.	AR	1840	Darcus J. Moss	Honry Moss	Martha Rogers	Howell Moss	Robert & Jane Rogeers
11843	Moss, Jennie	KY	1870	Charles Moss	Samuel Hinchee	Jane Ashbrooke	James Hinchee & Margret Smith	
13481	Moss, John	GA	39yrs	Louise Moss	Milton Moss	Rebecca Maney	Jeff & Margerett Moss	James & Barbere Maney
13937	Moss, John	NC	1882		George Moss	Mary Reider	James & Polly Moss	
20206	Moss, Luella	GA	1880	Bird Moss	Charles Mellow	Mandy Cash		Larry & Jane Cash
21099	Moss, Margaret	NC	1850	James Moss	M.Kizar Van	Jane Carn	James & Barbrey Kizar Van	Adam & Hanner Carn
13909 *	Moss, Mary	GA	1845	Willis Moss		Polly Whittler		Izzy & Jim Whittler

13482	Moss, Milus	NC	26yrs	Mary Moss	Milton Moss	Rebecca Maney	Jeff & Margerett Moss	James & Barbere Maney
18459	Moss, Nellie	MO	1884		John Mandy	Mahala Corbett	Ishmal & Bettie Mandy	
11331	Moss, Odessa	GA	1884		John Reece	Elizabeth Pool		John & Susan Pool
13926	Moss, Polly	NC	1826	James Moss	Thomas Lowe	Annie Harrington	Daniel Lowe	Martha Talent
957	Moss, Rebecca	NC		Milton Moss	James Maney	Barbara Barrett	Martin Maney & Kinziar Van	Wm & Betsy Barrett
311	Moss, Sallie gdn.	NC		Milty Moss	Milton Moss	Rebecca Moss	Jeff & Margaret Moss	James & Barbara Maney
18458	Moss, Thelma	MO			Fred Moss	Nellie Mandy	Levi & Mary Moss	John & Mahala Mandy
13918	Moss, Thomas	NC	1879		George Moss	Mary Reider	James & Polly Moss	
13908 *	Moss, W.B.	GA	1871	Hannah Moss	Willis Moss	Mary Whittler	Sharp Scism & Maria Heard	Polly Whittler
13483	Moss, William	NC	1872	Rhoda Moss	Milton Moss	Rebecca Maney	Jeff & Margerett Moss	James & Barbere Maney
13920	Moss, William	NC	1893		George Moss	Mary Reider	James & Polly Moss	
15321	Moss, William	GA	1905		Ceborn Moss	Odessie Reece		John & Elizabeth Reece
17401	Mote, Edderddanis	GA	1851	Mattie Mote	Dandy Mote	Saley Mote		
18677	Mouk, Miria	FL	1868		John Mouk	Silva Whitaker		
18676	Mouk, Robert	FL	1882	Julia Mouk	John Mouk	Silva Whitaker		
16914	Mounts, John	OK	1880		David Mounts	Carrie Thompson		Dick & Elizabeth Thompson
22001	Moyer, James	OK	1887	none	Jim Moyer	Jennie Luttrell	Jim Moyer	Andy & Margaret Luttrell
10239	Mulkey, Clerinda	GA	1874	A J Mulkey	W L Ingram	Jane Allen	Ruth Ingram	
20353	Mulkey, John	GA	1854	Cornelia Mulkey	William Mulkey	Lucinda Wooten	John & Esther Mulkey	Wm & Suckey Wooten
5138	Mulkey, Philip	KS	1840	Nancy Willis	Jessie Mulkey	Nancy Simpson	John Mulkey	Robert Simpson
14704	Mulkey, Rhoda	GA	1868	Bunyan Mulkey	Richard Evans	Eliza Loring	Wm & Stana Evans	Calvin & Elisabeth Loring
3665	Mull, James	NC	1873	Nettie Mull	W A Mull	Julian Right	Mershel & Eliseen Mull	Riley & Lousinda Right
3666	Mull, Julian	NC	1862	W A Mull	Riley Right	Lousinda Shope	John Right	Nick Shope
3664	Mull, Mary	NC	21yrs	none	William Mull	Johen Right	Meshal & Eliza Mull	Riley & Lourenda Right
21125	Mullen, Sarah	WI	1862	Charles Mullen	Edward Davis	Martha Washinton		Henry & Mary Washington
22572	Mullens, Brantley	GA	1851	Capitola Mullens	Green Mullins	Elizabeth Jemes	Mullow	Ridges
10137	Mullens, Pearl	WV	1898	none	Edward Mullins	Martelia Perdew	Richard & Sallie Mullins	Nathan & Sallie Perdew
18277 *	Mullin, Charles	GA	1833	Callie Mullin	Dick Culberson	Emilie Tatum		Tom & Millie Tatum
10480	Mullinax, Sarah	GA	1853	Hamilton Mullinax	James Helton	Tarrissa Sexton	John & Easter Helton	Russel & Ruth Sexton
14493	Mullinix, Amanda	GA	1851	T J Mullinix	S A Burrill	Margaret Hooper	Jessie & Mourning Burrill	Isaac & Sarah Hooper
15528	Mullinix, Asbury	GA	1892		Thomas Mullinix	Amanda Burrill	Ezekiel & Fannie Mullinix	Spencer & Margrett Burrill
15427	Mullinix, Eliza	GA	1879		Thomas Mullinix	Amanda Burrill	Ezekiel & Fannie Mullinix	Spencer & Margret Burrill

15426	Mullinix, Emma	GA	1893		Thomas Mullinix	Amanda Burrill	Ezekiel & Fannie Mullinix	Spencer & Margret Burrill
15425	Mullinix, George	GA	1890		Thomas Mullinix	Amanda Burrill	Ezekiel & Fannie Mullinix	Spencer & Margret Burrill
15424	Mullinix, Marion	GA	1877	Loula Mullinix	Thomas Mullinix	Amanda Burrill	Ezekiel & Fannie Mullinix	Spencer & Margret Burrill
15423	Mullinix, William	GA	1874		Thomas Mullinix	Amanda Burrill	Ezekiel & Fannie Mullinix	Spencer & Margret Burrill
2947	Mullins, Elizabeth	OK	1855	Ruben Mullins	Keener Gibson	Hetty Collins	Joe & Serkie Gibson	Martin & Betsey Collins
7613	Mullins, Lafayett	GA	1838	Martha Mullins	John Mullins	Francis Hubbard		
11634	Mullins, Louisa	WV	1865	H H Mullins	H C Cline	Virginia Sizemore		
9106	Mullins, Lydia	WV	1860	Harvey Mullins	Calvin Sizemore	Mary Brinegar	John & Jane Sizemore	Jacob & Sheba Brinegar
4980	Mullins, Minnie	GA	1877	T M Mullins	William Freeman	Phebe Jones		John & Lucinda Jones
10126	Mullins, Nathan	WV	1890	none	Edward Mullins	Martilia Perdew	Richard & Sallie Mullins	Nathan & Sallie Perdew
2946	Mullins, Ruben	OK	1855	Elizabeth Mullins	John Mullins	Mahala Collins	Jim & Clara Mullins	Solomon & Jincy Collins
3226	Mullins, Seborn	TN	1833	widower	John Mullins	Francis Mullinex	John Mullins	Andrew Mullinex
824	Mundon, Hannah	OK	1842	Frederick Mundon	J. Hugh Watkins	Margaret Clark		David & Nancy Clark
7264	Munn, Della	TX	1887	Pat Munn	Alford Williams	Fannie Curtis	Joseph & Rutha Williams	D B & Manery Curtis
10976	Munnick, Elizabeth	TN	1843	widow	William Jenkins	Eliza Woods	Henry & Francis Jenkins	John & Elizabeth Woods
22040	Munns, John	TX	1874		Mr. Munns	Mary Rimars		Francis & Binyan Rimar
9819	Murphy, Calvin	NC	1856	Rosa Murphy	James Murphy	Polly McMillan	Polly Murphy	Joe & Millie McMillan
6646	Murphy, Davud	NC	1828	Lucy Murphy	WhipLash	Polly Reilly	Bill & Rachel Rattler	
2013	Murphy, Emma	OK	1877	Albert Murphy	Bryce Smart	Ailcey Barber		Isaac & Joanah Barber
17409	Murphy, George Jr.	AL	1874	Mary Murphy	G.W. Murphy	Mary Alen		John & Nancy Alen
9825	Murphy, Henry	NC	1877	Eliza Murphy	Joseph Murphy		James & Polly Murphy	Wm & Rebecca Cole
21096	Murphy, Isaller	NC	1889	none	Saul Murphy	Jane Davis	Martin & Charlotte Murphy	William & Jane Davis
119	Murphy, James	NC	1847	Elizabeth Murphy	William Matoy	Martha Smith	Polly Murphy	
7609 *	Murphy, James	GA	1861	Lucy Murphy	George Terrel	Froney Murphy	Dickey	Sarah Santie
13260	Murphy, James	OK	41yrs		Joe Murphy	Polly Allen		
11399	Murphy, Jane	NC	1876		Leander Murphy	Easter Brown	Martin & Polly Murphy	
9828	Murphy, John	NC	1860	Tabitha Murphy	James Murphy	Polly McMillan	Polly Murphy	Joe & Millie McMillan
9822	Murphy, Joseph	NC	1853	Sarah Murphy	James Murphy	Polly McMillan	Polly Murphy	Joe & Millie McMillan
16475	Murphy, Laura	GA	1880	Oratia Murphy	Leroy Bettes	Laura Thompson	Wm Lettiner & Nancy Bettes	

6015	Murphy, Leander	NC	1854	Martha Canuth	Martin Murphy	Lottie Hart	WhipLash & Pollie Murphy	Enos & Nancy Hart
13261	Murphy, Lizzie	OK	1895		James Murphy	Jennie Car yar nur	Joe & Polly Murphy	
6014	Murphy, Martin	NC	1833	Lottie Hart	Whip Lash	Pollie Murphy		
3367	Murphy, Mary	AL	1870	George Murphy	William Dees	Annie Parte	Wm Dees & Hetty Shemack	Mary Parte
19155*	Murphy, May	GA	1862	Frank Murphy	Prince Terrell	Marenda Huckelby		Charles & Missouri Huckelby
7253	Murphy, Minnie	OK	1872	Sherman Murphy	Kinchen Matthews	Mary McBee	Lazarus Matthews	John & Katie McBee
21097	Murphy, Minnie	NC	1891	none	Calvin Murphy	Rosie	James & Polly Murphy	Dan & Betsy Goldsmith
6013	Murphy, Sallie	NC	1856	Jane Davis	Martin Murphy	Lottie Hart	Whiplash & Pollie Murphy	Enos Hooper & Nancy Hart
20348	Murray, Annie	TN	1888	William Murray	William Reed Jr.	Nancy Murray	McKenzie & Nancy Reed	James & Jane Murray
12688	Murray, Bandie	TX	1890		James Murray	Temperance Rushing	Wm & Lara Murray	James & Cornelia Rushing
12873	Murray, Benjamin	OK	1873	Lulu Murray	Christopher Murray	Elizabeth Pace	James & Yaurth Murray	John & Emily Pace
12876	Murray, Charles	MO	1861	Barbara Murray	Christopher Murray	Elizabeth Pace	James & Yaurth Murray	John & Emily Pace
12872	Murray, Elizabeth	MO	1863	James Murray	Christopher Murray	Elizabeth Pace	James & Yaurth Murray	John & Emily Pace
22708*	Murray, Fannie	IL	1849	Wilson Murray	Ocella Graves	Courtesy Glover	John Graves	John Straiter
12875	Murray, Fred	MO	1859	Elizabeth Murray	Christopher Murray	Elizabeth Pace	James & Yaurth Murray	John & Emily Pace
15932	Murray, James	OK	1832	Sarah Davis	James Murray	Jane Douglass		Thomas Douglass
12713	Murray, John	MO	1865	Catharine Murray	Daniel Murray	Tilitha Hines	Joshua & Mary Murray	Walter & Matilda Hines
12874	Murray, John	MO	1852	Mary Murray	Christopher Murray	Elizabeth Pace	James & Yaurth Murray	John & Emily Pace
12871	Murray, Joseph	MO	1855	Ellen Murray	Christopher Murray	Elizabeth Pace	James & Yaurth Murray	John & Emily Pace
21402	Murray, Mary	AL	1876	Doctor Murray	James Faught	Mariah Sides	Samuel & Elizabeth Faught	David & Sallie Sides
12712	Murray, Riley	MO	1870	Ida Murray	Daniel Murray	Tilitha Hines	Joshua & Mary Murray	Walter & Matilda Hines
8155	Murray, William	TN	1870	Eliza Murray	Joseph Murray	Nancy Hensley	Wm & Elizbeth Murray	Lewis & Elizbeth Hensley
12687	Murray, Willie	TX	1875	Alice Murray	James Murray	Temperance Rushing	Wm & Lara Murray	James & Cornelia Rushing
12516*	Murrell, Vina	IA	1867	Joseph Murrell	Alfred Weaver	Charity Revels		Macaga & Mornon Revels
16233	Musgrove, Margret	OK	1840	Levi Musgrove	David Lowe	Malinda McNeely		Ezekiel & Susana McNeely
21503	Myers, Delphia	AR	1879	W.M. Myers	Reuben Marcum	Sarah Berry	Robert & Polly Marcum	Wm & Nancy Berry
12187	Myers, Lura	NC	1882	Uriah Myers	Riley Stamper	Nancy Pruitt	Solomon & Elizebeth Stamper	Bedney Pruitt
21763	Myers, Martha	AL	1859	Abraham Myers	Elijah Sides	Nancy Brown	Henry & Susan Sides	John & Hannah Brown
10692	Myers, Orlena	TX	1859	Samuel Myers	John Ray	Mildred Hargrove		Isabel Hargrove
18804	Myers, Sam	GA	1872	Amanda Myers	Elijah Myers	Lydia Bates	Enoch & Charlotte Myers	Chas & Nancy Bates

#	Name	State	Year/Age	Parent/Spouse	Father	Mother	Paternal GP	Maternal GP
16753	Myres, Commodore	OK			Thomas Myres	M H Graham	Colnel Coffee	William Golden
15883	Myres, Eliza	NC	59yrs	Samuel Myres	W H Sawyer	Elizabeth Sawyer	Joel & Easter Sawyer	
14961	Nabors, Lila	AL	1861	W H Nabors	Eli Partain	Mary Morrisson		
8197	Nail, Eddie	KS		none	R M Nail	Mattie Gambill		Andrew & Mary Gambill
7787	Nail, Mattie	KS	1866	R M Nail	Andrew Gambill	Mary Hulsey	Wm & Sallie Gambill	
17076	Nakedhead, Katy	OK	1877	James Nakedhead	Cartah	Te car tu hi sty	Tobacco Pocket	Ol chee cloes
20074	Nall, Kansas	TN	1873	Jim Nall	John Yates	Mary Redin	Johny Yates	Drewey & Rebecca Chapel
7931	Nance, Rettie	NC	1881	William Nance	Eligha Hart	Amanda Blevins	Stephen & Rebecca Hart	
1044	Naranjo, Nancy	CO	1875	Sanpian Naranjo	Marlin Matthews	Sis		
21275	Narron, Eliza	MO	1885	John Narron	George Gordon	Emily Claws	James & Eliza Gordon	Joseph & Sallie Claws
1112	Nash, Lois	KS	1888	Poad Nash	Orvil Cavin	Margaret Burns	Wm & Bettie Cavin	Robert & Maria Burns
16912	Nash, Tookah	OK	1864	William Nash	Dick Thompson	Elizabeth Thornton	Jack Thompson	Amos & Betsey Thornton
2026	Nations, Laura	NC	41yrs		James Farley	Ingabo Hall		Jimison & Betsey Hall
8808	Nave, Julia	OK	48yrs	Andrew Nave	Eagle	Rolinar	Oo-loo-che	
9035	Neal, Alexander	WV		none	John Neal	Osburn	Alexander & Susan Neal	Wilburn & Permelia Osburn
2877	Neal, Anderson	GA	1832	Sarah Neal	Thomas Neal	Polly Smith	Elizabeth Neal	Wm & Susan Smith
22038	Neal, John	TX	1878	Anna Stinson	John Neal	Martha Crain		Jesse & Mary Crain
11004	Neal, Lutie	WV	1883	James Neal	Jessie Sizemore	Nancy Walker	Abram & Jane Sizemore	Milton & Martha Walker
438 *	Neal, Mattie	MN	1860	John Neal	Square Williamson	Harriett Adams	Elisha & Charity Williamson	Tony Adams
2881	Neal, Sarah	GA	1840	Anderson Neal	William Davis	Annie Cross	Mashack & Lydia Davis	Joseph & Sarah Cross
10617	Neal, Sidney	OK	1861	Ida Neal	William Neal	Theresa Green	Samuel Neal	James Green
10619	Neal, Squire	MO	1857	Amanda Neal	William Neal	Theresa Green	Samuel Neal	James Green
12053	Neal, Victoria	WV	1858	Jerry Neal	William Williams	Mary Sizemore	Wm & Mary Williams	Hiram & Jane Sizemore
5145	Neal, William	MO	1851	Martha Neal	William Neal	Terresa Green	William Neal	James & Peggy Green
22919 *	Neal, Willie	MN	1885		John Neal	Mattie Williamson		Square & Harritt Williamson
740	Neale, Amanda	PA	1842	widow	George Deckard	Charity Man		Chief & Sarah Man
2426	Needham, Harrison et al	MO	1889	none	John Needham	Susan Brown	Alfred & Mary Needham	William & Mary Brown
2424	Needham, Susan	MO	1906	John Needham	William Brown	Mary Stives	Tom & Polly Brown	Botts & Ferby Stives
3929	Neel, Emeline	OK	50yrs	D. Neel	John			

18835	Neff, Abram	MO	1870		Henry Neff	Hannah Hammonds		Martin Hammonds & Mary Elmore
10251	Neighbors, Elizabeth	GA	1835	Joseph Neighbors	James Helton	Camilla Southerland	Calvin & Sarah Helton	John & Martha Southerland
22077	Neighbors, Isaac	AR	1880	Ruth Neighbors	Louis Neighbors	Cintha Ragsdale		
2838	Nelms, Sara	OK	1841	widow	John Wheeler	Nancy Watie	John & Jane Wheeler	Daniel & Susanna Watie
8470	Nelson, Adam	KY		Susan Nelson	Ned Blevins	Susan	Armstrong Blevins	Catherine Blevins
19910	Nelson, Arthur et al	NC	1889		Leander Nelson	Adoshia Tilly	Leroy & Thena Nelson	Robert & Adaline
7274	Nelson, Eliza	MO	1851	William Nelson	James Foley	Rhoda Boatright		Benj & Elizabeth Boatright
10202	Nelson, Eliza	VA	1840	C L Nelson	Eli Stamper	Susanna Stamper	John & Sallie Stamper	Solomen & Elizabeth Stamper
19914	Nelson, Leander	NC	1834		Leroy Nelson	Thenia Flinchm		Wm & Martha Pinegar
21054	Nelson, Lindsay	TN	1831	Elizabeth Nelson	Edward Nelson	Polly Morton	William Nelson	Elizabeth Ware
10365	Nelson, Rebecca	NC	1882	Henry Nelson	John Postell	Sarah Head	James & Malissa Postell	
20985	Nelson, Sarah	AL		Cherious Nelson	David Beam	Mary Wilabay		Rebecca Wilabay
13788*	Nemons, Jack	GA	1850	Alice Nemons	Joe Nemons	Tannily Cobb		Winnie Cobb
14056*	Nesbitt, Archie	TN	1841	Tennessee Nesbitt	Henry Drake	Bettie Nesbitt	McCoy & Letha Nicey Drake	
14058*	Nesbitt, Elenora	TN	1852	John Nesbitt	Manuel Clemons	Fannie Gilbert	Granville & Sylvia Clemons	Wm & Violet Gilbert
20369	Newberry, George	TN	1860		Enoch Newberry	Emeline Quiet	Greenberry Newberry	Thomas Quiet
18805	Newbery, Millie	GA	1853	J.A. Newbery	William Jones	Mary Toney		Ira Toney & Ana Lanksly
17933	Newburry, Richard	GA	1870	Lillian Newburry	Enoch Newberry	Mary Auburn		Alex & Mary Auburn
3120	Newell, Mattie	MS	1880	E T Newell	John Hobgood	Mattie Coleman	Charles & Martha Hobgood	
6276	Newman, Emily	MO	1868	Willard Newman	Newell Bays	Carrie Heaton	Joshua & Emily Bays	
16363	Newman, James	TN	1863	Maggie Newman	Allomadon Newman	Charlotte Payne	Joshua Newman	Jane Payne
18919*	Newman, Mary	SD		Lincoln Newman	Henry Revels	Annis Winchel	McCaga & Mornon Revels	James & Jane Winchel
19156*	Newman, Mary	GA	1874	Jim Newman	Henry Hanes	Ann Wright		Jerry & Sally Wright
21674	Newman, Mary	AR	1884	Joseph Newman	Charly Spears	Susie Smith	Charlie Spears & Kith Locks	
18311	Newsom, Henry	IN	1852	Mary Newsom	Jessie Newsom	Charlotie Waldon	John & Martha Newsom	
18629	Newsom, Idella	KS	1881	Thomas Newsom	Napoleon Holt	Sarah White	George & Sarah Holt	Susan White
18628	Newsom, Lorene	KS	1905		Thomas Newsom	Idella Holt	Henry & Mary Newsom	Napoleon & Sarah Holt
5401	Newsom, LouElla	TX		Fletcher Newsom	John Avary	Harriett Whitten	W M & Talitha Avary	Jack & Nancy Whitten
17947*	Newsom, Lula	TN	1865	George Newsom	Frank Wycoff	Oma Wilson	Jonas Garrett & Nancy Montgomery	Joseph & Hannah Wycoff
2576	Newton, D. M.	GA	1874	John Newton	Willliam Postell	Disey Davenport		John & Elisabeth Davenport

20459	Newton, Eldrige	TN	1900		James Newton	Lula Ervin	George & Minerva Newton	Clay & Elizabeth Ervin
15670	Newville, Matilda	WI	1863	Warren Newville	Elijah Bass	Elizabeth Arnold	Elijah Bass & Matilda Dutten	Dewey & Emily Arnold
7546	Nicely, Bettie	NC	24yrs	Will Nicely	Waitsel Sutherd	Mary Hitchcock		Glen & Dovie Hitchcock
19429	Nicely, Mary	GA	1851	Cal Nicely	Pierce Cody	Jarrard		
3824	Nichols, Adline	GA	1863	Henderson Nichols	George Davis	Rebecca Garland	Isaac & Rhoda Davis	Ezekiel & Annie Garland
20300	Nichols, Clarissa	KS	1871	Walter Nichols	John Edmonds	Annaliza Herrell		Clarissa Herrell
12897	Nichols, Lona	MS	1887	Mark Nichols	J M Loveless	Mary Presley	Loveless & Nancy Townsand	Jim & Elizabeth Presley
2515	Nichols, Samantha	OK		Alex Nichols		Sherill Thompson	Thomas & Hester Black	Benj Hyde & Betsy Latham
14923	Nicholson, Estella	GA	9yrs		Andrew Nicholson	Laura Wright	Thos & Susan Nicholson	W A & Arminda Wright
14936	Nicholson, James	GA	1880	Neaty Nicholson	Andrew Nicholson	Louisa Wright	Thos & Susan Nicholson	W A & Arminda Wright
2261	Nicholson, John	NC	1866	Tina Nicholson	Nute Nicholson	Melvina McDonald	Alfred & Polly Nicholson	Sallie McDonald
14928	Nicholson, Laura	GA	1856	Andrew Nicholson	W A Wright	Arminda Orr	Thos & Ella Wright	
7275	Nicholson, Lela	TX		Andrew Nicholson	John Jolly	Amanda Ward	Wm & Martha Jolly	Jerry & Nancy Ward
1303	Nicholson, Melvina	NC	1845	N. D. Nicholson	Calhoun Morice	Sallie McDonald	Sid Morice	Anguish & Sallie McDonald
21778	Nicks, Nancy	OK	1853	Robert Nicks	James Puckett	Eliza True	James & Nancy Puckett	David & Martha True
21777	Nicks, William	OK	1874	Claudia Nicks	Robert Nicks	Nancy Puckett	Isaac & Nancy Nicks	James & Eliza Puckett
11982	Nilges, Mary	MO	1873	Ben Nilges	Andrew Sweaney	Sarah Rush	Levi & Myra Sweaney	Ephraim & Sarah Rush
14383	Nipper, Allis (decd)	AL		G W Nipper	John Mattor	Caroline Baker	Wm Mattor & Nancy Newman	Wm McIntosh
19988	Nix, Lillie	GA	1874		Francis Owen	Sarah Whitmire	Wiley & Mary Owen	James & Cassie Whitmire
4768	Nix, Nancy	IL			James Eddings		John & Frances Eddings	Weaver
21115	Noah, Arminda	NC	1873	K. Noah	G.M. Hiatt	Catherine Taylor	Jacob & Taba Hiatt	Tom & Mary Taylor
11184	Nobles, Annie	TX	1877		James Murray	Temperance Rushing	Wm & Cara Murray	James & Cornelia Rushing
6321	Nolen, Andrew	AL	1862		William Nolen	Lousinda Waginer		George & Matilda Waginer
14375	Nolen, Martha	AL		J G Nolen	John Otts	America Newell	Jasper & Delphia Otts	Mathis & Rebecca Newell
17520 ½	Noles, Louiza	OK	1865	Harry Noles				
15001	Noon, John	OK	1843	Polly Noon	Noon	Su sie	Ese tow ace	Too nigh
18375	Nored, Mrs. W.M.	FL	1875	W.M. Nored	J.A. Williams	Mary Hightower	James & Margretta Williams	James & Nancy Hightower
19275	Norman, Betty	TN	1870	Mathew Norman	Gilbert Gibson	Cordelia Maxell	Hiram Gibson	Salley Maxell
14888	Norman, Fathie	NC	1866	J I F Norman	T C M Poindexter	Margarett Wooten	Robt & Charlotte Poindexter	Thos & Alsie Wooten
17484	Norman, Sarah	NC	1857	David Norman	Thomas Poindexter	Margaret Wootin	Robert & Charlotte Poindexter	Thos & Elsie Wootin
14874	Norman, Susan	NC	1853	Ellis Norman	Thomas Poindexter	Margaret Wooten	Robt & Charlotte Poindexter	Thos & Alcie Wooten

19756	Norrell, Ninnie	GA	1885	T.J. Norrell	Acy Chambers	Elizabeth West		
17706	Norris, Elijah	TN	1851	Malinda Norris	Dempsee Wiley	Jane Hulsey		Selby Hulsey
14381	Norris, John	GA	1874	Sintha Norris	Ninniar Norris	Mary Evans	Isac & Barbary Norris	Pleasant & Mahala Evans
2453	Norris, M M Belle	NC	1882	Katie Norris	Jacob Dockery	Martha Kephart	A J & Martha Dockery	Andy & Dorcus Kephart
14380	Norris, Mary	GA	1836	Ninnian Norris	Pleasant Evans	Mahaly Carver	Wm Evans & Charlotte Allen	Thos & Agnes Carver
7273	Norris, Parallee	OK	1866	George Norris	James Brumley	Sarah Cantrell	James & Malinda Brumley	Hozell & Sintha Cantrell
14395	Norris, Stephen	GA	1877	Julia Norris	Ninnian Norris	Mary Evans	Isaac & Barbary Norris	Pleasant & Mahala Evans
17304	Northcutt, Martha	OK	1872	Luney Northcutt	Daniel Sizemore	Margarett Woods	Daniel & Anna Sizemore	Thomas & Juda Woods
9553	Norton, Edward	GA	1883	May Norton	W C Norton	Malissie Dockins	Edward & Elizabeth Norton	Benj & Amanda Dockins
2545	Norton, Elias	GA	1859	Martha Norton	Edward Norton	Elizabeth Wall	Barrack & Mary Norton	Wm & Rebecca Wall
9550	Norton, John	GA	1852	Mary Norton	Edward Norton	Elizabeth Wall	Barack & Mary Norton	Wm & Rebecca Wall
2544	Norton, Mary	GA	1850	none	Edward Norton	Elizabeth Wall		Wm & Rebecca Wall
9552	Norton, William	GA	1854	Malissie Norton	Edward Norton	Elizabeth Wall	Barrack & Mary Norton	Wm & Rebecca Wall
22138 *	Norwood, H.Turner	NC	54 yrs	Lucy Norwood	Elious Norwood	Eliza	Henry & Betty Lenoir	
22137 *	Norwood, Henry	NC	1855	Emma Norwood	Elias Norwood	Eliza	Henry & Betty Lenoir	
14756	Nuckolls, Margret	KY		Jackson Nuckolls	Solmon Blevins	Elizabeth Quinley		
11419	Null, Cora	VA	1888	Henry Null	Leander Peak	Jane Goins	Uriah & Carnealy Peak	
3121	Null, Willie	MS	1871	E D Null	R L McElroy	Nancy Hobgood		Charles & Martha Hobgood
13974	Nunly, Matilda	VA	1857	J J Nunly	Kiah Billips	Arenia Sizemore	James & Nancy Billips	George & Jennie Sizemore
17447	O Neal, Mary	AL	1835	James O Neal	Wm Hollinger	Hettie Manoc	Wm Hollinger	
17445	O Neal, William	AL	1851	Jane O Neal	James O Neal	Mary Hollinger	James & Settie O Neal	Wm & Hetta Hollinger
10227	O'Brian, Stella	WV	1881	Wm O'Brian	Keet Mills	Martha Walker	Robt & Lidda Mills	Newma Walker & Adaline Sizemore
1560	O'Fields, Moses adm.	OK	1848	none				
19200	O'Harrow, Elizabeth	OK	1880	W.H. O'Harrow	W.T. Cooper	Sary Woods	J.W. Cooper & Elizabeth McAdams	J.W. Woods
18307	O'Neal, Mary	AL	1859		James O'Neal	Mary Hollinger		Wm & Hetty Hollinger
19157 *	Obleton, Leathie	GA	1856	Sam Obleton	John Marshall	Harriatte Blanchard	Alec & Sallie Marshall	
19158 *	Obleton, Sam	GA	1847	Leathie Obleton	Peter Obleton	Julia Wynn	Austin Obleton	
7276	Odell, Mary	AR	1876	Lorenzo Odell	John Carbell	Mary Musgraves	Henry & Louise Corbell	Anderson & Millie Musgraves
17207	Odell, Minnie	OK	1884	John Odell	Lawson Runyon	Elsie	Robert Runyon	

9319	Odom, Eliza	GA	1848	John Odom	Franklin Orton	Tilda Rufly	James & Rebecca Orton	Cobble
21793	Odom, Maudie	AL	1889	Huel Odom	Abraham Myers	Martha Sides	Russell & Sarah Myers	Elijah & Nancy Sides
14249	Oelschlagel, Joseph	IN	1897		Christian Oelschlagel	Josephine Bogue		Joseph & Martha Bogue
14250	Oelschlagel, Josephine	IN	1869	widow	Joseph Bogue	Martha Allen	Charles & Sarah Bogue	Herman & Ann Allen
9567 *	Ogden, Ock	AL	71yrs	Darcus Ogden	Bil Brazies	Precilla Cook		
17978	Ohelsen, Samantha	TN	1848	Fredrick Ohelsen	Charles Morris	Mary Neal		
15926	Oldham, Leonia	TN	1881	Walter Oldham	J W Hargis	Frances Beasley	Jackson & Mary Hargis	Jesse & Matilda Beasley
21303	Oldham, Linzy	OK	1850	Sallie Oldham	William Oldham	Polly Rodgers	Jesse Oldham	John Rodgers
4153	Oliver, Frankie	OK	1886	William Oliver	Joel Barber	Attie Swinney	Isaac & Joanah Barber	
1666	Oliver, Mary	OK	184?	L.L. Oliver	Jefferson Latta	Harit Robertson		Elzira & Emzie Robertson
7277	Olmstead, Sallie	KS	1871	George Olmstead	John Boatright	Fannie Wylie	Benj & Julia Boatright	Harvey & Ruth Wylie
4957	Omstead, Etta	OK	1886	Frank Omstead	George Deckard	Matilda Brown	Ephram & Rachel Deckard	Robert & Esther Brown
22149	Oney, Susanna	KY	1839		William Sizemore	Martha Milam		
9278	Oowausuute, Nancy	OK	1878	none	George Oowausuute	Charlott John		
20276	Orr, James	TX			Samuel Orr	Christiana McDonald		Wm & Christiana McDonald
21708	Orr, Louis	GA	1870	Etta Orr	Samuel Orr	Christian McDonald		Christiana Bailey
1772	Orr, Martha	GA	45yrs	Robert Orr	Henry Summey	Mary Helton	George & Barbra Summy	John & Easter Helton
12860	Orsbon, George	NC	1867	Myrtie Orsbon	Ephram Orsbon	Cameria Bare	Jesse & Cyntha Orsbon	Joseph & Susie Bare
10019	Orsborn, Andrew	NC	1852	Zildia Orsborn	Jesse Orsborn	Lovinda Taylor	Elias Orsborn	
8583	Orsborn, Joseph	VA	1871	Isabel Orsborn	James Orsborn	Mensey Base	James & Mensey Orsborn	
12563	Orsborn, Zedrick	NC	1850	Catherine Orsborn	Jessie Orsborn	Cynthy Ketchum	Elias & Salley Orsborn	Johnathan & Sarah Ketchum
11470	Orten, Abner	GA	1840	Nancy Orten	Franklin Orten	Matilda Rufty		
20991	Orten, Alford	AL	1853	Martha Orten	Alford Orten	Tilda Rufty		
20994	Orten, David	AL	1861	Lockina Orten	Alford Orten	Tilda Rufty		
11469	Orten, George	GA	1838	Sarah Orten	Franklin Orten	Matilda Rufty		
20993	Orten, Samuel	AL	1857	Emma Orten	Alford Orten	Tilda Rufty		
14400	Orton, Sidney	GA	1845	Harriet Orton	Alfred Orton	Sofia Rufta		
1660	Osborn Jr., James	VA						
11809	Osborn, Aaron	NC	1851	Martha Osborn	Johnethan Osborn	Polly Stamper	Jessey & Cyntha Osborn	Jobe & Elizabeth Stamper
18156	Osborn, Aaron	NC			Aaron Osborn	Martha	Johnathan & Polly Osborn	
18600	Osborn, Benjaman	NC	1891			Tennessee Osborn		John & Polly Osborn
12856	Osborn, Calie et al	NC	1894 etc.		Cicero Osborne	Isabelle Reed	David & Susie Osborne	Andy & Carolina Reed

ID	Name	State	Year	Spouse	Father	Mother	Paternal Grandparents	Maternal Grandparents
12193	Osborn, Calvin	NC	1832	Francis Osborn	Jesse Osborn	Cynthia Ketchum	Elias & Sally Osborn	Jonathan & Sarah Ketchum
12184	Osborn, Eli	NC	1827		David Osborn	Lucy Billings	Jesse & Cyntha Osborn	Jasper & Nancy Billings
1852	Osborn, Emaline	VA	46yrs	none	James Osborn	Rachel Blevins	Elias & Sallie Osborn	
14728	Osborn, Enoch	VA	1876	Demmie Osborn	A M Osborn	Leanzy Penington		Stephen & Margaret Penington
10413	Osborn, Fielden	NC	1869	Cally Osborn	William Osborn	Sirena Lewis		Ephrim & Abbie Roark
12260	Osborn, Fields	NC	1857	Juliann Osborn	Johnathan Osborne	Polly Stamper	Jesse & Cyntha Osborne	Jobe & Elizbeth Stamper
14152	Osborn, Florence	NC	1884		Fields Osborn	Julia Richardson	Jonathan & Polly Osborn	Neil & Delpha Richardson
14149	Osborn, Frances	NC						
1851	Osborn, James	VA	1822	Rachel Osborn	Elias Osborn	Sally Sizemore	Ned & Ana Sizemore	
12192	Osborn, Jessee	VA	1868	Sarah Osborn	John Osborn	Polly Stamper	Jesse & Cynthia Osborn	Jobe & Elizbeth Stamper
14731	Osborn, Jettie	VA		A M Osborn	Cicero Spencer	Jettie Osborn		A M & Leazy Osborn
12181	Osborn, John	NC	1882		Reeves Osborn	Nan Stringer	John & Polly Osborn	Winston Stringer & Betty Murry
14729	Osborn, Leanzy	VA		A M Osborn	Stephen Penington	Malindia	Samuel & Elizabeth Penington	
18598	Osborn, Lester et al	VA			Jessie Osborn	Sarah Naris	John & Polly Osborn	
20084	Osborn, Lester, Mary	NC	1896 1894		Noah Osborn	May Andrews	Zedack & Catherine Osborn	John & Malinda Andrews
10411	Osborn, Lockie	NC	1880	none	William Osborn	Sirena Lewis		Ephrim & Abbie Roark
1805	Osborn, Maggie	VA	1878	Thomas Osborn	Levi Haga	Martha Faircloth	David & Rebecca Haga	T.A. & Christina Faircloth
12195	Osborn, Margaret	NC	1877		Calvin Osborn	Francis Candill	Jesse & Cynthia Osborn	Jesse & Sarah Candill
18727	Osborn, Martha	NC	1869	James Osborn	A.H. Scott	Ann Hunt	Leonard & Sally Scott	James & Temperance Hunt
1750	Osborn, Noah	VA	1842	Nancy Osborn	James Osborn	Rachel Baldwin	Elias & Eula Osborn	
12258	Osborn, Polly	NC	1835	John Osborn (decd)	Jobe Stamper	Elizbeth Rose	Johnathan & Polly Stamper	Franklin Rose
12180	Osborn, Reeves	NC	1855	Nan Osborn	Johnathan Osborn	Polly Stamper	Jesse & Cynthia Osborn	Jobe & Elizbeth Stamper
1857	Osborn, Roley	VA	1870	Laura Osborn	Jesse Osborn	Catharine Price	David & Cathrine Osborn	
18158	Osborn, Rufus	NC	1879	Carda Osborn	Osborn	Slyan Richardson		Noel Richardson
14150	Osborn, Rufus Jr	NC						
1803	Osborn, Thomas	VA	1873	Maggie Osborn	Robert Osborn	Mary Caldwell	James & Rachel Osborn	Nancy Caldwell
20996	Osborn, Thomas et al	NC	1892		Nelson Osborne	Milly Woodie	James & Clemminzy Osborne	Jackson & Sarah Woodie
12560	Osborne, Alexander	NC	1863	Sarah Osborne	Zedrick Osborne	Catherine Hoppers	Jesse & Cyntha Osborne	Jacob & Ekissia Hoppers
20999	Osborne, Beldon et al	NC	1895		David Osborne	Cora Sheets	James & Clemmenzy Osborne	Nelson & Martha Sheets

19641	Osborne, Calvin & Edna	NC	1898 1900			Margret Osborne		Calvin & Francis Osborne
12861	Osborne, Cicero	NC	1870	Isabel Osborne	Davie Osborne	Sousie Sheets	Elias & Sally Osborne	Jacob & Sally Sheets
12476	Osborne, David	NC	1826	Nancy Osborne	Jesse Osborne	Cynthia Ketchum	Elias & Sally Osborne	Jonathan & Sarah Ketchum
12477	Osborne, David	NC	1869	Cora Osborne	James Osborne	Clemmenzy Bare	David & Nancy Osborne	Joseph & Sousie Bare
12987	Osborne, Eliza	NC	1860	Emory Osborne	Alfred Sheets	Mary Osborne	John & Mary Sheets	James & Elisabeth Osborne
19626	Osborne, Emma et al	NC			Gideon Osborne	Celia Gulyan	Calvin & Francis Osborne	
12988	Osborne, Emory	NC	1873	Eliza Osborne		Emaline Osborne		James & Rachael Osborne
11819	Osborne, Ephraim	NC	1840	America Osborne	Jesse Osborne	Cynthy Ketchem	Elias & Sally Osborne	Johnathan & Sarah Ketchem
12554	Osborne, Felix	NC	1873	Mary Osborne	James Osborne	Clemminzy Bare	David & Nancy Osborne	Joseph & Sousie Bare
21841	Osborne, Georgia	KS	1882	Charles Osborne	Elijah Sloan	Lucy Mizener	A.C. Sloan & Mary Hamilton	
12469	Osborne, James	NC	1855		Washington Osborn	Mima Sheets	David & Lucy Osborne	Jacob & Sally Sheets
12470	Osborne, Jesse	NC	1849	Louisa Osborne	David Osborne	Nancy Woodie	Jesse & Cyntha Osborne	James & Margret Woodie
12473	Osborne, John	NC	1875	Malinda Osborne	James Osborne	Clemmenzy Bare	David & Nancy Osborne	Joseph & Sousie Bare
12251	Osborne, Marshall	NC	1883		Troy Osborne	Francis Pruitt	John & Polly Osborne	Joel & Elisa Pruitt
20997	Osborne, Nina & Chas	NC	1903 1905		John Osborne	Malinda Cox	James & Clemmenzy Osborne	Wm & Polly Cox
12857	Osborne, Nina et al	NC	1887 etc.		Rufus Osborne	Alice Cox	David & Nancy Osborne	Isam & Nancy Cox
12561	Osborne, Noah	NC	1871	Mary Osborne	Zedrick Osborne	Catherine Hoppers	Jesse & Cyntha Osborne	Jacob & Ekissia Hoppers
20998	Osborne, Pearl et al	NC	1900		Felix Osborne	Mary Baker	James & Clemmenzy Osborne	Wm Baker & Mary Sheets
12249	Osborne, Robert	NC	1882		Aaron Osborne	Martha Garel	John & Polly Osborne	
12858	Osborne, Rufus	NC	1862	Alice Osborne	David Osborne	Nancy Woodie	Jesse & Cynthia Osborne	James & Francis Woodie
12562	Osborne, Stephen	NC	1875	Ellen Osborne	Zedrick Osborne	Catherine Hoppers	Jesse & Cyntha Osborne	Jacob & Ekissia Hoppers
12472	Osborne, Tatton	NC	1882	Lizzie Osborne	James Osborne	Clemmenzy Bare	David & Nancy Osborne	Joseph & Sousie Bare
12257	Osborne, Tennessee	NC	1869		Johnathan Osborne	Polly Stamper	Jesse & Cyntha Osborne	Jobe & Elizbeth Stamper
12252	Osborne, Troy	NC	1863	Frankey Osborne	Johnathan Osborne	Polly Stamper	Jesse & Cyntha Osborne	Jobe & Elizbeth Stamper
12259	Osborne, Willie	NC	1882		Fields Osborn	Julyan Richardson	John & Polly Osborn	Noel & Delphy Richardson
12450	Osburn, David	WV	1865	Julia Pritt	Jefferson Osburn	Mary Kiger	Solomon & Patsey Osburn	John & Malinda Kiger
10872	Osburn, Emery	WV	1873	Glendora Osburn	John Osburn	Louana Keith	Solomon & Martha Osburn	Guy & Rachel Keith
10867	Osburn, George	WV			Solomon Osburn	Susan Nicholas	Elias & Sarah Osburn	
6376	Osburn, James	WV	1843	Nancy Osburn	Solomon Osburn	Patsy Arms	Elias & Sally Osburn	
10870	Osburn, James	WV	1883	Mary Osburn	John Osburn	Louana Keith	Solomon & Martha Osburn	Guy & Rachel Keith

12520	Osburn, James Jr.	WV	1865	Martha Osburn	William Osburn	Melia Dunford	Solomon & Martha Osburn	Thos & Honor Dunford
11623	Osburn, Jerome	WV	1876	Susan Osburn	Jefferson Osburn	Mary Kiger	Solomen & Patsy Osburn	John & Malinda Kiger
6408	Osburn, John	WV	1870	Rebecca Osburn	Jefferson Osburn	Mary Kiger	Solomon & Patsy Osburn	John Kiger & Malinda Ronsey
9102	Osburn, John	WV	1845	Louanna Osburn	Solomon Osburn	Martha Arms	Elias Osburn & Sarah Sizemore	Robert & Martha Arms
10876	Osburn, John	WV	1878		John Osburn	Louana Keith	Solomon & Martha Osburn	Guy & Rachel Keith
10878	Osburn, John	WV	1858	Martha Osburn	Willburn Osburn	Melia Dunford	Solomon & Martha Osburn	Thomas & Honor Dunford
14151	Osburn, Lura	NC						
10873	Osburn, Solomon Jr.	WV	1878	Amanda Osburn	Solomon Osburn	Susan Nicholas	Elias & Sarah Osburn	
9044	Osburn, Thomas	WV		Eliza Osburn	Wilburn Osburn	Parmelia Dunford	Solomon & Martha Osburn	Thomas & Honor Dunford
10877	Osburn, Willburn	WV	1876	Celia Osburn	John Osburn	Louana Keith	Solomon & Martha Osburn	Guy & Rachel Keith
19478	Osteen, Callie	AL	1887	John Osteen	Henry Ward	Emma Griffin	Henry & Carolina Ward	Clissen & Anne Griffin
19477	Osteen, Matilda	AL	1861	W.M. Osteen	H.L. Ward	Caroline Turner	Ely & Rebecca Ward	H.W. & Jensie Turner
14456	Otts, America	AL	1862	John Otts	Mathy Newell	Rebecca Brannon	James Newell	Nathan & Amanda Brannon
14377	Otts, Calvin	AL			John Otts	America Newell	Jasper & Delphia Otts	Mathis & Rebecca Newell
14376	Otts, Clint	AL	1887		John Otts	America Newell	Jasper & Delphia Otts	Mathis & Rebecca Newell
18873	Overby, Lewis	NC	1859	Christine Overby	Rufus Overby	Jane Hall		Mary Hall
22873	Overby, Mary	GA	1883	Walter Overby	Elias Reece	Sarah Franklin		Anderson & Elisebeth Franklin
15180	Overby, William	GA	1857	Lou Overby	Hiram Overby	Armindy Lewis	Freeland & Amanda Overby	
235	Overholser, Allie	OK	1878	Ed Overholser	G W Garrison	Martha Hunter	David & Mary Garrison	
18493	Overman, Isabella	AR	51yrs		Wm Thurman	Lane Shrum		
1961	Overtaker, James & Nelli	OK	1888 1890		James Overtaker	Maggie McKinney	Chas & Nelly Overtaker	
18128	Owen, Alice	GA	1874	Charlie Owen	Abijah Patterson	Jane Jones	Samuel & Nancy Patterson	Joseph & Elizabeth Jones
19991	Owen, George	GA	1868	Anna Owen	Francis Owen	Sarah Whitmire	Wiley & Mary Owen	James & Cassie Whitmire
594	Owen, Joseph	AR	1880	none	Larkin Owen	Mary Sackry		George Sackry
4803	Owen, Mary (decd)	AR	52yrs	Larkin Owen	George Zachary	Mahala Ballard	Jonah Zachary	Elijah Ballard
14878	Owen, Nancy	NC	1834		Henry Scott	Mary Hunter	Leonard Sr & Nancy Scott	Wm & Annie Hunter
19986	Owen, Sarah	GA	1839	Francis Owen	James Whitmire	Cassie Holland	Chris & Nancy Whitmire	Elijah Holland
5577	Owenby, Alice	NC	1874	Alfred Owenby	James Martin	Elizabeth Caylor	Abigail Martin	
17476	Owenby, Altha	GA			Lucian Owenby	Lenor Cowart	George & Sarah Owenby	Columbus Cowart & Marthene Henson
301	Owenby, Nancy	GA	25yrs	none	George Owenby	Sarah Anderson	Winter & Elenender Owenby	Lazrus & Nancy Anderson

#	Name	State	Year					
309	Owenby, Sarah	GA	61yrs	George Owenby	Laxrus Anderson	Nancy Maney	James Anderson & Franky Smerlin	James Maney & Barbara Barrett
22725	Owens, Benjamin	OK	1884	Dolly Owens	William Owens	Susan Butler	Henry & Mary Owens	John & Elizabeth Butler
21294	Owens, Charles	OK	1882	Fannie Owens	Benj Owens	Mary Biddy		George & Edna Biddy
16033 *	Owens, Cynthia	WI	1860	Nate Owens	Ishmael Roberts	Delaney Revels	Benj Roberts	McCaga Revels
20957 *	Owens, General	NC	1872	Emma Owens	John Owens	Lizzie Scott	John & Barbara Owens	Nancy Scott & Wm Abbott
20814	Owens, Georgian	GA	1880	Fayette Owens	John Godfrey	Margaret Findley	Jim Godfrey	Manuel & Linda Findley
15615	Owens, Henry	NC	1844	Melinda Owens	Payton Owens	Eliza Marion	Thomas & Pollie Owens	Jerry & Mary Marion
20528	Owens, Hixie	TN	1875	C.E. Owens	W.B. Smith	Nancy Colvard	Pleas & Mary Smith	Jesse & Sarah Colvard
18007	Owens, Jerry	NC	1870	Flo Owens	Payton Owens Jr.	Eliza Marion	Thomas & Mary Owens	Jerry & Mary Marion
18005	Owens, John	NC	1866	Laura Owens	Payton Owens Jr.	Eliza Marion	Thomas & Mary Owens	Jerry & Mary Marion
22722	Owens, John	OK	1882	Bina Owens	William Owens	Susan Butler	Henry & Mary Owens	John & Elizabeth Butler
22723	Owens, Joseph	OK	1872	Mollie Owens	William Owens	Susan Butler	Henry & Mary Owens	John & Elizabeth Butler
22724	Owens, Jr., William	OK	1879		William Owens	Susan Butler	Henry & Mary Owens	John & Elizabeth Butler
20956 *	Owens, Lizzie	NC	1855	John Owens	Jim Harnell	Nancy Scott		William Forney
6825	Owens, Malissa	VA	1881	G W Owens	James Orsborn	Mary Blevins	Elias & Sally Orsborn	
14057	Owens, Marion	TN	1880	Eddie Owens	Johnny Ownens	Emma Hall	John Owens	Matt & Missouri Hall
21735	Owens, Martha	TN	1868	John Owens	Joseph Vaughn	Mary Nickles	John & Patsy Vaughn	Henry & Nancy Nickles
14126	Owens, Mary	NC	1846	Thomas Owens	William Poindexter	Mary Taylor	Wm & Elizabeth Poindexter	Mart & Susan Taylor
22064	Owens, Mary	MO	1881	George Owens	David Taylor	Elizabeth Furgason	Zebadee & Mary Taylor	James & Martha Furgason
20815	Owens, May	GA	1894		Fayette Owens	Georgian Godfrey		John & Margaret Godfrey
9559	Owens, Milley	NC	1873	J A Meney	Jhonegan Ridley	Patsy Pritchard		Jessey & Dart Pritchard
15320	Owens, Nancy	GA	1848	Benj Owens	Edward Doss	Seleta Parker		Jesse & Lizzie Parker
20813	Owens, Ozzie	GA	1900		Fayette Owens	Georgian Godfrey		John & Margaret Godfrey
15611	Owens, Payton	NC	1852	Susan Owens	Payton Owens	Eliza Marion	Thomas & Pollie Owens	Jerry & Mary Marion
21021	Owens, Sarah	OK	1854	Frank Owens	William Foster	Susan Blackburn		Francis Blackburn
16048	Owens, Susan	OK	1853	William Owens	John Butler	Elizabeth Standle	Nedy & Amy Butler	John & Sooky Standle
18006	Owens, Thomas	NC	1846	M.S. Owens	Payton Owens Jr.	Eliza Marion	Thomas & Mary Owens	Jerry & Mary Marion
20109 *	Owens, Wilson	GA	1817	Emiline Owens	Dave Gearin	Sarah Walker		Fannie Walker
17825 *	Owensbee, Joe	GA	75yrs	Florence Owensbee	Joe Owensbee	Diley Lipscomb	Sucky	
12288	Owensby, Colby	GA	1882		Thomas Owensby	Mary Henson		William Henson
11317	Owensby, Francis	GA	1842	Mary Owensby	Ephram Owensby	Sallie Hunter	Arter & Polly Owensby	John Hunter

12284	Owensby, Ida	GA	1896		Thomas Owensby	Mary Henson	Author & Mary Owensby	Wm & Mary Henson
285	Owensby, Lucius	GA	37yrs	Lever Owensby	George Owensby	Sarah Anderson	Mintie & Ellender Owensby	Largrus & Nancy Anderson
12279	Owensby, Sarah	GA	1884		Thomas Owensby	Mary Henson		William Henson
17477	Ownby, Jesse	GA	1888		George Ownby	Sarah Anderson	Minter & Ellander Ownby	Thayers & Nancy Anderson
2641	Ownby, Joseph	GA	1880	none	Thomas Ownby	Mary Henson	Arthur & Mary Ownby	William & Mary Henson
21276	Owsley, Jennie	OK	1867	George Owsley	James Gordan	Deborah McAdams		Joseph & Delilah McAdams
21101	Oxendine, Arthur	CA	1883	Frankie Oxendine	Griffin Oxendine	Perline Lowery	Revel Oxendine	Mary Lowery
584	Oxendine, Griffin	NM	1848		James Oxendine	Lily Lowry	John Oxendine & Bettsey Revel	Daniel Lowry & Bettsey Locklear
396	Pace, Alexander	NC	1861	Susia Johnson	Stephen Pace	Dovey Martin	Wm & Harriett Pace	Joseph & Mary Martin
666	Pace, Charles	NC	1859	Emeline Pace	Stephen Pace	Dovey Martin	Wm & Harriett Pace	Joseph & Mary Martin
393	Pace, James P	NC	1865	Lizzie Pace	Stephen Pace	Dovey Martin	Wm & Harritt Pace	Joseph & Mary Martin
3311	Pace, John	MO	1866	Mollie Pace	John Pace	Jane Wallis	Robert & Annis Pace	Jehtha & Nancy Wallis
394	Pace, Lester A	NC	1887	Gertie Pace	Alexander Pace	Susie Johnson		Stephen & Dovey Pace
395	Pace, Loney F	NC	1883	May Pace	Alexander Pace	Susie Johnson		Stephen & Dovey Pace
22249	Pace, Marvin	CO	1884	George Payne	William Pace	Marina Alsup	John & Jane Pace	James & Mary Alsup
22387	Pace, Thomas	CO	1850	Mary Pace	William Pace	Jayne Bancom	Robert & Anne Pace	Thomas Bancom & Elizbeth Noble
3776	Pace, William	MO	1856	Marina Pace	John Pace	Jane Wallis	Robert & Annie Pace	Jeptha & Nancy Wallis
20185	Pack, Jackson	TN	1858	Elizabeth Pack	Jefferson Pack	Necie Hooper	Jessie & Nancy Pack	E.C. & Darkis Hooper
18208	Pack, Martha	TN	1853		Jeff Pack	Penice Hooper	Jeff Pack	Darcus Hooper
16209	Pack, Nancy	OK	1857	William Pack	Charley Mays	Polly Melton	James Mays	Reuben & Lena Melton
16050	Pack, William	OK	1844		John Pack	Clara Perkins	Smith & Margaret Pack	Levi Perkins
19352 *	Paden, Ed	GA	1877	Mattie Paden	Henry Paden	Jane Spears	Daniel & Kittie Fowler	Mack & Caresudie Spears
12047 *	Paden, Henry	GA	1838	Jane Paden	Daniel Fowler	Kittie Paden		
1142	Padget, James	AL	1859	none	Elijah Padget	Mary Gross	Padget & Bailey	Gross
3396	Padget, James	AL	1857	none	Elijah Padget	Mary Gross	Theodore Padget	Syntha Sizemore
3395	Padget, Mary	AL		none	Elijah Padget	Mary Gross	Theodore Padget	Syntha Sizemore
1145	Padget, Richard	AL	1857	Gima Hadley	Elijah Padget	Mary Gross	Padget & Bailey	Gross
14591	Padgett, Arthur	GA	1889		J W Padgett	Lillie Jones		Allison & Hester Jones
14590	Padgett, Cynthia	GA	1891		J W Padgett	Lillie Jones		Allison & Hester Jones

14589	Padgett, Dewey	GA	1906		J W Padgett	Lillie Jones		Allison & Hester Jones
3363	Padgett, Dora	AL	1886		Richard Padgett	Jemma Hadley	Elijah Padgett & Mary Gross	Thos Hadley & Isabella Bryars
14588	Padgett, Earley	GA	1893		J W Padgett	Lillie Jones		Allison & Hester Jones
9891	Padgett, Hannah	GA	1851	John Padgett	Ancil Roe	Ara Talley	Ancil Roe & Mary Tally	Pryor Talley & Elisbeth Hensley
14587	Padgett, Hillard	GA	1903		J W Padgett	Lillie Jones		Allison & Hester Jones
14586	Padgett, Jacob	GA	1885		J W Padgett	Lillie Jones		Allison & Hester Jones
17370	Padgett, Josephine	AL	1859	Levi Padgett	Abner Loveless	Nancy Townsand	Barton Loveless	Ned Townsand & Ann Taylor
17369	Padgett, Levi	GA	1855	Josephine Padgett	Berry Padgett	Lindy Denimore		
14585	Padgett, Lillie	GA	1868	J W Padgett	Allison Jones	Hester Prather		James & Parthenia Prather
3327	Padgett, Minnie	AL	1885	none	Richard Padgett	Jemima Hadley	Elijah Padgett & Mary Gross	Thos Hadley & Isabella Bryars
14584	Padgett, Ruby	GA	1897		J W Padgett	Lillie Jones		Allison & Hester Jones
21496	Page, Emily	CO	1853	William Page	Drury Wall	Elizabeth Moore	Dred Wall	Sarah Ross
9267	Page, Francis	OK	1845	Malinda Page	Joseph Page	Lucindy Johnson		
14364	Page, Martha (decd)	GA		Martin Page	Edward Norton	Elizabeth Wall	Edward & Elizabeth Norton	
21695	Page, Minnie	GA	1887	Robert Page	William Burkett	Mary Phillips	Isaac & Evaline Burkett	Wm & Martha Phillips
17876	Paine, J.	TN	1838	Mary Paine	Thos Paine	Cinthia Williamson	Thomas Paine	
17938	Palmer, Angeline	TN	1873	Henry Palmer	Marion Johnson	Lucinda Lusk	Marion & Hannah Johnson	
8486	Palmer, Bertie	VA	1885	Conly Palmer	John Fisher	Malinda Stamper	Levi & Nancy Fisher	Wiley & Eliza Stamper
14746	Palmer, Ida	GA	1869	J P Palmer	Wm Quarles	Tildy James	Wm & Artie Quarles	John & Lily James
9347	Palmer, James	NC	23yrs	none	Bailey Palmer	Sallie McDonald		Jonathan & Harritt McDonald
12680	Palmer, Margaret	OK	1879	Enlow Palmer	Jasper Chaney	Ellen Ragsdale		Isaac & Mary Ragsdale
20161	Palmer, Rhoda	GA	1842		Ephriam Sosebee	Sarah Church	Wm & Nancy Sosebee	Timothy & Mary Church
3024	Palmer, Sallie	NC	1851	Bart Palmer	Jonathan McDonald	Harret Smart	Anguish & Sarah McDonald	
9349	Palmer, William	NC	33yrs	Mollie Palmer	Bailey Palmer	Sallie McDonald		Jonathan & Harritt McDonald
20164	Palmer, William	GA	1866	Venie Palmer	Gideon Palmour	Rhoda Sosebee		Ephriam & Sarah Sosebee
3002	Pannell, John	OK	1850	Parlee	Victor Pannell	Barsheba Blaylock	Jediah Pannell	
16418	Panoski, Susie	OK	1869		Ganoski	Aley ?	Ganasini & Simhoyer Chinucqui	
15593	Panther, James	OK	1872		Tye cogy	Lucy Wesstan	Chieh qu lee	Wes stan
17570	Pappan, Grace	OK	1880	Harris Pappan	Frank Norman	May Wright		John & Anna Wright

4568	Pappin, Alex	OK	1859	Molly Pappin	Lafoss Pappin	Jennie Blythe		John & Justine Blythe
4331	Pappin, John	OK	1861	Susan & Mamie	Lafoss Pappin	Jennie Blythe	Osage	John & Justine Blythe
14006	Pardue, Robbert	GA	1865	Fannie Pardue	Rollin Pardue	Lissie Loggins	Albert & Ruth Pardue	James & Dicie Loggins
20921	Paris, Anna	GA	1840	Holt Paris	Ezekiel Townsend	Anna Patterson	Ed Townsend & Anna Taylor	
17379	Paris, Charley	GA	1881	Ella Paris	H.M. Paris	Anna Townsend		Ezekiel Townsend
17380	Paris, David	GA	1883		H.M. Paris	Anna Townsend		Ezekiel Townsend
17373	Paris, Edward	GA	1861	Fannie Paris	H.M. Paris	Anna Townsend		Ezekiel Townsend
17371	Paris, Elendar	GA	1861		Martin Paris	Nancy Townsend		Ezekial Townsend
17372	Paris, Ezekiel	GA			H.M. Paris	Anna Townsend		Ezekiel Townsend
19367	Paris, Hattie	GA	1877	Clinton Paris	John Anderson	Malinda Galaway	John & Emily Anderson	Robert & Mahala Galaway
17375	Paris, Henry	GA	1868	Glennie Paris	H.M. Paris	Anna Townsend		Ezekiel Townsend
17374	Paris, Indiana	GA	1866		H.M. Paris	Anna Townsend		Ezekiel Townsend
17378	Paris, James	AL	1876	Mattie Paris	H.M. Paris	Anna Townsend		Ezekiel Townsend
19368	Paris, Mattie	GA	1905		Clinton Paris	Hattie Anderson	Henry & Martha Paris	John & Malinda Anderson
17377	Paris, Samuel	GA	1875	Gussie Paris	H.M. Paris	Anna Townsend		Ezekiel Townsend
17376	Paris, William	GA	1870	Mamie Paris	H.M. Paris	Anna Townsend		Ezekiel Townsend
13011	Parish, Cynthia	NC	1866	Frank Parish	John Orsborn	Polly Stamper	Jerry & Cyntha Orsborn	Job & Betsy Stamper
13012	Parish, Lula	NC	1884	Lorenzo Drawn	Frank Parish	Cyntha Orsborn	Wesley & Betsy Parish	John & Polly Orsborn
6878	Parish, William	VA	1852	Ada Parish	William Parish	Ada Waters		
8490	Parker, Andrew	VA	1878	Ida Parker	William Parker	Mary Lewis		Andrew & Biddy Lewis
19586	Parker, Carrie	GA	1883	Augustus Parker	Robert Little	Alice Watson	Isaac & Jane Little	Hampton & Hulda Watson
4751	Parker, Clerinda	NC	1848	William Parker	John Adams	Leomy Parker	Price & Elizabeth Adams	Jonathan & Leomy Parker
21163	Parker, Daniel	TN	1842	Perneasa Parker	Dempsey Parker	Frances Hargis	Mills Parker	William & Jennie Hargis
4172	Parker, Don	OK	1860	Nannie Parker	James Parker	Eliza Cole	Dempsey & Fanny Parker	
11711	Parker, Emma	GA	1882		William Parker	Marcena Mears	Abner & Millie Parker	Marion & Lucy Mears
4067	Parker, George	GA	1859	Margaret Parker	Abner Parker	Minie McDonald	Wm & Peggy Parker	Washington & Mary McDonald
4173	Parker, Hattie	OK	1850	none	James Parker	Eliza Cole	Dempsey & Fannie Parker	
18938	Parker, Howard	TN	1874	Eliza Parker	Daniel Parker	Neice Burrow	Dempsy & Fannie Parker	Fannie Hargis
5044	Parker, J. L.	GA	1866	Emma Parker	Abner Parker	Millie McDonald	Wm & Peggy Parker	Washington & Mary McDonald

1138	Parker, James	NC	1832	Mary Parker	Jonathan Parker	Leomy Blythe		Jonathan & Annie Blythe
5042	Parker, James	GA	53yrs					
14911	Parker, Jasper	GA	1829	Emily Parker	Wm Parker	Edith Lindsey		Isaac Lindsey
12113	Parker, Jefferson	OK	1861	Alice Parker	Willis Parker	Adaline Vannoy	Jonathan & Leona Parker	Joel & Elizabeth Vannoy
11040	Parker, Jessie	OK	1883	William Parker	Tuxie Carey	Jessie Drew	Walker & Melinda Carey	Creeks
17924	Parker, Joe	TN	1846	Mary Parker	Robert Parker	Sallie Ballard	Anderson Parker	Cagen Ballard
3493	Parker, John	CO	1849	Nancy Parker	Joseph Parker	Rebeca Smith	Joseph Parker	Elisha Smith
8514	Parker, John	VA	1874	Nancy Parker	Wilburn Parker	Mary Lewis		A J & Biddy Lewis
8960	Parker, John	TN	1861	Mary Parker	Doctor Parker	Bettie Helton	Samuel & Sallie Parker	Peter & Mary Helton
19003	Parker, John	GA	1837	Rosa Parker	Julian Parker	Celia Moss	Wm & Edith Parker	
12114	Parker, Jonathan	OK	1867	Bertha Parker	Willis Parker	Adaline Vannoy	Jonathan & Leona Parker	Joel & Elizabeth Vannoy
2085	Parker, Joseph	OK	1837	Susan & Irene Parker	Jonathan Parker	Oma Blythe	Wm Parker	Jonathan & Almie Blythe
2638	Parker, Joseph	GA	1858	Sarah Parker	John Parker	Martha Maroney	Jonathan & Leomy Parker	Lucinda Maroney
6411	Parker, Joseph	NC	1856	Alice Parker	Willis Parker	Adaline Vanoy	Jonathan & Leoma Parker	Joel & Elizabeth Vanoy
6412	Parker, Joseph	NC	1861	Julia	James Parker	Mary Allison	Jonathan & Leoma Parker	
7538	Parker, Lida	GA	48yrs	Joe Parker	Marion Hayes	Martha Scott		Lon Scott
11683	Parker, Malinda	GA	1880		James Parker	Martha Ray	Abner & Lillie Parker	Thos & Julia Ray
20135	Parker, Margaret	FL	1863	John Parker	James Bryars	Lizzie Miles		James & Ellen Miles
5040	Parker, Martha	GA						
8515	Parker, Mary	VA	1849	Wilburn Parker	Andrew Lewis	Biddy Blevins		Wells & Elisabeth Blevins
4885	Parker, Nancy	TN	1856	Hiram Parker	John Buster	Matilda Bedwell	Daniel & Rebecca Buster	John & Sallie Bedwell
8556	Parker, Nancy	VA	1887	Willie Parker	William Lewis	Mary Caldwell		Nancy Caldwell
11712	Parker, Oscar	GA	1884	Rhoda Parker	William Parker	Marcena Mears	Abner & Millie Parker	Marion & Lucy Mears
22720	Parker, Portina	TX	1888	E.B. Rico	R.P. Parker	Sarrah Higdon		James & Rachel Higdon
6760	Parker, Samuel	NC	42yrs	Bettie Parker	James Parker	Mary Allison	Jonathan & Laura Parker	
9525	Parker, Sarah	GA	1875	James Parker	John Abernathy	Delphia Tidwell	Daniel Abernathy	Francis Tidwell
18748	Parker, Sarah	TX	1867	Robert Parker	James Higdon	Rachel Freeland	Joseph & Margret Higdon	Howell & Zilpha Freeland
21446	Parker, Savannah	TX	1867	J.D. Parker	Joseph Litchfield	Sarah Elder	Joseph Litchfield Sr.	Benj Elder
11598	Parker, Thomas	GA	1884	Mattie Parker	James Parker	Martha Ray	Abner & Mattie Parker	Thos & Julia Ray

845	Parker, William	NC	1846	Clerinda Parker	Willis Parker	Adaline Vanoy	Johnathan & Leomy Parker	Joel & Elizabeth Vanoy
2259	Parker, William	OK	1835	Nancy Parker	Jonathan Parker	Oma Blythe	William Parker	Jonathan & Annie Blythe
3599	Parker, William	GA		none	John Parker	Martha Maroney	Jonathan & Leomy Parker	
4068	Parker, William	GA	1857	Marcena Parker	Albner Parker	Millie McDonald	Wm & Peggy Parker	Washington & Mary McDonald
4653	Parker, William	TN	1865	Laura Parker	Hiram Parker	Nancy Kirby		Francis Kirby
8541	Parker, Willie	VA	1876	Nancy Parker	Wilburn Parker	Mary Lewis		Andrew & Biddy Lewis
20176	Parkison, Susie	TN	1867	S.F. Parkison	Alford Hanks	Lidia Crabtree	John & Bettie Hanks	Thomas & Susie Crabtree
15015 *	Parkman, Carrie	TN			Benj Parkman	Fannie Hale		
17759 *	Parks, John	TN	1876	Elizabeth Parks	Natan Parks	Caroline Coulter	Henry & Harriet Parks	David Coulter
16758	Parks, Margaret	OK	1855	John Parks	Robert Prather	Edith Rogers		Pleasant & Phoeba Rogers
19558	Parks, Mary	TN	1852	Joseph Parks	Andrew Payne	Jane Powell	John & Jane Payne	
18031 *	Parks, Richard	TN	1884	Chaney Parks	Nathan Parks	Caroline Coulter	Henry & Harriet Parks	David Coulter
17824 *	Parks, Squire	GA	67yrs		Squire Parks	Jennie Parks		Mochy Parks
7288	Parmley, Jennie	OK	1864	Giles Parmley	James Brumley	Sarrah Cantrell	James & Malinda Brumley	Hazel & Cintha Cantrell
7287	Parmley, Sam	OK	1883	Mary Parmley	Giles Parmley	Jinnie Brumley		James & Sarrah Brumley
20760	Parr, James	GA	1851	Annie Parr	William Parr	Mary Jenkins	John & Malinda Parr	Randolph & Nancy Jenkins
17640	Parr, Nancy	GA	1848		William Parr	Mary Jenkins	John & Malinda Parr	Randolph & Nancy Jenkins
20761	Parr, William	GA	1879	Gertie Parr	James Parr	Annie Goddard	Wm & Mary Parr	John & Edie Goddard
14389	Parris, Anna	GA		Hezekiah Parris	Ezekiel Townsend	Anna Patterson	Edward & Anna Townsend	
3915	Parris, Annie	OK	1877	George Parris	Walter Townsend	Katie	Jesse Townsend	
17713	Parris, Nancy	OK	1848	Jim Parris	Aaron Parris	Polly Irvin	George & Nancy Parris	
941	Parris, Susan	OK	1850	E.T. Parris	Jesse Townsend	Ailsey Cloud	John Townsend	Soo Kiney
18902	Parrish, James	AR	1853	Amandy Parrish	Asberry Parrish	Margarate Parrish	James & Nancy Parrish	
7279	Parsley, W F	TX	1875	Edna Parsley	W P Parsley	Mattie Boatright		J S Boatright
7280	Parsley, Henry	OK		Mary Parsley	William Parsley	Mattie Boatright		
7278	Parsley, W.P.	TX		Martha Parsley	W P Parsley	Mattie Boatright		J S Boatright
13158	Parsons, Hannah	OK	60yrs			Hannah Hawkins		
21745	Parsons, Henry	OK	1882	Joanne Parsons	Richard Parsons	Jane Logan	Hiram & Martha Parsons	John & Sarah Logan
21743	Parsons, Jane	OK	1856	Richard Parsons	John Logan	Jane Logan		

2148	Parsons, Malvina	NC	1867	William Parsons	J R Baldwin	Marilda James	Wm & Margaret Baldwin	
21770	Parsons, Thomas	OK	1877	Hattie Parsons	Richard Parsons	Jane Logan	Hiram Parsons & Martha Goode	John Logan & Sarah Goss
21773	Parsons, Thomas	OK	1877	Hattie Parsons	Richard Parsons	Jane Logan	Hiram Parsons & Martha Goode	John Logan & Sarah Goss
17429	Partain, John	GA	1887	Manda Partain	Elias Partain	Mary Ray	Martha Partain	Wadie Ray
21244	Parvin, Andrew	AL	1881	Jane Parvin	William Parvin	Lou Gilley	Starlin Parvin	Jordan & Ann Gilley
6031	Passmore, A. M.	GA	1851		Harden Passmore	Emoline Sanders	Enoch & Alesey Passmore	Wm Watson & Polly Sanders
13275	Passmore, George	GA	1859	Jessee Passmore	Harden Passmore	Elisabeth Watson	Enoch & Alesey Passmore	Wm Watson & Polly Sanders
14818	Patrick, Charles	TN	1823	Bettie Patrick	S W Patrick	Sarah Faris	Martha Patrick	H E & Elisa Faris
15422 *	Patrick, Maggie	GA	1888	Lester Patrick	Taylor Scuddurs	Mattie Hunter	Louis & Kitty Scuddurs	Henry & Delphia Hunter
21934 *	Patten, Emma	TN	1862	Rubin Patten	Lawson Sykes	Pheba Goss	Moses & Mary Sykes	Cella Goss
21935 *	Patten, Homer	TN			George Nichols	Emma Sykes		Moses & Phebe Sykes
17922 *	Patten, Jane	TN	1850		William Russell	Eliza Jones		Jonas Brown & Juda Jones
18125	Patterson, Abija	GA	1850	Jane Patterson	Samuel Patterson	Nancy Patterson	Wm & Martha Patterson	John & Jane Patterson
18127	Patterson, Benjamin	GA	1883	Azzie Patterson	Abijah Patterson	Jane Jones	Samuel & Nancy Patterson	Joseph & Elizabeth Jones
18781	Patterson, Carry	GA	1878		John Patterson	Eliza Mauldin	Samuel & Nancy Patterson	John & Caroline Mauldin
10767	Patterson, Charles	GA	1860	Mindy Patterson	Samuel Patterson	Nancy Patterson	Wm & Martha Patterson	John & Jane Patterson
15319	Patterson, Dillard	GA	1862	Louella Patterson	Ezekiel Patterson	Louisa Morris	Hix & Sallie Patterson	Joseph & Mahaly Morris
8412	Patterson, Edy	GA		Joseph Patterson	John Green		George Green	
9947	Patterson, Enoch	GA	1859	Laurene Patterson	Samuel Patterson	Nancy Patterson	Wm & Martha Patterson	John & Jane Patterson
18126	Patterson, Ida	GA	1878		Abijah Patterson	Jane Jones	Samuel & Nancy Patterson	Joseph & Elizabeth Jones
9950	Patterson, Iry	GA	1853	Sarie Patterson	Samuel Patterson	Nancy Patterson	Wm & Martha Patterson	John & Jane Patterson
13052	Patterson, James	GA	1857	Maggie Patterson	Samuel Patterson	Nancy Patterson	Wm & Martha Patterson	John & Jane Patterson
9948	Patterson, Jay	GA	1885	Adaline Patterson	Enoch Patterson	Laurene Smith	Saml & Nancy Patterson	Jonah & Betty Smith
13050	Patterson, Jemy	GA	1883	Lulu Patterson	William Patterson	Susan Tatum	Jemy & Sarah Patterson	Moses & Nancy Tatum
13051	Patterson, John	GA	1877	Donie Patterson	James Patterson	Maggie Ward	Samuel & Nancy Patterson	John & Sarah Ward
15658	Patterson, John	GA	1856	Eliza Patterson	Samuel Patterson	Nancy Patterson	William & Martha Patterson	John & Jane Patterson
9949	Patterson, Joseph	GA	1871	Sarah Patterson	Samuel Patterson	Nancy Patterson	Wm & Martha Patterson	John & Jane Patterson
18165	Patterson, Lillie	GA	1885		Jack Patterson	Sinda Chalmers	Samuel & Nancy Patterson	Jophel & Sarah Chalmers
20976	Patterson, Louisa	NC	1853		William Scott	Berthia Witherspoon		Sallie Scott
18779	Patterson, Lula	GA	1883		John Patterson	Eliza Mauldin	Samuel & Nancy Patterson	John & Caroline Mauldin
18116	Patterson, Lurenia	GA	1859	Enoch Patterson	Januk Smith	Bettie Clouts	Eli & Ruban Smith	John & Rene Clouts

14710	Patterson, Martha	NC	1865	John Patterson	Perkins Smitherman	Sarah Trulove	Andrew & Lucinda Smitherman	Auston & Patsy Trulove
15657	Patterson, Martha	GA	1863		Samuel Patterson	Nancy Patterson	William & Martha Patterson	John & Jane Patterson
2080	Patterson, Mary	NC	1876	Wm Patterson	Jesse Delozier	Mary Stillwell	Ed & Elizabeth Delozier	Wm & Maria Stillwell
20952*	Patterson, Mary	NC	1879	Peter Patterson	Marshall Strickland	Vinnie Brown	John Strickland	May Brown
15867*	Patterson, Matilda	TN	1842	Julius Patterson		Millie Jasper		Sidney
17847	Patterson, Mellie	GA	1888		Jack Patterson	Sinda Chalmurs	Samuel & Nancy Patterson	Jophus & Sarah Chalmurs
19581	Patterson, Minerva	MO	1842	Thomas Patterson	Thomas Poindexter	Amelia Dull	Wm & Elizabeth Poindexter	
15656	Patterson, Minnie	GA	1869		Samuel Patterson	Nancy Patterson	William & Martha Patterson	John & Jane Patterson
18918	Patterson, Miriam	GA	1875		Jack Patterson	Sinda Chamburs	Samuel & Nancy Patterson	Jophes & Sarah Chamburs
4961	Patterson, Nancy	GA	1829	Samuel Patterson	John Patterson	Jane Chapman		John & Christine Chapman
17846	Patterson, Nancy	GA			Jack Patterson	Sinda Chalmurs	Samuel & Nancy Patterson	Jophus & Sarah Chalmurs
17968	Patterson, Naomi	GA	1903		James Patterson	Maggie Ward	Samuel & Nancy Patterson	John & Sarah Ward
13152	Patterson, Nebraska	GA	1881	Feba Patterson	Charles Patterson	Arminda Key	Wm & Martha Patterson	John & Jane Patterson
19582	Patterson, Samuel	GA	1876	Nancy Patterson	William Patterson	Martha Tucker	John & Nancy Patterson	Sara Tucker
13151	Patterson, Truman	GA	1880	Lilley Patterson	Charles Patterson	Arminda Key	Wm & Martha Patterson	
18780	Patterson, Wesley	GA	1881	Nannie Patterson	John Patterson	Eliza Mauldin	Samuel & Nancy Patterson	John & Caroline Mauldin
9951	Patterson, William	GA	1859	Susana Patterson	Jerry Patterson	Sarah Davis	John & Jennie Patterson	Jackson & Elizabeth Davis
14089	Patterson, William	GA	1859	Susie Patterson	Jerry Patterson	Sarah Davis	John & Jane Patterson	Jackson & Mary Davis
19461	Patterson, William	CO	1872	Anna Patterson	Merideth Patterson	Perlina Bear		James & Polly Bear
19121	Paul, John	OK	1857	Olive Paul	Samuous Paul	Elizabeth Cobb	George & Bulah Paul	Jessie & Jeanetta Cobb
19120	Paul, Nellie	OK	1888		John Paul	Olive Hukill	Samuel & Elizabeth Paul	Wm & Louisa Hukill
19122	Paul, Nettie	OK	1885		John Paul	Olive Hukill	Samuel & Elizabeth Paul	Wm & Louisa Hukill
11253	Pauley, Clarisy	OK	1865	Robert Pauley	Joe Hall	Becky Burns		Clarisy Burns
21171	Pauly, Mattie	TX	1887	Henry Pauly	James Holt	Anna Rogers	Berry Holt	Susan Driskill
14492	Paurl, Lillas	GA	1883	Will Paurl	John Anglin	Mary Helton		Clark Helton & Nancy Hinkle
9900	Payne, Angus	OK	18yrs	none	John Payne	Elisebeth Swindle	Elisha & Malissa Payne	
13003	Payne, Benjamin	TN	1830		John Payne	Jane Walls	John & Jane Payne	
22413	Payne, Bruner	TN	1883	none	James Payne	Annice Parks	John & Mary Payne	
16493*	Payne, Cephus	NC	42yrs	Celia Payne				
9198	Payne, Delia	NC	1858		Joshua Payne	Patsy Hayden	Leonard & Sally Payne	Robert & Susanna Hayden
22416	Payne, Delores	TN	1875	none	James Payne	Annice Parks	John & Mary Payne	
9899	Payne, Edward	OK	20yrs	none	John Payne	Elisebeth Swendle	Elisha & Malissa Payne	
20954	Payne, Effie	OH	1906		Elijah Payne	Annie O'Neil		Patsy Hayden

2514	Payne, Elijah	OH	1871	Anna Neal	Joshua Payne	Patsey Hayden		
9925	Payne, Fletcher	OK	16yrs	none	John Payne	Elisebeth Swindle	Elisha & Malisa Payne	
22366	Payne, Geo	TN	1840	none				
9886	Payne, George	OK	1877	Joann Payne	John Payne	Elisebeth Swindle	Elisha & Malissa Payne	
18339	Payne, George	TN	1840		John Payne	Mary Hammontree	John & Jane Payne	Jake & Jane Hammontree
19560	Payne, George	TN	1819		Jack Payne	Jane Walls	John & Jane Payne	Henry Walls & Suse Powhatan
19562	Payne, George Jr.	TN	1856	Alice Payne	George Payne	Nancy Hooper	John & Jane Payne	Eanis & Margaret Hooper
11747	Payne, Hattie	OK	1869	Richard Trainor	Thomas Trainor	Lucy Williams		Lenord & Sarah Williams
22410	Payne, J.W.	TN		Annice Payne	John Payne	Mary Poindexter		
21175	Payne, James	TN	1846	Annos Payne	John Payne	Mary Hamentree	John & Jane Payne	Jacob Hamentree
10101	Payne, Joel	NC		Ellen Payne	Green Payne	Fannie Harkins	Acey & Nancy Payne	
10100	Payne, John	NC	1870	Laura Payne	Green Payne	Fannie Harkins	Acey & Nancy Payne	
7574	Payne, Joseph	OH	1867	Anna Payne	Joshua Payne	Patsie Hayden		Sukie Hayden
22409	Payne, Joseph	TN	1871		James Payne	Annice Parks	John & Mary Payne	
10098	Payne, L W	NC	1860	Aviline Payne	Green Payne	Fannie Harkins	Acey & Nancy Payne	
19563	Payne, Lemuel	TN	1850	Bethany Payne	George Payne	Nancy Hooper	John & Jane Payne	Eanis & Margaret Hooper
22096	Payne, Lucinda	AR	1876		James Rogers	Amanda Hodges	Henry & Mariah Rogers	John & Jemima Hodges
9554	Payne, Mack	NC	1869	Laura Payne		Mary Deck		Patsie Carson
12256	Payne, Malinda	NC	1859	Lee Payne	Johnathan Osborne	Polly Stamper	Jesse & Cyntha Osborne	Jobe & Elizabeth Stamper
2251	Payne, Mary	KS	1882	Oscar Payne	William Long	Lucena Cook		Jacob & Delana Cook
21507	Payne, Mattie	OK	1877	Albert Payne	Henry Jeter	Mary Fortson	Ealy Jeter	Elijah Fortson
22412	Payne, Nettie	TN	1877	none	J.W. Payne	Annice Parks	John & Mary Payne	
22415	Payne, Robert	TN	1879	none	James Payne	Annice Parks	John & Mary Payne	
21157	Payne, Rosa	OK	1870	Henry Payne	Charles Coody	Laura Haff	Archibald & Elizabeth Coody	
10241	Payne, S D	NC	1864	Sarah Payne	Green Payne	Fannie Harkins	Acey & Nancy Payne	
15062	Payne, Sallie	GA	1877	James Payne	Toliver Floyd	Ginsey King		W S & Rhoda King
15318	Payne, Seleta	GA	1869	William Payne	Benj Owens	Nancy Doss		Edward & Seleta Doss
10090	Payne, Tom	NC	1880	M A Payne	Green Payne	Fannie Harkins	Acey & Nancy Payne	
9901	Payne, Will	OK	1869	Laura Payne	John Payne	Elisebeth Swindle		
18605	Payne, Zada et al	NC			Leander Payne	Malinda Osborn	Walton & Rebecka Payne	John & Polly Osborn
8411	Payton, Eliza	MO	1856	John Payton	Thomas Johnston Jr	Eliza Bancum	Thos & Mary Johnston	Thos & Elizabeth Bancum
3323	Peacock, Rosa	AL	1880	John Peacock	William Dees	Annie Parte	William & Holly Dees	Mary Parte
9993	Peak, Alexander	NC	1875	none	Columbus Peak	Caroline Spencer	Hugh & Marga Peak	Solomon & Nellie Spencer

11418	Peak, Alexander	PA	1867	Lou Peak	Uriah Peak	Carnealy Hart		George & Polly Hart
9992	Peak, Alice	NC	1871	none	Columbus Peak	Caroline Spencer	Hugh & Marga Peak	Solomon & Nellie Spencer
18499	Peak, Andrew	MO	1868		Russel Peak	Nancy Reynolds	Jim & Judah Peak	John Reynolds
11420	Peak, Carnealy	VA	1828	Uriah Peak	George Hart	Polly Hart	James & Catherine Hart	
9991	Peak, Caroline	NC	1833	Columbus Peak	Solomon Spencer	Nellie Hash		Robert & Marga Hash
1116	Peak, Cephus	TN	1853	Feby Peak	Louis Peak	Matilda Griffith	Able Peak	Liddie Jones
11386	Peak, Clemon	OK	1861	Dollie Peak	Richard Peak	Susan Peak	James & Judy Peak	
11387	Peak, Dollie	OK	1873	Clemon Peak	Jess Murphy	Phoeba Murphy	Wm & Polly Murphy	
6427	Peak, Emma	VA	1883		Robert Peak	Sarah Pickle	Hugh & Margie Peak	
12958	Peak, Harvey	CA	1869		Richard Peak	Susan	James & Judy Peak	
6949	Peak, James	VA	1871	Winnie Peak	John Peak	Sarilda McGrady	Hugh & Marga Peak	
7932	Peak, James	NC	1864	Bethane Peak	Hugh Peak	Margo Hart		George & Polly Hart
10951	Peak, James	MO	1864	Susan Peak	Russel Peak	Nancy Reynolds	James & Judia Peak	Johnnie Reynolds
14232	Peak, James	OK	1856	Mary Peak	Richard Peak	Susan Lewis	James & Judy Peak	
6951	Peak, John	VA	1846	Sarelda Peak	Hugh Peak	Marga Hart		George & Polly Hart
6948	Peak, John Jr.	VA	1874	Augusta	John Peak Sr.	Sarilda McGrady	Hugh & Marga Peak	
6950	Peak, Joseph	VA	1879	Dora Peak	John Peak	Sarilda McGrady	Hugh & Marga Peak	
11421	Peak, Leander	VA	1858	Jane Peak	Uriah Peak	Carmealy Hart		George & Polly Hart
9754	Peak, Louvina	AL	1835	none	James Peak	Judy Henson	James Peak	Joseph & Rebecca Henson
16188	Peak, Richard	OK	1840	Susan Peak	James Peak	Judy Peak	Nathaniel Peak	
6428	Peak, Robert	VA	1860	Sarah Peak	Hugh Peak	Marga Hart		George & Polley Hart
6429	Peak, Rush	VA	1882	Girtie Peak	Robert Peak	Sarah Pickle	Hugh & Marga Peak	
15651*	Pearson, Mollie	GA	1866	John Pearson	Arthur Wolding	Clarisy Mohair		Charity Cash
20955	Pearson, Robert	AL	1840	Elizabeth Pearson	Charly Pearson	Boshuba Moore	Charly Pearson	
13587*	Pearson, William	GA	1879		John Pearson	Mollie Wolding		Arthur & Clara Wolding
19588	Peck, Mary	AL	1879	Ed Peck	John Garren	Nancy Cooper	Elizabeth Garren	Wm & Susan Cooper
4890	Peck, Susan	TN	1861	H.L. Peck	Thomas Wilson	Rebecca Hampton	Thomas & Sarah Wilson	Sarah Hampton
7788	Peebly, Eliza	MO	1841	widow	Sterling Carroll	Jane Clendenon	James & Polly Carroll	John & Mary Clendenen
20375*	Peek, Norah	TN	1857	Frank Peek	John Goldin	Vina Thornton	Shafers & Onie Goldin	Joseph & Cyntha Thornton

ID	Name	State	Year	Col5	Col6	Col7	Col8	Col9
18195	Peek, Ollie	GA	1882	Samuel Peek	Elijah Sprouse	Mary May	Terrett & Delila Sprouse	Thomas & Hannah May
16138	Peery, Lucy	TX	1891		C R Peery	Louisa Henson	Thomas Peery & Rebecca Whitley	Henry Henson & Mary Hardman
3062	Peetoom, Martha	OK	1877	John Peetoom	James Reed	Laura Jackson	Samuel & Francis Reed	Henry & Matilda Jackson
17595	Pendergraft, Mary	MO	1852	J.J. Pendergraft	Henry Shell	Elisabeth Yoakum		Jacob Yoakum
2308	Pendergrass, Linda	NC	1871	J D Pendergrass	W J Mason	Susie Benfield	Aaron & Pollie Robinson	Thomas & Lydia Benfield
18763	Pendergrass, Linda	GA	1871		W.A. Masan	Susie Benfield	John & Pelle Masan	Tom & Lydia Benfield
535	Pendergrass, Maggie	OK	1873	Jesse Pendergrass	Lew Mathews	Artie Sanders	Samuel & Elizabeth Mathews	John & Nancy Sanders
9836	Pendergrass, Nancy	NC	1838	John Pendergrass	John Rogers	Sallie Dills		Bartlett & Margaret Dills
20609	Pendleton, Ada	GA			John Pendleton	Nina Wilson	Simeon & Margaret Pendleton	Noah & Manerva Roper
20395	Pendleton, John	GA	1873	Nina Pendleton	Simeon Pendleton	Margaret Raper	Elijah & Salina Pendleton	Noah Raper & Jane Ward
20610	Pendleton, Mark	GA			John Pendleton	Nina Wilson	Simeon & Margaret Pendleton	Noah & Manerva Roper
20396	Pendleton, Ruth	GA			John Pendleton		Simeon & Margaret Pendleton	Noah & Minerva Roper
2475	Pendleton, Tyne	TN	1857	Simeon Pendleton	Noah Roper	Minerva Taylor	Thomas & Jane Roper	Hudson & Sallie Taylor
18638*	Penland, Ham	NC	1868	Mary Penland	Louis Penland	Rheno Rona		Tilda Wilburn
6886	Pennington, Abel	VA	1836	Emly & Sarah	Andrew Pennington	Hester Blevins		James & Lydia Blevins
8542	Pennington, Andrew	TN	1844	Eliza Pennington	Andrew Pennington	Hester Blevins		James & Lyddia Blevins
6892	Pennington, Asa	VA	1872	Katey Pennington	Eli Pennington	Emily Allens	Andrew & Hetty Pennington	
6826	Pennington, Asa (decd)	VA	1862	Emaline Pennington	Andrew Pennington	Hester Blevins		James & Lydia Blevins
6891	Pennington, Calaway	VA	1874	Malinda Pennington	Hiram Pennington	Margaret Huffman	Andrew & Hetty Pennington	
6812	Pennington, Cicero	VA	1871	Sary Pennington	Andrew Davis	Naomy Pennington		Andrew & Netty Pennington
5190	Pennington, Claborn	NC	1830	Charity Pennington	Samuel Pennington	Elizabeth Anderson	Andrew & Hattie Pennington	
6161	Pennington, D. Eli	VA	1874	Eadith Pennington	Hiram Pennington	Margaret Huffman	Andrew & Hetty Pennington	
6160	Pennington, Eady	VA	1883	David Pennington	Welborin Blevins	Susan Lewis	Edward & Nancy Blevins	
6811	Pennington, Effa	VA	5yrs		Edward Pennington	Nanny Owens	Asa & Emaline Pennington	
6890	Pennington, Eli	VA	1840	Emily Pennington	Andrew Pennington	Hetty Blevins		James & Lydia Blevins
6823	Pennington, Elic	VA	1874	Margree	Calaway Penington	Nancy Privell	Andrew & Hesther Pennington	Noah & Neoma Privill
6828	Pennington, Elijah	VA	1864	Martha Pennington	Eli Pennington	Emily Allen	Andrew & Hetty Pennington	
5194	Pennington, Elisebeth	VA		E C Pennington	W H Hart	Martha Miller	Stephen & Rebecca Hart	

6829	Pennington, Evaline	VA	1856	David Pennington	Andrew Pennington	Hetty Blevins		James & Lydia Blevins
6906	Pennington, Florence	VA	1876	Samuel Pennington	Shade Blevins	Oney Blevins	Tobias Blevins	Susan Blevins
6850	Pennington, Freeling	VA	1876	Carrie Pennington	Abel Pennington	Sarah Able	Andrew & Hesther Pennington	Leander Able
6883	Pennington, George	VA	1866	Amanda Pennington	Hyram Pennington	Margaret Huffman	Andrew & Hester Pennington	
6896	Pennington, Henry	VA	1876	Zara Pennington	Eli Pennington	Emily Allen	Andrew & Hetty Pennington	
6882	Pennington, Hiram	VA	60yrs	Margaret Pennington	Andrew Pennington	Hetty Blevins		James & Lydia Blevins
6821	Pennington, James	VA	1888	Florence Pennington	Abel Pennington	Sarah Able	Andrew & Hesther Pennington	Leander & Mary Able
6822	Pennington, James	VA	1848	Sela Pennington	Caloway Pennington	Nancy Duvitt	Andrew & Hester Pennington	
6110	Pennington, Laney	VA	1883	Samuel Pennington	Henderson Hart	Martha Miller		Stephen & Rebecca Hart
6820	Pennington, Leander	VA	1874	Ida Pennington	Abel Pennington	Sarah Abel	Andrew & Hesther Pennington	Leander Able
6813	Pennington, Lilley	VA	1874	none	Ceb Blevins	Naomy Pennington		Andrew & Netty Pennington
8455	Pennington, Lillie	TN	1876	none	Andrew Pennington	Eliza Gentry	Andrew & Hester Pennington	
9049	Pennington, Lydia	VA		Ambroes Pennington	William Miller	Eva Blevins		Riley & Agnes Blevins
9239	Pennington, Mary	VA	1867	McClelland Pennington	Jesse Blevins	Catharine Pennington	Eli & Milly Blevins	
8456	Pennington, Sally	TN		James Foryester	Andrew Pennington	Eliza Gentry	Andrew & Hester Pennington	
6118	Pennington, Samuel	VA	1845	Sarah Pennington	Andrew Pennington	Hetty Blevins		James & Lydia Blevins
6119	Pennington, Samuel	VA	1881	Laney Pennington	Samuel Pennington	Sarah Huffman	Andrew & Hetty Pennington	
6897	Pennington, Samuel	VA	1874	Florence Pennington	Eli Pennington	Emily Allen	Andrew & Hetty Pennington	
9083	Pennington, Sibby	VA	1883	Ambroes Pennington	Solomon Ham	Mary Blevins		Riley & Agnes Blevins
6120	Pennington, Siberious	VA	1871	Sarah Pennington	Samuel Pennington	Sarah Huffman	Andrew & Hetty Pennington	
8579	Pennington, Uriah	VA	1868	Ardelia Pennington	Hiram Pennington	Margaret Huffman	Andrew & Hetty Pennington	Uriah & Sally Huffman
6827	Pennington, Wells	VA	1883	Laura Pennington	David Pennington	Emaline Pennington	Andrew Pennington	Hetty Pennington
5188	Pennington, William	NC	1871	Essie Pennington	Claburn Pennington	Charity Perkins	Samuel & Elizabeth Pennington	
6109	Pennington, William	VA	1876	Mattie Pennington	Samuel Pennington	Sarah Huffman	Andrew & Hetty Pennington	
6817	Pennington, William	VA	1858	Phoebe Pennington	Calaway Pennington	Nancy Privette	Andrew & Hester Pennington	Noah & Naoma Privette
21551	Percer, Sarah	GA	1865	John Percer	Calieus Pruiett	Eliza Rainwaters	Wm & Darkey Pruiett	Gabriel & Nancy Rainwaters

22117	Perdew, Alice	WV	1875	Elzenia Perdew	Daniel Perdew	Clerinda	Nathaniel & Sallie Perdew	Jole & Sallie Cook
15161	Perdew, D.L.	WV	1845	Charlotte Perdew	Nathaniel Perdew	Sallie Sizemore	Jesse & Sarah Perdew	Ned & Annie Sizemore
3775	Perdew, Julia	GA	1845	J F Perdew	John Davis	Nancy Bird	Daniel & Rachel Davis	John & Nancy Bird
10141	Perdew, Leroy	WV	1848	Catharine Perdew	Nathaniel Perdew	Sallie Sizemore	Sallie Blankenship	Ned Sizemore & Annie Baldwin
9099	Perdew, Mary	WV	1867	Elbert Perdew	Adam Brinegar	Jane Hoppers	Jacob & Sheba Brinegar	Daniel & Sintha Hoppers
10135	Perdew, Mary	WV	1867	Tobias Perdew	David Brinegan	Sarah Osborne	Jacob & Sheba Brinegan	
9100	Perdew, Melvina	WV	1865	Nathaniel Perdew	Adam Brinegar	Jane Hoppers	Jacob & Sheba Brinegar	Daniel & Sintha Hoppers
18669	Perdue, J.L.	VA	1860	Lucy Perdue	Eli Perdue	Mary Mitchell	Zackariah Perdue	Sallie Wolf
22034*	Perdue, Leon	TX	1881	none	James Perdue	Mary Crawford	James & Carry Perdue	Watson & Margaret Crawford
22033	Perdue, Mary	TX	1842	widow	Watson Crawford	Margarett Starr	Calip Starr	Fenton Senton
10118	Perdue, Nathaniel	WV	1855	Nancy Perdue	Nathaniel Perdue	Sallie Sizemore	Jesse Perdue & Sallie Blankenship	Ned Sizemore & Annie Baldwin
22029	Perdue, Queen	TX	1878	none	James Perdue	Mary Crawford	James & Carry Perdue	Margaret Crawford
20669	Perin, John	TN	1844	Mary Perin		Mary Perin		James & Elizabeth Thomason
20671	Perin, Lucy	TN	1878		John Perin	Mary Perkinson	Mary Perin	Page & Matilda Perkinson
20359	Perin, Mary	TN	1856	John Perin	Page Perkinson	Matilda Owens	Jeremiah & Sophia Perkinson	John & Peggy Owens
20677	Perin, Page	TN	1887		John Perin	Mary Perkinson	Mary Perin	Page & Mildred Perkinson
20673	Perin, Samuel	TN	1870	Laura Perin	William Perin	Minnie Chaney	Boley & Elizabeth Perin	
17482	Perkins, Ida	OK	1876	F.L. Perkins	Wilkerson Lawson	Mahala Martin	Hennis Lawson	Wm & Susan Martin
4261	Perkins, James	MO	1854	widower	Jesse Perkins	Emaline Mason	Jack Perkins	James & Nancy Mason
11624	Perkins, Laura	TX	1877	Lee Perkins	Abraham Franklin	Lizzie Tapp	Anderson & Elisebeth Franklin	Hugh & Agnes Tapp
3603	Perkins, Lenox	MO	1882	none	J M Perkins	Laura Lenox	Jesse & Emaline Perkins	John & Susan Lenox
7286	Perkins, Maranda	MO	1840	Charles Perkins	James Carroll	Polly Bond		
10534	Perry, Anna	GA	1870	William Perry	Thomas Loyd	Susan Matthews	Thos & Susanna Loyd	Lewis & Elizabeth Matthews
3452	Perry, Augusta	OK		Sion Perry (decd)	James Perry	Susan Harlan		Ezekiel & Hannah Harlan
17480	Perry, Calvin	VA	1860		Maliciah Perry	Sarah Eldreth	Soloman Perry	
8621	Perry, Catherine	OK		none	William Perry	Susan Wheeler		John & Nannie Wheeler
19159	Perry, Francis	GA	1868	Vistory Perry	Merrida Perry	Sophronia Cheatwood	Emley Perry	
13348	Perry, Nancy	TN	1860	Thomas Perry	Alexander Cochran	Melvina Bradford	Thompson	James Everheart
3185	Perry, Stacey	OK		Oliver Perry (decd)	James Perry	Susan Harlan		Ezekiel & Hannah Harlan
9447	Perry, Susan	GA	1870	Calvin Perry	John Corn	Caroline Davis	Wm & Phebee Corn	John Davis & Nancy Bird

#	Name	State	Year	Spouse	Father	Mother	Paternal GP	Maternal GP
7516	Perry, Theodore	OK	1857	Cornelia Perry	William Perry	Susan Wheeler		John & Nannie Wheeler
21024	Peterson, Della	OK	1862	William Peterson	William Foster	Susan Blackburn		Francis Blackburn
21056 *	Peterson, Mary	IN	1848	widow	Alexander Mitchel	Rebecca Shoecraft		Silas & Mary Shoecraft
15916 ½ *	Pettiford, James	IN	1852	Sarah Pettiford	Osborn Jiles	Clarinda Pettiford		Edmund & Sarah Pettiford
5273	Pettit, Andrew	OK	1878	none	Sam Pettit	Susan Hampton	Wm & Maria Pettit	Francis & Delilah Hampton
19920	Pettitt, Augustine	NC	1884		Benj Pettitt	Ruth Bowen	Ben & Ruth Pettitt	Betty Bowen
19891	Pettitt, Benjamin	NC	1879		Benj Pettitt	Ruth Bowen		Betty Bowan
19890	Pettitt, Calvin	NC	1883	Callie Pettitt	Ben Pettitt	Ruth Bowen	Ben & Ruth Pettitt	
12729	Petty, Alexander	NC	1871	Ocy Petty	John Petty	Catherine Osborne		David & Lucy Osborne
12838	Petty, Bertie	NC	1884		John Petty	Catherine Osborne		David & Lucy Osborne
12725	Petty, Brady	NC	1875	Maggie Petty	John Petty	Catherine Osborne		David & Lucy Osborne
12798	Petty, Catherine	NC	1844	John Petty	David Osborne	Lucy Billings	Elias & Sally Osborne	Jasper & Nancy Billings
12428	Petty, Elijah	NC	1869	Alley Petty	John Petty	Catherine Osborn		David & Lucy Osborn
12731	Petty, Elizabeth	TN	1859	David Petty	Lemuel Michael	Mary Irvin	Jacob Michael	George & Phoebe Irvin
12430	Petty, Greeny	NC	1879	Eveline Petty	John Petty	Catherine Osborn		David & Lucy Osborn
18155	Petty, Jasper	NC	1861	Phoebe Petty	John Petty	Catharine Osborn		David & Lucinda Osborn
11182	Petty, John	OK	1838	Rachel Petty	Joseph Petty	Fannie Niland	Joseph & Polly Petty	
12970	Petty, John	GA		Sarah Petty	Isaac Petty	Parthenia	William Petty	
12429	Petty, Lee	NC	1869	Alley Petty	John Petty	Catherine Osborn		David & Lucy Osborn
15938 *	Pettyjohn, Victoria	GA	1876	William Pettyjohn	Arthur Wolding	Clarisy Mohair	Swept Cox	Charity Cash
19643 *	Peyton, Abraham	AR	1837	Mary Peyton	Abraham Peyton Sr.	Mary ?	Abraham & Betty Peyton	Tony & Arie
18324 *	Peyton, William	AR	1868	Eliza Peyton	Abraham Peyton	Sallie Spencer	Abraham & Mary Peyton	Wm & Louisa Clanton
21114	Phagan, Indiana	GA	1865	Washington Phagan	William Wade	Elizabeth Sosebee	William & Sarah Wade	Wm & Elizabeth Sosebee
20253	Phagans, Sallie	GA	1876	P.P. Phagans	J. P. Savage	Elisebeth Payne	Jimmina Hulsey & Elisebeth Savage	
10829	Pharis, Maggie	CO	1849	Oregon Pharis	Issac Jackson	Elizabeth Brock	Eliza Jackson	
20203	Phelps, Charles	NC	1877	Bessie Phelps	J.A.I. Phelps	Nancy Marion		Frank & Sallie Marion
16400	Philipps, Mary	NC	1828	William Philipps	Leonard Scott	Sally Hauser	Leonard & Nancy Scott	Adam & Peggy Hauser
22240	Philips, Malinda	AL		John Philips	John Warren	Fannie Sisemore	Jarrus & Abigal Grean	Henry & Martha Sisemore
16316	Phillip, Doyle	GA	1855	Sarah Phillip	Joel Phillips	Sallie Williams	Jonas Phillips & Betsie Hix	Dred Williams & Charlotta Honey
20647	Phillips, Abraham	TN	1851	Sarah Phillips	George Phillips	Mary Everett	Abraham Phillips	George Everett
17760	Phillips, Annie	TN	1833		Thomas Mansfield	Catharine Roberts	Thos & Susan Mansfield	James & Nancy Roberts
20252	Phillips, Eliza	TN	1877		John Lane	Louisa Phillips	Lindsey & Rebecca Lane	George & Mary Phillips

20646	Phillips, Eugene	TN	1867	Zaney Phillips	Isaac Phillips	Agnes Phillips	Abraham Phillips	George & Mary Phillips
8627	Phillips, George	OK	1857	Susa Phillips	Richard Phillips	Eliza Wilson	John & Sarah Phillips	
22681	Phillips, Gweney	IN	1870		Jessie Phillips	Jane Warnell		John & Jane Warnell
20251	Phillips, John	TN	1880	Eliza Phillips	George Phillips	Maggie Whittle		
21980	Phillips, John	TN	1882	none	Ab Phillips	Sarah Cogburn		
20061	Phillips, Laura	TN	1883	J.B. Phillips	Harvey Johnson	Mary Burch	Nathaniel & Nancy Johnson	Joseph & Polly Burch
21923	Phillips, Lula	TN	1850	Sarah Phillips	Ab Phillips	Sarah Cogburn	George & Mary Phillips	Moses & Isabel Cogburn
3990	Phillips, M A	NC	1866	Winfield Phillips	John Pendergrass	Elisabeth Ridle	Thomas & Margaret Pendergrass	Antny & Christina Ridle
17727	Phillips, Maggie	AL	1875	J.C. Phillips	W.G. Tidwell	Matilda Paine	W.G. Tidwell & Martha Shelton	Thos Paine & Miranda Watson
18175*	Phillips, Martha	OK	1850	Charles Phillips	Jack Thompson	Emily Brown	Wm Thompson & Betsy Fields	Joe & Debra Brown
18874	Phillips, Matthew	NC	1851	Margaret Phillips	Matthew Phillips	Ann Scott	Wm & Susan Phillips	Robert & Mary Scott
14004	Phillips, May	OK	1874	Walter Phillips	Levi Robbins	Sarah Stone		
6354	Phillips, Mrs J C	AL	45yrs	J C Phillips	John Steadham	Mary McGhee	Ned Steadham	Nancy McGhee
22269*	Phillips, Myrtle	OK	1883	Prince Phillips	James Fulse	Ruth Ratcliff		Ben Landrum & Winnie Ratcliff
12950	Phillips, Nora	OK	1885	Frank Phillips	Benjamin Courtney	Matilda Fender	Wm & Matilda Courtney	Daniel & Dicy Fender
17702*	Phillips, Richard	NC	1876	Margaret Phillips	Pleas Phillips	Nettie Eccles	Richard & Sarah Phillips	Alex & Lucinda Eccles
4758	Phillips, Rosa	MO	1880	William Phillips	William Presley	Malissa Fender	Isaac & Martha Presley	Michael & Martha Fender
14491	Phillips, Sarah	GA	1874	Robert Phillips	Thomas McClure	Amanda Millwood	J J & Maulda McClure	Hugh & Miram Millwood
16315	Phillips, Sarah	GA	1860	Doyle Phillips	Jonas Mills	Nancy Whitehead	George & Jennie Mills	Joseph & Annie Whitehead
18500*	Phillips, Stephen	GA	1807	Mary Phillips	Longtow Phillips	Josephine Phillips		
18351	Phillips, Sylvania	NC	1833	Wiley Phillips	Benj Hyde	Cynthia Sherrice	Benj Hyde	Elizabeth Leatherwood
5472	Phillips, Willard	MO	1873	Lovina Phillips	William Phillips	Nancy Pace		Robert & Annis Pace
13615	Phipps, Albert	IN	1874	Gertrude Phipps	Henderson Phipps	Phedelia Hash		James & Marjory Hash
9066	Phipps, B.F.	NC	1882	Cora Phipps	Nathan Phipps	Margrey Hash	Ahart & Maryann Phipps	John & Sarah Hash
6094	Phipps, Benjamin	NC	1880	Maud Phipps	Robbert Phipps	Caroline Yates	Benjamin & Ruthey Phipps	Eli & Nancy Yates
6170	Phipps, Bertha	NC	1889	none	Robert Phipps	Loudema Miller	Ahart & Maryan Phipps	Jackson & Elmira Miller
14795	Phipps, Bertie	VA	1882	Columbus Phipps	Rush Young	Ellen Phipps	Wm & Catherine Young	Elijah & Nellie Phipps
6095	Phipps, Caroline	NC	1849	Rpbbert Phipps	Eli Yates	Nancy Spencer	John & Elizabeth Yates	Solomon & Nellie Spencer
6096	Phipps, Clinton	NC	1883	none	Robert Phipps	Caroline Yates	Benjamin & Ruthey Phipps	Eli & Nancy Yates

6143	Phipps, Cora	NC	1869	none	Benjamin Phipps	Rebecca Plummer	Ahart & Maryan Phipps	Joseph Plummer
6173	Phipps, Corban	NC	1878	none	Robert Phipps	Loudema Miller	Ahart & Maryan Phipps	Jackson & Elmira Miller
6174	Phipps, Edward	NC	1881	none	Robert Phipps	Loudema Miller	Ahart & Maryan Phipps	Jackson & Elmira Miller
6188	Phipps, Eli	NC	1844	Joicey Phipps	Benjamin Phipps	Ruthy Hash	Wm & Nancy Phipps	Robbert & Margera Hash
6092	Phipps, Ellen	NC	1873	none	Robbert Phipps	Caroline Yates	Benjamin & Ruthey Phipps	Eli & Nancy Yates
6178	Phipps, Ennis	NC	1874	James Phipps	Robert Phipps	Loudema Miller	Ahart & Maryan Phipps	Jackson & Elmira Miller
13617	Phipps, Francis	IN			Henderson Phipps	Phedelia Hash		James & Marjory Hash
9065	Phipps, James	NC	1875	May Phipps	Nathan Phipps	Martha Hart	Ahart & Maryann Phipps	David & Nancy Hart
6166	Phipps, Joyce	NC	1851	Eli Phipps	James Blevins	Meacy Pennington	James & Lyddia Blevins	Abrum & Margera Pennington
6175	Phipps, Lester	NC	1888	none	Elihn Phipps	Alice Blevins	James & Eveline Phipps	Poindexter & Lyda Blevins
9067	Phipps, Margrey	NC	1844	Nathan Phipps	John Hash	Sarah Hash	Robert Hash	Margrey Hash
6091	Phipps, Mary	NC	1861		Ahart Phipps	Maryan Hash	Wm & Nancy Phipps	Robbert & Margera Hash
6097	Phipps, Nancy	NC	1872	none	Robbert Phipps	Caroline Yates	Benjamin & Ruthy Phipps	Eli & Nancy Yates
9064	Phipps, Nathan	NC	1837	Margrey Phipps	Ahart Phipps	Maryann Hash	Wm & Nancy Phipps	Robert & Margrey Hash
6093	Phipps, Rhoda	NC	1882	none	Robert Phipps	Caroline Yates	Benjamin & Ruthey Phipps	Eli & Nancy Yates
6089	Phipps, Robbert	NC	1850	Caroline Phipps	Benjamin Phipps	Ruthy Hash	William & Nancy Phipps	Robbert & Margera Hash
6167	Phipps, Rush	NC	1875	Gennie Phipps	Eli Phipps	Jeston Phipps	Benjamin & Ruthy Phipps	Ahart & Maryan Phipps
6177	Phipps, Stella	NC	1891	none	Elihus Phipps	Alice Blevins	James & Evaline Phipps	Poindexter & Lyda Blevins
6144	Phipps, Thomas	NC	1871	Louise Phipps	Eli Phipps	Jeston Phipps	Benjamin & Ruthy Phipps	Ahart & Maryann Phipps
6090	Phipps, William	VA	1841	Mary Phipps	Benjamin Phipps	Ruthy Hash	Wm & Nancy Phipps	Robbert & Margera Hash
13614	Phipps, William	IN	1880		Henderson Phipps	Phedelia Hash		James & Marjory Hash
15200	Phipps, William	GA	1873	Pearl Phipps	Uriah Phipps	Harriet Edwards		Lou Edwards
6171	Phipps, Worth	NC		none	Robert Phipps	Loudema Miller	Ahart & Maryan Phipps	Jackson & Elmira Miller
18750	Piccolini, Evaline	OK	1879	John Piccolini	James Higdon	Rachel Freeland	Joseph & Margret Higdon	Howell & Zilpha Freeland
11219	Pickard, Jeff	MO	1844		Thomas Pickard	Lucretia Johnson	Henry Pickard	James & Hester Johnson
15194	Pickel, Annie	GA			Jackson Pickel	Rena Mitchel	Isaac & Martha Pickel	Jackson & Polly Mitchel
12046	Pickens, Fannie	GA	1883	Robert Pickens	Membry Bramlett	Nancy Blalock	Miles & Annie Bramlett	George & Jane Blalock

#	Name	State	Year					
3125	Pickett, Jonnie	MS	1878	Joshua Pickett	Jerry Coleman	Mary Hobgood		Charley & Martha Hobgood
3124	Pickett, Mary	MS	1884	Nathan Pickett	Jerry Coleman	Mary Hobgood		Charles & Martha Hobgood
6840	Pickle, Martha	OK	1874	James Pickle	Andrew Hart	Rebbecca Pennington	Elisha & Nancy Hart	Andrew & Hesther Pennington
10454	Pierce, Mae	NC	1879	Robert Pierce	Catlett Greer	Charlotte Richardson		Wilborn & Esther Richardson
21663	Pierce, Mary	TN	1865	Ambrose Pierce	Almon Guinn	Sophia Arthur	Almon & Sarah Guinn	
10453	Pierce, Neva	NC	1890	none	Robert Pierce	Charlota Richardson	Andie & Jane Pierce	Wilborn & Easter Richardson
16926	Pigeon, Carrie	OK	1875	Jesse Pigeon	Will Blackfox	Elsie Smith	Blackfox & Neh chi li	Sanette & Ar yo gar
19888	Pike, Bailey	NC	1878	Aney Pike	James Pike	Elizabeth Hooker	Isac & Rebeca Pike	Sam & Sitha Hooker
19905	Pike, Edger & Nella	NC	4yrs 2 yrs		Joseph Pike	Kate Mears	James & Elizabeth Pike	
19903	Pike, Elizabeth	NC	1852	James Pike	Sam Hooker	Litha Beasly	Galee & Nancy Hooker	Harlen & Sally Beasly
19907	Pike, Elmer et al	NC			Sam Pike	Dosie Henderson	James & Elizabeth Pike	
19909	Pike, Joseph	NC	1879		James Pike	Elizabeth Hooker	Isaac & Rebecca Pike	Sam & Litha Hooker
19904	Pike, Rebeca et al	NC			James Pike	Elizabeth Hooker		James & Litha Hooker
19906	Pike, Sam	NC	1883	Dosey Pike	James Pike	Elizabeth Hooker	Isaac & Rebecca Pike	Sam & Litha Hooker
19908	Pike, Wm & Zely	NC	1902 1905		Bailey Pike	Ana Rains	James & Elizabeth Pike	
22176	Pilgrim, Emily	GA			Hezekiah Haney	Julayann Wilson	James Haney	Matilda McCluar
58	Pilgrim, Jeremiah	GA	1861	Mary Pilgrim	Elijah Pilgrim	Rhoda Ledbetter	Elijay & Betsey Pilgrim	Wm & Malinda Ledbetter
1348	Pinion, Charley	OK	1874	Flora Pinion	Jeptha Pinion	Nancy Donnell		Tally
7283	Pinkston, Ann	TX	1859	David Pinkston	Richard Poindexter	Mary Lollar	Sallie Poindexter	
11505	Pinson, Sarah	GA	1853		James Bridges	Elizabeth Carder	Aaron & Amy Bridges	Tom & Nancy Carder
9774	Pinyan, Jeptha	GA	1823	Nancy Pinyan	Stokes Pinyan	Nancy Tally	Ruben Pinyan	Elisabeth Hensley
22871	Pinyan, Jeptha	GA	1843		Jacob Piyan	Matilda Hyde	Stoken Pinyan & Nancy Tully	James & Susan Hyde
12348	Pinyan, Mattie	GA	1888	Jacob Pinyan	Oliver Howard	Susan Hillhouse	Samuel & Polly Howard	Samuel & Augusta Hillhouse
21627	Pippln, Margaret	OK	1878	Walter Pippin	James Lowry	Betsy Mainor	Isom & Syntha Lowry	Wm & Sally Mainor
11851	Pitman, William	GA	1888		Monroe Pitman	Eliza Stout	Jane Prince	
7649*	Pitner, Jennie	GA	1848	decd	Brown Kenyon	Phoebe Kenyon		Archaluke & Georgia Angels
12358	Pittman, Amanda	OK	1882		Joseph Coodey	Mary Hardage	Joseph & Jane Coodey	Joe & Muskogee Hardage
19982	Pitts, Elizabeth	GA	1848	William Pitts	Joshua Horton	Nancy Hightower	Joshua & Annie Horton	James & Mary Hightower
1636	Pitts, Harrett	OK	1846	Warren Pitts	Elaxander Walden	Monning Williams		John & Lucy Williams

7725	Pittsenborger, Francis	OK	1842	Sarah Pittsenborger	John Pittsenborger	Cathren Harman		Christopher Harman
1383	Pleasant, Jonia	OH	1878	John Pleasant	William Williamson	Emma Taborn	Square & Harriett Williamson	
4748	Pless, Sarah	GA	1853	Seabom Pless	Ellott Boling	Rosa Pruett	Thomas Boling	Polly McDonald
490	Plummer, Charles	CO	1880	none	Jesse Plummer	Frances Stamper	Plummer	Stamper
493	Plummer, Frances	TN	1850	Jesse Plummer	Eli Stamper	Susanna Stampler	Stamper	Betsy Stamper
417	Plummer, Geo Wash.	WY	1870	Ameline	Jesse Plummer	Frances Stamper	Plummer	Stamper
485	Plummer, Ophelia	VA	1898	none	Robt. Plummer	Callie Gentry	Plummer	Gentry
475	Plummer, Orley	VA	1900	none	Robt. Plummer	Callie Gentry	Plummer	Gentry
491	Plummer, Robt. E Lee	VA	1868	Callie Plummer	Jesse Plummer	Frances Stamper	Plummer	Stamper
476	Plummer, Thelmus	VA	1902	none	Robt. Plummer	Callie Gentry	Plummer	Gentry
6947	Plummer, Valeria	VA	1864	William Plummer	John Peak	Sarelda McGrady	Hugh & Marga Peak	
3974	Poe, Robert	MO	1886	Belle Poe	Henry Poe	Martha Sweckard		Isiah & Martha Hambelton
2028	Poe, Sarah	MO	1857	James Poe	Arnsan Harralson	Martha Hamilton		Alex Brown
4179	Poe, Thomas	MO		Gola Poe	Henry Poe	Martha Sweckard		Martha Hambelton
19271	Pogue, John	TN	1872	Sarah Pogue	Harve Mize	Sarah Jones		John & Martha
13485	Poindexter, Alex	NC	1844	Emma Poindexter	Denson Poindexter	Sarah Jones	Wm & Elizabeth Poindexter	Isaac & Bosheba Jones
18142	Poindexter, Andy	NC	1851	Alice Poindexter	Alex Poindexter	Sarah Douglas	John & Pollie Poindexter	John & Mary Douglas
16002	Poindexter, Augusta	NC	1850	Henry Poindexter	William Miller	Catherine Martin	John & Elizabeth Miller	Samuel & Elizabeth Martin
14677	Poindexter, Augustus	NC	1849	Mary Poindexter	Thomas Poindexter	Lucy Morlas	Denson & Sarah Poindexter	John & Mary Morlas
22694	Poindexter, Belva	NC	1891	Wiley Poindexter	Thomas Martin	Sarah Norman	John & Susan Martin	Ellis & Octava Norman
15014	Poindexter, Catherine	NC	1880		Henry Poindexter	Augusta Miller	Robert & Martha Poindexter	Wm & Catherine Miller
19636	Poindexter, Catherine	NC						
17501	Poindexter, Charlie	OR	1869		Robbert Poindexter	Martha Ward	Robbert & Charlotte Poindexter	
3971	Poindexter, Clayborn	OK	1853	Amanda Poindexter	James Murphy	Tildia Poindexter		Francis & Nancy Poindexter
19509	Poindexter, Columbia	NC	1861		George Poindexter	Eliza Herring	Thomas & Amelia Poindexter	Harding & Elizabeth Herring
22687	Poindexter, Comilar	NC	1871		Augustine Poindexter	Mary Davis		
18668 ½	Poindexter, Denson	NC	1834	Matilda Poindexter	Alex Poindexter	Sarah Douglas	John & Mary Poindexter	John & Mary Douglas
19508	Poindexter, Elizabeth	NC	1873		George Poindexter	Eliza Herring	Thomas & Amelia Poindexter	Harding & Elizabeth Herring

ID	Name	State	Year	Spouse	Father	Mother	Paternal Grandparents	Maternal Grandparents
2011	Poindexter, Etna	NC	35yrs	Frank Poindexter	James Fox	Etna Fox		
15999	Poindexter, Eva	NC	1882		Henry Poindexter	Augusta Miller	Robert & Martha Poindexter	Wm & Catherine Miller
15987 ½	Poindexter, Henry	NC	1849	Augusta Poindexter	Robert Poindexter	Martha Ward	Robert & Charlotte Poindexter	Wiley & Polly Ward
19231	Poindexter, Henry	NC	1878	Elah Poindexter	George Poindexter	Eliza Herring	Thomas & Amelia Poindexter	Harden & Elizabeth Herring
13609	Poindexter, Isaac	NC	1837	Mary Poindexter	Denson Poindexter	Sarah Jones	Wm & Elizbeth Poindexter	Isaac & Bosheba Jones
14891	Poindexter, James	NC		Emily Poindexter	Lewis Poindexter	Mary Sawyers		Solomon & Bitha Sawyers
18141	Poindexter, James	NC	1860	Nancy Poindexter	Alex Poindexter	Sarah Douglas	John & Pollie Poindexter	John & Mary Douglas
13522	Poindexter, John	NC		Julia Poindexter	Robert Poindexter	Charlotte Martin	Thos & Elizabeth Poindexter	Valentine & Elizabeth Martin
19232	Poindexter, John	NC	1866	Ludie Poindexter	George Poindexter	Eliza Herring	Thomas & Amelia Poindexter	Harden & Elizabeth Herring
14684	Poindexter, Joseph	NC	1854	Delilah Poindexter	Thomas Poindexter	Lucy Morlor	Denson & Sarah Poindexter	John & Mary Morlor
18668	Poindexter, Leroy	NC	1843	Sarah Poindexter	Tyrell Poindexter	Matilda Overby	John & Mary Poindexter	Wm & Susan Overby
18913	Poindexter, Lucrecia	NC	1833	David Poindexter	Louis Bledsoe	Mary Marsh	Larkin & Francis Bledsoe	Minor & Annie Marsh
22688	Poindexter, Lucy	NC	1878		Augustine Poindexter	Mary Davis		
15013	Poindexter, Margaret	NC	1875		Henry Poindexter	Augusta Miller	Robert & Martha Poindexter	Wm & Catherine Miller
14302	Poindexter, Mary	NC	1831	widow	Solomon Sawyer Jr	Bitha Evans	Solomon Sr & Polly Sawyer	Ben & Lucy Evans
15617	Poindexter, Nathaniel	NC	1859	Dora Poindexter	Simeon Poindexter	Nancy Woodley	John & Polly Poindexter	John & Matilda Woodley
21119	Poindexter, Neta	TX		none	James Poindexter	Mary Washburn	Richard & Mary Poindexter	
13489	Poindexter, Pleasant	NC	1837	Temperance Poindexter	Robert Poindexter	Charlotte Martin	Thos Poindexter & Elizabeth Pledge	Valentine Martin & Elizabeth Dalton
14685	Poindexter, Ray	NC	1864	Maurice Poindexter	Thomas Poindexter	Lucy Morlor	Denson & Sarah Poindexter	John & Mary Morlor
18814	Poindexter, Rebecca	NC	1842		Alex Poindexter	Sarah Douglas	John & Mary Poindexter	John & Mary Douglas
18567	Poindexter, Richard	NC	1853	Eliza Poindexter	William Poindexter	Mary Apperson	Thos & Amelia Poindexter	Thos & Luvitha Apperson
22692	Poindexter, Richard	NC	1874	Dollie Poindexter	Isaac Poindexter	Mary Hauser	Denson & Sarah Poindexter	Samuel & Nancy Hauser
16320	Poindexter, Robert	NC	1861	Amanda Poindexter	Anderson Poindexter	Mary Apperson	Thos & Millie Poindexter	
17417	Poindexter, Robert	NC	1865		Robbert Poindexter	Martha Ward	Robbert & Charlotte Poindexter	
19833	Poindexter, Robert	VA	1864	Ida, Laura Poindexter	George Poindexter	Eliza Herring	Thos & Amelia Poindexter	Harding & Elizabeth Herring
13597	Poindexter, Rufus	NC	1855		John Poindexter	Martha Ogburn	John & Sarah Poindexter	
16397	Poindexter, Sallie	NC	1865		Archie Poindexter	Elizabeth Ward	Robert & Mariam Poindexter	Wiley & Mary Ward
13491	Poindexter, Samuel	NC	1851	Sarah Poindexter	Robert Poindexter	Martha Ward	Robert & Charlotte Poindexter	Wiley & Polly Ward
22688 ½	Poindexter, Samuel	NC	1880	Lousey Poindexter	Augustine Poindexter	Mary Davis		
22693	Poindexter, Samuel	NC	1869	Cordelia Poindexter	Isaac Poindexter	Mary Hauser	Denson & Sarah Poindexter	Samuel & Nancy Hauser
14887	Poindexter, Sarah	NC	1856	Samuel Poindexter	Abner Smitherman	Sarah Trulove	Andrew & Lucinda Smitherman	Austin & Patsy Trulove

14307	Poindexter, Thomas	NC		widower	Thomas Poindexter	Amelia Dull	Wm & Elizabeth Poindexter	
14692	Poindexter, Thomas	NC	1863	Elizabeth Poindexter	Archibald Poindexter	Elizabeth Ward	Robt & Miriam Poindexter	Wiley & Polly Ward
17485	Poindexter, Thomas	NC	1850	Cora Poindexter	John Poindexter	Martha Ogbern	John & Sarah Poindexter	
18433	Poindexter, W. Van	VA	1865	Sallie Poindexter	Wm Poindexter	Mary Apperson	Thos & Amelia Poindexter	Thos & Levitha Apperson
15716	Poindexter, Wiley	NC	1866	Annie Poindexter	Robbert Poindexter	Martha Ward	Robt & Charlotte Poindexter	
22690	Poindexter, Wiley	NC	1880	Belva Poindexter	Isaac Poindexter	Mary Hauser	Denson & Sarah Poindexter	Samuel & Nancy Hauser
7281	Poindexter, William	OK	1874	Flora Poindexter	William Poindexter	Mary Harrell	Zedock & Sally Poindexter	Archie & Gila Harrell
7282	Poindexter, William	OK	1843	Mary Poindexter	Zaddock Poindexter	Sarah Anderson	Arche & Rebecca Poindexter	Wm & Nancy Anderson
14124	Poindexter, William	NC	1860	Jenie Poindexter	John Poindexter	Martha Ogburn	John Poindexter	Sarah James
18419	Poindexter, William	NC		Dora Poindexter	Wm Poindexter	Mary Apperson	Thos & Amelia Poindexter	Thos & Levitha Apperson
18815	Poindexter, William	NC	1837	Lellitie Poindexter	Alex Poindexter	Sarah Douglas	John & Mary Poindexter	John & Mary Douglas
18099	Poindexter, William Jr.	NC	1864	Louiza Poindexter		Rebecca Poindexter		Alex & Sarah Poindexter
21340	Polk, Alonzo	OK	1873	Mattie Polk	Crawford Polk	Arbela Jeter		Washing & Mary Jeter
21510	Polk, Arbelar	OK	1840	C.A. Polk	George Jeter	Mary West		
21364	Polk, Augustus	OK	1864	Dora Polk	Crawford Polk	Arbella Jeter		Washington & Mary Jeter
21270	Polk, James	OK	1878	Rattie Polk	C.A. Polk	Arbella Jeter	Wm & Catherine Polk	George & Mary Jeter
20510*	Polk, Mary	TN	1854	Nick Polk	Abraham Brown	Amanda Jones		Gabe & Gracie Jones
21504	Polk, Warren	OK	1884	Lula Polk	Crawford Polk	Arbela Jeter		Warshton & Mary Jeter
8191	Pollard, Hope	MO	1883	Earnest Pollard	Ed Boen	Olia Stockwell	James & Phoebe Boen	Miller & Mary Stockwell
21896	Pollard, Lucie	TN		Oscar Pollard				
14974	Ponder, Alonzo	GA	1880	Alice Ponder	T C Ponder	Parthena Wright	Menda & Elizabeth Ponder	W R & Manerva Wright
14843	Ponder, Martha	GA			Joseph Smith	Narcissus Wright		Thos & Parthena Ponder
14907	Ponder, Martha	GA	1868	W A Ponder	Joseph Smith	Narcissus Wright		Jesse & Lovici Wright
14975	Ponder, Mollie et al	GA			T C Ponder	Parthena Wright		W R & Manerva Wright
20816	Ponder, Oda	GA	1883	Earl Ponder	John Cook	Mary Ragan	James Cook & Louvica Carns	
14841	Ponder, Parthena	GA	1852	Thomas Ponder	W R Wright	Manerva Whelchel	Jesse & Louicie Wright	
14973	Ponder, Pearl et al	GA			Alonzo Ponder	Alice Keener	T C & Parthena Ponder	John Keener
14972	Ponder, W A	GA	1873	Martha Ponder	T C Ponder	Marthena Wright	Menda & Elizabeth Ponder	W R & Manerva Wright
19400	Pool Oliver	GA	1870	Belle Pool	William Pool	Martha Ferguson	Warren & Elizabeth Pool	
14583	Pool, Charlie	GA	1898		Dred Pool	Minda Fowler	John & Susan Pool	
11324	Pool, Dred	GA	1868	Armind Pool	John Pool	Susan Patterson	Clabom & Martha Pool	
14582	Pool, Effie	GA	1889		Dred Pool	Minda Fowler	John & Susan Pool	
14581	Pool, Ella	GA	1887		Dred Pool	Minda Fowler	John & Susan Pool	
14580	Pool, John	GA	1901		Dred Pool	Minda Fowler	John & Susan Pool	

18369	Pool, Leander	GA	1855	Lucy Pool	Marian Pool	Tilda Childers	Moses & Sarah Pool	Robt & Patience Childers
14579	Pool, Lillian	GA	1905		Dred Pool	Minda Fowler	John & Susan Pool	
14578	Pool, Pearl	GA	1891		Dred Pool	Minda Fowler	John & Susan Pool	
20058	Pool, Robert	GA	1878	Martha Pool	William Pool	Elizabeth Dearing	Francis & Matilda Pool	Robert & Polly Dearing
14577	Pool, Susie	GA	1895		Dred Pool	Minda Fowler	John & Susan Pool	
17960	Pool, William	GA	1854	Ida Pool	Francis Pool	Matilda Childers	Moses & Sarah Pool	Robert Childers
20059	Pool, William	GA	1882	Josey Pool	William Pool	Elizabeth Dearing	Francis & Matilda Pool	Robert & Polly Dearing
8814	Poole, Fannie	GA	1864	Roe Poole	Pickens Corley	Martha Whitemore		Spencer & Melissa Whitemore
22231	Poor, Polly	AR	1848	Nelson Poor	John Serat	Nancy Lane	Lynee Sarat	James Lane
1095 *	Poorboy, Belle	OK	1885	none	Josiah Poorboy	Sarah Ross	Eli & Temey Poorboy	Mose & Phillis Ross
4983	Pope, Daniel	GA	1872	none	John Pope	Sarah Jones		John & Lucinda Jones
4990	Pope, Henry	AL	1867	Ellen Pope	John Pope	Sarah Jones		John & Lucinda Jones
4987	Pope, Sarah	GA		John Pope	John Jones	Lucinda Spence		John & Fannie Watley
4985	Pope, Sarah gdn	GA		John Jones	John Jones	Lucinda Jones		
13919	Poplin, Charles	NC	1885		John Poplin	Mary Moss	Thomas & Julia Poplin	James & Polly Moss
13928	Poplin, James	NC	1872	Elizabeth Poplin	John Poplin	Mary Moss	Thomas & Julia Poplin	James & Polly Moss
13931	Poplin, John	NC	1874	Martha Poplin	John Poplin	Mary Moss	Thomas & Julia Poplin	James & Polly Moss
13915	Poplin, Mary	NC	1884	Henry Poplin	George Moss	Mary Reider	James & Polly Moss	
13935	Poplin, Mary	NC	1853	J A Poplin	James Moss	Polly Lowe		Thos & Annie Lowe
13923	Poplin, Samuel	NC	1882	Amanda Poplin	John Poplin	Mary Moss	Thomas & Julia Poplin	James & Polly Moss
13921	Poplin, William	NC	1879	Mary Poplin	John Poplin	Mary Moss	Thomas & Julia Poplin	James & Polly Moss
21873 *	Porter, Georgia	TN	1869	Taylor Porter	Daniel Oliver	Mary Cox	Henry & Juby Keith	Edie Shinoster
14306 *	Porter, John	NC	1873	Flora Porter	Jack Porter	Susana Williams	John & Emeline Porter	Dave & Phyllis Williams
14373	Porter, Julia	GA	1877	Rufus Porter	Albert Sison	Susan Barker	Lucy Sison	
19300	Porter, Mary	GA	1867	Harrison Porter	Hardy Bryant	Winnie Tatum	Wm & Fannie Bryant	James & Susie Tatum
12500	Porter, Minnie	GA	1875	John Porter	Kinibal Burrell	Elizabeth McClure	Morning Brown	
6122	Porter, Nancy	NC	1848	Leander Porter	James Hash	Margret Reedy	Robbert & Margera Hash	Crisley & Annie Reedy
20101 *	Porter, Pat	GA	1842	Mary Porter				
12215	Porter, Sallie	OK	55yrs	Charlie Porter	? Crane	Che yar ner nah		
10458	Posley, Goldie	NC	1888	B. Posley	Robert Pierce	Charlota Richardson	Andey & Jane Pierce	Wilborn & Easter Richardson
19371	Poss, Clarence	GA	1897		Thomas Poss	Edie Forrist	John & Judie Poss	James & Cinda Forrist
19372	Poss, Eddie	GA	1895		Thomas Poss	Edie Forrist	John & Judie Poss	James & Cinda Forrist
19373	Poss, Robert	GA	1900		Thomas Poss	Edie Forrist	John & Judie Poss	James & Cinda Forrist

19374	Poss, Thomas	GA	1874	Edie Poss		Judie Long	John Poss	Joe & Sarah Long
10367	Postell, Charles	NC	1888	Hettie Postell	John Postell	Sarah Head	James & Malissa Postell	
2572	Postell, Disey	GA	1838	W T Postell	John Davenport	Elisabeth Long		Josiah & Nancy Long
10319	Postell, John	NC	1849	Sarah Postell	James Postell	Malissie Stover	John & Lucilla Woody	
10366	Postell, Joseph	NC	1850	Hulda Postell	James Postell	Malissie Stover	John & Lucilla Woody	
9504	Postell, M.L.	GA	1864	Anjaline Postell	W.T. Postell	Disey Davenport		John & Elisabeth Davenport
2571	Postell, Mary	GA	1866	none	W T Postell	Disey Davenport		John & Elisabeth Davenport
2570	Postell, William	GA	1870	Mary Postell	W T Postell	Disey Davenport		John & Elisabeth Davenport
10368	Postell, William	NC	1857	Minnie Postell	William Postell	Mary Walker	James & Malissa Postell	
5378	Poston, Mattie	VA	1884	Fost Poston	Allen Clark	Clara Welch	Allen & Elisabeth Clark	James & Nancy Welch
22549	Potter, Laura	OK	1872	William Potter	John Maney	Jenan Moss	James & Jenan Maney	Jeff & Peggie Moss
7426	Potts, Pearl	OK	1885	John Potts	James Tanner	Susan Buttry		John & Margaret Buttry
1054 *	Potts, Scharlott	OK		Joseph Potts		Myra Scott		
16421	Potts, Susan & Jinnie	OK	10yrs 9yrs		Wilson Potts	Sallie Chamber	Ulisaligeda Ganigohe Potts	Nellie Chamber
20911 *	Powell, Elmoria	NC	1839	James Powell	Losen Jones	Emley Witherspoon	Joe & Hannah Jones	
11468	Powell, Ida	GA	1885		William Powell	Lucuisa Lail	Abe Powell	James Lail
4661	Powell, James	TN	1885	Sarah Powell	Abram Powell	Margaret Dooley	Daniel Powell	Thomas & Patsy Dooley
13210 *	Powell, Julius	GA	1833	Lizzie Powell	Louis Gillespie	Juna Gillespie		Jim Gillespie
10765	Powell, Rebecca	OK	1860	Lewis Powell	Benjamin Hinchee	Annie Walker	Jonnes & Margret Hinchee	
1347	Powell, Virginia	OK	1841	E M Powell	Wm Brazill	Margret Prater	Sarah Brazill	Aaron & Susan Prater
22951	Powell, William	OK	1870	Emma Powell	Elias Powell	Sherdan Braziell		Turner Braziell & Margret Prater
8585	Powers, Christian	VA	1861	Meacy Powers	James Powers	Susan Burkett		Armstrong & Catharine Blevins
18666	Powers, Malinda	TN	1856	John Powers	R.E.L. Blevins	Amanda Blevins	Hugh & Annie Blevins	Samuel & Sarah Blevins
14331	Powers, Margaret	TX	1858	J W Powers	William Gambill	Susan Ribble	Wm & Sarah Gambill	
6830	Powers, Mary	VA	1885	Ridaford Davis	Christian Powers	Meacy Blevins		W.H. & Nancy Blevins
18508	Powledge, Mattie	GA	1873	Rush Powledge	Wm Guthrey	Frances Lee	Robert & Mary Guthrey	
18358	Powledge, Sarah	TX	1866	Leonard Powledge	Wm Guthrey	E.Frances Lee	Robbert Guthrey & Mary Hardin	J.C. & Sarah Lee
19035	Prater, Barbra	GA	1872	A.J. Prater	Thomas Allison	Sarah Roberts	Ben & Beckey Allison	Wm & Rosa Roberts
18021 *	Prater, Charles	GA	1831			Martha Pitner		Rachel Pitner
14235 *	Prather, Brison	GA	1849	Clora Prather	Coleman Prather	Edie Tabor	Jessie Jarratt	Lott Tabor

14576	Prather, Elender	GA	1844		James Prather	Parthenia Pool		Clayborn & Martha Pool
16306	Prather, Elender	GA			James Prather	Parthana Pool	Edward Prather & Mary Jinkins	Thomas Pool & Martha Burton
11326	Prather, Georgia	GA	1873		Edward Prather	Mary Wofford	James & Parthenia Prather	
11325	Prather, Gideon	GA	1850	Nancy & Martha	James Prather	Parthenia Pool		Clabom & Martha Pool
19039	Prather, Joseph	GA	1881		John Prather	Laura Lumpkin		Joseph & Susan Lumpkin
11327	Prather, Lee	GA	1883		Edward Prather	Mary Wofford	James & Parthenia Prather	
16307	Prather, Ninena	GA	1887		James Prather	Mary Brand	James Prather & Parthana Pool	Z D Brand
14234*	Prather, Peggy & Sarah	GA	1850 1852	Anderson Prather	Elbert Prather	Drady Jarrett	Peter Jerrett	Jessie Jarrett
14038	Prather, Thomas	OK	1866	Henryetta Prather	Robert Prather	Edith Rogers		Pleasant & Phoeba Rogers
11320	Prather, Warren	GA	1846	Edie Prather	James Prather	Parthenia Burton		Clabom & Martha Pool
21467	Prator, Ava	TX	1855	John Prator	Watson Crawford	Margaret Starr		Fenton Senton
22031	Prator, Henry	TX	1883	none	John Prator	Ava Crawford	Henry & Carry Prator	Watson & Margarite Crawford
22030	Prator, Thomas	TX	1879	Nellie Prator	John Prator	Ava Crawford		Watson & Margarite Crawford
77	Presley, Barbara	TX	1835	Noah Presley	Abe Funderburk	Rachel Harget	Jake & Barbra Funderburk	Joe & Hanna Harget
1162	Presley, Exena	AL	22yrs	John Prestly	Wm Adams	Alice Gibson	Wm Adams	Bart & Peggy Gibson
2306	Presley, Fannie	GA	1884	Amos Presley	Allen Adams	Ellia Hudson	David & Clerinda Adams	James & Mary Hudson
3333	Presley, Gertrude	AL	1880	Olley Presley	William Adams	Alice Gibson	William & Peggy Adams	William & Peggy Gibson
22827	Presley, Hugh	MO	1881	Blanch Presley	Reuben Presley	Nancy Fanning		Joseph & Lucinda Fanning
2895	Presley, Melissa	MO	1858	W H Presley	Michael Fender	Martha Wallis	Daniel & Dicy Fender	Jeptha & Nancy Wallis
2305	Presley, Nancy	MO	1855	Reuben Presley	Joseph Fanning	Lucinda Brown	John & Jane Fanning	John & Nancy Brown
2016	Presley, Ollie	MO	1868	Hugh Presley	Michael Fender		Daniel & Dicy Fender	Jeptha & Nancy Wallis
3271	Presley, William	MO	1877	Florence Presley	William Presley	Malissa Fender	Isaac & Martha Presley	Michael & Martha Fender
22530	Pressley, Josephine	GA	1886	Sanford Pressley	Jasper Evans	Ada Parker	James & Mary Evans	Joseph & Irene Parker
15317	Pressley, Peggy	GA	1843		Jess Gravely	Elizabeth Warren		Anderson & Betsy Warren
13598	Pressnell, Hannah	NC	1871	Joseph Pressnell	W A Sharpe	Eliza Webb		Andrew & Hannah Webb
1945	Presson, Cecil	OK	1901		Wm Presson	Mary Eley Floyd	Wm & Sarah Presson	Wm & Sophie Floyd
1947	Presson, George	OK	1893		Wm Presson	Eley Floyd	Wm & Sarah Presson	Wm & Sophie Floyd
1946	Presson, Gracie	OK	1895		Wm Presson	Eley Floyd	Wm & Sarah Presson	Wm & Sophie Floyd
831	Presson, Mary	OK		Wm Presson	William Floyd	Sopha Pope	Mary Floyd	Liga & Mary Pope

1948	Presson, William	OK	1890		Wm Presson	Mary Floyd	Wm & Sarah Presson	Wm & Sophie Floyd
18379	Prestley, James	AL	20yrs	Zimmia Prestley	John Prestley	Matilda Gibson	James & Martha Prestley	W.D. & Peggy Gibson
18378	Prestley, Mrs. James	AL	19yrs	James Prestley	David Colbert	Bettie Hathcock	Wm & Bettie Colbert	
7284	Preston, Andrew	MO	1868	none	David Preston	Nancy Roberts		Andrew & Eliza Roberts
14969	Preston, Josie et al	NE		Wm Preston	Alfred Bays	Eva Hosse	Josiah & Letta Bays	
20187	Preston, Mary	AL	1847	Isac Preston	James Hall	Katherine Winkler		Henry Winkler
5074	Prewith, Catharine	VA	1884	A.J. Prewith	William Weaver	Frona Candill	Wm & Catharine Weaver	Wm & Sarah Candill
21361	Price, Anna	LA		J.J. Price	John Jeter	Susan Thompson	Washington & Mary Jeter	Amos Thompson
6048	Price, Candis	VA	1870	L C Price	Ira Stamper	Jaicy Blevins	Eli & Susanah Stamper	James & Necy Blevins
13007	Price, Howard	VA	1881		W C Price	Nancy Weaver	Thomas & Syntha Price	
17292	Price, Margaret	WV	1846	Henry Price	George Stewart	Peggie Cook	Ralph & Polly Stewart	Jack & Jennie Cook
20155	Price, Margaret	GA	1877	William Price	Robert Smith	Jane Fagan		James Fagan
10293	Price, Mary	TN	1848		Norman Mansfield	Jane Haney	William Mansfield	
4345	Price, Nancy	OK	1855	James Price	L L Smith	Mariam Colleirs	Adam Smith	Christian Young
22183	Price, Rebecca	NM	1840	James Price	Gabriel Keith	Cynthia Campbell		Campbell
136	Price, Sarah	AR	1837	Samuel Price	Martin Williams	Francis Smith		
4130	Price, William	VA	1838	Nancy Price	Thomas Price	Cyntha Cox	John Price	Nancy Richardson
18656	Prien, Manda	WV	1886	James Prien	Owen Sizemore	Lotty Belcher	Ned & Jane Sizemore	Wm & Polly Belcher
7543	Priest, Elizabeth	GA	1867	W T Priest	John Gibson	Mary Talley		
7535	Priest, J.W.	GA	1872	Magie Priest		Roda Pool		Moses & Sarah Pool
8415	Priest, James	GA	1876	none		Roda Pool		Moses & Sarah Pool
15421	Priest, James	GA	1868	Mary Priest	Pinkney Priest	Nancy Howell	Wesley & Cintha Priest	Frederic & Martha Howell
15420	Priest, Jasper	GA	1871	Emma Priest	Pinkney Priest	Nancy Howell	Wesley & Cintha Priest	Frederic & Martha Howell
8413	Priest, Kissey	GA		none	John Priest	Roda Pool		Moses & Sarah Pool
15419	Priest, Nancy	GA	1849	Pinkney Priest	Frederic Howell	Martha Grier	David & Nancy Howell	Aquilla & Bethamie Grier
7544	Priest, William	GA	1868	Elizabeth Priest		Roda Pool		Moses & Sarah Pool
3418	Priestly, Mrs John (decd)	AL	29yrs	John Priestly	Bart Gibson	Peggy Moniac		
19732*	Prigmore, Queen	TN	1877	Sam Prigmore	Jackson Cote	Jennie Macock		Sarah Jefferson
12929*	Prim, Cynthia	IN	1855	Joe Prim	Alfred Weaver	Charity Revels	Bird & Sarah Weaver	Macaga & Mornon Revels

15682	Prince, Church	GA	1883		Isaac Prince		Joseph & Nancy Prince	Al & Abagail Church
15944	Prince, Emma	GA	1885		Isaac Prince	Georgia Church	Joseph & Nancy Prince	A J & Abagail Church
13735	Prince, Isac	GA	1857	Mary Prince	Joseph Prince	Nancy English	John Prince	Haywood & Sallie English
13734	Prince, James	GA	1853		Joseph Prince		John Prince	Haywood & Sallie English
20990	Prince, James	GA	1862	Mary Prince	Kin Prince	Cinthia Keith	Gilbert & Pollie Prince	
22115	Prince, James	Ga`		Mary Prince	Kinrick Bruce	Cinthia Kieth	Gilbert Bruce	Pollie Hill
15943	Prince, Joe et al	GA	1886		Isaac Prince	Georgia Church	Joseph & Nancy Prince	A J & Abagail Church
14984	Prince, Margaret	GA		W A Prince	Davis Sinard	Sarah Ellenberg	James Jr & Margaret Sinard	John & Alice Ellenberg
20989	Prince, Sarah	GA	1855		Kindred Prince	Syntha Keath	Gilbert Prince & Polly Hill	James Keth & Sarah Butram
14983	Prince, Sarah & Harriett	GA	1888 1891		W A Prince	Margaret Sinard	Jack & Mahala Prince	David & Sarah Sinard
10297	Prince, Taylor	OK			Jackson Prince	Elsie Prince		
20966	Prince, Vinnie	GA	1887		Levi Stone	Sarah Prince		Kin & Cyntha Prince
17530	Prince, Wiley	GA	1851	Margaret Prince	Andrew Prince	Mahalie Cross	Josiah & Polly Prince	Dave Cross
19584 *	Pritchard, George	TN	1846		Peter Pritchard	Nellie Fitzgerald		
17918	Pritchet, Edna	GA	1881	Thomas Pritchet	Robert Landers	L.M. Partian	George & Betsey Landers	Henry & Nancy Partian
6671	Pritchett, Charles	OK	1856	Arley Pritchett	Mike Pritchett	Coh-tah-ga-we	Bear Chu-ke-yar-sken	
12096	Privett, Margret	WV	40yrs	Andrew Privett	Franklin Sizemore	Polly Workman	George & Jinney Sizemore	Joseph & Elizabeth Workman
4766	Proctor, Elizabeth	KY	1870	John Proctor	John Ragle	Mary Delosier	Henry Sr. & Mary Ragle	Edward & Elisabeth Delosier
2217	Proctor, Margret	OK	1847	Ezekiel Proctor	Ambers Downing	Gatsie Parris	Mose & Polly Downing	Bob & Hester Parris
20179	Proctor, Matilda	GA	1872	Dan Proctor	N.C. Tankersley	Eliza Lowe	Sarah Tankersley	
7285	Profitt, Lizzie	OK	1876	Ernest Profitt	John Boatright	Fannie Wylie	Benj & Julia Boatright	Harvey & Ruth Wylie
20844	Prueitt, Tantem	GA	1874	Linner Prueitt	Johnathan Bice	Angeline Prueitt		Calvin & Elizabeth Prueitt
11245	Pruett, Ephram	GA	1862	Mary Pruett	Benson Pruett	Tilda Sizemore	Recie & Phebe Pruett	James Sizemore
13009	Pruett, Everett	NC	1882	Hala Pruett	John Pruitt	Louisa Osborne	Mary Pruitt	David & Lucy Osborne
11246	Pruett, John	GA	1864	Dorthy Pruett	Benson Pruett	Tilda Sizemore	Recie & Phebe Pruett	James Sizemore
19921	Pruett, Joshua	NC	1863	Katherine Pruett	Joshua Pruett	Nancy Hensley	Martan & Polly Pruett	Henry & A. Hensley
19889	Pruett, Nancy	NC	1837	Joshua Pruett	Henry Hensley	Ann Haywood	Henry Hensley	Rachel Haywood
19902	Pruett, Taylor et al	NC			Joshua Pruett	Nancy Hensley	Joshua & Nancy Pruett	Henry Hensley
18730	Pruitt, J.M.	NC	1861	Mary Pruitt	J.W. Pruitt	Louisa Osborn	Abedingo & Mary Pruitt	David & Lucy Osborn
12466	Pruitt, Jacob	NC	1842	Tildy Pruitt	Bedney Pruitt	Mary Brinigan		
22737	Pruitt, John	NC	1812	Marth Pruitt	J.W. Pruitt	Louisa Osborn	Obeduago & Mary Pruitt	David & Lucy Osborn

12855	Pruitt, Louisa	NC	1848	John Pruitt	David Osborne	Lucy Billings	Elias & Sally Osborne	Jasper & Nancy Billings
12250	Pruitt, Rebecca	NC	1870	J F Pruitt	Wyatt Rose	Hesper Wood	Isaah Rose	Jesse Wood
12471	Pruitt, Sizemore	VA	1868	Mary Pruitt	Jacob Pruitt	Nancy Osburn	Bedney Pruitt	David Osburn
20095	Pruitt, Ular	AR	1887	Jessy Pruitt	William Rains	Lucinda Hollingsworth	Samuel & Mary Rains	Jerry & Jane Hollingsworth
22114	Pruitt, William	GA	1854	Milly Pruitt	Calvin Pruitt	Elizabeth Rainwater	William & Dorca Pruitt	Gabriel & Nancy Rainwater
20544	Pryor, Charles	GA	1889		Mitchel Pryor	Matilda Haney	Paul & Louiza Pryor	Hezekiah & Julia Haney
20542	Pryor, Clemens	GA	1892		Mitchel Pryor	Matilda Haney	Paul & Louiza Pryor	Hezekiah & Julia Haney
20543	Pryor, Henry	GA	1902		Mitchel Pryor	Matilda Haney	Paul & Louiza Pryor	Hezekiah & Julia Haney
18205	Pryor, Joseph	GA	1885		Mitchell Pryor	Matilda Haney	Paul & Catherine Pryor	Hezekiah & Julia Haney
18206	Pryor, Matilda	GA	1863	Mitchel Pryor	Hesekiah Haney	Julia Wilson	James & Matilda Haney	Wm & Caroline Wilson
20538	Pryor, Matilda	GA	1863		Mitchel Pryor	Matilda Haney	Paul & Louiza Pryor	Hezekiah & Julia Haney
20540	Pryor, Mattie	GA	1896		Mitchel Pryor	Matilda Haney	Paul & Louiza Pryor	Hezekiah & Julia Haney
20541	Pryor, Migah	GA	1899		Mitchel Pryor	Matilda Haney	Paul & Louiza Pryor	Hezekiah & Julia Haney
20548	Pryor, Paul	GA	1883	Ada Pryor	Mitchel Pryor	Matilda Haney	Paul & Louiza Pryor	Hezekiah & Julia Haney
20545	Pryor, Robert	GA	1906		Mitchel Pryor	Matilda Haney	Paul & Louiza Pryor	Hezekiah & Julia Haney
20546	Pryor, William	GA	1906		Paul Pryor	Ada Whitehead	Mitchel & Matilda Pryor	Wm & Jane Whitehead
15316	Puckett, Ella	GA	1883		Jeffrey Beck	Mandy Loggins	Coleman Davis & Elmira Beck	
5506	Pugh, Martha	NC	1860	William Pugh	Robert Davis	Darthula Weiss	Samiel & Jennie Davis	
22369	Pugh, Ruth	VA	1871	Roby Pugh	John Spencer	Martha Anderson	Solomon & Nellie Spencer	Elisha & Ruth Anderson
9574	Pugh, Sarah	GA	1850	Benj Pugh	Obedier Chastain	Maryan Keith	James Chastain & Sarah Butrum	James Keith & Jane Kelley
18026*	Pullen, Annie	TN	1858	Charles Pullen	William Hawkins	Mary Hawkins		Armstead & Mariah Johnson
10091	Pullium, Abbie	NC	28yrs	William Payne	David Taylor	Lucretia Adams		Posey & Jane Adams
18999	Punyear, Richard	NC	1845		Richard Punyear	Elizabeth Clingman	John & Sarah Punyear	Jacob & Jane Clingman
20553	Purcell, Abraham	AL	1836	Mary Purcell	John Purcell	Charity Crump	Jake & Mary Purcell	Robert & Agnes Crump
19468	Puryear, Henry	NC	1841		Richard Puryear	Elizabeth Clingman	John & Sarah Puryear	Jacob & Jane Clingman
19416	Puryear, Thomas	NC	1849		Richard Puryear	Elizabeth Clingman	John & Sarah Puryear	Jacob & Jane Clingman
15169	Pyle, Emeline	OK	1856	William Pyle	Lindsey Carter	Zaney Jones	Leonard & Lydia Carter	James & Charlotta Jones
4398	Pyle, Martha	OK	1855	W A Pyle	Lindsay Carter	Jona Jones	Leonard & Lydia Carter	
21853*	Pyron, Clara	TN	1853	Aaron Pyron	John Clark	Eveline Williams	Thomas & Martha Clark	Marian Triblett & Mariah Stewart
1526	Quarles, Delia	GA	1861	Montraw Quarles	Henry Summery	Mary Helton	Geo & Barby Summery	High & Easter Helton
351	Quarles, William R.	OK	1845	Sarah Morris Quarles decd			Jordan & Elizabeth Morris	James & Mary Dougherty

9034	Queen, Arayan	GA	1864	Albert Queen	George Claer	Annie Swanson	George & Mandy Claer	William Swanson
1308	Queen, Arzelia	GA	1847	John Queen	Thomas Thomas	Stacey Redmon	Thomas	Will & Nancy Redmon
14413	Queen, Erenea	GA	1863	M H Queen	David Ash	Elisabeth Davenport		John & Elisabeth Davenport
22712	Queen, Manda	TN	1861	W.H. Queen	Lafayette Stuart	Tilda Thomas	Isam Stuart	Elijah & Narsissas Thomas
7573	Quesenbury, Harriett	OK	1839	Argyle Quesenbury	John Wheeler	Nancy Watie		Oo-watie & Susannah
19511	Quick, Thomas	AR	1842	Bettie Quick	Nathan Quick	Pency Hubbard	Willis Quick	J.O. & Mary Hubbard
22235	Quinn, Mary	AL	1870	G.H. Quinn	Lafayett Bell	Manery Holcomb	Ira & Jane Bell	William & Sarah Holcomb
11260	Quinton, Sarah	OK	1880		Moses Quinton	Rebecca Lewis	Joseph & Lydia Quinton	William Lewis
22229	Quintrell, Amanda	TN	1865	S.H. Quintrell	Abraham Guinn	Cornelia Crawford	Allmon & Sara Guinn	Crawford & Prisilla Barnett
9763	Rabbit, Gent (decd)	OK	24yrs	none	Rabbit	Rhoda Lowe		Allan & Malinda Sizemore
4026	Raburn, Caroline	MS	1851	Jim Raburn	James Funderlurk	Ellaner Sureat	Abe & Rachel Funderlurk	
6769	Raby, Ruena	NC	1875	James Raby	William Rowland	Mary Trommel	Andy & Polly Rowland	Harriett Trommel
3432	Racard, Elisabeth	AL	43yrs	Aaron Racard	William Colbert	Mary Moniac	Bill & Cely Colbert	Sam & Susan Moniac
1067	Ragal, Henry	FL	1868	Mary Ragle	John Ragle	Mary Delozier	Henry & Mary Ragle	Ed & Elizabeth Delozier
20714	Ragan, Katie	TN	1878		James Hatcher	Mary Halbrook	John & Eliza Hatcher	Joseph & Catherine Halbrook
16225	Ragon, Frank	OK			Alfred Ragon	Lizzie Benner	Eli Ragon & Nancy Rodgers	Wm Benner & Anna Vymann
17638	Ragsdale, Berta	GA	1893		Joseph Ragsdale	Mary Parr	Larkin & Judie Ragsdale	Wm & Nancy Parr
20762	Ragsdale, Beulah	GA	1899		Calton Ragsdale Jr	Fannie McCollum	John & Adaline Ragsdale	Jesse & Matilda McCollum
20763	Ragsdale, Calton	GA	1858	Fannie Ragsdale	John Ragsdale	Adaline Smith	Calton & Susan Ragsdale	Wm & Harriett Smith
12347	Ragsdale, Claudie	GA	1885	Walter Ragsdale	Mack Cole	Francis Ingram	John & Betsy Cole	Isaac & Lottie Ingram
20764	Ragsdale, Daisy	GA	1897		Calton Ragsdale Jr	Fannie McCollum	John & Adaline Ragsdale	Jesse & Matilda McCollum
20765	Ragsdale, Earle	GA	1893		Calton Ragsdale Jr	Fannie McCollum	John & Adaline Ragsdale	Jesse & Matilda McCollum
1036	Ragsdale, Isaac	OK	1851	Johnsanna Ragsdale	Isaac Ragsdale	Mary Sanders	John & Nellie Ragsdale	Alex & Peggy Sanders
16740	Ragsdale, John	OK	1866	Francis Ragsdale	John Ragsdale	Adeline Smith	Calton & Sallie Ragsdale	
19369	Ragsdale, Jonah	GA	1904		Walter Ragsdale	Claudie Cole	Joseph & Mary Ragsdale	Mark & Frankie Cole
20766	Ragsdale, Ludie	GA	1895		Calton Ragsdale Jr	Fannie McCollum	John & Adaline Ragsdale	Jesse & Matilda McCollum
17639	Ragsdale, Mary	GA	1858	Joseph Ragsdale	William Parr	Mary Jenkins	John & Malinda Parr	Randolph & Nancy Jenkins
17637	Ragsdale, Owda	GA	1886		Joseph Ragsdale	Mary Parr	Larkin & Judie Ragsdale	Wm & Nancy Parr
17636	Ragsdale, Walter	GA	1881	Claudie Ragsdale	Joseph Ragsdale	Mary Parr	Larkin & Judie Ragsdale	Wm & Nancy Parr
15418	Raines, George	GA	1848	Louisa Raines	John Raines	Telisha Rakestraw	Thomas & Delilah Raines	Jack & Nancy Rakestraw

2193	Raines, Lifus	GA		Mary Raines	Wesley Raines	Talitha Rakestraw	Lila Raines	
1163	Raines, Nancy	GA		none	Wesley Raines	Talitha Rakestran	Lila Raines	
15417	Raines, William	GA	1874	Lula Raines	George Raines	Louisa Hyde	John & Talisha Raines	Ancel & Betsy Hyde
9865	Rains, Alma	GA	1898	none	Wesley Rains	Alice Jones	Wesley & Talitha Rains	Alfred & Elizabeth Jones
9866	Rains, Furmann	GA	1896	none	Wesley Rains	Alice Jones	Wesley & Talitha Rains	Alfred & Elizabeth Jones
9867	Rains, George	GA	1905	none	Wesley Rains	Alice Jones	Wesley & Talitha Rains	Alfred & Elizabeth Jones
9868	Rains, John	GA	1894	none	Wesley Rains	Alice Jones	Wesley & Talitha Rains	Alfred & Elizabeth Jones
8773	Rains, Mary	OK	1859	Isaac Rains	James Howard	Lidda Crabtree	Arington & Elizebeth Howard	Isaac & Mary Crabtree
9869	Rains, Mountee	GA	1901	none	Wesley Rains	Alice Jones	Wesley & Talitha Rains	Alfred & Elizabeth Jones
9870	Rains, Straund	GA	1903	none	Wesley Rains	Alice Jones	Wesley & Talitha Rains	Alfred & Elizabeth Jones
9864	Rains, Wesley	GA	1861	Alice Rains	Wesley Rains	Talitha Rakestraw	Delilah Rains	Jack & Nancy Rakestraw
20021	Rains, William	AR	1863	Lucindy Rains	Samuel Rains	Mary Sizemore	Wm & Fannie Rains	George & Juda Sizemore
17316	Rainwater, John	AL	1885	John Rainwater	Wm Rainwater	Virginia Sizemore		Wm & Minerva Sizemore
14464	Rainwater, Virginia	AL	1859	Wm Rainwater	William Sizemore	Minerva Hawkins	Felan Sizemore	Sarah Terry
19353	Rakestraw, Asby	GA	1865		Lifus Rakestraw	Malissa Raines	Jack & Nancy Rakestraw	Benj & Fannie Raines
15416	Rakestraw, Elsie	GA	1879	Lizzie Rakestraw	Lifus Rakestraw	Mellina Raines	Jack & Nancy Rakestraw	Fannie Raines
19354	Rakestraw, Julius	GA	1884	Teletha Rakestraw	Lifus Rakestraw	Malissa Raines	Jack & Nancy Rakestraw	Benj & Fannie Raines
18976	Rakestraw, Maude	KS	1885	Bert Rakestraw	Napolean Holt	Sarah White	George & Sarah Holt	Silas & Susan White
18806	Rakestraw, William	AL	1871		James Rakestraw	Delilah Raines	Wm & Telitha Rakestraw	Benj & Fannie Raines
2333	Ralings, Jane	GA	1882	Joe Ralings	W J Mason	Susie Benfield	John & Pollie Mason	Tom & Lydie Benfield
1114	Ralston, Eliza	OK	1843	Louis Ralston	James Postell	Melissa Stover	Postell	Jacob & Sallie Stover
21393	Ramey, Lula	OK	1875	E.H. Ramey	T.M. Gofford	Mary Marshall		J.L. Marshall
14401	Ramey, Martha	GA	1856	Isaac Ramey	Joe Blackwell	Mary Ridley		Wm & Mary Ridley
14637	Ramey, Mary	GA	1843	James Ramey	Washington Smith	Betsy Roach		
21138	Ramey, Thomas	GA	1863	Nancy Ramey	Mart Ramey	Elizabeth Swafford	Isaac Ramey	Elihu & Nancy Swafford
120 *	Ramsay, Albert	GA	1885	Blanche Ramsay	Robert Ramsay	Juda Colbert		Charly & Addie Colbert
415	Ramsey, Elizabeth	AR	1869	Favian Ramsey	James Groames	Delita Ramsey	Henry & Milley Groames	Thomas & Elisbeth Ramsey
7315	Ramsey, Eva	TX	1887	Wallace Ramsey	Alford Williams	Fannie Curtis	Joseph & Rutha Williams	Boone & Manervia Curtis
5898	Ramsey, Harriet	NC	1883		Samuel Shelton	Nancy Metcalf	Esaw & Sarry Shelton	James & Luvena Metcalf

ID	Name	State	Year	Col5	Col6	Col7	Col8	Col9
416	Ramsey, Mareyan	AR	1864	Thomas Ramsey	Gaberel Cadey	Moley Arington	Joseph Ray	Ludey Galashey Maired Arrngton
21919 *	Rankin, Grace	TN	1844	Joseph Rankin	Isaac McFarland	Flora McFarland	Hannah Hancock	Isaac McCloud
21976 *	Rankin, Joseph	TN	1844	Grace Rankin	Daniel Rankin	Mariah McFarland	David & Fanny Rankin	
21403	Rankins, Almeda	OK	1874	Emmett Rankins	Henry Evans	Emiline Russell		Woody Russell
19297	Ransom, Mary	GA	1890	Charles Robinson	Enoch Patterson	Lou Smith	Samuel & Nancy Patterson	Jonah & Bettie Smith
17495	Raper, Elijah	TN	1845	Ira Raper	James Raper	Margaret Tallent	James & Margaret Raper	
12739	Raper, Lazarus	TN	1856	Dunreath	Elijah Raper	Elizabeth Chadwick	Thos & Elizabeth Raper	Lazarus & Jensey Chadwick
13883	Raper, Robert	GA	1861	Mary Raper	Zir Raper	Polly Johnson	Jakey & Dosie Raper	
12740	Raper, William	TN	1852		Elijah Raper	Elizabeth Chadwick	Thos & Elizabeth Raper	Lazarus & Jensey Chadwick
4212	RattlingGourd, Looney	OK	1845	Dorthey RattlingGourd	Daniel RattlingGourd	Eliza Looney	RattlingGourd & Polly	
6054	Rattlingourd	OK	1852	George Rattlingourd	John Hendricks	Preshia Easky		Richard & Patsy Deasky
5385	Rattlingourd, John (decd)	OK	1850	Artemiss Rattlingourd	Daniel Rattlingourd	Eliza Looney	Gu-Natie & Pollie Rattlingourd	John Looney
15872	Rattlingourd, Susan	OK		Ellis Rattlingourd	Felix Riley	Annie Hendricks	John & Susan Rattlingourd	Wm & Susanna Hendricks
13825	Rawlings, Ruthie	MO	1855	J.M. Rawlings	George Haley	Abigail Rhea	George Jr & Luvisa Haley	
7598	Raxter, Catherine	NC	35yrs	William Raxter	Bailey Palmer	Sallie McDonald		Jonathen & Harriett McDonald
12604	Ray, Claud	GA	1891		Tate Ray	Ellen Sawyers	Wm & Julia Ray	Sarah Sawyers
15437	Ray, Dave	GA	1874		Robert Ray	Rachel Davis	Warren & Betsy Ray	Wm & Annie Davis
10533	Ray, Ed	GA		Minta Ray	Benj Ray	Nell Rakestraw	Sanford & Rachel Ray	
15038	Ray, Elijah	GA	1873	Nancy Ray	Thomas Ray	Julia Jackson	Wm & Antha Ray	Fed & Elisabeth Jackson
5039	Ray, Ellen	GA	1869	Fate Ray				
21231	Ray, Eva	TX	1884	Emit Ray	Richard Graham	Mittie Sisk	James & Martha Graham	
11607	Ray, Fletcher	GA	1888	Cena Ray	Fate Ray	Ellen Sawyers	Wm & Julia Ray	Sarah Sawyers
10532	Ray, George	GA	1860	Mary Ray	Robin Ray	Rachel Davis		Wm & Annie Davis
12603	Ray, George	GA	1890		Tate Ray	Ellen Sawyers	Wm & Julia Ray	Sarah Sawyers
12608	Ray, Grady	GA	1895		Tate Ray	Ellen Sawyers	Wm & Julia Ray	Sarah Sawyers
15039	Ray, Gus	GA	1864	Mandy Ray	William Ray	Nancy Crider	William Ray	
14979	Ray, Henry et al	GA			W H Ray	Rachel Call	J R & Elizabeth Ray	Joseph & Elizabeth Call
4655	Ray, James	TN	1873	Joanna Ray	James Ray	Polly Hildebrand		John & Nicey Hildebrand
11346	Ray, James	GA	1862	Dovey Ray (decd)	Sanford Ray	Rachel Corban		John & Delila Corban
10494	Ray, Joe	GA	1863	Louisa Ray	Robert Ray	Rachel Davis		Wm & Annie Davis
12742	Ray, John	TN	1862	Georgia Ray	Thomas Ray	Julia Jackson	Wm & Anthy Ray	Ted Jackson
12741	Ray, Julia	TN	1840	Thomas Ray	Ted Jackson	Elizabeth Martin	Bob Jackson	Stephen Martin
5041	Ray, Lafayette	GA	1866	Ellen Ray	Thomas Ray	Julia Jackson	Wm & Martha Ray	Federal Jackson & Elisabeth Warly
11682	Ray, Louisa	GA	1878		James Parker	Martha Ray	Abner & Lillie Parker	Thos & Julia Ray

#	Name	State	Year	Col5	Col6	Col7	Col8	Col9
12605	Ray, Luther	GA	1893		Tate Ray	Ellen Sawyers	Wm & Julia Ray	Sarah Sawyers
776	Ray, Malinda	GA	1856	William Ray	Nathaniel Dotson	Elizabeth Pen		William Dotson
4657	Ray, Mary	TN	1867	none	James Ray	Polly Hildebrand		John & Nicey Hildebrand
16146	Ray, Mary	MI	1883		Asberry Ray	Alice Ortrey	James & Mary Ray	Charles & Tabitha Ortrey
16571	Ray, Mary	GA	1871		William Ray	Malinda Dotson	Warren & Nancy Ray	Nathaniel & Elizabeth Dotson
16572	Ray, Nancy	GA	1873		William Ray	Malinda Dotson	Warren & Nancy Ray	Nathaniel & Elizabeth Dotson
690	Ray, Rachel	GA	1872	John Ray	Anderson Neal	Sarah Davis	Thomas Neal & Polly Smith	Wm Davis & Annie Cross
12012	Ray, Rachel	GA	1838	Robert Ray	William Davis	Anna Cross	Davis & Lydie Davis	Joseph Cross
14980	Ray, Rachel	GA	1867	W H Ray	Joseph Call	Elizabeth Teague	John & Nancy Call	Isaac & Rachel Teague
13815	Ray, Rolland	MI	1881		Asburry Ray	Alice Ortrey	James & Mary Ray	Charles & Tabitha Ortrey
15436	Ray, Sarah	GA			Joe Ray	Louisa Flowers	Robert & Rachel Ray	
15435	Ray, Sherman	GA	1867	Lillie Ray	Robert Ray	Rachel Davis	Warren & Betsy Ray	Wm & Annie Davis
16575	Ray, Sherman	GA	1866	Florence Ray	William Ray	Malinda Dotson	Warren & Nancy Ray	Nathaniel & Elizabeth Dotson
15434	Ray, Silvy	GA	1895		Jim Ray	Donie Ingram	Sanford & Rachel Ray	
4656	Ray, Stephen	TN	1871	none	James Ray	Polly Hildebrand		John & Nucey Hildebrand
2220	Ray, Taton	GA	1868	Ellen Ray	William Ray	Malinda Dotson	Warren & Nancy Ray	Nathaniel & Elizabeth Dotson
17754	Ray, Victoria	GA			John Holt	Manerva Baker	Rhoda Holt	James & Charlotte Baker
19401	Ray, Walter	GA			George Ray	Mary Knight	Robert & Rachel Ray	
898	Rayder, Margaret	TN	1852	widow	Jonas Linn	Dernerisa Kirkland	Thomas & Bettie Linn	Jim & Susan Kirkland
22836	Rayder, May	TN	1885		William Rayder	Margaret Lynn	Harvey & Katie Rayder	Jonas & Demerisa Lynn
20696	Reache, Ambrose	FL	1862	Marie Reache	Peter Reache	N.Helen Vaugham		Josephine Vaugham
18698	Reache, Ignatius	FL	1866	Edna Reache	Peter Reeache	Helen Vaughn		Ambrose & Tabitha Vaughn
19253	Reache, Lee	MS	1870		Peter Reache	Nancy Vaughan		Ambrose & Josephine Vaughan
21335	Reading, James	MO	1840	Sarah Reading	George Reading	Eliza Helton	Charles & Sarah Reading	James & Catherine Helton
21333	Reading, La Rue	MO	1867	Mattie Reading	James Reading	Sarah Eblen	George & Eliza Reading	Jesse & Rachel Eblen
20457	Readis, Esther	TN	1851		Dennis Higgins	Margaret Griscom		
4255	Reagan, Geo	OK	45yrs	Salina Reagan	Thomas Reagan	Harriett Roberts	James & Sarah Reagan	
18861	Reagan, Hixie	AL	1855		Braxton Harrison	Martha Williams		Josiah Williams
19328*	Reagan, Margaret	TN	1873	Isaac Reagan	Lorenzo Fore	Gemima McGill	Robert & Polly Hoyl	Rolan & Jane McGill
15756	Reagan, Michael	TN		Eliza Reagan	William Reagan	Emaline Wise		Henry Wise

4254	Reagan, Salina	OK	40yrs	Geo Reagan	Isaac Huskey	Lydia Lindsey	Wm & Dolly Huskey	
12941	Reagan, William et al	TN			William Reagan	Emaline Werse	William Reagan	Henry Werse
14475	Real, Eveline	AL	1864	Henry Real	Joel Sizemore	Sinthey Webster		
21493	Reames, Luvine	AR	1886	D.J. Reames	Henry Melton	Nancy Burnett		John & Lydia Burnett
15677	Reaves, Lizzie	GA	1842	John Reaves	Richard Redman	Malinda Reese	Sam & Genora Redman	Louis & Charity Reese
3276	Reavis, Charles	MO	1878	Harriet Reavis	John Reavis	Susan Fender		Daniel & Dicy Fender
3788	Reavis, Dovie	MO	1884	none	John Reavis	Susan Fender		Daniel & Dicy Fender
5410	Reavis, Evalena	MO	1892	none	John Reavis	Susan Fender		Daniel & Dicy Fender
5409	Reavis, Leona	MO	1892	none	John Reavis	Susan Fender		Daniel & Dicy Fender
3792	Reavis, Walt, Evalen, Leana	MO			John Reavis	Susan Fender		Daniel & Dicy Fender
19600	Rector, Stella	OR		Ralph Rector	William Coe	Mary	Andrew & Rhoda Coe	
11080	Redaford, Nancy	WV		Cany Redaford	Wilborn Blevins	Rosey Farmer	Washington Hart & Elizbeth Blevins	
19780	Redden, Martha	TN	1872	John Redden	James Choppell	Nancy Climer	John & Lucy Choppell	James & Nancy Climer
13886	Redding, Eliza	OK	58yrs	widow	Joe Ross	Percilla Gentry	Templeton Ross	Jesse & Susan Gentry
13997	Redding, Jesse	OK	1888		William Redding	Eliza Ross	John & Fannie Redding	Templeton & Percilla Ross
5889	Reece, Aaron	GA	1889	none	James Reece	Loduska Helton	Aaron & Nancy Reece	John & Mary Helton
8717	Reece, Ada	GA	1897	none	James Reece	Hattie Griffith	Wesley & Martha Reece	Budd & Mollie Griffith
17823	Reece, Albert	GA	1898		Kimsey Reece	Lissey Edwards	John & Elizabeth Reece	
11347	Reece, Allie	GA	1875		John Reece	Elizabeth Pool		John & Susan Pool
14902	Reece, Asa & Willie	GA	12yrs 9yrs		J W Reece	America Medaris	J M & Elizabeth Reece	H P & Nancy Medaris
14575	Reece, Bessie	GA	1903		Allie Reece	Daisy Green	John & Elizbeth Reece	
5888	Reece, Callie	GA	1892	none	James Reece	Loduska Helton	Aaron & Nancy Reece	John & Mary Helton
11348	Reece, Carter	GA	1869	Jane Reece	John Reece	Elizabeth Pool		John & Susan Pool
14574	Reece, Ceborn	GA	1906		Allie Reece	Daicy Green	John & Elizbeth Reece	
3084	Reece, Cicero	GA		Minnie Reece	James Reece	Loduska Helton	Aaron & Nancy Reece	John & Mary Helton
11345	Reece, Cicero	GA	1879	Shoshonie Reece	John Reece	Elizabeth Pool		John & Susan Pool
17822	Reece, Clarence	GA	1897		Monroe Reece	Callie Westbrook	John & Elizabeth Reece	
17821	Reece, Cleo	GA	1890		Kimsey Reece	Lissey Edwards	John & Elizabeth Reece	
15576	Reece, Dialphia	GA	1877	J W C Reece	Robert McClure	Mary Millwood	Jack & Marilda McClure	Hugh & Miram Millwood
8718	Reece, Dollie	GA	1889	none	James Reece	Hattie Griffith	Wesley & Martha Reece	Budd & Mollie Griffith

8608	Reece, Elizabeth	GA	1839	Marion Reece	James Newman	Sarah Davis	William Newman	Elisabeth Davis
14898	Reece, Elizabeth	GA	1839	J M Reece	James Newman	Sarah Davis	William Newman	John & Elizabeth Davis
15457	Reece, Ethel	GA	1889	Ottman Reece	John Fowler	Dora Hubbard		John & Sarah Hubbard
20539	Reece, Eva	GA	1889	Leslie Reece	Mitchel Pryor	Matilda Haney	Paul & Louiza Pryor	Hezekiah & Julia Haney
17820	Reece, Fredd	GA	1893		Kimsey Reece	Lissey Edwards	John & Elizabeth Reece	
8719	Reece, Freddie	GA	1899	none	James Reece	Hattie Griffith	Wesley & Martha Reece	Budd & Mollie Griffith
15314	Reece, Grover	GA	1892		John Reece	Elizabeth Pool		John & Susan Pool
14573	Reece, James	GA	1898		Allie Reece	Daisy Green	John & Elizbeth Reece	
8604	Reece, Jefferson	GA	1868	Miller Reece	Marion Reece	Elizabeth Newman	James & Mary Reece	James & Sarah Newman
14572	Reece, Jewel	GA	1900		Allie Reece	Daisy Green	John & Elizbeth Reece	
8606	Reece, John	GA	1875	Mollie Reece	Marion Reece	Elisabeth Newman	James & Mary Reece	James & Sarah Newman
14910	Reece, Johnson	GA	1871	America Reece	J M Reece	Elizabeth Newman	James & Mary Reece	James & Sarah Newman
15433	Reece, Julia	GA		W E Reece	W W James	Rhodia Dillard	Selena James	Wm & Nancy Dillard
21563	Reece, Julia	GA	1841	John Reece	Furiah Tidwell	Rachel Brown	Ben & Millie Tidwell	
11349	Reece, Kinsey	GA	1867	Lisey Reece	John Reece	Elizabeth Pool		John & Susan Pool
5887	Reece, Leslie	GA	1887	none	James Reece	Loduska Helton	Aaron & Nancy Reece	John & Mary Helton
14859	Reece, M.W.	GA	1864	Nancy Reece	J M Reece	Elizabeth Newman	James & Mary Reece	James & Sarah Newman
2782	Reece, Martha	GA	1847	John Reece	James Helton	Camilla Southerland	Calvin & Sarah Helton	John & Martha Southerland
22243	Reece, Mary	GA	1857		Anderson Franklin	Mary Bryan	Abraham & Elizabeth Franklin	Polly Bryan
14917	Reece, Matilda	GA	1867	J T Reece	C C Kelly	Rebecca Chastain	Richard & Frances Kelly	Wm & Elizabeth Chastain
8721	Reece, Mollie	GA	1895	none	James Reece	Hattie Griffith	Wesley & Martha Reece	Budd & Mollie Griffith
12011	Reece, Monroe	GA	1873		John Reece	Elizabeth Pool		John & Susan Pool
18084	Reece, Odessa	GA	1889		John Reece	Sarah Hughes	Alfred Reece	George & Margaret Hughes
18083	Reece, Otto	GA	1883	Ethel Reece	John Reece	Sarah Hughes	Alfred Reece	George & Margaret Hughes
15432	Reece, Patterson	GA	1887		John Reece	Elizabeth Pool		John & Susan Pool
10570	Reece, Paul	GA	1901		Robert Reece	Alice Wilson	Terrell & Lodusky Reece	Wm & Georgia Wilson
4351	Reece, Robert	GA	1881	Alice Reece	James Reece	Loduska Helton	Aaron & Nancy Reece	John & Mary Helton
8607	Reece, Robert	GA	1883	Addie Reece	Marion Reece	Elisabeth Newman	James & Mary Reece	James & Sarah Newman
8720	Reece, Roy	GA	1903	none	James Reece	Hattie Griffith	Wesley & Martha Reece	Budd & Mollie Griffith
315	Reece, Sarah	GA	1861	Elias Reece	Anderson Franklin	Elizabeth Bryan	Abraham & Elizabeth Franklin	Tarance & Mary Bryan
18082	Reece, Sarah	GA	1838	John Reece	George Hughes	Margaret Tannery	John & Milly Hughes	Joseph & Mary Tannery

11344	Reece, Shoshonie	GA	1887	Cicero Reece	John Corban	Arie King		Terrell & Susie King
14901	Reece, Thomas	GA	1903		J T Reece	Matilda Kelly	James & Mary Reece	C C & Rebecca Kelly
17819	Reece, Verni	GA	1904		Kimsey Reece	Lissey Edwards	John & Elizabeth Reece	
14903	Reece, Veva et al	GA			M W Reece	Nancy West	J M & Elizabeth Reece	J F M & Martha West
14717	Reece, Virginia	NC	1859	John Reece	Albert Overby	Malinda Hall	Howel & Elizabeth Overby	Lewis & Mary Hall
17818	Reece, Walter	GA	1903		Monroe Reece	Callie Nasthraak	John & Elizabeth Reece	
20676	Reed, Annie	TN	1887		James Reed	Lucinda Reed	Carrell & Elizabeth Reed	McKenzie & Nancy Reed
5405	Reed, Bertha	AR	1883	Elija Reed	William Buttry	Elizabeth Patterson	John & Margret Buttry	John & Susan Patterson
18310	Reed, Bertha	IN	1875	Wm Reed	Mymaduke Winburn	Timpie Brooks		Gilford & Dicie Brooks
11171	Reed, Capt. Dixon	FL	1843	Rosa Reed	Thomas Reed	Cinthia Robertson		Stewart Robinson & Peggy Bailey
11170	Reed, Dixon	FL	1874	none	Dixon Reed	Rosa Honica	Thos Reed & Cinthia Robertson	John Honica
11616	Reed, Elizabeth	WV		James Reed	Franklin Sizemore	Polly Workman	George & Jinney Sizemore	Joseph & Elizabeth Workman
7310	Reed, Ellender	MO	1848	Albert Reed (decd)	Joseph Dagley	Celina Keeney	Elias & Hannah Dagley	Wm & Elisabeth Keeney
17395	Reed, Emaline	AL	1843					Wm Weatherford & Nancy Fisher
17343*	Reed, Finley	NC	1876	Julay Reed	Waller Reed	Elisa Millar	Washington & Elisa Reed	
3063	Reed, Frank	OK	1875	Maggie Reed	James Reed	Laura Jackson	Samuel & Francis Reed	Henry & Matilda Jackson
20419	Reed, George	TN	1870	Mollie Reed	William Reed Jr	Nancy Murray	McKenzie & Nancy Reed	James & Jane Murray
20361	Reed, Gertie	TN			James Reed	Lucinda Reed	Camel & Elizabeth Reed	McKenzie & Nancy Reed
22358*	Reed, Harriet	OK	1870	George Reed	Simon Sanders	Sarah Rider	Daniel & Betsy Sanders	Jim & Esther Rider
7716	Reed, Isaac	OK	1860	Malinda Reed	Levi Reed	Mary Pittsinbor-ger		John & Cathrine Pittsenborger
3064	Reed, James	OK		Laura Reed	Samuel Reed	Francis Patterson		
7309	Reed, James	MO	1867	Pearl Reed	Albert Reed	Ellender Dagley	James & Emerine Reed	Joseph & Celina Dagley
20581	Reed, James	TN	1879	Kattie Reed	Joseph Reed	Amanda White	McKenzie & Nancy Reed	Lewis & Mahala White
20448	Reed, John	TN	1884	Flora Reed	Joseph Reed	Amanda White	McKenzie & Nancy Reed	Louis & Mahala White
20675	Reed, John	TN	1867	Millie Reed	William Reed Jr.	Nancy Murray	McKenzie & Nancy Reed	James & Jane Murray
3066	Reed, John gdn - Laura	OK	1886		Samuel Reed	Francis Patterson		
11165	Reed, Joseph	FL	26yrs	none	Dixon Reed	Rosa Honica	Thos Reed & Cinthia Robertson	John Honica
20580	Reed, Joseph	TN	1850	Amanda Reed	Joseph Reed	Amanda White	McKenzie & Nancy Reed	Lewis & Mahala White
20660	Reed, Joseph	TN	1850	Amanda Reed	McKenzie Reed	Nancy Hardin	Mitchel & Tempy Reed	Robert & Mary Hardin
17392	Reed, Lorinda	AL	1832		Weaver	Seceel Weatherford		Wm Weatherford & Nancy Fisher

20674	Reed, Nancy	TN	1823		Robert Hardin	Mary Hardin	James & Edie Hardin	Samuel & Nancy Boldin
20446	Reed, Pearl	TN	1897		Joseph Reed	Amanda White	McKenzie & Nancy Reed	Louis & Mahala White
20450	Reed, Robert	TN	1881	Cora Reed	Joseph Reed	Amanda White	McKenzie & Nancy Reed	Louis & Mahala White
20360	Reed, Sallie	TN	1887		James Reed	Lucinda Reed	Camel & Elizabeth Reed	McKenzie & Nancy Reed
20670	Reed, Sallie	TN	1894		William Reed Jr.	Nancy Murray	McKenzie & Nancy Reed	James & Jane Murray
18948	Reed, Sarah	GA	1855	G.W. Reed	Kinbrall Burrell	Elisabeth McClure	Jesse Burrell & Maring Brown	
10415	Reed, Susie	WV	1860	Eli Reed	John Sizemore	Marica Stanley	Georgia Sizemore	John Stanley
17393	Reed, Tiny	AL			David Weaver	Seceel Weatherford		Wm Weatherford & Nancy Fisher
20447	Reed, Verny	TN	1890		Joseph Reed	Amanda White	McKenzie & Nancy Reed	Louis & Mahala White
8631	Reed, William	OK	1869	Julia Reed	Thomas Reed	Almarinda Ezelle		Wm & Polly Ezelle
20449	Reed, William	TN	1876		Joseph Reed	Amanda White	McKenzie & Nancy Reed	Louis & Mahala White
20672	Reed, William	TN	1844	Nancy Reed	McKenzie Reed	Nancy Hardin	Mitchel Sr & Tempy Reed	Robert & Mary Hardin
18909	Reeder, Grace	AR	1888		James Reeder	Mary Glenn		James & Nancy Parrish
18911	Reeder, James	AR	1856		Andrew Reeder	Henretta Parrish		James & Nancy Parrish
9108	Reedy, Ellen	NC	1860	Calvin Reedy	Isham Blevins	Ann Edmonson	George & Lydia Blevins	
9107	Reedy, Orley	VA			Calvin Reedy	Ellen Blevins		Isham & Ann Blevins
11715	Rees, Niota	CA	1873	Eris Rees		Elizabeth Allen		Herman Allen
14471	Reese, Annie	AL	1879		William Sizemore	Margarett Black	Joel Sizemore	Mary Black
22304	Reese, Ben	OK	1877	Annie Reese	Jesse Reese	Betsy Muskrat		George & Sarah Drumgene
11321	Reese, Elizabeth	GA	1849	John Reese	John Pool	Susan Patterson	Clabom & Martha Pool	
22264	Reese, James	OK	1879	Savannah Reese	Jesse Reese	Betsy Muskrat		Lucy Muskrat
22089	Reese, John	GA	1872	Mary Reese	Wilburn Reese	Zepora Blalock	John & Polly Reese	William & Katy Blalock
11532	Reese, Nellie	OK	1850	Philo Harris	Tom Lott	Che nah sah Tony		Nelly Tony
9872	Reeve, Albert	GA	1903	none	Cicero Reeve	Minnie Perry	James & Loduska Reeve	George & Lee Perry
7844	Reeve, James	GA	1869	Hattie Reeve	John Reeve	Martha Helton	Aaron & Nancy Reeve	James & Camely Helton
20165	Reeves, Cenith	GA	1869	Elijah Reeves	William Martin	Rhoda Wade	Milton & Cynthia Martin	Wm & Elizabeth Wade
7846	Reeves, Estelle	GA	1904		Homer Reeves	Georgia Reeve	John & Mary Reeves	Wesley & Martha Reeve
7845	Reeves, Georgia	GA	1882	William Reeves	John Reeve	Martha Helton	Aaron & Nancy Reeve	James & Camely Helton
20845	Reeves, Martha	GA	1858	William Reeves	William Whitlock	Caroline Page	James & Sallie Whitlock	Jim & Sibbia Page
7847	Reeves, Pearl	GA	1902		Homer Reeves	Georgia Reeve	John & Mary Reeves	Wesley & Martha Reeve

12708	Reichel, Elizabeth	MO	1850	Henry Reichel	Robert Glenn	Martha Murray	James & Margaret Glenn	Joshua & Mary Murray
19892	Reid, Fred	NC	1845	Elizabeth Reid	Isaac Reid	Elizabeth McLaughlin	John & Mary Reid	Ephrim & Elizabeth McLaughlin
15894	Reid, Maggie	NC	1869	William Reid	William Apperson	Mary Edwards	Bennett & Nancy Apperson	Edward & Matilda Edwards
19402	Reinhardt, Janie	GA	1904		John Reinhardt	Sarah East		Francis & Peggy East
19403	Reinhardt, Sarah	GA	1873	John Reinhardt	Francis East	Peggy Cheatwood	Daniel & Betsey East	
19404	Reinhardt, Theophilus	GA	1899		John Reinhardt	Sarah East		Francis & Peggy East
19405	Reinhardt, Thomas	GA	1902		John Reinhardt	Sarah East		Francis & Peggy East
21922 *	Rells, James	TN	1849	Ella Rells	James Rells	Matilda Watts		
17518	Renfrow, Kittie	OK	1869		J.A. Hickman	Sarah Hicks	Fred & Polly Hickman	Linsey Hicks & Catherine Miller
7314	Ressler, Dora	TX	1871		William Black	Eliza Jackson		John Jackson & Elizabeth Caldwell
18400	Reveault, Adeline	AL	85yrs		Wm Sizemore	Lavitia Moniac	Arthur & Polly Sizemore	Samuel & Elizabeth Moniac
18398	Reveault, Charles	AL	44yrs		John Reveault	Adeline Sizemore		Wm & Lavitia Sizemore
14116 *	Revels, Addis	WI	1877	Alice Revels	Henry Revels	Annis Winchel	McCaga & Mornon Revels	James & Jane Winchel
22451 *	Revels, Albert	IN	1851	Lucy Revels	Aaron Revels	Martha Gilliam	Stephen & McCaga Revels	Joseph & Pernelia Lockler
14050	Revels, Alice	WI		Addis Revels	Elijah Bass Jr	Elizabeth Arnold	Elijah Sr & Elizabeth Bass	Andrew & Emily Arnold
14118	Revels, Alice	WI	1863	Mathew Revels	Burrel Murphy	Elizabeth Bass	Rebecha Murphy	Elijah Sr & Matilda Bass
19917	Revels, Amos	NC	1848	Mary Revels	Elias Revels	Emily Blanks	Burrell Revels	John & Mary Blanks
14112 *	Revels, Charles	WI			Henry Revels	Annis Winchel	McCaga & Mornon Revels	James & Jane Winchel
14159	Revels, Charles	NC	1878	Susan Revels	William Revels	Matilda Pace	Jordan & Polly Revels	Louise Pace
19913	Revels, David	NC	1878	Purly Revels	William Revels	Matildy Pare	Jordan & Polly Revels	Louesa Pare
14120	Revels, Della	WI	1875	Joseph Revels	Elijah Bass Jr	Elizabeth Arnold	Elijah Sr & Elizabeth Bass	Andrew & Emily Arnold
14117 *	Revels, Frank	WI		Ollie Revels	Henry Revels	Annis Winchel	McCaga & Mornon Revels	James & Jane Winchel
19836	Revels, Gladdie et al	NC			James Revels	Nora Evans	Wm & Caroline Revels	Lucy Evans
13445 *	Revels, Henry	WI			Henry Revels	Annis Winchel	McCaga & Mornon Revels	James & Jane Winchel
14110 *	Revels, Henry	WI		Annis Revels	McCaga Revels	Mornon Jakop	Stephen & Delilah Revels	Johnathan & Elizabeth Jakop
14254	Revels, Henry	NC	1860	Malissa Revels	Elios Revels	Emily Blaine	Burl & Vinie Revels	John Blaine
13443 *	Revels, James	WI		Lovina Revels	Aaron Revels	Elisebeth Walden	McCaga & Mornon Revels	Mike & Polly Walden
14174	Revels, James	NC	1873	Mattie Revels	William Revels	Matilda Pace	Jordan & Polly Revels	Louise Pace
13446 *	Revels, Jewell	WI			Aaron Revels	Elisabeth Walden	McCaga & Mornon Revels	Mike & Polly Walden
18726 *	Revels, John	OK	1845		McCaga Revels	Monon Jacobs	Stephen & Delila Revels	
19916	Revels, John	NC	15yrs		Amos Revels	Mary Revels	Elias & Emily Revels	Margaret Revels

14119 *	Revels, Joseph	WI	1861	Della Revels	Aaron Revels	Elizabeth Waldon	McCaga & Mornon Revels	Mike & Polly Waldon
22695	Revels, Lucy	IN	1851	Albert Revels	John Sweet	Olive Winbern		David Winbern
19918	Revels, Margaret	NC	1833		Jordan Revels	Polly Bryant	Jordan & Winnie Revels	Thomas & Sytha Bryant
14048 *	Revels, Mark	WI	1844	Cornelia Revels decd	McCaga Revels	Mornon Jakop	Stephen & Delila Revels	
19835	Revels, Mary	NC	1861	Amans Revels		Margret Revels		Jordan & Polly Revels
13531 ½ *	Revels, Mathew	WI	1859	Alice Revels	Aaron Revels	Elisebeth Walden	McCaga & Mornon Revels	Mike & Polly Walden
14293	Revels, William	NC	1838	Matilda Revels	Jordan Revels	Polly Bryant	Burl & Winnie Revels	Thomas & Scytha Bryant
7304	Reynolds, George	MO		none	John Reynolds	Mary Morgan	George & Elizabeth Reynolds	Nathan & Anna Morgan
7305	Reynolds, James	MO		Jamie Reynolds	John Reynolds	Mary Morgan	Geo & Elizabeth Reynolds	Nathan & Anna Morgan
19895	Reynolds, James	NC	1850	Elvira Reynolds	Martain Reynolds	Sally Adams	Thomas & Mariah Reynolds	Baily Ingram
7308	Reynolds, John	TX	1871	none	David Reynolds	Judith Holder	Henry & May Reynolds	Presley & Mary Holder
18474	Reynolds, Kansas	GA	1875	Wm Reynolds	William Bryant	Mary Hinton	Wm & Fannie Bryant	
20229 *	Reynolds, Louisa	TN	1850		Thomas Roberson	Parthenia Rice	Thomas & Zilpha Roberson	Ben & Sarah Rice
19893	Reynolds, Lucy	NC	1893		Thomas Reynolds	Augusta Holton	Martan & Sally Reynolds	James Holton
7306	Reynolds, Mary	MO	1847	John Reynolds	Nathan Morgan	Annie Massingale	James & Martha Morgan	Blakely & Polly Massingale
18172 *	Reynolds, Patsy	TN		Nelson Reynolds	Randle Moss	Rosie Toka		Sindy & Pashion Toka
19894	Reynolds, Sally	NC	1828	Martan Reynolds	Baily Adams	Charlotte	Joshua & Betsey Adams	
7307	Reynolds, Thomas	MO	1872	Ada Reynolds	John Reynolds	Mary Morgan	Geo & Elizabeth Reynolds	Nathan & Anna Morgan
19758 *	Rhea, Mary	TN	1826	Montgomery Rhea		Millie Crockett		John Chanklin
20022	Rhenark, Amanda	AR	1881	Amos Rhenark	Moses Colder	Mary Nelson	Peter & Liza Colder	Simon & Annie Nelson
19049	Rhine, Lizzie	TX	1872	Rinaldo Rhine	William Coe	Mary Smith	Andrew & Rhoda Coe	James Smith
22180 *	Rhoan Arrie	TN	1871	Thomas Rhoan	Samuel Goins	Sarah Bohanan	Jerry & Polly McReynolds	
19375	Rhodes, Carrie	GA	1883	Nathan Rhodes	John Anderson	Malinda Galoway	John & Emily Anderson	Robert & Mahala Galoway
7317	Rhodes, Fleatie	MO	1877	James Rhodes	John Williams	Mary Nichols	Minter & Frankie Williams	Henry & Mary Nichols
22402	Rhodes, Robert	TN	1885	Bertha Mason	Samuel Rhodes	Nancy Whaley	George & Vista Rhodes	
14164	Rhoten, Louisiana	TN	1872	Lemuel Rhoten	Elisha Rich	Mary Strong	John Rich	Mourning Strong
10573	Rice, Adlaid	GA	1903		John Rice	Julia Castile	Joseph & Emily Rice	James & Minta Castile
17635	Rice, Carrie	GA	1879	William Rice	Joseph Ragsdale	Mary Parr	Larkin & Judie Ragsdale	Wm & Nancy Parr
16134	Rice, Cynthia	GA	1867	Abraham Rice	Starling Vaughn	Sarah Fields	John Vaughn	Alex Fields
10571	Rice, Emily	GA	1849	Joseph Rice	John Cole	Betsy Whitlock		James & Sallie Whitlock
20332 *	Rice, George	GA	1876	Allice Rice	Singleton Rice	Mary Alexander	Levi & Bethie Alexander	Alec & Jane Green

10574	Rice, Gracie	GA	1905		John Rice	Julia Castile	Joseph & Emily Rice	James & Minta Castile
10575	Rice, Hansell	GA	1894		John Rice	Julia Castile	Joseph & Emily Rice	James & Minta Castile
10576	Rice, James	GA	1901		John Rice	Julia Castile	Joseph & Emily Rice	James & Minta Castile
17690	Rice, Jasper	TN	1844	Eliza Rice	Wilson Rice	Elizabeth Banks	Jesse Rice	
10572	Rice, John	GA	1872	Julia Rice	Joseph Rice Sr.	Emily Cole	Wm & Alester Rice	John & Betsy Cole
10577	Rice, Joseph Jr.	GA	1896		John Rice	Julia Castile	Joseph & Emily Rice	James & Minta Castile
10517	Rice, Leacie	GA	1891		John Rice	Julia Castile	Joseph & Emily Rice	James & Minta Castile
10578	Rice, Luther	GA	1899		John Rice	Julia Castile	Joseph & Emily Rice	James & Minta Castile
11587	Rice, Lydia	GA	1870	John Rice	Joseph Call	Elizabeth Teague	John & Nancy Call	Isaac & Rachel Teague
20846 *	Rice, Mary	GA	1831	Singleton Rice	George Tassel	Joyce Vernon		Robert & Lucy Vernon
15648 *	Rice, Orvelia	GA	1872		George Rice	Mandy Cowell		Rachel Cowell
11592	Rice, Rachel	GA	1890		J C Rice	Lydia Call	G W & Amanda Rice	Joseph & Elizabeth Call
20847 *	Rice, Singleton	GA	1831	Mary Rice	Joshua Rice	Mary Wooten	Reason & Mima Alexander	Henry & Annie Wooten
9873	Rice, William	GA	1874	Carrie Rice	Joseph Rice	Emily Cole	Wm & Aluster Rice	John & Betsy Cole
14304	Rich, Elisha	TN	1829	Mary Rich	John Rich	Jane Peak	Granse Rich	
14175	Rich, Elisha Jr	TN		Molly Rich	John Rich	M A Welch	Elisha & Mary Rich	
12673	Rich, James	KY	1846	Mary Rich	Elisha Rich	Mary Strong	John & Virginia Rich	Joseph & Morning Strong
14165	Rich, John	TN	1850		Elisha Rich	Mary Strong	John Rich	Mourning Strong
12220	Rich, Laura	NC	1858	Johnny Rich	William Poindexter		Denson Poindexter	Thomas Davis
14890	Rich, Laura	NC	1858	John Rich	William Poindexter	Lucinda Davis	Denson & Sarah Poindexter	Thos & Elizabeth Davis
21271	Rich, Mary	LA	1861	A.J. Rich	John Jeter	Susan Thompson	Washington & Mary Jeter	
14177	Rich, Roark	TN	1864	Alice Rich	Elisha Rich	Mary Strong	John Rich	Mourning Strong
3791	Richards, Amanda	MO	1844	Samuel Richards	Vinson Harralson	Martha Hambelton	David & Peachy Harralson	Elijah & Sarah Hambelton
8273	Richards, Gertrude	MO		none	Samuel Richards	Amanda Harralson	Martin & Lucy Richards	Vincin & Martha Harralson
8681	Richards, Lelia	OK	1879	Joe Richards	J. M. Tittle	Annie Prather	Dan & Rosana Tittle	Robert & Caroline Prather
3277	Richards, Samuel	MO	1883	Dollie Richards	Samuel Richards	Amanda Harralson	Martin & Lucy Richards	Vinson & Martha Harralson
442	Richardson, Alfred	NC	1847		Alfred Richardson	Eliza Silver	Hardy Richardson	Dorcas Boon
10502	Richardson, Allie	GA	1902		John Richardson	Maggie Brown	Nathan & Delilah Richardson	George & Mary Brown
10509	Richardson, Alva	GA	1894		Frank Richardson	Nancy Hopper	James & Nancy Richardson	Crawford & Martha Hopper
10510	Richardson, Alvin	GA	1894		Frank Richardson	Nancy Hopper	James & Nancy Richardson	Crawford & Martha Hopper
7852	Richardson, Annie	GA	1906		Harp Richardson	Elizabeth Brown	Nathan & Delilah Richardson	James & Lucy Brown
4878	Richardson, Catharine	VA		L.A. Richardson	John Hart	Polley Caldwell	George & Polley Hart	Joseph & Catharine Caldwell

10511	Richardson, Charlie	GA	1889		Frank Richardson	Nancy Hopper	James & Nancy Richardson	Crawford & Martha Hopper
10503	Richardson, Delilah	GA	1905		John Richardson	Maggie Brown	Nathan & Delilah Richardson	George & Mary Brown
19376	Richardson, Dora	GA	1886		Newton Richardson	Bettie Jordan	James & Nancy Richardson	Noah & Martha Jordan
4770	Richardson, Edward	MO	1874	none	Robert Richardson	Emeline Abney	Becky Beardon	
7848	Richardson, Ervin	GA	1873	Sallie Richardson	Nathan Richardson	Delilah Gibson	James & Nancy Richardson	John Gibson
6952	Richardson, Flora	VA	25yrs	Roby Richardson	John Peak	Sarilda McGrady	Hugh & Marga Hart	
19377	Richardson, Florida	GA	1888		Newton Richardson	Bettie Jordan	James & Nancy Richardson	Noah & Martha Jordan
18734	Richardson, Floyd	NC	1885	Louisa Richardson	B. Richardson	Mary Stamper	Clayburn & Nancy Richardson	Johnathan & Matilda Stamper
10508	Richardson, Frank	GA	1854	Nancy Richardson	James Richardson	Nancy Jordan	John & Ellender Richardson	Nathan & Annis Jordan
18732	Richardson, Frank	NC	1875	Nora Richardson	B. Richardson	Mary Stamper	Clayburn & Nancy Richardson	Johnathan & Matilda Stamper
10504	Richardson, Garnett	GA	1899		John Richardson	Maggie Brown	Nathan & Delilah Richardson	George & Mary Brown
10505	Richardson, George	GA	1891		John Richardson	Maggie Brown	Nathan & Delilah Richardson	George & Mary Brown
12346	Richardson, Glenn	GA	1905		Owda Richardson	Louella Dean	Nathan & Delilah Richardson	Zack & Jane Dean
7853	Richardson, Harp	GA	1870	Elizabeth Richardson	Nathan Richardson	Delilah Gibson	James & Nancy Richardson	John & Sarah Gibson
10516	Richardson, Harvey	GA	1882		Frank Richardson	Nancy Hopper	James & Nancy Richardson	Crawford & Martha Hopper
4775	Richardson, Henry	MO	1865	Della Richardson	Robert Richardson	Emeline Abney	Becky Beardon	
10512	Richardson, James	GA	1888		Frank Richardson	Nancy Hopper	James & Nancy Richardson	Crawford & Martha Hopper
4876	Richardson, John	VA	1885	none	Leander Richardson	Catharine Hart		John & Polly Hart
7849	Richardson, John	GA	38yrs	Maggie Richardson	Nathan Richardson	Delilah Gibson	James & Nancy Richardson	John Gibson
14330	Richardson, John	MO	1854	Ollie Richardson	John Richardson	Rowena Taylor	Harvey Richardson	
16202	Richardson, John	OK	1845	Margaret Richardson	John Richardson	Sarah Knight		Solom Knight
10513	Richardson, Lela	GA	1897		Frank Richardson	Nancy Hopper	James & Nancy Richardson	Crawford & Martha Hopper
12344	Richardson, Leon	GA	1901		Owda Richardson	Louella Dean	Nathan & Delilah Richardson	Zack & Jane Dean
19378	Richardson, Leroy	GA	1890		Newton Richardson	Bettie Jordan	James & Nancy Richardson	Noah & Martha Jordan
19379	Richardson, Levi	GA	1890		Newton Richardson	Bettie Jordan	James & Nancy Richardson	Noah & Martha Jordan
18157	Richardson, Lucinda	NC	1866	Caleb Richardson	John Petty	Catharine Osborn		David & Lucinda Osborn
19381	Richardson, Lum	GA	1882	Florida Richardson	Newton Richardson	Bettie Jordan	James & Nancy Richardson	Noah & Martha Jordan
10514	Richardson, Lutie	GA	1900		Frank Richardson	Nancy Hopper	James & Nancy Richardson	Crawford & Martha Hopper
7855	Richardson, Marshall	GA	1886		Nathan Richardson	Delilah Gibson	James & Nancy Richardson	John Gibson
11808	Richardson, Mary	NC	1855	B. Richardson	Johnethan Stamper	Matilda Osborn	Jobe & Elizabeth Stamper	David & Lucy Osborn

17709	Richardson, Mary	MO	1868	Thomas Richardson	Wiley Stephens	Malinda Cummins		Clarinda Cummins
10507	Richardson, Maud	GA	1896		John Richardson	Maggie Brown	Nathan & Delilah Richardson	George & Mary Brown
3373	Richardson, Mrs. O M	AL	1862	Olander Richardson	Sidney Lomax	Matilda Moniac		Sam & Susan Moniac
10501	Richardson, Nancy	GA	1817	James Richardson	Nathan Jordan	Annis Wyatt		John Wyatt
7850	Richardson, Nathan	GA	1835	Della Richardson	James Richardson	Nancy Wyatt	James Richardson	John & Annis Wyatt
7854	Richardson, Nellie	GA	1884		Nathan Richardson	Delilah Gibson	James & Nancy Richardson	John Gibson
19382	Richardson, Newton	GA	1845	Bettie Richardson	James Richardson	Nancy Jordan		Nathan & Annis Jordan
21452	Richardson, Ora	TX	1874		Frank Jeter	Adelia Thompson	George & Mary Jeter	
7851	Richardson, Owda	GA	1875	Luella Richardson	Nathan Richardson	Delilah Gibson	James & Nancy Richardson	John Gibson
7856	Richardson, Rebecca	GA	1881		Nathan Richardson	Delilah Gibson	James & Nancy Richardson	John Gibson
22721	Richardson, Rosa	OK	1877	Oscar Richardson	William Owens	Susan Butler	Henry & Mary Owens	John & Elizabeth Butler
4774	Richardson, Rufus	MO	1878	Tressia Richardson	Robert Richardson	Emeline Abney	Becky Beardon	
7857	Richardson, Russell	GA	1878	Lula Richardson	Nathan Richardson	Delilah Gibson	James & Nancy Richardson	
12330	Richardson, Sanford	GA	1899		Owen Richardson	Louella Dean	Nathan & Delilah Richardson	Jack & Jane Dean
4877	Richardson, Sarah	VA	1882	none	Leandre Richardson	Catharine Hart		John & Polly Hart
7858	Richardson, Thomas	GA	1889		Nathan Richardson	Delilah Gibson	James & Nancy Richardson	John Gibson
19383	Richardson, Walter	GA	1892		Newton Richardson	Bettie Jordan	James & Nancy Richardson	Noah & Martha Jordan
10515	Richardson, Wesley	GA	1892		Frank Richardson	Nancy Hopper	James & Nancy Richardson	Crawford & Martha Hopper
10506	Richardson, William	GA	1893		John Richardson	Maggie Brown	Nathan & Delilah Richardson	George & Mary Brown
19384	Richardson, Willie	GA	1900		Lum Richardson	Florence McPherson	Newton & Bettie Richardson	Asa McPherson
7859	Richerson, Dussie	GA	1892	Henry Richerson	William Wilson	Francis Helton	Hilyard & Lucinda Wilson	Clark & Mary Helton
18387	Rickard, Bell	AL	16yrs	John Rickard	John Prestley	Matilda Gibson	Tate & Marth Prestley	W.D. & Peggy Gibson
18386	Rickard, John	AL	20yrs	Bell Prestley	W.A. Richard	Lyzie Colbert	John & Elizabeth Richard	Wm & Mary Colbert
17864	Ricketts, Sarah	OK	1836		Alford McDonald	Lucindie Watley	Joshaway McDonald	
17455	Ricks, Mary	TX	1873	Wm Ricks	Robert Bell	Lucinda Hampton	J.W. & Elizabeth Bell	G.W. & Mary Hampton
18949 *	Ricksey, Josephine	GA	1857	P.R. Ricksey	Abb Price	Sarah Price		Tom & Harriet Price
21151	Riddle, James	KS	1887	none	James Riddle	Sarah Frazier	Benjamin Riddle	Emanuel & Laura Frazier
19252	Riddle, John	NC	1863	Elizabeth Riddle	William Riddle	Mary Sawyers	Sarah Riddle	
7318	Riddle, Sarrah	OK	1885	Wade Riddle	Giles Parmsley	Jennie Brumley		James & Sarah Brumley

19161*	Riddlespluger, Margrate	GA	1825	James Adams	George Harris	Missouri Dean	Celey Harris	Marinda Lambert
17579	Ridemour, Emma	OK		W.A. Ridemour	Milo Hoyt	Harriet Fulsom	Milo & Lydia Hoyt	Jacob Fulsom
17888	Rider, Bettie	MO			Robert Beeler	P.J. Shelton		Ralph & Annie Shelton
15431	Rider, Louranie	GA	1836	Berry Rider	Abram Crow	Feebie Townsend		Edward & Anna Townsend
10984	Ridge, Benjamin	TN	1873	Addie Ridge	David Ridge	Martha Baily	Thomas Ridge	Thomas & Nancy Baily
2197	Ridge, Charles	TN		Josephine Ridge		Martha Ridge		Jordan & Malinda Ridge
22351*	Ridge, Cornelius	OK	1850	Laura Ridge	Henry Ridge	Katie		Simon
10989	Ridge, Elizabeth	TN	1867		David Ridge	Martha Baily	Thomas Ridge	Thomas & Nancy Baily
2194	Ridge, G. Thomas	TN		Belle Ridge	Jordan Ridge	Malinda Bailey	Thomas Ridge	
10987	Ridge, Hiram	TN	1863	Deboria Ridge	David Ridge	Martha Baily	Thomas Ridge	Thomas & Nancy Baily
2195	Ridge, James	TN	1858	widower	Jordan Ridge	Malinda Bailey	Thomas Ridge	
10988	Ridge, James	TN	1870	Rebecca Ridge	David Ridge	Martha Baily	Thomas Ridge	Thomas & Nancy Baily
10985	Ridge, Joseph	TN	1865	Dora Ridge	David Ridge	Martha Baily	Thomas Ridge	Thomas & Nancy Baily
2196	Ridge, William	TN	1869	Ida Ridge	Jordan Ridge	Malinda Bailey	Thomas Ridge	
20431	Ridges, Robert	TN	1884		William Ridge	Ellen Wimberly	David & Martha Ridge	Thomas & Nancy Bailey
3989	Ridle, W M	NC	1865	Allice Rider	William Ridle	Mary Sawyer	Peter Gilley & Saley Ridle	Bird & Martha Sawyer
17559	Rieves, Maryan	VA	1871	Wm Rieves	Johnathan Miller	Louisa Blevins	Adam & Annia Miller	Daniel & Annia Blevins
21461	Riggs, William	OK	1864	Samantha Riggs	James Riggs	Louisa Deamon	Rubin Riggs	Gillian & Loukany Deamon
5200	Riley, Johnson	OK	1847	Sarah Riley	Lewis Riley	Nancy Tassel	James & Jennie Riley	Nee-ja-ka & Hou-te-u
4581	Riley, Mary	OK	1848	Samuel Riley	Roan Bowlin	Mary Jennan	Rodney & Lucy Bowlin	Wm & Margaret Jennan
20242*	Riley, Moses	OK	1851	Jane Riley	Riley McNair	Maria McNair	Samuel & Peggy McNair	Adam & Charlotte Martin
20316	Rinehart, Miza	MO		Ambrose Rinehart	Emerson Herrell	Clarisa Scruggs	Michael & Lucy Herrell	Lewis & Anne Scruggs
18048	Ring, Arthur	NC	1888		Henry Ring	Sarale Overby	Thos Poindexter	Betty Pledge
18046	Ring, Esther	NC	1899		Henry Ring	Sarale Overby	Thos Poindexter	Betty Pledge
18045	Ring, Henry	NC	1882		Henry Ring	Sarale Overby	Thos Poindexter	Betty Pledge
18044	Ring, Hubert	NC	1885		Henry Ring	Sarale Overby	Thos Poindexter	Betty Pledge
18047	Ring, Irvin	NC	1894		Henry Ring	Sarale Overby	Thos Poindexter	Betty Pledge
14876	Ring, Mary	NC	1857	Enoch Ring	Simson Poindexter	Nancy Woodley	John Poindexter & Rebecca Kerr	John Woodley & Matilda Mason
17642	Ring, Sarah	NC	1857	Henry Ring	Rufus Overby	Jane Hall		Thos Poindexter
871	Risner, William	OK		Luc Risner	Jack Risner	Elizabeth Perdue	George & Rebecca Risner	Dennis & Liza Perdue
17744	Rister, Francis	AL	1864	Jacob Rister	Josiah Chavis	Mary Davis	James & Becky Chavis	MaRee
8920	Ritchey, Nancy for children	OK	1837	S A Ritchey	Callaway Sizemore	Nancy	Edward & Polly Sizemore	
19729	Ritchie, James	TN	1887	Ellen Ritchie	Silas Ritchie	Polly Croye		

14490	Roach, Ida	GA	1875	Joe Roach	Thael DuPree	Francis Cole	Griffin & Juda DuPree	John & Betsy Cole
14718	Roach, Jennie	OK	1870	John Roach	Isaac Boyd	Ellen Mason	Frank Boyd	Isaac & Charity Justice
4263	Roads, Sarah	NC	1866	S B Roads	John More	Martha McDonald		James & Mima McDonald
8028	Robber, Joe	AR	1868	Lucy Robber	Robber	Unknown	Eagle McLemore	Unknown
20245	Robbins, Benjamin	OK	1859	Alice Robbins	Levi Robbins	Hester Quinton		Bill Quinton
5505	Robbins, Cessie	NC	1882	BrainIt Robbins	Wiliam Pugh	Martha Davis	Michael & Narcessa Pugh	Robert & Darthula Davis
20243	Robbins, James	OK	1876		Levi Robbins	Sarah Stone		
20244	Robbins, Levi	OK	1866	Roxie Robbins	Levi Robbins	Hester Quinton		Bill Quinton
2696	Robbins, Lotty	OK	1870	none	Jephus Robbins	Emma Critenton	Levi & Jane Robbins	Louis Critenton
11462	Robbins, Rebecca	OK	1845	widow	William Post	Elizabeth Chapman		
4459	Robbins, Sarah	MO	1842		Joseph Hubbard		Hardy Hubbard	
10344	Roberson, John	NC	1868		William Roberson	Polly Holcomb	Wiate & Patty Roberson	Robert & Sary Holcomb
10991	Roberson, Mollie	NC	1884	Thomas Roberson	Thomas Shepherd	Eliza Maney	John & Dorothy Shepherd	Martin & Matilda Maney
19657 *	Roberson, W.M.	TN	1843	Louisa Roberson	Bill Roberson	Mahalay Roberson	William Roberson	
16031 *	Roberts, Aaron	WI	1847	Rachel Roberts	Ishmael Roberts	Delany Revels	Benj & Sarah Roberts	McCoya & Momon Revels
12043	Roberts, Agnes	GA	1874	C N Roberts	Jerome Williams	Margaret Pressly	Henry & Agnes Williams	John & Elizabeth Pressly
13852 *	Roberts, Albert	IN	1861		Ismel Roberts	Delaney Revels	Benj & Sallie Roberts	Macaga & Mornon Revels
15387	Roberts, Annie	GA	1891		William Roberts	Sarah Harris	Joshua & Mary Roberts	Gillison & Martha Harris
7291	Roberts, Arthur	MT	1874	Ellie Roberts	William Roberts	Eliza Dagley	Andrew & Eliza Roberts	Joseph & Calina Dagley
16154 *	Roberts, Arthur	WI	1889	Sarah Roberts	Aaron Roberts	Martha Stewart	Ishmael & Delany Roberts	Walden & Nettie Stewart
12253	Roberts, Candace	NC	1874	James Roberts	Presley Brown	Lousanna Wagoner	Mason & Susie Brown	Henry & Charlotte Wagoner
21788	Roberts, Carry	AR	1866	Clark Roberts	William Haynes	Jane Thompson	Sarah Haynes	Wm & Estes Thompson
7293	Roberts, Charles	MO	1877	none	Jesse Roberts	Mary Wylie	Andrew & Eliza Roberts	Harvy & Rutha Wylie
10718	Roberts, Charlotte	NC	1870	James Roberts	Presley Brown	Lousiana Wagoner	Mason & Susie Brown	Henry & Charlotte Wagoner
19790	Roberts, Columbus	NC	1851	Callie Roberts	Gale Roberts	Octava Smith	Henry & Sinda Coleman	
10761	Roberts, Dolly	VA	1892	none	Elbert Roberts	Margret Welsh	John & Elizabeth Roberts	Harvy & Milly Hash
12042	Roberts, Dorothy	GA	1881	G W Roberts	Jerome Williams	Margaret Pressly	Henry & Agnes Williams	John & Elizabeth Pressly
22718	Roberts, Effie	MT	1874	Arthur Roberts	Elias Dagby	Mary Roberts	Joseph & Salina Dagby	
22488	Roberts, Eli	IN	1850	Laura Roberts	Wade Roberts	Mary Roberts	Hansel & Priscilla Roberts	Elijah & Keziah Roberts
7289	Roberts, Eliza	MO	1842	William Roberts	Joseph Dagley	Celina Keeney	Elias & Hannah Dagley	Wm & Elisabeth Keeney

7298	Roberts, Eliza	MO	1819	A Roberts (decd)	John Blackburn	Elizabeth Patterson	James & Rhoda Blackburn	John & Elizabeth Patterson
22485*	Roberts, Emily	GA	1858	Frank Roberts	Peter Waldon	Sarah Gilliam	Micajah & Mary Waldon	Moody & Mandy Gilliam
19247	Roberts, Emma	NC	1849		Thomas Martin	Ann Poindexter	Samuel & Elizabeth Martin	Francis & Rosana Poindexter
15144	Roberts, Florence	GA	1877	William Roberts	Henry Findley	Mary Whorton	Francis & Linnie Findley	
15386	Roberts, Francis	GA	1905		Luther Roberts	Mattie Chapman	Wm & Sarah Roberts	Asberry & Tot Chapman
22487	Roberts, Frank	IN	1863	Emily Roberts	Richard Roberts	Letitia Winburn	Elijah & Keziah Roberts	Bennett Winburn
15385	Roberts, Gladys	GA	1904		Luther Roberts	Mattie Chapman	Wm & Sarah Roberts	Asberry & Tot Chapman
15384	Roberts, Grace	GA	1888		William Roberts	Sarah Harris	Joshua & Mary Roberts	Gillison & Martha Harris
7292	Roberts, Henry	MN	1872	Irene Roberts	William Roberts	Eliza Dagley	Andrew & Eliza Roberts	Joseph & Calina Dagley
10760	Roberts, James	VA	1899	none	Elbert Roberts	Margret Welsh	John & Elizabeth Roberts	Harvy & Milly Hash
7297	Roberts, Jesse	MO	1839	Mary Roberts	Andrew Roberts	Eliza Blackburn	Wm & Margaret Roberts	John & Elizabeth Blackburn
14551	Roberts, Lee	GA	1884	James Roberts	Noah Cole	Mary Wimffy	John & Betsy Cole	Henley & Betsy Wimffy
15382	Roberts, Lois	GA	1902		Luther Roberts	Mattie Chapman	Wm & Sarah Roberts	Asberry & Ivy Chapman
18979*	Roberts, Lucy	WI	1890		Aaron Roberts	Rachel Bostwick	Ismael & Delany Roberts	Henry & Lucy Bostwick
15381	Roberts, Luther	GA	1876	Mattie Roberts	William Roberts	Sarah Fowler	Joshua & Mary Roberts	Gillison & Martha Harris
7294	Roberts, Lyman	MO	1884	Rosa Roberts	Jesse Roberts	Mary Wylie	Andrew & Eliza Roberts	Harvy & Rutha Wylie
7789	Roberts, Maggie	TX	1880	Wesley Roberts	James Webb	Lizzie Gambill		Jack Gambill
16153	Roberts, Malissie	WI		Richard Roberts	Sammie Bass	Eliza Murphy	Elijah & Matilda Bass	George & Becka Murphy
18317*	Roberts, Margurite	IN			Albert Roberts	Anna Holburt	Ishmal & Delaney Roberts	
18042	Roberts, Mary	TN	1849	Thomas Roberts	Abner Sayers	Nancy Scales	James Sayers	Nicholas & Mary Scales
19431	Roberts, Mary	IN	1845		Thomas Hammonds	Delany Smuthers	Markas Hammonds	
14114*	Roberts, Melbra	WI		Isaac Roberts	Mark Revels	Cornelia Winchel	McCaga & Mornon Revels	James & Jane Winchel
7290	Roberts, Oscar	CA	1881	Estrella Roberts	William Roberts	Eliza Dagley	Andrew & Eliza Roberts	Joseph & Calina Dagley
19430	Roberts, Oscar	IN	1840		Dudley Roberts	Elizabeth Hammonds		Thomas & Delany Hammonds
18988	Roberts, Rebecca	TN	1837	Jackson Roberts	Benj Kirkland	Rebecca Kirkland	John & Sarah Kirkland	James & Susie Kirkland
13278*	Roberts, Richard	WI	1866	Malissa Roberts	Ishmael Roberts	Delana Revels		McCaga & Mourning Revels
10759	Roberts, Robert	VA	1900	none	Elbert Roberts	Margret Welsh	John & Elizabeth Roberts	Harvy & Milly Hash
7296	Roberts, Rosa	MO	1885		Herman Knutter	Catharine Lockard	Ed & Lonesi Knutter	John & Nancy Lockard
5437	Roberts, Rozina	NC	1873	J P Roberts	Emanuel Sheets	Charity Orsborn	Jesse & Sarah Sheets	Jesse & Cynthy Orsborn
12866	Roberts, Sarah	MO	1847	Jesse Roberts	William Williams	Martha Murray	James & Phoebe Williams	James & Yaurth Murray

13742	Roberts, Sarah	GA	1871	Jeff Roberts	John Dean	Elizabeth Williams	Elisha & Sofie Dean	Absalom & Lucy Williams
15380	Roberts, Sarah	GA	1854	William Roberts	Gillison Harris	Martha Fowler	Lorenzo & Sarah Harris	Wm & Lucy Fowler
13023 *	Roberts, Simps	AL	1833	Mattie Roberts	John Roberts	Mattie Roberts		
18987	Roberts, Stonewall	TN	1862	Margret Roberts	Jackson Roberts	Rebecca Kirkland	Phillip & Nancy Roberts	Ben & Epsy Kirkland
13532 *	Roberts, Theoplis	WI			Ishamel Roberts	Delaney Revels	Benj & Sarah Roberts	McCaga & Mornon Revels
13850 *	Roberts, Wilbert	MI		Edith Roberts	Aaron Roberts	Martha Stewart	Ishmael & Delany Roberts	Walden & Hetta Stewart
9361	Roberts, Willard	IN	1889		Thomas Roberts	Narcissa Allen	Joseph & Amelia Roberts	Samuel & Martha Allen
7295	Roberts, William	MO	1865		Jesse Roberts	Mary Wylie	Andrew & Eliza Roberts	Harvy & Rutha Wylie
7299	Roberts, William	MO	1847	Eliza Roberts	Andrew Roberts	Eliza Blackburn	Wm & Margaret Roberts	John & Elizabeth Blackburn
22489	Roberts, William	IN	1843	Frances Roberts	Wade Roberts	Mary Roberts	Hansel & Priscilla Roberts	Elijah & Keziah Roberts
2082	Robertson, Alexander	MO	1850	none	Wm Robertson	Polly Cheek		Edmund Cheek
20919	Robertson, Amanda	AL	1868	D.H. Robertson	James Sizemore	Mary Black	Daniel Sizemore	
14419	Robertson, James	NC	1870	Ella Robertson	William Robertson	Mary Holcomb	Wyatt & Patty Robertson	Robert & Sallie Holcomb
20713	Robertson, Lottie	TN	1900		Hickman Robertson	Rittie Hatcher		James & Mary Hatcher
12130	Robertson, Lula	OK	1879	John Robertson	Thomas Redding	Eliza Ross		Joe & Percillia Ross
20716	Robertson, Lynus	TN	1901		Hickman Robertson	Rittie Hatcher		James & Mary Hatcher
20715	Robertson, Rittie	TN	1880	Hickman Robertson	James Hatcher	Mary Halbrook	John & Eliza Hatcher	Joseph & Catherine Halbrook
20368	Robinson, Agnes	TN	1891		John Robinson	Jennette Cooper	Thos & Louisa Robinson	Nathan & Nancy Cooper
11310	Robinson, Alice	GA	1872	J N Robinson	J S Garrett	Margret Dempsey		Porter & Charlotta Dempsey
20462	Robinson, Allen	GA	1870	Rosalind Robinson	Thomas Robinson	Louisa Roper	Thomas Robinson	Noah & Minerva Roper
13880	Robinson, Bedford	GA	1864	Lucy Robinson	John Robinson	Lucindy Leatherwood		Samuel & Elizabeth Leatherwood
20468	Robinson, Cora	GA	1894		Allen Robinson	Minnie Powell	Thomas & Louisa Robinson	B.T. & Rebecca Powell
17935	Robinson, Cornelius	TN	1886		Richard Robinson	Rachel Smith	John & Elizabeth Robinson	John & Nancy Smith
18113	Robinson, Edward	FL	1873	Bottie Robinson	Alex Robinson	Mary Gardner		Samuel Gardner & Eliza Barrios
11311	Robinson, Elle	GA	1869	W.J. Robinson	J S Garrett	Margret Dempsey		Porter & Charlotta Dempsey
18688	Robinson, Emanuel	FL	1858	Angeline Robinson	Thomas Robinson	Mary Harvel		Elizabeth Harvel
16199	Robinson, Florence	TX	1878	Ed Robinson	I D Harrell	Annie Davis	Thomas Paine	
17420	Robinson, Georgia	OK	1869	Leroy Robinson	Robert Prather	Edith Rogers		Pleasant & Phebe Rogers
18114	Robinson, Gilbert	FL	1879		Alex Robinson	Mary Gardner		Samuel Gardner & Eliza Barrios
20460	Robinson, Gordan	GA	1897		Allen Robinson	Minnie Powell	Thomas & Louisa Robinson	B.T. & Rebecca Powell
15732	Robinson, Ida	GA	1873	Amous Robinson	Jeff Lathem	Sufrona Bryant	George & Jane Lathem	Geber & Sallie Bryant

4776	Robinson, James	OK	1844	Marthy Robinson	William Robinson	Nancy Newberry	Risdon & Betsey Robinson	James & Liddie Newberry
19033	Robinson, James	TN		Mary Robinson	James Robinson	Louiza Hammontree	Wm & Nancy Robinson	Jacob & Jennie Hammontree
10479	Robinson, Jason	GA	1855	Sallie Robinson	John Robinson	Lucinda Leatherwood		Saml & Lizbeth Leatherwood
20394	Robinson, John	TN	1872	Jennette Robinson	Thomas Robinson	Louisa Roper	Thomas Robinson	Noah & Minerva Roper
10485	Robinson, Joseph	GA	1853	Sarah Robinson	John Robinson	Lucindy Leatherwood		Saml & Lizbeth Leatherwood
18687	Robinson, Joseph	FL	1847	Elizabeth Robinson	Thomas Robinson	Mary Harvel		Elizabeth Harvel
20441	Robinson, L. Bruce	GA	1903		Allen Robinson	Rosalind Russell	Thos & Louisa Robinson	G.D. & Victoria Russell
20662 *	Robinson, Laura	TN	1855		Dennis Fisher	Matilda Richardson	Kittie Fisher	Violet
20469	Robinson, Louisa	GA	1848		Noah Roper	Minerva Brown	Thomas & Katie Roper	John & Sallie Brown
14328	Robinson, Malinda	TX	1866	J T Robinson	Henry Dunaway	Susanne Savage	Benjamin Dunaway	Hiram & Polly Savage
19330	Robinson, Mary	AR	1874		Henry Lipe	Susan Rogers	Sandy & Elizabeth Lipe	Henry & Masah Rogers
20461	Robinson, Myrtle	GA	1898		Allen Robinson	Minnie Powell	Thomas & Louisa Robinson	B.T. & Rebecca Powell
21963 *	Robinson, Perry	TN	1844	widower	Mose Robinson	Delia	Robinson	
10474	Robinson, Robert	GA	1863	Alice Robinson	John Robinson	Lucindy Leatherwood		Saml & Lizbeth Leatherwood
18686	Robinson, Thomas	FL	1855	Isabelle Robinson	Thomas Robinson	Mary Harvel		Elizabeth Harvel
20520	Robinson, Thomas	GA	1895		Allen Robinson	Minnie Powell	Thos & Louisa Robinson	B.T. & Rebecca Powell
20522	Robinson, Walter	GA	1901		Allen Robinson	Rosalind Russell	Thos & Louisa Robinson	G.D. & Victory Russell
20123	Robison, Susan	OK	1876	Samuel Robison	Calvin Deaver	Melvina Mellican	Stephen & Jane Deaver	
21509	Robnett, Conalee	OK	1875	Joe Robnett	C.A. Polk	Arbella Jeter	Wm & Catherine Polk	George & Mary Jeter
13867	Rochester, Nora	NC	1886	Fayette Rochester	William Massey	Sarah Gibbs	Samuel Massey	Wm Gibbs & Ameline Battles
14463	Roden, Anna	AL	1853	W S Roden	William Sizemore	Martha Barker		
8204	Rodgers, Elissie	NC	1861	Levi Rodgers	Thos Ledbetter	Nellie Thomas	Phoeba Ledbetter	Thos & Hannah Thomas
542	Rodgers, Emma	TX	1855	Henry Rodgers	Larkin Weaver	Susan Harrison	David Weaver & Fannie Womack	
10495	Rodgers, George	OK	1865	Evaline Rodgers	Louis Rodgers	Rebecca	Johnacake	
19922	Rodgers, George	NC	1841	Sally Rodgers	George Rodgers	Lucy Newman	George & Lucy Rodgers	Winston & Lucy Newman
9039	Rodgers, Melia	WV	1874	Cornelius Rodgers	Solomon Osborn	Susan Nicholas	Elias & Sarah Osborn	Wm & Elizabeth Nicholas
6346	Rodgers, Mrs M.B.	AL	1883	M B Rodgers	Alex Boone	Minervy Moniac		David & Catherine Moniac
22714	Rodgers, Susan	TN	1883	Mat Rodgers	Lafayette Stuart	Tilda Thomas	Isam Stuart	Elijah & Narsis Thomas
22125	Roe, Alice	TX	1861	Peter Roe	Samuel Roe	Elizabeth Allen	Samuel & Rosana Roe	
16530	Roe, Amanda	GA	1860	James Roe	Elias Biddy	Polly Brooks	Meshack & Nancy Biddy	David & Susannah Brooks

5166 *	Roe, Billie	OK		Katie Roe	Jessie Roe	Lillie Roe	Roe	Roe
4346	Roe, Gale	TN	1837	Mollie Roe	William Roe	Lyda Frazier	Mary Roe	Gale & Sarah Frazier
9140	Roe, J.A.	GA	1853	Amanda Roe	Ancil Roe	Area	Horatio Tully & Ancil Roe	Mary Lovelace
13865	Roe, Laura	GA	1853	Solomon Roe	Terrell Collins	Rebecca Drake		Heartsell & Emeline Drake
17560	Roger, John	OK	1847	Hattie Rogers	George Rogers	Malinda Serimsher		Wm Serimsher
17334 *	Rogers, Annie	GA	1848	Newton Rogers	Wilson Parker	Pativi Winn		
10081	Rogers, Arther	OK	1880	Mary Rogers	N B Rogers	Annie Martin	Thos & Ellen Rogers	Joseph Martin & Sarah Childers
21771	Rogers, Bessie	OK	1886	Thomas Rogers	James Moore	Martha Parsons	John & Mary Moore	Hiram & Martha Parsons
1517	Rogers, Bettie	NC	1867	Edwards Rogers	Francis Adams	Mary Parker	Price & Elizabeth Adams	Jonathan & Lemy Parker
22098	Rogers, Calvin	AR	1868		Joseph Rogers	Mary Hodges	Henry & Mariah Rogers	John & Jemima Hodges
13954	Rogers, Charles	OK	1881	Mary Rogers	Charles Rogers	Jane Harland		Wilson Harland
9459	Rogers, Charlie	OK	35yrs	Lucy Rogers	Creek Charley	Mar-ley		
12216	Rogers, David	OK	1873	Janette Rogers	Jim Rogers	Polly Sanders		Mitchell & Polly Sanders
9724	Rogers, Edley	AR	1850	Harriet Rogers	Edley Rogers	Mahala Rodgers	Joseph & Susie Rogers	
10358	Rogers, Edley	AR	1875	Nancy Rogers	William Rogers	Sarah Figley	Edley & Mahala Rogers	
22316 *	Rogers, Eliza	OK	1881	Sam Rogers	Jack Baldridge	Nancy Barlow	Taloka Baldridge & Lettie Vann	John & Eliza Barlow
2360	Rogers, Ella	GA	1880	Charley Rogers	James McKinney	Cisco Adams	Allison & Fannie McKinney	David & Clerinda Adams
8816	Rogers, Ellie	GA		William Rogers	George King	Marilu Gray	John & Elisabeth King	Samuel Gray & Pollie Laudermilk
19660	Rogers, Franklin	GA	1853	Ammie Rogers	William Rogers	Marie Lamar	Henry Rogers	Elmire Lamar
15621	Rogers, Fredric	OK	1884		George Rogers	Elizabeth Foster	Robert Rogers	
9662	Rogers, George	AR	1855		Edley Rogers	Mahala Rodgers	Joseph & Susie Rogers	
19160 *	Rogers, Harriett	GA	1830	Rich Rogers	Sam Watts	Cloe		
15620	Rogers, Iola	OK	1865		George Rogers	Elizabeth Foster	Robert Rogers	
9629	Rogers, James	AR	1857		Edley Rogers	Mahala Rodgers	Joseph & Susan Rogers	
19337	Rogers, James	AR	1862		James Rogers	Amanda Hodges	Henry & Mariah Rogers	John & Jemima Hodges
22100	Rogers, James	AR	1867	Margaret Rogers	William Rogers	Melvina McBride	Henry & Mariah Rogers	John & Nancy McBride
5230	Rogers, Jesse	OK	1845	Mary Rogers	Jesse Rogers	Fereby Hill		
13397	Rogers, John	OK	1848	Emma Rogers	James Spaniard	Betsy Rogers		
9721	Rogers, Joseph	AR	1845		Henry Rogers	Mariah Rodgers		Joseph Rogers

10357	Rogers, Jug	AR	1868	Lizzie Rogers	John Rogers	Angiline Roe	Henry & Maria Rogers	
12697	Rogers, Levi	OK	1866	Susie Rogers	Jim Rogers	Polly Sanders		Mitchel & Polly Sanders
5033	Rogers, Lewis	OK	1842	Ellen Rogers	Nelson Rogers	Rosanna West	John Rogers	Jacob & Sarah West
593	Rogers, Mahala	AR	1888	A. C. Rogers	Larkin Owen	Mary Sackry		George Sackry
9630	Rogers, Maranda	AR	1852		Edley Rogers	Mahala Rogers	Joseph & Susan Rogers	
10356	Rogers, Matison	AR	1870	Kattie Rogers	John Rogers	Angaline Roe	Henry & Maria Rogers	
5525	Rogers, Nancy	OK	1848	Thomas Rogers	John Martin	Martha Chambers	Jack & Lucy Martin	John & Nancy Chambers
21150 *	Rogers, Rob	OK	1816	Rhody Rogers	Jessie Roe	Lucy Rogers	Little Nan	
7313	Rogers, Rosa	OK	1877	James Rogers	William Poindexter	Orlena Harrell	Zedock & Sallie Poindexter	Archie & Lila Harrell
9722	Rogers, Thomas	AR	1848		Edley Rogers	Mahala Rodgers	Joseph Rogers	
22095	Rogers, Thomas	AR	1870	Thomas Rogers	James Rogers	Amanda Hodges	Henry & Mariah Rogers	John & Jemima Hodges
9178	Rogers, Walter	OK	1871	Thula Rogers	George Rogers	Elizabeth Foster	Robert Rogers	
21620	Rogers, Walter	GA	1878	Mary Rogers	Edward Rogers	Luvenia Bagley	Jacariah Rogers	
19248	Rogers, Wellington	OK	1858	Emma Rogers	Nelson Rogers	Margaret Scrimsher		John & Edith Scrimsher
9725	Rogers, William	OK	1847	Melvina Rogers	Henry Rogers	Mariah Rodgers	Joseph Rogers	
20232	Rogers, William	OK	1859	Sarah Rogers	Thomas Rogers	Harriett Dickens	James & Betsy Rogers	Richard & Jennie Dickens
13243	Rolfe, Texie	OK			Henry Rolfe	Isabella Huff		John Huff
8965 *	Rolin, Walter	OK		none	Washington Rolan	Elijah Rauls	Tony & Charlotte Rolan	Dolphin & Rosella Druralls
21457	Rollen, Gordie	TX	1886	Henry Rollen	Tomas Mitchell	Deattha Busby	Enoch & Pheby Mitchell	Robbert & Elizabeth Busby
8414	Roller, Helen	MO	1871	Joshua Roller	Wilkerson Lawson	Mahala Martin	Hennis & Jula Lawson	Wm & Susan Martin
3402	Rollin, Alexander	AL	58yrs	Mary Hathcock	John Rollin	Polly Moniac		Betsey Moniac
3360	Rollin, Cleveland	AL	22yrs	Rhetta Galloway	Sam Rollin	Francis McGhee	Richard & Elizabeth McGhee	Jack & Polly Rollin
3419	Rollin, Dolly	AL	1879	Sam Rollin	John Poston	Ella Young	Jim & Elisabeth Poston	Wm & Litha Young
3410	Rollin, Elisa	AL		William Rollin	John McGhee	Polly Gibson	Richard McGhee & Elisabeth Henson	Bart Gibson & Peggy Moniac
6353	Rollin, George	AL	26yrs	none	George Hall	Mary Rollin	Wm & Maggie Hall	John & Polly Rollin
1143	Rollin, Henry	AL	1882	Aida Rollin	Gid Gibson	Peggy Rollin	Dixon Monia	Elisabeth Ellet
1149	Rollin, John	AL	1846	Rhoda Rollin	John Rolen	Polly Moniac	Dixon Moniac	Elizabeth Ellet
18393	Rollin, John	AL	1875	Ella Rollin	John Rollin	Rhody Taylor	John & Polly Rollin	Wash & Matilda Taylor

3408	Rollin, Lallie	AL	25yrs	none	Richard Rollin	Frances McGhee	Jack & Polly Coons	Jack & Maria McGhee
3428	Rollin, Levada	AL		Olly Rollin	John McGhee	Polly Gibson	Richard McGhee & Elisabeth Henson	Bart Gibson & Peggy Moniac
3411	Rollin, Martha	AL	38yrs	none	Richard Rollin	Frances McGhee	Jack & Polly Coon	Jack & Mariah McGhee
3404	Rollin, Mary	AL	60yrs	none	Jack Rollin	Polly Moniac		Betsy Moniac
3414	Rollin, Mary	AL		Alex Rollin	John Hathcock	Rosa McGhee	Thomas Hathcock	Betty McGhee
1151	Rollin, Oliver	AL	25yrs	Larada McGhee	Jim Padget	Mary Rollin	Rollin	Polly Moniac
3407	Rollin, Richard	AL	1884	Lucy Rollin		Jennie Rollin		Richard & Frances Rollin
3417	Rollin, Sam	AL	1856	Dolly Robbin	John Rollin	Polly Moniac		Betsy Moniac
1147	Rollin, William	AL	1857	Liza Rollin	Richard Rollin	Francis McGhee	Rollin	Rollin
18382	Rollin, William	AL	22yrs		John Rollin	Rhody Taylor	John & Polly Rollin	Wash & Matilda Taylor
21395	Romine, Margret	TX	1866	Lewis Romine	Thomas Marshall	Tiletha Martindale	Andrew Marshall	Mary Russell
20981	Rooks, Rosie	AL	1882	R.R. Rooks	Isaac Wilabay	Ruthie Lackey	John & Rebecca Wilabay	
21926*	Rooks, Susie	TN	1872	John Rooks	Willis Ware	Rachel Scott	Bob & Dafny Ware	Nathan & Rebecca Bates
8482	Roop, Elisha	VA	1859	Nancy Roop	Abram Roop	Catherine Hare		George Hare & Polly Blevins
5563	Roop, Ida	VA	1886	William Roop	Calvin Davis	Matildia Pennington	Jordan & Senie Davis	Andrew & Hettie Pennington
8481	Roop, James	WV	1882	Mary Houser	Elisha Roop	Nancy Poter	Aberham & Catherine Roop	James & Rebecka Poter
8528	Roop, James	VA	1882	none	Elisha Roop	Manda Osborn		James & Rachel Osborn
3993	Roop, John	NC	1857	Rebecca Roop	King Roop	Louisa Baldwin		Wm & Margret Baldwin
8526	Roop, John	VA	1882	Cordelia Roop	Elisha Roop	Manda Osborn		James & Rachel Osborn
3567	Roop, Louisa	VA	1832	King Roop	William Baldwin	Margret Stringer	Joseph Baldwin	Catherine Hart
8527	Roop, Luzilla	VA	1869	none	Elisha Roop	Manda Osborn		James & Rachel Osborn
8525	Roop, Mandy	VA	60yrs	Elisha Roop	James Osborn	Rachel Blevins	Elias & Sallie Osborn	
5562	Roop, Rebecca	NC	1862	John Roop	Calvin Davis	Matildia Pennington	Jordan & Senie Davis	Andrew & Hettie Pennington
11507	Roop, Wiley	TN	40yrs	Mandy Roop	King Roop	Louisa Baldwin		Wm & Margret Baldwin
5564	Roop, William	VA	1881	Ida Roop	William Roop	Mary Finley	King & Louisa Roop	
3994	Roop, Wm R	VA	1853	Mary Roop	King Roop	Louisa Baldwin		Wm & Margret Baldwin
15175	Roper, Carey	NC	68yrs	William Roper	Archey Fair	Clearcey Fair	James & Susanna Roper	Archer & Hollie Fair

6549	Roper, Delia	NC	1869	Charlie Roper	Wm Rowland	Mary Trammel	Andy & Polly Rowland	Harriet Trammel
22624	Roper, Emaline	TN	1871	Elijah Roper	Charley Surratt	Sarah Simmblehead		
13855	Roper, John	GA	1860	Rosetta Roper	John Roper	Lucinda Silver	Isaac & Sarah Roper	John & Elizabeth Silver
15168	Roper, John	NC	70yrs	Easter Roper		Elisabeth Roper		James & Elisabeth Roper
22478	Roper, John	TN	1871	Sarra Roper	Elijah Roper	Zilpha Willis	James & Margaret Roper	Berdite Willis
2007	Roper, Martha	NC	1881	W J Roper	John Thomason	Rodan McCoy	John Thomason	Arch & Polly McCoy
1028	Roper, William	NC	1874	Martha Roper	Eliza Roper	Zilpha Willis	Jim & Margaret Roper	Mat & Rachel Willis
15063	Rosburrow, Anna	GA	1850	John Rosburrow	Josh Hale	Emily Young		Jordan & Polly Young
4126	Rose Stokes	NC	1856	Frances Rose	Jackson Rose	Mary Brooks	Isiah & Mary Rose	Stokes & Clarisy Brooks
4127	Rose, A.J.	NC			Isiah Rose	Mary Boges	Samuel & Seidia Rose	Mary Boges
18224	Rose, Amanda	TN	1880	Al Strickland	Joshua Rose	Elizabeth Jeffries	John & Arabell Rose	Alex & Margaret Jeffries
12456	Rose, Edward	WV	1834	Elizabeth Rose	Joel Rose	Jennie Sizemore	Frank & Abbie Rose	Ned & Annie Sizemore
18223	Rose, Edward	TN	1891		Joshua Rose	Elizabeth Jeffries	John & Arabell Rose	Alex & Margaret Jeffries
10247	Rose, Eli	WV	1848	Lyda Rose	Joel Rose	Virginia Sizemore	Frank & Abby Rose	Ned & Annie Sizemore
12452	Rose, Elizabeth	WV	1839	Edward Rose	John Sizemore	Jennie Arms	Ned & Annie Sizemore	Bob & Frankie Arms
18225	Rose, John	TN	1893		Joshua Rose	Elizabeth Jeffries	John & Arabell Rose	Alex & Margaret Jeffries
21881	Rose, John	TN	1853	Minnie Rose	Dow Rose	Martha Owens		Sally Owens
18201	Rose, Julia	TN	1891		Joshua Rose	Elizabeth Jeffres	Joshua & Elizabeth Rose	Alex & Margaret Jeffres
8257	Rose, Lavicie	NC	1843	Q L Rose	Ben Hyde	Sintha Sherrill	Ben Sr & Elizabeth Hyde	
18200	Rose, Lilla	TN	1891		Joshua Rose	Elizabeth Jeffries	John & Elizabeth Rose	Alex & Margaret Jeffries
10246	Rose, Lyda	WV	1846	Eli Rose	John Sizemore	Jane Arms	Ned & Annie Sizemore	
13809	Rose, Martha	TN	1877	William Rose	Bradford Goins	Mary Newton	Jackson & Jennie Goins	Elijah Newton
6723	Rose, Nancy	TN	56 yrs		Frank Ables	Elvira Smith		
8730	Rose, Sallie	NC		David Rose	James Poe	July Ward	Adam Poe	Nathan Ward
10128	Rose, Sary	WV		James Rose	Nathaniel Perdew	Sallie Sizemore	Jesse Perdew	Ned Sizemore & Annie Blevins
10140	Rose, Tobias	WV	1882	Nancy Rose	Nathan Rose	Nancy Green	Joe & Virginia Rose	Polly Green
8729	Rose, Wyatt	NC	1830	Lora Rose	Isah Rose	Mary Bangus	Samuel Rose	Lydia Sizemore
9348	Rosner, Maggie	KS	1876	John Rosner	James Poe	Sarah Harralson		Vincent & Martha Harralson
18422	Ross, Bessie	AR	1890		Criss Adams	Alig Graham	Sampson & Nancy Adams	Alex & Margret Graham
22251*	Ross, Calvin	OK	1846	Maggie Ross	Andy Fields	Chany Ross		Sam & Betsy Ross

7303	Ross, Carl	MO	1881	Nell Ross	Charles Ross	Nannie Foley		James & Rhoda Foley
19311	Ross, Charles	OK	1851	Malinda Moten	William Ross	Mary Spears	Susan Ross	George Lowery
10254	Ross, Elzina	OK	1842	Oliver Ross	Thomas Genre	Nancy Campbell		
7301	Ross, Emma	MO	1887		Charley Ross	Nannie Foley		James & Rhoda Foley
21869	Ross, Hattie	TN	1874	John Ross	Joseph Dedmon	Martha Black	Jesse & Hannah Dedmon	John & Jane Black
19539	Ross, Isaac	TN	1824	Nancy Ross	John Ross	Nancy Taylor	John Ross	
5755	Ross, Jesse	OK	1851	Missouri Ross	Andrew Ross	Lucinda Gentry	Templeton & Eliza Ross	
4970	Ross, Julius	GA	1884	none	Wade Ross	Margaret Clouts		Mahala Clouts
4436	Ross, Luis	CA	1879	Anna Ross	Benj Ross Jr	Mary Montgomery	Benj Ross	G B Montgomery
2661	Ross, Margaret	GA	1852	W H Ross	John Clouts	Mahala Hambree		James Hambree
22434*	Ross, Mariah	OK	1862		Joshua Sheppard	Nancy Will		Tobacco & Maria Will
8793	Ross, Martin	OK	1855	Flora Ross	Alex Ross	Manervia Gofford	David Ross & Akiy Latimore	Allen & Nancy Gofford
22501*	Ross, Moses	OK	1854	widower	Jacob Ross	Lyddia Ross		Edmond & Winnie Ross
22107*	Ross, Nancy	OK	1840	Moses Ross	Cyrus Ross	Winnie Ross	Ned Hardrick	Lydia Holt
7302	Ross, Nannie	MO	1856	Charley Ross	James Foley	Rhoda Boatright		Benj & Elizabeth Boatright
11590	Ross, Neaty	GA	16yrs		W H Ross	Margaret Clouts	H P & Delila Ross	John & Mahala Clouts
6748	Ross, Orraona	OK	1877	Charley Ross	James Tittle	Annie Prather	Daniel & Rosanner Tittle	Robert & Caroline Prather
18833*	Ross, Polly	OK	51yrs	Henry Ross	Jack Thompson	Malinda Nivens		Nero & Sallie Smith
13459	Ross, Robert	OK	1853	Beulah Ross	Andrew Ross	Lucinda Gentry	W Templin & Eliza Ross	
7300	Ross, Roy	MO	1883	Elva Ross	Charles Ross	Nannie Foley		James & Rhoda Foley
11378	Ross, Samuel	OK	1867	Ollie Ross	George Ross	Mary Eddings		Richard Eddings
21812	Ross, William	TX	1866	Emma Ross	Melvin Ross	Julia Lumpkin	Akin & Martha Ross	Bushod & Mary Lumpkin
15921	Rougean, Minnie	OK	1884	Louis Rougean	James Cotter	Adaniza Malicoat	George Cotter	Daniel Malicoat
16172	Rounds, Adelia	OK	1850		John Wood	Equilla Haggard	John & Mary Wood	Noah & Sara Haggard
11691	Roup, John	NC	1862	Wadie Roup	John Roup	Sallie Osborn	John & Polley Roup	David & Lucy Osborn
4959	Rouse, Adaline	VA	1841	J R Rouse	John Heath	Alcie Powers	Abraham Heath & Vinie Redie	James Powers & Mimie Reed
14829	Rouse, W S	VA	1867		J P Rouse	Adaline Heath	Isaac & Margrete Rouse	John & Alcie Heath
14646	Routh, Gains	AZ	1869		A P Routh	Martha Sloan		A C & Mary Sloan
2496	Rowe, Daniel	OK	1853	Elisa Rowe	David Rowe	Elizabeth Vann	Dick Rowe	Avis Vann
22290*	Rowe, Eliza	OK	1860	Ben Vann	Louis Rowe	Chaney Landrum	Jesse & Delila Rowe	Clora Landrum

16203	Rowe, Freeman	OK	1875		George Rowe	Peggie Archie	Primus & Sara Bowleg	Root & Billy Vann
22305 *	Rowe, Jeff	OK	1857	Bettie Rowe	Daniel Rowe	Harriet Ross	Jesse & Lila Rowe	Isaac & Mary Ross
22293 *	Rowe, Jesse	OK	1863	Ben Vann	Louis Rowe	Chaney Landrum	Jesse & Delila Rowe	Clora Landrum
22331 *	Rowe, Jesse	OK	1847	Neely Rowe	Jesse Rowe	Katie Star		
190	Rowe, Napoleon	OK	1849	Leasta Rowe	David Rowe	Betsy Vann	Dick Rowe	Avi & Peggy Vann
7311	Rowell, David	OK	1869	Nora Rowell	William Rowell	Marth Terral	David Rowell & Mary Fountain	Joshaway & Matilda Terral
12074	Rowell, Emily	TX	1882		James Rowell	E J Partin	David Rowell	Mary Fountain
10828	Rowell, James	TX	1851	E. J. & Maggie	David Rowell	Polly Fountain	Jacob & Elizabeth Rowell	Owen Fountain
7312	Rowell, William	OK	1847	Martha	David Rowell	Mary Fountain	Jacob & Elizabeth Rowell	
21658	Rowland, America	KS	1881	Andrew Rowland	C.M. Gayler	Mary Sisemore	Calvin & Casandra Gayler	Wm & Susannah Sisemore
585	Rowland, Andrew	NC	1869	Addie Rowland	Robert Rowland	Margaret Pace		Stephen & Dovey Pace
634	Rowland, Charles	NC	1871	none	Robt. Rowland	Margaret Pace		Stephen & Dovey Pace
545	Rowland, John	NC	1873	Cally Rowland	Jake Rowland	Martha Pace		Stephen & Dovey Pace
6555	Rowland, Judson	NC	1889	none	Wm Rowland	Mary Trammel	Andy & Polly Rowland	Harriett Trammel
632	Rowland, Margaret	NC	1852	Robert Rowland	Stephen Pace	Dovey Martin	Wm & Harriett Pace	Joseph & Mary Martin
6548	Rowland, Mary	NC	1842			Harriett Trammel		Jacob & Polly Trammel
128	Rowland, Stephen	NC	1876	Sada Rowland	Jake Rowland	Martha Pace		Stephen & Dovey Pace
633	Rowland, William	NC	1875	none	Robt. Rowland	Margaret Pace		Stephen & Dovey Pace
11401	Roy, Mary	NC	1840	widow	William Dills	Elizabeth Morgan		
18179	Roy, Susie	GA	1872	John Roy	Anderson Neal	Sarah Davis	Thomas & Polly Neal	Wm & Annie Davis
13772 *	Rucker, Alfred	GA	1829	Sophia Rucker	Pleas Rucker	Alice Nails		John & Lattie Nails
13778 *	Rucker, Bradley	GA	1876	Rose Rucker	Alfred Rucker	Sophia Knox	Pleas & Amy Nails	
18807	Rucker, Naomi	GA	1878	Howard Rucker	James Evans	Nancy Rainwater	Robert & Sallie Evans	John & Julia Rainwater
13776 *	Rucker, Sophia	GA	1848	Alfred Rucker	Albert Knox	Minerva Terrell		Frank & Jane Terrell
13777 *	Rucker, Will	GA	1871	Jenny Rucker	Alfred Rucker	Sophia Knox	John & Lottie Nails	Albert Knox & Minerva Terrell
17040	Rude, William decd	OK	1848	Jinnie Guess	Pigeon Rude		Tee kaw le yes ky	
8174	Rudy, Callie	VA	1877	William Rudy	Joseph Dolinger	Nancy Blevins	John & Elisebeth Dolinger	Andrew & Charity Blevins
8824	Rumberg, Mollie	OK			Daniel Jordan	Susan James	Sarah Jordan	Johnathan & Amanda James
7630	Rumburg, America	WV			Daniel Jordan	Susan James	Sarah Jordan	Jonathan & Amanda James

16915	Runyon, Evaline	OK	1882		Dawson Runyon	Elsie Martin	Sally Runyon	Hercules & Permelia Martin
18933	Runyon, Nettie, & Lawson	OK	1890 1892		Lawson Runyon	Elsie Martin	Robert Runyon	Herciles & Permelia Martin
11904	Rupard, Amanda	TN	1861	Wiley Rupard	John Waters	Elizabeth Maab	Wm & Zilpha Waters	Lee & Mary Maab
12719	Rupard, Amanda	TN	1869	W R Rupard	John Waters	Elizabeth Maab	Wm & Zilpha Waters	Lee & Polly Maab
11906	Rupard, Mary	TN	1885	General Rupard	William Thompson	Matilda Miller	James & Caroline Thompson	Marion & Elizabeth Miller
22124	Ruple, Samantha	TX	1863		Samuel Roe	Elizabeth Allen	Samuel & Rosanna Roe	
12112	Rush, Martha	TN	1863	W.M. Rush	Andrew Harrison	Rachel Mathews	Samuel & Rosa Harrison	A.J. & Easter Mathews
6687	Rush, Mary	KS	1848	Anderson Rush	David Bullington	Mahulda McCandless	Josiah & Nancy Bullington	Alex & Francis McCandless
7316	Rush, Myrtle	MO	1882	Roy Rush	James Foley	Mary Osborne	James & Rhoda Foley	
10291	Rushing, James	OK	43yrs		James Rushing	Cornelia Mitchell		
18703	Russ, Charlotte	FL	1888	Isam Russ	Jasper Shanks	Victoria Barrios		Ferdinand Barrios & Eliza Reyer
49 *	Russell, David	OK	1852	Mattie Russell	Randle Russell	Celie Barton	Randle Russell	
22449	Russell, Edward	IN	1865	none	Harvey Russell	Mary Chandler		Samuel & Pearline Chandler
17784	Russell, Ellen	IN	1856		Barbershaw Bradley	Mancie		
2547	Russell, Mary	GA	1861	F M Russell	Jason Leadford	Lucinda Brown	Ely & Levey Leadford	
18836	Russell, Ollie	MO	1880	John Russell	Henry Neff	Hannah Hammonds		Martin Hammonds & Mary Elmore
19772	Russell, Samuel	TN	1872	Elizabeth Russell	Washington Russell	Adeline Lunsford		
11852	Ruster, Nellie	OK	1883		Nat Ruster			
16201	Ruth, John	OK	1844		H D Ruth	Milley Wheeler		
21733	Ruth, Robert	TN	1846	Rebecca Ruth	Hopkins, Ruth	Millie Wheeler		George & Martha Wheeler
22215	Ruth, Robert	OK	1871	Mary Ruth	John Ruth	Susia Prumley	H.D. & Millie Ruth	Charley Prumley
20638	Ruth, William	GA	1833	Catherine Ruth	Hopkins Ruth	Millie Wheeler		Charles & Frankie Wheeler
22214	Ruth, William	OK	1866		John Ruth	Suria Crumley	H.D. & Millie Ruth	Charley Crumley
22041	Rutherford, James	AL	1854	widower	James Rutherford	Margaret Young	William & Pru-dent Rutherford	Edmon & Fannie Young
11342	Rutledge, Joe	GA	1863		Tom Rutledge	Mary Clark		Jim & Tasey Clark
15313	Rutledge, Louisa	GA	1867	James Rutledge	Benj Owens	Nancy Doss		Edward & Seleta Doss
15312	Rutledge, William	GA	1865	Delia Rutledge	Tom Rutledge	Mary Clark		Jim & Tasey Clark
12463	Ryder, Edgar	CA	1874	Lillie Ryder	John Ryder	Susan Perkins	James & Edith Ryder	Jessie & Emaline Perkins
20866	Rymer heirs	TN				Mary Rymer		Abraham Gwinn
17341	Rymer, Mary	TN	1852	John Rymer	Abraham Guinn	Carnelia Crawford	Alman Guinn	
9823 *	Saddler, Amy	TN	1824	Cab Saddler	Berry Coleman	Elizabeth Coleman		
16055	Saddler, Mary	OK	1847	J S Saddler	James Gunter	Nancy Stewart		

22890	Sage, Gerara	VA	1883	Troy Sage	Jerome Hash	Nancy Peak	John & Sally Hash	Uriah & Carnelia Peak
18942	Sames, Dora	GA	1876	S.T. Sames	R.M. Whitmore	Mary Lyon	Hugh Whitmore & Sallie Chimler	Harry Lyon & Lucinda Harben
20817	Samples, Arzelle	GA	1902		Berry Samples	May Samples	Wesley & Francis Samples	
22079	Samples, Berry	GA	1881	May Samples	Wesley Samples	Francis Gaines	Thomas & Sallie Samples	
20818	Samples, Daniel	GA	1878	Alice Samples	Wesley Samples	Francis Goins	Thomas & Sallie Samples	
21536	Samples, Dock	GA	1874	Mollie Samples	Jim Samples	Malinda Handgard	Thomas & Sallie Samples	
21535	Samples, Ed	GA	1885	Minnie Samples	Levi Samples	Emma Hawkins	Thomas & Sallie Samples	
21537	Samples, Ezra & Mandel	GA	1889 1890		John Samples	Georgiana Bramblett	Thomas & Sallie Samples	
14571	Samples, Florence	GA	1880		Wesley Samples	Francis Ganes	Thomas & Sallie Samples	
22076	Samples, George	GA	1885	none	John Samples	Manda Poss	Thomas & Sallie Samples	
20819	Samples, Holbert	GA	1905		Berry Samples	May Samples	Wesley & Francis Samples	
20820	Samples, Hubert	GA	1907		Berry Samples	May Samples	Wesley & Francis Samples	
21539	Samples, John & Bill	GA	1835 1848	Georgiana & Nancy	Thomas Samples	Sallie Davis	John & Fannie Samples	Cul & Fannie Davis
21538	Samples, Maud et al	GA	1886		Bill Samples	Nancy Hawkins	Thomas & Sallie Samples	
20821	Samples, Robert	GA	1905		Daniel Samples	Alice Hawkins	Wesley & Francis Samples	
14570	Samples, Vader	GA	1883		Wesley Samples	Francis Ganes	Thomas & Sallie Samples	
15311	Samples, Wesley	GA	1844	Francis Samples	Thomas Samples	Sallie Davis		Cul & Fannie Davis
21220	Sampson, Lilly	OK	1884		James Sampson	Sarah Lumpkin	Wm & Mary Sampson	Bushsod & Mary Lumpkin
21225	Sampson, Sarah	OK	1851	James Sampson	Bushrod Lumpkin	Mary Martin	George & Mary Lumpkin	Joshua & Sarah Martin
21219	Sampson, Simpson	OK	1876	Nora Sampson	James Sampson	Sarah Lumpkin	Wm & Mary Sampson	Bushsod & Mary Lumpkin
21224	Sampson, William	OK	1874	Lue Sampson	James Sampson	Sarah Lumpkin	Wm & Mary Sampson	Bushsod & Mary Lumpkin
9860	Sams Jr., Columbus	GA	1892	none	Columbus Sams	Susan Mills	Wm & Mahala Sams	Wm & Annie Mills
19162	Sams, Bright	GA	1855	Ellen Sams	Asa Sams	Pernesia Baker	Lewis & Martha Sams	
9859	Sams, Columbus	GA	1856	Susan Sams	William Sams	Mahala Revis	Lewis & Peggie Sams	Wilson & Elizabeth Revis
9861	Sams, George	GA	1899	none	Columbus Sams	Susan Mills	Wm & Mahala Sams	Wm & Annie Mills
14067	Sams, James	GA	1882	Mary Sams		Margaret Sams		James & Caroline Sams
14068	Sams, James	GA	1860	Nancy Sams	James Sams	Caroline Biddy	Louis & Peggie Sams	Mashack & Nancy Biddy
12329	Sams, Louseille	GA	1906		Marion Sams	Minnie Goodson	Columbus & Susan Sams	Marion Goodson
12328	Sams, Marion	GA	1877	Minnie Sams	Columbus Sams	Susan Mills	Wm & Mahaley Sams	Joseph & Annie Mills
9862	Sams, Mattie	GA	1895	none	Columbus Sams	Susan Mills	Wm & Mahala Sams	Wm & Annie Mills
14066	Sams, Nancy	GA	1865	James Sams	Reuben Darby	Frances Mason	Charles & Nancy Darby	John & Polly Mason

14069	Sams, Samuel	GA	1856	Dora Sams	James Sams	Caroline Biddy	Louis & Peggie Sams	Mashack & Nancy Biddy
9863	Sams, Sanford	GA	1894	none	Columbus Sams	Susan Mills	Wm & Mahala Sams	Wm & Annie Mills
18013	Samuels, Nancy	WI	1862	G.W. Samuels	John Murphy	Elizabeth Bass	Willis & Rebecca Murphy	George Bass
10915	Sanburn, Florence	CA	1866	Charles Sanburn	John Carter	Rebecca Duncan		Charles & Mahala Duncan
13607	Sanders, Alfred	TN	1871		Andrew Sanders	Fannie Warty	John Poe	John & Fannie Warty
20633	Sanders, Alice	GA	1861	William Sanders	Madison Dodd	Annie Maples	Berry Dodd	
22406 *	Sanders, Anderson	OK	1870	Fannie Sanders	Simon Sanders	Sarah Chambers	Daniel Sanders	
20474	Sanders, Archibald	TN	1880		Joseph Sanders	Margaret Mason	Jackson & Margaret Sanders	Arch & Jane Mason
22359 *	Sanders, Ben	OK	1864	Lizzie Sanders	Simon Sanders	Sarah Rider	Daniel & Betsy Sanders	Jim & Esther Rider
1338	Sanders, Charlotte	OK	50yrs	Jesse Sanders		Ah-noo-yau-he	Johnson & Nannie	
15781 *	Sanders, Cudge	NC	1861	Polly Sanders	John Sanders	Eliza Sherrill	Tso go	
20473	Sanders, Edward	TN	1883		Joseph Sanders	Margaret Mason	Jackson & Margaret Sanders	Arch & Jane Mason
17811	Sanders, George	IL	1844	Mary Sanders	George Sanders	Harriet Singleton		John & Clara Singleton
18219	Sanders, George	TN	1856	Maranda Sanders	Alfred Sanders	Margaret Crowder		Overstreet & Elizabeth Crowder
20189	Sanders, J.R.	TN	1856	Lissie Sanders		Polly Sanders		James & Elizabeth Sanders
19316	Sanders, John	FL	1864	Sina Sanders	William Sanders	Prudence Grantham	John & Sarah Reyer	Mathew Grantham & Hattie Gardner
19313	Sanders, John Jr.	FL	1903		John Sanders	Sina Sanders	Wm & Prudence Sanders	
18218	Sanders, Joseph	TN	1857	Ella Sanders	Alfred Sanders	Margaret Crowder		Overstreet & Elizabeth Crowder
18220	Sanders, Lydia	TN	1872	John Sanders	Madison Dodd	Annie Maples	Berry Dodd	
20145 *	Sanders, Mariah	GA	1840	Berry Sanders	Squire Watters	Peggie Simmons	Ned Crow & Millie Simmons	
6824	Sanders, Martha	VA	1876	Walker Sanders	William Hollaway	Louisa Waters	David & Sarah Hollaway	Wm & Zilpha Waters
20600	Sanders, Mary	GA	1880	Aaron Sanders	Allen Avery	Agnis Purcell	John & Susan Avery	John & Charity Purcell
19315	Sanders, Oliver	AL	1856	Mandy Sanders	William Sanders	Prudence Grantham	John & Sarah Reyer	Mathew Grantham & Hattie Gardner
4979	Sanders, Rufus	GA		Maggie Sanders	Moses Sanders	Diana Jones		John & Fannle Watley
21243	Sanders, Sallie	OK	1874	Tom Sanders	Alfred Gilley	Rebecca Moon	Jordan & Leatha Gilley	James & Elizabeth Moon
18767	Sanders, Sarah	TX	1852	J.W. Sanders	Herod Foutch	Susan Williams		Albert Williams
10715	Sanders, Thomas	OK	1874	Elizabeth Sanders	Thomas Sanders	Mariah Gafford	Andrew & Betsy Sanders	Allen & Nancy Gafford
5297	Sanders, William	OK	1871	Ada Sanders	James Sanders	Kozzie James		
17849	Sanders, William	IL	1876	Ada Sanders	George Sanders	Mary Hollingsworth	George & Harriet Sanders	Eli & Mary Hollingworth
19317	Sanders, William	FL	1832		John Sanders	Sarah Mayo		

2256	Sandlin, Nancy	NC	1869	William Sandlin	Dalice Deheart	Sarah Delozier		Ed & Elizabeth Delozier
22178	Sands, Ollie	TN	46 yrs	Edmund Sands	Mathew Rodgers	Rebecca Billings	Jack Rodgers	
14871	Sanford, Rebecca	GA	1867	Ky Sanford	Vann Wright	Mary Smith	Jesse & Lovicie Wright	David & Lucy Smith
12111 *	Sapp, Frank	TN	1880	Eliza Sapp	Samuel Sapp	Mary Broyles		Long Jack & Sidney Broyles
10994 *	Sapp, Judson	GA	1874	Georgia Sapp	Samuel Sapp	Mary Broyles		Sidney Broyles
18043	Sapp, Lula	NC	1879	Robert Sapp	Henry Ring	Sarale Overby	Thos Poindexter	Betty Pledge
10996 *	Sapp, Mary	GA	1854		Frank Broyles	Sidney Broyles		Long Jack
10995 *	Sapp, Rosa	GA	1878	none	Samuel Sapp	Mary Broyles		Sidney Broyles
10130	Sarver, Neoma	WV	1873	Chas Sarver	Gideon Sizemore	Elizabeth Lambert	Geo Sizemore	Hiram & Neoma Lambert
11713	Satterfield, America	GA	1868	John Satterfield	Elliate Boling	Sarah Teague		Thos & Polly Boling
19105	Satterfield, Dora	GA	1867	James Satterfield	James Davis	Mary Morgan	Charles & Rebecca Davis	Samuel & Hannah Morgan
15288	Satterfield, Mattie	GA	1882	Amos Satterfield	George Spears	Mary Adams		Josiah & Martha Spears
17521	Satterfield, William	GA	1843	Mary Satterfield	John Satterfield	Adelpha Trammel	John & Sallie Satterfield	James & Delpha Trammel
19038	Saunders, Annie	GA	1880	W.E. Saunders	John Prather	Laura Lumpkin		Joseph & Susan Lumpkin
19037	Saunders, John	TN	1828		Jim	Sallie Roe		
14672	Saunders, Mary	NC	1883	R R Saunders	Sallamans Hauser	Jane Poindexter	Samuel & Nancy Hauser	Densan & Sallie Poindexter
7334	Saunders, Permelia	MT	1865	W A Saunders	George McMillen	Mary Boatright	Jonathan & Mary McMillen	Wm & Sallie Boatright
14020	Savage, Ader	GA	1882	Balie Savage	John Loggins	Martha Vandiver	Wm & Nancy Loggins	Sofonsky Crain
20254	Savage, Ader	GA	1882	M.K. Savage	Henry Cravens	Mary Popham	Armour Thorten	
20197	Savage, Charlie	GA	1882	Annie Savage	J.P. Savage	Elisebeth Payne		Elisebeth Savage
20152	Savage, Emley	GA	1843		? Hulsey	Elisebeth Savage		Sam Watkins & Jinnie Savage
20255	Savage, Guss	GA	1878		J.P. Savage	Elisebeth Payne		Jimmina Hulsey & Elisebeth Savage
20151	Savage, James	GA	1845	Elisebeth Savage	? Hulsey	Elisebeth Savage	Jessie Hulsey	Sam Watkins & Jinnie Savage
20150	Savage, M.K.	GA	1876	Ader Savage	Thomas Clark	Martha Savage		Elisebeth Savage
20150 ½	Savage, Martha	GA	1847		Wick Smallwood	Bettie Savage		Wash Tolbert & Jinnie Savage
14839	Savage, Sarah	GA	1872	J M Savage	J F Helton			
2021	Sawyer, James	NC	1848	Roxaner Sawyer	Jack Sawyer	Hester Thompson		Nathan & Ester Thompson
19421 *	Sawyer, John	NC	1845		Solomon Sawyer	Tabitha Evans	Solomon & Martha Sawyer	Ben & Lucy Evans
14154	Sawyer, Joseph	NC	1854	Louisa Sawyer	Solomon Sawyer	Betha Evans	Solomon & Polly Sawyer	Ben & Lucy Evans
5467	Sawyer, Nathan	NC	1835	Lucinda Sawyer	Joel Sawyer	Esther Thompson	Wm & Betsy Sawyer	Nathan & Hester Thompson
2005	Sawyer, Thomas	NC	1840	Margaret Sawyer	Joel Sawyer	Esther Thompson	Wm Sawyer	Nathan & Hester Thompson
18039 *	Sawyers, Adam	NC	1850	Lettie Sawyers	Solomon Sawyers	Tabitha Evans		Ben & Lucy Evans

16485 *	Sawyers, Edwin	NC	1838	Tolinda Sawyers	John Sawyers	Sallie Sawyers		
16481 *	Sawyers, Linda	NC	1843	Edwin Sawyers	Thomas Bitting	Anna Gordan	Nellie Betting	
19684	Sayers, Joab	TN	1854		Abner Sayers	Nancy Scales	James Sayers	Nicholas & Mary Scales
18809	Sayers, John	TN	1853	Addie Sayers	Abner Sayers	Nancy Scales	James Sayers	Nicholas & Mary Scales
7792	Saylors, Ralph	MO	1880	Grace Saylors	Zebedee Saylors	Sallie Madden	Thos & Nancy Saylors	George & Delila Madden
7793	Saylors, Reba	MO	1887		Zebedee Saylors	Mary Cravens	Thomas & Nancy Saylors	Jackson & Hulda Cravens
8825	Saylors, Thomas	AR	1850	Luvina Saylors	Jesse Saylors	Jane Parrin	Thomas Saylors	Price Parrin
7794	Saylors, Zebedee	MO	1843	Mary Saylors	Thomas Saylors	Nancy Elliott	Michael Saylors	Archie Elliott
19096	Scales, Bettie	TN	1856	John Scales	Abner Sayers	Nancy Scales	Jimmie & Mary Sayers	Nicholas Scales & Mary Coody
16484	Scales, Emily	NC	1837	Henry Scales	John Sawyer	Sallie Sawyer		
21388	Scales, Fannie	TX	1870	H.B. Scales	D.O. Brown	Amanda Graham	Fannie Brown	Perlina Graham
12371 *	Scales, James	NC	1866	Martha Scales	Harry Scales	Emily Sawyer		John & Sallie Sawyer
18617	Scales, John	KY	1885		John Scales	Bettie Sayers	John & Sallie Scales	Abner & Nancy Sayers
16487 *	Scales, Malinda	NC	1838	Abraham Scales	Solomon Sawyers	Tabitha Evans	John Sawyers	Benj Evans
16492	Scales, Martha	NC	1870	J R Scales	Samuel Shore	Lizzie Coe	Moses & Lucinda Shore	Jefferson & Susie Coe
21681 *	Scales, Viny	OK	1831	Clinton Scales	Sam Saul	Judy Ross		Juno & Joe Ross
20498	Scalf, Sarah	TN	1817		Samuel Keller	Katie Hicks	George & Nancy Keller	Joseph & Parlee Hicks
17619	Scarbrough, John	GA	1849	Tennie Scarbrough	John Scarbrough	Catherine Hanks		John Hanks & Nancy Weathers
17618	Scarbrough, Thomas	GA	1874	Nettie Scarbrough	John Scarbrough	Laura Cass	John Scarbrough & Catherine Hanks	Sarah & Thomas Cass
14805	Sceechowel, Thompson	OK	1852	Fannie Sceechowel	Wahee	Judie Teehee	Lawgi & Jennie	Charles Teehee
19538	Schaever, Sarah	TN	1865	Godfrey Schaever	Cornelius Long	Luraney Shoemake		John & Mary Shoemake
18390	Schram, Lorena	AL	19yrs	A. Schram	F.P. Cardwell	Frances Dees		Wm & Ann Dees
9155	Schrimsher, John	OK	1835	Juliette Schrimsher	Martin Schrimsher	Elizabeth Gunter		John Gunter
13786 *	Scism, Pink	GA	1851	James Scism	Simon Moore	Dinah Thompson	Patsy Padget	Tenny See
13637	Scites, Nancy	WV	1854	James Scites	Owen Sizemore	Rosie Baldwin	Ned & Ann Sizemore	Enoch & Vlcey Baldwin
15852	Scofield, Louisa	MO	1849	William Scofield	James Bennett	Lucinda Williams	Noah Bennett	Thomas & Liddie Williams
22122	Scofield, Riley	MO	1875	Annie Scofield	W.A. Scofield	Louisa Bennett	Walter & Susan Scofield	James & Lucinda Bennett
18081	Scoggins, Henry	GA	1874	Cassie Scoggins	Wm Scoggins	Emeline Sorrow	Washington & Sarah Scoggins	Harris & Adeline Sorrow
18080	Scoggins, John	GA	1872	Martha Scoggins	Wm Scoggins	Emeline Sorrow	Washington & Sarah Scoggins	Harris & Adeline Sorrow
18079	Scoggins, Newton	GA	1878	Lillie Scoggins	Wm Scoggins	Emeline Sorrow	Washington & Sarah Scoggins	Harris & Adeline Sorrow
18078	Scoggins, Samuel	GA	1868	Fannie Scoggins	Wm Scoggins	Emeline Sorrow	Washington & Sarah Scoggins	Harris & Adeline Sorrow

18077	Scoggins, Wesley	GA	1876		Wm Scoggins	Emeline Sorrow	Washington & Sarah Scoggins	Harris & Adeline Sorrow
22260 *	Scott, Abby	OK	1837	Major Scott	Ellis Bly	Mahala	Billy & Susie Bly	
14128	Scott, Adam	NC	1854		Samuel Scott	Mary Spainhour	Leonard & Sallie Scott	Jacob & Sallie Spainhour
20092	Scott, Adam	NC	1860	Philana Scott	Adam Scott	Angeline Hunt	Leonard & Sally Scott	
15645 *	Scott, Anna	GA	1871	Thomas Scott	Pett Lumpkin	Margarette Barrow		Dave & Bobbie Owl
19546	Scott, Arthur	TN	1897		Joshoway Scott	Sarah Goins	Wm & Katie Scott	John & Julia Goins
17533	Scott, Asa	NC	1860	Nervia Scott	Samuel Scott	Mary Spainhower	Leonard & Sally Scott	
14881	Scott, Benjaman	NC	1873	Sarah Scott	Samuel Scott	Mary Spainhower	Leonard Jr & Sally Scott	Jacob & Sally Spainhower
22329	Scott, Benjamin	NC	1878	Lonnie Scott	Thomas Scott	Jylphia Lowe	Benjamin & Thomas Scott	
22326	Scott, Bettie	NC	1880	none	Thomas Scott	Zyphia Snow	Benjamin & Thomas Scott	
8222	Scott, Cora	OK	1872	John Scott	Thomas Allen	Mary Stout	Martha Elmore	
10827	Scott, Cora	CO	1882	Arthur Scott	Oregon Pharis	Margaret Jackson	Onac Pharis	Elizabeth Jackson
14691	Scott, David	NC	1847	Naomi Scott	Samuel Scott	Mary Spainhower	Lenard Jr & Sallie Scott	Jacob & Sallie Spainhower
19552	Scott, Earnest	TN	1901		Joshoway Scott	Sarah Goins	Wm & Katie Scott	John & Julia Goins
21904	Scott, Edna	TN	1899		Samuel Scott	Kate Etter	John & Mary Scott	Jackson & Julia Etter
14703	Scott, Emanuel	NC			Winburn Scott		Samuel Scott & Mary Spainhour	Josey & Susan Flippins
18579	Scott, Franklin	NC	1856	Sarah Scott	Thomas Scott	Luzana Wall	Robert Scott	Adam & Polly Wall
4061	Scott, Georgian	OK	1843	Jack Walker (decd)		Amanda Lacy		Amanda Lacey
19550	Scott, Giles	TN	1888		Joshoway Scott	Sarah Goins	Wm & Katie Scott	John & Julia Goins
19545	Scott, Gracie	TN	1903		Joshoway Scott	Sarah Goins	Wm & Katie Scott	John & Julia Goins
17335	Scott, Hattie	AL	1880	J.D. Scott	John Metcalfe	Martha Jarrott		Allen & Maggie Grant
17608	Scott, Henry	NC	1843	Lucy Scott	Leonard Scott	Sarah Hauser	Leonard & Nancy Scott	
7319	Scott, Henryetta	TX		J W Scott	James Ward	Mary Ish	Jerry & Nancy Ward	John & Mary Ish
19548	Scott, Irre	TN	1887		Joshoway Scott	Sarah Goins	Wm & Katie Scott	John & Julia Goins
17919	Scott, James	TN	1844	Sarah Scott	Jack Scott	Polly Sumach		Samantha Sumach
20910	Scott, James	NC	1863	Carrie Scott	William Scott	Berthia Witherspoon	Sallie Scott	Millie Witherspoon
20975	Scott, James	NC	1837	Silia Scott	William Scott	? Gilbert		
22578	Scott, James	TN	1871	Mannie Scott	Reubin Scott	Fannie Parks	Nathan & Rebecca Bates	Abraham & Susie Scott
3065	Scott, Jemima	OK	1873	A J Scott	James Reed	Laura Jackson	Samuel & Francis Reed	Henry & Matilda Jackson
19547	Scott, Jennie	TN	1895		Joshoway Scott	Sarah Goins	Wm & Katie Scott	John & Julia Goins
6291	Scott, John	TN	1874	Minnie Scott	William Scott	Nancy Buster	Daniel & Margaret Scott	John & Matilda Buster
14122	Scott, John	NC	1885		Leonados Scott	Jennie Flippin	Samuel & May Scott	Joey & Suran Flippin

14722	Scott, John	NC	1859	Cordelia Scott	Leonard Scott	Elizabeth Smitherman	Leonard Jr & Sallie Scott	Andrew & Lucindy Smitherman
15021	Scott, John	NC	1860		John Scott	Sallie Trulove	Leonard & Sallie Scott	Susan Trulove
4887	Scott, Joseph	TN	1879	Mary Scott	William Scott	Nancy Buster	Daniel & Margaret Scott	John & Matilda Buster
17414	Scott, Joseph	AL	20yrs		Gladden Scott	Catherine Shomes	Charles & Annie Scott	Joseph Shomes & Mary Wheaden
19551	Scott, Julia	TN	1900		Joshoway Scott	Sarah Goins	Wm & Katie Scott	John & Julia Goins
17940	Scott, Kate	TN	1868	S.H. Scott	Jackson Etter	Julia Stancel	Peter & Frankie Etter	John & Sallie Stancel
16285	Scott, Laura	NC	1858	Solomon Scott	Adam Hauser	Catherine Scott	Adam & Margret Hauser	Daniel & Margret Scott
15673	Scott, Leonard	NC	1853	Bettie Scott	John Scott	Sallie Truelove	Leonard & Sallie Scott	Susan Truelove
17634	Scott, Leonard	OK	1852		Samuel Scott	Mary Spainhower	Leonard Scott	Jacob & Sally Spainhower
21905	Scott, Leonard	TN	1890		Samuel Scott	Kate Etter	John & Mary Scott	Jackson & Julia Etter
17817	Scott, Lewis	GA	1879	Lizzie Scott	Floyd Scott	Carrie Baxter		Nat & Mary Baxter
21929	Scott, Lillie	TN	1893		Samuel Scott	Kate Etter	John & Mary Scott	Jackson & Julia Etter
20205 *	Scott, Liza	GA	1876	Robert Scott	Bird Cash	Mary Wynn	Charles & Becy Cash	
9385	Scott, Lizzie	OK	1855	Son-e-qu-yah Scott	Dave Pea	Katie --		
20339 *	Scott, Lucie	TN	1877	William Scott	William Gray	Laura Russell	Anaca Gray	Hemon & Dicie Russell
21903	Scott, Maggie	TN	1889		Samuel Scott	Kate Etter	John & Mary Scott	Jackson & Julia Etter
4886	Scott, Malina	TN	1872	widow	William Scott	Nancy Buster	Daniel & Margaret Scott	John & Matilda Buster
6756	Scott, Mary	NC	42yrs	Fair Scott	Marion Hayes	Martha Scott	Lon Scott	
21116	Scott, Myrtle	NC	1891		K.T. Noah	Arminta Hiatt	G.W. & Cathen Hiatt	Tom & Mary Taylor
12494	Scott, Nannie	OK	1856	Walter Scott	William Ratliff	Martha Crossland	Richard & Nannie Ratliff	Samuel & Jane Crossland
14886	Scott, Naomi	NC	1856	Daniel Scott	William Apperson	Mary Edwards	Bennett & Nancy Apperson	Edward & Matilda Edwards
21902	Scott, Nora	TN	1896		Samuel Scott	Kate Etter	John & Mary Scott	Jackson & Julia Etter
14301	Scott, Perry	NC	1863		Samuel Scott	Mary Spainhour	Leonard & Sallie Scott	Jacob & Sallie Spainhour
19549	Scott, Rosa	TN	1901		Joshoway Scott	Sarah Goins	Wm & Katie Scott	John & Julia Goins
21908 *	Scott, Rubin	TN	1845		Nathan Bates	Rebecca Bates		Abram & Fanny Scott
19623	Scott, Rufus	NC	1859	Bettie Scott	H.H. Scott	Ann Hunt	Leonard & Sallie Scott	
18735	Scott, Samuel	NC	1877	Daisy Scott	A.H. Scott	Ann Hunt	Leonard & Sally Scott	James & Temperance Hunt
19517	Scott, Sarah	TN	1859	Joshowey Scott	John Goins	Julia Goins	Thomas & Sarah Goins	Tilman & Diane Goins
22327	Scott, Shade	NC	1884	Lurie Scott	Thomas Scott	Zylphia Lowe	Benjamin & Thomas Scott	
16412	Scott, Solomon	NC	1855	Laura Scott	John Scott	May Spiekle	Leonard & Nany Scott	Thomas Spiekle
21734	Scott, Susan	TN	1847		Edward Cox	Mary Corney	Joshoway & Mary Cox	Lot & Mary Corney

ID	Name	State	Year	Col5	Col6	Col7	Col8	Col9
12233	Scott, Susan, estate of	OK						
14155	Scott, Thomas	NC	1867	Letha Scott	Samuel Scott	Mary Spainburn	Leonard Jr & Sallie Scott	Jonah & Sallie Spainburn
20977*	Scott, Thomas	NC	1852	Sophia Scott		Sarah Scott		Alex & Charity Scott
22324	Scott, Thomas	NC	1855	Zylphia Scott	Benjamin Scott	Elizabeth Norman	Thomas & Donnieal Scott	Wm & Delila Norman
22129	Scott, W. Barham	NC	1859		William Scott	Bethiar Witherspoon	Sally Scott	
14109	Scott, Walter	NC	1863		Samuel Scott	Mary Spainhurs	Leonard & Sallie Scott	Jacob & Sallie Spainhurs
15020	Scott, William	NC	1857	Nancy Scott	John Scott	Sallie Trulove	Leonard & Sallie Scott	Susan Trulove
18875	Scott, William Jr.	NC	1857	Sarah Scott	William Scott Sr.	Amy Hunt	Henry & Polly Scott	James & Tempy Hunt
14838	Scott, Winburn	NC	1860	Celestia Scott	Samuel Scott	Mary Spainhower	Lenard Jr & Sallie Scott	Jacob & Sallie Spainhower
2640	Scroggs, Louisa	GA	1844	Joseph Scroggs	John Robinson	Lucindy Leatherwood	Samuel Leatherwood	Betsey Leatherwood
7501	Scruggs, James	OK		none	George Scruggs	Julia Pack	John & Mary Scruggs	Benson & Mary Pack
1171	Scruggs, Lewis	OK		none	Lewis Scruggs	Julia Shultz	Lewis Scruggs	Ann Parker
5827	Scruggs, Lewis	OK	1901	none	Lewis Scruggs Sr	Julia Shultz	Lewis & Ann Scruggs	
21381	Scruggs, Nathaniel	OK	1859	Belvia Scruggs	? Scruggs	Nancy King		
15575*	Scudders, Alexnder	GA	1882		Taylor Scudders	Mattie Hunter	Lewis & Kitty Scudders	Henry & Adelphe Hunter
15574*	Scudders, Lorrie	GA	1897		Taylor Scudders	Mattie Hunter	Lewis & Kitty Scudders	Henry & Adelphe Hunter
15573*	Scudders, Mary	GA	1890		Taylor Scudders	Mattie Hunter	Lewis & Kitty Scudders	Henry & Adelphe Hunter
14488*	Scudders, Mattie	GA	1850	Taylor Scudders	Henry Hunter	Delphia Hall	Joe Hunter & Katie Milbanks	Evon Hall
15572*	Scudders, Ora	GA	1898		Taylor Scudders	Mattie Hunter	Kitty Scudders	Henry & Adelphe Hunter
15571*	Scudders, Taylor	GA	1842	Mattie Scudders	Lewis Scudders	Kitty Scudders		Buzzard Flopper & Dorcas Scudders
15570*	Scudders, Willie	GA	1894		Taylor Scudders	Mattie Hunter	Kitty Scudders	Henry & Adelphe Hunter
7337	Seabery, Ethel	TX	1881	Tim Seabery	W P Parsly	Mattie Boatright		
18150	Seabolt, Liddie	GA	1844	William Seabolt	Jesse Stancel	Annie Brown	John & Millie Stancel	
18665	Seabolt, Martha	GA	1879	James Seabolt	Francis Griggle	Nancy Pruitt	Jack & Martha Griggle	David & Polly Pruitt
9879	Seabolt, Nancy	GA	1851	Nancy Seabolt	John Helton	Delila Hester	Joseph Helton	Benjamin Hester
17602	Seabolt, Nancy	GA	1881	G.L. Seabolt	John Jones	Caroline Helton	B.L. & Elizabeth Jones	John & Delila Helton
3448	Seals, James	AL	1869	Annie	James Seals	Louisa Hadley	Stewart Hollinger	
6327	Seals, Mrs. Seldon	AL	26yrs	Sheldon Seals	Tillman Lomax	Minnie Keller	Sidney Lomax & Marilda Moniac	Hank Keller & Elisabeth Gillaspy
18392	Seals, William	AL	32yrs	Ida Seals	James Seals	Louisa Hadley	Wm & Lucinda Seals	Simon & Caroline Hadley

15741*	Searcy, Sallie	GA	1870	Richard Searcy	Ansel Smith	Nancy Jenkins	Frank & Tena Hog	Sam & Lucy Jenkins
19205*	Sears, Dora et al	TX			Robert Sears	Lula Williams		Martha Stell
3283	Sears, Nettie	CA	1887	none	Ben Sears	Mary Kell		David & Dorcus Kell
4555	Seay, Eliza	NC		James Seay	Uriah Burns	Sallie Birchfield	Hezikiah & Betsey Burns	
19827	Seay, Myrtle	OK		G.M. Seay	David Shook	Amanda Colvard	Eli & Sara Shook	
6738	Sebastian, Jennie	VA	1860	Columbus Sebastian	T A Fancloth	Christien Hart		George & Polly Hart
8828	Sebastian, Leona	TX	1880	B E Sebastian	J R Reene	S A Yates	Henry Reene	Henrietta Yates
8699	Secor, Mary	OK	1860	Ed Secor	Benjamin Huddleston	Margurett Johnson	John & Susan Huddleston	
7325	Seever, Rhoda	KS	1875	Thomas Seever	J H Miller	Mary Foley	Wm & Susan Miller	James & Rhoda Foley
6134	Segraves, Lilley	NC	1872	Adolphus Segraves	Bartect Blevins	Ealine Carter	Eli & Milley Blevins	Daniel & Milley Carter
20576*	Seitz, Robert	TN	1861	Lucy Seitz	Lawson Seitz	Phoeba Peters		
20577*	Seitz, William	TN	1865	Alice Seitz	Lawson Seitz	Phoeba Peters		
22340*	Selane, Mary	OK	1870	Ruben Lane widow	Charley Pee	Susan Vann		Taloke & Lettie Vann
14214	Self, Adaline	GA	1848	William Self	William Pitts	Mary South	William & Mary Pitts	Luke & Elizabeth South
14489	Self, Cynthia	GA	1866	William Self	Francis Owensby	Mary Thompson	Ephriam & Sallie Owensby	Joseph & Irenia Thompson
10528	Session, Odessa	GA	1885	John Session	William Shaw	Susan Ashworth	Johny & Jane Shaw	George & Christiana Ashworth
16067	Settle, Mary	OK	1863	Anderson Setter	John Setter	Nancy Gaines		Frank & Anna Gaines
22458	Severance, Charley	KS	1901		Herbert Severance	Louisa Dunkin	George & Mary Severance	Daniel & Mary Dunkin
4569	Sexton, Henry	GA	1840	Sallie Sexton	Henry Sexton	Mary Axe	Eli & Mary Sexton	John & Phoebe Axe
5154	Sexton, Lydda	VA	1876	Preston Sexton	Allen Clark	Emaline McClure	Allen & Elizabeth Clark	Eleazer McClure
15081	Shafer, Rebecca	AR		Frank Shafer	James Davis	Mary Martin		Daniel & Sally Martin
19585	Shamblin, Sarah	TN	1851	George Shamblin	David Haskins	Ann Ferguson	Dennis Haskins & Myra Bryant	M.C. & Jane Ferguson
16112	Shamblin, Susan	KS	1873	George Shamblin	James Murphy	Esabelle Graham	David Murphy	Wm & Nancy Graham
19249	Shanahan, Charlotte	OK	1861	Patrick Shanahan	Nelson Rogers	Margaret Scrimsher		John & Edith Scrimsher
18701	Shanks, Julia	FL	1890		Jasper Shanks	Victoria Barrios		Ferdinand Barrios & Eliza Reyer
18702	Shanks, Paul	FL	1880		Jasper Shanks	Victoria Barrios		Ferdinand Barrios & Eliza Reyer
17903	Shanks, Victoria	FL	1850		Ferdinan Barris	Elisa Reyer	Sebastian Barris	John & Sarah Reyer
17923	Shannon, Lucinda	TN	1849		Jonathan Roach	Fannie Guy	Joel & Mary Roach	Marion & Fannie Guy
17122	Sharp, Charlotte	OK	1873		Ned Justice	Betsey Candy	Jack Justice	Tom & Susan Candy

3127	Sharp, Daisey	MS	25yrs	L M Sharp	Charles Hobgood	H E Henderson	Charles & Martha Hobgood	
19494	Sharp, George	MO	1883		Henry Sharp	Charlotta Auxies	Anderson & Martha Sharp	John & Nancy Auxies
19056	Sharp, Henry	OK	1849	Charlotta Sharp	Anderson Sharp	Martha Mazzies	Anderson & Susan Sharp	John & Susan Mazzies
21756	Sharp, John	TX	1870	George Sharp	Henry Sharp	Charlotta Auxies	Anderson & Martha Sharp	John & Nancy Auxies
19055	Sharp, Lena	OK	1906			Nancy Sharp		Henry & Charlotta Sharp
19163	Sharp, Lula	GA	1876	George Sharp	Dudley McIntosh	Lizzie Jones	Alex & Martha McIntosh	
19057	Sharp, Nancy	OK	1889		Henry Sharp	Charlotta Auzies	Anderson & Martha Sharp	John & Nancy Auxies
17576	Sharpe, Nancy	NC	1862	W.P. Sharpe	Isaac Sneed	Sarah Sneed	Ezekiel & Nancy Sneed	James & Elizabeth Sneed
19437	Shaves, James	NC	1854	Elan Shaves	Ned Welch	Charity Shepherd		Dick & Violet Shepherd
9114	Shaw, Adra	TN	45yrs	William Shaw	Leonard Cardin	Cinthia Henson		Lloyd & Sallie Henson
10529	Shaw, Amrose	GA	1888		William Shaw	Susan Ashworth	Johny & Jane Shaw	George & Christiana Ashworth
18340	Shaw, Bass	TN	1861	Jane Shaw	Bass Shaw	Rebecca Kirkland		James & Rebecca Kirkland
10526	Shaw, Ellis	GA	1876		William Shaw	Susan Ashworth	Johny & Jane Shaw	George & Christiana Ashworth
10527	Shaw, Jessie	GA	1868	Fannie Shaw	William Shaw	Susan Ashworth	Johny & Jane Shaw	George & Christiana Ashworth
10525	Shaw, Maud	GA	1890		William Shaw	Susan Ashworth	Johny & Jane Shaw	George & Christiana Ashworth
17652*	Shaw, Richard	GA	1838	Fannie Shaw	Dick Bell	Harriet Mitchell		Russel & Dicie Mitchell
10524	Shaw, Susan	GA	1852	William Shaw	George Ashworth	Christiana Shipp		Benj & Martha Shipp
16176	Shaw, W.F.	OK				Tom Novel		
10523	Shaw, William	GA	1880		William Shaw	Susan Ashworth	Johny & Jane Shaw	George & Christiana Ashworth
5436	Sheets, Calvin	NC	1866	Seanna Sheets	Emanuel Sheets	Charity Orsborn	Jesse & Sarah Sheets	Jesse & Cynthy Orsborn
10821	Sheets, Cecil	NC	1902		Ulysses Sheets	Margret Sheets	David & Martha Sheets	Adam & Susie Sheets
5439	Sheets, Charity	NC	1843	Emanuel Sheets	Jesse Orsborn	Cynthy Ketchem	Elias & Salley Orsborn	Johnathan & Sarah Ketchem
20908	Sheets, Clyde et al	NC	1892		Rufus Sheets	Mary Sheets	Alfred & Mary Sheets	Nelson & Martha Sheets
10812	Sheets, Cordovy	NC	1903		James Sheets	Alice Darnell	David & Martha Sheets	John Warden &Faney Darnell
10819	Sheets, Edna	NC	1896		Ulysses Sheets	Margret Sheets	David & Martha Sheets	Adam & Susie Sheets
8574	Sheets, Everett	VA	1881	Lydia Sheets	Otto Hart	Eliza Sheets		Alford & Mary Sheets
10813	Sheets, Forster	NC	1899		Ulysses Sheets	Margret Sheets	David & Martha Sheets	Adam & Susie Sheets
12999	Sheets, Franklin	NC	1863	Elisabeth Sheets	Alfred Sheets	Mary Osborne	John & Mary Sheets	James & Elizabeth Osborne

13013	Sheets, Hampton	NC	1905		Jesse Sheets	Mary Lowman	David & Martha Sheets	Wm & Alay Lowman
10817	Sheets, Hattie	NC	1894		Alvin Sheets	Luellen Sheets	Wiley & Bethany Sheets	David & Martha Sheets
10820	Sheets, Hester	NC	1906		James Sheets	Alice Darnell	David & Martha Sheets	John Warden &Faney Darnell
10816	Sheets, James	NC	1866	Alice Sheets	David Sheets	Martha Osborn	Jacob & Sallie Sheets	Jesse & Cynthia Osborn
5434	Sheets, Jesse	NC	1869	none	Emanuel Sheets	Charity Orsborn	Jesse & Sarah Sheets	Jesse & Cynthy Orsborn
13000	Sheets, Jesse	NC	1860	Jane Sheets	Alfred Sheets	Mary Osborne	John & Mary Sheets	James & Elisabeth Osborne
13015	Sheets, Jesse	NC	1871	Mary Sheets	David Sheets	Martha Osborne	Jacob & Sally Sheets	Jesse & Sinthy Osborne
22105	Sheets, Lester	NC	1890		Franklin Sheets	Bettie Bare	Alfred & Mary Sheets	Henry & Margaret Bare
10814	Sheets, Luaider	NC	1901		James Sheets	Alice Darnell	David & Martha Sheets	John Warden &Faney Darnell
10815	Sheets, Lue Ellen	NC	1863	Alvin Sheets	David Sheets	Martha Osborn	Jacob & Sallie Sheets	Jesse & Cynthia Osborn
10811	Sheets, Lula	NC	1894		Ulysses Sheets	Margret Sheets	David & Martha Sheets	Adam & Susie Sheets
10810	Sheets, Martha	NC	1838	David Sheets	Jesse Osborne	Cynthia Ketchem	Elias & Sally Osborne	Johnthan & Sarah Ketcham
13001	Sheets, Mary	NC	1840	Alfred Sheets	James Osborne	Elisabeth Ketchum	Elias & Sally Osborne	Jonathan & Sarah Ketchum
13002	Sheets, Rufus	NC	1868	Mary Sheets	Alfred Sheets	Mary Osborne	John & Mary Sheets	James & Elisabeth Osborne
5438	Sheets, Sarah	NC	1871	none	Emanuel Sheets	Charity Orsborn	Jesse & Sarah Sheets	Jesse & Cynthy Orsborn
5435	Sheets, Thomas	NC	1880	S M E Sheets	Emanuel Sheets	Charity Orsborn	Jesse & Sarah Sheets	Jesse & Cynthy Orsborn
10818	Sheets, Ulysses	NC	1868	Margaret Sheets	David Sheets	Martha Osborn	Jacob & Sallie Sheets	Jesse & Cynthia Osborn
13014	Sheets, Vale	NC	1900		Jesse Sheets	Mary Lowman	David & Martha Sheets	Wm & Alay Lowman
14550	Sheffield, Eva	GA	1893		John Sheffield	Jane Philgaw	Everett & Sarah Sheffield	Moses & Lucy Philgaw
5099	Sheffield, Marnie	OK	1854	Thomas Sheffield	John Tidwell	Lucretia Thompson	Young Deer	
7882	Sheffield, Martin	GA	1871		Martin Sheffield	Catharine Howard		Jane Howard
6003	Shelton, Effie	IL	1881	W L Shelton	Pleasant Blackburn	Caroline Frais	Andrew & Francis Blackburn	
18278	Shelton, Elizabeth	GA	1861	James Shelton	John Hicks	Susan Hancock	Elizabeth Hicks	
7791	Shelton, Guy	TX	1885	none	Joseph Shelton	Mollie Gambill	Joe Shelton & Nancy Gilespie	Benj & Mary Gambill
19638	Shelton, Jaala	TN	1856	Wm Shelton	Charles Kelly	Lucy Hudson	Charles Kelly	Obediah Hudson
19406	Shelton, James	GA	1882	Ida Shelton	James Shelton	Elizabeth Hicks		John & Susan Hicks
2517	Shelton, John	GA	1835	none	Lewis Shelton	Polly Harris		
18820*	Shelton, Mary	GA	72yrs			Lucy Spullock		Jerry & Matilda
8192	Shelton, Mollie	TX	1866	Joe Shelton	Benjamin Gambill	Mary Cooper	William Gambill	Milton & Charlotte Cooper
22277	Shelton, Nancy	OK	1879	John Shelton	Jack McGee	Tennessee Mitchell	Robert & Easter McGee	John & Polly Mitchell

11938	Shelton, Rose	VA	1882	C W Shelton	John Spencer	Martha ?	Solomon & Nellie Spencer	
7972	Shepard, Deler	NC	1902	none	Dalous Shepard	Poley Maney	Thomas & Eliza Shepard	George & Elisebeth Maney
7966	Shepard, Doney	NC	1901	none	Dalosis Shepard	Poley Maney	Thomas & Eliza Shepard	George & Elisebeth Maney
7971	Shepard, Poley	NC	1886	Dalous Shepard	George Maney	Elisebeth Anderson	John & Poley Maney	Jackson & Poley Anderson
11256	Shepherd, Eliza	NC		Thomas Shepherd	Martan Maney	Matilda ?	? & Polly Maney	Faney ?
9876	Shepherd, Ellen	GA	1883			Helton		
11254	Shepherd, George	NC	1880	Polly Shepherd	Thomas Shepherd	Eliza Maney	John & Dartha Shepherd	Martan & Matilda Maney
11248	Shepherd, Ida	NC			Thomas Shepherd	Eliza Maney	John & Dartha Shepherd	Martan & Matilda Maney
17937	Shepherd, Mary	GA	1866	Julius Shepherd	John Roach	Millie Roach		Robert & Mary Roach
11255	Shepherd, Mitty	NC	1882		Thomas Shepherd	Eliza Maney	John & Dartha Shepherd	Martan & Matilda Maney
10992	Shepherd, Robert	NC	1886		Thomas Shepherd	Eliza Maney	John & Dorothy Shepherd	Martin & Matilda Maney
11249	Shepherd, William	NC	1875	Lue Shepherd	Thomas Shepherd	Eliza Maney	John & Dartha Shepherd	Martan & Matilda Maney
18174	Shepherd, William	GA	1851	Luw Shepherd	William Shepherd	Sarah Short		Pollie Handcock
14634	Sheppard, Francis	MO	1879	Albert Sheppard	George Loveless	Percilla Brown		Wm & Amanda Brown
21630	Sheppard, Maggie	OK			John Horn	Maggie Sheppard	Jim & Rebecca Horn	
12270*	Sheppard, Robert	OK	1841	Mollisia Sheppard	Eliza Thompson			
7332	Shepperd, Daniel	TX			George Shepperd	Amanda Jordan		Daniel & Susan Jordan
14009	Sheridan, Ella	GA	1875	D W Sheridan	Rollin Pardue	Lissie Loggins	Albert & Ruth Pardue	James & Dicie Loggins
10338	Sherrel, May, Henry, & Fannie	NC			Henry Sherrel	Betsy Hyde		Elbert Hyde
13335	Sherrill, Elisha	NC	1851	Ibbie Sherrill	Jonas Sherrill	Mary Hyatt	George Sherrill	Elisha Hyatt
13860	Sherrill, George	NC	1859	Lizzie Sherrill	Jonas Sherrill	Mary Hyatt	George Sherrill	Elisha Hyatt
13882	Sherrill, Joseph	NC	1856	Nannie Sherrill	Jonas Sherrill	Mary Hyatt	George Sherrill	Elisha Hyatt
11379	Sherrill, William	NC	1848	Mary Sherrill	Jonas Sherrill	Mary Hyatt	George Sherrill	Elisha Hyatt
12073	Shewmake, William	TX	1867	Julia Shewmake	James Shewmake	Centelia McClelland	Edmund Shewmake	
18675	Shields, Charles	FL	1879		Isaac Shields	Clara Clara		Ignatius & Josphine Clara
18706	Shields, Domingo	FL	1875		Isaac Shields	Clara Clara		Ignatius & Josephine Clara
17905	Shields, Isaac	FL	58yrs		Elisha Clara	Josephine Hollinger		
18674	Shields, Isaac Jr.	FL	1877		Isaac Shields	Clara Clara		Ignatius & Josphine Clara
18705	Shields, John	FL	1885		Isaac Shields	Clara Clara		Ignatius & Josephine Clara
18708	Shields, Lino	FL	1872		Isaac Shields	Clara Clara		Ignatius & Josephine Clara
18707	Shields, Mark	FL	1872		Isaac Shields	Clara Clara		Ignatius & Josephine Clara

7323	Shinn, Carrie	KS	1874	Frank Shinn	Kinchen Matthews	Mary McBee	Lazarus & Mary Matthews	John & Katie McBee
7324	Shinn, Louis	KS	1878	Rosa Shinn	Charles Shinn	Matilda Allen		Louis & Maggie Allen
7322	Shinn, Matilda	OK	1853	Charles Shinn	Louis Allen	Margaret Logan	Joseph & Katie Allen	Wm & Matilda Logan
17513	Shipley, Addie	OK	1874	Frank Shipley	J.A. Hickman	Sarah Hicks	Fred & Polly Hickman	Linsey Hicks & Catherine Miller
18020	Shipp, Amanda	TN	1853	John Shipp	George Britt	Mary Britt		
9726	Shipp, John	AR		Fabia Shipp	Josiah Shipp	Susan Smith	Richard Shipp & Sarah McClanahan	
22002	Shipp, Poney	AR		Johnson Shipp	William Haynes	Jane Thompson		William & Esther Thompson
14650	Shirley, Lewis	GA	1840	Sibbie Shirley	Berriman Shirley	Bashaba Jones		
17655 *	Shivers, Alice	WI	18yrs		Thomas Shivers	Millie Revels	Edmund & Joann Shivers	Aaron & Elizabeth Revels
15084 *	Shivers, Cora	WI	1887		Thomas Shivers	Millie Revels		Aaron & Elisebeth Revels
11474 *	Shivers, Elen	WI	1862	Ashley Shivers	Samuel Waldron	Elizabeth Revels	Mike & Polly Waldron	Macaga & Mornon Revels
17658 *	Shivers, Herbert	WI	1884		Thomas Shivers	Millie Revels	Edmund & Joann Shivers	Aaron & Elizabeth Revels
13647	Shock, George	CA		Louisa Shock-decd	Caleb Duncan	Mary Hudson	Charles & Mahala Duncan	
13646	Shock, Ira et al	CA			George Shock	Louisa Duncan		Caleb & Mary Duncan
12062	Shock, Jane (decd)	CA	1860		James Braman	Pressia Wheeler		
19321	Shoecraft, Aurian	IN	1840		Silas Shoecraft	Hannah Currey	Silas & Mary Shoecraft	Mimie Currey
20216 *	Shoecraft, Cornelius	IN	1883		Elias Shoecraft	Jane White	Jeremiah & Patsey Shoecraft	
19256 *	Shoecraft, Daniel	IN	1845		Jeremiah Shoecraft	Patsey Miltan	Silas Shoecraft & May Lester	Anna Miltan
15914	Shoecraft, Jeremiah	IN	1822	Mary Shoecraft	Silas Shoecraft	Mary Jester	Wm Shoecraft & Bicia Nickens	John Raptert
20218 *	Shoecraft, John	IN	1866	Alice Shoecraft	Elias Shoecraft	Jane White	Jeremiah & Patsey Shoecraft	Dangerfield & Lottie White
19118	Shoecraft. Mary	IN	1829	Jeremiah Shoecraft	John Stewart	Virginia Tendley	Chas & Clara Stewart	Thos & Prisilla Tendley
15310	Shoemake, Georgia	GA	1862		Elias Whitmire	Louisa Owen	George & Mary Whitmire	
19681	Shoemake, Jackson	TN	1863		Morris Shoemake	Lourana Sampley	John Shoemake	Wm & Mary Sampley
18609	Shoemake, Morris	TN	1832		John Shoemake	Mary Shoemake	John Shoemake	
19682	Shoemake, Thomas	TN	1860	Laura Shoemake	Morris Shoemake	Lourana Sampley	John Shoemake	Wm & Mary Sampley
1257	Shoemaker, Lizzie	GA	1859	Jim Shoemaker	Wesley Rains	Talitha Rakistrand	Lila Raines	
5830	Shoemaker, Martha	OK	1854	James Shoemaker	John Blackburn	Sarah Miller	Andrew & Frances Blackburn	Frances Weaver
7333	Shoffner, Inez	IN	1875	John Shoffner	W Thorp	Mary Blackburn	John & Narcissa Thorp	John & Thena Blackburn
19604	Shook, Mandy	OK	1848	David Shook	William Colvard	Emily Campbell		John & Sallie Campbell
19824	Shook, Stephen	OK	1868	Dora Shook	David Shook	Amanda Colvard	Eli & Sara Shook	William Colvard

14826	Shore, Jennie	NC	1861	Henry Shore	Archie Poindexter	Elisabeth Ward	Robt & Miriam Poindexter	Wiley & Mary Ward
12821	Shores, Cora	NC	1877	Wiley Shores	John Petty	Catherine Osborne		David & Lucy Osborne
21246	Shores, Jinnie	AL	1876	John Shores	James Hilburn	Rebecca Kerbs		
21254	Short, Joseph	AL	1884	Amanda Short	David Short	Mary Gordon	George & Mary Short	James & Bethshe Gordon
10116	Short, Lydia	WV	1885	Joseph Short	B U Morgan	Elizabeth Smith	Jonathan & M E Morgan	David & Lydia Smith
21259	Short, Robert	AL	1883		David Short	Mary Gordon	George & Mary Short	James & Bathsobe Gordon
262	Shorter, Nellie	OK	1878	Thomas Shorter	James Wright	Mary Morgan	Bob Wright	Richard Morgan
12878	Shortridge, Frankie	OR	1875	Samuel Shortridge	William Thorn	Mary Wiles	Jacob & Malinda Thorn	James & Lucindia Wiles
2821	Shoupe, Eva	AR	1886	Matt Shoupe	William Keith	Mary Coghill	David & Mary Keith	Thomas & Sarah Coghill
22136 *	Shown, Alexander	NC	1853	Lear Shown	Daniel Shown	Melvina Vaught		
21359	Shreve, Sallie	OK	1867	Lafayette Shreve	Samuel Offutt	Mamie Barclay	Beason & Millie Offutt	
17863	Shue, Lottie	MO	1859	John Shue	Robert Sims	Margaret Kennedy	James & Mary Sims	John & Lucinda Kennedy
6426	Shuler, Catherine	NC	1856	George Shuler	Mike Cline	Cathrine Hyde		Ben & Elizabeth Hyde
4559	Shuler, Margaret	NC	1853	George Shuler	Uriah Burns	Sallie Birchfield	Hezekiah & Betsey Burns	
8483	Shuler, Margaret	VA	1884	Wiley Shular	William Dolinger	Selah Edmondson		Isaac & Martha Edmondson
11052	Shuler, Mary	VA	1890	Granvill Shuler	William Dolinger	Selah Edmondson		Isaac & Martha Edmondson
8256	Shuler, Susan	NC	1854	T D Shuler	Ben Hyde	Sintha Sherrill	Ben Sr & Elizabeth Hyde	
17983	Shull, Mary	TN	1829		Jeremiah Scott	Nicey Ward	Abraham & Nellie Scott	Benj & Elizabeth Ward
12247	Shultz, Pheby	VA	1882	Lyle Shultz	Levi Blevins	Evaline Hart	Ned & Nancy Blevins	
9194	Shumaker, Carl	OK	1879	widow	McBee	Katie Harnes	William & Rebecca McBee	Kate Harnes
13804	Shumate, Neva	NC	1887	Calaway Shumate	James Stamper	Sally Wagoner	Wilburn & Cathana Stamper	Henry & Charlotte Wagoner
11168	Shuttleworth, Mildred	FL	29yrs	J G Shuttleworth	Dixon Reed	Rosa Honica	Thos Reed & Cinthia Robertson	John Honica
18691	Sidberry, Ella	FL	1877	John Sidberry	Stephen Banks	Mima Tigner		Charles & Mima Tigner
21346	Sides, Eugene	AL	1883		Jeff Sides	Caroline Jones	Elijah & Nancy Sides	Wm & Naomia Jones
21347	Sides, Jeff	AL	1861	Caroline Sides	Elijah Sides	Nancy Brown	Henry & Susanah Sides	John & Hanah Brown
5163 *	Sills, Cap	OK		Hattie Sills	Jack Sills	Climmy Time	Monroo	Marlissy
20107 *	Silman, Mariah	GA	1829	John Silman	Benj Cheatham	Melvina Gaines		
14922	Silver, Elizabeth	GA	1843	Levi Silver	Julian Parker	Celia Moss	Wm & Edith Parker	
17362 *	Simalton, Antney	GA	1836	Lizzie Simalton	Geary Simalton	Ann Grimes		
10874	Simmons, Ella	WV	1886	Clark Simmons	Abraham Keith	Sarah Osburn	Guy & Rachel Keith	Solomon & Martha Osburn

12445	Simmons, George	OK	43yrs	Annie Simmons	George Simmons Sr	Doo ge	William Simmons	
8489	Simmons, Ida	VA	1875	W. H. Clark	William Simmons	Mary Blevins		Armstrong & Catharine Blevins
13606	Simmons, Ida	GA	1883	William Simmons	Geo Blaylock	Louisa Rice	Isam & Martha Blaylock	G W & Amanda Rice
13321	Simmons, John	OK	1882		Hully	Polly	Jess Simmons & La sah	Ah da yo he & A le sah
20325	Simmons, John	GA	1847	Hester Simmons	Willis Simmons	Cathrine Smith	John & Elisabeth Simmons	Samuel & Elsie Smith
21465	Simmons, Julia	TX	1873	Thomas Simmons	Francis Crawford	Nannie Cole	Watson Crawford & Margaret Starr	
9004	Simmons, Lewis	OK	1868	Lucy Simmons	James Simmons	Letitia Lilly		William & Nannie Lilly
11948	Simmons, Ransom	GA	1846	Ruthie Simmons	Willis Simmons	Catharine Smith	John & Elsie Simmons	Samuel Smith & Elsie Mattix
11946	Simmons, Ruthie	GA	1853	Ransom Simmons	James Smith	Rebecca Mealer	Samuel Smith & Elsie Mattix	Wm & Sallie Mealer
16036	Simmons, Sarah	GA	1856	R F Simmons	Walter McArthur	Mary Russell	Eleazer & Rosa McArthur	Elisha & Nancy Russell
13137	Simmons, Stealer	OK	1880	Ella Simmons	Hully	Polly	Jess Simmons	Ah da yo he
9875	Simmons, Steve	OK	1867	widow	Jess Long	Bessie	Adam	
11100	Simmons, Susan	IL	1850	Preston Simmons	Isham Blevins	Anna Edmondson	George & Lydia Blevins	
17806	Simmons, Waitie	OK	1887		George Simmons	Carline Elk	Sam Simmons & Goo weelten	Big & Betsy Elk
4171	Simms, George	OK	1855	Bertha Simms	John Simms	Angeline Stuinette		James & Elizabeth Stuinette
20456	Simms, Mary	TN	1873	J.Y. Simms	Joseph Reed	Amanda White	McKenzie & Nancy Reed	Lewis & Mahala White
19355	Simms, Nancy	GA	1851		Thomas Allen	Linda Minion	J & Fannie Allen	Thomas & Nancy Minion
21631	Simpson, Alice	AR	1870		W.J. Hartley	Mary McCauslin		James McCauslin & Jane Ross
12327	Simpson, Andrew	GA	1906		Charles Simpson	Angie Sams	Wm & Americus Simpson	Columbus & Susan Sams
12326	Simpson, Angie	GA	1888	Charles Simpson	Columbus Sams	Susan Mills	Wm & Mahaley Sams	Joseph & Annie Mills
21295	Simpson, Emma	AL	1883	William Simpson	Daniel Lamons	Delila Criscoe	James & Mary Lamons	G.W. & Emma Criscoe
9346	Simpson, Howard	WV	1887		James Simpson	Cordelia Osburn	J R & Annie Simpson	Solomen & Susan Osburn
20717	Simpson, Isabel	TN	1885	Alvie Simpson	James Hatcher	Mary Halbrook	John & Eliza Hatcher	Joseph & Catherine Halbrook
12325	Simpson, Lilli	GA	1905		Charles Simpson	Angie Sams	Wm & Americus Simpson	Columbus & Susan Sams
15080	Simpson, Maggie	OK	1881	John Simpson	A B West	Nann Rutheford	Isaac & Nancy West	
14853*	Sims, Angeline	GA	1844	Abe Sims	John Thornson	Mary Barnett		
20274	Sims, Cleo	MO	1880	Ethel Sims	Robert Sims	Margaret Kennedy	James & Mary Sims	John & Lucinda Kennedy
17862	Sims, George	MO	1859	Cora Sims	Robert Sims	Margaret Kennedy	James & Mary Sims	John & Lucinda Kennedy
13823	Sims, Hiram	GA	1857	Ellen Sims	John Sims	Mary Gibson	John Sims	Hiram Gibson
3527	Sims, James	AR	1854	Mollie Sims	George Sims	Jane Sinyard		Tomp & Mary Sinyard
17861	Sims, John	MO	1861	Florence Sims	Robert Sims	Margaret Kennedy	James & Mary Sims	John & Lucinda Kennedy

17859	Sims, Margaret	MO	1838	Robert Sims	John Kennedy	Lucinda Nicholson	David & Margaret Kennedy	John & Phoebe Nicholson
17860	Sims, Ol F.	MO	1877		Robert Sims	Margaret Kennedy	James & Mary Sims	John & Lucinda Kennedy
20275	Sims, Richard	MO	1865		Robert Sims	Margaret Kennedy	James & Mary Sims	John & Lucinda Kennedy
3526	Sims, Thomas	AR		Leathre Sims	George Sims	Jane Sinyard		Tomp & Mary Sinyard
14982	Sinard, Marcena	GA	1865		Davis Sinard	Sarah Ellenberg	James Jr & Margaret Sinard	John & Alice Ellenberg
14920	Sinard, Martha	GA	45yrs		Davis Sinard	Sarah Ellenberg	James & Margaret Sinard	John & Alice Ellenberg
14985	Sinard, Mary	GA	45yrs		Davis Sinard	Sarah Ellenberg	James Jr & Margaret Sinard	John & Alice Ellenberg
14987	Sinard, Nancy	GA	53yrs		David Sinard	Sarah Ellenberg	James & Margaret Sinard	John & Alice Ellenberg
14986	Sinard, Sarah	GA	1823	Davis Sinard	John Ellenberger	Alice Evett		
10845	Sinclair, Lizzie	NC	22yrs	Paul Sinclair	Billy Meacham	Helen Morse		Jesse & Littie Morse
21867*	Singway, Josie	TN	1881	Sam Singway	Thomas Colwell	Mary Glover	Joseph & Sarah Colwell	Wm & Clara Glover
21656	Sisemore, A. J.	KS	1855	Hester Sisemore	William Sisemore	Susannah Dockery	Richard & Elizabeth Sisemore	
21655	Sisemore, Richard	KS	1849	Agnes Sisemore	William Sisemore	Susannah Dockery	Richard & Elizabeth Sisemore	
14660	Sisk, Mary	WV		James Sisk	George Buchanon	Caroline Sizemore	Arthur & Ibby Buchanon	John & Jinny Sizemore
16711	Sisson, John	GA	54yrs	Kisey Sisson	Ervan Sisson	Kisey Robertson	Richard & Lucy Sisson	Jesse & Sally Robertson
16712	Sisson, Robert	GA		Henretta Sisson	Ervan Sisson	Kisey Robertson	Richard & Lucy Sisson	Jesse & Sally Robertson
11504	Sisson, Thomas	GA	1853	Lou Sisson	Erve Sisson	Lucy Franklin	Dickie & Lucy Sisson	Jesse & Patton Robertson
14687	Sisson, William	GA	1873	Margret Sisson	Seth Leatherwood	Emoline Sisson	Sam & Tersey Leatherwood	Richard & Lucy Sisson
2898	Sitton, Callie	NC		P L Sitton	John Constant	Elizabeth Delozier	Mollie Moore	Ed & Elizabeth Delozier
13487	Sixkiller, Minty	OK	54yrs		Tom Sixkiller	Betsey Sequoyah	Sixkiller & Oo loo jay	Sallie Sequoyah
6341	Sizemore, Alex	AL	70yrs	Mary Weatherford	William Sizemore	Lavittia Moniac	Arthur & Polly Sizemore	Sam & Betsey Moniac
19220	Sizemore, America	KS	1866		James Sizemore	Mary Abbott	Richard & Elizabeth Sizemore	Eliza Abbott
18660	Sizemore, Anderson	WV	1888		Owen Sizemore	Lotty Belcher	Ned & Jane Sizemore	Wm & Polly Belcher
14451	Sizemore, Andrew	AL	1881		William Sizemore	Margarett Black	Joel Sizemore	Joseph Black
14462	Sizemore, Andrew	AL	1883		William Sizemore	Mary Taylor	Wm & Martha Sizemore	Allen & Nancy Taylor
21665	Sizemore, Ben	AL	1878	Genevie Sizemore	George Sizemore	Mary Nobles	William Sizemore	
2560	Sizemore, Benjamin	AL	1878	Geneva Sizemore	G W Sizemore	Mary Nobles	Wm & Elizabeth Sizemore	Marion & Martha Nobles
12936	Sizemore, Bessie	WV	1891		Owen Sizemore	Julia Knight	Calvin & Mary Sizemore	Robert & Matilda Knight
7441	Sizemore, Caleb	WV	1866	Alice Sizemore	Hiram Sizemore	Frances Morton	Owen & Rebecca Sizemore	Thomas & Millie Morton
8051	Sizemore, Calvin	WV	1865	Kate Sizemore	Ned Sizemore	Jane Workmin	George & Jiney Sizemore	Joe & Betty Workmin

9089	Sizemore, Calvin	WV	1877	Effie Sizemore	Calvin Sizemore	Mary Brinegar	John & Jane Sizemore	Jacob & Sheba Brinegar
10129	Sizemore, Calvin	WV	1881	none	Gideon Sizemore	Elizabeth Lambert	John Sizemore	Hiram & Elizabeth Lambert
18657	Sizemore, Calvin	WA	1884	Emmer Sizemore	Owen Sizemore	Lotty Belcher	Ned & Jane Sizemore	Wm & Polly Belcher
6338	Sizemore, Charles	AL	44yrs	Margaret Sizemore	Alexander Sizemore	Mary Weatherford	Billy & Levitta Sizemore	Alex & Elisa Weatherford
15163	Sizemore, Charles	WV			Miles Sizemore	Mary Workman	Franklin & Polly Sizemore	Charles & Pheba Workman
20918	Sizemore, Columbus	AL	1884		Daniel Sizemore	Rebecca Markham	Joel & Catherine Sizemore	Andrew Markham
18653	Sizemore, Cosby	WV	1890		Owen Sizemore	Lotty Belcher	Ned & Jane Sizemore	Wm & Polly Belcher
17318	Sizemore, D.M.	AL	1879		Thos Sizemore		Daniel Sizemore	
9508	Sizemore, Dan	AL	1835		Daniel Sizemore		Wm & Mary Sizemore	John & Mary
12237	Sizemore, Daniel	AL	1876		Daniel Sizemore	M L Woods	Daniel & Anna Sizemore	Thos & Juda Woods
14452	Sizemore, Daniel	AL	1852	Rebecca Sizemore	Joel Sizemore	Catherine Webster	Daniel Sizemore & Anna Hawkins	
12935	Sizemore, Delphia	WV	1895		Owen Sizemore	Julia Knight	Calvin & Mary Sizemore	Robert & Matilda Knight
21424	Sizemore, Dollie	AL	1883		George Sizemore	Mary Nobles	Wm & Elizabeth Sizemore	Marion & Martha Nobles
2561	Sizemore, Dolly	AL	1883	none	G W Sizemore	Mary Nobles	Wm & Elizabeth Sizemore	Marion & Martha Nobles
13484	Sizemore, E.F.	AL	1877		Thomas Sizemore		Daniel Sizemore	
20914	Sizemore, Elder	AL	1888		Daniel Sizemore	Rebecca Markham	Joel & Catherine Sizemore	Andrew Markham
9103	Sizemore, Elizabeth	WV	1854	Gideon Sizemore	Hiram Lambert	Naoma Sizemore	Thomas & Rebecca Lambert	George & Jennie Sizemore
17272	Sizemore, Ephraim	GA	1868	Missouri Sizemore	Seaborn Sizemore	Mary Hayes	Ephraim Sizemore	
9513	Sizemore, Felin	OK	1839	Esther Sizemore	Daniel Sizemore	Anna Hankins	Wm Sizemore & Mary Moore	
18654	Sizemore, Floyd	WV	1892		Owen Sizemore	Lotty Belcher	Ned & Jane Sizemore	Wm & Polly Belcher
10133	Sizemore, Frank	WV	1867	Martha Sizemore	John Sizemore	Millie Green	George & Jennie Sizemore	Polly Green
12109	Sizemore, Frank	WV	1878	Alice Sizemore	George Sizemore	Elizabeth Mitchum	Owen & Nancy Sizemore	Francis & Christiana Mitchum
17154	Sizemore, Franklin	WV	1885		Miles Sizemore	Mary Workman	Franklin & Polly Sizemorre	Charles & Pheba Workman
2558	Sizemore, George	AL	1852	Mary Sizemore	William Sizemore	Elizabeth Barnett		Jno Barnett & Mary Steele
9511	Sizemore, George	AL	1879	none	W I Sizemore	Mary Taylor	Wm & Martha Sizemore	Allen & Nancy Taylor
12937	Sizemore, George	WV			Owen Sizemore	Julia Knight	Calvin & Mary Sizemore	Robert & Matilda Knight
15167	Sizemore, George	WV	27yrs		Miles Sizemore	Mary Workman	Franklin & Polly Sizemore	Charles & Pheba Workman
21667	Sizemore, George	AL	1852	Mary Sizemore	William Sizemore	Elizabeth Barnett	William Sizemore	
22716	Sizemore, George	VA	1874	Mary Sizemore	Hiram Sizemore	Jane Attizer	Wm & Mary Sizemore	
7440	Sizemore, H. H.	WV	1879		Hiram Sizemore	Frances Morton	Owen & Rebecca Sizemore	Thomas & Millie Morton

17317	Sizemore, H. H.	AL	1883		Thos Sizemore		Daniel Sizemore	
18658	Sizemore, Harden	WV	1881	Olie Sizemore	Owen Sizemore	Lotty Belcher	Ned & Jane Sizemore	Wm & Polly Belcher
9589	Sizemore, Harvey	WV		Jane Sizemore	Amon Sizemore	Nancy Backhouse	Hiram & Jane Sizemore	John & Pheeby Backhouse
9590	Sizemore, Hiram	WV	1861	Mary Sizemore	Amon Sizemore	Nancy Backhouse	Hiram & Jane Sizemore	John & Pheeby Backhouse
10122	Sizemore, Hiram	WV	1873	Respa Sizemore	Gideon Sizemore	Elizabeth Lambert	John & Jane Sizemore	Hiram & Oma Lambert
12117	Sizemore, Hiram	WV	1882	Vicy Sizemore	George Sizemore	Elizabeth Mitchum	Owen & Nancy Sizemore	Francis & Christiana Mitchum
12684	Sizemore, Hiram	VA	1852	Jane Sizemore	Anderson Sizemore	Mary Payton	Owen & Rebecca Sizemore	Jennie Payton
6344	Sizemore, Isaac	AL	25yrs	none	Alex Sizemore	Mary Weatherford	Billy & Lavittia Sizemore	Alex & Eliza Weatherford
10120	Sizemore, Isaac	WV	1875	Myrta Sizemore	John Sizemore	Millie Green	Geo & Jennie Sizemore	Polly Green
14661	Sizemore, James	WV	1866		Wiley Sizemore	Marinda Cook	Franklin & Polly Sizemore	James & Sarah Cook
18650	Sizemore, James	WV	1876	Nancy Sizemore		Leana Sizemore		Ned Sizemore & Jane Workman
10115	Sizemore, Jessie	WV	1840	Nancy Sizemore	Hiram Sizemore	Jane Dinkins	Owen & Rebecca Sizemore	
9512	Sizemore, Joel	AL	1867	Virgie Sizemore	Joel Sizemore	Sintha Webster	Daniel & Annie Sizemore	Samuel & Pollie Webster
9516	Sizemore, Joel	AL	1829	Sintha & Sary	Danil Sizemore	Annie Hankins	Wm & Mary Sizemore	John & Mary Hankins
14469	Sizemore, Joel	AL	1886		William Sizemore	Margarett Black	Joel Sizemore	Mary Black
17305	Sizemore, Joel	OK	1866		Daniel Sizemore	Margarett Woods	Daniel & Anna Sizemore	Thomas & Juda Woods
20913	Sizemore, Joel	OK	1873	Mollie Sizemore	Daniel Sizemore	Rebecca Markham	Joel & Catherine Sizemore	
2562	Sizemore, John	AL	1853	Nancy Sizemore	William Sizemore	Elizabeth Barnett		Jno Barnett & Mary Steele
9086	Sizemore, John	WV	1842	Lucy Sizemore	John Sizemore	Jane Arms	Ned & Anna Sizemore	Robert Arms
9509	Sizemore, John	AL	1869		Daniel Sizemore		Daniel Sizemore	
12104	Sizemore, John	WV	1877		Gideon Sizemore	Elizabeth Lambert	John Sizemore	Hiram & Oma Lambert
13005	Sizemore, John	WV	1873	Mannie Sizemore	George Sizemore	Elizabeth Mitchum	Owen & Nancy Sizemore	Francis & Christiana Mitchum
14457	Sizemore, John	AL	1872	Martha Sizemore	William Sizemore	Mary Taylor	Wm & Martha Sizemore	Allen & Nancy Taylor
21664	Sizemore, John	AL	1853	Nancy Sizemore			William Sizemore	
15162	Sizemore, Lewis	WV	1864		Wiley Sizemore	Marinda Cook	Franklin & Polly Sizemore	James & Sarah Cook
17102	Sizemore, Lissa	WV	1884		Miles Sizemore	Mary Workman	Franklin Sizemore	Charles Workman
18741	Sizemore, Lorence	WV	1890			Omey Sizemore		Ned & Jane Sizemore
2564	Sizemore, Luther	AL	1876	Martha Sizemore	W H Sizemore	Charlotte McGlathery	Wm & Elizabeth Sizemore	D H & Matilda McGlathery
21425	Sizemore, Luther	AL	1876	Martha Sizemore	W.H. Sizemore	Charlotte McGlathey	Wm & Elizabeth Sizemore	D.H. & Matilda McGlathey

#	Name	State	Year	Col5	Col6	Col7	Col8	Col9
6336	Sizemore, Margaret	AL	1866	Charles Sizemore	Charles Weatherford	Martha Staples	Charles Weatherford & Elizabeth Stiggins	Jason Staples & Margaret Powell
12235	Sizemore, Margaret	AL	1879		Daniel Sizemore	M L Woods	Daniel & Anna Sizemore	Thos & Juda Woods
14455	Sizemore, Martha	AL	1869	J M Sizemore	Brunson Hollis	Mary Wright	Berry & Mattie Hollis	John & Martha Wright
14468	Sizemore, Martha	AL	1877		William Sizemore	Margarett Black	Joel Sizemore	Mary Black
9094	Sizemore, Mary	WV	1840	Calvin Sizemore	Jacob Brinegar	Sheba Sizemore		Ned & Anna Sizemore
14466	Sizemore, Mary	AL	1875		William Sizemore	Margarett Black	Joel Sizemore	Mary Black
15165	Sizemore, Miles	WV			Franklin Sizemore	Polly Workman	George Sizemore	Joseph Workman
12234	Sizemore, Mirtie	AL	1885		Daniel Sizemore	M L Woods	Daniel & Anna Sizemore	Thos & Juda Woods
6340	Sizemore, Mrs Alex	AL	1843	Alex Sizemore	Alex Weatherford	Elliza Pollard	Billy Weatherford & Mary Higgins	Joice Pollard
12138	Sizemore, Nancy	WV	1886	Garret Carmea	George Sizemore	Elizabeth Mitchum	Owen & Nancy Sizemore	Francis & Christiana Mitchum
17097	Sizemore, Naomi	WV	1870	John Sizemore	Edward Sizemore	Malinda Workman	George & Jennie Sizemore	Joe & Betsy Workman
18655	Sizemore, Ned	WV	1877	Martha Sizemore	Owen Sizemore	Lotty Belcher	Ned & Jane Sizemore	Wm & Polly Belcher
18739	Sizemore, Ned	WV	1890		Calvin Sizemore	Kate Huffman	Ned & Jane Sizemore	George & Kathrine Huffman
2559	Sizemore, Odey	AL	1884	none	W H Sizemore	Charlotte McGlatheny	Wm & Elizabeth Sizemore	D H & Matilda McGlatheny
21668	Sizemore, Odey	AL	1884		Wade Sizemore	Charlotte McGlatheny	William Sizemore	D.H. McGlathery
20916	Sizemore, Ora	AL	1893		Daniel Sizemore	Rebecca Markham	Joel & Catherine Sizemore	Andrew Markham
21666	Sizemore, Otto	AL	1885		John Sizemore	Nancy Allrod	Wm & Elizabeth Sizemore	
8049	Sizemore, Owen	WV	1850	Charlotta Sizemore	Ned Sizemore	Jane Workmin	George & Jiney Sizemore	Joe & Betty Workmin
10131	Sizemore, Owen	WV	1886	Elizabeth Sizemore	John Sizemore	Millie Green	Geo & Jennie Sizemore	Polly Green
13329	Sizemore, Owen	WV		Nancy Sizemore	George Sizemore	Jenney Bauldin	George & Elizabeth Sizemore	John Bauldin
14799	Sizemore, Owen	WV	1869	Nany Sizemore	George Sizemore	Elizabeth Mitchum	Owen & Nancy Sizemore	Francis & Christiana Mitchum
9591	Sizemore, Philip	WV	1865	Cory Sizemore	Amon Sizemore	Nancy Backhouse	Hiram & Jane Sizemore	John & Pheeby Backhouse
10142	Sizemore, Phillip	WV	1884	Eddie Sizemore	Gideon Sizemore	Elizabeth Lambert	John Sizemore	Hiram & Elizabeth Lambert
18651	Sizemore, Phillip	WV	1878	Lola Sizemore		Leana Sizemore		Ned Sizemore & Jane Workmin
17452	Sizemore, Polly	WV	83yrs		Joseph Workman	Elizabeth Reed		
12105	Sizemore, Richard	WV		Ellen Sizemore	John Sizemore	Millie Green	Geo & Jennie Sizemore	
4915	Sizemore, Robert	TX	1868	Ikey Sizemore	Calloway Sizemore	Nancy Davis	Edward & Polley Sizemore	
12944	Sizemore, Robert	WV			Owen Sizemore	Julia Knight	Calvin & Mary Sizemore	Robert & Matilda Knight
14461	Sizemore, Robert	AL	1885	Maggie Sizemore	William Sizemore	Mary Taylor	Wm & Martha Sizemore	Allen & Nancy Taylor

6337	Sizemore, Ros	AL	22yrs	none	Alexander Sizemore	Mary Weatherford	Billy Sizemore & Levitta Moniac	Alex Weatherford & Elisa Pollard
12934	Sizemore, Rosa	WV	1893		Owen Sizemore	Julia Knight	Calvin & Mary Sizemore	Robert & Matilda Knight
21426	Sizemore, Roxie	AL	1878		George Sizemore	Mary Nobles	Wm & Elizabeth Sizemore	Marion & Martha Nobles
14467	Sizemore, Rozetta	AL	1876	W A Sizemore	James Sizemore	Mary Black	Daniel & Anna Sizemore	J C & Elizabeth Black
14479	Sizemore, Rufus	AL	1877	Ulamie Sizemore	Daniel Sizemore	Rebecca Markham	Joel Sizemore & Catherine Webster	Andrew Markham & Ulary Daniels
17320	Sizemore, S.E.	AL	1895		Thos Sizemore		Daniel Sizemore	
18740	Sizemore, Samson	WV	1897		Calvin Sizemore	Kate Huffman	Ned & Jane Sizemore	George & Kathrine Huffman
12528	Sizemore, Samuel	WV	1880	Barbra Sizemore	George Sizemore	Elizabeth Mitchum	Owen & Nancy Sizemore	Francis & Christana Mitchum
18659	Sizemore, Sean	WV	1894		Owen Sizemore	Lotty Belcher	Ned & Jane Sizemore	Wm & Polly Belcher
8052	Sizemore, Seanie	WV	1858	none	Ned Sizemore	Jane Workmin	George & Jiney Sizemore	Joe & Linda Workmin
20917	Sizemore, Shirley	AL	1891		Daniel Sizemore	Rebecca Markham	Joel & Catherine Sizemore	Andrew Markham
12943	Sizemore, Stella	WV	1897		Owen Sizemore	Julia Knight	Calvin & Mary Sizemore	Robert & Matilda Knight
12485	Sizemore, T.F.	AL	1885		Thomas Sizemore		Daniel Sizemore	
9104	Sizemore, Theodore	WV	1877		Calvin Sizemore	Mary Brinegar	John & Jane Sizemore	Jacob & Sheba Brinegar
14477	Sizemore, Thomas	AL	1840		Daniel Sizemore		William Sizemore	
17293	Sizemore, Thomas	AL			W.J. Sizemore	Mary		
12940	Sizemore, W T	WV	1877	M S Sizemore	Tobias Sizemore	Louisa Buchanan		Ned Sizemore & Anna Bladwin
17319	Sizemore, W.C.	AL	1881	Ethel Sizemore	Thos Sizemore		Daniel Sizemore	
2563	Sizemore, Wade	AL	1849	Charlotte McGlathery	William Sizemore	Elizabeth Barnett		
21669	Sizemore, Wade	AL	1898	Charlotte Sizemore	William Sizemore	Elizabeth Barnett	William Sizemore	
14638	Sizemore, Wiley	WV	1847		Franklin Sizemore	Polly Workman	George Sizemore	Joseph Workman
15164	Sizemore, Wiley	WV	1870		Wiley Sizemore	Marinda Cook	Franklin & Polly Sizemore	James & Sarah Cook
10110	Sizemore, William	WV	1876	Matildia Sizemore	Jessie Sizemore	Nancy Walker	Hiram & Jane Sizemore	Milton & Martha Walker
14450	Sizemore, William	AL	1854	Margarett Sizemore	Joel Sizemore	Sintha Webster	Daniel Sizemore	Anna Hawkins
14473	Sizemore, William	AL	1870	Rozeta Sizemore	William Sizemore	Mary Taylor	Wm & Martha Sizemore	Allen & Nancy Taylor
19222	Sizemore, William	KS	1861	Jennie Sizemore	James Sizemore	Mary Abbott	Richard & Elizabeth Sizemore	Eliza Abbott
20094	Sizemore, William	WV	1868	Lucinda Sizemore	John Sizemore	Matilda Lockhart	Anderson Sizemore	John & Mary Lockhart
20915	Sizemore, William	AL	1875	Cora Sizemore	Daniel Sizemore	Rebecca Markham	Joel & Catherine Sizemore	Andrew Markham
14225	Sizemore, Wood	WV	1852	Martha Sizemore	William Sizemore	Martha Milam		
12236	Sizemore, Woods	AL	1881	Addie Sizemore	Daniel Sizemore	M L Woods	Daniel & Anna Sizemore	Thos & Juda Woods
12455	Sizemore, Z.T.	WV	1848	Martha Sizemore	Tobias Sizemore	Lydia Mitchell	Edward Sizemore	Anna Baldwin

16110	Skidmore, Annie	OK	1857	Otis Skidmore	Luney Price	Letitie Coody	Luney Price	Joseph & Jennie Coody
15727 *	Skinner, Sallie	GA	1855		Sam Freeman	Nancy Welch		Billy & Precilla Welch
21721	Skipper, Virgie	TX	1886	Arthur Skipper	Richard Graham	Mittie Sisk	James & Martha Graham	
16068	Skipworth, George	OK	1832	Laura Skipworth	James Skipworth	Polly Rich		Jesse & Betsy Rich
19899	Slate, Andrew	NC		Sarah Slate	Joseph Slate	Nancy Moran	Peter Slate	Perlina Shelton
7328	Slate, Cora	KS	1888	Cal Slate	Charles Shinn	Matilda Allen		Louis & Maggie Allen
19900	Slate, John	VA	1847		Morrison Slate	Phebe Shelton	Isom Slate	Spencer Shelton
21418	Slate, Mollie	AL	1854	Jule Slate	Jack Talton	Lee Burns	Bettie Taultee	Jake Dunn
15309	Slatten, Ada	GA	1872	C Slatten	David Wallace	Ann Turner	Jesse & Liza Wallis	
1956	Slaughter, Alban	KS	183?	none	Harry Slaughter	Sarah Mongrain	Alban & Eunice Slaughter	Chas & Martha Mongrain
1958	Slaughter, Amanda	KS		none	Harry Slaughter	Sarah Mongrain	Alban & Eunice Slaughter	Chas & Martha Mongrain
1957	Slaughter, Harry Jr.	KS	1890	none	Harry Slaughter	Sarah Mongrain	Alban & Eunice Slaughter	Chas & Martha Mongrain
17685	Slaughter, Lou	TN	1863	Jordan Slaughter	Asa Murray	Martha Murray	Frank & Nannie Murray	Thomas & Lottie Hall
19898	Slawter, James	NC	1861	Elizabeth Slawter	Jerry Slawter	Ony Nelson	Jeremiah & Ony Slawter	
17795 *	Sligar, Charity	TN			Peter Sligar	Nancy Cazby		Jack & Rizzie Cazby
17798 *	Sligar, Partheain	TN			Peter Sligar	Nancy Cazby		Jack & Rizzie Cazby
17796 *	Sligar, Viannie	TN			Peter Sligar	Nancy Cazby		Jack & Rizzie Cazby
18620	Sliger, Luvaney	CO	1882	John Sliger		Seana Sizemore		Ned Sizemore & Jane Workmin
22584	Slimp, Mary	TN	1870	John Slimp	Charles Goodman	Elizabeth Streetton	Thomas & Elizabeth Goodman	Mahala Streetton
13873	Sloan, Barrett	AZ	1870	Maud Sloan	Jeremiah Sloan	Mary Lemmon	Absalom & Mary Sloan	
5429	Sloan, Charles	OK	1868	Nancy Sloan	Jeremiah Sloan	Mary Lemmon	Absalem Sloan & Mary Hambleton	Barrett Lemmon & Sarah Mcelhanan
22047	Sloan, Clarence	TX	1886	none	Sandford Sloan	Annie Davis	Absalom Sloan	Mary Sloan
9327	Sloan, Claude	MO	1889	none	Lewis Sloan	Emma Burros	A C & Mary Sloan	Frank & Eliza Burros
21843	Sloan, Edna	KS	1891		Elijah Sloan	Lucy Mizener	Absalom & Mary Sloan	
21840	Sloan, Elijah	KS	1855	Lucy Sloan	Absolom Sloan	Mary Hambelton	Jeremiah Sloan	Elijah & Sarah Hambelton
9329	Sloan, Harry	MO	1896	none	Lewis Sloan	Emma Burros	A C & Mary Sloan	Frank & Eliza Burros
8288	Sloan, Jacob	MO	1865	Deliah Sloan	A C Sloan	Mary Hornbelton		Sallie Hornbelton
11394	Sloan, James	MO	1867	S C Sloan	Jeremiah Sloan	Mary Lemmon	Absalom & Mary Sloan	
11223	Sloan, Orpha	CA	1869	Peter Sloan	Tayler Ridley	Vina Pope		
11395	Sloan, Roy	MO	1884		Jeremiah Sloan	Mary Lemmon	Absalom & Mary Sloan	
9328	Sloan, Ruby	MO	1890	none	Lewis Sloan	Emma Burros	A C & Mary Sloan	Frank & Eliza Burros

21844	Sloan, Vivian	TX	1892		Sandford Sloan	Annie Davis	Absalom & Mary Sloan	
22230	Sloan, Willard	MO	1878	Leatha Sloan	Absalom Sloan	Mary Hambelton	Jeremiah Sloan	Elijah & Sarah Hambelton
10848	Sloan, William	MO	1879		Jeremiah Sloan	Mary Lemmon	Absalom & Mary Sloan	
9827	Slocum, Sarah	OK	1861	R C Slocum	Charles Middleton	Mary Breeze	Wm & Nancy Middleton	
9841	Slocum, Zillah	OK	1866	George Slocum	Charles Middleton	Mary Breeze	Wm & Nancy Middleton	
15750	Slover, Mary	OK	1844	Thos Carter	David Carter	Jane Riley	Nathaniel & Jane Carter	Richard Riley
15749	Slusher, Ida	KS	1874	William Slusher	John Johnston	Mary Kimberman	Thomas & Mary Johnston	George & Mary Kimberman
21783	Slusher, John	CO	1868		Simeon Slusher	Kizzie Salyers		
13971	Sluss, Isabella	VA	1863	M C Sluss	Kiah Billips	Arenia Sizemore	James & Nancy Billips	George & Jennie Sizemore
20657	Smalley, Lillie	TN	1873	John Smalley	John Smith	Martha Hanson	George & Martha Smith	George & Emer Hansel
8033	Smalley, Willis	OK	1863	William Smalley	Feming Green	Margaret Clung	John Green	R J Clung
21255	Smallwood, Benton	AL	1840	Emmie Smallwood	Russell Smallwood	Sarah Clark		George & Hannah Clark
11384	Smallwood, M.I.	TN	1858	widow	James Helton	Tomasha Sexton	John & Easter Helton	Russell & Ruth Sexton
14019	Smallwood, Merry	GA	1851	Jackson Smallwood	William Loggins	Nancy Sears	James & Dicie Loggins	Bishop & Margrete Sears
9031	Smart, Alcey,	OK	1853	Bryce Smart	Isaac Barber	Joanah Petty		John & Elizabeth Petty
2837	Smart, Daisy	OK	1863	L P Smart	William Perry	Susan Wheeler		John & Nancy Wheeler
22313	Smedley, Nancy	TN	1875	John Smedley	Wesley Lewis	Sarah McClelland	Harry Lewis	Ephnoir McClelland
15587	Smith, A J	GA	1849	Mary Smith	Elijah Smith	Margrete Swaney		Nat & Jennie Swaney
6379	Smith, Alice	TN	1881	John Smith	Sol Murphy	Adeline Brown	Marton & Charlotta Murphy	Simon & Margret Brown
958	Smith, Amanda	NC	1843	Elisha Smith	Lazarus Anderson	Nancy Maney	Lazrus & Franky Anderson	James Maney & Barbara Barrett
14763	Smith, Amanda	KY	1858		Solmon Blevins	Elizabeth Quinley	Elisha & Rachel Blevins	
20549*	Smith, Amos	TN	1844	Amanda Smith	Jack Smith	Sallie Freeman		
2883	Smith, Anna	GA	1863	M L Smith	Anderson Neal	Sarah	Thomas & Polly Neal	William & Anna Davis
17934*	Smith, Anna	TN	1868	James Smith	Frank Wycoff	Omie Wilson	Jonas Garrett & NancyAnthony	Joseph & Hannah Wycoff
8840	Smith, Annis	IL	1828	widow	Harris Middleton	Nancy Eddings		John & Francis Eddings
15196	Smith, Arminda	GA	1858	Lafayette Smith	Elihu Randolph	Martha Magaha	Robert & Nancy Randolph	Wm & Rhody Magaha
21070	Smith, Asa	TN		Nancy Smith	Smith	Fania Cobb	Richard Smith	Jess Cobb
12572	Smith, Barbra	AR	63yrs		Frederick Fansler	Celia Monday		Isiam & Nancy Monday
2030	Smith, Benjamin	OK	1859	Sally & Ethel Smith	James Smith	Eliza Perrin	Benj Smith & Ellen Hill	Thos & Euphemia Perrin
9101	Smith, Benjamin	WV	1850	Emily Smith	David Smith	Lydia Sizemore		Ned Sizemore & Annie Baldwin

#	Name	State	Year	Col5	Col6	Col7	Col8	Col9
7790	Smith, Beulah	MO	1870	Thomas Smith	James Foley	Mary Osborn	James & Rhoda Foley	James Osborn & Nancy Lewis
21068	Smith, Bill	TN	1872		John Cobb	Amy Smith	Cobb	
9561	Smith, Bob	AR	1869	Addie Smith	Andrew Smith	Laura Southern	Robert Smith	Warren & Mary Southern
19680	Smith, Callie	AL	1872	James Smith	Wm Jenkins	Lucinda Cockrun	James Jenkins	James Ledbeter
12072	Smith, Catherine	OK		J B Smith	Anderson Elmore	Margret Modral	David & Elizabeth Elmore	
20495	Smith, Clara	AL	1871	Frank Smith	Gotlieb Zimmerman	Clarisa Countryman		Conrad & Catharine Countryman
17958 *	Smith, Clarissa	TN	1847		James Hunter	Lucy	James Hunter	
15561 *	Smith, Clinton	GA	1886	Cleo Smith	Sam Smith	Rhoda Jinks	Pink & Lizzie Smith	Joe Jinks & Elizabeth Morris
16178	Smith, Cora	OK	47yrs	Timothy Smith	Biley Brown	Bettie Laughlie		Hector Locklear
3201	Smith, Daniel	KS	1876	Mary Smith	John Smith	Julia Taylor	Pleasant & Pricilla Smith	Wiley & Rosamond Taylor
6796	Smith, Dave	OK	1882	none	Ben Smith	Cynthia Wicket		Mariah Wicket
20979 *	Smith, David	AL	1863	M.J. Smith	Willis Smith	Amanda Lee	Emious Lise	
20649	Smith, Della	TN	1896		John Smith	Elizabeth McCall	James Smith	Wm & Rebecca McCall
20848 *	Smith, Dennis	GA	1840		? Smith	? Smith	Isaac Boston	Sally Johnson
20652	Smith, Dovie	TN	1894		John Smith	Elizabeth McCall	James Smith	Wm & Rebecca McCall
13834	Smith, Ed	OK	1882		Willie Smith	Addie Hendricks	Ned & Susie Smith	Joe & Ruth Goldeman
19606	Smith, Edward	OK	1857	Lutitia Smith	Ned Smith	Susie Shelton	Ches-qua-neat & Jennie	Henry Shelton
14382	Smith, Eida	GA		James Smith	David Huggins	Jane Odle		James Odle & Elizabeth Chapman
10248	Smith, Elijah	WV	1855	Caroline Smith	David Smith	Lyda Sizemore		Ned & Ammie Sizemore
3813	Smith, Elizabeth	OK	1838	Hueston Smith (decd)	Frank Marrs	Delila Springston		Edly & Betsie Springston
11424	Smith, Elizabeth	OK	1855	McCoy Smith	Edward Butler	Elizabeth Nivens	John Butler	Wilson & Rachel Nivens
20630	Smith, Elizabeth	TN	1877	John Smith	Alexander McCall	Rebecca Frady	George & Caroline McCall	William Frady
21185	Smith, Ellie	TN	1873	widow	John Lindsey	Josie McKenney	David & Betsy Lindsey	James & Betsy McKenney
9576	Smith, Emeline	AL	1833	Ira Smith	Elexander Brashears	Emeline Wind	Samuel Brashears & Rachel Durant	Wm Wind & Sarah Pane
17217	Smith, Emma	AZ	1880	Robert Smith	Samuel Smith	Martha Green	John & Anna Smith	John & Eliza Green
20651	Smith, Emma	TN	1901		John Smith	Elizabeth McCall	James Smith	Wm & Rebecca McCall
12052	Smith, Esther	WV	1825	Andrew Smith	Hiram Sizemore	Jane Jenkins	Owen & Rebecca Sizemore	
7321	Smith, Evelina	OK	1884	Till Smith	Kinchen Mathews	Mary McBee	Lazarus Mathews	John McBee
13737	Smith, Fannie	GA	1853	W.S. Smith	Andrew Whitlock	Eliza Rowson	George & Nancy Whitlock	Elija & Millie Rowson
18279 *	Smith, Fannie	GA	1852		Ezekiel Roberson	Rosa McCarver		

22093	Smith, Flora	AR	1870		Joseph Rogers	Mary Hodges	Henry & Mariah Rogers	John & Jemima Hodges
21482	Smith, Frances	OK	1871	George Smith	Thomas Walker	Sarah Burnett	Sam & Catherine Walker	John & Lidia Burnett
19607	Smith, Frank	OK	1844		Ned Smith	Susie Shelton	Ches-qua-neat & Jennie	Henry Shelton
3826	Smith, Galdia	KS	1888		John Smith	Julia Taylor	Pleasant & Pricilla Smith	Wiley & Rosamond Taylor
18616	Smith, George	TN	1859	Matilda Smith	Charles Smith	Amy Finley	Harrison & Mary Smith	Sam & Matilda Finley
19481	Smith, George	SC	1835	Elizabeth Smith	Long Will	Betsy Smith		Betsy Smith
20079	Smith, George	TN		Georgia Smith	Eli Smith	Mary Curtis	Gipson & Edith Smith	Joshua & Elizabeth Curtis
20488	Smith, George	GA	1895		Frank Smith	Clara Zimmerman	Wm & Emily Smith	Gotlieb & Clarisa Zimmerman
21131	Smith, Georgia	TN	1877	Will Smith	Samuel Carver	Americus Sams	Andy Thacker & Seveilia Carver	Acy & Pernica Sams
20372	Smith, Gladdis	AL	1905		Frank Smith	Clara Zimmerman	Wm & Emily Smith	Gotlieb & Clarissa Zimmerman
6755	Smith, Hannah	NC	1867	widow	Monroe Franknum	Ann Judlis	John & Catherine Judlis	
9562	Smith, Harlan	OK	1873	Narcissus Smith	Andrew Smith	Laura Southern	Robert Smith	Warren & Mary Southern
15308	Smith, Harvey	GA			W.C. Smith	Minnie Whitmire		George & Jane Whitmire
20400	Smith, Hazel	GA	1895		Frank Smith	Clara Zimmerman	Wm & Emmy Smith	Gotlieb & Clarisa Zimmerman
3128	Smith, Helen	MS	1875	Joe Smith	Jerry Coleman	Mary Hobgood		Charley & Martha Hobgood
3828	Smith, Helen	KS	1901	none	John Smith	Julia Taylor	Pleasant & Pricilla Smith	Wiley & Rosamond Taylor
19717	Smith, Henry	TN	1865	Johney Smith	Eli Smith	Mary Curtis	Gip & Edith Smith	Joshua & Betsey Curtis
15307	Smith, Homer	GA			W.C. Smith	Minnie Whitmire		George & Jane Whitmire
15306	Smith, Howard	GA	1896		W.C. Smith	Minnie Whitmire		George & Jane Whitmire
3899	Smith, Ira Bell	GA	1878	J A Smith	Andrew York	Mary Rogers	John & Sarah York	Samuel Rogers
11950	Smith, J.C.	GA	1839	Catharine Smith	William Smith	Tempie Edmunds		Ellen Moss Smith
5862	Smith, James	OK	1856	Mary Smith	Pig Smith	Eliza Hildebrand		John Hildebrand
7745	Smith, James	NC	1857	Louvia Smith	Levi McToy	Mary Smith	Wm & Patsy McToy	
9362	Smith, James	OK	1881	Patsy Smith	John Smith	Catherine Elmore		Anderson Elmore
12425	Smith, James	WV	1853	Annie Smith	Andy Smith	Esther Sizemore		Owen Sizemore & Rebeca Anderson
15305	Smith, James	GA	1900		W.C. Smith	Minnie Whitmire		George & Jane Whitmire
15724*	Smith, James	GA	1872	Maggie Smith	Ansel Smith	Nancy Jenkins	Frank & Tena Hog	Sam & Lucy Jenkins
19719	Smith, James	TN	1863	Dovey Smith	Eli Smith	Mary Curtis	Gip & Edith Smith	Joshua & Betsey Curtis
20978*	Smith, James	AL	1886		Willis Smith	Amanda Lee	Emious Lise	
18280*	Smith, Jane	GA	1855	Monroe Smith	Major Campbell	Lucy Campbell		

1551	Smith, Jennie	AR	1874	widow	James Glass	Cor-hi-ni	Cou-see-ni & Tah-li-yi	All Kinny
19164	Smith, Jerry	GA	1884	Mattie Smith	William Smith	Nanny Niolin	Jerry & Juda Smith	
3827	Smith, Jess	KS	1884	none	John Smith	Julia Taylor	Pleasant & Pricilla Smith	Wiley & Rosamond Taylor
15304	Smith, Jessie	GA	1902		W.C. Smith	Minnie Whitmire		George & Jane Whitmire
10744	Smith, John	OK	1866	Nannie Smith	Matthew Smith	Martha Berry	Goodman & Sallie Smith	Michael & Mary Berry
15887	Smith, John	AL	1833	Lucinda Smith	John Smith	Kissie McNeir		
19442	Smith, John	GA	1848	Martha Smith	Jim Stovall	Eliza Bray		Lynda Bray
20650	Smith, John	TN	1905		John Smith	Elizabeth McCall	James Smith	Wm & Rebecca McCall
21358	Smith, Joseph	AL	1885		William Smith	Mary Cryor		
22732	Smith, Josephine	TN	1866	Thomas Smith	John Curtis	Amandy Hatcher	Joshua Curtis	William Hatcher
1680	Smith, Julia	KS	1858	John Smith	Wiley Taylor	Rosamond Stamper	Samuel & Hester Taylor	Eli & Susanna Stamper
15303	Smith, Julia	GA	1870	M D Smith	George Whitmire	Jane Reeves	James & Carrie Whitmire	
20849	Smith, Katie	GA	1885	Jesse Smith	Henry Wooten	Aley Sorrow	John Wooten	Harris Sorrow
20980	Smith, L.A.	AL	1884	Sis Smith	Willis Smith	Amanda Lee	Emmious Lise	
21564	Smith, Leah	GA	1861	L.T. Smith	Harrison Cooley	Adaline Jones		Harriette Jones
20850	Smith, Lena	GA	1889	Will Smith	Tyre Whitlock	Alice	Wm & Caroline Whitlock	
22203	Smith, Lena	CA	1879	widow	John Ryder	Susan Perkins	Dr & Edith Ryder	Jessie & Evaline Perkins
18974	Smith, Lidie	TN	33yrs		Moses Mayfield	Margret Green	Daniel Green	Anie
15554	Smith, Lilly	GA	1882	Robert Smith	Benj McConnell	Georgia Gregory	Frank & Liza McConnell	Ephraim & Caroline Gregory
2978	Smith, Lizzie	OK	1874	C H Smith decd				
17064	Smith, Lizzie	OK	1861		Harrison Smith	Jane Henson	Bu & Nelly Ragsdale	James & Elizabeth Henson
9834	Smith, Louis	AL		Nancy Smith	Oliver Smith	Zilley Ledbetter		Wm Ledbetter & Roda Williamson
7744	Smith, Louranie	NC	1862	James Smith	David Murphy	Caroline McMullen	WhipLash & Polly Murphy	Joseph & Nellie McMullen
15940	Smith, Luther	GA	1877	Emma Smith	Bob Smith	Jane Fagan	John & Betsy Smith	Terrell Fagan
3689	Smith, Maggie	CA	1873	W B Smith	S S Smith	Martha Green	John Smith & Anna Ernest	John Green & Eliza Snowden
17650	Smith, Malica	GA	1868	Merick Smith	Henry Hatcher	Betsey Parris	Wm & Charlotte Hatcher	Aaron Parris & Celia Tidwell
12930	Smith, Malinda	IN	1840	Anthony Smith	Samuel Waldron	Elizabeth Revels	Mike & Polly Waldron	Macaga & Mormon Revels
21110	Smith, Mandy	TN		Samuel Smith	T.J. Jefferson	Mary	T.J. Jason	Jefferson
16166	Smith, Manerva	OK	1845	Tom Smith	George Griffith	Margret Slaughter	Judi Griffith	John & Milly Slaughter
9364	Smith, Margaret	AR	1853	James Smith	Thomas McCollough	Lovicie Bays	Moses McCollough	Letta Bays
17950	Smith, Martha	TN	1850	John Smith	Samuel Porter	Irene Chastain	Hugh Porter	Wm & Mary Chastain
20731	Smith, Martha	TN			John Smith	Theodocie Cowen	Eli & Jane Smith	
20851	Smith, Martha	GA	1882	Luther Smith	Ebenezer Barnett	Haley Evans		Robert & Sallie Evans

12927 *	Smith, Mary	IN	1859	Thedore Smith	Alfred Weaver	Charity Revels	Bird & Sarah Weaver	Macaga & Mornon Revels
13331	Smith, Mary	WV	1879	John Smith	Gideon Sizemore	Elizabeth Lambert	John Sizemore & Jenne Armes	Hiram & Ima Lambert
15552	Smith, Mary	GA	1871	William Smith	James Millwood	Nancy Wimpey	Hugh & Miram Millwood	Henry & Betsy Wimpey
15553 *	Smith, Mary	GA	1889		Sam Smith	Rhoda Jinks	Pink & Lizzie Smith	Joe Jinks & Elizabeth Morris
19165	Smith, Mary	GA	1867	Charlie Smith	Jim Jones	Mary Cash		Billy Cash
19897	Smith, Mary	NC		Robert Smith	Wm Jackson	Laura Simmons	Pete Jackson & Sarah Thore	Gabriel & Emily Simmons
20081	Smith, Mary	TN	1836	Eli Smith	Joshua Curtis	Elizabeth Hatcher	Joshua & Jane Curtis	John & Rittie Hatcher
21293	Smith, Mary	OK	1860	James Smith	George Biddy	Edna McDonald	Elvin & Elizabeth Biddy	Tillman & Louise McDonald
22381	Smith, Mary	NC	1881	H P Smith	Jessie Isaacs	Mary Scott	Joseph & Frankie Isaacs	Benjamin & Bettie Scott
20489	Smith, Maud	GA	1893		Frank Smith	Clara Zimmerman	Wm & Emily Smith	Gotlieb & Clarisa Zimmerman
17189	Smith, Maude	OK	1876	John Smith	Thomas Houston	Martha Pierce	Charlotte Houston	Wm & Mary Pierce
13715	Smith, McCoy	OK	1847	Jennie Smith	Ned Smith	Susie Shelton	Ches qua neat & Jennie	Henry Shelton
15302	Smith, Minnie	GA	1876	W C Smith	George Whitmire	Jane Reeves		
18834	Smith, Minnie	MO	1882	Austin Smith	Henry Neff	Hannah Hammonds		Martin Hammonds & Mary Elmore
14163	Smith, Mourning	TN		C. Smith	Sam Strong	Margarite Rich	Johnie Rich	
20531	Smith, Nancy	TN	1854		Jesse Colvard	Sarah Cooper	Wm & Rachel Colvard	Pleasant & Delila Cooper
21030	Smith, Narcissa	OK	1850	J.M. Smith	Hercules Martin	Parmelia Griffin	Tuxie-oou-ste	
19896	Smith, Norma	NC	5 mos		William Smith	Mary Jackson	Cooper & Martha Smith	Wm & Lara Jackson
22094	Smith, Oliver	OK	1865	Mary Smith	Oliver Smith	Zillah Ledbetter		
5861	Smith, Redbird	OK	1850	Lucy Smith	Pig Smith	Eliza Hildebrand		John Hildebrand
15551 *	Smith, Rhoda	GA	1853	Sam Smith	Joe Jinks	Elizabeth Morris	Richard Roe & Sarah Ceasars	John & Eunice Leonard
19605	Smith, Roach et al	OK			Frank Smith	Sallie Young	Ned & Susie Smith	Joe & Polly Young
15550 *	Smith, Robert	GA	1880	Elizabeth Smith	Sam Smith	Rhoda Jenks	Pink & Lizzie Smith	Joe Jenks & Elizabeth Morris
7320	Smith, Rosa	OK	1887	Oliver Smith	Luther Burns	Allice French	Willis & Keziah Burns	Robert & Sarah French
15301	Smith, Rosa	GA	1904		W.C. Smith	Minnie Whitmire		George & Jane Whitmire
20527	Smith, Sallie	TN	1887		W.B. Smith	Nancy Colvard	Pleas & Mary Smith	Jesse & Sarah Colvard
8423	Smith, Sam	NC	43yrs	decd	Martin Murphy	Margaret Smith	Whiplash & Polly Murphy	Jonathan & Sally Smith
20080	Smith, Sam	TN	1868	Elizabeth Smith	Eli Smith	Mary Curtis	Gipson & Edith Smith	Joshua & Elizabeth Curtis
678	Smith, Sarah	OK	1871	Tomas Smith	Francis Houseman	Mary Garrett	James & Srophona Houseman	Hesikiah & Margrett Garrett
11579	Smith, Sarah	KY	1844	Jonas Smith	Elijah Baker	Margaret Caldwell	Elijah & Sallie Baker	Joseph & Catharine Caldwell
18170 *	Smith, Sarah	TN	54yrs	Tom Smith	Randle Moss	Rosie Toka		Sindy & Pashion Toka

ID	Name	State	Year	Spouse	Father	Mother	Paternal GP	Maternal GP
18215 *	Smith, Sarah	TN	1844	Benj Smith	George Moseley	Rachel Mitchel	James & Nancy Moseley	Henry & Sarah Woodside
20393	Smith, Sarah	TN	1844	Ben Smith	Jefferson Mitchel	Sarah Woodside		Polly Rodgers
13898	Smith, Simmie	OK	1872	William Smith	Levi Robbins	Sarah Stout		
6556	Smith, Susan	NC	29yrs	Ed Smith	Henry Whitaker	Martha Scott		Lon Scott
1309	Smith, Thomas	OK	1863	Cynthia Smith	James Smith	Eliza Perrin	Benj Smith & Ellen Hill	Thomas & Euphrmie Perrin
16168	Smith, Tim	OK	1852		Elex Smith	Jane Martain		Ebenezer & Elizabeth Martain
18700	Smith, Victoria	FL	1883	Horrac Smith	Jasper Shanks	Victoria Barrios		Ferdinand Barrios & Eliza Reyer
14384	Smith, Volcy	AL	1881		John Mattor	Caroline Baker	Wm Mattor & Nancy Newman	Wm McIntosh
3832	Smith, Walter	KS	1895	none	John Smith	Julia Taylor	Pleasant & Pricilla Smith	Wiley & Rosamond Taylor
19234	Smith, Wesley	TN	1874	Anie Smith	John Smith			
783	Smith, William	OK	1849	none	William Smith Sr.	Emma Brown		John & Elizabeth Brown
1768	Smith, William	OK	1861	Mary Smith	James Smith	Eliza Perrin	Benj Smith & Ellen Hill	Thomas & Euphemia Perrin
3831	Smith, William	KS	1890	none	John Smith	Julia Taylor	Pleasant & Pricilla Smith	Wiley & Rosamond Taylor
9363	Smith, William	OK	1870	Ida Smith	John Smith	Catherine Elmore		Anderson Elmore
19716	Smith, William	TN	1875	Mary Smith	Eli Smith	Mary Curtis	Gip & Edith Smith	Joshua & Betsey Curtis
20487	Smith, William	GA	1892		Frank Smith	Clara Zimmerman	Wm & Emily Smith	Gotlieb & Clarisa Zimmerman
21552	Smith, Willie	GA	1869		Robert Smith	Cornelia Hawkins	Robert Smith	Robert & Annie Hawkins
2451	Smith, Zillah	AL	1834		William Ledbetter	Malinda Williams	Johnson Ledbetter	John Williams
20912	Smitherman, Drucilla	AL	1882	James Smitherman	James Beasley	Emley Sims	Wm & Liza Beasley	John & Mary Sims
14121	Smitherman, Isabella	NC	1859	John Smitherman	William Martin	Margaret Houser	John & Jennie Martin	John & Elizabeth Houser
14895	Smitherman, James	NC	1862	Alice Smitherman	Abner Smitherman	Sarah Trulove	Andrew & Lucinda Smitherman	Austin & Patsie Trulove
14123	Smitherman, John	NC	1854	Isabel Smitherman	Abner Smitherman	Sarah Trulove	Andrew & Lucinda Smitherman	Austin & Patsie Trulove
14894	Smitherman, Robert	NC	1867	Cordelia Smitherman	Abner Smitherman	Sarah Trulove	Andrew & Lucinda Smitherman	Austin & Patsie Trulove
19625	Smitherman, Sarah	NC	1868	Abner Smitherman	Austin Trulove	Patsy Poindexter		John & Sarah Poindexter
14894 ½	Smitherman, Thomas	NC		M A Smitherman	Abner Smitherman	Sarah Trulove	Andrew & Lucinda Smitherman	Austin & Patsie Trulove
19659	Smoots, Elizabeth	MO	1849		Summus Smoots	Salla Buckley	James & Mary Smith	John Buckley & Hannah Tanna
21612	Smyth, Isaac	TN	1857	Margarette Smyth	John Smyth	Elizabeth Snavely	Jacob & Susan Smyth	George Snavely
21611	Smyth, Joseph	TN	1855	Mary Smyth	John Smyth	Elizabeth Snavely	Jacob & Susan Smyth	George Snavely
17964	Smyth, Sarah	VA	22yrs	Wm Smyth	James Hayes	Mary Blevins	Granville & Sarah Hayes	Tobias & Susan Blevins
20273	Snead, Maud	OK	1878	Orville Snead	Green McCollum	Martha Orr	John & Sofronia McCollum	Samuel & Christoina Orr

#	Name	State	Year	Spouse	Father	Mother	Paternal Grandparents	Maternal Grandparents
2433	Sneed, Cordelia	NC	1879	Harve Sneed	J M Davis	Lurane McDonald	Reason & Servilla Davis	Jim & Vina McDonald
22126	Sneed, Gertie	NC	1895	none	Robert Sneed	Lillie Dockery	Morgan & Jane Sneed	Andrew & Martha Dockery
2255	Sneed, Lillie	NC	1876	Bob Sneed	A J Dockery	Martha McLoud	James & Bitha Dockery	Harvie & Sallie McLoud
17575	Sneed, Meredith	NC	1879	Deda Sneed	Isaac Sneed	Sarah Sneed	Ezekiel & Nancy Sneed	James & Elizabeth Sneed
17574	Sneed, Sarah	NC	1836	Isaac Sneed	James Sneed	Elizabeth Veal		
11772	Sneed, Thomas	TX	1864	Martha Sneed	Isaac Sneed	Sarah Sneed		James & Elizabeth Sneed
11771	Sneed, Willliam	TX	1866	Ida Sneed	Isaac Sneed	Sarah Sneed		James & Elizabeth Sneed
5574	Snow, Laura	MO	1867	W P Snow	William Hagar	Sarah Fullerton	Anthony & Sarah Hagar	Taylor & Mary Fullerton
22323	Snow, Susan	NC	1875	Richard Snow	Thomas Scott	Jylphia Lowe	Benjamin & Thomas Scott	
12119	Snowden, Mary	KY	1854	Troy Snowden	James Baker	Etta Pitts	Elijah & Margaret Baker	Thomas & Mary Pitts
19507	Snyder, Orville	MO	1876	Pearl Snyder	James Snyder	Fannie Bunch	Pearson Snyder	Daniel & Delila Bunch
4355	Snyder, Susan	AR	1868	Samuel Snyder	Alfred Martin	Louisa Tillman	William & Susan Martin	John & Lydia Tillman
2716	Sorrells, Catherine	OK	1867	George Sorrells	Simon Lewis	Mary Hildebrand		David Hildebrand & Elizabeth Carter
22301*	Sorril, Morris	OK	1875	Ida Sorril	Morris Sorril Sr.	Dicy Sanders		Jack Corner & Ardie Coody
18711	Sosebee, Ada	GA	1880		John Sosebee	Nancy Popham	Ephram & Sarah Sosebee	A.M. & Elizabeth Popham
15430	Sosebee, Amanda	GA	1860	J H T Sosebee	Thomas Dooley	Martha Townsend		Tom Townsend
15646*	Sosebee, Emma	GA	1854	Seph Sosebee	Gilford Chandler	Mary Brown	Stokes & Hannah Chandler	Jenkins & Martha Hammonds
18850	Sosebee, Ephram	GA	1875	Ida Sosebee	John Sosebee	Nancy Popham	Ephram & Sarah Sosebee	A.M. & Elizabeth Popham
14487	Sosebee, George	GA	1891		Solomon Sosebee	Martha Millwood	Solomon & Polly Sosebee	Hugh & Miriam Millwood
18852	Sosebee, James	GA	1867	Nancy Sosebee	Drury Sosebee	Nancy Haney	Ephram & Sarah Sosebee	
14486	Sosebee, Jobe	GA	1882		Solomon Sosebee	Sarah Millwood	Solomon & Polly Sosebee	Hugh & Miriam Millwood
15736*	Sosebee, John	GA	1873	Nellie Sosebee	Ephriam Sosebee	Emma Brown	Sarah Sosebee	Guilford & Mary Chandler
18552	Sosebee, John	GA	1846	Nancy Sosebee	Ephriem Sosebee	Sarah Church	Wm & Nancy Sosebee	Timothy & Polly Church
18712	Sosebee, Julia	GA	1873		John Sosebee	Nancy Popham	Ephram & Sarah Sosebee	A.M. & Elizabeth Popham
14485	Sosebee, Katie	GA	1897	Solomon Sosebee	Solomon Sosebee	Mattie Millwood	Solomon & Polly Sosebee	Hugh & Miriam Millwood
11312	Sosebee, Mattie	GA	1858	Solomon Sosebee	Hugh Millwood	Miram Whitlock	Benj Malew & Rachel Millwood	Dock & Sallie Whitlock
18713	Sosebee, Minnie	GA	1884		John Sosebee	Nancy Popham	Ephram & Sarah Sosebee	A.M. & Elizabeth Popham
14484	Sosebee, William	GA	1878	Dora Sosebee	Solomon Sosebee	Sarah Millwood	Solomon & Polly Sosebee	Hugh & Miriam Millwood
18851	Sosebee, William	GA	1868	Mary Sosebee	John Sosebee	Nancy Popham	Ephram & Sarah Sosebee	A.M. & Elizabeth Popham
15740*	Sosebee, Willie	GA	1880	Mary Sosebee	Ephriam Sosebee	Emma Brown	Sarah Sosebee	Guilford & Mary Chandler
14483	Sosebee, Winnie	GA	1893		Solomon Sosebee	Mattie Millwood	Solomon & Polly Sosebee	Hugh & Miriam Millwood

14246	Soshee, Alfred	OK	1848	Sarah Soshee	Lafayette Sosbee	Temple Clark		Wm & Annie Clark
1514	South, Matilda	TX	1846		Thomas Barlow	Leta Grass	Joseph & Rachel Barlow	Richard & Rachel Gross
2656	South, Matilda	OK	1846	Granville South	Thomas Barlow	Letta Gross	Joseph & Rachel Barlow	Richard & Rachel Gross
19997	Souther, Elder	GA	1867	Joseph Souther	Francis Swaim	Matilda Dyer	Enoch & Cynthia Swaim	Elijah & Elizabeth Dyer
14860	Souther, Nancy	GA	1846	Noah Souther	Kimbell Burrell	Elizabeth McClure	Jesse & Morning Burrell	James & Sarah McClure
18470	Southerland, Benjamon	GA	1873	Mary Southerland				
11313	Southerlen, Cinthia	GA	1844	Marion Southerlen	Ephram Owensby	Sallie Hunter	Arter & Polly Owensby	John Hunter
15549	Southerlen, Ephraim	GA	1877	Pluma Southerlen	Francis Southerlen	Cynthia Owensby	Cas & Patsy Southerlen	Epraim & Sallie Owensby
15583	Southerlen, Robert	GA	1881	Roxie Southerlen	Francis Southerlen	Cynthia Owensby	Cas & Patsy Southerlen	Ephraim & Sallie Owensby
15582	Southerlen, Roxie	GA	1885	Robert Southerlen	Thomas Mullinix	Amanda Burrill	Ezekiel & Fannie Mullinix	Spence & Margret Burrill
15581	Southerlen, William	GA	1874	Manda Southerlen	Francis Southerlen	Cynthia Owensby	Cas & Patsy Southerlen	Ephraim & Sallie Owensby
18319	Spainhour, Laura	NC		Jacob Spainhour	Frank Marion	Sallie Hauser	Adam & Sallie Marion	Samuel & Nancy Hauser
13049	Spainhower, Margaret	NC	1856	E I Spainhower	Andrew Webb	Hannah Poindexter	John Webb & Mary Coe	John Poindexter & Sarah James
10439	Spaniard, Jack	OK	25yrs	Eliza Spaniard	Jack Spaniard	Chu-cau-nv-dv	Ger you cha he	Ner you cha he
17792	Spann, Jane	GA	1883		Charles Alford	Mary Wright		Phoebe Wright
15643*	Sparks, Dora	GA	1869	Pink Sparks	Colonel Jackson	Judy Mize		Charley & Edy Anderson
13546	Sparks, Sary	NM	1845	James Sparks	William Bandy	Dicy Gum	Edwin Jones	Shadrick Gum
14762	Speakes, Elijah	OH	1861	Sallie Speakes	Isaac Speaks	Rachel Blevins	Musentine Speaks	Wells Blevins
14758	Speakes, James	ID	1865	Florence Speakes	Isaac Speakes	Rachel Blevins	Musentine Speakes	Wells & Nancy Blevins
16090	Spear, George	OK	1849	Sidney Spear	Andrew Spear	Mary Colborn	Robert Spear & Polley Fair	
12297	Spear, Thomas	GA	1862		John Spear	Lizzie Otts	Jahugh & Sibbia Spear	George & Nancy Otts
18831	Spearman, Nathaniel	GA	1882		Benj Spearman	Hester Stevenson	John Spearman & Elizabeth Cameron	Joe Stevenson & Sibbbie Thompson
15300	Spears, Bessie	GA	1886		Joshua Spears	Mary Dean	Josiah & Martha Spears	
15299	Spears, Caldwell	GA	1884		Josiah Spears	Mary Dean	Josiah & Martha Spears	
15580	Spears, Carrie	GA	1858		Jehu Spears	Margret Foster	Hezekiah & Christlana Spears	Josiah & Polly Foster
15298	Spears, Charley	GA	1886	Ida Thompson	James Spears	Francis Dupree	Josiah & Martha Spears	
15296	Spears, George	GA	1857	Mary Spears	Josiah Spears	Martha McKissick	James & Docia Spears	
15297	Spears, George	GA	1878		James Spears	Francis Dupree	Josiah & Martha Spears	
15295	Spears, Henry	GA	1900		George Spears	Mary Adams	Josiah & Martha Spears	
15293	Spears, James	GA	1848	Francis Spears	Josiah Spears	Martha McKissick	James & Docia Spears	
15294	Spears, James	GA	1881		James Spears	Francis Dupree	Josiah & Martha Spears	
15292	Spears, Joshua	GA	1852	Mary Spears	Josiah Spears	Martha McKissick	James & Docia Spears	

15291	Spears, Josiah	GA	1873		James Spears	Francis Dupree	Josiah & Martha Spears	
15290	Spears, Leland	GA	1895		Joshua Spears	Mary Dean	Josiah & Martha Spears	
15579	Spears, Leon	GA	1898		R B Spears	Luella Dobbs	John & Margret Spears	Parks & Lena Dobbs
15289	Spears, Lester	GA	1893		George Spears	Mary Adams	Josiah & Martha Spears	
15287	Spears, May	GA	1892		James Spears	Francis Dupree	Josiah & Martha Spears	
15286	Spears, Minnie	GA	1889		James Spears	Francis Dupree	Josiah & Martha Spears	
15284	Spears, Pearl	GA	1889		George Spears	Mary Adams	Josiah & Martha Spears	
15577	Spears, R B	GA	1863	Luella Spears	Jehu Spears	Margret Foster	Hezekiah & Christiana Spears	Josiah & Polly Foster
15283	Spears, Rhoda	GA	1876		James Spears	Francis Dupree	Josiah & Martha Spears	
15282	Spears, Roscoe	GA	1886		Joshua Spears	Mary Dean	Josiah & Martha Spears	
15578	Spears, Sibbia	GA	1851		Jehu Spears	Margret Foster	Hezekiah & Christiana Spears	Josiah & Polly Foster
15281	Spears, Walter	GA	1880	Laura Spears	Joshua Spears	Mary Dean	Josiah & Martha Spears	
14161	Spears, William	AR	1852	Susan Spears	Manon Spears	Mary Bell		Cassie Bell
15142	Spears, William	GA	1883		James Spears	Francis Dupree	Josiah & Martha Spears	
15073	Speas, Mary	NC	1859	Wesley Speas	Thomas Houser	Lucinda Sprinkle	Samuel & Nancy Houser	Thos & Elizabeth Sprinkle
16488 *	Spease, Bettie	NC	1851	Eugene Spease	Solomon Sawyers	Tabitha Evans	John Sawyers	Benj & Lucy Evans
17071	Spease, Dorothy	NC	1857	Lewis Spease	Robbert Poindexter	Martha Ward	Robbert & Charlotte Poindexter	Wiley & Polly Ward
7335	Speed, Maude	MO	1873	James Speed	William Nelson	Eliza Foley	Henry & Catharine Nelson	James & Rhoda Foley
18812	Speer, Sarah	TX	1843	Henry Speer	Nipper Tekell	Eliza Bradley	John & Nancy Tekell	Joshua & Polly Bradley
21948	Spence, Charles	TN	1874	Florence Spence	James Spence	Martha Wilson	George & Amanda Spence	Thomas & Rebecca Wilson
4888	Spence, Martha	TN	1854	James Spence	Thomas Wilson	Rebecca Hampton	Thomas & Sarah Wilson	Sarah Hampton
10009	Spencer, Annie	NC	1878	Wiley Spencer	Benjamin Phipps	Rebecca Plummer	Ahart & Maryan Phipps	
10006	Spencer, Bessie	NC	1884	none	Robert Spencer	Mary Reeves	Solomon & Nellie Spencer	
14730	Spencer, C W, gdn.	VA	1866		C W Spencer	Jettie Osborn		A M & Leanzy Osborn
10008	Spencer, C.P.	NC	1876	Minnie Spencer	Robert Spencer	Mary Reeves	Solomon & Nellie Spencer	
10018	Spencer, Elisha	NC		Callie Spencer	John Spencer	Martha Anderson	Solomon & Nellie Spencer	
10011	Spencer, Elizabeth	NC	1879	none	Robert Spencer	Mary Reeves	Solomon & Nellie Spencer	
6125	Spencer, Emmer	NC	1884	Horton Spencer	Joseph Blevins	Nancy Hurley	Alford & Margera Blevins	Leander & Amandy Hurley
10004	Spencer, G.Frank	NC	1871	none	Robert Spencer	Mary Reeves	Solomon & Nellie Spencer	
10005	Spencer, Joseph	NC	1881	none	Robert Spencer	Mary Reeves	Solomon & Nellie Spencer	

9995	Spencer, Mattie	NC	1877	Arthur Spencer	Columbus Peak	Caroline Spencer	Hugh & Marga Peak	Solomon & Nellie Spencer
10007	Spencer, Robert	NC	1844	Mary Spencer	Solomon Spencer	Nellie Hash		Robert & Marga Hash
10017	Spencer, Solomon	NC	1874	Sarah Spencer	John Spencer	Martha Anderson	Solomon & Nellie Spencer	
10010	Spencer, Wiley	NC	1868	Annie Spencer	Robert Spencer	Mary Reeves	Solomon & Nellie Spencer	
3126	Spitchley, Sallie	MS	1885	Martin Spitchley	Ben White	Kibbie Hobgood		Charles & Martha Hobgood
2639	Spivey, Cordelia	GA	1841	Sully Spivey	John Robinson	Lucindy Leatherwood	Samuel Leatherwood	Betsey Leatherwood
17464	Spotswood, Sarah	IL	1858	James Spotswood	Wm Winslow	Cynthia Jackson	Peter Winslow	
22384	Spradlin, Lee Ann	TX	1863	Adolphus Spradlin	Henry Henson	Mary Hudman	James & Elizabeth Henson	Hezekiah & Martha Hudman
17245	Springer, Ed	TX	1874	Nora Springer	Loll Springer	Jensie Blue	Thursy Springer	Polly Blue
18187	Sprouse, Colonel	GA	1899		Elijah Sprouse	Mary May	Terrett & Delila Sprouse	Thomas & Hannah May
20063	Sprouse, Delilah	TN	1815	Terrell Sprouse	Evan Richards	Sarah Smith	Joshua Richards	William Smith
7329	Sprouse, Emma	OK	1882	James Sprouse	Willis Hunter	Sarrah Cantrell	Willis Brumley	Sallie Brumley
18199	Sprouse, Ida	GA			Elijah Sprouse	Mary May	Terrett & Delila Sprouse	Thomas & Hannah May
18186	Sprouse, John	GA	1889		Elijah Sprouse	Mary May	Terrett & Delila Sprouse	Thomas & Hannah May
18347	Sprouse, John	GA	52yrs	Emaline Sprouse	Teritt Sprouse	Delilah Richards	Vinson Sprouse	Evans Richards
18190	Sprouse, Luther	GA	1895		Elijah Sprouse	Mary May	Terrett & Delila Sprouse	Thomas & Hannah May
18188	Sprouse, Mary	GA	1886		Elijah Sprouse	Mary May	Terrett & Delila Sprouse	Thomas & Hannah May
18185	Sprouse, Pearl	GA	1891		Elijah Sprouse	Mary May	Terrett & Delila Sprouse	Thomas & Hannah May
18216	Sprouse, Thomas	GA	1880	Cnthia Sprouse	Eliphus Sprouse	Mary May	Territt & Delila Sprouse	Thomas & Hannah May
15036	Spruce, Adine	OK	1868		Wm Spruce	Helen Bailey	Homer & Martha Spruce	A C C & Nancy Bailey
15035	Spruce, William	OK	1870	Alice Spruce	Wm Spruce	Helen Bailey	Homer & Martha Spruce	A C C & Nancy Bailey
19771*	Spurgeon, Henry	TN	1830	Fannie Spurgeon	Dangerfield Wheeler	Sallie Spurgeon		
21349	Spurgeon, Margaret	OK	1863	W. Spurgeon	Francis Shulty	Annie Ford	Francis & Malinda Shulty	Alex & Margaret Ford
9577	Spurlin, Mattie	GA	1869	Wm Spurlin	Samuel Lowry	Catharine Rouse	Becky Lowry	William Rouse
18495	Stafford, Eliza	NC	1831	Pinkney Stafford	David Hendrix	Hannah Jones	Robertson & Hannah Stafford	Hesekiah & Martha Jones
20138	Stafford, Mary	FL	1865	Edward Stafford	Valentine Fillingim	Sarah Dukes	Robert & Ester Fillingim	Thomas & Ann Duke
12071*	Stagg, Anderson	OK		Ellen Stagg	Cope Stagg	Bethena Spivy		
12070*	Stagg, Ellen	OK	1851	Anderson Stagg	John Baker	Ann Baker		
12265	Stamper, Arthur	NC	1886		James Stamper	Mary Wagoner	Welborn & Cathana Stamper	Henry & Charlotte Wagoner
5994	Stamper, Caney	VA	1881	Betty Stamper	Ira Stamper	Jaicy Blevins	Eli & Susanah Stamper	James & Mecy Blevins
9081	Stamper, Elihu	NC	1836	Tamsey Stitt	Eli Stamper	Susanah Stamper	Solomon Stamper	Betsy Stamper

#	Name	State	Year	Spouse	Father	Mother	Paternal GP	Maternal GP
9046	Stamper, Gilmore	VA	1878	R. Stamper	Mack Stamper	Kizza Joins	Wiley & Eliza Stamper	
10205	Stamper, James	MO	1850	Callie Stamper	Eli Stamper	Susanna Stamper	John & Sallie Stamper	Solomen & Elizabeth Stamper
12264	Stamper, James	NC	1853	Sally Stamper	Welborn Stamper	Cathana Crause	Solomon & Bettie Stamper	
771	Stamper, John	TN	1844	Mary Stamper	Richard Stamper	Jane Byrd	Stamper & Benge	Byrd
5864	Stamper, John	VA	1867	Rachel Stamper	Ira Stamper	Docie Blevins	Eli & Susanna Stamper	James & Nancy Blevins
10925	Stamper, John	NC		Docy Stamper	James Stamper	Sally Wagoner	Wilborn Stamper	Henry Wagoner
11070	Stamper, John	VA	1860	Mattie Stamper	Wiley Stamper	Eliza Anderson	George & Naoma Stamper	
8488	Stamper, Mack	VA	1858	none	Wiley Stamper	Eliza Anderson	George & Naomi Stamper	
1587	Stamper, Madison	VA	1862	Franky Stamper	W.M. Weaver	Catherine Baldwin		Wm & Margret Baldwin
6165	Stamper, Maggie	NC	1876	Willey Stamper	Robbert Phipps	Ludeamy Miller	Ahart & Maryan Phipps	Jackson & Elmira Miller
772	Stamper, Mary	TN	1865		Thomas Spartook	Jennia Woodard	John & Nacy Spartook	John & Sally Woodard
10214	Stamper, Sally	NC	1857	James Stamper	Henry Wagoner	Charlotte Sizemore		Owen & Rebecha Sizemore
2457	Stamper, Wiley	VA	1833	Matilda Stamper	George Stamper	Naoma Stamper	Solomon Stamper	John Stamper
8536	Stamper, Willey	NC	1875	Magga Stamper	Ira Stamper	Joisey Blevins	Eli & Susanah Stamper	James & Meacy Blevins
20358	Stancel, Barbara	GA	1891		John Stancel	Sarah Man	Hillsman & Sarah Stancel	John & Barbara Man
18148	Stancel, Cader	GA	1837	Eliza Stancel	Jesse Stancel	Annie Brown	John & Millie Stancel	
20354	Stancel, George	GA	1888		John Stancel	Sarah Man	Hillsman & Sarah Stancel	John & Barbara Man
18149	Stancel, James	GA	1862	Fannie Stancel	Cader Stancel	Eliza Corbin	Jesse & Annie Stancel	
8708	Stancel, John	GA	1849	Sarah Stancel	Hillsman Stancel	Sarah Thompson	John & Catharine Stancel	James & Nancy Thompson
13813	Stancel, John	TN	1873	Eva Stancel	Caleb Stancel	Nancy McCauley	John & Sarah Stancel	G B & Nancy McCauley
20355	Stancel, John	GA	1884		John Stancel	Sarah Man	Hillsman & Sarah Stancel	John & Barbara Man
8707	Stancel, Sarah	GA	1861	John Stancel	John Mann	Barbra Owens		Henry & Mary Owens
13811	Stancel, Thomas	GA	1876	Hattie Stancel	Caleb Stancel	Nancy McCauley	John & Sarah Stancel	G B & Nancy McCauley
18151	Stancel, Wilson	GA	1884		Cader Stancel	Eliza Corbin	Jesse & Annie Stancel	
20823	Stancil, Charley et al	GA	1894		Tom Stancil	Martha Cook		Gazaway & Nellie Cook
18618	Stancil, George	GA	1879	Josephine Stancil	Cader Stancil	Eliza Corbin	Jesse & Annie Stancil	Bartley & Susie Corbin
13120	Stancil, Jodie	GA	1887	George Stancil	Joseph Hembree	Talitha Jones	Jack & Louisy Hembree	Wm & Beckey Jones
17612	Stancil, Lula	GA	1885		James Stancil	Sary Taylor	Major & Amanda Stancil	Dudley & Caroline Taylor
20822	Stancil, Martha	GA	1877	Tom Stancil	Gazaway Cook	Nellie Pemhards	Richard & Sarah Cook	

17611	Stancil, Sary	GA	1866	James Stancil	Dudley Taylor	Caroline York	C.C. & Susan Taylor	John & Sary York
8892	Stanfield, Malinda	GA	1840	Mason Stanfield	Reubin Emery	Sarah Lord	Nancy Emery	Courtis & Sarah Lord
17294	Stanford, Mary	AL			Samuel Brown	Sarah Sizemore		William Sizemore
19610	Stanly, Edward	NC	1861	Mary Stanley	Henry Stanly	Catherine Rutledge	Guaret & Jamima Stanly	
21092	Stanly, Emiline	NC	1849	Hiram Stanly	Garret Stanly	Jemina Smith	John & Polly Stanley	Edmund & Susan Smith
2024	Stansbury, Minnie	NC	1874	James Stansbury	John Ragle	Mary Delozier	Henry & Mary Ragle	Ed & Elizabeth Delozier
7457	Starbuck, Earnest	OK		none	Jim Starbuck	Goldey Bivins		Lewis & Catherine Bivins
8540	Starlin, Noah	NC	1846	Lear Starlin	Abraham Starlin	Sarah Thompson		John & Mary Thompson
8448	Starlin, Polley	NC	1880	none	Abraham Starlin	Sarah Thompson		John & Mary Thompson
8549	Starlin, Rebecky	NC	1883	none		Polley Starlin		Aberham & Sarah Starlin
11796	Starlin, Rosa	VA	1886		Marshall Farmer	Mary Starlin		Abraham & Sarah Starlin
17843	Starling, Delia	NC	1888		Wilburn Starling	Tamsey Powers	Abraham & Sarah Starling	
14035	Starling, Virginia	NC	1851		William Poindexter	Mary Taylor	Wm & Elizabeth Poindexter	Mart & Susanah Taylor
8551	Starling, Wilburn	NC	1856	Tamsey Starling	Abraham Starling	Sarah Thompson		John & Mary Thompson
6283	Starnes, John	TN	1852	Annie Starnes	James Starnes	Clarissa Echols	Lewis & Tempy Gorman	Abraham & Polly Echols
7611	Starns, Jasper	GA	73yrs	Elizabeth Starns	John Starns	Delpha Barber	Sliter Starns	
12362	Starr, Henry	OK	1873	Ollie Starr	George Starr	Mary Scott	Fields & Polly Starr	Sterlind & Jane Scott
16165*	Starr, Lafayette	OK	1858		Jess Mayfield	Gracy Hawk	Thom Starr	
10618	Starr, Louisa	MO	1851		William Neal	Theresa Green	Samuel Neal	James Green
17717	Starr, Mary	OK			Wm Starr	Lydice Pumpkin	George Starr & Oo-li-Cass	Jesse & Susan Pumpkin
3348	Steadham, Ausphera	AL	1879	none	John Steadham	Mary McGhee	Ned Steadham	Nancy McGhee
3346	Steadham, Benjamin	AL	1872	Ruthie	John Steadham	Mary McGhee	Ned Steadham	Nancy McGhee
3347	Steadham, Edward	AL	1870	none	John Steadham	Mary McGhee	Ned Steadham	Nancy McGhee
3349	Steadham, George	AL	1882	Bessie	John Steadham	Mary McGhee	Ned Steadham	Nancy McGhee
6318	Steadham, James	AL		Sudie Nettles	John Steadham	Mary McGhee	Ned Steadham	Nancy McGhee
3351	Steadham, John	AL	1858		John Steadham	Mary McGhee	Ned Steadham	Nancy McGhee
6364	Steadham, John	AL	21yrs	Liddia Parson	Rhueben Steadham	Margaret Woods	John & Mary Steadham	John Woods & Mary Weatherford
6319	Steadham, Leonard	AL	1870	Hattee Eddings	John Steadham	Mary McGhee	Ned Steadham	Nancy McGhee

#	Name	State	Year/Age	Spouse	Father	Mother	Paternal GP	Maternal GP
6315	Steadham, Mary	AL	40yrs	John Steadham	O.R. Boone	Susan Hathcock	John & Rena Boone	Thos Hathcock & Elisabeth Marlow
6317	Steadham, Mrs. Geo	AL	27yrs	George Steadham	James Moniac	Mary Williams	Sam & Susan Moniac	Seaburn Williams
3350	Steadham, Reuben	AL	1860	widow	John Steadham	Mary McGhee	Ned Steadham	Nancy McGhee
6355	Steadham, Robert	AL	39yrs	Emma Dinnis	John Steadham	Mary McGhee	Ned Steadham	Nancy McGhee
21619	Steddum, Nancy	TX	1841	Polsy Steddum	Thomas Williams	Mary Davis	Sam & Nancy Williams	
20122	Steed, Kathleen	TX	1888	Robert Steed	J.D. Harwell	Annie Davis	James & Nancy Harwell	W.P. & M.H. Davis
3708 *	Steele, Alice	OK	1875	Theodore Steele (decd)	Dock Parker	Mattie Lynch	Harriett Martin	Harry Martin & Sallie Starks
16779	Steeler, John & Wm	OK	14yrs 13yrs		Coo wee skoo wee Steeler	Nancy Rogers	Steeler & Sallie Steeler	
7795	Steelman, Willie	OK	1867		Nathan Steelman	Susan Gambill		A J Gambill
11322	Stegall, Mary	GA	1886	Charles Stegall	Edward Prather	Mary Wofford	James & Parthenia Prather	
21377	Stegall, Mollie	OK	1870	Lawrence Stegall	George Edwards	Loana Lumpkins	James & Elizabeth Edwards	Bushnod & Mary Lumpkins
18049 *	Stell, George	TX	1865	Ella Stell	Charlie Stell	Margaret Green	Burly Marshall	Delia Green
3757 *	Stell, John	TX	1869	Lula Stell	Charles Stell	Margeret Green	Burlie Marshal	
12324	Stells, Clara	GA	1901		William Stells	Peggy Sams	John & Eliza Stells	Columbus & Susan Sams
12323	Stells, Grady	GA	1897		William Stells	Peggy Sams	John & Eliza Stells	Columbus & Susan Sams
12298	Stells, Peggy	GA	1880	William Stells	Columbus Sams	Susan Mills	Wm & Mahaly Sams	Joseph & Annie Mills
12300	Stells, Ruby	GA	1905		William Stells	Peggy Sams	John & Eliza Stells	Columbus & Susan Sams
1194	Stephens, Alfred	OK	1887	Pearl Stephens	James Stephens	Mary Hall	Green & Nancy Stephens	Alfred & Mahala Hall
478	Stephens, Eliza	AL	1838	widow	Isom Henry	Dorcus Williams	unknown	Hubard Williams
18574	Stephens, Fannie	GA	1886		General Stephens	Jane Ledford	Canon Stephens	Silas & Armindia Ledford
18563	Stephens, Ferdinand	GA	1890		General Stephens	Jane Ledford	Canon & Jane Stephens	Silas & Arminda Ledford
19782	Stephens, Frank	MO	1865	Addie Stephens	Wiley Stephens	Malinda Cummins		
21499	Stephens, George	AR	1866	Minnie Stephens	John Stephens	Salua Malicoat	John & Sabia Stephens	
6697	Stephens, Jane	GA	1857	Geneme Stephens	Silas Ledford	Eliza Boling		Thos Boling & Polly McDonald
21497	Stephens, John	OK	1845	Salva Stephens	Benj Stephens	Elizabeth Brown		John Brown & Martha
21723	Stephens, John	OK	1874	Rhoda Stephens	John Stephens	Salera Malicoat	Benj & Elizabeth Stephens	
18716	Stephens, Lillie	TN	1862	Joseph Stephens	Willis Guy	Mahala Gibson	Edmund & Judie Guy	George & Viney Gibson
20329	Stephens, Martha	GA	1850	Joseph Stephens	Thomas Miles	Martha Payton	John & Winnie Miles	Moses & Nancy Bryant
18619	Stephens, Sarah	GA	1877	Sherman Stephens	Cader Stancil	Eliza Corbin	Jesse & Annie Stancil	Bartley & Susie Corbin

#	Name	State	Year					
10339	Stephens, William	GA	1878	none	General Stephens	Jane Ledford	Canon & Jane Stephens	Silas & Amanda Ledford
21500	Stephens, William	OK	1876	Rebecca Stephens	John Stephens	Salua Malicoat	John & Sabia Stephens	
21165	Stephenson, Myrtle	TX	1878	Martin Stephenson	Thomas Cordill	Sallie Baker	Rufus & Nancy Cordill	Seth & Lucy Baker
20909	Stephenson, Nellie	TN	1901		E. Lafayette Stephenson	Minnie Gwinn	Elijah & Elizabeth Stephenson	Newton & Alluion Gwinn
20920	Stephenson, Park	TN	1905		E. Lafayette Stephenson	Minnie Gwinn	Elijah & Elizabeth Stephenson	Newton & Forest Gwinn
21042	Stephenson, William	KS	1853	Martha Stephenson	John Stephenson	Sarilda Ritchie		Zachriah Ritchie & Elizabeth McDaniel
21282	Stepp, Hattie	TX	1882	Granville Stepp	? Cole	? Anderson	George Cole	Louis Anderson
8285	Stevens, Amy	TX	1861	Urlson Stevens	William Franklin	Amy Ledford	Abram & Elisabeth Franklin	Benjamin Ledford
13905 *	Stevens, Henry	GA	1861	Julia Stevens	Loyd Brown	Rebecca Brown	Steven & Cordelia Brown	Diana Schley
7336	Stevens, Rosa	OK	1874	Albert Stevens	Joel Massey	Laura Holcomb	Ephram & Mary Massey	Wm & Louisa Holcomb
6538	Stevens, Susan	OK	1850	John Stevens	Thomas Whitaker	Mary Teery	Jacob Whitaker & Poly Redden	John Teery & Rebeca Dickey
18646	Stevenson, Arah	OK	1866	Butler Stevenson	Richard Peak	Susan Lewis	James & Judy Peak	
19187	Stevenson, Nannie	OK	1877	George Stevenson	James Lue	Lizzie Goings	Walter Lue	Jess & Leucin Brown
2089	Steward, Dalton	IL	1830	Mary Steward	Walden Steward	Rebecca	Moses & Polly Steward	
3393	Steward, George	AL		Elisabeth Taylor	Sam Steward	Nancy Marlow		Jennie Marlow
18374	Steward, George	AL	29yrs	Beatrice Steward	George Steward	Mary Taylor	Jack & Liddie Steward	Wash & Lizzie Taylor
437 *	Steward, Margaret	IL	1861	Louis Steward	Square Williamson	Harriett Adams	Elish & Charity Williamson	Tony Adams
19023	Stewart, Annie	TN	1832	Thomas Stewart	Wm Cunningham	Nancy Newman	Thos Cunningham & Pollie Phincaster	James & Nancy Newman
21715	Stewart, Charles	OK	1881		Green Stewart	Charlotte Roach	Isaac & Mariah Stewart	Isaac & Lucindy Roach
19119	Stewart, Constantine	IN	1842		John Stewart	Virginia Tendley	Chas & Clara Stewart	Thos & Prisilla Tendley
3392	Stewart, Corine	AL		none	George Stewart	Elisabeth Taylor	Sam Steward	Nancy Marlow
21716	Stewart, Green	OK	1842	Charlotte Stewart	Isaac Stewart	Mariah Wyatt	Joshua Stewart	Nathan & Annis Jordan
21712	Stewart, Isaac	OK	1868		Green Stewart	Charlotte Roach	Isaac & Mariah Stewart	Isaac & Lucindy Roach
18112	Stewart, Lottie	FL	1868	Robert Stewart	Alex Robinson	Mary Gardner		Samuel Gardner & Eliza Barrios
10960	Stewart, Louisa	KS	1858	John Stewart	Duncan McDonald	Lucinda Smith		James Smith
16967	Stewart, Margret	OK	1875	W.W. Stewart	J M Hail	Nancy McKinzie		
18881 *	Stewart, Mima	GA	1867	Jim Stewart	Spencer Monroe	Mary White		
14815	Stewart, Minnie	NC	1881	Mitchell Stewart	Solomon Blevins	Louisa Wyatt	Wilburn & Rosa Blevins	
20228	Stewart, Robert	TN	1865	Nancy Stewart	James Stewart	Letha Parker	Matt & Nancy Stewart	Wm & Polly Parker
19117	Stewart, Samuel	IN	1844	Francis Stewart	John Stewart	Virginia Tendley	Chas & Clara Stewart	Thos & Prisilla Tendley

21714	Stewart, Samuel	OK	1883		Green Stewart	Charlotte Roach	Isaac & Mariah Stewart	Isaac & Lucindy Roach
4165	Stewart, Thomas	OK	1844	Lizzie Stewart	Cornelius Stewart	Maria Jourdan	Freddie Stewart	Nathan & Annie Jourdan
21713	Stewart, Thomas	OK	1879	Nina Stewart	Green Stewart	Charlotte Roach	Isaac & Mariah Stewart	Isaac & Lucindy Roach
18494*	Stewman, Caroline	GA	1846		David Thomas	Jane Morrison		John Morrison & Ruthey Land
22421	Stiles, Dorcus	TN	1881	Edgar Stiles	William Harris	Susan Payne	John & Mary Payne	
21309	Stiles, Ida	TX	1886	M.H. Stiles	Charles Graham	Mary Adkinson	James & Martha Graham	
2008	Stiles, Polly	NC	1851	Marion Stiles	Wm Gibbs	Avaline Battles	Hugh & Sallie Gibbs	Watson & Sallie Battles
9762	Still, Jane	OK	44yrs	Asbury Glenn	Martin Goins	Amanda Goins	James & Rhoda Goins	Malinda Bowlin
6360	Still, Jason	AL	1884	none	Isaac Still	Helen Staples	Richmond Still	Jason & Margaret Staples
6359	Still, Richard	AL	1883	none	Isaac Still	Helen Staples	Richmond Still	Jason Staples & Margaret Powel
6361	Still, William	AL	1887	none	Isaac Still	Helen Staples	Richmond Still	Jason & Margaret Staples
12069	Stillwell, Abigail	OK	1850	Elias Stillwell	Anderson Elmore	Margret Modrel	David & Elizabeth Elmore	
19470	Stillwell, Edward	NC	1888		Harrison Stillwell	Mary Hank	Henry & Angeline Stillwell	
14329	Stillwell, Jacob	OK	1875		Elias Stillwell	Abigal Elmore		Anderson Elmore
12068	Stillwell, Maney	OK	1881		Elias Stillwell	Abigal Elmore		Anderson Elmore
21796	Stillwell, Rosa	OK	1888	Louis Stillwell	Linzy Oldham	Sally Herrod	Wm Oldham & Mary Rodgers	Lancy Herrod
20235	Stilwell, Sarah	OK	1881	John Stillwell	Frank Corban	Mary Downing		
22430	Stilz, Susan	IL	1858	William Stilz	Henry Henson	Mary Hudman	James & Hezekiah Henson	Martha Hudman
22689	Stimpson, Martha	NC	1873		Augustine Poindexter	Mary Davis		
13942	Stingell, Charity	VA	1869	J A Stingell	Wilson Farmer	Elisebeth Blevins		Wm & Rosia Blevins
21283	Stinnett, Mollie	TX	1882	Harvey Stinnett	William Cole	Mary Anderson	George & Mattie Cole	Lewis & Nancy Anderson
19166	Stinson, Ethel	GA	1894		William Stinson	Francis Turner		Thomas & Launica Turner
19167	Stinson, Fannie	GA	1901		William Stinson	Francis Turner		Thomas & Launica Turner
18281	Stinson, Frances	GA	1882	William Stinson	Thomas Turner	Louvica Carner		Polly Carner
19168	Stinson, George	GA	1903		William Stinson	Francis Turner		Thomas & Launica Turner
19169	Stinson, Jim	GA	1892		William Stinson	Francis Turner		Thomas & Launica Turner
19170	Stinson, Lillie	GA	1887		William Stinson	Francis Turner		Thomas & Launica Turner
19171	Stinson, Mollie	GA	1890		William Stinson	Francis Turner		Thomas & Launica Turner
19172	Stinson, Samuel	GA	1885		William Stinson	Francis Turner		Thomas & Launica Turner
5000	Stitt, Carl	VA	1896	none	Eliga Stitt	Martha Wyatt	Jacob & Hylia Stitt	
4998	Stitt, Clyde	VA	1891	none	Elega Stitt	Martha Wyatt	Jacob & Hydia Stitt	

4999	Stitt, Dorsia	VA	1886	none	Elega Stitt	Martha Wyatt	Jacob & Hydia Stitt	
5001	Stitt, James	VA	1894	none	Eliga Stitt	Martha Wyatt	Jacob & Hylia Stitt	
18451	Stockton, Frances	NM	1868	J.E. Stockton	Thomas Avants	Frances Stoval		
19173	Stodard, Frances	GA	1889	Will Stodard	George Quarles	Clarinda Gilly		John & Nancy Gilly
10449	Stofford, Mary	GA	1840	Samuel Stofford	Jasper Lloyd	Tolitha Leiser	Thos & Susan Lloyd	
13465	Stokes, Georgia	OK	1866	James Stokes	Hugh Russell	Ruth Butler		Wm Riley & Mary Butler
3019	Stokes, Martha	MO	1881	George Stokes	Elijah Hambelton	Nancy Harralson	Isaiah & Martha Hambelton	Jas Harralson & Mary Lusk
11380	Stokes, Pina	MO	1879	Edward Stokes	James Doke	Jacky Harralson	Merritt & Mary Doke	Vincent & Martha Harralson
10093	Stokes, Virgie	MO	1882	Wesley Stokes	James Tindell	Percilla Brown	Wm & Susan Tindell	Wm & Amanda Brown
7326	Stone, Cordie	GA	1881	L W Stone	Martin Holcomb	Sarah Hayes	Wm & Louisa Holcomb	John & Louisa Hayes
15069 ½	Stone, Foster	OK	1887		Benjamin Stone	Emma Murphy		Jess & Phoeba Murphy
21286	Stone, George	TX	1866	Juliah Stone	James Stone	Sarah Coe	George & Delpha Stone	Andrew & Roda Coe
14371	Stone, Harriet	OK	1868	Alfred Stone	Martin Williamson	Margret Ledford		John & Nancy Ledford
19204 *	Stone, Ida et al	TX	1886		Tom Stone	Ann Stell		Charley Stell & Burby Marshall
13808	Stone, Jennie	TN	1879	Jesse Stone	Caleb Stancel	Nancy McCauley	John & Sarah Stancel	G B & Nancy McCauley
20091	Stone, John	OR	1868	Mathie Stone	Francis Stone	Sarah Poindexter	Enoch & Elizabeth Stone	Denson & Sally Poindexter
22569 *	Stone, Kate	IN	1853	Barny Stone	George Hardan	Violia Dickson		Josuth & Tabitha Bass
18973	Stone, Mamie	NC	1885	Ellis Stone	I. W. Crouse	Martha Scott	Henry & Henrietta Crouse	W.P. & Amy Scott
19270	Stone, Mary	KS	43yrs		Francis Stone	Sarah Poindexter		
19269	Stone, Mata et al	KS	18yrs		Wesley Stone	Mary Stone		
20090	Stone, Mattie & Francis	OR	1904 1906		John Stone	Mathie Waddill	Francis & Sarah Stone	James & Martha Waddill
21284	Stone, S.R.	TX	1868	Alma Stone	J.R. Stone	Elizabeth Coe		
7327	Stone, Sarah	TX	1860	James Stone	Willis Hunter	Sarrah Cantrell	Willis Brumley	Sallie Brumley
18564	Stone, Sarah	NC	1833	Francis Stone	Denson Poindexter	Sarah Jones	Wm & Elizabeth Poindexter	Isaac & Bashaba Jones
21287	Stone, William	TX	1863		J.R. Stone	Elizabeth Coe		
6021	Stonecipher, Nellie	IL	1886	Mont Stonecipher	James Jourdan	Lydia Friend	Joseph & Sarah Jourdan	
11323	Stoner, Mamie	GA	1877	Michael Stoner	Edward Prather	Mary Wofford	James & Parthenia Prather	
9564	Storey, Mary	AR	1885	James Storey	Andrew Smith	Laura Southern	Robert Smith	Warren & Mary Southern
22121	Stotts, Annie	MO	1878	Joseph Stotts	William Scofield	Louisa Bennett	Walter & Susan Scofield	James & Lucinda Bennett
1022	Stough, Gwynn	KS	1905		Wade Jones	Annie Dugas	Wm & Mary Jones	Joseph & Johanna Dugas

1021	Stough, Nancy	KS	1874	Wm Stough	Wm Jones	Mary Stamper	Wm & Martha Jones	Eli & Susanna Stamper
1020	Stough, Winnie	KS	1899		Stough	Nancy Jones	David Stough	Wm & Mary Jones
16179	Stout, Stephen	OK	1865	Virginnie Stout	Joseph Stout			
4199	Stovall, Ida	TX	1863	R B Stovall	- Sizemore	Nancy Davis	Edward & Polly Sizemore	
18967*	Stover, Abbie	OK	50yrs	Mayhugh		Charity Stover		
14416	Stover, Fannie	GA	1872	John Stover	David Lovell	Fannie Long		Wm & Mary Long
20119	Stover, Jasper	AR	1867		Jake Stover	Rebecca Ulen		
8196	Stover, Luevena	AR			John Flood	Angline Lucas		John Hash
18602	Stow, Abraham	AL	1847	Frances Stow	Abraham Stow	Frances Poindexter		Wm & Elizabeth Poindexter
21091	Stow, Isaac	AL	1850	Tilla Stow	Abraham Stow	Frances Poindexter	Wm & Elizabeth Poindexter	Isaac & Bashaba Jones
21942*	Stowers, Toliver	TN	1861	Mattie Stowers	Manee Stowers	Mary		
1307	Stratton, Jefferson	GA	1861	Kansas Stratton	Jackson Stratton	Eliza Russell	Dick Stratton	Woody & Barbara Russell
21159	Streeter, Rosie	OK		Albert Streeter	George McDaniel	Torrie Lumford	Redbird & Polly McDaniel	Calvin & Mary Lumford
13871	Streetman, John	GA	1866	Ida Streetman	Jehu Streetman	Emily Bagley	John & Francis Streetman	Francis & Lucretia Strickland
20472*	Strickland, Andrew	TN	1870		Squire Strickland	Harriet Spencer	Joyce	John & Cilla Spencer
22461	Strickland, Charley	TN	1856	none	James Strickland	Amanda Denton		Wm & Elizabeth Camp
12010	Strickland, Ella	GA	1885	Benjamin Strickland	Robert Lawrence	Eliza Brown		John & Loduska Brown
20852*	Strickland, George	GA	1859	Mary Strickland	Squire Strickland	Harriet Fields	George & Joyce Tassell	Sylla Fields
12009	Strickland, Mary	GA	1903		Ben Strickland	Ella Lawrence		Robert & Eliza Lawrence
12008	Strickland, Ronnie	GA	1905		Ben Strickland	Ella Lawrence		Robert & Eliza Lawrence
20853*	Strickland, Thomas	GA	1866	Julia Strickland	Squire Strickland	Harriet Fields	George & Joyce Tassell	Sylla Fields
21047*	Stricklin, Andrew	GA	1852	Eliza Stricklin	Andrew Stricklin	Esther Sanders		James Hayden & Thenia Sanders
7715	Stridebaker, Martha	OK		Moses Stridebaker	R. Branch	Nancy West		Isaac & Nancy West
11091	Stringer, Cora	OK	1884	W C Stringer	William Blevins	Elizabeth Blevins	Jessie & Catharine Blevins	James & Margaret Blevins
19993	Stripland, Tallulah	GA	1871		Lester Stripland	Malinda Wallis	Toliver Stripland	Eliza Wallace
7330	Stripling, Franklin	OK	1881	Grace Stripling	William Stripling	Louisa Davis		Richard & Martha Davis
7331	Stripling, Louisa	OK	1862	William Stripling	Richard Davis	Martha Holcomb		Wm Holcomb & Louisa Berry
22139*	Stripling, Virgil	GA	1842	Annie Stripling	Jack Joyce	Anna Duke	Virgil & Sarah Bell	Kugole
2310	Stroud, Maybell	GA	1888	Willey Stroud	Allen Adams	Ellia Hudson	David & Clerinda Adams	James & Mary Hudson
20621	Stroup, Fredrick	TN	1884		Andrew Stroup	Jennie Chase	Jacob & Elizabeth Stroup	Nathan & Narcissa Chase

20622	Stroup, Jessie	TN	1888		Andrew Stroup	Jennie Page	Jacob & Elizabeth Stroup	Nathan & Narcissa Chase
17568	Strutt, Disa	TN	1862	Bill Strutt	Bill Donnel	Nancy Ferguson	Disa Donnel	Jim & Polly Ferguson
6168	Stuard, Rutha	NC	1867	W E Stuart	Eli Phipps	Jeston Phipps	Benjamin & Rutha Phipps	Ahart & Maryan Phipps
6128	Stuart, Emma	NC	1874	John Stuart	Alfred Blevins	Marjary Sheets	James & Meacy Blevins	Joseph & Elizabeth Hudler
2095	Stuart, Lettie	NC	1886	Charley Stuart	Urvin Dickson	Mary Blevins		Alford & Marjary Blevins
22713	Stuart, Linda	TN	1889		Lafayette Stuart	Tilda Thomas	Isam Stuart	Elijah & Narsis Thomas
4742	Stuart, Mary	MO	1872	Carlos Stuart	William Doke	Sarah Hambelton	Merick & Mary Doke	Isariah & Martha Hambelton
14816	Stuart, Mitchell	NC			Elbert Stuart	Mazy Porter	William Stuart	Frank & Katy Porter
18376	Stuart, William	AL	30yrs	Claude Stuart	George Steward	Ann Taylor	Sam & Nancy Steward	Wash & Mary Taylor
11213	Stubblefield, Mollie	NC	1839	Francis Stubblefield	Jerry Roach	Pollie Kelley		James & Juda Kelley
14967	Stubbs, A.E.	OK	1853	S M Stubbs	W T Hill	Martha Allen		Martha Allen
11422	Stump, Caroline	PA	1865	Wiley Stump	Uriah Peak	Carmealy Hart		George & Polly Hart
9243 ½	Stump, Charles	VA	1885	Lucie Stump	W E Stump	Sarah Phipps	Christopher & Sallie Stump	Wm & Mary Phipps
9243	Stump, Sarah	NC	1867	W E Stump	William Phipps	Mary Matheny	Benj & Rutha Phipps	David & Febee Matheny
12448	Sturgeon, Annie	WV	1868	James Sturgeon	Jefferson Osburn	Mary Kiger	Solomon & Patsey Osburn	John & Malinda Kiger
9068	Sturgill, Cynthi	NC	1879	Wickliff Sturgill	Robert Gambill	Nancy Jones	Patsy Gambill	Samuel & Adaline Jones
9606	Sturgill, Dora	VA	1884	Luther Sturgill	Drury Hart	Laurinda Blevins	Riley & Emily Hart	Wesley & Nancy Blevins
11447	Sturgill, Ellon	VA	1884	Byron Sturgill	Levi Blevins	Evaline Hart	Ned & Nancy Blevins	
3772	Sturgill, James	NC	1883	Maud Sturgill	Byron Sturgill	Martha Pennington	John & Bidzy Sturgill	Stephen & Joanah Pennington
6899	Sturgill, Mandy	VA	1891	F E Sturgill	Alexander Huffman	Emeline	Alex & Sely Huffman	Samuel & Sarah Pennington
3773	Sturgill, Martha	NC	1856	Byran Sturgill	Stephen Pennington	Joanah Spencer	Sam & Elizabeth Pennington	Isaac & Joanah Spencer
11067	Sturgill, Milley	VA	1883	C W Sturgill	Leander Blevins	Elizabeth Hart		John & Polley Hart
3992	Sturgill, William	NC	1882	Dora Sturgill	Byron Sturgill	Martha Pennington	John & Bidy Sturgill	Stephen & Joanah Pennington
10897	Suagee, David (decd)	OK	1852	Louisa Suagee	Wilson Suagee	Dorcas Vann		
7527	Sudderth, Clara	NC	30yrs	Jim Sudderth	Elza Irving	Adaline Whitaker		
6761 *	Sudderth, Rachel	NC	35yrs	John Sudderth	Charles Siles	Rose Crawford		Sylla Crawford
12380 *	Sugg, Jesse	TN	1825	Winetta Sugg	Jacob Terry	Tina Sugg		
16319	Suggs, Elias	GA	57yrs		James Suggs	Polly Cox		John Cox
21779	Suggs, Lillie	OK	1877	James Suggs	Robert Nicks	Nancy Puckett	Isaac & Nancy Nicks	James & Eliza Puckett
18690	Suggs, Mrs. John	FL	1860	John Suggs	Thomas Robinson	Mary Harvel		Elizabeth Harvel

10392	Suggs, Polly	GA	89yrs	widow	John Cox	Sallie Cline	Absalom & Polly Cox	Jacob Cline
13591	Sullens, Charlotte	OK	1871	Enos Sullens	Daniel Loveall	Anna Sweaney		Levi & Myra Sweaney
3935	Sullens, Viola	41yrs	1866	E E Sullens	Daniel Loveall	Anna Sweaney	Johnathan Loveal & Ruth Allen	Levi Sweaney & Alyna Blackard
4134	Sullivan, William	NC	1873	Callie Sullivan	David Sullivan	Mary Roop		King & Louisa Roop
5256	Sullivan, Betty	NC	1873	Felix Sullivan	John Young	Orlean Pennington	Wm & Cathrine Young	Stephen & Johannah Pennington
4133	Sullivan, Callie	NC	1880	William Sillivan	J C Finley	Ider Hart	Washington & Elisabeth Finley	Eliazer & Nancy Hart
3623	Sullivan, Margret	VA	1874	Daniel Sullivan	Wm Weaver	Catharine Baldwin		Wm & Margret Baldwin
4316	Sullivan, Martha	NC	1878	none	David Sullivan	Mary Roop		King & Louisa Roop
5192	Sullivan, Martha	VA	1894	David Sullivan	Frank Walls	Malinda Blevins	G W & Malinda Walls	Allen & Malinda Blevins
4315	Sullivan, Mary	NC	1855	David Sullivan	King Roop	Louisa Baldwin		Wm & Margret Baldwin
5193	Sullivan, Mary	VA	1881	Roby Sullivan	Frank Walls	Malinda Blevins	G W & Malinda Walls	Alen & Malindia Blevins
5875	Sullivan, Rausa	NC	1855	Wesley Sullivan	Ebenezer Hart	Nancy Inghram	Washington & Elisabeth Hart	Richard & Jennie Ingham
4882	Sullivan, Roby	VA	1885	none	David Sullivan	Neala Hart		John & Polly Hart
20499*	Sullivan, Salena	TN	1854		George Moseley	Rachel Mitchel	James & Nancy Moseley	Jeff & Sarah Mitchel
13826	Sumerous, Florence	GA	1870	William Sumerous	Thompson Whitmore	Martha Lyon	Hugh & Polly Whitmore	Harvey & Susan Lyon
17338	Summer, Artilda	GA	1850	Linford Summer	Francis Tidwell	Margaret Gravitt	John Langley & Sally Tramle	Obidiah Gravitt
15415*	Summerhour, Agnes	GA	1902		Jordan Summerhour	Clarisy Royal	Phillis Hill	Summer Royal & Fanny Cole
15414*	Summerhour, Carl	GA	1898		Jordan Summerhour	Clarisy Royal	Phillis Hill	Summer Royal & Fanny Cole
20854*	Summerhour, Clarissy	GA	1828		Wm Summer Royal	Fannie Cole	Bill Bride	Phil & Creecy Cole
15413*	Summerhour, Furman	GA	1888		Jacob Summerhour	Octavia Blide	Jordan & Clarisy Summerhour	Bill Blide & Jane Jefferson
15412*	Summerhour, Jacob	GA	1843	Octavia Summerhour	Jordan Summerhour	Clarisy Royal	York & Phillis Hill	Summer Royal & Fanny Cole
15411*	Summerhour, Jordan	GA	1854	Fannie Summerhour	Jordan Summerhour	Clarisy Royal	Phillis Hill	Summer Royal & Fanny Cole
15410*	Summerhour, Lavonia	GA	1897		Jordan Summerhour	Clarisy Royal	Phillis Hill	Summer Royal & Fanny Cole
15409*	Summerhour, Luther	GA	1897		Jacob Summerhour	Octavia Blide	Jordan & Clarisy Summerhour	Bill Blide & Jane Jefferson
14482*	Summerhour, Octavia	GA	1860	Jacob Summerhour	Bill Blide	Jane Jefferson	Mary Blide	Lewis & Kitty Scudders
15408*	Summerhour, Octavia	GA	1894		Jacob Summerhour	Octavia Blide	Jordan & Clarisy Summerhour	Bill Blide & Jane Jefferson
15407*	Summerhour, Odell	GA	1891		Jacob Summerhour	Octavia Blide	Jordan & Clarisy Summerhour	Bill Blide & Jane Jefferson
15406*	Summerhour, Sherman	GA	1893		Jordan Summerhour	Clarisy Royal	Phillis Hill	Summer Royal & Fanny Cole
15405*	Summerhour, Tully	GA	1900		Jordan Summerhour	Clarisy Royal	Phillis Hill	Summer Royal & Fanny Cole

18907	Summers, Ben	AR	1859	Mary Summers	Wm Summers	Polley Pack		Jessie & Jennie Page
18906	Summers, Charles	AR	1852		Wm Summers	Polley Pack		Jessie & Jennie Page
7524	Summers, Lucinda	OK	1883	Lem Summers	David Swadley	Mary Fannin		Joseph & Jane Fannin
5411	Summey, Andrew	GA		Margrett Summey	Henry Summey	Marry Helton	George & Barbra Summey	Jake & Clarcey Helton
2623	Summing, Dock	GA	1886	Lula Summing	Linford Summing	Artilda Tidwell	F M & Sallie Tidwell	Margaret Grantt
2624	Summing, John	GA	1876	Katie Summing	Linford Summing	Artilda Tidwell	F M & Sallie Tidwell	Margaret Grantt
2620	Summing, Joseph	GA	1883	none	Linford Summing	Artilda Tidwell		Francis & Sallie Tidwell
2625	Summing, Linford	GA	1881	Bessie Summing	Linford Summing	Artilda Tidwell		FM & Sallie Tidwell
2621	Summing, Ophelia	GA	1878	none	Linford Summing	Artilda Tidwell	F M & Sallie Tidwell	Margaret Grantt
2622	Summing, William	GA	1873	Sallie Summing	Linford Summing	Artilda Tidwell		F M & Sallie Tidwell
15678 *	Sutton, Anna	GA	1872	Joe Sutton	Henry Winters	Jane Brown		Gilford & Mary Chandler
15728 *	Sutton, Ed	GA	1870	Willie Sutton	Balous Sutton	Adaline Welch		Sam & Nancy Freeman
13583 *	Sutton, Eugene	GA	1870	Cora Sutton	Ros Sutton	Francis Welch		Joe & Millie Welch
14849	Sutton, Hester	GA	1868	W P Sutton	W R Wright	Manerva Whelchel	Jesse & Lovicie Wright	
18322	Sutton, Isham	TN	1836		Thomas Sutton	Hanah Lawson		Drewry Lawson Sr. & Hanah Potes
15729 *	Sutton, Joe	GA	1873		Ron Sutton	Francis Welch		Joe & Millie Welch
19739	Sutton, Julia	GA	1868	Thomas Sutton	Robert Evans	Margaret Barnett	Robert & Sallie Evans	Richard & Rhoda Barnett
14840	Sutton, Wm, Lily, Wesley	GA	18, 17 15 yrs		W P Sutton	Hester Wright		W R & Manerva Wright
7525	Swadley, Joseph	OK	1880	Fronia Swadley	David Swadley	Mary Fannin		Joseph & Jane Fannin
7545	Swadley, Marion	OK	1887	none	David Swadley	Mary Fannin		Joseph & Jane Fannin
7521	Swadley, Mary	MO	1890	none	David Swadley	Mary Fannin		Joseph & Jane Fannin
3600	Swadley, Nettie	MO	1860	Thomas Swadley	Michael Fender	Martha Wallis	Daniel & Dicy Fender	Jeptha & Nancy Wallis
17942 *	Swan, Harriet	TN			Nathan Harris	Charlotte Parks		Jennie Houston
7712	Swaney, Harriet	MO	1860	James Swaney	Jesse Walker	Susan White		
15067	Swann, Margaret	GA	1880		W B Swann	Polly Kelly	James & Rebecca Swann	
16038	Swann, Serrena	GA	1847		W B Swann	Polly Kelly	James & Rebecca Swann	
5314	Sweaney, Andrew	MO	1849	Sarah Sweaney	Levi Sweaney	Myra Blackard		
11003	Sweaney, Andrew	MO	1881		Andrew Sweaney	Sarah Rush	Levi & Alyna Sweaney	Ephram & Sarah Rush
11986	Sweaney, Frank	MO	1896		Andrew Sweaney	Sarah Rush	Levi & Myra Sweaney	Ephraim & Sarah Rush

11515	Sweaney, Ira	MO	1886		Andrew Sweaney	Sarah Rush	Levi & Myra Sweaney	Ephraim & Sarah Rush
8233	Sweaney, John	MO	1874	Ollie Sweaney		Charlotte Sweaney		Levi & Myra Sweaney
12223	Sweaney, John	MO	1873	Athelia Sweaney				
11514	Sweaney, Sophronia	MO	1890		Andrew Sweaney	Sarah Rush	Levi & Myra Sweaney	Ephraim & Sarah Rush
11749	Sweaney, William	MO	1876	Mary Sweaney	Andrew Sweaney	Sarah Rush	Levi & Myra Sweaney	Ephraim & Sara Rush
18308	Sweat, Emery	IN	1863	Minnie Sweat	John Sweat	Olive Winburn		Hary Winburn
15006	Sweat, Marvel	GA	1853	Barbra Sweat	Jim Sweat	Mahaily Baggett	Ephram & Salie Sweat	
18309	Sweat, Minnie	IN	35yrs	Emery Sweat	Benson Russell	Nancy Simpson		Elic & Jamie Simpson
18312	Sweat, Olive	IN	1826	Oliver Sweat	Harry Winburn	Kizar James	David Winburn	Lula James
4164	Sweckard, Martha	MO	1852	Benjamin Sweckard	Isiah Hambelton	Martha Martin		
20434	Swicegood, Lou	TN	1872	William Swicegood	Richard McDuffy	Mary Nichols	Ceiley McDuffy	
17992	Swift, George	KS	1872	Daisy Swift	Nathan Swift	Adalaine Holt		Berry & Susanna Holt
17993	Swift, Jefferson	KS	1861	Loui Swift	Nathan Swift	Adalaine Holt		Berry & Susanna Holt
17991	Swift, John	KS	1865	Mary Swift	Nathan Swift	Adalaine Holt		Berry & Susanna Holt
17781	Swift, Nathan Jr.	MO	1868	Annie Swift	Nathan Swift	Adaline Holt		Berry & Susanna Holt
10763	Swinford, William	TN	1875	Mary Swinford	Markis Swinford	Margret Runions	Elijah & Celia Swinford	
7338	Swofford, Mamie	TX	1880		Moses William	Althea Cook	Joseph & Catharine Williams	Oscar Cook
20575*	Tabb, Artaway	TN	1855		John Tabb	Henriette Graves		
2904	Tabor, Bertha	AR		H A Tabor				
21120	Tadlock, Mary	OK	1861	John Tadlock	Leroy Martin	Mary Phillips	Taylor Martin	Daniel Phillips
21183	Talbert, William	TN	1866	widower	Russel Talbert	Mary Saunders	Jeptie Talbert	James & Betsy McKenney
12734	Talent, Emma	TN	1868	William Talent	Lemuel Michael	Mary Irvin	Jacob Michael	George & Phoebe Irvin
12730	Talent, Tennie	AL	1871	JamesTalent	Lemuel Michael	Mary Irvin	Jacob Michael	George & Phoebe Irvin
486	Taliferro, Lou Dorra	TN	1875		Jesse Plummer	Frances Stamper	Plummer	Stamper
21112	Tallent, Charley	TN	24 yrs	Rachel Tallent	J.M. Tallent	Sarah Wilcox		Joseph Wilcox
20521	Tallent, Mary	TN	1833			Elizabeth Sanders		
3466	Tally, Elizabeth	VA		John Tally	Alfred Blevins	Margia Huddler	James & Macy Blevins	Joseph & Elizabeth Huddler
940	Tally, Robert	GA	1829	none	Horatio Tally	Mary Lovelace	Elisabeth Henson	Pryor Tally
19984	Tangsley, Nancy	GA	1857	John Tangsley	David Anthony	Elizabeth Wade	Martin Anthony	Henry & Rebecca Wade
20170	Tankersley, Andrew	GA	1875	Ola Tankersley	N.C. Tankersley	Eliza Lowe	Sarah Tankersley	
20159	Tankersley, Emory	GA	1881		N.C. Tankersley	Eliza Lowe	Sarah Tankersley	

6277	Tanksley, N.C.	GA	1840	Eliza Tanksley		Sarah Tanksley		James & Polley Mohanee
2319	Tanner, Albert	OK	1878	Effie Tanner	James Tanner	Susan Buttry		John & Margarett Buttry
13743 ½ *	Tanner, Charley	GA	1885		Tom Tanner Sr.	Sallie Smith		Ned & Caoline Hay
13746 *	Tanner, Ida	GA	1876		Tom Tanner Sr.	Sallie Smith		Ned & Caoline Hay
9880	Tanner, Jane	GA	1856	A L Tanner	John Helton	Delila Hester	Joseph Helton	Benjamin Hester
2757	Tanner, John	OK		Mary Tanner	James Tanner	Susan Buttry		John & Margaret Buttry
2423	Tanner, Lafayette	OK	1877	Naancy Tanner	James Tanner	Susan Buttry		John & Margaret Buttry
17810	Tanner, Louisa	KS	1873	Thomas Tanner	Daniel Dunkin	Mary Golden		Alex Graham & Margret Golden
22457	Tanner, Ruby	KS	1906		Thomas Tanner	Louisa Dunkin	John & Elizabeth Tanner	Daniel & Mary Dunkin
13745 *	Tanner, Sally	GA	1849		Monroe Dickens Or Ned Hay	Caroline Smith		James & Bowlin Bradley
2247	Tanner, Susan	OK	1851	James Tanner	John Buttry	Margaret Martin	Wm & Luvica Buttry	Wm & Susan Martin
13744 *	Tanner, Tom Jr.	GA	1877		Tom Tanner Sr.	Sallie Smith		Ned & Caoline Hay
2257	Tanner, Vernon	OK	1880	none	James Tanner	Susan Buttry		John & Margaret Buttry
14436	Tarkinton, Charles	NC	1844		Arthur Tarkinton	Sylvia Harper		Charles Harper
12060	Tarpley, Charles	CA			Harve Tarpley	Mahala Kell		Tabiatha Dorcas Kell
12061	Tarpley, Edward	CA			Harve Tarpley	Mahala Kell		Tabiatha Dorcas Kell
12059	Tarpley, John	CA			Harve Tarpley	Mahala Kell		Tabiatha Dorcas Kell
3282	Tarpley, Nellie	CA	1883	none	Harvey Tarpley	Mary Kell		David & Dorcas Kell
948	Tarpley, Samuel	NM	1845	Jennie Tarpley	John Tarpley	Sarah Nicholson	Sterling & Lucresia Tarpley	Merriett & Mary Davis
19620	Tarpy, Nancy	TN	1857		Robert Hatcher	Mary Hooper	John & Henrietta Hatcher	
7694	Tarrapin, Charley	OK	1881	Polly Tarrapin	Little Tarrapin	Sallie	Eah da teck	Dul las teck
10916	Taster, Susie	OK	1885		Taster	Sallie		Johnson Fields & Junt-na-ha-go
19598	Tate, Burr	TN	1890		Tip Tate	Rutha Wilson	Isaac & Polley Tate	
20310	Tate, Emerson	MO			Ben Tate	Eliza Herrell		Emerson & Clarisa Herrell
19596	Tate, Estella	TN	1868		Tip Tate	Rutha Wilson	Isaac & Polly Tate	
2087	Tate, Ida	OK		John Tate	J.H. Hughs	Rebecca Wilson		Wilson
20534 *	Tate, William	TN	1850		Ellis Tate Raney	Mariah Tate		Beryson & Miney Tate
15141	Tatum, Bell	GA	1888		James Jackson	Nancy Wallis		Jesse & Liza Wallace
8389	Tatum, Emma	GA	1881	J L Tatum	Joseph Blalock	Georgia Rice	Isam & Martha Blalock	

20907	Tatum, Henrietta	GA	1885		S.S. Tatum	Freby Lindsy		George Lindsy & Serana Crow
263	Tatum, Leverda	GA	1882	Thomas Tatum	Richard Adams	Docia Sharp	David & Clarinda Adams	Richard & Elizabeth Sharp
18391	Taylor, Aida	AL	20yrs	Robert Taylor	Robert Freeman	Misomee Williams	Ross & Roxana Freeman	Wash & Edy Williams
19762	Taylor, Amanda	TN	1857	Rufus Taylor	Landon Duffield	Malinda Taylor	George & Charlotte Duffield	Jasper & Tena Taylor
22144	Taylor, Amos	GA	1855	Elizabeth Taylor	William Taylor	Sarah Joyce		Anna Kugole
20685	Taylor, Andrew	FL	1879		Jacob Taylor	Malissa Kimbrough	Richard & Susan Taylor	Hiram & Nancy Kimbrough
9758	Taylor, Ann	TN	1826	J B Taylor (decd)	Zachariah Crass	Sarah Hicks	Eli Crass	Marshall Hicks
7796	Taylor, Annie	TX	1882	Omer Taylor	James Eidson	Jinnie Avants	Orn & Mary Eidson	Thos & Francis Avants
1012	Taylor, Arabella	GA	1855	James Taylor	Augustus Williams	Sarah Ledbetter	John & Rhoda Williams	Johnston & Nancy Ledbetter
19841	Taylor, Arthur et al	NC			F.R. Stone	Sarah Poindexter	John & Susan Taylor	
1010	Taylor, Augustus	GA	1882	none	James Taylor	Arabella Williams	Aus & Jane Taylor	Augustus & Sarah Williams
7600	Taylor, Boney	VA		Noah Taylor	Wiley Farmer	Lydia Miller	Henry & Nancy Farmer	Irnat & Bashabe Miller
22067	Taylor, Camel	MO	1869	none	David Taylor	Elizabeth Furgason	Zebadee & Mary Taylor	James & Martha Furgason
18282	Taylor, Catherine	GA	1841	John Taylor	Drew Morris	Sallie Davenport	Billy & Julia Morris	
3591	Taylor, Charles	VA	25yrs	Lilly Taylor	R T Taylor	Mary Lyles	Robert & Catherine Taylor	George & Margret Lyles
17336	Taylor, Charles	GA	1874	Cleola Taylor	Ed Taylor	Judia Butler		Ben & Ester Butler
20118	Taylor, David	MO	1837	Elisabeth Taylor	Zebadee Taylor	Mary Grooms	Samuel & Mary Taylor	George & Millie Grooms
10201	Taylor, Eli	KY		Jane Taylor	Wiley Taylor	Rosamond Stamper	Danny & Hesse Taylor	Eli & Susanna Stamper
5431	Taylor, Eliza	OK	1874	W H Taylor	Johnson Wood	Martha Martin	Thompson Wood	Wm & Susan Martin
11088	Taylor, Elon	VA		Samuel Taylor	James Blevins	Margaret Edmondson	Wells & Betsy Blevins	Andy & Susan Blevins
20424*	Taylor, Elsy	TN	1856	Samuel Taylor	Allen Love	Eliza Burnett	Rosette Love	Julias & Caroline Burnett
5962	Taylor, Elzada	OK	1822	David Taylor				
20686	Taylor, Eugene	FL	1882		Jacob Taylor	Malissa Kimbrough	Richard & Susan Taylor	Hiram & Nancy Kimbrough
19761	Taylor, George	TN	1881		Rufus Taylor	Amanda Duffield	Rufus & Maria Taylor	Landon & Malinda Duffield
22070	Taylor, George	MO	1861	none	David Taylor	Elizabeth Furgason	Zebadee & Mary Taylor	James & Martha Furgason
2659	Taylor, Hattie	MO	1875	Ray Taylor	Samuel Anglen	Nancy Kirby	John & Vilettie Anglen	Henry & Rebecca Kirby
18969	Taylor, Henry	FL	36yrs		W.H. Taylor	Margie Smith	Richard & Susan Taylor	Maurice & Martha Smith
22120	Taylor, Jack	MO	1881	none	James Taylor	Annie Davison	Zebadee & Mary Taylor	Armstrong & Louisa Davison
20684	Taylor, Jacob	FL	1872		Jacob Taylor	Malissa Kimbrough	Richard & Susan Taylor	Hiram & Nancy Kimbrough
7343	Taylor, James	TX	1879	Netty Taylor	John Taylor	Cate Nolin	John Taylor	

ID	Name	State	Year	Spouse	Father	Mother	Father-in-law	Parents-in-law
22066	Taylor, James	MO	1858	widower	David Taylor	Elizabeth Furgason	Zebadee & Mary Taylor	James & Martha Furgason
22119	Taylor, James	OK	1843	Annie Taylor	Zebedee Taylor	Mary Grooms	Samuel & Mary Taylor	George & Millie Grooms
10204	Taylor, Jane	KY	1852	Eli Taylor	Wesley Brown	Sarah Stamper		Eli & Susanna Stamper
22068	Taylor, Jasper	MO	1873	none	David Taylor	Elizabeth Furgason	Zebadee & Mary Taylor	James & Martha Furgason
17621	Taylor, Jess	GA	1864	Mary Taylor	Dud Taylor	Caroline York	Cincinnath & Sersie Taylor	John & Sary York
6739	Taylor, John	NC	1844	Cyntha Taylor	Zeke Osborne	Polly Taylor	Elis Osborne	John Taylor
7960	Taylor, John	NC	1854	Nancy Taylor	Tobias Taylor	Milley		Hiram & Annie Stamper
2395	Taylor, Jonathan	NC	1874	Allie Taylor	James Taylor	Hannah Manchester	David Taylor	
14280*	Taylor, Julia	TN	1865	Henry Taylor	John Hardigan	Sina Jackson	Dave Hartigan	George & Juliet Bibb
14797	Taylor, Julia	WV	21yrs	H H Taylor	W W Walls	Emline Peak		Hugh & Marga Peak
10420	Taylor, Kate	OK	1855	Wm Taylor (decd)	William Wilkins	Lucinda Wood	John & Kate Wilkins	Michael & Mary Wood
4571	Taylor, Laura	VA	1880	Andy Taylor	Eli Hart	Jennie Sheets	Stephen & Rebecca Hart	Andrew & Katherine Sheets
21604	Taylor, Lawrence	NC	1881	Alice Taylor	Rostie Taylor	Virginia Stone	Andrew Taylor	Fouk & Elizabeth Stone
8533	Taylor, Lilley	VA	1884	John Taylor	William Hollaway	Louisa Waters		Wm & Zilpha Waters
21818	Taylor, Liza	FL	1865	Henry Taylor	Henry Sowell	Ann Chechee		Lydia Franklin Chechee
7345	Taylor, Maggie	TX	1881	none	John Taylor	Cate Nolin		
10206	Taylor, Martha	GA	1851	none	Wiley Taylor	Rosamond Stamper		Eli & Susanna Stamper
3438	Taylor, Mary	AL	73yrs	Washington Taylor	William Colbert	Cealy Sizemore	George Colbert	Wm Sizemore & Polly Bailey
3755	Taylor, Mary	VA	47yrs	R T Taylor	George Lyles	Margret Hart		John & Nancy Hart
7344	Taylor, Mary	TX				Ann Pinkston	Richard Poindexter	
7624	Taylor, Mary	GA	1846	Albert Taylor	James Watts	Deliza Rich	Joseph & Plesant Watts	Lidy Cargle
18143	Taylor, Mary	OK	1855	Marion Taylor	Jacob Cresson	Martha Cresson	Walter & Mary Cresson	Elijah & Elizabeth Cresson
20158	Taylor, Mary	NC	1873	W.H. Taylor	James Davis	Tennessee Taylor	Isaac & Rhoda Davis	Herald Taylor
13024	Taylor, Merrill	LA	1869	Mary Taylor	J P Lemplor	Rebecca Monk	Merrill Monk	Nancy Gray
19842	Taylor, Mrs. A.J.	NC	1859	A.J. Taylor	F.R. Stone	Sarah Poindexter	Enoch & Elizabeth Stone	Denson & Sally Poindexter
4545	Taylor, Nancy	VA	1877	Lee Taylor	Noah Baldwin	Mahala Blevins		W D & Margret Baldwin
10138	Taylor, Nancy	WV	1888	Andrew Taylor	Greensberry Green	Mary Perdew	Nancy Green	Nathaniel & Sallie Perdew
22084	Taylor, Olma	OK	1882	Levi Taylor	David Logan	Mary Akin	Thomas & Eliza Logan	Samuel Akin
15875	Taylor, Owen	NC	1825		Buck Taylor	Salley Collins	Bill & Polly Taylor	
18389	Taylor, Robert	AL	28yrs	Aida Taylor		Cealy Taylor		Wash & Matilda Taylor

22065	Taylor, Robert	MO	1875	none	David Taylor	Elizabeth Furgason	Zebadee & Mary Taylor	James & Martha Furgason
22992	Taylor, Robert	VA	1874	Alice Taylor		Martha Taylor		Rosey Taylor
3589	Taylor, Sanders	VA	24yrs	Claddie Taylor	R L Taylor	Mary Lyles	Robert & Catherine Taylor	George & Margret Lyles
19288	Taylor, Sarah	NC	1839	Wright Taylor	Isaac Davis	Rhoda James	Mashack & Lydia Davis	
21707	Taylor, Synthia	OK	1847	Robert Taylor	William Horn	Margaret Ledbetter	Jeramiah & Cynthia Horn	John & Cynthia Ledbetter
18970	Taylor, Walter	FL	21yrs	Ida Taylor	W.H. Taylor	Margie Smith	Richard & Susan Taylor	Maurice & Martha Smith
21775	Taylor, William	OK	1860	Dollie Taylor	Harm Taylor	Philby Nickles		John Nickles
22069	Taylor, Zebadee	MO	1856	none	David Taylor	Elizabeth Furgason	Zebadee & Mary Taylor	James & Martha Furgason
17516	Tayrien, Nellie	OK	1880	Charley Tayrien	J.A. Hickman	Sarah Hicks	Fred & Polly Hickman	Linsey Hicks & Catherine Miller
4279	Teague, Mary	OK	1872	Benjamin Teague	John Brown	Lodusky Tidwell	James & Nancy Brown	John & Lucrecia Tidwell
22866	Teague, Mollie	TN	1877	Jack Teague	William Headrick	Ella Haynes	Andrew & Eliza Headrick	Albert & Martha Haynes
20326*	Teasly, Lindsy	GA	1818	Julia Teasly	Newman Allen	Millie Allen		Ned Allen
19175	Teat, Wade	AL	1829		Edwin Teat	Ava Garner	Baner & Sallie Teat	
18283	Teat, William	GA	1839		Erwin Teat	Ava Garner	Boner & Sally Teat	
7341	Tedrow, George	OK	1881	none	John Tedrow	Harriett Beggs	David & Elisa Tedrow	Robert & Adeline Beggs
17180	Teechee, Wadee	OK	1847	Jack Teehee	Webber	Garkie lo wee star	Okie Oogarductie	
17179	Teehee, Jack	OK	1845	Wadee Techee	Charles Deehee	Wagigee Yoholar		Dulsy & Hogjarnee Yoholar
1393	Teel, Lafayette	OK	1858		John Teel	Minervia Fleetwood		Chas & Lucinda Fleetwood
13862	Teems, Susan	GA	1864	Miles Teems	G W Edwards	Catherine Bird	Thomas & Agnes Edwards	Robert & Polly Dowdy
12006	Temples, Annie	GA	1887		Thomas Temples	Harriett Gravely	Patrick & Mary Temples	
15140	Temples, Elizabeth	GA	1864	John Temples	Bailey White	Francis Ezall		
15139	Temples, Francis	GA	1842	William Temples	James Clark	Tasey Brewer	Patrick & Susie Clark	George & Tempie Brewer
12005	Temples, General	GA	1880		Thomas Temples	Harriett Gravely	Patrick & Mary Temples	
12004	Temples, Gertrude	GA	1894		Thomas Temples	Harriett Gravely	Patrick & Mary Temples	
12003	Temples, Lula	GA	1892		Thomas Temples	Harriett Gravely	Patrick & Mary Temples	
12002	Temples, Thomas	GA	1884	Jane Temples	Thomas Temples	Harriett Gravely	Patrick & Mary Temples	
12007	Temples, Thomas	GA	1850	Harriett Temples	Patrick Temples	Mary Stephens	Larkin & Susie Temples	
19407*	Terhune, Alford	GA	1890		Alford Terhune	Kizzie Fallen	Berry & Elcie Terhune	
22027	Terry, Alexander	OK	1855	Arminda Terry	William Terry	Mary Bailey	David & Lucinda Terry	
7797	Terry, Cerene	OK	1836	Thomas Terry	John Jackson	Elizabeth Caldwell		Andrew & Cerene Caldwell
16212	Terry, Dola	OK	1886		James Terry	Mollie Williams	Thos & Carene Terry	Wm & Mary Williams
7798	Terry, James	OK	1848	Mollie Terry	Thomas Terry	Cerene Jackson		John & Elizabeth Jackson

7342	Terry, Jasper	OK		Mary Terry	Thomas Terry			Elizabeth Jackson
18163	Terry, Martha	GA	1861	Thomas Terry	Wm Shephard	Sarah Short		Pollie Handcock
16214	Terry, Mollie	OK	1860	J W Terry	W A Williams	Mary Haynes	Joseph & Catherine Williams	
11024	Tester, Sarah	VA	1855		John Tester	Sarah Mofield		James Dolison & Polly Mofield
3516	Testerman, Laura	NC	1874	Barn	J R Baldwin	Marilda Jones	Wm & Marilda Baldwin	
5524	Testerman, Lucy	NC	1874	Carsen Testerman	Cicero Blevins	Elisabeth Childers	Daniel & Anna Blevins	Franklin & Susana Childers
14673	Testerman, Marthy	VA	1876		Henry Testerman	Catherine Spencer		Solomon & Ellen Spencer
11810	Testerman, Robert	VA	1874	Molly Testerman	Henry Testerman	Catharine Spencer		Ellen Spencer
4883	Tetters, Mary	VA	1883	Claud Tetters	David Sullivan	Neala Hart		John & Polly Hart
5473	Thomas, Bruce	GA	1869	Marousia Thomas	Thomas Green	Nancy Thomas		Sarah Thomas
9321	Thomas, Calvin decd	GA	1855	Caroline Thomas	Elisha Thomas	Pollie	Aaron & Sallie Thomas	
15066 *	Thomas, Darthula	TN	1834	Arthur Thomas	Harrison Houston	Catharine Abington	George & Elsy Houston	Clem & Ruth Abington
15138	Thomas, Donor	GA	1883	Charlie Thomas	Jeffrey Beck	Mandy Loggins	Coleman Davis & Elmina Beck	
18076	Thomas, Donor	GA	1882		Jeffrey Beck	Mandy Loggins	Coleman Davis & Elmira Beck	
19314	Thomas, Emily	FL	1871	John Thomas	William Sanders	Prudence Grantham	John & Sarah Reyer	Mathew Grantham & Hattie Gardner
22626	Thomas, Enoke	TN	1853	Mosuria Thomas	Elisha Thomas	Mary Lee	Aron & Sally Thomas	John & Elizabeth Lee
18664	Thomas, Ethel	GA	1887	Harry Thomas	Andrew Etter	Julia Stancel	Francis Etter	John Stancel
14830	Thomas, Fannie	VA	1880	R M Thomas	J P Rouse	Adaline Heath	Isaac & Margrete Rouse	John & Alcie Heath
17446	Thomas, Florence	MI	1876	Daniel Thomas	James Spottswood	Sarah Winslow	Peter & Lizzie Spottswood	Wm & Cynthia Winslow
22404 *	Thomas, Hannah	OK	1855	Henry Thomas	George Landrum	Peggy Walker	Jack & Charity Dixon	Mose & Lucy Walker
9238	Thomas, Lillie	AL	1880	J H Thomas	Noah Bare	Meacy Blevins		Jesse & Catharine Blevins
17072	Thomas, Lillie	NC	1876	W E Thomas	Andrew Davis	Silia Radford	John & Sintha Davis	
18704	Thomas, Mary	FL	1873	Alonzo Thomas	Jasper Shanks	Victoria Barrios		Ferdinand Barrios & Eliza Reyer
19326 *	Thomas, Mary	TN	1870	Wm Thomas	Lorenzo Fore	Gemima McGill	Robert & Polly Hoyl	Rolan & Jane McGill
10788 *	Thomas, Mattie	TN	1875	S T Thomas	Hairie Jefferson	Luciey Jackson		
19826	Thomas, Nora							
14327	Thomas, Pearl	TX		Rosser Thomas	James Jackson	Sarah Maloney	John & Elizabeth Jackson	
2569	Thomas, Rossetta	GA	1863	T W Thomas	Henry Campbell	Susanah Davenport		John & Elisabeth Davenport
5477	Thomas, Zara	GA	41yrs	none	Thomas Green	Nancy Thomas		Sarah Thomas
18412	Thompkins, Mrs. S.Y.	FL	1851	S.Y. Thompkins	James Williams	Margret Miles		James & Millie Miles
3653	Thompson, Alex	VA	23yrs	Lizzie Thompson		Milie Thompson		Sam & Margret Thompson

22142*	Thompson, Alfred	OK	1849		Sam Thompson	Hannah		
21265	Thompson, Amanda	TX	1872	William Thompson	T.B. Coulston	Mary Graham		James & Martha Graham
5693	Thompson, Andrew	VA	1890	none	James Thompson	Almeda Thompson	Calvin & Sinthy Thompson	Calvin & Elizabeth Thompson
5161	Thompson, Augustus	OK	1883	Lula Thompson	Mason Thompson	Flora Banko	Maria Swapshaw	Caroline Banks
22306*	Thompson, Berry	OK	1857	Annie Thompson	Dave Thompson	Mary Stover		
5740	Thompson, Calvin	VA	1846	Elizabeth Thompson	Samuel Thompson	Margret Blevins	John & Polley Thompson	Elizebeth Blevins
6698	Thompson, Charley	VA	1873	Mary Thompson	Calvin Thompson	Elizabeth Welch	Samuel & Margaret Thompson	James & Nancy Welch
5149	Thompson, Elijah	NC	1852	Malinda Thompson	Samuel Thompson	Marget Blevins	John & Mary Thompson	Elizabeth Blevins
15719	Thompson, Elizabeth	OK	1827		Amos Thornton	Betsey McIntosh		
8609	Thompson, Ella	GA	1885	William Thompson	Jefferson Reece	Miller Forest	Marion & Elizbeth Reece	William & Loucindia Forest
5835	Thompson, Ervin	VA	1881					
7635	Thompson, Evert	VA	1884	none	George Thompson	Levaniah Hart	James & Caroline Thompson	Eliazer & Nancy Hart
18373	Thompson, Frankie	KS		Wm Thompson	John Brock	Rebecca Langley	James & Sarah Brock	Matthew Langley
7638	Thompson, George	VA	1854	Levaniah Thompson	James Thompson	Caroline Head	John & Polly Thompson	Elexander & Liza Head
22005*	Thompson, George	OK		Roda Thompson		Mary Thompson		
4116	Thompson, Harvey	NC	1884	none	James Thompson	Melvine Sullivan	Samuel & Marget Thompson	
7636	Thompson, Henry	NC	1882	Louise Thompson	George Thompson	Levaniah Hart	James & Caroline Thompson	Eliazer & Nancy Hart
14748	Thompson, Henry	VA	1882	Martha Thompson	James Thompson	Caroline Thompson	John & Polly Thompson	Elexander & Liza Head
4115	Thompson, James	NC	1854	Melvina Thompson	Samuel Thompson	Marget Blevins	John & Mary Thompson	Elizabeth Blevins
7472	Thompson, James	OK	1877	Maggie Thompson	James Thompson	Elisabeth Treadwell	Matthew Thompson	
9572	Thompson, James	OK	1826	Nancy Thompson	Thompson	Millsap		
22812	Thompson, James	OK		Eigty Thompson	Nathan Thompson	? Milesap	Nathan Thompson	Hester Black
5741	Thompson, John	VA	1875	Minnie Thompson	Calvin Thompson	Elizebeth Welch	Samuel & Margaret Thompson	James & Nancy Welch
8569	Thompson, John	NC	1887	none	Felix Thompson	Rebecca Miller	Calvin & Nella Thompson	Betty & Marion Miller
17295	Thompson, John	OK		Sarah Thompson	Thompson	Betty Hyde		Benj & Betty Hyde
5112	Thompson, Joseph	TN	1879	none	Wilson Thompson	Eda Eldreth	Wesley & Amanda Thompson	John & Sarah Eldreth
22481	Thompson, Joseph	OK	1872	Bridie Thompson	Nathaniel Thompson	Mollie Lake		
21334	Thompson, Josie	MO	1869	Perry Thompson	James Reading	Sarah Eblen	George & Eliza Reading	Jesse & Rachel Eblen

7637	Thompson, Levaniah	VA	1862	George Thompson	Eliazer Hart	Nancy Inghram	Washington & Elisbeth Hart	Richard & Ginnie Inghram
20104 *	Thompson, Lillie	GA	1860	Tom Thompson	Calvin Luckey	Mary Smith		Sarah & Fedrick Smith
3652	Thompson, Lizzie	VA			James Thompson		Calvin & Elisabeth Thompson	Alvin & Vilene Thompson
4317	Thompson, Louisa	NC	1880	Lee Thompson	David Sullivan	Mary Roop		King & Louisa Roop
3610	Thompson, Marcella	NC	1865	widow	Andrew Hurly	Nancy Blackburn	Samuel & Marget Thompson	
5148	Thompson, Marget	NC	1824	Samuel Thompson	Daniel Blevins	Elizabeth Blevins		James & Lydia Blevins
117	Thompson, Mary	GA	1865	William Thompson	William Henson	Maryan Hood	Joseph & Nancy Henson	Enoch & Milly Hood
8386	Thompson, Mary	OK	1846	George Thompson	Benj Yeates	Elizabeth	Larkin & Nancy Yeates	
17442	Thompson, Mary	GA	1865	Wm Thompson	Wm Henson	Mary Hood	Joseph & Nancy Henson	Enoch & Milly Hood
18985 *	Thompson, Mary	IN	1844		Mathew Morgan	Nancy Bass		Joseph & Tempie Bass
11565	Thompson, Matilda	TN	1861	William Thompson	Marion Miller	Betty Blevins		Betsy Blevins
8451	Thompson, Milley	VA	1879	Frank Thompson	John Bone	Mary Blevins		Armstrong & Catharine Blevins
5833	Thompson, Minnie	VA			Winfield Thompson	Sarah	James Thompson	
9570	Thompson, Nancy	OK	80yrs	James Thompson	Watson Batle	Sarah Hyde		Benj Hyde & Betsy Leatherwood
19211	Thompson, Nancy	GA	1852		Hillsman Stansel	Sarah Thompson	John & Catharine Stansel	James & Nancy Thompson
22813	Thompson, Nancy	OK	1826	James Thompson	Watson Batte	? Hide		Benjamin Hide
13981	Thompson, Nellie	OK	1887	Oscar Thompson	John Horn	Mattie Harmon	Tom & Nelly Horn	
8145	Thompson, Nicholas	OK	1858	none	James Thompson	Polizia Martin		Joseph & Julia Martin
22058 *	Thompson, Rhoda	OK	1842	George Thompson	Harry Martin	Celia Martin		Amy Martin
21751 *	Thompson, Robin	OK	1865		Robin Thompson	Patsy Nevins		Sallie Baker
6040	Thompson, Samuel	VA	1864	Susan Mussler	Alvin Thompson	Syntha Cole	John & Mary Thompson	Charles & Elizabeth Cole
5147	Thompson, Sarah	NC	1884	none	Elijah Thompson	Malinda Testament	Samuel & Margot Thompson	James & Milley Testament
14670	Thompson, Sarah	NC	1808	J L Thompson	H G Cook	Mary Tucker	David & Mary Cook	David & Mahala Tucker
16227 *	Thompson, Taylor	TX	1858	Silvia Thompson	Mace Thompson	Flora Banks		Maria Olivor
5692	Thompson, William	VA	1878	Lydia Thompson	Calvin Thompson	Elizabeth Welch	Samuel & Margret Thompson	James & Nancy Welch
8531	Thompson, William	WV	1878	Milley Thompson	George Thompson	Miley Thompson	George & Miley Thompson	Samuel & Margaret Thompson
8568	Thompson, William	NC	1877	none	Felix Thompson	Rebecca Miller	Calvin & Nella Thompson	Betty & Marion Miller
11564	Thompson, William	TN	1859	Matilda Thompson	James Thompson	Caroline Head	John & Polley Thompson	Elexander & Liza Head

3613	Thompson, Wilson	NC	1855	Eady Thompson	Wesley Thompson	Amanda Powers	John & Polly Thompson	Joseph & Elizabeth Powers
5832	Thompson, Winfield	VA	1856	Sarah Thompson				
22642	Thompson, Zimri	AR	1845	E.L. Thompson	John Thompson	Dotia Foset	Zimri & Hannah Thompson	Polley Foset
3700	Thomson, Nana							
19853	Thore, Agnes	NC			G.R. Thore	Charity Hall	G.W. & Marget Thore	
19852	Thore, G.W.	NC	47yrs		Norfleet Thore	Frances Boon		
19837	Thore, George	NC	1878		G.M. Thore	Margret Joyce	Norflete Thore	
21113	Thore, James	WV	1876	Ella Thore	George Thore	Margaret Joyce	Norflet & Louisa Thore	John & Louisa Joyce
19838	Thore, Jessie	NC			George Thore	Margaret Joyce		
19839	Thore, John	NC	1880		George Thore	Margaret Joyce	Norfleet Thore	John Joyce
21111	Thore, Thomas	WV	1871	Perry Thore	George Thore	Margaret Joyce	Norflet & Louisa Thore	John & Louisa Joyce
19901	Thore, Walter	NC	1884	Bettie Thore	George Thore	Margaret Joyce		
19840	Thore, William	NC	66yrs	Polly Thore	Norfleet Thore	Francis Boone		John Boone
12880	Thorn, John	OR	1883		William Thorn	Mary Wiles	Jacob & Malinda Thorn	James & Lucindia Wiles
12879	Thorn, Mary	OR	1852	Wm Thorn (decd)	James Wiles	Lucinda		
12877	Thorn, Tessie	OR	1893		William Thorn	Mary Wiles	Jacob & Malinda Thorn	James & Lucindia Wiles
21037	Thornhill, Sopha	OK	1873	William Thornhill	Hugh Magners	Martha Beard	David Magners	Elisha Beard
1404	Thornsbery, Andrew	OK	1861	Mary Thornsbery	Ira Thornsbery	Martha Chambers		Grief & Didamay Chambers
21719 *	Thornton, Henrietta	OK	1876		Roswell Mackey	Sylvia Thornton	Lynn Smith & Joshua Mackey	John & Nancy Thornton
17741 *	Thornton, Winnie	TN	1863		Charles Lawrence	Matilda Kirkland		John & Fannie Kirkland
2246	Thorp, Emery	MO	1881	Mamie Thorp	John Thorp	Marvillia Fender	Jacob & Catharine Thorp	Michael & Martha Fender
2242	Thorp, Marvillia	MO	1856	John Thorp	Michael Fender	Martha Wallis	Daniel & Dicy Fender	Jeptha & Nancy Wallis
7346	Thorp, Mary	IN	1852	W L Thorp	John Blackburn	Thena Proctor	James & Nancy Blackburn	James & Elizabeth Proctor
13192	Thrower, Ella	OK	1872	Charlie Thrower	Mohawk Beaver	Mollie Simmons	Runabout	
22933	Thurman, Belle	OK	1872	John Thurman	Johnson Riley	Bettie Keys	Louis & Eghu-goo Riley	Wm & Sallie Keys
12896	Tice, Emma	MS	1885	Bob Tice	J M Loveless	Mary Presley	Loveless & Nancy Townsand	Jim & Elizabeth Presley
5237	Tic-kah-nee-skee, Emma & Ailcey	OK	1907		Tic-kah-nee-skee, Jefferson	Alcey Easkey	Tic-kah-nee-skee & Sallie	Richard & Patsey Easkey
17722	Tidwell, Edgar	TN	1880		W.G. Tidwell	Matilda Paine	W.G. Tidwell & Martha Shelton	Thos Paine & Miranda Watson
2618	Tidwell, Franklin	GA	1878	Mattie Tidwell	John Tidwell	Susan Abernathy	F M Tidwell	Isaiah Abernathy
2614	Tidwell, George	GA	1865	none	Richard Tidwell	Jane Mundy	John Langley	Elisabeth Mundy

15135	Tidwell, George	GA	1883		John Tidwell	Rachel Langford	John & Lucreasy Tidwell	
2613	Tidwell, Ida	GA	1870	John Tidwell	John Harris	Mollie Grasham		
2616	Tidwell, Jas	GA	1858	Susan Tidwell	Francis Tidwell	Margaret Grantt	John Langley & Sally Tidwell	Obediah Grantt
2619	Tidwell, John	GA	1848	Susan Tidwell	Francis Tidwell	Margaret Grantt	John Langley	Obediah Grantt
6421	Tidwell, John	OK	1815	Lucretia Thompson	Youngdeer	Winnie Tidwell		John Tidwell
12001	Tidwell, John	GA	1853	Rachel Tidwell	John Tidwell	Lucreasy Thompson		
13408	Tidwell, John	AL	1815	Luetia Tidwell	Youngdeer	Winnie Ridwell		John Tidwell
2617	Tidwell, Joseph	GA	1884	none	John Tidwell	Susan Abernathy	F M Tidwell	Isiah Abernathy
8659	Tidwell, Mancel	OK	1859	Rachel Tidwell	John Tidwell	Betsy Grovette	Young Deer	
2612	Tidwell, Marion	GA	1863	Ada Tidwell	Francis Tidwell	Margaret Grantt	John Langley & Sally Tidwell	Obidiah Grantt
17725	Tidwell, Matilda	TN	1837	Wm Tidwell	Thos Payne	Miranda Watson	Thos Payne	
10347	Tidwell, Minor	OK	1865	Alice Tidwell	John Tidwell	Lucrie Thompson	Young Deer	Winnie Goddard
6422	Tidwell, Pleasant	OK	1843	Martha Tidwell	John Tidwell	Loucretia Thompson	Youngdeer	Winnie Tidwell
14445	Tidwell, Richard	GA	1881		James Tidwell	Susan Tidwell	F M & Margaret Tidwell	Richard & Jane Tidwell
17726	Tidwell, Robert	TN		Maggie Tidwell	W.G. Tidwell	Matilda Paine	W.G. Tidwell & Martha Shelton	Thos Paine & Miranda Watson
17728	Tidwell, Samuel	TN	1870	Minnie Tidwell	W.G. Tidwell	Matilda Paine	W.G. Tidwell & Martha Shelton	Thos Paine & Miranda Watson
14447	Tidwell, Susan	GA	1855	James Tidwell	Mendy Tidwell	Jane Munday	John Langley & Sallie Tidwell	
137	Tidwell, Versa	OK	1850	none	John Tidwell	Loucrecia Thompson		
15134	Tidwell, Walter	GA	1887		John Tidwell	Rachel Langford	John & Lucreasy Tidwell	
15133	Tidwell, Willie	GA	1894		John Tidwell	Rachel Langford	John & Lucreasy Tidwell	
2615	Tidwll, John	GA	1882	Nancy Tidwell	Jas M Tidwell	Susan Tidwell	F M & Margaret Tidwell	Richard & Jane Tidwell
12841	Tigue, Nancy	TN	1830	Jacob Tigue	Richard Ingraham	Jenie Davis		John & Aner Davis
10225	Tiller, Rosa	WV	1876		Calvin Cook	Rebecca Bailey	Thos Cook & Rebecca Sizemore	Jamison Bailey & Polly McConnor
17793	Tillery, Annie	OK	1889	Charley Tillery	Gus Eppel	Ella Bibb		
18356	Tillery, John	OK	1852	Sarah Tillery	John Tillery	Nancy Rogers	Wm Tillery	Andrew & Sarah Rogers
7348	Tillery, Nora	MO	1875	none	Wyatte Tillery	Sarah Roberts	Noah & Jeanette Tillery	Andrew & Eliza Roberts
18355	Tillery, Sarah	OK	1853	John Tillery	Hickman Murry	Betsy McDaniel		Dan & Salie McDaniel
9087	Tilley, Mary	WV	1862	John Tilley	Calvin Sizemore	Mary Brinegar	John Sizemore & Jane Arms	Jacob & Shebe Brinegar
21268	Timmons, Etta	LA	1873	Mack Timmons	John Jeter	Susan Thompson	Washington & Mary Jeter	Amos Thompson

12067	Timmons, Litia	TX	1877	Henry Timmons	James Rowell	E J Pertin	David Rowell	Man Fountain
21267	Timmons, Sudie	LA	1879	James Timmons	John Jeter	Susan Thompson	Washington & Mary Jeter	Amos Thompson
3378	Timmothy, Jessie	AL	21yrs	none	Thomas Timmothy	Emaline Dees		
17407	Timothy, Alex	AL	1883		Tom Timothy	Emerline Dees		Martin & Elizabeth Dees
817	Tincup, Lucinda	OK	1853	James Tincup	John Vance	Manerva Fleetwood		Chas & Lucinda Fleetwood
12098	Tindell, Edward	MO	1884	Lucretia Tindell	James Tindell	Percilla Brown	Wm & Susan Tindell	Wm & Amanda Brown
10095	Tindell, James	MO	1859	Percilla Tindell	William Tindell	Susan Brown	William Tindell	John & Nancy Brown
12097	Tindell, Lucretia	MO	1884	Edward Tindell	James Norman	Susan Johnston	Thos & Lucretia Norman	Thos & Eliza Johnston
10094	Tindell, Percilla	MO	1861	James Tindell	William Brown	Amanda Harralson		Vincent & Martha Harralson
14252	Tinnis, Mattie	OK	1882	Mathias Tinnis	George McDaniel	Isadore Lunsford	Redbird & Polly McDaniel	Calvin & Mary Lunsford
13343	Tippens, L.O.	GA	1882	Cally Tippens	William Tippens	Matildia Floyed	Benj & Sally Tippens	A.J. & Harret Floyed
10240	Tippin, Nancy	KS		John Tippin	Benjamin Yeates	Elizabeth Klinkenbrand	Larkin & Nancy Yeates	
14140	Tise, Fannie	NC	1881		John Tise	Margaret Poindexter	Solomon & Loretta Tise	Thos & Jennie Poindexter
14308	Tise, Lora	NC	1880		John Tise	Margaret Poindexter	Solomon & Loretta Tise	Thos & Jennie Poindexter
14095	Tittle, Andy	OK	1865	Ollie Tittle	Bill Tittle	Sarah Latty		Nancy Latty
6305	Tittle, James	OK	1881	none	James Tittle	Annie Prather	Daniel & Rosanner Tittle	Robert & Caroline Prather
17337	Todd, Dell	AL	1879	Maynard Todd	J.S. Todd	Pollie Morris		
17344	Todd, James	AL	1877	Susie Todd	J.S. Todd	Missoura Morris	John & Lucinda Todd	John & Didama Morris
14432	Todd, John	MS		Alvie Todd	Jonathan Todd	Palistine Morris	John & Lucinda Todd	John & Didama Morris
14433	Todd, Palistine	MS	1859	J S Todd	John Morris	Didamie Trout	James & Katie Morris	James & Annie Trout
17111	Tolan, Sallie	OK	43yrs		Tolan	Justice		Ned & Rachel Justice
20973	Toles, James	TX	1884	Cora Toles	Robert Toles	Sibby Tidwell		Frances & Margaret Tidwell
14448	Toles, Sibly	TX	1867	Robert Toles	Francis Tidwell	Margaret Gravitt	John Langley & Sally Tidwell	
20974	Toles, William	TX	1886	Mary Toles	Robert Toles	Sibby Tidwell	Cathron Toles	Margaret Tidwell
17941*	Tolliver, Mattie	TN	1876	Henry Tolliver	Jasper Roach	Lula Patten	Perkins & Charlotte Roach	Randle Patten
53	Tompkins, Phenias	NY	1857	Mary Tompkins	Phenias Tompkins	Hannah Ross	Isaac Tompkins & Helen Backus	Templin Ross & Eliza Sevier
36	Tompkins, Robert	SC	1854	Nannie	Phineas Tompkins	Hannah Ross	Isaac Tompkins & Helen Backies	Templin Ross & Eliza Sevier
17268	Toney, Jennie	OK	1859	John Toney		Sophia		Ah-nu-we-gi
322	Toombs, Margaret	OK	1849	Gabriel Toombs	Mathew Smith	Martha Berry	Goodman & Sallie Smith	Michael & Mary Berry
22751	Toombs, Roy	OK	1881	Lizzie Toombs	G.J. Toombs	Margaret Smith	Owen & Lucinda Toombs	Mathew & Martha Smith
19174	Topley, Emma	GA	1882	Joe Topley	George Quarles	Clarinda Gilly		John & Nancy Gilly
20062	Toppins, Sarah	TN	1869	William Toppins	Andrew Barnes	Nancy Sisk	Wm & Lucinda Barnes	Alex & Jane Sisk

20507	Torbet, Margaret	TN	1885	Henry Torbet	Joseph Bales	Evaline Cagle	John & Fannie Bales	Peter & Elizabeth Cagle
12836	Torbett, Eliza	OK	1869	R B Torbett	Harry Burns	Olie Grant	Euriah & Charlottie Burns	John & Pollie Grant
14370	Totherow, Julia	NC	1885	Wm Totherow	Nathan Cento	Matilda Ledford	Thos & Francis Cento	E B & Eliza Ledford
14394	Totten Mahala	CA	1831	Jefferson Totten		Docie Oxendive		
18696	Touart, Clifford	FL	1884		Richart Touart	Annette Vaughn	Poucher Touart & Josephine Hollinger	Ambrose & Josephine Vaughn
18694	Touart, Frank	FL	1883	Williamina Touart	Richart Touart	Annette Vaughn	Poucher Touart & Josephine Hollinger	Ambrose & Josephine Vaughn
18697	Touart, Ignatius	FL	1875	Margaret Touart	Richart Touart	Annette Vaughn	Poucher Touart & Josephine Hollinger	Ambrose & Josephine Vaughn
18695	Touart, Joseph	FL	1878	Blanche Touart	Richart Touart	Annette Vaughn	Poucher Touart & Josephine Hollinger	Ambrose & Josephine Vaughn
17900	Touart, Richard	FL	1852	Richard Touart	Ambrose Vaughn	Josephine Reyer	Wm Vaughn	John & Sarah Reyer
17904	Touart, Richard	FL	54yrs	Annette Touart	Poncho Touart	Josephine Hollinger		
22266*	Towers, John	OK	1850	Mary Towers		Nellie Towers		Peter & Rose Maglarthen
15064*	Towns, Adeline	GA	1851	George Towns		Jane Martin		James Wahler
13774	Towns, Sanford	GA	1867	Fannie Towns	Sandyford Towns	Cinda Daniel	Wattie Towns & Mima Williford	Lenders Daniel
7347	Townsend, Deffie	TX	1891	Trumen Townsend	Alfred Williams	Fannie Curtis	Joseph & Rutha Williams	Boon & Minervia Curtis
20906	Townsend, Edward	AL	1844	Rhoda Townsend	Ezekiel Townsend	Anna Patterson		
17384	Townsend, Kinsey	GA	1851	Mary Townsend	Ezekiel Townsend	Anna Patterson	Edward & Anna Townsend	Rolla Patterson
20126	Townsend, Martha	TX	1895	Frank Townsend	James Higdon	Rachal Freland	Joseph & Marthey Higdon	Howell & Zilpha Freland
20219	Townsend, Meta	IN	1874	Edward Townsend	Richard Elmore	Rachel Reed	John & Mary Elmore	Isaac & Hannah Reed
20668	Townsend, Oscar	TN	1879	Amanda Townsend	John Townsend	Martha Worley		
17385	Townsend, Samuel	GA	1846	Catharine Townsend	Ezekiel Townsend	Annie Patterson	Ed Townsend & Annie Taylor	Rolla Patterson & Nancy Williams
8768	Tramel, Caroline	NC	1867	none	Van Tramel	Mary Morgan	Jake & Pollie Tramel	
17428	Tramel, Susie	GA	1856	Daniel Tramel	Jim Brown	Sarah Brown	Jim & Carrie Brown	
5458	Tramel, T.J.	NC	1850	Becky Tramel	Enick Cunningham	Harrett Tramel		Jackey Tramel & Pollie Hogsed
19428	Trammell, A.	GA	1838	Sarah Trammell	Jesse Step	Jane Trammell		
18290	Trammell, Dennis	GA	1856	Lizzie Trammell	Asa Trammell	Elizabeth Kirkham		Henry & Martha Kirkham
12093	Trantham, Ebbie	NC	20yrs	Lee Trantham	Joseph Adams	Lucretia Taylor	Posey & Jane Adams	David Taylor & Anna Adams
18362	Trantham, Rhoda	AR	1836	Martin Trantham	Daniel Fender	Dicie Brown	Michael & Winnie Fender	Alex & Viletty Brown
1346	Trapp, Joseph	OK	1850	none	Trapp	Katie McDanniel	Jay Bird	Thomas & Sallie McDanniel
22533	Traut, Stella	OK	1887	Henry Traut	William Lauchmen	Mary Millen	Charles & Margaret Lauchmen	Daniel & Mary Millen
2973	Trent, Edward	OK	1873	Minervia Trent	Charles Trent	Ella Ratcliff	Vance Trent	Wm & Margaret Ratcliff

12717	Trent, Mary	VA	1855	Isaac Trent	John Heath	Alcey Powers	John & Vina Heath	James & Mima Powers
11076	Trent, Waitie	VA	1875	Thomas Trent	Andrew Widener	Mary Blevins		Isham & Anna Blevins
22166	Trentham, Virgie	MS			Bornsun Hollis	Mary Wright		John & Martha Wright
14472	Trim, Amanda	AL		D S Trim	William Sizemore	Martha Barker		
15016*	Trimble, Elizabeth	TN	1874	James Trimble	Benj Parkman	Fannie Hale		
7339	Trimble, Gertrude	MO	1882	none	Benj Trimble	Mary Carroll	John & Maggie Trimble	Frances & Prudence Carroll
534	Trimble, Lizzie	OK	1884	William Trimble	Lew Mathews	Artie Sanders	Samuel & Elizabeth Mathews	John & Nancy Sanders
7340	Trimble, Oscar	CO	1884		Benj Trimble	Mary Carroll	Maggie Trimble	Frances & Prudence Carroll
20478	Trimby, Lula	TN	1860	Joseph Trimby	William Dover	Mary Whitice	John & Elizabeth Dover	Wm & Eliza Whitice
21081	Triplet, Georgia	TN	1886	Thomas Triplet	John Smith	Theodoria Cowen	Eli & Mary Smith	
20701	Triplet, James	TN	1883	Mandy Triplet	Robert Triplet	Elisabeth Hatcher	Jerry & Jane Triplet	William Hatcher
21079	Triplet, Thomas	TN	1879	Georgia Triplet	Robert Triplet	Elizabeth Hatcher	Jerry & Rebecca Triplet	Wm & Charlotte Hatcher
21580	Triplett, Mary	OK	1835	William Triplett	Nelson Riley	Lizzie Thompson	Sam Riley	
20661	Tripp, Elizabeth	TN	1886	John Tripp	William Reed Jr.	Nancy Murray	McKenzie & Nancy Reed	James & Jane Murray
8453	Trivett, Jennie	VA	1881	Jeff Trivett	Lee Blevins	Bethany Blevins	Edward Blevins	Nancy Blevins
11072	Trivett, Sarrah	VA	1875	N C Trivett	Leander Blevins	Elizabeth Hart		John & Polley Hart
11652	Troglin, David	OK	1854	Sarah Troglin	Millican Troglin	Susan Dines	Abner & Pacient Troglin	
11653	Troglin, Elihugh	OK	1863	Eva Troglin	Millican Troglin	Susan Dines	Abner & Pacient Troglin	
10947	Troglin, Isaac	OK	1851		Millican Troglin	Susan Dines	Abner & Pacient Troglin	
10948	Troglin, James	OK		Louisa	Millican Troglin	Susan Dines	Abner & Pacient Troglin	
10946	Troglin, John	OK	1874	Louisa Troglin	Millican Troglin	Susan Dines	Abner & Pacient Troglin	
20535	Trotter, Clarrissa	TN	1843	Benj Trotter	Henry Smith	Katie Ralston		Patsy Knew
7726	Trotter, Louisa	OK	1835	William Trotter	John Pittsenborger	Cathrine Harman		Christopher & Mary Harman
6561	Troy, Ollie	AR	1879	B E Troy	Thompson Wood	Eliza Martin	Johnson & Margaret Wood	Wm & Susan Martin
17898	True, Harvey	TN	1863	Nancy True	Watson True	Ruth Vann	Osey True	Hiram & Susan Vann
17897	True, Joseph	TN	1861	Nannie True	Watson True	Ruth Vann	Osey True	Hiram & Susan Vann
20682	True, Margaret	TN	1887		Joseph True	Nancy Cagle	Watson & Ruth True	Peter & Elizabeth Cagle
20471	True, Nancy	TN	1866	Joseph True	Peter Cagle	Elizabeth Henson	Jacob & Rutha Cagle	Thomas & Nancy Henson
15588	Truelove, M.C.	GA	1868	John Truelove	A J Smith	Patsy Bowen	Elijah & Margret Smith	Thomas & Elizabeth Bowen
14686	Truelove, Rufus	NC	1891		John Trulove	Fannie Steele	J G & Florina Trulove	W D & Francis Steele

ID	Name	State	Year	Spouse	Father	Mother	Paternal GP	Maternal GP
22903	Trull, James	GA	1885	Ella Trull	James Trull	Lillie Adams		John & Leomy Adams
724	Trull, Lillie	NC	1860	James Trull	John Adams	Leomy Parker	David & Elizabeth Adams	Johnathan & Leomy Parker
398	Trull, Mary	NC	1878	Columbus Trull	Thos J Wilson	Josephine Pace	Jack & Isibella Wilson	Stephen & Dovey Pace
22904	Trull, Willie	NC	1880		James Trull	Lillie Adams		John & Leomy Adams
14875	Trulove, John	NC	1862	Mary Trulove	Frank Trulove	Lucy Newson	Austin & Pattie Trulove	J Newson
14036	Trulove, Robert	NC	1860	F E Trulove	John Trulove	Florina Butner	Austin & Patsy Trulove	
19042	Trumbo, Maggie	GA	1863		Joseph Lumpkin	Susan Lloyd		Thomas & Susan Lloyd
12459	Trusty, Sherman	GA	1865	Sarah Trusty	John Trusty	Malinda Hoop	Trusty	
2241	Tuck, Ada	MO	1883	Benjamin Tuck	John Thorp	Fender	Jacob & Catherine Thorp	Michael & Marthy Fender
2301	Tuck, Flora	MO	1868	Robert Tuck	Michael Fender	Martha Wallis	Daniel & Dicy Fender	Jeptha & Nancy Wallis
22423	Tuck, Mayme	OK	1907		Joseph Tuck	Ellen Dudley		James & Latalde Hilderbrand
8523	Tucker, David	VA	1858	Elsina Tucker	David Tucker Sr.	Mahala Blevins	David & Polly Tucker	Wells & Elizabeth Blevins
18016	Tucker, Elijah	NC	1858	Ida Tucker	David Tucker	Mahala Blevins		Wells & Elizabeth Blevins
22252*	Tucker, Eliza	OK	1847	widow	Lewis Dixon	Winnie Ratcliff		Tom & Polly Ratcliff
11936	Tucker, George	OK	1867	Millie Tucker	William Tucker	Mary Spears		
12997	Tucker, John	NC	1822	Martha Tucker	David Tucker	Mahala Blevins	David & Polly Tucker	Wells & Elizabeth Blevins
2359	Tucker, Josephus	AR	1873	Rosa Tucker	Leonard Tucker	Margret Morton	Lewis & Patsey Tucker	Joseph & Margret Morton
20225	Tucker, Julia	GA	1876		Caleb Stancel	Nancy Mc	John Stancel & Sally Ellis	Benj Mc & Nancy Quinn
17467	Tucker, Liddia	OK	17yrs	Johnson Tucker	Nelson Glass	Peggie Money		
10107	Tucker, Malvina	VA	50yrs	Sidney Tucker	Eli Blevins	Elisabeth Sturgill	Wells & Elisabeth Blevins	
14727	Tucker, Rosa	NC	1883		John Tucker	Martha Goss	David & Mahala Tucker	John & Oala Goss
6420	Tucker, Roxey	NC	41yrs	David Tucker	William Darnel	Sarah York	John & Polley Hart	
10979	Tucker, Sallie	GA	1841	widow	John Stancel	Catharine Selcer	John & Millie Stancel	Mollie Selcer
2364	Tucker, Sarah	IN	1857		Daniel McDonall	Rachel McNeal		James & Lucy McNeal
14734	Tucker, Sidney	VA	1849	Malvina Tucker	David Tucker	Mahala Blevins	David Tucker	Wells & Elizabeth Blevins
6652	Tucker, Thomas	NC	1875	Octavia Tucker	William Tucker	Nancy Sheehan	Andy & Eliza Tucker	Ned & Dora Good
8554	Tuell, Cora	VA	1881	John Tuell	Eli Blevins	Margarett Ruper	Shubal & Ada Blevins	
16228	Tulk, John	TX	1855	Bettie Tulk	John Tulk	Delilah Vann		Jennie Vann
8593	Tumbleson, Donna	TX	1876	William Tumbleson	John Pollard	Joan Bishop		Hazeltine Bishop
17816*	Tumling, Romeo	TN	1843	Maggie Tumling	Nathan	Luda Cox		Indian Hunter

16229	Tunstall, Martha	OK	1838		Hugh Goodwin	Rebecca Adair	Thos Goodwin	Wm & Elizabeth Adair
19632	Turbeyville, Mabella	TN	1884	Arthur Turbeyville	Charles Brown	Jennie McCrary	Elizabeth Brown	Robert & Lizzie McCrary
12064	Turley, Precious	OK		Sherman Turley	Ephraim Willson	Anna Bays	Wm & Margret Willson	David & Precious Bays
18291	Turner, Agnes	GA	1893		John Turner	Clarinda Gilly		John & Nancy Gilly
18542	Turner, Annis	GA	1868	John Turner	Hampton Watson	Hulda Chapman		Rena Castle
22962	Turner, Arbozine	TX	1881	Si Turner	Lewis Gaines	Elizabeth Baxter	Caleb & Sallie Gaines	
14431	Turner, Areah	AL	1856			Elizabeth Trout		James & Annie Trout
19177	Turner, Arthur	AL	1896		James Turner	Mollie Frazier	Thomas & Launica Turner	
19178	Turner, Bernis	AL	1902		James Turner	Mollie Frazier	Thomas & Launica Turner	
15404	Turner, Carrie	GA	1881	L O Turner	Robert McClure	Mary Millwood	Jack & Marilda McClure	Hugh & Miram Millwood
19179	Turner, Charlie	AL	1896		James Turner	Mollie Frazier	Thomas & Launica Turner	
17537	Turner, Clarinda	GA	1861	John Turner	John Gilly	Nancy Locklear	Jordan & Lethy Gilly	Jesse & Mary Locklear
18292	Turner, David	GA	1900		John Turner	Clarinda Gilly		John & Nancy Gilly
19180	Turner, Fred	AL	1899		James Turner	Mollie Frazier	Thomas & Launica Turner	
18544	Turner, George	GA	1890		John Turner	Annis Watson	Jackson & Eliza Turner	Hampton & Hulda Watson
19181	Turner, Harry	AL	1888		James Turner	Mollie Frazier	Thomas & Launica Turner	
5456	Turner, Hassie	GA	1872	William Turner	Joseph Hughs	Martha Hampton	James & Anna Hughs	George & Mary Hampton
18293	Turner, James	AL	1860	Mollie Turner	Thomas Turner	Louvica Carner		Polly Carner
7349	Turner, Lizzie	MO	1861	J W Turner	Benage Smith	Elizabeth Blackburn	Nathan & Elizabeth Smith	James & Nancy Blackburn
18294	Turner, Mamie	GA	1897		John Turner	Clarinda Gilly		John & Nancy Gilly
17766	Turner, Martha	TN	1850		Tyree Kelley	Delila Emry	Johnathan & Mary Kelley	James & Nancy Emry
18432	Turner, Mary	NC	1857	John Turner	Archibald Poindexter	Elizabeth Ward		
12066	Turner, Ova	OK	1884	Fred Turner	Ephraim Willson	Anna Bays	Wm & Margret Willson	David & Precious Bays
18543	Turner, Rachel	GA	1893		John Turner	Annis Watson	Jackson & Eliza Turner	Hampton & Hulda Watson
19182	Turner, Ramon	AL	1905		James Turner	Mollie Frazier	Thomas & Launica Turner	
14958	Turner, Samuel	TN	1840	Martha Turner	Marion Turner	Cynthia Brannon		Mike & Nancy Brannon
22202	Turner, Tiney	GA	1880	Belton Turner	Hiram Smith	Nancy League	Job Smith	Henry & Nancy League
19183	Turner, Winfield	AL	1893		James Turner	Mollie Frazier	Thomas & Launica Turner	
14365	Turpen, Sarah (decd)	GA	1863	Jesse Turpen	Edward Norton	Elizabeth Wall		Wm & Rebecca Wall
14366	Turpin, John	GA	1885		Jesse Turpin	Sarah Norton		Edward & Elizabeth Norton
2262	Turpin, Lucy	GA	1871	Mart Turpin	Richard Adams	Docia Sharp	David & Clarinda Adams	Richard & Elizabeth Sharp
16946	Tweedy, Melissa	OK	1846	Arista Tweedy	Enoch Wood	Francis Allison	Elijah & Winnie Wood	Thos & Martha Allison

19654	Twitty, Hays	TN	1881	Cora Twitty	Frank Twitty	Cindy Wilson	Calvin & Martha Twitty	Nelson & Harriet Wilson
22902	Twomey, Eliza	TX	1839	William Twomey	James Henson	Elizabeth Tulley		
22918	Tyer, Mary	AR	1866	Wesley Tyer	Ransom Barlow	Mary Robertson	Samuel & Sarah Barlow	Thos & Hepsey Robertson
21203	Tyler, Albert	AL	1881	Georgie Tyler	Albert Tyler	Angeline	Gabriel Tyler & Celia Johnson	
4809	Tyler, Elisebeth	GA	1835	Daniel Tyler	William Nicholson	Elisa More	Isic & Laufrecia Nicholson	
21204	Tyler, Georgie	AL	1884	Albert Tyler	John Jennings	Charly Lamascus	Saul & Georgia Jennings	
21208	Tyler, William	AL	1883	Ada Tyler	A.J. Tyler	Angeline Kelly		Gabriel Kelly
16778	Tyner, Almyra	OK	56yrs	Reubin Tyner				
18540	Tyner, Amy & Jesse	AR	1894 1896		Dee Tyner	Nancy Helton	Jesse & Loucinda Tyner	Andrew & Martha Helton
18197	Tyree, Lurany	TN	1830	Reuben Tyree	Samuel Beverly	Rhodia Terry		Wm & Dina Terry
18196	Tyree, Reuben	TN	1829	Lurany Tyree	Zacharih Tyree	Polly Curry		Reuben & Mollie Curry
8815	Tyson, Louvina	GA	1871	William Tyson	Pickens Corley	Martha Whitemore		Spencer & Melissa Whitemore
16565	Uhls, Roxie	VA	1872	Frank Uhls	James Osburn	Ellen Dorsey	Solomen & Patsy Osburn	James & Margarett Dorsey
7350	Uland, Aaron	IN	1885	Myrtle Uland	John Uland	Vina Combs	John & Polly Uland	Aaron & Ruth Combs
7352	Uland, Jesse	IN	1877	Mary Uland	John Uland	Visa Combs	John & Polly Uland	Aaron & Ruth Combs
7351	Uland, John	IN	1854	Visa Uland	John Uland	Polly Bays		Walter & Lella Bays
7353	Uland, John	IN	1874	Leona Uland	John Uland	Visa Combs	John & Polly Uland	Aaron & Ruth Combs
9542	Underwood, Calvin	NC	1854	Susan Underwood	Lafayette Underwood	Margaret Jackson	Jo Vanoy	Moses & Sarah Jackson
11005	Underwood, Hiley	TN	1849	Jordan Underwood	Thomas Riggins	Hursy Pugh	Thomas Riggins	Nancy Hazzard
9544	Underwood, Jane	NC	1859	none	Lafayette Underwood	Margaret Jackson	Joseph Vanoy & Delia Underwood	Moses & Sarah Jackson
9540	Underwood, John	NC	1857	Delia Underwood	Lafayette Underwood	Margaret Jackson	Joseph Vanoy & Delia Underwood	Moses & Sarah Jackson
18964	Underwood, John	TN	1848	Martha Underwood	Wesley Underwood	Mary Dayley		
20047	Underwood, Margaret	GA	1876	Vaney Underwood	John Paniter	Rosany Shope		
9541	Underwood, Mary	NC	1856	none	Lafayette Underwood	Margaret Jackson	Joseph Vanoy & Delia Underwood	Moses & Sarah Jackson
13781*	Underwood, Mary	GA	1872	George Underwood	Crawford Little	Pink Wyley	Crawford Little & Sallie Strame	Simon & Dinah Moore
20117	Underwood, Millie	OK	1885	Emery Underwood	James Taylor	Anna Davison	Zebadee & Mary Taylor	Armstrong & Louisa Davison
16196	Underwood, Rosa	OK	1882	Eli Underwood	Peter Baize	Patience Hunley	Joseph & Mary Baize	Joseph & Mary Hunley
18345	Underwood, Sarah	TN	1835		Joel Underwood	Sency Loveless	Bill Doolen & Ann Underwood	Samuel & Anna Loveless
18346	Underwood, Seborn	TN	1833	Nancy Underwood	Joel Underwood	Sency Loveless	Bill Doolen & Ann Underwood	Samuel & Anna Loveless
15132	Underwood, Thomas	GA	1834	Selah Underwood	William Underwood	Margarette Wilson		Jim & Sallie Wilson

21063	Upchurch, Mosier	TN		none	G.T. Upchurch	Enceres		Joshua & Jane Evans
20892	Upchurch, Sarah	AL	1859	William Upchurch	Dempsey Fowler	Mary Rodgers	Sam & Lucy Fowler	John & Sallie Rodgers
14938	Upton, James	TN	1844	Safrona Upton	Thomas Upton			
14446	Upton, Lizzie	GA	1880		Thomas Upton	Milbary Dudley	Eli Upton	
19267	Usrey, Clarinda	TX	1880	John Usrey	Charlie Core	Betty Wright		
11688	Ussery, Jessie	TX	1855	Ellen Ussery	Anvel Ussery	Levina Gunter		
18994	Valentine, Lucy	IN	1861	Ches Valentine		Mary Morgan		Mathew & Nancy Morgan
21605	Valentine, Susan	NC	60yrs		Charles Valentine	Betty Wilson	John & Beayton Valentine	
7356	Van Trump, A.V.	MO	1857	Melissa Van Trump	Reuben Van Trump	Dyanna Carnes	John & Elisabeth Van Trump	Davie Carnes
7358	Van Trump, John	AR	1865	Minervie	Josiah Van Trump	Susan Heffly	John & Elizabeth Van Trump	Samuel & Mary Heffly
7359	Van Trump, John	MO	1852	Mollie Van Trump	Reuben Van Trump	Dyanna Carnes	John & Elizabeth Van Trump	Daniel Carnes
7355	Van Trump, Melissa	MO	1863	A V Van Trump	Josiah Van Trump	Susan Heffly	John & Elisabeth Van Trump	Samuel & Mary Heffly
7357	Van Trump, Osee	MO		none				
7354	Van Trump, Pomeroy	MO	1877	Alice Van Trump	Josiah Van Trump	Susan Heffly	John & Elizabeth Van Trump	Samuel & Mary Heffly
7362	Vance, Charles	MO	1878	Emma Vance	William Vance	Margaret Marlin	Wm & Emeline Vance	
13047	Vance, Elizabeth	NE			Alpherd Denton	Rody Burges		Wm & Polly Burges
4160	Vance, James	MO	1867	none	Harris Vance	Spicy Voss		William & Phoebe Voss
17288	Vance, Manda	VA	1867	W.A. Vance	John Cline	Louisa Sizemore	John & Polly Cline	Franklin & Polly Sizemore
7364	Vance, Ollie	MO	1880	Nancy Vance	William Vance	Margaret Marlin	Wm & Emeline Vance	
7363	Vance, Thomas	MO	1883	Sallie Vance	William Vance	Margaret Marlin	Wm & Emeline Vance	
7360	Vance, William	MO	1876	Annie Vance	William Vance	Margaret Marlin	Wm & Emeline Vance	
7361	Vance, William	MO	1853	Margaret Vance	William Vance	Emeline Watham		Richard Watham
20588	Vandergriff, Eliza	TN	1856	William Vandergriff	Wiley Burnett	Mary Looney	John & Susie Burnett	Robert & Polly Looney
18777	Vanderpool, John	MO	1900		Corbet Vanderpool	Mary Jones	Quincy & Mary Vanderpool	John & Sarah Jones
16226	Vanderpool, William	OK	1854	Mary Vanderpool	James Vanderpool	Annie Henderson		Pop Frost
19802	Vanhooser, Maggie	GA	1880	Alex Vanhooser	David Mozell	Mina Cordell		
22891	Vanhorn, Fannie	MO	1866	Edd Vanhorn	Arch Bridges	Catherine Harmon	William Bridges	Wilburn & Polley Harmon
13281	Vann, Annie	OK	1887	Hickory Vann	Mohawk Beaver	Mollie Simmons		
18782 *	Vann, Dennis	OK	1850	Annie Vann	William Vann	Caroline Vann	George Bruner & Sarah	Ebbie & Katie Vann
19486 *	Vann, Dunk	OK		Chick Vann	James Vann	Patsy Vann	Caesar & Lettie Vann	Raleigh & Nancy Vann

ID	Name	State	Year	Spouse	Father	Mother	Paternal Grandparents	Maternal Grandparents
18632 *	Vann, G.W.	OK	1813	Mary Vann	Joshoway McCamey	Charlotte Brown		John & Mary Brown
13316	Vann, George	OK	1852	Mary Vann	David Vann	Nancy Mackey	Joseph & Polly Vann	Samuel & Sally Mackey
22056 *	Vann, George	OK	1853	Ellen Vann	William Vann	Caroline Vann	George & Kattie Vann	Joe & Ebbie Vann
22257 *	Vann, Ibby	OK	1837	Lewis Lynch	Rufus Vann	Lucy	Nan Vann	Joe & Ibby Vann
17616	Vann, James	OK	1859	Alice Vann	James Vann	Mary Wadsworth		
18860 *	Vann, James	OK	52yrs	Rachel Vann	Neil Vann	Jennie Vann	Talakah Baldridge	Lett & Nann Vann
22352 *	Vann, Jesse	OK	1854	none	Bill Vann	Peggie Lynch	Esseck	
22314 *	Vann, Josh	KS	49yrs	Callie Vann	Cull Vann	Susan Pee Vann	Joe & Lizzie Vann	Teleque & Lettie Vann
20247 *	Vann, Katie	OK	1845	Emanuel Taylor	Jessie Roe	Melinda Harnige	Jesse & Malinda Roe	
22338 *	Vann, Louisa	OK	1849	Arthur Bean	Rufus Vann	Lucy Vann	Nan Vann	Ibby Vann
22500 *	Vann, Nicy	OK	1863	Jesse Vann decd	David Brown	Mary Mayfield		Benjamin & Ibby Bean
22495 *	Vann, Sam	OK		Rachel Vann	Rufus Vann	Lucy Vann	Squirrel & Nancy Vann	Ibby Vann
9236	Vann, William	OK	1845	Lottie Vann	David Vann	Nancy Mackey	Joseph & Mary Vann	Samuel & Sallie Mackey
18849	Vaughan, George	GA	1896		Wm Vaughan	Mary Hester	Alman & Anna Vaughan	Joseph & Rhoda Hester
18847	Vaughan, Jeddie	GA	1903		Wm Vaughan	Mary Hester	Alman & Anna Vaughan	Joseph & Rhoda Hester
8387	Vaughan, Maggie	OK	1867	Isaac Vaughan	Benj Yeates	Elizabeth Klinkenbeard	Larkin & Nancy Yeates	
2611	Vaughan, Mary	GA	1875	Alford Vaughn	John Tidwell	Susan Abernathy	F M Tidwell	Isaiah Abernathy
18846	Vaughan, Mary	GA	1872	Wm Vaughan	Joseph Hester	Rhoda Hester		Giddeon & Louiza Hester
18848	Vaughan, William	GA	1899		Wm Vaughan	Mary Hester	Alman & Anna Vaughan	Joseph & Rhoda Hester
22411	Vaughn, Gussie	TN	1885	Van Vaughn	James Payne	Annice Parks	John & Mary Payne	
9483 *	Vaughn, Jennie	OK	1859	Moses Vaughn	John Hemmitt	Celia Law	John & Bedie Hemmitt	Isaac & Jennie Law
5480	Vaughn, Lillie	MO	1875	Emory Vaughn	William Fender	Polly Stokes	Daniel & Dicy Fender	Richard & Malinda Stokes
8506	Vaughn, Lutetia	KY	1876	James Vaughn	Lemuel Faircloth	Mary Atwood	Thelbert & Cristeen Faircloth	George & Mahaly Atwood
18515	Vaughn, Nancy	NM	1877	S.W. Vaughn	Charles Middleton	Mary Breeze	Wm & Nancy Middleton	
2583	Vaughn, Nevada	GA	1872	Agater Vaughn	David Ash	Elisabeth Davenport		John & Elisabeth Davenport
21729	Vaughn, Will	TN	1875	Mattie Vaughn	Joseph Vaughn	Mary Nichols	John & Patsy Vaughn	Henry & Nancy Nichols
17731	Venable, Emma	TN	1847	Thomas Venable	George Fuller	Martha Higginbothin		Oliver & Nancy Higginbothin
12369 *	Venerable, Sarah	NC	1849	John Venerable	Solomon Sawyer	Tabitha Evans		Benjamin & Lucy Evans
5158 *	Venton, Josephus	KS	1863	none	Lice Stover	Melvina Berry	Bill Stover	Clara Berry
12296	Verhine, Annie	GA	1876	John Verhine	Frank Richardson	Susan Phillips	James & Nancy Richardson	James & Caroline Phillips

12295	Verhine, Elmo	GA	1896		John Verhine	Annie Richardson	Richard & Joicey Verhine	Frank & Susan Richardson
12294	Verhine, Ethel	GA	1901		John Verhine	Annie Richardson	Richard & Joicey Verhine	Frank & Susan Richardson
12293	Verhine, Howard	GA	1905		John Verhine	Annie Richardson	Richard & Joicey Verhine	Frank & Susan Richardson
12290	Verhine, Irene	GA	1903		John Verhine	Annie Richardson	Richard & Joicey Verhine	Frank & Susan Richardson
12331	Verhine, Ralph	GA	1898		John Verhine	Annie Verhine	Richard & Joicey Verhine	Frank & Susan Richardson
12343	Verhine, Roy	GA	1894		John Verhine	Annie Richardson	Richard & Joicey Verhine	Frank & Susan Richardson
15131	Vernon, Charley	GA	1884	Lula Vernon	William Vernon	Nancy Philips	Archie & Jane Vernon	
10493	Vernon, John	GA	1869	Nancy Vernon	Josiah Vernon	Evaline Phillips	Archie & Jane Vernon	
10492	Vernon, Josiah	GA	1849	Evaline Vernon	Archie Vernon	Jane Hays	Nehemiah & Elizabeth Vernon	Stephen & Nancy Hays
15130	Vernon, Mary	GA	1887		William Vernon	Nancy Philips	Archie & Jane Vernon	
11204	Vernon, Mittie	GA	1876	F.L. Vernon	Johnathan Maddox	Elizabeth Harrison	Dudley Maddox	Luther Dobbs
15129	Vernon, Nancy	GA	1851		Archie Vernon	Jane Hayes	Nehemiah & Elizabeth Vernon	Stephen & Nancy Hayes
14640	Vernon, Pulina	NC	1853		Thomas Doby	Eda Winkler	Alice Doby	
10491	Vernon, William	GA	1872	Dovie Vernon	Josiah Vernon	Evaline Phillips	Archie & Jane Vernon	
19798	Vest, Solomon	TN	1874		Lewis Vest	Mary Schaub	Nancy Vest	Eliza Schaub
21508	Vickery, Anna	TX	1864	Andrew Vickery	Ealy Jeter	Martha Bentley	George Jeter	
11770	Vicks, Mattie	TX	1877	Charles Vicks	Isaac Sneed	Sarah Sneed		James & Elizabeth Sneed
18689	Vidal, Elizabeth	FL	1837	Miguel Vidal	Thomas Robinson	Mary Harvel		Elizabeth Harvel
12479	Viers, Mint	OK	1872	Will Viers	Jim Goins	Francis McGill	Martin & Mandy Goins	Bill & Sally McGill
18869	Vincent, A.M.	AL	1877	V.R. Vincent	J.C. Vincent	A.C. Sammons	J.C. & Eliza Vincent	Oliver & Elizabeth Cleveland
20033	Vincent, Henry	GA	1854	Telulah Vincent	James Vincent	Louisa Lloyd		Thos Lloyd & Susan Parsons
20034	Vincent, Telulah	GA	1867	Henry Vincent	Thomas Lloyd	Lizzie Mathis	Thos Lloyd & Susan Parsons	
21512	Vines, Evie	AL	1890	Joe Vines	James Henderson	Selena Berry	James Haskin	George Berry
7365	Violett, Nora	MO	1869	Thomas Violett	Jesse Roberts	Mary Wylie	Andrew Roberts	Harvy Wylie
21440	Voekle, Iva	TX	1882	Samuel Voekle	J.D. Coe	Melissa Hestand	Rhoda Coe	Dicie Hestand
22431	Voss, Andrew	NC	1857	Francis Voss	James Voss	Nancy Lewis	Thomas Voss	Joel & Betsy Lewis
7861	Voyles, Clara	GA	1902		James Voyles	Mary Wilson	David & Mary Voyles	Wm & Francis Wilson
7860	Voyles, Mary	GA	1883	Everett Voyles	William Wilson	Francis Helton	Hilliard & Lucinda Wilson	Clark & Mary Helton
21304	Voyles, Mattie	AL	1888	Davis Voyles	William Pogue	Mollie Gilly		Jordan & Ann Gilly
22375	W W Lovill for minors	NC			Walter Lovill	Martha Jones	James & Bettie Lovill	Francis & Mary Jones
9287	Waddell, Emma	VA	1882	George Waddell	Joseph Hart	Jane More	Riley & Emily Hart	Wm & Isabella More
13990	Waddell, Lissie	NC	1871	B C Waddell	John Baldwin	Francis Kilby	Wm & Margret Baldwin	

#	Name	State	Year					
11181	Waddle, Lottie	GA	1839	George Waddle	John Cox	Sallie Cline		
17715 *	Waddy, Larkin Jr.	TX	1861	Maria Waddy	Larkin Waddy	Catherine Keel	Mark & Alsy Waddy	Wm & Lucinda Keel
16152	Wade, Harriet	GA	1848	H S Wade	James Roberts	Harriet Peyton		
11899	Wafford, Eliza	OK	1872	Nathaniel Wafford	Harrison Hughes	Elmira Sylcox		Burton & Farribee Sylcox
12263	Wagoner, John	NC	1869	Bettie Wagoner	Owen Wagoner	Polly Sturgill	Henry & Charlotte Wagoner	John Sturgill
12998	Wagoner, Laura	NC	1869	James Wagoner	John Tucker	Martha Goss	David & Mahala Tucker	John & Ala Goss
5502	Waitman, Henry	OK	1894	none	General Waitman	Dora Bacon		Tom & Martha Bacon
5501	Waitman, Ludie	OK	1888	none	General Waitman	Dora Bacon		Tom & Martha Bacon
14016	Walden, Almer	GA	1876	William Walden	Kinsey Loggins	Marry Smallwood	William & Nancy Loggins	Wilkenson & Sarrah Smallwood
7403	Walden, George	OK	1882	Ellen Walden	John Walden	Barbra Pennell	John & Nancy Walden	Bartly & Sislie Pennell
7401	Walden, John	OK	1880	none	John Walden	Barbra Pennell	John & Nancy Walden	Bartly & Sislie Pennell
7402	Walden, John	OK	1855	Barbra Walden	John Walden	Nancy Young	John Walden	John & Millie Young
7404	Walden, Nancy	OK	1878	Tom Gilmore	John Walden	Barbra Pennell	John & Nancy Walden	Bartly & Sislie Pennell
14024	Waldin, Dovey	GA	1881	Theodore Waldin	Mat Loggins	Matilda Smallwood	Wm & Nancy Loggins	Wilkerson & Sarah Smallwood
2591	Waldon, Ann	GA	1872	James Waldon	John Beaver	Mary Davenport		John & Elisabeth Davenport
16786 *	Waldon, Della	WI	1871	Sherida Waldon	Aaron Roberts	Martha Stewart	Ishmael & Delany Roberts	Walden & Hetta Stewart
13533 *	Waldon, Elsworth	WI	1873	Etta Waldon	Samuel Waldon	Elizabeth Revels	Mike & Polly Waldon	McCaga & Mornon Revels
13534 *	Waldon, Peter	WI	1875	Flora Waldon	Samuel Waldon	Elizabeth Revels	Mike & Polly Waldon	McCaga & Mornon Revels
17996 *	Waldon, Sheridan	WI	1865	Della Waldon	Samuel Waldon	Elizabeth Revels		Macaga Revels
22285 *	Waldon, Shery	WI	1887	none	Thomas Waldon	Minnie Bowles	Samuel & Elizabeth Waldon	Miller & Mary Bowles
11475 *	Waldron, Elizabeth	WI	1833	Samuel Waldron	Macaga Revels	Mornon Jackops	Stephen & Delilah Revels	
18169 *	Waldron, Flora	WI	1882	Peter Waldron	Matthew Revels	Alice Murphy	Aaron & Elizabeth Revels	Berlie & Elizabeth Murphy
18596 *	Waldron, Maria	WI	1876		Samuel Waldron	Elizabeth Revels	Mike Waldron	Macaga Revels
19665	Waldroup, Belzora	OK	1878	J.H. Waldroup	J.S. Bell	Emily Ditmore	J.M. & Elisabeth Bell	H.W. & Ellisabeth Ditmore
21759	Waldroup, Ida	OK	1886	Oscar Waldroup	J.S. Bell	Emily Ditmore	J.M. & Elisabeth Bell	Hen & Elisabeth Ditmore
6227 *	Walk, Bird	TN	1853	Mary Walk	John Walk	Rebecca Calerman		
12744	Walker Arminda	TN	1862	T L Walker	James Kelley	Charlotta Evans	Wm & Nancy Kelley	Meeley Evans
14435 *	Walker, Alonzo	FL	1869	George Walker	Archabal Walker	Annetta Holmes		Susan Holmes
10125	Walker, C.G.C.	WV	1869	Josephine Walker	Norma Walker	Martha Sizemore	Amos Walker & Frankey Peters	John Sizemore & Virginia Arms
17815 *	Walker, Calvin	GA	1852	Opelia Walker	Gabel Dawson	Crecy Dick	Ross & Jane Lavender	Benj Dick

3345	Walker, Carmon	AL	1878	Matilda Walker	Jay Walker	Treacie McGhee		Richard & Betsy McGhee
22102	Walker, Cassie	AR	1873		Joseph Rogers	Mary Hodges	Henry & Mariah Rogers	John & Jemima Hodges
8434	Walker, Charles	WV	1868	Mary Walker	William Walker	Susan Sizemore		Hiram & Jane Sizemore
6039	Walker, Daniel	VA	1869	Elsina Thompson				
17778	Walker, Daniel	TN	1841	Mary Walker	Riley Walker	Charlotte Reeves	Daniel Walker	Wiley & Lucinda Reeves
10487	Walker, Della	WV	1884	W A Walker	J W C Walker	Nancy Bailey	Newma & Martha Walker	Floyd Bailey
3409	Walker, Emma	AL	1884	Richard Walker	William McGhee	Julia McGhee	Richard & Betsy McGhee	Jack & Maria McGhee
17961	Walker, Emma	GA	1883	James Walker	Robert Landers	L.M. Partian	George & Betsy Landers	Henry & Nancy Partian
12366	Walker, Eula	OK	1877	Eddie Walker	Joseph Coodey	Mary Hardage	Joseph & Jane Coodey	Joe & Muskogee Hardage
6371	Walker, Fred	AL	36yrs	none	J A Walker	Creasy McGhee		Richard & Nancy McGhee
20529	Walker, Fredrick	TN	1889		John Walker	Lucinda Robinson	Henry & Elizabeth Walker	Eli & Tempy Robinson
10223	Walker, H.C.	WV	1877	Lillie Walker	J W C Walker	Nancy Bailey	Newma & Adaline Walker	Floyd & Zilphy Bailey
20523	Walker, Henry	TN	1888		John Walker	Lucinda Robinson	Henry & Elizabeth Walker	Eli & Tempy Robinson
3320	Walker, J G	AR	1840	Lovah Walker	John Walker	Sarah Walker	Joe & Emily Walker	
10124	Walker, J.W.C.	WV	1855	Nancy Walker	Norma Walker	Martha Sizemore	Amos Walker & Frankey Peters	John Sizemore & Virginia Arms
8408	Walker, James	AR	1840	Lovah Walker	John Walker	Sarah Walker	Ben Walker	John Walker
17776	Walker, James	GA	1861	Martha Walker	Riley Walker	Charlotte Reeves	Daniel Walker	Wiley & Lucinda Reeves
21343	Walker, James	OK	1880	Ida Walker	Thomas Walker	Sarah Burnett	Samuel & Catherine Walker	John & Lydia Burnett
20550	Walker, John	TN	1884	Willie Walker	John Walker	Lucinda Robinson	Henry & Elizabeth Walker	Eli & Tempy Robinson
21308	Walker, Josie	TX	1861	Jeff Walker	James Graham	Martha Glass		John & Pliny Glass
10228	Walker, L.M.C.	WV	1874	H.G. Walker	Newma Walker	Adaline Sizemore	Chris Walker & Frankie Peters	John Sizemore & Frankie Arms
15765	Walker, Leroy	WV	1880	Ardelia Walker	J W C Walker	Nancy Bailey	Noma & Martha Walker	Floyd & Z S Bailey
20558	Walker, Lillie	TN	1878	Joseph Walker	Henry Peck	Susan Wilson	John & Amanda Peck	Thos & Rebeca Wilson
3344	Walker, Lizzie	AL	1871		Jay Walker	Neacie McGee		Richard & Betsy McGee
7405	Walker, Louisa	TX	1861	Casino Walker	John King	Martha Foley		James & Rhoda Foley
20608	Walker, Lucinda	TN	1850	John Walker	Eli Robertson	Temperance Lewis	Wm & Mary Robertson	John & Temperance Lewis
3375	Walker, Lucretia	AL	58yrs	James Walker	Richard McGhee	Elisabeth Hinson	Lewis McGhee	
17814	Walker, Lula	GA	1841	Cabe Walker		Jane Carson		Rachel Carson
11797	Walker, Mahala	VA	1877	Willis Walker	John Tucker	Martha Goss	David & Mahala Tucker	John Goss
21746	Walker, Morgan	OK	1873		Thomas Walker	Sarah Burnett		Lydia & John Burnett

10235	Walker, N CC	WV	1856	Sarah Walker	Newma Walker	Adaline Sizemore	Chris Walker & Frankie Peters	John Sizemore & Frankie Arms
10224	Walker, N N C	WV	1879	G C Walker	Newma Walker	Adaline Sizemore	Chris Walker & Frankie Peters	John Sizemore & Frankie Arms
20103 *	Walker, Nathaniel	GA	1841	Hannah Walker	Jack Fain	Patsie Heard		Buck & Patsie Heard
15762	Walker, Opie et al	WV	17 yrs etc.		John W.C. Walker	Nancy Bailey	Numa & Martha Walker	Floyd & Y.S. Bailey
14952	Walker, Rebecca	OK	1842	S J Walker	Wm Boyd	Elisabeth Oxford		Abel & Eda Oxford
3416	Walker, Richard	AL	22yrs	Emma Walker	Jay Walker	Treacie McGhee		Richard & Betsy McGhee
21342	Walker, Robert	AR	1874	Martha Walker	Thomas Walker	Sarah Burnett	Samuel & Catherine Walker	John & Lydia Burnett
21344	Walker, Sarah	OK	1850	Thomas Walker	John Burnett	Lydia Griffith	John & Susanna Burnett	Arden & Delilah Griffith
15024	Wall, Lucinda	NC	1860	J B Wall	Abner Smitherman	Sarah Trulove	Andrew & Lucinda Smitherman	Auston & Patsy Trulove
19843	Wall, Maud et al	NC			O.C. Wall	Alice Whitaker	Miles & Betsy Wall	
19844	Wall, Miles	NC	1838		Michael Wall		Wm & Huba Wall	
18421	Wall, Nancy	NC	1867	Stanley Wall	Solomon Hauser	Louisa Poindexter	Samuel & Nancy Hauser	Denson & Sarah Poindexter
19846	Wall, Roxey	NC		Miles Wall	George Terry	Ruth Napier	Moses & Mary Terry	
15608	Wall, Stanley	NC	1861	Nancy Wall	Isarah Wall	Martha Scott	Adam & Pollie Wall	Robert & Mary Scott
19845	Wall, Ulysses	NC	1886		C.G. Wall	Whitaker	Miles & Betsy Wall	
18627	Wall, Wilburn	GA	1873	Etner Wall	Wilburn Wall	Harriet Ballew	Keneen & Mahala Wall	Robert & Margaret Ballew
15124	Wallace, David	GA	1853	Ann Wallace	Jesse Wallace	Liza Whitmire		Chris & Nancy Whitmire
15128	Wallace, Eliza	GA	1826	Jesse Wallace	Chris Whitmire	Nancy Reece	Samuel & Polly Whitmire	Jacob & Susan Reece
17610 *	Wallace, Henry	IN			John Wallace	Amanda Harris	Aaron & Esther Wallace	
17693	Wallace, Hiley	TN	1857	Hiram Wallace	James Heatherly	Elizabeth Evans	James & Mary Heatherly	
15915 *	Wallace, Jane	IN	1840		Alex Mitchell	Rebecca Shoecraft		Silas & Mary Shoecraft
4009	Wallace, Nancy	OK	1850	Charles Wallace	Felix Riley	Oma Vickory	John & Susanna Riley	Daniel & Taki Vickory
5050	Wallace, Sarah	NC	1867	Harlin Wallace	James Harrison	Elizabeth Hensley		Riley & Sarah Hensley
21023	Walldroop, Nancy	GA	1824	Hisakirah Walldroop	William Ridley	Poley Irby	Mathew Ridley	
20125	Walling, Early	TX	1852	Mary Walling	Thomas Walling	Nancy Price	John & Ana Walling	
15127	Wallis, Charley	GA	1877	May Wallis	David Wallis	Ann Turner	Jesse & Liza Wallis	
15126	Wallis, Claudie	GA	1883		David Wallis	Ann Turner	Jesse & Liza Wallis	
15125	Wallis, David	GA	1892		David Wallis	Ann Turner	Jesse & Liza Wallis	
15123	Wallis, Duffie	GA	1880	Ella Wallis	David Wallace	Ann Wallace	Jesse & Liza Wallace	
15122	Wallis, Ezra	GA	1893		David Wallis	Ann Turner	Jesse & Liza Wallis	
15121	Wallis, Flora	GA	1886		David Wallis	Ann Turner	Jesse & Liza Wallis	
15120	Wallis, James	GA	1874	Florence Wallis	David Wallis	Ann Turner	Jesse & Liza Wallis	
15119	Wallis, Robert	GA	1882		David Wallis	Ann Turner	Jesse & Liza Wallis	
15118	Wallis, Thomas	GA	1879	Minnie Wallis	David Wallis	Ann Turner	Jesse & Liza Wallis	
15117	Wallis, Willie	GA	1888		David Wallis	Ann Turner	Jesse & Liza Wallis	
6898	Walls, Bertha	VA	1888	none	Frank Walls	Malindia Blevins	G W & Malindia Walls	Alex & Malindia Blevins

ID	Name	State	Year	Spouse	Father	Mother	Paternal Grandparents	Maternal Grandparents
19847	Walls, Christopher	NC		Josephine Walls	Miles Walls	Elizabeth Barnes	Mike & Nancy Walls	
6894	Walls, Dorcy	VA	1868	Frank Walls	Eli Pennington	Emily Allens	Andrew & Hetty Pennington	
13887	Walls, Emeline	WV	1859	W W Walls	Hughie Peak	Margie Hart	Josiah & Annie Peak	Elijah & Polly Hart
19848	Walls, Emery	NC		Ora Walls	Miles Walls	Elizabeth Barnes	Mike & Nancy Walls	
13889	Walls, J.O.	WV	1880	Ruth Walls	W W Walls	Emeline Peak	Parks & Jane Walls	Hughie & Margie Peak
6885	Walls, James	VA	1889	none	Frank Walls	Malindia Blevins	G.W. & Malindia Walls	Alen & Malindia Blevins
19597	Walls, James	TN	1872	Sarah Walls	William Walls	Nancy Spurling	James & Martha Walls	Richard & Nancy Spurling
3129	Walls, Lottie	MS	1886	S T Walls	John Hobgood	Mattie Coleman	Charles & Martha Hobgood	
7933	Walls, Matilda	WV		W W Walls	Hugh Peak	Margo Hart		George & Polly Hart
14690	Walls, William	VA	1882		Frank Walls	Malinda Blevins	G W & Malinda Walls	Allen & Malinda Blevins
21098	Walls, William	NC	1851	Nancy Walls	James Walls	Martha Mosley	William & Rebecca Walls	Samuel Moseley
1550	Walls, Wm Dyer	NC	1842	Sarah Walls	Burell Walls	Charlotty Slaten	Wm & Rebecca Walls	
16139	Walters, Appleton	TX	1868	Louisa Walters	George Walters	Martha McManns	Davie & Elizabeth Walters	John McMann
16140	Walters, Aubraetta	TX	1900		Appleton Walters	Louisa Henson	George Walters & Martha McMann	Henry Henson & Mary Hardman
16245	Walters, Louisa	TX	1864	Appleton Walters	Henry Henson	Mary Hardman	James Henson	Elizabeth Kelly
16236	Walters, Louise	TX	1879	V B Walters	Charley Peery	Louise Henson		Henry Henson & Mary Hardman
16145	Walters, Marvin	TX	1895		Appleton Walters	Louisa Henson	George Walters & Martha McManns	Henry Henson & Mary Hardman
18731	Walters, Mary et al	NC	1874		J.W. Pruitt	Louisa Osborn	Abedingo & Mary Pruitt	David & Lucy Osborn
16063	Walters, Mattie	TX	1897		Appleton Walters	Louisa Henson	George Walters & Martha McManns	Henry Henson & Mary Hardman
7680 *	Walton, Abner	TN	1818	Mary Walton	Buck Walton	Mariah Dubose		Joe & Lucy Martin
9055	Walton, Amanda	VA	1882	R C Walton	Eli Blevins	Liza Bare	Jessie & Catherine Blevins	James & Ausley Bare
7679 *	Walton, Bettie	TN	1871	none	Anthony Walton	Martha Strong	Abner & Mary Walton	John & Betsy Strong
6853	Walton, Lockey	VA	1880	John Walton	Wells Blevins	Kisiah Walls	Allen & Fanny Blevins	
19685	Wannamaker, Margret	TN	1878	Ed Wannamaker	J. Curtis	Elizabeth Patrick	Joshua & Elizabeth Curtis	
3431	Ward, Mrs J P	AL	30yrs	J P Ward	William House	Martha Lambert	J G & Lavitia House	Joseph & Mary Lambert
20271	Ward, Andrew	TX	1861		A.J. Ward	Emily Jolly	Jeremiah & Nancy Ward	Wm & Martha Jolly
4277	Ward, Catherine	OK	1844	Samuel Ward (decd)				
19472	Ward, Daniel	AL	1877	Lizzie Ward	H.L. Ward	Caroline Turner	Ely & Rebecca Ward	H.W. & Jensie Turner
11512	Ward, Eliza	OK	1849	Willie Ward	Caleb Beck	Martha Smith		Suk Kinnie
20272	Ward, Flem et al	MO			Lovel Ward		Lovel Ward	

19565	Ward, Forest	AL	1885		William Ward	Emma Griffin	Henry & Carolina Ward	Glissen & Annie Griffin
22954	Ward, Francis	OK	19yrs		Jerry Ward	Sarah Fleetwood		Charles & Lucinda Fleetwood
7391	Ward, Fred	MO	1884	none	John Ward	Angeline Smith	Wm & Naomi Ward	Eddy & Mary Smith
7389	Ward, Henry	TX	1872	Bera Ward	Bedford Ward	Ellen Ward	Jerry Ward	Nancy Ward
19564	Ward, Henry	AL	1856	Bamma Ward	Henry Ward	Carolina Turner	Ely & Rebecca Ward	H.W. & Jensie Turner
19567	Ward, Henry	AL	1830	Caroline Ward	Ely Ward	Rebecca Hogg	Nancy Ward	H.M. & Polly Hogg
7408	Ward, Hugh	OK	1837	Eliza Ward	Green Ward	Elizabeth Anderson	William Ward	
7388	Ward, James	TX	1845	Mary Ward	Jerry Ward	Nancy Freeman	John Ward	Polly Wadoll
8194	Ward, James	TX	1873	Mollie Ward	W W Ward	Martha Richardson	Thomas & Elizabeth Ward	
19566	Ward, James	AL	1875	Emmie Ward	Henry Ward	Carolina Turner	Ely & Rebecca Ward	H.W. & Jensie Turner
7390	Ward, John	MO	1853	Angeline Ward	William Ward	Naomi		
19568	Ward, John	AL	1864	Itila Ward	Henry Ward	Carolina Turner	Ely & Rebecca Ward	H.W. & Jensie Turner
17538 *	Ward, Julia	GA	1847	Gus Ward	James Carson	Rhoda Huckerby		George & Tilda Huckerby
10292	Ward, Kattie	OK	1885		James Murray	Temperance Rushing	Wm & Cora Murray	James & Cornelia Rushing
9500	Ward, Mary	GA	1867	Albert Ward	George Hice	Margaret Davenport		John & Elisabeth Davenport
5823	Ward, McCauley	KS	1867	C A Ward	Johnson Wood	Martha Martin	Thompson Wood	Wm & Susan Martin
22719	Ward, Nathan et al	CO	1858		William Ward	Naoma Perkins		
16941	Ward, Otis	OK	1880	Maggie Ward	William Ward	Mary Webb	Enoch & Francis Ward	Wm & Polly Webb
21644 *	Ward, Peter	OK	1820	Louisa Ward	Abraham Ward	Isabell Ward		
3944	Ward, Sarah	GA	1844	John Ward (decd)	Jack Keenan	Mahaley Sanders		
3657	Ward, Susie	MO	1884	William Ward	Jonathan Hicks	Levinda Harralson	Hiram & Mary Hicks	Vinson & Martha Harralson
16940	Ward, Thomas	OK	1877		Wm Lindsay Ward	Mary Webb	Enoch & Francis Ward	Wm & Polly Webb
1098	Ward, William	OK	1862	Roxanna Ward	James Ward	Esther Hoyt	James Ward Sr.	Milo & Lydia Hoyt
8193	Ward, William	TX	1832	Martha Ward	Thomas Ward	Elizabeth Widick	John Ward	Polly Madole
19451	Ward, William	AL	1905		John Ward	Vicie House	James & Cynthia Ward	Wm & Martha House
16942	Ward, Wm E.	OK	1875	Helen Ward	William Ward	Mary Webb	Enoch & Francis Ward	Wm & Polly Webb
11203	Ward, Yell	AR	1857	July Ward	George Ward	Mary Townsen	James & Lucy Ward	Jessie & Alsie Townsen
17989	Ward. Nora	MO	1892		Jerry Ward	Louisa Dunkin		Daniel & Mary Dunkin
17357	Wardlow, Laura	MS	1886	W.E. Wardlow	J.S. Todd	M.P. Morris	Lucinda Todd	John & Didamie Morris

#	Name	State	Year	Spouse	Father	Mother	Paternal Grandparents	Maternal Grandparents
13060	Ware, Agnes	OK		Clark Ware	Alexander Martin	Rachel Sanders	Joseph & Julia Martin	Isaac & Jennie Sanders
7627*	Ware, Augustus	GA	1812	Adier Ware	Bush	Henrietta Lowry		
20110	Ware, Emily	GA	67yrs		Richard	Lucy Ware		
21868*	Ware, Mattie	TN	1884	Paul Ware	Thomas Colwell	Mary Glover	Joseph & Sarah Colwell	Wm & Clara Glover
889	Ware, Victoria	OK	1850	David Ware	Lewis Mongrain	Mary Fields	Nuel Mongrain	John & Elizabeth Fields
19679	Warfort, Nancy	TN	1873	Will Warfort	Charles Weaver	Eva Ellison		
19306	Warner, Parrie	NC	1868	M.E. Warner	Leonard Scott	Eunetta Dorsett	Charles & Rebecca Scott	Henry & Pathey Dorsett
13816	Warner, Sarah	LA	1885	Neson Warner	George Edwards	Cynthia Eads	Mathew & Sarah Edwards	Daniel & Elizabeth Eads
22172	Warren Major	AL	1890	none	Frank Warren	Mary Wiffer	John Warren	Harry Sizemore
10243	Warren, Allen	WA	1877	none	William Warren	Catharine Martin	George & Susan Warren	Wm & Susan Martin
7599	Warren, Catharine	AR	1843	William Warren	William Martin	Susan Wolf	Thomas & Elizabeth Martin	Dennis & Polly Wolf
17895*	Warren, Clara	TN	1836	Richard Warren	Peter Alexander	Ann Gaerdner	Simon & Easter Alexander	
7592	Warren, Claudis	AR	1888	none	William Warren	Catharine Martin	George & Susan Warren	Wm & Susan Martin
8171	Warren, Columbia	VA	39yrs	Elbert Warren	John Peak	Surilda McGacey		Hugh & Margie Peak
7593	Warren, Francis	MO	1870	Magnolia Warren	William Warren	Catharine Martin	George & Susan Warren	Wm & Susan Martin
10244	Warren, George	WA	1875	none	William Warren	Catharine Martin	George & Susan Warren	Wm & Susan Martin
8404	Warren, Jasper	AR	1886		Wm Warren	Catharine Martin	George & Susan Warren	Wm & Susan Martin
7590	Warren, Katie	AR	1880	none	William Warren	Catharine Martin	George & Susan Warren	Wm & Susan Martin
8405	Warren, Lula	AR	1882		Wm Warren	Catharine Martin	George & Susan Warren	Wm & Susan Martin
22276	Warren, Margaret	TN	1866	Benjamin Warren	William Hood	Elizabeth Gibbs	Lucas Hood	Sallie Hood
21975	Warren, Minnie	TN	1876	Sidney Warren	William Smith	Margaret Mills		Pleasant & Manerva Slay
6265	Warren, Nancy	VA	1848	John Warren	Uriah Peak	Cornelia Hart	Josiah & Anna Peak	George & Polly Hart
22173	Warren, Richard	AL	1884	none	Frank Warren	Mary Wiffer	John Warren	Harry Sizemore
22167	Warren, Ruben	AL	1882		Francis Warren	Marie Niper	John & Fannie Warren	
20313	Warren, Winnie	MO	1888	Elmer Warren	Peter Loveless	Ida Davis	Jonathan & Clarisa Loveless	James & Maude Davis
21565	Warsham, Nancy	GA	1857	John Warsham	William Edwards	Catherine Dowdy	Thomas & Agnes Edwards	
21566	Warsham, Robert	GA	1887	Bertha Warsham	John Warsham	Nancy Edwards		Wm & Catherine Edwards
21567	Warsham, Sallie	GA	1882		John Warsham	Nancy Edwards		Wm & Catherine Edwards
21568	Warsham, William	GA	1885		John Warsham	Nancy Edwards		Wm & Catherine Edwards
8867	Washaw, Ella	OK	1885		William Cochran	Hester	John & Betsy Cochran	

12711	Washburn, Barbara	MO	1874	George Washburn	Daniel Murray	Tilitha Hines	Joshua & Mary Murray	Walter & Matilda Hines
11956 *	Washburn, Bird	GA	1865	Cornelia Washburn	David Ax	Rachel Cash		Larry & Jane Cash
11945	Washburn, Cornelia	GA	1865	B J Washburn	Alfred Crow	Cassie Cash	Samuel & Mariah Farrow	Jordan & Martha Sisson
21123	Washington, Gertrude	WI	1871	Louis Washington	Edward Davis	Martha Washinton	Henry & Mary Washington	
11695 *	Washington, Guy	TN	1827	Emily Washington	Wm McNeal	Kittie ?		Chief Bob & Mary McNeal
18958 *	Washington, Laura	OK	1877	Walter Washington	Sam Starr	Nancy Starr		
21124	Washington, Mary	WI	1824	Henry Washington	Thomas Grop	Rachel Hodgesty		Samuel Hodgesty
4343	Washington, Mary Ella	GA	1877	C.E. Washington	James Owen	Amanda Dudley	T M & Millie Owen	David & Genettia Dudley
4233 *	Washington, Sarah	LA	1850	George Washington	Isac Gahiggin	Martha Neil		
21801	Wassom, John	AL	1858	Annie Wassom	Jonas Wassom	Mary Davis		David & Sallie Davis
12088	Waters, A.G.	TN		Rebecie Waters	William Waters	Zilpha Thompson	John & Eliza Waters	John Thompson
11902	Waters, Avery	TN	1865	Acenith Waters	John Waters	Elizabeth Maab	Wm & Zilpha Waters	Lee & Mary Maab
829	Waters, Henry	TN	1871	Martha Waters	John Waters	Elizabeth Maab	Wm & Zilpha Waters	Lee & Mary Maab
3565	Waters, Henry	KS		Phebe Waters	William Waters	Zilpha Thompson		John & Polly Thompson
11812	Waters, Henry	TN	1871		James Waters	Elizabeth	Wm Waters & Leander Maab	Zilpha
12086	Waters, James	TN			L.G. Waters	Mary	Wm & Zilpha Waters	
11838	Waters, John	TN	43yrs	Elizabeth Waters	William Waters		Jake & Elizabeth Waters	
22049	Waters, Linville	NC	1847	Martha Waters	Wesley Waters	Martha Kees	Wesley Waters	
12521	Waters, Martha	GA	1859	Coleman Waters	Thomas Howell	Elvira Elrod	Jackson & Cathrine Howell	Wm & Nancy Elrod
12089	Waters, Mary	TN					Wm & Zilpha Waters	
3005	Waters, Polly	TN	1835	James Ray & Samuel Water	John Hildebrand	Nicie Russell	Michael Hildebrand	Russell
11701	Waters, Sarah	OK	1865	Gustavis Waters	Isaac Avance	Malindy Blanton	Mae Sharp & Elisebeth Avance	
7582	Waters, Wade	VA	1869	Zilpha Waters		Martha Waters		Zilpha Waters
5 *	Waters, William	GA	1826	Maria Waters				
8873	Waters, William	TN	1867	Docia Waters	John Waters	Elizabeth Maab	Wm & Zilpha Waters	Lee & Mary Maab
7581	Waters, Zilpa	VA	1870	Wade Waters	William Hollaway	Louisa Waters	Daniel & Sarah Hollaway	Wm & Zilpha Waters
21167 *	Watie, Mary	OK	1859	Andrew Watie	Dick Whitmire	Louisa Davis	Lewis Downing	Stephen & Eddie Davis
11830	Watkins, Amanda	SC	1857	George Watkins	Elias Jones	Rachel Brady	Elias & Rachel Jones	
9747	Watkins, Eliza	OK	1856	P W Watkins	John Rogers	Angeline Row	Joseph Rogers	

22570	Watkins, John	OK	1856	Queen Watkins	Jack Watkins	Kizzie Sneed	Isaiah Watkins	
289	Watkins, Liddy	NC	31yrs	James Watkins	James Anderson	Mary Smith	Lazrus & Nancy Anderson	Wm & Margarette Smith
19004	Watkins, Luella	TN	1894		Willie Watkins	Cora Donoho	Rue Watkins & Eliza Thonelson	I.S. & M.F. Donoho
21027*	Watkins, Nick	GA	1855	Nancy Watkins	James Watkins	Polly Lewis	John Watkins	John & Amie Cannon
16223	Watkins, Tiff	AR	1861	Mary Watkins	Frances Watkins	Nancy Jones	John & Kiziar Watkins	Wm & Sarah Jones
11835	Watkins, William	SC	1880	Narcisa Watkins				
17719	Watson, Annettie	TN	1858	R.L. Watson	Wm Tidwell	Matilda Payne	Gasaway Tidwell & Martha Shelton	Thos Payne & Miranda Watson
17723	Watson, Berina	TN	1883		R.L. Watson	Annettie Tidwell	James Watson	Wm Tidwell
18912	Watson, Clorinda	OK	1848		Smith Bell	Elizabeth Carter	Smith Bell	Joseph & Susan Carter
2568	Watson, Coleman	GA	1882	Octava	C J Watson	Rosetta Campbell	Hendeson Campbell & Susannah Davenport	Thomas Watson
19575	Watson, David	MD	1860		Hampton Watson	Hulda Chapman		Joseph & Reba Chapman
21810	Watson, George	TX	1863		Perry Watson	Millie Hopgood		Hezekiah Hopgood
17721	Watson, James	TN	1885		R.L. Watson	Annettie Tidwell	James Watson	Wm Tidwell
20012	Watson, John	GA	1842	Emeline Watson	Joseph Watson	Catherine Motes	Hyder & Repekah Watson	John & Nancy Motes
2585	Watson, Julia	GA	1877	R W Watson	David Ash	Elisabeth Davenport		John & Elisabeth Davenport
14248	Watson, Louis	TX	1876	Etta Watson	Robert Watson	Annette Tidwell	James & Margaret Watson	Wm & Matilda Tidwell
21571	Watson, Lucy	FL	1867	George Watson	Henry Weatherford	Louisa Clark	Henry Weatherford	Abraham & Sallie Clark
17441	Watson, Malinda	OK	1863	Tom Watson	Jim Simmons	Lutetia Lilly		
2566	Watson, Manervy	GA	1872	Thomas Watson	W T Postell	Disey Davenport		John & Elisabeth Davenport
9505	Watson, Mary	GA	1878	George Watson	John Ash	Sarah Hall	David & Elisabeth Ash	
158	Watson, Sarah	IL	1852	Henry Watson	Alexander Merrit	Mariah Don	Will Merrit	Barnea Don & Harret Powell
8221	Watson, Tom	MO	1834		Amous Watson	Millie Bays	John Watson	Lettie Bays
18296	Watson, Walter	GA	1863	Susan Watson	Hampton Watson	Hulda Chapman		Joseph & Rena Chapman
8950 1/2	Watt, Edna	OK	1899		James Thornton	Polly Thornton		
16762	Watters, Mary	OK	1867	Charlie Watters	Sam Killer	Jennie To bac o wale		
15186	Watts, Andrew	GA	1875	Texanna Watts	Charles Watts	Eliza Williams	John Watts	George Williams
15753	Watts, Charles	GA	1866		Charles Watts	Eliza Williams	Joseph Watts	George Williams
15043	Watts, Claude	GA	27yrs	Minnie Watts	Martin Watts	Jossie Robertson	Pleasant Watts	
14652	Watts, Crayton	GA	1867	Dicey Watts	John Watts	Dicy Williams	John & Mary Watts	George & Polly Williams

ID	Name	State	Year	Spouse	Father	Mother	Paternal GP	Maternal GP
10622	Watts, Elisabeth	GA	1848	none	Hiram Good	Eliza Nickolson		Isaac & Luciecy Nickolson
16727	Watts, Elizabeth	OK	1860	Jacob Watts	Wilson Miller	Nancy Tony		Richard & Nellie Tony
15185	Watts, George	GA	1862	Lucy Watts	Charles Watts	Eliza Williams	Joseph Watts	George Williams
10364	Watts, James	GA	1860	Sarah Watts	John Watts	Catharine Alexander	James & Eliza Watts	
14653	Watts, John	GA	1860	Henrietta Watts	Charles Watts	Eliza Williams	Joseph Watts	George Williams
14655	Watts, John	GA	1864	Harriet Watts	John Watts	Dicy Williams	John & Mary Watts	George & Polly Williams
15172	Watts, John	GA	1838	Dicey Watts	John Watts	Mary Crow		
12434	Watts, Louisa	OK	1882	Wattie Watts	John Beamer	Annis Blevins	Jack Beamer	Jack Blevins
4988	Watts, Maggie	GA		Paul Watts	John Pope	Sarah Jones		John & Lucinda Jones
15170	Watts, Mary	GA	1854	Joseph Watts	Berriman Shevers	Basheba Jones		
12812	Watts, William	GA			Milton Watts	Lydia McCall	Plesant Watts	Wm McCall
14651	Watts, William	GA	1861	Eliza Watts	John Watts	Dicy Williams	John & Mary Watts	George & Polly Williams
16210 *	Watts, Willie	GA	1885	James Watts	Joseph Colton	Emeline Andrews		Allen & Lucinda Andrews
19770	Waugh, John	TN						
9829	Waybourn, Georgia	OK	1870	Wilson Waybourn	Bryce Smart	Alcey Barber	Wm & Polly Smart	Isaac & Joanah Barber
19609	Waybourn, Royal	OK	1877		W.L. Waybourn			
8580	Wayne, Mattie	VA	1886	Jesse Wayne	Alford Sheets	Mary Orsborn	John & Polly Sheets	James Orsborn & Lizzy Sheets
3829	Weare, Glenn	KS	1898	none	Eugene Weare	Rose Smith	William & Nancy Weare	John & Julia Smith
3830	Weare, Lloyd	KS	1894	none	Eugene Weare	Rose Smith	William & Nancy Weare	John & Julia Smith
1681	Weare, Rose	KS	1872	Eugene Weare	John Smith	Julia Taylor	Pleasant & Priscilla Smith	Wiley & Rosamond Taylor
6323	Weatherford, Charles	AL	18??	None	Charles Weatherford	Martha Staples	Charles Weatherford & Elisabeth Stiggers	Jason Staples & Margaret Powell
21569	Weatherford, Henry Jr.	FL	1874	Martha Weatherford	Henry Weatherford	Louisa Clark	Henry Weatherford	Abraham & Sallie Clark
21570	Weatherford, Louisa	FL	1876		Henry Weatherford	Louisa Clark	Henry Weatherford	Abraham & Sallie Clark
6330	Weatherford, Sidney	AL		Phene Ship	Charles Weatherford	Martha Staples	Charles Weatherford & Elisabeth Stiggins	Jason & Margies Staples
20637 *	Weathers, Malissa	TN	1834		Randle Carter	Nellie Walker	Della Carter	James & Dilla Walker
11270	Weaver, Abram	VA	1865	Rebecca Weaver	William Weaver	Catharine Baldwin		Wm & Margret Baldwin
20967	Weaver, Ada	MS	1883	William Weavers	? Todd	? Morris	John Todd	Didama Morris
10886 *	Weaver, Alaford	WI		Mamie Weaver	Alfred Weaver	Charity Revels		McGaga & Mornan Revels
17390	Weaver, Albert	AL	1847	Mary Weaver	David Weaver	Nancy Fisher	David Weaver	Nancy Fisher
17394	Weaver, Alfred	AL		Rose Weaver	David Weaver	Nancy Fisher		Wm Weatherford & Nancy Fisher
12511 *	Weaver, Bert	WI	1869	Carrie Weaver	Alfred Weaver	Charity Revels		Macaga & Mornon Revels
8818	Weaver, Bettie	GA		Andrew Weaber	George King	Mary Gray	John & Elisabeth King	Samuel Gray & Pollie Laudermilk

3624	Weaver, Catharine	VA	1838		Wm Baldwin	Margret Stringer	Joseph Baldwin	Catharine Hart
11621	Weaver, Conard	TN	1851	Sallie Weaver	Solomon Weaver	Elizabeth Fowler	Adam Weaver	Lona Fowler
17391	Weaver, David	AL			Weaver	Nancy Fisher		Wm Weatherford & Nancy Fisher
22709	Weaver, Elzina	VA	22yrs	S.H. Weaver	Eli Blevins	Nancy Ham	Riley & Agnes Blevins	
12926*	Weaver, Ezra	IN	1865		Alfred Weaver	Charity Revels	Bird & Sarah Weaver	Macaga & Mornon Revels
3566	Weaver, Frankey	VA	1863	Winton Weaver	King Roop	Louise Baldwin		William & Margaret Baldwin
3626	Weaver, Grant	VA	1868	Frona Weaver	Wm Weaver	Catharine Baldwin		Wm & Margret Baldwin
3621	Weaver, Jefferson	VA	1862	none	Wm Weaver	Catharine Baldwin		Wm & Margart Baldwin
3519	Weaver, Joe & Baby	OK			Bill Burgess	Jennie Weaver decd		
5076	Weaver, Lillie	VA	1886	none	Marion Weaver	Frona Roten	Wm & Catharine Weaver	W. & Catharine Roten
19578	Weaver, Mary	GA	1833	William Weaver	Peter Lewis	Nancy Land	Samuel Lewis & Stacy Wallace	Ellen Land
11239*	Weaver, Melvin	WI	1871	Alice Weaver	Alfred Weaver	Charity Revels		McCaga & Momon Revels
20619	Weaver, Rachel	TN	1850		Ephraim Jones	Sarah Oxford	Sally Jones	Jacob & Elizabeth Oxford
15889*	Weaver, Sarah	IN	1864	James Weaver	Alex Jones	Jane Mitchell	John & Rebecca Jones	Alex & Rebecca Mitchell
17613*	Weaver, Sarah	IN	1851	Alfred Weaver	John Wallace	Amanda Harris	Aaron & Esther Wallace	
3625	Weaver, Sherman	VA	1870	none	Wm Weaver	Catharine Baldwin		Wm & Margret Baldwin
13031	Weaver, Wade	NC	1871	Malleny Weaver	John Weaver	Celia Pennington		Samuel & Elizabeth Pennington
4541	Weaver, William	VA	1833	Trona Weaver	William Weaver	Catharine Baldwin		Wm & Margret Baldwin
3622	Weaver, Winfield	VA	1883	none	Wm Weaver	Catharine Baldwin		Wm & Margret Baldwin
2529	Webb, A.J. gdn.	NC	1850	Sarah Webb		Sarah Harris		Paten & Mary Harris
8200	Webb, Edgar	OK	1883	none	James Webb	Mary Gambill		Andrew & Sally Gambill
21429	Webb, Graham	TX		Mattie Webb	Jeremiah Webb	Francis Galleher		Charles & Eliza Galleher
17178	Webb, John	NC	1848	Mary Webb	Andy Webb	Hanner Poindexter	Andy & Mary Webb	John & Sarah Poindexter
17286	Webb, Lydia	VA		Joseph Webb	John Cline	Louisa Sizemore	John & Polly Cline	Franklin & Polly Sizemore
7530	Webb, Malissa	OK	1852	Elijah Webb	Jacob Cook	Delana Epperson		Thomas & Phebea Barnes
8195	Webb, Robert	OK	1877	none	James Webb	Mary Gambill		Andrew & Sally Gambill
1679	Webb, Sarah	ID	1834	widow	Calvin Hurst	Nancy Clark	Jesse & Winey Hurst	John & Sallie Clark
2528	Webb, Sarah	NC	1865	Aaron Webb	Pator Haris	Mary Underwood	Silvester & Nansey Haris	

#	Name	State	Year	Spouse	Father	Mother	Paternal GP	Maternal GP
14897	Webb, Thomas	NC	1842	Sarah Webb	Andy Webb	Hanner Poindexter	Andy & Mary Webb	John & Sarah Poindexter
13553	Webb, William	NC			Andrew Webb	Hannah Poindexter	Andrew & Mary Webb	John & Sarah Poindexter
20953	Webber, Walter	AL	1880	Bertie Webber	William Webber	Hannah Early	William Webber	Ned Early
16163	Webber, William	OK	1844		William Webber	Peggie ?	Watts & Agie Webber	Nah go me
22435	Weber, Malinda	OK	47yrs	Robert Jackson	Robsie Weber	Hannah Weber		
17525	Weddel, Lula	OK	1874	Huram Weddel	L.M. Douthitt	Nancy Dawson	Ambrose & Nancy Douthitt	Elbert & Sarah Dawson
14563	Weddington, Affie	GA	1890	Homer Weddington	John Carter	Jane McMain	Thomas & Nellie Carter	
9506	Weeks, Amanda	GA	1876	W H Weeks	John Davenport	Sarah Ross	John & Elisabeth Davenport	
5461	Weeks, Mary	NC	1866	J M Weeks	John Constant	Elisabeth Delozier		Edward & Elisabeth Delozier
21690	Weir, Mary	AR	1875	George Weir	William Page	Emily Wall	David & Ann Page	Drury & Elizabeth Wall
7809	Weiss, Charles	KS	1884	none	Albert Weiss	Mary Ballou	John & Maria Weiss	Hugh & Eliza Ballou
1789	Weiss, Mary Jane	KS	1862	Albert Weiss	Hugh Ballou	Eliza Stamper	Blake & Patsy Ballou	Eli & Susanna Stamper
1790	Weiss, Olive	KS	1882	none	Albert Weiss	Mary Ballou	John Weiss	Hugh & Eliza Ballou
1791	Weiss, Wave	KS	1891	none	Albert Weiss	Mary Ballou	John Weiss	Hugh & Eliza Ballou
5462	Welch, Amanda	NC	1860	none	Adolphus Welch	Sarah Sawyer	Joseph & Cathrine Welch	Joel & Esther Sawyer
14832	Welch, Charles	FL	1875		James Welch	Elizabeth Lewis	John & Arminda Welch	James & Sarah Lewis
12747	Welch, Elizabeth	GA	1850	Cornelius Welch	James Ford	Elizabeth Mantooth		Thos Mantooth & Lettie Dillon
44 *	Welch, Emma	GA	1872	Robert Welch	Abraham Angel	Amey Walker	James Guy & Rever Angel	
5465	Welch, Ida	NC	1879	none		Montera Welch		Adolphus & Sarah Welch
10324	Welch, Irena	OK	1872	J G Welch	Benj Kiper	Nancy Wood	Eliza Kiper	Luke & Mary Wood
5479	Welch, Jestiana	NC	1849	none	Adolphus Welch	Sarah Sawyer	Joseph & Cathrine Welch	Joel & Esther Sawyer
5469	Welch, Joseph	NC	1848	Emeline Welch	Adolphus Welch	Sarah Sawyer	Joseph & Cathrine Welch	Josel & Esther Sawyer
7631	Welch, Leahoma	VA	1883	Wm Welch	Calvin Thompson	Elizabeth Welch	Samuel & Margaret Thompson	James & Nancy Welch
6018	Welch, Lucinda (decd)	OK	1825	James Welch	Jonathan Parker	Oma Blythe	William Parker	Jonathan & Annie Blythe
3056	Welch, Mahaley	TX	1857	Edgar Welch	James Southerland	Mahaley Briggs		John Briggs
12809	Welch, Margaret	NC	1852	J M Welch	Watson Battle	Sallie Hyde		Benj & Elizabeth Hyde
843	Welch, Mary	NC	1865	John Welch	Willis Parker	Adaline Vanoy	Johnathan & Leomy Parker	Joel & Elizabeth Vanoy
18990	Welch, Mary	OK	1842	Thomas Welch	Barnabus Johnson	Phebe Boring	Barnabus Johnson	John Boring
15731	Welch, Reuben Jr.	GA			Billy Welch	Percilla Simmons	Reubin Welch	

5478	Welch, Samuel	NC	1862	none	Adolphus Welch	Sarah Sawyer	Joseph & Cathrine Welch	Joel & Esther Sawyer
16284	Welch, Samuel	GA	1867	Alice McLain	James Welch	Elizabeth Lewis	John & Armadel Welch	Wm & Sarah Lewis
17913	Welch, Thomas Sr.	OK		Mary Welch	Joseph Welch	Mary Brasie	John & Betsie Welch	Ephram Brasie
5464	Welch, William	NC	1852	Elizabeth Welch	Adolphus Welch	Sarah Sawyer	Joseph & Cathrine Welch	Joel & Esther Sawyer
9498	Welch, William	GA	1892		William Beaver	Altha Welch	John & Mary Beaver	
15002	Weller, Nellie	OK	1884	Joseph Weller	George Keys	Alice Sturm	Polly Noon	J J Sturm
21489	Welliver, Venny	OK	1879		Richard Parsons	Jane Logan	Hiram & Martha Parsons	John & Sarah Logan
22232 *	Wells, Lora	NC	53 yrs	James Wells	Isom Floid	Mariah Bockster		Simon & Eliza Bockster
7395	Wells, Mattie	MO	1873	W J Wells	William Vance	Margaret Marlin	Wm & Emeline Vance	
14708	Wells, May	AR	1885		Cyrus Hathaway	Cenie Bell	Cyrus & Ann Hathaway	Wm & Nancy Bell
17243	Welter, Siler	OK	1872	W.D. Welter	Thomas Redding	Eliza Ross	John & Percilla Redding	Templeton & Percilla Ross
22484	Werther, Charles	OK	1883	Annie Werther	Guenther Werther	Lucy Jones		
1166	Werther, Lucy	OK	1865	Guenther Werther	Jim Jones	Barbara Asher	Jones Pig	
21366	West, Catherine	OK	1867	J.F. West	Crofford Polk	Arabella Jeter		Mary Jeter
15078	West, Charles	OK	1885		A B West	Nann Rutheford	Isaac & Nancy West	
11391	West, Eller	NC	25yrs	Alyia West	Joseph Adams	Lucretia Taylor	Posey & Jane Adams	David & Anna Taylor
21640	West, James	TN	1825	Sophous West	John West	Betsy Miller		
7614	West, Mary	GA	1837	Thos West	John Baily	Sarah Mullins	Furdinand & Annie Baily	
18745	West, Minnie	TX	1875	Ed West	James Higdon	Rachel Freeland	Joseph & Marget Higdon	Howell & Zilpha Freeland
9487	West, Nancy	NC	1862	Calvin West	Van Tramel	Mary Morgan	Jake & Pollie Tramel	
20116	West, Zachriah	MO	1852	Lula West	Isaac West	Nancy Owens	Reuben & Rachael West	Philip & Rebecca Owens
20337 *	Westfield, Minnie	GA	1875	James Westfield	William Gray	Laura Russell	Annica Gray	Henson & Dicey Russell
18818	Westmoreland, James	GA	1846	Julia Westmoreland	Revis Westmoreland	Susie Allison	Robert Westmoreland	Wm Allison & Abigail Padget
18452	Westmoreland, Sarah	NC	1854	Seaton Westmoreland	Frank Marion	Sallie Hauser	Adam & Sallie Marion	Samuel & Nancy Hauser
18819	Westmoreland, William	GA	1858	Ida Westmoreland	Revis Westmoreland	Susie Allison	Robert Westmoreland	Wm Allison & Abigail Padget
19208	Wheatley, Eddie	OK	1877	J.H. Wheatley	W.T. Cooper	Sary Woods	J.W. Cooper & Elizabeth McAdams	J.W. Woods
7394	Wheeler, Ader	TX	1875	D P Wheeler	John Montgomery	Catharine Williams	Nathan & Martha Montgomery	Joseph & Catharine Williams
20167	Wheeler, George	GA	1845	Annis Wheeler	Larkin Wheeler	Charity Godard	Wm & Nancy Wheeler	John & Winnie Godard
19884	Wheeler, Lydia	TN	1882	Robert Wheeler	Charles Curtis	Eudora Smith	Joshua & Lucinda Curtis	Eli & Mary Smith

2781	Wheeler, Mary	GA	1855	Robert Wheeler	John Helton	Mary McElroy	James & Camilla Helton	
20168	Wheeler, Mary	GA	1877		George Wheeler	Annis Herrin	Larkin & Charity Wheeler	Wm & Eliza Herrin
8505	Wheeler, Susan	KY	1878	John Wheeler	Lemuel Faircloth	Mary Atwood	Thelbert & Cristeen Faircloth	George & Mahaly Atwood
20082	Wheeler, Theodocia	TN	1880	James Wheeler	Eli Smith	Mary Curtis	Gipson & Edith Smith	Joshua & Elizabeth Curtis
5912	Wheeler, William	OK	1847	Emma Wheeler	John Wheeler	Nancy Watie		Oo-watie & Susannah
10521	Wheeler, William	GA	1872	Kansas Wheeler	Robert Wheeler	Isabella Helton	Wm & Polly Wheeler	Clark & Mary Helton
20166	Wheeler, William	GA	1842		Larkin Wheeler	Charity Godard	Wm & Nancy Wheeler	John & Winnie Godard
20169	Wheeler, William	GA	1872	Ella Wheeler	George Wheeler	Annis Herrin	Larkin & Charity Wheeler	Wm & Eliza Herrin
7425	Whelchel, Francis	GA	1842	Margaret Whelchel	John Whelchel	Susan Buffington	Frank & Nancy Whelchel	Thomas Buffington & Nancy Eaton
20263	Whirley, Francis	OK	1883	Marian Whirley	James Fryar	Margarett Yates	Isaac & Rebecca Fryar	Lewis & Elizabeth Yates
20264	Whirley, Gertrude	TX	1885	John Whirley	James Fryar	Margarett Yates	Isaac & Rebecca Fryar	Lewis & Elizabeth Yates
21212	Whisenhunt, Bessie	OK	1886	Wiley Whisenhunt	John Cooper	Emma Simpson	J.W. & Elizabeth Cooper	Wm & Jemima Simpson
21215	Whiserhunt, Cora	OK	1878	A.B. Whiserhunt	John Cooper	Emma Simpson	J.W. & Elizabeth Cooper	Wm & Jemima Simpson
21216	Whiserhunt, Ollie	OK	1883	Y.E. Whiserhunt	John Cooper	Emma Simpson	J.W. & Elizabeth Cooper	Wm & Jemima Simpson
13743*	Whitaker, Henry	GA	1854	Rosa Whitaker	John Kearklin	Millie Howe		Jonney & Fannie Howe
13897	Whitaker, Mattie	KY	1882	Henry Whitaker	William Caldwell	Louisa Smith	Freland & Elizabeth Caldwell	Jonas & Sarah Smith
3132`	White, Ben	MS	1876	Gussie White	Ben White	Kibbie Hobgood		Charles & Martha Hobgood
21578	White, Benjaman	TN	1882	Myrtle White	Erve White	Liddie Hargrove	Dempsy & Nancy White	James & Serena Hargrove
21577	White, Bessie	TN	1890		Erve White	Liddie Hargrove	Dempsy & Nancy White	James & Serena Hargrove
21576	White, Ed	TN	1884	Lillie White	Erve White	Liddie Hargrove	Dempsy & Nancy White	James & Serena Hargrove
13903*	White, Edney	GA	1820		George Bell	Peggie		
3385	White, Ellen	AL		Harry White	John Woods	Mary Weatherford	John Woods	
3105	White, George	MS	1879	Ida White	Ben White	Kibbie Hobgood		Charles & Martha Hobgood
12600	White, Hay	WV	1885	R A White	J A Rodgers	Louisa Cline	J J & Mary Rodgers	H C & Virginia Cline
1	White, Isom	MO	1841	widower	William White	Malinda Durham	Henry Durham	Sarah Durham
21597	White, John	NC	1855	Milly White	Joseph White	Mary May	Joseph & Clara White	Proe & Rachel May
21584	White, John et al	NC			Joseph White	Mary Gordon	Joseph & Mary White	Lucy Gordon
21614	White, Joseph	NC	1879	Mary White	Joseph White	Mary May	Joseph & Clara White	Prior & Rachel May
7392	White, Katy	KS	1886	W B White	Jasper Wade	Lucinda Allen		Joseph & Margaret Allen

#	Name	State	Year	Spouse	Father	Mother	Paternal Grandparents	Maternal Grandparents
3131	White, Kibbie	MS	1858	Ben White	Charles Hobgood	Martha Lowe		Thomas & Annie Lowe
21572	White, Lawrence	TN	1886		Erve White	Liddie Hargrove	Dempsy & Nancy White	James & Serena Hargrove
22649	White, Lewis	OK	1881	Clorena White	William White	Mary Tidwell	Orsburn & Permelia White	John & Lucrecia Tidwell
16627	White, Lillie	NC			Johneth White	Sarah Roper		John & Elisabeth Roper
4249	White, Lula	MO	36yrs	William White	Robert Richardson	Emmaline Abney	Punctilhion & Becky Richardson	
569	White, M. F.	OK	1847	Elishey White	Auston Jeter	Mary Ann Bumbley	Buck & Sally Jeter	Wm & Elizabeth Bumbley
2315	White, Martha	NC	1875	Patton White		Melvina McDonald		Sallie McDonald
21184	White, Martha	TN	1879	Berry White	John Lindsey	Josie McKenney	David Lindsey	
16	White, Mary	OK	1847	Wiliam White	John Tidwell	Lucretia Thompson		
20335	White, Mary	TN	1869	Miniard White	Joseph Anderson	Caroline Jordan	Richard & Mary Anderson	Daniel & Julia Jordan
20515	White, Miniard	TN	1859	Mary White	John White	Rachel Jones	Ervin & Susan White	Ephraim & Sarah Jones
8846	White, Missouri	GA		James White	William Stokes	Margarett Harris	John Stokes	Ruben Harris
18414	White, Mrs. J.M.	AL	28yrs	J.M. White	James Seals	Louisa Hadley	Wm & Lucy Seals	Simon & Caroline Hadley
21573	White, Myrtle	TN	1893		Erve White	Liddie Hargrove	Dempsy & Nancy White	James & Serena Hargrove
22672	White, Myrtle	IN	1883	Grant White	Frank Henderson	Victoria Hammonds		Thomas & Delaney Hammonds
5834	White, Rebecca	VA	1877		Winfield Thompson			
21574	White, Sallie	TN	1880		Erve White	Liddie Hargrove	Dempsy & Nancy White	James & Serena Hargrove
13818	White, Sarah	GA	1849	Jacob White	James White	Adline Sutton	Luke White	William Sutton
16617	White, Sarah	NC	1865	Jontes White	John Roper	Easter Hughes	Wm Walker & Elisabeth Roper	Jackson & Elithebeth Hughes
22401	White, Sarah	TN	1870	John White	John Lyndsey	Josie McKennie		Betsey McKennie
11947	White, Susan	GA	1881	Amos White	Lee Branner	Margaret Deadwyler	Thomas Hicks	
15403	White, William	GA	1877		Henry White	Eliza White	Noah & Amanda White	Richard & Sylvia White
22788	White, William	OK	1872		William White	Mary Tidwell	Orsburn & Permelia White	John & Lucrecia Tidwell
15074	Whitely, Calpernia	KY	1841	John Whitely	Luke Wood	Mary Thornton	Wm & Elizabeth Wood	Seth & Nancy Thornton
17505	Whitely, George	OK	1850	Nanancy Whitely	Jesse Whitely	Elizabeth Harp	Samuel & Lucy Whitely	
19408	Whitener, Ary	GA	1888		Philip Whitener	Martha Hardin	Abram & Elizabeth Whitener	
19409	Whitener, Henry	GA	1896		Philip Whitener	Martha Hardin	Abram & Elizabeth Whitener	
19411	Whitener, Marion	GA	1888		Philip Whitener	Martha Hardin	Abram & Elizabeth Whitener	
19412	Whitener, Martha	GA	1857		John Hardin	Fenobee Moore		Alfred & Tempe Moore
19413	Whitener, Philip	GA	1844	Martha Whitener	Abram Whitener	Elizabeth Chambers	John & Margaret Whitener	

ID	Name	State	Year					
19414	Whitener, Virginia	GA	1884		Philip Whitener	Martha Hardin	Abram & Elizabeth Whitener	
16437	Whiteside, Mary	OK	1879	Charley Whiteside	William Henson	Josephine Mabry	Henry & Mary Henson	Joseph & Hester Athens
15429	Whitfield, Rozella	GA	1854	Caleb Whitfield	Tom Cantrell	Annie Crow		Edward & Annie Townsend
19020	Whitice, Alice	CA	1882		R.D. Whitice	S.A. Sherrill	Josiah Reid	
19019	Whitice, Belle	CA	1878		R.D. Whitice	S.A. Sherrill	Josiah Reid	
18193	Whitice, Fulsom	TN	1889		William Whitice	Flora Smith	Wm & Eliza Whitice	George & Mary Smith
19021	Whitice, Paul	CA	1888		R.D. Whitice	S.A. Sherrill	Josiah Reid	
19018	Whitice, Robert	CA	1855	S.A. Whitice	W.A. Whitice	Eliza Reid		Josiah Reid
18184	Whitice, Rolla	TN	1852		W.W. Whitice	Flora Smith	Wm & Eliza Whitice	George & Mary Smith
18030	Whitice, William	TN	1880	Sallie Whitice	Wm Whitice	Flora Smith	Wm & Eliza Whitice	John & Mary Smith
15116	Whitley, Joseph	GA	1828	Lucy Whitley	George Whitley	Mary Harvel	George & Elizabeth Whitley	
21367	Whitley, Lela	LA	1876	Eugene Whitley	John Jeter	Susan Thompson	Washington & Mary Jeter	
15115	Whitley, Lucy	GA	1840	Joseph Whitley	Griffin Barber	Mary Ward	Jim & Parmy Barber	Billie & Elizabeth Ward
22590	Whitlock, Alice	TN	1869	James Whitlock	James Helton	Martha Clark	Daniel & Patsy Helton	John & Peggy Clark
20855	Whitlock, Bennie	GA	1901		Tyre Whitlock	Alice Turner	Wm & Caroline Whitlock	Francis & Harriet Turner
20856	Whitlock, George	GA	1856		William Whitlock	Caroline Page	James & Sallie Whitlock	Jim & Sibbia Page
13740	Whitlock, John	GA	1856	Huldy Whitlock	Andrew Whitlock	Eliza Rowson	George & Nancy Whitlock	Elija & Millie Rowson
20857	Whitlock, John	GA	1896		John Whitlock	Mary Waters	Wm & Caroline Whitlock	Bailus & Elizabeth Waters
20858	Whitlock, John	GA	1854	Mary Whitlock	William Whitlock	Caroline Page	James & Sallie Whitlock	Jim & Sibbia Page
20859	Whitlock, Josephine	GA	1898		John Whitlock	Mary Waters	Wm & Caroline Whitlock	Bailus & Elizabeth Waters
20860	Whitlock, Lillie	GA	1891		John Whitlock	Lou Fowlers	Wm & Caroline Whitlock	Elbert & Susan Fowler
16060	Whitlock, Mary	OK	1857	J T Whitlock	Bishop	Elizabeth Bohanon		
20861	Whitlock, Ola	GA	1898		Tyre Whitlock	Alice Turner	Wm & Caroline Whitlock	Francis & Harriet Turner
20862	Whitlock, Tyre	GA	1863	Alice Whitlock	William Whitlock	Caroline Page	James & Sallie Whitlock	Jim & Sibbia Page
20863	Whitlock, Walter	GA	1892		Tyre Whitlock	Alice Turner	Wm & Caroline Whitlock	Francis & Harriet Turner
17607	Whitman, Rachel	MO	1849	W.W. Whitman	Manlove Cranon	Eleanor Lee		Elisabeth Little
15114	Whitmire, Avarilla	GA	1900		George Whitmire	Jane Reeves	James & Carrie Whitmire	
21149*	Whitmire, Betsy	OK	1844	Lewis Whitmire	Nick Sanders	Jennie Saunders		Daniel & Betsy Saunders
15112	Whitmire, Christopher	GA	1869		Elias Whitmire	Louisa Owen	George & Mary Whitmire	
15113	Whitmire, David	GA	1878	Elsie Whitmire	Elias Whitmire	Louisa Owen	George & Mary Whitmire	
15111	Whitmire, Earnest	GA	2mos		Thomas Whitmire	Myrtle Smith	George & Jane Whitmire	
15110	Whitmire, Elias	GA	1835	Louisa Whitmire	George Whitmire	Mary Smith	Chris & Nancy Whitmire	
19469	Whitmire, Emory	GA	1878	Ella Whitmire	John Whitmire	Sarah Moore	James & Cassie Whitmire	Watson & Charity Moore
15108	Whitmire, George	GA	1864		Elias Whitmire	Louisa Owen	George & Mary Whitmire	

15109	Whitmire, George	GA	1844	Mary Whitmire	James Whitmire	Cassie Holland	Chris & Nancy Whitmire	
15107	Whitmire, John	GA	1880		Elias Whitmire	Louisa Owen	George & Mary Whitmire	
19474	Whitmire, John	GA	1842	Sarah Whitmire	James Whitmire	Cassie Holland	Chris & Nancy Whitmire	Elijah Holland
15106	Whitmire, Lola	GA	1902		George Whitmire	Jane Reeves	James & Carrie Whitmire	
15105	Whitmire, Mary	GA	1889		George Whitmire	Jane Reeves	James & Carrie Whitmire	
18720	Whitmire, Ruth	TN	1850	Henderson Whitmire	Willis Guy	Mahala Gibson	Edmund & Judie Guy	George & Viney Gibson
15104	Whitmire, Samuel	GA	1875	Cansada Whitmire	Elias Whitmire	Louisa Owen	George & Mary Whitmire	
15103	Whitmire, Sanford	GA	1898		George Whitmire	Jane Reeves	James & Carrie Whitmire	
15101	Whitmire, Thomas	GA	1905		Thomas Whitmire	Myrtle Hall	George & Jane Whitmire	
15102	Whitmire, Thomas	GA	1882	Myrtle Whitmire	George Whitmire	Jane Reeves	James & Carrie Whitmire	
15100	Whitmire, Walter	GA	1871	Georgia Whitmire	Elias Whitmire	Louisa Owen	George & Mary Whitmire	
13856	Whitmire, William	GA	1839	Louisa Whitmire	Christopher Whitmire	Nancy Reese	Samuel Whitmire	Jacob & Betsey Reese
15099	Whitmire, Willie	GA	1895		George Whitmire	Jane Reeves	James & Carrie Whitmire	
15189	Whitmore, James	GA	1880	Catherine Whitmore	George Whitmore	Sarah Hood	Henry Whitmore & Kizzie Blalock	Moses Hendrick & Hannah Trout
20297	Whitney, Mattie	OK		John Whitney	Andrew Avants	Rebeckie Welsh	Peter & Mary Avants	
7367	Whitsett, Barna	MO	1861		William Whitsett	Piercy Perkins	James & Polly Whitsett	Aaron & Sealy Perkins
7366	Whitsett, Williamson	MO	1859	Perlina Whitsett	William Whitsett	Piercey Perkins	James & Polly Whitsett	Aaron & Celia Perkins
8446	Whitsitt, Lizzie	MO	1887	Nevel Whitsitt	Elias Dagley	Lois Craven	Alvis & Nancy Dagley	James & Sarah Craven
9200	Whitson, Ellen	NC	1864	C.D. Whitson	Joshua Payne	Patsy Hayden	London & Sally Payne	Robert & Susan Hayden
21391	Wicker, Laura	OK	1883	John Wicker	Abner Christopher	Nancie Rimare	John & Laura Christopher	Benj & Francis Rimare
18194	Wicks, Alice	TN	1874	Willis Wicks	King Phillips	Millie Cooper		Mordeca & Grnette Cooper
11082	Widener, Mary	VA	1852	Andrew Widener	Isham Blevins	Anna Edmondson	George & Lydia Blevins	
12967	Widener, Nancy	VA	1852	Samuel Widener	Elisha Hart	Nancy Stringer	George & Polly Hart	
11065	Widener, Robert	VA	1884	Myrtle Widener	Andrew Widener	Mary Blevins		Isham & Anna Blevins
10602	Wiegand, Lucy	OK	1820	widow	Thomas Starr	Nancy Foreman		Anthony & Wottie Foreman
17544	Wiggins, Ida	AR	1871	T.J. Wiggins	James Hamilton	Anna Denny	Wm & Matilda Hamilton	James & Margaret Denny
4557	Wiggins, Lillie	NC	1861	Ju Wiggins	Uriah Burns	Sallie Birchfield	Hezekiah & Betsey Burns	
3496	Wigington, Sarah	GA	1847	James Wigington	William Pinjan	Cyntha Davis	Stokes Pinjan	Nancy Tally
18808	Wigley, Bethany	GA	1862	Henry Wigley	Nathan Gunnin	Mary Maddox	Ezekiel & Mary Gunnin	Dudley & Ruth Maddox
8069	Wigton, Mary	IL	1886	Egbert Wigton	Robert Duncan	Nancy Peak	Joseph & Annie Duncan	Uriah & Carnelia Peak

ID	Name	State	Year	Col5	Col6	Col7	Col8	Col9
14378	Wilabay, Isaac	AL	1857	Elizabeth Wilabay	John Wilabay	Rebecca Davidson	James & Sarah Wilabay	James & Elizabeth Davidson
20984	Wilabay, James	AL	1891		Isaac Wilabay	Rutha Lackey	John Wilabay & Rebecca Davidson	
20982	Wilabay, Martha	AL	1884		Isaac Wilabay	Rutha Lackey	John Wilabay & Rebecca Davidson	
20983	Wilabay, Samuel	AL	1878	Susan Wilabay	Isaac Wilabay	Rutha Lackey	John Wilabay & Rebecca Davidson	
14379	Wilabay, Sarah	AL	1840		John Wilabay	Rebecca Davidson	James & Sarah Wilabay	James & Elizabeth Davidson
9517	Wilbert, Lena	TN	1877	A M Wilbert	C.N. Ledford	Eliza Alexander	Ealburn & Eliza Ledford	
19356 *	Wilborn, John	GA	1864	Alice Wilborn	Thomas Wilborn	Tama Hawkins	Philip & Aggie Wilborn	Alex & Lucy Hawkins
8839	Wilburn, Minerva	IL	1847	William Wilburn	James Eddings	Roda West	John & Francis Eddings	James West
1800	Wilcox, Rebecca	NC	1883	George Wilcox	Elijah Hart	Amanda Blevins	Stephen & Rebecca Hart	
17171	Wildcat, Ar-dar-lo-ee	OK	1902		Gee-yah-ha Wildcat	Elsy Buster	Willie Wildcat	Lyndie Buster
11161	Wilder, Charlotte	OK	1847	William Wilder	Ellis West	Clara Buffington	Jacob & Sallie West	
11160	Wilder, Nancy decd	OK		William Wilder	Joshua Bufffington	Elizabeth Welch	Thos & Mary Buffington	David & Elizabeth Welch
9057	Wiles, Cora	NC	1882	W H Wiles	William Caldwell	Celia Hash		John & Sarah Hash
13084	Wilkerson, Asa	OK	1852	Margaret Wilkerson	John Wilkerson	Nancy Blankenship	John & Annie Wilkerson	
20597 *	Wilkerson, Hattie	TN	1847	George Wilkerson	Frank Craven	Charity Craven		John & Gemima Craven
1730	Wilkerson, John	OK	1843	Rebecca Wilkerson	Geo Wilkerson	Susan		
8214	Wilkerson, John	OK	1848	Lizzie Wilkerson	Tom Wilkerson	Lucinda Childres	Peggy Wilkerson	Lemuel & Nancy Childers
8959	Wilkerson, Nora	TX	1876		James Wilkerson		Nancy Wilkerson	
14003	Wilkerson, Sarah	OK	1861	John Wilkerson	Levi Robbins	Hester Quinton	Ben & Rachel Robbins	
20653 *	Wilkes, Alice	TN	1873	William Wilkes	Richard Wofford	Eliza Quillan	Moses & Phebe Berry	Zilpha Quillan
20401 *	Wilkins, Hattie	TN	1860		Richard Hutchinson	Jane Hutchinson		Kisiah Coulter
18367	Wilkins, Martha	GA	1860	Jack Wilkins	Marian Pool	Tilda Childers	Moses & Sarah Pool	Robt & Pacience Childers
15098	Willbanks, Annie	GA	1882	Arthur Willbanks	Noah Jordan Jr	Susan Ragsdale	Noah & Adaline Jordan	
15097	Willbanks, Sever	GA	1861	Evaline Willbanks	Burt Wilbanks	Susan Crow	Wm & Bookie Wilbanks	Abram & Phoebe Crow
20486 *	Williams, Adaline	TN	1837		Green Henry	Malissa Hemphill	June Henry	Cato & Dollie Hemphill
7368	Williams, Albert	TX	1847	Rosa Williams	Louis Williams	Lucinda Privett	Martin Williams & Nancy Osborne	Noah & Neoma Privett
7380	Williams, Alford	TX	1858	Fannie Williams	Joseph Williams	Rutha Holland	Edward Williams	Peggie Crittenden
8370	Williams, Alford	OK	1872	Annie Williams	John Williams	Louisa Cope	Pleasant Williams	
9197	Williams, Alfred	TX	1878	Winnie Williams	Moses Williams	Alethea Cook	Joseph & Catherine Williams	Oscar & Nancy Cook

7378	Williams, Allie	MO	1864	widow	Rumbust Sullenger	Maranda Carroll	William Sullenger	James & Polly Carroll
14654	Williams, Andrew	GA	1845	Rebecca Williams	George Williams	Polly Sargleter		Free Will
16171	Williams, Ann	OK	1853		Thomas York	Minda Beans		Sandy Beans
7374	Williams, Beniah	MO	1871	none	Jeremiah Williams	Sarah Worthington	Beniah & Nancy Williams	Francis & Sarah Worthington
10825	Williams, Benjiman	TX	1886		Vergil Williams	Rebecca Loyd	Joseph & Catharine Williams	Benj & Elizabeth Loyd
20270	Williams, Carrie	MO	1880		Jeremiah Williams	Sarah Worthington	Beniah & Nancy Williams	Francis & Sarah Worthington
17858	Williams, Charles	MO	1860	Sudie Williams	Jeremiah Williams	Mary McGaugh	Beniah & Nancy Williams	Patton & Mary McGaugh
7800	Williams, Claud	MO	1887	none	Charles Williams	Mollie Dee	Jeremiah Williams	Patton & Mary McGaugh
13352	Williams, Dallas	OK	1878		W A Williams	Mary Haynes	Joseph & Catherine Williams	
12865	Williams, Davis	MO	1845	Josephine Williams	William Williams	Martha Murray	James & Phoebe Williams	James & Yaurth Murray
10668	Williams, Edward	MO	1840		John Williams	Nancy James	Edward Williams	Edward & Lazina James
12057	Williams, Elizabeth	WV	1860		William Williams	Mary Sizemore	Wm & Elizbeth Williams	Hiram & Jane Sizemore
22443	Williams, Ella	OK	1884	Darnell Williams	Edward McDonald	Annie Killgore	James & Annie McDonald	Charley Killgore
20571	Williams, Ellen	TN	1890	W.D. Williams	Elijah Lower	Louise Huffstuttler	John & Ellen Lower	Wm & Lucinda Huffstuttler
7376	Williams, Emma	MO	1882	none	Jeremiah Williams	Sarah Worthington	Beniah & Nancy Williams	Francis & Sarah Worthington
21253	Williams, Ettie	AR	1882		Joseph Williams	Isabell Cahoon	John & Patience Williams	
8199	Williams, Fannie	TX		O F Williams	James Pauly	Henritta Sessions	Andrew Caldwell	Margrett Sessions
20574 *	Williams, Forest	TN	1865	Mattie Williams	William Williams	Adaline Jones	Queen McConnell	Green & Malissa Henny
12044	Williams, George	GA	1876		Jerome Williams	Margaret Pressly	Henry & Agnes Williams	John & Elizabeth Pressly
12378 *	Williams, George	TN	1841	Alice Williams	George Morrow	Leona Williams		Lucy Williams
17906	Williams, Helen	FL	32yrs	Hunter Williams	Richard Touart	Annette Vaughn	Poncho Touart	Ambrose & Josephine Vaughn
1315	Williams, Ida	TX	1875	none	Lewis Williams	Mary Lovelady	Augustus & Sarah Williams	A J & Sarah Lovelady
20115	Williams, Ida	MO	1883	Jess Williams	James Taylor	Anna Davison	Zebadee & Mary Taylor	Armstrong & Louisa Davison
12868	Williams, Isaac	MO	1852	Lydia Williams	William Williams	Martha Murray	James & Phoebe Williams	James & Yaurth Murray
7382	Williams, J.P.	TX	1883	Stella Williams	Alford Williams	Fannie Curtis	Joseph & Rutha Williams	Boon & Minervia Curtis
16215	Williams, J.P.	OK	1867	Dollie Williams	W A Williams	Mary Haynes	Joseph & Catherine Williams	
18403	Williams, James	MS	26yrs		John Williams	Mary Hightower	James & Margrette Williams	James & Nancy Hightower
12272	Williams, Jane	TX	1884	Henry Williams	George Blair	Elvira Jones	George Blair	
7377	Williams, Jeremiah	MO	1865	none	Jeremiah Williams	Sarah Worthington	Beniah & Nancy Williams	Francis & Sarah Worthington
7381	Williams, Jerry	OK	18?9	Nannie Williams	Joseph Williams	Rutha Holland	Edward Williams	Peggie Crittenden

ID	Name	State	Year	Spouse	Father	Mother	Paternal GP	Maternal GP
7371	Williams, John	MO	1844	Mary Williams	Minter Williams	Frankie Lane	Beniah & Nancy Williams	
7372	Williams, John	MO	1872	Meade Williams	John Williams	Mary Nichols	Minter & Frankie Williams	
12867	Williams, John	MO	1842	Henrietta Williams	William Williams	Martha Murray	James & Phoebe Williams	James & Yaurth Murray
17854	Williams, John	OK	1875	Minnie Williams	W.A. Williams	Mary Haynes	Joseph & Catharine Williams	
18075	Williams, John	GA	1852	Nellie Williams	Andrew Williams	Lucinda King	John & Sallie Williams	Wm & Mary King
18406	Williams, John	FL	57yrs	Mary Williams	James Williams	Margret Miles		James & Millie Miles
20334 *	Williams, John	TN	1889		Taylor Knox	Katie Williams	Richard & Nancy Knox	Wm & Adaline Williams
20485	Williams, John	GA	1860	Alice Williams	Daniel Williams	Elizabeth Hargis	Martha Williams	Jackson & Mary Hargis
6964	Williams, Joseph	OK	1844	Julia Williams	Joseph Williams	Katherine Swafford	Ned & Peggy Williams	
7802	Williams, Joseph	TX	1873	Laura Williams	Virgil Williams	Mattie McClain		
16213	Williams, Joseph	OK	1869		W A Williams	Mary Haynes	Joseph & Catherine Williams	
20418 *	Williams, Joseph	TN	1878	Ida Williams	William Williams	Adaline Jones	Queen McConnell	Green & Malissa Henry
21252	Williams, Joseph	AR	1856	Isabell Williams	John Williams	Patience Man		Frederick & Sarah Man
20346 *	Williams, Katie	TN	1870		William Williams	Adaline Jones	Queen McConnell	Green & Malissa Henry
10785	Williams, Laura	GA	1875	Alfred Williams	Jerrymine Boling	Amanda Caldwell	James & Letty Boling	
4982	Williams, Lena	GA	1869	Jasper Williams	Andrew Sanders	Dianah Jones		
59	Williams, Lewis	GA	1849	Mary Williams	Augustus Williams	Sarah Ledbetter	John & Rhoda Williams	Lewis & Nancy Ledbetter
7370	Williams, Lewis	TX	1870	Belle Williams	Albert Williams	Rosa Shipley	Louis Williams & Lucinda Privett	Willis Shipley & Jane Harris
21442	Williams, Lizzie	KY	1876	Hardin Williams	Oliver Hutchens	Lucettie Martin	John & Elizabeth Hutchens	David & Lucinda Martin
17520	Williams, Louisa	OK		Freeman Williams	Orrell Couch	Nannie Wilson	John & Mary Couch	
16211	Williams, Lucinda	OK	1881	James Williams	William Pack	Polly Melton	John Pack & Clara Perkins	Charles Mays & Polly Melton
16405	Williams, Malisie	TN	1853	Marion Williams	William Swanson	Ellen Latch	William Swanson	
18405	Williams, Mallory	MS	30yrs	Lavonia Williams	John Williams	Mary Hightower	James & Margrette Williams	James & Nancy Hightower
12045	Williams, Margaret	GA	1842	Jerome Williams	John Pressly	Elizabeth Hooper	Dunigan & Jane Pressly	John & Margaret Hooper
21764	Williams, Margret	AL	1874	Harry Williams	James Faught	Mariah Sides	Samuel & Elizabeth Faught	David & Sabie Sides
19851	Williams, Martha	NC	1843	L.W. Williams	Benj Donathan	Marena Frazier	Jacob & Nancy Donathan	
7595	Williams, Mary	KS	1868	Henry Williams	William Warren	Catharine Martin	George & Susan Warren	Wm & Susan Martin
13584 *	Williams, Mary	GA	1866	Tom Williams	Charley Welch	Millie Lewison	Billy & Precilla Welch	
14326	Williams, Mattie	NE	1871	Frank Williams	E W Crane	Elizabeth Bays	Nathanie & Phebe Crane	James & Rachel Bays
12054	Williams, Melvin	WV	1866	Linnett Williams	William Williams	Mary Sizemore	Wm & Mary Williams	Hiram & Jane Sizemore

12058	Williams, Michael	WV	1873	Nora Williams	William Williams	Mary Sizemore	Wm & Elizbeth Williams	Hiram & Jane Sizemore
14564	Williams, Millie	GA	1882	Hiram Williams	John Carter	Jane McMain	Thomas & Nellie Carter	
20570 *	Williams, Minnie	TN			Taylor Knox	Katie Williams	Richard & Nancy Knox	Wm & Adaline Williams
8398	Williams, Miriam	OK	1859	Anderson Williams	Wm Franklin	Amy Ledford	Abram & Elisabeth Franklin	Benj & Grace Ledford
21397	Williams, Missouri	OK	1877	George Williams	Samuel Faught	Sarah Cowart	John & Alta Faught	Tom & Lydia Cowart
6356	Williams, Mrs James	AL	23yrs	James Williams	James Moniac	Mary Williams	Sam & Susan Moniac	Seaburn Williams
12474	Williams, Nancy	NC	1879	E.V. Williams	James Osborne	Clemmenzy Bare	David & Nancy Osborne	Joseph & Sousie Bare
7383	Williams, Noah	OK			Louis Williams	Lucinda Privett	Martin Williams	Neoma Privett
21251	Williams, Ora	AR	1884		Joseph Williams	Isabell Cahoon	John & Patience Williams	
10362	Williams, Robert	KY	1841	Amanda Williams	Jefferson Williams	Mary Griffie	Robert & Mary Williams	
18407	Williams, Robert	FL	22yrs		John Williams	Mary Hightower	James & Margrette Williams	James & Nancy Hightower
21946 *	Williams, Rosa	TN	1832		William Rolls	Charlotte		Sallie Rolls
22418	Williams, Rosa	TN	1876	Frank Williams	William Harris	Susan Payne	John & Mary Payne	
12869	Williams, Thomas	MO	1855	Barbara Williams	William Williams	Martha Murray	James & Phoebe Williams	James & Yaurth Murray
20269	Williams, Thomas	MO			Charles Williams	Mary Dees	Jeremiah & Sarah Williams	Julius & Marth Dees
7373	Williams, William	MO	1870	Frances Williams	John Williams	Mary Nichols	Minter & Frankie Williams	Henry & Mary Nichols
7375	Williams, William	MO	1864	Lettie Williams	Jeremiah Williams	Sarah Worthington	Beniah & Nancy Williams	Francis & Sarah Worthington
7801	Williams, William	TX	1871	Lizzie Williams	Virgil Williams	Mattie McClain		
12864	Williams, William	MO	1838	Anna Williams	William Williams	Martha Murray	James & Phoebe Williams	James & Yaurth Murray
17851	Williams, William	OK	1871		W.A. Williams	Mary Haynes	Joseph & Catharine Williams	
7369	Williams, Willie	TX	1869	Lucy Williams	Albert Williams	Rosa Shipley	Louis Williams & Lucinda Privett	Willis Shipley & Jane Harris
14325	Williamson, Annie	OK		James Williamson	Robert Elmore	Anna Wood	Amdersen & Margaret Elmore	Amiter & Nancy Wood
10826	Williamson, Bruce	MO	1881	Ida Williamson	Benj Williamson	Martha Logan	James & Polly Williamson	Wm & Matilda Logan
9532	Williamson, C. Mont	GA	1884	none	Martin Williamson	Margret Ledford		John & Nancy Ledford
22795	Williamson, Dora	GA	1884	John Williamson	Roe Poole	Fanny Corley	Pikens & Martha Corley	Spence & Melissa Whittenson
7385	Williamson, Elmer	KS	1885	Maggie Williamson	James Williamson	Rose Bell	Ben & Martha Williamson	
22885 *	Williamson, George	IL	1886	Bertha Williamson	John Williamson	Sarah Scott	Squire & Harriet Williamson	John & Marie Scott
7386	Williamson, John	KS	1869	Polly Williamson	Benj Williamson	Martha Logan	James & Polly Williamson	Wm & Matilda Logan
435 *	Williamson, John W.	IL	1857	Sadie Williamson	Square Williamson	Harriett Adams	Eliah & Charity Williamson	Tony Adams

ID	Name	State	Year	Spouse/Other	Father	Mother	Paternal Grandparents	Maternal Grandparents
9534	Williamson, Margret	GA	1847	Martin Williamson	John Leadford	Nancy Leadford	Ely Leadford	Levy Leadford
7387	Williamson, Martha	KS	1837	Benj Williamson	William Logan	Matilda Thaxton	Zachariah & Margaret Logan	
9533	Williamson, Mary	GA	1882	none	Mart Williamson	Margret Ledford		John & Nancy Ledford
7384	Williamson, Nellie	WA	1870	none	Benj Williamson	Martha Logan		Wm & Matilda Logan
9535	Williamson, Rebecca	GA	1874	none	Mart Williamson	Margret Ledford		John & Nancy Ledford
7379	Williamson, William	KS	1875	none	Benj Williamson	Martha Logan	James & Polly Williamson	Wm & Matilda Logan
18512	Williford, Asa	OK		May Williford	A.E. Williford	Eliza Stringer		Masurie Garner
20148 *	Willis, Loueaser	GA	1863	James Willis	George Steels	Mollie Brooks		
2322	Willis, Mary	OK	1887	Ben Willis	Thomas Crutchfield	Saran Piersall	Joseph & Lizzie Crutchfield	
13775 *	Willis, Oscar	GA	1857	Sallie Willis	Dave Willis	Rachel Shelton	Nelson & Amy Lottie	
2812	Willis, Pickens	GA	1851		William Willis	Mary Dougherty		Mary Dougherty
14892	Willis, Viney	GA	1858		John Green	Delila Henson	John Green	Charlie Henson
3631	Willison, Mary	OK	1852	James Willison	Wm Mackey	Nannie Drew	Samuel & Sallie Mackey	
16537	Wills, Jennie	WV	1878	W E Wills	Reece Milam	Mary Boman		
19476	Wills, Minnie	GA	1876	John Wills	John Whitmire	Sarah Moore	James & Cassie Whitmire	Watson & Charity Moore
14075	Willson, Arinnda	GA	1838	widow	Charles Darby	Nancy Biddy	Charles & Mary Darby	Jonathan & Mary Biddy
2780	Willson, Francis	GA	1863	William Willson	John Helton	Mary McElroy	James & Camilla Helton	
20327	Willson, Manda	GA	1872	B.A. Willson	Bart Taylor	Lucinda Jones	Jack & Pollie Taylor	Abram & Brincy Jones
2567	Willson, Margaret	TN	1881	Thomas Willson	John Campbell	Martha Earley	Henderson & Susey Campbell	
3969	Willson, Syntha	TN	1839	J G Willson	John Mason	Polly Roberson	Wm Mason & Sallie Miller	Aaron Roberson & Jane Deorman
14953	Willson, William	OK	1886		Ephriam Willson	Anna Bays	Wm & Marget Willson	David & Precious Bays
7399	Wilson, Agnes	KS	1870	A S Wilson	Joseph Allen	Margaret Logan	Joseph & Kate Allen	Wm & Matilda Logan
20988 *	Wilson, Augusta	GA	1879		George Wilson	Mary Morgan	Eliga & Martha Wilson	Elizabeth Morgan
4168	Wilson, Belle	NC	1887	Harve Wilson	James Davis	Lurana McDonald	Reason & Sevilla Davis	James & Minia McDonald
18671	Wilson, Carrie	GA	1869	Bonnie Wilson	Wm Martin	Rhoda Wade	Sinthy Martin	Wm & Elizabeth Wade
8722	Wilson, Cora	GA	1896	none	William Wilson	Francis Helton	Hilyard & Lucinda Wilson	Clark & Mary Helton
8723	Wilson, Edward	GA	1889	none	William Wilson	Francis Helton	Hilyard & Lucinda Wilson	Clark & Mary Helton
7398	Wilson, Edyth	MO	1887	none	Thomas Wilson Jr	Maggie Roberts	Thos Sr & Nancy Wilson	Andrew & Eliza Roberts
4810	Wilson, Elisa	GA	1852	James Wilson	Danial Tyler	Elisebeth Nicholson	Henry & Malindia Tyler	Wm Nicholson & Elisa Ore

ID	Name	State	Year	Col5	Col6	Col7	Col8	Col9
17162	Wilson, Elizabeth	GA	1856	Thomas Wilson	David Terrell	Rebeca Drake	Patsy & Jane Terrell	Heartsell & Nancy Drake
22321	Wilson, Elizabeth	VA	1860	Curren Wilson	Benjamin Scott	Elizabeth Norman	Thomas & Dannel Scott	
718	Wilson, Ella	NC	1883	none	Thos Wilson	Josephine Pace		Stephen & Dovey Pace
17953	Wilson, Ellen	OK	1878	Richard Wilson	Merritt Hill	Sarah Harrison		Oscar & Mary Harrison
21717	Wilson, Ernest	OK	1884	Maud Wilson	Samuel Wilson	Mariah Stewart	Joseph & Polly Wilson	Green & Charlotte Stewart
20987*	Wilson, George	GA	1849	Mary Wilson	Eliga Wilson	Martha Meyers	Young & Winnie Wilson	Nancy Meyers
7397	Wilson, Ida	OK	1863	Oliver Wilson	Roland Clark	Mary Baugh	James & Mildred Clark	Wm & Susan Baugh
2192	Wilson, Jacob	KS	1875	Lucinda Wilson	Elijah Wilson	Nancy Corn	Samuel & Julian Wilson	Timothy & Rachel Corn
6578	Wilson, James	KS	1855	Hannah Gilwiche	Samuel Wilson	Julian Guy	Robert & Polly Wilson	Richard Guy & Martha Whitmore
8092	Wilson, James	OK	1874	Evah Wilson	Hamilton Wilson	Elizabeth Maney		Martin & Polly Maney
21186	Wilson, James et al	NC	1888		William Wilson	Hulda Jones	Leeroy & Luly Wilson	William & Jane Jones
4110	Wilson, John	AR	1868	none	Hamilton Wilson	Elisabeth Maney	Rand Wilson	Martin Maney
6611	Wilson, John	OK	1879	Armindie Wilson	William Wilson	Susan Mathis		Allen & Jane Mathis
18746	Wilson, John	OK	1855	Laura Wilson	George Wilson	Carmilita Norigia	Samuel & Malinda Wilson	
18747	Wilson, John	OK	1854	Mary Wilson	John Wilson	Elizabeth Vance	Saver Wilson & Betsey Logan	
21586	Wilson, Josa	NC	1882	Joe Wilson	John Maney	Consuela Banks	Martin & Matilda Maney	
399	Wilson, Josephine	NC	1855	Thomas Wilson	Stephen Pace	Dovey Martin	Wm & Harriett Pace	Joseph & Mary Martin
21736	Wilson, Jossie	TN	1869	Morgan Wilson	Joseph Vaughn	Mary Nickles	John & Patsy Vaughn	Henry & Nancy Nickles
11589	Wilson, Laura	GA	1892		J W Wilson	Nancy Call	John & Laura Wilson	Joseph & Elizabeth Call
20986*	Wilson, Lizzie	GA	1876		George Wilson	Mary Morgan	Eliga & Martha Wilson	Elizabeth Morgan
20511*	Wilson, Lucinda	TN	1859	Dock Wilson	Samuel Green	Bettie Boyls		Lucinda Mack
17345	Wilson, Luneza	NC	1842	Alexander Wilson	Martin Maney	Matilda Holcombe	John & Polly Maney	Henry & Faney Holcombe
21962	Wilson, Mamie	TN	1890	Clyde Wilson	Willis Lindsey	Sallie Lewis	Hosey & Morning Lindsey	Isaac & Miram Lewis
19981	Wilson, Margret	TN	1874		John Lane	Louisa Phillips	Lindsey & Rebecca Lane	George & Mary Phillips
21718	Wilson, Mariah	OK	1863	Samuel Wilson	Green Stewart	Charlotte Roach	Isaac & Mariah Stewart	Isaac & Lucindy Roach
12870	Wilson, Martha	MO	1854	William Wilson	Christopher Murray	Elizabeth Pace	James & Yaurth Murray	John & Emily Pace
17929	Wilson, Martha	TN	1861	S.M. Wilson	Thomas Johnson	Eliza Robison		Mat Anderson & Polly Robison
20209	Wilson, Martha	GA	1852	George Wilson	William Suddith	Eliza Jordan		Alex & Mary Jordan
21516	Wilson, Mary	OK	1864	Stith Wilson	James Bowles	Malinda Nutt	Allen & Arraville Bowles	
22239	Wilson, Mary	NC	57 yrs	Bill Wilson	Wilson Scott	Mahalie Jackson		

#	Name	State	Year	Spouse	Father	Mother	Paternal Grandparents	Maternal Grandparents
3130	Wilson, Mattie	MS	1886	Allen Wilson	E G Moore	Dora Hobgood		Charles & Martha Hobgood
11591	Wilson, Nancy	GA	1873	James Wilson	Joseph Call	Elizabeth Teague	John & Nancy Call	Isaac & Rachel Teague
20681	Wilson, Nellie	TN	1888	William Wilson	Joseph Bales	Eveline Cagle	John & Francis Bales	Peter & Elizabeth Cagle
8724	Wilson, Nettie	GA	1899	none	William Wilson	Francis Helton	Hilyard & Lucinda Wilson	Clark & Mary Helton
8725	Wilson, Pearl	GA	1894	none	William Wilson	Francis Helton	Hilyard & Lucinda Wilson	Clark & Mary Helton
15428	Wilson, Polly	GA	1882	Head Wilson	Jack Elrodd	Sarah Dover	Peter & Kate Elrodd	Wm & Alantha Dover
19980	Wilson, Sam Jr.	TN	1904		Sam Wilson Sr.	Margret Lane	Thomas & Sallie Wilson	John & Louise Lane
5446	Wilson, Sarah	NC	1832	William Wilson	John Mason	Polly Robinson		Aaron & Jane Robinson
19114	Wilson, Sarah	TN	1863	Thomas Wilson	Abner Sayers	Nancy Scales	James Sayers	Nicholas & Mary Scales
7431	Wilson, Victoria	TN	1862	Henry Wilson	Ben Lacefield	Margaret Horn	Martin & Polly Lacefield	Richard & Annie Horn
2191	Wilson, William	KS	52yrs	none	Samuel Wilson	Julian Guy	Robert & Polly Wilson	Richard Guy & Marth Whitmore
4344	Wilson, William	AR	1872	none	Hamilton Wilson	Elisabeth Maney	Paul Wilson	Martin Maney
8726	Wilson, William	GA	1890	none	William Wilson	Francis Helton	Hilyard & Lucinda Wilson	Clark & Mary Helton
21187	Wilson, William	NC	1850	Hulda Wilson	Leeroy Wilson	Lucy Wilson	Dick & Ana Wilson	Willis & Sally Wilson
21188	Wilson, William	NC	1874	Elizabeth Wilson	William Wilson	Hulda Jones	Leroy & Lucy Wilson	William & Jane Jones
9727	Wimberly, Sarah	OK	1869	W A Wimberly	John Armstrong	Marandy Rogers		Henry & Mariah Rogers
9655	Wimer, Margarett	AR	1878		Henry Lipe	Susan Rogers	Sandy & Elizabeth Lipe	Henry & Mariah Rogers
22706	Winburn, Arthur	IN	1871	Jennie Winburn	Joshua Winburn	Mary Roberts	Louis & Kittie Winburn	
22486	Winburn, George	IN	1874	Mattie Winburn	Levi Winburn	Martha Roberts	Harry & Kesiah Winburn	Stephen & Marsha Roberts
22242	Winburn, Jennie	IN		Walter Winburn	William Burnett	Henrettie James	Ostan Burnett	Kisia James
13800	Winburn, Levi	IN	1849		Henry Winburn	Kesiah James		Henry James
14051*	Winchell, Emma	WI	1874	Charles Winchell	Henry Revels	Annis Winchel	McCaga & Mornon Revels	James & Jane Winchel
17069	Winder, Susan	OK	1871	S H Winder	William Reed	Celia Cochran		Jesse & Jane Cochran
12899	Windham, Della	MS	1889	Ed Windham	J M Loveless	Mary Presley	Loveless & Nancy Townsand	Jim & Elizabeth Presley
18299	Windsor, Elizabeth	NC	1848	James Windsor	Kingman	Eliza Hartgrave	James & Mary Kingman	Robert & Ann Hartgrave
7393	Wines, Geraldine	IN	1904	none	Elmer Wines	Grace Yingst	Simon & Margaret Wines	Jacob & Nancy Yingst
7400	Wines, Grace	IN	1880	Elmer Wines	Jacob Yingst	Nancy Blackburn	Lewis & Elizabeth Yingst	John & Thena Blackburn
17767	Winesburg, Catharine	TN	1857		Tyree Kelley	Delila Emry	Johnathan & Mary Kelley	James & Nancy Emry
5877	Wingler, Sinda	VA	1889	William Wingler	Eli Hart	Jennie Sheets	Stephen & Rebecca Hart	Andrew & Katherine Sheets

17500	Winkler, Annie	KS	1884	Van Winkler	Frank Doncarlos	Mary Cornwell		Isie & Mary Conrwell
20620 *	Winsett, Joseph	TN	1872	Maggie Winsett	William Winsett	Dellie Marshall	Miles Tate & Dido Hall	
19611 *	Winsett, Minos	TN	1877	Mattie Winsett	William Winsett	Dillie Marshall	Miles Tate & Dido Hall	Dick Manor & Matilia Pigg
15737 *	Winters, Ella	GA	1885		Henry Winters	Jane Brown		Gilford & Mary Chandler
15738 *	Winters, Emma	GA	1886		Henry Winters	Jane Brown		Gilford & Mary Chandler
1483	Winton, Stan	OK			William Winton	Martha Crittenden	James & Minerva Winton	Moses & Ede Crittenden
10111	Wiseman, Elizabeth	WV	1874	Henry Wiseman	Eli Rose	Mary Weavers	Joel & Virginia Rose	Lewis & Catherine Weavers
12185	Witherspoon, Ida	VA	1888		L H Witherspoon	Mary Jones	Sidney & Ellen Witherspoon	Thos & Tams Jones
12186	Witherspoon, Mary	VA	1867	L.H. Witherspoon	Thomas Jones	Tamsy Thompson	Johnathan & Nancy Jones	Christopher & Salli Thompson
12839	Witherspoon, Walter	VA	1884	Emaline Witherspoon	L H Witherspoon	Mary Jones	Sidney & Ellen Witherspoon	Thos & Tamsy Jones
21137	Witt, Cyrus	NC	1880	Ethel Witt	William Witt	Sophie Parker	Burgess & Matilda Witt	Willis & Adaline Parker
5110	Witt, Eula & Gladys	OK	1892 1896		Eugene Witt	Georgia Alberty		Jesse & Cathrine Alberty
15402 *	Witt, Jack	GA	1835		Joe Witt	Clay Chuck		Joe Chuck
22460	Witt, Nancy	TN	1873	none	William Witt	July Camp		Wm & Elizabeth Camp
18965	Witt, Nicy	TN	1860	J.P. Witt	John Foraster	Agnes Brooksher	John & Milly Foraster	Manering & Patsey Brooksher
1518	Witt, Sophie	NC	1850	William Witt	Willis Parker	Adaline Vaney	Jonathan & Lemy Parker	Joel & Elizabeth Vaney
21154	Wm & Ethel Guinn	TN			William Guinn	Abbie McCoy	Abraham & Cornelia Guinn	H.T. & M.E. McCoy
20567 *	Wofford, Arthur	TN	1893		William Wofford	Mattie McCanny	Eliza Wofford	Isaac & Mckie McCanny
20572 *	Wofford, Jane	TN	1856		Isiah Johnson	Elvira Shields	Isiah & Hager Johnson	Daniel & Harriet Shields
20345 *	Wofford, Mattie	TN	1896	William Wofford	Isaac McCarny	Mckie Thompson	Lindsay McCarny	Moses & Fashion Johnson
20422 *	Wofford, Maud	TN	1893		William Wofford	Mattie McCanny	Eliza Wofford	Isaac & Mckie McCanny
6794	Wofford, Nannie	OK	1870	Joseph Wofford	Charley Davis	Isadore Shelton	John Davis	Jesse & Nellie Shelton
20421 *	Wofford, Oney	TN	1888		William Wofford	Mattie McCanny	Eliza Wofford	Isaac & Mckie McCanny
19184 *	Wofford, Sarah	GA	1870	Will Wofford	Robert Anderson	Louisa Wooley	Addie Anderson	Charlie & Willie Wooley
20412 *	Wofford, William	TN	1852	Mattie Wofford	Nathaniel Wilkey	Eliza Hutchison		Zilpha Quillan
10308	Wolf, Linney	OK		none	Squirel Wolf	Jennie Beaver	Squirl Wolf	Charles Beaver
7799	Wolf, Mary	KS	1870	William Wolf	Wm Boatwright	Isabella Clark	James & Rebecca Boatwright	Thomas & Sarah Clark
14709	Wolfe, Belle	LA	1883	Lonis Wolfe	Cyrus Hathaway	Cenie Bell	Cyrus & Ann Hathaway	Wm & Nancy Bell
22377	Wolfe, Racheal	NC	1866	E K Wolfe	Jessie Isaacs	Mary Scott	Joseph & Frankie Isaacs	Benjamin & Bettie Scott
7548	Womack, Laura	TN	1860	James Womack	John Constant	Elizabeth Delozier	Wm & Siney Constant	Ed & Elizabeth Delozier
22506	Womack, Sarah	MO	1879	Jesse Womack	John McGuire	Judy Pendergrass	Jesse & Elizabeth McGuire	John & Martha Pendergrass

8834	Wood, Allice	TX	1885	Richard Wood	James Rowell	E J Partin	David Rowell	Mary Fountain
22554	Wood, Betty	TN	1867	John Wood	Joe Collett	Lucresia Watson	Joel Collett & Betsy Raburn	Thos Watson & Martha Patterson
16058	Wood, Clara	OK	1875	Ike Wood	William Pack	Nancy Melton	John Pack & Clara Perkins	Charles Mays & Polly Melton
8417	Wood, Edna	AR	1877	none	Thompson Wood	Eliza Martin	Johnson & Margret Wood	Wm & Susan Martin
6404	Wood, Eliza	AR	1848	Thompson Wood	Wm Martin	Susan Wolf	Thos & Elizabeth Martin	Dennis & Polly Wolf
3551	Wood, Frank	OK	1850	Rose Wood	Campbell Wood	Mary Hubbard	William & Lottie Wood	Uriah & Nellie Hubbard
4527	Wood, George	OK	1873	Etha Wood	Marcus Wood	Alcy Pinnell		Mary Pinnell
3553	Wood, John	OK	1848	Susan Wood	Campbell Wood	Mary Hubbard	William & Lettie Wood	Uriah & Nellie Hubbard
21912*	Wood, Joseph	TN	1875	Mary Wood	Alfred Wood	Mattie Pitman	Willis & Violet Wood	Sarah Pitman
6517	Wood, Josephine	OK	1857	Henry Wood	Paul Andre	Mary Scott	R M Andre	Harvey Woodword & Jessie Scott
5568	Wood, Leonidas	KS	1869	Cordelia Wood	Johnson Wood	Martha Martin	Thompson Wood	Wm & Susan Martin
6339	Wood, Marian	AL		Mary	John Woods	Mary Hadley	John Woods	Alex Weatherford & Jane Hadley
5432	Wood, Norman	KS	1877	Mamie Wood	Johnson Wood	Martha Martin	Thomas Wood	Wm & Susan Martin
8392	Wood, Robert	AR	1871	Hattie Wood	Thompson Wood	Eliza Martin	Johnson & Margaret Wood	Wm & Susan Martin
4526	Wood, William	OK	1884	none	Marcus Wood	Alcy Pinnell		Mary Pinnell
8390	Wood, William	AR	1885	none	Thompson Wood	Eliza Martin	Johnson & Margaret Wood	Wm & Susan Martin
19849	Wood, William	NC	1855	Jane Wood	Andrew Wood	Cindy Holyfield	Betsey Wood	John Holyfield
4525	Wood, Wyly	OK	1877	Hallie Wood	Marcus Wood	Alcy Pinnell		Mary Pinnell
21173	Woodall, Andrew	AL	1827		Isaiah Woodall	Sallie Bigan	Andrew Woodall	Dave & Phebin Bigan
15088	Woodall, Daniel	OK	1847	Nancy Woodall	Andrew Woodall	Margaret Hendricks	Betsy Woodall	Wm & Susan Hendricks
19488	Woodall, J.T.	OK	1837	Bettie Woodall	George Woodall	Ellen Moore		Charles & Eliza Moore
21727	Woodall, James	TN	1872	Nancy Woodall	Zophonor Woodall	Cyntha Carlock	Isaih & Sarah Woodall	Sarah Carlock
11977	Woodall, John	OK	1841	Maven Woodall	George Woodall	Ellen Moore		Charles & Oo lu tse Moore
21728	Woodall, John	TN	1848	Arminda Woodall	Andrew Woodall	Mary Wilson	Isaih & Sarah Woodall	Billy Wilson
4448	Woodall, Margaret	OK	1842	John Woodall	John Ridge	Sarah Northrup	Major & Susanna Ridge	
6711	Woodall, Mathis	OK	1867	Rosa Woodall	Andrew Woodall	Sarah McKinney	David Woodall & Amy Hicks	Lindsey McKinney
14993	Woodall, Pearl	SC	1868	Charlottie Woodall	John Woodall	Sarah Jones	John & Sarah Woodall	
11832	Woodall, Sarah	SC	1837		Elias Jones	Rachel Brady		

2979	Woodall, Thomas	MO	1850	Sarah Woodall	John Woodall	Annie Halcomb	John & Causby Woodall	John & Sarah Halcomb
21172	Woodall, Zephynor	AL	1847	Alline Woodall	Isaiah Woodall	Sallie Bigan	Andrew Woodall	
12171	Woodard, Jesse	AL	1872	Lucy Woodard	Siles Campbell	Sarah Woodard		Tobias & Linigar Woodard
20932	Woodie, Ben et al	NC	1892		Theophilus Woodie	Laura Blevins	Fulton & Mary Woodie	Leander & Peggy Blevins
20937	Woodie, Estel et al	NC	1891		George Woodie	Jane Blevins		Granville & Polly Blevins
20931	Woodie, Jane	NC	1872	George Woodie	Leander Blevins	Peggy Osborne	Granville & Polly Blevins	David & Nancy Osborne
20933	Woodie, Laura	NC	1871	Theophilus Woodie	Leander Blevins	Peggy Osborne	Granville & Polly Blevins	David & Nancy Osborne
11820	Woodie, Leona	NC	1871	C V Woodie	Ephrim Osborne	America Bare	Jesse & Cyntha Osborne	Joseph & Susie Bare
20930	Woodie, Mattie	NC	1878	Theo Woodie	Leander Blevins	Peggy Osborne	Granville & Polly Blevins	David & Nancy Osborne
20929	Woodie, Robert et al	NC	1899		Theo Woodie	Mattie Blevins	Jackson & Sarah Woodie	Leander & Peggy Blevins
11821	Woodie, Rozina	NC	1866	Thomas Woodie	Ephrim Osborne	America Bare	Jesse & Cyntha Osborne	Joseph & Susie Bare
10990	Woodring, Laura	OK	1870	Parbo Woodring	Benjaman Hinchee	Annie Walker	James & Margret Hinchee	
3397	Woods, Mrs. George	AL		George Woods	Ben Franklin	Frances Bryars		
9514	Woods, Adaline	AL	1847		Daniel Sizemore	Anna Hankins	William Sizemore	
9515	Woods, Amanda	AL	1844	W C Woods	Daniel Sizemore	Anna Hankins	William Sizemore	
10519	Woods, Ben	GA	1902		Henry Woods	Georgia Hillhouse	Winchester & Malinda Woods	Samuel & Augusta Hillhouse
7862	Woods, Carrie	GA	1886	Alonzo Woods	William Wilson	Francis Helton	Hilyard & Lucinda Wilson	Clark & Mary Helton
19990	Woods, Charity	GA	1845	John Woods	Russell Jones	Ellen Perdue	Bartley & Disa Jones	Ruth Perdue
8727	Woods, Coker	GA	1906		Alonzo Woods	Carrie Wilson	Charley & Eliza Woods	Wm & Francis Wilson
21938 *	Woods, Delia	TN	1859	James Woods	James Martin	Nancy Martin	Jennie Martin	Hannah Martin
14284	Woods, Frances	TN	1848	Rice Woods	Harry Jones	Mimie Gupton		
3381	Woods, George	AL		Jenner Franklin	John Woods	Mary Watherford	John Woods	Alex Watherford
10518	Woods, Georgia	GA	1879	Henry Woods	Samuel Hillhouse	Augusta Cole	Samuel & Annie Hillhouse	John & Betsy Cole
10520	Woods, Gradie	GA	1906		Henry Woods	Georgia Hillhouse	Winchester & Malinda Woods	Samuel & Augusta Hillhouse
5494	Woods, Luthenia	AR	1866	Rector Woods	Hamilton Wilson	Elizabeth Maney		Martin & Polly Maney
3390	Woods, Mary	AL	70yrs	John Woods	Alex Weatherford	Jane Hadley	Billy & Polly Weatherford	Betsy Kinnison
18643	Woods, Melvina	MO	1865	John Woods	George Forshey	Narcissus Halin	Hiram & Sarah Forshey	James & Mary Halin
11880	Woods, Nancy	TN	1849	Jesse Woods	Henry Hale	Sarah Hale	Michael Hale	
20301	Woods, Sarah	MO	1867	John Woods	John Edmonds	Anna Herrell		Emerson & Clarissa Herrell
8832	Woodward, Polly	TX	1880	Charles Woodward	James Rowell	E J Partin	David Rowell	Mary Fountain

15444	Woody, Maranda	GA	1880	Marion Woody	John Chambers	Alice Witherow	Martin & Elisbeth Chambers	Alfred & Nancy Witherow
5162	Woody, Robert	OK	1836	none	Woody			
3742	Woody, Rosa	NC	1881	Lee Woody	Solomon Ham	Mary Blevins	Solomon & Mary Ham	Riley & Agnes Blevins
1675	Woolly, James	OK	1879	Ada Woolly	James Woolly	Lydia Vaughan	Riley Woolly	
1674	Woolly, Lydia	OK	1851	James Woolly	James Vaughan	Lydia Duncan	John & Elizabeth Vaughan	Mary Duncan
19080	Woolsey, Margaret	AR	1875	Henry Woolsey	James Brown	Margaret Suggs	Silas & Surelda Brown	
18074	Wooten, Aley	GA	1843	Henry Wooten	Harris Sorrow	Adeline Kidd	Randall & Jennie Sorrow	Absalom & Elizabeth Kidd
17502	Wooton, Frank	MO	1866	Etta Wooton	Wm Wooton	Mary Wooton	Abner & Annie Wooton	
14324	Worel, Flora	OK	1875	John Worel	Jessie McGee	Jennie Gardnor	Robert & Easter McGee	
21041	Workman, Christina	WV	1878	Zack Workman	J.L. Sizemore	Elizabeth Mitchew	Oen Sizemore	Nancy Lambert
20240	Workman, Ribern	WA	1856	Emily Workman	James Workman	Elizabeth Webb	Joe Workman & Elizabeth Reed	George & Susannah Webb
17865	Workwardt, Annie	MO	1864	Charles Workwardt	Robert Beeles	P.J. Shelton		Ralph & Annie Shelton
22037	Worley, Addie	TX	1885	Elija Worley	John Freeman	Martha Crain	Hiram & Dillie Freeman	Jesse & Mary Crain
12197	Worley, Columbus	GA	1840	Elizabeth Worley	James Worley	Milley Donaldson	Wm & Susan Worley	Wm & Elizbeth Donaldson
6085	Worley, Dela	GA	1870	Ira Worley	Alpheus Key	Minerva Hembree	William Key	Reubin Emery
17594	Worley, Ellen	NC	1861	Joseph Worley	Wm Wilson	Sarah Mason		John & Polly Mason
16279	Worley, Emily	GA	1853	Jason Worley	James Darby	Caroline Hudgins	Charles & Nancy Darby	Jacob & Elizabeth Hudgins
12373	Worley, James	GA	1849	Elizabeth Worley	James Worley	Milley Donaldson	Wm & Susan Worley	Wm & Elizbeth Donaldson
9641	Worley, Rosa	TN	1881	Manson Worley	Allen Bryson	Angeline Williams	Daniel & Laurindia Bryson	Burdett & Polly Williams
12376	Worley, Timothy	GA	1842	Mary Worley	James Worley	Milley Donaldson	Wm & Susan Worley	Wm & Elizbeth Donaldson
12375	Worley, William	GA	1837		James Worley	Milley Donaldson	Wm & Susan Worley	Wm & Elizbeth Donaldson
21949	Worthington, Lee	TN	1877	Elizabeth Worthington	Fayett Worthington	Emaline Billingsley	Tim & Hannah Worthington	Jane Nedd
15890 *	Worthy, Mary Jane	GA	1853	Joe Worthy	John Thornton	Emeline Stoolo		
14848	Wright, A A et al	GA			R W Wright	Jerelia Thompson	W R & Manerva Wright	
14977	Wright, Charlie et al	GA			Henry Wright	Elizabeth Shepherd	W R & Manerva Wright	
14668	Wright, Cordelia	GA	1840	James Wright	Joseph Moreland	Cynthia Mooney		Daniel & Hannah Mooney
4158	Wright, Darlene	KS	1901		Zeb Wright	Nora Smith	John & Maggie Wright	John & Julia Smith
4147	Wright, Elsia	KS	1906		Zeb Wright	Nora Smith	John & Maggie Wright	John & Julia Smith
4146	Wright, Ernest	KS	1898		Zeb Wright	Nora Smith	John & Maggie Wright	John & Julia Smith
14868	Wright, Gallartan	GA	1870	Palistine Wright	Vann Wright	Mary Smith	Jesse & Lovicie Wright	David & Lucy Smith

14926	Wright, George	GA	1862	Martha Wright	Allen Wright	Permelia Suddeth	Jesse & Lovicie Wright	James & Lizzie Suddeth
7396	Wright, Granville	TX	1861	Joanna Wright	Phileman Wright	Mary Pierce	P W & Charity Wright	John & Nancy Pierce
14846	Wright, Henry	GA	1858	Elisabeth Wright	W R Wright	Manerva Whelchel	Jesse & Louicie Wright	
14845	Wright, Hiram	GA	1867	Alice Wright	W R Wright	Manerva Whelchel	Jesse & Louicie Wright	
3463	Wright, Ida	OK	1889	Frank Wright	Richard Young	Mary Young	Mary Young	Elisha & Nancy Young
11343	Wright, James	GA	1883	Bessie Wright	William Wright	Mary Atkins		Berryman & Martha Atkins
14844	Wright, James	GA	1863	Polly Wright	W R Wright	Manerva Whelchel	Jesse & Louicie Wright	
14929	Wright, James	GA	1878	Rachel Wright		Martha Wright		Allen & Permelia Wright
21937	Wright, Jefferson	TN	1833		Abram Wright	Barbara ?	Abram Sr. & Mary Wright	Juda Wright
14933	Wright, Jennie & George	GA	17yrs 16yrs			Martha Wright		Allen & Permelia Wright
14905	Wright, Jesse	GA	1853	Rachel Wright	Allen Wright	Permelia Suddeth	Jesse & Lovici Wright	
14927	Wright, John	GA	1856	Nancy Wright	Allen Wright	Permelia Suddeth	Jesse & Lovicie Wright	James & Lizzie Suddeth
15005	Wright, Joseph	GA	1868	Samantha Wright	Vann Wright	Mary Smith	Jesse & Lovicie Wright	David & Lucy Smith
17753	Wright, Lena	GA	1880		John Holt	Manerva Baker	Rhoda Holt	James & Charlotte Baker
14852	Wright, Lovicie	GA	1862		W R Wright	Manerva Whelchel	Jesse & Lovicie Wright	
14935	Wright, Lutitia	GA	1855		Allen Wright	Permelia Suddeth	Jessie & Lovicie Wright	James & Lizzie Suddeth
14847	Wright, M E et al	GA	17yrs		H H Wright	Alice Sawyer	W R & Manerva Wright	
19821	Wright, Maggie	AL		Dan Wright	George Quarles	Clarinda Gilly		John & Nancy Gilly
17297	Wright, Margaret	AL			John Wright	Martha Sizemore	Edward & Marget Wright	Wm & Mary Sizemore
11081	Wright, Martha	VA	1873	John Wright	Andrew Widener	Mary Blevins		Isham & Anna Blevins
14937	Wright, Martha	GA	1851		Allen Wright	Permelia Suddeth	Jessie & Lovicie Wright	
21202	Wright, Minnie	AL	1883		Bill Wright	Lettie Tyler		Gabrel Tyler & Celia Johnson
17298	Wright, Nancy	AL	1840		John Wright	Martha Sizemore	Ed & Marget Wright	Wm & Mary Sizemore
21182	Wright, Newton	TN	1888	none	John Wright	Martha Beaver	William & Lowenda Wright	Edly & Cintha Beaver
4157	Wright, Nora	KS	1879	Zeb Wright	John Smith	Julia Taylor	Pleasant & Pricilla Smith	Wiley & Rosamond Taylor
14978	Wright, Ola et al	GA			W T Wright	Beatrice Henderson	W R & Manerva Wright	
665	Wright, Ollie	NC	1882	Boone Wright	Charles Pace	Emeline Bryson	Stephen & Dovey Pace	Joe & Nancy Bryson
14930	Wright, Paralee	GA			J R Wright	Rachel Nicholson	Martha Wright	Andrew & Laura Nicholson
14906	Wright, R H et al	GA			J J Wright	R A Suddeth	Allen & Permelia Wright	
14842	Wright, Reuben	GA	1871	Jeretia Wright	W R Wright	Louicie Whelchel	Jesse & Louicie Wright	

4145	Wright, Robert	KS	1904	none	Zeb Wright	Nora Smith	John & Maggie Wright	John & Julia Smith
14976	Wright, Robert et al	GA			J S Wright	Ollie Ray	W R & Manerva Wright	
1562	Wright, Sarah	TX	1847	W.W. Wright	Jones Funderbunk	Elendon Sweat	Abe & Rachel Funderburk	Elija & Sarah Sweat
18295	Wright, Susan	GA	1858	Louis Wright	John Taylor	Catherine Morris		Drew & Sallie Morris
19483	Wright, Susan	NC						
14675	Wright, Thomas	GA	1861	Laura Wright	James Wright	Cordelia Moreland	Alcy Wright & Sarah Kell	Joseph & Cynthia Moreland
14850	Wright, William	GA	1830	Manerva Wright	Jesse Wright	Luvicie Grant	John & Kate Wright	J R Grant
14851	Wright, William	GA	1872	Beatrice Wright	W R Wright	Manerva Whelchel	Jesse & Lovicie Wright	
21179	Wright, William	GA	1885	Florence Wright	John Wright	Martha Beaver	William & Lowenda Wright	Edly & Cintha Beaver
8267	Wyatt, Alley	NC	1870	James Wyatt	Isaac Speaks	Rachel Blevins		Wills & Nancy Blevins
12179	Wyatt, David	NC	1874	Alice Wyatt	Calvin Wyatt	Phebe Stamper	David & Millie Wyatt	Jobe & Elizabeth Stamper
21525	Wyatt, George	OK	1880		George Wyatt	Mattie Bowles	Ruben & Mary Wyatt	James & Malinda Bowles
1856	Wyatt, Malissa	VA	1877	J.D. Wyatt				
21527	Wyatt, Mattie	OK	1858	George Wyatt	James Bowles	Malinda Nutt	Allen Bowles	Aberrila Broach
21526	Wyatt, Nellie	OK	1883		George Wyatt	Mattie Bowles	Ruben & Mary Wyatt	James & Malinda Bowles
8530	Wyatt, Sarah	VA	1880	John Wyatt	Elisha Roop	Mandy Osborn		James & Rachel Osborn
17920 *	Wycoff, Frank	TN	69yrs	Ornie Wycoff	Jonas Garrett	Nancy Anthony		
6403	Wylie, Hester	NC	27yrs	Mack Wiley	Eli Griswold	Martha Scott		
15739 *	Wyly, Hubbard	GA	1890		Oliver Wyly	Ann Brown	Prince & Ritta Wyly	Jack Turk & Martha Brown
13913 *	Wyly, Janey	GA	1860	John Wyly	Dan Cash	Katy Wells	Dan & Rachel Simpson	
2673	Wyly, Liza	OK	1875	John Wyly	William Winton	Martha Critendon	James & Marneva Winton	Moses & Edith Critendon
15652 *	Wyly, Mary Winters	GA	1878	Dolan Wyly	Henry Winters	Jane Brown		Gilford & Mary Chandler
15676 *	Wyly, Mattie	GA	1878	Shalls Wyly	Ephriam Sosebee	Emma Brown	Sarah Sosebee	Guilford & Mary Chandler
2504	Wynn, Mary	AL	1864	George Wynn	William Long	Mary Johnson		
21404	Wyse, Andrew	AR	1908	Docie Wyse	Johnathon Wyse	Elizabeth Jones	Peter Wyse & Susan Taylor	Stephen Jones & Betsy Wyse
21247	Wyse, George, & James	AR		Keenan Wyse	Howard Wyse	Docie Adkins	John & Betsy Wyse	
22083	Wyse, J.W.	AR		Minnie Wyse	Calvin Wyse	Clementine Duvall	John Wyse & Elizabeth Jones	
21297	Yancy, Delia	AL	1881	M.C. Yancy	Daniel Lamons	Delila Criscoe	James & Mary Lamons	G.W. & Emma Criscoe
21296	Yancy, Elzora	AL	1885	Rony Yancy	Daniel Lamons	Delila Criscoe	James & Mary Lamons	G.W. & Emma Criscoe
11758	Yarber, Sarah	TN	1873		Joseph Everett	Caroline Jordan	George & Easter Everett	Oyras & Susan Jordan

3031	Yarberry, Bessie	MO	1874	Walter Yarberry	Jeremiah Sloan	Mary Lemmon	A C & Mary Sloan	
7805	Yates, Albert	OK	1878	Ruby Yates	Thomas Yates	Cordelia Womack		Henrietta Yates
8831	Yates, Albert	OK	1860	Delila Yates	Albert Yates	Henrettie Ward		Jerry & Nancie Ward
7803	Yates, Elizabeth	TX			William Gambill	Sallie Ward		John Ward & Polly Madole
14305	Yates, Elzadia	TN	1882	T B Yates		Missouri Rich		Elisha & Marry Rich
7807	Yates, Henry	OK	1884	May Yates	Thomas Yates	Cordelia Womack		Henrietta Yates
6088	Yates, Jestin	NC	1874	Leander Yates	Robbert Phipps	Caroline Yates	Benjamin & Ruthy Phipps	Eli & Nancy Yates
11560	Yates, Lafayette	NC	1864	Susan Yates	Eli Yates	Nancy Spencer	John & Elizabeth Yates	Soloman & Nellia Spencer
9020	Yates, Martha	MO	1879	G T Yates	Elicy Stillwell	Abigal Elmore		Anderson Elmore
7804	Yates, Thomas	OK	1848	Cordelia Yates	Albert Yates	Henrietta Ward		Jeremiah & Nancy Ward
3494	Yather, Dovea	GA	1856	Andrew Yather	William Pinjan	Cyntha Davis	Stokes Pinjan	Nancy Tally
8384	Yeates, William	OK	1852	Julia Yeates	Benj Yeates	Elizabeth Klinkenbeard	Larkin & Nancy Yeates	
7406	Yoakum, Mirtie	MO	1879	J B Yoakum	Francis Preston	Sallie Smith	Gerusha Preston	Benaja & Elizabeth Smith
8598	Yonce, Susan	NC	1862	Archbald Yonce	Archibald Bateman	Mahala Tramel		Jake & Pollie Tramel
3901	York, Andrew	GA	1848	Mary York	John York	Sarah Chastain	Jefery York & Sallie Dunlap	Wm Chastain & Annie Motes
4754	York, Cordelia	GA	1857	none	John York	Sary Chastain	Jefrey & Sallie York	Wm & Annie Chastain
5407	York, George	GA	1875	Lillie York	Andrew York	Emaline Rodgers	John & Sary York	Sam & Catherine Rodgers
4749	York, John	GA	1853	Frances York	John York	Saryan Chastain	Jefrey & Sallie York	Wm & Annie Chastain
9642	York, Margret	TN	1873	J M York	Allen Bryson	Angeline Williams	Daniel & Laurindia Bryson	Burdett & Polly Williams
2332	York, Martin	AR	1836	Sarah York	John York	Precious Lake	William York	Elizabeth Kitchins
21396	York, Myrtle	TX	1881	Joseph York	Abner Christopher	Nancy Rimar	John Christopher & Mary Sydle	Binion Rimar & Frances Marshall
3656	York, Sary	GA	1828	John York	William Chastain	Annie Motes	Abner & Nancy Chastain	Hogeny & Nancy Motes
18482	Yother, B.F.	GA	1846	Hannah Yother	Adam Yother Jr.	Celia Hollifield	Adam Yother	Isaac Hollifield
15096	Young, Alexander	GA	1872	Minnie Young	John Young	Louisa Findley		Alex & Hulda Findley
20402*	Young, Amelia	TN	1878	Calvin Young	Paul Hendricks	Lydia Posey		Celia Posey
15095	Young, Cal	GA	1878	Mary Young	John Young	Louisa Findley		Alex & Hulda Findley
3006	Young, Caroline	TN	1850	Monroe Bain & Alex Young	John Mayfield	Malinda Bowlin	Mayfield	Bowlin
15445	Young, Daisy	GA	1902		Alexander Young	Minnie Samples	John & Louisa Young	

15446	Young, Dewey	GA	1901		Cal Young	Mary Taylor	John & Louisa Young	
15447	Young, Eddie	GA	1899		Cal Young	Mary Taylor	John & Louisa Young	
16411	Young, Elijah	VA	1879	Bessie Young	Jerome Young	Jone Phipps	Wm & Catharine Young	Elijah & Nellie Phipps
21819	Young, George	FL	1847	Helen Young	Edward Young	Ann Chechee		Lydia Franklin Chechee
15448	Young, Henry	GA	1903		Cal Young	Mary Taylor	John & Louisa Young	
8823	Young, Jacob	OK	1851	Sarah Young	James Young	Mary Stokes	John & Millie Young	
3462	Young, James	OK			Richard Young	Mary Young		Elisha & Nancy Young
5255	Young, John	NC	1842	Orlean Young	William Young	Cathrine Hash	Thomas & Milla Young	Robert & Margery Hash
15092	Young, Louisa	GA	1844	John Young	Alex Findley	Hulda Huggins	Bill & Elizabeth Findley	Hamilton & Linda Huggins
16051	Young, Luvery	AL	1866	Arch Young	Colman Conner	Lizzie Henley	Henry & Lillie Conner	
15798	Young, Maggie	VA	188?			? Phipps		Elijah Phipps
15449	Young, Mardel	GA	1896		Alexander Young	Minnie Samples	John & Louisa Young	
21466	Young, Margaret	TX	1882		Frank Crawford	Nannie Cole	Watson & Margaret Crawford	
10231	Young, Martha	WV	1880	J T Young	Aden Mills	Mahulda Walker	Robert & Lydia Mills	Newma & Adaline Walker
13586*	Young, Martha	GA		Jacob Young	George Whitlock	Nancy Barnes		Journer & Millery Barnes
2317	Young, Mary	NC	1878	Browneon Young	A J Dockery	Martha McLoud	James & Bitha Dockery	Harve & Sallie McLoud
2340	Young, Mary	OK	1859	Michael Young	Elisha Young	Nancy Musgrove	John & Millie Young	Quim Musgrove
20201	Young, Mary	OK	1858	Hiram Young	Josiah Davidson	Elisabeth Gilstrap	Mary Davidson	
20936	Young, Mary	GA	1847	Yac Young	Acie Keith	Libeckie Jackson		
15450	Young, Milton	GA	1898		Alexander Young	Minnie Samples	John & Louisa Young	
16569	Young, Mollie	GA	1873	Perry Young		Lula Langley		Lock Langley
15451	Young, Odessa	GA	1905		Cal Young	Mary Taylor	John & Louisa Young	
5258	Young, Orlean	NC	1850	John Young	Stephen Pennington	Joanah Spencer	Samuel & Elizabeth Pennington	Isaac & Joanah Spencer
14796	Young, Roby	VA	1880	Molly Young	Rush Young	Ellen Phipps	Wm & Catherine Young	Elijah & Nellie Phipps
15452	Young, Roy	GA	1900		Alexander Young	Minnie Samples	John & Louisa Young	
14323	Young, Sarah	OK	1850	Jacob Young	Anderson Musgrave	Millie Young	Thomas & Sallie Musgrave	John & Millie Young
5257	Young, William	NC	1875	Matildia Young	John Young	Orlean Pennington	Wm & Cathrine Young	Stephen & Johanah Pennington
15093	Young, William	GA	1876		John Young	Louisa Findley		Alex & Hulda Findley
15094	Young, Willie	GA	1906		William Young	Martha Garrison	John & Louise Young	
592	Zachary, James	AR	1869	Eliza Zachary	George Zachary	Mahalia Ballard	Josiah & Mariah Zachary	Elijah Ballard & Martha Bloodworth

674	Zachary, John	AR	1855	Missouri Zachary	George Zachery	Martha Massingille	Josiah & Mariah Zachary	Fisher & Nancy Massingille
12489	Zachary, Susan	CA	1875	John Zachary	William Hyde	Emily Battle		
8764	Zeigler, Nancy	OK	1850	Frank Zeigler	Allen Gofford	Nancy Foreman		Anthony & Wattie Foreman
20654	Zoll, Tina	TN	1885		Joseph True	Nancy Cagle	Watson & Ruth True	Peter & Elizabeth Cagle
20864	Zuber, John	GA	1867		Gus Lay	Fannie Zuber		

www.ingramcontent.com/pod-product-compliance
Ingram Content Group UK Ltd.
Pitfield, Milton Keynes, MK11 3LW, UK
UKHW051301180426
11947UKWH00020B/1836